An Introduction to

the Literature of the Old Testament

AN INTRODUCTION TO

the Literature of the Old Testament

by S. R. DRIVER

Meridian Books

THE WORLD PUBLISHING COMPANY

CLEVELAND AND NEW YORK

A MERIDIAN BOOK

Published by The World Publishing Company
2231 West 110th Street, Cleveland 2, Ohio

First Meridian printing September 1956
Seventh printing April 1963

Library of Congress Catalog Card Number: 56-10898
Printed in the United States of America   7MWP463

PREFACE.

—o—

THE aim of the present volume is to furnish an account, at once descriptive and historical, of the Literature of the Old Testament. It is not, I ought perhaps to explain, an Introduction to the *Theology*, or to the *History*, or even to the *Study*, of the Old Testament : in any of these cases, the treatment and contents would both have been very different. It is an Introduction to the *Literature* of the Old Testament ; and what I conceived this to include was an account of the contents and structure of the several books, together with such an indication of their general character and aim as I could find room for in the space at my disposal.* [xiii] The treatment of the material has been determined by the character of the different books. The contents of the prophetical and poetical books, for instance, which are less generally known than the history, properly so called, have been stated more fully than those of the historical books : the legislative parts of the Pentateuch have also been described with tolerable fulness. A *comparative* study of the writings of the Old Testament is indispensable, if their relation to one another is to be rightly apprehended : accordingly the literary and other characteristics which connect, or distinguish, as the case may be, particular groups of writings have been indicated with some care. Distinctive types of style prevail in different parts of the Old Testament ; and as these—apart from the interest independently attaching to them—have frequently a bearing upon questions of date or authorship, or throw light upon the influences under

* The Theology of the Old Testament forms the subject of a separate volume in the present series, which has been entrusted to the competent hands of Professor A. B. Davidson, of the New College, Edinburgh.

which particular books (or parts of books) were composed, I have been at pains to illustrate them as fully as space permitted. Especial care has been bestowed upon the lists of expressions characteristic of different writers. It was impossible to avoid altogether the introduction of Hebrew words ; nor indeed, as the needs of Hebrew students could not with fairness be entirely neglected, was it even desirable to do so ; but an endeavour has been made, by translation, to make the manner in which they are used intelligible to the English reader.

Completeness has not been attainable. Sometimes, indeed, the grounds for a conclusion have been stated with approximate completeness ; but generally it has been found impossible to mention more than the more salient or important ones. This is especially the case in the analysis of the Hexateuch. A full statement and discussion of the grounds for this belongs to a Commentary. Very often, however, it is believed, when the relation of different passages to each other has been pointed out briefly, a comparative study by the reader will suggest to him additional grounds for the conclusion indicated. A word should also be said on the method followed. A strict inductive method would have required a given conclusion to be preceded by an [xiv] enumeration of all the facts upon which it depends. This would have been impossible within the limits at the writer's disposal, as well as tedious. The method pursued has thus often been to assume (on grounds not fully stated, but which have satisfied the author) the conclusion to be established, and to point to particular salient facts, which exemplify it or presuppose its truth. The argument in the majority of cases is *cumulative*—a species of argument which is often both the strongest and also the most difficult to exhaust within reasonable compass.

In the critical study of the Old Testament, there is an important distinction, which should be kept in mind. It is that of *degrees of probability*. The probability of a conclusion depends upon the nature of the grounds on which it rests ; and some conclusions reached by critics of the Old Testament are for this reason more probable than others : the facts at our disposal being in the former case more numerous and decisive than in the latter. It is necessary to call attention to this difference, because writers who seek to maintain the traditional view of the structure of the Old Testament sometimes point to conclusions

which, from the nature of the case, are uncertain, or are propounded avowedly as provisional, with the view of discrediting
all, as though they rested upon a similar foundation. But this is
very far from being the case. It has been no part of my object
to represent conclusions as more certain than is authorized by
the facts upon which they depend; and I have striven (as I hope
successfully) to convey to the reader the differences in this
respect of which I am sensible myself. Where the premises
satisfy me, I have expressed myself without hesitation or doubt;
where the *data* do not justify (so far as I can judge) a confident
conclusion, I have indicated this by some qualifying phrase. I
desire what I have just said to be applied in particular to the
analysis of the Hexateuch. That the "Priests' Code" formed
a clearly defined document, distinct from the rest of the Hexateuch, appears to me to be more than sufficiently established by
a multitude of convergent indications; and I have nowhere
signified any doubt on this conclusion. On the other hand, in
the remainder of the narrative of Gen.-Numbers and of Joshua,
though there are facts which satisfy me that this also is not
homogeneous, I believe that the analysis (from the nature of
[**xv**] the criteria on which it depends) is frequently uncertain,*
and will, perhaps, always continue so. Accordingly, as regards
"JE," as I have more than once remarked, I do not desire to
lay equal stress upon all the particulars of the analysis, or to
be supposed to hold that the line of demarcation between its
component parts is at every point as clear and certain as it is
between P and other parts of the Hexateuch.

Another point necessary to be borne in mind is that many
results can only be approximate. Even where there is no question of the author, we can sometimes determine the date within
only comparatively wide limits (*e.g.* Nahum); and even where
the limits are narrower, there may still be room for difference of
opinion, on account of the different aspects of a passage which
most strongly impress different critics (*e.g.* in some of the
acknowledged prophecies of Isaiah). Elsewhere, again, grounds
may exist sufficient to justify the negative conclusion, that a
writing does not belong to a particular age or author, but not

* See pp. 16, 17, 19, 39, 116 f., &c. The same admission is constantly
made by Wellhausen, Kuenen, and other critics: see, for instance, p. xi of
the edition of Genesis by Kautzsch and Socin, mentioned below, p. 14 *n.*

definite enough to fix positively the age to which it does belong, except within broad and general limits. In all such cases we must be content with approximate results.

It is in the endeavour to reach definite conclusions upon the basis either of imperfect *data*, or of indications reasonably susceptible of divergent interpretations, that the principal disagreements between critics have their origin. Language is sometimes used implying that critics are in a state of internecine conflict with one another, or that their conclusions are "in a condition of perpetual flux." * Such statements are not in accordance with the facts. There is a large area on which the *data* are clear : here, accordingly, critics are agreed, and their conclusions are not likely to be ever reversed. And this area includes many of the most important results which criticism has reached. There is an area beyond this, where the *data* are complicated or ambiguous ; and here it is not more than natural that independent judges should differ. Perhaps future study may reduce this margin of uncertainty. I make no claim to have admitted into the present volume only those conclusions on which all critics are agreed ; for naturally [xvi] I have followed the guidance of my own judgment as to what was probable or not ; but where alternative views appeared to me to be tenable, or where the opinion towards which I inclined only partially satisfied me, I have been careful to indicate this to the reader. I have, moreover, made it my aim to avoid speculation upon slight and doubtful *data* ; or, at least, if I have been unable absolutely to avoid it, I have stated distinctly of what nature the *data* are.

Polemical references, with very few exceptions, I have avoided. It must not, however, be thought that, because I do not more frequently discuss divergent opinions, I am therefore unacquainted with them. I have been especially careful to acquaint myself with the views of Keil, and of other writers on the traditional side. I have also constantly, both before and since writing the present volume, followed closely the course of archæological research ; and I am aware of no instance in which its results are opposed to the conclusions which I have expressed. Upon no

* It may not be superfluous to remark that both the principles and the results of the critical study of the Old Testament are often seriously misrepresented, especially on the part of writers opposed to it, including even such as might from their position be supposed to be well informed.

occasion have I adopted what may be termed a critical as opposed to a conservative position, without weighing fully the arguments advanced in support of the latter, and satisfying myself that they were untenable.

Naturally a work like the present is founded largely on the labours of previous scholars. Since Gesenius, in the early years of this century, inaugurated a new epoch in the study of Hebrew, there has been a succession of scholars, of the highest and most varied ability, who have been fascinated by the literature of ancient Israel, and have dedicated their lives to its elucidation. Each has contributed of his best : and those who come after stand upon the vantage-ground won for them by their predecessors. In exegesis and textual criticism, not less than in literary criticism, there has been a steady advance.* The *historical* significance of different parts of the Old Testament—the aim and drift of individual prophecies, for instance, or the relation to one another of parallel groups of laws—has been far more carefully observed than was formerly the case. While in fairness to myself I think it right to state that my volume embodies the results of much independent work, for I accept conclusions, not on the authority of the critic who affirms them, but because I have satisfied myself, by personal study, that the grounds alleged in their support are adequate,—I desire at the same time to acknowledge gratefully my [xvii] indebtedness to those who have preceded me, and facilitated my labours. The references will generally indicate who the authorities are that have been principally of service to me ; naturally they vary in different parts of the Old Testament.

It does not fall within the scope of the present volume to deal with either the Theology or the History of the Old Testament, as such : nevertheless a few words may be permitted on them here.

It is impossible to doubt that the main conclusions of critics with reference to the authorship of the books of the Old Testament rest upon reasonings the cogency of which cannot be

---

* The progress in the two former may be measured approximately by the Revised Version, or (in some respects, more adequately) by the notes in the "Variorum Bible" of Eyre & Spottiswoode. See also the translation and notes (*Beilagen*, pp. 1–98) in Kautzsch's *Die Heilige Schrift des A.T.s* (below, p. 3).

denied without denying the ordinary principles by which history is judged and evidence estimated. Nor can it be doubted that the same conclusions, upon any neutral field of investigation, would have been accepted without hesitation by all conversant with the subject: they are opposed in the present instance by some theologians, only because they are supposed to conflict with the requirements of the Christian faith. But the history of astronomy, geology, and, more recently, of biology,* supplies a warning that the conclusions which satisfy the common unbiassed and unsophisticated reason of mankind prevail in the end. The price at which alone the traditional view can be maintained is too high.† Were the difficulties which beset it isolated or occasional, the case, it is true, would be different: it could then, for instance, be reasonably argued that a fuller knowledge of the times might afford the clue that would solve them. But the phenomena which the traditional view fails to explain are too numerous for such a solution to be admissible ; they recur so *systematically* that some cause or causes, for which that view makes no allowance, must be postulated to account for them. The hypothesis of glosses and marginal additions is a superficial remedy : the fundamental distinctions upon which the main conclusions of critics depend remain untouched.‡

The truth, however, is that apprehensions of the character [xviii] just indicated are unfounded. It is not the case that critical conclusions, such as those expressed in the present volume, are in conflict either with the Christian creeds or with the articles of the Christian faith. Those conclusions affect not the *fact* of revelation, but only its *form*. They help to determine the stages through which it passed, the different phases which it assumed, and the process by which the record of it was built up. They do not touch either the authority or the inspiration of the Scriptures of the Old Testament. They

---

* Comp. the luminous and able treatment of this subject, on its theological side, by the late lamented Aubrey L. Moore in *Science and the Faith* (1889), esp. pp. xi–xlvii, and pp. 163–235.

† Of course there are many points at which tradition is not affected by criticism. I allude naturally to those in which the case is different.

‡ The same may be said of Bishop Ellicott's "rectified traditional view." The distinctions referred to, it ought to be understood, in works written in defence of the traditional position, are, as a rule, very imperfectly stated, even where they are not ignored altogether.

imply no change in respect to the Divine attributes revealed in the Old Testament; no change in the lessons of human duty to be derived from it; no change as to the general position (apart from the interpretation of particular passages) that the Old Testament points forward prophetically to Christ.* That both the religion of Israel itself, and the record of its history embodied in the Old Testament, are the work of men whose hearts have been touched, and minds illumined, in different degrees,† by the Spirit of God, is manifest:‡ but the recognition of this truth does not decide the question of the author by whom, or the date at which, particular parts of the Old Testament were committed to writing; nor does it determine the precise literary character of a given narrative or book. No part of the Bible, nor even the Bible as a whole, is a logically articulated system of theology: the Bible is a "library," showing how men variously gifted by the Spirit of God cast the truth which they received into many different literary forms, as genius permitted or occasion demanded, —into poetry of various kinds, sometimes national, sometimes individual, sometimes even developing a truth in a form approaching that of the drama; into prophetical [xix] discourses, suggested mostly by some incident of the national life; into proverbs, prompted by the observation of life and manners; into laws, prescribing rules for the civil and religious government of the nation; into narratives, sometimes relating to a distant or a nearer past, sometimes autobiographical; and (to include the New Testament) into letters, designed, in the first instance, to meet the needs of particular churches or individuals. It is probable that every form of literary composition known to the

---

* Comp. Prof. Sanday's words in *The Oracles of God* (1891), p. 7—a volume which, with its counsels of wisdom and sobriety, I would gladly, if I might, adopt as the Preface to my own. See also the admirable work of Prof. A. F. Kirkpatrick, *The Divine Library of the Old Testament.*

† I say, in different degrees; for no one would attribute to the authors of some of the Proverbs, or of the Books of Esther or Ecclesiastes, the same degree of spiritual perception displayed *e.g.* in Isa. 40-66, or in the Psalms.

‡ So, for instance, Riehm, himself a critic, speaking of the Pentateuch as a record of revelation, remarks on the "immediate impression" of this character which it makes, and continues: "Every one who so reads the Pentateuch as to allow its contents to work upon his spirit, must receive the impression that a consciousness of God such as is here expressed cannot be derived from flesh and blood" (*Einleitung,* § 28, "Der Pentateuch als Offenbarungsurkunde").

ancient Hebrews was utilised as a vehicle of Divine truth, and is represented in the Old Testament.* Hence the character of a particular part of the Old Testament cannot be decided by an *à priori* argument as regards what it *must* be; it can only be determined by an application of the canons of evidence and probability universally employed in historical or literary investigation. None of the historians of the Bible claim supernatural enlightenment for the *materials* of their narrative : † it is reasonable, therefore, to conclude that these were derived by them from such human sources as were at the disposal of each particular writer; in some cases from a writer's own personal knowledge, in others from earlier documentary sources, in others, especially in those relating to a distant past, from popular tradition. It was the function of inspiration to guide the individual writer in the choice and disposition of his material, and in his use of it for the inculcation of special lessons. And in the production of some parts of the Old Testament different hands co-operated, and have left traces of their work more or less clearly discernible. The whole is subordinated to the controlling agency of the Spirit of God, causing the Scriptures of the Old Testament to be profitable [**xx**] "for teaching, for reproof, for correction, for instruction, which is in righteousness": but under this presiding influence scope is left for the exercise, in different modes and ways, of the faculties ordinarily

---

* Πολυμερῶς καὶ πολυτρόπως πάλαι ὁ Θεὸς λαλήσας τοῖς πατράσιν ἐν τοῖς προφήταις, Heb. I[1]. On the manifold Voice of God as heard in the Old Testament, the writer may be permitted to refer to the sixth of his *Sermons on Subjects connected with the OT.* (1892). In the seventh Sermon in the same volume he has developed more fully the view taken by him of Inspiration (cf. the *Contemp. Review*, Feb. 1890, p. 229 f.). He has pleasure also, in the same connexion, in referring to the very lucid and helpful "Bampton Lectures" for 1893 (ed. 3, 1896) on Inspiration, by his colleague, Prof. Sanday, especially Lectures ii.–v.

† The preface to St. Luke's Gospel (Luke I[1-4]) is instructive in this respect. St. Luke only claims for his narrative that he has used in its composition the care and research of an ordinary historian. Comp. Sanday, *Oracles of God*, pp. 72–75 : "In all that relates to the Revelation of God and of His Will, the writers [of the Bible] assert for themselves a definite inspiration ; they claim to speak with an authority higher than their own. But in regard to the narrative of events, and to processes of literary composition, there is nothing so exceptional about them as to exempt them from the conditions to which other works would be exposed at the same place and time."

employed in literary composition. There is a human factor in the Bible, which, though quickened and sustained by the informing Spirit, is never wholly absorbed or neutralized by it; and the limits of its operation cannot be ascertained by an arbitrary *à priori* determination of the methods of inspiration; the only means by which they can be ascertained is by an assiduous and comprehensive study of the facts presented by the Old Testament itself.*

* Two principles, once recognized, will be found to solve nearly all the difficulties which, upon the traditional view of the historical books of the Old Testament, are insuperable, viz.—(1) that in many parts of these books we have before us *traditions*, in which the original representation has been insensibly modified, and sometimes (especially in the later books) coloured by the associations of the age in which the author recording it lived; (2) that some freedom was used by ancient historians in placing speeches or discourses in the mouths of historical characters. In some cases, no doubt, such speeches agreed substantially with what was actually said; but often they merely develop at length, in the style and manner of the narrator, what was handed down only as a compendious report, or what was deemed to be consonant with the temper and aim of a given character on a particular occasion. No satisfactory conclusions with respect to the Old Testament will be arrived at without due account being taken of these two principles. Should it be feared that the first of these principles, if admitted, might imperil the foundations of the Christian faith, it is to be pointed out that the records of the New Testament were produced under very different historical conditions; that while in the Old Testament, for example, there are instances in which we can have no assurance that an event was recorded until many centuries after its occurrence, in the New Testament the interval at most is not more than 30–50 years. Viewed in the light of the unique personality of Christ, as depicted both in the common tradition embodied in the Synoptic Gospels and in the personal reminiscences underlying the fourth Gospel, and also as presupposed by the united testimony of the Apostolic writers belonging almost to the same generation, the circumstances are such as to forbid the supposition that the facts of our Lord's life on which the fundamental truths of Christianity depend can have been the growth of mere tradition, or are anything else than strictly historical. The same canon of historical criticism which authorizes the assumption of tradition in the Old Testament, forbids it—except within the narrowest limits, as in some of the divergences apparent between the parallel narratives of the Gospels—in the case of the New Testament.

It is an error to suppose, as appears sometimes to be done, that topographical exploration, or the testimony of Inscriptions, supplies a refutation of critical conclusions respecting the books of the Old Testament. The Biblical records possess exactly that degree of historical and topographical accuracy which would be expected from the circumstances under which all reasonable critics hold that they were composed. The original sources of

[**xxi**] It is objected, however, that some of the conclusions of critics respecting the Old Testament are incompatible with the authority of our blessed Lord, and that in loyalty to Him we are precluded from accepting them. That our Lord appealed to the Old Testament as the record of a revelation in the past, and as pointing forward to Himself, is undoubted; but these aspects of the Old Testament are perfectly consistent with a critical view of its structure and growth. That our Lord in so appealing to it designed to pronounce a verdict on the authorship and age of its different parts, and to foreclose all future inquiry into these subjects, is an assumption for which no sufficient ground can be alleged. Had such been His aim, it would have been out of harmony with the entire method and tenor of His teaching. In no single instance, so far as we are aware, did He anticipate the results of scientific inquiry or historical research. The aim of His teaching was a religious one; it was to set before men the pattern of a perfect life, to move them to imitate it, to bring them to Himself. He accepted, as the basis of His teaching, the opinions respecting the Old Testament current around Him : He assumed, in His allusions to it, the premises which His opponents recognised, and which could not have been questioned (even had it been necessary to question them) without raising issues for which the time was not yet ripe, and which, had they been raised, would have interfered seriously with the paramount purpose of His life.* There is no record of Samuel and Kings, for instance, being the work of men familiar with Palestine, describe localities there with precision : the chronology, being (in many cases) added subsequently, is in several respects in irreconcilable conflict with contemporary Inscriptions (cf. Sanday, *l.c.* p. 9 ; or the note in the writer's *Isaiah*, p. 13). Mr. Girdlestone, in *The Foundations of the Bible* (1890), partly from an inexact knowledge of the facts, partly through misapprehension of what critics really hold, employs himself largely in beating the air.

* On Ps. 110, see the note, p. 384 f.; and especially the discussion of our Lord's reference to this Psalm in the seventh of Mr. Gore's "Bampton Lectures." It does not seem requisite for the present purpose, as, indeed, within the limits of a Preface it would not be possible, to consider whether our Lord, as man, possessed all knowledge, or whether a limitation in this, as in other respects,—though not, of course, of such a kind as to render Him fallible as a teacher,—was involved in that gracious act of condescension, in virtue of which He was willing "in all things to be made like unto His brethren" (Heb. 2¹⁷). On this subject a reference to the sixth of the Lectures just mentioned must suffice. The questions touched upon in the

the question, whether a particular portion of the Old Testament was written by Moses, or David, or Isaiah, having been ever submitted to [xxii] Him; and had it been so submitted, we have no means of knowing what His answer would have been. The purposes for which our Lord appealed to the Old Testament, its prophetic significance, and the spiritual lessons deducible from it, are not, as has been already remarked above, affected by critical inquiries.* Criticism in the hands of Christian scholars does not banish or destroy the inspiration of the Old Testament; it *presupposes* it; it seeks only to determine the conditions under which it operates, and the literary forms through which it manifests itself; and it thus helps us to frame truer conceptions of the methods which it has pleased God to employ in revealing Himself to His ancient people of Israel, and in preparing the way for the fuller manifestation of Himself in Christ Jesus.

Six years have elapsed since the first edition of the present work was published, and the preceding preface written, substantially as it still stands. The favourable reception which the volume has received has much exceeded what I had ventured to anticipate; and many gratifying indications have reached me of the assistance which it has afforded to students of the Old Testament, in other countries, as well as at home. It has been a particular satisfaction to me to know that it has so largely won

present paragraph of the Preface are also thoughtfully handled by Bishop Moorhouse in his volume entitled, *The Teaching of Christ* (1891), Sermons i. and ii. And since this note was originally written, there have appeared two essays, one by A. Plummer, D.D., in the *Expositor* for July 1891, on "The Advance of Christ in Σοφία," the other *An Inquiry into the Nature of our Lord's knowledge as man*, by the Rev. W. S. Swayne, with a Preface by the Bishop of Salisbury, each meriting calm and serious consideration. The subject of our Lord's attitude towards the Old Testament is also discussed suggestively by J. Meinhold, *Jesus und das Alte Testament* (1896).

* In support of this statement, the writer may be allowed to refer to his *Sermons on Subjects connected with the Old Testament* (1892), to which is prefixed a paper read by him at the Church Congress at Folkestone (1892), " On the Permanent Moral and Devotional Value of the Old Testament for the Christian Church." For proof also that a spiritual appreciation of the Old Testament is fully compatible with a critical view of it, see Cheyne's *Commentary on the Psalms*, and the Sermons on the Psalms in his *Aids to the Devout Study of Criticism* (1892), Kirkpatrick's *Doctrine of the Prophets*, Sanday's " Bampton Lectures " (1893), etc. (cf. below, p. xvi).

the approval of those who have been workers themselves upon the same field, and who possess consequently a practical acquaintance with the ground which it traverses.* The study of the Old Testament does not, however, stand still ; and since 1891 many important books, or articles, dealing with different parts of it, have appeared. In the 2nd, 3rd, and 4th editions, such notices of these works as seemed needful were incorporated in the Addenda or elsewhere ; in the 5th edition (1894) an Appendix of twenty-one pages (which was also published separately) was added. Meanwhile it had been felt, by Prof. Kautzsch of Halle, and other scholars whose judgment possessed weight, that the lines upon which my *Introduction* was written were such as to render it valuable even in Germany : accordingly, in 1895, I was invited to sanction its translation into German. The translation was executed by the competent and practised hand of Prof. J. W. Rothstein of Halle,—the translator of Prof. Robertson Smith's *Old Testament in the Jewish Church,*—and appeared in 1896. For the translation I naturally incorporated into the text the material collected in the *Appendix* of the 5th English edition, and also added notes, taking account of the principal critical and exegetical literature which had appeared between 1891 and 1896 : the translator, also, in several cases, added notes of his own. When a sixth English edition was called for, it seemed to me that the new material had now outgrown the limits of an Appendix, and (though I regretted the disadvantage at which possessors of the previous editions would in consequence be placed) that there was no alternative but to have the work reset, and to introduce into the text, at the proper places, such additions as might be necessary. This has accordingly now been done. In all its main conclusions the present edition does not differ from the preceding ones, and the text is, as a rule, unchanged. I have, however, revised the work throughout ; and I have, in particular—(1) introduced from time to time verbal, and even, occasionally, slight material, improvements into the text ; † (2) brought the bibliographical notices,

---

* In support of this statement, notices by Professors A. B. Davidson, T. K. Cheyne, H. E. Ryle, A. R. S. Kennedy, and G. A. Smith, as well as reviews in the *Times* and *Guardian* newspapers, were referred to in the Prefaces to the 2nd–5th editions.

† As pp. 51 ff. (where I have sought to distinguish, more exactly than before, between H and the priestly additions), 71, 91, 93 f., 96 f., 98, 149-

as far as possible, up to date ; (3) given some account of the principal critical views which have been propounded, with reference to various parts of the OT., since 1891.* If I have seldom found myself able to accept definitely these newer views, it is because they have seemed to me to be based too largely either upon merely subjective criteria, or upon *data* of that imperfect or ambiguous kind alluded to above (p. vi), from which assured inferences cannot be drawn. Nevertheless, in spite of my own attitude towards the views in question, I have deemed it only proper to notice and describe them, so far as space permitted : for in a work dealing with the many problems which the Literature of the Old Testament presents, the student has a right to find some account of what the best and ablest thinkers of the day are saying about them : and even provisional or tentative solutions are not without their value, as indicating the directions along which a subject may be advantageously studied, and perhaps pointing the way towards truer solutions in the future.

The progress which critical opinion has made during recent years, especially in this country and in America, is remarkable. At first even the slightest concessions were viewed with alarm ; and though the same attitude is still maintained in some quarters, it has on the whole been largely overcome. The cogency of the reasonings upon which at least the broader and more important critical conclusions rest, is seen to be irresistible; and the truth of what was urged above, that critical conclusions are not really in conflict with the claims and truths of Christianity, has been widely recognized. So far as the Anglican Church is concerned, the Essay of Mr. (now Canon) Gore in *Lux Mundi* was one of the first indications of a change of front on the part of those who were not, so to say, critics by profession. The sympathetic review of the present work in the *Guardian* † was another significant symptom of the changed

151, 163, 215, 221 f., 271 f., 337 f., 349–351, 390 f., 410, 474, 498–500, 534, 538, 539 f., &c.

* The additional matter in the present edition does not correspond exactly to that in the German translation. Much of it is the same, but some of the notes are altered in form, and there are also considerable additions.

For convenience of reference, the pagination of the previous editions is inserted within square brackets.

† Nov. 18 and Dec. 2, 1891.

times. Other indications are not far to seek. In the *Expositor*, the *Expository Times*, and other theological periodicals, critical opinions are openly advocated and discussed. Scotland, which twenty years ago removed Prof. W. Robertson Smith from his chair, is now amongst the foremost to honour those upon whom it has devolved to carry on and develop his teaching. In America, a daily increasing number of the leading theological Professors avow their adhesion to the critical cause. In the Roman Catholic Church, the Abbé Loisy, and (in this country) Baron von Hügel, have urged that it is only the theological sense of Scripture which was defined by the Council of Trent, and that consequently in its critical and historical interpretation the theologian is free to follow the best guidance which modern research has provided for him.* And to mention but three representative names from among ourselves, Prof. Kirkpatrick, Prof. Sanday, and, most recently, Mr. R. L. Ottley, Bampton Lecturer for the present year, all men of cautious and well-balanced judgment, have signified, with the reservations which, considering the nature of the subject-matter, are only reasonable, but at the same time quite unambiguously, their acceptance of the critical position.† Mr. Ottley, in particular, has demonstrated, what many had before been conscious of, but had not developed upon the same comprehensive scale, the entire compatibility of a critical

---

* See the Abbé Loisy's two instructive brochures, *Les Études Bibliques* (Amiens, 1894), and *Les Mythes Chaldéens de la Création et du Déluge* (Amiens, 1892) ; and the Baron von Hügel's articles in the *Dublin Review*, Oct. 1894, April and Oct. 1895. Cf. the *Academy*, Oct. 17, 1896, p. 275 f.

† Kirkpatrick, *The Divine Library of the OT.* 1891, p. 41 (cf. pp. 46, 99, 100, 108 f., &c.) ; Sanday, *Bampton Lectures*, pp. 116, 121 f. I am unable to quote specific passages from Mr. Ottley's Lectures, as they have not yet been published. A full consideration of these aspects of the subject is beyond the scope of the present volume ; but it can hardly be doubted that to many minds the new historical setting in which criticism places many parts of the Old Testament, and the correlation which it establishes between the religious history of the Old Testament and the principle of a " progressive revelation," constitute a strong confirmation of the truth of the critical position. On Prof. J. Robertson's *Early Religion of Israel*, comp. the review by C. G. Montefiore in the *Jewish Quarterly Review*, Jan. 1893, p. 302 ff. The fact that the critical view of the literature and history of the OT. may be presented in an extreme and vulnerable form, is not evidence that it is unsound in itself, or that it cannot be presented with such limitations as free it from reasonable objection.

position with the truest and warmest spiritual perceptions, and
with the fullest loyalty to the Christian creed. At the present
moment, two new Dictionaries of the Bible, differing somewhat
in scale and design, but both representing an avowedly critical
standpoint, are in progress, and will, it is probable, be published
shortly.* And even as I write, the Committee appointed to
report upon the subject by the Conference of Bishops of the
Anglican Communion, held at Lambeth in July 1897, while
naturally passing no verdict itself upon critical questions, affirms
distinctly both the right and the duty " of the critical study
of every part of the Bible " on the part of "those Christian
teachers and theologians who are capable of undertaking it ";
and anticipates no disparagement of Scripture, but rather "an
increased and more vivid sense of the Divine revelation" contained in it, from the careful and reverent application to it of
critical methods.

The consensus of so many acute and able scholars, of different countries, of different communions, trained independently
in different schools, and approaching the subject with different
theological and intellectual prepossessions, cannot, as some
would have us believe, rest upon illusion: it can rest only
upon the fact that, whatever margin of uncertainty there may
be, within which, as explained above, critics differ, there is an
area within which their conclusions are deduced, by sound and
legitimate logical processes, from a groundwork of solid fact.†

* By Messrs. A. & C. Black and Messrs. T. & T. Clark respectively.

† It is remarkable how inexact and undiscriminating is the knowledge of
the critical position displayed frequently by those who come forward to
oppose it ; and how largely even the more prominent of its recent opponents
appear to rely upon rhetorical depreciation and invective. It is difficult to
understand what force such weapons can be supposed to possess. No serious
issue has ever yet been decided by their aid ; and the present one, it is
certain, will form no exception to the rule.

Readers of Maspero's *Struggle of the Nations*, and of Hommel's *Ancient
Hebrew Tradition*, published by the Society for the Promotion of Christian
Knowledge, ought to be aware that in the former the author's conclusions on
the history of Israel, and on critical questions connected with it, have been
systematically suppressed or altered, and that in the latter many of the terms
of disparagement and offence applied to certain scholars have been gratuitously
introduced: in both cases, without any notification being given of the liberties
taken by the translators. See particulars in the *Athenæum*, Jan. 2, 1897 ; or
the *Church Quarterly Review*, July 1897, pp. 462-473 ; and the *Athenæum*,
Aug. 28, 1897, p. 285 ; or the *Expository Times*, Sept. 1897, p. 557.

The attempt to refute the conclusions of criticism by means of archæology has signally failed. The archæological discoveries of recent years have indeed been of singular interest and value : they have thrown a flood of light, sometimes as surprising as it was unexpected, upon many a previously dark and unknown region of antiquity. But, in spite of the ingenious hypotheses which have been framed to prove the contrary, they have revealed nothing which is in conflict with the generally accepted conclusions of critics.* I readily allow that there are some critics who combine with their literary criticism of the Old Testament an *historical* criticism which appears to me to be unreasonable and extreme ; and I am not prepared to say that isolated instances do not exist, in which opinions expressed by one or another of these critics may have to be reconsidered in the light of recent discoveries ;† but the idea that the monuments furnish a refutation of the general critical position, is a pure illusion. By an irony of fate, the only two positions adopted in the first edition of the present work, which, if Prof. Sayce's *Verdict of the Monuments* be taken as the standard, must be deemed inconsistent, the one certainly, the other very probably, with the evidence of the inscriptions, are not critical, but *conservative* positions : the possibility, viz. that there may have been a ruler, such as Darius the Mede is represented as having been in the Book of Daniel, and a date as early as *c.* 586 B.C. for Ob.[10-21].‡ A more conclusive proof of the unreality of the supposed " refutation " could not be desired.

S. R. D.

September 1897.

---

* Comp. the remarks below, pp. 3 f., 158 f.

† Critics are, however, not unfrequently credited with opinions contradicting the evidence of archæology, which the present writer, at any rate, has never been able to discover that they have really expressed.

‡ See below, pp. 320 f., 499 *note* ‡.

CONTENTS

CHAPTER VI

CHAPTER VII

CHAPTER VIII

CHAPTER IX

CHAPTER X

CHAPTER XI

CHAPTER XII

ADDITIONS AND CORRECTIONS.

Preface, p. XVI, note *. Add Père Lagrange's article in the *Revue Biblique*, Jan. 1898, on "Les Sources du Pentateuque" (summarised in the *Expos. Times*, June 1898, p. 405 f.).

Preface, p. XVII, l. 5–6. The first volume of the Dictionary published by Messrs. Clark, extending as far as FEASTS, has appeared.

Preface. p. XVII, note †. The liberties taken in the translation of Maspero have been acknowledged by the General Literature Committee of the S.P.C.K., who have issued a leaf, containing corrections of several (though by no means of all), together with a note by the author, in which he expresses his surprise "que le traducteur ait altéré de parti pris le texte qu'il voulut rendre en anglais." It appears now, from official statements, that the alterations in question were made without the knowledge or sanction either of the Committee or of the author. Cf. the *Expos. Times*, 1898, pp. 147–149, 201, 434.

P. 1. Dillmann's *Ex. Lev.* appeared in a new edition, revised by V. Ryssel, in 1897.

P. 1. A "Kurzer Hand-Commentar zum A.T.," edited by K. Marti (somewhat briefer than Nowack's), has recently (1897) been commenced: Genesis by H. Holzinger, Judges by K. Budde, Ezekiel by A. Bertholet, Proverbs by G. Wildeboer, Job by B. Duhm, and the *Megilloth* (Song of Songs and Lam. by Budde, Ruth by Bertholet, Eccl. and Esther by Wildeboer) have appeared already.

P. 1, end of first paragraph. Add: *The Cosmogony of Genesis and its Reconcilers*, by President Henry Morton, of the Stevens Institute of Technology, Hoboken, N.J. (comparing the note in the *Expositor*, June 1898, pp. 464–469); and Principal Whitehouse's art. COSMOGONY, in Clark's *Dictionary of the Bible*.

P. 2. Add: W. E. Addis, *The Documents of the Hexateuch, translated and arranged in chronological order, with introduction and notes*, vol. i. 1892, vol. ii. 1898.

P. 2. A second and enlarged edition of Dr. Briggs' *Higher Criticism of the Hexateuch* appeared in 1897; and a fourth edition of his *Biblical Study*, with many additions, under the title, *A General Introduction to the Study of the Bible*, is expected shortly.

P. 3. In Haupt's "Sacred Books of the O.T." (also known as the "Polychrome Bible") the *English* editions of Leviticus (Driver and White), Judges (Moore), Isaiah (Cheyne), and the Psalms (Wellhausen) have appeared. The illustrations, designed for these volumes by the editor, form an instructive addition; and at the end of Wellhausen's *Psalms*, the appendix on the Music of the Ancient Hebrews (pp. 217–234), also with numerous illustrations, deserves notice.

P. 3 f. On the critical bearings of Sayce's *Early History of the Hebrews*, see G. B. Gray in the *Expositor*, May 1898, pp. 337–355.

P. 22. Add: R. Klopfer, "Zur Quellenscheidung in Exod. 19," in the *ZATW*, 1898, p. 197 ff.

Pp. 15, 159. With regard to Gen. 14, substantially the same judgement is expressed by the Assyriologist Zimmern in the *Theol. Rundschau*, for May 1898 (see the abstract in the *Expos. Times*, June 1898, p. 448 f.): the names of the four kings mentioned in v.[1] are historical; but at present nothing is proved from the monuments as to the historical character of the campaign described in the rest of the chapter.

P. 47. Add: L. B. Paton, "The Original form of Lev. xvii.–xix.," in *JBLit*. 1897, pp. 31–77 (also separately, Marburg, 1897).

P. 70. Add: C. Steuernagel (in Nowack's "Handkommentar"), 1898.

P. 130 *note**. See further, on the types of Hebrew laws, Briggs, *Higher Criticism of the Hexateuch* (ed. 2), App. x. p. 242 ff.

P. 172. Add: M. Löhr (in the *Kgf. Exeg. Handb.*), 1898; H. P. Smith (in the *International Critical Commentary*), 1898 (shortly).

P. 204. Add: J. Skinner (in the *Camb. Bible for Schools*), 1898 (on c. 40–66). Dillmann's Commentary has also appeared in a new edition, revised by R. Kittel (1898).

P. 205. Add: F. Giesebrecht, *Die Berufsbegabung der Alttestamentlichen Propheten*, 1897 (on the predictive element in prophecy).

P. 299. Add: W. Nowack, *Die Kleinen Propheten*, 1897 (very complete and useful. In the conclusion that many passages in these prophets are later additions, the author agrees largely with Wellhausen). Add also G. A. Smith, vol. ii. 1898.

P. 318. Giesebrecht, also (*l.c.* p. 107 f.), finds himself obliged to agree, though reluctantly ("schweren Herzens"), that Am. 9[8-15] is a post-exilic appendix to the genuine prophecies of Amos.

P. 320 f. G. A. Smith comes to the conclusion that Ob. is the work of a prophet writing during the exile, who in v.[1-6. 8-10] incorporated portions of an older, pre-exilic prophecy on Edom. He thinks (p. 176) that the Sephared of v.[21] may be the Median Shaparda, mentioned by Sargon (cf. *KAT*[2] *ad loc.* p. 447); or, if this should be shown to be impossible, that the word (or clause) may be a later addition to the prophecy.

P. 330. Nowack now (in his *Commentary*) assigns to Micah in c. 4–5 only 4[9-11] (without the Babylon-clause), 5[1] (Heb. 4[14]), 5[10-14] (Heb. [9-13]).

P. 337. Nowack, following, and in some cases improving upon, Gunkel and Bickell, seeks also to restore the supposed acrostich in Neh. 1: but the textual changes which his restoration in parts postulates, especially the inversions and transpositions, are violent, and decidedly in excess of what a comparison of such parallel texts as Ps. 14 and 53, Ps. 40[13-17] and Ps. 70, or Ps. 18 and 2 Sam. 22, would lead us to expect. (Cf. the present writer's notice in the *Expos. Times*, Dec. 1897, p. 119.) Mr. G. B. Gray (in the

Expositor, Sept. 1898, p. 207 ff.), while less ambitious, is more convincing ; and has certainly restored Nah. 1^{2-9} with probability in an acrostich form.

P. 342. In Zeph. 2–3, Nowack rejects $2^{7a\alpha.}$ $b\beta.8-11.15$ $3^{9-10.14-20}$. G. A. Smith suspects strongly Zeph.'s authorship of 2^{8-11} ; and regards 3^{14-20} as an epilogue, added during, or immediately after, the exile.

Pp. 349–351. Nowack also is of opinion that Zech. 9–11, 13^{7-9} belongs to the Greek age ; but remarks justly that the necessary materials do not exist for fixing its date more closely. G. A. Smith (who also treats 13^{7-9} as the sequel to c. 9–11) thinks (p. 463) that Zech. 9–14 consists of "a number of separate oracles, which their language and general conceptions lead us on the whole to believe were put together by one hand"; and agrees that, "with the possible exception of some older fragments [as 9^{1-5}], they reflect the troubled times in Palestine that followed the invasion of Alexander the Great." G. L. Robinson, in an elaborate study, *The Prophecies of Zechariah* (Chicago, 1896, —reprinted from the *American Journ. of Sem. Languages*, Oct. 1895—Jan. 1896), seeks to show that Zech. 9–14 is by the same author as Zech. 1–8.

P. 359. Add: S. R. Driver, *The Parallel Psalter, being the Prayer-Book Version of the Psalms and a new Version, arranged on opposite pages, with an Introduction and Glossaries*, 1898 ; B. Jacob, *ZATW*, 1897, p. 263 ff. (the Psalms and the Temple-worship), 1898, p. 99 ff. (the order of the Psalms).

P. 393. Add: W. Frankenberg (in Nowack's "Handkommentar"), 1898.

P. 401. On Pr. $30^{1ff.}$ cf. Cheyne's *Jewish Religious Life after the Exile* (1898), p. 173 ff.

P. 408. Add: G. Beer, *ZATW*, 1898, p. 257 ff. (ending the "Studien").

P. 436. Add: C. Siegfried (in Nowack's "Handkommentar"), 1898.

P. 452 f. Budde, in his *Commentary* in Marti's series, mentioned above (note on p. 1), develops in detail the view of the Song of Songs here described. He regards the book as a collection of songs, the unity of which he finds not in the consistent development of a plot, but in the unity of *place and occasion*, which they all display : the songs were essentially "Volkslieder," of a kind that might be heard at any Hebrew wedding, though naturally the poet to whom we owe this collection was a gifted one, who selected, or adapted, the choicest that he knew : all spring out of the festivities accompanying a wedding, and all depict, in an imaginative, poetical form, different phases, or stages, in the happiness of a single (typical) wedded pair, represented hyperbolically by "Solomon," and the Shulamite : as it is the poet's aim to delineate this as forcibly and vividly as possible, the poem, not unnaturally, assumes in parts a dramatic character. Siegfried takes substantially the same view of the book. The identification of Solomon with a shepherd, which (below, p. 444) is a serious difficulty, if the poem is understood literally, disappears, if "Solomon" be merely the typical name of the bridegroom, founded on the Syrian village-custom, explained on p. 452. Budde quotes as analogous, though they are briefer, two collections of old Egyptian love-poems, published recently by G. Maspero in his *Études Égyptiennes*, i. 217 ff., and by Spiegelberg in *Ægyptiaca* (Festschrift für G. Ebers), p. 117 ff., the resemblance of the former of which, in particular, to the Song of Songs had been pointed out (p. 258 f.) by the translator.—It is true, no interpretation of the poem can be said to be entirely free from difficulty. Ewald's view, attractive though it is, certainly requires a good deal to be read between the lines, which is not expressed. Budde presents his view forcibly and cleverly : but the reader, before accepting it, should satisfy himself that it does proper justice to the dialogue, and other dramatic elements which the poem undoubtedly contains, and that the hyperbole involved in passages such as 3^{6-10} $6^{8.\ 9d.\ e}$ is not greater than is probable.

P. 458, *note**. See, however, now, his *Commentary* (in Marti's series).

P. 464, lines 3-1 from bottom. Budde now (in his *Commentary*, pp. 75-77) ascribes c. 2 and c. 4 to a poet writing very shortly after the fall of Jerusalem (*c.* 580 B.C.), c. 1, with Löhr, on the ground, chiefly, of apparent literary dependence (v.[7. 9. 10. 15]) upon II Isaiah, to a second poet writing *c.* 530, or somewhat later [430 must be a misprint : see Löhr, p. xvii], and c. 5, in contents a kind of sequel to c. 2. 4, to *c.* 550 : c. 3 he considers to have been written much later, in the 3rd cent. B.C., *e persona Jeremiæ*, for the purpose of supplementing the other poems by giving expression to the feelings which an *individual* Israelite might be supposed to have experienced at the time of his country's great disaster.

P. 465. Add : C. Siegfried (in Nowack's ' Handkommentar '), 1898.

P. 485, *note*. Jensen, as quoted by Wildeboer (in Marti's series), pp. 173-175, adopts Zimmern's view of the origin of the Feast of Purim (though not his explanation of the word). See, further, the discriminating article by C. H. Toy, in the *New World*, March 1898, p. 130 ff.

P. 498, lines 4, 3 from bottom. Ed. Meyer (*ZATW*, 1898, p. 339 ff.) adduces strong reasons for believing that, in the passage (l. 12) fixing the month in which Sippar was taken, and Gubaru entered Babylon, *Tammuz* (June) is an error for *Tishri* (September): notice, especially, that *Elul* (August) has just preceded (l. 10). If this conclusion be correct, the "four months" of p. 499, l. 13, will be reduced to 17 or 18 days.

P. 501, *note*. The Persian prototype of רחבר, *dâtabâri*, occurs frequently in the cuneiform inscriptions of the reigns of Artaxerxes I. (B.C. 465-425), and Darius II. (424-405), found by the Pennsylvania Expedition at Nippur (Hilprecht, in the *Pal. Expl. Fund Quarterly Statement*, Jan. 1898, p. 55).

ABBREVIATIONS.

CIS. = *Corpus Inscriptionum Semiticarum* (Parisiis, 1881 ff.).

JBLit. = *Journal of Biblical Literature* (Boston, U.S.A.).

JPTh. = *Jahrbuch für Protestantische Theologie.*

JQR. = *Jewish Quarterly Review.*

KAT.[2] = (Eb. Schrader) *Die Keilinschriften und das AT.* (ed. 2, 1883), —translated under the title *The Cuneiform Inscriptions and the Old Testament,* London, 1885, 1888 (the standard work on the subject).

KB. = *Keilinschriftlichte Bibliothek* (translations of Assyrian and Babylonian Inscriptions), edited by Eb. Schrader.

OTJC.[2] = (W. R. Smith) *The Old Testament in the Jewish Church* (ed. 2, 1892).

QPB.[3] = *Queen's Printers' Bible* (otherwise called the *Variorum Bible*), ed. 3, 1889, published by Eyre and Spottiswoode :—the Old Testament edited by Prof. T. K. Cheyne and the present writer.

RV. = *Revised Version of the Old Testament* (1885).

SBOT. = (Haupt's) *Sacred Books of the Old Testament* (see p. 3).

ThT. = *Theologisch Tijdschrift* (Leiden).

ZATW. = *Zeitschrift für die Alttest. Wissenschaft,* edited by B. Stade.

ZDMG. = *Zeitschrift der Deutschen Morgenländischen Gesellschaft.*

ZKWL. = *Zeitschrift für kirchliche Wissenschaft und kirchliches Leben.*

The symbol P is explained on p. 10 ; J, E, and JE on p. 13 ; H on p. 48 ; D and D^2 on pp. 72, 104.

The arrow (↑), attached to a list of passages, indicates that it includes all instances of the word or phrase referred to, occurring in the OT.

In citations, the letters [a] and [b] denote respectively the first and second halves of the verse cited. Where the verse consists of three or more members, the letters [a], [b], [c], [d], [e], are employed sometimes to denote them similarly (as pp. 364 f., 439, 440). The *Greek* letters α, β denote the first and second parts, respectively, of the clauses indicated by [a] or [b].

A small "superior" figure, attached to the title of a book, or to an author's name, indicates the *edition* of the work referred to (as *KAT*[2]., above).

The citations of Biblical passages are accommodated throughout to the *English* version, except sometimes where the reference is more particularly to a Hebrew term. (The division of chapters is occasionally not the same in the Hebrew as in the English Bible ; and the title to a Psalm, where it consists of more than two words, is usually reckoned in the Hebrew as v.[1].)

An Introduction to

the Literature of the Old Testament

INTRODUCTION.

---o---

*THE ORIGIN OF THE BOOKS OF THE OLD TESTAMENT, AND
THE GROWTH OF THE CANON, ACCORDING TO THE JEWS.*

IT is sometimes supposed that conclusions such as those
expressed in the present volume on the age and authorship
of certain parts of the Old Testament are in conflict with trustworthy historical statements derived from ancient Jewish sources.
This, however, is not the case. On the authorship of the Books
of the OT., as on the completion of the Canon of the OT., the
Jews possess no *tradition* worthy of real credence or regard,
but only vague and uncertain reminiscences, intermingled often
with idle speculations.

Of the steps by which the Canon of the Old Testament was
formed, little definite is known.* It is, however, highly probable
that the tripartite division of the books, current from antiquity
among the Jews, has an historical basis, and corresponds to
three stages in the process; and it has accordingly been adopted
in the present volume. It ought only to be stated that, though
the books belonging to one division are never (by the Jews)
transferred to another, in the case of the Prophets and the
" Kethubim " (Hagiographa), certain differences of arrangement
have sometimes prevailed. In the Talmud (*Bâba bâthra* 14ᵇ)

---

* For further information on the subject of the following pages, the reader
is referred to the learned and elaborate article by Strack, " Kanon des Alten
Testaments," in Herzog's *Encykl.* (ed. 2) vol. vii. (1880). See also Dillmann,
" Über die Bildung u. Sammlung heiliger Schriften des AT.," in the *Jahrb. f.
Deutsche Theol.* 1858, pp. 419–491; Jul. Fürst, *Der Kanon des AT.s nach
Talmud u. Midrash,* 1868; G. Wildeboer, *Die Entstehung des Alttest.
Kanons,* 1891 (tr. by B. W. Bacon, 1895); F. Buhl, *Kanon u. Text des
AT.s* (translated); and esp. Prof. H. E. Ryle's valuable essay, *The Canon
of the OT.,* 1892 (published since the following pages were written), ² 1895.

the arrangement of the "Latter" Prophets is Jer. Ez. Isa. the XII ;
and this order is commonly observed in German and French
[**xxviii**] MSS.   The Massoretic scholars (7–9 cent.) placed
Isaiah first; and the order sanctioned by them is adopted in
the ancient MS., now at St. Petersburg, and bearing a date =
A.D. 916, in Spanish MSS., and in the printed editions of the
Hebrew Bible.   The Talmudic arrangement of the Hagiographa
is Ruth, Ps. Job, Prov. Eccl. Song of Songs, Lam. Dan. Est.
Ezr.-Neh. Chr.; and this order is found in MSS.; the Massorites,
followed (as a rule) by Spanish MSS., adopted the order Chr.
Ps. Job, Prov. Ruth, Song of Songs, Eccl. Lam. Est. Dan. Ezr.-
Neh.: German MSS. have generally the order followed in printed
editions of the Hebrew Bible (and in the present volume), Ps.
Prov. Job, the 5 *Megilloth*,* Dan. Ezr.-Neh. Chr. Other variations
in the arrangement of the Hagiographa are also to be found in
MSS.†   The following are the earliest and principal passages
bearing on the subject :—

1. The Proverbs of Jesus, the son of Sirach (*c.* 200 B.C.),
were translated into Greek by the grandson of the author, *c.* 130
B.C., who prefixed to them a preface, in which he speaks of "the
law and the prophets, and the others, who followed upon them"
(καὶ τῶν ἄλλων τῶν κατ' αὐτοὺς ἠκολουθηκότων), to the study of
whose writings his grandfather had devoted himself, "the law
and the prophets, and the other books of our fathers (καὶ τὰ
ἄλλα πάτρια βίβλια)," "the law, the prophets, and the rest of
the books (καὶ τὰ λοιπὰ τῶν βιβλίων)." This passage appears
to recognise the threefold division of the Jewish Canon, the
indefinite expression following "the prophets" representing
(presumably) the miscellaneous collection of writings known
now as the Hagiographa.   In view of the fact that the tripartite
division was afterwards generally recognised by the Jews, and
that two of the names are the same, it may be taken as a
tolerably decisive indication that this division was established
c. 130 B.C., if not in the days of the translator's grandfather himself.   It does not, however, show that the Hagiographa was
already completed, as we now have it ; it would be entirely consistent with the terms used, for instance, if particular books, as

---

* In the order in which they are read in the synagogue (p. 436 *n.*), viz.
Song of Songs, Ruth, Lam. Eccl. Est.

† See more fully Ryle, pp. 219–234, 281 f. (² pp. 230–246, 292 ff.).

Esther, or Daniel, or Ecclesiastes, were only added to the collection subsequently.

2. The Second Book of Maccabees opens with two letters (1^1–2^{18}), [**xxix**] purporting to have been sent by the Palestinian Jews in B.C. 144 to their brethren in Egypt. The second of these letters, after the mention of certain apocryphal anecdotes connected with Jeremiah and Nehemiah, continues as follows :—

"The same things were also reported in the public archives and in the records relating to Nehemiah ; and how, founding a library, he gathered together the things concerning the kings and prophets, and the (writings) of David, and letters of kings about sacred gifts.* And in like manner Judas also gathered together for us all those writings that had been scattered (τὰ διαπεπτωκότα) by reason of the war that we had ; and they remain with us. If, therefore, ye have need thereof, send some to fetch them unto you " (2^{13-15}).

These letters, whether they were prefixed to what follows by the author of the rest of the book, or by a later hand, are allowed on all hands to be spurious and full of untrustworthy matter ; † and the source referred to in the extract just cited—probably some pseudepigraphic writing—is in particular discredited by the legendary character of the other statements for which it is quoted as an authority. The passage *may*, however, contain an indistinct reminiscence of an early stage in the formation of a canon,—" the things relating to the kings and prophets" being a general designation of the writings (or some of them), now known as the " Former " and " Latter " Prophets, τὰ τοῦ Δαυεὶδ being some part of the Psalter, and the " letters of kings respecting offerings " being (possibly) documents, such as those excerpted in the Book of Ezra, respecting edicts issued by the Persian kings in favour of the Temple. But even though the statement be accepted as historical, manifestly the greater part of the Hagiographa would not be included in Nehemiah's collection. And from the expression "founding a *library*," it would naturally be inferred that Nehemiah's aim was the collection and preservation of ancient national literature generally, rather than

---

* ἐξηγοῦντο δὲ καὶ ἐν ταῖς ἀναγραφαῖς καὶ ἐν τοῖς ὑπομνηματισμοῖς τοῖς κατὰ τὸν Νεεμίαν τὰ αὐτά, καὶ ὡς καταβαλλόμενος βιβλιοθήκην ἐπισυνήγαγε τὰ περὶ τῶν βασιλέων καὶ προφητῶν καὶ τὰ τοῦ Δαυεὶδ καὶ ἐπιστολὰς βασιλέων περὶ ἀναθημάτων.

† *The Speaker's Comm. on the Apocrypha*, ii. p. 541 ; cf. Schürer, *Gesch. des Jüd. Volkes im Zeitalter Jesu Christi*, ii p. 741.

the determination, or selection, of such books as deserved the authority which we now express by the term "canonical." The utmost that follows from the passage is that, according to the [xxx] unknown author of the documents quoted, the books (or some of them) now constituting the second division of the Canon (the "Prophets"), and certain writings attributed to David, were collected together under Nehemiah, and that they formed part of a larger collection founded by him. But the origin of the statement is too uncertain, and its terms are too indefinite, for any far-reaching conclusion to be founded upon it.

3. The Fourth Book of Ezra. In this apocryphal book, written, as is generally agreed, towards the close of the 1st cent. A.D.,* Ezra, shortly before his death, is represented as lamenting to God that the Law is burnt, and as craving from Him the ability to re-write it, in order that after his decease men may not be left destitute of Divine instruction—" But if I have found grace in Thy sight, send the Holy Ghost into me, and I shall write all that hath been done in the world since the beginning, even the things which were written in Thy law, that men may find Thy path, and that they which will live in the latter days may live" ($14^{21f.}$). God grants Ezra's request: he prepares writing materials and five skilled scribes; the next day he hears a voice saying to him, "Ezra, open thy mouth, and drink that I give thee to drink" [cf. Ezek. 3^1], after which we read :—

"Then opened I my mouth, and, behold, He reached me a full cup, which was full, as it were, with water, but the colour of it was like fire. And I took it and drank ; and when I had drunk of it, my heart uttered understanding, and wisdom grew in my heart, for my spirit strengthened my memory ; and my mouth was opened, and shut no more. The Highest gave understanding unto the five men, and they wrote by course the things that were told them, in characters which they knew not,† and they sat forty days ; they wrote in the daytime, and at night they ate bread. As for me, I spake

---

* *Speaker's Comm. on the Apocrypha*, i. p. 81 ; Schürer, ii. 656 f.

† So the Syriac Version (the original text of 4 Ezr. is not extant): similarly the Ethiopic, Arabic, and Armenian (Hilgenfeld, *Messias Judæorum*, 1869, pp. 260, 321, 376, 432). The allusion is to the change of character, from the old type, known from the Siloam inscription and Phœnician inscriptions, to the so-called " square " type, which was attributed by tradition to Ezra. In point of fact, the transition was a gradual one, and not completed till long after Ezra's time. See the writer's *Notes on Samuel*, p. ix ff.

in the day, and by night I held not my tongue. In forty days they wrote 94 * books. And it came to pass, when the forty days were fulfilled, that the [xxxi] Highest spake, saying, The first that thou hast written † publish openly, that the worthy and the unworthy may read it : but keep the 70 last that thou mayest deliver them only to such as be wise among the people ; for in them is the spring of understanding, the fountain of wisdom, and the stream of knowledge. And I did so " (*ib.* v.[39-48]).

The same representation is frequently alluded to by the Fathers,‡ being derived in all probability from the passage of 4 Ezra just quoted. The point to be observed is that it contains no statement respecting either a completion of the Canon, or even a collection, or redaction, of such sacred books as were extant in Ezra's time: according to the representation of the writer, the books were actually *destroyed*, and Ezra re-wrote them by Divine inspiration. Moreover, not only did he re-write the 24 canonical books of the Old Testament, he re-wrote 70 apocryphal books as well, which are placed upon an equal, or, indeed (v.[46f.]), upon a higher level than the Old Testament itself ! No argument is needed for the purpose of showing that this legend is unworthy of credit : the crudely mechanical theory of inspiration which it implies is alone sufficient to condemn it. Nor can it be determined with any confidence what germ of fact, if any, underlies it. It is, however, observable that there are traces in the passage of a twofold representation: according to

---

* So the Syr. Eth. Arab. Arm. The Vulgate has " 204." Comp. W. R. Smith, *OTJC.* (ed. 1) p. 407 f. (more briefly, ed. 2, p. 151).

† *I.e.* the 24 canonical books of the OT., according to the regular Jewish computation (Strack, p. 434), viz. Gen. Ex. Lev. Num. Dt. Josh. Jud. Sam. Kings, Jer. Ez. Isa. the XII, Ruth, Ps. Job, Prov. Eccl. Song of Songs, Lam. Dan. Est. Ezr.-Neh. (below, p. 516), Chr.

‡ *E.g.* Iren. *adv. hær.* iii. 21. 2 (*ap.* Euseb. 5, 8) ; Clem. Al. i. 21, p. 392. See other references in Strack, p. 415. That the passage in Irenæus has no reference to a completion of the Canon by Ezra, and is based upon no independent source, is shown clearly by Strack, p. 415, from the context: after speaking of the marvellous manner in which, according to the legend, the LXX translators, working independently, agreed verbally in their results, ὥστε καὶ τὰ παρόντα ἔθνη γνῶναι ὅτι κατ' ἐπίπνοιαν τοῦ θεοῦ εἰσὶν ἡρμηνευμέναι αἱ γραφαί, Irenæus continues : "Nor is there anything remarkable in God's having thus acted ; for, *after the sacred writings had been destroyed* (διαφθαρεισῶν τῶν γραφῶν) in the exile under Nebuchadnezzar, when the Jews after 70 years had returned to their own country, He, in the days of Artaxerxes, inspired Ezra the priest, of the tribe of Levi, to rearrange (ἀνατάξασθαι) all the words of the prophets who had gone before, and to restore (ἀποκαταστῆσαι) to the people the legislation of Moses." Cf. Ryle, p. 239 ff. (² 250 ff.).

one (v.²⁰⁻³²), Ezra is regarded only as the restorer of the *Law*; according to the other (v.⁴⁴), he is regarded as the restorer of the entire Old Testament (and of the 70 apocryphal books besides). [xxxii] The first of these representations agrees with a tradition recorded elsewhere in Jewish literature, though expressed in much less extravagant language (*Succah* 20ᵃ): "The Law was forgotten out of Israel: Ezra came up [Ezr. 7⁶], and established it." * Whether this statement is simply based upon the phrase in Ezr. 7⁶, that Ezra was "a ready scribe in the law of Moses" (cf. v.¹¹· ²¹), or whether it embodies an independent tradition, may be uncertain: there exists no ground whatever for questioning the testimony of the compiler of the Book of Ezra, which *brings Ezra into connexion with the Law*. This, no doubt, is the historical basis of the entire representation: Ezra, the priest and scribe, was in some way noted for his services in connexion with the Law, the recollection of which was preserved by tradition, and (in 4 Ezr.) extended to the entire Old Testament. What these services were, we do not certainly know; they may have been merely directed towards promoting the observance of the law (cf. Neh. 8–10); but the term "scribe," and the form of the representation in 4 Ezr. (in so far as this may be supposed to rest upon an historical foundation), would suggest that they were of a literary character: it would not, for instance, be inconsistent with the terms in which he is spoken of in the OT. to suppose that the final redaction and completion of the Priests' Code, or even of the Pentateuch generally, was his work. But the passage supplies no historical support for the supposition that Ezra had any part either in the collection (or editing) of the OT. books generally, or in the completion of the OT. Canon.

4. The Talmud. Here the celebrated passage is in the *Bâba bâthra* 14ᵇ, which, after describing the *order* of the books of the OT., as cited above, continues thus :—

"And who wrote them? Moses wrote his own book and the section concerning Balaam,† and Job. Joshua wrote his own book and eight verses of the Law.‡ Samuel wrote his own book and Judges and Ruth. David

---

* Comp. Delitzsch, *Z. für Luth. Theol.* 1877, p. 446.

† Nu. 22²–25⁹. Named specially, as it seems, on account of its not being directly connected with the subject of the law (so Rashi [11th cent.] in his commentary on the passage).

‡ Dt. 34⁵⁻¹².

wrote the Book of Psalms, at the direction of * ten elders, viz. Adam,†
Melchizedek,‡ Abraham,§ Moses, Heman, Jeduthun, Asaph, and the three
sons of Korah. Jeremiah wrote his own book and the Book of Kings and
Lamentations. Hezekiah and his college wrote Isaiah, Proverbs, the Song
of Songs, and Qohéleth (Ecclesiastes). The Men of the Great Synagogue
wrote Ezekiel, the XII (Minor Prophets), Daniel, and Esther. Ezra wrote
his own book and the genealogies of the Book of Chronicles as far as himself." ‖

By the college, or company (סיעה), of Hezekiah, are meant,
no doubt, the literary associates of the king mentioned in Prov.
25¹. The "Great Synagogue," according to Jewish tradition,
was a permanent council, established by Ezra, which continued
to exercise authority in religious matters till about B.C. 300. But
the statements respecting it are obscure and vague; already
critics of the last century doubted whether such a permanent
body ever really existed; and in the opinion of many modern
scholars all that is told about it is fiction, the origin of which lies
in the (historical) narrative in Neh. 8–10 of the convocation
which met at Jerusalem and subscribed the covenant to observe
the law.¶ Into the further discussion of this question it is not
necessary for our present purpose to enter. The entire passage
is manifestly destitute of historical value. Not only is it late in

---

* על ידי. See p. 538, No. 34.   † Ps. 92, 139.   ‡ Ps. 110.

§ Ps. 89. Jewish exegesis understood (falsely) the "righteous man from
the East (ממזרח)" in Isa. 41² of Abraham : Ps. 89 is ascribed by the title to
Ethan the *Ezrahite* (האזרחי) ; and upon the supposition that the word אזרחי
is connected with מזרח "east" in Isa. 41², the Jews identified Ethan with
Abraham ! Ps. 89¹ Targ.: "Spoken by Abraham, who came from the
east." (There are other slightly different enumerations of the supposed
authors of Psalms : see the Midrash on Qohéleth, 7¹⁹, p. 105 f. of Wünsche's
translation, or on Cant. 4⁴ (substantially the same passage), *ap.* Neubauer,
Studia Biblica, vol. ii. p. 6 f., where Melchizedek is not named, and Ezra is
included ; also G. H. Dalman, *Traditio Rabbinorum veterrima de Libr.
V. T. ordine atque origine,* 1891, p. 44 f.).

‖ עד לו. Supposed to mean as far as the genealogies in 1 Ch. 6 (which
recites Ezra's ancestors, v.¹⁵, though not including himself). See especially
on this passage Dalman, *l.c.* pp. 14, 22 f., 41 ff. ; Ryle, p. 273 ff. (² 284 ff.).

¶ See J. E. Rau, *Diatribe de Synagoga Magna,* 1726 ; and esp. Kuenen,
"Over de Mannen der Groote Synagoge," tr. in his *Ges. Abhandlungen,* p.
125 ff. ; W. R. Smith, *OTJC.* p. 156 f. (² p. 169 f.) ; Buhl, § 9 ; Ryle, pp.
250-272 (² 261-283) ; and on the other side, J. Derenbourg, *Essai sur
l'hist. et la géogr. de la Palestine d'après les Thalmuds* (1867), p. 29 ff.; C.
H. H. Wright, *Ecclesiastes,* pp. 5 ff., 475 ff. Cf. also Taylor, *Sayings of the
Jewish Fathers* (the Mishnic treatise פרקי אבות), 1877, p. 124 f.

date; it is discredited by the character of its contents themselves. [**xxxiv**] What are we to think of the statement respecting the authorship of the Psalms? What opinion can we form
of the judgment of men who argue that because a person
(Melchizedek) happens to be mentioned in a particular poem,
he was therefore in some way connected personally with its composition?* or of the reasoning by which Abraham is brought
into relation with Ps. 89? Moreover, the word "wrote"†
(כתב) must plainly bear the same meaning throughout; what
sense then is to be attached to the statements about the college
of Hezekiah and the Men of the Great Synagogue? In what
sense can it be said that they "wrote" different books of the
Old Testament? The fact of so much of the passage being thus
unworthy of regard, discredits the whole. It is an indication
that it is not the embodiment of any genuine or trustworthy
tradition. In so far as the passage yields an intelligible sense,
it merely expresses inferences of the most superficial order :
it assigns books to prominent characters living at, or shortly
after, the times with which they deal.‡ The origin of the statements about the other books is uncertain. If any book bears the
impress of its author's hand, both in matter and in arrangement,
it is the Book of Ezekiel ; and yet it is said here to have been
"written" by the members of a body which (*ex hyp.*) did not
come into existence till a century after its author's death. If
some tradition of the manner in which the books referred to

---

* It is right, however, to mention that, according to some scholars (see
Wright, *l.c.* p. 453 ; Dalman, *Der Gottesname Adonaj*, 1889, p. 79), על ידי
means here *on behalf of* ; but even so, it will still be implied that the persons
named were in some sense the inspirers of the Psalms in question : for the
Jewish view, absurd as it may seem to be, is that the Psalms were composed
(lit. "spoken") by ten authors (עשרה בני אדם אמרו ספר תהלים), though in some
undefined way David gave form to their words (see the passages cited on p.
vii, *note* §, and similar statements elsewhere).

† Not "arranged," or edited," or even "inserted in the Canon." Rashi's
explanation (Strack, p. 418 ; Wright, p. 455 f.) is anything but satisfactory.
The supposition that the term means "wrote down" or "reduced to writing
what had previously been transmitted orally" is not probable, considering
the nature of the books referred to ; such a sense might be suitable in connexion with a body of law, or a system of traditional exegesis, perpetuated in
a school, but hardly, for instance, with reference to a volume of prophecies.

‡ Dalman, *Traditio Rabbinorum*, &c., p. 58, expresses a similar judgment.

were edited, or made generally available, for popular use underlies these statements, its character and source are far too doubtful
for any weight to be attached to it, where it [**xxxv**] conflicts
with the irrefragable testimony supplied by the books themselves
respecting their authorship or date.*

5. Josephus (1 cent. A.D.). In his work against Apion,
written to establish, against detractors, the antiquity of the Jews
and the trustworthiness of their history, Josephus, after remarking that the prophets were the only historians, continues (i. 8) :—

"For we have not myriads of discordant and conflicting books, but
twenty-two only, comprising the record of all time, and justly accredited as
Divine. Of these, five are the books of Moses, which embrace the laws and
the traditions of the origin of mankind, until his own death, a period of
almost 3000 years. From the death of Moses to the reign of Artaxerxes
[B.C. 465–425] the prophets who followed Moses narrated the events of their
own time in thirteen books.† The remaining four books ‡ consist of hymns
to God, and maxims of conduct for men. From Artaxerxes to our own age,
the history has been written in detail ; but it is not esteemed worthy of the
same credit, on account of the exact succession of the prophets having been
no longer maintained."

Josephus is dealing here primarily with the history, the
superior trustworthiness of which, as compared with that of the
Greeks, he desires to establish. He holds the prophets to be
the authors of the contemporary history : to the time of
Artaxerxes they form an unbroken series, hence to that date
the history is credible ; in the period which follows, the succession ceases, and the narratives relating to it are not equally
trustworthy. Upon what grounds this opinion rests does not
appear. Josephus appeals to no authority earlier than himself. His statements would be sufficiently accounted for by the
supposition that they rested upon a basis of fact, or reasonable
probability, in some cases (*e.g.* Hosea, Ezekiel, Kings), and were

---

* It should never be forgotten that, with regard especially to antiquity, the
Talmud and other late Jewish writings abound with idle conjectures and
unauthenticated statements.

† *I.e.* Joshua, Judges and Ruth, Sam., Kings, Chr., Ezra and Neh.,
Esther, Job, the Twelve Minor Prophets, Isaiah, Jer. and Lam., Ezek.,
Daniel.

‡ *I.e.* Psalms, Prov., Eccl., Song. Josephus disregards the more
historical tripartite division of the OT. accepted in Palestine, and follows
both the arrangement and the computation current in Alexandria (Strack,
p. 435 f.).

inferred to be true in other cases on the strength of assumed propriety, or of analogy: thus the books of Job, Joshua, and Daniel, for instance, would be written by men contemporary with the occurrences related in them. This inference, or theory, is the same as that drawn in the Talmud (p. viii), except that [**xxxvi**] it is applied more consistently. Josephus bears witness probably, to an opinion more or less current at the time: but the ultimate *source* of this opinion is not sufficiently certain for its authority to be regarded as decisive.*

For the opinion, often met with in modern books, that the Canon of the OT. was closed by Ezra, or his associates, there is no foundation in antiquity whatever. As has been shown above, all that can reasonably be treated as historical in the accounts of Ezra's literary labours is limited to the *Law*. The Men of the Great Synagogue—in so far as their services to Biblical literature may be accepted as historical—were a permanent body, which continued to act for more than a century after Ezra's time. The opinion referred to is not a tradition at all: it is a *conjecture*, based no doubt upon the passages that have been just cited, but inferring from them more than they actually express or justify. This conjecture was first distinctly propounded *in the* 16th *century* by Elias Levita, a learned Jew, the author of a work on the origin and nature of the Massorah, entitled *Massoreth ha-Massoreth*, written in 1538.† The reputation of Elias Levita caused this opinion to be adopted by the Protestant divines of the 17th and 18th centuries, Hottinger, Leusden, Carpzov, &c.; and it has thus acquired general currency. But it is destitute of historical foundation; and the authority of Ezra cannot, any more than that of the Great Synagogue, be invoked against the conclusions of critical investigation. The Canon of the Old Testament, in Loescher's words (quoted by Strack, p. 424), was "non uno, quod dicunt, actu ab hominibus, sed paulatim a Deo, animorum temporumque rectore, productus." The age and

---

* See further Wildeboer, pp. 40–43; Buhl, §§ 7, 9, 12; Ryle, p. 158 ff. (² 169 ff.).

† Edited, with an English translation and notes, by C. D. Ginsburg, London, 1867. See p. 120: "In Ezra's time the 24 books of the OT. were not yet united in a single volume; Ezra and his associates united them together, and divided them into three parts, the Law, the Prophets, and the Hagiographa." See further Strack, p. 416; Ryle, pp. 250–252 (² 261–264).

authorship of the books of the Old Testament can be determined (so far as this is possible) only upon the basis of the
internal evidence supplied by the books themselves, by methods
such as those followed in the present volume : no external
evidence worthy of credit exists.

AN INTRODUCTION

TO THE

LITERATURE OF THE OLD TESTAMENT.

CHAPTER I.

THE HEXATEUCH.

(Pentateuch and Joshua.)

LITERATURE.*—*a.* Commentaries:—A. Dillmann (in the *Kurzgefasstes Exegetisches Handbuch zum AT.*), *Die Genesis*[6], 1892; *Ex. und Lev.* 1880; *Numeri Deut. und Josua,* 1886; F. Delitzsch, *Neuer Commentar über die Genesis,* 1887 (translated: T. & T. Clark); C. F. Keil (in the *Biblischer Commentar über das AT.*, edited by himself and Delitzsch), *Gen. und Ex.*[3] 1878; *Lev. Num. und Deut.*[2] 1870; *Josua, Richter und Ruth*[2], 1874; M. Kalisch, *Hist. and Crit. Comm. on the OT.*, viz. *Genesis,* 1858; *Exodus,* 1855; *Leviticus,* 1867, 1872 (with much illustration from Jewish sources); Fr. Tuch, *Commentar über die Genesis*[2], 1871; G. J. Spurrell, *Notes on the Hebrew Text of Genesis*[2], Oxford, 1896; H. L. Strack (in Strack and Zöckler's *Kurzgefasster Kommentar*), 1892–94 (Gen.—Numbers: Dt. and Josh. by S. Oettli); G. A. Wade, *The Book of Genesis,* 1896; C. J. Ball in Haupt's *Sacred Books of the OT.* (see below) 1896. On the Cosmogony of Gen. i. (in its relation both to science and to the cosmogony of Babylonia) see Dillm. pp. 1–16; Riehm, *Der Biblische Schöpfungsbericht* (a Lecture), 1881; articles by the present writer in the *Expositor,* Jan. 1886 (where other literature is referred to), and the *Andover* (U.S.A.) *Review,* 1887, p. 639 ff. (a criticism of Prof. Dana's theory); C. Pritchard, *Occas. Notes of an Astronomer,* 1890, p. 257 ff.; Abbé Loisy, *Les Mythes Chaldéens de la Création et du Déluge* (Amiens, 1892); H. E. Ryle, *The Early Narratives of Genesis* (1892); H. Gunkel, *Schöpfung u. Chaos,* 1895.

b. Criticism:—H. Hupfeld, *Die Quellen der Genesis,* 1853; H. Ewald, *History of Israel*[3] (1864 ff. : translated, Longmans, 1869 ff.), i. pp. 63–132;

---

* Only the more important works can be named. The older literature, which has been largely superseded by more recent works, is of necessity omitted altogether

K. H. Graf, *Die geschichtlichen Bücher des AT.s*, 1866; Th. Nöldeke, *Die Alttestamentliche Literatur*, 1868; *Untersuchungen zur Kritik des AT.s*, 1869 (on the limits and characteristics of the document now generally styled P); J. Wellhausen, *Die Composition des Hexateuchs und der hist. Bücher des AT.s*, 1889 (the first part published originally in the *Jahrb. f. Deutsche Theol.* 1876, 1877; the second part in the same author's 1878 * edition of Bleek's *Einleitung*), *Gesch. Israels*, i. 1878, [2] under the title *Prolegomena zur Gesch. Israels*, 1883 ([4] 1895), translated under the title *History of Israel*, 1885; Ed. Reuss, *La Bible* (translation [2] with notes and Introductions), vol. i. 1879, pp. 1–271; F. Delitzsch, 12 *Pent.-kritische Studien* in the *ZKWL.* 1880, and *Urmosäisches im Pent., ib.* 1882, p. 113 ff. (on Nu. 6[22-7]), p. 226 ff. (Nu. 10[33-36]), p. 281 ff. (the Decalogue), p. 337 ff. (Nu. 21[14f.]), p. 449 ff. (Nu. 21[17f.]), p. 561 ff. (Nu 21[27-30]); also *ib.* 1888, p. 119 ff. (Balaam); A. Kuenen, *Bijdragen tot de critiek van Pent. en Josua* in the *Theol. Tijdschrift* xi.–xviii. (1877–84) [see the titles in Wellh. *Comp.* p. 312]; W. R. Smith, *The OT. in the Jewish Church* ([2]1892), esp. Lect. viii.–xiii.; David Castelli, *La Legge del Popolo Ebreo nel suo svolgimento storico*, 1884; W. H. Green, *The Hebrew Feasts*, 1886; R. Kittel, *Gesch. der Hebräer*, i. (Quellenkunde u. Geschichte der Zeit bis zum Tode Josuas [translated: follows Dillmann largely]), 1888; Vuilleumier in the *Rev. de Théol. et de Philos.* 1882 (pts. 1, 5, 7, 9, 11), 1883 (pts. 1, 3), 1884 (pt. 5); Prof. W. R. Harper's papers in *Hebraica*, v. (1888) 1, 4, vi. 1, 4, with Prof. W. H. Green's criticisms, *ib.* v. 2–3, vi. 2, 3, vii. 1, 2, viii. 1–2; the commentaries of Delitzsch [pp. 1–38 on the Hexateuch generally] and Dillmann (esp. the Schlussabhandlung, in *NDJ.* pp. 593–690), mentioned above; W. W. Graf Baudissin, *Die Gesch. des Alttest. Priesterthums* (1889), with Kautzsch's review in the *Stud. u. Krit.* 1890, p. 767 ff., and Kuenen's in the *Theol. T.* 1890, p. 1 ff. (=Kuenen's *Gesammelte Abhandlungen*, tr. by Budde, 1894, p. 465 ff.); C. G. Montefiore in the *Jewish Quarterly Review*, Jan. 1891, and "Hibbert Lectures" on *The Religion of the Ancient Hebrews* (1892); C. A. Briggs, *The Higher Crit. of the Hex.* (New York, 1893); Ed. König in the *Stud. u. Krit.* 1893, pp. 445–479, and the *Expositor*, Aug. 1896 (on the critical value of the argument from language); and the following "Introductions":—Eb. Schrader's edition (the 8th) of De Wette's *Einleitung*, 1869; Keil's *Einleitung*, 1873; E. C. Bissell, *The Pentateuch, its origin and structure*, 1885; Ed. Reuss, *Die Gesch. der Heiligen Schriften AT.s*[2], 1890; the very thorough work of A. Kuenen, *Hist.-crit. Onderzoek naar het Ontstaan en de Verzameling van de Boeken des Ouden Verbonds*[2], i.–iii. 1 (1885–1893: the first part tr. under the title *The Hexateuch*, 1886; and all tr. into German by Weber and Müller, 1887–1894; Ed. Riehm, *Einl. in das AT.* (published posthumously), 1889–90; C. H. Cornill, *Einleitung in das AT.* 1891,[3] 1896; Ed. König, *Einleitung in das AT. mit Einschluss der Apokryphen und der Pseudepigraphen Alten Testaments*, 1893; G. Wildeboer, *De Letterkunde des Ouden Verbonds naar de Tijdsorde van haar Ontstaan*, 1893 (tr. into German by F. Risch);

---

* In the editions of 1886 and 1893 *Bleek's* treatment of the OT. books mentioned is reprinted; and the only part written by Wellhausen is that relating to the Text and Versions.

Al. Westphal, *Les Sources du Pentateuque*, 1888, 1892; H. Holzinger, *Einleitung in den Hexateuch*, 1893; R. G. Moulton, *The Literary Study of the Bible*, 1896. In *Die Heilige Schrift des AT.s*, translated and edited by Em. Kautzsch, in conjunction with other scholars, the sources of the different books are marked by letters on the margin; the *Beilagen*, also, contain many useful notes on the criticism of the text, together with a synoptic chronological table, and a masterly "Abriss" of the history of OT. literature. A more elaborate work, designed for the same end, is *The Sacred Books of the OT.* (in parallel volumes, Hebrew and English), now in course of publication, under the editorship of Paul Haupt, consisting of a critically revised text, with short critical and exegetical notes, the structure of such books as are composite being indicated by the use of colours.

Books or articles dealing with special parts of the Hexateuch will be referred to as occasion arises. Of the works named, the most important (even for those who but partially accept its conclusions) is Wellhausen's essay *On the Composition of the Hexateuch*, partly on account of its lucid exposition of the subject, and partly on account of its forming the basis of all subsequent investigation and discussion. Next in importance come the writings of Dillmann, Delitzsch, and Kuenen. In Dillmann's commentaries, especially, details and references will usually be found, for which it has been impossible to find a place in the present volume. Kittel's work contains a useful synopsis and comparison of different views. The style and characteristics of the various sources of which the Hexateuch is composed are most abundantly illustrated in the papers of Prof. Harper, and in Holzinger's *Einleitung*. The chief question in dispute among critics concerns, not the *limits* of the several sources, but their relative dates (see below, § 7). Keil, Green, and Bissell represent the traditional view of the origin and structure of the Hexateuch. The reason why this cannot be maintained is, stated briefly, the presence in the Hexateuch (and in other parts of the Old Testament) of too many facts which conflict with it.

On the *history* of the critical study of the OT., see Cheyne, *Founders of OT. Criticism* (1893); Briggs, *Biblical Study*, chap. vii.: and with special reference to the Hexateuch, Westphal, *l.c.* i. pp. 45–228; Holzinger, pp. 25–70; Briggs, *The Higher Crit. of the Hex.* chaps. iv. vi.; Cornill, *Einl.* §§ 2, 6; Kuenen, *Hex.* pp. xi–xl (since 1860). The term "higher criticism" appears to have been first used in connexion with Biblical literature by Eichhorn; see the quotation from the 2nd ed. of his *Einleitung* (1787) in Dr. Briggs' *Biblical Study*, p. 204. The province of the "higher criticism" is to determine the origin, date, and literary structure of a writing: sometimes it is understood also to include the consideration of its historical value and credibility as well; but this is rather the work of the *historical* critic. The adjective (the sense of which is often misunderstood) has reference merely to the higher and more difficult class of problems, with which, as opposed to the "lower," or textual, criticism, the higher criticism deals (comp. Briggs, *l.c.* pp. 24, 86–92). Prof. Sayce, in his *"Higher Criticism" and the Verdict of the Monuments*, as well as in other recent writings, polemizes much against the "higher critics"; but his statements are often very inexact, and the defeats which he represents critics as constantly sustaining at the hands of archæology are purely imaginary, being obtained either by attributing to them opinions which they do not hold, or by basing upon the monuments more than they legitimately prove (see the articles by the present writer in the *Contemp. Rev.* March 1894, and the *Guardian*, Nov. 13, 1895, March 11 and Apr. 8, 1896). In point of fact, the general critical position has in no respect been affected unfavourably by recent archæological discovery, and in some cases it has been materially confirmed by it.   The standard work illustrating the OT. from Assyrian sources is Schrader's *Cuneiform Inscriptions and the OT.* (translated, 1885, 1888 : a new ed. of the German in preparation).   On some other aspects in which archæology has a bearing on the OT., see W. R. Smith, *Contemp. Rev.* Apr. and Oct. 1887.   The statements on biblical matters contained in Sir J. W. Dawson's *Modern Science in Bible Lands*, are to be received with distrust ; see the *Contemp. Rev.* March 1889, p. 399 ff.

On the *Texts* and *Versions* of the OT., the most recent information is to be found in Wellhausen's edition of Bleek's *Einleitung*, 1878, p. 563 ff. ; 1886 and 1893, p. 523 ff. ; or in König's *Einleitung*, pp. 14–133.   See also the present writer's *Notes on the Hebrew Text of Samuel*, 1890, p. xxxvi ff., with the references.   Of more general works, C. A. Briggs, *Biblical Study, its principles, methods, and history, together with a Catalogue of books of reference* (³1891); and G. T. Ladd, *What is the Bible?* (New York, 1890) may be recommended.

The historical books of the Old Testament form two series : [3] one consisting of the books from Genesis to 2 Kings,* embracing the period from the creation to the release of Jehoiachin from his imprisonment in Babylon, B.C. 562 ; the other, comprising the Books of Chronicles, Ezra, and Nehemiah, beginning with Adam and ending with the second visit of Nehemiah to Jerusalem in B.C. 432.† Though differing from each other materially in scope and manner of treatment, these two series are nevertheless both constructed upon a similar plan ; no entire book in either series consists of a single, original work ; but older writings, or sources, have been combined by a compiler in such a manner that the points of juncture are often plainly discernible, and the sources are in consequence capable of being separated from one another. The authors of the Hebrew historical books —except the shortest, as Ruth and Esther—do not, as a modern historian would do, *rewrite* the matter in their own language ; they excerpt from the sources at their disposal such passages as are suitable to their purpose, and incorporate them in their work,

---

* Exclusive of Ruth, which, at least in the Hebrew Canon, is treated as part of the כְּתוּבִים or *Hagiographa*.

† Though the genealogies are brought down to a later date.

sometimes adding matter of their own, but often (as it seems) introducing only such modifications of form as are necessary for the purpose of fitting them together, or accommodating them to their plan. The Hebrew historiographer, as we know him, is essentially a *compiler* or arranger of pre-existing documents, he is not himself an original author. Hebrew writers, however, exhibit, as a rule, such strongly marked individualities of style that the documents, or sources, thus combined can generally be distinguished from each other, and from the comments of the compiler, without difficulty. The literary differences are, moreover, frequently accompanied by differences of treatment or representation of the history, which, where they exist, confirm independently the conclusions of the literary analysis. Although, however, the historical books generally are constructed upon similar principles, the method on which these principles have been applied is not quite the same in all cases. The Books of Judges and Kings, for instance, resemble each other in their mode of composition : in each a series of older narratives has been taken by the compiler, and fitted into a framework supplied by himself, the framework in both cases being, moreover, composed of similar elements and [4] designed from the same point of view. The Books of Samuel are likewise constructed from pre-existing sources, but the compiler's hand is very much less conspicuous than is the case in Judges and Kings. The Pentateuch includes elements homogeneous, at least in large measure, with those of which the Book of Joshua is composed ; and the literary structure of both is more complex than that of either Samuel, or Judges and Kings. It will be our aim, in the following pages, to exhibit the structure of these different books by discovering, so far as this is possible, their component parts, and determining the relation which these parts hold in regard to each other.

§ 1. GENESIS.

The Book of Genesis is so called from the title given to it in the Septuagint Version, derived from the Greek rendering of 2⁴ᵃ αὕτη ἡ βίβλος γενέσεως οὐρανοῦ καὶ γῆς. By the Jews it is termed, from its opening word, בְּרֵאשִׁית *B'rēshīth*. It forms the first book in the *Hexateuch,*—as the literary whole formed by the

Pentateuch and Book of Joshua may conveniently be termed,—
the general object of which is to describe in their origin the
fundamental institutions of the Israelitish Theocracy (*i.e.* the civil
and ceremonial law), and to trace from the earliest past the course
of events which issued ultimately in the establishment of Israel
in Canaan.   The Book of Genesis comprises the introductory
period of this history, embracing the lives of the ancestors of
the Hebrew nation, and ending with the death of Joseph in
Egypt.   The aim of the book is, however, more than merely to
recount the ancestry of Israel itself; its aim is, at the same
time, to define the place occupied by Israel among other nations,
and to show how it gradually emerges into separate and distinct
existence.   Accordingly the line of its ancestors is traced back
beyond Abraham to the first appearance of man upon the earth;
and the relation, both to each other and to Israel, of the nations
descended from the second father of humanity — Noah — is
indicated by a genealogical scheme (c. 10).   The entire book
may thus be divided into two parts, of which the first, c. 1-11,
presents a general view of the *Early History of Mankind*,
explaining the presence of evil in the world (c. 3), sketching
[5] the beginnings of civilisation (c. 4), accounting for the existence of separate nations (c. 10. 11^{1-9}), and determining the position
occupied by Israel among them ($10^{1. 21. 22}$ 11^{10-26}); while the
second, c. 12-50, comprehends in particular the *History of
Israel's immediate ancestors, the Patriarchs*.

The narrative of Genesis is cast into a framework, or scheme,
marked by the recurring formula, *These are the generations*
(lit. *begettings*) *of* . . .   This phrase is strictly one proper to
genealogies, implying that the person to whose name it is prefixed
is of sufficient importance to mark a break in the genealogical
series, and that he and his descendants will form the subject
of the record which follows, until another name is reached
prominent enough to form the commencement of a new section.
By this means the Book of Genesis is articulated as follows :—

C. 1-4* (Creation of *heaven and earth*, 1^1-2^{4a}: second account of the
origin of man upon earth, followed by the story of the Fall, 2^{4b}-3^{24};

---

* The formula is here applied *metaphorically* to "heaven and earth," and
stands at 2^{4a}.   By analogy it will introduce an account of heaven and earth,
and of that which sprang from either, or could be regarded as its progeny.
This agrees with what is narrated in c. 1, but not with what follows in $2^{4bff.}$

growth of sin in the line of Cain, and progress of invention, 4^{1-24};
beginning of the line of Seth's descendants, $4^{25f.}$).

5^1–6^8 (*Adam* and his descendants, through Seth, to Noah, c. 5; the
increasing wickedness of the earth, 6^{1-8}).

6^9–9^{29} (History of *Noah* and his sons till their father's death, including, in
particular, the narrative of the Flood, 6^9–8^{22}; and the covenant made
by God with humanity in the person of Noah, 9^{1-17}).

10^1–11^9 (*Sons of Noah* and nations sprung from them, c. 10; the dispersion
of mankind over the earth, 11^{1-9}).

11^{10-26} (Line of *Shem* to Terah, the father of Abraham).

11^{27}–25^{11} (*Terah*, with the history of his descendants, Abram and Lot,
ending with the death of Abram).

25^{12-18} (*Ishmael*, with list of Arab tribes claiming descent from him).

25^{19}–35^{29} (Life of *Isaac*, with history of Esau and Jacob, until the time of
Isaac's death).

[6] C. 36 [see v.$^{1.\ 9}$] (*Esau* and his descendants, the rulers of the Edomites,
with a digression, v.$^{20-30}$, on the aboriginal inhabitants of Edom).

C. 37 [see v.^{2}]–50 (Life of *Jacob* subsequently to Isaac's death, and history
of his sons till the death of Joseph).*

With which of the component parts of Genesis this scheme
was originally connected, will appear subsequently. The entire
narrative, as now disposed, is accommodated to it. The attention of the reader is fixed upon Israel, which is gradually disengaged from the nations with which it is at first confused; at
each stage in the history, a brief general account of the collateral
branches having been given, they are dismissed, and the narrative
is limited more and more to the immediate line of Israel's
ancestors. Thus after c. 10 (the ethnographical Table) all the
descendants of Noah disappear except the line of Shem, $11^{10ff.}$;
after 25^{12-18} Ishmael disappears and Isaac alone remains; after
c. 36 Esau and his descendants disappear, and only Jacob is
left. The same method is adopted in the intermediate parts;
thus 19^{30-38} the relation to Israel of the collateral branches of

---

(for the narative here is silent respecting the *heavens*, the subject being the
formation of man, and the preparation of the earth to receive him). The
formula must here, therefore, contrary to usual custom, refer to what precedes. It is a plausible conjecture that originally it stood as the superscription to 1^1. (Dr. Green, *Hebraica*, v. 143–5, omits to observe that the
formula introduces some account of *the person himself* named in it, as well
as of his descendants.)

* The formula occurs next Nu. 3^1: see also Ru. 4^{18}, 1 Ch. 1^{29}↑ (from
Gen. 25^{12}). The close of one section is sometimes repeated so as to form the
starting-point of the section which follows: cf. Gen. $1^{27f.}$ with $5^{1t.}$; 5^{02} with
6^{10}; 11^{27} with 11^{26}.

Moab and Ammon is explained: 22²⁰⁻²⁴ (sons of Abraham's brother Nahor), and 25¹⁻⁴ (sons of Abraham's concubine Keturah), the relation to Israel of certain Aramaic and Arabian tribes is explained.

The unity of plan thus established for the Book of Genesis, and traceable in many other details, has long been recognised by critics. It is not, however, incompatible with the use by the compiler of pre-existing materials in the composition of his work. And as soon as the book is studied with sufficient attention, phenomena disclose themselves which show incontrovertibly that it is composed of distinct documents or sources, which have been welded together by a later compiler or redactor into a continuous whole. These phenomena are very numerous; but they may be reduced in the main to the two following heads: (1) the same event is doubly recorded; (2) the language, and frequently the representation as well, varies in different sections. Thus 1¹–2⁴ᵃ and 2⁴ᵇ⁻²⁵ contain a double narrative of the origin of man upon earth. It might, no doubt, [7] be argued *prima facie* that 2⁴ᵇᶠᶠ. is intended simply as a more detailed account of what is described summarily in 1²⁶⁻³⁰; and it is true that probably the present position of this section is due to the relation in which, speaking generally, it stands to the narrative of those verses; but upon closer examination differences reveal themselves which preclude the supposition that both sections are the work of the same hand. In 2⁴ᵇ ff. the order of creation is: 1. man (v.⁷); 2. vegetation (v.⁹; cf. v.⁵); 3. animals (v.¹⁹);* 4. woman (v.²¹ᶠ·). The separation made between the creation of woman and man, if it stood alone, might indeed be reasonably explained upon the supposition just referred to, that 2⁴ᵇᶠᶠ. viz. describes in detail what is stated succinctly in 1²⁷ᵇ; but the order in the other cases forms part of a progression evidently intentional on the part of the narrator here, and as evidently opposed to the order indicated in c. 1 (vegetation, animals, man). Not only, however, are there these *material* differences between the two narratives; they differ also in form. The style of 1¹–2⁴ᵃ is unornate, measured, precise, and particular phrases frequently recur. That of 2⁴ᵇᶠᶠ. is freer and more varied: the actions of God are described with some fulness and picturesqueness of

---

* The rendering "had formed" is contrary to idiom (see the writer's *Hebrew Tenses*, § 76 *Obs.*; and comp. also König, *Einl.* p. 173).

detail; instead of simply *speaking* or *creating*, as in c. 1, He *fashions, breathes* into man the breath of life, *plants, places, takes, sets, brings, closes up, builds,* &c. ($2^{7.\ 8.\ 15.\ 19.\ 21.\ 22}$), and even, in the allied c. 3 (v.[8]), *walks* in the garden: the recurring phrases are less marked, and *not the same* as those of 1^1-2^{4a}. In the narrative of the Deluge, 6^{9-13} (the wickedness of the earth) is a duplicate of 6^{5-8}, as is also 7^{1-5} of 6^{18-22}—the latter, with the difference that of every clean beast *seven* are to be taken into the ark, while in 6^{19} (cf. 7^{15}) *two* of every sort, without distinction, are prescribed; similarly $7^{22f.}$ (destruction of all flesh) repeats the substance of 7^{21}: there are also accompanying differences of representation and phraseology, one group of sections being akin to 1^1-2^{4a}, and displaying throughout the same phraseology, the other exhibiting a different phraseology, and being conceived in the spirit of $2^{4b}-3^{24}$ (comp. *e.g.* 7^{16} *shut in*, 8^{21} *smelled*, with $2^{7.\ 8.\ 15}$ &c.).* 17^{16-19} and 18^{9-15} the [8] promise of a son to Sarah is twice described, with an accompanying double explanation of the origin of the name *Isaac.*† The section $27^{46}-28^9$ differs appreciably in style from 27^{1-45}, and at the same time exhibits Rebekah as influenced by a different motive in suggesting Jacob's departure from Canaan, not as in 27^{42-4b} to escape his brother's anger, but to procure a wife agreeable to his parents' wishes (see $26^{34f.}$).‡ Further, in 28^{19} and 35^{15} we find two explanations of the origin of the name *Bethel*: 32^{28} and 35^{10}, two of *Israel*: 32^3 33^{16} Esau is described as already resident in Edom, while $36^{6f.}$ his migration thither is attributed to causes which could have come into operation only after Jacob's return to Canaan.§ The Book of Genesis presents a group of sections distinguished from the narrative on either side of them by differences of

---

* The composite character of the narrative of the Flood has been pointed out often; see the art. *Pentateuch*, by the present Bishop of Worcester, in Smith's *Dictionary of the Bible* ([1]1863), p. 776. On the phraseology see more fully below, pp. 129-125.

† There is a third explanation, from a third source (see below), in 21^0.

‡ Of course, men frequently act from more motives than one; and thus a difference of motive *in itself* is no ground for supposing that the narrative in which it appears is of composite authorship; but when, as here, it is *coincident* with a literary distinction, it tends, like the differences of representation just alluded to, to confirm the inferences deduced in the first instance from literary criteria alone.

§ Keil's explanation of this discrepancy is insufficient.

phraseology and style, and often by *concomitant* differences of representation : these differences, moreover, are not isolated, nor do they occur in the narrative indiscriminately : they are numerous, and reappear with singular persistency *in combination with each other*; they are, in a word, so marked that they can only be accounted for upon the supposition that the sections in which they occur are by a different hand from the rest of the book.

The sections homogeneous in style and character with 1^1–2^{4a} recur at intervals, not in Genesis only, but in the following books to Joshua inclusive; and when disengaged from the rest of the narrative, and read consecutively, are found to constitute a nearly complete whole, containing a systematic account of the *origines* of Israel, treating with particular minuteness the various ceremonial institutions of the ancient Hebrews (Sabbath, Circumcision, Passover, Tabernacle, Priesthood, Feasts, &c.), and displaying a consistent regard for chronological and other statistical data, which entitles it to be considered as the framework of our present Hexateuch. This source, or document, has received different names, suggested by one or other of the various characteristics attaching to it. [9] From its preference (till Ex. 6^3) for the absolute use of the name *God* ("Elohim") rather than *Jehovah*, it has been termed the *Elohistic* narrative, and its author has been called the *Elohist*; and these names are still sometimes employed. By Ewald it was termed the "Book of Origins";* by Tuch and Nöldeke, from the fact that it seemed to form the groundwork of our Hexateuch, the "Grundschrift"; by Wellhausen, and most other recent critics, it has been styled the "Priests' Code." This last designation is in strictness applicable only to the ceremonial sections in Ex.–Nu.; these, however, form such a large and characteristic portion of the work, that the title may not unsuitably be extended so as to embrace the whole; and it may be represented conveniently, for the sake of brevity, by the letter P.†

---

* *Ursprünge*,—Ewald's rendering of the Heb. תּוֹלְדוֹת ("generations"), the term (p. 6) characteristic of this source ; see his *Hist. of Israel*, i. 74–96.

† Dillmann uses the letter A. Wellhausen, who supposes the "Priests' Code" to have passed through more stages than one before it reached its present form, denotes the nucleus of it by the letter Q. This letter is chosen by him on account of the *four* (Quatuor) covenants described in it (with Adam, 1^{28-30}; Noah, 9^{1-17}; Abraham, c. 17 ; Israel, Ex. $6^{2ff.}$). The first of these, however, is not properly a covenant, but a blessing.

In Genesis, as regards the limits of P, there is practically no difference of opinion amongst critics. It embraces the description of the Creation of heaven and earth, and of God's rest upon the Sabbath ($1^1 2^{4a}$); the line of Adam's descendants through Seth to Noah ($5^{1-28. 30-32}$); the story of the Flood, with the subsequent blessing of Noah, and covenant established with him by God ($6^{9-22} 7^{6. 11. 13-16a. 17a}$ [except *forty days*] $^{18-21. 24} 8^{1-2a.}$ $^{3b,-5. 13a. 14-19} 9^{1-17. 28-29}$); an enumeration of nations descended from Japhet, Ham, and Shem ($10^{1-7. 20. 22-23. 31-32}$); the line of Shem's descendants to Terah (11^{10-26}); a brief account of Abraham's family ($11^{27. 31-32}$), of his migration to Canaan, and separation there from Lot ($12^{4b-5} 13^{6. 11b}$ [from *and they*] $^{-12a}$ [to *Plain*]), of the birth of Ishmael ($16^{1a. 3. 15-16}$), the institution of Circumcision (c. 17), the destruction of the Cities of the Plain (19^{29}), the birth of Isaac ($21^{1b. 2b-5}$), the purchase of the family burial-place at Machpelah in Hebron (c. 23), the death of Abraham and his burial by his sons at Machpelah ((25^{7-11a}); a list of tribes tracing their origin to Ishmael (25^{12-17}); Isaac's marriage with Rebekah, Esau's Hittite wives, Jacob's journey to Paddan-Aram to obtain a wife [10] agreeable to his mother's wishes ($25^{19-20. 26b} 26^{34-35} 27^{46}-28^9$), Jacob's marriage with Rachel, his return from Paddan-Aram to Canaan ($29^{24. 29} 31^{18b}$ [from *and all*] 33^{18a}), the refusal of his sons to sanction intermarriage with the Shechemites ($34^{1-2a. 4. 6. 8-10. 13-18. 20-24. 25}$ [partly] $^{27-29}$), his change of name to Israel at Bethel ($35^{9-13. 15}$), the death of Isaac (35^{22b-29}); the history of Esau (c. 36 [in the main]);* the migration of Jacob and his family to Egypt, and their settlement by Pharaoh in the land of Rameses (37^{1-2a} [to *Jacob*] $41^{46} 46^{6-27} 47^{5-6a.}$† $^{7-11. 27b}$ [from *and they*] ^{28}), Jacob's adoption of Ephraim and Manasseh ($48^{3-6. 7}$), the final charge

---

* For it is generally allowed that v.$^{2-5. 9-28}$ (though even here the framework appears to be that of P) include an element foreign to P : in particular, the names of Esau's wives differ from those given in $26^{34f.} 28^9$ (both P), and must thus have been derived, most probably by the compiler, from a different source.

† As read in LXX, where, though the substance is unaltered, the sequence is preferable : "And Jacob and his sons came into Egypt to Joseph ; and Pharaoh, king of Egypt, heard of it. And Pharaoh spake unto Joseph, saying, Thy father and thy brethren are come unto thee : behold, the land of Egypt is before thee ; in the best of the land make thy father and thy brethren to dwell." Then follows v.^{7}.

addressed by him to his sons, and his burial by them ($49^{1a.\ 28b-33}$ 50^{12-13}).

These passages present an outline of the antecedents and patri-archal history of Israel, in which only important occurrences—as the Creation, the Deluge, the Covenants with Noah and Abraham—are described with minuteness, but which is sufficient as an introduction to the systematic view of the theocratic insti-tutions which is to follow in Ex.–Nu., and which it is the main object of the author of this source to exhibit. In the earlier part of the book the narrative appears to be tolerably complete; but elsewhere there are evidently omissions (*e.g.* of the birth of Esau and Jacob, and of the events of Jacob's life in Paddan-Aram, presupposed by 31^{18}).* But these may be naturally attributed to the compiler who combined P with the other narrative used by him, and who in so doing not unfrequently gave a preference to the fuller and more picturesque descriptions contained in the latter. If the parts assigned to P be read attentively, even in a translation, and compared with the rest of the narrative, the peculiarities of its style will be apparent. Its language is [II] that of a jurist, rather than a historian; it is circumstantial, formal, and precise: a subject is developed systematically; and completeness of detail, even at the cost of some repetition, is regularly observed.† Sentences are cast with great frequency into the same mould; ‡ and particular formulæ are constantly repeated, especially such as articulate the progress of the narra-tive. § The attention paid by the author to numbers, chrono-logy, and other statistical data, will be evident. It will also be apparent that the scheme into which, as was pointed out above, the Book of Genesis, as a whole, is cast, is his work,—the formula by which its salient divisions are marked constituting an essential feature in the sections assigned to P.

The parts of Genesis which remain after the separation of P have next to be considered. These also, as it seems, are not homogeneous in structure. Especially from c. 20 onwards the

---

* Fragments of P's narrative may be preserved in $30^{1a.\ 4a.\ 9b.\ 22a}$.

† *E.g.* $7^{11.\ 13-16}$ $9^{9-11.\ 12-17}$ $17^{10-14.\ 23-27}$ $49^{29-30.\ 32}$.

‡ *E.g.* $1^{5b.\ 8b.\ 13}$ &c.; $5^{6-8.\ 9-11.\ 12-14}$ &c.; $11^{10-11.\ 12-13}$ &c.; 12^{4b} 16^{16} $17^{24.\ 25}$ 21^5 25^{26b} 41^{46a}, Ex. 7^7, Nu. 33^{39}.

§ " These are the generations of . . ." (above); $1^{5b.\ 8b.\ 13}$ &c.; 10^5 [see *QPB*³] $20.\ 31.\ 32$ 25^{16} $36^{40.\ 43}$ &c.; 6^{22} compared with Ex. 7^6 $12^{28.\ 50}$ (and else-where). See more fully p. 129 f.

narrative exhibits marks of composition; and the component parts, though not differing from one another in diction and style so widely as either differs from P, and being so welded together that the lines of demarcation between them frequently cannot be fixed with certainty, appear nevertheless to be plainly discernible. Thus in 20$^{1\text{-}17}$ our attention is arrested by the use of the term *God*, while in c. 18–19 (except 19^{29} P), and in the similar narrative 12$^{10\text{-}20}$, the term *Jehovah* is uniformly employed. The term *God* recurs similarly in 21$^{6\text{-}31}$ 22$^{1\text{-}13}$ and elsewhere, particularly in c. 40–42. 45. For such a variation in similar and consecutive chapters no plausible explanation can be assigned except diversity of authorship.* At the same time, the fact that *Elohim* is not here accompanied by the other criteria of P's style, forbids our assigning the sections thus characterized to that source. Other phraseological criteria are slight; [12] there are, however, not unfrequently differences of representation, some of which will be noticed below, which point decidedly in the same direction. It seems thus that the parts of Genesis which remain after the separation of P are formed by the combination of *two* narratives, originally independent, though covering largely the same ground, which have been united by a subsequent editor, who also contributed inconsiderable additions of his own, into a single, continuous narrative. One of these sources, from its use of the name *Jahweh*, is now generally denoted by the letter J; the other, in which the name *Elohim* is preferred, is denoted similarly by E; and the work formed by the combination of the two is referred to by the double letters JE. The method of the compiler, who combined J and E together, was sometimes, as it would seem, to extract an entire narrative from one or other of these sources (as 20$^{1\text{-}17}$ from E; c. 24 from J); sometimes, while taking a narrative as a whole from one source, to incorporate with it notices derived from the other; and sometimes to construct his narrative of materials derived from each source in nearly equal proportions.

* It is true that *Elohim* and *Jahweh* represent the Divine Nature under different aspects, viz. as the God of nature and the God of revelation respectively; but it is only in a comparatively small number of instances that this distinction can be applied without great artificiality to explain the variation between the two names in the Pentateuch.

In the *details* of the analysis of JE there is sometimes uncertainty, owing to the criteria being indecisive, and capable, consequently, of divergent interpretation. Points of minor importance being disregarded, the analysis, so far as it seems to the writer to be reasonably clear, is exhibited in the following tables. E first appears in the history of Abraham (c. 15 or 20).*

I. c. 1–11. *The beginnings of history.*

J 2^{4b}–3^{24} 4^{1-26} 5^{29} $6^{1-4.\ 5-8}$ $7^{1-5.\ 7-10}$ (in the main) † $^{12.\ 16b}$ [standing originally after v. ^{9}] $^{17b.}$ $^{22-23}$ $8^{2b-3a.\ 6-12.\ 13b.\ 20-22}$ 9^{18-27} $10^{8-19.\ 21.\ 24-30}$ $11^{1-9.\ 28-30}$.

[13] The rest belongs to P (above, p. 11 f.). 4^{25-26} 5^{29} are fragments of the line of Seth, as it was given in J, the final redactor of the Pentateuch (R) having preferred in the main the line as given by P ($5^{1-28.\ 30}$): notice that in point of fact the verses $4^{25f.}$ are *parallel* to $5^{3.\ 6}$: notice further the difference in style of 5^{29} from the rest of the ch., and the resemblance to $4^{25f.}$, as well as the allusion to $3^{16f.}$ (also J). In the account of the Flood, the main narrative is that of P, which has been enlarged by the addition of elements derived from J: here, however, these elements form a tolerably complete narrative, though there are omissions, *e.g.* between 6^8 and 7^1 of the instructions for making the ark, the redactor having preferred the account of P: and in what follows, the narrative of J, for a similar reason, is not perfectly complete. The distinguishing characteristics of the two narratives are well exhibited by Delitzsch (p. 164 f.): each viz. is marked by a series of *recurring features* which are absent from the other, and by which it is connected with other sections of the book, belonging respectively to the same source (comp. above, p. 9). The interchange of *Jehovah* and *God* is here specially noticeable. In c. 10 the scheme of P is singularly clear: v.^{1} is the title to the entire section, dealing with the "sons of Noah"; v.$^{2-5}$ sons of Japheth, with subscription: v.$^{6-7.\ 20}$ sons of Ham, with subscription: v.$^{22-23.\ 31}$ sons of Shem, with subscription: v.^{32} the subscription to the entire section. The framework of the

---

* The notes appended are not intended to do more than afford a partial indication of the grounds on which the analysis rests; for fuller details reference must be made to the more special works named, p. 1 f. The Book of Genesis has been published (in German), in a convenient form, with the different sources distinguished typographically, by Kautzsch and Socin (*Die Genesis mit äusserer Unterscheidung der Quellenschriften* ^{2}, 1891). Great pains and care have been bestowed upon the preparation of this work; but the details, so far as the line of demarcation between J and E, and the parts assigned to the redactor, are concerned, can in many cases not claim more than a *relative* probability, as the editors themselves avow. A more elaborate work of the same kind is B. W. Bacon, *The Genesis of Genesis* (Hartford, U.S.A., 1892): see also C. J. Ball's edition (above, pp. 1, 3).

† For v.$^{7-9}$ include two or three expressions ("two and two," "male and female," "God" [Sam. Targ. Vulg. "Jehovah"]) borrowed by the redactor from P.

ch. is thus supplied by P, and into it notices of the nations descended from Noah, derived from J, have been inserted by the final redactor. Observe that v.^{22} *begins* the third main division of the ch., and that v.^{21}, taken strictly, is out of place before it : v.$^{24f.}$ contain J's account of Shelah, Eber, and Peleg, parallel to that of P in 11$^{12-17}$ (comp. 4$^{25f.}$ beside 5$^{3-8}$).

Notice also that the genealogies in J (both here and elsewhere) are *cast in a different mould* from those of P, and are connected together by similarities of expression, which do not occur in P : thus in 4$^{17-26}$ 10$^{8-19.\ 21.\ 24-30}$ 19$^{37-38}$ 22$^{20-24}$ 25$^{1-6}$ notice the recurrence of the form of sentence, *Unto . . . was born* : of ילד (not הוליד, as in P) used of the father ; of נם הוא ; and of the phrase *the father of . . .* (see Budde, *Die Biblische Urgeschichte*, 1883, pp. 220–223). On the question whether J's narrative in c. 1–11 is really a literary unity, it must suffice to refer to Holzinger, *Einl.* p. 138 ff.

II. c. 12–26. *Abraham and Isaac.*

$$\begin{cases} J \\ E \end{cases} 12^{1-4a.\ 6-20}\ 13^{1-5.\ 7-11a} \text{ (to } East) \ ^{12b} \text{ (from } and\ moved) \ ^{13-18} \quad \text{c. } 15 \qquad 16^{1b-2.\ 4-14}$$

$$\begin{cases} J \\ E \end{cases} 18^1-19^{28.\ 30-38} \qquad 21^{1a.\ 2a} \qquad\qquad 33 \qquad\qquad 22^{15-18} \qquad 20-24 \\ \qquad\qquad\quad 20^{1-17.\ (18)} \qquad 21^{6-21.\ 22-32a.\ (32b)} \quad (34)\ 22^{1-14} \qquad 19$$

$$\begin{cases} J \\ E \end{cases} \text{c. } 24.\ 25^{1-6.\ 11b.\ 18.\ 21-26a.\ 27-34}\ 26^{1-14.\ (15).\ 16-17.\ (18).\ 19-33}$$

The verses enclosed in parentheses appear to be due to the compiler of JE. The parts not included in the table belong to P (p. 11 f.), with the exception of c. 14, the character of which points to its being taken from a [14] special source. The historical improbabilities of the narrative contained in this ch. have been exaggerated : but though the four names in v.^{1} correspond, more or less exactly, with those of kings (*c.* B.C. 2300) which have been discovered recently in the Inscriptions, there is at present (Dec. 1896) no monumental corroboration of any part of the following narrative (see the writer's articles in the *Guardian*, 1896, Mar. 11 and Apr. 8). C. 15 shows signs of composition ; but the criteria are indecisive, and no generally accepted analysis has been effected : it is therefore printed in the table *between* the J and E lines. Several recent critics have assigned to E v.$^{1.\ 3a.\ 2b.\ 5}$, and to J v.$^{2a.\ 3b.\ 4.\ 6-11.\ 17-18}$, regarding v.$^{12-16.\ 19-21}$ as expansions due to a later hand (or hands) ; see, further, Bacon, *Hebraica*, vii. (1890), p. 75 f.

19^{29} belongs to P. Observe (1) *God* twice, *Jehovah* having been regularly used before (*e.g.* v.$^{13.\ 14.\ 16.\ 24.\ 27}$) ; (2) *remembered* (see 8^1 in P ; and Ex. 2^{24}) ; (3) " cities of the Plain," as 13^{12} P. The verse further betrays itself as an insertion in its present context, in that it *repeats* in other words the substance of the preceding narrative ; and secondly in the *general* statement that Lot dwelt in " the cities of the Plain," which would fall naturally from a writer compiling a summary account of the occurrence (and is actually used by P in 13^{12}), but hardly so from one who had just before named Sodom repeatedly as the *particular* city in which Lot dwelt.

With 21^{33} (" called on the name of Jehovah ") comp. 4^{26} 12^8 13^4 26^{25}.

26^{3b-5} has probably (on grounds of style: see Del.) been expanded or recast by the compiler. The same may have been the case with 22^{15-18}. $26^{15.\ 18}$ appear to be additions made by the compiler for the purpose of harmonizing with $21^{25ff.}$. Observe in v.^{33} the different explanation of the name "Beersheba," as compared with 21^{31} (E). It has been plausibly conjectured that in c. 24–26 a transposition has taken place, and that the original order was $25^{1-6.\ 11b}$ c. 24 (observe that v.^{36} appears to *presuppose* 25^5) 26^{1-33} $25^{21-26a.\ 27-34}$, of which c. 27 is now the natural sequel.

III. c. 27–36. *Jacob and Esau.*

$$\begin{cases} J & 27^{1-45}\ 28^{10} & & ^{13-16} & ^{19} & & ^{2-14} & & ^{31-35} \\ E & & ^{11-12} & & ^{17-18} & ^{20-22}\ 29^1 & & ^{15-23.\ 25-28.\ 30.} & & 30^{1-3a}\ (\text{to } knees) \end{cases}$$

$$\begin{cases} J & 30^{3b-5} & ^7 & ^{9-16} & ^{20b}\ (now \ldots sons) & & ^{22b\beta} & ^{24}-31^1 & ^3 \\ E & & ^6 & ^8 & ^{17-20a} & ^{20c-22b\alpha} & ^{23} & & 31^2 & ^{4-18a.\ 19-45} \end{cases}$$

$$\begin{cases} J & 31^{46} & ^{48-50} & & 32^{3-13a} & ^{22} & ^{24-32} & 33^{1-17} & & 34^{2b-3.\ 5.\ 7.\ 11-12.\ 19} \\ E & & ^{47} & ^{51}-32^2 & & ^{13b-21} & ^{23} & & ^{18b-20} & \end{cases}$$

$$\begin{cases} J & 34^{25}\ (\text{partly})\ ^{26.\ 30-31} & & 35^{14} & ^{21-22a} \\ E & & 35^{1-8} & ^{16-20} & \end{cases}$$

In 27^{1-45} some critics discover the traces of a double narrative, and consider accordingly that the narrative of J has been supplemented by details taken from E; but it is doubtful whether the grounds alleged are decisive.

In 28^{10-22} the main narrative is E, v.$^{13-16}$ being inserted from J. Both narratives contained the account of the theophany at Luz, E giving prominence to the dream and vision of the ladder, which made the place one "where heaven and earth meet" (v.^{17} being the sequel to v.^{12}), J to the words of promise addressed to Jacob; the compiler has united the two [15] accounts, as mutually supplementing each other. The promise in v.$^{13t.}$, as elsewhere in J ($13^{14-16}\ 12^3$), accommodated in v.^{15} to Jacob's present situation. Render v.^{13} as RV *marg.* (see 18^2 Heb.): in J Jehovah appears *standing beside* Jacob as he slept.

In 29^{31}–30^{24} (births of Jacob's children) the main narrative is J, with short notices from E. Notice *God* interchanging with *Jehovah*, and the *double etymologies* in $30^{16.\ 18}$, $30^{20a.b}$, 30^{23} (with *God*) ^{24} (with *Jehovah*). But in c. 29–32 it must remain an open question whether the points of separation between J and E have in all cases been rightly determined (see also p. 12 *note**).

In 30^{25}–31^{18a} (the parting of Jacob and Laban), 30^{25}–31^1 is mainly J, 31^{2-18a} mainly E. The two sources give a different account of the arrangement between Jacob and Laban, and of the manner in which, nevertheless, Jacob prospered. The success which in $30^{35ff.}$ is attributed to Jacob's stratagem, with the effect of the striped rods upon the ewes in the flock, is in 31^{7-12} attributed to the frustration by Providence of Laban's attempt, by repeatedly altering his terms, to overreach Jacob, and to the fact that only the striped he-goats leaped upon the ewes. Each account, however, appears also to contain notices incorporated from the other, which, in some cases, harmonize imperfectly with their present context, and complicate the interpretation (for details see Dillmann or Delitzsch).

31$^{45-54}$ may have been in parts expanded or glossed by the compiler; v.$^{45. 47. 51-54}$ appear to embody E's account of the covenant between Jacob and Laban; v.$^{46. 48-50}$ the account given by J. Observe that the covenant in v.^{50} is *different* in its terms from the covenant in v.^{52}.

In c. 34 the analysis is not throughout equally certain; but marks of P's style appear unmistakably in some parts, while they are absent in others, and the motives and aims of the actors seem not to be uniformly the same (cf. p. 9 *n.*). In v.$^{3. 11-12}$ Shechem himself is the spokesman, and his aim is the *personal* one of securing Dinah as his wife; in v.$^{8-10}$ (cf. v.$^{16. 21-23}$) his father Hamor is spokesman, and his aim is to secure an amalgamation between his people and Jacob's: observe also the similarity in the terms in which circumcision is mentioned v.$^{15b. 22b. 24b}$ and 17^{10b} (P), and between v.^{24} and 23$^{10b. 18b}$ (also P). But it is not impossible that P here is based upon elements derived from E; see Wellh. *Comp.* p. 312 ff.; Cornill, *ZATW.* 1891, p. 1 ff.; and cf. 35^5 48^{22} (both E). In 35^{21-22a} notice *Israel* for *Jacob* (cf. p. 19).

IV. c. 37–50. *Joseph.*

$$\begin{cases} J \\ E \end{cases}$$ 37^{2b} (from *Joseph*) $\begin{matrix} & & 12\text{-}18 & & 21 & & 25\text{-}27 & & & & 28b \text{ (to } silver) & & 31\text{-}35 \\ ^{3\text{-}11} & & 19\text{-}20 & & 22\text{-}24 & & 28a \text{ (to } pit) & & & & 28c\text{-}30 & & 36 \end{matrix}$

[16]

$$\begin{cases} J \\ E \end{cases}$$ c. 38 c. 39 $\begin{matrix} & & & & 42^{38}\text{-}44^{34} \dagger & & & 46^{28}\text{-}47^{4. \ 6b} \ddagger \\ \text{c. } 40 * \ 41^{1\text{-}45}. * \ 47\text{-}57 \ 42^{1\text{-}37} & & & 45^1\text{-}46^5 * & & \end{matrix}$ 12

$$\begin{cases} J \\ E \end{cases}$$ $\begin{matrix} 47^{13\text{-}26. \ 27a} \text{ (to } Goshen) & 29\text{-}31 & & 49^{1b\text{-}28a} \ 50^{1\text{-}11. \ 14} \\ & 48^{1\text{-}2. \ 8\text{-}22} \S & & 15\text{-}26 \end{matrix}$

Though the analysis of c. 37 is in parts uncertain, the differences of representation which it exhibits show that it is of composite origin. Thus v.^{28} is not the continuation of v.$^{25-27}$: notice the indefinite expression, "and there passed by Midianites, merchantmen," which evidently describes the *first* appearance of merchants upon the scene: the *sequel* to v.^{25} would have

---

* With traces of J, as 40$^{1b. \ 3b. \ 15b}$ 41^{14} ("and they brought him quickly from the dungeon") 42$^{27-28}$ 45^4 ("whom ye sold into Egypt") ^{5} ("that ye sold me thither") 45^{10} (to *Goshen*) ^{28} 46^1 ("*Israel*"). Here, as in other cases, the details of the analysis (subject to the reservation which is sometimes necessary) may be seen most conveniently in Kautzsch and Socin's edition of Genesis, or in the edition of Mr. Ball.

† With traces of E (43$^{14. \ 23b}$ "and he brought Simeon out unto them").

‡ As read in LXX, viz. (directly answering v.^{4}): "And Pharaoh said unto Joseph, Let them dwell in the land of Goshen; and if thou knowest that there are able men amongst them, then make them," &c. Then follows v.$^{5-6a}$ (P), as given above, p. 11 *note.*

§ In the main, probably; but the two narratives cannot here be disengaged with certainty. Perhaps v.$^{13-14. \ 17-19}$ are from J.

been expressed by "and *the* Ishmaelites drew near" (or some similar verb, but with the subject *definite*): v.[28] is thus *parallel* to v.[25-27], not the sequel to it. Notice, further, that it is *twice* said that Joseph was brought into Egypt and sold there; once, 37[36], by the *Midianites*, in agreement with v.[28a. c]; the other time, 39[1], by the *Ishmaelites*, in agreement with v.[28b]. Again, if in v.[28] the subject of "they drew" be Joseph's brethren, it is strange, as Reuben appears clearly to be in their company, that, going afterwards to the pit, he should be surprised at not finding Joseph in it; on the other hand, if "they" refer to the Midianite merchants passing by, who *drew up Joseph from the pit* without his brothers' knowledge, the surprise of Reuben is at once explained, and the expression in 40[15] "for I was *stolen* out of the land of the Hebrews" exactly describes what had occurred. If 37[21. 25-27. 28b] (And they sold . . . silver) [31-35] 39[1] &c., on the one hand, and 37[22-24. 28a. c. 29-30. 36], on the other, be read consecutively, they will be found to form two complete *parallel* accounts of the manner in which Joseph was taken into Egypt, each (as will appear presently) connecting with two corresponding narratives in the chapters following: in one (J) Joseph is *sold* by his brethren to *Ishmaelites*, in the other (E) he is cast by his brethren into a pit, and *stolen* thence by the *Midianites* without his brothers' knowledge. V.[21] is tautologous beside v.[22a], but forms an excellent introduction to v.[25-27]. Notice that in J *Judah* takes the lead (so 43[3] 44[14ff.]); in E *Reuben* (so 42[22. 37]): it is considered by many critics that "Reuben" in v.[21] was originally "Judah."

The narrative of Joseph in c. 39 ff. consists, as it seems, of long passages excerpted alternately from J and E, each, however, embodying traits derived from the other. The ground of this conclusion is the observation—(*a*) that the representation in different parts of the narrative varies; (*b*) that in each of these long passages occur short, isolated notices, not in entire harmony with the context in which they are embedded, but *presupposing different circumstances*. Thus (*a*) in c. 42 Joseph's brethren are charged with being spies, and in reply volunteer the information about their younger brother (v. [17] [7-13. 30-32]); in the report of what had occurred given in c. 43, there is no allusion to such a charge, and Joseph is expressly said to have *asked* them if they had a brother (v.[6-7]: so 44[19]); (*b*) 42[35] comes unexpectedly after v.[27t.], but agrees with v.[25]: having been given special provision for the way (v.[25]), the brethren naturally make the discovery that the money is in their sacks only at the end of the journey. On the other hand, 42[27t.] harmonizes with 43[19t.], where the discovery is made *at the lodging place*. The former is E's account, the latter J's, 42[27t.] being inserted in E from J. Further, in 42[19-24. 33-37] the detention of Simeon is an essential feature of the narrative; but in 42[38]–43[10], and again in 44[18-34], there is entire silence respecting him; his release is not one of the objects for which the brethren return to Egypt. Had the whole narrative been by one hand, it would have been natural to find Simeon mentioned *in the parts of c.* 43-44 *where he is unnoticed*. The notices of Simeon in 43[14. 23b], agreeing thus imperfectly with their immediate context (J), appear to have been inserted in it from the parallel narrative (E). (A similar point connected with c. 39 is noticed by the commentators.) Phraseological indications pointing to the same conclusion are—(*a*) *Jehovah* in 39[2. 3. 5. 21. 23], *God* in 41[51. 52] 45[5b. 7-9] 46[2]. (The use of *God* elsewhere in these sections, in converse with Egyptians, or between Joseph, whilst in disguise, and his brethren, is naturally inconclusive either *for* E, 40^8 41^{16} &c., or *against* J, 43^{29} 44^{16}.) (*b*) A preference for *Israel* as the name of the patriarch in one group of passages ($37^{3.\ 13}$ $43^{6.\ 8.\ 11}$ $46^{29.\ 30}$ $47^{29.\ 31}$ $48^{8.\ 10.\ 13.\ 14}$ 50^2 : J), and for *Jacob* in the other ($42^{1.\ 4.\ 29.\ 36}$ $45^{25.\ 27}$ $46^{2.\ 5}$ 48^2 : E),—a preference so decided as to make it probable that in the few passages where, in the context of J, *Jacob* occurs (37^{34}), or, in the context of E, *Israel* (45^{28} $46^{1.\ 2}$ $48^{2b.\ 11.\ 21}$), the variation is either a change made by the compiler, or is due to the use by him of the other source. The unusual word אמתחת *sack* occurs thirteen times in c. 43–44 (J): by a remarkable coincidence it also occurs twice in the two verses $42^{27f.}$, which, on independent grounds, were assigned above to the same source; E uses the more ordinary term שׂק $42^{25.\ 35}$ (also v. ^{27a} J).

In c. 49 the Blessing of Jacob is, of course, incorporated by J from an independent source. The historical and geographical conditions reflected in it are those of the period of the Judges, Samuel, and David; and this is the age in which the ancient tradition of the patriarch's blessing must have been cast into its present poetical form (cf. Dillm. p. 454 f.).

That P and JE form two clearly definable, independent sources, is a conclusion abundantly justified by the facts. As regards the analysis of JE, the criteria (as said above) are fewer and less definite; and the points of demarcation cannot in all cases be determined with the same confidence. Nevertheless the indications that the narrative is composite are of a nature which it is not easy to gainsay; and the difficulty which sometimes presents itself of disengaging the two sources is but a natural consequence of the greater similarity of style subsisting [18] between them than between JE, as a whole, and P.* In the history of Joseph the harmonizing additions which the analysis attributes to the compiler may be felt by some to constitute an objection to it. In estimating the force of such an objection, we must, however, balance the probabilities: is it more probable, in the light of what appears from other parts of the Pentateuch, that the work of one and the same writer should exhibit the incongruities pointed to above, or that a redactor in combining

---

* Dillmann attempts to separate J and E with great minuteness. But it is often questionable if the phraseological criteria upon which he mainly relies warrant the conclusions which he draws from them. He is apt (as the present writer ventures to think) not to allow sufficiently for the probability that two writers, whose general styles were such as those of J and E are known to have been, would make use of the same expressions, where these expressions are not (as in the case of P) of a peculiar, strongly marked type, but are such as might be used, so far as we can judge, by any writer of the best historiographical style.

two parallel narratives should have introduced into one traits borrowed from the other? The narrative of Joseph cannot be judged entirely by itself; it must be judged in the light of the presumption derived from the study of JE as a whole. And this presumption is of a nature which tends to confirm the conclusion that it is composite.

The distinction between P and JE—in particular, between P and J—may be instructively illustrated from the *blessings* and *promises* which form a conspicuous feature in the Book of Genesis, and, in virtue of the progressive limitation of their scope, harmonize with its general plan (p. 7). To P belong 1^{28-30} (Adam); 9^{1-7} (Noah); 17^{6-8} (Abraham); $28^{3f.}$ and $35^{11f.}$ [quoted 48^{3}] (Jacob): to JE 3^{15} (the Protevangelium); 9^{26} (Shem); 12^{1-3} (Abraham: also 13^{14-17} $15^{5.\ 18}$ 18^{18} 22^{15-18}); $26^{2-5.\ 24}$ (Isaac); 27^{27-29} 28^{13-15} (Jacob); 49^{10} (Judah). Let the reader notice how those assigned to P are cast in the same phraseology, and express frequently the same thoughts: those assigned to J exhibit greater variety; and such common features as they present (especially those addressed to the three patriarchs) are different from those that mark the other series. In P, it may be observed, the promises are limited to Israel itself; in J the prophetical outlook embraces other nations as well. Comp. the writer's *Sermons on the Old Testament* (1892), pp. 52-55.

The process by which, probably, the Book of Genesis assumed its present form may be represented approximately as follows. First, the two independent, but parallel, narratives of the patriarchal age, J and E, were combined into a whole by a compiler whose method of work, sometimes incorporating long sections [19] of each intact (or nearly so), sometimes fusing the parallel accounts into a single narrative, has been sufficiently illustrated. The whole thus formed (JE) was afterwards combined with the narrative P by a second compiler, who, adopting P as his framework, accommodated JE to it, omitting in either what was necessary in order to avoid needless repetition, and making such slight redactional adjustments as the unity of his work required. Thus he naturally assigned $1^{1}-2^{3}$ the first place, — perhaps at the same time removing 2^{4a} from its original position as superscription to 1^{1} and placing it where it now stands. In appending next, from J, the narrative of Paradise, he omitted probably the opening words (for the narrative begins abruptly), and to *Jahweh* added the defining adjunct *Elohim*,* "God," for

---

* Producing an unusual and emphatic phrase (=Jahweh, who is God), occurring again in the Pentateuch only Ex. 9^{30}.

the purpose of identifying expressly the Author of life in $2^{4b\,ff.}$ with God, the Creator, in $1^{1ff.}$ Still following J, he took from it the history of Cain and his descendants (4^{1-24}), but rejected the list of Seth's descendants (which the fragments that remain show that J must have once contained) except the first two names ($4^{25f.}$), and the etymology of *Noah* (5^{29}), in favour of the genealogy and chronological details of P ($5^{1-28.\ 30-32}$). In 6^{1} -9^{17} he combines into one the double narrative of the Flood, preserving, however, more from both narratives than was usually his practice, and in parts slightly modifying the phraseology In 9^{18-27} he introduces from J the prophetical glance at the character and capabilities of the three great ethnic groups descended from Noah, following it by the account, from P, of the close of Noah's life ($9^{28f.}$). C. 10 (the Table of nations) includes elements derived from both sources (p. 14 f.); it is succeeded by the account from J of the dispersion of mankind (11^{1-9}). C. 11^{10-25} carries on the line of Israel's ancestors from Shem to Terah, from P; 11^{26-32} states particulars respecting Abram's immediate relations, taken partly from P, partly from J, and necessary as an introduction to the history of Abram in c. 12 ff. *Mutatis mutandis*, a similar method is followed in the rest of the book. The narrative of Genesis, though composite, is constructed upon a definite plan, and to the development of this plan the details that are incorporated from the different sources employed are throughout subservient.

[20] Twice in P ($17^{1}\ 21^{1b}$) the name *Jehovah* appears in place of the name *God*; and the variation, it has been argued, is subversive of the grounds upon which the critical analysis of Genesis rests. But this argument attaches undue significance to an *isolated* phenomenon. We must weigh the alternatives, and ask which is the more probable : that an inference, dependent upon an *abundance* of criteria, extending throughout the entire Pentateuch, should be a mistaken one, or that the compiler, or even a scribe, should *twice* have substituted the more usual *Jehovah* for *Elohim* under the influence of the usage of the verses preceding. To this question there can surely be but one answer. The compiler of Chronicles changes conversely *Jehovah* of his original source into *God*, neither consistently nor with apparent reason, except that when writing independently, he evinces a preference for the latter term himself; comp. *e.g.* 2 Ch. $22^{12}\ 23^{9}\ 25^{24}\ 33^{7}\ 34^{9.\ 27}$ with 2 Ki. $11^{3.\ 10}\ 14^{14}\ 21^{7}\ 22^{4.\ 19}$ respectively.

The more special characteristics of J, E, and P, and the question of their probable dates, will be considered when they have been reviewed in their entirety at the end of the Book of Joshua.

§ 2. EXODUS.

LITERATURE (in addition to the works mentioned above, p. 1 f.).—Ad. Jülicher, *Die Quellen von Exodus* i.–vii. 7, Halis Sax. 1880, and *Die Quellen von Exodus* vii. 8–xxiv. 11, in the *Jahrbücher für Protestantische Theologie*, 1882, pp. 79–127, 272–315; C. A. Briggs, "The Little Book of the Covenant" [Ex. 34$^{11-26}$] in *The Hebrew Student* (Chicago), May 1883, p. 264 ff. ; "The Greater Book of the Covenant" [Ex. 20^{22}–c. 23], *ib.* June 1883, p. 289 ff. ; J. W. Rothstein, *Das Bundesbuch u. die rel.-gesch. Entwicklung Isr.* 1888; B. W. Bacon in the *Journ. of Bibl. Lit.* 1890, p. 161 ff. (on Ex. 7^{14}–12^{36}) ; 1891, p. 107 ff. (on Ex. 1–7) ; 1892, p. 177 ff. (on Ex. 12^{37}–17^{16}) ; 1893, p. 23 ff. (on Ex. 18–34); K. Budde, *ZATW.* 1891, p. 99 ff. (Bemerkungen zum Bundesbuch), p. 193 ff. (chiefly on the analysis of Ex. 12–34) ; B. Baentsch, *Das Bundesbuch, seine ursprungliche Gestalt, u.s.w.* (1892); B. W. Bacon, *The Triple Tradition of the Exodus* (Hartford, U.S.A. 1894) [distinguishes typographically J, E, and P, to the end of the Pent., with explanatory introductions and notes ; but the grounds of the analysis (in Ex.) are stated more fully in the articles just referred to].

The Book of Exodus (called by the Jews, from its opening words, וְאֵלֶּה שְׁמוֹת, or more briefly שְׁמוֹת) carries on the history of the Israelitish nation from the death of Joseph to the erection of the Tabernacle by Moses in the second year of the exodus (40$^{1.17}$). The structure of the book is essentially similar to that of Genesis, the same sources, P and JE, appearing still side by side, and exhibiting the same distinctive peculiarities. It will be convenient, in analysing the book, to divide it into sections, which may be briefer than was the case in Genesis.

I. c. 1–11. *Events leading to the deliverance of the Israelites from Egypt.*

C. 1–2. The continued increase of Jacob's posterity in Egypt, and the measures instituted for the purpose of checking it by a "new king," unmindful of the benefits conferred previously upon [21] his country by Joseph (c. 1). The birth and education of Moses, and his flight from Egypt into the land of Midian (c. 2).

$$
\begin{cases}
\text{P } 1^{1-5} \quad 7 \qquad 13\text{-}14 \qquad\qquad\qquad\qquad 2^{23\text{b}\text{-}25} \\
\hline
\begin{cases}
\text{J} \qquad 1^6 \quad {}^{8\text{-}12} \qquad\qquad\qquad 2^{15\text{-}23\text{a}} \text{ (to \textit{died})} \\
\text{E} \qquad\qquad\qquad 1^{15\text{-}22} \; 2^{1\text{-}14}
\end{cases}
\end{cases}
$$

1$^{1-5}$ repeats the substance of Gen. 46$^{8-27}$ (cf. p. 7). As regards 2^{15-23a}, it is true, in J, Moses' father-in-law is called Hobab (Nu 10^{29}, cf. Jud. 4^{11}) ; but as no name is mentioned when he is first introduced (v.^{16}), *Reuel* in v.^{18} is very probably a gloss, due to a misconception of Nu 10²⁹. In 3¹ 4¹⁸, c. 18 (E), he is called *Jethro*: the variation is a good example of the divergent traditions to be found in the Pentateuch.

C. 3¹–7¹³. Moses is commissioned by Jehovah to be the deliverer of his people; his preliminary negotiations with the Israelites and with Pharaoh.

P						6^2–7^{13}
J	7-8	16-20	4^{1-16}	19-20a	4^{22}–6^1	
E	3^{1-6}	9-15	21-22	17-18	20b-21	

In c. 3 the main narrative is E (notice the frequency of *God* v.$^{4.\ 6b.\ 11.\ 12.\ 13a.\ 14a.\ 15a}$), with short passages from J; in c. 4–6¹, on the contrary, the main narrative is J, with short passages from E. The verses 4¹⁷⁻¹⁸. ²⁰ᵇ⁻²¹ are assigned to E on account of their imperfect connexion with the context: 4¹⁷ speaks of "*the* signs" to be done with the rod, whereas only *one* sign to be performed with it has been described v.¹⁻⁹; 4²¹ mentions wonders to be done before *Pharaoh*, whereas v.¹⁻⁹ speaks only of wonders to be wrought for the satisfaction of the *people*. The two verses read, in fact, like fragments from another narrative, which once, of course, contained the explanations which are now missing. Further, in the existing narrative, v.¹⁹, from its contents, is not fitted to be the *sequel* of v.¹⁸: it, in fact, states an alternative ground for Moses' return into Egypt; and the name *Jethro* makes it probable that v.¹⁸ belongs to the same current of narrative as 3¹ and c. 18 (*i.e.* E); hence v.¹⁹ will be referred to J. V.²⁰ᵇ goes naturally with v.¹⁷ (the rod).

Passing now to the consideration of the passage assigned to P (6^2–7^{13}), and comparing it with JE as a whole, we observe that it does not describe the *sequel* of 3¹–6¹, but is *parallel* to it, and contains a partly divergent account of the commission of Moses, and of the preliminary steps taken by him to secure the release of his people. This will be apparent if the narrative [22] be followed attentively. 3¹–6¹ describes the call and commission of Moses, the nomination of Aaron as his spokesman *with the people* (3¹⁶ 4¹. ¹⁶), and three signs given to him for the satisfaction of the people if they should demand his credentials: Moses and Aaron have satisfied the people (4³⁰. ³¹), but their application to Pharaoh has proved unsuccessful (c. 5) and something further is threatened (6¹). The continuation of 6¹ is, however, 7¹⁴; for though the revelation and commission contained in 6^{2-8} might *in itself* be treated as a repetition of that in c. 3, its different style points to P as its source, and the sequel shows that in fact it is part of a *parallel* narrative of Moses' call and commission, in which, *unlike* 4^{31}, the people refuse to listen to the promises conveyed to them (6^9), and in which, upon Moses' protesting his inability to plead, not, as before, with the people, but with *Pharaoh*, Aaron is appointed to be his spokesman *with him* ($6^{11-12. \ 29-30} \ 7^{1-2}$). If Pharaoh had already refused to hear him (as he would have done, had c. 5–6 formed a continuous narrative), it is scarcely possible that Moses should allege (6^{12}) a different, *à priori* ground—a ground, moreover, inconsistent with 4^{31}—for his hesitation. Aaron having been thus appointed Moses' spokesman with Pharaoh, the case of the king's requiring a guarantee is next provided for: Aaron's rod is to be thrown down that it may become a reptile * $7^{8f.}$. Pharaoh's heart, however, is hardened; and the narrative at 7^{13} has reached just the same point which was reached in 6^1. The parallelism of details which prevails between the two narratives is remarkable; comp. 6^{2-8} and $3^{6-9. \ 14-15}$; 6^{12b} $^{(=30)}$ and 4^{10}; 7^1 and 4^{16}; $7^{4f.}$ and $3^{19f.} \ 6^1$.

C. 7^{14}–11^{10}. The narrative of the plagues.

P	7^{19-20a} (to *commanded*)				21b-22			8⁵⁻⁷
J	7^{14-18}					23	25	8^{1-4} †
E	17 (partly)			20b-21a (to *river*)			24	

P	8^{15b-19}		9^{8-12}						
J	8^{8-15a}	8^{20}–9^7		13-21	23b-34	10^{1-7}		13b-19	
E					9^{22-23a} 24a 35		10^{8-13a} 14a		20-27

[23]

P				11^{9-10}
J	10^{28-29}		11^{4-8}	
E		11^{1-3}		

The grounds of the analysis depend, in the first instance, upon literary criteria; which, however, are remarkably supported by corresponding differences in the representation. Reserving for the present the consideration of the few passages referred to E, and confining our attention to P and J, we observe that the narrative of the plagues is marked by a series of *systematic* differ-

---

* צְפַרְדֵּעַ *a reptile*, not נָחָשׁ *a serpent*, as in 4^3.
† The verses are numbered as in the *English* version.

ences, relating to four distinct points—viz. 1. the terms of the command addressed to Moses; 2. the demand made of Pharaoh; 3. the description of the plague; 4. the formula expressive of Pharaoh's obstinacy: and further, that these differences *agree frequently with corresponding differences* in the parts of the preceding narrative, 3^1–6^1, which have been assigned (on independent grounds) to P and JE respectively. Thus in P Aaron *co-operates* with Moses, and the command is *Say unto Aaron* (7^{19} $8^{5.\ 16}$; so before, in 7^9: even 9^8, where Moses acts, both are expressly addressed); no demand is ever made of Pharaoh, the plagues being viewed rather as signs, or proofs of power, than as having the practical object of securing Israel's release; the description of the plague is brief, seldom extending beyond the compass of two or three verses; the success or failure of the Egyptian magicians (who are mentioned only in this narrative) is noted; the hardening of Pharaoh's heart is expressed by the verb חָזַק, חָזֵק (*was strong, made strong,* RV. *marg.*) 7^{22} 8^{19} 9^{12} 11^{10} (so 7^{13}), and the closing formula * is *And he hearkened not unto them, as Jehovah had spoken* (7^{22} $8^{15b.\ 19}$ 9^{12} (so 7^{13}). In J, on the contrary, Moses alone (without Aaron) is commissioned to present himself before Pharaoh: he addresses Pharaoh himself † (in agreement with 4^{10-16}, where Aaron is appointed expressly to be Moses' spokesman *with the people*); a formal demand is uniformly made, *Let my people go, that they may serve me* (7^{16} 8^1 $9^{1.\ 13}$ 10^3: compare before 4^{23} in the corresponding narrative); upon Pharaoh's refusal, the plague is announced, and takes [24] effect, either without further human intervention (8^{24} 9^6), or at a signal given by Moses (not by Aaron) (7^{20} $9^{22f.}$ $10^{12f.\ 22}$); the interview with Pharaoh is prolonged, and described in some detail; sometimes also the king sends for Moses and Aaron to crave their intercession for the removal of the plague ($8^{8.\ 25}$ 9^{27} 10^{16}); the term used to express the hardening of Pharaoh's heart is *was heavy* (כבד) or *made heavy* (הכביד) 7^{14} $8^{15.\ 32}$ $9^{7.\ 34}$ 10^1.‡ The

* Except the last time, 11^{10} (cf. 6^{11b} 7^{2b}; and with v.^{9}, $7^{4.\ 3b}$).

† Aaron, if he appears at all, is only Moses' silent companion: 8^8 (see v.$^{9.\ 10}$) ^{25} (see v.$^{26.\ 29}$) 9^{27} (see v.^{29}). In 10^3 it is doubtful if the plural "and *they* said" is original: notice in v.^{6b} "and *he* turned."

‡ The two words חזק *hard, strong,* and כבד *heavy,* really express different ideas: the former means *firm,* in a bad sense *stubborn, defiant* (cf. Ez. 3^{7-9}), the latter *slow to move* or *be affected, unimpressionable* (cf. of the ear, Is. 6^{10} 59^1, Zech. 7^{11}; of the eye, Gen. 48^{10}; of the tongue, Ex. 4^{10}).

narrative generally is written in a more picturesque and varied style than that of P ; there are frequent descriptive touches, and the dialogue is abundant. In a word, the two currents of narrative display just the same contrasted literary characteristics which they exhibit in the Book of Genesis.

Recurring phrases which mark this narrative and distinguish it from that of P are (besides "Let my people go," &c., and כבד, הכביד of the heart, just noted) *refuseth* (מאן), esp. followed by "to let the people go," 7¹⁴ 8² 9² 10³· ⁴ (so before 4²³) ; 7¹⁵ *serpent* (נחש), see 4³ ; *Thus saith Jehovah*, said regularly to Pharaoh (so 4²² 5¹) ; *behold* . . . with the participle in the announcement of the plague 7¹⁷ 8². ²¹ 9³· ¹⁸ 10⁴ (so 4²³) ; *border* 8⁹ 10⁴· ¹⁴· ¹⁹ ; *thou, thy people, and thy servants* 8³· ⁴· ⁹· ¹¹· ²¹· ²⁹ 9¹⁴,* cf. 10⁶ 12³⁰ ; *God of the Hebrews* 7¹⁶ 9¹· ¹³ 10³ (so 3¹⁸ 5³) ; *to intreat* 8³· ⁹· ²⁸· ²⁹ 9²⁸ 10¹⁷ ; *such as hath not been* &c. 9¹⁸· ²⁴ 11⁶, cf. 10⁶· ¹⁴ ; *to sever* (הִפְלָה) 8²² 9⁴ 11⁷ ; the end or object of the plague (or circumstance attending it) stated 8¹⁰· ²² 9¹⁴· ¹⁶· ²⁹ᵇ 10²ᵇ 11⁷.

The grounds for believing that what remains in the narrative of the plagues after the separation of P is not perfectly homogeneous, but contains elements due to E, are, stated briefly, as follows. Reasons were given above (p. 23) for concluding that the two verses 4¹⁷⁻¹⁸, which speak of the *rod* of Moses, were not originally part of the context in which they are now found, and they were assigned accordingly to E. Now, in the narrative of the plagues, the effect in certain cases is brought about not immediately by God, but by the intervention of *Moses' rod* (7¹⁷· ²⁰ᵇ 9²³ 10¹³). It is difficult not to connect the passages in which the rod is thus named with 4¹⁷⁻¹⁸, and to treat both as notices derived from the same source E. The opinion that the parts of the narrative which remain after the [25] separation of P are to some extent composite, is confirmed by other indications. Thus in 7¹⁷ the transition from the "I" of God to the "I" of Moses is abrupt and (in the historical books) unusual ; hence the suspicion arises that originally the subject of *I will smite* was Jehovah (cf. v.²⁵ᵇ), and that the words "with the rod that is in mine hand" were introduced by the compiler of JE from the other source used by him. By the side of 9³⁴ᵇ, v.³⁵ᵃ would seem to be superfluous.

The analysis of JE is often difficult, and that there are points in it at which finality has not been reached, is generally admitted by critics (cf. p. 14) ; and Bacon (who handles the subject with much ability), in the

---

* The symmetry of this verse is much improved, if, with Hitzig, for אל לבך we read אֵלֶּה בְּךָ.

articles mentioned on p. 22, has made important contributions towards the separation of J and E, especially in Ex. 7–11. The writer hesitates to adopt absolutely results on which at present (Dec. 1896) no judgment has been expressed by other scholars ; but Bacon's analysis of JE in Ex. 1–11 ought not to be withheld from the reader (in c. 3 and c. 4, according to the *Triple Tradition*, p. 16 ff.) :—

$$\begin{cases} J \\ E \end{cases}$$ Ex. $1^{6.\ 8\text{-}12}$ 20b   15-23a   2-4a (to *see*)   5   7-8   16-18

      15-20a   21-22 $2^{1\text{-}14}$ 3^{1} 4b   6   9-15   19-22

$$\begin{cases} J \\ E \end{cases}$$ $4^{1\text{-}14a}$ 15-16   19-20a (to *Egypt*)   22-26   29-31   3   5-23 7^{14}

      14b   17-18   20b-21   27-28 $5^{1\text{-}2}$ 4 6^{1}

$$\begin{cases} J \\ E \end{cases}$$ 16. 17 *   18   21a (to *from the river*)   24-25

7^{15} 17 †   20 (from *and he lifted*)   23

$$\begin{cases} J \\ E \end{cases}$$ $8^{1\text{-}4.\ 8\text{-}15a}$ (to *heart*) $^{20\text{-}32}$ $9^{1\text{-}7.\ 13\text{-}21}$ 23b-24   25b-34

      $9^{22\text{-}23a}$ (to *earth*)   25a (to *beast*)

$$\begin{cases} J \\ E \end{cases}$$ $10^{1\text{-}11}$ 13b   14b-15a (to *darkened*)

9^{35a} (to *go*)   12-13a (to *Egypt*)   14a (to *land of Egypt*)

$$\begin{cases} J \\ E \end{cases}$$ 15c-19   24-26   28-29   4-8

10^{15b} (to *left*)   20-23   27 $11^{1\text{-}3}$

The parts not included in this table belong to P. $12^{29\text{-}30}$ is the sequel to $11^{4\text{-}8}$ in J, and $12^{35\text{-}36}$ the sequel to $11^{1\text{-}3}$ in E. 3^{15} $4^{22\text{-}23}$ 7^{17a} ("In this thou shalt know that I am Jehovah") 8^{10b} ("to the end," &c.) ^{22b} $9^{14b\text{-}16.\ 19\text{-}21.\ 29b}$ ("that," &c.) ^{30} 10^{1b} ("for I," &c.) $^{2\text{-}3a}$ (to "Pharaoh," the next words being supposed to have read originally *and say*) 11^{7b}, which are of the nature of didactic comments, are regarded (after other critics) as probably editorial additions ; and 9^{35b} ("as Jehovah," &c.) is borrowed by the compiler from P's formula 7^{13} 8^{19} &c.). In 7^{15} the words "which was turned to a serpent" are a harmonistic insertion (cf. 4^{17} LXX).

The variations from previous critics are deliberate, and supported by argument : as Bacon shows, his predecessors had at certain points (notably at $10^{24\text{-}26}$) failed to discover the true clues. The effect of this analysis is to disengage two narratives, each (substantially) complete, and each (as Bacon is careful to point out) consistent with itself, and dominated by a distinctive unity of character and representation ; in the hands of previous critics, E's narrative has been mostly fragmentary. Thus, upon Bacon's view, E preserves more closely than J does the connexion with the patriarchal period : there are only 3-4 generations from Joseph to Moses (Gen. 50^{23}, cf. Nu. 32^{40}) ; he pictures the Israelites accordingly as a relatively small clan, capable of being served by two midwives : in J, Israel is a populous nation ; Ex 1^{6} covers the gap between the patriarchs and Moses, and allows time for the multiplication of Jacob's descendants. In E, again, the Israelites are "royal pensioners,"

---

* Reading, "Thus saith Jehovah, Behold, I will smite the river" ; cf. v. ^{25}.

† Reading, "And thou shalt smite with the rod that is in thine hand upon the waters which are in the river, and they shall become blood."

dependent upon Pharaoh's bounty (comp. Gen. 45[11] 47[12], cf. 50[21]; 45[19] 46[5]), and they live side by side with the Egyptians (Ex 3[22] 11[2]); in J they are independent owners of cattle (9[4. 6] 10[9. 24. 26] 12[32. 38]; cf. Gen. 45[10] 46[32]), and they reside apart in the pastoral district of Goshen (Ex. 8[22] 9[26]; cf. Gen. 45[10] 46[28. 29. 34] 47[1. 4. 6b. 27a]). In E, further, Pharaoh is depicted as stubborn and defiant, his refusal is peremptory and complete; in J he is weak-minded and deceitful (8[29]), he promises release, and craves Moses' intercession, but afterwards evades his promise. Other characteristics of the two representations are also pointed out by Bacon. The literary distinctions between the two narratives remain substantially as before; J is graphic, and abounds in colloquy; E, though complete, is brief and ungarnished. The concluding formula in E is *and Pharaoh's heart was hardened* [חזק lit. *was strong*] (or *and Jehovah hardened Pharaoh's heart*), *and he did not let the children of Israel* (or *them*) *go* 9[35] (contrast J's phrase, v.[34b]) 10[20. 27] (cf. 4[21] E). P uses the same verb חזק, but follows it usually by *and he hearkened not unto them, as Jehovah had spoken*.

II. c. 12–19[2]. *The last plague, the departure of the Israelites from Egypt, and their journey to Sinai.*

C. 12–13. The institution of the Passover, and the Feast of Unleavened Cakes. The death of the first-born of the Egyptians, and journey of the Israelites from Rameses to Succoth. The law respecting the dedication of the first-born (12[1]–13[16]). March of the Israelites from Succoth to Etham, on the border of the wilderness (13[17-22]).

	P 12[1-20]	28		37a	40-51	13[1f.]		20
J		21-27	29f.				3-16		21f.
E				31-36	37b-39	42a*		13[17-19]	

In c. 12–13 the double treatment is peculiarly evident. We have (*a*) 12[1-13] (Passover); v.[14-20]† (*Mazzoth* or Unleavened Cakes); v.[28. 37a. 40-41. 51] (narrative); v.[43-50] (Passover—supplementary); 13[1f.] (first-born): (*b*) 12[21-27] (Passover); v.[29-36. 37b-39. 42a] (narrative,—continuation of 11[4-8]); 13[3-10] (Unleavened Cakes); v.[11-16] (first-born): the former narrative exhibits throughout the marks of P; the latter, those of JE. The Passover, it is to be observed, though followed by the Feast of *Mazzoth* (Unleavened Cakes), is distinct from it both in its origin and in its observance; and the distinction is recognised in both [**26**] narratives, especially in that of JE. The injunction in P respecting the first-born (13[1f.]) is here isolated; the full explanation is first given Nu. 3[12f.] 8[16-19].

---

* 12[42b], the Hebrew of which is very strange (הוא הלילה הזה), appears to be a gloss (Budde, *ZATW*. 1891, p. 200; Bacon).

† V.[14] refers to the first day of *Mazzoth* (Lev. 23[6]), not to the Passover.

The distinction between P and JE in c. 12 is sufficiently established upon literary grounds ; but a material justification of the analysis is to be found in the fact that 12^{21-27} cannot be the original sequel of 12^{1-20} (or rather, of 12^{1-13} ; for v.$^{14-20}$ does not concern the *Passover* at all). The verses do not describe the *execution* of the commands received by Moses in v.$^{1-13}$. Moses does not repeat to the people, even in an abridged form, the injunctions before received by him ; but while several points of importance (*e.g.* the character of the lamb, and the manner in which it was to be eaten) are omitted, *fresh* points (the hyssop, the basin, none to leave the house), not mentioned before, are added. The inference is irresistible that 12^{21-27} is really part of a different account of the institution of the Passover, which " stands to 12^{3-13} in the same relation that the regulations respecting *Mazzoth* in 13^{3-10} stand to those in 12^{14-20} " (Dillm. p. 100). V.$^{25-27}$ is conceived entirely in the spirit of parts of 13^{3-16} (see v.$^{5.\,8.\,10.\,14f.}$) ; it is probable, therefore, that both passages are of similar origin, and may be referred either to J (Dillm.) or to the compiler of JE expanding materials derived from J (so Wellh., at least for 13^{3-16}).

A noticeable difference between P and JE is the greater specialization and strictness of the provisions contained in the former narrative (*e.g.* $12^{15f.\,18f.\,43-49}$). As regards the parts assigned to E, with v.^{31b} comp. 3^{12} $10^{8.\,11.\,24a}$; with v.^{32}, $10^{9.\,24b}$; with v.$^{35f.}$, $3^{21f.}$ $11^{2f.}$ (all E) ; in 13^{17-19} notice *God* (not *Jehovah*) four times ; and with v.^{19} comp. Gen. 50^{24}, in a context which (on independent grounds) is assigned to the same source. $12^{34.\,39}$ deserve attention, being evidently intended as an explanation of the origin of the Feast of "Unleavened Cakes." See further, on c. 12–13, Delitzsch, *Studien*, vii. p. 337 ff.

C. 14–15. The passage of the Red Sea ; Moses' Song of Triumph ; the journey of the Israelites to Marah and Elim.

[27]

P 14^{1-4}	8-9		15-18	21a (to *over the sea*)
J	5-7	10a (to *afraid*)	11-14	19b-20
E			10b	19a

P		21c. 22-23	26-27a (to *over the sea*)	28-29
J 21b (to *dry land*)		24-25	27b	30-31
E				

P	(15^{19})		
J		22-27	
E 15^{1-18}	20-21		

The passages assigned to P will be found to be connected both with each other and with other parts of the Pentateuch belonging to the same source : thus "harden (חזק) the heart" v.[4] recurs v.[8. 17], and is the same term that is used by P in the narrative of the plagues (p. 25) ; "get me honour" *ib.* recurs v.[17. 18] Lev. 10[3] ; comp. also v.[4. 18] "and the Egyptians shall know," &c. (cf. 6[7] 7[5] 16[12]) ; v.[9. 23] "and the Egyptians pursued" ; v.[22. 29] "the dry land" and "the wall" ; v.[16. 21] "divide" ; the *repetitions* (in the manner of P) in v.[17f.] as compared with v.[4], in v.[28a] as compared with v.[23], in v.[29] as compared with v.[22]. The particulars of the analysis depend to a certain extent upon the apparently *double* character of the narrative in some parts of the chapter. As regards the parts attributed to E, with v.[10b] comp. Josh. 24[7] (E) ; with v.[19], Gen. 21[17] 31[11] (the "angel of *God*"). It is possible that other traits in the narrative also have their source in E (*e.g.* v.[16] "lift up thy *rod*" ; comp. above, p. 26). 14[28b] may be a notice derived from J (comp. 8[31] 9[7] 10[19]).

In c. 15 the *Song* (v.[1b-18], cf. v.[20-21]) is, of course, incorporated by E from an earlier source—perhaps from a collection of national poems. V.[19] appears to be a later redactional addition, reverting, in terms borrowed from P (see 14[23. 26. 29b]), to the occasion of the Song. The Song itself appears to have undergone some expansion, or modification of form, at a later age ; for v.[13] ("Thou *hast guided them* to Thy holy habitation") appears clearly to describe a *past* event, and v.[17b] points to some *fixed* abode of the ark—the temple at Shiloh (1 Sa. 1[9]), if not (Riehm, *Einl.* i. 299 f.) the temple at Jerusalem (the verbs in v.[17a] may be translated as pasts or futures indifferently). In v.[1b-3] we seem indeed (to use Dillmann's expression) to hear Moses himself speaking ; and both Dillm. and Delitzsch (*Gen.* p. 29) agree with Ewald (*Die Dichter des A.B.s*, i. 1, p. 175 ; cf. *Hist.* ii. 354) in supposing that the Song, as a whole, is a later expansion of the Mosaic theme contained in v.[1b-3],— perhaps designed originally as a festal Passover-song (Is. 30[29]). Probably, however, the greater part of the Song is Mosaic, and the modification, or expansion, is limited to the closing verses ; for the general style is antique, and the triumphant tone which pervades it is just such as might naturally have been inspired by the event which it celebrates.

C. 16–19[2]. The journey of the Israelites from Elim to Sinai, including particulars respecting the quails and manna given to the people in the wilderness of Sinai (c. 16) ; the miraculous supply of water at Rephidim, and the conflict with Amalek at the same place (c. 17) ; the meeting with Jethro, and the counsel given by him to Moses (c. 18).

[28]

P 16[1-3]	6-24	31-36 17[1a] (to *Rephidim*)		19[1-2a]
J	4-5	25-30	17[1b-2] 7	
E			3-6 8-16 c. 18	19[2b]

In c. 16 the parts assigned to P have many marks of his style which are absent from the rest of the chap. (cf. p. 131 ff. There are also corresponding differences of representation: thus in v.$^{6-7}$ (*evening* and *morning*, agreeing with v.$^{8.\ 12}$ *flesh* at evening, and *bread* at morning) the communication made to the people is different in its terms from that given in v.$^{4-5}$ to Moses (*bread* alone, with no distinction of morning and evening); and v.$^{25-30}$ agrees with v.$^{4-5}$. In the text of P a transposition appears to have taken place; for v.$^{11-19}$ the command to speak to the people *follows* the account v.$^{6-8}$ of the actual delivery to them of the message; probably the original order was v.$^{1-3.\ 9-12.\ 6-8.\ 13}$ &c.

C. 18, though in one or two places (as in parts of v.$^{2-4.\ 8-10}$) there may be traces of the hand of the compiler of JE, is otherwise an excerpt from E; notice the preponderance in the chapter of *God* (not *Jehovah*). The chapter is one of great historical interest; it exhibits to us a picture of *Moses legislating*. Disputes arise among the people; the contending parties come to Moses to have them settled; he adjudicates between them; and his judgments are termed "the statutes and directions (*Tôrōth*) of God" (v.^{16}). It was the historic function of the priests to *give direction* (תורה, הורה) upon cases submitted to them, in matters both of civil right (Dt. 17^{11}) and ceremonial observance (*ib.* 24^8)* ; and here Moses himself appears discharging the same function, and so laying the foundation of Hebrew law.

III. 19^3–c. 40. *Israel at Sinai.*

(*a*) The solemn establishment of the theocracy at Sinai (see 19$^{5-8}$ 24$^{3-8}$) on the basis of the Ten Commandments (20$^{1-17}$), and of a Code of laws (20^{23}–23^{33}) regulating the social life and religious observances of the people, and called the "Book of the Covenant" (24^7); (*b*) the giving of directions to Moses on Mount Sinai for the construction of the Tabernacle, with the vessels and appointments belonging to it, for the consecration of Aaron and his sons as priests, the selection of Bezaleel and Oholiab to execute the skilled work that was necessary, and the delivering to Moses of the two Tables of the Law (24^{12}–31^{18}); (*c*) the incident of the Golden Calf, Moses' intercession [29] on behalf of the people, and the renewal of the covenant (c. 32–34); (*d*) the construction of the Tabernacle and its appurtenances in accordance with the directions prescribed in c. 25–31, and its erection (40^{17}) on the first day of the second year of the exodus (c. 35–40).

	P				
J		19$^{20-25}$		24$^{1-2}$	9-11
E 19$^{3-19}$ (in the main)		20$^{1-21}$ 20^{22}–23^{33}		3-8	12-14

* Cf. Mic. 3^{11} (give *direction*); Hag. 2^{11} (ask now *direction* of the priests).

$$\left\{ \begin{array}{l} \text{P } 24^{15\text{-}18a} \text{ (to } cloud\text{)} \qquad 25^1\text{-}31^{18a} \text{ (to } testimony\text{)} \\ \hline \left\{ \begin{array}{l} \text{J} \\ \text{E} \qquad\qquad\quad 24^{18b} \qquad\qquad\qquad\qquad 31^{18b} \; 32^{1\text{-}8} \qquad\qquad 32^{9\text{-}14} \end{array} \right. \end{array} \right.$$

$$\left\{ \begin{array}{l} \text{P} \qquad\qquad\qquad\qquad\qquad 34^{29\text{-}35} \text{ c. } 35\text{-}40 \\ \hline \left\{ \begin{array}{l} \text{J} \\ \text{E } 32^{15}\text{-}33^6 * \; 33^{7\text{-}11} \; 33^{12}\text{-}34^{28} \end{array} \right. \end{array} \right.$$

The structure of JE's narrative of the transactions at Sinai 19^3–$24^{14\text{-}18b}$ and 31^{18b}–34^{28} is complicated, and there are parts in which the analysis (so far as concerns J and E) must be regarded as provisional only. Nevertheless, the composite character of the narrative seems to be unmistakable. Thus in c. 19 the natural sequel of v.[3] *went up* would be, not v.[7] *came*, but v.[14] *went down* : v.[9] is superfluous after v.[8b] (if, indeed, it be more than an accidental repetition of it) : v.[13b] is isolated, and not explained by anything which follows (for the "trumpet" of v.[16-19] is not the "ram's-horn" of this verse). In the latter part of the chapter v.[20-25] interrupt the connexion : v.[20] is a repetition of v.[18a] ("descended"), and v.[21] of v.[12] ; the priests and Aaron are introduced without preparation : v.[25] "and *said* (ויאמר) *unto* them" (not "and *told* them") should be followed by a statement of the words reported, and is quite disconnected with 20[1] : on the other hand, 20[1] is the natural continuation of 19[19]. It is evident that *two* parallel narratives of the theophany on Sinai have been combined together, though it is no longer possible to determine throughout the precise limits of each. 19[3-19] (though parts of v.[3-8] may [30] be derived from J) belongs in the main to E ; the sequel (as just said) is formed by 20[1], introducing the Decalogue (20[2-17]), and the following verses 20[18-21] † (notice *God* in 19[3. 17. 19b] 20[1. 19. 20. 21]) &c. In c. 24, v.[3-8] is manifestly the sequel to c. 23. V.[1-2. 9-11] interrupt the connexion : their origin has been disputed ; but they are probably to be referred to J.

According to Bacon, they form the sequel to 19[2b] (from *and there*) [18. 22-24. 24] [rendering, "and Aaron with thee, and the priests ; but let not the people," &c.], [11b] (from *for*), [12-13] [the emph. המה "they" in v.[13b] obtaining by the transposition a suitable antecedent in *the priests* of v.[24]], [25] (20[1-21] being the

---

* In the main.

† Whether Kuenen is right in his suggestion (*Th. Tijdschr.* 1884, p. 190) that 20[18-21] stood originally in E between 19[15-19] and 20[1], may be doubted, notwithstanding the assent of Wellh. *Comp.* 327 f., and Budde, *ZATW.* 1891, p. 229 : Dt. 5[23-28] appears to show the contrary.

sequel to 19^{3-11a. 14-17. 19} in E). On the attribution of the Book of the Covenant
to E, see Dillm. p. 220; Jülicher, *JPTh.* 1882, p. 205 f. ; Budde, *ZATW.*
1891, p. 215 f. ; Wellh. *Comp.* p. 327.

The Decalogue was, of course, derived by E from a pre-
existing source, at least the substance of it being engraven on
the tables in the Ark, and incorporated by him in his narrative.
Some interesting critical questions arise from a comparison of
the Decalogue as here given with the form in which it is repeated
in Dt. (5⁶⁻²¹), where, although it is introduced ostensibly (v.^{5. 22}) as
a verbal quotation, it presents considerable differences from the
text of Exodus. The differences are most remarkable in the
4th, 5th, and 10th Commandments, which are here printed in
parallel columns, the variations being indicated by italics :—

<table>
<tr><td align="center">Ex. 20.</td><td align="center">Dt. 5.</td></tr>
<tr><td>8. Remember the sabbath day to keep it holy.</td><td>12. *Observe* the sabbath day to keep it holy, *as Jehovah thy God commanded thee.* 13. Six days shalt thou</td></tr>
</table>

Ex. 20.

8. Remember the sabbath day to
keep it holy.

9. Six days shalt thou
labour, and do all thy work : 10. but
the seventh day is a sabbath unto
Jehovah thy God : in it thou shalt not
do any work, thou, nor thy son, nor
thy daughter,   thy man-servant,
nor thy maid-servant, nor
                              thy cattle,
nor thy stranger that is within thy
gates :

11. For in six days Jehovah made
heaven, and earth, the sea, and all
that in them is, and rested the seventh
day : therefore Jehovah blessed the
sabbath day, and hallowed it.

[31] 12. Honour thy father and thy
mother,
              that thy days may be
long
        upon the land which Jehovah
thy God is giving thee.

.   .   .   .   .

17.   Thou shalt not covet thy
neighbour's house,   thou shalt not
covet thy neighbour's wife,

Dt. 5.

12. *Observe* the sabbath day to
keep it holy, *as Jehovah thy God commanded thee.* 13. Six days shalt thou
labour, and do all thy work : 14. but
the seventh day is a sabbath unto
Jehovah thy God : in it thou shalt not
do any work, thou, nor thy son, nor
thy daughter, *nor* thy man-servant,
nor thy maid-servant, nor *thine ox,
nor thine ass, nor any of* thy cattle,
nor thy stranger that is within thy
gates : *in order that thy man-servant
and thy maid-servant may rest as well
as thou.* 15. *And thou shalt remember that thou wast a servant in the
land of Egypt, and Jehovah thy God
brought thee out thence by a mighty
hand, and by a stretched out arm :
therefore Jehovah thy God commanded
thee to keep the sabbath day.*

16. Honour thy father and thy
mother, *as Jehovah thy God commanded thee :* that thy days may be
long, *and that it may be well with
thee,* upon the land which Jehovah
thy God is giving thee.

.   .   .   .   .

21. *And* thou shalt not covet thy
neighbour's *wife, and* thou shalt not
desire thy neighbour's *house, his field,*

or his man-servant, or his maid-servant, *or* his ox, or his ass, or anything that is thy neighbour's.	or his man-servant, or his maid-servant, his ox, or his ass, or anything that is thy neighbour's.

The principal variations are in agreement with the style of Dt., and the author's hand is recognisable in them. Thus with *Observe* v.[12] comp. Dt. 16[1]; with *as Jehovah thy God commanded thee* (which is not strictly appropriate in what purports to be a *report* of the words spoken), 20[17] 24[8] 26[18]; with the spirit of v.[14b], 14[29] 15[10]; with the motive of gratitude in v.[15], 15[15] 16[11. 12] 24[18. 22]; and with the addition in v.[16b], 5[29] [Heb. [26]] 6[18] 12[25. 28] 22[7]. Does, however, even the text of Ex. exhibit the Decalogue in its primitive form? It is an old and probable supposition,* suggested in part by the fact of this varying text, that in its original form the Decalogue consisted merely of the Commandments themselves, and that the explanatory comments appended in certain cases were only added subsequently. Thus, according to this view, the 2nd, 4th, and 5th Commandments read originally—

" Thou shalt not make to thyself any graven image."
" Remember the sabbath day to keep it holy."
" Honour thy father and thy mother."

All the Commandments would thus be moulded in uniform shape, and would be expressed in the same terse and simple form in which the 1st, and the 6th to the 9th, appear now. It has further been conjectured that, as the comments in v.[9. 10. 12] bear a singular resemblance to the style of Dt., they were in the first instance added in that book, and thence transferred subsequently to Ex.; and that, as it is scarcely probable that the author of Dt. would *omit* part of the Decalogue (though he might [32] for the purpose of explanation *add* clauses), v.[11] may have been only introduced into the text of Ex. after Dt. was written. As regards the first of these conjectures, it is no doubt attractive and plausible. In the phrase "them that *love* me" v.[6] there is embodied a thought which in the Pent. is confined to Dt., viz. the love of God, which in that book is made the foundation of all human action (*e.g.* 6[5] 10[12] 11[1] *al.*); the expression "within thy gates" v.[10] (= in thy cities) is all but peculiar to Dt., occurring in it twenty-nine times; the expressions in v.[12] "that thy days may be long," and "the land which Jehovah thy God

* Ewald, *Hist.* ii. 159; *Speaker's Comm.* p. 336; Dillmann, p. 201.

is giving thee," are also (especially the latter) of repeated occurrence in the same book (neither occurring elsewhere in the Pent.).
These facts possess undoubtedly considerable weight. It is,
however, some objection to the inference which they appear to
authorize, that the clauses in question (as a glance at the parallel
columns will show) are not incorporated *entire* in Exodus. If the
clauses were transferred to Ex. from Dt., it is not apparent why
portions of them were omitted. On the whole, therefore, the
more probable view appears to be that these clauses are in their
original place in Exodus, and that they are of the same character
as certain other sections in Ex., chiefly of a parenetic or hortatory
character (as $13^{3\text{-}16}$ $23^{20\text{-}33}$), which do exhibit an approximation
to the style of Dt., and which are the source of certain of the
expressions which were adopted afterwards by the author of
Dt., and became part of his phraseology.* Certainly, the expression "within thy gates," and the phrases in v.[12], read more
distinctively Deuteronomic than those occurring in the sections
referred to ; but (unless the text of the Decalogue has passed
through phases respecting which we can but speculate) the
explanation proposed seems to be the most reasonable one. If
it be correct, the additions in Dt. will, of course, be of the nature
of *further* comments upon the text of Exodus. V.[11], however,
stands upon a different footing : not only does it supply no
elements for the style of Dt., but it is dissimilar in style to JE :
in its first clause it resembles closely 31^{17b}, and in its second
Gen. 2^{2b}—both passages belonging to P. As there is force in
the remark that the author of Dt. is not likely to have omitted
the verse had it formed part of the Decalogue at the time when
he wrote, it is not improbable that [33] it was introduced into the
text of Exodus subsequently, upon the basis of the two verses
of P just cited.

The laws contained in the "Book of the Covenant" (20^{22}–
23^{33}) comprise two elements (24^3), the "words" (or commands)
and the "judgments": the latter, expressed all hypothetically,
occupy 21^1–$22^{17. \ 25a. \ 26}$ $23^{4f.}$; the former occupy the rest of the
section to 23^{19}; what follows, $23^{20\text{-}33}$, annexing a *promise* in case
of obedience, as Wellh. observes, imparts to the preceding law-
book the character of a "covenant" (cf. 24^7). The laws themselves are taken naturally from a pre-existing source, though their

* The expressions referred to are noted below, p. 99 f.

form, in particular cases, may be due to the compiler who united J and E into a whole. The main body of the "judgments," 21¹–22¹⁷, seems to have undergone no alteration of form; but in the following parts of the section most critics are of opinion that slight parenetic additions have been made by the compiler, *e.g.* 22²¹ᵇ⁻²² (observe in v.²³ [Heb. ²²] *him, he, his* in the Hebrew, pointing back to the *singular* "sojourner" in v.²¹); and in the final exhortation, 23²³⁻²⁵ᵃ * (which anticipates unduly v.²⁷ᶠ·, and disguises the *conditional* character of the promises v.²⁵ᵇ· ²⁶ᶠᶠ·, which are dependent on v.²²): the *substance* of this passage may have been derived from 34¹¹· ¹³. The verses 23⁴ᶠ· can hardly be in their original position; for the context (on both sides) relates to a subject of a different kind, viz. just judgment.

The laws themselves are designed to regulate the life of a community living under simple conditions of society, and chiefly occupied in *agriculture*.† They may be grouped as follows :— (1) 20²²⁻²⁶ prohibition of graven images, and regulations for the construction of altars ; (2) 21²⁻¹¹ regulations respecting Hebrew male and female slaves ; (3) 21¹²⁻¹⁷ capital offences ; (4) 21¹⁸⁻³² injuries to life or limb ; (5) 21³³–22⁶ cases of danger caused by culpable negligence, or theft ; (6) 22⁷⁻¹⁷ deposits, loans, and seduction (which is here treated, not as a moral offence, but as a wrong done to the father, and demanding pecuniary compensation); (7) 22¹⁸⁻³¹, and 23⁴ᶠ·(not to refuse help to an *enemy* in his need), miscellaneous religious and moral injunctions; (8) 23¹⁻³· ⁶⁻⁹ veracity, and equity in the [34] administration of judgment ; (9) 23¹⁰⁻¹⁹ on the Sabbatical year, the Sabbath, the three annual pilgrimages, and sacrifice ; (10) 23²⁰⁻³³ the concluding exhortation. That the community for whose use the Code was designed had made *some* progress in civilisation, is evident from the many restrictions imposed on the arbitrary action of the individual ; on the other hand, that it was still in a relatively archaic condition appears from such regulations as 21¹⁸ᶠ· ²³⁻²⁵ (the *lex talionis*), or the conception of God as the immediate source of judgment (21⁶ 22⁸⁻⁹: cf. 1 S. 2²⁵). Notice also the rudimentary character of the *ceremonial* injunctions respecting altars 20²⁴⁻²⁶, the right of asylum 21¹³ᶠ·, first-fruits and firstlings 22²⁹ᶠ· 23¹⁹, prohibition to eat טרפה 22³¹, the observance of the sacred seasons 23¹⁰⁻¹⁷, sacrifice 23¹⁸ ; comp. 20²³ 22²⁰

---

* To *God*, v.²⁵ᵇ beginning originally "And *I* will bless " (LXX. Vulg.).

† Notice the prominence of the *ox, ass,* and *sheep,* 21²⁸–22¹⁰.

against the worship of idols or false gods. Just and equitable
motives are insisted on (*e.g.* 22$^{21.\ 27}$ 23$^{4f.\ 9}$); but religious institutions, it is evident, are still in a simple, undeveloped stage.*

In c. 24, v.^{18b} ('and he went up,' &c.) is E's introduction to 31^{18b}, c. 32;
and v.$^{15-18a}$ is P's introduction to c. 25–31.

C. 25–31^{18a} forms P's account of the instructions given to
Moses respecting the Tabernacle and the priesthood. These
instructions fall into two parts : (1) c. 25–29; (2) c. 30–31. In
c. 25–29 the following subjects are dealt with :—(*a*) the vessels
of the Sanctuary, named naturally first, as being of central
interest and importance (c. 25); (*b*) the Tabernacle, designed to
contain and guard them (c. 26); (*c*) the Court round the Tabernacle containing the Altar of the daily Burnt-offering (c. 27);
(*d*) the dress (c. 28) and consecration (29$^{1-37}$) of the priests who
are to serve in the Sanctuary; (*e*) the daily Burnt-offering, the
maintenance of which is a primary duty of the Priesthood (29$^{38-42}$),
followed by what is apparently the final close of the entire body
of instructions, 29$^{43-46}$, in which Jehovah promises that He will
bless the Sanctuary thus established with His presence. C. 30–31
relate to (*a*) the Altar of Incense (30$^{1-10}$); (*b*) the maintenance of
public service (30$^{11-16}$); (*c*) the Brazen Laver (30$^{17-21}$); (*d*) the
holy Anointing Oil (30$^{22-33}$); (*e*) the Incense (30$^{34-38}$); (*f*) the
nomination of Bezaleel and Oholiab (31$^{1-11}$); (*g*) the observance
of the Sabbath (31$^{12-17}$).

[35] A question arises here whether the whole of this group of chapters
belongs to the original legislation of P. It is remarkable that the *Altar of
Incense*, which, from its importance, might have seemed to demand a place in c.
26–29 (among the other vessels of the Tabernacle), is mentioned for the first time
in 30$^{1-10}$, when the directions respecting the essential parts of the Tabernacle
are apparently complete (see 29$^{43-46}$): even in 26$^{34f.}$ (where the position of the
vessels of the sanctuary is defined) it is not included. Moreover, the annual
rite prescribed in Ex. 30^{10} is not noticed in the detailed account of the Day
of Atonement in Lev. 16, and only one altar, the Altar of Burnt-offering,
appears to be named throughout the chapter. Further, the ceremony of
anointing, which in 29^7 Lev. 8^{12} is confined to the Chief priest (Aaron), is in
30^{30} extended to the ordinary priests (his "sons"), although the original
limitation to Aaron alone would seem to be confirmed by the title "the
anointed priest," applied to the Chief priest (Lev. 4$^{3.\ 5.\ 16}$ 6^{22} [Heb. ^{15}]: cf.
16^{b2} 21$^{10.\ 12}$, Ex. 29$^{29t.}$, Nu. 35^{25}), which, if the priests generally were anointed,

* Comp. further on this code W. R. Smith, *OTJC.* p. 336 ff. (² p. 340 ff.).

would be destitute of any distinctive significance. On these grounds (chiefly) it is argued that c. 30–31, together with certain other passages in which the same phenomena occur, form part of a secondary and posterior stratum of P, representing a later phase of ceremonial usage. Space forbids the question being considered here as fully as it deserves; and it must suffice to refer to Wellh. *Comp.* 139 ff.; Kuen. *Hex.* § 6. 13; Del. *Studien*, iii.; Dillm. *EL.* p. 263 f., *NDJ.* p. 635; and Smith's *Dict. of the Bible* (ed.²), art. EXODUS.

The section on the Sabbath (31¹²⁻¹⁷), as has been often observed (*e.g.* by Delitzsch, *Studien*, xii. p. 622), has in v.¹³⁻¹⁴ᵃ affinities with the code of which extracts have been preserved in Lev. 17–26 (see p. 47 ff.); and it is probable that these verses have been excerpted thence, and adapted here as the nucleus of a law inculcating the observance of the Sabbath in connexion with an occasion on which the temptation might arise to disregard it.

In the narrative of the Golden Calf (31¹⁸ –34²⁸), c. 32, as a whole, may be assigned plausibly to E; only v.⁹⁻¹⁴ appears to have been expanded by the compiler of JE (comp. Gen. 22¹⁶⁻¹⁸, to which in v.¹³ allusion is made). 32³⁴–33⁶ exhibits traces of a double narrative: thus v.⁵ᵇ the people are commanded to do what, according to v.⁴ᵇ, *they had already done*—which confirms the *prima facie* view that v.⁵⁻⁶ is a doublet of v.³ᵇ⁻⁴. No satisfactory analysis of the entire passage has, however, been effected. All that can be said is that if E be the basis of 33¹⁻⁶, it has been amplified by the compiler, possibly with elements derived from J.

33⁷⁻¹¹, which (as the tenses in the original show) describes throughout Moses' *practice* (v.⁷ "*used* to take and pitch," &c.), was preceded, it may be conjectured, in its original connexion by an account of the construction of the Tent of Meeting and of [36] the Ark,* which was no doubt the purpose to which the ornaments, v.⁴⁻⁶, were put; when the narrative was combined with that of P, this part of it (being superfluous by the side of c. 25. 35, &c.) was probably omitted, only v.⁷⁻¹¹ being regarded as of sufficient interest to be retained.

33¹²–34⁹ forms a continuous whole, though whether belonging to J (Dillm.) or to the compiler of JE (Wellh.) can scarcely be definitely determined; in 34¹⁻³ there may be traces of E. It is a plausible conjecture of Dillmann's that 33¹⁴⁻¹⁷ originally followed 34⁹: where this passage now stands, it breaks the connexion between 33¹³ and 33¹⁸; while as stating the issue of the whole intercession, and directly responding to 34⁹, it would be

---

* See especially Dt. 10¹, which a comparison with the text of Ex. shows must refer to something *omitted* in the existing narrative (see below, § 5).

entirely in place. 34^{10-26} introduces the terms of the covenant, v.^{27}. These agree substantially—often even verbally *—with the theocratic section of the "Book of the Covenant" ($23^{10ff.}$); the essential parts of which appear to be repeated, with some enlarge ment (especially in the warning against idolatry v.$^{12-17}$), as consti tuting the conditions for the *renewal* of the covenant.

In the preceding pages no attempt has been made to give more than an outline of the structure of JE's narrative in c. 19–24. 32–34. Much has been written upon it; but though it displays plain marks of composition, it fails to supply the criteria requisite for distributing it in detail between the different narrators, and more than one hypothesis may be framed which will account, at least apparently, for the facts demanding ex planation. It is probable that it reached its present form by a series of stages which can no longer, in their entirety, be dis tinguished with certainty. The relation of the Code of Laws in 34^{11-26} to the very similar Code in $23^{10ff.}$ is also capable of dif ferent explanations. Hence beyond a certain point the conclu sions of critics are divergent. Under the circumstances, it seemed wisest to the writer not to include in his analysis more than appeared to him to be reasonably probable.

Those who desire to pursue the subject further should consult Wellh. *Comp.* pp. 83 ff., 327–333; Dillmann, *Comm.* pp. 189 ff., 331 ff. (who in some [37] respects takes a very different view from Wellh.); Montefiore, *JQR.* Jan. 1891, p. 276 ff.; Jülicher, *JPTh.* 1882, pp. 295–315; and the discussions of Budde, Bacon, and Baentsch, cited p. 22. See also *OTJC.*^{2} p. 332 ff.

By the author—or redactor—of 34^{1-28} in its present form (see v.^{1b}; and cf. Dt. 10^{1-4}) the "ten commandments" (Heb. "words") of v.^{28b} are manifestly intended to be the Decalogue of 20^{1-17}; on the other hand, the natural subject of ויכתב v.^{28b} seems to be Moses (cf. also v.^{27a}): hence it has been inferred by many that, in the original context of v.^{28}, the "ten words" were the body of laws contained in the preceding verses (v.$^{10-26}$), which, though now expanded by the compiler, will in that case have comprised originally ten particular injunctions. Wellh. (*l.c.* p. 331 f.; cf. Stade, *Gesch.* i. 510) supposes this second Decalogue to have consisted of $34^{14.~17.~18a}$ (to *keep*) $^{19a.~22a.~22c.~25a.~25b}$ [in the form of 23^{18b}] $^{26a.~26b}$. Those who adopt this view consider v.^{1} from כראשנים, and v.^{4a} to כראשנים—or כראשנים alone—to be additions made by the compiler: note in v.^{4b} אבנים, not האבנים,—unless indeed this be merely a textual error.

On the other hand, it has long been noticed—as by Bertheau (1840), Ewald

---

* Cf. v.$^{18.~20b.~21.~22-23.~25-26}$ with $23^{15.~12.~16-19}$. V.$^{19-20a}$, however, agrees with an earlier part of JE, viz. 13^{12-13}.

(*Hist.* ii. 166 ff.), Dillmann, Briggs (*Higher Crit. of the Hex.* 1893, p. 211 ff.) —that many of the laws in the Book of the Covenant seem to fall into groups of *ten*; and L. B. Paton (*JBLit.* 1893, p. 79 ff.), developing further the views expressed by these scholars, and comparing partly the (largely) parallel laws in 34$^{12-26}$, partly the laws in Dt. (which, as will be shown in § 5, depend in many cases upon those of Ex.), argues with some force that Ex. 20^{22}–23^{33} and 34$^{12-26}$ are both abbreviations, and in part rearrangements, of a common longer original, which consisted of *eight*, or perhaps even of *ten*, groups of ten laws each, each group being comprised of laws closely related in their subject-matter, and being systematically divided into two tables of five laws each.   The decades are : — 1. On slavery, 21$^{2.\ 3a.\ 3b.\ 4.\ 5-6}$ (males), 21$^{7-11}$ (females) ; 2. On assaults, 21$^{12-16}$ (punishable with death), 21$^{18-19.\ 20.\ 21.\ 26.\ 27}$ (punishable with lighter penalties) ; 3. On domestic animals, 21$^{28-32}$ (injuries done *by* them), 21$^{33-34.\ 35.\ 36}$ 22$^{1.\ 4}$ (injuries done *to* them) ; 4. On property, 22$^{5-9}$ (in general), 22$^{10-11.\ 13.\ 14.\ 15a.\ 15b}$ (property in *cattle*) ; 5. On injustice, 23$^{1a.\ 1b.\ 2a.\ 2b.\ 3}$ (among equals), 23$^{6.\ 7a.\ 7b.\ 7c}$ LXX [And *thou* shalt not justify the wicked] ^{8} (on the part of those in authority) ; 6. On the sacred seasons and the manner of their observance, 23$^{10-11.\ 12.\ 15a.\ 16a.\ 16b}$, 23$^{17.\ 18a.\ 18b.}$ $^{19a.\ 19b}$ (all but the first of this decade being repeated in 34$^{21.\ 18a.\ 22a.\ 22b}$, 34$^{23.\ 25a.\ 25b.\ 26a.\ 26b}$) ; 7. On certain religious duties, 34$^{12.\ 13.\ 14}$ (cf. 20^{23a}) 15. 16. 17 (cf. 20^{23b}), 20$^{24a.\ 24b.\ 25.\ 26}$; 8. (do.) 22$^{28a.\ 28b.\ 29a.\ 29b}$ (cf. 34^{19a}) ^{30} (cf. 34^{19b}), 34$^{20a.\ 20b.\ 20c.\ 20d}$ (=23^{15c}) 22^{31} ; 9. On purity, Dt. 22$^{13-19.\ 20-21.\ 22.\ 23-24.\ 25-27}$ 22$^{28-29}$ (cf. Ex. 22^{16}), Ex. 22$^{17.\ 18.\ 19.\ 20}$; 10. On kindness, Ex. 22$^{21.\ 22.\ 25a.\ 25b.}$ $^{26-27}$ (towards men), 23^4 (=Dt. 22^1), Dt. 22$^{2.\ 3.\ 4}$ (=Ex. 23^5) $^{6-7}$ (towards animals).   The passages omitted are either laws which cohere badly with the context, and have probably been introduced from some different source by a later hand (Ex. 21$^{17.\ 22-25}$ 22$^{2-3.\ 12}$ 23$^{9.\ 13.\ 14.\ 15c}$), or parenetic additions ; the original form of many of the laws, especially those in Ex. 34 and Dt., was also probably much terser than it is now.   The scheme is attractive ; but it may be doubted whether all the decades are quite clearly and naturally constituted.

C. 35–40 form the sequel to c. 25–31, narrating the execution of the instructions there communicated to Moses.   The relation of these chapters to c. 25–31 will be best learnt from the following synopsis, extracted (with slight modifications) from Kuenen's *Onderzoek* (§ 6. 15), which exhibits at the same time the corresponding passages of the LXX (the *order* of which in several cases differs remarkably from that of the Hebrew) :—

Hebrew Text.	Greek Text.	Ex. 25–31.
35$^{1-3}$ (the Sabbath : v.^{3} added).	35$^{1-3}$.	31^{15}.
$^{4-9}$ (the people are invited to bring free-will offerings).	35$^{4-8}$ (v.^{8} Heb. omitted).	25$^{1-9}$.
$^{10-19}$ (all skilled workmen invited to assist).	35$^{9-19}$ (with variations).	

Hebrew Text.	Greek Text.	Ex. 25-31.
35^{20-29} (the offerings are presented).	35^{20-29}.	
^{30}-36^1 (Moses announces to the people the appointment of Bezaleel and Oholiab).	35^{30}-36^1.	31^{1-11}.
36^{2-7} (the presentation of offerings completed).	36^{2-7}.	
$^{8-19}$ (Curtains made for the "tabernacle" (the משכן), and the	cf. 37^{1-2}.	$26^{1-11. 14}$.
[38] tent over it).		
$^{20-34}$ (Boards for the framework of the "tabernacle").	cf. 38^{18-21}.	26^{15-29}.
$^{35-38}$ (Veil for the Holy of holies, and Screen for the entrance to the Tent).	37^{3-6}.	$26^{31-32. 36-37}$.
37^{1-9} (the Ark).	38^{1-8}.	25^{10-20}.
$^{10-16}$ (Table of Shewbread).	38^{9-12}.	25^{23-29}.
$^{17-24}$ (Candlestick).	38^{13-17}.	25^{31-39}.
$^{25-28}$ (Altar of Incense).	*Wanting.*	30^{1-5}.
^{29} (Anointing Oil and Incense).	38^{25}.	$30^{22-33. 34-38}$.
38^{1-7} (Altar of Burnt-offering).	cf. 38^{22-24}.	27^{1-8}.
^{8} (Brazen Laver).	38^{26}.	30^{17-18a}.
$^{9-20}$ (Court of the Tabernacle).	37^{7-18}.	27^{9-19}.
$^{21-23}$ (Superscription to the account of metal employed).	37^{19-21}.	
$^{24-31}$ (the account itself).	39^{1-10}.	cf. 30^{11-16}.
39^{1-31} (Vestments for the High Priest and the Priests).	36^{8b-40}.	28^{1-43}.
$^{32-43}$ (Delivery to Moses of the completed work of the Tabernacle).	$39^{11. 14-23}$.	
40^{1-16} (Moses commanded to rear up the Tabernacle and to consecrate the priests).	40^{1-13} (v. $^{6-8}$ Heb. omitted in part, v. ^{11} altogether).	
$^{17-33}$ (the Tabernacle erected, and the sacred vessels arranged in their places).	40^{14-26} 38^{27} 40^{27} (v$^{28. 29b}$ Heb. omitted).	
$^{34-38}$ (the Cloud and Pillar of Fire).	40^{28-32}.	

In the main, the narrative is repeated *verbatim* from the instructions in c. 25-31, with the simple substitution of past tenses for future; in two or three cases, however, a phrase is altered, and there are also some instances of omission or abridgment. Thus a few verses (as $25^{15. 22. 40}$ 26^{12-13} $28^{29. 35}$ 29^{43-46} 30^{7-10}) are omitted, as not needing repetition; others (as $25^{16. 21.}$ $^{30. 37b}$ $26^{30. 33. 34-35}$ $30^{6. 18b. 19-21}$, chiefly relating to the *position* of the different vessels named) are incorporated in c. 40^{17-33}, the account of the erection of the Tabernacle, where they naturally belong;

and the sections on the Anointing Oil and the Incense ($30^{22\text{-}33.}$ $^{34\text{-}38}$) are merely referred to briefly in a single verse, 37^{29}. In c. 39 there are also some noticeable cases of abbreviation. The only material omissions are the Urim and Thummim (28^{30}), [39] and the consecration of priests ($29^{1\text{-}37}$), which follow in Lev. 8, the oil for the lamps ($27^{20f.}$), and the daily Burnt-offering ($29^{38\text{-}42}$) : with these exceptions the execution of the instructions contained in c. 25–31 is related systematically.* The change of order is in most cases intelligible. The injunction to observe the Sabbath, which closes the series of instructions, stands here in the first place. This is followed by the presentation of offerings, and the nomination of Bezaleel and Oholiab ; after which is narrated the construction of the Tabernacle, of the sacred vessels to be placed in it, and of the Altar and Laver, with the Court surrounding them. The Sanctuary having been thus completed, the dress of the priests is prepared, the work, complete in its different parts, delivered to Moses, and the Tabernacle erected and set in order. The Altar of Incense and the Brazen Laver, which appear in the Appendix to c. 25–29 (viz. in c. 30), are here enumerated in accordance with the place which they properly hold, in the Tabernacle (c. 37) and Court (c. 38) respectively.

C. 35–40 raise the same question of relationship to the main body of P which was stated above on c. 30 f. If c. 30 f. be allowed to belong to a secondary stratum of P, the same conclusion will follow for these chapters as a necessary corollary ; for in c. 35–39 the notices referring to c. 30–31 are introduced *in their proper order*, and c. 40 alludes to the Altar of Incense. † Dillm., though he disputes Wellh.'s conclusions with regard to c. 30-31, agrees with him virtually as regards c. 35–40 (*NDJ.* p. 635).

§ 3. LEVITICUS.

LITERATURE.—See above, p. 1 f. ; and add S. R. Driver and H. A. White in Haupt's *Sacred Books of the OT.*

The Book of Leviticus is called by the Jews, from its opening word, וַיִּקְרָא. It forms throughout part of the Priests' Code, in which, however, c. 17–26 constitute a section marked by certain

* $38^{24\text{-}31}$ differs, however, somewhat remarkably from $30^{11\text{-}16}$.

† For some other grounds, peculiar to these chapters, which are held to point in the same direction, see Kuenen, *Hex.* § 6. 15.

special features of its own, and standing apart from the rest of the book.

I. C. 1–16. *Fundamental Laws of Sacrifice, Purification, and Atonement.*

(i.) 1¹–6⁷ (c. 1–5 Heb.). *Law of the five principal types of sacrifice.*

[40] C. 1. The Burnt-offering (ritual of sacrifice).

C. 2. The Meal-offering (ritual of sacrifice).

The *second* pers. in 2⁴⁻¹⁶ (unlike the rest of these chapters) is noticeable, and may be an indication that the ch. is formed out of a combination of elements originally distinct.

C. 3. The Peace-offering (ritual of sacrifice).

C. 4. The Sin-offering (ritual of sacrifice for the four cases of unintentional sin, committed by 1. the "anointed priest" (*i.e.* the Chief priest); 2. the whole people; 3. a ruler; 4. an ordinary Israelite).

It is not impossible that Lev. 4 may represent a more advanced stage in the growth of the sacrificial system than Ex.²⁹ Lev. 8–9; for here the blood of the Sin-offering for the Chief priest and for the people is treated with special solemnity, being sprinkled against the veil, and applied to the horns of the Incense-altar; whereas in Ex. 29¹² Lev. 8¹⁵ 9⁹. ¹⁵ it is treated precisely as prescribed here in the case of the ordinary Sin-offering, v.²⁵. ³⁰. ³⁴ (see Wellh. *Comp.* p. 138 f.).—A law for the Sin-offering both of the people and of an individual is contained also in Nu. 15²²⁻³¹.

5¹⁻¹³. Appendix to c. 4, containing (1) examples of unintentional sins, requiring a Sin-offering, v.¹⁻⁶; (2) provision for the case of those whose means did not suffice for the ordinary sin-offering, v.⁷⁻¹³.

5¹⁴–6⁷ (5¹⁴⁻²⁶ Heb.). The Guilt-offering (three cases, or groups of cases—viz. different cases of *fraud*, or sacrilege —defined, in which the Guilt-offering is incurred).

On 5¹⁷⁻¹⁹, which enjoins a *Guilt*-offering for (apparently) the same case for which in 4²²ᶠᶠ· a *Sin*-offering is prescribed, see Dillm. *ad loc.*; Stade, *Gesch.* ii. 256 f.

(ii.) 6⁸–c. 7 (c. 6–7 Heb.). *A manual of priestly directions under eight heads.*

6⁸⁻¹³. Regulations to be observed by the priest in sacrificing the Burnt-offering.

6^{14-18}. Regulations to be observed by the priest in sacrificing the Meal-offering.

$^{19-23}$. The High Priest's daily Meal-offering.

$^{24-30}$. Regulations to be observed in sacrificing the Sin-offering.

7^{1-7}. Ritual of the Guilt-offering (which is not defined in 5^{14}–6^7), with an appendix, v.$^{8-10}$ (arising out of v.^{7}), on the priests' share in the Burnt- and Meal-offering.

[41] $^{11-21}$. On the *species* of Peace-offering (the Thank-offering, v.$^{12-15}$; the Vow- and the Voluntary-offering, v.$^{16ff.}$), with the conditions to be observed by the worshipper in eating the flesh.

$^{22-27}$. Fat (of ox, sheep, and goat in all cases, and of other animals dying naturally or torn of beasts) and blood (generally) not to be eaten.

$^{28-34}$. The priests' share of the Peace-offering, viz. the "heave-leg" and the "wave-breast."

$^{35-36}$. First subscription to the preceding section, 6^8–7^{34} (in so far as this comprises regulations respecting the priests' share in the different offerings).

$^{37-38}$. Second more general subscription.

This subscription relates to 6^8–c. 7 only, which forms an independent collection of laws linked together by the same formula that is used here, viz. *This is the law of* . . . ($6^{9.\ 14.\ 25}$ $7^{1.\ 11}$); only the laws thus introduced are recognised in the subscription, where they occur in the same order: * 6^{19-23} (otherwise introduced, and not, as it seems, recognised in the subscription) was perhaps not originally part of the collection; 7^{22-27} (regulating the conditions under which animals might be used for food) may be regarded as an appendix to 7^{11-21}, being probably placed here on account of the Peace-offering being accompanied by a sacrificial meal; the subject of 7^{28-34} is also closely connected with the Peace-offering, and may be fairly regarded as comprehended in the heading 7^{11}.

The main distinction between c. 1–6^7 and 6^8–c. 7 is that while the laws of the former group relate, as a rule, to the manner in which *the sacrifice itself* is to be offered, the latter contain regulations *ancillary* to this, *e.g.* concerning the dress of the officiating priest, the fire on the altar, the portions to be eaten by the priest or the worshipper (as the case may be), the disposal of the flesh of the Peace-offerings (as opposed to the parts which went upon the

---

* In the existing text of Lev. 6^8–c. 7 nothing corresponds to the "consecration" offering of 7^{37}; either the expression rests on a misinterpretation of 6^{19-23}, or a law on this subject may have been omitted by the compiler of P in view of the fuller treatment in Ex. 29.

altar, c. 3), etc. The treatment is not, however, perfectly uniform through-out : on the analogy of c. 1–4, 7$^{1-7}$ (the *ritual* of the Guilt-offering) should occupy the place of—or, at least, precede (cf. c. 4 before 5$^{1-6}$)—5^{14}–6^7 (the *cases* in which the Guilt-offering is to be paid).

(iii.) C. 8–10. *The consecration of the priests, and their solemn entry upon office.*

C. 8. Aaron and his sons consecrated to the priesthood in accordance with the instructions Ex. 29$^{1-37}$.

[42] C. 9. Aaron and his sons solemnly enter upon their office.

C. 10$^{1-7}$. Nadab and Abihu punished for offering strange fire : the priests forbidden to mourn for them.

8-9 (10-11). Priests forbidden to drink wine while officiating.

12-15. The priests' share in the Meal-offerings and Peace offerings.

16-20. A law in narrative form determining that, in the people's Sin-offering (the blood of which was not v.^{18} (cf. 9$^{15,\ 9}$) brought within the Tabernacle), the flesh should be eaten by the priest, not burnt without the camp (as had been done 9^{15}, cf. v.^{11}).

This law is a correction of the usage followed in 9^{15b} (see 9^{11})—which is in agreement with the analogy of the injunction Ex. 29^{14}, and its execution Lev. 8^{17}—on the ground of the regulation in c. 4, according to which the flesh of only those Sin-offerings was to be *burnt*, of which the blood had been brought within the Tabernacle and applied to the Altar of Incense (4$^{1-21}$; cf. 6^{80}). The connexion of 10$^{10f.}$ with 10^9 is imperfect, the subject treated being in reality a different one (see 11^{47} ; and comp. Ez. 44^{23} beside v.^{21}). Unless the rendering of RV. *marg.* be adopted—which, though gram-matically possible, is somewhat artificial—it would almost seem as if 10$^{10f.}$ had been transplanted from its original context.

(iv.) C. 11–16. *Laws of Purification and Atonement.*

C. 11. Clean and unclean animals.

(1) Animals unclean as food : (*a*) Quadrupeds (בהמה), v.$^{2-8}$; (*b*) aquatic creatures (שרץ המים " swarming * things of the waters "), v. $^{9-12}$; (*c*) flying creatures (עוף), a. birds, v.$^{13-19}$; β. flying insects (שרץ העוף " swarming things that fly "), v.$^{20-23}$; (*d*) creeping insects and reptiles (הַשֶּׁרֶץ הַשֹּׁרֵץ עַל הָאָרֶץ " swarming things that swarm upon the earth "), v.$^{41-42}$, with conclusion, v.$^{43-45.}$ (2) On the pollution caused by contact with the carcases of certain animals, v.$^{24-40.}$ V.$^{46-47}$ subscription.

* On this rendering, see Clark s *Bible Dict. s.v.* CREEPING THINGS.

V.[2b-23] recurs, with verbal differences (the two texts are printed in parallel columns in the writer's *Deut.* pp. 157–159), in Dt. 14[4-20]. The law, in its primitive form, is, no doubt, older than either Lev. or Dt., and appears (Paton, *Journ. of Bibl. Lit.* 1895, p. 48 ff.) to be preserved on the whole more exactly in Dt. than in Lev., the variations in Lev. betokening generally the hand of the priestly author (or editor) of P. The original law may be read probably in Dt. 14[4a. 6-8a] (to *you*) [9-12], Lev. 11[14-19], Dt. 14[19], Lev. 11[21-22. 41. 43-45]. (On "abomination" in this ch., cf. Clark's *Bible Dict. s.v.*)

V.[24-40] appears also to be a later insertion in the chapter ; for the subscription, v.[46f.], notices only the four classes of creatures not to be *eaten* (v.[2-8] ; [13-23] ; [9-12] ; [41-45]), and ignores the contents of v.[24-40] (creatures whose carcases are not to be *touched*) ; these verses, moreover, differ from the rest of the ch., in that they define the purification rendered necessary by non-observance of the regulations prescribed.

[**43**] C. 12. Purification after child-birth.

This ch. would more suitably follow c. 15, with which it is connected in subject, and which, indeed, it presupposes in v.[2] (see 15[19]).

C. 13–14. Leprosy.

Diagnosis of leprosy in man, 13[1-46] ; leprosy in clothing and leather, v.[47-59] ; purification of the leper, 14[1-32] ; leprosy in a house, v.[33-53] ; subscription to the whole, v.[54-57].

C. 15. Purification after certain natural secretions.

C. 11–15 are linked together by the recurring colophon *This is the law of* . . . 11[46] 12[7] 13[59] 14[32. (54). 57] 15[32].

C. 16. Ceremonial of the Day of Atonement.

V.[1-2] Historical introduction.—V.[3-10] Preparations for the ceremonial prescribed in v.[11-28] (Aaron's dress, selection of animals, &c.).—V.[11-14] Aaron to offer the *sin-offering* (a bullock) for himself.—V.[15-19] Aaron to make atonement for the sanctuary (v.[15f.]), and the Altar of Burnt-offering (v.[18f.]), with the *sin-offering* (a goat) offered on behalf of the people.—V.[20-22] The sins of the people to be confessed over the other goat (v.[8. 10]), which is then to be led away into the wilderness for Azazel.—V.[23-24] Aaron to offer the *burnt-offerings* (two rams) for himself and for the people.—V.[25-28] Subordinate instructions.—V.[29-34] The people, on the day on which atonement is made for them, to practise self-denial, and to abstain from all labour.

The introduction, v.[1], directly connects this ch. with c. 10. Whether it was originally separated from c. 10 by c. 11–15 (esp. when the different character of the introductions 11[1] 13[1] 14[33] 15[1] is considered) may be doubtful. At the same time, the position which c. 11–15 now occupy is a thoroughly appropriate one : "They come *after* the consecration of the priests, whose functions concerning the 'clean' and 'unclean' they regulate, and *before* the law of the Day of Atonement, on which the sanctuary is cleansed from the pollutions caused by involuntary uncleanness of priests and people" (Kuen. p. 82 ; so Wellh. p. 150).

The ch. deals in reality with two subjects, viz. (1) the conditions under which the high priest might enter the Holy of holies (see v.²), and (2) an atoning ceremony, to be enacted once annually, on behalf of the nation. As here treated, these subjects are imperfectly connected together ; and hence Benzinger (*ZATW.* 1889, pp. 65–89), with whom Nowack (*Hebr. Arch.* ll. 187 ff.) agrees, argues that the ch. is of composite authorship, its nucleus, as he supposes, consisting of v.¹⁻⁴. ⁶ (=11). 12–13. 34b (conditions of the high priest's entering the Holy of holies), and v.²⁹⁻³⁴ᵃ (an independent law, prescribing a relatively simple annual rite of atonement : cf. 23²⁶⁻³²), while v.⁵. ⁷⁻¹⁰. ¹⁴⁻²⁸ present a subsequent development of the older rite, which was introduced into the ch. by a later hand, and interwoven, as it now stands, with directions relating to Aaron alone, on account of its having become the custom for the high priest to enter the Holy of holies on the Day of Atonement only. It is highly probable that the ritual of the Day of Atonement (cf. Ez. 45¹⁸⁻²⁰) was once simpler than that now prescribed in this ch.; but, though the proposed analysis is very suggestive, it may be doubted whether the stages through which the ritual passed are fully represented by it : v.³³ (cf. 23²⁸ᵇ) appears to presuppose more special rites than the nucleus of the ch., as thus defined, makes provision for. Comp. ATONEMENT, DAY OF, in Clark's *Bible Dictionary*, p. 200.

II. C. 17–26. *The Law of Holiness.*

LITÉRATURE.—Graf, *Die Geschichtlichen Bücher des AT.s* (1866), pp. 75–83 ; Nöldeke, *Untersuchungen* (1869), pp. 62–71 ; Kayser, *Das Vorexilische Buch der Urgeschichte Isr.* (1874), pp. 176–184 ; Klostermann, *Hat Ezechiel die in Lev.* 18–26 *am deutlichsten erkennbare Gesetzessammlung verfasst?* in the *Z. für Luth. Theologie*, 1877, pp. 406–445 (reprinted in *Der Pentateuch*, 1893, p. 368 ff.) ; Wellhausen, *Comp.* pp. 151–175 ; Delitzsch, *Studien* (1880), xii. p. 617 ff. ; Horst, *Leviticus* xvii.–xxvi. *und Hezekiel* (Colmar, 1881) ; Wurster in the *ZATW*. 1884, pp. 112–133 ; Kuenen, *Hexateuch*, §§ 6. 24–28 ; 14. 6 ; 15. 5–10 ; Riehm, *Einleitung* (1889), i. 177–202 ; Baentsch, *Das Heiligkeits-Gesetz*, 1893.

We arrive here at a group of chapters which stand by themselves in P. While in general form and scope appertaining to P, they differ from the main body of P by the presence of a *foreign element*, which manifests itself partly in the style and phraseology, partly in the motives which here become prominent. The phenomena which the chapters present are explained by the supposition that [44] first an independent collection of laws was edited, with parenetic additions, by a compiler (Rʰ), and that afterwards the whole thus formed was incorporated in P, either by the author of P, or by a redactor writing under the influence of P (Rᴾ),—sometimes with modifications introduced for the purpose of adjusting it more completely to the spirit and system of P, at other times interwoven with elements derived from P. The elements thus united with P are distinguished from it, partly by the predominance of certain expressions never, or very rarely, found in P (or indeed in the Hexateuch generally), partly by the prominence given to particular principles and motives : the parenetic framework with which the laws have, in certain cases, been provided is also contrary to P.'s usual style. The principle which determines most conspicuously the character of the entire section is that of *holiness*—partly ceremonial, partly moral—as a quality distinguishing Israel, demanded of Israel by Jehovah (19^2 $20^{7.\ 8.\ 26}$ $21^{6-8.\ 15.\ 23}$ $22^{9.\ 16.\ 32}$), and regulating the Israelite's life. Holiness is, indeed, a duty laid upon Israel in other parts of the Pent. ;* but while elsewhere it appears merely as one injunction among many, it is here insisted on with an emphasis and frequency which constitute it the leading motive of the entire section. In consequence of this very prominent characteristic, the present group of chapters received from Klostermann in 1877 the happily-chosen title of *Das Heiligkeitsgesetz*, or "The Law of Holiness," which it has since retained.

That these chapters of Lev. are rightly treated as containing an independent body of laws, appears not merely from the distinctive character thus belonging to them, but, further, from the somewhat miscellaneous nature of their contents (as compared with Lev. $1-16^{27}$), from the recurrence in them of subjects that have been dealt with before, not only in Ex. 20-23, but also in P (comp. 17^{10-14} and $7^{26f.}$; 19^{6-8} and 7^{15-18}; 20^{25} and c. 11), and from the fact that they open with instructions respecting the place of sacrifice, and close with a parenetic exhortation, exactly in the manner of the two other Pentateuchal Codes, the "Book of the Covenant" (Ex. 20^{24-26} $23^{20ff.}$) and the code in Deuteronomy (Dt. 12 and 28). The laws, no doubt, in substance, if not also in form, date in general from a much older time than that of the collector (R^h) who [45] first fitted them into their present framework. It will be convenient to denote the laws thus incorporated in P, with their parenetic framework, by the abbreviation *H*.† H has points of contact with P, but lacks many of its most character-

---

* In JE Ex. 22^{31} (though in a ceremonial rather than in a moral connexion) ; and in Dt. $14^{2.\ 21}$.

† Kuenen uses the symbol P^1, distinguishing different strata of the Priests' Code (denoted by P in the present volume) as P^2 and P^3.

istic features. Ezekiel, the priestly prophet, has affinities with P, but his affinities with H are peculiarly striking and numerous : the laws comprised in H are frequently quoted by him, and the parenetic passages contain many expressions—sometimes remarkable ones—which otherwise occur in Ezekiel alone.

List of phrases characteristic of c. 17-26 :—

1. אני יהוה *I am Jehovah*, esp. at the end of an injunction or series of injunctions (nearly fifty times) : $18^{2. * 4. * 5. 6. 21. 30 *}$ $19^{3. * 4. * 10. * 12. 14.}$ $16. 18. 25. * 28. 30. 31. * 32. 34. * 36. * 37$ $20^{7. * 8. + 24 ‡}$ $21^{12. 15. + 23 +}$ $22^{2. 3. 8. 9. +}$ $16. + 30. 31. 32. + 33$ $23^{22 * 43 *}$ $24^{22 *}$ $25^{17. * 38. + 55 *}$ $26^{1 * 2. 13. + 44. * 45}$. So Ex. $6^{(2. 6.) 8. 29}$ 12^{12b} $29^{46b} *$ (cf. 31^{13b} †), Nu. $3^{13 end. 41. 45}$ $10^{10 *}$ $15^{41a. ‡}$ $41b$ *.

2. כי קדוש אני יהוה *For I Jehovah am holy* : $19^2 *$ 20^{26} $21^{8}.$† Cf. $11^{44. 45}$, (For I am holy).

3. *That sanctify you (them, &c.)* : 20^8 $21^{8. 15. 23}$ $22^{9. 16. 32}$. So Ex. 31^{13}, Ez. 20^{12} $37^{28}.$↑

4. איש איש for *whoever* : $17^{3. 8. 10. 13}$ 18^6 $20^{2. 9}$ $22^{4. 18}$ 24^{15}. So 15^2, Nu. 5^{12} 9^{10}, Ez. $14^{4. 7}$ (with מבית ישראל as ch. $17^{3. 8. 10}$).

5. *I will set* (ונתתי) *my face against* . . . : 17^{10} $20^{3. 5}$ (ושמתי אני) 6 26^{17}. So Ez. 14^8 $15^{7a. 7b}$ (שם), Jer. 21^{10} (שם), 44^{11} (שם).↑

6. *I will cut off from the midst of his (its, their) people* : 17^{10} $20^{3. 5. 6}.$§ Cf. Ez. 14^8 (. . . מתוך : in Lev. מקרב).

[46] 7. הלך בחקות *to walk in the statutes* : 18^3 20^{23} 26^3. Also 1 Ki. 3^9 6^{12}, 2 Ki. $17^{8. 19}$; but chiefly in Ez., viz. $5^{6. 7}$ 11^{20} $18^{9. 17}$ $20^{13. 16. 19. 21}$ 33^{15} : cf. Jer. 44^{10} (בחוקתי ובחקתי).↑

8. חקתי ומשפטי *my statutes and my judgments* : 18^4 (inverted) $5. 26$ 19^{37} 20^{22} 25^{18} $26^{15. 43}$.

9. *To observe and do* : 18^4 19^{37} $20^{8. 22}$ 22^{31} 25^{18} 26^3.

10. שְׁאֵר *flesh = next-of-kin* : $18^{12. 13. 17}$ (שארה) 20^{19} 21^2, Nu. 27^{11} ; שְׁאֵרוֹ בִּ 18^6 25^{49}. Not so elsewhere.

11. ומה *evil purpose* (of unchastity) : 18^{17} 19^{29} $20^{14 bis}$. So Jud. 20^6, Hos. 6^9 (?), Jer. 13^{27}, Ez. $16^{27. 43. 58}$ $22^{9. 11}$ $23^{21. 27. 29. 35. 44. 48. 48. 49}$ 24^{13}, Job 31^{11}. (In RV. often *lewdness*.)

12. עמית *neighbour* : 18^{20} $19^{11. 15. 17}$ 24^{19} $25^{14 bis. 15. 17}$ $5^{21 bis}$, Zech. 13^7.↑ A peculiar term ; not the one in ordinary use.

---

* Followed by *your (their) God*.

† Followed by the participial clause *that sanctify you (him, &c.)*.

‡ Followed by a relative clause.

↑ The arrow (both here and elsewhere) denotes that all instances of the word or phrase referred to that occur in the OT. have been cited. The *distinctive* character of an expression is evidently the more marked, and the agreement between two writers who use it is the more striking, in proportion to the rarity with which it occurs in the OT. generally.

§ In P always "*shall be* cut off" (see p. 133). In general the Divine "I" appears here with a prominence which it never assumes in the laws of P.

13. *To profane*—*the name of Jehovah* 18²¹ 19¹² 20³ 21⁶ 22². ³² (Am. 2⁷, Isa. 48¹¹) : a *holy thing* or *sanctuary* 19⁸ 21¹². ²³ 22¹⁵ (so Nu. 18³²) : in other connexions 19²⁹ 21⁹ᵇ. ¹⁵ 22⁹ : comp. 21⁴. ⁹ᵃ. So Ex. 31¹⁴ (of the Sabbath). So often in Ezek. : of *Jehovah* 13¹⁹ 22²⁶ ; *His name* 20⁹. ¹⁴. ²². ³⁹ 36²⁰⁻²³ 39⁷ ; *His sabbaths* 20¹³. ¹⁶. ²¹. ²⁴ 22⁸ 23³⁸ (Isa. 56². ⁶) ; *His holy things* or *sanctuary* 22²⁶ 23³⁹ 44⁷ ; cf. also 7²¹. ²². ²⁴ 22¹⁶ 24²¹ 25³ 28⁷. ¹⁶. ¹⁸. Obviously the correlative of Nos. 2, 3.

14. *My sabbaths* : 19³. ³⁰ 26², Ex. 31¹³, Ez. 20¹². ¹³. ¹⁶. ²⁰. ²¹. ²⁴ 22⁸. ²⁶ 23³⁸ 44²⁴, Isa. 56⁴.↑

15. אֱלִילִים *things of nought*=*vain gods* : 19⁴ 26¹. Not elsewhere in Pent. Chiefly besides in Isaiah (9 times, and הָאֱלִיל once).

16. וְיָרֵאתָ מֵאֱלֹהֶיךָ *and thou shalt be afraid of thy God* : 19¹⁴. ³² 25¹⁷. ³⁶. ⁴³.

17. (רמיו בו (דמיהם בם *his* (*their*) *blood shall be upon him* (*them*) : 20⁹. ¹¹. ¹². ¹³. ¹⁶. ²⁷, Ez. 18¹³ (רמיו בו יהיה) 33⁵ (רמו בו יהיה).↑ (The ordinary phrase is רמו על (ב)ראשו.)

18. *The bread of* (*their*) *God* : 21⁶. ⁸. ¹⁷. ²¹. ²² 22²⁵, Nu. 28² (cf. v.²⁴, Lev. 3¹¹. ¹⁶), Ez. 44⁷.↑ (Ez. 16¹⁹ differently.)

19ᵃ. נשא חטא *to bear sin* : 19¹⁷ 22⁹, Nu. 18²². ³² ; cf. Ez. 23⁴⁹.↑

19ᵇ. (נשא(ו) חטא(ם *to bear his* (*their*) *sin* : 20²⁰ 24¹⁵, Nu. 9¹³.↑

20ᵃ. (נשא(ו) עונו(ם *to bear his* (*their*) *iniquity* : 17¹⁶ 19⁸ 20¹⁷. ¹⁹. So 5¹. ¹⁷ 7¹⁸, Nu. 5³¹ 14³⁴ (cf. 15³¹ עונה בה), Ez. 14¹⁹ 44¹⁰. ¹².↑

20ᵇ. נשא עון *to bear iniquity* : Ex. 28⁴³ ; cf. Lev. 22¹⁶.↑

20ᶜ. . . . נשא עֲוֹן *to bear the iniquity of* . . . (=*be responsible for*) : Ex. 28³⁸, Nu. 18¹. ¹ ; so *bear their iniquity*, v.²⁸ (see Dillm. ; and comp. Wellh. *Comp.* p. 341).↑

20ᵈ. . . . *to bear the iniquity of* another : Lev. 10¹⁷ 16²², Nu. 30¹⁵ [H.¹⁶], Ez. 4⁴. ⁴. ⁵. ⁶ (not always in the same application). So נשא חטא *to bear the sin of* many, Is. 53¹².

[47] The distinctive prominence attached in this group of chapters to the ideas of holiness, and of the reverence due to Jehovah or to a holy thing, will be evident from this collection of characteristic expressions. Amongst the expressions quoted, several instances of agreement with Ezekiel will have been observed; others will be noticed subsequently (§ 7), when the nature of the relation subsisting between Ezekiel and the "Law of Holiness" comes to be considered more particularly. The principal critical problem which the chapters present is the separation of their original nucleus from the subsequent priestly additions.

We may now proceed to examine c. 17–26 in detail.

C. 17 treats of *four* subjects:—

　　　　1. Animals (of a kind offered in sacrifice), when slain for *food*, to be presented at the central sanctuary, and their flesh eaten there as a Peace-offering, v.¹⁻⁷.

2. Animals slain for *sacrifice* to be offered only to Jehovah, and at the central sanctuary, v.[8-9].

3. Blood not to be eaten : in the case of animals of a kind not offered in sacrifice, it is to be poured upon the earth, v.[10-14].

4. The flesh of animals dying naturally, or torn by beasts, not to be eaten, v.[15-16].

C. 17 belongs in the main to H ; but the text is mixed, the regulations in their original form having received additions at the hands of the priestly compiler (Rᴾ), for the purpose of bringing them into greater conformity with P : viz. (Paton) v.[1-2] (the editorial title), v.[3] (the words "in the camp . . . without the camp"), v.[4. 9] ("unto (at) the door of the tent of meeting"), v.[5] ("even that . . . unto the priest," and "of peace-offerings"), v.[6] (the whole), v.[7b] v.[15-16] ("whether . . . his flesh, then he" ; according to others, the whole of v.[15-16] is a priestly addition). Whether what remains in v.[5-7], after these additions have been removed, is in its proper place, is also doubtful ; for it states in reality a motive not for v.[3-4] but for v.[8-9]. Comp. the analysis and notes in Haupt's *SBOT*; Baentsch, pp. 13-23 ; Paton, *l.c.* [p. 46], pp. 52-55.

On 17[1-7], and its relation to Dt 12[15ff.], see (1) Wellh. *Comp.* 152-154, *Hist.* 50 f. 377 ; Horst, 60 ; Kuen. § 6. 27, 28 ; 14. 6 ; 15. 5, 9 ; and esp. Baentsch, p. 116 f., who argue that the injunction belongs historically to the period intermediate between Dt. and P (*i.e.* to the exile) ; (2) Del. *Studien*, 447 f., 622, who argues that it is older than Dt., and abrogated by it (so Dillm. *EL.* 535) ; (3) Kittel, *Theol. Studien aus Württemberg*, 1881, 42 ff., *Gesch.* 99, and Baudissin, *Priesterthum*, 47, following Kayser and Diestel (cf. also Dillm. *EL.* 536; W. R. Smith, *OTJC.* 249; *Answer to the Amended Libel* (Edin. 1879), 61-64, 72, 73), who think that in its original form the law contained no reference to the central sanctuary, but presupposed a *plurality* of legal sanctuaries (Ex. 20[24]; cf. 1 Sa. 14[32-35]), and was accommodated to the single sanctuary only when it was incorporated in P. The law is not strictly consistent with P ; for in P (Lev. 7[22-27]) the slaughtering of animals for food is freely permitted, the only restriction being that their fat and blood are not to be eaten. The third of the opinions quoted appears to be the most probable.

To many of the laws in H there are parallels in the other Codes. See the passages quoted in the Synopsis of Dt., p. 73 ff.

C. 18. Unlawful marriages and unchastity; and Molech worship, v.[21].

[48] Entirely H. Observe the plan of the chapter : the laws themselves occupy the central part v.[6-23] ; v.[1-5. 24-30] form respectively a parenetic introduction and conclusion. The characteristics of H are very evident in the style of the parenetic portion, and also in the refrain "I am Jehovah," both there (v.[2b. 4b. 5b. 30b]) and in the laws (v.[6b. 21b]). No doubt the laws themselves were found by the compiler of H already formulated, and he merely provided

them with the parenetic setting. The *laws*, it may be observed, are in the 2nd pers. *sing.*, the parenetic portions in the 2nd pers. *plural.* V.[25-30], where (see the Heb.) the standpoint changes, and the conquest is looked back upon as past, may be (Paton) "a later editor's sermon upon v.[24] as a text."

C. 19. A collection of miscellaneous laws, regulating (chiefly) the religious and moral behaviour of the Israelites, in the manner of parts of Ex. 20–23, but with a more distinct predominance of the ethical element.

Likewise H, except, probably, v.[21f.]. V.[2b] ("Ye shall be holy," &c.) states the fundamental principle from which the special precepts which follow are deduced. The ch. (excluding v.[5-8]) may be divided into three parts : (1) v.[3-4] laws analogous to the *first* table of the Decalogue ; (2) v.[9-22] laws analogous to the *second* table. Here, however, v.[19] deals with a different subject, viz. unnatural mixtures, in three precepts, with a new introduction. And v.[20], treating of a very special case of unchastity, and (unlike v.[3-19]) in the *third* person, belongs rather to c. 20, where it would stand suitably after v.[10]. Either it has been removed here by accident, or it was once accompanied by other laws on the same subject, omitted by the compiler in view of c. 18 and 20. V.[21f.] is alien to the general tenor of either this ch. or c. 20, and appears to be an addition from the point of view of P. (3) V.[23-37], a kind of supplement to v.[2-19], with a special introduction, v.[23], and containing injunctions of a somewhat more general character ; notice in v.[34] the extension of the principle of v.[18] ("thou shalt love thy neighbour as thyself" [viz. among the "children of thy people "]) to the "stranger" (the רג, or resident foreigner). The 2nd pers. sing. preponderates (though it is not used exclusively) in v.[9-19], the 2nd pers. plural in v.[2-8. 23-37]. In v.[2-19] the laws appear often to be arranged in *Pentads*, or groups of five, each closed by the refrain (implying the ground of their observance) *I am Jehovah* : see v.[9-10. 11-12. 13-14. 15-16. 17-18. 19] (incomplete).

V.[5-8] deals with a point of ritual, viz. the period within which the flesh of the peace-offerings might be consumed. The law laid down here is in 7[15-18] (P) retained only for two of the three species into which the peace-offering is there divided, viz. the Vow and the Voluntary-offering ; for the third species, the Thanksgiving-offering, the stricter rule of 22[29f.] is prescribed. The solution of the discrepancy is to be found in the fact that in H the Peace-offering and the Thanksgiving-offering are *co*-ordinate (22[21. 29]), while in P the latter has been *sub*-ordinated to the Peace-offering, as one of its three species.

C. 20. Penalties enjoined for certain offences specified in c. 18 and 19[3a. 31] : viz. (1) Molech worship, and consultation of ghosts or familiar spirits, v.[1-7] ; (2) (chiefly) unlawful marriages and unchastity, v.[8-21], with conclusion, v.[22-26], and supplement, v.[27] (a man or woman, in whom is a ghost, or a familiar spirit, to be put to death).

[49] The laws forming the body of the ch. are provided with a parenetic introduction and conclusion (v.$^{2-6}$ partly, v.$^{7-8}$, v.$^{22-26}$) in the same style as c. 18, and evidently by the same hand (R^h). It is commonly considered that c. 18 states the prohibitions, and c. 20 prescribes the penalties incurred by disobedience to them ; but though this may be the relation between the two chapters which guided the compiler in placing them where they now stand, it may be doubted whether it is the principle which determined their original composition ; for the correspondence is imperfect ; not only does the order of cases differ, but four of the cases named in c. 18 (v.$^{7.\ 10.\ 17b.\ 18}$) are not noticed here. Nevertheless, the two lists have many features in common ; and they may well have been drawn up by the same writer, though not with the definite intention of their supplementing one another. As in the case of c. 18, the parenetic framework is probably all that is due to the compiler of H. V.^{24b} introduces a short injunction (v.^{25}) on the distinction of clean and unclean food, which, to judge from the general character of the "Law of Holiness," must once have been accompanied by fuller definitions on the same subject (analogous to those which now stand in c. 11):* v.$^{24b-26}$ has features in common with 11$^{43-45}$. V.^{27} is supplementary to v.^{6}.

C. 21-22. Regulations touching priests and offerings, under five main heads—(1) Ceremonial restrictions obligatory in domestic life upon (*a*) the ordinary priests, 21$^{1-9}$; (*b*) the high priest, 21$^{10-15}$: (2) the conditions of bodily perfection to be satisfied by those discharging priestly duties, 21$^{16-24}$: (3) the two conditions for partaking in the sacrificial food, viz. ceremonial purity and membership in a priest's family, 22$^{1-16}$: (4) animals offered in sacrifice to be free from imperfections, 22$^{17-25}$: (5) three special injunctions respecting sacrifices, 22$^{26-30}$, with concluding exhortation, 22$^{31-33}$.

The contents of both chapters are evidently determined by the main idea of the code ; they show how the "Law of Holiness" is to be observed in its application to the priesthood and to sacrifices. Both also exhibit repeatedly the characteristic phraseology and motives of H ; the only question is whether they belong to it entirely. In the laws themselves there is little that is akin to P ; it is probable, therefore, that these are derived mainly from H, the parts exhibiting the ideas of P being chiefly redactional additions. Thus the laws themselves use the uncommon expressions "*seed* of Aaron" 21$^{17.\ 21}$ 22$^{3.\ 4}$, and "the priest that is chief among his brethren" (for the "chief priest ") ; the superscriptions and subscriptions use the more fixed phraseology of P, "the sons of Aaron," 21$^{1.\ 24}$ 22$^{2.\ 18}$, and were probably added later : in 21$^{1-15}$ there is, further, a disagreement between the superscription (in which the *priests* are addressed) and the laws that follow (in which the priests are spoken of in the 3rd pers., and the *people*, v.^{8}, are addressed), [50] which

---

* Wellh. p. 158 ; Klost. *Der Pent.* p. 377 ; Riehm, p. 184.

supports the same conclusion. Other isolated phrases which may be assigned to R^p are 21^{10} (" upon . . . garments "), v.^{12b} (" for . . . him "), v.^{22b} (see p. 58n.), v.^{23} (" go in . . . nor "), see Wellh. p. 160 f. ; in the original law, also, the priests, probably, were not brought into relation with Aaron, *seed of Aaron* having been altered from *seed of the priests.* Cf. Baentsch, p. 39 ff., according to whom the original nucleus of c. 21–22 consisted of 21$^{1b-7.\ 9.\ 10-22}$ 22$^{3-7.\ 10-14.\ 18-25}$. The conclusion 22$^{31-33}$ is in the style of 18$^{26-30}$ 19^{37} 20$^{22-26}$ (H).

C. 23. A calendar of sacred seasons,* in particular (v.$^{2.\ 37}$) of the days on which "holy convocations," *i.e.* religious assemblies, were appointed to be held, with particulars respecting the manner of their observance. The days stated are the following : all Sabbaths, the 1st and 7th days of *Mazzoth*, the Feast of Weeks, New Year's Day, the Day of Atonement, the 1st and 8th (or super-numerary) day of the Feast of Booths.

The elements of which the ch. is composed consist of excerpts from two sources ; laws from H and P having been combined so as mutually to supplement one another,—in all probability by a compiler (R^p) living subsequently to both, and representing the principles of P.

$$\begin{cases} \text{H} & \text{9-20} & \text{22} & \text{39b} & \text{40-43} \\ \text{P 23}^{1-8} & \text{21} & \text{23-38. 39a} & \text{39c} & \text{44} \end{cases}$$

Our guide in analysing the chapter must be the *title* (v.$^{2.\ 4}$) and *subscription* (v.$^{37f.}$), which authorize us to expect an enumeration of "holy convocations." V.$^{3.\ 5-8}$ correspond with the terms of the title ; the Sabbath, and the first and seventh days of *Mazzoth*, were observed by "holy convocations." (It is true that the Passover-day v.^{5} was not so observed ; but the Passover appears to be mentioned here, not on its own account, but rather as introductory to *Mazzoth*, v.$^{6-8}$.) V.$^{9-14}$ prescribes an offering of a sheaf, as the first-fruits of the harvest, on " the morrow after the Sabbath." This injunction (1) falls outside the scope of the calendar, as fixed by the title ; it relates [51] to an offering to be made on a day for which no convocation is pre-scribed ; moreover, in its present connexion (2) there is nothing to fix the day which is meant, an indication — as Delitzsch remarks — that the passage no longer stands in its original

---

* מוֹעֲדִים " stated times," RV. (usually) " set (*or* appointed) feasts," a wider term than חג " pilgrimage," which denotes the three " feasts " observed as pilgrimages, viz. *Mazzoth*, Weeks, and Ingathering (Ex. 23$^{14-17}$).

context (which must naturally have specified the "Sabbath" intended).* V.[9-14] (in the main : cf. p. 56 *n.*) belongs thus to H.

V.[15-22] (Feast of Weeks). Here only v.[21] falls within the scope of the title ; the rest (1) depends upon the same computation from the undefined "Sabbath" as v.[9-14] ; (2) prescribes an offering of similar kind to that in v.[11], viz. of the wave-loaf, which falls outside the category of the sacrifices named in the subscription, v.[37]. V.[15-20. 22] (in the main) will belong accordingly to H ; with v.[22] comp. 19[9f.] (also. H).

V.[23-25] (New Year's Day), v.[26-32] (Day of Atonement), v.[33-36] (Feast of Booths, with a supernumerary eighth day), agree with the terms of the title, prescribing observances for the days on which the "holy convocations" were to be held. V.[37f.] is the subscription corresponding to the title, v.[2. 4]. According, now, to v.[2. 4. 37-38] the subject to be dealt with in the chapter is completed ; it is surprising, therefore, *after* the subscription, v.[37f.], to find a group of additional regulations, v.[39-43]. These verses, enjoining certain usages in connexion with the Feast of Booths, and explaining the significance of this name, form an appendix, derived from H (notice the refrain in [43b]), but accommodated to P by slight additions introduced by a later hand. (1) In H—to judge by the analogy of v.[10] ("when ye reap the harvest") and v.[15] (the date in which *depends* upon that fixed in v.[10])—the date of the Feast of Booths was fixed only in general terms by the close of the period of harvest ("when ye have gathered in the increase of the land") ; it is probable, therefore, that the words, "on the 15th day of the 7th month," are an insertion in the original law, made with the object of harmonizing it more completely with the definite date of P in v.[34] ; (2) v.[39], after stating that the feast is to last for *seven* days, proceeds to add, "on the first day *and on the eighth day* shall be a solemn rest ; " in v.[40-43], however, this eighth day [52] is consistently ignored, though the *seven* days are spoken of repeatedly. It can scarcely be doubted that in v.[39] the words, "on the first day shall be a solemn rest, and on the eighth day shall be a solemn rest," are a second insertion, made by a later

---

* It is understood traditionally of the 1st day of *Mazzoth* (so that the " morrow " would be Nisan 16) ; but this is not the usual sense of " Sabbath." In its original connexion, the " Sabbath " meant was probably the ordinary weekly Sabbath that fell during the seven days of *Mazzoth*.

hand for the purpose of bringing the appendix into formal agreement with v.[36], where, it is to be noticed, the eighth day is introduced in a natural and orderly manner, after the seven have been dealt with, expressly as an additional observance. In point of fact, under Solomon this feast was observed for seven days—on the eighth day the king sending the people away (1 Ki. 8[66]); in post-exilic times, a supernumerary eighth day is mentioned, with express reference to the law of P here, Neh. 8[18]; 2 Ch. 7[9] (where the text of Kings is altered).*

The common characteristic of the parts of this calendar which belong to H is the relation in which the feasts stand to the *land* and to *agriculture* : the "morrow after the Sabbath" during *Mazzoth*, the Feast of Weeks, and the Feast of Booths, all alike mark stages in the ripening of the produce of the soil; the first cut sheaf, the completed barley and wheat harvest (the loaf), the end of the vintage. The feasts are significant in the same manner in JE and Deut. (Ex. 23[15. 16] 34[18. 22] Dt. 16[1. 9. 13]); in P this point of view has become obscured, and they are treated rather as occasions, fixed arbitrarily, for religious observances.

C. 24. 1. On the lamps in the Tabernacle, v.[1-4] (v.[2-3] = Ex. 27[20f.] almost *verbatim*).

2. On the Shewbread, v.[5-9].

3. Laws on blasphemy, and certain cases of injury to the person, arising out of a particular incident, v.[10-23].

The analysis of the ch. is not difficult. The laws in v.[15-22] belong to H, the marks of whose style they show (*e.g.* איש איש v.[15] ; עמית v.[19] ; the refrain v.[22b]) : the tradition respecting the occasion which gave rise to [53] them has been cast into form by P (or R[p]), v.[10-14. 23] (comp. the similar narrative, Nu. 15[32-36]), who has also, probably, added two or three clauses in v.[16] (from "all"), and v.[22] (to "for "). The injunctions contained in v.[1-9] belong likewise to P.

C. 25. 1. The Sabbatical year, v.[1-7. 20-22].

2. The year of Jubile, v.[8-19. 23-55].

V.[8-13]. General character and object of the institution.
V.[14-19. 23]. Land not to be alienated beyond the next Jubile.

---

* The analysis given above agrees with that of Delitzsch, *Studien*, p. 621 f.; but probably v.[41b] and parts of v.[9-20] are due to R[p] as well : according to Baentsch (pp. 47–50), v.[9. 10a] (the title) [13-14. 15b. 16] (והספן), one or two phrases in v.[17], v.[18-19] (*seven* to *sin-offering, and*), v.[20] (*with two lambs*). In v.[18-20] the words *seven* to *even*, *And ye* to *sin-offering*, and *with two lambs*, are generally recognised as being late (and inexact) interpolations, founded on Nu. 28[27-30].

V.$^{24\text{-}28}$. On the redemption of *lands*.

V.$^{29\text{-}34}$. On the redemption of *houses*.

V.$^{35\text{-}38}$. Usury not to be exacted of an impoverished Israelite.

V.$^{39\text{-}46}$. An Israelite not to be sold into servitude to another Israelite beyond the next Jubile.

V.$^{47\text{-}55}$. On the redemption of Israelites enslaved to resident foreigners.

As in c. 23, the reference to agriculture is prominent, especially in v.$^{1\text{-}7}$ (which seems plainly to be based upon Ex. 23$^{10.\ 11}$), v.$^{19\text{-}22}$. Note that the provisions in v.$^{25.\ 35.\ 39.\ 47}$ are all introduced as designed for the relief of the impoverished Israelite.

V.$^{20\text{-}22}$ interrupts the connection; for v.^{23} is evidently the sequel to v.$^{8\text{-}19}$. The verses were probably placed where they now stand by the redactor, who desired their contents to be referred to the Jubile year as well as to the Sabbatical year. In explanation of them, see Riehm, *HWB.*[1] p. 1313^{b}, [2] p. 1331^{a}; or Nowack, *Arch.* ii. 164 *n*.

The marks of H are most evident in v.$^{1\text{-}7.\ 14f.}$ (עמית) $^{17\text{-}22.\ 35\text{-}38.\ 42.\ 43.\ 55}$ (comp. also v.$^{1.\ 2;\ 8}$ with 23$^{9.\ 10;\ 15}$); they are least prominent in v.$^{29\text{-}34}$. The analysis is, however, difficult in particulars; and critics differ. In Haupt's *Sacred Books of the OT.* the following analysis is proposed :—

H	25$^{2b\text{-}7.\ 8\text{-}9a}$	10a		13-15	17-22	24-25	35-40a	43
P	25$^{1\text{-}2a}$		9b	10b-12	16	23	26-34	40b-42 *

H	47	53	55
P	25$^{44\text{-}46}$	48-52	54

It is impossible to think that (as has sometimes been supposed) the institution of the Jubile is a mere paper-law,—a theoretical completion of the system of seven; at least so far as concerns the *land* (for the periodical redistribution of which there are analogies in other nations), it must date from ancient times in Israel. On the other hand, the regulations for the manumission of *slaves* in the 50th year, differ (see p. 82, below) from those of Dt. 15$^{12\text{-}18}$; and both laws can hardly have been in operation at the same time. In the preceding analysis an endeavour is made to take account of both these facts. The older Jubile law of H, it is assumed, provided (1) that land should not be sold beyond the next Jubile (v.$^{13\text{-}15}$); and (2) contained four regulations for the relief of the impoverished Israelite,—(*a*) his land might be redeemed for him (v.^{25}), (*b*) usury was not to be exacted of him (v.$^{35\text{-}38}$), (*c*) and (*d*) when in servitude, either with a brother-Israelite (v.$^{39\text{-}40a.\ 43}$) or with a resident foreigner (v.$^{47.\ 53.\ 55}$), he was to be treated humanely. This law of H was afterwards incorporated into the priestly law-book P, with additions (1) containing closer definitions, especially in regard to the redemption of land (v.$^{9b.\ 10b\text{-}12.\ 23.\ 26\text{-}34}$); and (2) extending the benefits of the Jubile from land to *persons* (v.$^{40b\text{-}42.\ 44\text{-}46.\ 48\text{-}52.\ 54}$), at a time when experience had shown (cf. Jer. 34$^{8\text{-}16}$) that the law of Dt. 15$^{12\text{-}18}$ could not be enforced.†

---

* V.^{42} adapted by the compiler from v.$^{55.}$

† According to Baentsch (pp. 53-63), the original nucleus of c. 25 consisted of v.$^{1\text{-}7.\ 14.\ 17\text{-}24.\ 35\text{-}40a.\ 43.\ 46b.\ 53.\ 55}$, and belonged, like the nucleus of c. 23 and c. 24, to the same collection of laws as c. 18-20.

C. 26. Prohibition of idolatry, and injunction to observe the Sabbath, v.$^{1-2}$ (v.^{2} = 19^{30}); hortatory conclusion to the preceding code, v.$^{3-45}$, with subscription (R^p), v.^{46}.

This conclusion is in the general style of Ex. 23$^{20ff.}$ and Dt. 28, but expresses the ideas and principles peculiar to the Law of Holiness, and is evidently the work of the same compiler. "The *land* and *agriculture* have here the same fundamental significance for religion as in c. 19. 23. 25. The threat of expulsion, 18$^{27f.}$ 20^{22}, is repeated here in greater detail. The one commandment expressly named is that of allowing the land to lie fallow in the Sabbatical year, 26^{34}." It begins, as it also ends, with one of the characteristic expressions of H ("if ye *walk in my statutes*": "*I am Jehovah*"). As the list, p. 49 f., will have shown, many of the other characteristic expressions of H also occur in it.* [54] It contains, however, in addition, many words and phrases which are original, several recurring remarkably in Ezekiel (see p. 147).

In Lev. 17–26, then, we have before us elements derived from P, combined with excerpts from an earlier and independent collection of laws (H), the latter exhibiting a characteristic phraseology, and marked by the preponderance of certain characteristic principles and motives.† In some of its features this Code of laws resembles the "Book of the Covenant." As there, the commands (in the main) are addressed to the people, not to the priest; as there, they are also largely (cf. esp. Lev. 19) cast into an abrupt, concise form, without comments or motives (except "I am Jehovah"). The moral commands cover also much of the same ground. It differs from Ex. 21–23 chiefly in the greater amount of detail, and in dealing with the ceremonial, rather than with the civil, side of an Israelite's life. That this collection of laws is not preserved in its original integrity is

---

* Comp. also v.^{5b} with 25$^{18b.\ 19b}$; v.^{10} (esp. יָשַׁע) with 25^{22}.

† For a systematic exposition of the legislation of H, see Baentsch, pp. 131–152. When it is compared carefully with P, differences of standpoint disclose themselves. For instance, H seems not to recognise the distinction of "Holy" and "Most holy" (Wellh. *Comp.* p. 160f.); it mentions עולה and זבח (17^8 22$^{17f.}$), but not חטאת and אשם; it forbids (what P allows) the slaughter of domestic animals for food, without a sacrifice at the central sanctuary; and the hierarchical system, especially in what concerns the distinctive pre-eminence of the high priest, is not so fully developed as in P (see Baentsch, pp. 22 f., 39, 42, 106 f.).

evident from many indications : some subjects are treated incompletely ; * elsewhere the arrangement is imperfect,† and there are several instances of repetition.‡ The question arises whether other excerpts from this collection of laws are preserved elsewhere in the Pentateuch. If the list on p. 49 f. be considered carefully, it will appear that several of the expressions characteristic of the " Law of Holiness " are combined remarkably in the short ordinance on the Sabbath in Ex. 31^{13-14a}, which may accordingly, with great probability, be regarded as an excerpt from it (so Del., Dillm., Horst). Lev. 11^{43-45} (cf. both the phraseology and 20^{25}) may be another excerpt : Horst, Kuenen, and Dillm. (partly) would even include the entire body of law with which 11^{43-45} was primarily connected, viz. $11^{1-23.\ 41-47}$.§ A third passage that may be plausibly assigned to it is the law of " Tassels," Nu. 15^{37-41} (Del., Horst, Dillm., Kuen.).‖ When the collection existed as a complete whole, the different subjects [55] which it embraced were no doubt treated in accordance with a definite plan ; at present only excerpts exist, which show what some of the subjects included in it were, but do not enable us to determine what principle of arrangement was followed in it.

III. C. 27. On the commutation of vows and tithes. (1) Of *vows*; which might consist of persons, v.$^{2-8}$, cattle, v.$^{9-13}$, houses, v.$^{14f.}$, fields, v.$^{16-25}$, but not of firstlings, v.$^{26f.}$, and if consisting in some object banned or " devoted," ¶ could not be commuted, v.$^{28f.}$; (2) of *tithes*, v.$^{30-33}$.

The chapter belongs to P, and presupposes c. 25 (v.$^{17ff.}$ the year of Jubile).

* *Eg.* 19^{5-8} (which almost necessarily implies that laws respecting *other* species of sacrifices must once have formed part of the code) ; 20^{25}.

† As 19^{5-8}, just quoted ; $19^{20.\ 21-22}$ 20^{27}.

‡ $19^{3.\ 30}$ 26^{2} ; 19^{4} 26^{1} ; 19^{9} 23^{22} ; 19^{31} 20^{6}. From the facts just noted it is inferred by Dillm. (*NDJ.* p. 639) that the collection, before it reached its present form, passed through several hands.

§ Or (Paton) the nucleus of 11^{1-23} (above, p. 46), and 11^{43-45}.

‖ Dillm. (*NDJ.* p. 640) considers that H is also the basis of Lev. 5^{1-6} (cf. ונשא עונו) $^{21-24a}$ (עמית), Nu. $10^{9f.}$. Baentsch, on the contrary (p. 4 ff.), does not find sufficient reason for referring to H any of the passages mentioned, except Lev. 11^{43-45} (the close of a brief list of clean and unclean animals, which once followed 20^{24}) and Nu. 15^{37-41}. See further below, p. 151 f.

¶ The חרם : see the author's *Notes on Samuel* (1890), pp. 100–102 ; or more fully Ewald, *Antiquities of Israel*, pp. 101–106 (Eng. tr. pp. 75 78) ; Nowack, *Heb. Arch.* ii. 266 ff.

§ 4. Numbers.

LITERATURE.—See above, p. 1 f.

The Book of Numbers (called by the Jews, from its fifth word, בְּמִדְבַּר) carries on the narrative of the Pentateuch to the 40th year of the exodus. The book opens on the 1st day of the 2nd month in the 2nd year; the departure from Sinai, in the 20th day of the 2nd month, is related in 10^{11-28}; the arrival in the wilderness of Paran (or Kadesh), the mission of the spies, and subsequent defeat at Hormah are narrated in c. 13–14; the arrival in the desert of Zin (or Kadesh), in the 40th year, is recorded 20^1; Aaron's death (on the 1st day of the 5th month of the 40th year, 33^{38}) is related in 20^{23-29}.

In structure the Book of Numbers resembles Exodus, JE reappearing by the side of P, though, as a rule, not being so closely interwoven with it. It begins with a long extract from P, extending from 1^1 to 10^{28}, the main topics of which are *the disposition of the camp and the duties of the Levites.*

C. 1. The census of the twelve tribes, exclusive of the tribe of Levi (v.$^{47-54}$), who are to be appointed guardians of the Tabernacle, and to be located around it in the centre of the camp, apart from the other tribes. The number of males above 20 years old (exclusive of Levites) is given at 603,550.

C. 2. The position of the tribes in the camp, and their order on the march.

[56] C. 3–4. The Levites taken to assist the priests, in lieu of the first-born, in doing the service of the Tent of Meeting. Their numbers, their position in the centre of the camp about the Tabernacle, and their duties.

3^{1-4} the priests (recapitulation); v.$^{5-10}$ the Levites appointed to assist the priests in subordinate duties; v.$^{11-13}$ they are taken for this purpose in lieu of the first-born in Israel; v.$^{14-20}$ the Levites (from one month old) to be numbered; v.$^{21-37}$ the numbers, position, and charge of the three Levitical families—the Gershonites, Kohathites, and Merarites; v.^{38} the priests to be on the east of the Tabernacles; v.^{39} the whole number of Levites 22,000; v.$^{40-51}$ the first-born numbered (22,273), and a ransom taken on behalf of the 273 in excess of the number of the Levites.

C. 4. Particulars (in fuller detail than in c. 3) respecting the duties of the Kohathites v.$^{1-20}$, Gershonites v.$^{21-28}$, Merarites v.$^{29-33}$; and their numbers (from 30 to 50 years of age), viz. Kohathites v.$^{34-37}$ (2750), Gershonites v.$^{38-41}$ (2630), and Merarites v.$^{42-45}$ (3200),—in all (v.$^{46-49}$) 8580.

The style of c. 1–4 is more than usually diffuse. Thus in c. 2 all that is essentially new as compared with c. 1 are the statements 2[3a. 5a. 7a. 9b] &c. respecting the *order* of the tribes ; and in c. 3–4, 4[4-33] is largely an expansion of what is stated more succinctly in 3[24-38]. It is observable that 3[40-51] exemplifies by actual numerical computation the more general thought of 3[12], that the Levites are *representative* of the first-born of Israel. The systematic development of a subject, capable in itself of being stated more simply and succinctly, is characteristic of the narrative-sections of P.

C. 5–6. Laws on different subjects :—(*a*) 5[1-4] exclusion of the leprous and unclean from the camp; (*b*) 5[5-10] the officiating priest to receive the compensation for fraud, in case the injured person be dead, and have no next-of-kin, as also all heave-offerings and dedicatory offerings : (*c*) 5[11-31] law of ordeal prescribed for the woman suspected by her husband of unfaithfulness; (*d*) 6[1-21] the law of the Nazirite; (*e*) 6[22-27] the formula of priestly benediction.

C. 7. The offerings of the 12 princes of the tribes at the consecration of the Tent of Meeting and of the altar, viz. (1) 6 "covered wagons," or litters, for the transport of the fabric of the Tabernacle by the Gershonites and Merarites, v.[1-9] ; (2) vessels for use at the altar, and animals for sacrifice, v.[10-89].

The ch. (in the names of the 12 princes, and the use of the 6 wagons) presupposes cc. 1. 4 ; and yet the occasion to which it relates *precedes* Nu. 1[1] (comp. 7[1. 10. 84] with Ex. 40[17], Lev. 8[10-11]). The origin of this incongruity must remain uncertain. The particularity of detail which characterizes P generally here reaches its climax, 5 entire verses being [57] repeated *verbatim* 12 times. But the aim of the writer, no doubt, was to dilate upon the example of liberality displayed upon the occasion by the heads of the people.

C. 8. (*a*) V.[1-4] instructions for fixing (see RV. *marg.*) the lamps upon the golden candlestick ; (*b*) v.[5-22] consecration of the Levites to their duties (connecting with 3[5-13]) ; (*c*) v.[23-26] the period of the Levites' service (from 25 to 50 years of age).

In 4[3. 23. 30] the limits are from *thirty* to fifty years of age. The law here must represent the practice (or theory) of a different time from that of c. 4, and is in all probability a later modification of that law. The supposition that the regulations in c. 4 are temporary and refer only to the transport of the Tabernacle in the wilderness, while the regulation here is permanent, relating to the service of the Levites generally, introduces an arbitrary distinction : the terms used in the text are precisely the same in both cases (8[24b] and 4[3b-4. 23b. 30b]). In the time of the Chronicler (*c.* 300 B.C.) liability to service began in the 20th year (2 Ch. 31[17], Ezr. 3[8]) : the change from the 30th year is attributed (1 Ch. 23[3. 24-27]) to David.

C. 9. (a) The Passover of the second year, followed by the institution of a supplementary or "Little" Passover, a month afterwards, for the sake of those hindered accidentally from keeping the Passover at the regular time, v.$^{1-14}$; (b) the signals given by the cloud for the marching and halting of the camp, v.$^{15-23}$.

C. 10. (a) The use of the silver trumpets in starting the several camps, and on other occasions, v.$^{1-10}$; (b) the departure of the Israelites from Sinai, and order of their camps on the march, v.$^{11-28}$; (c) (JE) the services of Hobab secured for the guidance of the Israelites in the wilderness; and the functions of the ark in directing the movements of the Israelites, v.$^{29-36}$.

C. 11–12 (JE). The murmuring of the people at Taberah and Kibroth-hattaavah. Appointment of seventy elders to assist Moses. Quails given to satisfy the people. Miriam's leprosy.

C. 11 appears to show marks of composition (see Dillm.), though, as is often the case in JE, the data do not exist for separating the sources employed with confidence. Bacon (agreeing nearly with Wellh.) refers v.$^{1-3. \ 16-17. \ 24-30}$ to E, v.$^{4-15. \ 18-23. \ 31-35}$ to J. C. 12 belongs probably to E.

C. 13–14. The narrative of the spies.

$\begin{cases} P \\ JE \end{cases}$ 13^{1-17a} $\quad$ 17b-20 $\quad$ 21 $\quad$ 22-24 $\quad$ 25-26a to *Paran*) $\quad$ 26b-31 $\quad$ 32a $\quad$ 32b-33

$\begin{cases} P \\ JE \end{cases}$ 14$^{1-2}$ (in the main) $\quad$ 3-4 $\quad$ 5-7 $\quad$ 8-9 $\quad$ 10 $\quad$ 11-25 $\quad$ 26-30 $\quad$ 31-33 $\quad$ 34-38 $\quad$ 39-45

[58] The double character of the narrative is very evident. Observe (1) that 13^{22} is *parallel* to v.^{21}, v.^{32} to v.$^{27-31}$, and 14$^{26-30}$ to 14$^{11. \ 22-25}$; observe (2) the difference of representation which characterizes the two accounts: in JE the spies go only as far as the neighbourhood of *Hebron*, in the south of Judah (13$^{22-24}$); in P they explore *the whole country*, to Rehob (Jud. 18^{28}) in the far north (13^{21}: with this agrees the expression in 13^{32} and 14^{7} "*through which we have passed*"); in JE, upon their return, they represent the land as a fertile one, but one which the Israelites have not the means of conquering (13$^{27-31}$); in P they represent it as one that "eateth up its inhabitants," *i.e.* as an impoverished land (see Lev. 26^{38}, Ezek. 36^{13}), not worth conquering (13^{32}): in JE Joshua is not named as one of the spies, and *Caleb alone* stills the people, and is exempted in consequence from the sentence of exclusion from Palestine (13^{30} 14^{24}); in P Joshua as well as Caleb is among the spies; *both* are named as pacifying the

people, and are exempted accordingly from the sentence of exclusion ($14^{6.\ 30.\ 38}$; cf. 26^{65} P). This last difference is remarkable, and will meet us again : had the whole narrative been by a single writer, who thought of Joshua as acting in concert with Caleb, it is difficult not to think that Joshua would have been mentioned beside Caleb—not, possibly, in 13^{30}, but—in 14^{24}, when *the exemption from the sentence of exclusion from Palestine is first promised.* In P the spies start from the "wilderness of Paran" (13^3; cf. v.^{26}): in JE, though it is not here so stated, it may be inferred from Nu. 32^8 (cf. Dt. 1^{19}, Josh. 14^6) that they started from *Kadesh*; and with this agree the words *to Kadesh* in 13^{26}. If the passages assigned to the two narratives be read continuously, it will be found that each is nearly as complete as in the case of the narrative of the Flood in Genesis : only the beginning in JE is replaced by the fuller particulars from P. The phraseology of the two narratives differs as usual.*

C. 15 (P). (*a*) V.$^{1-16}$ the Meal- and Drink-offering appointed to accompany every Burnt-offering and Peace-offering; (*b*) v.$^{17-21}$ a cake of the first dough of the year to be offered as a Heave-offering; (*c*) v.$^{22-31}$ the Sin-offering of the community, or of an individual, for accidental derelictions of duty; (*d*) v.$^{32-36}$ narrative of the punishment inflicted upon a Sabbath-breaker; (*e*) v.$^{37-41}$ the law of "Tassels."

[59] V.$^{22-31}$ belong to the general subject of Lev 4^1–5^{13}; the Sin-offering of the congregation having been already prescribed there (4^{13-21}), but the animal being a different one, viz. a bullock. The language of v.^{22} supports the view that here sins of omission are referred to, while in Lev. 4 the reference is to sins of commission. Those who are not satisfied with this explanation suppose that the two laws represent the practice of different times (so Dillm., remarking that in v.^{24} the language of *com*mission is used, and in Lev. 5^1 that of *o*mission). On v.$^{37-41}$ see p. 59.

C. 16–17. The rebellion of Korah, Dathan, and Abiram. Confirmation of the priestly prerogatives enjoyed by the tribe of Levi.

| P | 16^{1a} | | $2b$-$7a$. ($7b$-11) | | (16-17). 18-24 | | $27a$ | | $32b$ | 35. (36-40). 41-50 | c. 17 |
| JE | | 1b-2a | | 12-15 | | 25-26 | | 27b-34 | | | |

Here two, if not three, narratives have been combined. If the parts assigned to each in the table be read continuously, the following will appear as their several characteristics :—

1. In JE Dathan and Abiram, Reubenites, give vent to their

* On JE in Nu. 13-14, see also Bacon, *Hebraica*, xi. (1895) p. 234 ff.

dissatisfaction with *Moses*, complaining (v.[14]) that his promises have been unfulfilled, and resenting the authority (v.[13b]) and judgeship (v.[15b]) possessed by him ; they, with their tents and households, are swallowed up by the earth v.[27-34]. This is a rebellion of *laymen* against the *civil* authority claimed by Moses. The narrative is nearly complete, there being only some slight omissions at the beginning.

2. In P there appear to be two strata of narrative. In the parts not enclosed within parentheses, Korah, at the head of 250 princes of the congregation, not themselves all Levites,* opposes Moses and Aaron in the interests of the community at large, protesting against the limitation of priestly rights to the tribe of Levi, on the ground (v.[3]) that "*all* the congregation are holy." Invited by Moses to establish their claim by appearing with censers at the sanctuary, they are consumed by fire from Jehovah. With this representation agrees 16[41-50] c. 17, the point of [60] which is to confirm—not the exclusive rights of Aaron, as against the rest of the tribe of Levi, but—the exclusive right to the priesthood possessed by Levi, against Israel generally (the opposition is clearly not between Aaron and the other Levites, but between Levi and the other tribes ; the words in 17[12f.], also, are spoken from the point of view of the *people at large*).

3. This narrative appears to have been afterwards enlarged by additions (the parts enclosed within parentheses), emphasizing a somewhat different point of view, and exhibiting Korah, at the head of 250 *Levites*, as setting himself in opposition to *Aaron*, and protesting on behalf of the tribe of Levi generally against the exclusive rights claimed by the sons of Aaron (observe v.[7b] *ye sons of Levi*, and v.[9ff.] where Korah's company are described as dissatisfied with their menial position, and claiming equal rights with *Aaron*). With this representation agrees 16[36-40] (see v.[40] "that no stranger that is *not of the seed of Aaron*," &c.).

Thus JE mentions only Dathan and Abiram, P only Korah ; and the motives and aims of the malcontents are in each case different. The phraseology of the two main currents of the

---

* As appears, partly from the *general* expression in v.[2] (" princes of the congregation," with no limitation to Levites), partly from the fact that in 27[3] *Manassites* disown, on behalf of their father, complicity in the insurrection of Korah, which, if all his company had consisted of Levites, would evidently have been unnecessary.

narrative is that of JE and P respectively. A more general ground, tending to show the composite character of the narrative, is the inequality of the manner in which Korah, Dathan, and Abiram appear in it : whereas in v.[1f.] they are represented as taking part in a *common* conspiracy, they afterwards continually act separately ; Moses speaks to Korah without Dathan and Abiram, and to Dathan and Abiram without Korah (v.[4-11], v.[12-14], v.[16-22], v.[25f.]) ; Dathan and Abiram do not act in concert with Korah v.[16-22], but remain in their tents at a distance v.[20-27] ; finally, their fate is different. Of course, an alliance between an ecclesiastical and a civil party is, in itself, nothing incredible ; but such a representation of their *common* action is not probable, except upon the supposition of a combination of two narratives describing the course of it from different sides, or points of view.

The important distinction between the two strata of P is that in the main narrative there is no indication of any opposition between Aaron and Levi (*i.e.* between priests and Levites), while in the secondary narrative this opposition is palpable, and the gulf separating priests and Levites is strongly emphasized (cf. the emphasis laid on the same distinction in Nu. 3. 4. 8).

[61] The analysis is that of Wellh. (*Comp.* p. 339 f.), Dillmann (p. 89), and Baudissin (*Priesterthum*, p. 35). In v.[24. 27] it is highly probable that the original reading was "the tabernacle of *Jehovah*" (as 17[13]) ; not only is the *sing.* "tabernacle" remarkable, but the word (משכן) is never in *prose* (whether in the Pent. or elsewhere) applied to a *human* habitation, whereas it is used repeatedly of "the Tabernacle." LXX (each time) has only "the tabernacle of Korah."

C. 18 (P). (*a*) V.[1-7] duties, and relative position, of priests and Levites : the sons of Aaron to act as priests, to be responsible for the service of the Sanctuary and Altar ; the other Levites to assist them in subordinate offices ; (*b*) v.[18-19] the revenues of the priests defined ; (*c*) v.[20-24] the tithe to be paid by the people to the Levites ; but v.[25-32], a tithe of the tithe to be paid by the Levites to the priests.

The ch. stands in close connexion with the main narrative of P in c. 16–17, 17[12f.] forming the transition to it : notice how, as there, the rights of the tribe of Levi (whether in the persons of "priests" or "Levites") are protected against the "stranger" belonging to another tribe, v.[4h. 5h. 7h. 22] (with evident allusion to 16[35. 46] 17[13]). In v.[1] "bear the iniquity of the sanctuary "=be liable for any damage or desecration which may befall it through their neglect, in one word, *be responsible for it* (cf. p. 50, No. 20c). In v.[2] "joined" there is in the Hebrew a play on the name *Levi*.

C. 19 (P). The rite of purification (by means of water mingled with the ashes of a red heifer) after defilement with a corpse, v.[1-13]; with directions for the application of the rite in particular cases, v.[14-22].

C. 20–22[1] (P and JE). Israel at Kadesh; with their journeyings thence to the plains of Moab.

20[1-13] death of Miriam; murmurings of the people for water, and sin of Moses and Aaron at Meribah; v.[14-21] refusal of Edom to permit the Israelites to pass through their territory; v.[22-29] death of Aaron, and investiture of Eleazar as his successor, on Mount Hor. 21[1-3] defeat of the king of Arad; v.[4-9] impatience of the people while making the circuit of the land of Edom; the brazen serpent; v.[10-20] their itinerary to the "field of Moab" at Pisgah; v.[21-23] refusal of Sihon to allow Israel to cross his border; v.[24-35] conquest by the Israelites of the territory of Sihon, and of Og the king of Bashan; 22[1] arrival at the plains of Moab.

```
⎧P  20¹ᵃ (to month)    2    3b-4    6-13      22-29         21⁴ᵃ (to Hor)
⎨
⎩JE             1b    3a    5        14-21    21¹-³                  4b-9

⎧P  21¹⁰-¹¹      22¹
⎨
⎩JE       12-35
```

On c. 20 comp. Cornill, *ZATW*. 1891, p. 20 ff.; Bacon, *JBLit.* 1892, p. 197, and *Triple Tradition of the Exodus*, pp. 195–197, 203 f. [62] 20[14-21.] 21[4b-9. 12-30] may belong in particular to E.

In 21[10ff.] it is observable that the form of the itinerary in P and JE is slightly different. In P (v.[10f.]) the *verb* stands first; in JE (v.[12. 13. 16. 19. 20]) the *place* stands first ("from . . . they journeyed," &c.). The same distinction recurs elsewhere: contrast c. 33 (P) *passim* with 11[35]. 21[33-35] recurs (largely *verbatim*) in Dt. 3[1-3], and is so Deuteronomic in style that Dillm. and Bacon (*l.c.* p. 211) may be right in thinking the passage to be introduced here from Dt. (observe that the conquest of Og is not alluded to in 22²).

C. 22[2]–36[13]. Israel in the steppes of Moab.

22[2]–c. 24. The history of Balaam (JE).

22[2-41] (except v.[22-35a]) may be assigned with some confidence to E; observe *God* almost uniformly (not *Jehovah*); and comp. v.[9a. 20a] with Gen. 20³ 31[24] (both E). V.[22-35a] (the episode of the ass) is taken from a different source, viz. J; notice (*a*) in v.[21] Balaam goes "with the princes of Moab," in v.[22ff.] he is evidently alone; (*b*) in the main narrative of the ch. Balaam, at the second message from Balak, receives permission to go, provided only that he speaks what is put into his mouth by God; the episode implies that no permission to go had been given to him, and he is first taught by the angel on the way that he is only to speak what is put into his mouth; (c) *Jehovah* (not *God*). The narrative at v.[35a] reaches the same point as v.[20b]: v.[35b] (repeating v.[21h]) appears to have been added by the compiler for the purpose of leading back into the text of E. It is uncertain whether c. 23–24 belong to J or E, or whether they are the work of the compiler who has made use of both sources: critics differ, and it is wisest to leave the question undetermined. The early part of c. 22 seems to contain elements derived from a different source from the main body of the ch.: thus v.[2] is superfluous before v.[4b], v.[3a] and v.[3b] are different statements of substantially the same fact; and the notices of the "elders of Midian" in v.[4. 7] (and not afterwards) suggest the inference that they are derived from a narrative which told more fully how the Midianites made common cause with Moab against Israel.

C. 25. The Israelites seduced at Shittim into idolatry and immorality: the zeal of Phinehas rewarded with the promise of the permanency of the priesthood in his family. V.[1-5] belongs to JE; v.[6-18] to P.

The beginning of P's narrative has been omitted in favour of that of JE. From 31[16] it may be inferred that it contained some account of the treacherous (see v.[18]) "counsel of Balaam," given with the view of seducing the men of Israel into sin, and so of bringing them into disfavour with Jehovah. Of the two narratives, one (JE) names the Moabites, the other (P) the Midianites, as those who led Israel into sin; the latter supplies the [63] motive for the war against Midian described in c. 31 (comp. Delitzsch, *ZKWL*. 1888, p. 121). For Midianites in the neighbourhood of Moab, cf. 22[4. 7] Gen. 36[35].

C. 26–31 all belong to P.

C. 26. The second census of Israel (see c. 1 f.) during the wanderings. The sum-total of males (from 20 years old) is given at 601,730, exclusive of the Levites (from one month old), 23,000.

V.[9-11], which are based upon c. 16 in its present (composite) form, are probably an insertion in the orginal text of the ch.: likewise v.[58a] (the details of which are not in harmony with P's genealogy of Levi in Ex. 6[17-19] Nu. 3[20. 21. 27. 33], and are disregarded in the verses that follow).

C. 27. (a) V.[1-11] the law of the inheritance of daughters, in families in which there was no son, arising out of the case of the daughters of Zelophehad; (b) v.[12-23] Moses commanded to view Palestine before his death; and Joshua instituted as his successor.

C. 28–29. A priestly calendar, defining the public sacrifices proper for each season.

28$^{1-2}$ introduction; v.$^{3-8}$ the daily morning and evening Burnt-offering; v.$^{9-10}$ the Sabbath; v.$^{11-15}$ the New Moons; v.^{16} the Passover; v.$^{17-25}$ *Mazzoth*; v.$^{26-31}$ the Day of First-fruits [*i.e.* the Feast of Weeks: so called only here, cf. Ex. 23^{16a} 34^{22a}]; 29$^{1-6}$ New Year's Day; v.$^{7-11}$ Day of Atonement; v.$^{12-34}$ the seven days of the Feast of Booths, with the supernumerary eighth day v.$^{35-38}$; v.$^{39-40}$ subscription.

28$^{3-8}$ is largely a verbal repetition of Ex. 29$^{38-42}$. For the rest, the ch. is supplementary to the calendar in Lev. 23 (which, as a rule, alludes to, but does not describe in detail, the special sacrifices), from which some of the particulars are repeated (as 28$^{17. 18. 25. 26b}$ 29$^{1. 7. 12. 35}$; cf. Lev. 23$^{6-8. 21. 24f. 27. 34. 36}$). The New Moons (28$^{11-15}$) are not mentioned in Lev. 23.

C. 30. The law of vows.

V.^{2} a vow made by a man to be in all cases binding: v.$^{3ff.}$ conditions for the validity of vows made by women.

C. 31. The war of vengeance against Midian (see 25$^{16-18}$).

Though cast into narrative form, the ch. has really a legislative object, viz. to prescribe a principle for the distribution of booty taken in war. Of the place, circumstances, and other details of the war we learn nothing: we [64] are told only of the issue, how, viz., 12,000 Israelite warriors, without losing a man (v.^{49}), slew all the males and married women of Midian, took captive 32,000 virgins, and brought back 800,000 head of cattle, besides other booty. In the high figures, and absence of specific details, the narrative resembles the descriptions of wars in the Chronicles or in Jud. 20. The account, as we have it, contains elements which are not easy to reconcile with historical probability. The difficulties of the section are mitigated by the supposition that the simpler materials supplied by tradition have here been elaborated by the compiler, in accordance with his love of system, into an ideal picture of the manner in which a sacred war must have been conducted by Israel.

C. 32. Allotment by Moses of the trans-Jordanic region to the tribes of Gad, Reuben, and the half-tribe of Manasseh.

$\begin{cases} P \\ JE \end{cases}$ 32$^{1-17}$ (in the main) $^{18-19}$ $^{20-27}$ in the main) $^{24-32. (33)}$ $^{34-42}$

Throughout v.$^{1-32}$ the negotiations with Moses are conducted on the part of *Gad* and *Reuben* alone: the half-tribe of Manasseh is named for the first time—and apparently only for the sake of completeness—in the summary statement, v.^{33}. As regards the structure of the ch., in some parts the style of P is manifest throughout, in others only in traces. It would seem that the compiler has combined P and JE, sometimes following P exclusively, sometimes following in the main JE, but introducing elements from P.

Thus in v.[1-4] "Eleazar the priest," the "princes," and the "congregation" (*i.e.* v.[2b] and part of v.[4]) belong to P: in v.[5-15] the expressions are chiefly those of JE, and the allusions are nearly entirely to JE's narrative in c. 13–14; but isolated phrases appear to have been introduced from P (v.[5] "for a possession"; v.[11] "from 20 years old and upward"; v.[12] "Joshua"; v.[13] cf. 14[33] P); similarly in v.[20-27], where the phrases suggestive of P might even be removed without injury to the narrative (v.[22a] to *before the Lord*; v.[22b] from *and this land* [the preceding "then afterward . . . and be" may, of course, with equal propriety be rendered "and afterward . . . ye shall be guiltless"]; perhaps v.[24b] (cf. 30[9b] P); v.[27] "every one that is armed for war"). On the other hand, v.[34-38] evidently points back to v.[3. 16f. 24a] (JE). It is not impossible that v.[33] is a late addition to the ch. On v.[39-42] comp. Wellh. *Comp.* p. 117; Dillm. p. 200; and Budde, as cited below, p. 163, *note* ¶.

C. 33. P's itinerary of the journeyings of the Israelites from Rameses to the plains of Moab, v.[1-49]; followed by directions respecting the occupation of Canaan, v.[50-56] (introductory to c. 34).

[65] In v.[50-56] directions from P relative to the method of allotment of Canaan, v.[50. 51. 54], have been combined, as it seems, with two excerpts from H respecting the extirpation of Canaanitish idolatry, v.[52-53. 55-56]. Observe the two rather noticeable terms במה and משכית (v.[52]), occurring elsewhere in the Pent. only Lev. 26[1. 30] (H).

C. 34 (P). The borders of Israel's territory W. of Jordan, v.[1-15], with the names of those appointed for the purpose of assisting Joshua and Eleazar in its allotment, v.[16-29].

C. 35 (P). Appointment of 48 cities for the residence of the Levites, v.[1-8]; and of 6 among them, 3 on each side of Jordan, as cities of refuge for the manslayer, with conditions regulating their use, v.[9-34].

C. 36 (P). Heiresses possessing landed property to marry into their own tribe (in order, viz., to preserve the inheritance of each tribe intact).

A provision rendered necessary by the ordinance of 27[6-11].

§ 5. DEUTERONOMY.

LITERATURE.—See p. 1 f.; and add: Ed. Riehm, *Gesetzgebung Mose's im Lande Moab*, 1854 (cf. also *Einl.* i. 233–248, 311–318); F. W. Schultz,

Das Deut. erklärt, 1859 (the Mosaic authorship here maintained was afterwards abandoned by the author, being no longer considered by him to be
required by the terms of 31⁹) ; P. Kleinert, *Das Deut. u. der Deuteronomiker*,
1872, with Riehm's review in the *Stud. u. Krit.* 1873, pp. 165–200 ; Aug.
Kayser, *Das Vorexilische Buch der Urgeschichte Israels*, 1874 (deals in
particular with the relation of Dt. to Gen.–Nu.) ; J. Hollenberg in the *Stud.
u. Krit.* 1874, pp. 472–506 (on the "margins" of Dt. [*i.e.* Dt. 1–4, 29–34],
and their relation to the Deuteronomic sections of Joshua) ; W. R. Smith,
OTJC. p. 352 ff. : T. K. Cheyne, *Jeremiah, his Life and Times*, pp. 48–86 ;
Westphal, *Les Sources du Pent.* 1892, ii. 33–132, 262–318 ; S. Oettli (in
Strack and Zöckler's *Kgf. Kommentar*), 1893 ; S. R. Driver (in the "International Critical Commentary"), Edinb. 1895 ; also W. Staerk, *Das Deut., sein
Inhalt, u. seine litt. Form*, 1894, and C. Steuernagel, *Der Rahmen des Deut.*,
1894, *Die Entstehung des Deut. Gesetzes*, 1896 (both attempts to analyse Dt.
into pre-existing groups of laws).

On c. 32 the monograph of Ad. Kamphausen, *Das Lied Moses*, 1862 ; and
on c. 33 K. H. Graf, *Der Segen Mose's*, 1857 ; A. van der Flier, *Deuteronom-
ium* 33, Leiden, 1895.

Deuteronomy is called by the Jews (from the opening words)
אֵלֶּה הַדְּבָרִים, or more briefly דְּבָרִים. The English name is derived
from the (inexact) rendering of 17¹⁸ מִשְׁנֵה הַתּוֹרָה הַזֹּאת* in the [66]
LXX τὸ δευτερονόμιον τοῦτο. It records the events of the last
month (1³ 34⁸) of the forty years' wanderings of the children of
Israel. The greater part of the book is occupied by the discourse in which Moses, before his death, sets before the Israelites
the laws which they are to obey, and the spirit in which they are
to obey them, when they are settled in the Promised Land. This
is preceded and followed by other matter, the nature of which
will appear from the following table of contents :—

1¹⁻⁵. Historical introduction, stating the place and time at which the
discourses following were delivered.

1⁶–4⁴⁰. Moses' *first* discourse, consisting of a review of the circumstances under which the Israelites had reached the border of the
Promised Land, and concluding with an eloquent practical appeal
(c. 4) not to forget the great truths impressed upon them at
Horeb.

4⁴¹⁻⁴³. Historical account of the appointment by Moses of three cities of
refuge east of Jordan.

4⁴⁴⁻⁴⁹. Superscription to Moses' *second* discourse, forming the legislation
proper.

---

* Which signifies *a repetition* (i.e. *copy*) *of this law*, not *this repetition of
the law.*

C 5-26. The Exposition of the Law, consisting of two parts: (1) c. 5-11 hortatory introduction, developing the first commandment of the Decalogue, and inculcating the *general* theocratic principles by which Israel, as a nation, is to be guided; (2) c. 12-26 the Code of special laws.

C. 27. Injunctions (interrupting the discourse of Moses, and narrated in the third person) relative to a symbolical acceptance by the nation of the preceding Code, after entering Canaan.

C. 28-29^1. Conclusion to the Code (connected closely with 26^{19}), and consisting of a solemn declaration of the consequences to follow its observance or neglect.

29^2-30^{20}. Moses' *third* discourse, of the nature of a supplement, insisting afresh upon the fundamental duty of loyalty to Jehovah, and embracing (1) an appeal to Israel to accept the terms of the Deuteronomic covenant, with a renewed warning of the disastrous consequences of a lapse into idolatry (c. 29); (2) a promise of restoration, even after the abandonment threatened in c. 28, if the nation should then exhibit due tokens of penitence (30$^{1-10}$); (3) the choice set before Israel (30$^{11-20}$).

31$^{1-13}$. Moses' last words of encouragement to the people and Joshua. His delivery of the Deuteronomic law to the Levitical priests.

31^{14}-32^{47}. Institution of Joshua by Jehovah (31$^{14-15.\ 23}$). The Song of Moses (32$^{1-43}$), with accompanying historical notices (31$^{16-22.\ 24-30}$, 32$^{44-47}$).

32^{48}-34^{12}. Conclusion of the whole book, containing the Blessing of Moses (c. 33), and describing the circumstances of his death.

Throughout, the author's aim is *parenetic*: he does not merely collect, or repeat, a series of laws, he "expounds" them (1^5), *i.e.* he develops them with reference to the moral purposes which they subserve, and the motives by which the Israelite should feel prompted to obey them.

The structure of Dt. is relatively simple. The main part of the book is pervaded throughout by a single purpose, and bears the marks of being the work of a single writer, who has taken as the basis of his discourses, partly the narrative and laws of JE as they exist in the previous books of the Pentateuch, partly laws derived [67] from other sources. Towards the end of the book either the same author, or a writer imbued with the same spirit, has incorporated extracts from JE, and other sources, recording incidents connected with the death of Moses. One of the final redactors of the Pentateuch has brought the whole thus constituted into relation with the literary framework of the Hexateuch, by the addition of excerpts from P. The analytical scheme of the book is accordingly as follows:—

P	1^3						27^{5-7a}
JE							
D	1^{1-2}	1^4-3^{13}	$3^{18}-4^{28}$	4^{32-40}		5^1-26^{19}	
D²			3^{14-17}	4^{29-31}	$4^{41-43.\ 44-49}$		27^{1-4}

P							31^{14-15}
JE							
D		27^{9-10}		c. 28. 29^{1-9}		30^{11-20} 31^{1-13}	
D²	27^{7b-8}		11-13. (14-26)		29^{10-29} 30^{1-10}		

P			32^{48-52}	
JE	31^{23}			(c. 33*) 34^{1a}†
D		31^{24-27}	32^{45-47}	
D²	$(31^{16-22}*)$	31^{28-30} $(32^{1-43}*)$ 44		

P	34^{1a}‡	5b	7-9
JE	34^{1b-5a}	6	10
D			
D²		11-12	

On c. 1–4. 27. 29–34 see more fully pp. 93–98. Certain parts of Dt., while displaying the general Deut. style, connect imperfectly with the context, or present differences of representation, which make it probable that they are the work of a later Deuteronomic hand (or hands), by whom the original Dt. was supplemented or enlarged: these are indicated in the Table by the symbol D². (The line dividing D and D² cannot in every case, especially in c. 29–34, be fixed with confidence.)

It will be convenient to consider first the character and scope of the central part of the book, c. 5–26, and c. 28.

As will be seen from the table of contents, the Deuteronomic *legislation*, properly so called, is contained in c. 12–26, to which c. 5–11 form an introduction, and c. 27, 28 a conclusion. In Dt. itself the Code (including c. 28) is referred to frequently $(1^5\ 4^8\ 17^{18.\ 19}\ 27^{\ 3.\ 8.\ 26}\ 28^{58.\ 61}\ 29^{29}\ 31^{9.\ 11.\ 12.\ 24}\ 32^{46})$ as *this law*, or as *this book of the law* $(29^{21}\ 30^{10}\ 31^{26}$; cf. Josh. $1^8)$.

That these expressions refer to Dt. alone (or to the Code of laws contained in it), and not to the entire Pent., appears (1) from the terms of $1^5\ 4^8$, which point to a law about to be, or actually being, set forth ; (2) from the parallel phrases, *this commandment, these statutes, these judgments*, often spoken of as inculcated *to-day* $(7^{12}$, see v.[11]; $15^5\ 19^9\ 26^{16}\ 30^{11})$, and *this covenant* $(29^{9.\ 14})$, which clearly alludes to the Deuteronomic legislation (cf. v. [19. 20] "the curse written *in this book*," *i.e.* in c. 28), and is distinguished from the covenant made before at Sinai (29^1).

---

* Incorporated from independent sources.

† The words, "And Moses went up to the top of Pisgah."

‡ The rest of clause ᵃ (to *Jericho*).

In order rightly to estimate the character of Dt., it is necessary to compare it carefully with the previous books of the Pentateuch. The accompanying synopsis of *laws* in Dt. will show immediately which of the enactments in it relate to subjects not dealt with in the legislations of JE and P, and which are parallel to provisions contained in either of those codes.

[68] SYNOPSIS OF LAWS IN DEUTERONOMY.

JE.	DEUTERONOMY.	P (INCLUDING H).
Ex. 20$^{2-17}$.	5$^{6-21}$ (the Decalogue).	
20^{24}.*	12$^{1-28}$ (place of sacrifice).	Lev. 17$^{1-9}$.*
23^{24} 34$^{12. 15f.}$.	,, $^{29-32}$ (not to imitate Canaanite rites).	Nu. 33^{52}.
	13 (seduction to idolatry).	
	14$^{1f.}$ (disfigurement in mourning).	Lev. 19^{28}.
	,, $^{3-20}$ (clean and unclean animals).	,, 11$^{2-22}$; 20^{25}.
22^{31}.	,, ^{21a} (food improperly killed).	,, 17^{15}; 11^{40}.
23^{19b}; 34^{26b}.	,, ^{21b} (kid in mother's milk).	
	,, $^{22-29}$ (tithes).	,, 27$^{30-33}$; Nu. 18$^{21-32}$.*
23$^{10f.}$.*	15$^{1-11}$ (Year of Release).	,, 25$^{1-7}$.*
21$^{2-11}$.*	,, $^{12-18}$ (Hebrew slaves).	,, 25$^{39-46}$.*
22^{30}; 13$^{11-12}$; 34^{19}.	,, $^{19-23}$ (firstlings of ox and sheep: cf. 12$^{6. 17f.}$; 14^{23}).	Nu. 18$^{17f.}$*(cf. Ex. 13$^{1f.}$; Lev. 27^{26}; Nu. 3^{13}; 8^{17}).
23$^{14-17}$; 34$^{18. 20b}$. 22-25	16$^{1-17}$ (the three annual pilgrimages).	Lev. 23*; Nu. 28–29.*
	,, ^{18} (appointment of judges).	
23$^{1-3. 6-8}$.	,, $^{19f.}$ (just judgment).	,, 19^{15}.
	,, $^{21f.}$ (erection of Ashérahs and "pillars" prohibited).	,, 26^{1a}.
	17^1 (sacrifices to be without blemish: cf. 15^{21}).	,, 22$^{17-24}$.
22^{20}.	,, $^{2-7}$ (idolatry, especially worship of the "host of heaven").	
	,, $^{8-13}$ (supreme tribunal).	
	,, $^{14-20}$ (law of the king).	
	18$^{1-8}$ (rights and revenues of the tribe of Levi).	,, 7$^{32-34}$*; Nu. 18$^{1-20}$.*
	,, $^{9-22}$ (law of the prophet).	
	,, ^{10a} (Molech-worship; cf. 12^{31}).	,, 18^{21}; 20$^{2-5}$.
22^{18} (sorceress alone).	,, $^{10b-11}$ (different kinds of divination).	,, 19$^{26b. 31}$; 20$^{6. 27}$.
21$^{12-14}$.	19$^{1-13}$ (asylum for manslaughter: murder).	Nu. 35; Lev. 24$^{17. 21}$.
	,, ^{14} (the landmark).	
23^1.	,, $^{15-21}$ (law of witnesses).	Lev. 19^{16b}.

[69] JE.	DEUTERONOMY.	P (INCLUDING Ḥ).
	20 (military service and war: cf. 24^5).	
	21$^{1-9}$ (expiation of untraced murder).	
	,, $^{10-14}$ (treatment of female captives).	
	,, $^{15-17}$ (primogeniture).	
Ex. 21$^{15.\ 17}$.	,, $^{18-21}$ (undutiful son).	Lev. 20^9.
	,, $^{22f.}$ (body of malefactor).	
23$^{4f.}$.	22$^{1-4}$ (animals straying or fallen).	
	,, ^{5} (sexes not to interchange garments).	
	,, $^{6f.}$ (bird's nest).	
	,, ^{8} (battlement).	
	,, $^{9-11}$ (against non-natural mixtures).	,, 19^{19}.
	,, ^{12} (law of " tassels ").	Nu. 15$^{37-41}$.
	,, $^{13-21}$ (slander against a maiden).	
	,, $^{22-27}$ (adultery).	Lev. 18^{20} ; 20^{10}.
22$^{16f.}$.	,, $^{28f.}$ (seduction).	
	,, ^{30} (incest with step-mother).	,, 18^8 ; 20^{11}.
	23$^{1-8}$ (conditions of admittance into the theocratic community).	
	,, $^{9-14}$ (cleanliness in the camp).	Nu. 5$^{1-4}$.*
	,, $^{15f.}$ (humanity to escaped slave).	
	,, $^{17f.}$ (against religious prostitution).	
22^{25}.	,, ^{19} (usury).	Lev. 25$^{35-37}$.
	,, $^{21-23}$ (vows).	Nu. 30$^{2ff.}$.
	,, $^{24f.}$ (regard for neighbour's crops).	
22$^{26f.}$.	24$^{1-4}$ (divorce).	
21^{16}.	,, $^{6.\ 10-13}$ (pledges).	
	,, ^{7} (man-stealing).	
	,, $^{8f.}$ (leprosy).	Lev. 13–14.
	,, $^{14f.}$ (justice towards hired servants).	,, 19^{13}.
	,, ^{16} (the family of a criminal not to suffer with him).	
22$^{21-24}$; 23^9.	,, $^{17f.}$ (justice towards stranger, widow, and orphan).	,, 19$^{33f.}$.
	,, $^{19f.}$ (gleanings).	,, 19$^{9f.}$; 23^{22}.
	25$^{1-3}$ (moderation in the infliction of the bastinado).	
	,, ^{4} (ox not to be muzzled while threshing).	
	,, $^{5-10}$ (law of the levirate).	
	,, $^{11f.}$ (modesty).	
	,, $^{13-16}$ (just weights).	,, 19$^{35f.}$.
17^{14}.	,, $^{17-19}$ (Amalek !).	
cf. 22^{29a} ; 23^{19a} ; 34^{26a}.	26$^{1-11}$ (thanksgiving at the offering of first-fruits).	cf. Nu. 18$^{12f.}$.
	,, $^{12-15}$ (thanksgiving at the offering of triennial tithes).	
[70]		
20$^{4.\ 23}$; 34^{17}.	27^{15} [cf. 4$^{16.\ 23.\ 25}$; 7^{25}].	Lev. 19^4 ; 26^{1a}.
20^{12} ; 21^{17}.	,, ^{16} [cf. 21$^{18-21}$].	,, 20^9.
	,, ^{17} [19^{14}].	,, 19^{14}.
	,, ^{18}	,, 19$^{33f.}$.
22$^{21-24}$; 23^9	,, ^{19} [24^{17}].	

JE.	DEUTERONOMY.	P (INCLUDING H).
Ex. 22^{19}.	27^{20} [22^{30}].	Lev. 18^{8}; 20^{11}.
	,, 21.	,, 18^{23}; 20^{15}.
	,, 22.	,, 18^{9}; 20^{17}.
	,, 23.	,, 18^{17}; 20^{14}.
20^{13}; 21^{12}.	,, 24.	,, 24^{17}.
23^{8}.	,, 25 [16^{19b}].	
23$^{20-33}$.	28 (closing exhortation).	,, 26$^{3-45}$.

JE.	DEUTERONOMY.	P (INCLUDING H).
20$^{4.\ 23}$; 34^{17}.	4$^{16-18.\ 23}$; 7^{25} (against images).	Lev. 19^{4b}; 26^{1}.
23^{12}.	5^{14b} (object of Sabbath).	
cf. 13$^{9.\ 16}$.	6^{8}; 11^{18} (law of frontlets).	
20^{3}; 23^{13}; 34^{14}.	6^{14}; 11^{16} (against "other gods").	,, 19^{4a}.
12$^{26f.}$; 13^{14}.	6$^{20f.}$ (instruction to children).	
23$^{32f.}$; 34$^{12.\ 15f.}$.	7$^{2-4.\ 16}$ (no compact with Canaanites).	Nu. 33^{55}.
23^{24}; 34^{13}.	7^{5}; 12^{3} (Canaanite altars, "pillars," &c. to be destroyed).	,, 33^{52}.
19^{6}; 22^{30}.	7^{6}; 14$^{2.\ 21}$; 26^{19}; 28^{9} (Israel a holy people), (in different connexions).	Lev. 11$^{44f.}$; 19^{2}; 20$^{7.\ 26}$; Nu. 15^{40}.
22^{21}; 23^{9}.	10^{19} (to love the stranger).	,, 19^{34}.
	12$^{16.\ 23}$; 15^{23} (blood not to be eaten).	,, 17$^{10-14}$; 19^{26a}; (cf. 3^{17}; 7$^{26f.}$; Gen. 9^{4}).
23^{18a}; 34^{25a}.	16^{3a} (no leavened bread with Passover).	Ex. 12^{8}.
13$^{6f.}$; 23^{15}; 34^{18}.	16$^{3b.\ 4a.\ 8}$ (unleavened cakes for seven days afterwards).	,, 12$^{15.\ 18-20}$; Lev. 23^{6}.
23^{18b}; 34^{25b}.	16^{4b} (flesh of Passover not to remain till morning).	,, 12^{10}; Nu. 9^{12}.
	16$^{13.\ 15}$ (feast of "booths," "seven days").	Lev. 23$^{34.\ 39.\ 41-43}$.
	17^{6}; 19^{15} ("two or three witnesses").	Nu. 35^{30}.
21$^{23-25}$.	19^{21} (*lex talionis*) (but *in a different application* in each case).	Lev. 24$^{19f.}$.

The passages should be examined individually: for sometimes, especially in the case of the right-hand column, the parallelism extends only to the subject-matter, the details being different, or even actually discrepant. The instances in which the divergence is most marked are indicated by an asterisk (*). The first important fact that results from such an examination is this, that *the laws in JE*, viz. Ex. 20–23 (repeated, partially, in 34$^{10-26}$), and the kindred section 13$^{3-16}$, *form the foundation of the Deutero-*

nomic legislation. This is evident as well from the numerous verbal coincidences * as from the fact which is plain from the [71] left-hand column, viz. that nearly the whole ground covered by Ex. 20–23 is included in it, almost the only exception being the special compensations to be paid for various injuries (Ex. 21[18]–22[15]), which would be less necessary in a manual intended for the people. In a few cases the entire law is repeated *verbatim*, elsewhere only particular clauses (*e.g.* 6[8. 20] 7[2] 15[12. 16. 17]), more commonly it is explained (16[19b] 22[4b]) or expanded; fresh definitions being added (16[1-17]), or a principle applied so as to cover expressly particular cases (17[2-7] 18[10b. 11]). Sometimes even the earlier law is modified; discrepancies arising from this cause will be noticed subsequently. The additional civil and social enactments make provision chiefly for cases likely to arise in a more complex and developed community than is contemplated in the legislation of Ex. 20–23.

In the right-hand column most of the parallels are with Lev. 17–26 (the Law of Holiness). These consist principally of specific moral injunctions; but it cannot be said that the legislation in Dt. is based upon this code, or connected with it organically, as it is with Ex. 20–23. With the other parts of Lev.–Nu. the parallels are less complete, the only remarkable verbal one being afforded by the description of clean and unclean animals in 14[4a. 6-19a] (= Lev. 11[2b-20], with immaterial differences †): in some other cases the differences are great,—in fact, so great as to be incapable of being harmonized.

An example or two will illustrate the different relation in which Dt. stands to the other Pentateuchal codes. If 16[1-17] be compared with the parallels in JE, it will be seen to be an *expansion* of them, several clauses being quoted verbally (see below, note *), and only placed in a new setting. If it be compared with Lev. 23, the general scope will be seen to be very different, though, with the parts of Lev. 23 which belong to H, there are two or three expressions in common, viz. in 16[11a. 13. 15]. With the table of sacrifices in Nu. 28 f. there is no point of contact in Dt. The laws in 14[22-29] 15[19-23] 18[1-8] diverge most remarkably from those on the same subjects in Lev.–Nu. In other instances, also, there are differences, though less considerable.

The different relation in which Dt. stands to the other codes may be thus expressed. It is an *expansion* of that in JE (Ex. 20–23); it is, in several features, *parallel* to that in H (Lev.

" *E.g.* Dt. 6[8] 7[5] 10[19] 16[3. 4. 16. 19], with the parallels cited in the Table.

† 14[9-10. 20] are *briefer* than Lev. 11[9-12. 21-22]; 14[4b-5] is not in Lev. (cf. p. 46).

17-26); it contains *allusions* to laws such as those codified in [72] some parts of P, while from those contained in other parts its provisions differ widely.*

In so far as it is a law-book, Dt. may be described as a manual, which without entering into technical details (almost the only exception is 14^{3-20}, which explains itself) would instruct the Israelite in the ordinary duties of life. It gives general directions as to the way in which the annual feasts are to be kept and the principal offerings paid. It lays down a few fundamental rules concerning sacrifice ($12^{5f. 20. 23}$ 15^{23} 17^1) : for a case in which technical skill would be required, it refers to the priests (24^8). It prescribes the general principles by which family and domestic life is to be regulated, specifying a number of the cases most likely to occur. Justice is to be equitably and impartially administered (16^{18-20}). It prescribes a due position in the community to the prophet (13^{1-5} 18^{9-22}), and shows how even the monarchy may be so established as not to contravene the fundamental principles of the theocracy ($17^{14ff.}$).

Deuteronomy is, however, more than a mere code of laws ; it is the expression of a profound ethical and religious spirit, which determines its character in every part. The author wrote, it is evident, under a keen sense of the perils of idolatry ; and to guard Israel against this by insisting earnestly on the debt of gratitude and obedience which it owes to its Sovereign Lord, is the fundamental teaching of the book. Accordingly at the head of the hortatory introduction (c. 5-11) stands the Decalogue ; and the First Commandment forms the text of the chapters which follow. Having already ($4^{12ff.}$) dwelt on the *spirituality* of the God of Israel, the lawgiver emphasizes here, far more distinctly than had been before done, His *unity* and *unique* *Godhead* (6^4 10^{17} : cf. 3^{24} $4^{35. 39}$), drawing from this truth the practical consequence that He must be the sole object of the Israelite's reverence (6^{13} 10^{20}). He exhorts the people to keep His statutes ever in remembrance (5^1 $6^{6-9. 17f.}$ &c.), warning them again and again, upon peril of the consequences, not to follow after "other gods" (6^{12-15} 7^4 8^{11-20} $11^{16f. 28}$ $30^{17f.}$: cf. 4^{23-28} 29^{25-28} $31^{16f. 20f. 29}$), not to be tempted, even by the most

* From what has been said in the text, it will be apparent how incorrect is the common description of Deuteronomy as a "recapitulation" of the laws contained in the preceding books.

specious representations, to the practice of idolatry (13^{1-11}), and declaring emphatically that obedience to Jehovah's will will bring with it the Divine blessing, and be the sure avenue to national prosperity (cf. the passages cited, p. 99 f., Nos. 3, 13, 21). He reminds them of the noble privileges, undeserved on their part ($7^{7f.}$ 9^{4-6}; and the retrospect following, as far as 10^{11}), which had been bestowed [73] upon them ($10^{14f.\ 22}$; so 4^{37}); and reasserts with fresh emphasis the old idea (Ex. 19^5 24^8 34^{10}) of the covenant subsisting between the people and God ($5^{2.\ 3}$ 26^{16-19} : so $4^{23.\ 31}$ $29^{9.\ 12-15.\ 25}$), assuring them that if they are true on their side God will be true likewise (7^{9-13} 8^{18} 11^{22-28}). Particularly he emphasizes the love of God ($7^{8.\ 13}$ 10^{15} 23^{5b} : so 4^{37}), tracing even in his people's affliction the chastening hand of a father ($8^{2f.\ 5.\ 16}$), and dwelling on the providential purposes which His dealings with Israel exemplified.

Duties, however, are not to be performed from secondary motives, such as fear, or dread of consequences : they are to be the spontaneous outcome of a heart penetrated by an all-absorbing sense of personal devotion to God ("with *all* the heart, and with *all* the soul"; see p. 101), and prepared to renounce everything inconsistent with loyalty to Him. Love to God, as the motive of human action, is the characteristic doctrine of Deuteronomy (6^5 10^{12} $11^{1.\ 13.\ 22}$ 13^3 19^9 $30^{6.\ 16.\ 20}$) : as here dwelt upon and expanded, the old phrase *those that love me* is filled with a moral significance which the passing use of it, in passages like Ex. 20^6, Jud. 5^{31} would scarcely suggest. The true principle of human action cannot be stated more profoundly than is here done : it was a true instinct which in later times selected Dt. 6^{4-9} for daily recitation by every Israelite ; * and it is at once intelligible that our Lord should have pointed to the same text, both as the "first commandment of all" (Matt. $22^{37f.}$ Mark $12^{29f.}$), and as embodying the primary condition for the inheritance of eternal life (Luke $10^{27f.}$).

The code of special laws (c. 12–26) is dominated by similar principles. Sometimes, indeed, the legislator is satisfied to leave an enactment to explain itself : more commonly he insists upon the object which it is to subserve (*e.g.* 14^{23} 21^{23} &c.) or the motive which should be operative in its observance. An ethical and religious aim should underlie the entire life of the com-

---

* The *Shěmá'* : Schürer, *Gesch. d. Jüd. Volkes*, ii. 377 f., 382 f.

munity. Local sanctuaries were apt to be abused, and to degenerate into homes of superstition and idolatry : all offerings and public worship generally are to take place at the central sanctuary, " the place which Jehovah thy God shall choose" (c. 12, and often). Old enactments are repeated (12^3 ; cf. 7^5), [74] and fresh enactments to meet special cases (c. 13. 20^{16-18}) are added, for the purpose of neutralizing every inducement to worship "other gods." The holiness of the nation is to be its standard of behaviour, even in matters which might appear indifferent ($14^{1f.\ 3-20.\ 21}$) ; its perfect devotion to its God is to exclude all customs or observances inconsistent with this (18^{9-14}). In particular the duties of humanity, philanthropy, and benevolence are insisted on, towards those in difficulty or want (12^{19} 15^{7-11} 22^{1-4} $24^{12f.\ 14f.}$ 27^{18}), and towards slaves ($15^{13f.}$ $23^{15f.}$), especially upon occasion of the great annual pilgrimages ($12^{12.\ 18}$ $14^{27.\ 29}$ $16^{11.\ 14}$ $26^{11.\ 13}$). Gratitude and a sense of sympathy evoked by the recollection of their own past, are the motives again and again inculcated : two forms of thanksgiving form the termination of the code (c. 26). Already in the Decalogue the reason assigned for the observance of the fourth commandment, " that thy man-servant and thy maid-servant may rest as well as thou," and the motive, "And thou shalt remember that thou wast a bondman in the land of Egypt" ($5^{14b.\ 15}$), indicate the lines along which the legislator moves, and the principles which it is his desire to impress (add $13^{5.\ 10}$ 15^{15} $16^{3b.\ 12}$ 23^7 $24^{18.\ 22}$). Forbearance, equity, and forethought underlie the regulations $20^{5-11.\ 19f.}$ $21^{10-14.\ 15-17}$ 22^8 $23^{24.\ 25}$ $24^{5.\ 6.\ 16.\ 19-22}$ 25^3 ; humanity towards animals, those in 22^7 25^4. Not indeed that similar considerations are absent from the older legislation (see *e.g.* Ex. $22^{21-24.\ 27}$ $23^{9.\ 11.\ 12}$), and (as the table will have shown) some of the enactments which have been cited are even borrowed from it ; but they are developed in Dt. with an emphasis and distinctness which give a character to the entire work. Nowhere else in the OT. do we breathe such an atmosphere of generous devotion to God, and of large-hearted benevolence towards man; and nowhere else is it shown with the same fulness of detail how these principles may be made to permeate the entire life of the community.*

Dt. contains, however, two historical retrospects, 1^6–3^{22} and

---

* See further, on the leading principles of Deut., Holzinger, *Einl.* p. 313 ff., and the writer's *Commentary*, pp. xix–xxxiv.

9^6-10^{11}, besides allusions to the history in other places ; and the relation of these to the four preceding books must next be examined. The following table of *verbal coincidences* shows that in the history Dt. is even more closely dependent upon the earlier narrative than in the laws. The reader who will be at [75] the pains to underline (or, if he uses the Hebrew, to *over*line) in his text of Dt. the passages in common, will be able to see at a glance (1) the passages of Ex.–Nu. passed over in Dt., (2) the variations and additions in Dt.

Dt.	1^{7a}	(Nu. 14^{25}).*
,,	$9b$	(Nu. 11^{14}).
,,	12	(Nu. 11^{17b}).
,,	$13a$	Cf. Ex. 18^{21a}.
,,	15	Ex. 18^{25}.
,,	$17b$	,, $18^{22.\,26}$.
,,	9^6 *end*	,, $32^9\,33^{3.\,5}\,34^9$.
,,	$9a$	,, 24^{12}.
,,	9 *middle*	,, 24^{18b}.
,,	9 *end*	(Ex. 34^{28a}).
,,	$10a$	Ex. 31^{18b}.
,,	12	,, $32^{7.\,8a}$.
,,	13	,, 32^9
,,	$14b$	,, 32^{10b} (Nu. 14^{12b}).
,,	15	,, 32^{15}.
,,	16	,, $32^{19a.\,8a}$.
,,	17	,, 32^{19b}.
,,	18-19	,, 34^{28} (cf. v.^{9}).
,,	20	. . .
,,	21 †	,, 32^{20}.
,,	22	See Nu. 11^{1-3} Ex. 17^7 Nu. $11^{4.\,34}$.
,,	23-24	[See Dt. 1^{19} *end*. $26.\,32$].
,,	25	(Resumption of Dt. 9^{18}).
,,	26 ‡	(Ex. 32^{11b}).

---

* The parenthesis indicates that, though there is a coincidence in the language, the passage quoted does not describe the same event, but is borrowed from *another part of the narrative.* Thus Dt. 1^{9-17} alludes to the appointment of judges to assist Moses, described in Ex. 18 ; but some of the phrases are borrowed from the narrative of the 70 elders in Nu. 11. So in $2^{27b.\,28b.\,29b}$, alluding to Nu. 21^{22} (the message to *Sihon*), the expressions are borrowed from Nu. $20^{17.\,19}$ (the message to *Edom*).

† This verse does not necessarily describe the *sequel* of v.^{20} ; it may be rendered : " And your sin . . . I took (= *had taken*)."

‡ V. $^{26-29}$ cannot refer *actually* to Ex. 32^{11-13}, because the intercession there recorded was made *before* Moses' first descent from the mount, whereas in Dt. v.^{25} points back to v.^{18}, which clearly relates what took place *after* it.

Dt.	9^{27a}	(Ex. 32^{13}).
,,	28	(Nu. 14^{16}; cf. Ex. 32^{12}).
,,	$29b$	(Ex. 32^{11b}).
,,	10^{1a}	Ex. 34^{1a}.
[76]	,,	$1b$	,, 34^2.
,,	$1c$ (the *ark*)	. . .
,,	$2a$	Ex. 34^{1b}.
,,	$2b$-$3a$ (the *ark*)	. . .
,,	$3b$	Ex. 34^4.
,,	4	,, 34^{28b}.
,,	5. 6-9	. . .
,,	10 ($=9^{18}$)	Cf. Ex. $34^{9f. \ 28}$.
,,	11	(Ex. 33^1).

The dependence of Dt. $1^{24\text{-}40. \ 41\text{-}46}$ on Nu. 13^{17}–14^{25} $14^{40\text{-}45}$ 20^1 and of 2^1–3^3 on Nu. $21^{4\text{-}35a}$ ($3^{4\text{-}11}$ being an expansion of Nu. 21^{35b}),* it must be left to the reader to work out for himself. Apart from the verbal coincidences, while there are sometimes omissions, as a rule the substance of the earlier narrative is reproduced freely with amplificatory additions. A singular characteristic of both retrospects is the manner in which, on several occasions, a phrase describing originally one incident *is applied in Dt. to another.* Allusions to the narrative of Gen.-Nu. occur also in other parts of Dt.† But the remarkable circumstance is that, as in the laws, so in the history, Dt. *is dependent upon JE.* Throughout the parallels just tabulated (as well as in the others occurring in the book), not the allusions only, but the words cited, will be found, all but uniformly, to be in JE, not in P. An important conclusion follows from this fact. Inasmuch as, in our existing Pent., JE and P repeatedly cross one another, the constant absence of any reference to P can only be reasonably explained by one supposition, viz. that when Dt. was composed *JE and P were not yet united into a single work, and JE alone formed the basis of Dt.*‡

* Unless indeed Dillm.'s view of Nu. $21^{33\text{-}35}$ (above, p. 66) be correct.

† As 1^8 6^{10} and often (the *oath*) to Gen. $22^{16f.}$ 24^7 26^3; 6^{16} to Ex. 17^7; 11^6 to Nu. $16^{1b. \ 32a}$; 24^9 to Nu. 12^{10}. Comp. also $7^{14. \ 20}$ (the hornet) ^{22} and Ex. $23^{28. \ 28. \ 30. \ 29b}$; 7^{16b} and Ex. 23^{33b}; 9^{3b} and Ex. $23^{23. \ 27. \ 31b}$; $11^{23. \ 25}$ and Ex. 23^{27}; 12^{20} and Ex. 34^{24}; &c.

‡ Notice esp. the transition from Dt. 1^{40} ($=$Nu. 14^{25b}) to Dt. 1^{41} ($=$Nu. 14^{40}), the intervening passage, v. $^{26\text{-}39}$, which belongs in the main to P, being disregarded. A single instance of this kind would not be conclusive; but the *consistent* disregard of P in Dt. admits of but one interpretation.

This conclusion, derived primarily from the two retrospects, is confirmed by other indications. Dt. speaks regularly, not of *Sinai*, but of *Horeb* (as Ex. 3^1 17^6 33^6), a term never used by P : Dt. names Dathan and Abiram (11^6), but is silent as to Korah ; in the composite narrative of Nu. 16 Dathan and [77] Abiram alone (p. 64) belong to JE. Similarly the exception of Caleb alone (without Joshua) in 1^{36} agrees with JE, Nu. 14^{24} (p. 63). The allusions to Gen.–Ex. are likewise consistently to JE : thus, while the promise (1^8) is found both in JE and P, the *oath* is peculiar to JE. If the author of Dt. was acquainted with P, he can only have referred to it occasionally, and certainly did not make it the basis of his work. The verdict of the *historical* allusions in Dt. thus confirms that of the *laws* (p. 75 f.).*

Authorship and date of Deuteronomy.

Even though it were clear that the first four books of the Pent. were written by Moses, it would be difficult to sustain the Mosaic authorship of Deuteronomy. For, to say nothing of the remarkable difference of style, Dt. conflicts with the *legislation* of Ex.–Nu. in a manner that would not be credible were the legislator in both one and the same. Even in Dt. 15^{17b} compared with Ex. $21^{2ff.}$ and Dt. 15^{1-11} compared with Ex. $23^{10f.}$ (both JE), there are variations difficult to reconcile with both being the work of a single legislator (for they are of a character that cannot reasonably be attributed to the altered prospects of the nation at the close of the 40 years' wanderings, and point rather to the people having passed during the interval into changed social conditions) ; but when the laws of Dt. are compared with those of P, such a supposition becomes impossible. For in Dt. language is used implying that *fundamental institutions of P are unknown to the author*. Thus, while Lev. 25^{39-43} enjoins the release of the Hebrew slave in the year of Jubile, in Dt. 15^{12-18} the legislator, *without bringing his new law into relation* with the different one of Lev., prescribes the release of the Hebrew slave in the 7th year of his service. In the laws of P in Leviticus and Numbers a sharp distinction is drawn between the priests and the common Levites : in Dt. it is implied (18^{1a}) that *all* members of the tribe of Levi are qualified to exercise priestly functions ; and regulations are laid down (18^{6-8})

---

* The dependence of Dt. upon JE is generally recognised by critics ; see *e.g.* Delitzsch, *ZKWL.* 1882, p. 227 ; Dillm. *NDJ.* p. 609.

to meet the case of any member coming from the country to the central sanctuary, and claiming to officiate there as priest.* Moreover, in P particular [78] provision is made for the maintenance of both priests and Levites, and in Nu. 35 (cf. Josh. 21) 48 cities are appointed for their residence. In Dt., under both heads, the provisions are very different. Dt. 18³ is in conflict with Lev. 7³²⁻³⁴ ; and Dt. 18⁶ is inconsistent with the institution of Levitical cities prescribed in Nu. 35 : it implies that the Levite has no settled residence, but is a "sojourner" in one or other of the cities ("gates," see p. 99) of Israel. The terms of the verse are indeed entirely compatible with the institution of Levitical cities, supposing it to have been imperfectly put in force ; but they fall strangely from one who, *ex hypothesi*, had only 6 months previously assigned to the Levites permanent dwelling-places. The same representation recurs in other parts of Dt. : the Levites are frequently alluded to as scattered about the land, and are earnestly commended to the Israelite's charity (12¹².¹⁸.¹⁹ 14²⁷.²⁹ 16¹¹.¹⁴ 26¹¹.¹²⁻¹³). Further, Dt. 12⁶.¹⁷ᶠ. 15¹⁹ᶠ. conflict with Nu. 18¹⁸ : in Nu. the firstlings of oxen and sheep are assigned expressly and absolutely to the *priest*; in Dt. they are to be *eaten by the owner himself* at the central sanctuary. Lastly, the law of tithes in Dt. is in conflict with that of P on the same subject. In Nu. 18²¹⁻²⁴ the tithes—viz. both animal and vegetable alike (Lev. 27³⁰.³²)—are definitely assigned to the Levites, who, in their turn, pay a tenth to the priests (Nu. 18²⁶⁻²⁸) : in Dt. there appears to be no injunction respecting the tithes of animal produce ; but the reservation of a tithe of vegetable produce (12¹⁷ᶠ. 14²²ᶠ.) is enjoined, which is to be consumed by the offerer, like the firstlings, at a sacrificial feast, in which the Levite shares only in company with others as the recipient of a charitable benevolence. A large proportion, therefore, of what is assigned in Nu. to the Levites remains implicitly the property of the lay Israelite in Dt.† It is held,

---

* The terms used in v.⁷ to describe the Levites' services are those used elsewhere regularly of *priestly* duties. שרת בשם *to minister in the name*, as 18⁵ (of the priest : cf. 17¹² 21⁵) ; עמר לפני *to stand before—i.e.* to wait on (see *e.g.* 1 Ki. 10⁸)—*Jehovah*, as Ez. 44¹⁵ Jud. 20²⁸, cf. Dt. 17¹² 18⁵. (The Levites " stand before "—*i.e.* wait upon—*the congregation* Nu. 16⁹ Ez. 44¹¹ᵇ. In 2 Ch. 29¹¹ *priests* are present : see v.⁴.)

† The common assumption that in Dt. a *second* tithe, on vegetable produce only, in addition to that referred to in Nu. is meant, is inconsistent with the

then, that these [79] differences of detail between the laws of
Dt. and those of P are greater than could arise were the legislator the same in both, and that they can only be explained by
the supposition that the two systems of law represent the usage
of two distinct periods of the nation's life.   For though it is no
doubt thoroughly conceivable that Moses may have foreseen
the neglect of his own institution, this will not explain his
enjoining observances in conflict with those which he had
already prescribed; while, as regards the impoverished condition of the Levites, there is no indication that this is merely
a *future* contingency for which the legislator is making provision; it is represented throughout as the condition *which the
writer sees around him* (cf. Jud. $17^{7f.}$ $19^{1ff.}$).

There are also discrepancies between Dt. and other parts of P, as 1^{22} (the
people suggest spying out the land of Canaan) and Nu. $13^{1ff.}$ (the same suggestion referred to Jehovah); 10^3 (*Moses* makes the ark *before* ascending Sinai
the second time) and Ex. 37^1 (*Bezaleel* makes it *after* Moses' return from the
mount); 10^6 and Nu. $33^{31.\,38}$; 10^8 and Ex. 28 f. Lev. 8 &c.   In the light of
the *demonstrated* dependence of Dt. upon JE, it can scarcely be doubted
that the real solution of these discrepancies is that the representation in Dt. is
based upon parts of the narrative of JE, which were still read by the author
of Dt., but which, when JE was afterwards combined with P, were not
retained by the compiler.   Notice that in 10^7 the form of the itinerary *agrees
with that of JE* (p. 66).

There are, moreover, expressions in the retrospects (esp. the
repeated "at that time" 2^{34} $3^{4.\,8.\,12.\,18.\,21.\,23}$, and "unto this day"
3^{14}) implying that a longer interval of time than 6 months (1^3
compared with Nu. 33^{38} and 20^{22-28}) had elapsed since the
events referred to had taken place.*   And the use of the phrase
"beyond Jordan" for Eastern Palestine in $1^{1.\,5}$ 3^8 $4^{41.\,46f.\,49}$,

manner in which it is spoken of in Dt.: even supposing the first tithe to be
taken for granted as an established usage, it is not credible that a second tithe
should be thus *for the first time instituted* without a word to indicate that it
was an innovation, or in any respect different from what would be ordinarily
understood by the word "tithe."   And if a larger and more important tithe
had to be paid, it is scarcely possible that there should be no reference to it in
the solemn profession $26^{12f.}$.

* The curious transition in 1^{37} from the 2nd to the 40th year of the exodus,
and back again to the 2nd year in 1^{39} points in the same direction—unless,
indeed (which is quite possible), the solution suggested above be here also the
true one, and the reference be to some incident of the second year recorded in
JE, but not preserved in our existing Pentateuch.

exactly as in Josh. 2^{10} 7^7 9^{10} &c. Jud. 5^{17} 10^8, implies that the
author was resident in Western Palestine (the same usage, im-
plying the same fact, in Nu. 22^1 34^{15}).*

[80] But in fact the Mosaic authorship of Gen.–Nu. cannot
be sustained. P, at any rate, must belong to a widely different
age from JE. Can any one read the injunctions respecting
sacrifices and feasts in Ex. 23^{14-19} beside those in P (Lev. 1–7,
Nu. 28–29, for instance), and not feel that some centuries must
have intervened between the simplicity which characterizes the
one and the minute specialization which is the mark of the
other? The earliest of the Pentateuchal sources, it seems clear,
is JE : but at whatever date this be placed, Dt. must follow it at
a considerable interval ; for the legislation of Dt. implies a more
elaborately organized civil community than that for which provision is made in the legislation of JE. Nor is this more
elaborate organization merely anticipated in Dt.; it is presupposed
as already existing. And in fact the historical books afford a
strong presumption that the law of Dt. did not originate until after
the establishment of the monarchy. In Dt. the law respecting
sacrifice is unambiguous and strict : it is not to be offered in
Canaan "in every place that thou seest" (12^{13}), but only at the
place chosen by God "out of all thy tribes to set his name there"
($12^{5. 14. 18}$ 14^{23} and often), *i.e.* at some central sanctuary. Now
in Ex. it is said (20^{24b}), "in every place where I record my
name, I will come unto thee and bless thee"; and with the
principle here laid down the practice of Josh.–1 Ki. 6 conforms :
in these books sacrifices are frequently described as offered in
different parts of the land, without any indication (and this is
the important fact) on the part of either the actor or the narrator
that a law such as that of Dt. is being infringed. After the
exclusion of all uncertain or exceptional cases, such as Jud. 2^5
6^{20-24}, where the theophany may be held to have justified the
erection of an altar, there remain as instances of either altars or
local sanctuaries Josh. $24^{1b. 26b}$ 1 Sa. $7^{9f. 17}$ 9^{12-14} $10^{3. 5. 8}$ ($13^{9f.}$),
11^{15} 14^{35} 20^6 2 Sa. $15^{12. 32}$.

* The variations between Dt. and Ex.–Nu., in connexion with the
attempts that have been made to reconcile them, as well as other features
inconsistent with Moses' authorship, are considered more fully in an article on
Dt. by the author in Smith's *Dict. of the Bible*,[2] §§ 11, 14, 16–18, 20, 31–33 :
and in his *Commentary*, pp. xxxiv–xliv, lxii–lxiv.

The inference which appears to follow from these passages is sometimes met by the contention that the period from the abandonment of Shiloh to the erection of the Temple was an exceptional one. The nation was in disgrace, and undergoing a course of discipline, its spiritual privileges being withheld till it was ripe to have them restored ; and, in so far as Samuel appears often [81] as the agent, his function was an extraordinary one, limited to himself. It may be doubted whether this answer is satisfactory. There is no trace in the narrative of such disciplinary motives having actuated Samuel ; and the narrator betrays no consciousness of anything irregular or abnormal having occurred. See especially 1 Sa. $9^{12ff.}$ 10^{3-5}, where ordinary and regular customs are evidently described ; and 14^{35}, which implies that Saul was in the habit of building altars to Jehovah.

The sanctuary at which the Ark was for the time located had doubtless the pre-eminence (cf. Ex. 23^{19}, 1 Sa. 1–3) ; but, so far as the evidence before us goes, sacrifice was habitually offered at other places, the only limitation being that they should be properly sanctioned and approved ("in every place *where I record my name*").* The non-observance of a law does not, of course, imply necessarily its non-existence ; still, when men who might fairly be presumed to know of it, if it existed, not only make no attempt to put it in force, but disregard it without explanation or excuse, it must be allowed that such an inference is not altogether an unreasonable one.

The history thus appears to corroborate the inference derived above from c. 1–4 &c., and to throw the composition of Dt. to a period considerably later than the Mosaic age. Can its date be determined more precisely? The *terminus ad quem* is not difficult to fix : it must have been written prior to the 18th year of King Josiah (B.C. 621), the year in which Hilkiah made his memorable discovery of the "book of the law" in the Temple (2 Ki. $22^{8ff.}$). For it is clear from the narrative of 2 Ki. 22–23 that that book must have contained Deuteronomy ; for although the bare description of its contents, and of the effect produced by it upon those who heard it read ($22^{11. 13. 19}$) might suit Lev. 26 equally with Dt. 28, yet the allusions to the *covenant* contained in it ($23^{2. 3}$), which refer evidently to Dt. ($29^{1. 9. 21. 25}$: cf. 27^{26}), and the fact that in the reformation based upon it Josiah carries out, step by step (2 Ki. $22^{13. 19}$

---

* The expression בכל המקום may include equally places conceived as existing contemporaneously (cf. the same idiomatic use of כל, Lev. 15^{24b} Dt. 11^{24} &c.), or selected successively.

23[3-5. 7. 9-11. 24] &c.), the principles of Dt., leave no doubt upon the matter.

How much earlier than B.C. 621 it may be is more difficult to determine. The supposition that Hilkiah himself was concerned in the composition of it is not probable : for a book compiled by the high priest could hardly fail to emphasize the interests of the [82] priestly body at Jerusalem, which Dt. does not do (18[6-8]).* The book is stated to have been found while some repairs were being carried on in the Temple : and there is force in the argument that it could hardly have been lost during the early years of Josiah (who appears to have been throughout devoted to the service of Jehovah); but this might easily have happened during the heathen reaction under Manasseh. Hence it is probable that its composition is not later than the reign of Manasseh.†

The conclusion that Dt. belongs, at least approximately, to this age, is in agreement with the contents of the book.

(1.) The differences between Dt. and Ex. 21–23, point with some cogency to a period considerably removed from that at which the Israelites took possession of Canaan, and presuppose a changed social condition of the people.

(2.) The law of the kingdom, 17[14ff.], is coloured by reminis-

---

* W. R. Smith, *OTJC.*[2] p. 363 ; Dillm. p. 614. Colenso's opinion, that Jeremiah was the author, has found no favour with critics, and is certainly incorrect ; it is true, the language of Jeremiah often remarkably resembles that of Dt., but when the two are compared minutely, it appears that many of the *characteristic* expressions of each are absent from the other (cf. Kleinert, pp. 185–190, 235, and the writer's *Commentary*, pp. xciii, xciv).

† So Ewald, *Hist.* i. 127, iv. 221; W. R. Smith, *Add. Answer* (Edin. 1878), p. 78 (cf. *OTJC.*[2] p. 355); Kittel, pp. 57–59; Kautzsch, *Abriss*, p. 168 ; Wildeboer, *Letterkunde des O. V.* § 11. 10. Reuss, *La Bible* (1879), i. 156 ff. ; Kuenen, *Hex.* p. 214 ; Dillmann, *NDJ.* p. 613 f. (less confidently); Stade, *G.* i. 650 ff. ; Holzinger, p. 327 f., prefer the reign of Josiah : Cornill, *Einl.*[3] p. 30, "not long before 621." Delitzsch, *Studien*, x. 509 ; Riehm, *Einl.* p. 246 f.; König, p. 217 ; Westphal (i. 278 ff.); Oettli (p. 19 f.), assign it to the reign of Hezekiah, considering that it was in its origin connected with, or even gave the impulse to, the reform of 2 Ki. 18[4. 22]. G. A. Smith (*Crit. Rev.* 1895, p. 341 f.) assigns it to the close of the same reign, remarking that if it had been written later, it might have been expected to exhibit traces of the opposition and persecution to which faithful Israelites were then exposed. It is true, the data showing Dt. to be post-Mosaic are more definite and distinct than those which we possess for fixing the *precise* part of the century before B.C. 621 to which it is to be assigned.

cences of the monarchy of Solomon. The argument does not deny that Moses may have made provision for the establishment of a monarchy in Israel, but affirms that the form in which the provision is here cast bears traces of a later age.

(3.) The forms of idolatry alluded to, specially the worship of the "host of heaven" (4^{19} 17^3), seem to point to the middle period of the monarchy. It is true, the worship of the sun and moon is ancient, as is attested even by the names of places in Canaan; but in the notices (which are frequent) of idolatrous practices in Jud.–Kings no mention occurs of "the host of heaven" till the period of the later kings.* That the cult is *presupposed* in Dt. and not merely anticipated prophetically, seems clear from the terms in which it is referred to. While we are not in a position to affirm positively that the danger was [83] not felt earlier, the law, as formulated in Dt., seems designed to meet the form which the cult assumed at a later age.

(4.) The influence of Dt. upon subsequent writers is clear and indisputable. It is remarkable, now, that the early prophets, Amos, Hosea, and the undisputed portions of Isaiah, show no certain traces of this influence; Jeremiah exhibits marks of it on nearly every page; Ezekiel and II Isaiah are also evidently influenced by it. If Dt. were composed in the period between Isaiah and Jeremiah, these facts would be exactly accounted for.

(5.) The language and style of Dt., clear and flowing, free from archaisms, but purer than that of Jeremiah, would suit the same period. It is difficult in this connexion not to feel the force of Dillmann's remark (p. 611), that "the style of Dt. implies a long development of the art of public oratory, and is not of a character to belong to the first age of Israelitish literature."

(6.) The *prophetic teaching* of Dt., the dominant theological ideas, the point of view from which the laws are presented, the principles by which conduct is estimated, presuppose a relatively advanced stage of theological reflexion, as they also approximate to what is found in Jeremiah and Ezekiel.

(7.) In Dt. 16^{22} we read, "Thou shalt not set thee up a

* 2 Ki. 23^{12} names Ahaz (cf. Is. $17^{8\,end}$, belonging to the same reign); 2 Ki. $21^{3.\,5}$ [cf. $23^{4.\,5}$] Manasseh; 17^{16} is vague; Zeph. 1^5, Jer. 7^{18} 8^2 19^{13} 44^{17}, Ezek. 8^{16} belong to a somewhat later period.

mazzêbah (obelisk or pillar), which the Lord thy God hateth."
Had Isaiah known of this law he would hardly have adopted the
mazzêbah (19^{19}) as a symbol of the conversion of Egypt to the
true faith. The supposition that *heathen* pillars are meant in Dt.
is not favoured by the context (v.^{21b}); the use of these has, moreover, been proscribed before (7^5 12^3).

When once Deuteronomy is viewed in the light of the age
which gave it birth, its true significance appears. It was a great
manifesto against the dominant tendencies of the time. It laid
down the lines of a great religious reform. Whether written in
the dark days of Manasseh, or during the brighter years which
followed the accession of Josiah, it was a nobly-conceived endeavour to provide in anticipation a spiritual rallying-point, round
which, when circumstances favoured, the disorganized forces of
the national religion might range themselves again. It was an
emphatic reaffirmation of the fundamental principles which
Moses had long ago insisted on, loyalty to Jehovah and repudia-
tion of all false gods : it was an endeavour to realize in practice
the ideals of the prophets, especially of Hosea and Isaiah, to
transform the Judah demoralized by Manasseh into the "holy
nation" pictured in Isaiah's vision, and to awaken in it that
devotion to God, and love for man, which Hosea had declared
to be the first of human duties. In setting forth these truths the
author exhausts all his eloquence : in impressive and melodious
periods, he dilates upon the claims which Jehovah has upon the
Israelite's allegiance, and seeks, by ever appealing to the most
generous and powerful motives, to stir Israel's heart to respond
with undivided loyalty and affection.

If, however, it be true that Deuteronomy is the composition
of another than Moses, in what light are we to regard it? In
particular, does this view of its origin detract from its value and
authority as a part of the Old Testament Canon? The objection
is commonly made, that if this be the origin of the book it is a
"forgery": the author, it is said, has sought to shelter himself
under a great name, and to secure by a fiction recognition or
authority for a number of laws devised by himself. In estimating this objection, there are two or three important distinctions
which must be kept in mind. In the first place, though it may
appear paradoxical to say so, Dt. *does not claim to be written by
Moses :* whenever the author speaks himself, he purports to give

a [84] description *in the third person* of what Moses did or said.*
The true " author " of Dt. is thus the writer who *introduces Moses
in the third person*; and the discourses which he is represented
as having spoken fall in consequence into the same category as
the speeches in the historical books, some of which largely, and
others entirely, are the composition of the compilers, and are
placed by them in the mouths of historical characters. This
freedom in ascribing speeches to historical personages is characteristic, more or less, of ancient historians generally †; and it
certainly was followed by the Hebrew historians. The proof
lies in the great similarity of style which these speeches constantly exhibit to the parts of the narrative which are evidently
the work of the compiler himself. In some cases the writers may
no doubt have had information as to what was actually said on
the occasions referred to, which they recast in their own words;
but very often they merely give articulate expression to the
thoughts and feelings which it was presumed that the persons in
question would have entertained. The practice is exemplified
with particular clearness in the Book of Chronicles, where David,
Solomon, and different prophets constantly express ideas and use
idioms which are distinctively late, and are mostly peculiar to
the compiler of Chronicles himself; but there are many instances
in other books as well.‡ An author, therefore, in framing discourses appropriate to Moses' situation, and embodying principles which (see p. 91) he would have cordially approved,
especially if (as is probable) the elements were provided for him
by tradition, would be doing nothing inconsistent with the literary
usages of his age and people.

Secondly, it is an altogether false view of the laws in Dt. to
treat them as the author's "inventions." Many are repeated
from the Book of the Covenant; the existence of others is independently attested by the "Law of Holiness"; others, upon
intrinsic grounds, are clearly ancient. In some cases, no doubt,
an aim formerly indistinctly expressed is more sharply formulated,

* See 1^{1-5} 4^{41-49} 5^1 $27^{1.\ 9.\ 11}$ 29^2 (Heb.[1]) 31^{1-30}. Undoubtedly, the third
person *may* have been used by Moses; but it is unreasonable to assert that he
must have used it, or to contend that passages in which it occurs could *only*
have been written by him. See Delitzsch, *Studien*, x. p. 503 f.; or, more
briefly, *Genesis* (1887), p. 22. On *wrote* in Dt. 31^9, see below, p. 124 *n.*

† See Arnold's *Thucydides*, on i. 22 (ed. 5, 1861, vol. i. p. 28).

‡ See below, under Joshua, Kings, and Chronicles.

as in others modifications or adaptations are introduced which the tendencies of the age required; but, on the whole, the laws of [85] Dt. are unquestionably derived from *pre-existent usage*; and the object of the author is to insist upon their importance, and to supply motives for their observance. The new element in Dt. is thus not the laws, but their *parenetic setting*. And even this is new, not in substance, but only in form. The point of capital importance in Dt. is the attitude of the nation towards Jehovah : throughout the discourses the author's aim is to provide motives, by which to secure loyalty to Him. But Moses also (as critics themselves do not doubt *) laid the greatest stress upon Jehovah's being the sole and exclusive object of Israel's reverence : the principles on which Dt. insists are thus in substance Mosaic; all that belongs to the post-Mosaic author is the rhetorical form in which they are presented. Deuteronomy may be described as the *prophetic re-formulation, and adaptation to new needs, of an older legislation.* It is highly probable that there existed the tradition of a final legislative address delivered by Moses in the plains of Moab : there would be a more obvious motive for the plan followed by the author, if it could be supposed that he worked thus upon a traditional basis. But be that as it may, the bulk of the laws contained in Dt. is undoubtedly far more ancient than the time of the author himself : and in dealing with them as he has done, in combining them into a manual for the guidance of the people, and providing them with hortatory introductions and comments, conceived in the spirit of Moses himself, he cannot, in the light of the parallels that have been referred to, be held to be guilty of dishonesty or literary fraud. There is nothing in Dt. implying an interested or dishonest motive on the part of the (post-Mosaic) author : and this being so, its moral and spiritual greatness remains unimpaired; its inspired authority is in no respect less than that of any other part of the Old Testament Scriptures which happens to be anonymous.

The view of Dt. as the re-formulation, with a view to new needs, of an older legislation, meets the objection that is sometimes urged against the date assigned to it by critics, viz. that it contains provisions that would be nugatory in the 7th cent. B.C.; for instance, the injunction to give no quarter to the inhabitants of

* Cornill, *Der Isr. Prophetismus* (1894), p. 25 f.

Canaan ($7^{1\text{-}5}$ $20^{16\text{-}18}$). Of course, as the *creation* of that age, such an injunction would be absurd : but it is *repeated* from Ex. $23^{31\text{-}33}$; in a recapitulation of Mosaic principles, supposed to be addressed to the people when they were about to enter Canaan, it would be naturally included ; and so far from being nugatory in the 7th cent. B.C., it would indirectly have a real value : occurring, as it does, in close connexion with the prohibition of all intercourse with the Canaanites, it would be an emphatic protest against tendencies which, under Ahaz and Manasseh, became disastrously strong. The injunction respecting Amalek [86] ($25^{17\text{-}19}$) is repeated for a similar reason ; it formed an indisputable part of the older legislation (Ex. 17^{16}), and would be suitable in Moses' mouth at the time when the discourses in Dt. are represented as having been spoken.

The much-debated "law of the kingdom" ($17^{14\text{-}20}$) appears also in its kernel to be old. It will be observed that the limitations laid down are all *theocratic*: the law does not define a political constitution, or limit the autocracy of the king in civil matters. It stands thus out of relation with 1 Sam. $8^{11\text{-}17}$ 10^{25}. Its object is to show how the monarchy, if established, is to conform to the same Mosaic principles which govern other departments of the theocracy. V.^{15} asserts the primary condition which the monarchy must satisfy,—"Thou mayest not set a foreigner to be king over thee" : a condition conceived thoroughly in the spirit of Ex. $23^{32\text{f.}}$, and designed to secure Israel's distinctive nationality against the intrusion of a heathen element in this most important dignity. The prohibitions, v.$^{16\text{f.}}$, guard against the distractions too often caused by riches and luxury at an Oriental Court ; danger from this source may well have been foreseen by Moses : still, these verses certainly wear the appearance of being coloured by recollections of the court of Solomon (1 Ki. $10^{25\text{-}28}$ $11^{2\text{-}4}$), or even of the eagerness of a powerful party in the days of Isaiah to induce the king to strengthen himself by means of Egyptian cavalry (Isa. 30^{16} 31^1 ; cf. Jer. $2^{18,\ 36}$). The injunctions, v.$^{18\text{ff.}}$, secure the king's personal familiarity with the principles of the Deuteronomic law, for the reason assigned in v.^{20}. As the re-formulation of an older law, embodying the theocratic ideal of the monarchy, the law of the kingdom contains nothing that is ill-adapted to a date in the 7th cent. B.C., or that would have sounded "absurd" to the author's contemporaries, supposing that to have been the period in which he lived.*

For reasons that have been stated, the law of the Central Sanctuary appears, in its *exclusiveness*, to be of comparatively modern origin; but this law in reality only accentuates the old *pre-eminence* in the interests of a principle which is often insisted [87] on in JE, viz. the segregation of Israel from heathen influences. History had shown that it was impossible to secure the local sanctuaries against abuse, and to free them from contamination by Canaanitish idolatry. The prophets had more and more distinctly taught that Zion was emphatically Jehovah's seat; and it became gradually more and more plain that the progress of spiritual religion demanded the unconditional abolition of the local shrines. It was not enough (Ex. 23[24] 34[13]) to demolish heathen sanctuaries: other sanctuaries, even though erected ostensibly for the worship of Jehovah, must not be allowed to take their place. Hezekiah, supported, it may be presumed, by prophetical authority, sought to give practical effect to this teaching (2 Ki. 18[4, 22] 21[3]). But he was unable to bring it really home to the nation's heart; and the heathen reaction under Manasseh ensued. Naturally, this result only impressed the prophetical party more strongly with the importance of the principle which Hezekiah had sought to enforce; and it is accordingly codified, and energetically inculcated, in Deuteronomy. Josiah (2 Ki. 22–23), acting under the influence of Dt., abolished the high places with a strong hand; but even he, as Jeremiah witnesses (*passim*), could not change radically the habits of the people; and the ends aimed at in Dt. were only finally secured after the nation's return from the Babylonian captivity.

It has been shown above that the legislation proper of Dt. is comprised in c. 5–26, to which 4[44-49] forms a superscription and c. 28 a conclusion. What relation, now, do the other parts of Dt., sometimes called its "margins," bear to this? By the majority of recent critics c. 1–4[40] is held—partly on account of

---

* With the last three paragraphs comp. Delitzsch, *Studien*, xi. *passim*. That the legislation of Dt. is based generally upon pre-existing sources is fully recognised by critics; see *e.g.* Graf, *Gesch. Bücher*, pp. 20, 22, 24; Reuss, *La Bible*, i. 159 f.; Dillmann in his commentary, *passim*, esp. p. 604 ff. On the relation of Dt. 17[14ff.] to 1 Sa. 8, 10[17-27a] 12, cf. Kön. p. 217, and the writer's *Deut.* p. 213 (the law may have been known to the *author* of the narrative, but it was clearly unknown to the *actors* in the incidents described).

slight disagreements in representation and expression with c. 5–26 which it exhibits, partly on account of the separate heading 4^{44-49}, which appears to be superfluous after $1^{1-2. 4-5}$—to be not part of the original Dt., but to have been added, as an introduction, by a somewhat later hand, for the purpose, partly of supplying the reader with an account of the antecedents of the Dt. legislation (c. 1–3), partly of inculcating fresh motives for its observance (4^{1-40}). It is doubtful if this view is correct. The inconsistencies,* though they no doubt exist, are scarcely sufficiently serious to outweigh the strong impression produced by the predominant linguistic character of c. $1-4^{40}$, that it is by the same hand as c. 5 ff. But the separate heading, especially if its circumstantiality be considered, can hardly be due to the same author who had already prefaced his work with $1^{1-2. 4-5}$. A heading, however, lends itself readily to expansion; and there is nothing unreasonable in the supposition that, as formulated by the original author, this title was considerably briefer than it now is, and not longer than sufficed to mark the commencement of the "exposition" of the law, after the introduction, 1^6-4^{40}.†

[88] C. 27. This chapter, which enjoins certain ceremonies to be performed after the Israelites have entered Canaan, interrupts the connexion between c. 26 and c. 28, and has probably been removed from the position which it originally occupied. $V.^{9-10}$ may have once formed the connecting link between c. 26 and c. 28. In the rest of the ch. four distinct ceremonies are enjoined—(1) the inscription of the Deuteronomic law on stones upon Mount Ebal $v.^{1-4. 8}$; (2) the erection of an altar and offering of sacrifices on the same spot $v.^{5-7}$; (3) the ratification of the new covenant by the people standing on *both* Ebal and Gerizim $v.^{11-13}$; (4) the twelve curses uttered by the Levites and responded to by the whole people $v.^{14-26}$. $V.^{1-8}$ appears to

---

* The most noticeable is that between 2^{14-16} and 5^{2-3} 11^{2-7}. The question whether c. $1-4^{40}$ is by the same hand as c. 5 ff. was made recently the subject of an interesting discussion between A. Van Hoonacker (affirming it), in *Le Muséon*, vii. (1888) p. 464 ff., viii. (1889) pp. 67 ff., 141 ff., and L. Horst (denying it), in the *Rev. de l'Hist. des Religions*, xxiii. (1891), p. 184 ff. See an outline of the arguments on both sides in the writer's *Deuteronomy*, pp. lxvii–lxxii.

† 4^{49} is based upon 3^{17}: so that, if it be true (cf. p. 72; and see Dillm., or the author's *Comm. ad loc.*) that 3^{14-17} is an insertion in c. 1–3, 4^{44-49} *must*, in its present form, be of later origin than c. 1–3.

be based upon an older narrative, which has been expanded and recast by the author of Dt. V.[11-13] is disconnected with [1-8], the situation and circumstances being both different; but it must be taken in connexion with 11[29f.], and understood to particularize the symbolical ceremony which is there contemplated. The connexion of v.[14-26] with v.[11-13] is very imperfect. V.[12f.] represents six of the tribes (including Levi, which is reckoned here as a lay-tribe, Ephraim and Manasseh being treated as *one*) on Gerizim and six on Ebal—in tolerable accordance with Josh. 8[33]; and we expect (cf. 11[29]) some invocation of blessings and curses on the two mountains respectively. V.[14ff.], on the contrary, describe only a series of *curses*, uttered by the *Levites*, to which *all* Israel respond. The two representations are evidently divergent, and give an inconsistent picture of the entire scene. Either something which made the transition clear has dropped out between v.[13] and v.[14], or v.[14ff.] have been incorporated from some independent source (see Dillmann, pp. 367–9): the imprecations, namely, do not present an epitome of the sins most earnestly warned against in Dt. (as might have been expected, were they drawn up by the same author), but correspond closely to some of the laws of H (see p. 74 f.).

29[2]–30[20]. Here the standpoint is not throughout the same as in Dt. generally; for whereas in c. 5–26, 28, the alternatives of national obedience and disobedience are balanced one against the other, and one is not represented as more likely to follow than the other, in 29[22ff.], and esp. in 30[1-10], the latter is assumed to have definitely taken place, and the writer even contemplates the conditions of Israel's restoration from exile: the connexion is also in parts imperfect (notice the transition from the individual in 29[19-21] to the nation in 29[22ff.]; and *for* in 30[11], introducing the reason for a *present* duty, whereas in 30[1-10] Israel is represented as being in exile); hence it is probable that 29[2]–30[20] is a supplement, embracing original Deuteronomic material (esp. 30[11-20]), but due, in its present form, to a later Deuteronomic hand.

31[1]–32[47], including the "Song of Moses" (32[1-43]).

Argument of the Song. After an exordium (v.[1-3]), the poet states his theme (v.[4a] *As for the Rock, His work is perfect*), the uprightness and faithfulness of Jehovah, as illustrated in His dealings with a corrupt and ungrateful nation (v.[4-6]). He dwells on the providential care with which the [89] people had been guided to the home reserved for them, how prosperity had there tempted it to be untrue to its ideal ("Jeshurun") character, until the punishment decreed for this had all but issued in national extinction, and the final step had only been arrested by Jehovah's "dread" of the foe's malicious triumph (v.$^{7-27}$). Now, therefore, in His people's extremity, Jehovah will interpose on their behalf; and when the gods whom they have chosen are powerless to aid them, will Himself take up and avenge His servants' cause (v.$^{28-43}$). Thus the main idea of the poem is the rescue of the people by an act of grace, at a moment when ruin seemed imminent. The poem begins reproachfully; but throughout tenderness prevails above severity, and at the end the strain becomes wholly one of consolation and hope.

The Song shows great originality in form, being a presentation of prophetical thoughts in a poetical dress, which is unique in the OT. Nothing in the poem points to Moses as the author. The period of the Exodus, and of the occupation of Canaan, lies in a distant past (v.$^{7-12}$); Israel is settled in Palestine, has lapsed into idolatry, and been brought in consequence to the verge of ruin (v.$^{13-30}$); all that is future is its deliverance (v.$^{34ff.}$). The thought, and the style of composition, exhibit also a maturity which points to a period considerably later than that of Moses. The style of treatment, as a historical retrospect, is in the manner of Hos. 2, Jer. 2, Ezek. 20, Ps. 106. The theme is developed with great literary and artistic skill; the images are varied and expressive; the parallelism is usually regular, and very forcible.

It would be going too far to affirm that the Song *cannot* be by the same hand as the body of Deut. At the same time, most of the characteristic expressions are different, and it presents many fresh thoughts; so that internal evidence, though it does not absolutely preclude its being by the same author, does not favour such a supposition, and the context hardly leaves it a possibility. For if 31$^{14ff.}$ be examined carefully, it will be seen that there are really *two* introductions to the Song, viz. v.$^{16-22}$ and v.$^{24-30}$. These are evidently by different hands; the first exhibiting several phrases not found elsewhere in Dt., the second being in the general style of the body of the book. By many critics it has been taken for granted that v.$^{16-22}$ (with the concluding notice 32^{44}) formed part of JE, the author of which, finding the Song attributed to Moses, incorporated it as such in his work, whence it was excerpted afterwards by the author (or redactor) of Dt., who, adding 31$^{24-30}$ and 32$^{45-47}$, gave it the place that it now holds. Upon this view, the date of the poem will be earlier than the compilation of JE ; and Israel's foe, the "not people" of v.[21], will have been either (Ew. Kamp.) the Assyrians, or (Schrader, Dillm., Oettli) the Syrians,—Dillm. referring the poem to the interval in the Syrian wars (c. 800 B.C.) between 2 Ki. 13[4, 7] and 13[23, 25] 14[25f.], when Israel under Jehoahaz was reduced to the utmost straits by the successes of Hazael. It has, however, been observed that in its theological standpoint— for instance, in the terms in which idolatry is reprobated, the contrasts drawn between Jehovah and other gods, the thought of Israel's lapse, punishment, and subsequent restoration—as well as in its literary characteristics, the Song presents far greater affinities with the prophets of the Chaldæan than with those of the Assyrian age ; and hence Kuenen (§ 13. 30) may be right in assigning it to the age of Jer. and Ezek., and treating it as a prophetic meditation on the lessons to be deduced from Israel's national history. As v.[16-22] (the introduction to the Song) separates awkwardly v.[14-15] from its sequel in v.[23], and displays also literary differences from the usual style of JE, the supposition is a reasonable one that the Song once formed part of a separate source (later than JE), whence (together with 31[16-22] and 32[44]) it was inserted in Dt. by a second Deuteronomic hand,—the same, no doubt, which (p. 72) supplemented the original Dt. by various other additions in c. 29–34.

[90] C. 32[48-52]. This short passage bears evident marks of P's style ; it is a slightly expanded duplicate of Nu. 27[12-14].

C. 33. *The Blessing of Moses.* This offers even fewer points of contact with the discourses of Dt. than the Song. It was probably handed down independently, and inserted here, when Dt. as a whole was incorporated in the Pent. It should be compared with the Blessing of Jacob in Gen. 49 ; for though (with the exception of the blessing on Joseph, which contains reminiscences from Gen. 49[25f.]) the thoughts here are original, there is a general similarity of character and structure between the two blessings. A difference in external form may be noted : each blessing here is introduced by the narrator separately, speaking in his own person. Compared, as a whole, with the Blessing of Jacob, it may be said to be pitched in a higher key : the tone is more buoyant ; while the former in the main has in view the *actual* characteristics of the different tribes, the Blessing of Moses contemplates them in their ideal glories, and views them both separately and collectively (v.[26-29]) as exercising theocratic functions and enjoying theocratic privileges. The most salient features are the (apparent) isolation and depression of Judah, the honour and respect with which Levi is viewed, the strength and splendour of the double tribe of Joseph, and the burst of grateful enthusiasm with which (v.[26-29]) the poet celebrates the fortune of his nation, settled and secure, with the aid of its God, in its fertile Palestinian home. There is also a special exordium (v.[2-5]), describing how Jehovah, coming *from* [not *to*] Sinai, gave His people a law through Moses, and held the tribes together under His sovereignty.

[91] V.[4], if not also v.[27b. 28] (*drave out, said, dwelt*), implies a date later than Moses ; as regards the rest of the Blessing, opinions differ, and, in fact, conclusive criteria fail us. The external evidence afforded by the title (v.[1]) is slight. Internal evidence, from the obscure nature of some of the allusions, is indecisive, and offers scope for diverging conclusions. Kleinert (pp. 169–175), urging v.[7] (Judah's isolation, in agreement with its non-mention in Deborah's song), assigns it to the period of the Judges. Graf, understanding v.[7] differently, and remarking the allusion to the Temple in v.[12], and the terms in which the power of Joseph is described in v.[17], thinks of the prosperous age of Jeroboam II. (2 Ki. 14[25]), which is accepted by Kuenen, Reuss, Stade (*Gesch.* i. 150, 152), Cornill (§ 13. 6), and others. Dillmann (p. 415 f.), interpreting v.[7. 12] similarly, considers that the terms in which Levi and Judah are spoken of are better satisfied by a date very shortly after the division of the kingdom, in the reign of Jeroboam I., and remarks that the sympathy shown in it for the northern tribes may be taken as an indication that the author was a poet of the northern kingdom (so also Westphal, ii. 50 : cf. the writer's *Deut.* p. 388). V.[7] "And bring him—not, unto his *land*, but—unto his *people*" is very difficult. Perhaps the allusion is to some circumstance on which the historical books are silent : in default of a better explanation, it is interpreted by many as a prayer, uttered from the point of view of an Ephraimite, for the reunion of Judah and Israel, either, viz. after the rupture of the kingdom under Jeroboam I. (Dillm. &c.), or (Riehm, *Einl.* p. 313) during the rivalry between the two kingdoms of David and Ishbosheth (2 Sa. 2-4), or (Graf, &c.) under Jeroboam II. The style of c. 33 suggests a higher antiquity than c. 32. The Blessing is best regarded — like the poems attributed to Balaam in Nu. 22-24 — as the poetical development of an ancient popular tradition ; and as having been (Dillm.) "written from the first under Moses' name, in order to rally the nation anew under the banner of the Mosaic institutions, and to awaken in it a fresh and vivid consciousness of the privileges enjoyed by it as Jehovah's people."

Style of Deuteronomy. The literary style of Dt. is very marked and individual. In vocabulary, indeed, it presents comparatively few exceptional words; but particular words and phrases, consisting sometimes of entire clauses, recur with extraordinary frequency, giving a *distinctive colouring* to every part of the work. In its predominant features the phraseology is strongly original, but in certain particulars it is based upon that of the parenetic sections of JE in the Book of Exodus (esp. 13[3-16] 15[26] 19[3-8], parts of 20[2-17] 23[20ff.] 34[10-26]). The possibility must, however, be admitted (cf. p. 35) that some of these passages owe in reality their present form to Deuteronomic influence.

In the following select list of phrases characteristic of Dt., the first 10 appear to have been adopted by the author from these sections of JE; those which follow are original, or occur so rarely in JE, that there is no ground to suppose them to have been borrowed thence. For the convenience of the synopsis, the occurrences in the Deuteronomic sections of *Joshua* are annexed in brackets.

1. אהב *to love*, with God as object: 6[5] 7[9] 10[12] 11[1. 13. 22] 13[3] [Heb. 4]. 19[9] 30[6. 16. 20]. [Josh. 22[5] 23[11].] So Ex. 20[6] (=Dt. 5[10]). A characteristic principle of Dt. Of God's love to [92] His people: 4[37] 7[8. 13] 10[15] 23[5] [Heb. 6]. Not so before. Otherwise first in Hos. 3[1] 9[15] 11[1], cf. v.[4] 14[4] [Heb. 5].

2. אלהים אחרים *other gods*: 6[14] 7[4] 8[19] 11[16. 28] 13[2. 6. 13] [Heb. 3. 7. 14] 17[3] 18[20] 28[14. 36. 64] 29[26] [Heb. 25] 30[17] 31[18. 20]. [Josh. 23[16] 24[2. 16].] So Ex. 20[3] (=Dt. 5[7]) 23[13]; cf. 34[14] (אל אחר). Always in Dt. (except 5[7] 18[20] 31[18. 20]) with *to serve* or *go after*. Often in Kings and Jeremiah, but (as Kleinert remarks) usually with other verbs.

3. *That your (thy) days may be long* [or *to prolong days*]: 4[26. 40] 5[33] [Heb. 30] 6[2b] 11[9] 17[20] 22[7] 25[15] 30[18] 32[47]. So Ex. 20[12] (=Dt. 5[16]). Elsewhere, only Is. 53[10], Prov. 28[16], Eccl. 8[13]; and, rather differently, Josh. 24[31]=Jud. 2[7].†

4. *The land* (הארץ: less frequently *the ground*, האדמה) *which Jehovah thy God is giving thee* (also *us, you, them*, 1[20] &c.): 4[40] 15[7], and constantly. So Ex. 20[12] (=Dt. 5[16]) האדמה.

5. בית עבדים *house of bondage* (lit. *of slaves*): 6[12] 7[8] 8[14] 13[5. 10] [Heb. 6. 11]. [Josh. 24[17].] So Jud. 6[8], Mic. 6[4], Jer. 34[13]. From Ex. 13[3. 14] 20[2] (=Dt. 5[6]).†

6. *In thy gates* (of the cities of Israel): 12[12. 15. 17. 18. 21] 14[21. 27-29] 15[7. 22] 16[5. 11. 14. 18] 17[2. 8] 18[6] 23[16] [Heb. 17] 24[14] 26[12] 28[52. 55. 57] 31[12]. So Ex. 20[10] (=Dt. 5[14]). Hence 1 Ki. 8[37]=2 Ch. 6[28].† Cf. (perhaps) Jer. 14[2].

7a. עם סגלה *a people of special possession*: 7[6] 14[2] 26[18].† Cf. Ex. 19[5] והייתם לי סגלה.

7b. עם קדוש *a holy people*: 7[6] 14[2. 21] 26[19] 28[9].† Varied from Ex. 19[6] גוי קדוש *a holy nation*: cf. 22[30] and *holy men* shall ye be unto me.

8. *Which I am commanding thee this day* : 4^{40} 6^6 7^{11}, and repeatedly. So Ex. 34^{11}.

9. *Take heed to thyself* (*yourselves*) *lest*, &c. : $4^{9.\ 23}$ 6^{12} 8^{11} 11^{16} $12^{13.\ 19.\ 30}$ 15^9 (cf. 24^8) ; comp. 2^4 4^{15}. [Josh. 23^{11}.] So Ex. 34^{12} ; cf. 19^{12}. (Also Ex. 10^{28}, Gen. 24^6 31^{24}, cf. v.^{29} ; but with no special force.)

10. *A mighty hand and a stretched out arm* : 4^{34} 5^{15} 7^{19} 11^2 26^8. The *combination* occurs first in Dt. *Mighty hand* alone : Dt. 3^{24} 6^{21} 7^8 9^{26} 34^{12} [cf. Josh. 4^{24}]. So in JE Ex. 3^{19} 6^1 13^9 32^{11}. (Nu. 20^{20} differently.) *Stretched out arm* alone : Dt. 9^{29} (varied from Ex. 32^{11}. So Ex. 6^6 P.

11. בחר *to choose* : of Israel 4^{37} $7^{6.\ 7}$ 10^{15} 14^2,—the priests 18^5 21^5,—of the future king 17^{15},—and especially in the phrase " the place which Jehovah shall choose to place (*or* set) His name there," $12^{5.\ 11.\ 21}$ $14^{23.\ 24}$ 15^{20} $16^{2.\ 6.\ 11}$ 26^2, or "the place which Jehovah shall choose," $12^{14.\ 18.\ 26}$ 14^{25} $16^{7.\ 15.\ 16}$ $17^{8.\ 10}$ 18^6 31^{11}. [Josh. 9^{27}.] Very characteristic of Dt. : not applied before to God's choice of Israel ; often in Kings of Jerusalem (1 Ki. 8^{44} 11^{32} &c.) ; in Jeremiah once, 33^{24}, of Israel. Also charact. of II Isaiah ($41^{8.\ 9}$ 43^{10} $44^{1.\ 2}$: cf. *chosen* [93] 43^{20} 45^4. Of the *future*, 14^1 $65^{9.\ 15.\ 22}$: and applied to Jehovah's ideal Servant, 42^1 49^7).

12. ובערת הרע מקרבך (מישראל) *and thou shalt extirpate the evil from thy midst* (or *from Israel*) : 13^5 [Heb. ^{6}] $17^{7.\ 12}$ 19^{19} 21^{21} $22^{21.\ 22.\ 24}$ 24^7.↑ This phrase is peculiar to Dt.; but Jud. 20^{13} is similar.

13. *That the Lord thy God may* (or *Because He will*) *bless thee* : $14^{24.\ 29}$ $15^{4.\ 10}$ $16^{10.\ 15}$ 23^{20} [Heb. ^{21}] 24^{19} : cf. 12^7 $15^{6.\ 14}$.

14. *The stranger, the fatherless, and the widow* : 10^{18} $24^{17.\ 19.\ 20.\ 21}$ 27^{19}. Cf. Ex. $22^{21f.}$. Hence Jer. 7^6 22^3, Ezek. 22^7. Together with *the Levite* : 14^{29} $16^{11.\ 14}$ $26^{12.\ 13}$.

15. דבק *to cleave,* of devotion to God : 10^{20} 11^{22} 13^4 [Heb. ^{5}] 30^{20} : the corresponding adjective, 4^4. [Josh. 22^5 23^8.] So 2 Ki. 18^6 : cf. 3^3 (of devotion to sin), 1 Ki. 11^2 (to false gods).↑

16. *And remember that thou wast a bondman in the land of Egypt* : 5^{15} 15^{15} 16^{12} $24^{18.\ 22}$.↑

17. לא תחוס עינך (עליו) *thine eye shall not spare* (*him*) : 7^{16} 13^8 [Heb. ^{9}] $19^{13.\ 21}$ 25^{12}. Also Gen. 45^{20}, Is. 13^{18}, and frequently in Ezek.

18. והיה בך חטא *and it be sin in thee* : 15^{19} 23^{21} [Heb. ^{22}] 24^{15} : cf. 21^{22} : with *not*, 23^{22} [Heb. ^{23}].

19, הארץ הטובה *the good land* (of Canaan) : 1^{35} 3^{25} $4^{21.\ 22}$ 6^{18} 8^{10} (cf. v.^{7}) 9^6 11^{17}. [Josh. 23^{16}.] So 1 Ch. 28^8.↑ Dt. 1^{25} (Nu. 14^7) and Ex. 3^8 are rather different.

20. *Which thou* (*ye*) *knowest* (or *knewest*) *not* : $8^{3.\ 16}$ 11^{28} $13^{2.\ 6.\ 13}$ [Heb. $^{3.\ 7.\ 14}$] $28^{33.\ 36.\ 64}$ 29^{26} [Heb. ^{25}]. Chiefly with reference to strange gods, or a foreign people. Cf. 32^{17}.

21. *That it may be well with thee* : (אשר ייטב לך or למען or : 4^{40} $5^{16.\ 29}$ [Heb. ^{26}] $6^{3.\ 18}$ $12^{25.\ 28}$ 22^7. Similarly (וטוב לך (לכם) : 5^{33} [Heb. ^{30}] 19^{13} and למוב 6^{24} 10^{13}.

22. היטיב, *inf. abs.*, used adverbially=*thoroughly* : 9^{21} 13^{14} [Heb. ^{15}] 17^4 19^{18} 27^8. Elsewhere, as thus applied, only 2 Ki. 11^{18}.↑

23. *To fear God* (ליראה) : often with *that they may learn* prefixed): 4^{10} 5^{29}
   [Heb. ^{26}] 6^{24} 8^6 10^{12} 14^{23} 17^{19} 28^{58} 31^{13}, cf. v.^{12}.

24. (יוכל) לא תוכל, in the sense of *not to be allowed* : 7^{22} 12^{17} 16^5 17^{15} 21^{16}
   $22^{8.\ 19.\ 29}$ 24^4.   A very uncommon use ; cf. Gen. 43^{32}.

25. *To do that which is right* (הישר) *in the eyes of Jehovah* : 12^{25} 13^{18}
   [Heb. ^{19}] 21^9 : with הטוב *that which is good* added, 6^{18} 12^{28}.   So
   Ex. 15^{26}, then Jer. 34^{15}, and several times in the Deuteronomic
   framework of Kings and in the parallel passages of Chronicles.

26. *To do that which is evil* (הרע) *in the eyes of Jehovah* : 4^{25} 9^{18} 17^2 31^{29}.
   So Nu. 32^{13} ; often in the framework of Judges and Kings,
   Jeremiah, and occasionally elsewhere.   Both 25 and 26 gained
   currency through Dt., and are rare except in passages written
   under its influence.

[94] 27. *The priests the Levites* (=the Levitical priests) : 17^9 18^1 24^8 27^9 :
   the priests the sons of Levi, 21^5 31^9. [Josh. 3^3 8^{33}.] So Jer. 33^{18},
   Ezek. 43^{19} 44^{15}, 2 Ch. 5^5 23^{18} 30^{27}. P's expression " sons of Aaron "
   is never used in Dt.

28. *With all thy* (*your*) *heart and with all thy* (*your*) *soul* : 4^{29} 6^5 10^{12}
   11^{13} 13^3 [Heb. ^{4}] 26^{16} $30^{2.\ 6.\ 10}$. [Josh. 22^5 23^{14}.] A genuine
   expression of the spirit of the book (p. 78).   Only besides (in the
   third person) 1 Ki. 2^4 8^{48} (=2 Ch. 6^{38}), 2 Ki. 23^3 (=2 Ch. 34^{31}) ^{25},
   2 Ch. 15^{12} ; and (in the first person, of God) Jer. 32^{41}.

29. נתן לפני, in the sense of *delivering up* to : $1^{8.\ 21}$ $2^{31.\ 33.\ 36}$ $7^{2.\ 23}$ 23^{14}
   [Heb. ^{15}] 28^7 and ^{25} (with נִתֵּן) 31^5. [Josh. 10^{12} 11^6.] Also Jud.
   11^9 1 Ki. 8^{46}, Is. 41^2.↑ The usual phrase in this sense is נתן ביד.

30. *To turn* (סר) *neither to the right hand nor to the left* : 2^{27} *lit.* (Nu. 20^{17}
   has (נטה : so 1 Sa. 6^{12}. *Metaph.* 5^{32} [Heb. ^{29}] $17^{11.\ 20}$ 28^{14}. [Josh.
   1^7 23^6.] So 2 Ki. 22^2 (=2 Ch. 34^2).↑

31. מעשה ידים *the work of the hands* (=enterprise) : 2^7 14^{29} 16^{15} 24^{19} 28^{12}
   30^9 : in a bad sense, 31^{29}.

32. פדה, of the *redemption* from Egypt : 7^8 (Mic. 6^4) 9^{26} 13^5 [Heb. ^{6}] 15^{15}
   21^8 24^{18}.   Not so before : Ex. 15^{13} (the Song of Moses) uses גאל
   (to *reclaim*).

33. קרב *midst*, in different connexions, especially בקרבך, מקרבך. A favourite
   word in Dt., though naturally occurring in JE, as also elsewhere.
   In P תוך is preferred.

34. *To rejoice before Jehovah* : $12^{7.\ 12.\ 18}$ 14^{26} $16^{11.\ 14}$ (cf. Lev. 23^{40}) 26^{11} 27^7.

35. *To make His name dwell there* (שֵׁם, לְשַׁכֵּן) : 12^{11} 14^{23} $16^{2.\ 6.\ 11}$ 26^2.   Only
   besides Jer. 7^{12}, Ezr. 6^{12}, Neh. 1^9.↑ With לָשׂוּם (to *set*) : $12^{5.\ 21}$
   14^{24}.   This occurs also in Kings : see below, at the end of Kings,
   in the list of phrases, No. 14.

36. (ידכם, ידך) *that to which thy* (*your*) *hand is put* : $12^{7.\ 18}$ 15^{10}
   23^{20} [Heb. ^{21}] $28^{8.\ 20}$.↑

37. *And . . . shall hear and fear* (of the deterrent effect of punishment) :
   13^{11} [Heb. ^{12}] 17^{13} 19^{20} 21^{21}.↑

38. *To observe to do* (שמר לעשות) : $5^{1.\ 32}$ [Heb. ^{29}] $6^{3.\ 25}$ 7^{11} 8^1 &c. (seventeen
   times : also three times with an object intervening). [Josh. $1^{7.\ 8}$
   22^5.] Also 2 Ki. 17^{37} 21^8 (=2 Ch. 33^8 : hence also 1 Ch. 22^{13}).

39. *To observe and do*: 4^6 7^{12} 16^{12} 23^{23} [Heb. ^{24}] 24^8 26^{16} 28^{13} ; cf. 29^9 [Heb. ^{8}]. [Josh. 23^6.]

40. *The land whither ye are going over* (or *entering in*) *to possess it* : $4^{5.\ 14}$ and repeatedly. Hence Ezr. 9^{11}. לרשתה *to possess it* follows also *which Jehovah is giving thee* (No. 4) : 12^1 $19^{2.\ 14}$ 21^1. [Josh. 1^{11b}.] Cf. Gen. 15^7. In P, with similar clauses, לאחוז is used : Lev. 14^{34} 25^{45}, Nu. 32^{29}, Dt. 32^{49}.

41. *a.* תועבת יהוה *Jehovah's abomination*, esp. as the final ground of a
[95] prohibition : 7^{25} (cf. ^{26}) 12^{31} 17^1 18^{12a} 22^5 23^{18} [Heb. ^{19}] 24^4 25^{16} 27^{15} : *b.* תועבה alone, chiefly of heathen or idolatrous customs, 13^{14} [Heb. ^{15}] 14^3 17^4 $18^{9.\ 12b}$ 20^{18} 32^{16}. *a.* So often in Prov. ; comp. in H, Lev. $18^{22.\ 26f.\ 29f.}$ 20^{13} (but *only* of sins of unchastity). *

There are one or two points of contact between Dt. and H (*e.g.* in the use of the term *thy brother*, $15^{3.\ 7.\ 9.\ 11.\ 12}$ 17^{15} 22^{1-4} $23^{19f.}$ 25^3 (cf. *his brother*, $19^{18.\ 19}$), as Lev. 19^{17} $25^{25.\ 35.\ 36.\ 39.\ 47}$) ; but with P generally it shows no phraseological connexion whatever. In the few laws covering common ground, identical expressions occur (as c. 14 מין, 24^8 נגע הצרעת) ; but these are either quotations or technical expressions, and do not constitute any real phraseological similarity between the two writings ; they are not *recurrent* in Dt.

Most of the expressions noted above occur seldom or never besides, or only in passages modelled upon the style of Dt. In addition, other recurring features will be noticed by the attentive reader, which combine with those that have been cited to give a unity of style to the whole work. The original features preponderate decidedly above those that are derived. The strong and impressive individuality of the writer colours whatever he writes ; and even a sentence, borrowed from elsewhere, assumes, by the setting in which it is placed, a new character, and impresses the reader differently (so especially in the retrospects, c. 1–3. 9–10). His power as an orator is shown in the long and stately periods with which his work abounds : at the same time the parenetic treatment, which his subject often demands, always maintains its freshness, and is never monotonous or prolix. In his command of a chaste, yet warm and persuasive eloquence, he stands unique among the writers of the Old Testament.

The influence of Dt. upon subsequent books of the OT. is very great. As it fixed for long the standard by which men and actions were to be judged, so it provided the formulæ in

* See further Holzinger, *Einl.* p. 283 ff.

which these judgments were expressed; in other words, it provided a religious terminology which readily lent itself to adoption by subsequent writers. Its influence upon parts of Joshua, Judges, Kings will be apparent when the structure of those books comes to be examined: in a later age it shows itself in such passages as Neh. 1⁵ff. 9⁶ff.; Dan. 9. Among the prophets, Jeremiah's phraseology is modelled most evidently [96] upon that of Dt.; and reminiscences may frequently be traced in Ezekiel and Deutero-Isaiah.

Differences should, however, be noted, as well as resemblances; for instance, the Deuteronomic passages in the historical books contain *new* expressions not found in Dt. (*e.g.* Josh. 24²³ *to incline the heart*; 1 Ki. 2⁴ *to observe their way*; 8⁶¹ *a perfect heart*, &c.): on Jeremiah, comp. p. 87, *note*.

§ 6. JOSHUA.

LITERATURE.—See p. 1 f.; and add: Hollenberg in the *Studien und Kritiken*, 1874, pp. 462–506; and *Der Charakter der Alexandrinischen Uebersetzung des Buches Josua*, Moers, 1876; Budde, *Richter und Samuel*, 1890, pp. 1–89; Albers, *Die Quellenberichte in Josua* i-xii, 1891; W. H. Bennett in Haupt's *SBOT.* Comp. Delitzsch, *Genesis* (1887), pp. 30–33.

The Book of Joshua is separated by the Jews from the Pentateuch (the *Tōrāh* or Law), and forms with them the first of the group of writings called the "Former Prophets" (*i.e.* Joshua, Judges, Samuel, and Kings). This distinction is, however, an artificial one, depending on the fact that the book could not be regarded, like the Pentateuch, as containing an authoritative rule of life; its contents, and, still more, its literary structure, show that it is intimately connected with the Pentateuch, and describes the final stage in the history of the *Origines* of the Hebrew nation.

The book divides itself naturally into two parts, the first (c. 1–12) narrating the passage of Jordan by the Israelites, and the subsequent series of successes by which they won their way into Canaan; the second (c. 13–24) describing the allotment of the country among the tribes, and ending with an account of the closing events in Joshua's life. Chronological notes in the book are rare (4¹⁹ 5¹⁰; and incidentally 14¹⁰). The period of time covered by the book can be determined only approximately; for though Joshua is stated to have died at the age of 110 years,

there is no distinct note of his age on any previous occasion.*
From a comparison of 14^{10} with Dt. 2^{14} it would seem that in
the view of the writer of the section 14^{6-15} the war of conquest
occupied about 7 years.

The Book of Joshua consists, at least in large measure, of a
continuation of the documents used in the formation of the Pentateuch. In c. 1–12 the main narrative consists of a work, itself
[97] also in parts composite, which appears to be the continuation of JE, though whether its component parts are definitely
J and E, or whether it is rather the work of the writer who
combined J and E into a whole, and in this book, perhaps, permitted himself the use of other independent sources, may be an
open question. The use of P in these chapters is rare. In
c. 13–24, on the contrary, especially in the topographical descriptions, the work of P predominates, and the passages derived
from JE are decidedly less numerous than in the first part of
the book. There is, however, another element in the Book of
Joshua besides JE and P. In this book, JE, before it was
combined with P, passed through the hands of a writer who
expanded it in different ways, and who, being strongly imbued
with the spirit of Deuteronomy, may be termed the Deuteronomic
editor, and denoted by the abbreviation D^2.† The parts added
by this writer are in most cases readily recognised by their
characteristic style. The chief aim of these Deuteronomic
additions to JE is to illustrate and emphasize the zeal shown by
Joshua in fulfilling Mosaic ordinances, especially the command
to extirpate the native population of Canaan, and the success
which in consequence crowned his efforts.‡ In point of fact, as
other passages show (p. 115), the conquest was by no means
effected with the rapidity and completeness which some of the
passages quoted imply; but the writer, as it seems, generalizes
with some freedom. Another characteristic of the same additions is the frequent reference to the occupation of the
trans-Jordanic territory by Reuben, Gad, and the half-tribe of
Manasseh, not merely in $1^{12ff.}$ and 22^{1-6}, but also 2^{10} 9^{10} 12^{2-6}
13^{8-12} 18^{7b}.

---

* He is called a "young man," Ex. 33^{11}, in the first year of the exodus.

† No account is here taken of the distinction drawn by Kittel, p. 60.

‡ See 1^{1-9} $3^{7.\ 10}$ 4^{14} 5^1 6^2 $8^{1.\ 29}$ (Dt. 21^{23}) $^{30-35}$ 10^{40-42} $11^{14f.\ 16-23}$ 21^{43-45} $23^{3.\ 9.}$
^{14b} 24^{11} *middle*. 13.

I. 1–12. *The Conquest of Palestine.*

C. 1–2. Preparations for the passage of the Jordan and conquest of Canaan. Joshua is encouraged by God for the task imposed upon him, and receives (according to the stipulation, Nu. 32$^{20-27}$) the promise of assistance from the 2½ tribes whose territory had already been allotted to them on the E. of Jordan (c. 1). The mission of the spies to Jericho and the compact with Rahab (c. 2).

[98] {JE   2$^{1-9}$ 12-24
     {D^2 c. 1   2$^{10-11}$

C. 1 is based probably upon an earlier and shorter narrative, from which, for instance, the substance of v.$^{1. 2. 10. 11}$ may be derived, but in its present form it is the composition of D^2. It is constructed almost entirely of phrases borrowed from Dt.: comp. v.$^{3-5a}$ and Dt. 11$^{24. 25a}$; v.$^{5b-6}$ Dt. 31$^{23 end. 6. 7b. 8}$ (also 1^{38} 3^{28}); v.^{7} Dt. 5^{32} (Heb. ^{29}) 29^9 (Heb. ^{8}); v.^{9} Dt. 31^6, also *ib.* 1^{29} 7^{21} 20^3 (the uncommon יַעֲרֹץ); v.^{11b} Dt. 11^{31}; v.$^{13b-15}$ Dt. 3$^{18-20}$; v.^{17b} as v.^{5}; v.^{18b} as v.^{6a}. Even where the phrases do not actually occur in Dt., the tone and style are those of Dt.

The greater part of c. 2 shows no traces of the Deut. style; it is, however, very evident in the two verses v.$^{10-11}$; see Dt. 31^4 1^{28}, and esp. 4^{39} (the phrase *He is God in heaven above,* &c. occurring nowhere else in the OT.); comp. also Josh. 4^{23} 5^1 (both D^2). V.^{9} contains reminiscences from the Song in Ex. 15 (v.$^{16. 15}$).

C. 3–4. The passage of the Jordan, and the erection of two monuments in commemoration of the event, consisting of two cairns of stones, one set up in the bed of the river itself, the other at the first camping-place on the West side, Gilgal, which henceforth becomes the headquarters of the Israelites till the conquest is complete.

P								4^{13}		19	
JE {a	3^1	5	10-11	13-17	4$^{1-3}$	8					20
{b				12			4-7	9-11a		15-18	
D^2	3$^{2-4}$	6-9						11b-12	14		21-24

The composite structure of c. 3–4 is apparent from the following considerations. (1) After it has been stated, 3^{17}, in express terms, that the passage of the Jordan was completed, the language of 4$^{4. 5. 10b}$ implies, not less distinctly, that the people have not yet crossed; in fact, at 4^{11} the narrative is at precisely the same point which was reached at 3^{17}. (2) 4^8 and 4^9 speak of two *different* ceremonies—the location of stones, taken from

Jordan, at *Gilgal,* and the erection of stones *in the bed of the river itself*: v.[8], now, is plainly the sequel of v.[3], while v.[9] coheres with v.[4-7], which, on the other hand, interrupts the connexion of v.[3] with v.[8].   (3) 3[12] is superfluous, if it and 4[2] belong to the same narrative; it is, however, required [99] for 4[4].   The verses assigned to *a* form a consecutive narrative, relating to the stones deposited at Gilgal.   The narrative *b* is not complete, part having been omitted when the two accounts were combined together. In the parts which remain, 4[4] is the sequel to 3[12]; the twelve men pass over before the ark into Jordan 4[4-7]; the stones are erected *in* the river v.[9]; after this, the people "hasten and pass over" (v.[10b]): in the other narrative the people have "clean passed over" before the ceremony is even enjoined.   The combined narrative *a b* has been slightly amplified by D[2] in the verses assigned to him in the analysis—in 3[2-4. 6-9], probably, upon the basis of notices belonging to JE.   It is not, however, clear that the two main narratives are J and E respectively; and hence the letters *a* and *b* have been used to designate them. With 4[21] (אשר) comp. Dt. 11[27] 18[22]; with v.[23b], c. 2[10] 5[1]; with v.[24], Dt. 28[10] 4[10b]; and above, p. 100, No. 10.

C. 5–8. Joshua circumcises the people at Gilgal; and the Passover is kept there (5[1-12]).   He receives instructions respecting the conquest of Jericho: the city is taken and "devoted" (Dt. 7[2. 25f.]), Rahab and her household being spared according to the compact of c. 2.   After this Joshua advances against Ai, in the heart of the land, near Bethel; he is at first repulsed in consequence of Achan's offence in having appropriated a portion of the spoil, which had been "devoted" at Jericho.   Achan having been punished, the Israelites succeed in obtaining possession of the city by a stratagem (7[1]–8[29]).   Joshua erects an altar on Ebal, the mountain on the north of Shechem, and fulfils the injunctions Dt. 27[2-8].

$$\begin{cases} \text{P} & 5^{10\text{-}12} & 7^1 \\ \begin{cases} \text{JE} & \text{2-3} & \text{8-9} & 5^{13}\text{-}6^{27} & 7^{2\text{-}26}\ 8^{1\text{-}29} \\ \text{D}^2\ 5^1 & \text{4-7} & & 8^{30\text{-}35} \end{cases} \end{cases}$$

6[2. 27] shows signs of the hand of D[2]: with v.[2a] comp. 8[1] Dt. 2[24]; with v.[2b], c. 1[14] 8[3] 10[7]; v.[27] recalls 1[5. 9. 17] 9[9b].   On the question (which cannot here be properly considered) whether the rest of c. 6 exhibits marks of composition, reference must be made to Wellh. (*Comp.* pp. 121–124) and the Commentary of Dillm.

In 8[1-29] short additions or expansions due to D[2] are v.[1] ("Fear not, neither be thou dismayed " : cf. Dt. 1^{21} 31^8, c. 10^{25}) $2^{b.\ 27}$ (cf. Dt. 2^{35}), and probably a few phrases besides, both here and in c. 7. (Comp. the additions often made by the *Chronicler* in his excerpts from Sam. and Kings, [**100**] *e.g.* 1 Ch. 21^{11b} [2 Sa. 24^{13}], 2 Ch. $7^{12b-16a}$ 8^{11b} 18^{31b} [1 Ki. $9^{3.\ 24}$ 22^{32}].) On the rest of 8^{1-29}, see Wellh. *Comp.* 125 f., and Dillm. p. 472 ff.

With regard to 8^{30-35} a difficulty arises from the position which it occupies in the book. Ebal lies considerably to the *north* of Ai, and until the intervening territory was conquered (respecting which, however, the narrative is silent) it is difficult to understand how Joshua could have advanced thither. Either the narrative is misplaced, and (as has been suggested) should follow 11^{23}; or (Dillm.) JE has been curtailed by the compiler of the book, and the details which, no doubt, it once contained respecting the conquest of Central Palestine—similar to those respecting that of the South (c. 10) and of the North (c. 11)— have been omitted.

8^{30-32} agrees with Dt. 27^{1-8}; v.^{33} also agrees tolerably with Dt. 11^{29} 27^{11-13}, but not completely, there being no mention of the *curse*. The *reading* of the law v.$^{34f.}$ is not enjoined in Dt. In v.^{34} the words "the blessing and the curse" (which, though they *seem* to be epexegetical of "*all* the words of the law," cannot be so in reality) may be a late insertion, designed to rectify the apparent omission in v.^{33}. With the expressions in v.^{35} cf. 11^{15}, Dt. 31^{30} 29^{10}: notice also in v.^{33} the Deut. phrase, "the priests the Levites" (p. 101, No. 27).

C. 9. The Gibeonites, by a stratagem which disarms the suspicions of the Israelites, secure immunity for their lives, and are permitted to retain a position within the community as slaves, performing menial offices for the sanctuary (ἱερόδουλοι).

			15b	17-21		
P						
JE	3-9a	11-15a	16	22-23	26-27a (to *day*)	
D² 9^{1-2}	9b-10				24-25	27b

V.$^{22.\ 23.\ 26f.}$ form evidently part of a narrative *parallel* to that of v.$^{17-21}$, and not the sequel of it; and the style of the latter shows that it belongs to P (notice especially "the congregation," and "the princes" [p. 133 f.], who here take the lead rather than Joshua). In v.^{27} "for the congregation, and," and perhaps in v.$^{23.\ 27}$ "(both) hewers of wood and drawers of water," will likewise be elements derived from P.

C. 10. The conquest of *Southern* Canaan : Joshua first defeats at Beth-horon the five kings of Jerusalem, Hebron, Jarmuth, Lachish, Eglon, and afterwards gains possession of Makkedah, Libnah, Lachish, Gezer, Eglon, Hebron, Debir : further particulars are not given, but Joshua's successes in this direction are generalized, v.[40-43].

[101] { JE 10[1-7]   9-11   12b-14a   15-24   26-27
       { D²   8   12a   14b   25   28-43

10[1-14] forms a whole from JE, with additions (to which the middle clause of v.[1] may be added) revealing the hand of D², and similar in style to those made by him in c. 6 and c. 8. V.[12b-13a] (to *enemies*) is an extract from an ancient collection of national songs, called the *Book of Jashar* or *of the Upright* (see also 2 Sa. 1[18]): v.[13b-14a] is the comment of the narrator (here, perhaps, E) upon it. In v.[12a] and v.[14b] notice the phraseology: *delivered up* (lit. *gave before*) as 11[6] and frequently in Dt. (p. 101); לעיני ישראל as Dt. 31[7]; *fought for Israel* as v.[42] 23[3], Dt. 1[30] 3[22] 20[4]. As regards the account in v.[28-43] of the manner in which Joshua pursued his victory, it is to be observed that in Jud. 1[1-20] the conquest of the South of Palestine is attributed to *Judah*; and Hebron and Debir are represented in Josh. 15[14-19] (= Jud. 1[10-15]) as having been taken under circumstances very different from those here presupposed. It seems that these verses are a generalization by D², in the style of some of the latter parts of the book, attached to the victory at Gibeon, and ascribing to Joshua more than was actually accomplished by him in person. With v.[40] comp. 11[11, 14], Dt. 20[16].

C. 11. The conquest of *Northern* Canaan; Joshua defeats Jabin, king of Hazor, with his allies, at the waters of Merom, and captures the towns belonging to him (v.[1-15]). The ch. closes (v.[16-23]) with a view of the entire series of Joshua's successes, in the South as well as in the North of Canaan. V.[1-9] is from JE, amplified by D² in parts of v.[2, 3, 6, 7, 8b]: v.[10-23] belongs to D².

In v.[10-15] the consequences of the victory by the waters of Merom are generalized by D² in the same manner as those of the victory at Beth-horon in 10[28-39]. The survey in v.[16-23] is also in the style of D². In v.[21f.] " what in other accounts (14[12] 15[15-19], Jud. 1[10-15]) is referred to Caleb and Judah is generalized and attributed to Joshua " (Dillmann).

C. 12. A supplementary list of the kings smitten by the Israelites—Sihon and Og (with a notice of the territory belonging to them) on the East of Jordan, and 31 kings slain under Joshua, on the West of Jordan.

Another generalizing review by D². The retrospective notice of Sihon and Og is in the manner of this writer (p. 104). Of the 31 (or, if v.[18] be [102] corrected after the LXX, 30) kings named, 16 (15) are not mentioned elsewhere, at least explicitly, among those conquered under Joshua, viz. the kings of Geder, Adullam, Bethel, Tappuah, Hepher, Aphek of the Sharon (LXX), Taanach, Megiddo, Kedesh, Jokneam, Dor, the nations of Galilee (LXX), Tirzah (on Hormah and Arad, comp. Jud. 1[17], Nu. 21[1-3]); hence, probably, either omissions have been made in the narrative of JE (comp. what was said above on 8[30-35]) in the process of incorporation by the compiler, or this list is derived from an independent source.

II. C. 13–24. *The Distribution of the Territory.*

C. 13. (1) V.[1-14]. Joshua receives instructions to proceed with the allotment of the conquered territory, v.[1. 7]. V.[2-6] contains a parenthetic notice of the districts, chiefly in the South-West and in Lebanon, not yet conquered. V.[8-12] describes the limits of the territory assigned by Moses to the 2½ trans-Jordanic tribes ; v.[13] is a notice of tribes on the East of Jordan not dispossessed by the Israelites. (2) V.[15-33] the borders and cities of the trans-Jordanic tribes, Reuben, Gad, and the half-tribe of Manasseh. V.[15-32] belongs to P (except, probably, parts of v.[29-31]), v.[13] to JE, v.[1-12. 14. 33] to D².

V.[1. 7] may also be derived from JE. For a difficult question arising out of v.[7] in connexion with v.[2-6], it must suffice to refer to Wellh. p. 130 f., or Kuen. *Hex.* § 7. 27. At the beginning of v.[8] the text (which yields an incorrect sense) must be imperfect ; see Dillm., or QPB[3]. V.[33] is a repetition of v.[14], added probably by a late hand : it is not found in LXX.

In the parts of this ch. assigned to P, observe the recurring superscriptions and subscriptions v.[15. 23. 24. 28. 29. 32] ; similarly 15[20] 16[8] 19[1. 8. 10. 16] &c. The framework is that of P ; but the details are in some cases (especially in c. 16) derived from JE.

C. 14. Preparations for the division of the land by lot by Joshua and Eleazar (v.[1-5]) ; Caleb receives from Joshua his portion at Hebron in accordance with the promise Dt. 1[36] (v.[6-15]). V.[1-5] belongs to P, v.[6-15] may be a narrative of JE, expanded or recast, in parts, by D².

In introducing his account of the division of West Palestine among the tribes, the compiler of the book has followed P ; v.[1-5] being evidently dependent on Nu. 34[13-17] 35[1-8], and showing, moreover, the usual marks of P's style. The corresponding subscription, from the same source, is 19[51].

Wellh. Kuen. Dillm. agree in supposing that 18[1] (which certainly reads more appropriately as an introduction to the narrative of the partition of the *whole* land than to that of a part only) stood originally before 14¹⁻⁵.

[103] V.⁶⁻¹⁵ display traits pointing to D², though not so numerous as is usually the case. They also contain allusions to phrases found in Dt., but *not* in Nu. 13–14; as v.⁷ᵃ לרגל *to spy out* to Dt. 1²⁴ (the idea is expressed by other words in Nu. 13–14; v.⁸ᵃ to Dt. 1²⁸; v.⁹ᵃ to Dt. 1³⁶; v.¹² ענקים to Dt. 1²⁸ בני ענקים (Nu. 13²². ²⁸ ילידי הענק); v.¹⁴ᵇ to Dt. 1³⁶. The passage in its original form appears, like JE in Nu. 13–14 (p. 62f.), to have presupposed *Caleb alone as a spy*: for the terms used in v.⁷· ⁸ ("sent *me*," "went up with *me*") are not those of a person addressing another *who was his companion on the occasion referred to*; so that in v.⁶ the words "and concerning thee," it seems, must have been added for the purpose of accommodating the narrative to that of P in Nu. 13–14.

C. 15. *Judah.* The borders of Judah, v.¹⁻¹²; Caleb's conquest of Hebron, and Othniel's of Kirjath-sepher (Debir), v.¹³⁻¹⁹; the cities of Judah, arranged by districts, v.²⁰⁻⁶³.

$$\begin{cases} \text{P } 15^{1-13} & 20\text{-}44 \quad (45\text{-}47) \quad 48\text{-}62 \\ \text{JE} \qquad\qquad 14\text{-}19 \qquad\qquad\qquad\qquad\qquad 63 \end{cases}$$

V.⁴⁵⁻⁴⁷ seem to be a late insertion in P, designed to conform the territory of Judah to the ideal limits of v.¹²: they are difficult historically (contrast Jud. 1¹⁹; and cf. p. 163 *n.*‡); and *daughters*, in the sense of dependent towns, is not one of P's expressions (on 15²⁸ LXX, cf. Dillm. p. 528). On v.¹⁴⁻¹⁹· ⁶³, see below, pp. 115, 162 f.

C. 16–17. The children of *Joseph* (*i.e.* the west half of Manasseh, and Ephraim). The description is less complete than in the case of Judah, and also less clearly arranged. 16¹⁻³ describes the south border (but only this) of the 2 tribes treated as a whole; 16⁵⁻¹⁰ describes the borders of *Ephraim*, with a notice (v.⁹) of certain cities belonging to Ephraim, but situated in the territory of Manasseh, and (v.¹⁰ = Jud. 1²⁹) of the fact that the Israelites did not succeed in dispossessing the Canaanites from Gezer. C. 17 describes the borders of *Manasseh*, with a notice of the cities belonging to it in Issachar and Asher (v.¹⁻¹³), concluding (v.¹⁴⁻¹⁸) with an account of the complaint of insufficient territory made by the joint tribes to Joshua, and of the permission given to them by him to extend their territory for themselves.

$$\begin{cases} \text{P} \qquad\quad 4\text{-}8 \quad\quad 17^{1a} \quad\quad 3\text{-}4 \quad\quad 7 \quad 9a \quad 9c\text{-}10a \\ \text{JE } 16^{1-3} \quad 9\text{-}10 \qquad 17^{1b-2} \quad 5. (6) \quad 8 \quad 9b \quad\quad 10b\text{-}18 \end{cases}$$

The main description is that of JE, the compiler having here followed P less than usual. Two indications of compilation

may be noted. (1) In JE the lot of the two sons of Joseph is
[**104**] consistently spoken of as *one* (16¹ 17¹⁴⁻¹⁸ ; so 18⁵) ; in P it
is expressly described as twofold (16⁵· ⁸ 17¹ᵃ), Manasseh being
named *first* (16⁴) in accordance with 14⁴ Nu. 26²⁸ by the same
narrator ; * (2) after the description of the southern border alone
of " Joseph " 16¹⁻³, the narrative starts afresh 16⁴, the description
first given being in great part repeated (v.⁵⁻⁸).   V.⁸ᵇ is the regular
subscription of P (19⁸· ¹⁶ &c.).

JE's original narrative is thus restored in outline by Wellh. (p. 133) :
"The two divisions of Joseph receive but one territory (16¹, cf. 17¹⁴), the
borders of which are defined (16¹⁻³ : the north border is now missing).   In
this territory Ephraim receives we do not know how many portions, and
Manasseh ten (17⁵).   The more important Ephraimite cities are enumerated,
and a limitation follows (16⁹).   Next, Manasseh's territory is described, and
it is mentioned that some important cities situate in it belong to Ephraim
(17⁸· ⁹ᵇ) ; but that, on the other hand, Manasseh also extended northwards
into Asher and Zebulun, though the cities belonging to it there remained
Canaanitish (17¹⁰ᵇ⁻¹³).   The account is concluded by 17¹⁴⁻¹⁸, which is of the
nature of an appendix."   The narrative of JE is continued by 18²⁻¹⁰.

C. 18. (1) V.¹⁻¹⁰ the Israelites assemble at Shiloh, and set up
the Tent of Meeting : at Joshua's direction a survey (" describe "
lit. write) of the land yet undivided is made, and its distribution
by lot to the seven remaining tribes is proceeded with at Shiloh ;
(2) v.¹¹⁻²⁸ the tribe of *Benjamin*, its borders (v.¹¹⁻²⁰), and cities
(v.²¹⁻²⁸).   V.¹· ¹¹⁻²⁸ belong to P, v.²⁻⁶· ⁸⁻¹⁰ to JE, v.⁷ to D².

On 18¹ comp. above on c. 14.   With the notice in v.⁷ᵃ, cf. 13¹⁴· ³³ Dt.
10⁹ 18¹ᵇ· ² ; with that in v.⁷ᵇ, 2¹⁰ &c. (p. 104).

C. 19. The lots of *Simeon* (v.¹⁻⁹), *Zebulun* (v.¹⁰⁻¹⁶), *Issachar*
(v.¹⁷⁻²³), *Asher* (v.²⁴⁻³¹), *Naphtali* (v.³²⁻³⁹), and *Dan* (v.⁴⁰⁻⁴⁸), with
a notice of the assignment of Timnath-serah, in Ephraim, to
Joshua (v.⁴⁹ᶠ·), and subscription, v.⁵¹.

P 19¹⁻⁸	10-46	48	51
JE	9	47	49-50

V.³⁵⁻³⁸, where the enumeration differs in form from the rest of the ch.,
may be an excerpt from JE, which, to judge from 18⁹, would appear to have
contained a description of the tribal allotments *by cities*—now mostly superseded by the text of P.   The notice v.⁴⁹ᶠ· is parallel to 15¹³ (Caleb), and is
presupposed in 24³⁰ (both JE).   V.⁵¹ is the final subscription to [**105**] P's

* With 17¹ᵃ· ³⁻⁴, cf. Nu. 27¹⁻¹¹ (P).   V.¹ᵇ⁻⁹ differs from P in representation
(Nu. 26²⁸⁻³⁴) : cf. Kuenen, *Th. T.* xi. 484–488 ; Dillm. p. 542.

whole account of the division of the land, 18¹ 14¹ᶠᶠ·, following the *particular* subscription, v.⁴⁸, relating to Dan, just as Gen. 10³² follows Gen. 10³¹, or as c. 21⁴¹ᶠ· follows 21⁴⁰.

C. 20. The appointment of ₜcities of refuge, in accordance with Nu. 35⁹ᶠᶠ· and Dt. 19 ; Dt. 4⁴¹⁻⁴³ (the appointment of the three trans-Jordanic cities by Moses) being disregarded.

$$\left\{ \begin{matrix} P & 20^{1-3} * & & {}^{6a}\ (to\ judgment) & 7\text{-}9 \\ (D^2) & & (4\text{-}5) & & (6b) \end{matrix} \right.$$

The ch., as a whole, is in the style of P, but it exhibits in parts points of contact with Dt. It is remarkable, now, that just these passages *are omitted in the LXX* (v.³ " (and) unawares " ; v.⁴⁻⁵ ; v.⁶ from " (and) until " to " whence he fled " ; also v.⁸ " at Jericho eastward "). As no reason can be assigned for the omission of these passages by the LXX translators, had they formed a part of the Hebrew text which they used, it is probable that the ch. in its original form (P) has been enlarged by additions from the law of homicide in Dt. (c. 19) at a comparatively late date, so that they were still wanting in the MSS. used by the LXX translators. Cf. Hollenberg, *Alex. Uebers.* p. 15.

In v.⁸ observe that בשגגה *unwittingly* (lit. *in error*) is the phrase of P (Nu. 35¹¹· ¹⁵, Lev. 4² &c.) ; בבלי רעת *unawares* is the phrase of Dt. (4⁴² 19⁴ : not so elsewhere) : it is the latter which LXX do not recognise.

C. 21. Forty-eight cities assigned by the Israelites to the tribe of *Levi*, in accordance with the injunctions contained in Nu. 35¹⁻⁸. V.¹⁻⁴² belongs to P, v.⁴³⁻⁴⁵ to D².

V.⁴³⁻⁴⁵ forms D²'s subscription, not to 21¹⁻⁴², but to D²'s entire account of the division of the land, as 19⁴⁹ᶠ· is JE's, and 19⁵¹ P's.

C. 22. The division of the land being thus completed, Joshua dismisses the 2½ tribes to their homes on the east of Jordan, v.¹⁻⁸. The incident of the altar erected by them at the point where they crossed the Jordan, v.⁹⁻³⁴.

$$\left\{ \begin{matrix} P & & (22^{9\text{-}34}) \\ D^2\ 22^{1\text{-}6.}\ (7\text{-}8) & & \end{matrix} \right.$$

V.⁷⁻⁸ is a fragment of uncertain origin, attached, as it seems, to v.⁶ by a later hand.† The source of v.⁹⁻³⁴ is also uncertain. The phraseology [106]

---

* Except " (and) unawares " (בבלי רעת) in v.³.

† נכסים *riches*, in 22⁸ is a word otherwise only in the latest parts of the OT. (Eccl. 5¹⁸ 6², 2 Ch. 1¹¹· ¹²), and in Aramaic (Ezr. 6⁸ 7²⁶ ; also in the Targums and in Syriac).

is in the main that of P (cf. the citations, p. 131 ff.*) ; but the narrative does not display throughout the characteristic style of P, and in some parts of it † there occur expressions which are not those of P. Either a narrative of P has been combined with elements from another source ‡ in a manner which makes it difficult to effect a satisfactory analysis, or the whole is the work of a distinct writer, whose phraseology is in part that of P, but not entirely.

C. 23. The *first* of the two closing addresses of Joshua to the people, in which he exhorts them to adhere faithfully to the principles of the Deuteronomic law, and in particular to refrain from all intercourse with the native inhabitants of Canaan.

C. 24. (*a*) The *second* of Joshua's closing addresses to the people, delivered at Shechem, differing in scope from that in c. 23, and consisting of a review of the mercies shown by God to His people from the patriarchal days, upon which is based the duty of discarding all false gods, and cleaving to Him alone. The people, responding to Joshua's example, pledge themselves solemnly to obedience ; and a stone, in attestation of their act, is erected in the sanctuary at Shechem, v.[1-28] ; (*b*) notices of the death and burial of Joshua, of the burial of Joseph's bones at Shechem, and of the death and burial of Eleazar, v.[29-33].

$$\begin{cases} E \\ D^2 \text{ c. 23} \end{cases} \quad 24^{1-11a} \text{ (to } you) \qquad \begin{matrix} 11c. 12 \\ 11b \text{ (to } Jebusite) \end{matrix} \quad \begin{matrix} 14-30 \\ 13 \end{matrix} \quad \begin{matrix} 32-33 \\ 31 \end{matrix}$$

C. 23 shows throughout the hand of D²: comp. c. 1 and 22[1-6] ; its object apparently being to supplement 24[1ff.] by inculcating more particularly the principles of the Deuteronomic law. C. 24 is generally admitted to belong to E ; it is incorporated here, with slight additions, by D². In v.[11] the words "the Amorite . . . the Jebusite" (cf. Dt. 7[1]) in point of fact interrupt the connexion : the context speaks only of the contest with the "lords" of Jericho. With v.[13] comp. Dt. 6[10b. 11] ; with v.[31] Dt. 11[7]. Other similar

---

* Which, however, do not include all the marks of P's style which the section contains.

† Esp. v.[22-29], and in the expression שבט (ה)מנשה v.[7. 9. 10. 11. 13. 15. 21], which, though common in D and D² (*e.g.* 1[12]), occurs, in lieu of P's regular term מטה מנשה, only in two doubtful passages of P (13[29a], Nu. 32[33]).

‡ The sense of v.[11b] is uncertain. מול ארץ כנען is usually rendered *opposite to the land of Canaan* ; but W. A. Wright, *Journ. of Philology*, xiii. 117 ff. argues that מול means *in front of* (viz. on the same side : cf. Ex. 34[3] אל מול ההר, *i.e.* on the sides of the mountain itself, not opposite to it : so Jos. 8[33]) : if this rendering be correct, one chief reason for treating the narrative as composite—viz. that the altar is represented in v.[10] as on the west side of Jordan, and in v.[11] on its east side—disappears.

slight additions by D[2] are probably v.[1] middle clause (cf. Dt. 29[10]), v.[12a] to *before you* (cf. Ex. 23[28], Dt. 7[20]). In v.[12] *twelve* for *two* should certainly be read with LXX. The context requires imperatively a reference [**107**] to some event *subsequent* to the capture of Jericho ; so that the *two* kings of the Amorites on the east of Jordan (Sihon and Og)—who have, moreover, been noticed in v.[8]—are here out of place. This retrospect differs in some respects from the previous narrative, and mentions incidents not otherwise recorded, *e.g.* the worship of " other gods " beyond the Euphrates v.[2. 14] ; the *war* of Balak with Israel v.[9] ; the " lords " or citizens of Jericho *fighting* against Israel v.[11] ; the number of the kings in v.[12], which, whether two or twelve, disagrees in either case with the 31 (or 30) of 12[24].

Points of contact with E : v.[1] " before *God*," cf. Ex 18[12] ; v.[12. 15. 18] " the Amorite " (p. 119) ; v.[25b], cf. Ex. 15[25] ; further, with v.[2b. 23a. 26b] (the oak) comp. Gen. 35[2-4] ; with v.[26], Gen. 28[18] ; with v.[27], Gen. 31[44f. 52] ; and with v.[32], Gen. 33[19] 50[25], Ex. 13[19].

The Book of Joshua thus assumed the form in which we have it by a series of stages. First, the compiler of JE (or a kindred hand), utilizing older materials, completed his work : this was afterwards amplified by the elements contributed by D[2] : finally, the whole thus formed was combined with P.* From a historical point of view, it is of importance to distinguish the different elements of which the narrative is composed. Historical matter, as such, is not that in which D[2] is primarily interested ; except in his allusions to the 2½ trans-Jordanic tribes (which are of the nature of a retrospect), the elements contributed by him either give prominence to the motives actuating Joshua, or generalize and magnify the successes achieved by him. Looking at JE, we observe that it narrated the story of the spies sent to explore Jericho, the passage of the Jordan (in two versions), the circumcision of the Israelites at Gibeath-araloth (5[2f.]) or Gilgal (5[8f.]), the capture of Jericho and of Ai (c. 6; 7–8), in each of which accounts traces are perhaps discernible of an earlier and simpler story than that which forms the body of the existing narrative, the compact made with the Gibeonites, the defeat at Beth-horon of the five kings who advanced to attack Gibeon, with their execution at Makkedah, and Joshua's victory over the kings of the North at the waters of Merom. From this point the narrative of JE is considerably more fragmentary, consisting of little more than partial notices of the territory occupied by the tribes (parts of c. 16–17), and anecdotes of the manner in which, in particular cases, they completed, or failed to complete, the conquest of

* This view is preferred deliberately to that of Dillmann.

the districts allotted to them.* [**108**] The account of the close
of Joshua's life is preserved more fully c. 24 (E).

That JE's narrative is incomplete is apparent from many
indications, *e.g.* the *isolated* notice of Bethel assisting Ai in 8^{17},
the entire absence of any mention of the conquest of Central
Palestine (p. 107), the fragmentary character of the notices of the
conquest of Judah, &c. It is, however, remarkable that a series
of notices, similar in form and representation, and sometimes in
great measure verbally identical with those found in the Book
of Joshua, occur in the first chapter of Judges ; and the resemblance is of such a character as to leave little doubt that the two
series are mutually supplementary, both originally forming part
of one and the same continuous account of the conquest of
Palestine (see below, under Judges). From the entire group of
these notices, narrating, partly the successes, partly the failures,
of individual tribes, we learn that the oldest Israelitish tradition
represented the conquest of Palestine as having been in a far
greater degree due to the exertions of the separate tribes, and as
having been effected, in the first instance, much less completely
than would be judged to have been the case from the existing
Book of Joshua, in which the generalizing summaries of D^2
(*e.g.* $10^{40\text{-}43}$; $11^{16\text{-}23}$; $21^{43\text{-}45}$) form a frequent and prominent
feature. The source of the notices in question is supposed by
many critics (Budde, p. 73 f.) to be J, though not of $18^{2\text{-}6.\ 8\text{-}10}$,
where the survey of Canaan is represented as being carried out
as though no unfriendly population were still holding its own
in the land. C. 24 also stands on a different footing from the
notices referred to J, the conquest, as it seems, being conceived
as more completely effected (v.$^{12b.\ 18}$) than in the representation
contained in these notices. C. 24, however, is assigned, upon
independent grounds, to the source E, which might almost be
said to be written from a standpoint approaching (in this respect)
that of D^2.

P entertains the same view of the conquest as D^2 (18^{1b}),
and carries it to its logical consequences : Eleazar and Joshua
formally divide the conquered territory among the tribes (18^1 ;
$14^{1\text{-}5}$). The limits of the different tribes, and the cities belonging to them, are no doubt described as they existed in a later

* 13^{13} ; perhaps the nucleus of $14^{6\text{-}15}$: $15^{14\text{-}19}$; ^{63} ; 16^{10} ; $17^{12f.}$; $^{14\text{-}18}$;
$18^{2\text{-}6}$; $^{8\text{-}10}$; 19^{47}.

day; but the partition of the land being conceived as *ideally*
effected by Joshua, its complete distribution and occupation
[109] by the tribes are treated as his work, and as accomplished
in his lifetime. A difference between P and JE may here be
noted. P mentions Eleazar the priest as co-operating with
Joshua, and even gives him the precedence (14^1 17^4 19^{51} 21^1;
cf. Nu. $27^{19.\ 21}$ 34^{17} P); in JE Joshua always acts alone (14^6 17^{14}
$18^{3.\ 8.\ 10}$ 24^1).

On the phraseology of D^2 see, besides the citations pp. 99 ff., 105 ff.,
JOSHUA, in Smith's *Dict. of the Bible* (ed. 2), § 5. It has, in particular,
affinities with the *margins* of Dt. (cf. Hollenberg, *Stud. u. Krit.* 1874, p.
472 ff.); and includes also a few expressions not found in Dt. One term,
frequent in D^2's summaries, may be here noted, החרים *to ban* or *devote*, 2^{10}
$10^{1.\ 28.\ 35.\ 37.\ 39f.}$ $11^{11f.\ 20f.}$: see Dt. 2^{34} 3^6, and esp. in the injunctions (cf. p. 104,
note) 7^2 13^{15} 20^{17}. But the חרם (p. 59 *n.*) must be a very old institution in
Israel: it is mentioned in JE Ex. 22^{20}, Nu. $21^{2f.}$, Josh. 6-7. Note also *the
servant of Jehovah*, of Moses: $1^{1.\ 2.\ 7.\ 13.\ 15}$ $8^{31.\ 33}$ 9^{24} $11^{12.\ 15}$ 12^6 13^8 14^7 18^7
$22^{2.\ 4.\ 5}$ (Dt. 34^5).

§ 7.

Our analysis of the Hexateuch is completed, and the time has
arrived for reviewing the characteristics of its several sources, and
for discussing the question of their probable date. Deuteronomy,
indeed, has been considered at sufficient length; but there
remain J, E, and P. Have we done rightly, it will perhaps be
asked, in distinguishing J and E? That P and "JE" formed
originally two separate writings will probably be granted; the
distinguishing criteria are palpable and abundant: but is this
established in the case of J and E? is it probable that there
should have been two narratives of the patriarchal and Mosaic
ages, independent, yet largely resembling each other, and that
these narratives should have been combined together into a
single whole at a relatively early period of the history of Israel
(approximately, in the 8th century B.C.)? The writer has often
considered these questions; but, while readily admitting the
liability to error, which, from the literary character of the narrative, accompanies the assignment of particular verses to J or E,
and which warns the critic to express his judgment with reserve,
he must own that he has always risen from the study of "JE"
with the conviction that it *is* composite; and that passages
occur frequently in juxtaposition which nevertheless contain

indications of not being the work of one and the same hand. [110] It is no doubt possible that some scholars may have sought to analyse JE with too great minuteness; but the admission of this fact does not neutralize inferences drawn from broader and more obvious marks of composition. The similarity of the two narratives, such as it is, is sufficiently explained by the fact that their subject-matter is (approximately) the same, and that they both originated in the same general period of Israelitish literature. Specimens have already been given of the grounds upon which the analysis of JE mainly rests, of the cogency of which the reader will be able to form his own opinion: as the notes appended will have shown, the writer does not hold the particulars, even in the Book of Genesis, to be throughout equally assured. If, however, minuter, more problematical details be not unduly insisted on, there does not seem to be any inherent improbability in the conclusion, stated thus generally, that "JE" is of the nature of a compilation, and that in some parts, even if not so frequently as some critics have supposed, the independent sources used by the compiler are still more or less clearly discernible.

J and E, then (assuming them to be rightly distinguished), appear to have cast into a literary form the traditions respecting the beginnings of the nation that were current among the people,—approximately, as it would seem, in the early centuries of the monarchy. In view of the principles which predominate in it, and in contradistinction to the "Priests' Code," JE, as a whole, may be termed the *prophetical* narrative of the Hexateuch. In so far as the analysis contained in the preceding pages is accepted, the following features may be noted as characteristic of J and E respectively. In the Book of Genesis both narratives deal largely with the antiquities of the *sacred sites* of Palestine. The people loved to think of their ancestors, the patriarchs, as frequenting the spots which they themselves held sacred: and the traditions attached to these localities are recounted by the two writers in question.

Thus in J Abraham builds altars at Shechem, Bethel, and Hebron ($12^{7.8}$; $13^{4.18}$), Isaac at Beer-sheba (26^{25}), and Jacob erects a "pillar" at Bethel (35^{14}): in E Abraham builds an altar on Moriah (22^{9}); Jacob erects and anoints a "pillar" ($28^{18.22}$ 31^{13}) at Bethel, and afterwards builds an altar there ($35^{1.3.7}$); another pillar is built by him near Bethel, over Rachel's grave (35^{20}); and an altar, on ground bought by himself, at Shechem ($33^{19f.}$); he also sacrifices at Beer-sheba (46^{1}). Jacob and Laban, moreover, erect a "pillar," marking a boundary, in Gilead (31^{45} [**111**] $^{51-52}$); and Joshua sets up a "great stone" in the sanctuary at Shechem (Josh. 24^{26}). J explains the origin of the names Beer-lahai-roi Gen. 16^{14}, Beer-sheba 26^{33}, Bethel 28^{19}, Penuel 32^{30}, Succoth 33^{17}, Abel-Mizraim 50^{11} : E those of Beer-sheba $21^{31f.}$, Mahanaim 32^2, Allon-bachuth (near Bethel), the burial-place of Deborah, 35^8. In J Abraham journeys through the district of Shechem and Bethel, and also visits Beer-sheba (21^{33}), but his principal residence appears to be Hebron, afterwards the great *Judaic* sanctuary (13^{18} 18^1); in E he dwells chiefly in Beer-sheba (the sanctuary frequented by *Ephraimites*, Am 5^5 8^{14}) and the neighbourhood (20^1 21^{14} 22^{19}). Isaac's home is in or near Beer-sheba ($25^{11b.}$ $^{21-23}$ $26^{6.\ 23-25.\ 33}$: J). Jacob's original home is Beer-sheba ($25^{11b.\ 21ff.}$ 28^{10} : J), and he at least passes through it in 46^{1-5} (prob. E); but the places with which he is chiefly associated are Bethel $28^{11ff.}$ J and E, $35^{1ff.}$ E, and Shechem $33^{19f.}$ E, 48^{22} E (alluded to here as assigned expressly to Joseph, *i.e.* to northern Israel). Only once, 37^{14} (J or E?), is he mentioned, exceptionally, as being at Hebron. Allusions to sacred trees (mostly terebinths or oaks), which, it may be supposed, were pointed to in the narrator's own day, occur in both J (12^6 13^{18} 18^1 21^{33}) and E ($35^{4.\ 8}$, Josh. 24^{26}), as also in Gen. 14^{13} (cf. Jud. 4^{11} $6^{11.\ 19}$ $9^{6.\ 37}$, 1 S. 10^3).

As compared with J, E frequently states more particulars: he is "best informed on Egyptian matters" (Dillm.); the names Eliezer (probably), Deborah, Potiphar, "Abrekh," Zaphenath-Pa'neach, Asenath, Potiphera (Gen. 15^2 [contrast 24^2 J] 35^8 [contrast 24^{59} J] 37^{36} $41^{43.\ 45}$), Pithom and Raamses(?), Puah, Shiphrah, Hur (Ex. 1^{11}(?) ^{15} $17^{10.\ 12}$ 24^{14}), are preserved by him: to the details mentioned above, add those respecting the burial-places of Joshua, Eleazar (Josh. $24^{30.\ 33}$), and Joseph (*ib.* 24^{32}; cf. Gen. 50^{25}, Ex. 13^{19}). The allusions to the teraphim-worship and polytheism of the Aramæan connexions of the patriarchs (Gen. $31^{19.\ 30.\ 53}$ [see the Heb.] 35^4 Josh. $24^{2.\ 15}$) are all due to him, as well as, probably, the notices of Miriam (Ex. $2^{4ff.}$ $15^{20f.}$, Nu. 12. 20^1), of Joshua as the minister and attendant of Moses (Ex. $17^{9f.}$ 24^{13} 32^{17} 33^{11}, Nu. 11^{28}; cf. Josh. 1^1), and of the rod in Moses' hand (Ex. $4^{17.\ 20b}$ 7^{17b} $9^{22f.}$ $10^{12f.}$ 14^{16} 17^5).

The standpoint of E is the prophetical, though it is not brought so prominently forward as in J, and in general the narrative is more "objective," less consciously tinged by ethical and theological reflexion than that of J. Though E mentions the local sanctuaries, and alludes to the "pillars" without offence, he lends no countenance to unspiritual service: the putting away of "strange gods" is noticed by him with manifest approval Gen. 35^{2-4}, Josh. 24^{14-25}. Abraham is styled by him a "prophet," possessing the power of effectual intercession (Gen. 20^7); Moses, though not expressly so termed, as by Hosea (12^{14}), is represented by him essentially as a prophet, entrusted [**112**] by God with a prophet's mission (Ex. 3), and holding exceptionally intimate communion with Him (Ex. 33^{11}, Nu. 12^{6-8};

cf. Dt. 34[10]). In his narrative of Joseph, the *didactic* import of the history is brought out 50[20] : the lesson which he makes it teach is the manner in which God effects His purposes through human means, even though it be without the knowledge, and contrary to the wishes, of the agents who actually bring them about (cf. also 45[5-8]).

Other features that have been noticed in E are: אלהים construed as a *plural* (Gen. 20[13] 35[7], Josh. 24[19]); God's *coming* in a dream (Gen. 20[3] 31[24], Nu. 22[8f. 20] : not so elsewhere), and generally the frequency of the dream as a channel of revelation in his representations (add Gen. 28[11f.] 31[10f.] c. 40–41. 46[2] : cf. 37[5-11] 42[9] ; probably also 15[1] 21[12] [see v.[14]] 22[1] [see v.[8]]) ; * the *double* call Gen. 22[11] 46[2], Ex. 3[4] ; Jethro, not Hobab (Nu. 10[29] : see p. 22 f.), as the name of Moses' father-in-law Ex. 3[1] 4[18] 18[1ff.] ; and (if the passages quoted are all rightly derived from E) "Horeb" † (Ex. 3[2] 17[6] 33[6]) in preference to "Sinai"; "mountain of God" (Ex. 3[2] [cf. 1 Ki. 19[8]] 4[27] 18[5] 24[13]); "Amorite," as the general name of the pre-Israelitish population not only of the land of Sihon, E. of Jordan (Nu. 21[21. 31f.]), but also of the territory W. of Jordan (Gen. 15[16] 48[22], Josh. 24[12] [read with LXX *twelve* for *two*, of the kings W. of Jordan] [15. 18] [so 2 Sa. 21[2], Am. 2[9. 10] : cf. Jud. 6[10], 1 Sa. 7[14]]) ; J prefers "Canaanite" (Gen. 10[19] 12[6] 13[7] 24[3. 37] 34[30] 50[11], Ex. 13[11] ; cf. Jud. 1[4. 5]). ‡

J, if he dwells less than E upon concrete particulars, excels in the power of delineating life and character. His touch is singularly light : with a few strokes he paints a scene which, before he has finished, is impressed indelibly upon his reader's memory. In ease and grace his narratives are unsurpassed ; everything is told with precisely the amount of detail that is required ; the narrative never lingers, and the reader's interest is sustained to the end. His dialogues especially (which are frequent) are remarkable for the delicacy and truthfulness with which character and emotions find expression in them : who can ever forget the pathos and supreme beauty of Judah's intercession, Gen. 44[18ff.]? Other noteworthy specimens of his style are afforded by Gen. 2–3, 11[1-9], c. 18–19. 24. 27 [113] [1-46] (which is mostly, if not entirely, the work of J) Ex. 4[1-16]. The char-

* Much less frequently in J : 26[24] 28[13-16].

† As in Dt. (1[2. 6. 19] 4[10. 15] 5[2] 9[8] 18[16] 29[1] [28[69] Heb.]) : not elsewhere in the Pent.

‡ The *lists* of nations Gen. 15[19-21], Ex. 3[8. 17] 13[5] 23[23. 28] 33[2] 34[11], Josh. 3[10] 9[1] 11[3] 12[8] 24[11] (cf. Dt. 7[1] 20[17], Jud. 3[5]) stand upon a different footing, and are probably due mostly to the compiler of JE (or to D[2], as the case may be). Comp. Budde, *Die Bibl. Urgeschichte*, p. 345 ff.; and the writer's *Deut.* pp. 11, 97.

acter of Moses is pourtrayed by him with singular attractiveness
and force. In J, further, the prophetical element is conspicuously
prominent. Indeed, his characteristic features may be said to
be the fine vein of ethical and theological reflexion which pervades his work throughout, and the manner in which his narrative,
even more than that of E, becomes the vehicle of religious
teaching. "He deals with the problem of the origin of sin and
evil in the world, and follows its growth (Gen. 2–4. 6$^{1-8}$); he
notices the evil condition of man's heart even after the Flood
(8^{21}), traces the development of heathen feeling and heathen
manners (11$^{1ff.}$ 9$^{22ff.}$ 19$^{1ff. 31ff.}$), and emphasizes strongly the want
of faith and disobedience visible even in the Israel of Moses'
days (Ex. 16$^{4-5. 25-30}$ 17$^{2. 7}$ 14$^{11f.}$ 32$^{9-14}$ 33^{12}–34^{28}, Nu. 11. 14. 25$^{1ff.}$,
Dt. 31$^{16-22}$). He shows in opposition to this how God works for
the purpose of. counteracting the ruin incident to man, partly by
punishment, partly by choosing and educating, first Israel's forefathers to live as godlike men, and finally Israel itself to become
the holy people of God. He represents Abraham's migration
into Canaan as the result of a divine call and promise (Gen. 12$^{1-3}$
24^{7}); expresses clearly the aim and object of this call (18$^{18f.}$);
exhibits in strong contrast to human sin the Divine mercy, long-
suffering, and faithfulness (Gen. 6^{8} 8$^{21f.}$ 18$^{23ff.}$, Ex. 32$^{9-14}$ 33$^{12ff.}$);
recognizes the universal significance of Israel in the midst of the
nations of the world (Gen. 12$^{2f.}$ 27^{29}, Ex. 4$^{22f.}$ 19$^{5f.}$, Nu. 24^{9});
declares in classical words the final end of Israel's education
(Nu. 11^{29}; cf. Gen. 18^{19} RV., Ex. 19$^{5f.}$); and formulates under
the term *belief* the spirit in which man should respond to the
revealing work of God (Gen. 15^{6}, Ex. 4$^{1. 5. 8f. 31}$ 14^{31} 19^{9}; cf. Nu.
14^{11}; and also Dt. 1^{32} 9^{23}). And in order to illustrate the divine
purposes of grace, as manifested in history, he introduces, at
points" fixed by tradition, "prophetic glances into the future
(Gen. 3^{15} 5^{29} 8^{21} 9$^{25-27}$ 12$^{2f.}$ 18$^{18f.}$ 28^{14}, Nu. 24$^{17f.}$), as he also loves
to point to the character of nations or tribes as foreshadowed in
their beginnings (Gen. 9$^{22ff.}$ 16^{12} 19$^{31ff.}$ 25$^{25ff.}$ 34$^{25ff.}$ 35^{22} [see
Dillm.'s note here]; cf. 49$^{9ff.}$)" (Dillm. *NDJ.* p. 629 f.).

It is a peculiarity of J that his representations of the Deity
are [114] highly anthropomorphic. He represents Jehovah not
only (as the prophets generally, even the latest, do) as expressing
human resolutions and swayed by human emotions, but as performing sensible acts. Some illustrations from J's narrative in

Gen. 2–3. 7–8 were quoted above (p. 9); but the instances are not confined to the childhood of the world. Thus He *comes down* to see the tower built by men, and to confound their speech 11$^{5.7}$ (so 18^{21}, Ex. 3^8: rather differently Nu. 11$^{17.25}$ 12^5), visits the earth in visible form Gen. 18–19, *meets* Moses and seeks to slay him Ex. 4^{24}, *takes off* the chariot wheels of the Egyptians 14^{25}. Elsewhere, He *is grieved*, *repents* (Gen. 6$^{6f.}$, Ex. 32^{14}), *swears* (Gen. 24^7, Nu. 11^{12}), *is angry* (Ex. 4^{14} *al.*); but these less material anthropomorphisms are not so characteristic as those just noticed, being met with often in other historical books and in the prophets (*e.g.* 1 Sa. 15^{11}, 2 Sa. 24^{16}, Jer. 18$^{8-10}$, 26^{19}).

How far other sources were employed by J and E must remain uncertain, though the fact that such are sometimes actually quoted, at least by E, makes it far from improbable that they were used on other occasions likewise. The sources cited are mostly poetical: no doubt in Israel, as in many other nations, literature began with poetry. Thus E cites the "Book of the Wars of Jehovah" (Nu. 21$^{14f.}$), and the "Book of Jashar" (Josh. 10$^{12f.}$), from each of which an extract is given. The former book can only have been a collection of songs celebrating ancient victories gained by Israel over its enemies.* The poems themselves will naturally, at least in most cases, have been composed shortly after the events to which they refer. At what date they were formed into a collection must remain matter of conjecture: the age of David or Solomon has been suggested. The Book of Jashar, or "the Upright" (in which David's lament over Saul also stood 2 Sa. 1^{18}), was probably of a similar character,—a national collection of songs celebrating the deeds of worthy Israelites. This, at least, was not completed before the time of David, though the nucleus of the collection may obviously have been formed earlier. E, moreover, on other occasions, quotes lyric poems (or fragments of poems), viz. the Song of Moses (Ex. 15$^{1ff.}$), the Song of the Well (Nu. 21$^{17f.}$), and the Song of triumph over Sihon (*ib.* v.$^{27-30}$). There is no express statement [115] that these were taken by him from one of the same sources; but in the light of his actual quotations this is not improbable, at least for the first two: the Song of Deborah, Jud. 5$^{1ff.}$, may also have had a place in one of these collections. Further, the

* For the expression, cf. 1 Sa. 18^{17} 25^{28}.

command to write "in a book"* the threat to extirpate Amalek (Ex. 17[14]), makes it probable that some written statement existed of the combat of Israel with Amalek, and of the oath sworn then by Jehovah to exterminate His people's foe. The poetical phrases that occur in the context may suggest that this too was in the form of a poem, reminiscences of which were interwoven by E in his narrative. And the Ten Commandments, which E incorporates, of course existed already in a written form. The Blessing of Jacob (Gen. 49) may have been derived by J from a source such as the Book of Jashar : the Song of Moses in Dt. 32 (which is very different in style) was taken probably from an independent source. The ordinances which form the basis of the "Book of the Covenant" must also have existed in a written shape before they were incorporated in the narrative of E ; as well as the "Words of the Covenant," which, probably in an enlarged form, are preserved in Ex. 34[10ff.] (cf. v.[27f.]). The existence of written laws *c.* 750 B.C. is implied by Hos. 8[12].

Critics of different schools—Dillmann, Kittel, and Riehm, not less than Wellh. and Kuen.—agree in supposing that E was a native of the Northern kingdom. His narrative bears, indeed, an Ephraimitic tinge. Localities belonging to the Northern kingdom (see above) are prominent in it, especially Shechem and Bethel (the custom of paying tithes at which—cf. Am. 4[4]— appears to be explained in Gen. 28[21f.]). Hebron is subordinate : Abraham is brought more into connexion with Beersheba. Reuben, not Judah (as in J), takes the lead in the history of Joseph. Joshua, the Ephraimite hero, is already prominent before the death of Moses ; the burial-places of famous personages of antiquity, as of Deborah, Rachel, Joshua, Joseph, Eleazar, when they were shown in Ephraimite territory, are noticed by him (Gen. 35[8. 19f.] Josh. 24[30. 32. 33]). J is commonly regarded as having belonged to the Southern kingdom. [116] The general Israelitish tradition treated Reuben as the first-born ; but in J's narrative of Joseph, Judah is represented as the leader of the brethren. Gen. 38 (J) records traditions relating to the history of Judahite families which would be of subordinate interest for one who was not a member of the tribe. Abraham's

---

* Heb. בַּסֵּפֶר, of which, however, the English equivalent is "in *a* book" : comp. Nu. 5[23], Job 19[23]. The Hebrew idiom is explained in Ges.-Kautzsch (ed. 26), § 126. 4 ; or in the writer's *Notes on Samuel,* on 1 Sa. 1[4] 19[3].

home is at Hebron. The grounds alleged may seem to be slight in themselves, but in the absence of stronger grounds on the opposite side, they make it at least *relatively* probable that E and J belonged to the Northern and Southern kingdoms respectively, and represent the special form which Israelitish tradition assumed in each locality.

On the relative date of E and J, the opinions of critics differ. Dillm., Kittel, and Riehm assign the priority to E, placing him 900–850 B.C., and J *c.* 750 (Dillm.), 830–800 (Kittel), or *c.* 850 (Riehm).* Wellhausen, Kuenen, and Stade, on the other hand, assign the priority to J, placing him 850–800 B.C., and E *c.* 750.†

The grounds of this difference of opinion cannot be here fully discussed. It turns in part upon a different conception of the limits of J. Dillm.'s "J" embraces more than Wellh.'s "J," including, for instance, Ex. 13^{3-16} $19^{5f.}$ 32^{7-14}, and much of 34^{1-28}, which approximate in tone to Dt., and which Wellh. ascribes to the compiler of JE. Dillm.'s date, *c.* 750 (p. 630), is assigned to J largely on the ground of just those passages which form no part of Wellh.'s J. It is true, these passages display a tone and style (often parenetic) which is not that which prevails generally in J; and as the anthropomorphisms of J favour, moreover, an earlier date, it is possible that they are rightly assigned to the compiler of JE rather than to J (as, indeed, is admitted by Dillm. (p. 681) for the similar passages, Gen. 22^{15-18} 26^{9b-5}, Ex. 15^{26}, Nu. 14^{11-23}). Dillm. allows the presence in his "J" of archaic elements, but attributes them to the use of special sources; his opinion that E is one of these sources is not probable. On the possibility of the existence of later strata in J, see Holzinger, pp. 138–160.

Although, however, critics differ as to the *relative* date of J and E, they agree that neither is later than *c.* 750 B.C.; and most are of opinion that one (if not both) is decidedly earlier. The *terminus ad quem* is fixed by the general consideration that the prophetic tone and point of view of J and E alike are not so definitely marked as in the canonical prophets (Amos, Hosea, &c.), the earliest of whose writings date from *c.* 760–750. It is [**117**] probable, also, though not quite certain (for the passages *may* be based upon unwritten tradition), that Am. 2^9, Hos. $12^{3f.}$ $12^f.$ contain allusions to the narrative of JE. The *terminus a quo* is more difficult to fix with confidence: in fact, conclusive criteria fail us. We can only argue upon grounds of probability derived

* So most previous critics, as Nöldeke (J *c.* 900), Schrader (E 975–950; J 825–800), Kayser (*c.* 800), Reuss (J 850–800; E " perhaps still earlier ").

† In the same order, H. Schultz, *OT. Theology* (transl.), i. 66 f. (" B," *i.e.* J, to the reign of Solomon; " C," *i.e.* E, 850–800).

from our view of the progress of the art of writing, or of literary
composition, or of the rise and growth of the prophetic tone and
feeling in ancient Israel, or of the period at which the traditions
contained in the narratives might have taken shape, or of the
probability that they would have been written down before the
impetus given to culture by the monarchy had taken effect, and
similar considerations, for estimating most of which, though
plausible arguments, on one side or the other, may be advanced,
a standard on which we can confidently rely scarcely admits of
being fixed.   Nor does the language of J and E bring us to any
more definite conclusion.   Both belong to the golden period of
Hebrew literature.   They resemble the best parts of Judges and
Samuel (much of which cannot be greatly later than David's own
time) ; but whether they are actually earlier or later than these,
the language and style do not enable us to say.   There is at
least no *archaic* flavour perceptible in the style of JE.   And
there are certainly passages (which cannot all be treated as
glosses), in which language is used implying that the period of
the exodus lay in the past, and that Israel is established in
Canaan.*   The [118] manner also in which *songs* are appealed
to (Nu. 21¹⁴· ²⁷), in support of historical statements, is scarcely that

---

* See (in JE) Gen. 12⁶ 13⁷ 34⁷ ("in Israel" : comp. Dt. 22²¹, Jud. 20⁶· ¹⁰, 2
Sa. 13¹²); 40¹⁵ ("the land *of the Hebrews*"); Nu. 32⁴¹ (as Dt. 3¹⁴: see Jud. 10⁴).
In the other sources of the Pent. comp. similarly Gen. 14¹⁴, Dt. 34¹
("Dan"; see Josh. 19⁴⁷, Jud. 18²⁹); Gen. 36³¹; Lev. 18²⁷ᶠ·; Nu. 22¹ 34¹⁵
(p. 84 f.); Dt. 2¹²ᵇ; 3¹¹ (Og's bedstead a relic of antiquity); as well as the
passages of Dt. quoted p. 82 f. &c.   Dt. 2¹² 3¹¹· ¹⁴ might, indeed, in themselves be treated as glosses (though they harmonize in style with the rest of
Dt. 1–3) ; but the attempts that have been made to reconcile the other
passages with Moses' authorship must strike every impartial reader as forced
and artificial.   The laws, also, in many of their details, presuppose (and do
not merely *anticipate*) institutions and social relations, which can hardly have
grown up except among a people which had been for some time settled in a
permanent home.   Cf. Dillm. *NDJ.* 593–6 ; Riehm, *Einl.* § 12.
It must be remembered that there is no passage of the OT. which ascribes
the composition of the Pent. to Moses, or even to Moses' age ; so that we
are thrown back upon independent grounds for the purpose of determining its
date.   The "law of Moses" is indeed frequently spoken of ; and it is un-
questioned that Israelitish law did originate with him : but this expression is
not evidence that Moses was the *writer* of the Pent., or even that the laws
which the Pent. contains represent throughout his unmodified legislation.
Dt. 31⁹· ²⁴ may be referred reasonably to the more ancient legal nucleus of
Deut. (cf. 27³· ⁸, Josh. 8³²).   Comp. Delitzsch, *Genesis*, pp. 23 f., 34.

of a contemporary. All things considered, both J and E may be assigned with the greatest probability to the early centuries of the monarchy. The date at which an event, or institution, is first mentioned in writing, must not, however, be confused with that at which it occurred, or originated : in the early stages of a nation's history the memory of the past is preserved habitually by oral tradition ; and the Jews, long after they were possessed of a literature, were still apt to depend much upon tradition.

On some of the supposed " archaisms " of the Pent. see Delitzsch, *Genesis* (1887), p. 27 f. ; the present writer's art. " Deuteronomy " in Smith's *Dict. of the Bible*, § 31, or his *Comm. on Deut.* p. lxxxviii-xc. The remains of ancient case-endings (though without the force of cases) occurring in the Pent., which have been appealed to as evidence of its antiquity, are too isolated (Gen. 1²⁴ 31³⁹· ³⁹ ; and in poetry 49¹¹· ¹¹, Ex. 15⁶, Nu. 23¹⁸ 24³· ¹⁵, Dt. 33¹⁶ being all that exist), and too closely analogous to those which appear in admittedly later books (*i* about 25 times, Hos. 10¹¹, Is. 1²¹ 22¹⁶, Mic. 7¹⁴, Jer. 10¹⁷ 22²³· ²³ 49¹⁶· ¹⁶ 51¹³ &c ; *o* 8 times, viz. Zeph. 2¹⁴, Is. 56⁹· ⁹, Ps. 50¹⁰ 79² 104¹¹· ²⁰ 114⁸ : cf. Ges.-Kautzsch, § 90. 3), for an argument of any value to be founded upon them. Were the occurrence of these and a few other exceptional forms,—such as הָאֵל 8 times (against הָאֵלֶּה and אֵלֶּה some 260 times), and the term. ‏‏‎ן‎‏‏- in the 2nd and 3rd pers. plur. of the impf.,*—really due to antiquity, they must have been both more constant, and also accompanied by *other marks of an ancient style*. This, however, is not the case : the general literary style of the Pent. contains nothing more suggestive of antiquity than books written confessedly under the monarchy, and the affinities of P are with writings belonging quite to the close of this period. The words peculiar to the Pent., collected by Keil and others as evidence of its superior antiquity, do not establish the required conclusion ; for we possess no proof of the antiquity of these words, other than the assumption that the books in which they occur are ancient : the argument is consequently circular. Every book of the OT. has words and expressions peculiar to itself ; and the number of these is greater in the Pent. than in any other single book, simply on account of its greater length and the large amount of technical matter comprised in the Laws. Nor are there *Egyptian* words occurring in the Pent. sufficiently numerous to imply that the author was born and bred in Egypt : such as they are, they are simply words which were either naturalized in Hebrew, or could not be avoided in describing scenes in Egypt (as איפה, תבה, שעטנז, שש, אחו, יאר, סוף, נמא ; perhaps מנא) : most of these, also, are not confined to the Pent., but occur in books written subsequently (איפה, סוף, and יאר repeatedly ; אחו Job 8¹¹ ; נמא *ib.* Is. 18² 35⁷ ; שש *linen*, Ezek. 16¹⁰· ¹³ 27⁷ Pr. 31²²) ; and the same is the case with סיר, חבן (*pot*), &c., *if* it be true that

---

* See the writer's note on 1 Sa. 2¹⁵, or on Dt. 1¹⁷. It is the older form ; but it occurs in Heb. 202 out of 305 times in books other than the Pent., being used chiefly for emphasis. האל is shown by the cognate languages to be, not archaism, but simply an irregular orthography for הָאֵל.

these are Egyptian in origin. Other words that have been alleged to be Egyptian are shown by the cognate languages to be really Semitic. The assertion in the Oxford *Helps* that "the language of Exodus shows a large infusion of Egyptian words" is extraordinarily false ; the author of it appears to have accepted, without verification, the very exaggerated and inaccurate statements in the *Speaker's Commentary*, i. 244, 488 ff.

Space forbids here an examination of the styles of J and E : careful and instructive synopses will be found in Holzinger, pp. 93–110, 177, 181–191. They have much in common ; indeed, stylistic criteria alone would not generally suffice to distinguish J and E ; though, when the distinction has been effected by other means, slight differences of style appear to disclose themselves ; for instance, particular expressions are more common in J than in E, and E is apt to employ somewhat unusual words.* Whether, however, the expressions noted by Dillm. *NDJ.* pp. 618, 625 f., are all cited justly as characteristic of E and J respectively, may be questioned (cf. Holzinger, *l.c.*) ; they depend in part upon *details* of the analysis which are not throughout equally assured. Both J and E bear a far closer *general* resemblance than P does to the earlier narratives of Jud. Sam. Kings : J especially resembles Jud. 6[11-24] 13[2-24] c. 19.

P, both in method and literary style, offers a striking contrast to either J or E. P is not satisfied to cast into a literary form what may be termed the *popular* conception of the patriarchal and Mosaic age : his aim is to give a *systematic* view, from a priestly standpoint, of the origin and chief institutions of the Israelitish theocracy. For this purpose, an *abstract* of the history is sufficient : to judge from the parts that remain, the narrative of the patriarchal age, even when complete, cannot have been more than a bare outline ; it only becomes detailed at important epochs, or where the origin of some existing institution has to [**119**] be explained (Gen. 9[1ff.], c. 17. 23) ; the intervals are bridged frequently by genealogical lists, and are always measured by exact chronological standards. Similarly in the Mosaic age, the commission of Moses, and events connected with the exodus, are narrated with some fulness ; but only the description of the Tabernacle and ceremonial system can be termed comprehensive ; even. of the incidents in the wilderness, many appear to be introduced chiefly on account of some law or important consequence arising out of them.† But even here the writer is careful not to leave

---

* *E.g.* קְשִׂיטָה Gen. 33[19], Josh. 24[32] (Job 42[11]) ↑ ; מֹנִים Gen. 31[7. 41] ↑ ; Ex. 18[9] ; חרה v.[21] חוה (very uncommon in *prose*) ; 32[18] חלושה ; v.[25] לשמצה בקמיהם (poetical) ; כה in a *local* sense (see below, under Ruth).

† Ex. 16[1-3. 6-24], see v.[32-34] ; Lev. 10[1ff.]; 24[10-14. 23] ; Nu. 9[1ff.]; 15[32-36]; c. 17 ; 20[2. 3b. 6], see v.[12-13. 22-29] ; 25[6-9], see v.[10-13] ; 27[1ff.] 36[1ff.].

an absolute gap in his narrative ; as in the patriarchal period the intervals are bridged by genealogical lists, so here the 40 years in the wilderness—the greater part of which is a blank in JE—are distributed between 40 stations (Nu. 33). In the Book of Joshua the account of the conquest—though largely superseded by that of JE—appears to have been told summarily : on the other hand, the allotment of land among the tribes—arising out of the instructions in Nu. 34, and the basis of the territorial subdivision existing under the monarchy—is narrated at some length (the greater part of Josh. 15–21). Other statistical data, besides genealogies, are a conspicuous feature in his narrative ; for instance, the lists of names and enumerations in Gen. 46, Nu. 1–4. 7. 13$^{1-15}$, c. 26. 34.

In the arrangement of his material, system and circumstantiality are the guiding principles ; and their influence may be traced both in the plan of his narrative as a whole, and in his treatment of individual sections. Not only is the narrative constructed with a careful and uniform regard to chronology, but the history advances along a well-defined line, marked by a gradually diminishing length of human life, by the revelation of God under three distinct names, *Elohim, El Shaddai,** and *Jehovah,* by the blessing of Adam, with its characteristic conditions, and by the subsequent covenants with Noah, Abraham, and Israel, each with its special " sign," the rainbow, the rite of circumcision, and the Sabbath (Gen. 9$^{12f.}$ 17^{11}, Ex. 31$^{18.}$ [120] ^{17}). In his picture of the Mosaic age, the systematic marshalling of the nation by tribes and families, its orderly distribution in the camp and upon the march, the unity of purpose and action which in consequence regulates its movements, are the most conspicuous features (Nu. 1–4. 10$^{11-28}$ &c.). In the age of Joshua stress is similarly laid upon the complete and methodical division of the entire land among the tribes. Further, wherever possible, P seeks to set before his readers a *concrete* picture, with definite figures and proportions : consider, for example, his precise measurements of the ark of Noah, or of the Tabernacle ; his representation, just noticed, of the arrangement of the tribes in the camp and on the march ; his double census of the tribes (Nu. 1. 26) ; his exact estimate of the amount of gold and other

* Gen. 17^1 28^3 35^{11} 48^3, Ex. 6^3 ; also Gen. 43^{14} in E : comp. in poetry 49^{25}, Nu. 24$^{4.\ 16}$. Gen. 49^{25} shows that the title *Shaddai* is an ancient one.

materials offered by the people for the construction of the
Tabernacle (Ex. 38²⁴⁻³¹), of the offerings of the princes (Nu. 7),
and of the spoil taken from the Midianites (Nu. 31). It is
probable, indeed, that in many of these cases only particular
elements of the representation were supplied to him by tradition :
his representation, as a whole, seems to be the result of a
systematizing process working upon these materials, and perhaps,
also, seeking to give sensible expression to certain ideas or truths
(as, for instance, to the truth of Jehovah's presence *in the midst
of His people*, symbolized by the " Tent of Meeting," surrounded
by its immediate attendants, in the centre of the camp).* His
aim seems to have been to present an ideal picture of the
Mosaic age, constructed, indeed, upon a genuine traditional
basis, but so conceived as to exemplify the principles by which
an ideal theocracy should be regulated.† That he does not [121]
wilfully desert or falsify tradition, appears from the fact that even
where it set antiquity in an unfavourable light, he still does not
shrink from recording it (Ex. 16², Lev. 10¹, Nu. 20¹². ²⁴ 27¹³ᶠ·).
It is probable that, being a priest himself, he recorded traditions,
at least to a certain extent, in the form in which they were
current in priestly circles.

His representations of God are less anthropomorphic than
those of J (p. 120 f.), or even of E. No angels or dreams are
mentioned by him. "Certainly he speaks of God as 'appearing'
to men, and as 'going up' from them (Gen. 17¹. ²²ᶠ· 35⁹. ¹³ 48³,
Ex. 6³), at important moments of the history, but he gives no
further description of His appearance : usually the revelation of

---

* In JE the " Tent of Meeting" is represented regularly as *outside* the
camp, Ex. 33⁷⁻¹¹ (where the tenses used express what was Moses' *habit* ; see
Ges.-Kautzsch, ed. 26, § 112. 3), Nu. 10³³ 11²⁶⁻²⁷ 12⁴ (" come out "), only
once as being within it (Nu. 14⁴⁴). The general *impression*, also, derived
from the narrative of JE, is that it was simpler in its structure and appointments than as represented in P.

† It is difficult to escape the conclusion that the representation of P
includes elements, not, in the ordinary sense of the term, historical. His
chronological scheme appears to have been deduced by him by calculation
from data of a nature now no longer known to us, but in part artificial. It
is remarkable, for instance, that the entire number of years from the Creation
to the Exodus is 2666 (=⅔ of 4000) years. There are also difficulties connected with the numbers of the Israelites (esp. in Nu. 1-4) ; here, likewise,
as it seems, the figures cannot all be historical, but must have been obtained
in some manner by computation.

God to men takes with him the form of simple *speaking* to them
(Gen. 1²⁹ 6¹³ 7¹ 8¹⁵ 9¹, Ex. 6². ¹³ *al.*) ; only in the supreme revelation on Sinai (Ex. 24¹⁶ᶠ· cf. 34²⁹ᵇ), and when He is present in
the Tent of Meeting (Ex. 40³⁴ᶠ·), does he describe Him as
manifesting Himself in a form of light and fire (כבוד *glory*), and
as speaking there with Moses (Nu. 7⁸⁹, Ex. 25²²), as man to man,
or in order that the people may recognise Him (Ex. 16¹⁰, Lev.
9⁶. ²³ᶠ·, Nu. 14¹⁰ 16¹⁹. ⁴² 20⁶). Wrath also proceeds forth from
Him (Nu. 16⁴⁶), or destroying fire and death (Lev. 10², Nu. 14³⁷
16³⁵. ⁴⁵ᶠᶠ· 25⁸ᶠ·). But anthropopathic expressions of God he
avoids scrupulously ; even anthropomorphic expressions are rare
(Gen. 2²ᶠ·, cf. Ex. 31¹⁷ᵇ), so that a purpose is here unmistakable.
It may be that as a priest he was accustomed to think and speak
of God more strictly and circumspectly than other writers, even
those who were prophets. On the other hand, he nowhere
touches on the deeper problems of theology. On such subjects
as the justice of the Divine government of the world, the origin
of sin and evil, the insufficiency of all human righteousness
(see, on the contrary, Gen. 5²⁴ 6⁹), he does not pause to reflect ;
the free Divine choice, though not unknown to him (Nu. 3¹²ᶠ·
8¹⁶ 17⁵ᶠᶠ· 18⁶), is at least not so designedly opposed to human
claims as in J. His work contains no Messianic outlooks into
the future : his ideal lies in the theocracy, as he conceives it
realized by Moses and Joshua " (Dillm. *NDJ.* p. 653). In P the
promises to the patriarchs, unlike those of J, are *limited to Israel
itself* (see above, p. 20 ; and add Ex. 6⁴. ⁶⁻⁷). The substance of
these promises is the future growth and glory [**122**] ("*kings* shall
come out of thee ") of the Abrahamic clan ; the establishment of
a covenant with its members, implying a special relation between
them and God (Gen. 17⁷ᵇ, Ex. 6⁷ᵃ), and the confirmation of the
land of Canaan as their possession. The Israelitish theocracy is
the writer's ideal ; and the culminating promise is that in Ex. 29⁴³⁻⁴⁶,
declaring the *abiding presence of God with His people Israel.*

The literary style of P is strongly marked. If JE—and especially J—be free, flowing, and picturesque, P is stereotyped,
measured, and prosaic. The narrative, both as a whole and in
its several parts, is articulated systematically ; the beginning and
close of an enumeration are regularly marked by stated formulæ.*

* Comp. p. 12, *notes* † and ‡ ; and add Nu. 1²⁰⁻²¹. ²²⁻²³ &c. ; 2³⁻⁹. ¹⁰⁻¹⁶ &c. ;
10¹⁴⁻²⁸ ; 26¹²⁻¹⁴. ¹⁵⁻¹⁸ &c. See also p. 134, No. 44.

The descriptions of P are methodical and precise. When they embrace details, emphasis * and completeness † are studied; hence a thought is often repeated in slightly different words.‡ There is a tendency to describe an object in full each time that it is mentioned; § a direction is followed, as a rule, by an account of its execution, usually in the same words.‖ Sometimes the circumstantiality leads to diffuseness, as in parts of Nu. 1–4 and (an extreme case) Nu. 7 (p. 61). Metaphors, similes, &c., are eschewed (Nu. 27[17b] is an exception), and there is generally an absence of the poetical or dramatic element, which is frequently conspicuous in the other historical books of the OT. (including J and E). To a greater degree than in any other part of the OT. is a preference shown in P for *standing formulæ and expressions*; some of these recur with great frequency, and are apparent in a translation. Particularly noticeable is an otherwise uncommon mode of expression, producing a peculiar rhythm, by which a statement is first made in general terms, and then partly repeated, for the purpose of receiving closer limitation or definition.¶ [123] It seems as though the habits of thought and expression, which the author had contracted through his practical acquaintance with the law, were carried by him into his treatment of purely historical subjects. The writer who exhibits the greatest stylistic affinities with P, and agrees with him sometimes in the use of uncommon expressions, is the priestly prophet Ezekiel.

The following is a select list of some of the most noticeable expressions characteristic of P; many occurring rarely or never besides, some only in Ezekiel. The list could readily be increased, especially if terms occurring *only* in the laws had been added; ** these, however, have been excluded, as the object of

---

* Gen. 1[29] 6[17] 9[3].

† Notice the precision of definition and description in Gen. 10[5. 20. 31] 36[40]; 6[18] 7[13f.] 23[17] 36[6] 46[6-7] Ex. 7[19], Nu. 1[2. 20. 22] &c.

‡ Comp. p. 12, *note* *; add Gen. 2[2-3] 23[17-20], Ex. 12[18-20].

§ Comp. Gen. 1[7] beside v.[6]; v.[11] beside v.[10]; 8[18f.] beside v.[16f.].

‖ Gen. 1[6f.]; v.[11f.]; v.[24f.]; 6[18-20] 7[13-16]; 8[16-19]; Ex. 8[16f.]; 9[8-10]; Nu. 17[2. 6]. ¶ Gen. 1[27] 6[14] 8[5] 9[5] 23[11] 49[29b-30], Ex. 12[4. 8] 16[16. 35] 25[2. 11. 18. 19] 26[1], Lev. 25[22], Nu. 2[2] 18[18] 36[11-12] (Heb.) &c.

** *E.g.* "savour of satisfaction," "fire-sacrifice," "statute for ever." But the laws of P, it is worth remarking, are, as a rule, formulated differently from those of either JE or D (contrast *e.g.* the איש או אשה כי, נפש כי, אדם כי

the list is rather to show that the *historical* sections of P exhibit the same literary features as the *legal* ones, and that the same habits of thought and expression pervade both.* References to Lev. 17-26 have been included in the list. It will be recollected that these chapters do not consist wholly of excerpts from H, but comprise elements belonging to P (p. 47 f.). H itself also, as was remarked, is related to P, representing likewise priestly usage, though in an earlier phase; so that it is but natural that its phraseology should exhibit points of contact with that of P.

1. *God*, not *Jehovah*: Gen. 1¹ and uniformly, except Gen. 17¹ 21¹ᵇ [above, p. 21], until Ex. 6².

2. *Kind* (מין): Gen. 1¹¹· ¹² *bis.* ²¹ *bis.* ²⁴ *bis.* ²⁵ *ter* 6²⁰ *ter* 7¹⁴ *quater*, Lev. 11¹⁴· ¹⁵· ¹⁶· ¹⁹ [hence Dt. 14¹³· ¹⁴· ¹⁵· ¹⁸] ²² *quater.* ²⁹, Ez. 47¹⁰.†

3. *To swarm* (שרץ): Gen. 1²⁰· ²¹ 7²¹ 8¹⁷, Ex. 7²⁸ [hence Ps. 105³⁰], Lev. 11²⁹· ⁴¹· ⁴²· ⁴³· ⁴⁶, Ez. 47⁹. *Fig.* of men: Gen. 9⁷, Ex. 1⁷.†

[124] 4. *Swarming things* (שרץ): Gen. 1²⁰ 7²¹, Lev. 5² 11¹⁰· ²⁰ [hence Dt. 14¹⁹] ²¹· ²³· ²⁹· ³¹· ⁴¹· ⁴²· ⁴³· ⁴⁴ 22⁵.†

5. *To be fruitful and multiply* (פרה ורבה): Gen. 1²²· ²⁸ 8¹⁷ 9¹· ⁷ 17²⁰ (cf. v.²· ⁶) 28³ 35¹¹ 47²⁷ 48⁴, Ex. 1⁷, Lev. 26⁹. Also Jer. 23³; and (inverted) 3¹⁶, Ez. 36¹¹.†

6. *For food* (לאכלה): Gen. 1²⁹· ³⁰ 6²¹ 9³, Ex. 16¹⁵, Lev. 11³⁹ 25⁶, Ez. 15⁴· ⁶ 21³⁷ 23³⁷ 29⁵ 34⁵· ⁸· ¹⁰· ¹² 39⁴.† (In Jer. 12⁹ לאכלה is an infin.)

7. *Generations* (תולדות):
    (*a*) In the phrase *These are the generations of* . . . (see p. 6 f.).
    (*b*) Otherwise: Gen. 10³² 25¹³, Ex. 6¹⁶· ¹⁹ 28¹⁰, Nu. 1 (12 times), 1 Ch. 5⁷ 7²· ⁴· ⁹ 8²⁸ 9⁹· ³⁴ 26³¹.†

8. מאת in the *st. c.*, in cases where ordinarily מאה would be said: Gen. 5³· ⁶· ¹⁸· ²⁵· ²⁸ 7²⁴ 8³ 11¹⁰· ²⁵ 21⁵ 25⁷· ¹⁷ 35²⁸ 47⁹· ²⁸, Ex. 6¹⁶· ¹⁸· ²⁰ 38²⁵· ²⁷ (thrice), Nu. 2⁹· ¹⁶· ²⁴· ³¹ 33⁸⁹. So besides only Neh. 5¹¹ (prob. corrupt), 2 Ch. 25⁹ Qrê, Est. 1⁴.† (Peculiar. P uses מאה in such cases only twice, Gen. 17¹⁷ 23¹.)

9. *To expire* (גוע): Gen. 6¹⁷ 7²¹ 25⁸· ¹⁷ 35²⁹ 49³³, Nu. 17¹²· ¹³ 20³ *bis.* ²⁹, Josh. 22²⁰. (Only besides in poetry: Zech. 13⁸, Ps. 88¹⁶ 104²⁹, Lam. 1¹⁹; and 8 times in Job.)†

&c. of Lev. 1² 4² 5¹· ¹⁵ 13²· ²⁹· ³⁸, Nu. 5⁶ 6² *al.* with the וכי איש of Ex. 21⁷· ¹⁴· ²⁰· ²⁶ &c.), and show besides differences of terminology, which, however, the reader must be left to note for himself.

* Were these expressions *confined* to the legal sections, it might be argued that they were the work of the same hand as JE, who, with a change of subject, adopted naturally an altered phraseology; but they are found repeatedly in the *narrative* parts of the Hexateuch, where the peculiar phraseology cannot be attributed to the special character of the subject (*e.g.* Gen. 6-9, Ex. 6²-7¹³, c. 16, Nu. 13-14. 16-17, Josh. 22⁹ᶠᶠ·).

10. *With thee* (*him*, &c.) appended to an enumeration: Gen. 6¹⁸ 7⁷· ¹³ 8¹⁶· ¹⁸ 9⁸ 28⁴ 46⁶· ⁷, Ex. 28¹· ⁴¹ 29²¹ *bis*, Lev. 8²· ³⁰ 10⁹· ¹⁴· ¹⁵ (25⁴¹· ⁵⁴ עם), Nu. 18¹· ²· ⁷· ¹¹· ¹⁹ *bis*. Similarly *after you* (*thee*, &c.) appended to "seed": Gen. 9⁹ 17⁷ *bis.* ⁸· ⁹· ¹⁰· ¹⁹ 35¹² 48⁴, Ex. 28⁴³, Nu. 25¹³.

11. *And Noah did* (*so*)*; according to*, &c.: Gen. 6²²: exactly the same form of sentence, Ex. 7⁶ 12²⁸· ⁵⁰ 39³²ᵇ 40¹⁶, Nu. 1⁵⁴ 2³⁴ 8²⁰ 17¹¹ [Heb. ²⁶]: cf. Ex. 39⁴³, Nu. 5⁴ 9⁵.

12. *This selfsame day* (עצם היום הוה): Gen. 7¹³ 17²³· ²⁶, Ex. 12¹⁷· ⁴¹· ⁵¹, Lev. 23¹⁴· ²¹· ²⁸· ²⁹· ³⁰, Dt. 32⁴⁸, Josh. 5¹¹ 10²⁷ (not P: probably the compiler). Ez. 2³ 24² *bis*. 40¹.↑

13. *After their families* (למשפחותם ־יהם): Gen. 8¹⁹ 10⁵· ²⁰· ³¹ 36⁴⁰, Ex. 6¹⁷· ²⁵ 12²¹,* Nu. 1 (13 times) 2³⁴ 3-4 (15 times) 11¹⁰ (JE) 26 (16 times) 29¹² 33⁵⁴, Josh. 13¹⁵· ²³· ²⁴· ²⁸· ²⁹· ³¹ 15¹· ¹²· ²⁰ 16⁵· ⁸ 17² *bis* 18¹¹· ²⁰· ²¹· ²⁸ 19 (12 times) 21⁷· ³³· ⁴⁰ (Heb. ³⁸), 1 Sa. 10²¹, 1 Ch. 5⁷ 6⁶²· ⁶³ (Heb. ⁴⁷· ⁴⁸, from Josh. 21³³· ⁴⁰).↑

[125] 14. לכל *as regards all*, with a generalizing force = *namely*, *I mean* (Ewald, § 310ᵃ): Gen. 9¹⁰ᵇ 23¹⁰ᵇ, Ex. 14²⁸ (cf. v.⁹ וחילו) 27³· ¹⁹ (si vera l.), 28³⁸ 36¹ᵇ, Lev. 5³ 11²⁶· ⁴² 16¹⁶· ²¹ 22¹⁸, Nu. 4²⁷· ³¹· ³² 5⁹ 18⁴· ⁸· ⁹, Ez. 44⁹. (Prob. a juristic use. Occasionally elsewhere, esp. in Ch.)

15. *An everlasting covenant*: Gen. 9¹⁶ 17⁷· ¹³· ¹⁹, Ex. 31¹⁶, Lev. 24⁸; cf. Nu. 18¹⁹ 25¹³.↑↑ †

16. *Exceedingly* (במאד מאר, not the usual phrase): Gen. 17²· ⁶· ²⁰, Ex. 1⁷, Ez. 9⁹ 16¹³.↑

17. *Substance* (רכש): Gen. 12⁵ 13⁶ 31¹⁸ 36⁷ 46⁶, Nu. 16³² *end* 35³. Elsewhere (not P): Gen. 14¹¹· ¹²· ¹⁶ *bis.* ²¹ 15¹⁴; and in Ch. Ezr. Dan. (15 times).↑

18. *To gather* (רכש—cognate with "substance"): Gen. 12⁵ 31¹⁸ *bis* 36⁶ 46⁶.↑

19. *Soul* (נפש) in the sense of *person*: Gen. 12⁵ 36⁶ 46¹⁵· ¹⁸· ²²· ²⁵· ²⁶· ²⁷, Ex. 1⁵ 12⁴· ¹⁶ (RV. *man*) ¹⁹ 16¹⁶ (RV. *persons*), Lev. 2¹ (RV. *one*) 4²· ²⁷ 5¹· ²; and often in the legal parts of Lev. Nu. (as Lev. 17¹² 22¹¹ 27²), Nu. 31²⁸· ³⁵· ⁴⁰· ⁴⁶ (in the account of the war with Midian), Josh. 20³· ⁹ (from Nu. 35¹¹· ¹⁵). See also below, No. 25ᵃ. A usage not confined to P, but much more frequent in P than elsewhere.

20. *Throughout your* (*their*) *generations* (לדרתם לדרתיכם): Gen. 17⁷· ⁹· ¹², Ex. 12¹⁴· ¹⁷· ⁴² 16³²· ³³ 27²¹ 29⁴² 30⁸· ¹⁰· ²¹· ³¹ 31¹³· ¹⁶ 40¹⁵, Lev. 3¹⁷ 6¹¹ 7³⁶ 10⁹ 17⁷ 21¹⁷ 22³ 23¹⁴· ²¹· ³¹· ⁴¹ 24³ 25³⁰ (*his*), Nu. 9¹⁰ 10⁸ 15¹⁴· ¹⁵· ²¹· ²³· ³⁸ 18²³ 35²⁹.↑

---

* The isolated occurrence of this expression in JE does not make it the less characteristic of P. Of course the writer of Ex. 12²¹ was acquainted with the word משפחה, and could use it, if he pleased, in combination with ל. It is the *frequency* of the combination which causes it to be characteristic of a particular author. For the same reason εὐθύς is characteristic of St. Mark's style, nothwithstanding the fact that the other evangelists employ it occasionally. The same remark holds good of Nos. 12, 15, 17, 22, 38, 41, &c.

† The double arrow indicates that all passages of the Hexateuch in which the word or phrase quoted occurs are cited or referred to.

21. *Sojournings* (מגורים), with *land* : Gen. 17^8 28^4 36^7 37^1, Ex. 6^4, Ez. 20^{38} ; with *days* : Gen. 47$^{9 \ bis}$.   Only besides Ps. 119^{54} ; and rather differently 55^{16}, Job 18^{19}.↑

22. *Possession* (אחזה) : Gen. 17^8 23$^{4. \ 9. \ 20}$ 36^{43} 47^{11} 48^4 49^{30} 50^{13}, Lev. 14^{34} 25$^{10-46}$ 27$^{16. \ 21. \ 22. \ 24. \ 28}$, Nu. 27$^{4. \ 7}$ 32$^{5. \ 22. \ 29. \ 32}$ 35$^{2. \ 8. \ 28}$, Dt. 32^{49}, Josh. 21$^{12. \ 39}$ 22^4 (D^2) $^{9. \ 19 \ bis}$.   Elsewhere only in Ezekiel (44$^{28 \ bis}$ 45$^{5. \ 6. \ 7 \ bis. \ 8}$ 46$^{16. \ 18 \ ter}$ 48$^{20. \ 21. \ 22 \ bis}$) ; Ps. 2^8 ; 1 Ch. 7^{28} 9^2 (=Neh. 11^3), 2 Ch. 11^{14} 31^1.↑

23. The cognate verb *to get possessions* (נאחז), rather a peculiar word : Gen. 34^{10} 47^{27}, Nu. 32^{30}, Josh. 22$^{9. \ 19}$.↑

24. *Purchase, purchased possession* (מקנה) : Gen. 17$^{12. \ 13. \ 23. \ 27}$ 23^{18}, Ex. 12^{44}, Lev. 25$^{16 \ bis. \ 51}$ 27^{22}.   (Prob. a legal term.   Only besides Jer. 22$^{11. \ 12. \ 14. \ 16}$.)↑

25. *Peoples* (עמים) in the sense of *kinsfolk* * (peculiar) :
  (*a*) *That soul* (or *that man*) *shall be cut off from his kinsfolk* : Gen. 17^{14}, Ex. 30$^{33. \ 38}$ 31^{14}, Lev. 7$^{20. \ 21. \ 25. \ 27}$ 17^9 19^8 [**126**] 23^{29}, Nu. 9^{13}↑.   (In Lev. 17$^{4. \ 10}$ 18^{29} 20$^{3. \ 5. \ 6. \ 18}$ 23^{30}, Nu. 15^{30} the noun is *singular*.)
  (*b*) *To be gathered to one's kinsfolk* : Gen. 25$^{8. \ 17}$ 35^{29} 49^{33}, Nu. 20^{24} 27^{13} 31^2, Dt. 32$^{50 \ bis}$.↑
  (*c*) Lev. 19^{16} 21$^{1. \ 4. \ 14. \ 15}$, Ez. 18^{18} : perhaps Jud. 5^{14}, Hos. 10^{14}.↑

26. *Settler* or *sojourner* (תושב) : Gen. 23^4 (hence fig. Ps. 39^{13}, 1 Ch. 29^{15}), Ex. 12^{45}, Lev. 22^{10} 25$^{6. \ 23}$ (fig.) $^{35. \ 40. \ 45. \ 47 \ bis}$, Nu. 35^{15}.   Also 1 Ki. 17^1 (text doubtful).↑

27. *Getting, acquisition* (קנין) : Gen. 31^{18} 34^{23} 36^6, Lev. 22^{11}, Josh. 14^4 : cf. Ez. 38$^{12f.}$; also Pr. 4^7, Ps. 104^{24} 105^{21}.↑

28. *Rigour* (פרך) : Ex. 1$^{13. \ 14}$, Lev. 25$^{43. \ 46. \ 53}$, Ez. 34^4.↑

29. *Judgments* (שפטים [not the usual word]) : Ex. 6^6 7^4 12^{12}, Nu. 33^4, Ez. 5$^{10. \ 15}$ 11^9 14^{21} 16^{41} 25^{11} 28$^{22. \ 26}$ 30$^{14. \ 19}$, Pr. 19^{29}, 2 Ch. 24^{24}.↑

30. *Fathers' houses* (=families : בית אבות, or sometimes אבות alone) : Ex. 6$^{14. \ 25}$ 12^3, Nu. 1-4 (often). 17$^{2. \ 3. \ 6}$ 26^2 31^{26} 32^{28} 34^{14} 36^1, Josh. 14^1 19^{51} 21^1 22^{14}.

31. *Hosts* (צבאות) of the Israelites : Ex. 6^{26} 7^4 12$^{17. \ 41. \ 51}$, Nu. 1$^{3. \ 52}$ 2$^{3. \ 9. \ 10. \ 16. \ 18. \ 24. \ 25. \ 32}$ 10$^{14. \ 18. \ 22. \ 25. \ 28}$ 33^1.↑↑   (Dt. 20^9 differently.)

32. *Congregation* (עדה) of the Israelites : Ex. 12$^{3. \ 6. \ 19. \ 47}$ 16$^{1. \ 2. \ 9. \ 10. \ 22}$ 17^1 34^{31} 35$^{1. \ 4. \ 20}$ 38^{25}, Lev. 4$^{13. \ 15}$ 8$^{3-5}$ 9^5 10$^{6. \ 17}$ 16^5 19^2 24$^{14. \ 16}$, Nu. 13$^{26 \ bis}$ 14$^{1. \ 2. \ 5. \ 7. \ 10. \ 27. \ 35. \ 36}$ 16$^{2. \ 3. \ 9 \ bis. \ 19 \ bis. \ 21. \ 22}$ (Lev. 10^6) 24$^{26. \ 41.}$ 42. 45. 46 [Heb. 17$^{6. \ 7. \ 10. \ 11}$] 20$^{1. \ 2. \ 8 \ bis. \ 11. \ 22. \ 27. \ 29}$ 25$^{6. \ 7}$ 31$^{12. \ 16. \ 26. \ 27. \ 43}$ (as well as often in the other chapters of Nu. assigned wholly to P) 32$^{2. \ 4}$, Josh. 9$^{15. \ 18 \ bis. \ 19. \ 21. \ 27}$ 18^1 20$^{6. \ 9}$ 22$^{12. \ 16. \ 17. \ 18}$ (Nu. 16^{22}) 20. 30. (Cf. No. 39.)   Never in JE or Dt., and rare in the other hist. books : Jud. 20^1 21$^{10. \ 13. \ 16}$, 1 Ki. 8^5 (=2 Ch. 5^6) 12^{20} (cf. p. 143 f.).

33. *Between the two evenings* (a technical expression) : Ex. 12^6 16^{12} 29$^{39. \ 41}$ 30^8, Lev. 23^5, Nu. 9$^{3. \ 5. \ 11}$ 28$^{4. \ 8}$.↑

---

* Properly *father's kin* (Wellh. in the *Gött. Nachrichten*, 1893, p. 480)

34. *In all your dwellings* (בכל מושבותיכם) : Ex. 12²⁰ 35³, Lev. 3¹⁷ 7²⁶ 23³· ¹⁴· ²¹· ³¹, Nu. 35²⁹ (cf. 15² 31¹⁰), Ez. 6⁶· ¹⁴.

35. *This is the thing which Jehovah hath commanded* : Ex. 16¹⁶· ³² 35⁴, Lev. 8⁵ 9⁶ 17², Nu. 30² 36⁶.†

36. *A head* (גלגלת lit. *skull*), in enumerations : Ex. 16¹⁶ 38²⁶, Nu. 1²· ¹⁸· ²⁰· ²² 3⁴⁷, 1 Ch. 23³· ²⁴.†

37. *To remain over* (ערף : not the usual word) : Ex. 16¹⁸· ²³ 26¹² *bis.* ¹³, Lev. 25²⁷, Nu. 3⁴⁶· ⁴⁸· ⁴⁹.†

38. *Ruler* or *prince* (נשיא), among the Israelites : Ex. 16²² 35²⁷, Lev. 4²², Nu. 1¹⁶· ⁴⁴ cc. 2. 3. and 7 (repeatedly) 4⁴⁶ 10⁴ 13² 17²· ⁶ (Heb. ¹⁷· ²¹) 25¹⁴· ¹⁸ 34¹⁸⁻²⁸, Josh. 22¹⁴. In JE once only, Ex. 22²⁷ : never in Dt. Jud. Sam.: in Kings only 1 Ki. 8¹ [p. 144], and in a semi-poetical passage, 11³⁴. Cf. Gen. 17²⁰ 23⁶ 25¹⁶ 34². Often in Ez., even of the king (see below, in the list of phrases at the end of Ezekiel).

[127] 39. *Rulers* (*princes*) *of* (or *in*) *the congregation* : Ex. 16²² 34³¹, Nu. 4³⁴ 16² 31¹³ 32², Josh. 9¹⁵· ¹⁸ (cf. v.¹⁹· ²¹) 22³⁰ (cf. v.³²) : cf. Nu. 27² 36¹ Josh. 17⁴.†

40. *Deep rest* (שבתון): Ex. 16²³ 31¹⁵ 35², Lev. 16³¹ 23³· ²⁴· ³²· ³⁹ *bis* 25⁴· ⁵.†

41. *According to the command* (lit. *mouth*) *of Jehovah* (על פי יהוה) : Ex. 17¹, Lev. 24¹², Nu. 3¹⁶· ³⁹· ⁵¹ 4³⁷· ⁴¹· ⁴⁵· ⁴⁹ 9¹⁸· ²⁰· ²³ 10¹³ 13³ 33²· ³⁸ 36⁵, Josh. 15¹³ (אל) 17⁴ (אל) 19⁵⁰ 21³ (אל) 22⁹. Very uncommon elsewhere : Dt. 34⁵ᵇ (probably from P : cf. Nu. 33³⁸), 2 Ki. 24³.

42. *Half* (מחצית : not the usual word) : Ex. 30¹³ *bis.* ¹⁵· ²³ 38²⁶, Lev. 6¹³ *bis*, Nu. 31²⁹· ³⁰· ⁴²· ⁴⁷, Josh. 21²⁵ (=1 Ch. 6⁵⁵). Only besides 1 Ki. 16⁹, Neh. 8³, 1 Ch. 6⁴⁶.†

43. מעל *to trespass* and מעל *trespass* (often combined, and then rendered in RV. *to commit a trespass*) : Lev. 5¹⁵ 6² [Heb. 5²¹] 26⁴⁰, Nu. 5⁶· ¹²· ²⁷ 31¹⁶, Dt. 32⁵¹, Josh. 7¹ 22¹⁶· ²⁰· ²²· ³¹,†† Ez. 14¹³ 15⁸ 17²⁰ 18²⁴ 20²⁷ 39²³· ²⁶. (A word belonging to the priestly terminology. Never in Jud. Sam. Kgs., or other prophets [except Dan. 9⁷] ; and chiefly elsewhere in Ch.; see the list at the end of this book, No. 3.)

44. The methodical form of *subscription* and *superscription* : Gen. 10 [5]· ²⁰· ³¹· ³² 25¹⁶ 36¹⁹· ²⁰· ³⁰· ³¹· ⁴⁰· ⁴³ 46⁸· ¹⁵· ¹⁸· ²²· ²⁵, Ex. 1¹ 6¹⁴· ¹⁶· ¹⁹ᵇ· ²⁵ᵇ· ²⁶, Nu. 1⁴⁴ 4²⁸· ³³· ³⁷· ⁴¹· ⁴⁵ 7¹⁷ᵇ· ²³ᵇ· ²⁹ᵇ &c. ⁸⁴ 33¹, Josh. 13²³ᵇ· ²⁸· ³² 14¹ 15¹²ᵇ· ²⁰ 16⁸ᵇ 18²⁰· ²⁸ᵇ 19⁸ᵇ· ¹⁶· ²³· ³¹· ³⁹· ⁴⁸· ⁵¹ [cf. Gen. 10³¹· ³²] 21¹⁹· ²⁶· ³³· ⁴⁰· ⁴¹⁻⁴². (Not a complete enumeration.)

45. For *tribe* P has nearly always מטה, very rarely שבט ; for *to beget* הוליד (Gen. 5³⁻³² 6¹⁰ 11¹¹⁻²⁷ 17²⁰ 25¹⁹ 48⁶, Lev. 25⁴⁵, Nu. 26²⁹· ⁵⁸), not ילד (as in the genealogies of J : Gen. 4¹⁸ *ter* 10⁸· ¹³· ¹⁵· ²⁴ *bis.* ²⁶ 22²³ 25³) ; for *to be hard* or *to harden* (of the heart) חזק, חזק lit. *to be or make strong* (Ex. 7¹³· ²² 8¹⁹ [Heb. ¹⁵] 9¹² 11¹⁰ 14⁴· ⁸· ¹⁷), not כבד, הכביד *to be* or *make heavy* (Ex. 7¹⁴ 8¹⁵· ³² [Heb. ¹¹· ²⁸] 9⁷· ³⁴ 10¹) ; for *to stone* רגם (Lev. 20²· ²⁷ 24¹⁴· ¹⁶ *bis.* ²³, Nu. 14¹⁰ 15³⁵· ³⁶ : also Dt. 21²¹, Josh. 7²⁵ᵃ [?P]††), not סקל (Ex. 8²⁶ [Heb. ²²] 17⁴ 19¹³ *bis* 21²⁸ *bis.* ²⁹· ³² Dt. 13¹⁰ [Heb. ¹¹] 17⁵ 22²¹· ²⁴, Josh. 7²⁵ᵇ ††) ; for *to spy* תור (Nu. 13²· ¹⁶· ¹⁷· ²¹· ²⁵· ³² *bis* 14⁶· ⁷· ³⁴· ³⁶· ³⁸ 15³⁹ : also 10³³ JE, Dt. 1³³ ††), not רגל (Nu. 21³², Dt. 1²⁴, Josh. 2¹ 6²²· ²³· ²⁵ 7² *bis* 14⁷) ; and for the pron.

of 1 pers. sing. אני * (nearly 130 times ; אנכי once only Gen. 23⁴ : comp. in Ez. אני 138 times, אנכי once 36²⁸).†

[128]   The following geographical terms are found only in P :

46. *Kirjath-Arba* for *Hebron* : Gen. 23² 35²⁷, Josh. 15¹³· ⁵⁴ 20⁷ 21¹¹. (The same name is referred to, but not used, in Josh. 14¹⁵=Jud. 1¹⁰ JE : see also Neh. 11²⁵.)

47. *Machpelah* : Gen. 23⁹· ¹⁷· ¹⁹ 25⁹ 49³⁰ 50¹³.†

48. *Paddan-Aram* : Gen. 25²⁰ 28²· ⁵· ⁶· ⁷ 31¹⁸ 33¹⁸ 35⁹· ²⁶ 46¹⁵.† (48⁷ *Padaan* alone. J says *Aram-naharaim* 24¹⁰, as Dt. 23⁴ [Heb. ⁵], Jud. 3⁸.)

49. *The Desert of Zin* (צן) : Nu. 13²¹ 20¹ᵃ 27¹⁴ 33³⁶ 34³, Dt. 32⁵¹, Josh. 15¹ : cf. *Zin*, Nu. 34⁴, Josh. 15³.

50. *The Steppes of Moab* (ערבות מואב) : Nu. 22¹ 26³· ⁶³ 31¹² 33⁴⁸⁻⁵⁰ 35¹ 36¹³, Dt. 34¹· ⁸, Josh. 13³².†

Eleazar the priest, though not unmentioned in the other sources (Dt. 10⁶, Josh. 24³³), is specially prominent in P, esp. after the death of Aaron (Nu. 20²⁵⁻²⁸), as Nu. 26¹ &c. 31¹² &c. 32²· ²⁸ 34¹⁷, Josh. 14¹ 17⁴ 19⁵¹ 21¹. The priestly tradition also records incidents in which his son Phinehas (Ex. 6²⁵) took part : Nu. 25⁷· ¹¹ 31⁶, Josh. 22¹³· ³⁰⁻³² (in JE 24³³ ; cf. Jud. 20²⁸).

Under the circumstances, the statement in the *Speaker's Commentary*, i. p. 28ᵃ, that the peculiarities of the Elohistic phraseology "are greatly magnified, if they exist at all," is a surprising one. In point of fact, the style of P (even in the historical sections) stands apart, not only from that of J, E, and Dt., but also from that which prevails in any part of Jud. Sam. Kings, and has substantial resemblances only with that of Ezekiel.

It remains to consider the date of P. Formerly this was assumed tacitly to be the earliest of the Pentateuchal sources ; and there are still scholars who assign at least the main stock of it to 9–8 cent. B.C. No doubt the fact that in virtue of its systematic plan and consistent regard to chronology, it constitutes, as it were, the groundwork (see p. 10) of the history, into which the narratives taken from the other sources are fitted, gave to this view a *prima facie* plausibility. No *à priori* reason, however, exists why these narratives should not have been drawn up first, and their chronological framework have been added to them afterwards ; and a comparative study of the intrinsic character of P in its relation to these other sources has led the principal critics of more recent years to adopt a different view of its origin

* In Dt., on the contrary, אנכי is regularly employed, except (1) 12³⁰ *after* the verb, according to usual custom (*Journ. of Phil.* 1882, p. 223) ; (2) 29⁶ [Heb. ⁵] in a stereotyped formula (Ex. 7¹⁷ *al.*) ; (3) in the *Song*, 32²¹· ³⁹ (4 times) ; (4) in the passage assigned to P, 32⁴⁹· ⁵²—9 times in all.

† See further Budde, *ZATW.* 1891, p. 203 ff. ; Holzinger, p. 338 ff. ; and the instructive comparative table of the usage of E, J, D, P, H, in Strack's *Einleitung*⁴ (1895), pp. 42 51.

and date.   The earlier criticism of the Pent. was mostly literary ; and literary criteria, though they enable us to effect the analysis of a document into its component parts, do not always afford decisive evidence as to the date to which the component parts are severally to be assigned.   A comparison of P, both in its historical and legal sections, (*a*) with the other Hexateuchal [**129**] sources, (*b*) with other parts of the OT., brings to light facts which seem to show that, though the elements which it embodies originated themselves, in many cases, at a much earlier age, it is itself the latest of the sources of which the Hexateuch is composed, and belongs approximately to the period of the Babylonian captivity.

The following, stated briefly, are the principal grounds upon which this opinion rests.

The pre-exilic period shows no indications of the legislation of P as being in operation.   Thus the place of sacrifice is in P strictly limited ; and severe penalties are imposed upon any except priests who presume to officiate at the altar.   In Jud. Sam. sacrifice is frequently offered at spots not consecrated by the presence of the Ark, and laymen are repeatedly represented as officiating,—in both cases without any hint of disapproval on the part of the narrator, and without any apparent sense, even on the part of men like Samuel and David, that an irregularity was being committed.   Further, the incidental allusions in books belonging to the same time create the impression that the ritual in use was simpler than that enjoined in P : in P, for instance, elaborate provisions are laid down for the maintenance and safety of the Tabernacle, and for the reverent handling of the Ark and other sacred vessels ; in 1 Sam. the arrangements relating to both are evidently much simpler : the establishment at Shiloh (1 Sa. 1–3) is clearly not upon the scale implied by the regulations Ex. 35–40, Nu. 3–4 : the Ark is sent for and taken into battle, as a matter calling for no comment ; when it is brought back to Kirjath-jearim, instead of the persons authorized by P being summoned to take charge of it, it is placed in the house of a native of the place, whose son is consecrated by the men of Kirjath-jearim themselves for the purpose of guarding it.   In 2 Sa. 6 the narrative of the solemn transference of the Ark by David to Zion, the priests and Levites, the proper guardians of it according to P (Nu. 3^{31} 4$^{1-15}$), are both conspicuous by their absence; David offers sacrifice (as seems evident) with his own hand, and certainly performs the solemn priestly (Dt. 10^8 21^5; cf. Nu. $6^{23\text{-}27}$) function of blessing (2 Sa. $6^{13.\ 17.\ 18}$; cf. 1 Ki. 8^{55} 9^{25} of Solomon). That many of the distinctive institutions of P are not alluded to—the Day of Atonement, the Jubile year, the Levitical cities, the Sin-offering, the system of sacrifices [130] prescribed for particular days—is of less importance: the writers of these books may have found no occasion to mention them. But the different *tone of feeling*, and the different *spirit* which animates the narratives of the historical books, cannot be disguised: both the actors and the narrators in Jud. Sam. move in an atmosphere into which the spirit of P has not penetrated. Nor do the allusions in the pre-exilic prophets supply the deficiency, or imply that the theocratic system of P was in operation. The prophets attack formalism and unspiritual service; they therefore show that in their day *some* importance was attached by the priests, and by the people who were guided by them, to ritual observances; but to the institutions specially characteristic of P they allude no more distinctly than do the contemporary historians.

Nor is the legislation of P presupposed by *Deuteronomy*. This indeed follows almost directly from the contents and character of Dt. as described above (pp. 75 f., 82–84). As was there shown, Dt., in both its historical and legal sections, is based consistently upon JE: language, moreover, is used, not once only, but repeatedly, implying that some of the fundamental institutions of P are not in operation. Had a code, as extensive as P is, been in force when Dt. was written, it is difficult not to think that allusions to it would have been both abundant and distinct, and that, in fact, it would have determined the attitude and point of view adopted by the writer in a manner which certainly is not the case.

And when P is compared with Dt. in detail, the differences tend to show that it is *later* than Dt.

Thus (*a*) in Dt. the centralization of worship at one sanctuary is *enjoined*, it is insisted on with much emphasis as an end aimed at, but not yet realized: in P it is *presupposed* as already existing. (*b*) In Dt. any member of the tribe of Levi possesses the right to exercise priestly functions, contingent only upon his residence at the Central Sanctuary: in P this right is strictly limited to the descendants of Aaron. (*c*) In Dt. the members of the tribe of Levi are commended to the charity of the Israelites generally, and only share the tithe, at a sacrificial feast, in company with other indigent persons: in P definite provision is made for their maintenance (the 48 cities, with their "suburbs"), and the tithes are formally assigned to the tribe as a specific due; similarly, while in Dt. firstlings are to be consumed at sacrificial feasts, in which the Levite is only to have his share among others, in P they are reserved solely and explicitly for the priests. In each case the stricter limitation is on the side of P. (*d*) The entire system of feasts and sacrifices [**131**] is much more complex and precisely defined in P than in Dt. True, the plan of Dt. would not naturally include an enumeration of minute details; but the silence of Dt. is nevertheless significant; and the *impression* which a reader derives from Dt. is that the liturgical institutions under which the author lived were of a simpler character than those prescribed in P.

It is possible, indeed, that, considered in themselves, some of the cases quoted might be regarded as relaxations, sanctioned by D, of observances that were originally stricter. But this view lacks support in fact. The ritual legislation of JE, which, it is not disputed, is earlier than D, is in every respect simpler than that of D; and a presumption hence arises, that that of D is similarly earlier than the more complex legislation of P. This presumption is supported by the evidence of the history. The legislation of JE is in harmony with, and, in fact, sanctions, the practice of the period of the Judges and early Kings, with its relative freedom, for instance, as to the place of sacrifice (p. 85) and the persons authorized to offer it;* during which, moreover, a simple ritual appears to have prevailed, and the Ark was guarded, till it was transferred by Solomon to the Temple, by a small band of attendants, in a modest structure, quite in accordance with the representation of JE (p. 128, *note*). The legislation of D harmonizes with the reforming tendencies of the age in which it was promulgated, and sanctions the practice of the age that immediately followed: it inculcates a centralized worship, in agreement with a movement arising naturally out of the existence of the Temple at Jerusalem, strengthened, no doubt, by the fall of the Northern kingdom, and enforced practically by Josiah; its attitude towards the high places determines that of the compiler of Kings, who wrote in the closing years of the monarchy; it contains regulations touching other matters (*e.g.* the worship of the "host of heaven") which assumed prominence at the same time; the revenues and functions of the priests are more closely defined than in JE, but the priesthood is still open

* Ex. 20²⁴⁻²⁶, it seems clear, is addressed to the *lay* Israelite (cf. 24⁵).

to every member of the tribe of Levi. The legislation of P is
in harmony with the spirit which shows itself in Ezekiel, and
sanctions the practice of the period beginning with the return
from Babylon; and the principles to which P gives expression
appear (at a later date), in a still more developed form, as forming the standard by which the Chronicler consistently judges the
[132] earlier history. The position into which the legislation of P
appears to fall is thus *intermediate between Dt. and the Chronicler*.

But further, P appears, at least in some of its elements, to
be later than *Ezekiel*. The arguments are supplied chiefly by
c. 40–48, where Ez. prescribes the constitution of the restored
community, and in particular regulates with some minuteness
the details of the Temple worship. The most important passage
is 44⁶⁻¹⁶. Here the Israelites are rebuked for having admitted
foreigners, uncircumcised aliens, into the inner Court of the
Temple to assist the priest when officiating at the altar (v.⁶⁻⁸);
and it is laid down that no such foreigners are to perform these
services for the future (v.⁹)—

" ¹⁰ But the Levites that went far from me, when Israel went astray, which
went astray from me after their idols ; they shall bear their iniquity.   ¹¹ And
they shall be ministers in my sanctuary, having oversight at the gates of the
house, and ministering in the house ; they shall slay the burnt-offering and
the sacrifice for the people, and they shall stand before them [see p. 83, *note*]
to minister unto them . . .   ¹³ And they shall not come near unto me, to
execute the office of priest unto me, nor to come near to any of my holy things,
unto the things that are most holy : but they shall bear their shame, and their
abominations which they have committed.   ¹⁴ Yet will I make them keepers
of the charge of the house, for all the service thereof, and for all that shall
be done therein.   ¹⁵ But the priests the Levites, the sons of Zadok, that kept
the charge of my sanctuary when the children of Israel went astray from me,
they shall come near to me to minister unto me ; and they shall stand before
me [see *ib.*] to offer unto me the fat and the blood, saith the Lord Jehovah :
¹⁶ they shall enter into my sanctuary, and they shall come near to my table,
to minister unto me, and they shall keep my charge " (v.¹⁰⁻¹⁶: cf. 48¹¹).

From this passage it seems to follow incontrovertibly that the
Levites generally had heretofore (in direct conflict with the provisions of P) *enjoyed priestly rights* (v.¹³): for the future, however, such as had participated in the idolatrous worship of the
high places are to be deprived of these rights, and condemned
to perform the menial offices which had hitherto been performed
by foreigners (v.¹⁰ᶠ· ¹⁴) ; only those Levites who had been faithful
in their loyalty to Jehovah, viz. the sons of Zadok, are hence-

forth to retain priestly privileges (v.[15f.]). Had the Levites not enjoyed such rights, the prohibition in v.[13] would be superfluous. The supposition that they may have merely *usurped* them is inconsistent with the passage as a whole, which charges the Levites, not with *usurping* rights which they did not possess, but with *abusing* rights which they did possess. If Ez., then, [133] treats the Levites generally as qualified to act as priests, and degrades them to a menial rank, without so much as a hint that this degradation was but the restoration of a *status quo* fixed by immemorial Mosaic custom, could he have been acquainted with the legislation of P?*

This is the most noteworthy difference between Ez. and P. There are, however, other points in which Ez.'s regulations deviate from P's in a manner that is difficult to explain, had the legislation of P, in its entirety, been recognized by him. In particular, while more complex than those of Dt., the provisions of Ez. are frequently simpler than those of P; so that the inference that the system of P is a development of that of Ez., as Ez.'s is of that of D, naturally suggests itself. Comp. in particular Ez. 43[18-27] 45[18-20] (RV. *marg.*) 21-24. 25 46[13-15. 4-7] with Ex. 29[1-37], Lev. 16, Nu. 28–29. If the rites prescribed in these passages of P had been in operation, and were invested with the authority of antiquity, it seems improbable that Ez. would have deviated fròm them as largely as he has done. It is true that, as a prophet, his attitude towards the sacrificial system may have been a free one; and hence this argument, taken by itself, would not perhaps be a decisive one: still, when it is seen to be in harmony with other facts pointing in the same direction, it is not to be lightly ignored, the more so, as Ez. plainly attached a value to ceremonial observances, and is thus the less likely to have introduced a simplification of established ritual.

The later date for P, suggested by a comparison of it with JE, D, and Ez., is confirmed, as it seems, by the character of the religious conceptions which it presents. No doubt all representations of the Deity must be anthropomorphic; but contrast the anthropomorphism of Gen. 2[4bff.] with that of 1[1]–2[4a]: in the former, Jehovah is brought into close connexion with earth, and *sensible* acts are attributed to Him (above, p. 121): in the latter, His transcendence above nature is conspicuous throughout: He

---

* The suggestion made by Delitzsch (*Studien*, vi. p. 288) does not really mitigate the difficulty; for the terms of v.[10] do not admit of being *restricted* to the descendants of Aaron's other son Ithamar. Cf. König, *Offenbarungsbegriff des AT.s*, ii. p. 325; Kautzsch, *Stud. u. Krit.* 1890, p. 767 ff.; and Kuenen, *Gesammelte Abhandlungen* (1894), p. 472 ff. Paton's argument (*JBLit.* 1893, p. 10) is not conclusive (the root-meaning of כהן, as given *ib.* p. 3, is highly questionable: Arab. *kāhin* means a *seer*.

conducts His work of creation from a distance; there are no anthropomorphisms which might be misunderstood in a material sense.   Contrast, again, the genealogies in JE (Gen. 4) with those in P (Gen. 5), does not JE display them in their fresher, more original form, while in P they have been reduced to bare lists of names, devoid of all imaginative colouring?   In JE the growth of sin in the line of Cain leads up suitably to the narrative of the Flood; in P no explanation is given of the [134] corruption overspreading the earth, and rendering necessary the destruction of its inhabitants.   In JE the patriarchs are men of flesh and blood; the incidents of their history arise naturally out of their antecedents, and the character of the circumstances in which they are placed.   Moreover, in the topics dwelt upon, such as the rivalries of Jacob and Esau, and of Laban and Jacob, or the connexion of the patriarchs with places famed in later days as sanctuaries, the interests of the narrator's own age are reflected: in P we have a skeleton from which such touches of life and nature are absent, an outline in which legislative (Gen. 17), statistical, chronological elements are the sole conspicuous feature.*   There is also a tendency to treat the history theoretically (p. 128), which is itself the mark of a later age. The representations of the patriarchal age seem, moreover, not to be so primitive as in JE: the patriarchs, for instance, are never represented as building altars or sacrificing; and Noah receives permission to slaughter animals for food without any reference to sacrifice, notwithstanding the intimate connexion subsisting in early times between slaughtering and sacrifice.†

Dillm. and Kittel seek to explain the contradiction, or silence, of Dt. &c. by the hypothesis that P was originally a " private document," representing, not the actual practice of the priests, but *claims* raised by them,—an ideal theocratic constitution, which they had for the time no means of enforcing,

---

* In the earlier historical narratives precise chronological data are scarce; in Jud. Sam. Kings they are admitted to belong to the latest element in the books, viz. the post-Deuteronomic redaction.

† The subject of pp. 136–141 is treated at length by Wellhausen, *Hist. of Israel*, chaps. i.–v., viii. (or, more succinctly, in his art. " Pentateuch " in the *Encycl. Britannica*, ed. 9), where, in spite of some questionable assumptions, and exaggerations in detail, many true points are undoubtedly seized. See also W. R. Smith, *OTJC*.[2] Lect. xii. xiii. ; and König, *op. cit.* ii. pp. 321–332, where some of the principal grounds for the opinion expressed in the text are concisely and forcibly stated.

and which consequently might well have either remained unknown to prophetic writers, or not been recognized by them as authoritative. " It is a literary peculiarity of P to represent his ideal as already existing in the Mosaic age ; hence from his representation of an institution it cannot be argued that it actually existed, but only that it was an object of his aims and claims " (Kittel, pp. 91–93 ; Dillm. *NDJ.* pp. 666, 667, 669 ; similarly Baudissin, *Priesterthum*, p. 280). But such a conception of P is highly artificial ; and there is an antecedent improbability in the supposition that a system like that of P would be propounded when (as is admitted) there was [135] no hope of its realization, and in an age which shows no acquaintance with it,—for Dillm. places it *c.* 800, between E and J,—and whose most representative men evince very different religious sympathies.

As regards the distinction between priests and Levites, it is observed by Kittel that there are parts of P in which this is not treated as *established.* Thus in the main narrative of P in Nu. 16–17 (p. 64) there is no sign of opposition between priests and Levites ; the tribe is regarded as one ; and the standpoint is thus that of Dt. : while in the insertions 16⁷ᵇ⁻¹¹. ¹⁶⁻¹⁷. ³⁶⁻⁴⁰ (*ib.*) the distinction, so far from being universally accepted, appears as a matter of dispute. (Similarly Baudissin, pp. 34 f., 276 f.) He further argues that there are grounds for supposing that many passages of P (esp. Lev. 1–7. 11–15 ; parts of Nu. 5–6 ; and H) where now " Aaron " or " Aaron and his sons " (implying the clearly-felt distinction of priests and Levites) stands, originally there stood " the priest " alone (as is actually still the case in most of c. 13). The recognition of the distinction in other strata of P he reconciles with their earlier date by the same supposition as Dillm., viz. that it was not really in force when they were written, but assumed by the author to be so, " in order to set vividly before his contemporaries the ideal which he sought to see realized " (p. 109).

These arguments are cogent, and combine to make it probable that the *completed* Priests' Code is the work of the age subsequent to Ezekiel. When, however, this is said, it is very far from being implied that all the institutions of P are the *creation* of this age. The contradiction of the pre-exilic literature does not extend to the *whole* of the Priests' Code indiscriminately. The Priests' Code embodies some elements with which the earlier literature is in harmony, and which indeed it presupposes : it embodies other elements with which the same literature is in conflict, and the existence of which it even seems to preclude. This double aspect of the Priests' Code is reconciled by the supposition that the chief ceremonial institutions of Israel are *in their origin* of great antiquity; but that the laws respecting them were gradually developed and elaborated, and *in the shape in which they are formulated in the Priests' Code* that they belong to the exilic or early post-exilic period. In its main stock, the legislation of P was thus not (as the critical view of it is sometimes represented by its opponents as teaching) "manufactured" by the priests during the Exile : it is based upon *pre-existing Temple usage*, and exhibits the form which that finally assumed.* Hebrew legislation took shape gradually; and the codes of [**136**] JE (Ex. 20–23; 34[10-26]), Dt., and P represent three successive phases of it.

From this point of view, the allusions to priestly usage in the pre-exilic literature may be consistently explained. They attest the existence of certain institutions : they do not attest the existence of the particular document (P) in which the regulations touching those institutions are now codified. Thus Gen. 8[21] (J) uses the term "savour of satisfaction" (Lev. 1[9] and often in P); Jud. 13[4. 7] alludes to "unclean" food; Jud. 13[5. 7] 16[17], Am. 2[11f.] to Nazirites (cf. Nu. 6[2ff.]); 1 Sa. 2[28] speaks of "fire-sacrifices" (Lev. 1[9] &c.); 3[3] of the "lamp of God" (Ex. 27[20]); 6[3ff.] names a "guilt-offering"; 21[6] the shewbread (Lev. 24[8f.]); Amos (4[4. 5]) mentions tithes and free-will offerings.† These passages are proof that the institutions in question are ancient in Israel, but not that they were observed *with the precise formalities prescribed in P*; indeed, the manner in which they are referred to appears not unfrequently to imply that they were much simpler and less systematically organized than is the case in P.

Other allusions to priestly usage or terminology may be found in Am. 4[5] (Lev. 2[11] 7[12]); Is. 1[13] (מקרא a "convocation," Lev. 23[2. 3] &c.); Jer. 2[9] (Lev. 22[10. 16]); 6[28] 9[3] (הלך רכיל Lev. 19[16]); 30[21] (נגש Lev. 21[21. 23]; הקריב Nu. 16[5b. 9. 10]); 34[8. 15. 17] (קרא דרור to "proclaim liberty," Lev. 25[10], but in Jer. of the liberty granted to slaves in the seventh year of service, in Lev. of the year of Jubile) ; perhaps also in Am. 2[7] (p. 50, No. 13), though this expression is of a kind which might have been used independently.

Whether, however, Jud. 20–21, 1 Sa. 2[22b] (see Ex. 38[8]), 1 Ki. 8[1. 5] are evidence of the early existence of the conceptions of P is doubtful. Jud. 20–21 shows in parts the phraseology of P,‡ but (as will appear when these

---

* Even a critic as radical as Stade refers to Lev. 1–7. 11–15. Nu. 5. 6. 9. 15. 19, as well as the Law of Holiness, as embodying for the most part pre-exilic usage (*Gesch.* ii. 66) : comp. Wellh. *Hist.* pp. 366, 404.

† There are other similar allusions. *e.g.* to Burnt- and Peace-offerings, 1 Sa. 6[14] 10[8] &c. ; the Urim and Thummim, and the Ephod, Dt. 33[8], 1 Sa. 14[3. 41] LXX (see *QPB*[3]) 28[6] &c.

‡ 20[1] 21[16. 13. 16] the "congregation" [see p. 133, No. 32] ; with the verb ותקהל 20[1] cf. Lev. 8[4], Nu. 16[42] [Heb. 17[7]] 20[2], Josh. 18[1] 22[12]; 20[6] כי עשו זמה

chapters come to be considered) there are independent grounds for concluding that this narrative is composite, and that the parts in which this phraseology appears are of later origin than the rest. In 1 Sa. 2²²ᵇ it is remarkable (a) that the LXX omits this half-verse ; (b) that it disagrees with the rest of the narrative, representing the sanctuary as a *tent*, rather than as [**137**] a "temple" with doors and door-posts (1⁹ 3³· ¹⁵). Thus *two* grounds, neither connected with its relation to P, converge in favour of the conclusion that this passage is an insertion in the original narrative, of uncertain date. In 1 Ki. 8¹· ⁵ * the terms agreeing with the usage of P are isolated in Kings, and *omitted in the LXX* (comp. below, p.191 *n.*).

It is admitted by Dillm. (p. 667) that the passages alleged to show the *literary* use of P in pre-exilic times are insufficient : either the resemblance is too slight to establish the use of P, or the origin of the passages adduced is doubtful.

Thus Hos. 12⁴ᵇ [Heb.⁵ᵇ] is not evidence of the use of Gen. 35⁹⁻¹³· ¹⁵ ; the terms of the reference are satisfied by the narrative of J, of which an extract is still preserved in Gen. 35¹⁴,—a view which is the more probable, as Hos. 12³⁻⁴ᵃ· ¹²ᵇ [Heb.⁴⁻⁵ᵃ· ¹³ᵇ] is admitted to be based upon JE, see Gen. 25²⁶ 32²⁸ [Heb.²⁹] 27⁴³ [in 27⁴⁶⁻28⁹ P Jacob does not *take flight*] 29²⁰· ³⁰: Hos. 12¹²ᵃ [Heb.¹³ᵃ] the "field" of Aram is supposed to be a variation of "*Paddan*-Aram," which is peculiar to P (see p. 135, No. 48); but there is no substantial ground for this hypothesis, and the fact just mentioned that in P Jacob does not *flee* from Esau is against it: Am. 7⁴ and Gen. 7¹¹ the "great deep," Jer. 4²³ and Gen. 1² תהו ובהו (cf. Is. 34¹¹), Jer. 23³ and Gen. 1²² &c. "be fruitful and multiply," may have been phrases in current use, but not necessarily derived from the passages of P. (A few other similar instances exist.)

In Dt. the following parallels may be noted :—

5¹⁵, Ex. 31¹⁶ (עשה, lit. *make*, of *holding* the Sabbath↑).—12²³ᵃ, Lev. 17¹¹· ¹⁴. —14⁴⁻²⁰, Lev. 11²ᵇ⁻²³ (permitted and forbidden animals).—16⁸ᵇ, Ex. 12¹⁶ᵇ.— 17¹ (cf. 15²¹), Lev. 22¹⁷⁻²⁴ (animals offered in sacrifice to be without blemish). —18¹ᵇ ("fire-sacrifices," as 1 Sa. 2²⁸).—19⁸ᵇ (לנוס שמה כל רצח), Nu. 35⁶· ¹¹.— 19¹² (the "avenger of blood"), Nu. 35¹⁹· ²¹.—20⁶ 28³⁰ ("use the fruit thereof," lit. *profane it* : cf. Lev. 19²³⁻²⁵).—22⁹ᵃ, Lev. 19¹⁹ᵃ.—22⁹ᵇ RV. *marg.* (the same priestly penalty which is found Lev. 6¹⁸ᵇ [Heb.¹¹ᵇ], Ex. 29³⁷ᵇ 30²⁹ᵇ).—22¹¹, Lev. 19¹⁹ᵇ (שעטנו).—23²³ [Heb.²⁴], Nu. 30¹³ (מוצא שפתיך ; also Jer. 17¹⁶, Ps. 89³⁵, but not specially of a *vow*).—24⁸, Lev. 13-14.—25¹⁶, Lev. 19³⁵ (עשה עול ; unusual).

_____

[p. 49, No. 11] ; 20¹⁵· ¹⁷ 21⁹↑ התפקרו (see Nu. 1⁴⁷ 2³³ 26⁶² הָתִפקרו ; also 1 Ki. 20²⁷↑) ; 21¹¹ "every male," as often in P, see (in a similar context) Gen. 34²⁵, Nu. 31⁷· ¹⁷ ; *ib.* ידעת משכב זכר ¹², אשר לא ידעה איש למשכב זכר (Nu. 31¹⁷· ¹⁸· ³⁵).

* "All the *congregation* of Israel," "*gathered together*" (נועדים Nu. 10³· ⁴ 14³⁵ 16¹¹ 27³), "*heads* of the *tribes*" [Nu. 30² ; cf. 32²⁸ Josh. 14¹ 19⁵¹], "the *princes* of the *fathers*" [pp. 134, 133, Nos. 38, 30].

There are also allusions to Burnt- and Peace-offerings, tithes (but with regulations very different from those of P), "heave"-offerings, vows, free-will-
offerings (12[6. 11. 17] *al.*), the sanctity of firstlings (*ib.*) and of firstfruits (18[4]
26[2. 10]), the distinction of clean and unclean (12[15] 21[23] *al.*), the prohibition to
eat blood (12[16. 23]), and the flesh of animals dying of themselves (14[21]).

Of these the most important is 14[4-20]. Here is a long passage
in great measure verbally identical in Dt. and Lev., and a critical
comparison of the two texts makes it probable (p. 46) that both
are divergent recensions of a common original, which in each
case, but especially in Lev., has been modified in accordance
with the spirit of the book in which it was incorporated. It is
thus apparent that at least one collection of priestly *Tôrôth*,
which now forms part of P, [138] was in existence when Dt.
was written; and a presumption at once arises that other parts
were in existence also. Now, the tenor of Dt. as a whole conflicts with the supposition that *all* the institutions of the Priests'
Code were in force when D wrote; but the list of passages
just quoted shows that *some* were, and that the terminology used
in connexion with them was known to D. Dt. thus corrobor-
ates the conclusions drawn from the prophetical and historical
books. Institutions or usages, such as the distinction of clean
and unclean, the prohibition to eat with the blood, sacrifices to
be without blemish, regulations determining the treatment of
leprosy, vows, the avenger of blood, etc., were ancient in Israel,
and as such are alluded to in the earlier literature, though the
allusions do not show that the laws respecting them had yet
been codified precisely as they now appear in P.

The following historical passages of Dt. also deserve notice, and will be
referred to again :—16[3], Ex. 12[11] (חִפָּזוֹן "haste"; only besides Is. 52[12]).—26[6],
Ex. 1[14] 6[9] ("hard bondage"; also 1 Ki. 12[4], Is. 14[3]).—26[8], Ex. 6[6] ("out-
stretched arm").—27[9] 29[13] [Heb. 12], Ex. 6[7] (Israel to become a people to Jehovah
[expressed, however, by different verbs]); cf. Lev. 26[12] ("to be to you a
God" occurs elsewhere in P, but not "to be to me a people"; cf. the writer's
Deut. p. 293).

The same phenomena are repeated in Ezekiel. However
doubtful it may be whether Ezekiel presupposes the *completed*
Priests' Code, it is difficult not to conclude that he presupposes
parts of it. In particular, his book appears to contain clear
evidence that he was acquainted with the "Law of Holiness."
Thus, when in c. 4 he resents the command to eat food prepared
in such a manner as to be unclean; when in c. 18[20. 22] he lays

down the principles of a righteous life, or reproaches the nation or Jerusalem with its sin; when in c. 44 he prescribes laws regulating the life of the priests in the restored community,—in each instance he expresses himself in terms agreeing with the Law of Holiness in such a manner as only to be reasonably explained by the supposition that it formed a body of precepts with which he was familiar, and which he regarded as an [139] authoritative basis of moral and religious life. Let the following passages be compared :*—

4[14a], Lev. 11[44b].—4[14b], Lev. 22[8].—6[9], cf. Nu. 15[39] ("heart and eyes," "go a whoring").—14[4. 7a], Lev. 17[3. 8. 10] (see p. 49, No. 4).—14[8] (see *ib.* Nos. 5, 6 [with מקרב, which Ez. does not use in this sense, *altered* to [מתוך]).—18[6b. 11. 15], Lev. 18[20. 19].—18[7a. 12a. 16a. 18a], Lev. 19[33] 25[14b. 17a].—*ib.* Lev. 19[13] ("spoil by violence").—18[8a. 13a], Lev. 25[37].—18[8b. 24. 26], Lev. 19[15. 35] (עול *iniquity*: cf. Ez. 3[20] 28[18] 33[13. 15. 18]: rare elsewhere).—18[9a. 17], Lev. 18[3] 26[3].—18[13b] 33[5], Lev. 20[9. 11. 12. 13. 16. 27]↑ (the concise phrase of Lev. *amplified* in Ez. by the addition of יהיה).—18[19b], Lev. 18[4] 19[37] *al.*—20[5] ("lifted up my hand" [also v.[6. 15. 23. 28. 42] 36[7] 47[14], Nu. 14[30] (P)], "made myself known," "I am Jehovah"), Ex. 6[8. 3. 6].—20[7], cf. Lev. 18[3].—20[11. 13. 21], Lev. 18[5] ("which if a man do, he shall live in them").—20[12. 20], Ex. 31[13] (nearly the whole verse).—20[28a. 42b], Ex. 6[8].—20[38], Ex. 6[4] *al.* (p. 133, No. 21)[7].—22[7a], Lev. 20[9].—22[5] ("profaned," "my sabbaths," p. 50, Nos. 13, 14).—22[9a], Lev. 19[16].—22[9 end] (זמה; *ib.* No. 11).—22[10], cf. Lev. 18[7. 19].—22[11], Lev. 20[10. 12. 17].—22[12], Lev. 25[37].—22[26], Lev. 22[15a] 10[10].—24[7b], Lev. 17[13].—33[25], Lev. 19[26].—44[7] ("my bread," see p. 50, No. 18).—44[20], cf. Lev. 21[10] (long locks forbidden, but to the *chief* priest only).—44[21a], Lev. 10[9].—44[22], cf. Lev. 21[14] (of the *chief* priest).—44[23], Lev. 10[10].—44[25a], Lev. 21[1].—44[25b], Lev. 21[2b-3] (abridged in Ez.). —44[28a], Nu. 18[20] ("I am their inheritance").—44[29b], Nu. 18[14].—44[30b], Nu. 15[21].—44[31], Lev. 22[8].—45[10] Lev. 19[36].†

The following are technical expressions, borrowed (as seems clear) from priestly terminology, but not sufficient to prove Ez.'s acquaintance with the codified laws in the form in which we now have them : 4[14b] פגול "abomination" [or "refuse meat," used technically of stale sacrificial flesh ‡] (Lev. 7[18] 19[7], Is. 65[4]↑).—8[10] שקץ "detestation" [used technically of forbidden animals ‡] (Lev. 7[21] 11[10-13. 20f. 23. 41f.], Is. 66[17]↑).—14[7] "separateth himself" (Lev. 22[2]).—14[10] 44[10. 12b] "bear their iniquity" (p. 50, No. 20[a]).—14[13a], Lev. 5[15] (form of sentence ; and מעל מעל, p. 134, No. 43).—16[40] 23[47] רגם for *to stone*

---

* The passages, both here and in other similar instances, would have been transcribed in full, had not the exigencies of space forbidden it.

† But expressions such as 1[9] (cf. Ex. 26[8]) 1[27b] (cf. Nu. 9[15]) 1[28a] (Gen. 9[14]) 8[17] (Gen. 6[11]) 10[2] (Lev. 16[12]) 24[17] (Lev. 13[45]: see Mic. 3[7]) 24[23] (Ex. 12[11]), &c. appear to *arise out of the narrative in which they occur*, and are not necessarily reminiscences of the passages cited.

‡ Comp. Clark's *Bible Dictionary*, *s.v.* ABOMINATION.

(p. 134, No. 45).—21^{23} [Heb. ^{28}] 29^{16} "bringeth iniquity to remembrance" (Nu. 5^{15}).—36^{25}, cf. Nu. 19^{13}.—40$^{45.\ 46}$ 44^{14} "keep the charge of" (Nu. 18$^{4.\ 5}$).—46^{7} "as his hand shall attain unto" (Lev. 5^{11} 14$^{21f.\ 30\text{-}32}$ 25$^{26.\ 47.\ 49}$ 27^{8}, Nu. 6^{21}).—47^{9a}, Gen. 1^{21}, Lev. 11^{46}; and Nos. 2, 12, 14, 25c, 28, and perhaps 6, 22, 34, in the list, p. 131 ff.

[140] The parallels with Lev. 26$^{3ff.}$ are peculiarly numerous and striking, including several expressions not occurring elsewhere in the Old Testament :—

Ez. 4^{16} 5^{16} 14^{13} ("break the staff of bread") : Lev. 26^{26}.

4^{16} ("bread by weight") : ib.

4^{17} 24^{23}, cf. 33^{10} ("pine away in their iniquities") : v.^{39}.

5$^{2.\ 12}$ 12^{14} ("scatter," "draw out a sword after them") : v.^{33}.

5^{6} 20^{16} ("rejected my judgments") : v.^{43}.

5$^{6.\ 7}$ $al.$ [see p. 49, No. 7] ("walk in my statutes") : v.^{3}.

5^{8} 20$^{9.\ 14.\ 22.\ 41}$ 22^{16} 28^{25}, cf. 38^{23} 39^{27} ("before the eyes of the nations" ; 20$^{14.\ 22}$ "brought out") : v.^{45}.

5^{17} 14^{15} ("send upon you . . . beasts . . . and they will bereave thee") : v.^{22}.

5^{17} 6^{3} 11^{8} 14^{17} 29^{8} ("and I will bring a sword upon you") : v.^{25}. (Not a phrase used by other prophets.)

6$^{4.\ 6}$ ("your sun-pillars") : v.^{30}.

6^{5} ("lay the carcases . . . before their idol-blocks [גלולים]") : v.^{30}.

11^{20a} ("walk in my statutes, and keep my ordinances, and do them") : v.^{3}.

13^{10} 36^{3} (יען וביען "*because and by the cause that*" . . . a peculiar phrase, not found elsewhere) : v.^{43}.

16$^{60.\ 62a}$ ("remember," "establish my covenant") : v.$^{42.\ 45.\ 9b}$.

24^{21} 30$^{6.\ 18}$ 33^{28}, cf. 7^{24} ("pride of your power") : v.^{19}.

34^{25} ("and I will cause evil beasts to cease out of the land") : v.^{6}.

34^{26} ("the heavy rain . . . in its season") : v.^{4}.

34^{27a} ("and the tree of the field shall yield its fruit, and the earth shall yield her increase") : $ib.$ cf. v.^{20b}.

34^{27b} ("when I shall have broken the bars of their yoke") : v.^{13}.

34^{28b} 39^{26b} ("they shall dwell securely, none making them afraid") : v.$^{5b\text{-}6a}$.

36$^{9\text{-}10a}$ ("and I will turn unto you, and multiply, &c.) : v.^{9}.

37^{26b} ("and I will set my sanctuary in the midst of them") : v.^{11}.

37^{27} ("they shall be to me a people, and I will be to them a God"), and in inverted order, v.^{33} 11^{20} 14^{11} 36^{28} : v.^{12} (cf. Ex. 6^{7}).

39^{27} ("their enemies' lands") : v.$^{36.\ 39}$, cf. v.$^{34.\ 41.\ 44}$.

Cf. 5$^{7.\ 8}$ 11^{12} ("nations that are round about you") : 25^{44}.

These phraseological resemblances between Ez. and H (the number of which is not exhausted by this list*) are, in truth,

* See Baentsch, *Das Heiligkeits-Gesetz*, p. 121 ff.; or the excellent article of L. B. Paton, *Presbyterian and Reformed Review*, Jan. 1896, p. 98 ff.

evidence of a wider and more general fact, viz. the fundamental identity of interest and point of view which shows itself in Ez. and the "Law of Holiness." Both breathe the same spirit; both are actuated largely by the same principles, and aim at realizing the same ends. Thus both evince a special regard for the "sanctuary" (Lev. 19³⁰ 20³ 21¹². ²³ 26², Ez. 5¹¹ 8⁶ 23³⁸ᶠ. [141] 25³ 43⁷ᶠᶠ.), and prescribe rules to guard it against profanation; both allude similarly to Israel's idolatry in *Egypt* (Lev. 18³, Ez. 20⁷ᶠᶠ.), and to the "abominations" of which Israel has since been guilty; both emphasize the duty of observing the Sabbath; both attach a high value to ceremonial cleanness, especially on the part of the priests; both lay stress on abstaining from blood, and from food improperly killed (נבלה וטרפה); and both further insist on the same moral virtues, as reverence to parents, just judgment, commercial honesty, and denounce usury and slander (Ez. 18⁶ᶠᶠ. 22⁷ᶠᶠ., with the parallels).*

The similarities between Ez. and the Law of Holiness, especially Lev. 26³ᶠᶠ., are so great that it has been held by some critics that the prophet himself was the author, or, at least (Horst), the redactor of this collection of laws.† But there are *differences*, as well as resemblances, between Ez. and H, of which this hypothesis gives no sufficient explanation; and from the time when it was first propounded there have always been critics who opposed it.‡ Nöldeke pointed to stylistic differences;§ Klostermann, comparing in greater detail Ez. and H, showed further that the prophet seemed everywhere to be expanding or emphasizing a simpler original;‖ Wellh. and Kuenen appealed to material differences as likewise precluding the authorship of Ez. It is thus agreed by the best critics that Ez. is not the

---

* Comp. Smend, *Ezechiel*, p. xxv f.

† Graf, *Gesch. B.* pp. 81–83 ; Colenso ; Kayser ; Horst, pp. 69–96.

‡ Nöldeke, *Untersuchungen*, p. 67 ff. ; Wellh. *Hist.* 376–384 ; Klostermann, *Der Pent.* p. 368 ff.; Smend, *Ezechiel*, pp. xxvii, 314 f.; Delitzsch, *Studien*, p. 617 ff.; Kuenen, *Hex.* § 15. 10.

§ Thus in H we never find Ez.'s standing title "Lord Jehovah": in Ez. we never find עמית, and only once עמיו (p. 49, No. 11 ; p. 133, No. 25).

‖ Ez. never uses the phrase "I am Jehovah" alone : he always says, "And ye (thou, they) shall know that I am J.," sometimes adding besides a further clause introduced by "when . . ." ; or he attaches some epithet, or predicate, "I am Jehovah your God," or "I Jehovah have spoken." See further Paton, pp. 102–106.

author, or even the compiler, of the Law of Holiness.   It may further be taken as granted that the laws of H—at least the principal and most characteristic laws—are prior to Ez. : the manner in which he takes as his standard, or point of departure, laws identical with those of H, is admitted to establish this point.*

[142] The age of the writer who fitted these laws into their parenetic framework is, however, disputed.   The principal clue appears to be afforded by the closing exhortation, 26[3ff.].   This, it seems clear, must have been written at a time when Israel had *already* worshipped at "high places," and erected sun-pillars (v.[30]) ; but beyond this it is thought by many to presuppose the *exile*.   Especially, it is argued, the hopes of national penitence and the promise of restoration (v.[40-45]) are unsuitable in a discourse designed to move the nation to obedience by exhibiting vividly (v.[14-39]) the penal consequences of transgression of the law, whereas they spring naturally from an age in which the penalties of transgression have been actually incurred (Dillm. *NDJ.* p. 645 f. ; Baentsch, p. 126 f.).   Wellh. (*Hist.* p. 383 f.), Kuenen (§ 15. 9), Smend (p. xxvi f.), and others assign accord-

---

* Kuenen (*Hex.* § 15. 10, 5) allowed this for the *laws* of Lev. 18–20 ; Baentsch (pp. 81–91), after a careful comparison, affirms it, very decidedly, for their parenetic setting as well, and for the nucleus (above, pp. 56 *n.*, 57 *n.*) of c. 23–25.   As regards the ceremonial legislation of Lev. 21–22, Ez. is in most respects clearly in advance of H, but in one or two, especially in the distinctive position assigned (21[10-15]) to the high priest, H is in advance of Ez. ; the legislation of Ez., namely, recognizes no high priest, the domestic restrictions imposed upon the priests in general (44[20. 22. 25]) being greater than those imposed by H upon the ordinary priests (Lev. 21[1-9]), but less than those imposed by it upon the high priest ("the priest that is greater than his brethren," 21[10-15]).   Baentsch (pp. 108–115) attaches such weight to this difference that he separates Lev. 21–22 from Lev. 18–20, and places the compilation of the former after Ez., allowing indeed that elsewhere in this section the compiler (R[h]) followed older laws, but thinking that 21[10-15] was formulated by himself for the first time.   However, the principal priest appears in the later parts of Kings (2 Ki. 24[4. 8] 23[4] ; 25[18]) with a distinctive title, and may have held therefore a distinctive position, such as might have been marked by the additional restrictions of Lev. 21[10-15].   And Ez.'s ideal constitution (c. 40–48), though based upon existing institutions, is not an exact copy of them ; his "prince" is more than a mere secular head of the community ; he is in certain particulars its theocratic head as well ; and by his side Ez. may have deemed a "high" priest (in the sense of H) no longer necessary (cf. Paton, p. 107).

ingly 26[3ff.], and, with it, the compilation of H as a whole, to the
exile.* Klost. and Del., on the contrary, place it prior to the
exile, the former, in particular, arguing at some length that the
resemblances between Ez. and Lev. 26[3ff.] are of a character that
shows Ez. to be dependent on Lev. 26[3ff.], rather than the author
of Lev. 26[3ff.] on Ezekiel.† On the whole, while fully admitting
the great difficulty of determining questions of priority by the mere
comparison[143] of parallel passages, the view that gives the priority
to 26[3ff.] seems to the present writer to be the more probable.‡
Nor is this inference modified by the considerations referred to
above. On the one hand, the certainty of *approaching* exile
(which was unquestionably realized by the prophets of Jeremiah's
age) would, not less than the actual exile, form a sufficient basis
on which to found the promise of v.[40-45]; on the other hand,

* Dillm. does not question the pre-exilic origin of 26[3ff.] as a whole ; but
points (*EL.* 620 ; *NDJ.* 647) to the loose connexion with the context, and
the unusual heaviness of the style, in v.[34-35. 39. 40-45], as indicating that the
parts which have been thought to suggest most strongly an exilic date did not
belong to the original discourse, but were added to it subsequently. The
verses in question present, however, indications of being by the same hand as
the rest of the discourse (Kuen. *l.c.*). Baentsch (though he treats the whole
of 26[3ff.] as exilic) agrees (p. 66 ff.) with Dillm., so far as regards the secondary
origin of v.[34-35. 39-43].

† It is Ez.'s custom to combine reminiscences from his predecessors (Dt.,
or other prophets) with expressions peculiar to himself ; and Klost. seeks to
show that he deals similarly with Lev. 26[3ff.]. Thus he argues that in 4[17]
"pine away in their iniquity" is a reminiscence from Lev. 26[39], to which
Ez. has prefixed his own expression (cf. 30[7]) "be astonied one with another"
(comp. 34[4b] with Lev. 25[43. 46. 53] ["with force" added]). Whether all Klost.'s
arguments are cogent may be doubted ; nevertheless there seem to the writer
to be considerations which support the view taken in the text. Lev.
26[3ff.] is in style terse and forcible ; Ez. is diffuse : Lev. also appears to have
the advantage in originality of expression (contrast *e.g.* "the pride of your
power" in Lev. 26[19] and in Ez. 7[24] (LXX) 24[21] 30[6. 18] 33[28]), and in the connexion of thought (contrast Lev. 26[4-ñ. 13] with Ez. 34[25-29]). The opposite
view, which is also that of Smend (pp. xxvi f., 315), Wellh. (p. 384), Cornill
(§ 13. 9), and others, is maintained strongly by Baentsch (p. 124 f.), who
urges the improbability that an author of the originality and scope of Ez.
would have adopted so largely the thoughts and phraseology of a single
chapter. In *expression*, however (Nöld. *l.c.* p. 68), Ez. is far from original ;
and if, as Baentsch himself allows (p. 84 ff.), he is dependent largely upon
Lev. 18-20, and moves in the same circle of ideas, the presumption is considerably lessened that he should not be dependent also upon another section
of the same legislative *corpus*.

‡ See further, in support of the same view, Paton, p. 109 ff.

hardly any subsequent promise, least of all one so indefinite in its terms as that of v.$^{40\text{-}45}$, could neutralize the deterrent effect of such a denunciation of disaster and exile as that contained in v.$^{14\text{-}39}$. But the parenetic framework of H, while it may thus be earlier than Ez., will hardly be much earlier; for though isolated passages in Lev. 26 resemble, for instance, passages of Amos or Micah,* the tone of the whole is unlike that of any earlier prophet; on the other hand, its tone is akin to that of Jeremiah, and still more (even apart from the phrases common to both) to that of Ezekiel. The language and style are compatible with the same age, even if they do not actually favour it.† The *laws* of H date in the main from a considerably earlier time; but it seems that they were arranged in their present parenetic framework, by an author who was at once a priest and a prophet, probably towards the closing years of the monarchy. And if H formed still, in Ez.'s day, a separate body of law, which was not combined with the rest of the Priests' Code till subsequently, the prophet's special familiarity with it would be at once naturally explained.

While the majority of the parallels in Ez. are with the excerpts of the Law of Holiness embedded in Lev. 17–26, it will be observed that there are others, sometimes remarkable ones, with certain other passages of the Pent., especially with Ex. 6$^{6\text{-}8}$ 12$^{12\text{-}13}$ 31$^{13\text{-}14a}$, Lev. 10$^{9a.\ 10\text{-}11}$ 11^{44}, Nu. 15$^{37\text{-}41}$, several of which have been already referred, on *independent* grounds (p. 59), to H. The evidence of Ez. thus confirms the conclusion stated above, that a considerable body of priestly *Tôrôth* existed, permeated by the same dominant principles, and embracing, not only the continuous extracts preserved in Lev. 17–26, but also fragments—perhaps not confined to those just cited—embedded in other parts of the Pentateuch. And if Ex. 6$^{6\text{-}8}$ be rightly assigned to this collection of laws, it may be conjectured that it was prefaced by a short historical introduction, setting forth its origin and scope. And several at least of [144] these *Tôrôth* seem clearly to be older than Dt. Not only do some of the passages just quoted appear to be presupposed by Dt. (p. 145), but the instances in which the laws of D are *parallel* to those of

---

* As v.^{5a}, Am. 9^{13a} ; v.$^{16b.\ 26b}$, Mic. 6$^{14a.\ 15a}$. Riehm's argument (*Einl.* i. p. 202) is far from conclusive.

† Comp. Dillm. *EL.* p. 619.

H (see the table, p. 73 ff.) are most reasonably explained by the supposition that both D and the compiler of H drew from the same more ancient source, the language of which has been, perhaps, least changed in H, while D has allowed himself greater freedom of adaptation.*

The argument of the preceding pages meets by anticipation—for it was completed before the writer had seen either—objections such as those urged in the *British Quarterly Rev.* vol. 79 (1884), p. 115 ff., or by Principal Cave, *The Inspiration of the OT.* p. 263 ff., and places, it is believed, the relation of the Priests' Code to the pre-exilic literature in a just light.   An unbiassed comparison of P with this literature shows, namely, that there are elements of truth *both* in Dillm.'s view of the origin of P, *and* in Wellh.'s.   The passages appealed to in proof of the existence of the *completed* Priests' Code under the earlier kings lack the necessary cogency, on account of the *general* contradiction which the pre-exilic literature opposes to the conclusion that the system of P was then in operation, and because the hypothesis that P had a "latent" existence, as an unrealizable priestly ideal (p. 142), does not seem a probable one.   On the other hand, as said above, these passages are good evidence that the principal institutions of P are not a *creation* of the exilic period, but that they existed in Israel in a more rudimentary form from a remote period.   It is not so much the institutions in themselves as the system with which they are associated, and the principles of which in P they are made more distinctly the expression, which bear the marks of a more advanced stage of ceremonial observance.

The consideration of the probable age of the several institutions of P is an archæological rather than a literary question, and hence does not fall properly within the scope of the present volume.   A few general remarks may, however, be permitted. It cannot be doubted that Moses was the ultimate founder of both the national and the religious life of Israel ; † and that he provided his people not only with at least the nucleus of a system of civil ordinances (such as would, in fact, arise directly out of his judicial functions, as described in Ex. 18), but also (as the necessary correlative of the primary truth that *Jehovah was the God of Israel*) with some system of ceremonial observances, [145] designed as the expression and concomitant of the religious and ethical duties involved in the people's relation to its national God.   It is reasonable to suppose that the teaching of Moses on

* It is remarkable that, while clauses from JE are often excerpted in Dt. *verbatim*, in the parallels with H the language is hardly ever identical.

† Comp. Wellh. *Hist.* pp. 432, 434, 438 f., endorsed by Kuenen, *Th. T.* 1883, p. 199.

these subjects is preserved, in its least modified form, in the Decalogue and the "Book of the Covenant" (Ex. 20-23). It by no means, however, follows from the view treated above as probable that the Mosaic legislation was *limited* to the subjects dealt with in Ex. 20-23 : amongst the enactments peculiar to Dt.—which tradition, as it seems, ascribed to a later period of the legislator's life—there are many which likewise may well have formed part of it. It is further in analogy with ancient custom to suppose that some form of *priesthood* would be established by Moses ; that this priesthood would be hereditary ; and that the priesthood would also inherit from their founder some traditionary lore (beyond what is contained in Ex. 20-23) on matters of ceremonial observance. And accordingly we find that JE both mentions repeatedly an Ark and "Tent of Meeting" as existing in the Mosaic age (Ex. 33^{7-11}, Nu. $11^{24ff.}$ $12^{4ff.}$, Dt. $31^{14ff.}$), and assigns to Aaron a prominent and, indeed, an official position (Ex. 4^4 "Aaron *the Levite*"; 18^{12}; $24^{1.9}$); further, that in Dt. (10^{6b}) a hereditary priesthood descended from him is expressly recognized ; and also that there are early allusions to the "tribe of Levi" as enjoying priestly privileges and exercising priestly functions (Dt. 33^{10}, Mic. 3^{11}; cf. Jud. 17^{13}).* The principles by which the priesthood was to be guided were laid down, it may be supposed, in outline by Moses. In process of time, however, as national life grew more complex, and fresh cases requiring to be dealt with arose, these principles would be found no longer to suffice, and their extension would become a necessity. Especially in matters of ceremonial observance, which would remain naturally within the control of the priests, regulations such as those enjoined in Ex. 20^{24-26} 22^{29-31} 23^{14-19} would not long continue in the same [146] rudimentary state ; fresh definitions and distinctions would be introduced, more precise rules would be prescribed for the method of sacrifice, the ritual to be observed by the priests, the dues which they were authorized

---

* These functions consisted largely in pronouncing *Tôrāh*, i.e. *pointing out* (הורה) what was to be done in some special case ; giving direction in cases submitted to them—declaring, *e.g.*, whether or not a man was "unclean," whether or not he had the leprosy, &c. ; and also imparting authoritative *moral* instruction. See a good note on the term in Kuen. *Hex.* § 10. 4 ; comp. also the writer's Commentary on Joel and Amos, in the *Cambridge Bible for Schools*, p. 230 f. In civil matters, it is the function which Moses himself is represented as discharging in Ex. 18 (above, p. 31).

to receive from the people, and other similar matters. After the priesthood had acquired, through the foundation of Solomon's Temple, a permanent centre, it is probable that the process of development and systematization advanced more rapidly than before. And thus the allusions in Dt. imply the existence of usages beyond those which fall directly within the scope of the book, and belonging specially to the jurisdiction of the priests (*e.g.* 17[11] 24[8]) : Ezekiel, being a priest himself, alludes to such usages more distinctly. Although, therefore, there are reasons for supposing that the Priests' Code assumed finally the shape in which we have it in the age subsequent to Ez., it rests ultimately upon an ancient traditional basis ; * and many of the institutions prominent in it are recognized, in various stages of their growth, by the earlier pre-exilic literature, by Dt., and by Ezekiel. The laws of P, even when they included later elements, were still referred to Moses,—no doubt because in its basis and origin Hebrew legislation was actually derived from him, and was only modified gradually.†

The institution which was among the last to reach a settled state, appears to have been the *priesthood*. Till the age of Dt., the right of exercising priestly offices must have been enjoyed by every member of the tribe of Levi (p. 83, *n.* 2) ; but this right on the part of the tribe generally is evidently not incompatible with the *pre-eminence* of a particular family (that of Aaron : cf. Dt. 10[6]), which, in the line of Zadok, held the chief rank at the Central Sanctuary. After the abolition of the high places by Josiah, however, the central priesthood refused to acknowledge the right which (according to the law of Dt.) the Levitical priests of the high places must have possessed.‡   The action of the

---

* And indeed (like Dt.) includes some elements evidently *archaic*.

† A similar view of the gradual expansion of the legislation of P from a Mosaic nucleus is expressed by Delitzsch, *Genesis*, p. 26 f. Indeed, it is a question whether even in form P is throughout perfectly homogeneous. There are other parts as well as those including the Law of Holiness, which, when examined closely, seem to consist of *strata*, exhibiting side by side the usage of different periods. The stereotyped terminology may (to a certain extent) be the characteristic, not of an individual, but of the priestly style generally.

‡ See 2 Ki. 23[9], where it is said of the disestablished Levitical priests that they "came not up to the altar of Jehovah in Jerusalem, but they did eat unleavened cakes among their brethren," *i.e.* they were not deprived of the

central priesthood [**147**] was endorsed by Ezekiel (44[6ff.]) : the priesthood, he declared, was for the future to be confined to the descendants of Zadok ; the priests of the high places (or their descendants) were condemned by him to discharge subordinate offices, as menials in attendance upon the worshippers. As it proved, however, the event did not altogether accord with Ez.'s declaration ; the descendants of Ithamar succeeded in maintaining their right to officiate as priests, by the side of the sons of Zadok (1 Ch. 24[4] &c.). But the action of the central priesthood under Josiah, and the sanction given to it by Ezekiel, combined, if not to create, yet to sharpen and accentuate * the distinction of " priests " and " Levites." It is possible that those parts of P which emphasize this distinction (Nu. 1–4, &c.) are of later origin than the rest, and date from a time when—probably after a struggle on the part of some of the disestablished Levitical priests—it was generally accepted.

The language of P † is not opposed to the date here assigned

maintenance due to them as priests by the law of Dt. 18[8], but they were not admitted to the exercise of priestly functions.

* For it is difficult not to think that among the families permanently connected with the Temple, which belonged, or were reputed to belong, to the priestly tribe, there must have been some whose members failed to maintain the right which they technically possessed, and were obliged to be content with a menial position ; so that this exclusion of the priests of the high places from the priesthood probably only emphasized a distinction which already *de facto* existed, and which is recognised explicitly in B.C. 536 (Neh. 7[39, 43] &c.).

† See V. Ryssel, *De Elohistae Pentateuchi Sermone* (1878) ; F. Giesebrecht, *Der Sprachgebrauch des hexateuchischen Elohisten* in the *ZATW.* 1881, 177–276, with the critique of the latter by the present writer in the *Journal of Philology*, xi. 201–236 (cf. the synopsis in Holzinger, pp. 457–465) ; Kuenen, *Hex.* § 15. 11. The present position of the writer is not inconsistent with that adopted as the basis of his critique in 1882. The aim of that article was not to discuss the general question of the date of P, or even to show that the language of P was incompatible with a date in or near the exile (see p. 204) ; its aim was avowedly limited to an examination of *particular* data which had been alleged, and an inquiry whether they had been interpreted correctly (*ib.*). In the philology of the article the writer has nothing of consequence to modify or correct. In his etymology of משה, p. 205, he was led into error through following Ges. too implicitly (see Dillm. *ad loc.*) ; and the discussion of הוליד, p. 209, is incomplete (see König, *Offenb. des AT.s*, ii. 324 f.). The writer is also now of opinion that, although in particular cases P's use of אני might be explained consistently with an early date, yet his all but *uniform* preference for it above אנכי, taken in conjunction with his resemblance in this respect to Ez. (p. 134, No. 45), and other later

[148] to it. To be sure, Giesebrecht, in his endeavour to demonstrate the lateness of P, overshoots the mark, and detects many Aramaisms and other signs of lateness in P which do not exist; indeed, in some cases the words alleged by him form part of the older laws which P embodies. But it is true (as is admitted in the *Journal of Philology*, p. 232) that there is a residuum of words which possess this character, and show affinities with writings of the age of Ez. That these are less numerous than might perhaps be expected, may be explained partly by the fact that P's phraseology is largely traditional, partly by the fact that the real change in Hebrew style does not begin till a later age altogether; many parts of Ez. (*e.g.* c. 20), and even Haggai and Zechariah, do not show more substantial signs of lateness than P. The change is beginning (*c.* 450) in the memoirs of Nehemiah and in Malachi; but Aramaisms and other marks of lateness (ésp. in syntax) are abundant only in works written after this date—Esther, Chr., Eccl., &c. The phraseology of P, it is natural to suppose, is one which had gradually formed; hence it contains elements which are no doubt ancient side by side

writers (as Lam., Zech. 1-8, Hag., Est., Eccl., Dan., Ezr., Neh., Chr., in all of which אנכי occurs only Neh. 1⁶, Dan. 10¹¹, and 1 Chr. 17¹ [from 2 Sam. 7¹], against some 120 occurrences of אני), constitutes a presumption, difficult to neutralize, that he wrote in the later period of the language (cf. König, *Stud. u. Krit.* 1893, pp. 464-8, 478, *Einl.* pp. 168, 227, 229, *Expositor*, Aug. 1896, p. 97). At the same time he does not doubt that there is a larger traditional element in the phraseology of P than Giesebrecht's argument appears to allow for.

There are also other features, in which it is remarkable that the usage of P agrees with that of the later parts of the OT. Two may be noticed here :—

1. The months not distinguished by *names*, but *numbered*, Gen. 7¹¹ 8⁴· ⁵· ¹⁴, Ex. 16¹ 40²· ¹⁷ &c. (uniformly), as 1 Ki. 12⁸²· ³³ (compiler), 2 Ki. 25¹· ⁸· ²⁵· ²⁷, and regularly in Jer., Ez., Hag., Chr. In the earlier literature the months are *named*, Ex. 13¹⁴ 23¹⁵ 34¹⁸, Dt. 16¹ (Abib); 1 Ki. 6¹· ³⁷ (Ziv), v.³⁸ (Bul), 8² (Ethanim),—the last three being *explained* by the terms current in the compiler's own day, viz. the "second," "eighth," and "seventh" months respectively. (These are the old Phœnician names, *Bul* and *Ethanim* being found on Phœnician inscriptions : Nisan (1st), Sivan (3rd), Elul (6th), Kislev (9th), Tebeth (10th), Shebat (11th), Adar (12th), found in Zech. 1⁷ 7¹, Neh. 1¹ 2¹ 6¹⁵, Ezr. 6¹⁵, and in Esther, are of Babylonian origin.)

2. *Eleven* expressed by עשׁתי עשׂר, Ex. 26⁷· ⁸ (=36¹⁴· ¹⁵), Nu. 7⁷² 29²⁰, Dt. 1³ (P), as in 2 Ki. 25² (=Jer. 52⁵), Jer. 1³ 39², Ez. 26¹ 33²¹ (LXX) 40⁴⁹, Zech. 1⁷, 1 Ch. 12¹³ 24¹² 25¹⁸ 27¹⁴† ; not by אחד עשׂר, as Gen. 32²³ 37⁹, Dt. 1², 1 Ki. 6³⁸ *al.*

with those which were introduced later.   The priests of each
successive generation would adopt, as a matter of course, the
technical formulæ, and other stereotyped expressions, which they
learnt from their seniors, new terms, when they were introduced,
being accommodated to the old moulds.   Hence, no doubt, the
similarity of Ez.'s style to P, even where a definite law is not
quoted by him : although, from the greater variety of subjects
which he deals with as a prophet, the vocabulary of P is not
sufficient for him, he still frequently uses expressions belonging
to the priestly terminology, with which he was familiar.*

After the illustrations which have been given above (p. 8, &c.) of the
grounds upon which the analysis of Exodus and the following books depends,
the inadequacies of the "Journal theory" of the Pentateuch, advocated by
[149] Principal Cave in the work cited on p. 152, will be manifest.   This theory
fails, in a word, *to account for the phaenomena which the Pent. presents.*
Thus (1) it offers no explanation of the phraseological variations which Ex.
&c. display : these (as the list, p. 131 ff., will have shown) are quite as
marked as those in Genesis, which nevertheless Principal Cave *accepts*
(p. 171 ff.) as proof of its composite origin.   If these variations were so
distributed as to distinguish consistently the *laws* on the one hand from
the *narratives* on the other, the theory might possess some plausibility ; the
laws, for instance, might be supposed to have required naturally a different
style from the narrative, or Moses might have compiled the one and an
amanuensis the other : but, as a fact, the variations are *not* so distributed ;
not only do the different groups of laws show differences of terminology, but
the narratives themselves present *the same variations of phraseology as in
Genesis,* some parts having numerous features in common with the sections
assigned to "P" in that book, and with the laws contained in Ex. 25, &c.,
and other parts being marked by an entire absence of those features.†   The
Journal theory cannot account for these variations *in the narrative sections of
Ex.–Dt.*   (2) The Journal theory is unable to account for the many and
cogent indications which the different codes in the Pent. contain, that they
took shape at different periods of the history, or to solve the very great
difficulties which both the historical (esp. c. 1–3, 9–10) and legal parts of Dt.
present, if they are regarded as the work of the same contemporary writer as

---

* The incorrectnesses which appear from time to time in Ez. are due probably, partly to the fact that, as a prophet mingling with the people, he was
exposed to influences from which the priests generally were free, partly to
errors originating in the transmission of his text.

† See further the *Contemp. Review,* Feb. 1892, p. 262 ff., where the
writer has shown by a series of excerpted passages, that whatever grounds exist
for holding Genesis to be of composite authorship, the same (or precisely
similar) grounds exist for holding the rest of the Hexateuch to be of composite
authorship likewise.

Ex.-Nu. (3) The Journal theory takes a false view of the Book of Joshua, which is not severed from the following books, and connected with the Pentateuch, for the purpose of satisfying the exigencies of a theory, but because this view of the book *is required by the facts*—a simple comparison of it with the Pent. showing viz. that it is *really homogeneous with it*, and (especially in the P sections) that it differs entirely from Jud., Sam., Kings. But Principal Cave's treatment of the 'books from Ex. to Josh. is manifestly slight and incomplete.

In ch. vi. of Principal Cave's book there are many just observations on the theological truths which find expression in the Mosaic law ; but it is an *ignoratio elenchi* to suppose them to be a refutation of the opinion that Hebrew legislation reached its final form by successive stages, except upon the assumption that all progress must proceed from purely natural causes,—an assumption both unfounded in itself and opposed to the general sense of theologians, who speak, for instance, habitually of a " progressive revelation " (so " Revelation " and " Evolution," p. 251,—though the latter is not a very suitable term to use in this connexion,—are not antagonistic except upon a similar assumption). Prof. Bissell's *Pentateuch* fails to establish the points which it was written to prove, partly for the same reason, partly for a different one. The author is singularly unable to distinguish between a good argument and a bad one. Thus the passages adduced (chiefly in chaps. viii.-x.) to prove the existence of the Pent. in the Mosaic age all, upon one ground or another (comp. above, p. 144, lines 11-14), fall short of the mark ; and while his volume contains many sound and true observations on the deep spiritual teaching both of the law and also of other parts of the OT., [150] he has not shown that this teaching must stand or fall with the traditional view of the origin of the OT. books, or that the critical view of their origin cannot be stated in a form entirely compatible with the reality of the supernatural enlightenment vouchsafed to the ancient people of God. (On the Pent. as a channel of revelation, cf. further Riehm's *Einl.* §§ 28, 29.)

It may not be superfluous to remark that the assertion, now not unfrequently made, that the primary basis of Pentateuchal criticism is the assumption that Moses was unacquainted with the art of writing, and that this has been completely overthrown by the Tel el-Amarna tablets, rests upon an entire misapprehension of the facts. As the absence of all mention of the supposed basis in the preceding pages will have shown, it is *not* the premiss upon which the criticism of the Pentateuch depends : the antiquity of writing was known long before the Tel el-Amarna tablets were discovered ; and these tablets (though deeply interesting on account of their historical contents) have no bearing on the question either of the composite structure of the Pentateuch, or of the date of the documents of which it is composed.

On Prof. Hommel's recently (May, 1897) published volume, *The Ancient Hebrew Tradition as illustrated by the Monuments*, see the notices by Prof. Margoliouth in the *Expository Times*, Aug. 1897, by Principal Whitehouse in the *Expositor*, Sept. 1897, and by G. B. Gray in the *Expos. Times*, Sept. 1897, and (specially on the argument founded upon the proper names in P) in the *Expositor*, Sept. 1897. All these writers agree that, while Prof. Hommel has collected much interesting material from the Inscriptions, especially those of Babylonia and Southern Arabia, as a refutation of the critical position his work is a failure. The reason of his failure lies in the fact—(1) that the positive evidence afforded by the OT. itself in support of the critical position is very much underrated ; (2) that the monumental evidence arrayed against it is far too indirect and hypothetical to possess the required cogency : the author makes no attempt to distinguish logically between fact and imagination ; and what he really brings into the field against the conclusions of critics are not facts, attested directly by the monuments, but a series of *hypotheses*, framed indeed with great ingenuity, but often resting upon the slenderest possible foundation, and most insufficiently supported by the *data* actually contained in the Inscriptions. His treatment of Gen. 14, while containing much that is arbitrary (the date of Khammurabi, the supposed name *Ammu-rapaltu*, &c.), does not really establish anything beyond what was stated by the present writer in the articles referred to above, p. 15, and in the *Expos. Times*, Dec. 1896, p. 143 f. It is nowhere maintained (or implied) in the present volume that in the writer's opinion "firm historical ground" begins for Israelitish history in the age of Solomon (Hommel, p. 4) ; and hence, even should Prof. Hommel have made it probable (as Mr. Gray had done before him) that ancient material is preserved amongst the names of P, the conclusion would be in no kind of conflict with the principles of the present work. It should be added that Prof. Hommel himself does not question the composite structure of the Pentateuch (pp. 12, 19 f.), and that until quite recently (*Neue Kirchliche Ztschr.* 1890, pp. 62–66) he accepted for J, E, and P, Wellh.'s dates.

THE PRIESTS' CODE.

Genesis 1^1–2^{4a} $5^{1-28. \ 30-32}$ 6^{9-22} $7^{6. \ 11. \ 13-16a. \ 17a}$ (except *forty days*) $^{18-21. \ 24}$ $8^{1-2a. \ 3b-5. \ 13a. \ 14-19}$ $9^{1-17. \ 28-29}$ $10^{1-7. \ 20. \ 22-23. \ 31-32}$ $11^{10-27. \ 31-32}$ 12^{4b-5} $13^{6. \ 11b-12a}$ $16^{1a. \ 3. \ 15-16}$ c. $17.$ 19^{29} $21^{1b. \ 2b-5}$ c. $23.$ $25^{7-11a. \ 12-17. \ 19-20. \ 26b}$ 26^{34-35} 27^{46}–28^9 $29^{24. \ 29}$ * 31^{18b} 33^{18a} $34^{1-2a. \ 4. \ 6. \ 8-10. \ 13-18. \ 20-24. \ 25}$ (partly) $^{27-29}$ $35^{9-13. \ 15. \ 22b-29}$ c. $36.$† 37^{1-2a} 41^{46} 46^{6-27} 47^{5-6a} (LXX) $^{7-11. \ 27b-28}$ $48^{3-6. \ 7 \ \dagger}$ $49^{1a. \ 28b-33}$ 50^{12-13}.

Exodus $1^{1-5. \ 7. \ 13-14}$ 2^{23b-25} 6^2–$7^{13. \ 19-20a. \ 21b-22}$ $8^{5-7. \ 15b-19}$ 9^{8-12} 11^{9-10} $12^{1-20. \ 28. \ 37a. \ 40-41. \ 43-51}$ $13^{1-2. \ 20}$ $14^{1-4. \ 8-9. \ 15-18. \ 21a. \ 21c-23. \ 26-27a. \ 28a. \ 29}$ $16^{1-3. \ 6-24. \ 31-36}$ 17^{1a} 19^{1-2a} 24^{15-18a} 25^1–31^{18a} 34^{29-35} c. 35–40.

Leviticus c. 1–16 (c. 17–26) c. 27.

Numbers 1^1–10^{28} $13^{1-17a. \ 21. \ 25-26a}$ (to *Paran*) ^{32a} $14^{1-2. \dagger \ 5-7. \ 10. \ 26-30. \ 34-38}$ c. $15.$ $16^{1a. \ 2b-7a. \ (7b-11). \ (16-17). \ 18-24. \ 27a. \ 32b. \ 35. \ (36-40). \ 41-50}$ c. 17–19. 20^{1a} (to *month*) $^{2. \ 3b-4. \ 6-13. \ 22-29}$ 21^{4a} (to *Hor*) $^{10-11}$ 22^1 25^{6-18} c. 26–31. $32^{18-19. \ 28-32}$ ‡ c. 33–36.

Deuteronomy 1^3 32^{48-52} 34^{1a} (largely) $^{5b. \ 7-9}$.

Joshua $4^{13. \ 19}$ 5^{10-12} 7^1 $9^{15b. \ 17-21}$ 13^{15-32} 14^{1-5} $15^{1-13. \ 20-44. \ (45-47). \ 48-62}$ 16^{4-8} $17^{1a. \ 3-4. \ 7. \ 9a. \ 9c-10a}$ 18^1 $18^{. \ 11-28}$ $19^{1-8. \ 10-46. \ 48. \ 51}$ 20^{1-3} (except "*and* unawares") ^{6a} (to *judgment*) $^{7-9}$ [cf. LXX] 21^{1-42} (22^{9-34}).

---

* With perhaps fragments in $30^{1a. \ 4a. \ 9b. \ 22a}$.
† In the main.   ‡ With traces in $32^{1. \ 17. \ 20-27}$.

CHAPTER II.

JUDGES, SAMUEL, AND KINGS.

§ 1. The Book of Judges.

LITERATURE.—G. L. Studer, *Das Buch der Richter*, 1842 ; E. Bertheau (in the *Kurzgef. Exeg. Handb.*), ² 1883 ; Keil in *Josua, Richter u. Ruth*,² 1874 ; Wellhausen in Bleek's *Einl.* (1878) pp. 181–205 [= *Comp.* 213–238] ; *Hist.* pp. 228–245 ; A. van Doorninck, *Bijdrage tot de tekst-kritiek van Richt.* i–xvi (1879), with K. Budde's review, *Th. Lit.-zt.* 1884, col. 211–216 ; Aug. Müller, *Das Lied der Deb.* 1887 ; K. Budde, *Die Bücher Richter u. Samuel*, 1890, pp. 1–166 ; J. S. Black (in the *Smaller Camb. Bible for Schools*), 1892 ; R. Kittel, *Gesch.* i. 239 ff. [E.T. i. 264 ff.] ; W. R. Smith, *OTJC.*² pp. 120–124, 431–433 ; G. A. Cooke, *The History and Song of Deborah*, Oxford, 1892 ; S. Oettli (in Strack and Zöckler's *Kgf. Komm.*), 1893 ; G. F. Moore (in the " International Crit. Comm."), 1895 (very thorough).

The Book of Judges derives its name from the heroes whose exploits form the subject of its central and principal part (2⁶–c. 16). It consists of three well-defined portions : (1) an introduction 1¹–2⁵, presenting a view of the condition of the country at the time when the period of the Judges begins ; (2) the history of the Judges, 2⁶–c. 16 ; (3) an appendix, c. 17–21, describing in some detail two incidents belonging to the period, viz. the migration of a part of the tribe of Dan to the north, c. 17–18, and the war of the Israelites against Benjamin, arising out of the outrage of Gibeah, c. 19–21.

The Judges whose exploits the book records are 13 in number, or, if Abimelech (who is not termed a judge) be not reckoned, 12, viz.: Othniel (3⁷⁻¹¹) ; Ehud (3¹²⁻³⁰) ; Shamgar (3³¹) ; Barak [Deborah] (c. 4–5) ; Gideon (6¹–8³²) ; Abimelech (8³³–9⁵⁷) ; Tola (10¹⁻²) ; Jair (10³⁻⁵) ; Jephthah (10⁶–12⁷) ; Ibzan (12⁸⁻¹⁰) ; Elon (12¹¹⁻¹²) ; Abdon (12¹³⁻¹⁵) ; Samson (c. 13–16). Shamgar, Tola, Jair, Ibzan, Elon, Abdon, whose exploits are told only summarily, are sometimes called the "minor" Judges. According to the chronology of the book itself, the period of the Judges embraced 410 years ; thus :—

[152]		years.
3 [8] Israel serves Cushan-Rishathaim	8	years.
3[11] Deliverance by Othniel : the land rests	40	,,
3[14] Israel serves Eglon	18	,,
3[30] Deliverance by Ehud : the land rests	80	,,
4 [2] Oppression by Jabin	20	,,
5[31] Deliverance by Deborah : the land rests	40	,,
6 [1] Oppression by Midian	7	,,
8[28] Deliverance by Gideon : the land rests	40	,,
9[22] Abimelech reigns over Israel	3	,,
10 [2] Tola judges Israel	23	,,
10 [3] Jair judges Israel	22	,,
10 [8] Oppression by Ammon	18	,,
12 [7] Jephthah judges Israel	6	,,
12 [9] Ibzan judges Israel	7	,,
12[11] Elon judges Israel	10	,,
12[14] Abdon judges Israel	8	,,
13 [1] Oppression by Philistines	40	,,
15[20] = 16[31] Samson judges Israel	20	,,

Total,	410 years.

This total, however, appears to be too high ; and it is at any rate inconsistent with 1 Ki. 6[1], which assigns 480 years * to the period from the exodus to the 4th year of Solomon, whereas, if the Judges be reckoned at 410 years, this period, which must embrace in addition the 40 years of the wilderness, 7 years of the conquest (p. 104), 20 years of Samuel (1 Sa. 7[2]), 20 (?) years of Saul, 40 years of David, and 4 of Solomon, would extend (at the least) to 541 years. Many attempts have been made to reduce the chronology of the Judges, by the assumption, for instance, that some of the periods named in it are synchronous, or the figures meant to be treated as round ones (especially 40 and 80 = 40 × 2) ; † but it must be admitted (with Bertheau, pp. xv, xvii) that no certain results can be reached by the use of such methods, and that, as matters stand, an exact chronology of the period is unattainable.

The three parts of which the Book of Judges consists differ

---

* Though this is open to the suspicion of having been reached artificially (= 40 × 12).

† Comp. Bertheau, pp. xii xvii ; Wellh. *Hist.* p. 229 f. ; *Comp.* p. 356 ; Kuenen, *Onderzoek*, i. 2 (1887), § 18. 4, 6, 7.

considerably in structure and character, and must be considered separately.

I. 1^1–2^5. This section of the book consists of fragments [153] of an old account of the conquest of Canaan—not by united Israel under the leadership of Joshua, but — by the individual efforts of the separate tribes. The fragments, however, narrate the positive successes of Judah and Simeon (1^{1-20}) and the "House of Joseph" (1^{22-26}) only. There follows a series of notices describing how particular tribes, viz. Manasseh, Ephraim, Zebulun, Asher, Naphtali, and Dan, failed to dispossess the native inhabitants. By the opening words : "And it came to pass after the death of Joshua," the section is attached to the Book of Joshua, and the events narrated in it are assigned to the period after the close of that book. But it has long been suspected * that these words are, in fact, merely a redactional addition, and that the account is, in reality, *parallel*, at least in part, with the narrative in Joshua, and not a continuation of it. The Book of Joshua (as we now have it) describes how the whole land was subdued by the Israelites, and taken possession of by the individual tribes (see *e.g.* 21^{43-45} 23^1: both D^2). In Jud. I the Israelites are still at Gilgal (2^1), or close by at Jericho (1^{16}); and hence the tribes "go up" (*i.e.* from the Jordan Valley to the high ground of Central Palestine), as at the beginning of the Book of Joshua (5^9), Judah first, to conquer their respective territories ($1^{1, 2, 3}$).

As was remarked above (p. 115), these notices display a strong similarity of style, and in some cases even verbal identity, with a series of passages, somewhat loosely attached to the context, preserved in the older strata of the Book of Joshua. Thus Jud. 1^{21} (the Benjaminites' failure to conquer Jerusalem) agrees almost verbally with Josh. 15^{63}, except that there what is no doubt the original reading is preserved, and the failure is laid to the charge, not of Benjamin, but of *Judah*; $1^{20b, 10b-15}$ agrees, in the main verbally, with Josh. 15^{14-19}; 1^{27-28} with Josh. 17^{12-13}; 1^{29} with Josh. 16^{10}. Most of the verbal differences are due simply to the different relations which the fragments hold in the two books to the contiguous narrative. Josh. 17^{14-18} (complaint of the "House of Joseph") and 19^{47} (Dan) are very similar in representation (implying the *separate* action taken by individual

* Comp. the *Speaker's Comm.* ii. p. 123 f.

tribes) and in phraseology.* It can hardly be doubted that both Jud. 1 and [154] these notices in Joshua are excerpts from what was once a detailed survey of the conquest of Canaan : of these excerpts some have been fitted in with the narrative of Joshua, others have been combined in Jud. 1 so as to form, with the addition of the opening words, *After the death of Joshua,* an introduction to the period of the Judges. The survey is incomplete ; but the parts which remain may have stood once somewhat in the following order : *a.* (Judah and Simeon) Jud. 1^1 (from "*and the children of Israel asked*"), v.$^{2-3.}$† $^{5-7.}$‡ $^{19.}$ ^{21} (with *Judah* twice for *Benjamin,* as Josh. 15^{63}), v.$^{20a.}$ ^{10a} (with *Caleb* for *Judah* §), Josh. 15^{14} (to *Talmai*), v.$^{15-19}$ (= Jud. 1^{11-15} ; cf. Josh. $14^{13b.}$ $^{15a\,\alpha}$), Jud. $1^{16-17.}$ ^{36} ; ‖ *b.* (Joseph) Jud. $1^{22-26.}$ $^{27-28}$ (= Josh. 17^{12} [the names of the towns are stated here in v.^{11}, and so not repeated]$^{-13}$), v.^{29} (= Josh. 16^{10}), Josh. 17^{14-18} ¶ 13^{13} ; *c.* (the other tribes) Jud. 1^{30-34}, Josh. 19^{47},** Jud. 1^{35}.††

II. 2^6–c. 16. This, the central and principal part of the book, comprising the history of the Judges properly so called, consists essentially of a series of older narratives, fitted into a

---

* Notice "House of Joseph" (unusual), Josh. 17^{17}, Jud. $1^{22.}$ $^{23.}$ ^{35} ; "daughters" for dependent towns, Josh. $17^{11.}$ ^{16}, Jud. 1^{27} ; "*would* dwell," Josh. 17^{12}, Jud. $1^{27.}$ ^{35} ; the "chariots of iron," Josh. 17^{16}, Jud. 1^{19}.

† V.^{4} agrees indifferently with the context, and is in all probability a redactional addition (Budde ; Kittel, *Gesch.* p. 241 [E.T. p. 266] ; Moore).

‡ V.^{8}, which cannot be reasonably reconciled with v.^{21} (see Moore, p. 21), appears to be a gloss, due to a misunderstanding of v.^{7} (cf. Budde, pp. 4, 8 f.; Kittel, *Hist. ib.*) : v.^{9} seems to be a generalizing introduction to v.$^{10ff.}$, made by the redactor ; v.^{18} (contrast v.^{19} 3^3, Josh. 13^3) is also probably due to him,—unless indeed ולא לכד "and took *not*" (cf. LXX) be the true reading instead of וילכד.

§ The context (cf. v.$^{11a.}$ ^{12a}) requires the conquest to be referred to Caleb, not to Judah. V.$^{10.}$ ^{20} and Josh. 15^{14} are different excerpts from the same common source ; and in v.^{10} the redactor generalizes ("*Judah*" ; "*they* smote ").

‖ Where *Amorites* is probably an error for *Edomites,* as in 1^{16} *the people* (העם) for *the Amalekite* (העמלקי) : cf. *QPB^3*.

¶ According to Budde (pp. 38 f., 60) 13^{13} was preceded in its original context by Nu. $32^{39.}$ $^{41.}$ ^{42} (which then would describe the conquest of Gilead from the *West* of Jordan).

** Read (as suggested by LXX) "*was too narrow* for them" for "went out beyond them " (ויצר for ויצא) : cf. 2 Ki. 6^1 (Heb.).

†† Comp. Budde, p. 84 ff. (where the passages, in somewhat different order, are printed consecutively) ; Kittel, *Gesch.* i. 239 ff. [E.T. p. 265 ff.].

framework by a later editor, or redactor, and provided by him, where necessary, with introductory and concluding comments. This editor, or redactor, is imbued strongly with the spirit of Deuteronomy. His additions exhibit a phraseology and colouring different from that of the rest of the book ; all contain the same recurring expressions, and many are cast in the same type or form of words, so that they are recognisable without difficulty. Thus the history of each of the six greater Judges is fitted into a framework as follows—the details vary slightly, but the general resemblance is unmistakable : 3^{7-11} (Othniel) "And the children of Israel did that which was evil in the sight of Jehovah, . . . and the anger of Jehovah was kindled against Israel, and He sold them into the hand of Cushan-rishathaim, . . . and they served Cushan-rishathaim eight years ; . . . and the children of Israel cried unto Jehovah, and He raised up unto them a saviour, . . . and the land had rest forty years." 3^{12-30} (Ehud) "And the children of Israel again did that which was evil in the sight of Jehovah, and Jehovah strengthened Eglon king of Moab against Israel, . . . and they served Eglon eighteen [155] years ; and the children of Israel cried unto Jehovah, and Jehovah raised up to them a saviour ; . . . and Moab was subdued, . . . and the land had rest eighty years." The scheme is similar in the case of Barak (4^1–5^{31}), Gideon (6^{1-7} ; 8^{28}), Jephthah ($10^{6.\,7.\,10}$; 11^{33b} ; 12^7), Samson (13^1 ; 15^{20} [twenty years] $16^{31\,end}$). In all we have the same succession of apostasy, subjugation, the cry for help, deliverance, described often in the same, always in similar, phraseology. Let the reader notice how frequently at or near the *beginning* and *close* of the narrative of each of the greater Judges the following expressions occur : *did that which was evil in the sight of Jehovah, sold** or *delivered them into the hand of . . ., cried unto Jehovah, subdued, and the land had rest . . .* ($3^{7.\,8.\,9.\,11}$; $3^{12.\,15.\,30}$; $4^{1.\,2.\,3.\,23}$ 5^{31b} ; $6^{1.\,6b}$ 8^{28} ; $10^{6.\,7.\,10}$ 11^{33b} ; 13^1 $16^{31\,end}$). It is evident that in this part of the book a series of independent narratives has been taken by the compiler and arranged by him in a framework, designed with the purpose of stating the chronology of the period, and exhibiting a theory of the occasion and nature of

---

* This figure is almost peculiar to the compiler of this book (2^{14} 3^8 4^2 10^7 ; rather differently in the older narrative 4^9) and the kindred author of 1 Sa. 12 (v.^{9}) ; it is a point of contact with Dt. 32^{30} (the Song).

the work which the Judges generally were called to undertake. In the case of the six minor Judges (Shamgar, Tola, Jair, Ibzan, Elon, Abdon) detailed particulars were probably not accessible to the compiler; hence the narratives are much briefer, though here also they show much mutual similarity of literary form (3^{31}; 10^{1-2}; 10^{3-5}; 12^{8-10}; 12^{11-12}; 12^{13-15}).

To this history of the Judges 2^6–3^6 forms an introduction, the nature of which must next be examined. Is this introduction the work of the compiler also? In parts of it we trace his hand at once ($2^{11.\ 12.\ 14}$; in v.$^{16.\ 18.\ 19}$ also notice the expressions *raised up, saved, oppressed,* comparing $3^{9.\ 15}$; 4^3; 6^9; $10^{12.\ 13}$; and the general similarity of tone). But the whole cannot be his work: for 2^{6-9} is repeated with slight verbal differences from Josh. $24^{28.\ 31.\ 29.\ 30}$ (LXX: $^{28.\ 29.\ 30.\ 31}$); elsewhere also *the point of view frequently changes,* and the details harmonize imperfectly with each other, authorizing the inference that he has here incorporated in his work *older materials.*

Thus 2^{23} cannot be the original sequel of 2^{20-22}; the fact that the Canaanites were not delivered "into the hand of Joshua" (v.^{23}), cannot be [156] a consequence of what happened (v.^{21}) *after Joshua's death.* In 3^{1-3} the ground for which the Canaanites were not driven out is that the Israelites might learn the art of war; in 2^{22} and 3^4 it is that they might be tested *morally,* that it might be seen whether they would adhere to the service of Jehovah or not. The list of nations in 3^3 is scarcely consistent with that in 3^5; the nations named in 3^3 are just those occupying *particular* districts in or near Canaan, the six named in 3^5 are representative of the *entire* population of Western Palestine (Ex. 33^2, Dt. 7^1 &c.: cf. p. 119, *n.*).

The oldest part of this section is, no doubt, 3^{1-3},—or rather its nucleus, for it has pretty clearly been expanded,—describing how the Israelites became trained in warfare through the inhabitants of particular districts continuing to dwell among or near them. As a whole, 2^6–3^6 may be analysed as follows:— 2^{6-10} (repeated, except v.^{10}, from Joshua) describes the death of Joshua, and the change which in the view of the compiler came over the nation in the following generation; 2^{11-19} states the compiler's theory of the period of the Judges, which he intends to be illustrated by the narratives following; 2^{20-22} deals with a different subject, not, as v.$^{11-19}$, the punishment of Israel for its apostasy by its being sold into the hand of one after another of the nations *around* it, but Jehovah's determination to spare the remnant of the nations *in its midst,* for the purpose of testing its moral strength; the sequel of 2^{20-22} is 3^{5-6}, stating how the Israelites intermarried with the Canaanites, and thus failed to endure the test. The nucleus of 3^{1-3} is the older fragment, enumerating the nations that were instrumental in training Israel in warfare; when this, in its expanded form, was incorporated, 2^{23} (attaching loosely and imperfectly to 2^{22}) was prefixed as an introduction, 3^4 being appended, for the purpose of leading back to the general thought of 2^{20-22} and its sequel 3^{5-6}. 2^{20-22} 3^{5-6} displays affinity with the Hexateuchal E; 3^{1-3}, in its original form, was probably the continuation of 1^1-2^5.*

It is not impossible that 10^{6-16}, the introduction to the narrative of Jephthah, which is much longer than the other introductions, may be the expansion of an earlier and briefer narrative allied to E (Stade, *ZATW*. 1881, p. 341 f.; Budde, p. 128; Moore), to which in particular v.$^{6b. 8}$ (partly) $^{10. 13-16}$ may [157] belong. The particulars in v.$^{17f.}$ appear to be simply derived from c. 11, the two verses being prefixed here as an introduction, after the notice of the Ammonites in $10^{7. 8}$.† That the author of c. 11 wrote independently of 10^{6-18}, and could not have had these verses before him, appears from the wording of 11^4, which, as it stands, is evidently the *first* mention of the Ammonites, and must have been differently expressed had 10^{6-18} preceded.

It is possible that the *Deuteronomic* compiler (as in view of his prevalent thought and tone we may now term him) was not the first who arranged together the separate histories of the Judges, but that he adopted as the basis of his work a continuous narrative, which he found ready to his hand. Some of the narratives are not adapted to illustrate the theory of the Judges, as expounded in 2^{11-19}; so, for instance, the accounts of the minor Judges (3^{31}; 10^{1-5}; 12^{8-15}), in which no allusion is made to the nation's apostasy, but which, nevertheless, as remarked above, are cast mainly in one and the same mould, and the narrative of Abimelech in c. 9: a lesson is indeed deduced from the history of Abimelech, $9^{24. 56. 57}$, but not the lesson of 2^{11-19}. It is very possible, therefore, that there was a *pre-Deuteronomic collection* of histories of Judges, which the Deuteronomic compiler set in a new framework, embodying his theory of the history of the period. Perhaps one or two of the recurring phrases noted

---

* So substantially Budde (see the grounds more fully in his work, pp. 91 f., 156 ff.): somewhat differently Moore, p. 63 ff.

† So in c. 8 the main contents of v.$^{33-35}$ seem derived from c. 9, and placed where they now stand, as a link of connexion between c. 8 and c. 9.

above, such as "subdued" (3^{30}; 4^{23}; 8^{28}; 11^{33}), which seem to form a more integral part of the narratives proper than the rest, may mark the portions due to the pre-Deuteronomic compiler. There is also a more noticeable feature of the book which may be rightly attributed to him. It is clear that the Judges were, in fact, merely local heroes; they formed temporary heads in particular centres, or over particular groups of tribes—Barak in the north of Israel; Gideon in the centre; Jephthah on the east of Jordan; Samson in the extreme south-west. Nevertheless, the Judges are consistently represented as exercising jurisdiction over Israel as a whole (3^{10}; 4^4; 9^{22}; $10^{2.3}$; $12^{8.9}$; 16^{31}; and elsewhere); and this generalization of their position and influence is so associated with the individual narratives that it must have formed a feature in them before they came into the hands of the Deuteronomic compiler: hence, if it was not a conception shared in common by the authors of the [158] separate narratives, it must be a trait due to the first compiler of this portion of the book. The question, however, whether the Deuteronomic compiler had before him a number of separate narratives, or a continuous work, is a subordinate one: the important distinction is undoubtedly that between the narratives generally and the framework in which they are set.

The parts, then, of 2^6–c. 16, which either belong wholly to the Deuteronomic compiler, or consist of elements which have been expanded or largely recast by him, are—$2^{7.11-23}$; 3^{4-6}; 3^{7-11} (almost entirely: there are no *details* of Othniel's judgeship such as constitute the narratives respecting Ehud, Barak, &c.); $3^{12-15a. 30b}$; 4^{1-3}; 5^{31b}; $6^{1. 7-10}$; * 8^{27b} (probably) $^{28b. 33-34. 35}$ (based on c. 9); $10^{6-16. 17f.}$ (based on c. 11); 13^1; 15^{20}; 16^{31b}. All these parts are connected together by a similarity of tone and phraseology, which stamps them as the work of a different hand

---

* Excerpted probably, to judge from the style (Budde, p. 107 f.; Moore), from a source akin to the Hexateuchal E (cf. above, p. 166). 11^{12-28}, containing the defence of Israel's title to Gilead, is considered by most recent critics (as Kuenen, Wellh., Budde, Moore) to be an insertion in the original narrative. It is remarkable that, while purporting to be an answer to the claim of the Ammonites (v. ^{13}), it in reality deals with Israel's relation to the *Moabites* (v. $^{17. 18}$, cf. v. ^{24} [Chemosh], v. $^{25. 26}$). Notice that the author has constructed Jephthah's message largely on the basis of JE's narrative : thus with v. $^{17-22. 26}$ comp. Nu. $20^{14. 17}$ $21^{4. 13. 21-24. 25}$ (where the agreement is often verbal).

from that of the author (or authors) of the histories of the Judges themselves.

III. C. 17-21. This division of the book differs again in character from either of the other two. It consists of two continuous narratives, not describing the exploits of any judge, but relating two incidents belonging to the same period of history. C. 17-18 introduces us to an archaic state of Israelitish life : the tribe of Dan (18¹) is still without a possession in Canaan : Micah's "house of God," with its instruments of divination, "the ephod and the teraphim," and its owner's satisfaction at securing a Levite as his priest (17^{5-13}), are vividly portrayed ; nor does any disapproval of what Micah had instituted appear to be entertained. The narrative as a whole exhibits the particulars of what is briefly stated in one of the notices mentioned p. 163, Josh. 19^{47} (cf. Jud. 1^{34}), though the latter can scarcely be derived from it on account of the different orthography of the name Laish (Leshem, or rather, probably, Lêshām). The two chapters contain indications which have led some to suppose that they have been formed by the combination of two parallel narratives. But [159] the inference is here a questionable one, and it is rejected by both Wellh. and Kuenen, who will only admit that in two or three places the narrative is in disorder or has suffered interpolation.*

With the second narrative (c. 19-21), on the other hand, the case appears to be different. In c. 20, not only does the description in parts appear to be in duplicate (as in v.$^{36b-46}$ by the side of v.$^{29-36a}$) ; † but the account, as we have it, can hardly be historical. The figures are incredibly large : Deborah (5⁸) places the number of warriors in *entire* Israel at not more than 40,000 ; here 400,000 advance against 25,000 + 700 Benjaminites,

---

* Wellh. *Comp.* p. 232 ; Kuenen, *Onderzoek*, i. 2 (1887), § 20. 3, 4 (see, however, on the other side, Budde, p. 138 ff., Moore, p. 367 f.). The *two* chronological notes, 18$^{30.\ 31}$, for instance, can hardly both be by one hand ; and had the original narrator desired to state the name of the Levite, he would almost certainly have done so where he was first mentioned, 17$^{7ff.}$. V.^{30} is a notice added by a later hand, intended to supply this deficiency. The "day of the captivity (properly *exile*) of the land" can denote only the exile of the ten tribes in 722 B.C.,—or, at least, of the N. tribes in 734 (2 K. 15^{29}).

† Comp. v.^{31} and v.^{39} (in each 30 Israelites smitten): v.^{35} (25,100 Benjaminites smitten) and v.$^{44-46}$ (18,000 + 5000 + 2000 = 25,000 smitten): the *whole* number of Benjaminites, as stated in v.^{15}, was but 25,000 + 700.

and the latter slay of the former on the first day 22,000, on the second day 18,000; on these two days not one of the 25,000 + 700 of the Benjaminites falls, but on the third day 10,000 Israelites slay 25,100 of them (20[2. 15] [LXX, Cod. A; RV. *marg.*] [17. 21. 25. 34. 35]). Secondly, whereas in the rest of the book the tribes are represented uniformly as acting separately, and only combining temporarily and partially, in this narrative Israel is represented as entirely centralized, assembling and taking action *as one man* (20[1. 8. 11]: similarly 21[5. 10. 13. 16]), with a unanimity which, in fact, was gained only—and even then imperfectly—after the establishment of the monarchy. This joint action of the " congregation " contradicts the notices of all except the initial stages in the conquest of Palestine, not less than every other picture which we possess of the condition of Israel during this period. The motives prompting the people's action, and the manner in which they are collected together, are unlike what appears in any other part of either Judges or Samuel : elsewhere the people are impelled to action by the initiative of an individual leader; here they move, in vast numbers, automatically; there is not even mention of the head, who must have been needful for the purpose of directing the military operations. [160] However keenly the rest of Israel may have felt its indignation aroused by the deed of Gibeah, and the readiness of the Benjaminites to screen the perpetrators (20[13]), the combination can hardly have taken place on the scale depicted. Nor is there any trace either in Judges (5[14])—if this incident (comp. 20[27] *) be prior to the time of Deborah—or in Samuel— if it be subsequent to it—of the tribe of Benjamin having been reduced to one-fortieth of its numbers, or in the narrative of 1 Sa. 11 of the virtual extermination (21[10-12]) of the population of Jabesh Gilead.

These difficulties attach only to c. 20–21, not to c. 19. The conclusion to which they point is this, that c. 20–21 are *not homogeneous* : parts are decidedly later than c. 19, and exhibit the tradition respecting the action of the Israelites against

---

* Which, however, is pretty clearly a gloss, and so no real indication of the period to which the incident was assigned by the original narrator. Had v.[27b-28a] been an explanation made by the original narrator, the notice would almost certainly have stood in v.[18], where the inquiry is mentioned for the first time.

Benjamin in the shape which it has assumed in the course of a long period of oral transmission. The story of the vengeance taken by the Israelites against the guilty tribe offered scope for expansion and embellishment, as it was handed on in the mouth of the people; and the literary form in which we have it exhibits the last stage of the process. Hence the exaggeration both in the numbers and in the scale upon which the tribes combined and executed their vengeance upon Benjamin and Jabesh Gilead. The narrative of the outrage in c. 19 is old in style and representation; it has affinities with c. 17–18, and in all probability has come down to us with very little, if any, alteration of form. The narrative of the vengeance, on the contrary, in c. 20, has been expanded; as it was first written down, the incidents were simpler, and the scale on which they were represented as having taken place was smaller than is now the case. But the original narrative has been combined with the additions in such a manner that it cannot be disengaged with certainty, and is now, in all probability, as Kuenen observes, not recoverable.* In c. 21 the narrative of the rape of the maidens at Shiloh wears the appearance [161] of antiquity, and stands, no doubt, on the same footing as c. 19; v.$^{5-14}$, on the contrary, have affinities with the later parts of c. 20. The remark, "In those days there was no king in Israel," connects the two narratives of the appendix together (17^6; 18^1; 19^1; 21^{25}: in 17^6 and 21^{25}, with the addition, "Every man did that which was right in his own eyes"): this, from its character, must certainly be pre-exilic, and stamps the narratives of which it forms a part as pre-exilic likewise. In c. 19–21 the phrase belongs to that part of the narrative, which there are independent reasons for supposing to be earlier than the rest. The object of the narrative in its present form appears to have been to give an *ideal* representation of the community as inspired throughout by a keen sense of right, and as acting harmoniously in concert for the purpose of giving effect to the dictates of morality.

In the first and third divisions of the book no traces are to

* Similarly Kittel, *Gesch.* ii. 21 ; Moore, pp. 405, 408 *top*. Bertheau's attempted analysis is admitted to be unsuccessful, being dependent upon insufficient criteria. Another tentative solution is offered by Budde, p. 150 ff. (see Moore, p. 407). The parts to which the difficulties attach have points of contact with P (p. 143).

be found of the hand of the Deuteronomic redactor of the middle division ; there are no marks either of his distinctive phraseology or of his view of the history, as set forth in 2^{11-19}. Hence it is probable that these divisions did not pass through his hand ; but were added by a later hand (or hands) after 2^6–c. 16 had reached its present shape.

On the historical value of the Book of Judges, reference may be made to an article by Prof. A. B. Davidson on Deborah in the *Expositor*, Jan. 1887, pp. 48–50, who, after remarking on the difference in point of view between the histories and the framework, observes that the regular movement of apostasy, subjugation, penitence, and deliverance, described in the latter, is hardly strict history, but rather the religious philosophy of the history. "The author speaks of Israel as an ideal unity, and attributes to this unity defection, which no doubt characterized only fragments of the whole. . . . The histories preserved in the book are probably traditions preserved among the individual tribes. That in some instances we have duplicates exhibiting divergences in details is natural, and does not detract from the general historical worth of the whole. The story of Deborah is given in a prose form (c. 4) as well as in the poem (c. 5), and the divergences can be accounted for only on the supposition that c. 4 is an independent tradition." Thus the Song speaks of a combination of *kings* of Canaan (5^{19}), of whom Sisera is the head—his mother (5^{29}) is attended by *princesses* (not *ladies*, AV. : see 1 Ki. 11^3, Is. 49^{13}) ; c. 4 speaks of Jabin, who is described as himself "king of Canaan," reigning at Hazor, and of Sisera, his general. Further, while in c. 4 Deborah dwells at Bethel in Ephraim, and Barak at Kedesh in Naphtali, and, in addition to his own tribe, summons only Zebulun (4^{10}), in 5^{15} both leaders are brought into close connexion with Issachar, and the [162] language employed creates at least the *impression* that they belonged to that tribe. In $5^{14.\ 15.\ 18}$ Ephraim, Benjamin, Machir (*i.e.* Manasseh), and Issachar, as well as Naphtali and Zebulun, are alluded to as assisting in the struggle. No doubt the points of agreement between the narrative and the poem are greater than the points of divergence ; but there is sufficient divergence to show that the narrative embodies a tradition which had become modified, and in parts obscured, in the course of oral transmission. In fact, it is not impossible that tradition (as is its wont) may have combined two distinct occurrences, and that, with the victory of Barak and Deborah over the kings of Canaan, with Sisera at their head, may have been intermingled elements belonging properly to an old Israelitish victory over Jabin, a king in the far north of Palestine, reigning at Hazor. On the narrative of Gideon (c. 6–8), comp. Wellh. *Comp.* p. 223 ff. ; Bertheau, p. 158 ff. ; Budde, p. 107 ff. ; Moore, p. 175 ff. ; all of whom, though differing in details of the analysis (which is admitted to be very difficult), agree that the narrative exhibits signs of composition. On the question whether E or J is traceable in Judges, see Kuen. § 19. 13 ; Kittel, *Stud. u. Krit.* 1892, p. 44 ff., *Gesch.* ii. 15–18 [E.T. 14–18] ; König, *Einl.* § 51. $2^{a.b}$; Moore, pp. xxv–xxviii, and elsewhere (*v.* Index), who answers the question in the affirmative, but only in the sense (p. xxvii) that J and E represent, "not individual authors, but a succession of writers, the historiography of a certain period and school."

§ 2. 1-2 SAMUEL.

LITERATURE.—Otto Thenius in the *Kgf. Exeg. Handb.*[2] 1864 (in some respects antiquated) ; Wellhausen, *Der Text der Bücher Samuelis*, 1871 (important for the criticism of the text) ; Keil, *Die Bücher Samuels*,[2] 1875 ; Wellhausen in Bleek's *Einleitung*, 1878, pp. 206-231 [= *Comp.* pp. 238-266]; *Hist.* pp. 245-272 ; A. F. Kirkpatrick in the *Cambridge Bible for Schools and Colleges* ; Aug. Klostermann in Strack and Zöckler's *Kgf. Kommentar*, 1887 (to be constantly distrusted in its treatment of the text); K. Budde, *Richter u. Sam.* 1890, pp. 167-276 ; and in Haupt's *SBOT.* 1895 ; S. R. Driver, *Notes on the Hebrew Text of the Books of Samuel, with an Introduction on Hebrew Palæography and the ancient Versions, and facsimiles of Inscriptions* (1890) ; T. K. Cheyne, *Aids to the Devout Study of Criticism* (1892), pp. 1-126 (on the David-narratives) ; Kittel, *Gesch.* ii. (1892) pp. 22-45 [E.T. pp. 22-49].

The two Books of Samuel, like the two Books of Kings, formed originally a single book. The Book of Samuel and the Book of Kings were treated by the LXX as a complete history of the two kingdoms of Israel and Judah ; and the work was divided by them into four books, termed accordingly βίβλοι βασιλειῶν.* The same division was followed by Jerome in the Vulgate, though for the title "Books of *Kingdoms*," he preferred to substitute "Books of *Kings*." † It hence passed generally into Christian Bibles, and was adopted from them in the printed editions of the Hebrew text, with the difference, however, that each pair of books retained the general title which it bore in [163] Hebrew MSS., and 1-4 βασιλειῶν or *Regum* became 1-2 *Samuel* and 1-2 *Kings*.

The Book owes its title to the circumstance that Samuel is the prominent figure both at its opening and for some time subsequently, and from the part taken by him in the consecration of both Saul and David, may be said in a measure to have determined the history during the entire period embraced by it.

The period of history included by 1-2 Sam. begins with the

---

* The case is similar with 1-2 Chronicles, and with Ezra and Nehemiah, each of which originally formed in the Hebrew one book. Comp. Origen, *ap.* Euseb. vi. 25.

† See his Preface to the Books of Kings (called also the *Prologus Galeatus*), printed at the beginning of ordinary editions of the Vulgate.

circumstances leading to the birth of Samuel, and extends to the close of David's public life—1 Kings opening with the picture of David lying on his deathbed, and passing at once to the events which resulted in the nomination of Solomon as his successor. The death of Saul marks the division between 1 and 2 Sam. The contents of the books may be grouped for convenience under the four heads: 1. Samuel and the establishment of the monarchy (I 1–14); 2. Saul and David (I 15–31); 3. David (II 1–20); 4. an appendix (II 21–24) of miscellaneous contents. The division possesses, however, only a relative value, the first two parts especially running into and presupposing each other. Some of the narratives contained in 1–2 Sam. point forwards, or backwards, to one another, and are in other ways so connected together as to show that they are the work of one and the same writer: this is not, however, the case in all; and it will be the aim of the following pages to indicate, where this is sufficiently clear, the different elements of which the two books are composed.

The reader will notice three *concluding summaries*, which occur in the course of the two books, I 14$^{47-51}$ (Saul's wars; his family and principal officer); II 8 (summary account of David's wars, v.$^{1-14}$, followed by a list of his ministers, v.$^{15-18}$); 20$^{23-26}$ (list of ministers repeated, with one addition, that of Adoram). These summaries show that the narrative to which each is attached has reached a definite halting point, and support (as will appear) certain inferences respecting its relation to the parts which follow.*

I. 1 Sa. 1–14. *Samuel and the Monarchy.*

(1) C. 1–7. Birth and youth of Samuel, including (2$^{17-36}$ 3$^{11-14}$) the announcement of the fall of Eli's house (1^{1}–4^{1a}); defeat of Israel by the Philistines: capture and restoration of the Ark (4^{1b}–7^{1}); Samuel's judgeship, and victory over the Philistines at Eben-ezer (7$^{2-17}$).

It is doubtful whether 4^{1b}–7^{1} was intended in the first [164] instance as a continuation of c. 1–4^{1a}. For, whereas the general tenor of c. 1–4^{1a} would lead us to expect the fall of Eli's house to be the prominent feature in the sequel, in point of fact the fortunes of the Ark form the principal topic in 4^{1b}–7^{1}, and the

---

* Comp. Wellh. *Comp.* pp. 247, 257 f.; Kuen. § 21. 1. I 14$^{47.\ 48}$ may have been expanded by a later Deuteronomic hand (cf. v.^{48b} with Jud. 2$^{14.\ 16}$, 2 Ki. 17^{20}); but the entire summary will hardly be redactional, as Budde (pp. 206–208) and Cornill (*Einl.*^{3} § 17. 4) argue.

fate of Eli and his sons is but a particular incident in the
national disaster : thus a different interest prevails in the two
narratives ; and c. 1–4[1a] appears to have been written as an
introduction to 4[1b]–7[1] (stating particulars of the previous history
of Eli and his sons, and accounting for the prophetical importance
of Samuel) by a somewhat later hand.

The Song of Hannah (2[1-10]) is not early in style, and is unsuited to
Hannah's position : its theme is the humiliation of the lofty and the exaltation of the lowly, which is developed with no special reference to Hannah's
circumstances ; * and v.[10] presupposes the establishment of the monarchy.
The Song was probably composed in celebration of some national success :
it may have been attributed to Hannah on account of v.[5b]. 2[27-36] (announcement to Eli by the unnamed prophet), which has affinities with II 7,
must have been recast by the narrator, and in its new form coloured by
the associations with which he was himself familiar ; for v.[35] (like 2[10])
presupposes the monarchy ("shall walk *before mine anointed* for ever ").
The prophecy relates to the supersession of the priesthood of Eli's family
by that of Zadok (1 Ki. 2[27]), which is to enjoy permanently (v.[35]) the
favour of the royal dynasty.   In point of fact, from the time of Solomon
onwards, Zadok's line held uninterrupted supremacy in the priesthood at
Jerusalem.   Observe that 6[6] alludes to the narrative of J (Ex. 8[82] [Heb.[28]] ;
10[2] התעלל ; 12[33]).

7[2-17] is a section of later origin than either c. 1–4[1a] or 4[1b]–7[1],
homogeneous (see below) with c. 8, 10[17-27a], c. 12.   Hitherto
Samuel has appeared only as a prophet : here he is represented
as a "judge" (7[3b. 6b. 10ff.] ; cf. 12[11]) under whom the Israelites
are delivered from their oppressors, much in the manner of the
deliverances recorded in the Book of Judges.   The consequences
of the victory at Eben-ezer are in 7[13] generalized in terms
hardly reconcilable with the subsequent history : contrast the
picture of the Philistines' ascendency immediately afterwards
(10[5] 13[3. 19ff.] &c.).

It is probable that the original sequel of 4[1b]–7[1] has here been omitted to
make room for 7[2ff.] ; for the existing narrative does not explain (1) how the
Philistines reached Gibeah (10[5] &c.), and secured the ascendency implied
13[19ff.] ; or (2) how Shiloh suddenly disappears from history, and the priesthood [165] located there reappears shortly afterwards at Nob (c. 22).   That
some signal disaster befell Shiloh may be inferred with certainty from the
allusion in Jer. 7[14] 26[6] (comp. Ps. 78[60] ; and Cheyne, *Jeremiah, his life and
times*, p. 117).

---

* It differs in this respect from the *Magnificat* (see v.[2] of this, Luke 1[48]),
which is sometimes quoted as parallel.

(2) C. 8–14. Circumstances leading to the appointment of Saul as king (c. 8–12); Saul's measures of defence against the Philistines; Jonathan's exploit at Michmash (13^1–14^{46}); summary of Saul's wars, and notice of his family (14^{47-52}).

C. 8–12 are formed by the combination of two *independent* [*] narratives of the manner in which Saul became king, differing in their representation both of Samuel and of his relation to Saul. The older narrative comprises 9^1–10^{16}; 10^{27b} [as in LXX: see RV. *marg.*]; $11^{1-11, 15}$ (nomination of Saul as king by Samuel; his success against Nahash king of Ammon, and coronation by the people at Gilgal), of which the continuation is c. 13–14. The other and later narrative consists of c. 8 (request of the people for a king); 10^{17-27a} (election of Saul by lot at Mizpah); c. 12 (Samuel's farewell address to the people). In the older narrative Samuel the seer, famous in a particular district, anoints Saul in accordance with Jehovah's instruction, in order that Israel may have a leader to deliver it from the Philistine yoke (9^{16}), inspiring him at the same time to do "as his hand shall find" (10^7) when occasion arises. The occasion comes in the peril to which Jabesh of Gilead a month (10^{27b} LXX) afterwards is exposed. Saul rescues it successfully (11^{1-11}); and Samuel's choice is confirmed by the people with acclamation (11^{15}). In $13^{2-7a, 15b}$–14^{46} Saul fulfils the object of his nomination by his successes against the Philistines; and 14^{47-52} closes the narrative. C. 11 does not appear to presuppose the election of Saul by the people, 10^{17-27a}. The messengers of Jabesh do not come to Gibeah (v.⁴) on Saul's account: Saul only hears the tidings accidentally upon his return from the field; and in what follows he acts, not in virtue of an office publicly conferred upon him, but in virtue of the impulse seizing him (v.⁶); whereupon, mindful of Samuel's injunction to "do as his hand shall find," he assumes the command of the people (on 11^{14}, see below). Throughout this narrative, also, the appointment of Saul is regarded favourably (see especially 9^{16b}); nor is there any indication of reluctance on Samuel's part to see the monarchy established.

[166] On the other hand, in the other narrative, in which this older account is incorporated, the point of view is different. Samuel exercises the functions, not of a seer or prophet, but of

* So Budde, p. 174, &c., against Wellh., Stade, and Kuenen.

a judge, in agreement with the representation of $7^{2ff.}$; and he rules the people in Jehovah's name (8^{7b}). The proposal for a king originates with the people; and the request addressed to Samuel is based, not on the need of deliverance from foreign foes, but on the injustice of Samuel's sons in their capacity as their father's deputies, and on the desire of the people to have the same visible head as other nations (8^{3-5}). The request is viewed with disfavour by Samuel, and treated as a renunciation of Jehovah. He seeks to dissuade the people from persisting in it, by enumerating to them the exactions which their king will impose upon them, and yields in the end unwillingly (8^{6-22}). The same tone prevails in 10^{17-27a}, and in the farewell address of Samuel c. 12 (v.$^{12.\,17.\,19}$). It is not, of course, necessary to suppose that this narrative is destitute of historical foundation; but the emphasis laid in it upon aspects on which the other narrative is silent, and the difference of tone pervading it, show not the less clearly that it is the work of a different hand. 11^{14}, in which the ceremony at Gilgal is viewed as a *renewal* of the kingdom, is probably a redactional adjustment, made for the purpose of harmonizing the two narratives; for in 11^{1-11}, as said above, Saul does not appear to act as one already recognised as king. Perhaps $11^{12f.}$ are inserted likewise; but the precise relation of these verses to 10^{25-27a} is uncertain. The notice $9^{2b} = 10^{23b}$ has been introduced in *one* of these passages from the other. The second narrative is in style and character homogeneous with 7^{2ff}, and with this may be regarded in a sense as forming the conclusion to the history of the Judges contained in Jud. 2^6–c. 16. In both the general point of view is similar: Israel's apostasy and obedience are contrasted in similar terms; and the task of delivering Israel from the Philistines, "begun" (Jud. 13^5) by Samson, is continued under Samuel ($7^{3b.\,13f.}$; cf. 12^{11}).

In the older narrative, 10^8 and 13^{7b-15a} are held by many to be subsequent insertions. The grounds for this opinion (which are based chiefly upon the imperfect connexion of the two passages with their context) may be seen in Wellh. *Hist.* 257 f.; Budde, pp. 191–193. According to the intention of the insertion, the meeting of Samuel and Saul related in it is the *first* after 10^8; [167] hence it is earlier than 11^{14} (if not than $11^{12f.}$ as well), *i.e.* earlier than the union of the two accounts of Saul's elevation to the throne.

The earlier narrative is an example of the best style of

Hebrew historiography: the scenes are brought vividly before the reader, and are full of minute incident.* The later narrative has been usually regarded as Deuteronomic; but the Deuteronomic style is by no means so pronounced as in the case of the framework of Judges and Kings. Budde (p. 180 ff.) has pointed out that it presents noticeable affinities with E, and has made it probable that it is a *pre*-Deuteronomic work, which in parts has been expanded by a subsequent editor.

Stylistically, the following features, connecting the different parts of the narrative with each other, or with E and Judges, deserve notice :—

7^3 $12^{20. \ 24}$ *with all your heart* [in Dt. always "with all your heart, *and with all your soul*"].

7^3 *put away the strange gods*: Gen. 35^2 (cf. v.⁴), Josh. $24^{14b. \ 23}$ (cf. v.²⁰), Jud. 10^{16}.

7^3 *prepare your hearts unto Jehovah* : Josh. 24^{23} ("incline").

7^4 12^{10} *Baal* and '*Ashtoreth* : Jud. 2^{13} 3^7 (the 'Ashērahs) 10^6.

7^5 $12^{19. \ 23}$ *pray for you* : cf. Gen. $20^{7. \ 17}$, Nu. 11^2 21^7.

7^6 12^{10} *we have sinned* : † cf. Jud. 10^{10} (notice the whole v.) ¹⁵.

7^8 *cry* and *save* : Jud. 3^9 $10^{10. \ 12}$ (*cry* also 3^{15} $6^{6. \ 7}$, 1 Sa. $12^{8. \ 10}$).

7^{13} *to be subdued* (נכנע) : Jud. 3^{30} 4^{23} (הכניע) 8^{28} 11^{33}.

7^{13} 12^{15} *the hand of J. was against them* : Jud. 2^{15}, Dt. 2^{15} *al.*

7^{14} *Amorite*, of the non-Israelite inhabitants of W. Palestine (p. 119). $8^{5b. \ 20a}$ $10^{19. \ 24a}$: Dt. $17^{14b-15a}$.

8^{7b} 10^{19} $12^{12b. \ 17b. \ 19b}$ (Jehovah the nation's king).

8^8 *to forsake Jehovah, and serve other gods* : Josh. 24^{16} (cf. v.²⁰), Jud. 10^{13} ; cf. c. 12^{10}, Jud. $2^{12. \ 13}$ 10^{10}.

8^{18} 12^{13} (whom *ye have chosen*).

10^{18b}, Jud. $6^{8f.}$ $10^{11f.}$: לחץ *to oppress* also Jud. 2^{18} 4^3 ; and Ex. 3^9 (E).

10^{19b} *present yourselves* (התיצב) *before Jehovah* : Josh. 24^1.

$12^{6. \ 8}$ (allusion to Moses and the exodus) : cf. Josh. $24^{4-6. \ 17}$.

12^9 *sold* : Jud. 2^{14} 3^8 4^2 10^7.

[168] 12^{11} *enemies on every side* (מסביב) : Dt. 12^{10} 25^{19}, Josh. 23^1 (D²), Jud. 2^{14} 8^{34} ; cf. Josh. 21^{44} (42) (also D²).

$12^{14. \ 24}$ *to fear and serve Jehovah* : Josh. 24^{14a}.

12^{16} *do before your eyes* : Dt. 1^{30b} 4^{34b} 29^{2b}, Josh. 24^{17b}.

12^{23} חלילה לי : cf. Josh. 24^{16}.

---

* It contains several somewhat remarkable and unusual words : 9^7 אול and תשורה ; v.¹⁷ עצר ; v.²⁵ LXX (διέστρωσαν) רבד ; 10^3 חלף = *to advance* ; 13^6 צריח ; 14^1 הלז ; v.⁶ מעצור ; v.³² עשה. Peculiar to this narrative also is the title נגיר *leader* or *prince* 9^{16} 10^1 (so 13^{14} and subsequently [below, p. 184]). In the other narrative *king* is the term always employed.

† The argument from style is *cumulative* : hence expressions which, if they stood alone, would have no appreciable weight, may help to support an inference, when they are combined with others pointing in the same direction.

The similarities, partly with E (esp. Josh. 24), partly with the redaction of Judges, are evident. The entire phenomena appear to be best explained by the supposition that the basis consists of a narrative allied to that of E,[*] which was afterwards expanded, esp. in 12[9ff.], by a writer whose style and point of view were similar to those of Dt. and the compiler of the Book of Judges. To this second writer may be attributed the strange mention of Samuel by himself in 12[11], and the notice in 12[12] of Nahash, derived, indeed, from c. 11, but so applied as to conflict with the representation in 8[4ff.]. The original narrative[†] may be an excerpt from the same source as Jud. 6[7-10] 10[6-16] (pp. 166, 167 *n.*), which perhaps carried on the history of E to the time of Samuel. Graf pointed out the resemblance of 1 Sa. 12 to Josh. 24; and remarked that the discourse in the one seems "to close the history of the Judges, as the discourse in the other closes that of the conquest of Palestine" (*Gesch. B.* p. 97 : cf. Del. *Gen.* p. 33). That this narrative—or at least the representation contained in it—was known to Jeremiah may be certainly inferred from Jer. 15[1]; for it is only here (and not in the other narrative of Saul's appointment as king) that mention is made of Samuel as *interceding* for the people (Cornill, *ap.* Budde, p. 178).

II. C. 15-31. *Saul and David.*

(1) C. 15–18. Rejection of Saul. Introduction of David to the history. Saul's jealousy aroused by his successes against the Philistines.

C. 15 (Saul and Amalek) was evidently not written originally in continuation of c. 14 : for (1) it would be out of place after the narrator of c. 14 had finished his account of Saul's reign (v.[47-51]); (2) the style and representation differ.

In c. 14, for instance, the history is narrated, so to say, objectively : Amalek, v.[48], is smitten (it is implied) because they spoiled the Israelites : here a theoretical *motive* is assigned for the expedition, v.[2, 6], and supreme importance is attached to the *principle* actuating Saul in his conduct of it (v.[10ff.]) : the circumstances, also, of Saul's rejection are so told as to inculcate at the same time the prophetic lesson (Jer. 7[21-26]) that Jehovah demands obedience in preference to sacrifice. Of course, the fact that the history is thus told with a purpose does not invalidate its general truth : "that Saul actually smote the Amalekites, and that Samuel actually slew Agag at Gilgal before Jehovah, are historical facts, which no ground exists for calling in question" (Wellh. *Comp.* p. 249).

C. 15 holds, in fact, an intermediate position between the two [169] currents of narrative 9[1] &c. and c. 8 &c. ; it presupposes the

---

[*] But hardly written by the same hand : see Kittel, *St. u. Krit.* 1892, pp. 66, 71, *Gesch.* ii. 25–28 ; and cf. above, pp. 171 *bottom*, 172 *top.*

[†] Which, especially in the view taken in it of the monarchy, presents affinities with *Hosea* (Budde, p. 184 f.).

former (for v.[1] points back to 10[1], and a phrase in v.[19b] appears to be borrowed from 14[32]), but approximates in its prophetic tone to the latter.* Its contents adapt it for the position which it now holds in the book, *after* the formal close of the history of Saul's reign, 14[47-51], and *before* the introduction of David: note in particular v.[28], which explains how, in what follows, David is the principal figure even during the lifetime of Saul.

In c. 16–18 there are *two* accounts of David's introduction to the history. According to one account, 16[14-23], he is of mature age, "a man of war, and clever in speech [*or* in business]," on account of his skill with the harp brought into Saul's service at the time of the king's mental distress, and quickly appointed his armour-bearer (v.[18, 21]). According to the other account, 17[1]–18[5], he is a shepherd lad, inexperienced in warfare, who first attracts the king's attention by an act of heroism against the Philistines: in this account, moreover, the inquiry 17[55-58] comes strangely from one who, according to 16[14-23], had not merely been told who his father was, but had manifested a marked affection for David, and had repeatedly been waited on by him (v.[21, 23]).† Allusions to David's exploit against Goliath occur, however, in subsequent parts of the narrative (see 19[5] 21[9] [Heb. [10]] 22[10b, 13]); so that the victory over Goliath must have formed a prominent element in the popular tradition respecting David,‡ and it is only the literary form in which 17[1]–18[5] here appears, and its collision with 16[14-23], which forbid the supposition that it was written originally for the place which it now occupies. But that the following section must from the first have been preceded by *some* account of David's military prowess is evident from 18[7], which implies that he had achieved some success (or successes) against the Philistines.

In the section 17[1]–18[5] the genuine text of LXX (cod. Vat.) omits [170] v.[12-31, 41, 50, 55]–18[5]. By the omission of these verses the elements which conflict

---

* Budde (pp. 188–191) treats it definitely as the sequel of I 12.

† Contrast also 18[2] ("did not let him go back") with 16[21-23]; and observe that the terms of 17[12] introduce David as a *new* character in the history (comp. 9[1]; 25[9]; 1 Ki. 11[26]). The latter circumstance shows, further, that 16[1-13] (David anointed at Bethlehem) and 17[1]–18[5] do not both belong to the same stratum of narrative.

† It is remarkable that in II 21[19] Goliath is stated to have been slain by *Elhanan* of Bethlehem (the text of 1 Ch. 20[5] is plainly less original).

with 16[14-23] are greatly reduced (*e.g.* David is no longer represented as *unknown* to Saul), but they are not removed altogether (comp. 17[33, 38ff.] with 16[18, 21b]). It is doubtful, therefore, whether the text of LXX is here really to be preferred to the Heb. : Wellh. (*Comp.* 250), Kuenen (*Onderz.* § 23. 7), and Budde (p. 212 f.) agree that either the translators, or, as Kuenen supposes, the scribe of the MS. used by them, omitted the verses in question from harmonistic motives, without, however, entirely securing the end desired; on the other hand, W. R. Smith, *OTJC.*[2] pp. 120 ff., 431 ff., and Cornill, *Einl.* § 17. 5, maintain the superior originality of the LXX text. It is to be observed that the covenant with Jonathan, 18[3], is presupposed by 20[8]. The verses 17[12, 15] have probably been modified in form, for the purpose of harmonizing the representation with that of 16[14-23].

In 18[6-30] (Saul's growing jealousy of David), the continuation of 16[14-23] (the evil spirit vexing Saul), there are again considerable omissions in LXX (cod. Vat.), the text of LXX reading as follows :—v.[6b] (And women dancing came forth out of all the cities to meet David with timbrels, with joy, &c.), [7, 8a] (to *but thousands*), [9] [see Swete], [12a] (And Saul was afraid of David), [13-16, 20-21a] (to *against him*), [22-26a] (to *son-in-law*), [27-29a] (reading in v.[28b] " and *that all Israel* loved him "). In this instance it is generally admitted that the LXX text deserves the preference : the sequence of events is clearer, and the stages in the gradual growth of Saul's enmity towards David are distinctly marked (comp. v.[12a, 15b, 29] 19[1]). See Kirkpatrick on 1 Samuel, p. 242 ; *OTJC.*[2] p. 122 f. ; or the writer's *Notes on Samuel*, p. 121 : on the other hand, Budde, p. 217 ff., prefers the Heb. text.

(2) C. 19–22. David finds himself obliged to flee from Saul. He visits Samuel at Ramah (19[18-24]), learns through Jonathan that Saul's enmity towards him is confirmed (c. 20), and repairs in consequence first to Abimelech at Nob, then to Achish at Gath (c. 21), and finally takes refuge in the cave of Adullam (c. 22).

19[18-24] is parallel with 10[10-13]. Two explanations must have been current respecting the origin of the proverb, Is Saul also among the prophets ? both, however, bringing the incident into connexion with *Samuel*. The account here cannot be by the same hand as that in 10[10-13], though both were deemed worthy of retention by the compiler of the book. C. 20 has been supposed to be a doublet to 19[1-7], partly on account of some resemblance in the situation (19[1-3] and 20[1b-3, 11, 24]), partly on account of the apparent incompatibility of David's uncertainty as to Saul's feeling towards him with the declared hostility of 19[1, 10ff.]. The resemblance is, however, very partial ; and Saul's attitude was probably apt to fluctuate from day to day with his changeful temper (comp. 19[6f.] after v.[1]).

(3) C. 23–26. David as an outlaw: (*a*) at Keilah (23[1-13]) ; (*b*) in the wilderness of Ziph (23[14-29]); (*c*) in En-gedi, where he cuts off Saul's skirt in the cave (c. 24); (*d*) in Carmel (David

and Nabal) (c. 25) ; (e) in the wilderness of Ziph again, where he steals by night Saul's spear and cruse of water (c. 26). C. 24 [171] and c. 26 recount two anecdotes of David's outlaw life. It is, however, a question whether the two narratives really relate to two different occasions, and whether they are not rather merely different versions of the same occurrence. There are remarkable resemblances between the two accounts ; and though there are also differences of detail, these are hardly greater than might have grown up in a story current among the people for some time before it was committed to writing. If the occasion in c. 26 is a different one from that in c. 24, it is singular that it contains no allusion, on either David's part or Saul's, to David's having spared Saul's life, under similar circumstances, before.

As regards the resemblances between the two accounts, compare 26[1] and 23[19] ; 26[2] and 24[2] ; 26[8] and 24[4, 18b] ; 26[9b, 11a] and 24[6, 10b] ; 26[17] and 24[16] ("Is this thy voice, my son David?") ; 26[18] and 24[9, 11] ; 26[19a] and 24[9] (Saul adjured not to listen to men who may have calumniated David); 26[20] * and 24[14] ; 26[21] and 24[17] ; 26[23] and 24[12, 15] ; 26[25a] and 24[19f.] ; 26[25b] and 24[22]. By those who hold the two narratives to be different versions of the same event, that in c. 26 is generally considered to be the earlier and the more original (notice the antique conception underlying 26[19] ; and in 24[17-21] the more explicit terms of Saul's answer as compared with 26[21, 25]) : otherwise, however, Budde, p. 228 f.

(4) C. 27–31. David seeks refuge in the country of the Philistines with Achish (c. 27). The Philistines resolve to attack Israel (28[1f.]). Saul consults the witch at En-dor (28[3-25]). David is dismissed by Achish on account of the suspicions of the Philistine lords (c. 29). His vengeance on the Amalekites who had smitten Ziklag (c. 30). Death of Saul and Jonathan on Mount Gilboa (c. 31).

28[1f.] attaches immediately to c. 27, and is continued by c. 29-31. 28[3-25] appears to have been misplaced. 28[4] the Philistines have advanced to Shunem (in the plain of Jezreel) ; 29[1] they are still at Aphek, in the Sharon (Josh. 12[18] LXX, Dillm.; G. A. Smith, PEFQuSt. 1895, p. 252 f., Geogr.[4] p. 675), and only reach Jezreel in 29[11]. Thus the situation in 28[4] anticipates c. 29-30. The narrative will be in its right order if 28[3-25] be read after c. 29-30. 28[3-25] is treated by Wellh. (Hist. pp. 258-262) as belonging to the same stratum of narrative as c. 15 : Budde (pp. 233-235) points out the resemblances in style and representation with I 9[1]-10[16] &c., and regards v. [17-19a] (to Philistines), which is the passage connecting it with c. 15, as a later amplification of the original text.

---

* Where, however, my life should probably be read with LXX for a flea.

III. 2 Sa. 1–20. *David*.

(1) C. 1–8. Lament of David over Saul and Jonathan (c. 1). David is made king at Hebron over Judah, and subsequently, after the murder of Ishbosheth, over all Israel (c. 2–5³). **[172]** Capture of the stronghold of Jebus, which David henceforth makes his residence (5⁴⁻¹⁶). Successes against the Philistines (5¹⁷⁻²⁵). The removal of the Ark to the "city of David" (c. 6). The prophecy of Nathan (7¹⁻¹⁷), arising out of David's desire to build a Temple for the Ark, with David's prayer consequent upon it (7¹⁸⁻²⁹). Summary of David's wars, and list of his ministers (c. 8).

The thread of the history is here carried forward without interruption. Only the notices in 2¹⁰ᵃ· ¹¹ are, probably, later insertions: for v.¹⁰ᵇ is the natural sequel of v.⁹, and v.¹² of v.¹⁰ᵇ. And 5¹⁷⁻²⁵ can scarcely have been written originally as the sequel of 5⁶⁻¹²; for were the entire ch. a continuous narrative, "the hold" (המצודה) of v.¹⁷ (cf. 23¹⁴) could hardly denote any other spot than "the hold" (same word) of v.⁹ (*i.e.* Zion), which, nevertheless, is evidently not the case. V.¹⁷ᵃ is the natural sequel of v.³ᵇ: it is conjectured plausibly by Budde (p. 243) that the original place of 5⁶⁻¹² was between 6¹ and 6².

C. 8 marks a break in the book, and closes the chief account of David's *public* doings. It should be compared with the conclusion of the history of Saul's reign, I 14⁴⁶⁻⁵¹. In some respects it anticipates what follows, just as that does (Amalek, c. 15), comp. v.³· ⁵· ¹² (Ammon), with c. 10–12. The oldest narrative of the two reigns is constructed upon a similar model. First is described the manner in which Saul and David respectively reach the throne; then their accomplishment of the military task in the first instance entrusted to them (I 9¹⁶; II 3¹⁸ 19⁹): then follows a survey of other memorable achievements; and so the history is concluded.

(2) C. 9–20 [of which 1 Ki. 1–2 is the continuation]. History of events in David's *court*-life, showing how Amnon, Absalom, and Adonijah failed in turn to secure the succession to the throne: viz. the friendly regard shown by David to Jonathan's son, Mephibosheth (c. 9); the war with Ammon; David and Bathsheba; the birth of Solomon (c. 10–12); Amnon's rape of his half-sister Tamar, and his murder by order of Absalom (c. 13); the rebellion and death of Absalom (c. 14–19); the revolt of Sheba (20¹⁻²²) (an incident springing out of the revolt of Absalom); list of David's ministers (20²³⁻²⁶).

The parts of this narrative are mutually connected together, and are marked by unity of plan : thus c. 9 is required for the purpose of explaining the notices 16^{1-4} 19^{24-30} (see 9^{10}), and [**173**] 17^{27} (see 9^5) ; the account of the war with Ammon is needed for the purpose of showing how David became acquainted with Bathsheba, the future mother of Solomon ; the following chapters describe in detail how one after another of Solomon's elder brothers failed to obtain the throne. The abundance and particularity of detail show that the narrative must date from a period very little later than that of the events related. The style is singularly bright, flowing, and picturesque.

IV. C. 21–24. An appendix to the main narrative of the book, of miscellaneous contents : viz. (*a*) the famine in Israel stopped through the sacrifice of the sons of Saul by the Gibeonites (21^{1-14}) ; (*b*) exploits against the Philistines (21^{15-22}) ; (*c*) David's Hymn of Triumph (c. 22 = Ps. 18) ; (*d*) David's "Last Words" (23^{1-7}) ; (*e*) further exploits against the Philistines, and list of David's heroes (23^{8-39}) ; (*f*) David's census of the people (c. 24).

Here *a* and *f* are in style and manner closely related (24^1 is evidently the sequel to 21^{14b} : comp. also 21^{14b} 24^{25}), as are also *b* and *e*. The four chapters interrupt the continuous narrative, c. 9–20. 1 Ki. 1–2 ; whence it may be inferred that they were placed where they now stand *after* the separation had been effected between the Books of Samuel and Kings. The sources made use of by the compiler exhibit no affinity with c. 9–20. 1 K. 1–2. The list of heroes (like the previous lists, 3^{2-5} 5^{14-16} 8^{15-18} &c.) may be derived from the register of the "recorder" (8^{16}) ; cf. below, p. 187.

Looking at 1–2 Sa. as a whole, relatively the latest passages will be Hannah's Song, and I 2^{27-36} 7^2–c. 8. 10^{17-27a} 11^{14} c. 12. c. 15. II 7, most of which, in their present form, have *some* affinities in thought and expression with Dt., though decidedly less marked than those observable in the redaction of Kings, so that —except in so far as I 7. 8. 12 may have been in parts expanded by a Deuteronomic hand—they will be *pre*-Deuteronomic, and hardly later than c. 700 B.C. The rest, it is plain, is not throughout the work of one hand, or written *uno tenore* (cf. what was said above on I $1-4^{1a}$; 17^1-18^5 ; 19^{18-24} ; c. 24 and 26 ; II 5^{17-25}) : but in all probability it is mostly earlier than the passages just quoted, and in some parts (esp. II 9 20) nearly contemporary with the events recorded. The most considerable part which appears plainly to be the work of a single author, is II 9–20 : many parts of the preceding history of David (I 15–II 5), especially those which, as Wellh. has shown, are mutually connected together,* [174] and form a continuous thread, are also, probably, by the same hand, though whether by the same as II 9–20, must remain here undetermined.

Budde (in Haupt's *SBOT*) thus connects together, and attributes to the oldest source,† 1 Sa. 9^1–10^7 $10^{9\text{-}16a}$ $11^{1\text{-}11.\ 14\text{-}15}$ $13^{2\text{-}7a.\ 15b\text{-}18.\ 23}$ $14^{1\text{-}46.\ 52}$ $16^{14\text{-}23}$ $18^{5.\ 6}$ (partly), $^{7\text{-}11.\ 20\text{-}21a.\ 22\text{-}30}$ $20^{1\text{-}3.\ 18\text{-}39.\ 42b}$ [21^1 H.] $22^{1\text{-}4.\ 6\text{-}10a.\ 11\text{-}18.\ 20\text{-}22}$ $23^{1\text{-}14a.}$ $^{19\text{-}29}$ $24^{1\text{-}19.\ 22b}$ c. 25. 27. $28^{1\text{-}2}$ c. 29–30. $28^{4\text{-}16.\ 19b\text{-}25}$ c. 31. 2 Sa. $1^{1\text{-}4.\ 11\text{-}12.\ 17\text{-}23}$ c. 2–4. $5^{1\text{-}3.\ 17\text{-}25}$ $21^{15\text{-}22}$ $23^{8\text{-}12.\ 17b\text{-}39.\ 13\text{-}17a}$ 6^1 $5^{6.\ 7a.\ 8a.\ 9\text{-}12}$ $6^{2\text{-}23}$ $8^{7\text{-}10.\ 13\text{-}14a}$ $3^{2\text{-}5}$ $5^{13\text{-}16}$ $8^{16\text{-}18}$ c. 24. $21^{1\text{-}2a.\ 3\text{-}6.\ 8\text{-}14}$ c. 9–11. $12^{1\text{-}7a.9\ b.\ 13\text{-}31}$ c. 13–19. $20^{1\text{-}22}$; cf. the criticism of Stade, *Th. Lit.-Zeit.* 1896, No. 1.

There are a certain number of expressions which occur frequently in 1–2 Sa.; but some are evidently colloquialisms, and many occur likewise in the narrative parts of Jud. Kgs., so that they appear to have formed part of the phraseology current at the time, and their use does not imply necessarily identity of author.   The following are the most noticeable :—

1. *As thy soul liveth* : I 1^{26} 17^{55}, II 11^{11} 14^{19} : preceded by *As Jehovah liveth* I 20^3 25^{26} 2 Ki. $2^{2.\ 4.\ 6}$ 4^{30}.†

2. בני בליעל : Dt. 13^{14}, Jud. 19^{22} 20^{13} I 1^{16} (בת בליעל) 2^{12} 10^{27} 25^{17}, 1 Ki. $21^{10.\ 13}$, 2 Ch. 13^7 : בליעל (אנשי) איש, I 25^{25} 30^{22}, II 16^7 20^1, 1 Ki. 21^{13}.†

3. *Jehovah of Hosts* : I $1^{3.\ 11}$ 4^4 15^2 17^{45}, II 5^{10} (י׳ אלהי צ׳) $6^{2.\ 18}$ $7^{8.\ 26.\ 27}$, 1 Ki. 18^{15} $19^{10.\ 14}$, 2 Ki. 3^{14} 19^{31} [=Is. 37^{32}]. (All in Gen.-Kings. Often in the prophets, except Joel, Obadiah, Jonah, and Ezekiel.)

4. *So may God do (to me) and more also* : I 3^{17} 14^{44} 20^{13} 25^{22}, II $3^{9.\ 35}$ 19^{14}, 1 Ki. 2^{23}, 2 Ki. 6^{31}, Ru. 1^{17} : with a plur. verb (in the mouth of a non-Israelite), 1 Ki. 19^2 20^{10}.†

5. *From Dan even to Beersheba* : I 3^{20}, II 3^{10} 17^{11} $24^{2.\ 15}$, Jud. 20^1 (. . . למדן), 1 Ki. 4^{25}.   *From B. even to Dan* : 1 Ch. 21^2, 2 Ch. 30^5.†

6. *Prince* or *leader* (נגיד), of the chief ruler of Israel : I 9^{16} 10^1 13^{14} 25^{30}, II 5^2 6^{21} 7^8, 1 Ki. 1^{35} 14^7 16^2, 2 Ki. 20^5. (All in Gen.-Kings.)

7. צלח *to come mightily* (of a spirit) : I $10^{6.\ 10}$ 11^6 16^{13} 18^{10} (of an evil spirit), Jud. $14^{6.\ 19}$ 15^{14}.   Not so elsewhere.

8. *As Jehovah liveth* : I $14^{39.\ 45}$ 19^6 $20^{3.\ 21}$ $25^{26.\ 34}$ $26^{10.\ 16}$ 28^{10} 29^6, II 2^{27} (*God*) 4^9 12^5 14^{11} 15^{21} (22^{47}), 1 Ki. 1^{29} (followed by *who redeemed my soul*, as II 4^9) 2^{24} $17^{1.\ 12}$ $18^{10.\ 15}$ 22^{14}‖, 2 Ki. $2^{2.\ 4.\ 6}$ 3^{14} 4^{30} $5^{16.\ 20}$. (All in the hist. books.   In the Pent. only *As I live* thrice : Nu. $14^{21.\ 28}$ [חי אני], Dt. 32^{40} [חי אנכי].)

---

* Cf. *e.g.* I 18^7 29^5 ; $18^{25.\ 27}$ (LXX), II 3^{14} ; $22^{20ff.}$ $23^{9ff.}$; 23^2 30^8, II 2^1 5^{19} ; I $25^{2ff.}$ $30^{26ff.}$; 27^3 30^5.

† Though whether this source is rightly identified with J is very questionable : the present writer agrees here with Kittel, *St. u. Krit.* 1892, p. 61 ff.

9. *Blessed be thou* (*ye*) *of J.* : I 15¹³ 23²¹, II 2⁵, Ruth 3¹⁰.   Only Ps. 115¹⁵
besides ; but cf. Jud. 17², Ru. 2²⁰.

10. פשט *to spread out, deploy* : I 23²⁷ 27⁸· ¹⁰ 30¹· ¹⁴, Jud. 9³³· ⁴⁴ 20³⁷.   (All
in Gen.-Kings.)

11. משתין בקיר : I 25²²· ³⁴, I Ki. 14¹⁰ 16¹¹ 21²¹, 2 Ki. 9⁸.†

Peculiar, or nearly so, to 1-2 Sa. are—אתמול (I 4⁷ 10¹¹ 14²¹ 19⁷, II 5².
The usual form is תמול).—ואדמה על ראשו (I 4¹², II 1² 15³²†).—מה היה הדבר (I 4¹⁶,
II 1⁴†).—מאיש (ו)עד אשה מעולל ועד יונק (I 15³ 22¹⁹†).—שמע in the *piel*=to
summon (I 15⁴ 23⁸†).—עלם *youth*, the masc. of עלמה (I 17⁵⁶ 20²²†).—*Battles of
Jehovah* [175] (I 18¹⁷ 25²⁸ ; rather differently Nu. 21¹⁴†).—ולא שנה לו and not
repeat it to him (I 26⁸, II 20¹⁰†).—The comparison to an *angel of God* (I 29⁹, II
14¹⁷· ²⁰ 19²⁷†).—ויהי אחרי כן as a link of transition (II 2¹ 8¹ 10¹ 13¹ 21¹⁸ : rather
differently I 24⁶.   Never in Hex. : in Jud. only 16⁴ ; in Ki. only II 6²⁴).—
חמש *belly* (II 2²³ 3²⁷ 4⁶ [not LXX] 20¹⁰†).—ברה *to eat,* הברה *to give food to,*
בריה *food* (II 3³⁵ 12¹⁷ 13⁵⁻⁷· ¹⁰.   An uncommon word : elsewhere only in the
piel, Lam, 4¹⁰ ; and ברות *food,* Ps. 69²²).

§ 3. 1-2 KINGS.

LITERATURE.—K. C. W. F. Bähr in Lange's *Bibelwerk*, 1868 ; Otto
Thenius in the *Kgf. Exeg. Handb.*[2] 1873 ; C. F. Keil,[2] 1876 ; Wellhausen in
Bleek's *Einl.* (1878) pp. 231-266 [= *Comp.* pp. 266-302, 359-361] ; *Hist.*
p. 272 ff. ; Stade, *Der text des Berichtes über Salomo's Bauten* in the *ZATW.*
1883, pp. 129-177 (important : see the chief results in *QPB.*,[3] also Stade's
Gesch. Isr. i. pp. 311-343, with illustrations) ; *ib.* 1884, p. 271 ff. ; 1885,
pp. 165 ff., 178, 275 ff. ; 1886, p. 156 ff. (on other passages of Kings) ;
Klostermann (see p. 172, with the caution) ; Kittel, *Gesch.* ii. pp. 45 ff., 177 ff. ;
F. W. Farrar (in the "Expositor's Bible "), 1893-4.

The two Books of Kings embrace the history of Israel from
the period of David's nomination of Solomon as his successor,
consequent upon the rebellion of Adonijah, to the release of
Jehoiachin from prison in Babylon by Evil-merodach, 562 B.C.
The structure of the two books is essentially similar to that of
the central part of the Book of Judges : materials derived from
older sources have been arranged together, and sometimes expanded at the same time, in a framework supplied by the compiler. The framework of the compiler is in general readily
distinguishable. It comprises the chronological details, references to authorities, and judgments on the character of the
various kings, especially with reference to their attitude to the
worship at the high places,—all cast in the same literary mould,
and marked by the same characteristic phraseology. Both in
point of view and in phraseology, the compiler shows himself to
be strongly influenced by *Deuteronomy.*

The Books of Kings may be treated conveniently in three parts :—(1) I 1–11 *Solomon*; (2) I 12–II 17 *Israel and Judah*; (3) II 18–25 *Judah*. Each part shows abundant marks of the compiler's hand; but the scheme or plan of his work, from the nature of the case, is most evident in the second part, where the compiler has to arrange and bring into mutual relation with one another the successive reigns in the two contemporary kingdoms. [176] For each reign he adopts an introductory and concluding formula, couched in similar terms throughout, between which are described the events belonging to the reign in question, only very rarely an isolated notice being allowed to appear after the closing formula (I 16^7 II 15^{16}; cf. 24^7).

These formulæ are too well known to need quotation. The opening formula, in the case of the kings of Judah (*e.g.* I $15^{9f.}$), consists of two sentences, the first defining the synchronism with the kingdom of Israel, the second stating the age, the length of reign, and the name of the king's mother. In the case of the kings of Israel (*e.g.* I 15^{33}), it consists usually of a single sentence, in which the synchronism with the kingdom of Judah and the length of reign are alone stated. The closing formula for the kings of Judah (*e.g.* II $8^{23f.}$) consists of two sentences, the first containing the compiler's reference to his source, the second—rarely separated from the first by an intervening notice (I 14^{30} $15^{7.\ 23b}$ 22^{46-49}, II 15^{37})—mentioning the death and burial of the king, and the name of his successor. In the case of the kings of Israel (*e.g.* I $16^{27f.}$) the formula is similar, except that the words "was buried with his fathers" are never used. Slight deviations from these formulæ occasionally occur, arising mostly out of the circumstances of the case: thus the clause "and slept with his fathers" is omitted in the case of those kings who came to a violent end, II 12^{21} 14^{20} 21^{26} 23^{30}. The repetition of the closing formula in the case of Jehoash II $13^{12f.}$ $14^{15f.}$ is no doubt the result of some error: its position in $13^{12f.}$, immediately after the opening formula (v.$^{10f.}$), is contrary to analogy.

The *judgments* on the several kings ("And he did that which was right—*or* that which was evil—in the eyes of Jehovah"; in the case of Israel, always "that which was evil") usually follow the opening formula, and are mostly confined to a single verse (as I 15^{26}). Occasionally, however, they are longer, and embrace fuller particulars (as I 14^{22-24} 15^{11-14} 16^{30-33}, II 16^{3-4}).

The Book of Kings differs from all the preceding historical books, in the fact that the compiler refers habitually to certain authorities for particulars not contained in his own work. These authorities are (1) for the reign of Solomon, the "Book of the acts of Solomon" (1 Ki. 11^{41}); (2) for the Northern kingdom, the "Book of the chronicles of the kings of Israel" (17 times—for all the kings except Jehoram and Hoshea); (3) for the

Southern kingdom, the "Book of the chronicles of the kings of Judah" (15 times—for all except Ahaziah, Athaliah, Jehoahaz, Jehoiachin, and Zedekiah). These authorities, it is to be noticed, are always referred to for information respecting the *kings*, their buildings, warlike enterprises, and other undertakings; for instance, [177] "And the rest of the acts of Solomon, and *all that he did*, *and his wisdom*, are they not written in the Book of the acts of Solomon?" * It may be safely inferred from the character of these references that the "Books of chronicles" were of a *political* character: they contained notices of the public and official doings of the several kings.† The Book of the acts of Solomon included, in addition, some specimens or notices of his "wisdom." The name by which the Books are quoted points to the same conclusion. The expression *chronicles* (lit. *words*, or *acts*, *of days*) is the proper term used to denote an official *journal*, or minutes of events: 1 Ch. 27^{24} it is implied that the results of David's census would in the ordinary course of things have been included in the "chronicles" of his reign; Neh. 12^{23} a "book of chronicles" is mentioned, in which the heads of Levitical families were registered. Now, it appears from 2 Sa. 8^{16} 20^{24}, 1 Ki. 4^{3}, 2 Ki. $18^{18.\ 37}$, 2 Ch. 34^{8} that David, Solomon, Hezekiah, and Josiah had among their ministers one who bore the title of *recorder* (lit. *remembrancer*: מזכיר, LXX ὁ ὑπομιμνήσκων, ὁ ὑπομνηματογράφος, ὁ ἐπὶ τῶν ὑπομνημάτων); and it may reasonably be inferred that the other kings as well had a similar minister. It can hardly be doubted that the function of this minister was to keep an official record of the public events of the reign,‡ such as

* Other phrases used are: "how he warred, and how he reigned" (I 14^{19}), "and all that he did" (I 14^{29} *al.*), "and all his might, and all that he did, and the cities that he built" (I 15^{23}), "and his treason that he wrought" (I 16^{20}, II 15^{15}), "and all that he did, and the ivory house which he built, and all the cities that he built" (I 22^{39}), "and his might, and how he fought against Amaziah king of Judah" (II 14^{15}), "and all that he did, and his might, how he warred, and how he recovered Damascus and Hamath" (v.^{28}), "and all his might, and how he made the pool, and the conduit, and brought water into the city" (II 20^{20}), "and all that he did, and his sin that he sinned" (II 21^{17}).

† The sin of Manasseh would be no doubt his public recognition of idolatry.

‡ Comp. Est. 2^{23} 6^{1}, in which last passage "chronicles" is in apposition with "book of records" (ספר הזכרנות), a term used in the Aramaic sections of Ezra to denote the Persian official archives (Ezr. 4^{15}; cf. 6^{2}).

would be denoted by דברי הימים or "chronicles." It has been
questioned whether the "Books" referred to in Kings are the
actual official records of the two kingdoms, or two independent
historical works *based* upon them. Modern scholars, though not
upon very decisive grounds, prefer generally [**178**] the latter
alternative. The difference is not important. In either case
the two books were digests or summaries of events of national
importance, with names and lists of officers, &c. The book
dealing with the reign of Solomon appears to have been distinct
from either of the two containing the annals of the two kingdoms
subsequent to the rupture.

In the *narrative* of Kings (apart from the compiler's framework) two elements are distinguishable—(1) brief, statistical
notices, sometimes called the "Epitome," relating chiefly to
events of political importance; (2) longer, continuous narratives,
describing usually occurrences in which the *prophets* were more
or less directly concerned. In form the Epitome is no doubt
the work of the compiler; but the particulars embraced in it,
after what has been said, may reasonably be regarded as derived
by him from the two books named. The longer narratives,
which there is no reason to suppose formed part of the official
annals (for these are uniformly referred to in connexion with the
public doings of the *kings*), will have been taken by him from
various independent sources. These narratives are written
mostly in a bright and chaste Hebrew style, though some of them
exhibit slight peculiarities of diction,* due doubtless (in part)
to their North Israelitish origin. Their authors were in all

---

* *E.g.* in the Elisha-narratives, אתי for אַתְּ *thou* (fem.) II 4[16. 23] 8[1] (also
I 14[2], Jud. 17[2], Jer. 4[30], Ez. 36[13]↑), and the other fems. in ‑ 4[2. 3. 7. 23]: the
prep. ‑אֶת *with*, written ‑אוֹת (as often in Jer., Ez.) 12 times between I 20 and
II 8 (I 20[25 *bis*] 22[7. 8] (מֵאֹתוֹ) [24] II 1[15]   3[11. 12. 26] 6[16] 8[8]); and slight solecisms
of form or expression, as בהשתחוָיתִי II 5[18]; ש in מִשֶּׁלָּנוּ 6[11] (Klost., however,
after LXX, מִנַּלֶּנוּ); איכה *where?* 6[13] Kt. (=אֵיכָה); זו *fem.* (Aram. רא) 6[19];
בהשרה 7[12]; עד־הם 9[18]; עד־אליהם 9[20]; the verb. (Aram.) השלה 4[28]. Comp. also
שפף *to suffice* (Aram. ספף), I Ki. 20[10] (in normal Hebrew מצא, Nu. 11[22], Jud.
21[14]); חֹרִים *nobles* (lit. *free*, a common Aram. word) 21[8. 11]. (‑אוֹת, however,
will hardly have been the pronunciation of the original author: notice the
frequent *plena scriptio*; and the occurrence several times in the same chapters
of the usual form ‑אַתְּ.) As the book approaches its close, some deterioration
of style is noticeable, though mostly (as it seems) in the parts due to the compiler, *e.g.* II 17. c. 21-25.

probability prophets,—in most cases, prophets belonging to the Northern kingdom ; though the data do not exist for identifying them, in individual cases, either with any of the prophets named incidentally in the narrative of Kings, or with those mentioned from time to time in the Chronicles in connexion with the history [179] of particular reigns.* These prophetical narratives appear in most cases to have been transferred by the compiler to his work without material alteration. Sometimes, however, especially where speeches or prophecies are concerned, the style and thought so closely resemble those of the framework, that it is impossible not to conclude that the original text has been expanded or developed by him.

From the fulness of particulars respecting the history of the Temple (II. 1 1⁴ff. ; 12⁴⁻¹⁶ ; 16¹⁰⁻¹⁸ ; 22³ff.), it has been conjectured, not improbably, that the Temple archives were also among the sources employed by the compiler. In the chronology, the age at accession and regnal years of the several kings are generally considered to be derived from the two official "chronicles": but the synchronisms will hardly have been taken from the same sources ; for it is not probable that in each kingdom the accessions would be dated regularly by the regnal years of the other. The author of a joint history of *both* kingdoms would, however, have a sufficient inducement to notice such synchronisms ; so that they may be reasonably attributed to the compiler, who may be supposed to have arrived at them by computation from the regnal years of the successive kings.†

In the arrangement of the reigns of the two series of kings a definite principle is followed by the compiler. When the narrative of a reign (in either series) has once been begun, it is continued to its close,—even the contemporary incidents of a prophet's career, which stand in no immediate relation to public events, being included in it : when it is ended, the reign or reigns of the other series, which have synchronized with it, are dealt with ; the reign overlapping it at the end having been completed, the compiler resumes his narrative of the first series with the reign next following, and so on.

We may now proceed to consider the Books of Kings in detail.

I. 1 Ki. 1-11. *Solomon.*—Here c. 1-2 is the continuation

---

* 2 Ch. 9²⁹ 12¹⁵ 13²² 20³⁴ 26²² 32³² 33¹⁹ (?).

† See the note in the writer's *Isaiah, his life and times*, p. 12 ff., with the references (esp. Wellh. *Jahrb. für Deutsche Theol.* 1875, pp. 607–640).

of 2 Sa. 9–20 (p. 182), forming at once the close of the history
of David and the introduction to that of Solomon.   Only 2^{2-4},
as the phraseology unmistakably shows (see p. 200), owes its
present form to the compiler; and the two notices respecting
David's death, and the length of his reign, in 2^{10-11}, may be
due to his hand also.   In other respects c. 1–2 is entirely in
[180] the style of 2 Sa. 9–20, and appears to be the work of the
same author.   Solomon's throne being now secured, the account
of his reign follows, c. 3–11.   The principle upon which the
narrative is here arranged has been pointed out by Wellh.   The
central point is the description of Solomon's buildings, the
Temple and the royal palace contiguous,* c. 6–7.   On each side
of this the compiler has placed a group of narratives and shorter
notices, with the view of illustrating Solomon's wisdom and magnificence.   At the close, c. 11, comes some account of Solomon's
political opponents, preparatory to the narrative, c. 12, of the
division of his kingdom.   Thus 3^{4-15} describes Solomon's
choice of wisdom, which is at once followed by an illustration of
it as afforded by his judgment on the two children.   C. 4 gives
a picture of the character and extent of his empire; c. 5 (negotiations with Hiram, king of Tyre, and preparations for the work
of building the Temple) is introductory to c. 6–7, as 8^{1}–9^{9}
(prayer of dedication, and warning for the future) forms the conclusion to it. 9^{10-28} consists of notices relating indirectly to
Solomon's buildings (the cities offered by him to Hiram in
acknowledgment of his services; the levy raised by Solomon
from among the Canaanites for the purpose of constructing his
buildings; his navy bringing gold from Ophir).   In 10^{1-13} (the
narrative of the visit of the Queen of Sheba) another even
more dazzling picture is presented of Solomon's wisdom and
royal splendour. 10^{14-29} the notices of the wealth which Solomon's
wide commercial relations brought in to him (9^{26-28}), which had
been interrupted by the episode of the Queen of Sheba, are
resumed.   It will be evident from this survey how homogeneous,
speaking generally, c. 3–4 is with 9^{10}–10^{29}.   C. 11, in terms
ominous of the future, describes how, in the judgment of the
compiler, Solomon's reign had been clouded, partly by his own
declension in religion, partly through the troubles occasioned by
political opponents.

* See the art. "Jerusalem," Part ii., in the *Encycl. Britannica* (ed. 9).

The parts of c. 3–11 which have been added, or expanded, by the compiler are distinguishable without much difficulty, viz. 3[2-3] (which agrees with the disapproval of the high places expressed elsewhere by him: the narrator of 3[4ff.], on the contrary, does not seem to consider any excuse to be necessary); 3[14] (notice the Deuteronomic phraseology: see p. 200 f., Nos. 2, [181] 3, 22b); 6[11-13]; 8[1-5].[*] [6-11] (expanded probably from a narrative originally briefer); 8[23-61] (the prayer of dedication, which in its present form is clearly the work of the compiler); 9[1-9] (the Deuteronomic phrases are here even more strongly marked than in the prayer: see below); 11[1-13] (in its present form), and parts of v.[32-39]: perhaps also 5[1-5], 8[15-19], though these two sections, which are kindred in character and import with the prophecy of Nathan, 2 Sa. 7, may be the work of an earlier prophetical narrator. All these passages are, on the one hand, so different in style from the main current of narrative, and, on the other hand, have such affinities both in style and in point of view with the subsequent parts of the two books which are plainly the work of the compiler, that no hesitation need be felt in attributing them to his hand. What remains is (in the main) *the pre-Deuteronomic narrative of Solomon's reign*, though probably not entirely in its original order, and including a few additions made to it subsequently. 3[4-13. 15. 16-28] 10[1-13] will be prophetical narratives of relatively early origin. The list of officers in 4[1-19], with the sequel (describing their *duties*) in 4[27-28], may naturally be supposed to be derived from the State-annals (the "Book of the acts of Solomon," 11[41]). The intermediate verses, 4[20-26], interrupt the connexion,[†] and seem to be an insertion, which the expression in v.[24] "*beyond* the River" [*i.e.* the Euphrates], applied to the country *west* of the Euphrates, and implying consequently a Babylonian standpoint (see Ezr. 4[10ff.] 5[3] &c.), shows cannot be earlier than the period of the exile.

In 5[15f.] the numbers are larger than is probable; and the entire notice

---

[*] 6[11-13] and parts of 8[1-5] are not in LXX; and as 6[11-13] and the parts of 8[1-5] not in LXX contain phrases of H and P (with 6[12a] cf. Lev. 18[4] 26[3]; with 6[13a] cf. Ex. 25[8] 29[45]: on 8[1-5] see p. 144 n.), it is probable that they are not the work of the principal compiler, but were added at a later date by a writer (or writers) influenced by P (comp. on Josh. 20, p. 112).

[†] The Heb. word rendered *those* in v.[27] (אלה) should properly be *these*. In the LXX, 4[27f.] immediately follows 4[19] (4[20f.] standing after 2[46]).

(in spite of the explanation proffered in 2 Ch. $2^{17f.}$) is in imperfect relation with v.$^{13f.}$. 9^{10-28} consists of a series of notices, imperfectly connected together : v.^{14}, for instance, appears, in fact, to refer to an incident *anterior* to v.$^{11b-13}$: the "account" of the levy, promised in v.^{15}, only follows in v.^{20}, the intermediate verses being parenthetic : 9^{24a} (Pharaoh's daughter and Millo) has no point of contact either with what precedes or with what follows. And 9^{22} (no levy of Israelites) conflicts with $5^{13f.}$, cf. 11^{28} (which speaks of the "burden of the house of Joseph"). The literary form of 9^{10-28} is, for some reason, less complete than that of any other portion of the Books of Kings. In the LXX many of the notices are [182] differently arranged, and the text is sometimes briefer : it seems, therefore, that in the MSS. used by them the Hebrew text here had not yet reached the form in which we now have it.*

$8^{12f.}$ has a poetical tinge. It is remarkable, now, that in LXX (where it stands after v.^{53}) it appears in a fuller form, with the addition οὐκ ἰδοὺ αὕτη γέγραπται ἐν βιβλίῳ τῆς ᾠδῆς ; *i.e.* (as can hardly be doubted : cf. Josh. 10^{13} Pesh.†) הלא היא כתובה על ספר הישר (comp. Wellh. *Comp.* 271 ; *Encycl. Brit.*^{9} xiv. p. 84). The original Hebrew cannot be represented quite exactly by the Greek text, and Cheyne's restoration (*Origin of the Psalter*, p. 212) ‡ is no doubt preferable to Wellh.'s : but the words just quoted cannot have been invented by the translators ; it appears therefore that the "Book of Jashar" (p. 121) contained a poetical account of the foundation of Solomon's Temple, and was still cited by name in the text of Kings used by the LXX.

The kernel of c. 11 is old ; but the narrative must, in parts, have been recast, and placed in a different light. In v.$^{1-13}$, v.^{7} —where אז *then* connects imperfectly with v.$^{5-6}$—and the notice v.^{3} respecting the number of Solomon's wives, are no doubt excerpts from the older narrative : the emphasis laid on the declension caused thereby in Solomon's religion is expressed in phrases which betoken the hand of the compiler. In what follows, the original purport of the narrative can hardly be that which now appears. In the narrative in its present form, the "adversaries" in v.$^{14ff.}$ are described as "raised up" by way of punishment for the sins of Solomon's later days (v.$^{3. 4. 9}$) : but,

---

* Compare the last two notes. So $5^{17. 18a}$ 6^{37-38a} take the place in LXX of 6^{1b} : 6^{11-14} and 9^{15-25} are omitted : on the other hand, $9^{24f. 23. 17}$ appear (with $4^{29f.}$ 3^{1b} 5^{15}) after 2^{35} ; $9^{16. 17a}$ (with 3^1) after 4^{34} ; 9^{24a} after 9^9 ; $9^{15. 17b-22}$ after 10^{22} : there are also several additions. In some cases (but by no means in all) there is good reason to suppose that the recension represented by the LXX has preserved better readings than the Hebrew ; see examples in QPB^3.

† Where הישר is similarly confused with השיר *the song* (مَصْدَر).

‡ שָׁמֶשׁ הֵכִין בַּשָּׁמַיִם יְהוָה אָמַר לִשְׁכֹּן בָּעֲרָפֶל :
בָּנֹה בָנִיתִי בֵּית זְבֻל לָךְ מָכוֹן לְשִׁבְתְּךָ עוֹלָמִים :

in point of fact, the incidents described in v.[21-22. 24-25] (note the expression "*all* the days of Solomon"), if not also in v.[26-28], occurred early in his reign ; hence, if the view of the compiler be that of the original narrator, the punishment will have preceded the sin which occasioned it. It seems clear that the narrative itself (v.[14ff.]) is ancient, but that the setting (v.[9-13]), which represents the events narrated as the punishment for the idolatry of v.[1-8], was added subsequently by the compiler. In the narrative of Ahijah (v.[29-39]), v.[32-39] must have been [183] expanded by the compiler, as they abound with marks of his style (see p. 200 ff.). 11[41-43] is the concluding formula of Solomon's reign, in the compiler's usual manner.

The work which lay at the basis of the pre-Deuteronomic account of Solomon's reign must have been one in which the arrangement of material was determined less by chronological sequence than by community of subject. In other words, it was not so much a chronicle as a series of detached notices. The description of the buildings forming the central feature in it, particulars respecting the preparations or materials required for them, and notices, or short narratives, illustrating Solomon's wisdom, or splendour, or the organization of his empire, were placed on either side of it. At the close came c. 11 (in its original form), containing some account of the political opponents who from time to time disturbed the tranquillity of his reign. Throughout, the author evinces a warm admiration for Solomon : he recounts with manifest satisfaction the evidences of his wisdom, and dwells with pride on the details of his imperial magnificence, on the wealth which streamed into Jerusalem from all quarters, on his successful alliances and commercial undertakings, and on the manner in which his fame commanded the wonder and respect of distant nations. The darker shades in the picture seem largely, though not, perhaps, entirely, to be due to the Deuteronomic compiler.

II. 1 Ki. 12–2 Ki. 17. *Israel and Judah.* — Here we have alternately short notices and long continuous narratives—the latter now and then expanded by the compiler—arranged in a chronological framework, in the manner indicated above. The longer narratives are sometimes slightly modified at the beginning and end for the purpose of establishing a connexion with the history on either side of them. C. 12 contains the older

narrative of the defection of the ten tribes from the dynasty of
David; v.[26-33] (Jeroboam's calves, and the worship instituted
in connexion with them) may be due, in their present form, to
the compiler; 12[33] introduces the account of the prophecy
against the altar of Bethel—a narrative not probably of very
early origin, as it seems to date from a time when the names both
of the prophet of Judah and of the " old prophet " were no longer
remembered. 13[33-34] lead back to the main thread of the history.
14[1-18] (the wife of Jeroboam and the prophet Ahijah) [184] is in
its substance, no doubt, ancient; but the answer of Ahijah has
certainly in parts been recast in the phraseology of the compiler
(esp. v.[8. 9. 10. 15. 16]).

Observe the standing phrases of the compiler in these verses (see p. 200 ff.);
and the anachronism in 14[9] (as addressed to *Jeroboam*), "above all *that were
before thee*" (16[25. 30] (cf. v.[33] II 17[2] 18[5]) show besides that this phrase is the
compiler's).   In some of its other features the prophecy bears a striking
resemblance to those of Jehu son of Hanani 16[1-4], Elijah 21[20b-22], the unnamed prophet 21[24], and the disciple of Elisha II 9[7-10] (comp. 14[7] with 16[2];
משתין בקיר 14[10] 16[11] 21[21], II 9[8] [1 Sa. 25[22. 34]]; עצור ועזוב 14[10] 21[21], II 9[8] 14[26]
[in a notice of the compiler's]; בער אחר 14[10] 16[3] [אחרי] 21[21]; *Him that dieth*,
&c., 14[11] 16[4] 21[24]): but it is quite possible that these phrases are original
here, and have been adopted thence by the compiler when he recast, or
amplified, the other later prophecies quoted.   (That the prophecies in the
Books of Kings have really, in parts, been amplified by the compiler may
be inferred upon two grounds: not only do the parts in question exhibit
common features, connecting them with the compiler, but in style and expression they have no parallel in the prophecies of Amos, Hosea, or other
prophets, whose writings have been preserved independently, prior to
Jeremiah.)

From 14[19] to c. 16 the history consists chiefly of a collection
of short notices (14[25-28] 15[6. 7b. 12-13. 15. 16-22. 27-28] &c.) arranged in
the schematism of the compiler (the chronology and judgments
on the kings), as 14[19-20. 21-24. 29-31] 15[1-2. 3-5. 7a. 8. 9-11. 14. 23-24. 25-26.
29-32. 33-34] 16[1-4] (recast), &c.   (On the phraseology of these passages, see below, p. 200 ff.)

C. 16 ended, the framework expands for the purpose of
admitting the narratives respecting Elijah and Elisha.   It is
doubtful whether all these narratives are by the same hand: but
all appear to be of North Israelitish origin; and all, especially
those dealing with Elijah, exhibit the ease, and grace, and vividness which belong to the best style of Hebrew historical narrative.
The beginning of the history of Elijah has probably been omitted

by the compiler: the place *whence* Elijah is to depart, 17³, the ground for which he is persecuted and addressed as the "Troubler of Israel," 18¹⁰· ¹⁷, and particulars respecting the murder of the prophets by Jezebel, alluded to 18¹³, are not stated in the existing narrative. The suddenness, however, with which Elijah is introduced upon the scene, and the abruptness of his first utterance in 17¹, are in harmony with the character which everywhere belongs to the prophet's movements, and the dramatic form in which the narrative is cast. C. 17 the drama opens: [185] the severity of the famine foretold by Elijah is left to be inferred by the reader from the picture of the privations to which the prophet himself is exposed. C. 18 recounts the triumph of Elijah upon Carmel; c. 19 the reaction experienced by him afterwards; his withdrawal to Horeb; the mysterious vision there; the commission (v.¹⁵⁻¹⁸) assuring him of the final triumph of his cause. The events to which this commission correspond are related in 2 Ki. 8⁷⁻¹⁵ c. 9–10, but with a different motive, from a political rather than a religious standpoint and without reference to Elijah,—an indication that these narratives, together with I 20. 22 (where likewise the predominant interest is political), did not originally form part of the same *literary* whole as I 17–19. I 21, however (Ahab and Naboth), is in the style of I 17–19: Elijah, as before, suddenly intercepts Ahab with his unwelcome presence; and the close of the struggle between the prophet and the king looms in view (v.¹⁹· ²⁰). But the narrative which records actually the death of Ahab, though designed by the compiler to describe the end of Ahab foretold by Elijah, was not, perhaps, *written* as the sequel to c. 21: in particular, the *place* 22³⁷⁻³⁸ (Samaria), where the dogs licked the blood of Ahab, does not accord with the prediction in 21¹⁹ (Jezreel). II 1 presents an impressive picture of Elijah's inviolable greatness; II 2 (the ascension of Elijah) is at once the close of the history of Elijah and the introduction to that of Elisha; from a literary point of view it is more closely connected with the latter than with the former.

To the same hand to which are due I 20. 22 may also, perhaps, be ascribed II 3⁴⁻²⁷ (Jehoram and Jehoshaphat against Moab); 6²⁴–7²⁰ (siege of Samaria by Benhadad: its relief in accordance with Elisha's prediction); and 9¹–10²⁸ (the "photographic picture" of the accession of Jehu). In all these narratives the political interest predominates above the biographical; and some noticeable similarities of form and expression also occur.*

The history of Elisha is comprised in a series of short narratives, describing particular incidents in his life : these are introduced by II 2[1-18] (Elisha succeeds to the inheritance of Elijah), the rest consisting of 2[19-22] (the bitter waters [**186**] sweetened); v.[23-25] (the mocking children rent by bears); 4[1-7] (the widow's oil multiplied); v.[8-37] (the Shunammite woman); v.[38-41] (the poisoned pot rendered harmless); v.[42-44] (the barley loaves multiplied); c. 5 (Naaman); 6[1-7] (the iron axe-head made to swim); v.[8-23] (attempt of the Syrians to capture Elisha); 8[1-6] (Gehazi recounts Elisha's wonders to the king); v.[7-15] (Elisha and Hazael); 13[14-19] (Elisha and Joash); v.[20-21] (miracle wrought by Elisha's bones). These narratives no doubt exhibit the traditions respecting Elisha as they were current in prophetic circles in the 9–8 cent. B.C. : their immediate source may have been a work narrating anecdotes from the life of Elisha (and perhaps from the lives of other prophets as well).

The narratives of Elijah and Elisha appear to have been incorporated by the compiler without substantial alteration : only here and there has one of them been expanded by an insertion which, by its manner, betrays the compiler's hand (I 21[20b-26] : notice the phrases in v.[20b-24], and the awkward parenthesis in v.[25-26]; II 9[7-10a], where not only do the phrases of the compiler abound (p. 200 ff.), but it is difficult not to think that v.[10b] "and he opened the door and fled," in agreement with the command v.[8b], should follow immediately the announcement of v.[6]).

In contrast with the sections dealing with the N. kingdom, in which the prophets play such a considerable part, the longer narratives relating to the S. kingdom II 11[1]–12[16] (elevation of Joash to the throne, and his measures regarding the Temple), 16[10-18] (the altar of Ahaz) place the Temple and priesthood of Jerusalem in the foreground. These narratives are evidently of Judæan origin, and (to judge from the minuteness in the details) based probably upon official documents. The section 13[14-19] (Elisha and Joash) has been noticed above : 14[8-14] (Amaziah's challenge of Joash), it may be inferred from v.[11] "Beth-shemesh *which belongeth to Judah*" (cf. I 19[3]), is of Israelitish origin. The narrative in the following chapters is

* Comp. I 20[18], II 7[12] 10[14]; I 20[30] *end* (חדר בחדר) 22[25], II 9[2]↑; I 22[4b, 5, 7], II 3[7b, 11]; חפך ידיו I 22[34], II 9[23].

composed chiefly of short notices—even the long and important reigns of Jeroboam and Azariah (Uzziah) receiving each hardly more than a single verse of independent detail ($14^{22, 25}$ [v.$^{26-27}$ is comment] 15^5). After the close of the N. kingdom (17^6), the compiler introduces a long survey of the causes which, in his judgment, led to its fall (17^{7-23}), and explains (v.$^{24-41}$) the origin of the mixed population and religion of the country of Samaria at the time in which he lived.

[187] III. 2 Ki. 18–25. *Judah.*

With c. 18 begins the reign of Hezekiah. 18^{1-12} is the composition of the compiler, though the particulars in v.$^{2, 4, 8}$ are doubtless derived by him from his sources ; v.$^{9-12}$ repeats, in brief, the account of the close of the N. kingdom. 18^{18}–19^{37} comprises the narrative of the invasion of Judah by Sennacherib in his campaign of 701, and the miraculous occurrence which obliged his retreat. Here the brief notices in 18^{14-16} differ in character from the circumstantial narrative commencing with v.^{17}; it is also remarkable that the name of the king, which v.$^{17ff.}$ is uniformly written חזקיהו, is here spelt חזקיה : it is fair to infer, therefore, that they are derived from a different source, which may well be the State-annals. 18^{17}–19^{37} is the one long narrative in the Book of Kings relating to *Judah*, and similar in general character to the prophetical narratives of the N. kingdom. It includes a prophecy, 19^{21-31}, attributed to Isaiah, and unquestionably his ; but there is no ground for supposing that the narrative as a whole, though it stands also (together with 20^{1-19}) in the Book of Isaiah (c. 36–39), is from Isaiah's hand ; as will be shown (under Isaiah), there are reasons for concluding it to be the work of a prophet writing in the subsequent generation, which was incorporated, with slight additions, in his work by the compiler of Kings.

As the narrative approaches the time in which the compiler himself lived (c. 21 ff.), and in which, therefore, the writer's personal knowledge, or information derived from the generation immediately preceding, would be available, his own share in the work appears to increase. In the account of the reign of Manasseh (c. 21), the narration of concrete facts scarcely extends beyond v.$^{3, 4a, 5, 6a, 7a, 16a}$: the rest is the comment of the compiler, v.$^{11-15}$, which is not assigned to any *individual* prophet, though it agrees remarkably with parts of Jeremiah (see below,

p. 203), being probably the compiler's summary of the teaching of contemporary prophets.

The reign of Josiah (22^1–23^{30}), including the two important events, the discovery of the Book of the Law and the reformation based upon it, engrosses naturally the interest of the compiler, and is described by him at some length : the parts in which his own style is specially prominent are $22^{13b.\ 16ff.}$ and $23^{3.\ 21-28}$ (especially v.^{25b} from Dt. 6^5; and v.$^{26-27}$). [188] 25^{22-26} is an abridgment of Jer. 40^{7-9} $41^{1f.\ 17f.}$ 42^1 $43^{3ff.}$: 25^{27-30} cannot, of course, have been written before the year of Jehoiachin's release, B.C. 562.

According to Wellh. and Kuenen, the compilation of the Book of Kings was completed substantially *before* the exile (c. 600 B.C.),* only short passages which imply an exilic standpoint being introduced afterwards.

These passages, as given by Kuenen (p. 420), are I 4^{20-26} [Heb. 4^{20}–5^6] (see v.^{24}); 9^{1-9} 11^{9-13} (in their present form); II 17^{19-20}; 20^{17-18}; 21^{10-15}; 22^{15-20}; 23^{26-27}; 24^{2-4}; 24^{18}–25^{30}.

I 4^{20-26} has been discussed above (p. 191): as the passage seems clearly to be an *insertion* in the text of c. 4, v.^{24} does not (cf. Keil, *Einl.* § 58. 3) show that the Book of Kings, as a whole, was only compiled during the exile. II $17^{19f.}$ likewise interrupts the connexion. The original writer is dealing only with the causes of the declension of the kingdom of *Israel*: in v.^{18} he remarks that in consequence of Israel's rejection Judah only was left; and the sequel to this is v.$^{21-23}$, describing how this result came about ("*For* he rent Israel from the house of David," &c.). V.$^{19-20}$, commenting on the faithlessness of *Judah*, and the rejection and exile of the *entire* seed of Israel, is plainly an insertion made by a subsequent writer, who desiderated a notice of the same causes producing a similar effect in the case of Judah. II $24^{18ff.}$ can, of course, only have been written after the exile had commenced. The other passages are either such as are thought to presuppose the fall of the city and temple, or contain references to passages which do this (I 11^{9b} to 9^{1-9}; II 23^{26} 24^8 to 21^{10-15} [Manasseh]): but very similar anticipations are expressed by Jeremiah before the exile ; so that no sufficient reason exists, at least on the ground of the contents of these passages, for attributing them to a different hand from that of the main compiler of the Book. But it must be admitted that II 21^{10-15} 23^{26-27} interfere with the con-

---

* Notice the expression *to this day*, II 8^{22} 16^6, in passages belonging clearly to the compiler, and not taken by him from his sources, and of which at least the first appears to imply that the Jewish State was still existing when it was written ; also the precise information respecting the Samaritans, 17^{24-34} (*unto this day*, v.^{34}), which a writer near at hand would be more likely to possess than one resident in Babylonia.

nexion, and wear the appearance of being insertions made after the original narrative was completed, so that upon literary grounds this view of their origin is not untenable. On the whole, it is highly probable that the redaction of Kings was not entirely completed by the main compiler; though it is only occasionally possible to point with confidence to the passages which belong to a subsequent stage of it.

That it is one and the same compiler who formulated the short notices or "Epitome," and at the same time combined them with the longer narratives, is shown (against Thenius) by Wellh. p. 298 (after Kuen. *Onderzoek*,[1] i. 266 f.) : there are cases in which each *presupposes* the other ; and the contents [189] of the Epitome are much too fragmentary for it to have ever constituted an independent history.

The compiler of Kings, though not, probably (as has sometimes been supposed), Jeremiah himself, was nevertheless a man like-minded with Jeremiah, and almost certainly a contemporary who lived and wrote under the same influences. Deuteronomy is the standard by which the compiler judges both men and actions ; and the history, from the beginning of Solomon's reign, is presented, not in a purely "objective" form (as *e.g.* in 2 Sa. 9–20), but from the point of view of the Deuteronomic code. It is a characteristic of the passages added by the compiler (so far as they are not notices based upon his sources) that they do not usually add to the historic contents of the narratives, but (like the corresponding additions in Judges) present comments upon it, sometimes introduced as such, sometimes introduced indirectly in the shape of prophetic glances at the future, at different stages of the history. The principles which, in his view, the history as a whole is to exemplify, are already expressed succinctly in the charge which he represents David as giving to his son Solomon (I 2^{3-4}) : they are stated by him again in 3^{14}, and more distinctly in 9^{1-9}. Obedience to the Deuteronomic law is the qualification for an approving verdict : deviation from it is the source of ill success (I 11^{9-13} 14^{7-11} 16^2, II 17^{7-18} &c.), and the sure prelude to condemnation. Every king of the Northern kingdom is characterized as doing "that which was evil in the eyes of Jehovah" : in the Southern kingdom the exceptions are Asa, Jehoshaphat, Jehoash, Amaziah, Uzziah, Jotham, Hezekiah, Josiah,—usually, however, with the limitation that "the high places were not removed," as demanded by the Deuteronomic law. The writer viewed Jeroboam as the author of a schism, and the founder of a worship which contravened the first principle of the Deuteronomic code, the law of the Central Sanctuary, and lent itself readily to contamination by heathen cults : hence his uniformly unfavourable verdict on the rulers of the N. kingdom. He does not, however, place *all* deviations from the law of Dt. in the same category : he views, indeed, the worship (of Jehovah) at the high places with disfavour, but the kings who permit it are not thereby disqualified from receiving a verdict of approval, as are those who patronized, or encouraged, practices actually heathen.

[190] *Phrases characteristic of the compiler of Kings.*   In many of these the influence of Dt. is directly traceable ; others, though not actually occurring in it, frequently express thoughts in harmony with its spirit.

1. *To keep the charge of Jehovah* : I 2³, Dt. 11¹ ; cf. Josh. 22³ (D²).
2. *To walk in the ways of Jehovah* : I 2³ 3¹⁴ 8⁵⁸ 11³³. ³⁸, Dt. 8⁶ 10¹² 11²² 19⁹ 26¹⁷ 28⁹ 30¹⁶, Josh. 22⁵.
3. *To keep* (or *execute*) *his statutes and commandments and judgments* (sometimes with one term omitted, or even *commandments* alone) : I 2³ 3¹⁴ 8⁵⁸. ⁶¹ 9⁴. ⁶ 11³³. ³⁴. ³⁸ 14⁸, II 17¹³ (cf. v.³⁷) 19 18⁶ 23³.   In Dt. constantly.   (The reference throughout is specially to *Deuteronomy*. So generally, where the law, or Moses, is alluded to : I 8⁹ (Dt. 10⁵ 29¹), ⁵³ (Dt. 4²⁰ 7⁶ [also Lev. 20²⁶]), ⁵⁶ (Dt. 12⁹ᶠ· 25¹⁹), II 10³¹ 14⁶ (Dt. 24¹⁶), 18¹² 21⁸ 22⁸ 23²¹. ²⁵.)
4. *Testimonies* (עֵדָוֹת) : I 2³ II 17¹⁵ 23³ (in Dt. pointed עֵדֹות : 4⁴⁵ 6¹⁷. ²⁰).
5. *That thou mayest prosper*, &c. : I 2³, Dt. 29⁹, Josh. 1⁷ᵇ.
6. *To establish his* (*my*) *word* : I 2⁴ 6¹² 8²⁰ 12¹⁵ ; cf. Dt. 9⁵.
7. *To walk before me* (*in truth, uprightness*, &c.) : I 2⁴ 3⁶ 8²³. ²⁵ 9⁴ (II 20⁸ the Hithp.).
8. *There shall not fail* (lit. *be cut off*) *to thee* : I 2⁴ 8²⁵ 9⁵.   Cf. Jer. 33¹⁷. ¹⁸ 35¹⁹ ; and with מִן (*from*) 2 Sa. 3²⁹, Josh. 9²³.
9. *With all the heart and with all the soul* : I 2⁴ 8⁴⁸, II 23³. ²⁵, as often in Dt. (in II 23²⁵ with מאד in the rare sense of "might," only besides in Dt. 6⁵) : see p. 101.   Cf. *with all the heart* (alone) : I 8²³ 14⁸, II 10³¹.
10. *To build an house to the name of J* : I 3² 5³. ⁵ 8¹⁷. ¹⁸. ¹⁹. ²⁰. ⁴⁴. ⁴⁸ (cf. 9⁷) : dependent on 2 Sa. 7¹³ (the prophecy of Nathan).
11. *As it is this day* (pointing out agreement of promise with event) : I 3⁶ 8²⁴. ⁶¹, Dt. 2³⁰ [see the writer's note], 4²⁰. ³⁸ 8¹⁸ 10¹⁵ 29²⁸ [Heb.²⁷].
12. *Given me rest on every side* : I 5⁴ [Heb.¹⁸], Dt. 12¹⁰ 25¹⁹, Josh. 21⁴² 23¹ (D²), 2 Sa. 7¹.
13. *Chose out of all the tribes of Israel* : I 8¹⁶ 11³² 14²¹, II 21⁷.
14. *That my name might be there* : I 8¹⁶. ²⁹, II 23²⁷.   Elsewhere with *to put* (שׂם) : I 9³ 11³⁶ 14²¹, II 21⁴. ⁷ (=2 Ch. 33⁷), as in Dt. (p. 101, No. 35) : so also 2 Ch. 6²⁰ 12¹³.

In 8²²ᶠᶠ· and 9¹⁻⁹, the reminiscences from Dt., or the Deut. sections of Joshua, are remarkably abundant :—

8²³, Dt. 4³⁹, Josh. 2¹¹ᵇ (D²).—v.²⁵ רק אם (*yet so that*), II 21⁸, Dt. 15

(peculiar. Not elsewhere, except in the parallels 2 Ch. 6^{16} 33^8).—v.^{27} (*the heaven of heavens*), Dt. 10^{14}.—v.^{32}, Dt. 25^1.—v.^{33a}, Dt. 28^{25}.—v.^{35a} Dt. 11^{17}. —v.^{37a}, Dt. $28^{22.\,38}$.—v.^{37b}, *ib.* v.^{52} (comp. esp. "gates"; p. 99, No. 6).— v.^{40a}, Dt. 4^{10b} 12^1 31^{13}.—v.^{41a}, Dt. 29^{21}. v.^{42a}, Dt. 11^2 and often.—v.^{43} (*peoples of the earth*) $^{53.\,60}$, Dt. 28^{10}, Josh. 4^{24} (D^2).—v.^{43b} (*thy name is called over*, viz. in token of ownership [see 2 Sa. 12^{28} RV. *marg.*]), Dt. 28^{10} (esp. in Jer., as $7^{10f.}$ 25^{29} *al.*).—v.^{44a}, Dt. 20^1 21^{10}.—v.^{46} (*deliver up before*: see p. 101, No. 29).—v.^{47a}, Dt. 30^1.—[191] v.^{48a}, Dt. 30^2.—v.^{51}, Dt. 9^{29}.—*ib.* (*iron-furnace*), Dt. 4^{20}, Jer. 11^4.↑—v.^{52b}, Dt. 4^7.—v.^{56}, Josh. 21^{43} 23^{14} (D^2).—v.^{58} (see above, Nos. 2, 3).—v.^{60a}, Josh. 4^{24} (D^2).—v.^{60b}, Dt. 4^{39}.—9^3 (*to put my name there*: see above, No. 14).—v.^{4} (see Nos. 7, 3).—v.^{6b}, Dt. 29^{26}.—v.^{7b}, Dt. 28^{37}.—v.$^{8b-9}$, Dt. 29^{24-26} (Jer. 22^{8-9}; cf. 5^{19} $16^{10f.}$).

15. *Perfect*= wholly devoted (of the heart): I 8^{61} 11^4 $15^{3.\,14}$, II 20^3=Is. 38^3. Only so besides in Ch.

16. *To cut off from upon the ground*: I 9^7 13^{34} (*to destroy*) 14^{15} (*to root up*): with the same, or similar, verbs, Dt. 4^{26} 6^{15} 11^{17} $28^{21.\,63}$ 29^{28}, Jer. 12^{14} 24^{10} 27^{10} 28^{16}.

17. *To dismiss* (שלח) *from before my* (*his*) *face*: I 9^7, Jer. 15^1: so with *cast away* (השליך), II 13^{23} 17^{20} [מן, not מעל] 24^{20}, Jer. 7^{15}; with *remove* (הסיר), II $17^{18.\,23}$ 23^{27} 24^3, Jer. 32^{31}; with *cast off* (נטש), Jer. 23^{39}. Not in Dt.

18. 11^2: Josh. 23^{12b} (Dt^2); cf. Dt. $7^{3.\,4a}$.

19. שקוצים *detestable things* (of false gods): I $11^{5.\,7}$, II $23^{13.\,24}$, Dt. 29^{17} [Heb. ^{16}] (cf. the writer's note here; or Clark's *Bible Dict.*, *s.v.* ABOMINATION, 4). So Jer. 4^1 7^{30} 13^{27} 16^{18} 32^{34}, Ez. 5^{11} 7^{20} $11^{18.\,21}$ $20^{7.\,8.\,30}$ 37^{23}, Is 66^3.

20. *To do that which is evil in the eyes of Jehovah*: I 11^6, and more than thirty times besides (p. 101, No. 26).

21. התאנף *to be angered*: I 11^9, II 17^{18}, Dt. 1^{37} 4^{21} $9^{8.\,20}$.↑

22^a. *For the sake of David thy father* (or *my servant*): I $11^{12.\,13.\,32.\,34}$ (cf. v.^{36}) 15^4, II 8^{19} 19^{34} 20^6.

22^b. Other references to David as a standard of piety are also frequent: I $3^{3.\,6.\,14}$ 9^4 $11^{4.\,6.\,33.\,38}$ 14^8 $15^{3.\,5.\,11}$, II 14^3 16^2 18^3 22^2.

23. *Chosen*, with reference to Jerusalem: I $11^{13.\,32.\,36}$ $8^{44.\,48}$ (cf. v.^{16}) 14^{21}, II 21^7 23^{27}. Based on Dt. (p. 100, No. 11).

24. *To do that which is right in the eyes of Jehovah*: I $11^{33.\,38}$ 14^8 $15^{5.\,11}$ 22^{43}, II 10^{30} 12^2 14^3 15^3 16^2 (p. 101, No. 25).

25. *A lamp* (for David): I 11^{36} 15^4, II 8^{19}=2 Ch. 21^7.

26. *To provoke Jehovah to anger* [rather, to *vex* Him, הכעים]: I $14^{9.\,15}$ 15^{30} $16^{2.\,7.\,13.\,26.\,33}$ 21^{22} 22^{53}, II $17^{11.\,17}$ $21^{6.\,15}$ 22^{17} $23^{19.\,26}$, Dt. 4^{25} (see the writer's note here), 9^{18} 31^{29} $32^{16.\,21}$, Jer. $7^{18.\,19}$ 8^{19} 11^{17} $25^{6.\,7}$ $32^{29.\,30.\,32}$ $44^{3.\,8}$.

27. *Behold, I bring evil upon* . . . : I 14^{10} 21^{21}, II 21^{12} 22^{16} (=2 Ch. 34^{24}), Jer. 6^{19} 11^{11} $19^{3.\,15}$ 35^{17} 45^5.↑ *To bring evil upon* also I 9^9 21^{29}, II 22^{20}, and often in Jer.: not common elsewhere.

28. *The fettered and the free* (an alliterative proverbial phrase, denoting "all"): I 14^{10} 21^{21}, II 9^8 14^{26}, Dt. 32^{36} (the Song).↑

29. *Who made Israel to sin* (of Jeroboam): I 14^{16} $15^{26.\,30.\,34}$ 16^{26} 22^{52},

II 3^3 $10^{29.\ 31}$ $13^{2.\ 6}$ 14^{24} $15^{9.\ 18.\ 24.\ 28}$ 23^{15} : comp. 21^{16} (of Manasseh and Judah). Cf. I 12^{30} 13^{34}, II $17^{21.\ 22}$.

30. *Upon every high hill and under every spreading tree* : I 14^{23} 17^{10}, Jer. 2^{20} (the first clause varied from Dt. 12^{2b}: the second precisely as there) ; similarly II 16^4 (=2 Ch. 28^4), Jer. 3^6 17^2, Ez. 6^{13}: the second clause also (alone) Jer. 3^{13}, Is. 57^5.↑

[192] 31. *Abominations of the nations* : I 14^{24}, II 16^3 21^2. Cf. Dt. $18^{9.\ 12}$.

32. *Whom Jehovah dispossessed from before the children of Israel* : I 14^{24} 21^{26}, II 16^3 17^8 21^2. Cf. Dt. $9^{4.\ 5}$ 11^{23}, Josh. 23^5.

33. *Idol-blocks* (גלולים) : I 15^{12} 21^{26}, II 17^{12} $21^{11.\ 21}$ 23^{24}. Also Lev. 26^{30}, Dt. 29^{16}, Jer. 50^2, and esp. in Ezek. [39 times].↑

34. *Turned not aside from* . . . : I 15^5 22^{43}, II 3^3 10^{29} (מאחרי) ^{31} (מעל) $13^{2.\ 6.\ 11}$ 14^{24} $15^{9.\ 18}$ (מעל) $^{24.\ 28}$ 17^{22} 18^6 (מאחרי).

35. *Vanities* הבלים (of idols) : I $16^{13.\ 26}$, Dt. 32^{21} ; cf. Jer. 8^{19} 14^{22}. Unusual. Cf. II 17^{15}, Jer. 2^5 (the same phrase,—וילכו אחרי ההבל ויהבלו).

36. *Did sell himself* (to do evil) : I $21^{20.\ 25}$, II 17^7. Only so here.

37. *The people still sacrificed and burnt incense in the high places* : I 22^{43}, II 12^4 14^4 $15^{4.\ 35}$: similarly I 3^2 11^8, II 16^4 17^{11} 23^5 : *burnt incense* also, in a similar connexion, II 18^4 22^{17} 23^8, and often in Jer. (1^{16} $11^{12.\ 13.\ 17}$ 18^{15} $19^{4.\ 13}$ 32^{29} $44^{3.\ 8.\ 15.\ 17\text{-}25}$).

38. *Would not destroy* : II 8^{19} 13^{23}, Dt. 10^{10}.

39. *My (his) servants the prophets* : II 9^7 $17^{13.\ 23}$ 21^{10} 24^2 : in Jer. six times (7^{25} 25^4 26^5 29^{19} 35^{15} 44^4). First in Am. 3^7. Also Zech. 1^6, Ezr. 9^{11}, Dan. 9^{10}.↑

40. *To blot out the name from under heaven* : II 14^{27}, Dt. 9^{14} 29^{19} ; cf. 7^{24} 25^{19}.

41. *The "host of heaven"* venerated : II 17^{16} 21^3 [=2 Ch. 33^3] $^{4.\ 5}$ [=2 Ch. 33^5], Jer. 8^2 19^{13}, Zeph. 1^5. Forbidden Dt. 4^{19} 17^3.↑

42. *To cleave to Jehovah* : II 18^6 (cf. the same word in 3^3, I 11^2), as in Dt. (p. 100, No. 15).*

If the reader will be at the pains of *underlining* in his text the phrases here cited, he will not only realize how numerous they are, but also perceive how they seldom occur indiscriminately in the narrative as such, but are generally *aggregated* in particular passages (mostly comments on the history, or speeches), which are thereby distinguished from their context, and shown to be presumably the work of a different hand.

The following modes adopted by the compiler for introducing historical notices are observable :—

43. *In his days* . . . I 16^{34}, II 8^{20} 15^{19} LXX (see *QPB.*³) 23^{29} 24^1.

44. *In those days* . . . II 10^{32} 15^{37} 20^1.

45. *At that time* . . . I 14^1, II 16^6 18^{16} 20^{12} 24^{10}.

46. *He* (הוא : emphatic) . . . II $14^{7.\ 22.\ 25}$ 15^{35b} $18^{4.\ 8}$.

47. *Then* (או) . . . I 3^{16} $8^{1.\ 12}$ $9^{11b.\ 24b}$ 11^7 16^{21} 22^{49} (Heb. ^{50}), II 8^{22b} 12^{17} (Heb. ^{18}) 14^8 15^{16} 16^5. Comp. τότε 9^9 LXX (=9^{24} Heb.).

---

* Comp. also II $17^{36.\ 38}$ and Dt. 9^{29} 6^{13} 4^{23} ; $19^{15.\ 19}$ (kingdoms of the earth) and Dt. 28^{25} (also Jer. 15^4 24^9 25^{26} [but omit here הארץ with LXX : notice the incorrect syntax], 29^{18} 34^{17}) ; 19^{15b} and Jer. 32^{17} ; 19^{18b} and Dt. 4^{28}.

This use of אז is noticeable. In many cases, the notices introduced by it [193] lack any definite point of attachment in the preceding narrative : at the same time, their directness of statement and terseness of form suggest the inference that they may be derived immediately from the contemporary annalistic records (Ewald, *Hist.* i. 168 ; Wellh. *Hist.* p. 286). The same may be the case with some of the other notices just cited.

48. The frequency with which the prophecies in 1-2 Ki. are introduced by the same term (כי) אשר יען *Forasmuch as* . . . is also noticeable : I 3^{11} 8^{18} 11^{11} 13^{21} 14^7 16^2 $20^{28.\ 36.\ 42}$ 21^{20} (יען c. infin.) ^{29}, II 1^{16} 10^{30} 19^{28} (Isaiah), 21^{11} 22^{19}.

The resemblances with Jer. are most marked towards the end of the two books, esp. in II 17^{13-20} 21^{11-15} 22^{16-19} :—

II 17^{13} *testified* : Jer. 11^7.

> *Turn ye*, &c. : cf. Jer. 18^{11} 25^5 35^{15}.
> *my servants the prophets* : see above, No. 39 (esp. 7^{25} 25^{41}).

v.$^{14.\ 40}$ 18^{12} 21^9 *hearkened not* : Jer. 7^{26} 11^7, and often besides.

> *hardened their necks* : Jer. 7^{26} 17^{23} 19^{15} (from Dt. 10^{16}).

v.^{15} *followed vanity and became vain* : Jer. 2^5.

v.^{16} *the host of heaven* : see above, No. 41.

v.$^{18.\ 23}$ *removed from before his face* : see above, No. 17.

v.^{20} *rejected all the seed of Israel* : cf. Jer. 31^{37} If . . ., I will also reject all the seed of Israel.

21^{11} (effect of Manasseh's guilt) : Jer. 15^4.

v.^{12} *both his ears shall tingle* : Jer. 19^3 (probably from I Sa. 3^{11}†).

v.^{14} *for a prey and a spoil* : cf. Jer. 30^{16}.

v.^{15} : cf. Jer. $25^{6.\ 7}$ 32^{32} ; 7^{25} (למן).

v.^{16} 24^4 *innocent blood* (or *the blood of innocents*) *in Jerusalem* : Jer. 19^4 22^{17} (of Jehoiakim).

$22^{16a.\ 17a}$: Jer. 19^{3b-4}. "This place" is also very common elsewhere in Jer., as $7^{6.\ 7.\ 20}$ 16^9.

v.^{17a} *to vex me with the work of their hands* (so I 16^7) : Jer. $25^{6b.\ 7b}$ 32^{30b} 44^8 (from Dt. 31^{29}).

v.^{17b} *and my wrath shall be kindled*, &c. : Jer. 7^{20}.

v.^{19} *for a desolation and a curse* : Jer. 42^{18b} 44^{22b}.

But these parallels are not sufficient to show that Jeremiah is the *compiler* of Kings. The passages quoted consist rather of summaries of the prophetic teaching of the time, which was based ultimately upon Dt., and of which the most influential representative was no doubt Jeremiah : hence it is not unlikely that his phraseology acquired general currency, and would be naturally employed by the compiler in framing his summaries.

It is remarked by König (*Einl.* p. 268), as a small but significant indication that Jer. was not the compiler of Kings, that הִדִּיחַ *to drive out*, used often in Jer. of the expulsion of Israel into exile (8^3 16^{15} $23^{3.\ 8}$ 24^9 $27^{10.\ 15}$ $29^{14.\ 18.}$ 32^{37} 46^{28} ; in the pass., 30^{17} 40^{19} 43^5, cf. $49^{5.\ 30}$ 50^{17} : so Dt. $30^{1.\ 4}$), is never so found in Kings.

CHAPTER III.

ISAIAH.

LITERATURE.—W. Gesenius, *Der Proph. Jesaja übersetzt mit einem vollst. phil. krit. u. hist. Commentar*, 1820–21 ; F. Hitzig, *Der Proph. Jes. übers. u. ausgelegt*, 1833 (the source of much that is best exegetically in more recent commentaries) ; H. Ewald in the *Propheten des Alten Bundes*, 1840–41, ²1867–68 (parts of vols. ii., iv., v. of the translation) ; A. Knobel (in the *Kgf. Exeg. Handb.*), 1843, ⁴ revised by L. Diestel, 1872 ; ⁵ (rewritten) by A. Dillmann, 1890 ; C. P. Caspari, *Beiträge zur Einl. in das Buch Jes.* 1848 ; S. D. Luzzatto, *il prof. Isaia volgarizato e commentato* [in Hebrew] *ad uso degli Israeliti*, Padova, 1856–67 ; F. Delitzsch, *Bibl. Comm. über das Buch Jes.* 1866, ⁴1889 (transl. T. & T. Clark, 1890) ; T. K. Cheyne, *The Book of Isaiah chronologically arranged*, 1870, *The Prophecies of Isaiah*, 1880, ³1884 ; W. Kay in the *Speaker's Comm.*; E. Reuss in *La Bible*, 1876 ; C. W. E. Nägelsbach (in Lange's *Bibelwerk*), 1877 ; H. Guthe, *Das Zukunftsbild des Jes.* 1885 ; C. J. Bredenkamp, *Der Proph. Jes. erläutert*, 1886–87 ; Kuenen, *Einl.* ii. (ed. 2), 1889, pp. 28–157 ; F. Giesebrecht, *Beiträge zur Jesaiakritik* (with notes on some of the other prophets), 1890 ; B. Duhm (in Nowack's "Hand-kommentar"), 1892 ; H. Hackmann, *Die Zukunftserwartung des Jesaia*, 1893 ; T. K. Cheyne, *Introduction to the Book of Isaiah*, 1895 (very full and thorough), and in Haupt's *SBOT*. ; M. L. Kellner, *The Prophecies of Isaiah*, Cambridge, U.S.A. 1895 (36 pp.: a convenient analysis of the prophecies, with synoptic tables of Ass. synchronisms, and transl. of Inscriptions, &c.) ; J. Skinner (in the *Cambridge Bible for Schools*), 1896. Of a more general character are—F. H. Krüger, *Essai sur la théologie d'Ésaie xl–lxvi*, 1881 ; W. R. Smith, *The Prophets of Israel and their place in history to the close of the 8th cent.* B.C., 1882, ²1895, Lectures v.–viii. ; A. B. Davidson in the *Expositor*, 1883, Aug., Sept. ; 1884, Feb., Apr., Oct., Nov., Dec. (on c. 40–66) ; S. R. Driver, *Isaiah ; his life and times, and the writings which bear his name* (in the " Men of the Bible " series), ²1893 ; G. A. Smith, *The Book of Isaiah* (in the " Expositor's Bible "), 1889–90 (historical and homiletic). For other literature, see Delitzsch, p. 34 ff. (E.T. 45 ff.) ; Dillm. p. xviii f.; and the authorities referred to in Kuenen, *l.c.*

On the *Prophets* generally, the character of prophecy, their relation to the history, their theology, &c., the following works may be consulted : Aug. Tholuck, *Die Propheten u. ihre Weissagungen*, 1860, ²1867 ; G. F. Oehler, *Die Theologie des AT.s*, 1873 (translated), § 205 ff.; B. Duhm, *Die Theologie der Propheten*, 1875 ; A. Kuenen, *Prophets and prophecy in Israel* (very full of information on the prophets and their work, but written from an avowedly naturalistic standpoint), 1877 ; F. E. König, *Der Offenbarungsbegriff des A T. s*, 2 vols. 1882 (an exhaustive discussion of the nature of prophecy, and the views that have been held of it) ; [195] C. von Orelli, *Die alttest. Weiss. von der Vollendung des Gottesreiches*, 1882 (translated under the title *Old Test. Prophecy*) ; Ed. Riehm, *Die Messianische Weissagung*, ²1885, transl. Edinb. 1891 (to be recommended) ; C. A. Briggs, *Messianic Prophecy*, 1886 ; H. Schultz, *Alttest. Theologie*,⁴ 1889, p. 213 ff. (translated, Edinb. 1892), ⁵1895; F. Delitzsch, *Mess. Weissagungen in Gesch. Folge*, 1890 (transl. Edinb. 1891) ; F. W. Farrar, *The Minor Prophets*, 1890, chaps. i.–iv. ; A. F. Kirkpatrick, *The Doctrine of the Prophets*, 1892 ; C. G. Montefiore, the "Hibbert Lectures" for 1892 ; R. Smend, *Lehrb. der Alttest. Rel.-gesch.* 1893 ; W. Sanday, "Bampton Lectures" for 1893 (on Inspiration), esp. Lect. iii.; parts of Wellhausen's *Isr. und Jüd. Geschichte*, 1894, ²1895 ; C. H. Cornill, *Der Isr. Prophetismus* (five Lectures),² 1896 (transl. Chicago, 1895); Dillmann, *Alttest. Theol.* 1895, p. 474 ff.; G. A. Smith, *The Book of the Twelve Prophets*, 1896, i. 11–30, 44–58 ; F. H. Woods, *The Hope of Israel* (1896).

B.C.	*Chronological Table.*
745.	TIGLATH-PILESER III.
740.	*Uzziah* named (probably) in Assyrian Inscription. Call of Isaiah.
734.*	*Pekah* deposed and slain ; *Hoshea* (with Assyrian help) raised to the throne of Samaria. N. and E. tribes exiled by Tiglath-Pileser.
732.	Damascus taken by Tiglath-Pileser.
727.	SHALMANESER IV.
722.	SARGON. Fall of Samaria, and end of the Northern Kingdom.
711.	Siege and capture of Ashdod by the troops of Sargon.
710.	Sargon defeats Merodach-baladan, and enters Babylon.
705.	SENNACHERIB.
703.	Sennacherib defeats Merodach-baladan, and spoils his palace.
701.	Campaign of Sennacherib against Phœnicia, Philistia, and Judah.
681.	Sennacherib succeeded by ESARHADDON.
607.	Nineveh destroyed by the Medes and Babylonians.
586.	Destruction of Jerusalem by NEBUCHADNEZZAR.
549–38.	Period of CYRUS' successes in Western and Central Asia.
538.	Cyrus captures Babylon, and releases the Jewish exiles.

Isaiah, Jeremiah, Ezekiel, and "the Twelve" (*i.e.* the Minor Prophets) form the concluding part of the second great division of the Hebrew Canon, "The Prophets," being called specially, in contradistinction to the "Former Prophets" (p. 103), the "Latter Prophets."

Isaiah, son of Amoz, received the prophetic call in the last year of King Uzziah's reign (6¹), *i.e.* (according to the chronology,

* 733-2, according to Rost, *Die Keilschrifttexte T.-P.'s III.* (1893), pp. xxix, xxxv f.

corrected from Assyrian data *) B.C. 740; and he prophesied in Jerusalem during the reigns of the three succeeding kings, Jotham, Ahaz, and Hezekiah. He was married (8^3); and two sons are alluded to, Shear-jashub (7^3) and Maher-shalal-hash-baz (8^{1-4}). The scene of his labours appears to have been chiefly, if not exclusively, Jerusalem; and from the position which was evidently accorded to him by both Ahaz and Hezekiah, it has been ⌊196⌋ conjectured that he was of noble blood. Few particulars of his life are recorded; the chief being connected with the part taken by him at the two crises through which during his lifetime Judah passed (c. 7-8; 36-37). For how many years he survived the second of these crises (B.C. 701) is not known: in 2 cent. A.D. there was a tradition current among the Jews, and alluded to also by Christian writers, that he suffered martyrdom by being sawn asunder in the persecutions which followed the accession of Manasseh. According to 2 Ch. 26^{22} Isaiah was the author of a history of the reign of Uzziah; and *ib.* 32^{32} mention is made of a "Vision of Isaiah," containing an account of the reign of Hezekiah, which formed part of the (lost) "Book of the Kings of Judah and Israel" (see below, under Chronicles); but nothing further is known of either of these works.

The Book of Isaiah may be divided conveniently as follows: —c. 1-12. 13-23. 24-27. 28-33. 34-35. 36-39. 40-66. Among these prophecies there are some which, as will appear, are not the work of Isaiah himself, but belong to a different, and later, period of Israelitish history.

I. C. 1-12. The first collection of Isaiah's prophecies, relating to the kingdoms of Judah and Israel, and belonging to various occasions from B.C. 740 to B.C. 701.

C. 1. The "Great Arraignment" (Ewald). V.$^{2-9}$ the prophet charges his people with unfaithfulness and ingratitude: he compares them to unnatural children who have disowned their father; and traces to their want of discernment the troubles from which they are at present suffering. V.$^{10-17}$ the defence which they are supposed to offer, that the Temple services are maintained with splendour and regularity, is indignantly dis-

---

* See the writer's *Isaiah*, pp. 8, 13 f. (with the references); Schrader, *KAT*.^{2} p. 465 ff.; or the *Beilagen* to Kautzsch, *Die heil. Schrift des A T.s* (above, p. 3), p. 121 ff.

allowed by him : their religious observances are not the expression of a right heart. V.$^{18-23}$ an offer of pardon is made, on God's part, to the guilty nation,—an offer, however, which it speedily appears will not be accepted by it. V.$^{24-31}$ the prophet passes sentence. Jehovah will take the judgment into His own hands, and by a severe discipline purge away evil-doers, and restore the people to its pristine and ideal character.

The date of c. 1 is uncertain, but it must have been written (notice in v.^{7} the *ptcp.* אכלים) whilst a foe was ravaging the territory of Judah. According to some (Ges. Del. Dillm. Hackm.), these foes are the allied troops of Syria and Israel (2 Ki. 15^{37}), and the ch. belongs to the beginning of Ahaz' reign, [197] being the first (or one of the first) of Isaiah's prophecies after his call (c. 6) : according to others (Hitz., W. R. Smith, Duhm, Cheyne) they are the Assyrians (*ib.* 18^{13}), and the ch.—or, at least (Cheyne), v.$^{5-26}$—belongs to the reign of Hezekiah (B.C. 701), its position at the beginning of Isaiah's prophecies being explained from the general character of much of its contents fitting it to form an introduction to the following discourses.

C. 2–5. Here Isaiah dwells in greater detail on the judgment which he sees imminent upon Judah. He opens, 2$^{2-4}$, with an impressive picture of the pre-eminence to be accorded in the future, by the nations of the world, to Israel's religion. V.$^{5-8}$ he contrasts therewith the very different condition of his people, which he sees about him ; and announces, v.$^{9-22}$, the judgment about to fall upon every object of human pride and strength. 3$^{1-11}$ a collapse of all existing society is approaching, the cause of which is referred, v.$^{12-15}$, to the selfish and thoughtless behaviour of the nation's guides. 3^{16}–4^1 Isaiah attacks the luxurious dress of the women, declaring how in the day when disaster overtakes the city, and her warriors are defeated by the foe, it will have to be exchanged for a captive's garb. This, however, is not the end. For those who *escape* the judgment a brighter future will then commence, which is described 4$^{2-6}$. C. 5, in its general scope, is parallel to c. 2–4. V.$^{1-7}$ the parable of the vineyard shows how Judah has disappointed its Lord and Owner : v.$^{8-24}$ the prophet denounces, in a series of "Woes," the chief national sins ; ending, v.$^{25-30}$, with a more distinct allusion to what may shortly be expected at the hands of an unnamed but formidable foe (the Assyrians).

Probably a summary of discourses delivered at the end of Jotham's reign, or beginning of that of Ahaz. 3^{19} implies that the throne was occupied by a weak king, such as Ahaz was : from 2^{16} ("ships of Tarshish") it may perhaps be inferred that the seaport of Elath, which Uzziah had recovered for Judah (2 Ki. 14^{22}), had not yet been captured by the Syrians (*ib.* 16^6). The idea of a national catastrophe, extirpating evil-doers, but preserving a remnant, worthy to form the nucleus of a renovated community in the future (4$^{3ff.}$), is characteristic of Isaiah ; it is foreshadowed at the time of his call (6^{13b}), and recurs often afterwards, 1$^{26f.}$ 10$^{21f.}$ 17$^{5-8}$ (of Ephraim), 28^5 37^{32}. The "Day of Jehovah" (2$^{12ff.}$) is the figure—first, as it seems, so applied by Amos (5$^{18.\ 20}$) —under which, with varying imagery, the prophets represent Jehovah's manifestation at important moments of history (see W. R. Smith, *Proph.* 131 f., 396 f. ; *Isaiah*, p. 27 f.).

By many recent critics, following Ewald, it has been supposed, chiefly on the ground of the common refrain (5^{25b} 9$^{12.\ 17.\ 21}$ 10^4), that 5$^{25-30}$ belonged originally to the prophecy 9^8–10^4, 5$^{26-30}$ forming the climax. Ewald (cf. Smith, *Proph.* p. 238) supposed the original order to have been 5^{25} 9^8–10^4 5$^{26-30}$; Dillm. (p. 43) 9^8–10^4 5^{25} (the close of a strophe, now incomplete), 5$^{26-30}$ (cf. Skinner, p. 40) ; Cheyne (*Introd.* pp. 25 f., 46, 393, 398 f.), 9^8–10^4 5$^{26-29}$ (5$^{25.\ 30}$ being editorial additions).

C. 6. Isaiah's call (year of Uzziah's death—not later than 740 B.C.). The vision, with its impressive symbolism, is described by Isaiah in chaste and dignified language. The terms of his prophetic [198] commission are stated in v.$^{10-13}$. He is to be the preacher and teacher of his people ; but his work, whatever it may accomplish secretly, is to be in appearance fruitless. And this is to continue until the desolating tide of invasion has swept over the land, and purged to the utmost the sin-stricken nation. He is not, however, left without a gleam of hope : the core of the Jewish nation will survive the judgment, and burst out afterwards into new life : it is a "holy seed," and as such is indestructible (v.^{13b} : for the figure of the reviving tree, cf. Job 14$^{7-9}$).

C. 7^1–9^7. Prophecies uttered during the Syro-Ephraimitish war (B.C. 735–734). An alliance had been concluded between Pekah, king of Israel, and Rezin, king of Damascus, for the purpose of opposing a barrier to the aggression of the Assyrians ; and the object of the present invasion of Judah was to force that country to join the coalition : the intention of the allies being to depose Ahaz (who cherished Assyrian proclivities), and to substitute for him a more subservient ruler, the son of one Tabeel (7^6). The invasion caused great alarm in Judah (7^2) ; and Ahaz meditated casting himself upon the Assyrians for help,—a policy of which Isaiah strongly disapproved. Isaiah, being directed to go and accost Ahaz, assures him that his fears are groundless : the power of the two allied kingdoms is doomed to extinction ;

their plan for the ruin of Judah will not succeed, 7^{4-9}. To meet Ahaz' distrust, Isaiah announces the birth of the child, who, in spite of the destitution (v.^{15} cf. v.^{22}) through which his country must first pass, is still the mysterious pledge and symbol of its deliverance, v.$^{13-16}$. The thought which has hitherto been in the background is now no longer concealed: and Isaiah confronts Ahaz with the naked truth, declaring how his plan for invoking Assyrian help will issue in unforeseen consequences: Judah will become the arena of a conflict between Assyria and Egypt, and will be desolated by their contending armies, v.$^{17-25}$. In 8^{1-4} Isaiah reaffirms, in a symbolical form, the prediction of $7^{8f. 16}$. 8^{5-15} are words of consolation addressed to his immediate friends and disciples. The tide of invasion will indeed inundate Israel; it will even pass on and threaten to engulph Judah: but it will be suddenly arrested, v.$^{5-10}$: do not regard Rezin and Pekah with unreasoning fear; do not desert principle in the presence of imagined danger, v.$^{11-15}$. Dark times are coming, when [199] men will wish that they had followed the "direction and admonition" (v.^{20}; see v.^{16}) of Isaiah, v.$^{16-22}$. But nevertheless Jehovah has a brighter future in store for His people: the North and North-east districts, which had just been depopulated (in 734) by Tiglath-pileser (2 Ki. 15^{29}), will be the first to experience it; and the prophecy closes with an impressive picture of the restoration and triumph of the shattered nation, of the end of its oppressors, and of its security and prosperity under the wondrous rule of its ideal King, 9^{1-7}.

9^8-10^4 (written probably shortly before the outbreak of the same war, but addressed to *Israel*, not Judah). The prophet in four strophes, each closing with the same ominous refrain (cf. Am. 4^{6-11}), draws a picture of the approaching collapse of the N. kingdom, which he traces to its moral and social disintegration. (1) 9^{8-12}. The Ephraimites' proud, but inconsiderate, superiority to danger has resulted in their country being beset on all sides by its foes. (2) 9^{13-17}. A great and sudden disaster befalls Ephraim, defeating the plans of its statesmen, and leaving it defenceless. (3) 9^{18-21}. Rival factions contending with one another insidiously undermine Ephraim's strength. (4) 10^{1-4}. The rulers of the nation have demoralized both the people and themselves: in the day when misfortune comes they will be unable to cope with it, and will perish helplessly on the battlefield.

10⁵–12⁶. A picture of the pride and ambition of the Assyrians, of their sudden ruin, of the release of Jerusalem from its peril, and of the ensuing rule of the Messianic king. This prophecy is one of the most striking creations of Isaiah's genius : in power and originality of conception it stands unsurpassed. The Assyrian is in reality an instrument in the hands of Providence, but he fails to recognize the truth; and Isaiah describes his overweening pretensions, 10⁵⁻¹⁵, and their sudden collapse, v.¹⁶⁻¹⁹. The fall of the Assyrian will not indeed leave Israel unscathed; but those who escape, though but a remnant, will have their understanding enlightened, and will look to Jehovah alone, v.²⁰⁻²³. Let Judah, then, be reassured : though the Assyrian draw near, and even swing his arm audaciously against the citadel of Zion, in the moment when victory seems secure he will be foiled, v.²⁴⁻³⁴ ; Jerusalem will be delivered, and a reign of peace, under the gracious rule of the ideal Prince of David's line, will be inaugurated, [200] 11¹⁻¹⁰ : Israel's exiles from all quarters will return ; the rivalry of Judah and Ephraim will be at an end, v.¹¹⁻¹⁶ ; and the restored nation will express its gratitude to its Deliverer in a hymn of thanksgiving and praise, c. 12.

In 10²⁸⁻³² Isaiah represents the Assyrian as advancing against Jerusalem by the usual line of approach from the north. It does not appear, however, that either Sargon or Sennacherib actually followed this route; and the prophet, it is probable, intends merely to draw an effective *imaginative* picture of the danger threatening Jerusalem, and of the manner in which (v.³³ᶠ·) it would be suddenly averted. The historical situation implied by the prophecy agrees with that of the year 701 B.C., when Sennacherib, having completed the reduction of the rebellious cities of Phœnicia, was starting for the south, intending to reduce similarly Jerusalem, and the Philistine cities of Ashkelon and Ekron : at a time when the Assyrians were actually approaching from the north, their intended attack might readily take shape in the prophet's imagination in the manner represented in 10²⁸⁻³² (comp. *Isaiah*,² pp. 66 f., 70–73, 213 f. Similarly Ew. ; Schrader, *KAT*.² p. 386; Stade, *Gesch*. i. 614 f.; Kittel, *Gesch*. ii. 313 ; Duhm, at least for 10⁵⁻⁹· ¹³⁻¹⁴ ; Hackmann).

Prof. W. R. Smith (*Proph*. 297 ff.) places the prophecy at the beginning of Sargon's reign, regarding 10⁵ᶠᶠ· as an ideal representation of the ambitious pretensions of the Assyrians, and of the failure to which they were doomed, not suggested by any *special* historical occasion. Similarly Dillm. ; Guthe, Giesebrecht (in 711). Kuen. § 43. 5 places it towards the end of Sargon's reign ; Cheyne (*Introd*. pp. 50 f., 55), abandoning the unity of the prophecy, assigns 10⁹⁻⁹· ¹³⁻¹⁴ to 711, and 10²⁷ᵇ⁻³² to 722, during the siege of Samaria.

Isaiah's authorship of c. 12 is, however, questioned by an increasing number of modern critics, who hold it to be a psalm of thanksgiving, attached to the original prophecy after the return from exile : so, for instance, Ewald, Cheyne, Stade, Kuenen (§ 43. 6), Prof. Fr. Brown (*Journ. of Bibl. Lit.* 1890, p. 128 ff.), Dillm. (p. 124 f.), Cornill, König (§ 62. 5*b*). This conclusion is based partly upon the contents of the chapter, partly upon its phraseology, both of which present deviations from Isaiah's usual manner, and resemblances with the usage of a later age ; the details will be found noted most fully by Brown and Dillmann (cf. also Cheyne, p. 58 f.).—11[10-16], also, on account of the ideas contained in it (which are in some respects in advance of those found elsewhere in Isaiah : note also the contrast between v.[14] and v.[6-9]), and the historical conditions presupposed by it (see more fully *Isaiah*,[2] p. 214 f.), has been considered by many recent critics to have been added in the post-exilic period, as a supplement to 11[1-9] (Kuen. § 43. 7 ; Giesebr. pp. 25–52 ; Cheyne, pp. 59–62 ; cf. Skinner, p. 95). Dillm. (p. 121) defends Isaiah's authorship.

II. c. 13–23. Prophecies dealing (chiefly) with foreign nations. C. 1–12 centre entirely round either Judah or Israel ; the present group comprises prophecies, in which though there is often an indirect reference to one of these countries, the primary interest lies, as a rule, in the nation which they respectively concern. The prophets observed closely the movements of history : they saw in the rise and fall of nations the exhibition of a Divine purpose ; and the varying fortunes of Israel's nearer or more distant neighbours often materially affected Israel itself. These nations were, moreover, related to Israel and Judah in different ways : sometimes, for instance, they were united by ties of sympathy and alliance ; in other cases they viewed one another with mutual jealousy and distrust. The neighbouring nations, especially, being thus in various ways viewed with interest by their own people, the Hebrew prophets not unnaturally included them in their prophetic survey. The foreign prophecies of Isaiah are distinguished by great individuality of character. The prophet displays a remarkable familiarity with [201] the condition, social or physical, of the countries with which he deals : and seizes in each instance some characteristic aspect, or feature, for notice (*e.g.* the haughty independence of Moab, the tall and handsome physique of the Ethiopians, the local and other peculiarities of Egypt, the commerce and colonies of Tyre).

13[1]–14[23]. On Babylon. In this prophecy the Jews are represented as in *exile*, held in thraldom by the Babylonians, but shortly to be released in consequence of the capture of Babylon by the Medes (13[17]). C. 13 describes the mustering of the assailing forces on the mountains, the terror of their approach, the capture and sack of the city, the fewness of the survivors (v.[12]), and the desolation which will mark thereafter the site of Babylon. 14[1-2] states the reason of this, viz. because the time has arrived for Israel to be released from exile : " For Jehovah will have compassion upon Jacob, and *will again choose Israel*, and settle them in their own land." 14[3-20] the prophet provides Israel with an ode of triumph, to be sung in the day of its deliverance, depicting, with extreme beauty of imagery, and not without a delicate under-current of irony, the fall of the Babylonian monarch from his proud estate : v.[21-23] he reasserts the irretrievable ruin of the great city.

The situation presupposed by this prophecy is not that of Isaiah's age. The Jews are not warned, as Isaiah (39[6]) might warn them, against the folly of concluding an alliance with Babylon, or reminded of the disastrous consequences which such an alliance might entail; nor are they threatened, as Jeremiah threatens them, with impending exile : they are represented as *in exile*, and as about to be delivered from it (14[1-2]). It was the office of the prophet of Israel to address himself to the needs of his own age, to announce to his contemporaries the judgments, or consolations, which arose out of the circumstances of their own time, to interpret for them their own history. To base a promise upon a condition of things *not yet existent*, and without any point of contact with the circumstances or situation of those to whom it is addressed, is alien to the genius of prophecy. Upon grounds of analogy the prophecy 13[2]–14[23] can only be attributed to an author living towards the close of the exile and holding out to his contemporaries the prospect of release from Babylon, as Isaiah held out to *his* contemporaries the prospect of deliverance from [202] Assyria. (Comp. below, p. 230.) The best commentary on it is the long prophecy against Babylon, contained in Jer. 50–51[58], and written towards the closing years of the exile, which views the approaching fall of Babylon from the same standpoint, and manifests the same spirit as this does. As the prophecy names only the Medes, and contains no allusion to Cyrus or the Persians, it is probable that it was written shortly before 549 B.C. (in which year Cyrus overthrew the Median empire of Astyages : the Persians uniting with the Medes, after successes in Asia Minor and elsewhere, captured Babylon in 538).

14$^{24\text{-}27}$. On the Assyrian. A short prophecy declaring Jehovah's purpose to overthrow the Assyrian army upon the "mountains" of Judah.

The date is no doubt during the period of Sennacherib's campaign against Judah in 701. The prophecy has no connexion with what precedes. It is directed against *Assyria*, not Babylon ; and it anticipates, not the capture of the city of Babylon, but the overthrow of the hosts of Assyria in Judah.

14$^{28\text{-}32}$. On the Philistines. The Philistines are in exultation at the fall of some dreaded foe : Isaiah warns them that their rejoicing is premature, that the power which they dreaded will recover itself, and prove even more formidable than before. The Assyrian is approaching in the distance (v.$^{31\text{b}}$) ; Philistia will suffer severely at his hands (v.$^{30\text{b. }31\text{a}}$), though Zion, in the strength of its God, will be secure (v.$^{30\text{a. }32\text{b}}$).

The title (v.^{28}) suggests that "the rod which smote" Philistia was Ahaz, and assigns the prophecy to 728 [or, as others calculate, 715] B.C. But the connexion of thought appears to require the foe alluded to in v.^{29} to be identical with the foe alluded to, more directly, in v.^{31}, *i.e.* the Assyrian. If so, Sargon will be the "snake" of v.^{29}, and Sennacherib the more formidable "serpent flying about," and the date will be some short time after Sargon's death in 705. The Philistines might naturally feel elated upon receiving news of the murder of Sargon, who had defeated Hanno of Gaza at Raphia in 720, and captured Ashdod in 711. That Sennacherib severely punished the Philistines, appears from his own inscription (*Isaiah*, p. 67 f.). Cheyne refers the prophecy to 720, supposing the occasion to be disturbances in Syria and Palestine shortly after the accession of Sargon (*Introd.* p. 81 f.).

C. 15–16. On Moab. The prophet sees a great and terrible disaster about to fall upon Moab, desolating the country, and obliging the flight of its inhabitants, c. 15. He bids the fugitives seek safety in the protection of the house of David, and send tokens of their submission to Jerusalem ; for there, as he knows, the violence of the Assyrian aggressor will soon be stilled (cf. 29^{20}), and a just and righteous king will be sitting on David's [203] throne (cf. 9$^{5\text{-}7}$), 16$^{1\text{-}5}$. But the haughty independence of the Moabites prevents their accepting the prophet's advice ; and the judgment must accordingly run its course, 16$^{6\text{-}12}$. V.$^{13\text{-}14}$ forms an epilogue. The prophecy, as a whole, had been delivered on some previous occasion : Isaiah, in the epilogue, affirms solemnly its speedy fulfilment.

The dates both of the original prophecy and of the epilogue are matter of conjecture. The epilogue may be assigned plausibly to a period shortly before Sargon's campaign against Ashdod in 711, when Moab is mentioned as intriguing with Philistia and Egypt (*Isaiah*, p. 45). But to what date the prophecy itself belongs is very uncertain. The expression *heretofore* in v.[13] is ambiguous : it may denote a comparatively short interval of time (2 Sa. 15[34]), or one that is much longer (Ps. 93[2]). The prophecy may have been written by Isaiah some 25 years before, in anticipation of the foray made by Tiglath-pileser upon the districts east of Jordan in 734, which (according to the notice 1 Ch. 5[26]) extended as far south as Reuben. But the style and tone of 15[1]–16[12] impress many critics as different from those of Isaiah ; and hence they suppose it to have been delivered originally by some earlier prophet, but to have been adopted and reinforced by Isaiah. The terms of 16[13] (which in no way connect the preceding prophecy with Isaiah himself) rather support this view. There are analogies for the reproduction (and partial modification) by one prophet of a passage written by another : comp. 2[2-4] with Micah 4[1-3] ; Jer. 49[7-16] and Obad. v.[1-9. 16] ; and the use made by Jer. himself of this prophecy (see the reff. on RV. *marg.* of Jer. 48[5. 29-34]). The invasion (as the Moabites flee in the direction of Edom) appears to take place from the North ; Judah is represented as strong enough to defend the fugitives ; and the territory N. of the Arnon (*i.e.* Reuben and part of Gad) is occupied by the Moabites. This combination of circumstances suits the reign of Jeroboam II.; and the original prophecy has accordingly been referred to the occasion of the subjugation of Moab by that king, presupposed by 2 Ki. 14[25], when the powerful monarch Uzziah was ruling over Judah—the author being supposed to be a prophet of Judah who sympathized (15[5] 16[10f]). with the suffering Moabites (so Hitzig, Reuss, Wellh. in the *Encycl. Brit.*[9] xvi. 535, W. R. Smith, *Proph.* pp. 91 f., 392, Dillm.). Ges., Ew., Kuen. (§ 44), Baudissin, also, attribute 15[1]–16[12] to an earlier prophet than Isaiah, but without attempting to define its occasion more particularly. 16[4b-5] (which is in harmony with Isaiah's style and thought) may be conjectured, if this view be adopted, to be an addition made to the original prophecy by Isaiah himself (Cheyne formerly).

17[1-11]. On Damascus. Isaiah declares the impending fall of Damascus, to be followed shortly by that of Ephraim as well, v.[1-5]. A remnant will, however, escape, who will be spiritually transformed, and recognise Jehovah as the sole source of their strength, v.[6-8]. The ground of Ephraim's ruin is its forgetfulness of Jehovah, and its adoption of foreign cults, v.[9-11].

[204] The prophecy is parallel in thought to 8[4], though, from its containing no allusion to hostilities with Judah, it may be inferred (Ew. Del. Ch. Kuen. Dillm.) that it was written before the Syro-Ephraimitish war had commenced.

17[12-14]. A short but singularly graphic prophecy, describing the ocean-like roar of the advancing Assyrian hosts, and their sudden dispersion.

In general conception (though the figures used are different) the prophecy resembles 14$^{24-27}$, and may be assigned to the same period. Cheyne thinks that it was written to reassure Judah during the siege of Samaria, *c.* 723.

C. 18. On Ethiopia [Heb. Cush]. The Ethiopians, alarmed by intelligence of the advance of the Assyrians, have just sent ambassadors to the king of Judah to induce him to combine with them in an anti-Assyrian league (v.$^{1-2a\,\alpha}$). Isaiah sends them back with the assurance that their anxiety is needless : the plans of the Assyrians will be intercepted, and their hosts overthrown, independently of the arms of Ethiopia, v.$^{2a\,\beta-6}$. Hereupon the Ethiopians will do homage to the God of Israel, v.^{7}.

The prophecy may be assigned, like the last, to the year 701. An advance upon Egypt lay always within the plans of the Assyrians : and the Ethiopians might well fear that Sennacherib, when he had conquered Judah and the Philistines, would pursue his successes, and make an endeavour to add not Egypt only, but Ethiopia as well, to his empire. In point of fact, Sennacherib was advancing towards Egypt when his army (at Pelusium) was smitten by a pestilence (Hdt. ii. 141 ; *Isaiah*, p. 81 f.).

C. 19. On Egypt. A period of unexampled collapse and decay, affecting every grade and class of society, is about to commence for Egypt, v.$^{1-17}$, to be succeeded by the nation's conversion and spiritual renovation, v.$^{18-25}$.

The prophecy is a remarkable one, both on account of its many allusions to the characteristic habits of the people and features of the country, and for the grand catholicity of the picture with which it closes (Assyria and Egypt, the one Judah's oppressor, the other its untrue friend, to be incorporated, on an equality with Israel itself, in the kingdom of God).

The date of the prophecy is not certain ; but it is at least a plausible con-jecture that it was written in 720 B.C., when Sargon defeated the Egyptians at Raphia. Sargon did not "rule over" Egypt (v.^{4}) ; but it is not necessary to suppose that Isaiah has here a definite person in view ; he probably merely means to say that, in the political disorganization which he sees to be imminent, the country will fall a prey to the first ambitious and determined man who invades it. In point of fact, Sargon defeated the Egyptian arms both in 720 and in 711 ; Sennacherib did the same in 701 : Esarhaddon penetrated into Egypt, and reduced it to the condition of an Assyrian province, *c.* 672 ; Psammetichus, a Libyan, made himself master of it shortly afterwards, *c.* 660, and revolutionized the policy of its former kings by opening it for the first time to the Greeks. Others think that the lofty hopes of the prophecy are most consistent with the period after 701, when the prophet could contemplate more calmly his country's foe : so Ewald (i. 481 f. [E.T. ii. 267 f.]), who describes this prophecy as Isaiah's last and noblest "testament to posterity," Stade, Dillm., Kuen. (§ 43. 23–25). Isaiah's authorship of v.$^{16-25}$ (or of v.[18-25]) has been questioned (see Cheyne, p. 100 ff.): in defence of it, see Kuen. § 43. 25; Dillm. p. 173.

[205] C. 20. On Egypt and Ethiopia. While Ashdod was besieged by the Assyrian troops in 711, Isaiah walks the street of Jerusalem in a captive's garb, continuing to do so for three years, in order to prefigure the shameful fate that would befall Egypt and Ethiopia at the hands of the victorious Assyrians.

The date is fixed by Sargon's inscriptions, which allude to the siege of Ashdod, and imply that the revolt of the Philistines, which led to it, was carried through with promises of help from Egypt. Isaiah's symbolical act was doubtless meant indirectly as a protest against the Egyptianizing party in Jerusalem, and intended to impress forcibly upon the people of the capital the folly of reliance upon Egypt.

21[1-10]. On Babylon. The prophet in imagination sees Babylon besieged by an eager and impetuous foe, v.[1-2]: the vision agitates and appals him, v.[3-4]: the issue, for a while, appears uncertain, but in the end he is assured that the city has fallen, v.[5-9]; and he announces the result to his people, v.[10].

In order to determine the date of the prophecy, it is necessary to consider what is the siege of Babylon alluded to in it. The mention of Elam (*i.e.*, substantially, Persia) and Media, among the assailing forces, appeared to point naturally to the attack upon Babylon by Cyrus, B.C. 538, as the occasion of the prophecy; and as no intelligible purpose would be subserved by Isaiah's announcing to the generation of Hezekiah an occurrence lying nearly 200 years in the future, and *having no bearing on contemporary interests*, it has been generally supposed by critics (Ewald, Hitzig, &c.) to be the work of an author living towards the close of the Babylonian captivity, and writing from the same general standpoint as the author of 13[2]–14[23]. The decypherment of the Assyrian Inscriptions has, however, shown that Merodach-Baladan, who bore from B.C. 721 to 710 the title "king of Babylon" (Schrader, *Keilinschriftliche Bibliothek*, iii. 1, 1892, p. 185 ff.; cf. Is. 39[1]), made repeated efforts to free his country from the Assyrian yoke, and that the Assyrians, on three separate occasions, in Isaiah's own lifetime, B.C. 710, 703, and 696, besieged and entered the rebellious city (*Isaiah*, pp. 45, 55, 106). Hence Kleinert (*Stud. u. Krit.* 1877, p. 174 ff.) sought to show that the prophecy had reference to the first of these sieges, the interest with which the issue was watched by Isaiah being explained by him from the fact that Merodach-Baladan had probably some understanding with Hezekiah (cf. c. 39), and that the success of the Assyrians would mean the punishment of those suspected of being his allies. This view was adopted formerly by Cheyne (*Isaiah*, ed. 3), and the present writer (*Isaiah*, p. 96 ff.); but it has not met with the support of recent writers on Isaiah (Delitzsch, ed. 4; Kuen. § 43. 10; Dillm.; &c.); and even Cheyne has abandoned it (*Introd.* p. 124). It seems, in fact, that the judgment of Ewald and the older critics was correct. The capture of Babylon by the Assyrians in 710 did not in reality (so far as we know) affect Judah at all ; [206] nor was it, like the conquest of Cyrus in 538, followed by momentous consequences for the Jews. See, more fully, the note in the writer's *Isaiah*, ed. 2, pp. 216–219 ; Cheyne, *Introd.* p. 121 ff.

21[11-12]. On Dumah (*i.e.* Edom). A call of inquiry reaches the prophet from Seir (Gen. 36[8f.]) : he replies, in dark and enigmatic terms, that though the " morning " (*i.e.* brighter days) may dawn for Edom, it will quickly be followed by a " night " of trouble ; for the present no more favourable answer can be given.

21[13-17]. On 'Arāb. A tide of invasion is about to overflow the region inhabited by 'Arāb and Kedar (v.[17]) ; the Dedanite caravans passing through it have to seek refuge in the woods : the people of Têma bring supplies to the fugitive traders. Within a year Kedar will be so reduced in numbers, that only an insignificant remnant will survive.

'Arāb denotes not Arabia (in our sense of the word), but a particular nomad tribe inhabiting the N. of the Peninsula, and mentioned Ez. 27[20f.], with Dedan and Kedar, as engaged in commerce with Tyre. Kedar was a wealthy pastoral tribe, 60[7], Jer. 49[29]. Têma lay some 250 miles S.-E. of Edom. Sargon's troops were engaged in war with the Philistines in both 720 and 711 : and it may be conjectured that these two prophecies were delivered in view of an expected campaign of the Assyrians in the neighbouring regions in one of these years.

22[1-14]. A rebuke, addressed by Isaiah to the inhabitants of the capital, on account of the undignified temper displayed by them when their city was threatened with an assault by the foe. V.[1] describes the demeanour of the people ; v.[2-3] the events which had preceded ; v.[4-5] the grief and shame overwhelming the prophet in consequence ; v.[6-12] the hasty measures of defence which had been taken by the people, and the inappropriate temper manifested by them at the time and subsequently ; v.[13] is the prophet's rebuke.

The prophecy belongs probably to either 711 or 701 B.C. In 711 B.C. Sargon's troops were in the neighbourhood of Judah (engaged upon the siege of Ashdod) ; and as Judah is mentioned at the same time (*Isaiah*, p. 45 ; Schrader, *op. cit.* ii. 64 f.) as " speaking treason " against him, it is possible that some collision may have taken place with Sargon's soldiers, resulting in a panic and defeat, such as Isaiah describes.* The objection to referring it to

---

* But Sayce's hypothesis that Sargon gained a series of successes, and even ended by capturing Jerusalem, lacks adequate historical foundation, and

701, the year of Sennacherib's invasion, is its minatory tone ; for in the other prophecies belonging undoubtedly to this period, Isaiah makes it his aim to encourage and sustain [207] his people : but this difficulty may be overcome by referring it to an *episode* in this invasion—by supposing it to allude, for instance, to a panic occasioned by the first conflict with the Assyrians (W. R. Smith, *Proph.* p. 346 ; Dillm.), or else to have been spoken by the prophet immediately *after* Sennacherib's retreat, in condemnation of the temper shown by the people while the invasion was in progress (Guthe, Sörensen, Kuenen, § 43. 19–21, Cheyne, *Introd.* p. 135 f.).

22$^{15-25}$. On Shebna.   Shebna, a minister holding in Jerusalem the influential office of Governor or Comptroller of the Palace, is threatened by Isaiah with disgrace and banishment ; and Eliakim, a man of approved views, is nominated as his successor.

It is evident that Shebna represented a policy obnoxious to Isaiah— probably he was one of the friends of Egypt.   The prophecy must date from before 701 ; for in that year (36^3 37^2) Eliakim is mentioned as holding the office here promised him by Isaiah, and Shebna occupies the subordinate position of "Scribe," or secretary.

C. 23. On Tyre.   In picturesque and effective imagery, the approaching fall of Tyre, the great commercial and colonizing city of antiquity, is described, v.$^{1-14}$.   After seventy years of enforced quiescence, however, Tyre will revive, and resume her former occupation ; but her gains, instead of being applied to her own profit or adornment, will be consecrated to the service of Jehovah, v.$^{15-18}$.

Isaiah expresses here, in a form consonant with the special character of Tyre—as before, in the case of Ethopia, 18^7, and Egypt, 19$^{18ff.}$—the thought of its future acknowledgment of the true God : the commercial spirit, by which it is actuated, will not be discarded, but it will be elevated and ennobled.

The date of the prophecy depends partly upon v.^{13}.   This verse is difficult and uncertain : but if the rendering of RV. be correct, the prophet points, as a warning to Tyre, to the punishment recently inflicted upon Chaldæa by the Assyrians—probably in 710–709 or 703 (p. 216) ; and the prophecy will have been written shortly before Sennacherib's invasion of Phœnicia in 701 * (Smith, *Proph.* p. 333 ; cf. *Isaiah*, p. 106).   But the terms of v.^{13} appear to describe a graver disaster than that which befell Babylon in either 710 or 703 (see Schrader, *Keilinschr. Bibliothek*, ii. 69–73, 83–85 [*KAT.*^{2} 346 f.]) ; the

---

must be rejected (see W. R. Smith, *Proph.* p. 295 ff. ; *Isaiah*, p. 101 f. ; Schrader, *KAT.*^{2} p. 407 f.; Kuen. § 41. 4c ; Dillm. pp. 3, 103, 197).

* Though *Tyre* is not mentioned among the cities then attacked by him.

"Chaldæans" are introduced abruptly, and Ewald's emendation, כנענים
Canaanites for כשרים (adopted by Schrader, *KAT*.² p. 409 f., and Orelli,
and viewed favourably by Delitzsch), is an attractive one ; the verse will
then refer simply to the fate impending on Phœnicia itself, and the prophecy
may be assigned plausibly, with Ew. Schrad. Kuen. (§ 42. 23), Dillm. Orelli,
Cheyne (*l.c.* p. 143 f.), to the period of Shalmaneser's siege of Tyre (between
727 and 723 B.C.), related by Josephus (*Arch.* ix. 14. 2).

III. C. 24–27. These chapters are intimately connected
[208] together, and form a single prophecy. They present a
vivid picture of a great world-judgment, and of the happy escape
from it of God's faithful people. In particular, they declare the
overthrow of some proud, tyrannical city (the name of which is
not stated), and depict the felicity, and spiritual blessedness,
which Israel will afterwards enjoy.

24¹⁻¹³ announces a great convulsion about to overwhelm a
large portion of the earth, obliterating every distinction of class,
and spreading desolation far and wide. For a moment, however, the vision of ruin is interrupted ; and the praises of the
redeemed Israelites are heard, borne from afar over the Western
waters, v.¹⁴ ᶠ.: but such rejoicings, the prophet declares, are
premature ; another and more terrible scene in the drama of
judgment has still to be enacted, v.¹⁶⁻²⁴. In c. 25 the deliverance is supposed to have been effected, and the hostile city
overthrown : and the prophet puts into the mouth of the
redeemed community two hymns of thanksgiving, 21¹⁻⁵. ⁹ ; 25⁶⁻⁸
he pictures the blessedness of which Zion will then be the centre
for *all* nations ; while haughty Moab, 25¹⁰⁻¹², will be ignomini-
ously humbled. 26¹⁻¹⁰ is a third hymn of thanksgiving ; 26¹¹⁻¹⁹
is a retrospect (supposed likewise to be spoken *after* the deliverance) : the nation looks back to the period of distress preceding
its deliverance, and confesses that this had been accomplished,
not by any power of its own, but by Divine aid. 26²⁰⁻²¹ the
prophet returns to his own present, and addresses words of
comfort to his contemporaries in view of the approaching
"indignation" (*i.e.* 24¹ᶠᶠ·). C. 27 contains further descriptions
of the fall of the hostile power, with a fourth hymn (v.²⁻⁵), and of
the restoration of God's own people.

Modern critics agree generally in the opinion that this
prophecy is not Isaiah's : and (chiefly) for the following reasons :
—1. It lacks a suitable *occasion* in Isaiah's age. It cannot be
plausibly assigned to the period of the Assyrian crisis of 701 ;

for we possess a long series of discourses belonging to the years
702–701 : in all Isaiah views similarly the coming overthrow of
Assyria ; but in the present prophecy both the structure and the
point of view are throughout different (contrast *e.g.* c. 29–32
with these chapters). Thus Isaiah never connects either the
aggressions or the ruin of the Assyrian power with movements
of the dimensions here contemplated : the Assyrian forces are
broken "upon [209] the mountains" of Judah (14^{25}) ; but the
earth generally is untouched (contrast $24^{1-12.\ 17-20}$). Isaiah always
speaks of the *army*, or *king* of Assyria : here the oppressing
power is some great *city* (25^{2-3} 26^{5}). In Isaiah, again, the
"remnant" which escapes is saved in Judah or Jerusalem (4^{3}
37^{32}) : here the voices of the redeemed are first heard from
distant quarters of the earth (24^{14-16}).

2. The literary treatment (in spite of certain phraseological
points of contact with Isaiah) is in many respects unlike Isaiah's.

3. There are features in the representation and contents of
the prophecy which seem to spring out of a different (and later)
vein of thought from Isaiah's.

Thus * the style is more artificial than that of Isaiah, as appears, for instance, in the frequent combination of nearly synonymous clauses, often ἀσυν-
δέτως ($24^{3ff.}$), the repetition of a word (24^{16} 25^{1b} $26^{3.\ 5.\ 15}$ 27^{5}), the numerous
alliterations and word-plays ($24^{1.\ 3.\ 4.\ 6.\ 16.\ 17.\ 18.\ 19}$ $25^{6.\ 10b}$ 26^{3} 27^{7}), the tendency to rhyme ($24^{1.\ 8.\ 16}$ $25^{1.\ 6.\ 7}$ $26^{2.\ 13.\ 20.\ 21}$ $27^{3.\ 5}$),—all features, which,
though they may be found occasionally in Isaiah, are never aggregated in his
writings as they are here. There are, moreover, many unusual expressions,
the *combination* of which points similarly to an author other than Isaiah.
Traits connected with the representation, not in the manner of Isaiah, are
e.g. $24^{16.\ 21-22}$ 25^{6} $26^{18f.}$ (the resurrection), 27^{1} (the animal symbolism), the reflexions $26^{7ff.}$. The principal points of contact with Isaiah are 24^{6} (מוֹעֵר),
v.^{10b} (23^{1}), v.^{13} (17^{6}), v.^{16b} (21^{2} 33^{1}), v.^{20} (1^{8} מְלוּנָה), 25^{2} (17^{1} מַפָּלָה), v.^{4} (14^{30} דלים
ואביונים), v.^{5} (32^{2} צִיּוֹן), 27^{4} (9^{17} שָׁמִיר וָשַׁיִת), v.^{7} (10^{20} מכהו), v.^{9} (17^{8} חמנים), v.^{11b} ($17^{1f.}$
22^{11b}), v.^{13} (11^{11} the wide dispersion) ; but, in the light of the general differ-
ence, these are not sufficient to establish Isaiah's authorship : they do not
show more than that the author was familiar with Isaiah's writings, and
sometimes borrowed expressions from them. His prophecy contains similarly
reminiscences from other prophets, as 24^{1} (Nah. 2^{11}) ; $24^{2.\ 4}$ 27^{6} (Hos. $4^{9.\ 3}$
$14^{7ff.}$) ; 24^{17-18a} (Jer. 48^{43-44a}) ; 24^{20b} (Am. 5^{2}) ; 26^{1} (Isa. 60^{18}) ; 26^{21} (Micah
1^{3}). It is true, the author follows Isaiah more than other prophets ; but it is
difficult not to feel the justice of Delitzsch's remark (*Isaiah*, ed. 4, p. 286),
"that the prophecy, in order to find a place in the history of the OT.
knowledge of salvation, must be referred to an age subsequent to Isaiah's."

---

* See more fully Cheyne, *Introd.* p. 147 ff.

But if it be not Isaiah's, to what period is the prophecy to be assigned? The absence of *distinct* historical allusions makes this question a difficult one to answer. 27^1 alludes (as it seems) to Assyria, Babylon, and Egypt; hence it will not be earlier than the time when Babylon became formidable to the Jews, [210] and there are features in which it is in advance not merely of Isaiah, but even of Deutero-Isaiah. It may be referred most plausibly to the early post-exilic period.*

The unnamed city is, most probably, Babylon, which, though conquered by Cyrus, was not destroyed by him, and remained an important city till the close of the Persian empire (B.C. 332). It is doubtful, however, whether the literal Babylon is intended by the author. The lineaments of the city which he depicts are so indistinct and unsubstantial that the picture seems rather to be an ideal one: Babylon becomes a type of the powers of heathenism, which the prophet imagines as entrenched behind the walls of a great city, strongly fortified indeed, but destined in God's good time to be overthrown. Israel is in a depressed condition, tyrannized over by this unfriendly power; and he depicts, with great imaginative power, the feelings with which the people of God will watch the course of its overthrow, and the sacred joy and gratitude which its fall will evoke in their hearts. In doing this, he reaffirms older, but as yet unfulfilled prophecies: he employs largely the materials supplied to him by the writings of earlier prophets; but these are generalized and idealized by him, as he recombines them into a new picture, designed upon a grander scale. The representation partakes in fact of an apocalyptic, or eschatological, character: the ideal, or symbolic, element is much larger than in the pre-exilic prophecies generally; and the closest parallels are Ez. 38–39, Joel 3$^{9-21}$, Zech. 12–14. The aim of the prophecy will have been to revive and invigorate Israel's hope in the age of depression which followed the restoration to Palestine, when even faithful souls, contrasting the meagre reality with the brilliant visions of Is. 40–66, must have found it hard to resist the temptation to despair.

* So Ewald, Delitzsch (*Mess. Weiss.* § 44), Dillm., Kirkpatrick, *The Doctrine of the Prophets* (1892), p. 475 ff. Smend (*ZATW*. 1884, p. 161 ff.) and Kuenen (§ 46. 20) place it later, in the 4th cent. B.C., but upon grounds of doubtful cogency.

The *precise* circumstances under which the prophecy was written must, however, remain matter of conjecture. From Neh. 1³ it may be inferred (cf. Bertheau, *ad loc.*) that some calamity, on which the historical books are otherwise silent, had befallen the restored community ; and perhaps this prophecy was designed for the encouragement [211] of the people at the time when that disaster was imminent, the author (in some cases) basing his representations upon those of Isaiah, and developing lines of thought suggested by him. Possibly, indeed, it may owe its place in the Book of Isaiah to the fact that it was from the first intended as a supplement to Isaiah's prophecies against foreign nations, applying some of the truths and principles on which Isaiah insisted to the circumstances of the age in which the author wrote (comp. Dillm. p. 222).

Cheyne (*Introd.* pp. xxvii, 155-160 ; cf. 358-363) seeks to fix the date more closely. It is stated (1) by Diodorus Siculus (xvi. 40-52) that under Artaxerxes (III.) Ochus (B.C. 359-339), there was a great revolt of Phœnicia, Cyprus, and Egypt, against Persia, which was suppressed by Ochus in 348-344 with much cruelty and bloodshed, and the capture, under tragic circumstances, of Sidon ; (2) by Eusebius, *Chron.* ii. 112 Schöne (=Sync. i. 486 ; similarly Orosius, iii. 7) that Ochus εἰς Αἴγυπτον στρατεύων μερικὴν αἰχμαλωσίαν εἷλεν Ἰουδαίων, ὧν τοὺς μὲν ἐν Ὑρκανίᾳ κατῴκισε πρὸς τῇ Κασπίᾳ θαλάσσῃ, τοὺς δὲ ἐν Βαβυλῶνι, οἳ καὶ μέχρι νῦν εἰσὶ αὐτόθι, ὡς πολλοὶ τῶν Ἑλλήνων ἱστοροῦσι ; (3) by Josephus (*Arch.* xi. 7. 1 : cf. Ewald, *Hist.* v. 205 f.), that Bagoses—no doubt the same as Bagoas, who quelled for Ochus (Diod. xvi. 47 ff.) the revolt in Egypt—the general τοῦ ἄλλου Ἀρταξέρξου, on account of a murder committed by the high priest John (Neh. 12²²) in the Temple, forced his way into the sanctuary, and laid a tax for 7 years of 50 drachms upon every lamb offered in the daily sacrifice ; (4) by Solinus, xxxv. 4 (in a brief description of the country) : Judaeae caput fuit Hierosolyma, sed excisa est. Successit Hierichus ; et hæc desivit Artaxerxis bello subacta.

Cheyne, combining * the events thus recorded, and observing (cf. W. R. Smith, *OTJC.*² p. 438 f. ; Wellhausen, *Isr. u. jüd. Gesch.*¹ p. 146, ²p. 181 f.) that a captivity implies a revolt, argues that the Jews at this time must have passed through a severe national and religious crisis, in the course of which he *conjectures* that Jerusalem was even taken by the Persians, and the Temple burnt : the memory of these events, he thinks, explains the language not only of the present prophecy, but also (see below) of 63⁷-c. 64, and of several Psalms. The original prophecy, promising the downfall of the powers hostile to Israel, and describing in glowing colours the glories to follow, consisted of c. 24, 25⁶⁻⁸ 26²⁰ᶠ· 27¹· ¹²ᶠ·, and dated from *c.* B.C. 334 : it was supplemented, shortly after Alexander's victory at Issus (B.C. 333), by 27⁷⁻¹¹, declaring that, terribly as the capital had been punished (v.¹⁰ᶠ·) by Ochus,

---

* The exact chronology is uncertain : see for particulars Judeich, *Kleinasiatische Studien*, p. 170 ff. Ochus invaded Egypt more than once : Judeich, (pp. 170 *n.*, 176 *n.*) connects the destruction of Jericho and deportation of Jewish captives with his expedition of 354-353, and places the interposition of Bagoses (Bagoas) in Jerusalem during his suppression of the revolt mentioned above, *c.* 346.

Israel nevertheless had not been smitten by him as severely as the Persians had been smitten now (v.⁷) at Issus: the lyrical passages were inserted yet later, and are not written from an ideal standpoint in the future, but depict the actual feelings of the nation ; 26¹⁻¹⁹ is the expression of Israel's gratitude for its delivery from Persian tyranny ; 25¹⁻⁶⋅ ⁰⁻¹¹ 27⁹ ⁶ testify to the satisfaction with which the pious Jews saw the fulfilment of ancient prophecies (25¹ᵇ) in Alexander's capture of Tyre (B.C. 332), and watched the humiliation of their heathen foes (comp. Skinner, p. 203 f.). This explanation of the prophecy is clever and suggestive : it must not be forgotten, however, that it rests upon a hypothetical basis ; however accurately such an event would harmonize with the terms of 27¹⁰ᶠ⋅ 64¹⁰ᶠ⋅, no destruction, or even capture of Jerusalem at the time is related by the ancients, although, had the disaster been of the magnitude which the passages quoted (if referred to it) imply, it is difficult not to think that some independent notice of it would have survived.

Of course the ascription of the prophecy to this age in no degree impairs its religious value. On the contrary, " c. 24–27 stand in the front rank of Evangelical prophecy. In their experience of religion, their characterizations of God's people, their expressions of faith, their missionary hopes, and hopes of immortality, they are very rich and edifying." *

The prophecy in some respects stands alone in the OT. It is remarkable on account of the width of area which the prophet's imagination traverses, the novelty and variety of the imagery which he employs, the music of language and rhythm which impressed Delitzsch's ear so forcibly, and the beautiful lyric hymns in which the redeemed community declares its gratitude.

IV. C. 28–33. A group of discourses, dealing (all but entirely) with the relation of Judah to Assyria,—the earlier insisting on the shortsightedness of revolting from Assyria, and trusting to Egypt for effectual help ; the later foretelling the trouble in which, through the neglect of Isaiah's warnings, Judah and Jerusalem would be involved, and their subsequent deliverance.

C. 28. V.¹⁻⁶ the prophet begins by declaring the approaching fall of the proud capital of Samaria. He then turns aside, v.⁷, to address Jerusalem. Here also there is the same self-indulgence and reluctance to listen to better counsels : the political leaders of the nation scorn the prophet's message, and trust to Egyptian help to free themselves from the yoke of Assyria ; but the day will come when they will find how terribly their calculations are at fault, v.⁷⁻²². V.²³⁻²⁹ are words of consolation addressed to

* G. A. Smith, *Isaiah*, i. 431 f.

Isaiah's own disciples and followers, teaching by a parable God's purposes in His discipline of His people.

It is evident that v.[1-6] was written shortly before 722, the year of the fall of Samaria.   The historical situation presupposed in v.[7-29], however,—*e.g.* the scheme of a revolt from Assyria, upon the strength of an alliance with Egypt,—resembles so closely that implied in c. 29-32, that it is doubtful whether an interval of 20 years should be assumed between them: in all probability v.[7-29] was written originally not long before 702, and adjusted afterwards by Isaiah (or an editor) so as to follow v.[1-7].

C. 29–32. A series of prophecies belonging (if 29[1] be [212] rightly interpreted) to the year before Sennacherib's invasion of Judah, *i.e.* to 702 B.C.

C. 29. Within a year Jerusalem will be besieged, and reduced to extremities by her foes ; but in a moment the hostile throng pressing around her will be dispersed, and vanish like a dream, v.[1-8]. To the people, however, all seems secure : the prospect opened by Isaiah appears to them incredible : they view his words with astonishment, v.[9a]. He reproaches them with their want of discernment, declaring that ere long the event will prove the truth of what he has said, and the wisdom of their counsellors will stand abashed, v.[9b-16]. He closes with a picture of the ideal future that will follow the downfall of the Assyrian (v.[20a]), and of the altered character and temper which will then manifest itself in the nation, v.[17-24].

C. 30. The negotiations with Egypt have here reached a further stage. An embassy, despatched for the purpose of concluding a treaty, is already on its way thither. Isaiah predicts the disappointment in which the project will assuredly end, and in a brief but pithy motto sums up the character of Egypt,— boastful in the offer of promises, procrastinating and inefficient in the performance of them, v.[1-7]. He paints the terrible results in which the political shortsightedness of the people's leaders will ultimately land them, v.[8-17] ; though afterwards his tone changes into one of reassurance, and he draws a picture (similar to that in in 29[17ff.]) of the ideal future that is to follow, of the glorification of external nature, corresponding to the nation's transformed character, which is to accompany it, v.[18-26], and of the triumphant overthrow of the Assyrian invader, by which it will be inaugurated, v.[27-33].

C. 31–32[8] reiterates, under fresh figures, substantially the same thoughts : the disappointment to be expected from Egypt, 31[1-3] ; Jehovah's deliverance of His city, v.[4f.]; the people's altered character afterwards, v.[6f.] ; the fall of the Assyrian, v.[8f.] : 32[1-8] the prophet delineates once more the ideal commonwealth of the future, dwelling in particular on the regeneration of society, and the recovery of a clear and firm moral judgment, which are to signalize its advent.

32[9-20] is addressed specially to the women, whose indifference and unconcern had attracted the notice of the prophet. Their careless assurance, Isaiah tells them, is misplaced : trouble [213] is impending over the land ; it is about to be ravaged by the foe ; and next year's harvest will be looked for in vain, v.[10-12]. And the state of desolation will continue, until a vivifying spirit is poured upon it from on high, altering the face of external nature, and transforming, morally and religiously, the character of the inhabitants, v.[13-20].

C. 33. The end of the Assyrian is at length approaching : the country is indeed a picture of desolation and misery (v.[7-9]) ; but the moment has arrived for Jehovah to arise and defend His city : and already the prophet sees the hosts of the Assyrians dispersed, and the Jews seizing the spoil (v.[3f.]), v.[1-12]. Ere long the present distress will be "mused on" only as a thing that is past : Zion, safe in the protection of her Divine Lord, will be at peace ; and no sickness, or sin, will disturb the felicity which thenceforth her citizens will enjoy, v.[13-24].

The date of this prophecy is a year later than c. 29–32, *i.e.* B.C. 701, apparently shortly after the incidents related in 2 Ki. 18[13b-16]. Sennacherib had taken many fenced cities of Judah, and laid a fine upon Hezekiah ; but had afterwards, upon whatever pretext, made a fresh demand for the surrender of Jerusalem ; and the messengers who had been sent to Lachish to purchase peace of him had returned without accomplishing their purpose (v.[7f.]). Isaiah, abandoning the tone of alarm which he had adopted a year previously, when the foe was still in the distance (*e.g.* 29[1-4]), sets himself here to calm and reassure his people (comp. 37[22-32]).

V. C. 34–35. The contrasted future of Edom and of Israel. The prophet declares a judgment to be approaching, which will embrace all nations : specially in Edom is "a great sacrifice" prepared, which will strip the country of its inhabitants, and leave it a desolation, the haunt of desert animals, for ever (c. 34). Far different will be the future of the ransomed Israelites. For them the desert soil will bring forth abundantly ;

human infirmities will cease to vex, human needs will be relieved ; secure from molestation the exiles will return to Zion, and obtain there never-ending joys (c. 35).

The most prominent characteristic of this prophecy is the glow of passion which prevades c. 34, recalling that which animates the prophecies against Babylon in 13[2ff.] and Jer. 50–51. The author, or the people whom he represents, must have been smarting from some severe provocation, as, indeed, is intimated unambiguously in 34[8] "For unto Jehovah belongeth a day of vengeance, and a year of recompense *for the quarrel of Zion.*" The hostile feeling which prevailed generally between Israel and Edom broke out most strongly at the time when Jerusalem was captured by the Chaldæans in 586 ; [214] then the Edomites manifested an open and malicious exultation at the fall of their rival, which, as contemporary (Ob.[10-16] ; Ez. 25[12ff.], c. 35 ; Lam. 4[21f.]) and even later (Ps. 137[7], cf. Mal. 1[3f.]) writers show, was bitterly resented by the Jews. It is extremely probable that c. 34 was written while this resentment was still keenly felt : the ground of Zion's "quarrel" may be illustrated from Ez. 35[10-13]. The literary style of the prophecy is also not Isaiah's ; and both in tone and in representation it presents affinities with prophecies (13[2ff.], c. 40 ff.) which, upon independent grounds, must be referred to the closing years of the exile (cf. Dillm. p. 301 f.).

VI. C. 36–39. An historical section, differing (except by the addition of the Song of Hezekiah, 38[9-20]) only verbally from 2 Ki. 18[13] 18[17]–20[19], and narrating certain important events in which Isaiah was concerned, viz. : (1) the double demand (36[2ff.] ; 37[7ff.]) made by Sennacherib for the surrender of Jerusalem ; Isaiah's final predictions of its deliverance, and their fulfilment, c. 36–37 ; (2) Hezekiah's sickness ; his cure, and the promise made to him by Isaiah, followed by his Song of thanksgiving, c. 38 ; (3) the embassy sent by Merodach-Baladan, king of Babylon, to Hezekiah ; Isaiah's reproof of Hezekiah for having displayed to them his treasures, and his prediction of future spoliation by the Babylonians, c. 39.

The original place of these narratives was not the Book of Isaiah, but the Book of Kings, whence they were excerpted (with slight abridgments) by the compiler of the Book of Isaiah (as Jer. 52 was excerpted from 2 Ki. 24[18ff.] by the compiler of the Book of Jeremiah), on account, no doubt, of the particulars contained in them respecting Isaiah's prophetical work, and the fulfilment of some of his most remarkable prophecies,* the Song of Hezekiah being added by him from an independent source.

* With 37[36f.] comp. not only 37[7. 22. 29], but also 10[33f.] 14[25] 17[13f.] 18[5f.] 29[6f.] 30[27ff.] 31[8f.] 33[3. 10-12] (*Isaiah*, p. 82 f.).

This is apparent—(1) from a comparison of the two *texts*. Thus (minor verbal differences being disregarded)*—

2 Ki. 18¹³ = Is. 36¹.

18¹⁴⁻¹⁶ = * * *

18¹⁷⁻19³⁷ − 36² 37³⁸.

20¹⁻⁶ = 38¹⁻⁶ (v.⁴⁻⁶ abridged).

20⁷⁻⁸ = 38²¹⁻²² (out of place).

20⁹⁻¹¹ = 38⁷⁻⁸ (abridged).

* * * = 38⁹⁻²⁰ (Hezekiah's Song).

20¹²⁻¹⁹ = c. 39 (Merodach-Baladan's embassy).

If the places in which the two texts differ be compared, it will be seen that [215] that of Kings has the *fuller* details, that of Isaiah being evidently abridged from it : notice especially Is. 38⁴· ⁷⁻⁸ by the side of 2 Ki. 20⁴· ⁹⁻¹¹ (Is. 36²⁻³ᵃ· ¹⁷⁻¹⁸ᵃ are related similarly to 2 Ki. 18¹⁷⁻¹⁸ᵃ· ³²) : Is. 38²¹⁻²² (where it is to be observed that the only legitimate version of the Hebrew ויאמר ישעיהו is " And Isaiah said " [not " *had* said "] is also clearly in its proper position in the text of Kings. Further (2) the narrative, as it stands in Isaiah, shows manifest traces of having passed through the hand of the compiler of Kings, especially in the form in which Hezekiah's prayer is cast (Is. 37¹⁵⁻²⁰=2 Ki. 19¹⁵⁻¹⁹), in 37³⁵ᵇ, where the reference to David is a motive without parallel in Isaiah, but of great frequency in Kings (p. 201, No. 22), and in c. 38–39 (*e.g.* 38¹ *In those days*, p. 202, No. 44 ; 38⁸, cf. 1 Ki. 2⁴, and p. 200, No. 7 ; 39¹ *At that time*, p. 202, No. 45). From what source the prophetical narrative, c. 36–37, was derived by the compiler of Kings, we have no means of determining. The *prophecy*, 37²²⁻³², bears, indeed, unmistakable marks of Isaiah's hand ; but the surrounding narrative (which shows no literary traits pointing to him as its author) seems to be the work of a writer belonging to the subsequent generation : for a contemporary of the events related would hardly have attributed the successes against Hamath, Arpad, and Samaria (36¹⁹), which were, in fact, achieved by Tiglath-Pileser or Sargon, to *Sennacherib*, or have expressed himself (37³⁸) without any indication—and apparently without any consciousness—that Sennacherib's assassination (B.C. 681) was separated from his invasion of Judah (B.C. 701) by an interval of 20 years. The absence in 37³⁶ of all particulars as to time and place points to the same conclusion. On 39⁶· ⁷, cf. Skinner. The Song 38⁹⁻²⁰, to judge from the title (cf. the titles of Ps. 3. 51. 52. 54, &c.), was taken from a collection of sacred psalmody, designed (v.²⁰) for liturgical use, in which it was already ascribed to Hezekiah. Hezekiah's authorship is questioned by Kuen. (§ 45. 6), Cheyne (*Introd.* pp. 224–226), and others : it is defended by Dillmann (p. 335).

Isaiah's † poetical genius is superb. His characteristics are

---

* See an exhaustive tabular comparison of the two texts in Kuenen, § 45. 3.

† For an estimate of Isaiah's position as a prophet, and an exposition of the leading principles of his teaching, the writer must refer either to what he has himself said on these subjects elsewhere (*Isaiah*, p. 107 ff.), or to what has been said on them, ably and fully, by other writers,—for example, by Dillm. pp. ix–xix (esp. xv–xix).

grandeur and beauty of conception, wealth of imagination, vividness of illustration, compressed energy and splendour of diction.
These characteristics, as is natural, frequently accompany each
other; and passages which exemplify one will be found to
exemplify another. Examples of picturesque and impressive
imagery are indeed so abundant that selection is difficult. These
may be instanced, however: the banner raised aloft upon the
mountains (5^{26} 11^{10} 18^3 30^{17},—in different connexions); the
restless roar of the sea (5^{30}); the waters rising with irresistible
might ($8^{7f.}$); the forest consumed rapidly in the circling flames,
or stripped of its foliage by an unseen hand ($10^{16f.\ 33f.}$); the
raised way (11^{16} 19^{23}); the rushing of many waters ($17^{12f.}$); the
storm driving or beating down all before it (28^2 29^6 $30^{27f.\ 30f.}$);
the monster funeral pyre (30^{33}); [216] Jehovah's hand "stretched
out," or "swung," over the earth, and bearing consternation
with it (5^{25} $14^{26f.}$ 23^{11} 31^3; 11^{15} 19^{16} 30^{32}). Especially grand
are the figures under which he conceives Jehovah as "rising
up," being "exalted," or otherwise asserting His majesty against
those who would treat it with disregard or disdain (2^{12-21} 3^{13} 5^{16}
$10^{16f.\ 26}$ 19^1 28^{21} 31^2 $33^{3.\ 10}$). The blissful future which he foresees, when the troubles of the present are past, he delineates in
colours of surpassing purity and beauty: with mingled wonder
and delight we read, and read again, those marvellous pictures
of serenity and peace, which are the creations of his inspired
imagination (2^{2-4} 4^{2-6} 9^{1-7} 11^{1-10} 16^{4b-5} $29^{18ff.}$ 30^{21-26} $32^{1-8.\ 15-18}$
$33^{5f.\ 20ff.}$). The brilliancy and power of Isaiah's genius appear
further in the sudden contrasts, and pointed antitheses and
retorts, in which he delights; as 8^{22}–9^1 17^{14} 29^5 $31^{4f.}$; $1^{3.\ 10}$
(Jerusalem apostrophized as *Sodom* and *Gomorrah*), $1^{19f.}$ $2^{20f.}$
(the idols and Jehovah), 3^{24} $5^{8f.\ 14}$ (the pomp of the busy city
sinking into Sheol), 5^{24} $10^{14f.}$ (the wonderful image of the helplessness of the entire earth before Sennacherib, followed by the
taunting comparison of the tyrant to an inanimate implement),
17^{13} 23^9 $28^{14ff.}$ 29^{16} 31^3 33^{10-12} 37^{29}.

Isaiah's literary style shows similar characteristics. It is
chaste and dignified: the language is choice, but devoid of all
artificiality or stiffness; every sentence is compact and forcible;
the rhythm is stately; the periods are finely rounded (*e.g.* $2^{12ff.}$;
$5^{26ff.}$; 11^{1-9}). Isaiah indulges occasionally—in the manner of
his people—in tone-painting ($17^{12f.}$ $28^{7f.\ 10}$ 29^6), and sometimes

enforces his meaning by an effective assonance (5^7 10^{16} $17^{1. 2}$ 22^5 $29^{2. 9}$ 30^{16} $32^{7. 19}$), but never to excess, or as a meretricious ornament. His style is never diffuse: even his longest discourses are not monotonous or prolix; he knows how to treat his subject fruitfully, and, as he moves along, to bring before his reader new and varied aspects of it: thus he seizes a number of salient points, and presents each singly in a vivid picture ($5^{8ff.}$; $7^{18ff.}$; $9^{8ff.}$; $19^{16ff.}$). Isaiah has the true classical sense of πέρας; his prophecies always form artistic wholes, adequate to the effect intended, and having no feature overdrawn. He, moreover, possesses a rare power of adapting his language to the occasion, and of bringing home to his hearers [217] what he would have them understand: thus, with a few sentences, he can shatter the fairest idols, or dissipate the fondest illusions ($1^{2. 3. 4}$; $2^{6ff.}$; $3^{14f.}$; $5^{8ff.}$; $22^{1ff.}$; $22^{15ff.}$; $28^{14ff.}$; $29^{12ff.}$; 31^3 &c.), or win his hearer's attention by the delicate irony of a parable ($5^{1ff.}$), or by the stimulus of a significant name (8^1 19^{18} 30^7), or enable them to gaze with him upon the majesty of the Divine Glory ($6^{1ff.}$), or to wander in imagination ($11^{1ff.}$, and elsewhere) over the transformed earth of the Messianic future. And he can always point the truth which he desires to impress by some apt figure or illustration: for instance, the scene of desperation in $3^{6f.}$, or $8^{21f.}$, the proverb in 9^{10}, the child in 10^{19} (cf. 11^6), the suggestive similes in $17^{5. 6}$, the uneasy couch 28^{20}, the disappointing dream 29^8, the subtle flaw, spreading insidiously through a wall, $30^{13f.}$ No prophet has Isaiah's power either of conception or of expression; none has the same command of noble thoughts, or can present them in the same noble and attractive language.

Among recent critics, the opinion has gained ground that the writings of the prophets have in many cases not been handed down to us in their original form, but that they were expanded, supplemented, and otherwise adjusted to the needs of a later age, by the scribes or editors through whose hands they passed in the centuries after the exile. Differences in the circumstances presupposed, in the beliefs and ideas, and in the style and phraseology are pointed to as establishing this position. It has, of course, been long recognized that certain prophecies, now forming part of the Book of Isaiah (13^1-14^{23}; 21^{1-10}; c. 24–27; c. 34–36; c. 40–66), are not by Isaiah's hand; but considerable portions of the prophecies hitherto commonly accepted as Isaiah's are attributed by the critics in question to literary activity of the kind indicated. "The fragmentary remains of the old prophet Isaiah," writes

Cheyne (*Introd. to Is.* p. xix), "had to be filled up when they were imperfect, and completed by the insertion of fresh passages, inspired by the 'holy spirit' of prophecy," the aim of which was chiefly either to mitigate Isaiah's threatenings by promise, or to enrich his pictures of the approaching ideal future with traits more closely expressive of the hopes and aspirations of the post-exilic age. Even Ewald ascribed c. 33 to a disciple of Isaiah: Stade (*ZATW.* 1884, p. 256 ff.; *G.* i. 586 ff. in the notes: cf. ii. 205–212) treated 2^{2-4} 4^{5-6} 5^{15-16} $7^{8-9a. 15. 17-25}$ 9^{1-7} 11^{5-12^6}, and c. 32–33, as additions made in the post-exilic period from the motives that have been described. Kuenen (in 1889) abandoned Isaiah's authorship of 11^{10}–12^6 23^{15-18}, and c. 32–33. The two most recent commentators, Duhm and Cheyne, go much further in the ascription of passages to later hands. According to Duhm, the genuine prophecies of Isaiah are limited to $1^{2-26. 29-31}$; $2^{2-4. 6-19. 21}$; $3^{1-9. 12. 13}$–4^1; $5^{1-14. 17-29}$; 6^{1-13} (to *remaineth*); $7^{2-8a. 9-14. 16. 18-20}$; $8^{1-18. 21-22}$; 9^{2-7}; $9^{8-14. 17}$–10^4; $10^{5-9. 13-14}$; 11^{1-8}; $14^{24-25a. 26-27}$; $17^{1-6. 9-14}$; 18^{1-6}; $20^{1. 3-6}$; 21^{16-17}; $22^{1-9a. 11b-14. 15a. 16-18}$; $28^{1-4. 7-29}$; $29^{1-4a. 5b-7. 9-10. 13-15}$; $30^{1-7a. 8-17. 27-33}$; 31^{1-4} (to *of them*) ^{5} (from *so*) $^{8a. 9b}$; $32^{1-5. 9-18. 20}$. Cheyne limits the genuine prophecies to $1^{5-26. 29-31}$; $2^{6-10. 18-21. 11-17}$ $3^{1. 4-5. 8-9. 12-15. 16-17. 24}$ 4^1; $5^{1-14. 17-22. 23.*}$ $^{24. 25b}$; 6^{1-13} (to *remaineth*); $7^{2-8a. 9-14. 16. 18-20}$ $8^{1-18. 20b-22}$; $9^{8-13. 16}$–10^4 5^{26-29} (the conclusion to 9^{8}–10^4); $10^{5-9. 13-14. 27-32}$; $14^{24-25a. 26-27}$; $^{29-32}$; 16^{14} (from *within*); $17^{1-6. 9-14}$; 18^{1-6}; $20^{1. 3-6}$; 21^{16-17}; $22^{1-9a. 11b-14. 15a. 16-18}$; $23^{1-2. 3? 4. 6-12. 14}$; $28^{1-4. 7-19. 21-22}$; $29^{1-4a. 6. 9-10. 13-15}$; $30^{1-7a. 8-17}$; 31^{1-5a} (to *birds*): † all that remains consists either of editorial additions (as $1^{2-4. 27-28}$ $3^{10-11. 18-23}$ &c.), marginal glosses (as 2^{22} 5^{15-16} 7^{8b} &c.), or post-exilic insertions or appendices (4^{2-6} 6^{13b} 10^{16-23} 11^{10-16} 12^{1-6} 18^7, c. 19. 23^{15-18} $28^{5-6. 23-29}$ $29^{5. 16-24}$ $30^{18-26. 27-33}$ 31^{5b-9}, c. 32–33. 37^{22-32}; and *perhaps* 9^{1-7} [Heb. 8^{23}–9^6] 11^{1-8}). It is impossible to condense into a note the grounds upon which these conclusions rest: they will be found stated with marked ability and acuteness, and with exhaustive references to all previous critics (including Duhm and Hackmann), in Cheyne's *Introduction to the Book of Isaiah*.

VII. C. 40–66. These chapters form a continuous prophecy, dealing throughout with a common theme, viz. *Israel's restoration from exile in Babylon.* There is no thought in this prophecy of the troubles or dangers to which Judah was exposed at the hands of Sargon or Sennacherib; the empire of *Assyria* has been succeeded (B.C. 607) by that of *Babylon*; Jerusalem and the Temple have been for long in ruins (58^{12}; 61^4 "the old waste places"; 64^{10}); Israel is in exile (47^6 48^{20} &c.). And the power of the Chaldæans is to all appearance as secure as ever: the Jewish exiles are in despair or indifferent; they think that God has forgotten them, and have ceased to expect, or desire, their release (40^{27} $49^{14. 24}$). This is the situation to which the present prophecy is addressed: its aim is to arouse the indifferent, to

---

* Probably introduced from another context.

† $3^{2-8. 6-7}$ 7^{21-25} 10^{16-19} $29^{7. 11-12}$ may have an Isaianic basis.

reassure the wavering, to expostulate with the doubting, to announce with triumphant confidence the certainty of the approaching restoration.

The Jews went into exile in two detachments : the flower of the nation with Jehoiachin in B.C. 597 ; the rest, after the revolt of Zedekiah, in 586, when the city was taken and the Temple burnt. Cyrus, who was to prove the instrument of their restoration, first appears shortly before 550 ; uniting and organizing the different tribes of Persian origin, he overthrows the Median empire of Astyages in 549 ; and, at the head of the combined [218] armies of both nations, advances to further conquests. Having captured Sardis, the capital of Crœsus, king of Lydia, and left his general Harpagus to complete the subjugation of Asia Minor, he next (Herod. i. 177) reduces one after another the tribes of Upper (or Inner) Asia, and ultimately prepares to attack Babylon. His own inscription * narrates his success (B.C. 538) : in the following year the exiled Jews receive permission from him to return to Palestine (Ezr. 1^{1-3}).

The prophecy opens at some date between 549 and 538 : for the conquest of Babylon is still future ; but the union of the Medes with the Persians appears to have already taken place.† It introduces us therefore to the time while Cyrus is pursuing his career of conquest in N.W. and Central Asia. The prophet's eye marks him in the distance as the coming deliverer of his nation : he stimulates the flagging courage of the people by pointing to his successes (41^{2-4}), and declares that he is God's appointed agent, both for the overthrow of the Babylonian empire and for the restoration of the chosen people to Palestine (41^{25} 44^{28} $45^{1-6.\ 13}$ 46^{11}).

The following is an outline of the argument of this great prophecy. It may be divided into three parts : (1) c. 40–48 ; (2) c. 49–59 ; (3) c. 60–66.

(1.) Here the prophet's aim is to demonstrate to the people *the certainty of the coming release,* and to convince them that no obstacles, real or imagined, will avail to hinder their deliverance. For this purpose he uses different arguments, designed to establish the *power* of Jehovah, and His ability to fulfil His promises.

---

* *Isaiah,* p. 136 f. ; Sayce, *Monuments,* p. 504 ff. ; more exactly in Delitzsch and Haupt's *Beiträge zur Assyriologie,* ii. part 1 (1891), p. 209 ff.

† 41^{25} " from the *east,*" *i.e.* Persia ; " from the *north,*" *i.e.* Media.

C. 40, after the exordium v.[1f.], stating the general theme of the entire prophecy, the prophet bids a way be prepared through the wilderness for the triumphal progress of Israel's king, who is figured as a Conqueror about to return to Zion, leading before Him His prize of war, the recovered nation itself. V.[12-26] the prophet demonstrates at length, chiefly from the works of nature, the omnipotence of Israel's Divine Deliverer : no finite spirit can compare with Him (v.[12-17]); no human conception can express Him (v.[18-26]). 41[1-7] he dramatically imagines a judgment scene. The nations are invited to come forward and plead their case with Jehovah. The question is, [219] *Who has stirred up the great conqueror, Cyrus ? who has led him upon his career of victory ?* (v.[2f.]). Only one answer is possible : not the heathen gods, but Jehovah, the Creator of history. A digression follows, v.[8-20], designed for the encouragement of Israel, which has been chosen by Jehovah as His " servant," and cannot therefore be discarded by Him. The judgment scene, interrupted after v.[4], is now resumed ; and the second proof of Jehovah's Godhead is adduced : *He alone knows the future* (v.[21-29]). 42[1-6] Jehovah's " servant " appears under a new aspect, and with new functions, —no longer the historic nation of Israel (as 41[8f.]), but an *ideal* figure, reproducing in their perfection the best and truest characteristics of the actual nation, and invested by the prophet with a far-reaching prophetic mission. Here his mission is described as twofold : (1) *to teach the world true religion*; (2) *to be the medium of Israel's restoration* (to be a " covenant of the people "), v.[6]. The prospect of the speedy realization of his present announcement (v.[9]) evokes from the prophet a short lyric ode of thanksgiving, v.[10-12] ; after which he depicts, in splendid anthropomorphic imagery, Jehovah's approaching manifestation for the deliverance of His people, and the discomfiture of the Babylonian idolaters, v.[13-17]. But some of those who listen to him are blind and deaf : Jehovah's " servant " (Israel, as 41[8]) has fallen short of the ideal which the titles bestowed upon it implied : it has not responded to Jehovah's gracious purpose ; hence the troubles which have fallen upon it, and the bondage in which it is at present enthralled, v.[18-25]. But now, Israel need fear no longer ; Egypt, Ethiopia, and Seba shall take its place as Cyrus' vassals ; from all quarters the exiles shall return, 43[1-7].

Another judgment scene, between Israel and the heathen, is here imagined. The question is the same as before : which of the two can point to predictions in proof of the divinity of their God ? But Israel is Jehovah's witness, 43$^{8-13}$; and Israel shall now speedily be redeemed, though of God's free pardon, and not for any merit on its part : a glorious and blessed future awaits it, a future in which the nations will press forward to dedicate themselves to Jehovah, and to claim the honour of membership in His people, 43^{14}–44^5. 44^6–45^{25} the prophet again brings forward the evidence of Jehovah's Godhead ; and the promises of deliverance given already are made [220] more definite. In particular, as the prophet shows by a satirical description of the manner in which they were manufactured in his day, 44$^{9-20}$, Jehovah is immeasurably superior to all idols, who are impotent to thwart His purpose, or impede His people's freedom : by His free grace He has blotted out Israel's sin, and nominated Cyrus as the conqueror of Babylon and the agent of His people's restoration, 44^{21}–45^{17} : His promises have been given openly, and will assuredly be fulfilled, 45^{18ff}. C. 46–47 the prophet dwells upon the near prospect of the fall of the oppressing city, —in c. 46 drawing an ironical picture of its humiliated idols ; in c. 47 contemplating the city itself, which he personifies as a lady of queenly rank, obliged to relinquish the position which she has long proudly held, and powerless to avert the fate which threatens her. C. 48 consists mainly of a repetition and reinforcement of the arguments insisted on in the previous parts of the prophecy : it ends with a jubilant cry addressed to the exiles, bidding them depart from Babylon, and proclaim to the utmost quarters of the earth the wondrous story of their return.

(2.) In this division of the prophecy a further stage is reached in the development of the author's theme. The controversial tone, the repeated comparisons between Jehovah and the idols, with the arguments founded upon them, disappear : the prophet feels that, as regards these points, he has made his position sufficiently secure. For the same reason, allusions to Cyrus and his conquest of Babylon cease also : that, likewise, is now taken for granted. He exhorts the people to fit themselves morally to take part in the return, and to share the blessings which will accompany it, or which it will inaugurate ; he contemplates more exclusively the future in store for Israel, if it will respond to Jehovah's call; and he adds fresh features to the portrait of Jehovah's ideal Servant. C. 49 introduces Jehovah's ideal Servant, describing dramatically his person and experiences, and announcing more distinctly than before (42^6) the twofold nature of his mission, v.$^{1-13}$: v.$^{14-26}$ the prophet meets objections arising out of Israel's want of faith. 50^{4-9} the ideal Servant is again introduced, recounting in a soliloquy the manner in which he discharges his prophetic mission, and the trials which attend it; v.$^{10f.}$ is the prophet's own exhortation to his fellow-countrymen. 51^1-52^{12} the [221] prospect of the approaching return is that which chiefly occupies the prophet's thoughts; and his confidence finds exultant expression in the thrice-repeated jubilant apostrophe, $51^{9. 17}$ 52^1: $52^{7f.}$ he sees in imagination the messengers bearing tidings of Israel's deliverance arrive upon the mountains of Judah, and hears the watchmen, whom he pictures as looking out eagerly from the city walls, announcing with gladness the joyous news: $52^{11f.}$ he repeats (cf. 48^{20}) the cry, "Depart."

$52^{13}-53^{12}$ deals again with the figure of Jehovah's ideal Servant, and develops under a new aspect his character and work. It represents, namely, his great and surprising exaltation, after an antecedent period of humiliation, suffering, and death, in which, it is repeatedly stated, he suffered, not (as those who saw him mistakenly imagined) for his own sins, but for the sins *of others.* 54^1-56^8 fresh promises of restoration are addressed to the exiles: c. 54 Zion, now distressed and afflicted, will ere long be at peace, with her children, the "disciples of Jehovah," about her; c. 55 let all prepare themselves to receive the prophet's invitation and share the approaching redemption; $56^{1f.}$ the moral conditions which they must satisfy are once again emphasized; 56^{3-8} all merely technical disqualifications will henceforth be abolished. 56^9–c. 57 the strain alters: the prophet turns aside from the glorious future, which is elsewhere uppermost in his thoughts, to attack the faults and shortcomings which Israel had shown itself only too reluctant to abandon, and which would necessitate in the end a divine interposition for their removal. 56^9-57^2 he denounces the unworthy rulers of the nation, who, like careless shepherds (cf. Jer. 2^8 $23^{1f.}$, Ez. 34), had neglected their people, and left them to perish. 57^{3-11a} he reproaches Israel with its idolatry, drawing a picture of strange

heathen rites, such as Jeremiah and Ezekiel show to have prevailed in Judah till the very eve of the exile, and the tendency
to which no doubt was still far from extirpated among the
people at large (cf. $65^{3-5, 11}$): 57^{11b-21} Israel's sole hope is penitence and trust in God—"he that taketh refuge in me shall
inherit the land, and take my holy mountain into possession."
C. 58 the prophet repeats that the moral impediments which
disqualify Israel for the enjoyment of the promised blessings
must be removed : especially he finds fault with the hollow unreality with which fasts [222] were observed, and draws a contrasted picture of the true fast in which Jehovah delights, viz.
deeds of philanthropy, unselfishness, liberality, and mercy : if
Israel will devote itself to these works, and at the same time
show a cheerful reverence towards its God (v.^{13}), then Jehovah
will shower down His blessings upon it, and it will triumphantly
resume possession of its ancient home.   C. 59 the prophet
represents the people as confessing the chief sins of which they
have been guilty : unable to rescue themselves, Jehovah will now
interpose on their behalf, and manifest Himself as a redeemer in
Zion, not indeed to all without distinction, but to those who
satisfy the needful moral conditions, and have "turned from
rebellion in Jacob."

(3.) Here the prophet depicts, in still brighter hues, the
felicity of the ideal Zion of the future.   As before, a progress
may be observed in the development of his thought.   In c.
40–48, when Israel's release was foremost in his thoughts, the
judgment was conceived as falling solely upon Israel's *foes* : in
c. 57–59, however, he evinces a more vivid consciousness of
Israel's sinfulness, and of the obstacle which that presents to the
restoration of the *entire* nation ; and in the chapters which now
follow, he announces a judgment to be enacted *in Israel* itself,
distinguishing Jehovah's faithful "servants" ($65^{8, 9, 13, 14, 15}$) from
those disloyal to him, and excluding the latter from the promised
blessings.   C. 60 the longed for "light" (59^9) bursts upon the
prophet's eye : the dark cloud of night that shrouds the rest of
the world has been lifted over the Holy City ; and he gathers
the features belonging to Zion restored into a single dazzling
vision. 61^{1-3} Jehovah's ideal Servant is once more introduced,
describing the gracious mission entrusted to him, to "bring
good tidings to the afflicted," and to "proclaim liberty to the

captives" (cf. 42³˙⁷ 49⁹), which is followed, as before (49⁹⁻¹²), by the promise of Jerusalem's restoration (61⁴): in the rest of c. 61–62 the prophet dwells upon the new and signal marks of Jehovah's favour, resting visibly upon the restored nation, and its own grateful appreciation (61¹⁰ᶠ˙) of the blessedness thus bestowed upon it. 63¹⁻⁶ is a dramatic dialogue between Jehovah, depicted as a victor returning from Edom, and the prophet, in which, under the form of an ideal humiliation of nations, marshalled upon the territory of Israel's inveterate foe, is expressed the thought of Israel's triumph over its enemies. [223] The dialogue ended, the prophet's tone changes; and 63⁷–64¹², in the assurance that the redemption guaranteed by Jehovah's triumph will be wrought out, he supplies faithful Israel with a hymn of thanksgiving, supplication, and confession, expressive of the frame of mind worthy to receive it, and couched in a strain of surpassing pathos and beauty. C. 65 appears to be intended as an answer to the supplication of c. 64,—an answer, however, in which the distinction, alluded to above, is drawn between the worthy and unworthy Israelites. God has ever, he says, been accessible to His people, and ready to renew intercourse with them; it was they who would not respond, but provoked Him with their idolatries. Israel, however, is not to be rejected on account of the presence within it of unworthy members; a seed of "chosen ones" will be brought out of Jacob, who shall again inherit the mountains of Palestine. A new order of things (v.¹⁷; cf. 51¹⁶) is about to be created, in which Jerusalem and her people will be to Jehovah a source of unalloyed delight, and in which care and disappointment will cease to vex. 66¹⁻⁵ the prophet, in view probably of the anticipated restoration of the Temple, reminds the Jews that no earthly habitation is really adequate to Jehovah's majesty, and that His regard is to be won, neither by the magnificence of a material temple, nor by unspiritual service, but by humility and the devotion of the heart. He concludes, v.⁶⁻²⁴, by two contrasted pictures of the glorious blessedness in store for Jerusalem, and the terrible judgment impending over her foes.

Authorship of c. 40–66. Three independent lines of argument converge to show that this prophecy is not the work of Isaiah, but, like 13²–14²³, has for its author a prophet writing towards the close of the Babylonian captivity. (1) The *internal evidence* supplied by the prophecy itself points to this period as that at which it was written. It alludes repeatedly to Jerusalem as ruined and deserted (*e.g.* 44^{26b} 58^{12} 61^4 63^{18} $64^{10f.}$); to the sufferings which the Jews have experienced, or are experiencing, at the hands of the Chaldæans ($42^{22.\ 25}$ 43^{28} [RV. *marg.*], 47^6 52^5); to the prospect of return, which, as the prophet speaks, is imminent (40^2 46^{13} 48^{20} &c.). Those whom the prophet addresses, and, moreover, addresses *in person*—arguing with them, appealing to them, striving to win their assent by his warm and impassioned rhetoric ($40^{21.\ 26.\ 28}$ 43^{10} [**224**] 48^8 $50^{10f.}$ $51^{6.\ 12f.}$ $58^{8ff.}$ &c.)—are not the men of Jerusalem, contemporaries of Ahaz and Hezekiah, or even of Manasseh; they are the exiles in Babylonia. Judged by the *analogy of prophecy*, this constitutes the strongest possible presumption that the author actually *lived* in the period which he thus describes, and is not merely (as has been supposed) Isaiah immersed in spirit in the future, and holding converse, as it were, with the generations yet unborn. Such an immersion in the future would be not only without parallel in the OT., it would be contrary to the nature of prophecy. The prophet speaks always, in the first instance, to his own contemporaries: the message which he brings is intimately related with the circumstances of his time: his promises and predictions, however far they reach into the future, nevertheless rest upon the basis of the history of his own age, and correspond to the needs which are then felt. The prophet never abandons his own historical position, but speaks from it. So Jeremiah and Ezekiel, for instance, predict first the exile, then the restoration; both are contemplated by them as still future; both are viewed from the period in which they themselves live. In the present prophecy there is no *prediction* of exile: the exile is not announced as something still future; it is *presupposed*, and only the *release* from it is *predicted*. By analogy, therefore, the author will have lived in the situation which he thus presupposes, and to which he continually alludes.

It is true, passages occur in which the prophets throw themselves forward to an ideal standpoint, and describe from it events future to themselves, as though they were past (*e.g.* 5^{13-15} 9^{1-6} $23^{1.\ 14}$); but these are not really parallel: the transference to the future, which they imply, is but *transient*; in the immediate context, the prophet uses future tenses, and speaks from his own standpoint (alluding, for instance, plainly to the events or circumstances of his own age); the expressions, moreover, are general, and the language is figurative. The writings of the prophets supply no analogy for such a *sustained* transference to the future as would be implied if these chapers were by Isaiah, or for the *detailed* and *definite* description of the circumstances of a distant age.

(2) The argument derived from the historic function of prophecy is confirmed by the *literary style* of c. 40–66, which is very different from that of Isaiah. Isaiah shows strongly marked individualities of style: he is fond of particular images and phrases, many of which are used by no other writer of the OT. Now, in the chapters which contain evident allusions to the [225] age of Isaiah himself, these expressions occur repeatedly; in the chapters which are without such allusions, and which thus authorize *primâ facie* the inference that they belong to a different age, *they are absent, and new images and phrases appear instead.* This coincidence cannot be accidental. The subject of c. 40–66 is not *so* different from that of Isaiah's prophecies (*e.g.*) against the Assyrians, as to necessitate a new phraseology and rhetorical form: the differences can only be reasonably explained by the supposition of a change of author. Isaiah in his earliest, as in his latest prophecies (c. 29–33; 37$^{22-32}$, written when he must have been at least sixty years of age), uses the same style, and shows a preference for the same figures; and the change of subject in c. 40–66 is not sufficiently great to account for the marked differences which here show themselves, and which indeed often relate to points, such as the form and construction of sentences, which stand in no appreciable relation to the subject treated.

The following are examples of words, or forms of expression, used repeatedly in c. 40–66 (sometimes also in c. 13 f. and c. 34 f.), but never in the prophecies which contain independent evidence of belonging to Isaiah's own age :—

1. *To choose*, of God's choice of Israel : 41$^{8.\ 9}$ 43^{10} 44$^{1.\ 2}$ (cf. 42^{1} 49^{7}, of the *ideal*, individualized nation); *my chosen*, 43^{20} 45^{4} 65$^{9.\ 15.\ 22}$. So 14^{1}.

2. *Praise* (subst. and verb : תהלה, הלל) : 42$^{8.\ 10.\ 12}$ 43^{21} 48^{9} 60$^{6.\ 18}$ 61$^{3.\ 11}$ 62$^{7.\ 9}$ 63^{7} 64^{10}.

3. *To shoot* or *spring forth* (צמח) : 44^{4} 55^{10} 61^{11a} ; esp. metaphorically— (*a*) of a moral state, 45^{8} 58^{8} 61^{11b} ; (*b*) of an event manifesting itself in history (not so elsewhere), 42^{9} 43^{19}.

4. *To break out* (פצח) *into singing* : 44^{23} 49^{13} 52^{9} 54^{1} 55^{12}. Also 14^{7}. Only Ps. 98^{4} besides.

5. *Pleasure* (חפץ) : (*a*) of Jehovah's purpose, 44^{28} 46^{10} 48^{14} 53^{10} ; (*b*) of human purpose or business, 58$^{3.\ 13}$. More generally, 54^{12} 62^{4}.

6. *Good will, acceptance* (God's) (רָצוֹן : 49⁸ 56⁷ 58⁵ 60⁷ ¹⁰ 61⁹.

7. *Thy sons*—the pronoun being feminine and referring to Zion : 49¹⁷·
²². ²⁵ 51²⁰ 54¹³ 60⁴· ⁹ 62⁵ ; cf. 66⁸. Isaiah, when he uses the same
word, always says *sons* absolutely, the implicit reference being to
God (Dt. 14¹) : so 1²· ⁴ 30¹· ⁹.

8. *To rejoice* (שׂושׂ) : 61¹⁰ 62⁵ 64⁴ 65¹⁸· ¹⁹ 66¹⁰· ¹⁴. Also 35¹.

9. The phrases, *I am Jehovah, and there is none else* (or *besides*) : 45⁵·
⁶· ¹⁸· ²¹· ²² ; *I am the first, and I am the last* : 44⁶ 48¹² ; cf. 41⁴ ; *I
am thy God, thy Saviour*, &c. : 41¹⁰· ¹³ 43³ 48¹⁷ᵇ [226] 61⁸ ; *I am
He, i.e.* He who *is*, opp. to the unreal gods of the heathen (from
Dt. 32³⁹) : 41⁴ᵇ 43¹⁰ᵇ· ¹³ 46⁴ 48¹². No such phrases are ever used by
Isaiah.

10. The combination of the Divine name with a participial epithet (in the
English version often represented by a relative clause) : *e.g. Creator*
(or *stretcher out*) *of the heavens* or *the earth* : 40²⁸ 42⁵ 44²⁴ᵇ 45⁷· ¹⁸
51¹³ ; *creator* or *former of Israel* : 43¹· ¹⁵ 44²· ²⁴ 45¹¹ 49⁵ ; *thy
Saviour* : 49²⁶ 60¹⁶ ; *thy* (*your, Israel's*) *redeemer* : 43¹⁴ 44²⁴ᵃ 48¹⁷ᵃ
49⁷ 54⁸ ; comp. 40²²ᶠ· 43¹⁶ᶠ· 44²⁵⁻²⁸ 46¹⁰ᶠ· 51¹⁵ 56⁸ 63¹²ᶠ·. Isaiah
never casts his thought into this form.

The following words, though found once or twice each in Isaiah (cf. p.
132, *n.*), are destitute there of any special force or significance, whereas in
c. 40–66 they occur frequently, sometimes with a particular *nuance*, or shade
of meaning, which is foreign to the usage of Isaiah :—

1. *Isles* or *coasts* (אִיִּים), used *representatively* of distant regions of the
earth : 40¹⁵ 41¹· ⁵ 42⁴· ¹⁰· ¹²· ¹⁵ 49¹ 51⁵ 59¹⁸ 60⁹ 66¹⁹. In Isaiah, 11¹¹
(also 24¹⁵), where it is used in its primary sense (Gen. 10⁵) of the
isles and coasts of the Mediterranean Sea. The application in
c. 40–66 is a marked extension of the usage of Isaiah.

2. *Nought* (אֶפֶס : not the ordinary word) : 40¹⁷ 41¹²· ²⁹ 45⁶· ¹⁴ 46⁹ 47⁸· ¹⁰
52⁴ 54¹⁵. Also 34¹². In Isaiah, 5⁸ only (where, however, the
original signification of the word is still perceptible).

3. *To create* : 40²⁶· ²⁸ 41²⁰ 42⁵ 43¹· ⁷· ¹⁵ 45⁷· ⁸· ¹²· ¹⁸ 54¹⁶ 57¹⁹ 65¹⁷· ¹⁸·
In Isaiah, only 4⁵ in a limited application. The prominence
given to the idea of creation in c. 40–66 is very noticeable (cf.
p. 242).

4. *Offspring* (צֶאֱצָאִים) : 42⁵ 44³ 48¹⁹ 61⁹ 65²³. In Isaiah, 22²⁴. Also 34¹.
Rather a peculiar word. The usage in c. 40–66 is wider and more
general than that in 22²⁴, and agrees with the usage of the Book of
Job, 5²⁵ 21⁸ 27¹⁴ 31⁸. The word does not occur elsewhere.

5. *Justice* emphasized as a principle guiding and determining God's
action : 41²· ¹⁰ᵇ 42²¹ 45¹³· ¹⁹ 51⁵ ; cf. 58²ᵇ. The peculiar stress laid
upon this principle is almost confined to these chapters ; comp.
however, Hos. 2¹⁹ [Heb. ²¹].

6. *The arm of Jehovah* : 51⁵ᵇ· ⁹ 52¹⁰ 53¹ 59¹⁶ᵇ (cf. 40¹⁰), 62⁸ 63⁵· ¹². Hence
Ps. 98¹ (see 59¹⁶ 52¹⁰). In Isaiah, 30³⁰. But observe the greater
independence of the figure as applied in c. 40–66.

7. *To deck* (פָּאַר), or (in the reflexive conjugation) *to deck oneself, i.e. to
glory*, especially of Jehovah, either glorifying Israel, or glorying

Himself in Israel: 44²³ 49³ 55⁵ 60⁷· ⁹· ¹³· ²¹ 61³.   In Isaiah, only 10¹⁵ of the saw *vaunting itself* against its user.

8. The future gracious relation of Jehovah to Israel represented as a *covenant*: 42⁶ (=49⁸) 54¹⁰ 55³ 59²¹ 61⁸.   In 28¹⁵· ¹⁸ 33⁸ the word is used merely in the sense of a treaty or compact.   Isaiah, often as he speaks of a future state of grace, to be [**227**] enjoyed by his people, never represents it under the form of a *covenant*.

9. *Yea* (אף), used with strong rhetorical force 25 times from 40²⁴ to 48¹⁵. In Isaiah, only 33².   Elsewhere in the book, 26⁸· ⁹· ¹¹ 35².

There are in addition several words and idioms occurring in c. 40–66 which point to a later period of the language than Isaiah's age, for which it must suffice to refer to Cheyne, *Isaiah*, ii. 257 f. (more fully *Introd.* pp. 255–270), or Dillm. p. 353.   A remarkable instance is afforded by 65²⁵, which is a condensed quotation from 11⁶⁻⁹, and where יחדו, the common Hebrew word for *together*, is replaced by כאחד, an expression modelled upon the Aram. כחדא, and occurring besides only in the latest books of the OT. 2 Ch. 5¹³ Ezr. 2⁶⁴ (=Neh. 7⁶⁶) 3⁹ 6²⁰, Eccl. 11⁶†).

As features of style may be noticed—

1. The *duplication of words*, significant of the impassioned ardour of the preacher: 40¹ 43¹¹· ²⁵ 48¹¹· ¹⁵ 51⁹· ¹²· ¹⁷ 52¹· ¹¹ 57⁶· ¹⁴· ¹⁹ 62¹⁰ *bis* 65¹. Very characteristic of this prophecy ; in Isaiah the only examples— and those but partly parallel—are 8⁹ᵇ [21⁹] 29¹.

2. A habit of repeating the same word or words in adjacent clauses or verses ; thus 40¹²ᶠ· (regulated) ; v.¹³ *end* and v.¹⁴ *end* (taught him) ; v.¹⁴ (instructed him) ; 40⁸¹ and 41¹ (renew strength) ; v.⁶ᶠ· (courage, encourage) ; v.⁸ᶠ· (have chosen thee) ; v.¹³ᶠ· (I have holpen thee) ; 45⁴ᶠ· (hast not known me) ; v.⁵ᶠ· (and none else) ; 50⁷ and ⁹ (will help me) ; 53³ (despised) ; v.³ᶠ· (esteemed him) ; v.⁷ (opened not his mouth) ; 58¹³ (thine own pleasure) ; 59⁸ (peace) ; 61⁷ (double). The attentive reader of the Hebrew will notice further instances. Very rare indeed in Isaiah ; cf. 1⁷ (desolate) ; 17⁵ (ears) ; 32¹⁷ᵗ· (peace).

3. Differences in the structure of sentences, *e.g.* the relative particle omitted with much greater frequency than by Isaiah.*

There are also literary features of a more general character, which differentiate the author of c. 40–66 from Isaiah.   Isaiah's style is terse and compact : the movement of his periods is stately and measured : his rhetoric is grave and restrained.   In these chapters a subject is often developed at considerable length :

* For examples of expressions used, on the other hand, repeatedly by Isaiah, but never found in c. 40–66, see *Isaiah*, pp. 194–196. Especially noticeable is the all but entire absence from c. 40–66 of the two expressions, *And it shall come to pass*, and *In that day*, by which Isaiah loves to introduce scenes or traits in his descriptions of the future (*e.g.* 4³ 7¹⁸· ²¹· ²³ 8²¹ 10²⁰· ²⁷ 11¹⁰· ¹¹ &c.; 3¹⁸ 4¹· ² 7¹⁸· ²⁰· ²¹· ²³ 19¹⁶⁻²⁴ &c.), but which occur here only 65²⁴ 66²³ ; 52⁶ (somewhat peculiarly).

the style is much more flowing : the rhetoric is warm and impassioned ; and the prophet often bursts out into a lyric strain ($42^{10f.}$ 44^{23} 45^8 49^{13}), in a manner to which even Is. 12 affords no parallel. Force is the predominant feature of Isaiah's oratory : persuasion sits upon the lips of the prophet who here [228] speaks ; the music of his eloquence, as it rolls magnificently along, thrills and captivates the soul of its hearer. So, again, if the most conspicuous characteristic of Isaiah's imagination be *grandeur*, that of the prophet to whom we are here listening is *pathos*. The storms, the inundations, the sudden catastrophes, which Isaiah loves to depict, are scarcely to be found in this prophecy. The author's imagery is drawn by preference from a different region of nature altogether, viz. from the animate world, in particular from the sphere of *human emotion*. It is largely the figures drawn from the latter which impart to his prophecy its peculiar pathos and warmth (see $49^{15.\ 18}$ 61^{10b} 62^5 66^{13}).* His fondness for such figures is, however, most evident in the numerous examples of *personification* which his prophecy contains. Since Amos (5^2) it became habitual with the prophets to personify a city or community as a *maiden*, especially where it was desired to represent it as vividly conscious of some keen emotion.† This figure is applied in these chapters with remarkable independence and originality. Zion is represented as a bride, a mother, a widow, *i.e.* under just those relations of life in which the deepest feelings of humanity come into play ; and the personification is continued sometimes through a long series of verses.‡ Nor is this all. The prophet personifies *nature* : he bids heaven and earth shout at the restoration of God's people (44^{23} 49^{13} ; cf. 52^9 55^{12}) ; he hears in imagination the voices of invisible beings sounding across the desert ($40^{3.\ 6}$ 57^{14}) ; he peoples Jerusalem with ideal watchmen (52^8) and guardians (62^6).§ Akin to these personifications is the *dramatic* character

* The prophecy abounds also with other passages of exquisite softness and beauty, as c. 51. c. 54–55. 61^{10} 63^7–64^{12} &c.

† Is. 1^8 23^4 (Sidon lamenting her bereavement), $29^{1\text{-}6}$ (*fem.* pronouns in the Hebrew), 37^{22} (Zion disdainfully mocking the retreating invader), Zeph. 3^{14} and Zech. 9^9 (Zion exultant), Jer. 4^{31} 6^{26} $46^{11.\ 19.\ 24}$ 50^{42} 51^{33}, Mic. $4^{8.\ 10.\ 13}$ *al.*

‡ See $49^{18\text{-}23}$ $51^{17\text{-}23}$ (Zion prostrate and dazed by trouble, but now bidden to lift herself up), $52^{1f.}$ $54^{1\text{-}6}$ $60^{1\text{-}5}$ 62^5 ; $47^{1\text{-}15}$ (Babylon).

§ Add the personification of Jehovah's arm, $51^{9f.}$. Isaiah, unlike the author of c. 40–66, evinces no *exceptional* preference for personification.

of the representation, which also prevails to a remarkable extent in the prophecy: see 40[3ff.] 49[1ff.] 50[4-9] 53[1ff.] 58[3a] 61[10f.] 63[1-6].

(3) The *theological ideas* of c. 40–66 (in so far as they are [229] not of that fundamental kind common to the prophets generally) differ remarkably from those which appear, from c. 1–39, to be distinctive of Isaiah. Thus, on the nature of God generally, the ideas expressed are much larger and fuller. Isaiah, for instance, depicts the majesty of Jehovah: in c. 40–66 the prophet emphasizes His *infinitude*; He is the Creator, the Sustainer of the universe, the Life-Giver, the Author of history (41[4]), the First and the Last, the Incomparable One. This is a real difference. And yet it cannot be argued that opportunities for such assertions of Jehovah's power and Godhead would not have presented themselves naturally to Isaiah whilst he was engaged in defying the armies of Assyria. But, in truth, c. 40–66 show an advance upon Isaiah, not only in the substance of their theology, but also in the form in which it is presented; truths which are merely *affirmed* in Isaiah being here made the subject of reflexion and argument. Again, the doctrine of the preservation from judgment of a faithful remnant is characteristic of Isaiah. It appears both in his first prophecy and in his last (6[13]; 37[31f.]): in c. 40–66, if it is present once or twice by implication (59[20] 65[8f.]), it is no *distinctive* element in the author's teaching; it is not expressed in Isaiah's terminology,* and it is not more prominent than in the writings of many other prophets. The relation of Israel to Jehovah—its choice by Him, its destiny, the purpose of its call—is developed in different terms and under different conceptions † from those used by Isaiah: the figure of the Messianic *king* (Is. 9[6-7] 11[1ff.]) is absent; the prophet associates his view of the future with a figure of very different character, Jehovah's righteous Servant,‡ which is closely connected with his own distinctive view of Israel's destiny.§ The Divine purpose in relation to the nations,

---

* שאר (10[20-22] 11[11. 16] 16[4] 17[3] 21[17] 28[5]; cf. 7[3]).

† Israel is Jehovah's "servant," entrusted by Him with the discharge of a sacred mission, and hence cannot now be disowned by its Divine Lord (41[8-10] 42[19f.] 43[10] 44[1f. 21] 45[4] 48[20]).

‡ 42[1ff.] 49[1ff.] 50[4-9] 52[13]–53[12] 61[1-3].

§ To say that the figure of the ideal Servant of c. 40–66 is an *advance* upon that of the Messianic king of Isaiah is not correct: it starts from a different origin altogether; it is *parallel* to it, not a continuation of it. Both

especially in connexion with the prophetic mission of [230] Israel, is more comprehensively developed.* The prophet, in a word, in whatever elements of his teaching are distinctive, moves *in a different region of thought* from Isaiah ; he apprehends and emphasizes different aspects of Divine truth.

C. 40–66 thus displays, in conception not less than in literary style, a *combination* of features, which confirm the conclusion based on the subject-matter of the prophecy, that it is the work of an author writing towards the close of the exile, and predicting the approaching conquest of Babylon by Cyrus, and the restoration of the Jews, just as Isaiah predicted the failure of Rezin and Pekah, or the deliverance of Jerusalem from Sennacherib. It need only be added (for the purpose of precluding misconception) that this view of its date and authorship in no way impairs the theological value of the prophecy, or reduces it to a *vaticinium ex eventu* : on the one hand, the whole tone of the prophecy shows that it is written *prior* to the events which it declares to be approaching ; on the other, it nowhere claims either to be written by Isaiah, or to have originated in his age. Nor upon the same view of it is any claim made by its author to prevision of the future disallowed or weakened.†

The attempt is sometimes made to meet the force of the argument derived from differences of phraseology and style by pointing to the examples of similarities observable between c. 40–66 and the acknowledged prophecies of Isaiah. No doubt a certain number of such similarities exist ; but they are very far from being numerous or decisive enough to establish the conclusion for which they are alleged. It is the *difference* between authors which are characteristic, and form consequently a test of authorship : similarities, unless they are exceedingly numerous and minute, may be due to other causes

representations meet, and are fulfilled, in the person of our Lord Jesus Christ, but in the Old Testament they are distinct (*Isaiah*, pp. 175–180).

* Israel in its *ideal* character is to be the medium of religious instruction to the world (42[1b. 4. 6] 49[6b]) : comp. 45[22f.] 51[4b. 5b] 56[7b].

† There is no ground for supposing that the *fulfilled predictions* frequently alluded to (41[26] 42[9] 43[8-10] 48[3-8]) are those constituting the prophecy itself ; on the contrary, 42[9] shows that they are, in fact, *prior* prophecies, on the strength of the fulfilment of which the prophet claims to be heard in the *new* announcements now made by him (*Isaiah*, p. 188 f.). And in 44[28] 45[1ff.] the prophet does not claim foreknowledge of *Cyrus*, but only of *what he will accomplish* : he is *already* "stirred up," and "come" (41[2. 25a] 45[13a]), and the prophet promises that he *will* prosper in his further undertakings (41[25b] 45[1-3. 13b]).

than identity of authorship. They may be due, for instance, to community of subject - matter, to the independent adoption by different writers of a current terminology, to an affinity of genius or mental habit prompting an [231] author to borrow the ideas or phraseology of a predecessor, to involuntary reminiscence. But the differences between c. 40-66 and the acknowledged prophecies of Isaiah are both more numerous and of a more fundamental character than the similarities. A large number of the latter that have been alleged will indeed be found, when examined, to be *not distinctive, i.e.* they are not the peculiar possession of the Book of Isaiah, but occur in other writers as well. And there are none which may not be naturally and reasonably accounted for upon one or other of the four principles that have just been mentioned. The fallaciousness of arguing from similarities alone ought to have been apparent from the case of Jeremiah and Dt., in which the resemblances are much more abundant and remarkable than those between the two parts of the Book of Isaiah, and yet are admitted—on all hands— not to establish identity of authorship (p. 87 *n.*).*

It will be found that the chief objections to the critical date of c. 40-66 have their root in an imperfect apprehension of the *historical situation* to which criticism assigns it, and which is required (in parts) by the *argument* of the prophecy : see in particular, on the latter point, G. A. Smith, ii. pp. 9-12, who shows that the prophet's reasoning in c. 41-48 implies that the early successes of Cyrus must have been already historical facts.

The *literary* unity of Is. 40-66 is undoubtedly imperfect, especially in its later chapters : naturally the whole will not have been delivered by the prophet continuously, but some alteration, and advance, in the historical situation may be presupposed for its later parts. Thus Dillm. (p. 363 f.) supposes c. 40-48 to have been written in the midst of Cyrus' successes, *c.* 545 B.C., c. 46-62 between 545 and 539-538 ; while c. 63-66 are, he considers, of the nature of an appendix, dealing with questions which arose when the return to Palestine was imminent, and added therefore nearly at the time of the edict of Cyrus ;—c. 66 may in parts (esp. in v.$^{18-24}$) have been expanded by a subsequent hand (p. 534). But other critics are of opinion that this view does not do justice to the difference of tone which marks certain parts of the prophecy, and which, they consider, points to a greater change both in the historical standpoint of the writer and in the circumstances of those addressed. As regards two passages, 56^9-57^{11a} and 59$^{3-15}$, which (esp. the former) recall strongly descriptions in Jer. and Ez. of the condition of Judah under the later kings, it is generally allowed (cf. the writer's *Isaiah*, p. 187 f.) that they were written originally in the age of Jer., and that the

---

* See more fully, both on the characteristic teaching of c. 40-66 and on the authorship, the papers of Prof. Davidson, cited above, p. 204 ; the writer's *Isaiah*, pp. 168-212 ; Dillm. pp. 347-362, 469-474 ; Kirkpatrick, *Doctrine of the Prophets*, pp. 349-406 ; also, on the figure of Jehovah's ideal servant, Riehm, *Alttest. Theol.* (1890), § 84.

author of c. 40–66, finding that they taught a lesson appropriate to his contemporaries, incorporated them, with or without some slight modifications of form, in his own work, accommodating them at the same time (see $57^{13b.\ 14}$; 59^{16-21}) to the situation of the exiles. Ewald held that the whole of c. 58–59 (as well as 56^9-57^{11a}) was borrowed by II Isaiah from a contemporary of Ez.: he considered further (as did also Bleek) that 63^7–c. 66 was added by the author *after* the return. Kuenen (§ 49. 5–7, 11–15) limited (in 1889) the prophecy of the restoration to c. 40–49, 52^{1-12}, and perhaps $52^{13}-53^{12}$; the rest, he argued, upon internal grounds, presupposed an author (or authors) living after the return in Palestine; and hence he concluded that these parts were added, after B.C. 536, either by II Isaiah himself, or (mostly) by subsequent writers belonging to the same school; $64^{10f.}$ he thought, in particular, alluded "either to the facts described in Neh. 1^3 [above, p. 222], or to still later occurrences of a similar kind" (cf. below). Cornill (§ 20 [³ § 24]. 19, 20), and Wildeboer (§ 17. 5), also agree that the greater part of c. 49–62 presupposes a writer living in Palestine; but they do not suppose this writer to have been different from the author of c. 40–48, and they find the marks of a later hand only in parts of c. 63–66.

Duhm and Cheyne, by a closer study of the historical circumstances presupposed, the ideas, and the phraseology, seek to fix the authorship and age of the prophecy more precisely. Duhm thus limits the original work of II Isaiah to $40^{1-4.\ 9-11.\ 6-8.\ 12-19}$ 41^{6-7} 40^{20-31a} $41^{1-4.\ 8-29}$ $42^{5-11.\ 13.\ 14.\ 25}$ $43^{1-20a.\ 22-28}$ $44^{1-8.\ 21-28a}$ $45^{1-9.\ 11-13a.\ 14-25}$ $46^{1-5.\ 9-13}$ $47^{1-2.\ 3b-14a.\ 15}$ 48^{1a} (to *Jacob*) $3.\ 5a.\ 6-7a.\ 8a.\ 11-16a$ (to *there am I*) $20-21$ 49^{7-26} 50^{1-3} $51^{1-10.\ 12-14.\ 17.\ 19-23}$ $52^{1-2.\ 7-12}$ $54^{1-14.\ 16-17a}$ $55^{1-2.\ 3b-6.\ 8-13}$. Duhm refers the "servant"-passages (42^{1-4} 49^{1-6} 50^{4-9} $52^{13}-53^{12}$) to a distinct writer, living B.C. 500–450: c. 56–66 he assigns to another writer ("Tritojesaia"), living a little later, at the beginning of the age of Ezra and Nehemiah, who stood in greater sympathy than II Isaiah had done with the legal school founded by Ezek., and promoted by Haggai and Malachi, and who attached greater importance to ritual observances: thus 56^{1-8}, in the interest with which it views the duty of Sabbath-keeping and the question of the separation of Israel from the heathen, places us in the age of Ezr. $9^{1f.}$ c. 10, Neh. 9^2 $10^{30f.}$ $13^{1-3.\ 23-30}$; the author is only less exclusive than Ezr. and Neh., in that he is willing to admit such foreigners and others, who conform (v.$^{4.\ 6}$) to the necessary moral and spiritual conditions: 56^9-57^{13a} is not pre-exilic, but alludes to the persecutions and idolatries practised by Samaritans, and disloyal Jews, in the same age; $65^{3f.\ 11}$ $66^{5.\ 17}$ &c., refer likewise to the same persistent adversaries of the faithful "servants" of Jehovah, whose future fate, here ($65^{6f.\ 11f.}$ $66^{4.\ 15ff.}$) and elsewhere (as 59^{16-20}), the prophet declares. C. 58–59 portray the besetting moral and religious faults of the same period. Cheyne agrees largely with Duhm. In his analysis of c. 40–55 he differs only in assigning the "servant"-passages, and 40^{31b} 42^{12} $45^{10.\ 13b}$ 47^{3a} 51^{18} 54^{17b} 55^{3a}, to II Isaiah, and by excluding 42^{24b} $44^{21b.\ 22b}$ 45^{25} $48^{3b.\ 16a}$. C. 56–66 he treats as a group of prophecies belonging similarly (except 63^7–c. 64) to the age of Ezr. and Neh., the religious characteristics of which (esp. the opposition of the Samaritans and false Jews) he considers that they accurately reflect; he assigns these, however, not to an individual, but to a school of writers, who fell under the literary spell of II Isaiah, and loved to perpetuate his teaching, and develop his ideas. C. 60–62 he regards as an appendix to the original prophecy of II Isaiah, giving expression to the high hopes raised in B.C. 432 by the arrival of Ezra and his fellow-exiles with rich gifts for the temple from Babylonia.   63[7]–c. 64 is of later origin : it reflects the conflicting emotions aroused in the breasts of pious Israelites, by the destruction of the temple (64[10f.]), and other calamities, conjectured (above, p. 222) to have taken place under Artaxerxes Ochus (c. B.C. 347).

CHAPTER IV.

JEREMIAH.

LITERATURE.—H. Ewald in his *Prophets of the OT.* 1840–41, [2]1867–68 (in the translation, vols. 3 and [c. 50–51] 5, p. 1 ff.) ; F. Hitzig (in the *Kgf. Exeg. Handb.*), [2]1866 ; K. H. Graf, *Der Proph. Jer. erklärt,* 1862 ; C. W. E. Nägelsbach in Lange's *Bibelwerk,* 1868 ; C. F. Keil in the *Bibl. Commentar,* 1872 ; Payne Smith in the *Speaker's Commentary,* 1875 ; T. K. Cheyne in the *Pulpit Commentary* (exposition of the text), 1883–85 ; *Jeremiah, his life and times* (in the "Men of the Bible" series), 1888 ; C. von Orelli in Strack and Zöckler's *Kgf. Kommentar,* 1887 ; C. J. Ball (vol. i.) and W. H. Bennett (vol. ii.) in the "Expositor's Bible," 1890, 1895 ; Stade, *ZATW.* 1885, p. 175 ff. (on 32[11-14]), 1892, p. 276 ff. (on c. 21. 24–29) ; Giesebrecht (in Nowack's "Handkommentar"), 1894 ; C. H. Cornill (in Haupt's *SBOT.*). On c. 25. 46–49, Schwally, *ZATW.* 1888, p. 177 ff.; Smend, *AT. Rel.-gesch.* p. 238 ; L. H. K. Bleeker, *Jer.'s Profetieën tegen de Volkeren,* Groningen, 1894 (with many text.-crit. and exeg. notes) ; and on c. 50–51, C. Budde in the *Jahrb. f. deutsche Theol.* 1878, pp. 428–470, 529–562.

B.C.   *Chronological Table.*

639. JOSIAH.
626. Call of Jeremiah.
621. Discovery of Deuteronomy ; Josiah's reformation.
609. JEHOAHAZ.
608. JEHOIAKIM.
604. Victory of Nebuchadnezzar over Pharaoh Necho at Carchemish.
597. JEHOIACHIN.
597. First siege of Jerusalem, and deportation of Jewish exiles.
596. ZEDEKIAH.
586. Destruction of Jerusalem by the Chaldæans, and *second* deportation of Jewish exiles.

The prophet Jeremiah was of priestly descent. He was sprung (1[1]) from a little community of priests settled at Anathoth (cf. 1 Ki. 2[26], Josh. 21[18]), a town not far north of Jerusalem, in the tribe of Benjamin, with which he continued to maintain a connexion (cf. 11[21] 37[12]), though the main scene of his prophetic ministry was Jerusalem. His first public appearance as a prophet was in the 13th year of king Josiah (1[2] 25[3]), *i.e.* 626 B.C., 5 years

before the memorable year in which the " Book of the Law "
was found by Hilkiah in the Temple. Of his life during the
reign of Josiah no further particulars are known : but [233] his
book contains abundant notices of the part played by him in the
anxious times which began soon after the accession of Jehoiakim,
and did not cease till the destruction of Jerusalem by the
Chaldæans in 586. Politically, the 4th year of Jehoiakim, in
which Nebuchadnezzar won his great victory over Pharaoh
Necho at Carchemish on the Euphrates, was the turning-point
of the age. Jeremiah at once grasped the situation : he saw
that Nebuchadnezzar was destined to achieve further successes ;
he greeted him with the ode of triumph in c. 46, and declared
that the whole of W. Asia would fall under his sway (c. 25),
implying thereby what he afterwards taught explicitly, that the
safety of Judah lay in yielding to the inevitable, and accepting
the condition of dependence upon Babylon. In the end, however, Jehoiakim revolted ; and under his son and successor
Jehoiachin the penalty for his imprudence fell severely upon
the nation : Jerusalem was besieged ; and after 100 days' reign,
the king " went out " (2 Ki. 24^{12}), *i.e.* surrendered at discretion,
to the enemy : he himself, the queen mother Nehushta, the
principal members of the court, and the *élite* of Jerusalem
generally, were condemned to exile in Babylonia. Zedekiah,
having sworn (Ez. 17$^{11-18}$) a solemn oath of allegiance to
Nebuchadnezzar, was nominated king over those who remained
in Jerusalem. After a few years, however, Zedekiah compro-
mised himself by treasonable negotiations with Pharaoh Hophra ;
and in his 9th year the second siege of Jerusalem by the
Chaldæans began. Jeremiah now (21$^{1-10}$: cf. 38$^{17f.}$) declares
unambiguously that the besiegers will prevail, adding, as a piece
of practical advice to the people generally, that desertion to
them was the sole guarantee of personal safety. This counsel
did not proceed from any unpatriotic motive, though it is easy
to see that it might be so interpreted : Zedekiah, in revolting at
all, had been guilty of a gross breach of faith (see Ez. 17), and
the position taken now by Jeremiah was but the corollary of that
adopted by him in 604 (c. 25). Jeremiah's experiences during
the siege—how he was arrested in the north gate of the city on
a charge of deserting to the Chaldæans, and thrown into the
common dungeon ; how he was released thence in consequence

of the king's anxiety to learn from him the final issue of the siege ; how Zedekiah was compelled to relinquish him into the hands of his courtiers; and how he was only rescued from death by starvation through the [234] intercession of a friendly foreigner, an Ethiopian, Ebed-melech—are related in vivid detail in c. 37–38. After the capture of Jerusalem, Jeremiah was treated with consideration by the Chaldæans, and allowed to remain where he pleased : he was carried against his will by some of the Jews who had been left in Palestine into Egypt (c. 42–44).

Respecting the composition of the Book of Jeremiah, we have, at least as regards its oldest portions, information considerably more specific than is usual in the case of the writings of the prophets. His prophecies, we learn from c. 36, were first committed to writing in the 4th year of Jehoiakim, when Jeremiah received the command to take a roll, and write therein "all the words" which Jehovah had spoken to him "against Israel, and against Judah, and against all the nations" from the days of Josiah onwards. Accordingly, we read, Jeremiah dictated them to his scribe Baruch, who wrote them "from his mouth" (v.[4. 6. 17. 18. 27]) in a roll. In the following year, in the 9th month (36[9f.]), Baruch read the contents of the roll publicly before the people at the gate leading into the upper court of the Temple. Jehoiakim, being informed by his princes of what Baruch was doing, ordered the roll to be brought to him, and read before him. After three or four leaves had been read, the king, in a passion, seized the roll, rent it with his penknife, and cast it into the fire. After the roll had been thus destroyed, Jeremiah was directed to rewrite its contents in a second roll (v.[28]), which was done in the same manner as before, Baruch writing at the prophet's dictation ; and, it is stated, not merely were the contents of the first roll repeated, but " *there were added besides unto them many like words* " (v.[32]). Whether, even in the first roll, Jeremiah's discourses were reproduced *verbatim* as they were delivered, or merely in general substance, coloured, perhaps, in parts by the course of subsequent events, it is impossible to say ; but in the second roll, which evidently must form the basis of the prophecies as we have them, they were reproduced *with additions*. Thus, as regards the prophecies belonging to the first twenty-three years of Jeremiah's ministry, there must always be some uncertainty as to what portions strictly reproduce the original discourses, and what portions belong to the additions made by the prophet in the fifth year of Jehoiakim. It is, however, not unreasonable to suppose that among these [235] additions are included some of the more definite and distinct denunciations of the nation's sin and of the coming judgment.

The earlier prophecies of Jeremiah's book, unlike the later ones, are usually without specific dates (comp. 3^6 the indeterminate expression, "In the days of Josiah"), and often, also, somewhat general in their contents, so that probably they are not so much the actual text of particular discourses, as a reproduction of their substance, made by the prophet on the basis of notes and recollections of his teaching at the time.

C. 1. The vision of the prophet's call, in the 13th year of Josiah, B.C. 626. Jeremiah, while still a youth (v.^{6}), is consecrated to be a prophet : it is to be his mission to announce the weal or woe (v.^{10}), not of Judah only, but of other nations as well; in particular, however, he is to bear the tidings of woe to his own people (v.$^{11\text{-}16}$); he must expect, in the discharge of his mission, to encounter great opposition, but is divinely strengthened for the purpose of overcoming it (v.$^{17\text{-}19}$).

C. 2–6 form presumably Jeremiah's first prophetical discourse, as it was reproduced in a written form in the 5th year of Jehoiakim. The discourse consists of four parts, in each of which the general theme, viz. the nation's sin, is treated under a distinct aspect, viz. (1) c. 2 ; (2) $3^{1\text{-}5}$ (continued by 3^{19}–4^2) ; (3) $3^{6\text{-}18}$; (4) 4^3–6^{30}. C. 2 the dominant subject is Judah's idolatry. The prophecy opens with a touching picture of the nation's innocency in the ideal period of its youth, $2^{2\text{-}3}$; v.$^{4\text{-}13}$ describes its ingratitude and defection from Jehovah, and v.$^{14\text{-}17}$ the punishment which ensued : next the people are reproached with leaning for help alternately upon Egypt and Assyria, and with their devotion to gods which, in the time of need, will be powerless to aid them, v.$^{18\text{-}28}$; and finally, v.$^{29\text{-}37}$, with their self-complacency (v.^{35}), and persistent refusal to listen to wiser counsels. (2) $3^{1\text{-}5}$ 3^{19}–4^2 the subject is still Judah's idolatry, but there is held out the prospect of a better future ; Judah has been like a faithless wife, $3^{1\text{-}3}$, whose promises of amendment, v.$^{4f.}$, are but as empty words. Yet Jehovah had thought to honour her, expecting love and faithfulness in return, but His purpose had been frustrated, $3^{19f.}$. This, however, will not continue for

ever: the offer of pardon is freely made: and the prophecy
closes with a picture of the penitent nation confessing its sin
($3^{21.\ 22b-25}$), and of the benefits accruing from the spectacle of its
loyalty to the nations of the earth [236] (4^{1-2}). (3) 3^{6-18}. *Judah
contrasted unfavourably with Israel.* Judah has witnessed the
fate which overtook her sister, the N. kingdom, in her sin, but
has derived no warning from it: hence, relatively, Israel is more
righteous than Judah, v.^{11}; and the offer of pardon and promise
of restoration are addressed in the first instance to it, v.$^{12-14}$;
only when the ideal Zion of the future has been established by
the restoration of *Israel*, so that even heathen nations flock
towards it (v.$^{15-17}$), will *Judah* abandon its sin and return from
banishment (which the prophet here presupposes) to dwell with
Israel upon its own land, v.^{18}.

It is almost certain that this section is misplaced. (1) It interrupts the
connexion, for the words in 3^{19}, " *But I* said," are not antithetical to anything
in v.^{18}, while they are obviously so to the thought of 3^5 : 3^{1-5} depicts Judah's
faithlessness and empty promises of amendment, to which the declaration,
v.^{19}, of Jehovah's purpose, which had been frustrated, forms a natural
contrast. (2) The *contrasted view* of the behaviour of the two kingdoms
is peculiar to this section, and is foreign to both 3^{1-5} and 3^{19}–4^2: notice, also,
that whereas in 2^1–3^5 and 3^{19}–4^2, "Israel" designates *Judah*, in 3^{6-18} it
denotes the N. kingdom as *opposed* to Judah. (3) The section is complete in
itself: for v.^{6} evidently marks a genuine beginning; and the promises, v.$^{15-18}$,
form a natural close, and one thoroughly in harmony with the analogy of
prophecy. Thus, though the prophecy belongs no doubt to the same period
as the rest of c. 2–6 (for it has many figures and thoughts in common, *e.g.*
v.$^{6.\ 13}$ and 2^{20b}; the figure in v.^{8} and 2^2 $3^{1ff.}$; 3^9 and $2^{20.\ 27}$ $3^{1b.\ 2}$; v.^{14} and
v.^{22}), it has probably, through some accident of transmission, been displaced
from its original position (Cornill places it after c. 6). See further Stade,
ZATW. 1884, pp. 151–154; Kuen. § 52. 10. Giesebr. leaves v.$^{6-13}$ where
it is, but treats v.$^{14-18}$ as a later addition (v.$^{14-16}$ being taken from another
context in Jer. himself, probably c. 31): v.$^{21-25}$, however, reads far more like
a confession placed in the mouth of *Judah* in its own home (and therefore
the continuation of 3^{1-5}), than like one supposed to be spoken by *Israel* in
the land of exile.

(4) 4^3–6^{30}. Here the coming judgment is depicted more distinctly: it is to be inflicted by *a foe from the north.* The
prophet begins by exhorting earnestly to penitence, if perchance
the future which he foresees can be averted, v.$^{3f.}$; afterwards, he
bids the people betake themselves for safety into the fenced
cities, for the destroyer is approaching from the north; soon he
sees him close at hand, and the capital itself invested by the foe,

v.[5-18]. Speaking in the name of his people, he gives expression to the sense of terror which thrills through him as the alarm of war draws nearer : the vision of desolation embraces the whole land : in vain does Zion seek the favour of her "lovers," they are turned against her, v.[19-31]. Does this severe judgment seem unmerited ? Gladly would Jehovah have pardoned, had the nation shown itself worthy of forgiveness ; but all, high and low alike ($5^{4f.}$), are corrupt, 5^{1-9}. Let the appointed [237] ministers of judgment, then, complete their task : the only restriction is this, that Israel must not be exterminated (v.[10. 18] : cf. 4^{27}) ; and a picture follows of the terrible and cruel invader, who will desolate the land, slay the inhabitants, and carry the survivors into exile, v.[10-19]. V.[20-29] revert to the thought of v.[1-9], dwelling afresh upon the moral cause of the coming disaster : prophets and priests unite in the furtherance of evil. In c. 6 the danger is depicted as still nearer : the capital itself must now be abandoned (contrast 4^6) : for the enemy is preparing to storm it (v.[5]). Jehovah's offer, even now, to spare Zion is made in vain : worldliness and the illusion of security engross the people's thoughts ; and the judgment must therefore take its course, v.[6-21]. Still another description follows of the approach of the invader ; and the section closes with a significant figure of the reprobate condition of the nation, v.[22-30].

The foe from the north constitutes a feature in which 4^3–6^{30} advances beyond 2^1–4^2 : so that it is reasonable to suppose that 4^3–6^{30} belongs to a somewhat later date. The invader is mentioned, or alluded to, $4^{6-7. 13. 15-17.}$ [21. 29] $5^{6. 15-17}$ $6^{1-6. 12. 22-25}$: as no name is specified, it is disputed who is meant. Herodotus (I. 103 ff.) speaks of a great irruption into Asia at this time of *Scythians*, a wild and fierce people, whose home was north of the Crimea, but who, like the Huns and Bulgarians of a later day, were apt to make predatory incursions into the more favoured regions of the south. On the present occasion their invasion is thus described (Rawlinson, *Anc. Monarchies*, Bk. II. ch. ix.; ed. 1879, vol. ii. p. 225 f.) :—" Pouring through the passes of the Caucasus, horde after horde of Scythians blackened the rich plains of the south. On they came like a flight of locusts, countless, irresistible, . . . finding the land before them a garden, and leaving it behind them a howling wilderness. Neither age nor sex would be spared. The inhabitants of the open country and of the villages, if they did not make their escape to high mountain tops or other strongholds, would be ruthlessly massacred by the invaders, or, at best, forced to become their slaves. The crops would be consumed, the herds swept off or destroyed, the villages and homesteads burnt, the whole country made a scene of desolation. . . . The tide then swept on. Wandering from district to district, plundering everywhere, settling nowhere, the clouds of horse passed over Mesopotamia, the force of the invasion becoming weaker as it spread itself, until in Syria it reached its term by the policy of the Egyptian king Psammetichus," who, hearing that the Scythian hordes had advanced as far as Ashkelon, and were threatening to invade Egypt, prevailed upon them by rich gifts to abstain from their enterprise. Herodotus, who states that they were masters of Western Asia from the Caucasus to the border of Egypt for 28 years (B.C. 635–607), may have exaggerated the extent and nature of their ἀρχή, but the fact of such an irruption having taken place cannot be doubted. It is probable that the present prophecy, in its *original* intention, alluded to these [238] Scythian hordes, whom some of the descriptions remarkably suit (5^{17} $6^{22t.}$), and who may well have ended by including Judah in their ravages ; though afterwards, when it was committed to writing, and, as it were, *re-edited* in the 5th year of Jehoiakim, it was accommodated by the prophet to the Chaldæans, who in the interval had become Judah's most formidable foe, the phraseology being possibly modified in parts so as to describe them more appropriately (*e.g.* 4^7 the " lion " and " destroyer of nations " are terms better suited to an individual as Nebuchadnezzar than to a horde ; comp. the " lion," 49^{19} of Nebuchadnezzar, 50^{44} of Cyrus : 6^{22} " from the uttermost parts of the earth," and " from the north " would be appropriate either to the Scythians or to the Chaldæans, cf. 25^{32} : 10^{22} 13^{20} 25^9 47^2). Comp. Ew. *Hist.* iv. 226–231 ; *Prophets*, iii. 70 ; Hitzig, *Jerem.* p. 31 f.; Graf, pp. 16–19 ; Wellhausen in Bleek's *Einleitung*, 1878, p. 335 ; Kuenen, § 52. 12.

C. 7–10 (excluding 10^{1-16}) form a second group of prophecies. The scene described in c. 7 is a striking one. The prophet is commanded to station himself at the gate leading to the upper court immediately surrounding the Temple, and there to address the people entering in to worship. V.[3] states the theme of his discourse : *Amend your ways and your doings, and I will cause you to dwell in this place.* The people of Jeremiah's day, appropriating, in a one-sided sense, Isaiah's teaching of the inviolability of Zion, pointed to the Temple, standing in their midst, as the palladium of their security. The prophet indignantly retorts that they mistake the conditions of security (v.[9-11]). So long as the people follow dishonesty, immorality, and idolatry, Jehovah will as little spare Zion as he spared Shiloh of old : the fate of Ephraim will be also the fate of Judah, 7^{1-20}. 7^{21}–8^{22} the subjects are substantially the same : the people's refusal to listen to the warnings of their prophets, their persistency in idolatry, the ruin imminent, the foe already in the midst of the land, the vain cry for help raised by the people in their distress, and the prophet's wail of sympathy. In c. 9 the plaintive strain of 8^{18-22} is continued : the prophet bewails the corruption of the people, which is rendering this judgment necessary, 9^{1-9} (the refrain, 9^9 as $5^{9, 29}$) : he dwells anew, and with livelier sympathy, upon the troubles about to fall upon the people, 9^{10-26} ; he bids (10^{17-25}) the inhabitants of the capital, which he already in spirit sees invested by the foe, prepare to depart into exile, only at the end ($10^{24f.}$) supplicating in the name of his people for a mitigation of the coming disaster.

[239] The date of this prophecy is disputed. Some, arguing from its position and the general similarity of tone with 4^3-c. 6, assign it to the same period, before Josiah's 18th year (Hitz., Bleek, *Einl.* ed. 4, p. 360, Keil); others, on account of the great resemblance with 26^{1-6}, regard the occasion as the same, and assign it to the beginning of the reign of Jehoiakim (Ew. Graf, Näg. Kuen. § 53. 6, 7, Payne Smith, Cheyne, p. 115, Wellh. *ap.* Bleek, *l.c.,* Delitzsch, *ap.* Workman [see p. 269, *note*], p. xix.

10^{1-16}. Against idolatry. The "house of Israel" are warned against standing in awe of the idols of the heathen, which, however splendid and imposing in appearance, are powerless to defend their worshippers (v.$^{14f.}$) : on the other hand, Jehovah, who is Jacob's portion, is the true and living God.

This section is misplaced, even if Jeremiah be the author. (1) It is foreign to the context : the context on both sides deals with the judgment impending upon Jerusalem, and the people are represented as *already* abandoned to idolatry, in particular, to the worship of the Queen of Heaven and Baal ($7^{18, 31}$): 10^{1-16} deals entirely with the contrast between Jehovah and idols, and warns the nation against *learning* idolatry (v.^{2}). (2) Jeremiah's argument is "Expect no help from vain gods ; they cannot *save* you" (2^{28} 11^{12}); here the argument is "Do not fear them, they cannot *harm* you." And yet, according to Jeremiah's teaching, at the very time to which from its position this section would be referred, Jeremiah was prophesying that Judah would shortly be ruined by a nation of idolaters. The descriptions in v.$^{3-5, 9}$ imply that the "house of Israel" addressed is in the presence of an elaborate idol-worship carried on—not by themselves, but—by the *heathen*, which, they are emphatically taught, deserves no consideration at their hands. The situation is that of *the exiles in Babylonia.* Either (Bleek) the prophecy belongs to the latter part of Jeremiah's career, and was addressed by him (cf. the letter in c. 29) to those of his fellow-countrymen who went into exile in 597 ; or (Movers, Hitz., Graf, Kuen. § 53. 8, 9, Ball, p. 215 ff.) it is the work of a later prophet, writing towards the close of the exile, when (as we know from II Isaiah) the magnificence of the Babylonian idols severely tried the faith of the exiles : both the descriptions of idolatry and the argument ("Do not stand in awe of the idols around you; they are a thing of nought; it is Jehovah who made heaven and earth") are in II Isaiah (Is. 40^{19-22} $41^{7, 29}$ 44^{9-20} 46^{5-7} &c.) strikingly similar. In the phraseology the only noticeable point of contact with Jeremiah's style is in v.^{15}, בעת פקדתם (p. 275, No. 14).

V.[11] is in Aramaic, with certain peculiarities showing that its author must have spoken a particular Aramaic dialect : * from the fact that it interrupts the connexion between v.[10] and v.[12] (for v.[12] in the Hebrew [240] begins with a *participle*, connecting immediately with v.[10]), it is probable that it was originally a note written upon the margin of v.[12], as a comment—perhaps taken from some independent writing—on the argument of the text. Those who attribute it to Jeremiah, generally view it as a reply with which he provides the exiles, to be used by them when invited to take part in idol-worship : Aramaic was understood, and used both commercially and officially, by Assyrians, Babylonians, and Persians (the inscriptions referred to in the note, however, have regularly ז, not as here די, for the relative particle).

C. 11–12. (*a*) 11[1-8]. This, with evident allusion to the lawbook discovered in Josiah's 18th year (v.[2] "Hear ye the words of *this* covenant" : v.[3b] almost *verbatim* = Dt. 27[26a] : with v.[5b] cf. *ib*. v.[26b]), relates, no doubt, what took place shortly after that event. Jeremiah was instructed to go and "proclaim" (or "recite") "*in the cities of Judah* and in the streets of Jerusalem " (v.[6]) the words of the covenant, *i.e.* probably to undertake an itinerating mission in Judah for the purpose of setting forth the principles of Dt., and exhorting men to live accordingly. (*b*) 11[9-17] appears to describe what happened some time subsequently—possibly as late as the reign of Jehoiakim—when the amendment of the people had been shown to be superficial (v.[10] "they have *returned* to the former iniquities of their fathers "), and when the prophet accordingly reaffirms the sentence of judgment, which neither his own intercession (v.[14]) nor the people's hypocritical repentance (v.[15] R.V. *marg*.) will be able to avert. (*c*) 11[18]–12[6]. In 11[18-23] Jer. relates how he had been apprised of a plot formed against his life by the men of

* The form ארקא occurs in the Aramaic inscriptions on weights from Nineveh of the 8th cent. B.C. (*Corp. Inscr. Sem.* II. i. Nos. 1, 2, 3, &c.), in Mandaic (Nöldeke, *Mand. Gr.* p. 73), and in the recently discovered Inscriptions from Zinjirli (near Aleppo), of the 8th cent. B.C. (together with מוקא = מוצא, cf. مَكَلَ, وَضًا, [*Heb. Tenses*,[3] § 178] ; and רקי = רצה = أَكَلَ = (رَضَيَ) : see D. H. Müller, *Die Altsem. Inschr. von Sendschirli* (1893), pp. 41, 54 ; and cf. Nöldeke, *ZDMG*. 1893, p. 96 ff.; the *jussive* without ן (יאבדו) in the Aram. of Têma (*C.I.S. ib*. No. 113*a*, l. 14), Egypt (*ib*. 137 B[3]), Nerab near Aleppo (*Rev. Sém.* 1896, p. 280 ff.), and Dan. 5[10] (cf. the same form in the indic., Ezra 4[12], and Müller, *l.c.* p. 50) ; אלה (for אלין) in the Nabatæan Inscriptions (Euting, *Nab. Inschriften*, 1887, p. 77). In להום (with *m*) Jer. 10[11] agrees with the Aram. of Ezra (which has *m*, as well as *n*, while that of Dan. has *n* only), as with that of Egypt (*C.I.S.* II. i. 145), of the Nabatæan Inscriptions (Euting, p. 77), and of Zinjirli (Müller, pp. 44, 50).

his native place, Anathoth, and the judgment which he had pronounced upon them in consequence : 12$^{1-6}$ he expostulates with Jehovah on account of the impunity which the conspirators nevertheless for the time enjoyed, and demands upon them summary vengeance : in reply he is rebuked for his impatience, and reminded that his faith may have in the future yet greater trials to endure.   (*d*) 12$^{7-17}$ deals with a different subject, and dates probably from a later time, when Judah, viz. after Jehoiakim's revolt from Nebuchadnezzar, was overrun by bands of Syrians, Moabites, and Ammonites (2 Ki. 24$^{1f.}$), alluded to here in the expression " my evil neighbours," v.^{14}.   They, as well as Judah, are threatened with exile ; but a gracious prospect of restoration afterwards is held out to them (v.$^{15f.}$), if they adopt from the heart the religion of Israel.

C. 13 contains—(*a*) the description of a symbolical act performed [241] by the prophet for the purpose of illustrating the corrupt condition of the people and its consequences, v.$^{1-11}$; (*b*) a parable, declaring significantly the disaster about to come upon them, v.$^{12-14}$; (*c*) a renewed exhortation to amendment, v.$^{15-17}$, followed v.$^{18-27}$, by the prophet's lamentation, as the dark reality forces itself upon him, that the exhortation will only be disregarded.

From v.^{18} " Say ye to the king, *and to the queen-mother*, Sit ye down lowly," it is generally inferred by commentators (Graf and Keil being nearly the only dissentients) that this prophecy belongs to the reign of Jehoiachin, whose mother, Nehushta (2 Ki. 24^8), is also specially mentioned in another prophecy of Jeremiah's 22^{26}, as well as in the narrative of the exile of Jehoiachin (29^2 ; 2 Ki. 24$^{12. \ 15}$), so that she probably exercised some unusual influence at the time.

14^1–17^{18}. (*a*) c. 14–15. The immediate occasion of c. 14 was a drought (v.$^{2-6}$), which was viewed by the prophet as a token of Jehovah's anger, and elicited from him accordingly the supplication following, v.$^{7-9}$: Jehovah's answer follows ; and the dialogue is continued to the end of c. 15. Jer.'s intercession is refused, 14$^{10-12}$ (with v.^{11} comp. 7^{16} 11^{14} ; with v.^{12a}, 6^{20b} 11^{11b}) ; he seeks to excuse the people on the ground that they have been deluded by their prophets, v.^{13} (cf. 5^{12} 6^{14}) ; but the excuse is not accepted ; prophets and people must perish alike, v.$^{14-18}$. In more beseeching tones, Jeremiah renews his intercession, v.$^{19-22}$; but is answered even more decisively than before : Even

Moses and Samuel would not avail to avert the coming doom, or undo the evil which Manasseh wrought for Judah, 15¹⁻⁹ (with v.⁴ cf. 2 Ki. 21¹¹⁻¹⁵ 24^{8f.}). Hereupon the prophet vents his grief and despair at the fate which (through the message which he bears) obliges him to encounter the hatred and ill-will of all men, v.¹⁰; v.^{11f.} Jehovah reassures him: the time will come when his opponents will be glad to implore his help, crushed by the irresistible might of the "iron from the north" (the "northern colossus," the Chaldæans);* once again, v.¹⁵⁻¹⁸, he bewails the hard fate imposed upon him of having to predict the ruin of [242] his country: v.¹⁹⁻²¹ he is finally taught that his success and happiness depend upon his abandoning the false path of mistrust and despair. (b) 16¹–17¹⁸. In 16¹–17⁴ the coming disaster, with its cause, the people's sin, is set forth in still plainer terms than in c. 14 f.: in 17⁵⁻¹³ the prophet points to Jehovah as the sole source of strength in the hour of trouble; and concludes, v.¹⁴⁻¹⁸, with a prayer that he himself may experience Jehovah's salvation, and be delivered from the enemies who taunt and persecute him.

The intensity of feeling which Jeremiah displays throughout 14¹–17¹⁸, the persistency and earnestness with which he steps forward again and again to intercede on behalf of his nation, the emphasis with which the doom is declared to be irrevocable, authorise the inference that the prophecy belongs to the time when the crisis was approaching, i.e. to the latter part of the reign of Jehoiakim, when the prophet felt moved to make every effort to avert, if it were possible, the inevitable. 17¹¹ has even been thought to contain an allusion to Jehoiakim's unjust and avaricious treatment of his subjects, described more directly in 22^{13f. 17}; but this is uncertain.

C. 17¹⁹⁻²⁷. An exhortation on the *Sabbath*, to the strict observance of which a promise of prosperity and the continued existence of the monarchy (v.²⁵: cf. 22⁴) is attached.

* Such is the most probable sense of the difficult v.¹² (Ewald, Keil). V.^{13. 14} [to be read as RV. *second marg.*], as they stand, must carry on the same line of thought: Jeremiah's enemies will be taken into exile, so as no longer to be able to trouble him. But the thought would be very obscurely and indirectly expressed: for just before (v.¹¹) the pron. of the 2 ps. denotes Jeremiah, here it would denote the nation, *to the exclusion of* Jeremiah! There is high probability in Ewald's view, that v.¹²⁻¹⁴ is accidentally misplaced, and ought properly to follow v.⁹, where the passage is in harmony with the context, and where the change of person would be far less abrupt (comp. the second person of the nation in v.⁶).

This prophecy is unconnected with what precedes : and from the difference in tone—for the doom which in 14^1–17^{18} is declared to be irrevocable, is here conceived as capable of being averted, upon one condition being observed—it may be inferred that it belongs to a different and earlier period, perhaps (Orelli) to the time of Josiah's reformation (cf. $11^{1ff.}$). The importance attached in it to the Sabbath, and the appreciation expressed in v.[26] for sacrifice, are not in the usual spirit of Jer.; and hence several recent critics (including Kuenen, § 52. 16; cf. Cheyne, *Introd. to Is.* pp. 311 f., 324) attribute it to a later prophet, belonging to the age of Nehemiah (cf. Neh. 10^{31} 13^{15-22}). The style is, however, thoroughly that of Jer.; and although no doubt Jer. speaks disparagingly of sacrifice offered by impure hands ($6^{19f.}$ $7^{9f.}$ $^{21-26}$ 14^{10-12}), it may be questioned whether he would have rejected it, when (as is the case implicitly in 17^{26}) it is conceived as the expression of a right heart (cf. 33^{11}; also Dt. 12^{11}, Is. 56^7 60^7).

C. 18–20. *Lessons from the potter.* In c. 18 Jeremiah is made to teach, by observation of the method followed by the potter, the great principle of the *conditional* nature of prophecy. The doom pronounced against a nation may, if the nation alters its course, be modified or reversed : God's purpose, *as declared*, is not of necessity absolute and unconditional, v.$^{1-10}$. The practical application follows : the Jews are invited to amend their ways, in order that the threatened evil may be averted; they are represented as declining; and the judgment originally pronounced is reaffirmed, v.$^{11-17}$. The people, proud in the possession of inviolable privileges [243] (v.^{18}), resent this unwelcome conclusion of the prophet's, and proceed to form plots against his life (cf. $26^{10f.}$), with a vehement prayer for the frustration of which the chapter closes, v.$^{19-23}$. This prophecy, in which the fate of Judah is represented as still undecided, and as depending on the people's choice, would seem to be earlier than 14^1–17^{18}, where it is treated as irrevocably fixed. C. 19, by a symbolical act, the breaking of the potter's *finished* work, the earthen bottle, in the valley of the son of Hinnom, the conclusion expressed in c. 18 is repeated and reinforced : the nation has reached a point at which amendment is no longer possible : and the disaster, when it comes, will be final and irretrievable, v.$^{1-13}$. V.$^{14-15}$ Jeremiah repeats in the Temple Court the substance of what he had said, the consequence of which was that Pashhur, son of Immer, the superintendent of the Temple, had the prophet thrown into the stocks till the following day : after his release, he pronounces upon the entire nation formal sentence of exile to Babylon, 20^{1-6}. The incident is followed, v.[7-18], by an outburst of deep emotion on the part of Jeremiah (comp. 15[10. 15-18] 17[15-18]): the impulse to be a prophet had been an irresistible one (cf. Am. 3[8]); but he had been rewarded by nothing but hostility and detraction; and though he is sensible that Jehovah is with him (cf. 1[19]), and will in the end grant him justice against his persecutors, he still cannot repress the passionate wish that he had never seen the light.

C. 21[1-10] places us in Zedekiah's reign, during the period (v.[2]) when Nebuchadnezzar's troops were investing the city, at the end of Zedekiah's ninth year. The passage contains the answer given by Jeremiah to the message of inquiry addressed to him by Zedekiah respecting the issue of the siege.

21[11]–23[8]. An important group of prophecies, containing Jeremiah's judgments on the successive rulers who occupied in his day the throne of David. 21[11-14] is introductory; 22[1-9] is an admonition impressing upon the king the paramount importance of justice. There follow the special judgments on the kings— on Shallum (Jehoahaz), v.[10-12], whose exile is pathetically foretold; on Jehoiakim, whose exactions are pointedly contrasted with the fair and honourable dealings of his father Josiah, and for whom an ignominious end is predicted, v.[13-19]; and on Jehoiachin, whose banishment to a foreign [244] land is emphatically announced, v.[20-30]. The climax of the entire prophecy is 23[1-8]. V.[1-2] is a denunciation of the unworthy shepherds— i.e. rulers, comp. 2[8] 10[21]—generally, who have neglected and ruined the flock entrusted to them: v.[3-8] the prophecy closes with a promise of ultimate restoration, and a picture of the rule of the ideal Prince of Jesse's line, which in every respect forms a contrast with that exercised by the imperfect rulers of Jeremiah's own day (v.[5b] the opposite of 22[13, 17]; v.[6a] the opposite of 23[1-2]; with v.[4] comp. 3[15]).

21[12] 22[3f.] (implying that the fate of Judah is not yet irrevocably fixed) appear to belong to the earlier part of Jeremiah's career (cf. 17[25]); the judgments which follow (as the terms of v.[11f. 19. 25f.] show) must have been originally pronounced during the reigns of the kings to whom they severally relate; the whole being arranged together subsequently, on account of the community of subject.

23[9-40] is directed against the *prophets*, who were influential in Jerusalem * in Zedekiah's reign (see 27[14f.] 28[1ff.]), and who

* And also among those carried into exile with Jehoiachin, 29[8f. 20ff.]

represented a policy the reverse of that counselled by Jeremiah, and misled the people by false promises of security. Jeremiah denounces them with much vehemence, charging them even with immorality and profaneness (comp. 29[23]), and declaring that their unauthorized prophesyings will avail neither the people nor themselves.

C. 24 was written shortly after the exile of Jehoiachin. As has been said (p. 248), the companions of Jehoiachin included the flower of the nation: among those who were left in Jerusalem must have been many who hitherto had occupied a humble station in life, but who now found themselves suddenly called to fill state offices: these in many cases were elated by their new dignities; and proud of the confidence placed in them by Nebuchadnezzar, they treated their brethren in exile with no small contempt, declaring loudly that "the land was given to *them*" (see Ez. 11[15] 33[24]). In this chapter Jeremiah passes a comparative estimate upon the two divisions of the nation: under the significant figure of the good and bad figs, he expresses emphatically the different character of each, and the different future in store for them.

C. 25 belongs to the critical year of the battle of Carchemish, the fourth year of Jehoiakim (B.C. 604). In it Jeremiah first [245] declares, v.[1-14], that Judah and the neighbouring nations must fall under the sway of the king of Babylon for seventy years, at the end of which time his empire will come to an end; afterwards, v.[15-38], extending the range of his survey, he views his empire as destined to embrace practically the then known world.

It is extremely doubtful whether v.[11-14, 26b] are genuine; nearly all modern critics are of opinion that the original prophecy has here been expanded by a writer, who had the entire book (including c. 50-51, to which v.[13] alludes) before him, for the purpose of emphasizing the judgment destined to fall upon Babylon ultimately: cf. pp. 270, 273.

C. 26 is assigned to "the beginning of the reign of Jehoiakim": no doubt, therefore, it dates from an earlier period than c. 25. It recounts Jeremiah's attempt to lead his people to better counsels, by warning them that, unless they amend their ways, Jerusalem will share the fate which overtook Shiloh of old (cf. c. 7); and describes the prophet's narrow escape from death in consequence of the indignation aroused by his words.

C. 27-29 belong to the beginning of the reign of Zedekiah. C. 27 relates how Jeremiah frustrated the attempt made by the five neighbouring nations—Edom, Moab, Ammon, Tyre, and Zidon—to induce Zedekiah to join them in a league for the purpose of revolting from the Chaldæans: it was the design of Providence that the entire known earth should fall under the rule of the king of Babylon ; and the prophets who promised the speedy restoration of the sacred vessels, which Nebuchadnezzar had carried away, simply deluded the people with vain hopes. C. 28 narrates how he opposed Hananiah, who was one of the prophets alluded to in c. 27, and who promised the return, within two years, of the sacred vessels (the loss of which was evidently keenly felt in Jerusalem), as well as the restoration of Jehoiachin and the other exiles. C. 29 contains the letter sent by Jeremiah to the exiles (who had been disquieted by prophets announcing confidently their speedy return to Judah) exhorting them to settle down contentedly where they were, to "build houses, and plant gardens," for no restoration would take place until the seventy years of Babylonian dominion had been accomplished, v.$^{1-23}$. This letter so enraged the false prophets in Babylonia, that one of them—Shemaiah—sent to Jerusalem with the view of procuring Jeremiah's arrest: the failure of his plot, and Jeremiah's reply, form the subject of v.$^{24-32}$.

C. 30-33 embrace Jeremiah's principal prophecies dealing with Israel's *restoration*. The thought has been expressed before incidentally (*e.g.* 3^{14-18}; 23^{3-8}); but it is here developed connectedly. The general import of c. 30, after the introductory words v.$^{1-4}$, is to assure Israel, that, though the present distress is severe, the nation will not wholly perish: in due time it [246] will be restored, Jerusalem will be rebuilt (v.^{18}), and ruled again by an independent prince of David's line, who will enjoy in particular the privilege of close access to Jehovah (v.$^{9, 21}$). In this chapter the two verses $^{10-11}$ (= 46^{27-28}) are especially noticeable: the title of honour, "My servant," here given to Israel for the first time (and applied to the *actual* nation), appears to have formed the basis upon which II Isaiah constructs his great conception of Jehovah's ideal Servant (p. 242). C. 31 holds out the hope of the restoration of *Ephraim*, v.$^{1-9}$, as well as of Judah, v.$^{10-14}$: at present Rachel (the mother of *Joseph, i.e.* Ephraim)—so the prophet's imagination pictures her—is watching from her tomb at Ramah, and tenderly bewailing the desolation of her children; but the mother may stay her grief; Ephraim will yet show penitence, v.[15-20], and both Ephraim and Judah will return together, v.[21-30]. There follows the great prophecy of the "New Covenant," by which the restored community will then be ruled, a covenant which is to consist not in an external system of laws, but in a law *written in the heart*, a principle operative from within, filling all men with the knowledge of Jehovah, and prompting them to immediate and spontaneous obedience, v.[31-34]. C. 32 describes how Jeremiah, as a sign that, though the exile of the entire nation was imminent, the Jews should still once again possess the soil of Canaan, both purchased fields belonging to his cousin at Anathoth, and took special means to ensure the preservation of the title-deeds, v.[1-15]: v.[16-25] he records how his heart afterwards misgave him, and v.[26-44] how he was reassured by Jehovah. In c. 33 the prophet, looking out beyond the troubles of the present (v.[4f.]), depicts afresh the subsequent purification and restoration of the nation (note v.[11], the reversal of 7[34] 16[9] 25[10]), v.[1-13]; closing with a repetition (in a slightly varied form *) of the Messianic prophecy of 23[5f.], and a solemn assurance of the perpetual validity of Jehovah's covenant with the house of David and the Levitical priests, v.[14-26].

[247] C. 32–33 are assigned expressly (32[2] 33[1]) to the period of Jeremiah's honourable confinement in the "court of the guard," *i.e.* to the second part of the siege, in Zedekiah's tenth year, after it had been interrupted by the temporary withdrawal of the Chaldæans : the composition of c. 30–31 belongs probably to the same time, though from the tenor of 30[2] ("Write thee all *the words that I have spoken unto thee* in a book") it is more than possible that the contents had in part been originally uttered previously, but, as 32[2] "then" shows, that they were not committed to writing till subsequently, probably after the fall of the city. 33[17-26] is not in LXX ; and the majority of recent critics, partly on account of the prominence assigned in it to the priests (cf., however, 31[14]), partly on other grounds (see Kuen. § 54. 21 ; Giesebr. p. 183 f.), question Jer.'s authorship of it.

---

* The symbolical name "Jehovah is our righteousness," which in 23[6] is given to the Messianic King, is here, 33[16], assigned to the restored, ideal city. The name is intended, of course, to symbolize the fact that Jehovah is the source of righteousness to the restored community. In the one case, this is indicated by the name being given to the *king* who rules over it (and who therefore is doubtless viewed as *mediating* the righteousness) ; in the other, by its being given to the *city* in which the community dwells (cf. Isa. 1[26]).

The chapters which follow are largely historical, though naturally confined to incidents in which Jeremiah was more or less directly concerned.

C. 34$^{1-7}$ relates the message which Jeremiah was instructed to bear to Zedekiah respecting the future fate as well of the city as of the king himself.

The occasion was probably during the first investment of Jerusalem by the Chaldæans (Hitz. Keil, Kuen. PS.), a little subsequent to 21$^{1-10}$; though others, from the fact that the prophecy is the one quoted in 32$^{3-5}$ during the second part of the siege, have referred it by preference to this period (Ew., Graf, Stade, *G.* i. 647).

34$^{8-22}$. The inhabitants of Jerusalem, under pressure of the siege, had solemnly engaged to emancipate their Hebrew slaves; but afterwards, when the siege was temporarily raised, had treacherously disregarded the engagement. Jeremiah denounces them for their breach of faith, with bitter irony proclaiming "liberty" to the sword, the pestilence, and the famine, and declaring that the Chaldæans will ere long return, and not depart until they have reduced the city.

C. 35–36 bring us back into the reign of Jehoiakim. The date of c. 35 is towards the close of Jehoiakim's reign, when, the territory of Judah being overrun by marauding bands (2 Ki. 24^2), the nomad tribe of Rechabites took refuge in Jerusalem: Jeremiah, from the example of their staunch adherence to the precepts of their ancestor, points a lesson for his own fellow-countrymen. C. 36 narrates the memorable incident of the fifth year of Jehoiakim, when the roll of Jeremiah's prophecies was burnt by the king in a fit of passion (p. 249).

C. 37–38^{28a} describe Jeremiah's personal history during the siege of Jerusalem by the Chaldæans (comp. p. 248 f.).

38^{28b}–c. 43 state particulars respecting the events of Jeremiah's life after the capture of Jerusalem, the favour shown to him by [248] Nebuchadnezzar, the murder of Gedaliah, and the circumstances under which the prophet, against his will, was brought into Egypt: 43$^{8-13}$ is a prophecy uttered by him upon the arrival of the refugees at Tahpanhes (Daphnae), declaring the future conquest of Egypt by Nebuchadnezzar.

38^{28b}–39^{14} connects imperfectly with 38^{1-28a}, 39^1 going back to the *beginning* of the siege. It seems (in spite of its being in the LXX) that 39$^{1-2}$ (which cannot be legitimately treated as a parenthesis) is an interpolation on the basis of 2 Ki. 25[1. 3. 4aα]. 39[4-13] is omitted in LXX, and it is doubtful if it forms part of the original narrative : the connexion of v.[4] with v.[3] is imperfect, and in any case v.[4-10] is merely *abridged* from 2 Ki. 25[4-12] (comp. esp. v.[8] with 2 Ki. 25[8-10]), according to the purer and more original text still preserved in Jer. 52[7-16]. Most probably the original text had only 38[28b] 39[3] [with *and* for *that*, as in the Heb.] v.[14] [Heb. *and they sent*] : these words form a continuous narrative, the particulars in which are *not* borrowed from c. 52 (so Ew. Hitz. Graf, Kuen. Orelli,—Hitz. and Or., however, including v.[11f.] as well). 39[15-18] is a supplement to c. 38, promising a reward to Ebed-melech on account of the services rendered by him to Jeremiah.

C. 44. Jeremiah here rebukes the fugitives in Egypt for relapsing into their old idolatries : they excuse themselves : the prophet, in reply, repeats his previous denunciations, declaring that of their entire body, a handful only should return into the land of Judah.

C. 45 is a supplement to 36[1-8], "these words" in v.[1] referring directly to the roll there mentioned. It consists of a short prophecy, containing words of mingled reassurance and reproof, addressed to Baruch in the depression and disappointment which overcame him, after writing the roll of the 4th year of Jehoiakim, at the near and certain prospect of his country's ruin. He is reminded that the age is one in which he must not expect great things for himself, but must be content if he escapes with his bare life.

C. 46-51 form the book of Jeremiah's prophecies concerning foreign nations, grouped together, as in the case of the similar prophecies in the Books of Isaiah (c. 13—23) and Ezekiel (c. 25–32). The prophecies are closely connected with c. 25 (most of the nations to which they refer being named in 25[19-26]), and no doubt in the first draft of Jeremiah's prophecies (see p. 271) immediately followed it.*

C. 46. On *Egypt*. This falls into two parts : (1) v.[3-12] an [249] ode of triumph on the defeat of Pharaoh Necho at Carchemish (v.[2]), B.C. 604 ; (2) v.[14-26] a prophecy written in the same strain as v.[3-12], foretelling the successful invasion of Egypt by Nebuchadnezzar.

---

* In the text of the LXX they are inserted *in* this chapter, after 25[13], the words in 25[13b] "which," &c., in the form, "The things which Jeremiah prophesied against the nations," forming a superscription ; v.[14] being omitted ; and v.[15] (in the form, "*Thus said* Jehovah," &c.) [16-38] following at the end.

V.$^{27f.}$ (words of reassurance addressed to Israel) are all but identical with 30$^{10f.}$. They appear to imply that the captivity has *begun*, and it is at least doubtful (in spite of 3^{18} 16^{15}) whether Jer. would have so expressed himself in B.C. 604. On the other hand, they are in their place in c. 30, which appears (p. 262) to have received its present form after the fall of Jerusalem. Perhaps they were attached here subsequently, either by Jer. himself, or by a reader, or editor, of his prophecies.

C. 47 is directed against the *Philistines*, indirectly also (v.^{4}) against Tyre and Sidon : their country is to be wasted by a foe whose attack is compared to waters rising up out of the north and inundating the land.

The foe meant is unquestionably the Chaldæans (cf. 13^{20} 25^9 46^{20}), and the occasion is no doubt the same as that of c. 46. The note of time in v.^{1b} is obscure ; but probably the allusion is to a capture of Gaza by the Egyptians not otherwise known to us, either on their retreat from Carchemish, or possibly in connexion with the movements mentioned in 37^5. The note *may*, however, be due to one who supposed the Egyptians to be meant in v.^{2}.

C. 48 is a long prophecy directed against *Moab*, for the inhabitants of which desolation and exile are foretold. The prophet develops his theme in considerable detail, in connexion with the topography of Moab : he closes, v.^{47}, with a prospect of restoration in the future.

The prophecy, in v.$^{5, 29-38}$, has numerous reminiscences from Isaiah's prophecy (c. 15–16) on the same nation (see RV. *marg.*), but the style and manner of the whole are very different : the treatment is more diffuse ; and it is marked by greater vehemence (*e.g.* v.$^{10, 20ff. 26. 39}$).

49$^{1-6}$ is on the *Ammonites*, a prophecy of similar import to that on Moab, but briefer; v.$^{7-22}$ is on *Edom*, whose mountain defences will form no protection against the attack of the Chaldæan king (figured by the " lion " of v.^{19}, and the " eagle " of v.^{22}) ; v.$^{23-27}$ is on *Damascus*, whose warriors, when the critical moment arrives, will be seized with panic, and perish helplessly in the streets ; v.$^{28-33}$ is on the great pastoral (Is. 42^{11} 60^7) tribe of *Kedar*, who are to be rudely disturbed in their security, and scattered " to every wind " by Nebuchadnezzar ; v.$^{34-39}$ is on *Elam* (assigned by the title to the beginning of the reign of Zedekiah), against which a fate similar to that of Kedar is predicted.

[250] It is probable that all these prophecies, except the last, belong to the 4th year of Jehoiakim, and reflect the profound impression which Nebuchadnezzar's victory at Carchemish produced upon the prophet. On

the remarkable similarities between the prophecy upon Edom and that of Obadiah, see below, under Obadiah. In the case of Ammon and Elam (49[6. 39]) the prophecy closes with a promise of restoration similar to that given to Moab (48[47]) : comp. 12[15f.].

Schwally and Smend (above, p. 247) argue, upon internal grounds, that c. 46–49 are not Jeremiah's : Giesebr. agrees partly, but admits c. 47, and a nucleus in 46[2-12] 49[7-11]. Against this view, see (at length) Bleeker (above, p. 247), who, however, allows that considerable parts—viz. 46[7-10. 25-28] 48[4-5. 8-9. 14-47] 49[6. 12. 14-17. 34-39]—are interpolated ; Cornill, *Einl.* § 21 (³ § 25). 9–10 ; Wildeboer, § 13 (p. 251 f.). Jeremiah was not the man to regulate the flow of his thought by literary canons ; and care must be taken not to limit arbitrarily either the terms or the manner in which he might express himself.

C. 50–51. A long and impassioned prophecy against *Babylon*, 50[1]–51[58], followed by a short historical notice, 51[59-64a], describing how, when Seraiah—probably the brother of Jeremiah's friend and assistant Baruch—in the 4th year of Zedekiah (B.C. 593) accompanied the king on a journey to Babylon, Jeremiah sent by his hand a scroll, containing a prophecy against the city, with instructions to read it upon his arrival there, and afterwards to sink it in the Euphrates, as a sign that Babylon would sink in like manner, and not rise again. The prophecy itself (50[2ff.]) declares the approaching capture of Babylon, and the speedy end of the power of the Chaldæans ; the time has come for the violence done by them to Israel to be requited (50[11f. 17-20. 33f.] 51[5. 24. 34f. 44. 56]) ; a people from the north, even the Medes, are about to be " stirred up " (cf. Is. 13[17]) against them (50[3. 9. 25. 41ff.] 51[2. 11. 20-23] [Cyrus]) ; again and again the prophet with eager vehemence invites the foe to begin the fray (50[14-16. 21. 26f.] 51[11f. 27f.]), while he bids the exiles escape betimes from the doomed city (50[8] 51[6. 45f. 50]), the future fate of which he contemplates with manifest delight (50[2b. 13. 23f. 35-38. 46] 51[13f. 25ff. 30ff. 33ff. 47ff.]).

It does not seem that this prophecy (50[1]–51[58]) is Jeremiah's. The grounds for this conclusion do not consist in the announcement *per se* which the prophecy contains of the end of the Babylonian power—for this was certainly foreseen by Jer. (25[12] 27[7. 22] 29[10])—or in the phraseology, which has much in common with Jer.'s ; but in the *manner* in which the announcement is made, and especially in the contradiction which it evinces with the position which Jer. is known to have taken in the year to which it is assigned by 51[59]. (1) The standpoint of the prophecy is later than Zedekiah's 4th year. The destruction of the *Temple* is presupposed (50[28] 51[11. 51]) ; the Jews are in exile, suffering for their sins (50[4f. 7. 17. 33] 51[34f.] " hath made me *an empty vessel* ") ; but Jehovah is now ready to pardon and deliver them (50[20. 34] 51[33b. 36]) ; the hour of retribution is at hand for their foes, and they themselves are bidden

prepare to leave Babylon (see the passages cited above). But in B.C. 593 it
was the measure of *Israel's* wickedness which, in Jer.'s estimation, was not
yet filled up ; the Chaldæans had yet to complete against Jerusalem the work
allotted to them [251] by Providence (c. 24, &c.); only when this had been
accomplished does the prophet expect the end of the Babylonian monarchy,
and the restoration of Israel (25^{12} 27^{7} 29^{10}). Thus the *situation* postulated
by the prophecy—Israel's sin forgiven, and the Chaldæans' work accomplished—had *not arrived* while Zedekiah was still reigning : on the other
hand, the coming destruction of Jerusalem, which is foremost in Jer.'s
thoughts throughout the prophecies belonging to Zedekiah's reign, and which
he views as necessarily *preceding* the restoration, is here alluded to as *past*.
(2) The *point of view* is not that of Jer. either in or about the year 593. At
that time, as we know from c. 27–29, Jer. was opposing earnestly the
prophets who were promising that shortly Babylon would fall, and the exiles
be restored ; he was even (c. 29) exhorting the exiles to settle down contentedly in their new home. But the prophet who speaks in c. 50–51, so far
from counselling patience, uses all the arts of language for the purpose of
inspiring the exiles with the hopes of a speedy release, for doing which the
"false prophets" were so severely denounced by Jer. The line of thought
adopted in the prophecy is thus inconsistent with the attitude of Jer. in
B.C. 593. (3) The prophecy is not a *mere* declaration of the end of the
Chaldæan rule, such as Jer. undoubtedly made : it is animated by a temper,
which, if it be Jer.'s, is not adequately accounted for. The vein of strong
feeling which pervades it, the manifest satisfaction with which the prophet
who utters it contemplates, under every imaginable aspect, the fate which he
sees imminent upon Babylon, show it to be the work of one who felt far more
keenly against the Chaldæans than Jer. did, who indeed, after the capture
of Jerusalem, was treated by Nebuchadnezzar with marked consideration
(c. 39, &c.), and who, even when in Egypt, still regarded the Babylonian
king as carrying out the purposes of Providence (43$^{10ff.}$ 44^{30}).* There
breathes in this prophecy the spirit of an Israelite, whose experiences had
been far other than Jer.'s, who had smarted under the vexatious yoke of the
Chaldæans (cf. Is. 47$^{6f.}$ 52^{5}), and whose thoughts were full of vengeance for
the sufferings which his fellow-countrymen had endured at their hands.
Other indications, not sufficient, if they stood alone, to authorise the conclusion thus reached, nevertheless support it. Jer. is not, indeed, like Isaiah,
a master of literary style : but the repetitions and the unmethodical development of the subject which characterise c. 50–51 are both in excess of his
usual manner. Jer. also, it is true, sometimes repeats his own words (p. 276),
but not to the extent which would be the case here if he were the author of
c. 50–51 (50$^{30-32.\ 40-46}$ 51$^{15-19}$).

On the whole, the most probable view of c. 50 f. is the following. The notice in 51^{59-64a}, that Jeremiah took the occasion of

---

* To suppose the prophet inspired to express *emotions* which (to judge
from the general tenor of his book) he did not feel, would imply a very
mechanical theory of inspiration.

Seraiah's visit to Babylon to record by a symbolical act his conviction that the Chaldæan dominion would in time be brought to its end, is thoroughly credible : it is in accordance with Jer.'s [252] manner on other occasions ($13^{1ff.}$ $19^{1ff.}$ $27^{2ff.}$) : and a *general* declaration similar to that contained in v.[62] is perfectly consistent with Jer.'s attitude at the time (25^{12} 29^{10}). The prophecy, 50^2–51^{58}, is the work of a follower of Jeremiah, familiar with his writings, and accustomed to the use of similar phraseology, who wrote no very long time before the fall of Babylon, from the same general standpoint as Is. 13^2–14^{23} c. 40–66. In a later age the prophecy came to be attributed to Jeremiah, and was identified with the "scroll" sent by him to Babylon. In its original form, the notice, $51^{59ff.}$, contained no reference to 50^1–51^{58}, but only to the words written on the scroll sunk in the Euphrates, v.[60] ended at "Babylon" (in the Heb. at אל ספר אחד : notice how awkwardly, in the Hebrew, clause *b* is attached to clause *a*) : when 50^1–51^{58} was incorporated in the volume of Jer.'s prophecies, v.[60b] was added for the purpose of identifying it with the contents of the scroll.*

The superscriptions to the longer independent prophecies in Jer.'s book fall into one or two well-defined types, *from which that in* 50^1 *differs*, which would agree with the conclusion that the prophecy following was not part of the original collection, but came into Jer.'s book by a different channel. The usual types are (1) "The word which came to Jer. from Jehovah (saying)" : 7^1 11^1 18^1 21^1 25^1 *al.*; (2) "That which came (of) the word of Jehovah to Jer." (p. 276, No. 27) : 14^1 46^1 47^1 49^{34}. The subject of a prophecy is also sometimes indicated briefly by the prep. ל : 23^9 46^2 48^1 $49^{1.\ 7.\ 23.\ 28}$; 21^{11} (?).

In 51^{64} the clause "and they shall be weary," which is evidently out of place where it stands, is repeated from v.[58]—either through some error, or (Budde) by the compiler, who prefixed it to the note, "Thus far are the words of Jeremiah," as an indication that he understood these "words" to extend, not as far as v.[59-64a], but only to ויעפו, the last word of the preceding prophecy.

C. 52. Historical account of the capture of Jerusalem by the Chaldæans, and exile of the inhabitants.

This narrative is excerpted by the compiler of the Book of Jeremiah from 2 Ki. 24^{18}–25^{30}—with the omission of 2 Ki. 25^{22-26} (which had either not yet been introduced into the text of Kings, or, being simply condensed from Jer.

---

* See, further, Tiele, *Bab.-Ass. Gesch.* p. 481 f.; and the careful discussion of Kuenen, § 57. Sayce's reasons (*Monuments*, pp. 484 ff., 521) for dating the prophecy before 561 are far from cogent, especially as he now (*Acad.* Sept. 7, 1895, p. 189) places Kastarit under Esarhaddon I., a century earlier.

40[7-9] 41[1-2. 17f.] 42[1] 43[3ff.], did not need to be repeated), and the addition of Jer. 52[28-30] (though these verses, which are not in the LXX, and the chronology of which differs from that of v.[12], were perhaps not introduced till a later stage in the redaction of the book) from some other source—on account, no doubt, of its containing detailed particulars of the manner in which Jer.'s principal and most constant [253] prediction was fulfilled. The *text* of this section has, in several places, been preserved here more purely than in Kings.

*The two texts of Jeremiah.** In the Book of Jeremiah the text of the LXX differs more widely from the Hebrew than is the case in any other part of the OT., even in Sam., Kings, or Ezekiel. In the text of the LXX, as compared with the Hebrew, there are very numerous omissions, sometimes of single words, sometimes of particular clauses or passages, there are occasionally additions, there are variations of expression, there are also transpositions. The number of words in the Hebrew text not represented in the LXX has been calculated at 2700, or one-eighth of the entire book. Very many of these omissions are, however, unimportant, consisting only of such words as the title *the prophet* attached to the name Jeremiah, or the parenthetic *Saith Jehovah*, &c.; but others are more substantial, as 10[6-8. 10] 11[7-8] (except v.[8b] "but they did them not"), 29[14] (except "and I will be found of you"), [16-20] 33[14-20] 39[4-13] 52[28-30]: sometimes, also, a chapter, though the substance is not materially altered, appears in a briefer form in the LXX (as c. 27. 28). The most considerable transposition is in the different place assigned to the prophecies on foreign nations (p. 264, *note*): the order of these prophecies among themselves is also changed. Different causes have been assigned in explanation of these variations. By some they have been attributed to the incompetence and arbitrariness of the LXX translators; by others they have been supposed to arise from the fact that the existing Hebrew text, and the text from which the LXX translation was made, exhibit *two different recensions* of Jeremiah's writings. A careful comparison of the two texts in the light of (*a*) Hebrew idiom, (*b*) intrinsic probability, shows that both

* See F. C. Movers, *De utriusque recens. vatic. Jeremiæ Græc. Alex. et Masor. indole et origine*, 1837; Hitzig, p. xv ff.; Graf, p. xl ff.; A. Scholz, *Der Mass. Text u. die LXX-Uebers. des Buches Jer.* 1875; E. C. Workman, *The Text of Jeremiah*, Edinburgh, 1889, with the reviews by the present writer in the *Expositor*, May 1889, and by H. P. Smith in the *Journ. of Bibl. Lit.* 1890, p. 107 ff.; Kuenen, § 58 (a very fair and impartial statement of the question); Giesebrecht, pp. xix–xxxiv; A. W. Streane, *The double Text of Jeremiah*, 1896.

these views contain elements of truth, though neither is true exclusively; the variations of the LXX are in part "recensional," *i.e.* they are due to the fact that the Hebrew text used by the translators deviated in some particulars from that which we at present possess; but in part, also, they are due to [254] the faulty manner in which the translators executed their work. The claims of each text to represent the prophet's autograph have been greatly exaggerated by their respective advocates; * *on the whole*, the Massoretic text deserves the preference; but it is impossible to uphold the unconditional superiority of either. To determine *which* readings of the LXX are more original than those of the Hebrew is often a task of no small difficulty and delicacy; and commentators and critics differ accordingly.

It is obviously impossible for the writer to enter here into details: he must content himself with the two general observations (1) that there are certainly many individual cases in which the purer reading has been preserved by the LXX; (2) that it is at least probable that there are passages in which the text has been glossed, or expanded, in the Hebrew, and is expressed by the LXX in its more original form (see examples in *QPB.*[3]). Thus in c. 25 words are omitted in LXX in v.[1. 2. 6. 7. 9. 11-13. 14](wholly) [18. 20. 24-26. 29. 33]. With respect to some of these, opinions may differ; but v.[18 *end*] "as it is this day" clearly cannot have been part of the original text of B.C. 604 (25[1]), but must have been added after the fulfilment. In c. 27–29 the omissions in LXX (or additions in the Heb., as the case may be) are, from some cause, peculiarly numerous: Kuenen, § 54. 6, here prefers the LXX almost throughout (except $34^{10\text{-}12}$ LXX = $27^{12\text{-}15}$ Heb., and 36 (29) [24-32], where the translators have entirely missed the sense); in c. 27 W. R. Smith, *OTJC.* p. 113 ff. (ed. 2, p. 104 ff.), also urges strongly the superiority of the LXX (cf. p. 273).

It is remarked by Kuenen that the two texts of Jer. are not so much two recensions, as the same recension *in different stages of its history*. The different positions of the foreign prophecies in the two texts may be accounted for by various hypotheses, which cannot here be discussed: in all probability, however, their position in the LXX (*in* c. 25) is less original than their position in the Hebrew (*after* it; cf. pp. 271, 272).

The redaction of the Book of Jeremiah, though details must necessarily in many cases remain hypothetical, must have passed

* Especially by Graf and Keil on the one side, and by Workman on the other. The last-named scholar has formed a raise view of the method followed by the translators, and has made, in consequence, the great mistake of not distinguishing between deviations due only to the translators, and those having their source in the MSS. used by them; thus in his elaborate "Synopsis of Variations," the majority were never in any Hebrew MS., but are simply imaginary originals of the translators' paraphrases.

through at least five distinct stages.* The *first* of these stages will have been represented by the roll of Jehoiakim's fourth year, in which the prophet, dictating to Baruch, committed for the first time to writing the prophecies delivered by him during the preceding twenty-three years (above, p. 249). The *second* stage was represented by the roll of Jehoiakim's fifth year, in which the same prophecies, after the first roll had been burnt, were re-written, *with many additions* (36^{22}): this roll, it may be reasonably supposed, embraced (allowing for possible glosses and expansions, introduced subsequently) $1^{1-2.\ 4-19}$; c. 2–6; $7^{1}-9^{26}$; 10^{17-25}; 11^{1-8}; $11^{9}-12^{6}$; $21^{11}-22^{19}$; c. 25; $46^{1}-49^{33}$.† The *third* stage will have corresponded to the title 1^{3}, and have included in addition the prophecies, delivered during the seventeen years following, down to the capture of Jerusalem in 586: for instance, c. 13; 21^{1-10}; $22^{20}-23^{8}$; 23^{9-40}; c. 24; c. 30–33 (in the main); 49^{34-39}; 51^{59-64a}. In the *fourth* stage, the narratives relating to events after B.C. 586 will have been added, viz. 38^{28b} $39^{3.\ 14}$, c. 40–44: to what stages the other biographical narratives, viz. c. 26, 35, 36, 45 (relating to Jehoiakim's reign), and c. 27–29, 34, $37^{1}-38^{28a}$ 39^{15-18} (Zedekiah's), are to be referred, must remain uncertain; the chronological disorder makes it improbable that they were all added at one and the same stage. To a *fifth* stage—spread, probably, over a series of years, and not completed by a single hand—will belong such additions as 10^{1-16} $50^{1}-51^{58}$; $39^{1-2.\ 4-13}$ (v.$^{1.\ 2.\ 4-10}$ abridged from 2 Ki. $25^{1.\ 3.\ 4-12}$), c. 52 (the historical appendix, excerpted from 2 Ki. $24^{18ff.}$, and presupposing consequently the completion of the Book of Kings), as also the insertions, or glosses, which are traceable, with greater or less probability, in various parts of the book (cf. pp. 270, 272 f.). The fourth stage will hardly have been completed till towards the close of the exile, and the fifth not till considerably later. Some of the biographical narratives may be the work of Baruch, though he will hardly have been responsible for the imperfect chronological order in which many of them are now arranged. The large amount of variation between the LXX and the Massoretic text constitutes an independent ground for supposing that, in

---

* Cf. Kautzsch, *Abriss der Gesch. des alttest. Schrifttums* (above, p. 3), p. 177 f. (in the separate reprint of 1897, p. 75 f.).

† Possibly also c. 14–17, 18–20 formed part of the same roll; but these prophecies *may* have been added in the third stage.

some cases, the writings composing the Book of Jer. circulated
for a while in separate small collections,* in which variations
might more easily arise than after they were collected into a
volume. As regards the position of individual prophecies, it
seems that as the original nucleus (the roll of Jehoiakim's fifth
year) was gradually enlarged, the prophecies relating to Judah
were placed (as a rule) *before* those dealing [255] with foreign
nations (c. 25, 46¹–49³³), while the narratives which were rather of
a biographical character were made to follow c. 25, the foreign
prophecies themselves being kept at the end. C. 30–33 (prophecies of restoration) may have been placed where they now
stand, on account of their being connected (like c. 27–29, 34)
with the reign of Zedekiah: c. 45 (supplement to 36¹⁻⁸) may
have been placed after c. 37–44 (which form a tolerably continuous narrative), and so separated from c. 36, on account of
its subordinate character. 49³⁴⁻³⁹ (on Elam), though belonging
to Zedekiah's reign, would naturally be attached to the other
foreign prophecies: the same would be the case with c. 50–51
(Babylon). Even so, however, there are several prophecies of
which the position remains unexplained: it is clear that in
many particulars the arrangement of the book is due to causes
respecting the nature of which we must confess our ignorance.

That the text of Jer. was liable to modification in the process of redaction
may be inferred, partly from some of the variations in the LXX (cf. p. 270),
partly from other indications. Thus 25¹³ᵇ cannot have been written by Jer.,
as it stands, in 604 (25¹), but must have been added by one who had the whole
book before him: for "even all that is written in this book" presupposes
a prophecy against Babylon; and c. 50 f. (or the prophecy implied [256] in
51⁵⁹ᶠ·) is expressly dated some years afterwards. And the verses 39¹ᶠ· ⁴⁻¹³,
being *abridged* from 2 Ki. 25, can have been inserted where they now stand
only after the compilation of the Book of Kings was completed. And this,
if 2 Ki. 25²²⁻²⁶ formed part of the original text of Kings (p. 268 f.), was subsequent to the composition of Jer. 40–43; so that in that case the existence
of *stages* in the formation of the present Book of Jeremiah will be palpable.

It ought to be stated that, in addition to 10¹⁻¹⁶ 39⁴⁻¹³ (p. 264), 50¹–51⁵⁸
(which are generally agreed not to be from Jeremiah's hand), there are several
other passages in Jer., mostly short ones, which, in some cases on the ground

---

* Thus c. 27–29, to judge from the unusual orthography of some of the
proper names (ירמיה, not ירמיהו, and some other names similarly; *Nebuchadnezzar*, not as commonly (and correctly) in Jer., *Nebuchadrezzar*), probably
have a history of their own (if we but knew it), and reached the compiler
through some special channel (comp. p. 270).

that they are not recognised in the LXX, in others on the ground that they are repetitions of previous passages, or that they interrupt the connexion, or contain ideas foreign to Jer.'s usual point of view (so especially 17^{19-27} 33^{17-26}), are considered by recent critics to be additions to the original text of the book. Thus Kuenen (partly after Stade, *ZATW.* 1883, p. 15 f., *Gesch.* i. 646 f.) treated as such $16^{14f.}$ (§ 53. 19), 17^{19-27} (§ 52. 15, 16), 29^{16-20} (§ 54. 6: not in LXX), $30^{10f.}$ (not in LXX) $= 46^{27f.}$ (in LXX : § 54. 25 ; 56. 7), 30^{22-24} ("perhaps," § 54. 23 : v.^{22} not in LXX), 31^{35-37} (§ 54. 25), $33^{2f.}$ (§ 54. 20), 33^{14-26} (§ 54. 21 ; not in LXX) ; in c. 25, he read (§ 56. 1–3) v.$^{1. 2. 7. 9a. 18 end}$ [above, p. 270] $^{20. 24. 25a}$ as in LXX, omitting besides v.$^{11b-14. 26b}$ (v.$^{14. 26b}$ omitted also in LXX) ; in $27^{7. 8b. 16-17. 19-22}$ he preferred (§ 54. 6) the shorter text of the LXX ; he regarded $9^{23f. 25f.}$ also as "very doubtful" (§ 53. 11) ; and allowed (§ 56. 9) that c. 48 might be in parts interpolated, esp. in v.$^{40-46}$ (v.$^{40a\beta b. 41b. 45-47}$ not in LXX) ; but he defended (against Stade) $3^{17f.}$ (§ 52. 10), 5^{20-22} (*ib.*), 32^{17-23} (§ 54. 22). The two most recent writers on Jer., Cornill and Giesebrecht, go, however, much beyond Kuenen in the assumption of such additions, each, namely, rejecting several other passages independently, and agreeing in the case of 1^3 $3^{17f.}$ 15^{11-14} $16^{14f.}$ $17^{12. 19-27}$ 21^{11-12} 23^{19-20} $30^{10f. 22-24.}$ $31^{10-14. 35-37}$ $32^{1b. 2b-5. 17-23}$ $33^{2f. 11a\beta}$ ("the voice of them . . . house of Jehovah"), 33^{14-26} $46^{27f.}$, and (largely) in 25^{1-26} (Corn. here, in particular, reads v.^{11b} as in LXX, and omits v.$^{12. 13b}$ (from *even all*) $^{14. 18 end. 26b}$; Giesebr. reads v.^{11b} as in the Heb., and omits v.$^{12-14. 18 end. 26b}$) ; in c. 27 Corn. omits (with LXX) v.^{7} and much of v.$^{19-22}$, while Giesebr. omits v.^{7} only : in c. 29 Corn. omits v.$^{2. 16-20}$ (not in LXX) $^{22-31}$ (from *saying* to *captivity, saying*), while Giesebr. retains here v.$^{16-20}$, neutralizing the difficulty which these verses occasion by placing them (with Luc. and other MSS. of LXX) *before* v.^{15}. In view of the omissions and variations in the LXX, and of the disarrangement which manifestly prevails in parts of Jer.'s prophecies (pp. 269–272), the possibility of such insertions must be granted ; though it may be greatly doubted whether there are sufficient grounds for holding them to be as numerous as Corn. and Giesebr. suppose (cf. König, *Einl.* § 65. 2b) : it may have been characteristic of Jer. to repeat himself (as it certainly was to be diffuse), as well as to follow the impulse of his feeling in introducing passages not in strict logical harmony with the context. The decision in individual cases is, however, sometimes difficult, and hard to keep free from subjective considerations. In c. 25 the critical verses are v.$^{11-14. 26b}$, the chief question being whether the original prophecy spoke here more (Heb. text) or less (LXX) distinctly, or (Kuen. Corn. &c.) not at all, of the future close of the Babylonian empire (cf. p. 260) ; in 27^{19-22} (p. 270) it is whether Jer. foretold the restoration, or only the captivity, of the furniture and vessels of the Temple, which had been left by Nebuchadnezzar in 597.

Jeremiah's was a susceptible, deeply emotional nature. The adverse course of events impresses him profoundly; and he utters without reserve the emotions which in consequence are stirred within him. The trials which he experienced in the discharge of his prophetic office, the persecution and detraction

which he encountered from those to whom his words were unwelcome, the disappointments which, in spite of the promises
given him at his call ($1^{10.\ 18}$), were nevertheless his lot in life,
the ruin to which, as he saw too truly, his country was hastening,
overpowered his sensitive, highly-strung organism : he breaks out
into bitter lamentations and complaints, he calls for vengeance
upon his persecutors, he accuses the Almighty of injustice, he
wishes himself unborn.* Yet he does not flinch from the call of
duty : he contends fearlessly against the forces opposed to him ;
he struggles even to avert the inevitable.   Love for his country
is powerful within him : through two long chapters (c. 14 f.) he
pleads on behalf of his erring nation : the aim of his life is to
lead his people to better things.   But the sharp conflict has left
its scar upon his soul.   Isaiah's voice never falters with emotion :
Jeremiah bewails with tears of grief the times in which his lot is
cast ; † the strain of his thoughts imparts naturally to his periods
a melancholy cadence ; in pathetic tones he bids his country
prepare to meet its doom.‡

And thus the tragic pathos of Jeremiah's life is reflected in his
book.   His writings disclose to us his inmost thoughts.   And as
the thoughts of an emotional spirit resent all artificial restraint,
so Jeremiah's style is essentially artless ; its only adornment consisting in the figures which a poetical temperament, in an Eastern
clime, would spontaneously choose as the vehicle of feeling.
His prophecies have neither the artistic finish of those of Amos
or Isaiah, nor the laboured completeness of Ezekiel's.   In his
[257] treatment of a subject he obeys no literary canons ; he
pursues it just as long as his feelings flow, or the occasion
prompts him.   His language lacks the terseness and energy
which is generally characteristic of the earlier prophets : sentences
are drawn out at greater length ; even where the style is poetical,
the parallelism of thought is less perfectly sustained ; and there
is a decided tendency to adopt the rhetorical prose style of
Deuteronomy (*e.g.* c. 7, 11, 34, 44), by which it is evident that
Jeremiah is greatly influenced.   More than any other prophet,
also, Jeremiah not only uses favourite phrases, but (like other

---

* 11^{20} 12^3 $15^{10ff.}$ 17^{15-18} $18^{19ff.}$ $20^{7ff.\ 14ff.}$.

† 4^{19} $8^{18}-9^1$ $10^{19ff.}$ 13^{17} 23^9.

‡ *E.g.* 6^{26} 7^{29} $9^{17f.}$ $22^{10.\ 20ff.}$: cf. $3^{14.\ 22}$ 4^{14} 6^8 31^{15-20}.   Comp. further
Wellh. *Isr. u. Jüd. Gesch.*, chap. x. (ed. I, pp. 103–106).

writers of the Deuteronomic school) is apt to *repeat* clauses and combinations of words, and sometimes (p. 276 f.) even whole verses. His foreign prophecies (c. 46–49), though not so striking as Isaiah's, display considerable variety of imagery and expression, as well as greater poetic vigour than most of his other writings. By his conception of the "New Covenant" ($31^{31\text{-}34}$), he surpasses in spirituality and profundity of insight every other prophet of the Old Testament.

Expressions characteristic of Jeremiah :

1. רעים *shepherds*, fig. of kings or rulers : 2^8 3^{15} 10^{21} 12^{10} 22^{22} $23^{1.\ 2.\ 4}$ $25^{34\text{-}36}$ 50^6. A favourite term in Jer., even when the figure of the flock is not explicitly drawn out.

2. The type of sentence, expressive of mingled pathos and surprise : מרוע . . . אם . . . ה $2^{14.\ 31}$ $8^{4f.\ 19.\ 22}$ 14^{19} 22^{28} 49^1↑ ; cf. 30^6.

3. משובה, משובות *backsliding(s)* : 2^{19} 3^{22} (=Hos 14^5) 5^6 8^5 14^7, Hos. 11^7, Pr. 1^{32} : in the combination משובה ישראל, $3^{6.\ 8.\ 11.\ 12}$.↑

4. פנה ערף ולא פנים *to turn the neck and not the face* : 2^{27} 18^{17} 32^{33}.↑

5. לקח מוסר *to receive correction* : 2^{30} 5^3 7^{28} 17^{23} 32^{33} 35^{13}, Zeph. $3^{2.\ 7}$, Pr. 1^3 8^{10} 24^{32}.↑

6. עלה על לב lit. *to come up upon the heart* (often ‖ to *remember*) : 3^{16} 7^{31} 19^5 32^{35} 44^{21b}. Rare besides, Is. 65^{17}, 2 Ki. 12^5.

7. שרירות *stubbornness* : 3^{17} 7^{24} 9^{13} 11^8 13^{10} 16^{12} 18^{12} 23^{17}, Dt. 29^{18}, Ps. 81^{13}.↑ Always followed by "of heart".

8. *From the land of the north* : (as the place whence evil or invasion arises) 6^{22} 10^{22} 50^9 : *from the north*, 1^{14} 4^6 6^1 13^{20} 15^{12} 46^{20} 47^2 $50^{3.\ 41}$ 51^{48} ; cf. 1^{15} $25^{9.\ 26}$ $46^{6.\ 10.\ 24}$: (as the place of Israel's banishment, whence it will be brought back) 3^{18} (cf. v.^{12}), 16^{15} 23^8 31^8.

9. *Men* (איש) *of Judah and inhabitants of Jerusalem* : 4^4 $11^{2.\ 9}$ 17^{25} 18^{11} 32^{32} 35^{13} 36^{31}. Elsewhere only 2 Ki. 23^2=2 Chr. 34^{30}, Dan. 9^7 (a reminiscence from Jer.: cf. 32^{37}).

[258] 10. שבר גדול *great destruction* : 4^6 6^1 14^{17} 48^3 50^{22} 51^{54}, Zeph. 1^{10}.↑

11. An idea strengthened by the negation of its opposite : 4^{22} 7^{24} 21^{10} (*for evil and not for good* : so 39^{16} 44^{27}, Am. 9^4) 24^{6b} 42^{10} (cf. Ps. 28^5). Cf. above No. 4. Not common elsewhere.

12. כלה עשה *to make a full end* : 4^{27} $5^{10.\ 18}$ 30^{11}=46^{28}.

13. מביא (or הנני אנכי, הנה הנני) *Behold I bring* . . . ! 5^{15} 6^{19} 11^{11} $19^{3.\ 15}$ 31^8 35^{17} 39^{16} 45^5 49^5, 1 Ki. 14^{10} 21^{21}, 2 Ki. 21^{12} 22^{16}=2 Ch. 34^{24} (cf. above, p. 201, No. 27). In other prophets, only three or four times in Ez.

14. [ם]עֵת פְּקֻדְּתִי *the time that I visit them* (*thee, him*) : 6^{15} 49^8 50^{31} : in the slightly varied forms עֵת פְּקֻדָּתָם *the time of their visitation*, 8^{12} 10^{15} (= 51^{18}) 46^{21} 50^{27} ; שנת פקדתם *the year of their visitation*, 11^{23} 23^{12} 48^{44}.↑

15. מגור מסביב *Terror on every side* : 6^{25} $20^{3.\ 10}$ 46^5 49^{29}, Ps. 31^{14}.↑ Cf. Lam. 2^{22} *my terrors on every side*.

16. אשר נקרא שמי עליו *over which my name is called* (in token of ownership) : of the temple or city, $7^{10.\ 11.\ 14.\ 30}$ 25^{29} 32^{34} 34^{15} ; of the people, 14^9 ;

of Jeremiah himself, 15^{16}. Similarly Dt. 28^{10}, 1 Ki. 8^{43} (=2 Ch. 6^{33}), 2 Ch. 7^{14}, Am. 9^{12}, Is. 63^{19}, Dan. 9$^{18. 19}$ (the original meaning of the phrase may be learnt from 2 Sa. 12^{28}; cf. Is. 4^{1b}).↑

17. . . . . הַשְׁכֵּם *rising up and* . . . (speaking) 7^{13} 25^3 35^{14}: (sending) 7^{25} 25^4 26^5 29^{19} 35^{15} 44^4, 2 Ch. 36^{15}; (testifying) 11^7; (teaching) 32^{33}.↑

18. *The cities of Judah and the streets of Jerusalem*: 7$^{17. 34}$ 11^6 33^{10} 44$^{6. 9}$ (with "land of Judah"), 17^{21}: *streets of Jerusalem*, also, 5^1 11^{13} 14^{16}. Not expressions used by other prophets.

19. המה און *to incline the ear*: 7$^{24. 26}$ 11^8 17^{23} 25^4 34^{14} 35^{15} 44^5 (not in Dt., or in any other prophet, except Is. 55^3).

20. *Behold, the days come, and* . . .: 7^{32} 9^{24} 16^{14} 19^6 23$^{5. 7}$ 30^3 31$^{27. 31. 38}$ 33^{14} 48^{12} 49^2 51$^{47. 52}$. Elsewhere only Am. 4^2 8^{11} 9^{13}, 1 Sa. 2^{31}, 2 Ki. 20^{17} = Isa. 39^6.

21. *The voice of mirth and the voice of gladness, the voice of the bridegroom and the voice of the bride*: 7^{34} 16^9 25^{10} 33^{11}.

22. מעון תנים *habitation of jackals*: 9^{11} (Heb. ^{10}) 10^{22} 49^{33} 51^{37}.↑

23. קצוצי פאה *corner-clipt* (*i.e.* shaved about the temples: an epithet of certain Arab tribes): 9^{25} 25^{23} 49^{32}.

24. A verb strengthened by the addition of its passive: 11^{18} (הודיעני וָאֵדָע) 17^{14} 20^7 31$^{4. 18}$.

25. *The sword, the pestilence, and the famine* (sometimes in changed order): 14^{12} 21$^{7. 9}$ 24^{10} 27$^{8. 13}$ 29$^{17. 18}$ 32$^{24. 36}$ 34^{17} 38^2 42$^{17. 22}$ 44^{13}; *the sword and the famine*: 5^{12} 11^{22} 14$^{13. 15. 16. 18}$ 16^4 18^{21} 42^{16} 44$^{12. 18. 27}$; cf. 15^2.

[259] 26. הנני פוקד על *Behold I visit upon* . . .: 11^{22} 23^2 29^{32} 46^{25} 50^{18} (אל). The verb itself is also much more frequent in Jer. than in any other prophet.

27. . . . . אשר היה דבר י״י אל (a very peculiar type of sentence: Ewald, *Syntax*, § 334^a): 14^1 46^1 47^1 49^{34}.↑

28. לועוה לכל ממלכות הארץ *for a shuddering unto all kingdoms of the earth*: 15^4 24^9 29^{18} 34^{17}. From. Dt. 28^{25}.

29. Sentences of the type "fishers, and they shall fish them": 16^{16} 23^4 48^{12} 51^2.

30. *And I will kindle a fire in* . . . *and it shall devour* . . .: 17^{27b} 21^{14b} 49^{27} 50^{32b}. From the refrain in Am. 1^{14}, varied from "And I will *send*," &c., Am. 1$^{4. 7. 10. 12}$ 2$^{2. 5}$, Hos. 8^{14}.↑

31. *To return each one from his evil way*: 18^{11} 25^5 26^3 35^{15} 36$^{3. 7}$, Jon. 3^8. Cf. 1 Ki. 13^{33}, 2 Ki. 17^{13}, 2 Ch. 7^{14}, Ez. 13^{22} 33^{11}, Jon. 3^{10}, Zech. 1^4.

32. *His* (*thy*) *soul shall be to him* (*thee*) *for a prey*: 21^9 38^2 39^{18}: cf. 45^5.

33. *Thus saith Jehovah* (often + *of hosts*), *the God of Israel*: a standing formula with Jeremiah, as 6$^{6. 9}$ 7$^{3. 21}$ 11^3 &c., but extremely rare in other prophets (not unfrequently, without *of hosts*, in Kings).

The principal cases of the *repetition* of passages, noted on p. 275, are the following (sometimes with slight variations in the phraseology):—1^{10b} and 18$^{7b. 9b}$.—1$^{18a. 19}$ 15^{20}.—2^{15b} 4^{7b}.—2^{28b} 11^{13a}.—4^{4b} 21^{12b}.—4^6 6^1.—5$^{9. 29}$ 9^9 (Heb. ^{8}).—6$^{13-15}$ 8$^{10-12}$.—6$^{22-24}$ 50$^{41-43}$.—6^{22b} 26^{32b}.—7^{16} 11^{14a}.—7$^{23a. 24-25}$ 11^{4b}.

8a. 7b.—7^{31-33} 19^{5. 6. 11b. 7b}.—8^{2b} 16^4 25^{33b}.—8^{15} 14^{19b}.—9^{15b} (Heb. 14b) 23^{15}.—9^{16b} (Heb. 15b) 49^{37b}.—10^{12-16} 51^{15-19}.—11^{20} 20^{12}.—11^{23b} 23^{12h} 48^{44b} 49^{8b}.—15^{2b} 43^{11b}.—15^{13-14} 17^{3. 4b}.—16^{14f.} 23^{7f.}.—17^{20} 19^{3a}.—17^{25} 22^4.—19^8 49^{17} (Edom) 50^{13b} (Babylon); cf. 18^{16}.—21^9 38^2.—21^{13f.} 50^{31f.}.—23^{5f.} 33^{15f.}.—23^{19f.} 30^{23f.}.—30^{10f.} 46^{27f.}.—31^{36f.} ; cf. 33^{20f.}.—46^{21b} 50^{97b}.—48^{40. 41b} 49^{22}.—49^{18} 50^{40}.—49^{19-21} 50^{44-46}.—49^{26} 50^{30}.—50^{13b} 19^8 49^{17}.—50^{27b} 46^{21b}.—50^{30} 49^{26}.—50^{31-32} 21^{13-14}.—50^{40} 49^{18}.—50^{41-43} 6^{22-24}.—50^{44-46} 49^{19-21}.—51^{15-19} 10^{12-16}. See also above, Nos. 21, 30. It is, of course, a question whether all these are due to Jer. himself: if the view adopted above be correct, this will certainly not be the case with those in c. 50-51; and probably it is not so in some of the others as well. The instances of the repetition of shorter clauses and phrases are too numerous to specify.

CHAPTER V.

EZEKIEL.

LITERATURE.—H. Ewald in *Die Propheten des AB.s* (vol. iv. of the translation); F. Hitzig in the *Kgf. Exeg. Handb.* 1847, ed. 2 (rewritten) by R. Smend, 1880 [does not altogether supersede Hitzig's work]; C. F. Keil, *Der Proph. Ez.* 1868, (ed. 2) 1882; C. H. Cornill, *Der Proph. Ez. geschildert*, 1882, and *Das Buch des Proph. Ez.* 1886 (Prolegomena, and *apparatus criticus*, remarkably thorough : text apt to be arbitrary); C. von Orelli (in Strack and Zöckler's *Kgf. Kommentar*), 1888; L. Gautier, *La mission du proph. Ezech.* 1891; A. B. Davidson in the *Cambridge Bible for Schools*, 1892 (to be recommended); D. H. Müller, *Ezechiel-Studien*, Wien, 1894; J. Skinner (in the "Expositor's Bible"), 1895. On the Temple in c. 40–42, &c., see also E. Kühn in the *Stud. u. Krit.* 1882, pp. 601–688. The Heb. text of Ez. is often corrupt, and needs correction from the LXX (cf. *QPB.*[3]).

Ezekiel, the son of Buzi, was one of the captives * who were carried with Jehoiachin in 597 into Babylonia, and was settled with others at Tel-abib (3^{15}), by the river Chebar ($1^{1.3}$ 3^{15} &c.). He was a priest, and as such belonged to the aristocracy of Jerusalem, who formed the bulk of the first captivity under Jehoiachin. The exiles at Tel-abib must have formed a considerable community. Though their circumstances could hardly have been affluent, they do not appear to have been in actual want: Ezekiel lived in his own "house" (3^{24} 8^1 $12^{3ff.}$), where the elders of the Israelites are represented as coming to sit and listen to his words (8^1; cf. 14^1 20^1); and the houses of others are alluded to, 33^{30} (cf. Jer. 29^5). It was in the fifth year of the exile of Jehoiachin (B.C. 592) that Ezekiel received his prophetic call ($1^{2ff.}$); and the latest date in his book (29^{17}) is 22 years afterwards (B.C. 570).

The home of Ezekiel's prophetic life was thus on the banks of

---

* He reckons by the years of "*our* captivity," 33^{21} 40^1. The epoch from which the "30th year," 1^1, is dated, is uncertain.

coils!

the Chebar. There he watched from a distance the toils closing round Jerusalem; and there he declared, in every variety of symbolism and imagery, the approaching fall of the city, the ruin of ancient Israel (c. 1-24). Israel's chief crime is its idolatry. [261] This has vitiated its history from the beginning (c. 16. 20. 23), and it is rife in it even now. It would seem that in this judgment Ezekiel is not wholly just to the past, and that he has transferred to it unconsciously the associations of the present. But be that as it may, the corruption of Jerusalem is incurable now; and therefore, as he repeatedly insists, Jerusalem must perish. But even the exiles fall far short of what they should be; exile has not yet wrought upon them the moral change (Hos. 2$^{14f.}$) which it was to effect. Hence his conviction that further judgments were imminent for them in the future: and his anxiety to win at least the souls of individuals (3$^{16ff.}$ 33$^{6ff.}$), who might form the nucleus of the purified Israel of the future. His advances were received with coldness: he was even, as it seems, obliged to refrain from speaking openly among the exiles, and to confine himself to addressing those who visited him specially in his own house (3$^{24f.}$; cf. c. 8. 14. 20), until the fall of Jerusalem sealed the truth of his predictions, and assured for him a credit which otherwise he would never have attained (24^{27} 33^{22}). The antagonism between Ezekiel and the exiles is manifest; he addresses them repeatedly as a "rebellious house" (see p. 297). How they felt towards him, and how he viewed them, appears further from such passages as 12$^{21ff.}$ 14$^{1ff.}$ 20$^{1ff.}$. Nevertheless, like Jeremiah (p. 260), he fixed his hopes for the future upon them: Zedekiah and the Jews in Jerusalem he gave up entirely (9$^{9f.}$ c. 12. 17$^{1-21}$ 21$^{25-27}$ c. 22): the exiles, when purged, would form the foundation of a better Israel in the future (11$^{17ff.}$ 17$^{22-24}$ 20$^{37f.}$ 36$^{25ff.}$).

The Book of Ezekiel consists of three sections, dealing with three different subjects:—I. c. 1-24. The approaching fall of Jerusalem; II. c. 25-32. Prophecies on foreign nations; III. c. 33-48. Israel's future restoration.

The dates of the several prophecies are in many cases stated with precision. No critical question arises in connexion with the authorship of the book, the whole from beginning to end bearing unmistakably the stamp of a single mind.

I. C. 1-24. The approaching fall of Jerusalem.

1. C. 1–3²¹. Ezekiel's call, and the beginnings of his ministry. In c. 1 Ezekiel relates how in the fifth year of his [262] exile (= B.C. 592) he fell into a prophetic trance or ecstasy;* and describes at length the vision which he then saw.

Out of a storm-cloud appearing in the north there gradually emerged the likeness of four living creatures (cherubim), each with four wings and four faces, and all moving harmoniously together, v.⁵⁻¹⁴. Looking more closely, he perceived that they enclosed a kind of quadrangular chariot, resting on four wheels, which had an independent motion of their own, though always in perfect harmony with that of the four cherubim, for one spirit actuated both, v.¹⁵⁻²¹; the four cherubim supported on their heads a firmament, v.²²⁻²⁵; and on the firmament was a throne, with a Divine Form seated upon it.

It is the supreme majesty of Jehovah which thus takes shape in the prophet's imagination; and it approaches "from the north" (not from Zion), as an omen that His abode is no longer in the city of His choice (cf. also Jer. 1¹³⁻¹⁵).

The main elements of the symbolism are suggested, no doubt, partly by the two colossal cherubim in the Temple at Jerusalem, partly by the composite winged figures which formed such an impressive feature in the palaces of Babylonia; but the prophet's imagination—the faculty which, when the outer senses, as in an ecstasy, are dormant, is abnormally active—combines the materials with which, while in a waking state, observation or reflection had stored his mind, into a new form,† which both as a whole and in its individual parts is, no doubt, meant to be significant (*e.g.* the four hands, one on each side of each cherub, and the wheels full of eyes, to symbolize the universality of the Divine presence).

2¹⁻⁷. Ezekiel hears the voice of Jehovah speaking from the throne, and commissioning him to be the prophet of His people, though at the same time warning him of the opposition and ill-success which he is likely to encounter. Nevertheless, he is bidden not to fear; and after the commission to preach has been repeated to him in a symbolic form, 2⁸–3³, he is encouraged with the further assurance that he will be enabled to bear up against his opponents, 3⁴⁻¹¹ (comp. Jer. 1). Hereupon the vision leaves him, v.¹²⁻¹⁴, and he proceeds to the scene of his mission among the exiles, v.¹⁵. After seven days he is commanded to com-

---

* 1³ᵇ "the hand of Jehovah came there upon him,"—a phrase describing the sense of overmastery by a power beyond their own control, of which the prophets were conscious when seized by the prophetic trance: cf. 3¹⁴· ²² 8¹ 33²² 37¹ 40¹, Isa. 8¹¹, Jer. 15¹⁷, 2 Ki. 3¹⁵.

† Lee, *Inspiration of Holy Scripture* (ed. 4), pp. 173–183.

mence his ministry, and is reminded of the nature of the [263] responsibility placed upon him: he is a "watchman," appointed to warn every sinner of the danger in which he stands, and, in case he fails to do so, liable to bear the consequences of his neglect, v.$^{16-21}$.

2. 3^{22}–c. 7. The impending ruin of Judah and Jerusalem.

3^{22-27}. Ezek. in a second trance sees again the same vision as in c. 1. On account of the temper in which the people will meet him, he is released temporarily from the obligation of speaking openly among them as a prophet (cf. 24^{27} 33^{22}).

C. 4–5. The destruction of Jerusalem portrayed symbolically. (*a*) 4^{1-3}, the prophet, representing *Jehovah*, lays mimic siege to Jerusalem; (*b*) 4^{4-17}, representing *the people*, he enacts figuratively the privations undergone by them during the siege, and the misery to be experienced by them in exile afterwards; (*c*) 5^{1-4}, representing *the city*, he significantly shows how the inhabitants (symbolized by his hair) will in different ways be scattered and perish. There follows, 5^{5-17}, an exposition, in unmetaphorical language, of the guilt of Jerusalem, and of the judgment imminent upon her.

C. 6. Ezek. here apostrophizes *the land*. Not the city only, but the land of Judah generally, has been desecrated by idolatrous rites, which can effectually be rooted out only by a desolation, and depopulation, of the entire territory.

C. 7. A final denunciation directed against the kingdom generally, describing in still stronger terms the certainty of the coming disaster, and the inability of prophet, priest, or elder to avert it. In v.$^{5-7. 10-12}$ the prophecy assumes a lyric strain, such as is unwonted in Ezekiel.

3. C. 8–11. Vision of the guilt and punishment of Jerusalem (sixth year of the exile of Jehoiachin = B.C. 591).

C. 8. Ezekiel, in the presence of the elders, who are sitting in his house, falls into a prophetic trance, and is brought in his vision to Jerusalem, where he sees different forms of idolatry carried on in the precincts of the Temple. C. 9 the threat expressed in 8^{18} is carried out. Jehovah, having left the throne borne by the cherubim, stands at the entrance of the Temple to superintend, as it were, the execution of His purpose: at His command His ministers pass through the city, and destroy all who have not previously been marked on the forehead by an

angel in token of their loyalty to Jehovah. C. 10 Jehovah reappears upon the [264] throne, and commands burning coals,
taken from the fire between the cherubim, to be scattered over
the city, v.[1-3]. He again leaves His throne and stands beside
the Temple while this is being done, v.[4-17], but resumes His seat
as soon as it is completed, preparatory to taking His final departure from His sanctuary. He pauses for a while at the east
gate of the outer Court, v.[18-22]. C. 11 the prophet sees 25 men
standing in the east gate, who "gave wicked counsel in the city,"
i.e., no doubt, who were planning revolt from Nebuchadnezzar,
confident (v.[3b]) in the strength of the city to resist reprisals.
Their confidence, it is declared, is misplaced; for the city will
be given into the hands of its foes, v.[1-12]. Even as Ezekiel
spoke, one of the ringleaders dropped down dead. The prophet
(cf. 9[8]), dreading the omen, is moved to intercede on behalf of
the "remnant of Israel," and receives in reply the assurance that
Israel will not perish: the exiles, however contemptuously the
Jerusalemites may view them (comp. p. 260), will return to their
former home, and again enjoy the tokens of Divine favour,
v.[14-22]. After this, the cherubim, bearing Jehovah's glory, finally
leave Jerusalem: the prophet watches them in their course as
far as the Mount of Olives, when the vision suddenly leaves him,
and he awakes from his prophetic trance to find himself again
among the captives of Tel-abib.

4. C. 12–19. The certainty of the fall of Jerusalem, and its
ground in the nation's sinfulness, further established.

12[1-20]. The exiles descrediting the announcement recently
made to them by the prophet, he firstly (v.[1-16]) enacts in their
sight a dumb show, symbolizing the approaching exile of
Zedekiah and the people; and secondly (v.[17-20]) represents under
a figure the privations which they will suffer during the siege and
subsequently.

12[21]–14[11]. On the prophets and their announcements. The
non-fulfilment of oracles uttered by the false prophets, and the
fact that Ezek.'s own prophecies, in consequence of their not
relating to the immediate future, did not admit of being tested
by the result, led the people to distrust all prophecies. But
Jehovah's word will not fail of its accomplishment, 12[21-28]: the
false prophets will not only be silenced by the logic of facts, but
they will themselves be swept away in the coming destruction,

13^{1-16}. V.$^{17-23}$ is directed against certain prophetesses, [265] whose influence among the exiles is described as particularly pernicious. The prophets alluded to are no doubt those who lulled the people of Jerusalem into false security, and who unsettled the exiles with delusive promises of a speedy return (see Jer. c. 28; 29$^{15ff.}$ &c.). There follows a specification of the conditions (abandonment of idolatry, and loyalty to Himself) under which alone Jehovah will be consulted by His people, or permit His prophet to answer them, 14$^{1-11}$.

14$^{12-23}$. An exception explained. When once Jehovah has passed His decree against a land, the righteous who may be therein will alone be delivered : * in the case of Jerusalem, however, a remnant, against this rule, will escape, in order, *viz.*, by the spectacle of their godlessness, to satisfy the exiles, among whom they are brought, of the justice of the judgment accomplished upon the city (cf. 12^{16}).

C. 15–17. Allegories, exhibiting from different points of view the nation's ripeness for judgment.

C. 15. Israel is compared to a vine-branch—not at its best the most valuable of woods, and now, already half-burnt by the fire (alluding to the exile under Jehoiachin) : can there be any question what use will be found.for the remainder? The unfavourable comparison is suggested by reflection on the history and temper of the nation : and from what has already happened, the prophet asks his hearers to infer what the final issue is likely to be.

C. 16. Jerusalem an adulteress. Jerusalem is depicted as a woman who, in spite of the care and attention which Jehovah had shown toward her, v.$^{1-14}$, had requited Him with persistent ingratitude and infidelity, v.$^{15-34}$,† and has merited accordingly the punishment of the adulteress, v.$^{35-43}$. In her sinfulness she has even exceeded Samaria and Sodom, v.$^{44-52}$; so low, accordingly, has she fallen in Jehovah's favour, that her restoration (for a prospect of this, however distant, is still held out) can take place only *after* that of Samaria and Sodom.

C. 17. Zedekiah's disloyalty to his Babylonian masters, and the consequences which may be expected to result from it, v.$^{1-21}$. In v.$^{3-10}$ the circumstances are stated in the form of an allegory

---

* Cf. the theory of strict (temporal) retribution expounded in c. 18.

† The same figure as in Hos. 2$^{7ff.}$, Jer. 2$^{20ff.}$ 3$^{1f.}$, cf. Isa. 57$^{1-9}$.

(or as it is termed in v.[2], a "riddle"), the sense of which is explained in v.[11-21]. The prophecy closes, v.[22-24], with [266] a glance at brighter days to come, and the restoration of the Davidic kingdom in the future.

C. 18. The moral freedom and responsibility of the individual before God. Ezek.'s contemporaries complained that they were suffering for sins committed by their forefathers : "the fathers," they said, "have eaten sour grapes, and the children's teeth are set on edge." The prophet, in opposition to this one-sided view, expounds a strongly individualistic theory of retribution : every one is rewarded according to his doings : the righteous man lives, the unrighteous man dies,—each entirely irrespectively of his father's merits or demerits, v.[1-20]. Similarly, the wicked man who repents of his wickedness lives ; the righteous man who turns from his righteousness dies, v.[21-29]. The practical lesson follows : let each one repent while there is time : for Jehovah "hath no pleasure in the death of him that dieth," v.[30-32].

The same proverb is quoted by Jeremiah (31[29f.]), who admits that it expresses a reality, but rests his hopes upon the advent of a better future, when the conditions of society will be so altered that the evil consequences of sin will be confined to the perpetrator, and not extend to the innocent. Ezek.'s theory is prompted by the desire to exert a practical influence upon his contemporaries ; hence he emphasizes that aspect of the question which they neglected, and which, though not the *sole* truth, is nevertheless a very important aspect of the truth, viz. that individual responsibility never entirely ceases, and that the individual soul, if it exerts itself aright, can emancipate itself from a moral doom entailed upon it, either by the faults of its ancestors, or by its own evil past. See further the notes of Prof. Davidson, pp. l, li, 124–134.

C. 19. A lamentation on the "princes" (*i.e.* the Jewish kings), and on the fall of the kingdom. Two other allegories :— (1) the Davidic stock is likened to a lioness : her two whelps are Jehoahaz (v.[3-4]) and Jehoiachin (v.[5-9]), whose different fates are described, v.[1-9] ; (2) it is likened to a vine planted in a fertile soil, and putting forth strong branches (the Davidic kings) ; but now the vine is forcibly uprooted : its strong rods (Jehoahaz and Jehoiachin) are broken and destroyed ; it is itself planted in the wilderness (the exiles with Jehoiachin) ; and fire is gone forth out of the rod of its branches, destroying its fruit (the suicidal policy of Zedekiah).

5. C. 20–24. The same theme further developed.

20[1-44] (= c. 20 Heb.). (the 7th year of the exile, *i.e.* the 4th before the fall of Jerusalem = B.C. 590). The elders of Israel come (as 14[1]) to consult Ezekiel. He answers them in similar [267] terms : while Israel's idolatry continues, Jehovah will not be consulted by them. This answer is justified by a review of the nation's history, showing how it had been continuously addicted to idolatry, and Jehovah had only been restrained from destroying it by the thought that, if He did so, His name would be profaned in the eyes of the heathen. And still the nation's heart is unchanged : even exile has not eradicated the impulse to idolatry ; hence (v.[33ff.]) further purifying judgments must yet pass over it, ere Jehovah (as He still will do) can acknowledge it again as His own.

But Ezekiel sees the end of Jerusalem advancing rapidly ; and, 20[45]–c. 24, his thoughts turn thither.

20[45-49] (= 21[1-5] Heb.). A great and all-devouring conflagration is to be kindled in the forest of the South (the " Negeb," *i.e.* the southern tract of Judah ; Gen. 12[9] RV. *marg.*). The meaning of the allegory is transparent.

C. 21 (= 21[6-37] Heb.). The sword of Jehovah against Jerusalem. Jehovah threatens to draw His sword from its sheath, and to cut off from Jerusalem " righteous and wicked " alike, v.[1-7]. In v.[8-17] the sword is represented as already drawn ; and the prophet adopts almost a lyric strain, as he pictures its glittering blade, darting hither and thither about the gates of Jerusalem. Next Ezekiel imagines Nebuchadnezzar to have already started, and to be debating whether first to attack Jerusalem or Ammon : at the point where the roads diverge, he consults his oracles; the lot falls for him to proceed to Jerusalem, v.[18-23] ; and the prophet describes, not without satisfaction, the consequent abasement of the unworthy Zedekiah, v.[24-27]. But though Jerusalem suffers first, Ammon will not long glory in its escape : in vain may Ammon furbish its sword in rivalry, as it were, to Jehovah's : it must return into its sheath, and leave Ammon defenceless before the foe, v.[28-32].

The Ammonites had previously (2 Ki. 24[2]) co-operated with Nebuchadnezzar, but they had afterwards intrigued to procure a general insurrection against the Chaldæan power (see Jer. 27[8f. 9]), and now were acting probably in concert with Zedekiah. It was doubtless expected in Jerusalem that

Nebuchadnezzar would attack the Ammonites first : Ezek. declares the speedy advent of the Chaldæans before Jerusalem. V.[23] alludes to the incredulity with which his prophecy would be received. The general sense of the sword-song is clear ; but the text in parts is very corrupt (esp. v.[10. 13] [Heb. [15. 18]] : see *QPB.*[3]).

[268] C. 22. The guilt of Jerusalem. The prophet draws an appalling picture of the crime rampant in the capital ; dwelling in particular, not (as c. 5, 16) on the idolatry, but on the moral offences of which the inhabitants had been guilty, v.[1-22]. The corruption extends to all classes, v.[23-31].

C. 23. Oholah and Oholibah. In c. 22 the prophet drew a picture of the present generation : here he draws one of those that had passed. Under an allegory, similar in character to that in c. 16, he describes the past history of Samaria and Jerusalem. Jehovah, in Egypt, took to Himself two women who were harlots : one became at length intolerable, so that she was put away, v.[1-11] ; the other, instead of taking warning by her sister's fate, excelled her in unholy practices, v.[12-21] (cf. Jer. 3[6-11]) : she must therefore be equally punished, v.[22-35], upon grounds which, that none may doubt their sufficiency, are stated again at length, v.[36-49].

C. 24 (the ninth year of the exile, B.C. 588, the 10th day of the 10th month, being the day on which Jerusalem was invested by the Chaldæans, 2 Ki. 25[1]; cf. Zech. 8[19]). V.[1-14]. By the parable of the rusty caldron the prophet sets forth, firstly, the siege now commencing ; secondly, its final issue, viz. the forced evacuation of Jerusalem by its inhabitants on account of the defilement which they have contracted through their sins.

V.[15-27] an incident in Ezek.'s family life is made the vehicle of a lesson. The prophet's wife suddenly dies : but he is commanded to refrain from all public manifestation of grief, in order thereby to prefigure the paralysing shock of surprise which will seize his countrymen when the tidings reaches them that the city to which they still turned with longing eyes has really fallen. And when this has taken place, the truth of Ezek.'s prophetic word will be demonstrated, and the need for his enforced silence (3[22ff.]) will have passed away.

II. C. 25–32. Prophecies on foreign nations.

Ezekiel, like Amos, Isaiah, and Jeremiah, embraced other nations besides Israel in his prophetic survey : but his point of view is one peculiar to himself, and determined naturally by the circumstances of his age. The fall of Jerusalem wore the appearance of a triumph for heathenism : Jehovah, so it seemed, had been unable in the end to defend His city : the nations around viewed Him with scorn, and His name was profaned amongst [269] them. To reassert the majesty and honour of Jehovah by declaring emphatically that He held in reserve a like fate over Israel's neighbours, is the main scope of the following chapters. Seven nations form the subject of the prophecies, viz. Ammon, Moab, Edom, the Philistines, Tyre, Sidon, and Egypt : most are comparatively brief ; only those on Tyre and Egypt being more elaborated.

1. 25^{1-7}. On Ammon (cf. 21^{28-32}). Though the Ammonites had seemingly combined with Judah in rebellion against Nebuchadnezzar, when Jerusalem was the first to fall, they had not delayed to give malicious expression to their delight : Ezek. declares that they shall be invaded in consequence by the "children of the east" (Jud. 6^3, Jer. 49^{28}), *i.e.* by nomad Arab tribes, who would plunder and appropriate the Ammonite territory.

2. 25^{8-11}. On Moab. A similar prospect, upon substantially the same ground, is held out to Moab.

3. 25^{12-14}. On Edom. The Edomites are charged with taking advantage of the opportunity of Judah's extremity to pay off old scores : in this instance, Jehovah's vengeance will be exacted of them by the hand of Israel itself.

4. 25^{15-17}. On the Philistines. The Philistines were always ready, when occasion offered, to manifest their hatred or contempt ($16^{27, \ 57}$) for Judah ; and it may be inferred from the present passage that they did so after the great misfortune which had now befallen it. For this they are threatened by Jehovah with extinction.

5. 26^1-28^{19}. On Tyre. In the eleventh year of the exile, B.C. 586, shortly after the fall of Jerusalem (alluded to in 26^2).

The number of the month has dropped out in 26^1 : it must have been one later than the fourth, the month in which Jerusalem was taken, Jer. $52^{6f.}$. The Phœnicians appear as vassals of Nebuchadnezzar in Jer. $27^{3ff.}$ (*c.* 593). Afterwards they carried into effect what they were already then planning, and revolted—doubtless in concert with Judah and other neighbouring states. At the time of Jerusalem's fall, Nebuchadnezzar was in the land of Hamath

(Jer. 52⁹) ; and he must soon afterwards have begun his famous siege of Tyre, the commencement of which Ezek. here anticipates, and which, according to Josephus (quoting from Phœnician sources), lasted for 13 years. Nebuchadnezzar, though he must have seriously crippled the resources and trade of Tyre, did not, as Ezek. himself owns (29¹⁸), succeed in reducing it. Tyre was always less important politically than commercially ; and the fame which the Tyrians enjoyed as the great seafaring nation of antiquity, and as [**270**] owning, moreover, an ancient and illustrious city, is no doubt the reason why Ezek. deals with them at such length. He devotes to them, in fact, three distinct prophecies, treating the Tyrian power under different aspects.

(*a*) C. 26. The rich merchant-city, which rejoices over the ruin of Jerusalem, and hopes to turn it to her own profit, will feel Jehovah's anger : the nations will come up against her and destroy her, v.²⁻⁶, even Nebuchadnezzar, with his hosts and implements of war, v.⁷⁻¹⁴ ; the tidings of her fall will produce a profound impression upon the seafaring nations of the world, v.¹⁵⁻²¹. (*b*) C. 27. A vivid and striking picture of the commercial greatness of Tyre, soon to come to an end. Tyre is here represented as a *ship*, to the equipment of which every quarter of the world has contributed its best, which is manned by skilful mariners and defended by brave warriors (v.¹⁻¹¹), but which, nevertheless (v.²⁶⁻³⁶), to the astonishment and horror of all beholders, is wrecked, and founders on the high seas. The figure is not, however, consistently maintained throughout ; already in v.⁹ᵇᶠᶠ· the language shows that the city is in the prophet's mind ; and v.¹²⁻²⁵ is devoted to a graphic and powerful description of the many nations who flocked to Tyre with their different wares. The contrast between the splendour depicted in v.¹⁻²⁵ and the ruin of v.²⁶ᶠᶠ· is tragically conceived. The chapter is one of peculiar archæological and historical interest. (*c*) 28¹⁻¹⁹. Against the king of Tyre. The king of Tyre is represented as claiming to be a god, and to possess Divine prerogatives ; but he will be powerless, Ezek. declares, in the day when the nations, at Jehovah's summons, advance against him, v.¹⁻¹⁰. In a second paragraph Ezek., with sarcastic allusion to these pretensions of the Tyrian king, describes him as a glorious being,* decked with gold and precious ornaments, and placed in Eden, the garden of God (or, of the gods) ; but now, for his crimes, to be expelled from his proud position, and made a mockery to all men, v.¹¹⁻¹⁹.

* In the Heb. text, a cherub. But see Davidson's notes.

6. 28²⁰⁻²⁶. On Sidon.   A short prophecy, threatening Sidon
with siege and invasion, and closing with a promise addressed to
Israel.

7. C. 29–32. A group of six prophecies on Egypt.

Zedekiah's revolt from the Chaldæans had been accomplished in reliance
upon Egyptian help (17¹⁵) ; but the army which they despatched to the relief
of Jerusalem, and which even necessitated Nebuchadnezzar's raising the [271]
siege (Jer. 37⁵ff· 34²¹f·), speedily withdrew : and the Chaldæans, as Jer. foresaw
would be the case, reinvested the city.   Ezek. here declares the ignominious
humiliation of the boastful, but incapable power (cf. Is. 30⁷), which had so
often exerted a seductive influence over Israel, but had ever failed it in the
time of need.

(a) C. 29¹⁻¹⁶ (10th month of the 10th year of the exile, 6
months before the fall of Jerusalem).   The humiliation of Egypt.
Pharaoh Hophra, king of Egypt, is figured as a river-monster
(the crocodile), secure in its native haunts, but soon to be drawn
thence by Jehovah, and left to perish miserably on the open
field, v.¹⁻⁷.   An invading foe will depopulate Egypt; and the
country will be desolate for 40 years, v.⁸⁻¹²; at the end of that
time the Egyptian exiles will return, and a new Egyptian kingdom will be established, but one too weak and unimportant to
inspire Israel again with false confidence, v.¹³⁻¹⁶.   (b) 29¹⁷⁻²¹. An
appendix to v.¹⁻¹⁶, added 16 years afterwards, in the 27th year of
the exile (= B.C. 570).   Nebuchadnezzar, though in his attack
upon Tyre he was carrying out Jehovah's purpose (cf. Jer. 25⁹),
had failed to capture it; and the conquest of Egypt is here
promised him as compensation for his unrewarded service.   (c)
30¹⁻¹⁹ (sequel to 29¹⁻¹⁶).   The ruin imminent upon Egypt will
affect the nation in its entirety : her army, her people, her idols,
her cities, will all suffer alike.   (d) 30²⁰⁻²⁶ (first month of the
11th year of the exile, i.e. 3 months before the fall of Jerusalem).
Ezek., alluding to the recent failure of the Egyptian army to
relieve Jerusalem (v.²¹· ²² the " broken arm "), predicts for Egypt
still further disaster.   (e) C. 31 (3rd month of the 11th year
of the exile, 5 weeks before the fall of Jerusalem).   The proud
cedar-tree.   The king of Egypt in his greatness is compared to
a spreading and majestic cedar : the fall of this cedar, and the
dismay which it will occasion in the world, are picturesquely
described.   (f) C. 32¹⁻¹⁶ (12th month of the 12th year of the
exile, i.e. 20 months after the fall of Jerusalem, B.C. 584).   A
lamentation on Egypt's approaching disgrace.   Pharaoh, repre-

senting Egypt, is compared, as in c. 29, to a crocodile dragged
far from its accustomed haunts, and cast upon the dry land : its
giant body covers hill and vale, and blood streaming from it
stains the earth : heaven and earth are aghast at the spectacle.
(g) 32$^{17-32}$ (fourteen days after v.$^{1-16}$: in v.^{17} "in the twelfth
month" has probably dropped out).   An [272] elegy, describing
the final end of the king of Egypt and all his multitude.   Their
corpses lying unburied on the battlefield, the prophet pictures
their shades descending to the under-world (Sheol), and imagines
the ironical greeting which they will there receive from the
various peoples who once spread terror in the earth, but who now
repose in their several resting-places in the recesses of Sheol :
Egypt is at length become like one of them.

III. C. 33–48. Israel's restoration.

1. C. 33–39. The land and people.

C. 33. The prophet.   By the fall of Jerusalem the truth of
Ezek.'s predictions was brilliantly confirmed : the exiles would
now be no longer unwilling to hear him.   Accordingly the responsibility of the prophetic office is again (see 3$^{16-21}$) impressed
upon him, v.$^{1-9}$; and he reaffirms publicly (v.^{10}) his doctrine
of individual responsibility (see c. 18), with the object of showing that no one, if he repents in time, need despair of the Divine
mercy.   These truths had been borne in upon him (v.^{22}) during
a prophetic trance into which he had fallen on the evening before
the tidings of the fall of Jerusalem reached the exiles.*   It was
the crucial date, which had been indicated to him before (24$^{25-27}$),
as that after which his mouth would be no longer closed.   V.$^{23-29}$
is directed against the remnant who were left in Judah, and
who cherished the vain hope that they would be able to maintain
themselves there in something like their former state.

C. 34. The advent of the Messianic kingdom.   The responsible rulers of the nation have woefully neglected their trust.
The people consequently have in different ways suffered violence,
and even been driven forcibly from their home : Jehovah Himself will take them by the hand and restore them.   The thought
(and figure) of Jer. 23$^{1-4}$ is here developed by Ezek. in detail.

C. 35–36. The land.   After the fall of Jerusalem, the Edomites
had obtained possession of a portion of the territory of Judah,

* In v.^{21} read, with MSS., LXX (MSS.), Pesh., *eleventh* for *twelfth* ; the
tidings of the fall of the city would hardly take 18 months to reach Babylon.

and manifested an ill-natured delight in their rival's humiliation. The prophet declares that for this unseemly ebullition of hatred, Edom shall become a perpetual desolation (c. 35), while Judah, which is now the reproach and derision of its neighbours, will be repeopled, and receive of Jehovah's hand an abundant blessing, 36¹⁻¹⁵. In 36¹⁶⁻³⁸ the prophet draws out the ultimate ground of Israel's restoration: Israel's dispersion, viz., caused Jehovah's power to be doubted, and His honour sullied, among [273] the heathen: that this might not endure for ever, but that the heathen might be morally impressed by the spectacle of Israel regenerate (cf. Jer. 4¹⁻²), Jehovah Himself brings His people back, at the same time, by an act of grace, purging its guilt, imparting to it a new heart, and ruling it by His spirit (v.²⁵⁻²⁷).

C. 37. The people. (a) V.¹⁻¹⁴. The vision of the valley of dry bones. Israel had in appearance ceased to be a nation; the people distrusted the future, and had abandoned all hope of restoration (v.¹¹ᵇ). By the striking symbolism of this vision they are taught that God can endow the seemingly dead nation with fresh life, and plant it again in its old land (v.¹⁴). (b) V¹⁵⁻²⁸. Judah, however, will not be restored alone; Ephraim also will share in the blessings promised for the future; and both houses of Israel will be united in the dominion of the Messianic king. Jehovah's dwelling will be over them, and the nations will acknowledge His presence in Israel.

The thought of the restoration of Ephraim as well as Judah occurs frequently elsewhere in the prophets (Hos. 1¹¹ 3⁵, Is. 11¹³, Mic. 2¹² 5³, Jer. 3¹⁸ 31⁵ᶠᶠ·; cf. also Am. 9⁸ᶠ· ¹⁴ᶠ·, Hos. 11¹⁰ᶠ· 14⁴⁻⁸), and in Ezek. himself (4⁴· ⁵ (Orelli), 16⁵³ᶠᶠ· 37¹¹⁻¹⁴ 39²⁵ 47¹³ᶠᶠ·). V.²⁷⁻²⁸ is a prelude of c. 40 ff. (esp. 43⁷⁻⁹).

C. 38–39. Jehovah's final triumph over the world. Ezek. here develops in a new form his fundamental thought that Jehovah's "name" must be vindicated in history, and acknowleged in its greatness by the nations of the earth. He imagines an attack of hordes from the north, organized upon a gigantic scale, against the restored nation, but ending, through Jehovah's intervention, in their total and ignominious discomfiture, 38¹⁻ 39¹⁶. The spectacle will afford ocular evidence to the world of Jehovah's power, and of the favourable regard which He will henceforth bestow upon His restored and renovated people, 39¹⁷⁻²⁹.

The imagery of 38⁴ᶠᶠ· may have been suggested to Ezek. by the hordes of

Scythians, which had poured into Asia during the reign of Josiah, spreading consternation far and wide (see p. 252). The same representation of an *ideal* defeat of nations, assembled for the purpose of annihilating Israel, will meet us again in Joel and Zechariah. Comp. on this prophecy C. H. H. Wright, *Biblical Essays*, pp. 99–137.

2. C. 40–48. The constitution of the restored theocracy (25th year of the exile = 572 B.C.). Ezek. is brought in a vision to Jerusalem, where he sees the Temple rebuilt. He describes at length its structure and arrangements; and lays down directions respecting its services and ministers, and the distribution of the reoccupied territory. Ezek., as a priest, and as one to whom [274] the associations of the Temple were evidently dear, attaches greater weight to the ceremonial observances of religion than was usually done by the prophets; and he here defines the principles by which he would have the ritual of the restored community regulated. Both the arrangements of the Temple and the ritual to be observed are evidently founded upon pre-exilic practice, the modifications which Ezek. introduces being designed with the view of better securing certain ends which he deems of paramount importance. The Temple is Jehovah's earthly residence: in the restored community, which Ezek. imagines to be so transformed as to be truly worthy of Him (36^{22-36}), He will manifest His presence more fully than He had done before (37^{25-28}); His re-entry into the Temple, and His abiding presence there, are the two thoughts in which c. 40–48 culminate (43^{1-9} 48^{35}); to maintain, on the one hand the sanctity of the Temple, and on the other the holiness of the people, is the aim of the entire system of regulations. Accordingly special precautions are taken to guard the Temple, the holy things, and the officiating priests, from profanation. The inner Court of the Temple is to be entered by none of the laity, not even by the "prince" ($46^{1ff.}$); no foreigners are for the future to assist the priests in their ministrations; instead of the Temple buildings being (as those of the pre-exilic Temple were) in close proximity to the city and royal palace (so that the residence, and even the burial-ground, of the kings encroached upon them, 43^{7-9}), they are to be surrounded by the domain of the priests, the city lying altogether to the south of this. The redistribution of the territories of the tribes has the effect of bringing the Temple more completely into the centre of the land. The rights of the

"prince" are limited : he is no longer to enjoy the prerogatives of the old Davidic king, who treated the Temple almost as his private chapel, entered its precincts as he pleased, and obliged the priests to give effect to his wishes. He has, however, certain religious duties to perform ; but his political signficance is reduced to a minimum : he is, in fact, little more than the representative of the nation in matters of religion. Though the details are realistically conceived, it is evident that there is an ideal element in Ezek.'s representations, which in many respects it was found in the event impossible to put into practice.

(1.) The Temple, c. 40–43. (a) Description and measurements [275] of the *outer* Court, with its gateways and chambers, 40^{5-27} ; (b) description and measurements of the *inner* Court, with its gateways and chambers, 40^{28-47} ; (c) the Temple—the dimensions of its various parts, the "side-chambers" (cf. 1 Ki. 6^5) surrounding it, and its decorations, $40^{48}-41^{26}$; * (d) the chambers north and south of the Temple (between the outer and inner Courts) to serve as sacristies or vestries for the priests, 42^{1-14} ; (e) the external measurements of the whole complex of buildings, 42^{15-20} ; (f) the Temple being thus represented as complete, Jehovah, under the same symbolical representation as before (c. 1, c. 8–10), solemnly resumes possession of it, entering by the same east gate of the outer Court by which Ezek., nearly nineteen years previously, had seen Him leave it (10^{19}), 43^{1-12} ; (g) the altar of Burnt-offering (noticed briefly, 40^{47}), with instructions for the ceremonial to be observed at its consecration, 43^{18-27}.

(2.) The Temple and the people, c. 44–46. The central aim of the regulations contained in these chapters is to maintain the sanctity of the Temple inviolate. (a) The east gate of the outer Court, by which Jehovah entered, to be permanently shut, 44^{1-3} ; (b) no foreigner to be admitted for the future to the precincts of the Temple, even for the performance of subordinate offices ; menial services for the worshippers (44^{11b}) are to be performed henceforth by those members of the tribe of Levi who had acted as priests at the high places, the right to exercise priestly functions being confined strictly to the sons of Zadok, 44^{4-16} ; (c) regulations on the dress, habits, duties, and revenues of the priests, 44^{17-31} ; (d) the "oblation," or sacred territory, occupied

---

* The "separate place," with the "building," 41^{12-14}, was a kind of yard with outhouses, at the back of the Temple, for the removal of refuse, &c.

by the Temple area, and by the domains of the priests and Levites; and the possessions reserved for the city, and "prince," respectively, 45^{1-8}; (*e*) specified dues, to be paid to the "prince," for the purpose of enabling him, without arbitrary exactions, to maintain, in the name of the community, the public services of the Temple, 45^{9-17}; (*f*) the half-yearly ($45^{18. 20}$ RV. *marg.*) rite of atonement for the Temple; and the sacrifices to be offered by the "prince" on various occasions, with regulations respecting the manner in which the outer Court of the Temple is to be entered by the laity, 45^{18}–46^{15}.

[276] $46^{1ff.}$ the east gate of the inner Court is to be opened on Sabbaths and New Moons, but the "prince" is to have no right of entry within it; at most, he may mount the steps to the threshold of the gate leading into it, and worship there while the priest is offering the sacrifice; on high festivals he is to enter and leave the outer Court, just like the people generally.

(*g*) (Appendix to $45^{7f.}$) Limitation of the rights to be exercised by the "prince" over his own and his subjects' landed possessions, 46^{16-18}; (*h*) (Appendix to $42^{13f.}$) the places reserved in the inner and outer Courts for cooking the sacrifices appertaining to the priests and people respectively, 46^{19-24}.

(3.) The Temple and the land, c. 47–48. (*a*) The barren parts of the land (in the neighbourhood of the Dead Sea) to be fertilized, and the waters of the Dead Sea to be sweetened, by a stream issuing forth from underneath the Temple, 47^{1-12}.

V.^{11}. An exception, showing the practical turn of the prophet's mind: the marshes beside the Dead Sea to remain as they are on account of the excellent salt which they furnish.

(*b*) The borders of the land to be occupied by the restored community, 47^{13-23}. (*c*) Disposition of the tribes—the 7 north of the Temple, 48^{1-7}; the "oblation," or strip of sacred land south of these, with the Temple, surrounded by the priests' possessions, in the centre, the Levites' land and the city on the north and south of these respectively, and with the domain of the prince (in two parts) on the east and west, v.$^{8-22}$ (cf. 45^{1-8}); the 5 tribes south of the Temple, v.$^{23-29}$; the 12 gates of the city, and its name, *Jehovah is there*, symbolizing the central thought of the entire prophecy, v.$^{30-35}$ (contrast c. 22).

Ezekiel emphasizes in particular the *power* and *holiness* of God. His standing designation of God is "Lord Jehovah," for which the title "God of Israel"—which Jeremiah, for instance, uses constantly—only appears on special occasions (c. 8–11, 43³ 44²); and in His presence, he is himself only a "son of man." The dominant motive of the Divine action is the dread lest His holy name should be profaned: on the other hand, in His people's restoration or in an act of judgment, His name is sanctified, *i.e.* its holiness is vindicated (p. 298, No. 28). These truths find expression in <u>Ezekiel's most characteristic phrase,</u> "And they (*or* ye) shall know that I am Jehovah" (above 50 times). This phrase is most commonly attached to the [277] announcement of a judgment,* but sometimes it follows a promise of restoration. It strikes the keynote of Ezek.'s prophecies. To the unbelieving mass of the people, as to the heathen, it must have seemed that in the fall of Jerusalem, Jehovah had proved Himself unable to cope with the enemies of His people: Ezek. sees in it a manifestation of Jehovah's holiness visiting Israel for its sins (cf. 39²³ᶠ·), and he insists that the course of history will bring with it other, not less striking, manifestations of His Godhead. Thus in his prophecies on foreign nations the same refrain constantly occurs (25⁵· ⁷· ¹¹· ¹⁷ 28²⁴ &c.): the judgment on each is a fresh proof of Jehovah's power, which is finally vindicated most signally in the ideal defeat of nations, whom Ezek. pictures as marshalled against the restored nation in the future (38²³; 39⁶ᶠ· ²²). To His faithful people, on the other hand, the blessings which Jehovah will pour upon them are an additional and special evidence of the same truth (20⁴² 34²⁷ 36¹¹· ³⁸ 37¹³· ¹⁴ 39²⁸). In His attitude towards His people, Jehovah is the righteous Judge, who is merciful towards the repentant sinner, but deals sternly with the rebellious (3¹⁶ᶠᶠ· c. 18, 33). But the prophet's exertions to gain the hearts of his fellow-countrymen were indifferently rewarded; hence, Israel's restoration in the last resort depends upon Jehovah alone, who will work in the future, as He had done in the past (20⁹· ¹⁴· ²²· ⁴⁴), *for His name's sake* (36²³; cf. 39⁷· ²⁵). "Jehovah *must* restore Israel, for so only can His sole Godhead, which the ruin of His people had caused to be questioned (c. 25–32), be generally acknowledged in the world; He *can* restore Israel, for of His free grace He forgives His people's sin and by the workings of His Spirit transforms their hard heart (36²⁶ᶠ· 39²⁹)." For the future which Ezek. thus anticipates, the prophet's chief aim is to

* 6⁷· ¹⁰· ¹³· ¹⁴ 7⁴· ⁹· ²⁷ 11¹⁰· ¹² &c.

make provision that Israel should not lapse again into its former sins; and hence the new constitution which he projects for it, c. 40–48. Ezek. is very far, indeed, from depreciating moral ordinances (c. 18, 33 &c.); but he finds the best guarantee for their observance, as well as the best preventive against all forms of idolatry, in a well-ordered ceremonial system; and this he develops in c. 40–48. The restored Temple assumes a central significance; to guard it, and all connected with it, from a repetition of the profanation which [278] it had experienced in the past (5^{11} c. 8–11, $43^{7f.}$), to teach the nation to reverence it aright, to render Israel worthy of the God who would thus make His dwelling in their midst, is the aim and scope of the concluding chapters of his book.*

The literary style of Ezek. is strongly marked. He uses many peculiar words; and stereotyped phrases occur in his book with great frequency. He is fond of artificial kinds of composition, especially symbol, allegory, and parable, which he sometimes develops at great length (*e.g.* c. 16, 23, 31), and elaborates in much greater detail than is done by other prophets. He has imagination, but not poetical talent. He is the most uniformly prosaic of the earlier prophets, Jeremiah, though often also adopting a prose style (*e.g.* c. 7), rising much more frequently into the form of poetry, and displaying genuine poetic feeling. The style of poetry which Ezek. principally affects is the *Qinah*, or lamentation, the rhythmical form of which is sometimes distinctly audible in his prophecies.† Only very rarely does he essay a lyric strain ($7^{5-7.\ 10f.}$ $21^{9ff.}$), of a species peculiar to himself. His allegories and long descriptive passages are, as a rule, skilfully and lucidly arranged: the obscurities which some of them present (especially c. 40 ff.) are probably due chiefly to corruption of the text. Most of the prophets display spontaneity: Ezek.'s book evinces reflection and study: his prophecies seem often to be the fruit of meditations, thought out in the retirement of his chamber. The volume of his prophecies is methodically arranged, evidently by his own hand: his book in this respect forms a striking contrast with those of Isaiah or Jeremiah.

* Comp. further Davidson, pp. xxxi–lii.

† C. 19, 26^{17-18} $28^{18f.}$, and parts of 32^{17-32}. See Budde, *ZATW.* 1882, pp. 15–22, and below, under Lamentations.

Examples of expressions characteristic of Ezekiel :—

1. *Son of man* (בן אדם), in addressing the prophet : 2[1] 3[1.3.4], **and** constantly (nearly 100 times) ; often in the phrase, *And thou, son of man* : 2[6.8] 3[25] 4[1] 5[1] &c. Elsewhere (as a title), only Dan. 8[17].

2. *Lord Jehovah* (אדני יהוה) : 2[4] 3[11.27] &c. (more than 200 times altogether. In other prophets occasionally, but far less frequently : *e.g.* about 14 times in Jer.). In AV., RV., "Lord God."

3. *House of rebelliousness* (בית מרי), of Israel : 2[5.6.8] 3[9.26.27] 12[2.3.9.25] 17[12] 24[3]↑ : *rebelliousness* alone (LXX *house of*), 2[7] 44[6]. Comp. Nu. 17[10] [Heb. 16[35]] P בני מרי ; Is. 30[9].

4. ארצות *lands* : 5[9] 6[8], and often (in all 27 times). The plur. of [279] this word greatly *preponderates* in later writers : Gen. 10[5.20.31] (P) 26[3.4] (R), 41[54], Lev. 26[36.39] (H) ; then not till 2 Ki. 18[35] 19[11] ; never in other prophets except Jer. 7 times, Dan. 3 times ; in Chr. Ezr. Neh. 22 times.

5. *Behold, I am against* . . . usually *thee* or *you* (אל or הנני על) : 5[8] 13[8.20] 21[3] [Heb.[8]] 26[3] 28[22] 29[3.10] 30[22] 34[10] 35[3] 36[9] (*toward*,—in a favourable sense) 38[3] 39[1]. So Nah. 2[14] 3[5], Jer. 21[13] 23[30.31.32] 50[31] 51[25]↑.

6. *To do judgments* (שפטים) *on* : 5[10.15] 11[9] 16[41] 25[11] 28[22.26] 30[14.19] ; also Ex. 12[12], Nu. 33[4] (both P), cf. 2 Ch. 24[24] (את) : שפטים also (a rare word) Ez. 14[21], Ex. 6[6] 7[4] (both P), Pr. 19[29]↑.

7. *To scatter to every wind* : 5[10.12] (cf. v.[2]), 12[14] (cf. 17[21]) ; Jer. 49[32].

8. *(My) eye shall not spare* (usu. followed by *neither will (I) have pity*), 5[11] 7[4.9] 8[18] 9[5.10] 16[5] 20[17] (cf. p. 100, No. 17).

9. *To satisfy* (lit. *bring to rest*) *my fury upon* . . . : 5[13] 16[42] 21[17] [Heb.[22]] 24[13]↑. Cf. Zech. 6[8].

10. *I, Jehovah, have spoken it*, usually as a closing asseveration : 5[13] 15[17] 17[21] 21[17.32] [Heb.[22.37]] 24[14] 26[14] 30[12] 34[24] ; followed by ועשיתי *and have done it* (or *will do it*), 17[24] 22[14] 36[36] 37[14]. So *I have spoken it* : 23[34] 26[5] 28[10] 39[5]. Comp. Nu. 14[35]. Not so in any other prophet.

11. *To finish my fury* (or *wrath*) *upon* . . . : 5[13b] 6[12] 7[8] 13[15] 20[8.21] ; cf. 5[13a] (*be finished*). So Lam. 4[11]↑.

12. *Set thy face toward* or *against* (. . . שים פניך) : 6[2] 13[17] 20[46] 21[2] [Heb. 21[2.7]] 25[2] 28[21] 29[2] 35[2] 38[2].

13. *The mountains of Israel* : 6[2.3] 19[9] 33[28] 34[13.14] 35[12] 36[1 bis.4.8] 37[22] 38[8] 39[2.4.17] ; cf. 34[14]. A combination peculiar to Ez.

14. אפיקים *water-courses* (often joined with *mountains, hills,* and *valleys,* as a rhetorical designation of a country) : 6[3] 31[12] 32[6] 34[13] 35[8] 36[4.6].

15. גלולים *idol-blocks* : 6[4.5.6.9.13] 8[10] 14[3-7] 16[36] 18[6.12.15] 20[7.8.16.18], and often (39 times) ; see p. 202, No. 33.

16. *And . . . shall know that I am Jehovah* (see p. 295). Comp. in P, Ex. 6[7] 7[5] 14[4.8] 16[12] 29[46] ; cf. 31[13b] (H). Occasionally besides, Ex. 10[2], 1 Ki. 20[13.28], Is. 49[23.26] 60[16], Joel 3[17].

17. *To scatter* (זרה) *among the lands* : 6[8] 12[15] 20[23] 22[15] 29[12] 30[23.26] 36[19] ; cf. with *to disperse* 11[16.17] 20[34.41]. Cf. No. 25.

18. *To stretch out my hand upon* . . . : 6^{14} $14^{9. 13}$ 16^{27} $25^{7. 13. 16}$ 35^3.

19. *To pour out my fury upon* . . . : 7^8 9^8 14^{19} $20^{8. 13. 21}$ 22^{22} 30^{15} 36^{18} cf. $20^{33. 34}$.

20. *Stumbling-block of iniquity* : 7^{19} $14^{3. 4. 7}$ 18^{30} 44^{12}.

21. נשׂיא *ruler* or *prince* (applied sometimes to the king) : 7^{27} $12^{10. 12}$ 19^1 21^{12} (Heb.[17]) ^{25} (Heb.[30]) 22^6 34^{24} 37^{25} $45^{8. 9}$; and (in the sing.) 44^3 $45^{6. 16. 17. 22}$ $46^{2. 4. 8. 10. 12. 16-18}$ $48^{21. 22}$.   Not of Israel, 26^{16} 27^{21} 30^{13} 32^{29} $38^{2. 3}$ $39^{1. 18}$.   This term is used by no other prophet, and is very rare elsewhere, except in P (p. 134).

22. A subject opened by means of a *question* : $8^{6. 12. 15. 17}$ (so 47^6), 12^{22} $15^{2 ff.}$ 18^2 19^2 $20^{3. 4}$ 22^2 23^{36} $31^{2. 18}$ 32^{19} 37^3; cf. $17^{9. 10. 15}$.

23. *To put a person's way upon his head* (*i.e.* to requite him) : נתן דרך בראש : 9^{10} 11^{21} 16^{43} 22^{31}; cf. 17^{19}.   Only besides 1 Ki. 8^{32} (=2 Ch. 6^{23}).   השיב רעה בראש is the more common synonym.

24. אנפים *wings* : 12^{14} 17^{21} $38^{6 \ bis. \ 9. \ 22}$ 39^4†.

25. *To disperse* (הפיץ) *among the nations* : 12^{15} 20^{23} 22^{15} 29^{12} $30^{23. 26}$ 36^{19}; cf. 28^{25} 29^{13}.   Cf. No. 17.

26. *To bear shame* (כלמה) : $16^{52. 54}$ $32^{24. 25. 30}$ 34^{29} $36^{6. 7. 15}$ 39^{26} 44^{13}.

27. שׁאט *contempt*, שׁוט *to contemn* (Aram.) : 16^{57} $25^{6. 15}$ $28^{24. 26}$ 36^5.

28. *To be sanctified* (or *get me holiness*) *in* : 20^{41} $28^{22. 25}$ 36^{23} 38^{16} (cf. v.^{23}), 39^{27}; cf. Lev. 10^3 22^{32}, Nu. 20^{13} (all P).   Cf. the stress laid on Jehovah's *holy name*, 20^{39} 36^{20-22} $39^{7. 25}$ $43^{7. 8}$ (cf. 36^{23}; and *for my name's sake*, $20^{9. 14. 22. 44}$).   Comp. Davidson, pp. xxxix–xli; 149, 279.

29. *In the time of the iniquity of the end* : $21^{25. 29}$ (Heb.[30. 34]) 35^5.

30. *The fire of my indignation* : 21^{31} $22^{21. 31}$ 38^{19}.

On Ezek.'s affinities with the priestly terminology, esp. with the Law of Holiness, see above, pp. 49 f., 130 ff., 145 ff. $37^{27 f.}$ $43^{7. 9}$, it is to be noted, express a fundamental thought of the Priests' Code (p. 129).

CHAPTER VI.

THE MINOR PROPHETS.

LITERATURE.—F. Hitzig (in the *Kgf. Exeg. Handb.*), 1838, [3] 1863, [4] by H. Steiner (substantially unchanged), 1881 ; H. Ewald in his *Propheten des AB.s*, 1840–41, [2] 1867–68 (translated) ; C. F. Keil, 1866, [2] 1888 ; E. B. Pusey, *The Minor Prophets, with a Commentary explanatory and practical* ; C. von Orelli (p. 278) ; F. W. Farrar, *The Minor Prophets, their lives and times*, in the " Men of the Bible " series, 1890 (useful) ; J. Wellhausen, *Die Kleinen Propheten übersetzt, mit Noten*, 1892 ; G. A. Smith, *The Book of the Twelve Prophets* (in the " Expositor's Bible "), i. 1896 (very suggestive). The articles in the *Encycl. Brit.* (ed. 9) may also often be consulted with advantage.

On particular prophets the following may be especially noticed :—

Hosea :—Ed. Pocock (Regius Professor of Hebrew in Oxford), *Comm. on Hosea*, 1685 (exhaustive, for the date at which it was written) ; Aug. Wünsche, *Der Proph. Hosea*, 1868 (with copious quotations from Jewish authorities) ; W. Nowack, *Der Proph. Hosea erklärt*, 1880 ; A. B. Davidson in the *Expositor*, 1879, p. 241 ff.; W. R. Smith, *Prophets of Israel*, Lect. iv.; T. K. Cheyne in the *Camb. Bible for Schools*, 1884 ; J. J. P. Valeton, *Amos en Hosea* (an exegetical and historical study), 1894.

Joel :—Ed. Pocock, *Comm. on Joel*, 1691 ; K. A. Credner, *Der Proph. Joel*, 1831 ; Aug. Wünsche, *Die Weiss. des Proph. Joel*, 1872 ; A. Merx, *Die Proph. des Joel u. ihre Ausleger*, 1879 (with an elaborate historical account of the interpretation of the book) ; J. C. Matthes, *ThT.* 1885, pp. 34 ff., 129 ff., 1887, p. 357 ff.; A. B. Davidson in the *Expositor*, March 1888 ; H. Holzinger, *Sprachkarakter u. Abfassungszeit des Buches Joel*, in the *ZATW.* 1889, pp. 89–131 ; S. R. Driver, *Joel and Amos*, in the *Camb. Bible for Schools*, 1897.

Amos :—G. Baur, *Der Proph. Amos erklärt*, 1847 ; J. H. Gunning, *De godspraken van Amos*, 1885 ; W. R. Smith, *Prophets*, Lect. iii.; A. B. Davidson, *Expositor*, March and Sept. 1887 ; H. G. Mitchell, *Amos* (Boston, U.S.A., 1893) ; L. B. Paton, *JBLit.* 1894, p. 80 ff.; S. R. Driver, as above.

Obadiah :—C. P. Caspari, *Der Proph. Ob. ausgelegt*, 1842.

Jonah :—M. Kalisch, *Bible Studies*, Part ii. 1878 ; T. K. Cheyne, *Theol. Review*, 1877, p. 291 ff.; C. H. H. Wright, *Biblical Essays* (1886), pp. 34–98 ; Delitzsch, *Mess. Weissagungen*, 1890, p. 88.

Micah :—Ed. Pocock, *Comm. on Micah*, 1677 ; C. P. Caspari, *Über*

Micha den Morasthiten u. seine proph. Schrift, 1851-52 (very elaborate) ; W. R. Smith, *Proph.* p. 287 ff.; T. K. Cheyne in the *Camb. Bible for Schools*, 1882, [2] 1895 ; V. Ryssel, *Untersuchungen über die Textgestalt u. die Echtheit des B. Micha*, 1887 ; J. Taylor, *The Mass. text and the ancient versions of Micah*, 1891 ; H. J. Elhorst, *De profetie van Micha* (Arnhem, 1891) ; W. H. Kosters, *ThT.* 1893, p. 249 ff. On c. 4 f. Kuenen, *ThT.* 1872, p. 285 ff.

Nahum :—O. Strauss, *Nahumi de Nino Vaticinium*, 1853 ; A. Billerbeck u. A. Jeremias, *Der Untergang Nineveh's u. die Weissagungsschrift des Nahum*, in Delitzsch and Haupt's "Beiträge zur Assyriologie," 1895, pp. 87-188 ; A. B. Davidson, *Nah. Hab. and Zeph.*, in the *Camb. Bible for Schools*, 1896.

[281] Habakkuk :—F. Delitzsch, *De Hab. Proph. vita atque ætate*, 1842, ed. 2, 1844 ; and *Der Proph. Hab. ausgelegt*, 1843 ; K. Budde, *St. u. Krit.* 1893, p. 383 ff.; J. W. Rothstein, *ib.* 1894, p. 51 ff.; K. Budde, *Expositor*, May 1895, p. 372 ff.; A. B. Davidson, as above.

Zephaniah :—F. A. Strauss, *Vaticinia Zephaniæ*, 1843 ; F. Schwally in the *ZATW.* 1890, pp. 165-240 (including a Comm. on the text) ; Budde, *St. u. Kr.* 1893, p. 393 ff. ; A. B. Davidson, as above.

Haggai :—A. Köhler, *Die nachexilischen Propheten erklärt* (I. *Haggai*, 1860 ; II. *Sachariah i.-viii.*, 1861 ; III. *Sachariah ix.-xiv.*, 1863 ; IV. *Malachi*, 1865) ; T. T. Perowne, *Hagg. and Zech.* in the *Camb. Bible*, 1886.

Zechariah :—A. Köhler, as above ; C. H. H. Wright, *Zechariah and his Prophecies*, 1879 (the "Bampton Lectures" for 1878, with crit. and exeg. notes) ; C. J. Bredenkamp, 1879 ; W. H. Lowe, *Comm. on Zech. Heb. and LXX*, 1882 ; K. Marti, 1892 (also *St. u. Kr.* 1892, p. 207 ff. [c. 3], 716 ff. [6⁹⁻¹⁵] ; cf. Ley, 1893, p. 771 ff.). From the abundant literature dealing specially with c. 9-14 may be selected, in addition, Abp. Newcome, *Minor Prophets*, London, 1785 ; Hengstenberg, *Beiträge zur Einl. ins AT.* 1831, i. p. 361 ff.; *Christology of the OT.* (Clark's transl.) iii. 329-iv. 138 ; Bleek, *Stud. u. Krit.* 1852, p. 247 ff., and in his *Introduction* ; Stähelin, *Einl. in die kan. Bb. des AT.* 1862, p. 315 ff.; J. J. S. Perowne, article ZECHARIAH in Smith's *Dict. of the Bible*, 1863 ; B. Stade in the *ZATW.* 1881, pp. 1-96 ; 1882, pp. 151-172, 275-309, with Kuenen's criticisms in his *Onderzoek* (ed. 2), §§ 81-83 ; T. K. Cheyne, *JQR.* 1888, pp. 76-83 ; A. F. Kirkpatrick, *Doctrine of the Prophets*, p. 438 ff.; Eckardt, *ZATW.* 1893, p. 76 ff.; A. K. Kuiper, *Zach. ix.-xiv., eene exeg.-krit. studie* (Utrecht, 1894).

Malachi :—Ed. Pocock, *Comm. on Malachi*, 1677 ; A. Köhler, as above ; B. Stade, *Gesch. Isr.* ii. 128-138 ; T. T. Perowne in the *Camb. Bible*, 1890.

§ 1. HOSEA.

Chronological Table.

786.	Jeroboam II.	737. Pekahiah.
746.	Zechariah.	735. Pekah.
745.	Shallum.	733. Hoshea.
745.	Menahem.	722. Fall of Samaria.

Hosea prophesied in the Northern kingdom under Jeroboam II. and succeeding kings. Jeroboam II. was the fourth and most successful ruler (2 Ki. 14$^{23-29}$) of the dynasty founded by Jehu, who overthrew the dynasty of Omri, and destroyed the public worship of Baal (to which Ahab had given the patronage of the court). The dynasty of Jehu had not, however, satisfied the expectations of the prophets by whose sanction and aid it had been established (2 Ki. 9–10); and hence almost the opening words of Hosea's prophecy are a denunciation of judgment upon it (1$^{4f.}$: the allusion is to 2 Ki. 10^{11}). The reign of Jeroboam II. was a long one, marked by successes without and prosperity within (comp. the picture of material welfare drawn in c. 2): the luxury, selfishness, oppression of the poor, and kindred vices which it engendered are rebuked in stern tones by Hosea's elder contemporary Amos. After the death of Jeroboam II. party [282] spirit, which there was now no strong hand to hold in check, broke out: Zechariah could not maintain his throne, and was murdered after a six months' reign by a conspiracy. With him the dynasty of Jehu came to an end. There followed a period of anarchy of which Hosea (7$^{3-7}$ 8^4) supplies a picture: phantom kings coming forward in rapid succession, with the form, but without the reality, of royal power; the aid of Assyria and Egypt alternately invoked by rival factions (Hos. 5^{13} 7^{11} 8^9 12^1: the corresponding penalty, 9$^{3.\ 6}$ 10^6 11^5). Thus Shallum, after a month, was overthrown by Menahem, who sought to strengthen his position by buying the support of the Assyrian monarch Pul (Tiglath-Pileser),* 2 Ki. 15$^{19f.}$. This application to Assyria appears to be alluded to in Hos. 8$^{9f.}$: at the same time, or shortly after, another party was seeking help in the opposite direction, from Egypt, 12^{1b}. Menahem reigned for 10 (8) years: his son Pekahiah succeeded him, but after two years was murdered by Pekah, a rough soldier from Gilead, whom we hear of in Is. 7 as engaged with Rezin, king of Damascus, in an attack upon the dynasty of David in Jerusalem. Pekah,—whose reign, to judge from the Inscriptions, must have been considerably shorter than is represented in the Book of Kings,—in his turn, was deposed and murdered by Hoshea, with the connivance and support of the Assyrian king Tiglath-

* See Schrader, *KAT.*² 227 ff.; *KB.* ii. 277, 291, compared with pp. 287, 290; or *Records of the Past*, 2nd series, i. 18, 23.

Pileser (B.C. 734). Hoshea, however, ultimately broke with the power to which he owed his throne, and opened treasonable negotiations with So or Sevé (*i.e.* Sabako), king of Egypt, with the result that Shalmaneser, Tiglath-Pileser's successor, laid siege to Samaria, which, after holding out for three years, capitulated to Sargon. Large numbers of the inhabitants were transported by Sargon to different parts of Assyria; and the kingdom of Ephraim was thus brought to its close.

It is probable that the title (1¹) has not come down to us in its original form: for (1) it is clear from internal evidence that c. 1–3 belong to the reign of Jeroboam II. and that c. 4–14 relate to the troubles that followed; this being so, it is strange that the later date (Uzziah, &c.) should *precede* the earlier one (Jeroboam); (2) it is hardly likely that Hosea, writing in and for the Northern kingdom, would date his book by reigns of the kings of *Judah*; (3) it is doubtful if any of Hosea's prophecies date from the period after 734, the year in which Tiglath-Pileser deported the inhabitants of the trans-Jordanic region (2 Ki. 15²⁹) to Assyria: for Gilead is alluded to as Israelitish (6⁸ 12¹¹; cf. 5¹), without any reference to a judgment having [283] fallen upon it; nor is there any allusion to Pekah's attack upon Judah in 735 B.C. Probably the original title had simply " in the days of Jeroboam," and was intended to refer only to c. 1–3: when a title had to be found for the whole book, in order to indicate that the latter part referred to a later period, the names of the Judæan kings contemporary with, and subsequent to, Jeroboam II. were added.

The *terminus a quo* of Hosea's prophecies will thus be shortly before B.C. 746: the *terminus ad quem*, B.C. 735–734.

The Book of Hosea falls naturally into two parts: (1) c. 1–3, belonging to the latter part of the reign of Jeroboam II.; (2) c. 4–14, belonging to the period of the kings following.

I. C. 1–3. This part of the book consists of three sections, 1²–2¹; 2²⁻²³; c. 3. The *first* of these contains a symbolical representation of Israel's unfaithfulness to Jehovah, and the consequences of it: Hosea gives to the three children borne by his unchaste wife Gomer, the symbolical names, *Jezreel*, in anticipation of the vengeance to be exacted of the house of Jehu on the spot where formerly Jehu had massacred the house of Ahab, 2 Ki. 10¹¹; *Lo-ruhamah*, "Uncompassionated," and *Lo-ammi*, "Not my people," in token of Jehovah's rejection of Ephraim, v.²⁻⁹. Yet this rejection is not final: a promise of the union of Judah and Israel and restoration of the latter to favour follows. Jezreel, the scene of defeat in 1⁵, becomes the scene of an ideal victory, marking the return of the nation from exile, and its

reconquest of Palestine; and its members are invited to resume
the use of the title which had just been discarded, and to accost
one another in terms implying their entire restoration to Jehovah's favour, 1^{10}–2^1 [Heb. 2^{1-3}].

The *second* section, 2^{2-23}, states in plain language the meaning which the prophet attaches to the narrative of 1^2–2^1. V.$^{2-13}$
the prophet dwells upon the impending punishment, and the
cause of it, viz. Ephraim's ingratitude to Jehovah, and her for-
saking him for the Baals; and v.$^{14-23}$ he shows how this period of
punishment will be also a means of reformation, and [284] will
result in the bestowal upon the nation of fresh marks of confidence and love at the hands of her Divine husband ("Jezreel,"
typifying Israel, is now to verify her name by being *sown* anew in
the earth). And thus the interpretation ends, 2^{23}, at the same
point which the original prophecy had reached in 2^1.

2^1 is the close of 1^{10-11}, and should be included in c. 1. The "mother"
in 2^2 is, of course, the community conceived as a whole, the "children" being
the individual members.

In the *third* section (c. 3) Hosea appears again, as in c. 1,
enacting the part of Jehovah towards His people. His love for
his faithless wife, and his behaviour towards her (v.$^{1-3}$), are, as
he says himself (v.$^{1b, 5}$), symbols of Jehovah's love towards the
unfaithful Israelites, and of the means employed by Him (de-
privation for a season of civil and religious institutions) to win
them back to purity and holiness.

II. C. 4–14. These chapters consist of a series of discourses,
a summary, arranged probably by the prophet himself at the close
of his ministry, of the prophecies delivered by him in the years
following the death of Jeroboam II. Though the argument is
not continuous, or systematically developed, they may be divided
into three sections: c. 4–8, in which the thought of Israel's *guilt*
predominates; c. 9–11^{11}, in which the prevailing thought is that
of Israel's *punishment*; 11^{12}–c. 14, in which these two lines of
thought are both continued (c. 12–13), but are followed (c. 14)
by a glance at the brighter future which may ensue, provided
Israel repents. The following is an outline of the subjects
treated:—(i.) C. 4. Israel's gross moral corruption (v.^{2}), abetted
and increased by the worldliness and indifference of the priests.
C. 5–7. The self-indulgence and sensuality of the leaders of the
nation, resulting in the degradation of public life, and decay of

national strength, intermingled with descriptions of the bitter consequences which must inevitably ensue. C. 8. The prophet announces the fate imminent on northern Israel, with its cause, viz. idolatry and schism, v.[1-7]: already, indeed, has the judgment begun; Israel has drawn it upon itself, by dallying with Assyria, by religious abuses, and by a vain confidence in fortified cities, v.[8-14]. (ii.) C. 9–11[11]. The approaching judgment is described more distinctly: disaster, ruin, exile (9[3]),—even the idols of Beth-el will not be able to avert it, but will be carried off themselves to Assyria (10[5f.]),—with passing allusions [285] to its ground, viz. the nation's ingratitude and sin, and with a glance at the end (11[8-11]) at the possibility of a change in the Divine purpose, resulting in Ephraim's restoration. (iii.) 11[12]– c. 14. The thought of Israel's sin again forces itself upon the prophet: they had fallen short of the example set them by their ancestor: in vain had Jehovah sought to reform them by His prophets; the more He warned them, the more He blessed them, the more persistently they turned from Him: the judgment therefore must take its course (13[15f.]). There follows an invitation to Israel to repent, and renounce its besetting sins; and with a description of the blessings which Jehovah will confer, in case Israel responds, the prophecy closes (c. 14).

Hosea is thus in a pre-eminent degree, especially in c. 4–14, the prophet of the decline and fall of the Northern kingdom : * what Amos perceived in the distance, Hosea sees approaching with rapid steps, accelerated by the internal decay and disorganization of the kingdom. Not only the moral corruption of the nation generally, including even the priests (4[1f. 8] 6[8-10] 7[1] 9[9]), but the thoughtless ambition of the nobles, the weakness of its kings, the conflict of opposing factions, are vividly depicted by him (4[18] 5[1] 7[3-7. 16] 9[15] 10[3] 13[10]). He alludes frequently to Israel's idolatry, both their attachment to sensuous Canaanitish cults and their devotion to the unspiritual calf-worship (4[12-14. 15. 17] 5[1-3] 8[4-6. 11] 9[1. 10. 15] 10[1. 5. 8. 15] 11[2] 12[11] 13[1f.]): idols are satirized by him as made by the hands of men, in a form devised by human minds, of the silver and gold which they owed to Jehovah (2[8] 8[4-6] 13[2]); hence the folly of trusting in them or worshipping

* *Judah* is alluded to only incidentally, 4[15] 5[5. 10. 12. 13. 14] 6[4. 11] 8[14] 10[11] 11[12] (obscure: text doubtful), 12[2]: usually in unfavourable terms; otherwise, however, in 1[7] and (by implication) 1[11] 3[5] (cf. p. 306).

them (8^4 ironically—"they are made *only to be cut off*": $10^{5f.}$ 14^3). Hosea urges Israel to repent, grounding his appeal upon the many tokens of Jehovah's love to which its history had borne witness (9^{10} $11^{1.\ 3\text{-}4}$ $12^{9.\ 13}$ $13^{4.\ 5}$; cf. 6^7 8^1), in virtue of which Israel was bound to the observance of a multitude of duties, comprised in the "Tôrāh" of Jehovah ($8^{1b.\ 12}$), which it was the office of the priests (4^6) to inculcate and uphold. Through Israel's neglect of the duties thus laid upon it, Jehovah has the right to enter into judgment [286] with it (4^1 5^1). These duties, for the non-observance of which the prophet rebukes Israel, are primarily *moral* ones, as appears in particular from $4^{1\text{-}8}$, where he attributes the moral degeneration of the people (v.$^{1\text{-}2}$) to the priests' forgetfulness of the "Tôrāh" of their God. The people, however, think to propitiate Jehovah with their offerings (8^{13}; cf. 5^6), forgetting that His delight is in "mercy, and not sacrifice," and in the (practical) "knowledge of God" (see Jer. 22^{16}) more than in burnt-offerings (6^6); and in spite of the love shown to them in the past, repay Him with ingratitude, and slight the commands on the observance of which He sets the highest value. Hence He is become their enemy ($5^{12.\ 14}$ $7^{12.\ 13}$ 8^{14} $9^{9.\ 15f.}$ $13^{7f.}$); and the prospect of invasion (5^8 $8^{1.\ 3}$ 11^6 13^{16}), and exile to a foreign land (8^{13} $9^{3.\ 6.\ 17}$ 11^5), is held out before them by the prophet with ever-increasing distinctness and force. Particularly noticeable is Hosea's conception of *love* as the bond uniting Jehovah and Israel (3^1 9^{15} $11^{1.\ 4}$ 14^4), as well as individual Israelites with one another (6^6).*

Style of Hosea. "Osee commaticus est [is broken up into clauses], et quasi per sententias loquens," said Jerome long ago; and his words exactly describe the style of the prophet, short, abrupt sentences, very frequently unconnected by any copula, full of force and compressed feeling, pregnant with meaning, the thought sometimes so condensed as to be ambiguous or obscure. The style of Hosea is unique among the prophets: his elder contemporary Amos writes in much more flowing and regular periods. But Hosea's style seems to be the expression of the emotion which is stirring in his heart: his sensitive soul is full of love and sympathy for his people; and his keen perception of their moral decay, and of the destruction towards which they

---

* See more fully on Hosea's prevailing lines of thought, W. R. Smith, *OTJC.* Lect. iv.; Cheyne, p. 22 ff.; Farrar, chap. viii.

are hastening, produces in consequence a conflict of emotions, which is reflected in the pathos, and force, and "artless rhythm of sighs and sobs," which characterise his prophecy (notice *e.g.* the pathos of such verses as 6^4 7^{13} $9^{12.\ 14}$ $11^{2-4.\ 8f.}$). The figures used are suggestive; they are, however, in agreement with his general style, indicated by a word, and not, as a rule, worked out (4^{16} 5^{14} $6^{4b.\ 5b}$ $7^{4.\ 6.\ 7.\ 11.\ 16}$ 8^7 9^{10} 10^7 13^3 $14^{5.\ 6.\ 8}$): Jehovah, on His terrible side, is compared [287] to a lion, a panther, a bear (5^{14} $13^{7.\ 8}$: in a different application, 11^{10}), and even to a moth or rottenness (5^{12}); on His gracious side, to the refreshing and invigorating "latter rain" (6^3), and to the dew (14^5).

Hosea is also fond of paronomasias $2^{22b-23a}$ ("sow"), 8^7 $9^{15\ end}$ 11^5 (double sense of "return"), 12^{11} [Heb. ^{12}]; comp. the allusion to the derivation of "Ephraim," 9^{16} 13^{15} 14^8 [Heb. ^{9}] ^{end}; and the use of "Beth-Aven" for "Beth-el," 4^{15} 10^5 (cf. v. ^{8}). The construction of clauses ἀσυνδέτως is more common in him than in any other prophet: *e.g.* $4^{7.\ 18}$ $5^{3b.\ 6b.\ 10}$ 6^{10} $7^{12.\ 16}$ $9^{6.\ 9.\ 15}$ $10^{1.\ 2b.\ 6.\ 11b}$ 14^4 (Heb. ^{5}), &c.: clauses with עַתָּה ("now") similarly, 4^{16} 5^7 7^2 $8^{8.\ 13b}$ (hence Jer. 14^{10}), 10^{2a} (uncommon).

There are several passages in Hosea, which, partly on the ground that they are thought to express ideas alien to Hosea's historical or theological position, partly because they interrupt the connexion of thought, have been held by recent critics to be later additions to the original text of his prophecies. Thus Stade (*Gesch.* i. 577 *n.*) questioned 1^7 $1^{10}-2^1$ 3^5 (the words "and David their king") 4^{15a} 8^{14}; Cornill (*Einl.*^{3} § 27. 3) agrees (except for 8^{14}); the originality of these, with the exception of 1^7, was defended by Kuenen (in 1889), *Onderzoek*, § 67. 8–10. More recently, Wellh. rejected in addition 2^{16} 6^{11} 7^1 (to *Israel, then*) 10^{13b}, most of 14^{1-9}, as well as a few less important phrases elsewhere: Cheyne (in W. R. Smith, *Proph.*^{2} p. xvii ff.) cites as the "most probable" later insertions 1^7 $1^{10}-2^1$ 3^5 ("and David their king") 4^{15a} $5^{15}-6^4$ 6^{11} 7^1 (to *Israel, then*) 8^{14} 14^{1-9} (entirely). G. A. Smith rejects 1^7 (p. 213), $4^{15f.}$ 8^{14} (pp. 224, 259), and doubts 2^{16} (p. 248), 5^5 $6^{10f.}$ (p. 225), $11^{6-7.\ 10-11}$ (p. 297 f.), 14^9 (p. 317), but seems to accept $1^{10}-2^1$ (though allowing that it must be misplaced), and the suspected words in 3^5 (p. 213 f.), and defends at length 14^{1-8} (pp. 309–312). The question (which will occur again in the case of Amos, Micah, Hab., and Zeph.) is analogous to that which has arisen before with reference to Is. Jer. and II Is.: it may no doubt occasionally happen (esp. in the case of a prophet like Jer., whose text has manifestly passed through many hands) that a prophecy has been expanded or supplemented at a later date: but the grounds ought to be very clear before it can be deemed probable that this has taken place upon the extensive scale which is sometimes supposed. It may be questioned whether recent criticism has not shown a tendency to limit unduly the spiritual capabilities, and imaginative power, of the pre-exilic prophets; and whether, the prophets being *poets*, guided often, as is clear, by impulse and feeling, rather than by strict logic, imperfect connexion with the context (except in extreme cases, or when supported by linguistic or other independent indications) forms a sufficient ground for judging a passage to be a later insertion. It is also not improbable that the discourses of the prophets have often been transmitted to us in a condensed form, in which mediating links may have been omitted. And a picture of restoration, at the end of a prophecy, does not neutralize previous threatenings : such pictures are always *ideal* ones ; they do not exempt those whom the prophet in question is addressing from the judgment of exile or disaster which has been pronounced upon them ; the judgment takes effect : but out of the national ruin which it implies, the prophet pictures in the undefined future a renovated community arising—he does not pause to ask by what historical process the renovation has been effected, though sometimes (esp. in Isaiah) the godly Israelites who escape the disaster are conceived as forming its nucleus—which shall carry on the historical continuity of the nation, and remain the recipient of Jehovah's blessings. See generally, on the subject of "the alternation of threatening and promise in the prophets," the discriminating study of Giesebrecht, *Beiträge*, pp. 187–220, who confesses himself unable to maintain the originality of some passages (including in particular Hos. 1^7 1^{10}–2^1), but insists that there is no sufficient ground for suspecting promises which come at the *close* of announcements of disaster.

§ 2. JOEL.

The title of this prophecy mentions nothing beyond the names of the prophet and of his father Pethuel. The prophecy consists of two parts, 1^2–2^{17}, and 2^{18} to the end. 1^{2-7} states, in graphic language, the occasion of the prophecy, viz. a visitation of locusts, accompanied by a drought, which caused the severest distress throughout the country, $1^{10-12.\ 16-20}$; the prophet exhorts the people to fasting, supplication, and mourning, $1^{13f.}$ $2^{1.\ 12f.}$; for the present visitation of locusts is to him a symbol of the approaching "Day of Jehovah" (1^{15}), to be ushered in by another visitation of terrible and unprecedented intensity, 2^{2-11}, which timely repentance may perchance avert, 2^{12-17}. The people, we must suppose, responded to the prophet's invitation : $2^{18f.}$ describes in narrative form (see RV.) Jehovah's gracious change of purpose, which thereupon ensued ; and what follows, to the end of the book, is His answer to the people's prayer. The answer begins with a promise of deliverance from the famine : rain will again descend upon the parched soil ; fruitful seasons will compensate for the locusts' ravages ; and all will know that Jehovah is Israel's God, 2^{20-27}. Then the spirit of prophecy will be poured out upon all flesh : and the "Day of Jehovah" will draw near, with dread-inspiring signs in heaven and earth.   But the terrors of that day are not now for the Jews, but for their enemies : in the judgment which marks its arrival, those who *trust* in Jehovah will escape, 2²⁸⁻³² ; but upon the heathen, who have "scattered Israel among the nations, and parted my land," besides otherwise ill-treating the people of God, summary vengeance will be taken : they are invited to arm themselves, and come up to the valley of [288] Jehoshaphat ("Jehovah judges"), ostensibly for battle against the Jews, in reality to be annihilated by the heavenly ministers of Jehovah's wrath (3¹¹ᵇ). The scene of carnage which ensues is pictured under suggestive figures, 3¹³ᶠ· ; but "Jehovah will be a refuge unto His people, and a stronghold to the children of Israel."   Then the soil of Judah will be preternaturally fertilised ; and "a fountain shall come forth of the house of Jehovah, and shall water the wādy of the Acacias " (symbolizing the arid and barren regions of Judah) : Egypt, on the other hand, and Edom, as a punishment for the wrongs inflicted by them upon the people of Judah, will be changed into wildernesses (3¹⁸⁻²¹).

The locusts in c. 1 (though this has been questioned) are, no doubt, to be understood literally ; there is nothing in the language used to suggest anything but an *actual* visitation of locusts, from which the country has been suffering.   The *actual* locusts suggest to Joel the imagery by which he describes, 2¹ᶠᶠ·, the approach of the "Day of Jehovah" : here the locusts are *idealized* ; they are creatures of the imagination, invested with appalling size and power, the prototype of the "apocalyptic" locusts of Rev. 9³⁻¹⁰ (where, however, the *ideal* delineation is carried much further than here). As the locusts in c. 2 are *compared* to an army, they can hardly (as some have supposed) be themselves merely symbolical of an army.   The meaning of "the northern one" in 2²⁰ is disputed, and uncertain.   From the connexion with v.¹⁹·²⁵ it would naturally be understood to denote the locusts, the removal of which follows the people's repentance.   But locusts never (or scarcely ever) enter Palestine from the north ; so that (unless the occasion was *one of the exceptions*) "the northern one" would be an unsuitable designation for them ; hence by some the term is considered to be descriptive of a *human* foe (see p. 311 *n.*).

For determining the date of Joel (the title being silent) we are dependent entirely upon internal evidence ; and as this is interpreted differently by different critics, much diversity of opinion exists on the subject.   The principal criteria afforded by the prophecy are the following :—(1) Joel mentions Tyre, Zidon, the Philistines, the Greeks (" Javan," *i.e. Ionians*), Sabeans, Egypt, and Edom ; (2) he is silent—not even noticing them allusively—on the Syrians, Assyrians, and Chaldæans; (3) he nowhere mentions or alludes to the Ten Tribes; even when speaking most generally, *e.g.* of the future restoration, or of Israelites sold as slaves ($3^{1.\ 6.\ 18}$), he names only "Judah and Jerusalem": "Israel," where the term occurs (2^{27}; 3^{16}: 3^2 is ambiguous), is used simply as the generic name of Judah; (4) Jehovah's people is "a reproach among the nations" (2^{19}); [289] and it is said of "all nations" that they have "scattered" His "heritage among the nations, and parted" His "land," and "cast lots over" His "people" (3^{2b-3a}); the return of the captivity of Judah and Jerusalem is also anticipated by the prophet (3^1); (5) the Tyrians, Zidonians, and Philistines are charged with having plundered the gold and silver and treasures belonging to Jehovah, and selling captive Judahites to the Greeks (3^{4-6}); (6) Egypt and Edom are threatened with desolation for the violence done to Judah in murdering innocent Judahites in their land (3^{19}); (7) there is no allusion to any kind of *idolatry*; the services of the Temple are conducted regularly; the priests take a prominent position, and are evidently held in respect ($1^{9.\ 13}$ 2^{17}); the cessation, through the locusts and drought, of the means of providing the daily Meal- and Drink-offering is treated as a grave calamity; (8) the prophet is silent as to the king, and even as to the princes; the *elders*, on the contrary, are alluded to (1^{14}) as prominent in a public gathering; (9) mention is made ($3^{2.\ 12}$) of the "valley of Jehoshaphat," presumably so called from the king of that name; (10) there are resemblances between Joel and Amos which show that one of the two prophets must have imitated or borrowed from the other (Joel 3^{16} and Amos 1^2; 3^{18} and Amos 9^{13b}).

It was argued by Credner in 1831 that the conditions implied by these criteria were satisfied by a date in the early part of the reign of King Joash, B.C. 878–839 [rather *c.* 837–801] (2 Ki. 12), *after* the invasion of Judah by Shishak (1 Ki. $14^{25.\ 26}$), which is supposed to be alluded to in 3^{17b} (no *strangers to pass through* Jerusalem any more), and 3^{19} ("*violence against the children of Judah*"), the reign of Jehoshaphat (No. 9), and the revolt of the Edomites under Jehoram (2 Ki. 8^{20-22}), to the murder by whom of Judahites settled in their territory 3^{19} may refer, and not long after the plundering of the royal treasures (No. 5) by marauding Philistines and Arabians during the same reign (2 Ch. $21^{16.\ 17}$

22¹), but *before* the time when the Syrians under Hazael threatened Jerusalem, and had to be bought off at the cost of the Temple treasures by Joash (2 Ki. 12¹⁷ᶠ·), and *à fortiori* before the time when Judah suffered at the hands of Assyrians or Chaldæans (cf. No. 2). Upon this view 3²⁻³· ⁶ are referred to the loss of territory suffered by Judah at the time of the revolt of Edom (which was followed quickly [290] by that of Libnah, 2 Ki. 8²²), and to the sale of prisoners, whom the Philistines and Arabians might be presumed to have taken, to other nations, such as is laid by Amos (1⁶· ⁹) to the charge of Gaza and Tyre. Joash (2 Ki. 11²¹) was only seven years old when he came to the throne : if Joel's prophecy dated from the period of his minority, the non-mention of the king (No. 8), it is urged, would be explained, while the position of the priests, and the regularity of the Temple services (No. 7), would be a natural consequence of the influence exerted by the priest Jehoiada.

Credner's arguments were specious ; and most scholars until recently acquiesced in his conclusion. At the same time, he can hardly be considered to have done justice to 3² : the strong expressions here used respecting the dispersion of Israel among the nations, and the allotment of the Holy Land to new occupants, cannot fairly be referred to any calamity less than that of the Babylonian captivity. Keil felt this objection so strongly, that he supposed the words in question to be spoken by Joel with reference to the future ; but if the passage be read in connexion with the context, it seems plain that the prophet alludes to sufferings which have been *already* undergone by the nation. And when the criteria noted by Credner are considered carefully, it appears that many of them are equally consistent with a date *after* the captivity, while other features exhibited by the prophecy even agree with such a date better.

Thus* (1) the enemies of Judah are *the nations collectively*, who are assembled for a signal defeat outside the walls of Jerusalem. This is a feature prominent in later prophets, as Ez. 38–39, Zech. 14 : the earlier prophets speak of *definite* enemies of Judah (as the Assyrians). (2) The book implies a nation united religiously, and free from any of those tendencies to heathenism which call forth the constant rebuke of the pre-exilic prophets. (3) No king is mentioned : the nation possesses a municipal organisation with

---

* Comp. W. R. Smith, *s.v.* JOEL, in the *Encycl. Brit.*⁹ (reprinted in Black's *Bible Dictionary*). The form in which the arguments on the same side are stated by Merx is not free from exaggeration.

a priestly aristocracy, which accords with the constitution that prevailed after the exile. That the Persians do not appear as the enemies of Israel is not more than natural, they were hard masters, but not invaders; and under their rule (comp. Neh.) the enemies of the Jews were their neighbours, precisely as appears in Joel. (4) Edom's hostility to Judah was not confined to the period of the reign of Joash: it was habitual; and a bitter feeling against [291] Edom often manifests itself in Jewish writers after the events of B.C. 586 (cf. p. 226). (5) Egypt is probably mentioned merely as the typical example of a power hostile to Judah: even on Credner's theory the allusion is to an incident which happened *a century before*. And 3[17b] is much more pointed if spoken after the desecration of the Temple by the Chaldæans (cf. Isa. 52[1]), than after the invasion of Shishak (who is not stated to have entered Jerusalem at all). (6) 2 Chr. 21 mentions Philistines and Arabians, but is silent altogether as to the Phœnicians, who appear here as the offenders. There is no ground for limiting the traffic in slaves to the age of Amos; and the notice of Javan (Greece) better suits a later time, when Syrian slaves were in request in Greece. (7) Judah and the people of Jehovah are convertible terms: northern Israel has disappeared. This is not the case in the earlier prophets; the prophets of Israel do not exclude Judah, at least from their promises, nor do the prophets of Judah exclude Israel. (8) The importance attached to the daily offering is not less characteristic of the post-exilic age (Neh. 10[33]; cf. Dan. 8[11] 11[31] 12[11]). (9) Joel's eschatological picture consists largely of a combination of elements derived from older unfulfilled prophecies. Its central feature, the assembling of the nations to judgment, already appears in Zeph. 3[8], and in Ezekiel's prophecy concerning Gog and Magog, where the wonders of fire and blood are also mentioned (Ezek. 38[22]). The picture of the fertility of the land (3[18]) is based on Am. 9[13] (comp. below); that of the stream issuing from the Temple, and fertilizing the Wādy of Acacias, upon Ezek. 47[1-12] (cf. Zech. 14[8]); the outpouring of the Spirit, upon Ezek. 39[29].*

These arguments are forcible. In particular, *the terms of* 3[1-2] (cf. 2[19b]), the relation of Israel to "the nations" which these passages presuppose, and the general resemblance of the repre-

---

* See also Farrar, pp. 105–112, 120–123. Those who adopt this date for Joel often suppose that "the northern one" of 2[20] is an allusion to the imagery of Ez. 38[15] 39[2], where the ideal hosts that threaten Judah are represented as coming from the north. But it is very doubtful if this is right: the fate of the "northerner" is distinctively that of a swarm of locusts.

Prof. J. W. Rothstein, in a note in the German translation of the present work (p. 333 f.), argues, on account of differences in the political situation presupposed, and in the literary originality displayed, that the book is not throughout the work of a single hand: 1[1]–2[27], he thinks, may well be pre-exilic; 2[28]–3[21] is a supplement, reflecting the situation and conceptions of the post-exilic age (cf. Ob. [10-21] by the side of v.[1-9]), added by one who, interpreting (incorrectly) the locusts of 1[1]–2[27] as a symbolical designation of the foes who were overrunning the land when he wrote, introduced at the same time 2[20] for the purpose of announcing their destruction.

sentation·in c. 3 to those found in the later prophets, must be allowed to turn the balance of evidence somewhat strongly in favour of the later date. Joel's imagery and language are fine : but he can scarcely be said to exhibit the originality and breadth of view which are generally characteristic of the earlier prophets. He seems to move "in the circle of moral convictions and eschatological hopes which had been marked out for him by his great predecessors " : though he calls to repentance ($1^{13f.}$ $2^{12f.\ 15}$), the stress lies with him not upon his people's sin, but upon the distinction between Israel and other nations ; Israel, at least in so far as it responds to Jehovah's call (2^{32}), is to be saved and glorified, the nations are annihilated. It seems as if Joel re-affirmed, in a form suited to the temper and needs of his age, the promises of the older prophets, which it was impossible [292] to regard as adequately accomplished in the actual condition of the restored exiles.*

The principal literary parallels between Joel and other prophets are the following :—1^{15}, Isa. 13^6.—2^2, Zeph. 1^{15} (and Ex. 10^{14b}).—2^8, Ez. 36^{35} (the " garden of Eden ").—2^{6b}, Nah. 2^{10b} [H. ^{11b}] (קבצו פארור ↑).—2^{10}, Isa. 13^{10}, Ez. 32^7.—2^{17b}, Ps. 79^{10} 115^2; cf. $42^{3.\ 10}$, Mic. 7^{10}.—2^{27}, Ez. 36^{11} 39^{28}, Isa. $45^{5.\ 6.\ 18}$.—2^{28}, Ez. 39^{29} (cf. 36^{27}).—2^{32}, Ob. ^{17}.—3^2, Ez. 38^{22}.—3^{3a}, Ob. ^{11} (ידו גורל : only Nah. 3^{10} besides).—$3^{4.\ 14}$, Ob.^{15}.—3^{10}, Isa. 2^4 (=Mic. 4^3).—3^{16}, Am. 1^2.—3^{17b}, Ob.^{17}, Isa. 52^{1b}.—3^{18}, Am. 9^{13}.—3^{19}, Ob.^{10}.

Von Orelli argues that some of these parallels are decisive for the pre-exilic date of Joel (p. 237) : "Ez. $30^{2f.}$ is unmistakably dependent upon Joel 1^{15} $2^{1f.}$; similarly Jer. $25^{30f.}$ on Joel $3^{11.\ 16}$. So Isa. 66^{18} presupposes Joel 3^2. Ez. $47^{1ff.}$ develops further the imagery of Joel 3^{18} ; and Ez. 38^{17} 39^8 allude in all probability especially to Joel 3. The dependency of Isa. $13^{6.\ 9}$ on Joel 1^{15} is palpable. And the parallels with Amos show incontrovertibly that he is earlier than this prophet. Am. 1^2 is taken certainly from Joel 3^{16} : accordingly Am. 9^{13} also is dependent on Joel 3^{18}." But that this is the true relation between the passages quoted is by no means self-evident. Nothing is more difficult (except under specially favourable circumstances) than from a *mere* comparison of parallel passages to determine on which side the priority lies ;† and if those cited by von Orelli be examined, it will be seen that there is no reason (apart from the assumption, upon other grounds, that Joel is the earlier) why the relation should not be inverted, why, in other words, it should not be Joel who is the borrower. And as regards the parallels with Amos, it is to be noticed that in each case the picture in Joel is more highly coloured than in Amos : especially (as Kuen. § 68. 15 observes)

---

* See further *Joel and Amos*, p. 30 ff.

† Hence the failure of the attempts made by Küper, Caspari, and others to show that Isa. 13^2-14^{23}, 34–35, 40–66 are prior to Jer., Nah., and Zeph.

it seems unlikely that Amos, if he had been borrowing from a passage which described Jehovah's thunder as shaking *heaven and earth,* would have limited its effects to the pastures of the shepherds and the top of Carmel. But even if this argument be not accepted as decisive, there is still nothing inherent either in these or in the other passages to show that the priority is with Joel : in other words, the parallels cannot be used for *determining* the date of Joel ; we can only, *after having determined his date on independent grounds,* point to the parallels for the purpose of *illustrating* (as the case may be) either his dependence upon the other prophets, or their dependence upon him. In 2^{32} [Heb. 3^5], however, Ob. [17], " And in mount Zion shall be those that escape," does appear to be expressly cited : " And in mount Zion and in Jerusalem shall be those that escape, *as Jehovah hath said.*" G. B. Gray, in the *Expositor,* Sept. 1893, p. 208 ff., after a careful and independent study of the parallel passages, reaches the same conclusion that Joel is the quoter (comp. the writer's *Joel and Amos,* pp. 19–23, 24 f.).

The style of Joel is bright and flowing ; and the contrast, which is palpable, with Haggai or Malachi is no doubt felt by many as a reason against the view that his prophecy dates from the same general period of the history. [293] But it is a question whether our knowledge of this period is of a character authorizing us to affirm that a style such as Joel's could not have been written then ; at least, if Zech. 12–14 dates from the post-exilic age, it is difficult to argue that Joel cannot date from it likewise. The phraseology, viewed as a whole, can hardly be cited as positively favouring the later date, though it is true that it includes some words and expressions which are more common in the later than in the earlier literature : thus 1^2 4^4 ואם . . . ה (the usual form is אם . . . ה) ; 1^9 2^{17} " ministers of Jehovah " (cf. Jer. $33^{21f.}$, Isa. 61^6, 1 Ch. 16^4 2 Ch. 13^{10} 29^{11}, Ezr. 8^{17}, Neh. $10^{87b. 40}$) ; 2^2 4^{20} דור ודור ; 2^8 שלח *weapon* (Job [Elihu], Neh. Chr.) ; 2^{20} סוף *end* (Aram.: 2 Ch. 20^{16}, Eccl. 3^{11} 7^2 12^{13} ↑) ; $3(4)^2$ Jehovah's *litigating* (נשפט) with His enemies (Jer. 2^{35} 25^{31}, Ez. 17^{20} $20^{35. 36}$ 38^{22}, Isa. 66^{16}) ; $3(4)^4$ נמל על (2 Ch. 20^{11}) ; $3(4)^{10}$ רמח *lance* ; $3(4)^{11}$ הנחת *cause to come down* (Aram.).

§ 3. AMOS.

Amos, as the title to his book informs us, was " among the shepherds of Tekoa," *i.e.* he belonged to a settlement of shepherds who had their home at Tekoa, and who, as the word used implies, reared a special breed of sheep, of small and stunted growth, but prized on account of their wool. From 7^{14} we learn that he had under his charge herds of larger cattle as well ; and that he was employed besides in the cultivation of sycomore trees. Although this has been questioned, the Tekoa meant is no doubt the place of that name about 12 miles south of Jerusalem : Amos, therefore, will have been a native of Judah, though he received a commission—being taken, as he describes it, "from after the flock" (7^{15})—to go and prophesy to the people of Israel. In connexion with the nature of prophecy, it is to be noticed that Amos disclaims (7^{14}) being a prophet by profession or education : he is no "son of a prophet," *i.e.* no member of a prophetic guild (2 Ki. 4^{1} &c.) ; his inspiration is independent of any artificial training. The year of Uzziah's reign, in which the "earthquake," mentioned in 1^{1} (cf. Zech. 14^{5}), took place, is not known ; but internal evidence points to the latter part of Jeroboam II.'s reign, *after* the successes alluded to in 2 Ki. 14^{25}, *i.e.* about 760–746 B.C., as that to which Amos' prophetic ministry belongs. The reign of Jeroboam II., though passed by briefly in the historical books (2 Ki. 14^{23-29}), was the culminating point in the history of the Northern kingdom. Jeroboam had been successful in recovering for Israel territory which it had lost (2 Ki. 14^{25}) ; and the allusions in Amos [294] show us the nation reposing in opulence and ease (*e.g.* 6^{1-5}) ; the ritual of the calf worship at Beth-el, Gilgal, and elsewhere was splendidly and punctiliously maintained ($4^{4f.}$ 5^{21-23} 7^{13} 8^{14}) : general satisfaction reigned : the proud citizen of Ephraim felt that he could defy any adversary (6^{13}). Such was the condition and temper of the people when Amos, arriving at the great national sanctuary of Beth-el as a stranger (7^{10-17}), interrupted the rejoicings there with his forebodings of woe.

The book falls naturally into three parts, c. 1–2, c. 3–6, c. 7–9, each dominated by the same fundamental thoughts, and the whole pervaded by a unity of plan which leaves no reasonable doubt that the arrangement is the author's own. I. The *first* part, c. 1–2, is introductory. Here, after the fine exordium (1^{2}), so graphically descriptive of Jehovah's power, Amos takes a survey of the principal nations bordering on Israel,—Damascus, Gaza, Tyre, Edom, Ammon, Moab, Judah,—with the object of showing that as none of these will escape retribution for having broken the common and universally regarded dictates of morality; so Israel, for similar or greater sins (2^{6-8}), aggravated, indeed, in its case by ingratitude (v.$^{9-12}$), will not be exempt from the same law of righteous government : a disaster darkly hinted at (v.$^{13-16}$) will undo all the conquests achieved by Jeroboam II. ! The enumeration of countries is evidently intended to lead up to Israel, and is arranged skilfully : the Israelite would listen with some inward satisfaction whilst his neighbours' faults, with the

judgments that they would incur, were being pointed out; in the
end, however, he is measured himself by exactly the same
standard that is applied to others, and is threatened with retribution not less severe.

II. C. 3–6. This part consists of three discourses, each
introduced by the emphatic *Hear ye this word* (3^1 4^1 5^1).
Here the indictment and sentence of 2^{6-16} are further justified
and expanded. The Israelites argued that the fact of Jehovah's
having chosen the nation was a guarantee of its safety. Amos
replies: That is not the case; you have mistaken the conditions
of His choice: for that very reason He will visit your iniquities
upon you ($3^{1f.}$) Nor, he continues, does the prophet say this
without a real power constraining him: for does any effect in
nature take place without its due and adequate cause? (v.$^{3-8}$).
Call the heathen themselves to witness whether *justice* rules in
[295] Samaria (v.$^{9f.}$). The toils will ere long have closed about
the land (v.$^{11-15}$). C. 4 begins by denouncing the thoughtless
cruelty and frivolity of the women (v.$^{1-3}$): the prophet next asks
the Israelites ironically whether their punctiliously performed
ritual will save them (v.$^{4f.}$): the fivefold warning has passed un-
heeded (v.$^{6-11}$): prepare thyself, then, for judgment! In c. 5–6
the grounds of the judgment are repeated with greater emphasis
($5^{7,\ 10,\ 11f.}$ 6^{3-6}): the infatuation of the people is exposed in
desiring the "Day of Jehovah," as though that could be anything but an interposition in their favour (5^{18-20}); a ritual un-
accompanied by any sense of moral obligation is indignantly
rejected (5^{21-24}); the nature of the coming disaster is described
more distinctly (exile, 5^{26} [RV. *marg.*] ^{27} 6^7), and the enemy
indicated, though not named (the Assyrians), which should
"afflict" Israel over the entire limits of the territory which
Jeroboam had not long since regained (6^{14}: see 2 Ki. 14^{25}).

III. C. 7–9, consisting of a series of visions, with an historical
interlude (7^{10-17}), and an epilogue (9^{7-15}). The visions reinforce,
under a simple but effective symbolism, the lesson of the previous discourses: in the first two (7^{1-6}), the threatened judgment
is interrupted at the prophet's intercession; the third, which
spoke without any concealment or ambiguity, aroused the alarm
and opposition of Amaziah, the priest of the golden calf at
Beth-el, and is the occasion of the historical notice, 7^{10-17}. The
fourth vision is the text of a fresh and more detailed denuncia-

tion of judgment (c. 8): the fifth depicts the desolation falling upon the people as they are assembled for worship in their own temple, and emphasizes the hopelessness of every effort to escape (9$^{1-6}$). The prophecy closes, 9$^{7-15}$, with brighter anticipations for a more distant future. Israel, indeed, for its sins will be dealt with as any other nation (v.^{7}): but only the *sinners* will perish utterly: a faithful remnant will escape (v.$^{8-10}$); the house of David will be restored to its former splendour and power,* and the blessings of unity and prosperity will be shared by the entire nation (v.$^{13-15}$).

The unity of plan governing the arrangement of the book will be manifest: the main theme, gradually introduced in c. 1–2, is developed with increasing [296] distinctness in the chapters which follow, till it gives place to the outlook upon a happier future at the close. The allusions of Amos to the social condition and religious life of the Northern kingdom do not present such a dark picture as that drawn by Hosea a few years later (c. 4–14), during the anarchy and misrule which prevailed after the dynasty of Jehu had fallen: nevertheless the amendment, which was still viewed by him as a possibility (5$^{14f.}$), never came; and almost before a generation had passed away, his forebodings of invasion, disaster, and exile (2$^{13-16}$ 3$^{11-15}$ 4^{12} 5$^{2f.}$ $^{16f.}$ ^{27} 6^{14} 7$^{9.\ 17}$ 8$^{2f.}$ 9$^{1-4}$) were amply realized by Tiglath-Pileser, Shalmaneser, and Sargon (2 Ki. 15^{29} 17$^{3-6}$). *Judah* is alluded to by Amos only incidentally: 2$^{4f.}$ 3^1 (" the *whole* family ") 6^1 9^{11}.

Amos is the earliest of the prophets whose writings are extant and of undisputed date; and hence, like those of his younger contemporary Hosea, his writings are of importance as witnessing to the religious beliefs current in the eighth century B.C. It is clear, for instance, that he recognised (2^4) an authoritative Divine teaching or *Tôrāh*, by which, however, like Hosea (4^6 compared with 4$^{1f.}$; 8$^{1.\ 12}$, cf. 6^6), he appears to have understood primarily the *moral* precepts of Jehovah (comp. 5$^{21-27}$, where he rebukes the people with neglecting the *moral* demands of God, and trusting to sacrifice to indemnify them). The broad moral standard by which he judges Israel is particularly noticeable. It is not a standard peculiar to Israel, it is the common moral standard recognised as binding by it and by other nations alike. Jehovah is God of the whole earth, of other nations not less than of Israel (c. 1; 9^7), and will only be Israel's God in so far as the same morality is practised in its

* V.^{12} alludes to the nations conquered by David, and so owned by Jehovah as His subjects (see p. 275, No. 16): 2 Sa. 8$^{1-14}$, Ps. 18^{43}.

midst. Jehovah had been pleased to enter into a special personal relation with Israel : this fact, to which the common people pointed as their security ($5^{14\ end}$), in the eyes of Amos only aggravates their guilt (3^2). Disregard of the moral law is the first charge which he brings against Israel itself (2^{6-8}) ; and his indignation against every form of moral wrong is vehemently expressed (comp. *e.g.* the outburst against deceit in commercial dealings 8^{4-8} ; notice also the *oath*, $8^7\ 4^2\ 6^8$: each time elicited by the same fault). The observances of religion are no substitute for honesty, and will not be accepted by Jehovah in lieu of righteousness of heart (5^{21-24}).

On the "Day of Jehovah" (5^{18-20}), and the manner in which Amos reverses the popular conception of it, see W. R. Smith, *Proph.* p. 131 f., who also (p. 120 ff.) draws out suggestively many other characteristics of Amos' teaching. In noticing the fortunes and deserts of the nations bordering [297] on Palestine, Amos adopted a precedent which was followed afterwards by Isaiah, Jeremiah, and Ezekiel. Amos was a man naturally shrewd and observant : alike in his survey of foreign nations (comp. also $6^2\ 8^8\ 9^7$), and in his allusions to Israelitish life and manners, he reveals a width of knowledge and precision of detail which are remarkable. He was enlightened by the true light that enlightens every man ʃnlʒ

Jerome (Pref. to Amos), speaking of Amos with reference to his style, describes him as " imperitus sermone, sed non scientia"; and, though the context suggests that he is merely arguing *à priori* from the prophet's antecedents, it has hence been sometimes the custom to attribute to his style a peculiar homeliness and "rusticity." But this judgment is not borne out by the facts. His language, with three or four insignificant exceptions, is pure, his style classical and refined. His literary power is shown in the regularity of structure, which often characterizes his periods, as 1^3–$2^6\ 4^{6-11}$ (the fivefold refrain), and the visions ($7^{1.\ 4.\ 7}\ 8^1$) ; in the fine climax 3^{3-8} ; in the balanced clauses, the well-chosen images, the effective contrasts, in such passages as $3^{15}\ 5^{2.\ 21-24}\ 6^{11}\ 8^{10}\ 9^{2-4}$: as well as in the ease with which he evidently writes, and the skill with which (as shown above) his theme is introduced and developed. Anything of the nature of roughness or rusticity is wholly absent from his writings. His regular, flowing sentences form a remarkable contrast with the short, abrupt clauses which Hosea loves. It is true, in the command of grand and picturesque imagery he is not the equal of Isaiah ; nevertheless his thought is often finely expressed

(1^2 5^{24} 8^8 $9^{5f.}$); and if, as compared with other prophets, images derived from rural life somewhat preponderate, they are always applied by him aptly (*e.g.* $3^{4.\ 8}$ $5^{8.\ 16.\ 17.\ 19}$ 9^9), and never strike the reader as occurring too frequently, or as out of place.

In Amos, as in Hosea, (p. 306 f.), there are passages which have been supposed by recent critics, upon similar grounds, to be later additions to the original text of the prophecy. Duhm (*Theol. der Proph.* 1875, p. 119) questioned thus 2^{4-5} 4^{13} 5^{8-9} 9^{5-6} (so Stade, *G.* i. 571 *n.*); Wellh. (1892) rejects in addition 1^{9-12}, 3^{14b} 5^{26} 6^2 8^{6},$^{8.\ 11-12}$ 9^{8-15}; Cheyne (in W. R. Smith, *Proph.*[2] 1895, p. xv f.; on 5^{26} 9^{8-15}, see also *Expositor*, Jan. 1897, p. 42 ff.) rejects 1^2 2^{4-5} 4^{13} $5^{8-9.\ 26}$ 8^{11-12} $9^{5-6.\ 8-15}$; and G. A. Smith (1896) at least suspects 1^{11-12} (p. 129 f.), 2^{4-5} (p. 135 f.), 4^{13} 5^{8-9} 9^{5-6} (p. 201 ff.), 5^{14-15} (p. 168 f.), 6^2 (p. 173, *n.* 2), 8^{13} (p. 185), and decidedly rejects 9^{8-15} (pp. 190 ff., 308 f.). Of these passages, 2^{4-5} 4^{13} 5^{8-9} 9^{5-6} were defended by W. R. Smith in 1882 (*Proph.* p. 398 f.), and by Kuenen in 1889 (*Onderz.* § 71. 6). In some cases, the grounds alleged are not devoid of force; but, as before, in similar instances, there is the same doubt whether they can be deemed conclusive. Space forbids any fuller discussion here; and the writer must be content to refer to what he has said in *Joel and Amos*, p. 117 ff. (on 4^{13} 5^{8-9} 9^{5-6}, also, cf. L. B. Paton, *JBLit.* 1894, p. 84 ff.).

§ 4. OBADIAH.

The short prophecy of Obadiah is concerned almost entirely with Edom. V.[1-9] the prophet declares the ruin impending on Edom: her lofty rock-hewn dwellings will this time be penetrated by the invader; her allies will abandon her; the "wisdom" for which Edom was proverbial will fail her in the hour of her need. V.[10-11] states the ground of the preceding denunciation, viz. the violence and outrage of which Edom had been [298] guilty in the day of Jerusalem's calamity; v.[12-14] he bids them emphatically desist from their inhuman delight; v.[15-21] he returns to dwell upon the retribution which awaits them. A "Day of Jehovah" is near upon all nations: the escaped of Judah, united (as it appears) with the restored "House of Joseph" (cf. Jer. $31^{5.\ 27}$ &c.), and endued with irresistible might, will exterminate the "House of Esau"; the territory of Judah will be enlarged on all sides, the inhabitants of the South possessing Edom, and Benjamin overflowing into Gilead; "saviours"— such as the judges (Jud. 2^{16} $3^{9.\ 15}$)—will defend Zion against its foes, and Jehovah's kingdom will be established.

For determining the date of Obadiah the two chief criteria

are (1) the expressions in v.[11-14]; (2) the relation of Ob. to
Jeremiah's prophecy on Edom, 49[7-22]. (1) In v.[11-14] Ob. speaks
of a day of "disaster," "calamity," and "distress" which has
befallen Jerusalem, on which "foreigners" entered the city and
"cast lots" upon it; and when the Edomites not only exulted
at the humiliation of the Jews, but actively assisted their foes,
and sought to intercept and cut off the fugitives. These expressions are most naturally referred to the destruction of Jerusalem by the Chaldæans in 586, and to the hostile temper
evinced then by the Edomites, which (see p. 226) was profoundly
resented by the Jews.* (2) Jer. 49[7-22] and Ob. display such a
large element common to both as to make it evident either that
one borrowed from the other, or that both are dependent upon
the same earlier original : comp. Ob.[1-4]; v.[5-6]; v.[8] with Jer. 49[14-16];
v.[9-10a]; v.[7] (respectively). There are reasons for supposing the
second of these alternatives to be the correct one. For, when
the two texts are compared carefully together, it appears that the
prophecy, viewed as a whole, *is in its more original form in Ob.*†
And yet, as the date of Jer. 49[7ff.] seems [299] fixed, not only by
46[1f.] (B.C. 604), but by internal evidence as well,‡ to a period
prior to the capture of Jerusalem by the Chaldæans, the prophecy of Ob., if it alludes to the conduct of the Edomites *after*
that event, cannot evidently have formed the model for Jer.;
and the resemblances between the two prophecies can only be
explained by the supposition that the common elements have
been derived by both *from a prophecy older than either*, which
Ob. has incorporated with least alteration, while Jer. has treated
it with greater freedom. § This older prophecy will consist of
Ob.[1-9], which contains no allusion to the *special* circumstances of

* So Ewald, Meyrick (in the *Speaker's Comm.*), Kuenen, Farrar, &c.

† The sequence in Ob. is better : thus "We (I) have heard tidings from
Jehovah" is in a more suitable place at the beginning, as in Ob., than in the
middle, as in Jer.; the language is terser and more forcible (Jer., in several
instances, appears to *expand* the text of Ob. by introducing words); and, in
particular, the parts of Jer. which have no parallel in Ob. have affinities with
Jer.'s own style, showing that Jer. took materials from an older prophecy,
which he embedded in elements contributed by himself. (This is shown in
detail by Caspari, pp. 7–13, whose argument is generally admitted to be
conclusive, *e.g.* by Graf, *Jer.* p. 559 ff.).

‡ 49[12a] RV. the punishment of Jerusalem is still *future*.

§ So Ewald, *Prophets*, ii. 277 ff.; Graf (*l.c.*); Kuenen; Briggs (*Mess.
Proph.* p. 315 f.). Meyrick, p. 564, appears to have overlooked Jer. 49[12].

B.C. 586 : * in Jer. the order of these verses is changed, and v.⁷ (Edom's abandonment by its allies,—an allusion apparently to some circumstance of the time when the original prophecy was written), and v.⁹, are omitted.   In favour of this supposition it is remarked, that though, on the whole, the prophecy is in its more original form in Ob., in particular instances more original elements seem to have been preserved by Jer. (49⁹· ¹⁵ᵇ· ¹⁶ [תפלצתך], as compared with Ob.⁵· ²ᵇ· ³ [תפלצתך omitted]).

The date and occasion of the earlier prophecy must remain uncertain ; Ewald (*Hist.* iii. 159 f.) conjectured that it may have been when Elath, the port on the Red Sea which had been occupied by the Jews under Uzziah (2 Ki. 14²²), was restored by Rezin to the Edomites (*ib.* 16⁶ RV. *marg.* [לאדם for לארם, and וארומים for וארמים] : cf. 2 Ch. 28¹⁷).

Other scholars (Delitzsch, Keil, von Orelli, Kirkpatrick) have sought to explain the relation of Jer. to Ob. more simply by referring the prophecy of Ob. to an earlier occasion altogether, viz. to the plundering incursion of "Philistines and Arabians," who apparently, according to 2 Ch. 21¹⁶ᶠ·, penetrated into Jerusalem in the reign of Jehoram (B.C. 851–844 [Kamphausen]), in which case, of course, Jer. would borrow from it directly.   The expressions, however, which Ob. uses (notice esp. "*cast lots* upon Jerusalem") appear to be too strong to be referred with probability to this invasion, which, to judge from the silence of the Book of Kings, was little more than a predatory incursion, from the effects of which Judah speedily [300] recovered ; and at least v.¹⁵⁻²¹ seems to display the tone and thought of a much later age (the exile of the northern tribes is presupposed in v.¹⁹).   In the taunting speech of v.⁷ᵃ notice the peculiar (elegiac) rhythm (see below, under Lamentations), and compare Jer. 38²²ᵇ : one of these passages must have served as the model for the other.

Kuenen (§ 72. 3–4) and Cornill (*Einl.*³ § 30) both adopt the same view of Ob.¹⁻⁹ which is given in the text, and agree that v.¹⁰⁻¹⁴ refers to the events of B.C. 586 ; but they argue that there is nothing in v.¹⁵⁻²¹ to imply that the city is still waste and uninhabited, and conclude accordingly that the author who added v.¹⁰⁻²¹, and so gave the prophecy its present form, wrote at some date after the return—probably in the 5th cent. B.C.   A further clue to the date has been sought in the name *Sĕphārēd* (" Sepharad " is the pausal form) in v.²⁰.   This, Cheyne (*Founders of O.T. Crit.* 311 f.) and Sayce (*Monuments*, pp. 482–484) agree, must be the Çparda or 'Saparda of the inscriptions, in Bithynia or Galatia (Sayce, *l.c.*), a region not owned by the Assyrians or Babylonians, but first held by Cyrus, and organized by Darius Hystaspis into a satrapy (cf. Schrader, *KAT.*² *ad loc.*).   This fact points to "a comparatively late date" (Sayce) for the prophecy : Cheyne would assign it

---

* And from which the sequel differs also in representation ; in v.¹⁻⁹ Edom is destroyed by the nations (v.¹) and its treacherous allies ; in v.¹⁵ᶠᶠ· it falls *with* other nations in the day of universal retribution (cf. Is. 34²· ⁵) before the victorious Israelites.

definitely to the occasion (*c.* B.C. 350) when Artaxerxes Ochus transported many Jews into Hyrcania and Babylonia (above, p. 222).   Wellh. (p. 204 f.) agrees that v. [10-14] looks back upon the events of B.C. 586 ; but he thinks that the whole of v.[1-14] is post-exilic, the occasion of the prophecy being the expulsion of the Edomites from their ancient home early in the 5th cent. D.C. (cf. Mal., 1[1-5]) by the Nabatæan Arabs (in whose possession their country appears, in B.C. 312 : Schürer, *Gesch. des Jüd. Volkes*, i. 612 [App. ii.]) ; v.[15-21] he regards as an appendix, added afterwards, in which the fate of Edom is represented as an episode in Jehovah's judgment on the heathen generally.

§ 5. JONAH.

Jonah, the son of Amittai, as we learn from 2 Ki. 14[25], was a native of Gath-hepher, in the tribe of Zebulun (Josh. 19[13]), who lived in the reign of Jeroboam II., and predicted to that king the successful issue of his struggle with the Syrians, which ended with his restoration of the territory of Israel to its ancient limits.   These prophecies must have been delivered in the early part of Jeroboam II.'s long reign ; it would have been interesting, had they been preserved, to compare them with the prophecies of Amos, uttered towards the close of the same reign, which announced how Jeroboam's successes would ere long be fatally undone (see Am. 6[14]).   The Book of Jonah, however (unlike the books of all the other prophets), consists almost entirely of narrative, being devoted to the description of a particular incident in the prophet's life.   The story is too well known to need repetition in detail.   Jonah, commissioned to preach at Nineveh Jehovah's judgment against the great city, seeks to avoid the necessity of obeying the command, fearing (as appears from 4[2]) that Jehovah might in the end be moved to have mercy upon the Ninevites, so that his predictions of judgment would be frustrated.   Accordingly, he takes ship at Joppa, with the view of escaping to Tarshish (Tartessus in Spain).   A violent storm overtakes the ship : the sailors, deeming that one of those on board is the cause of it, cast lots to discover who it is : the lot falls upon Jonah, who consents to be cast into the sea.   Thereupon the sea becomes calm.   Jonah is swallowed by a great fish, which, after three days, casts him forth, uninjured, upon the land.   Again the prophet receives the commission to preach at Nineveh.   This time he proceeds thither : but at his preaching the Ninevites repent, and Jehovah rescinds the decree which He had passed against them.   Displeased at the seeming failure of his mission, [301] Jonah sits down outside the city, and asks to be allowed to die; but a gourd quickly springing up and sheltering him from the sun, and as quickly dying and leaving him exposed to its rays, by exciting his sympathy, is made the means of justifying in his eyes Jehovah's merciful change of purpose with respect to Nineveh.

Both in form and contents the Book of Jonah resembles the biographical narratives of Elijah and Elisha (1 Ki. 17-19, 2 Ki. 4-6, &c.), though it is pervaded by a more distinctly didactic aim. It cannot, however, have been written until long after the lifetime of Jonah himself.

This appears (1) from the style, which has several Aramaisms, or other marks of a later age: as 1⁵ ספינה; 1⁶ התעשׁת to think (=Heb. חשׁב Ps. 40¹⁸); cf. עשׁתנת Ps. 146⁴; and in Aram., Dan. 6⁴ and the Targums; 1⁷· ¹² 4¹⁰ שׁ for אשׁר—esp. in the compound form in which it occurs in 1⁷· ¹²; 1⁹ the title "God of heaven," as in Neh. 1⁵ and other post-exilic writings (see below, under Ezra and Nehemiah); 1¹² שׁתק; 2¹ 4⁶· ⁷ ⁸ מְנָה as Dan. 1¹⁰· ¹¹ 1 Ch. 9²⁹, and in Aram.; מְעָם 3⁷ as in Aram., Ezr. 6¹⁴ 7²³; עמל to labour 4¹⁰ (in ordinary Hebrew ינע): also 1⁸ באשׁר למי (cf. p. 475, n.), if the clause "for whose cause this evil is upon us" be genuine; but it is omitted in Codd. B א of LXX, and is regarded by some modern scholars as a gloss explanatory of בשׁלמי in v.⁷. The diction is, however, purer generally than that of Esther or the Chronicles. (2) From the Psalm in c. 2, which consists largely of reminiscences of other Psalms (in the manner of Ps. 142, 143, 144¹⁻¹¹), many of them not of early origin (comp. v.² Ps. 18⁶· ⁵ 120¹; v.³ Ps. 18⁴ 42⁷; v.⁴ Ps. 31²² Lam. 3⁵⁴; v.⁵ᵃ Ps. 18⁴ 116³ 69¹; v.⁶ Ps. 30³; v.⁷ Ps. 142³ 18⁶; v.⁸ Ps. 31⁶; v.⁹ Ps. 50¹⁴ 116¹⁷ᶠ· 3⁸): a Psalm of Jonah's own age would certainly have been more original, as it would also have shown a more antique colouring. (3) From the general thought and tenor of the book, which presupposes the teaching of the great prophets (comp. esp. 3¹⁰ with Jer. 18⁷ᶠ·). (4) The non-mention of the name of the Assyrian king, who plays such a prominent part in c. 3, may be taken as an indication that it was not known to the author of the book. The title "king of Nineveh" (3⁶) is one, remarks Sayce (*Monuments*, p. 487), which could never have been applied to him while the Assyrian empire was still in existence.

Some of the linguistic features might (possibly) be compatible with a pre-exilic origin in northern Israel (though they are more pronounced than those referred to, p. 188 *n.*): but, taken as a whole, they can only be consistently explained by the supposition that the book is a work of the post-exilic period, to which the other considerations adduced point with some cogency. A date in the 5th cent. B.C. will probably not be far wide of the truth.*

* Like other late writings, the narrative itself is also dependent in parts

[302] *The aim of the book.* Although it is apparent that the book is written with a didactic purpose, opinions have differed as to what this purpose precisely was. According to Ewald, its main purpose is to show that only true fear and repentance can bring salvation from Jehovah,—a truth which is exemplified, first in the case of the foreign sailors (1^{14}), then in that of Jonah himself (c. 2), and lastly in that of the Ninevites (3^{5-9}), and which, in the last resort, rests upon the *Divine love* (3^{10} 4^{11}). According to Riehm, its aim is partly to teach that it is wrong in a prophet, as it is also useless, to attempt to evade a duty once imposed upon him by God, partly to develop and emphasize the teaching of Jer. $18^{7f.}$, that prophecy viz. is *conditional*; and to show that even when a Divinely-inspired judgment has been uttered by a prophet, it may yet be possible by repentance to avert its fulfilment; and, if this be done, objection must not be taken that God's word is made of none effect. But though these, and other lessons, are, no doubt, included in the book, the climax in c. 4 is an indication that the thought which is most prominent in the author's mind is a different one. The real design of the narrative is to teach, in opposition to the narrow, exclusive view, which was too apt to be popular with the Jews, that God's purposes of grace are not limited to Israel alone, but that they are open to the heathen as well, if only they abandon their sinful courses, and turn to Him in true penitence. It is true, the great prophets had often taught the future reception of the heathen into the kingdom of God: but their predominant theme had been the denunciation of judgment; and the Israelites themselves had suffered so much at the hands of foreign oppressors that they came to look upon the heathen as their natural foes, and were impatient when they saw the judgments uttered against them unfulfilled. Jonah appears as the representative of the popular Israelitish creed. He resists at the outset the commission to preach to Nineveh at all: and when his preaching there has been successful in a manner which he did not anticipate, he murmurs because the sentence which he had been commanded to pronounce is revoked. That repentance might avert punishment had often been taught with reference to [303] Israel; and

upon models: comp. 1^{14}, Jer. 26^{15}; 3^{8b}, Jer. 18^{11} 26^3; 3^{9a}, Joel 2^{14}; 3^{9b}, Ex. 32^{12b}; 3^{10b}, Ex. 32^{14}; 4^{2b}, Joel 2^{13b}, Ex. 34^{6b} (but in Ex. without ונחם על הרעה); $4^{3a.8b}$, 1 Ki. 19^{4b}.

Jeremiah lays down the same truth with reference to the nations generally in 18⁷ᶠ. The aim of the book is thus to supply a *a practical illustration of Jeremiah's teaching*: and in the rebuke with which the book closes, the exclusive spirit of the author's own contemporaries stands condemned. " In no book of the OT.," remarks Bleek, " is the all-embracing fatherly love of God, which has no respect for person or nation, but is moved to mercy on all who turn to Him, exhibited with equal impressiveness, or in a manner so nearly approaching the spirit of Christianity."

On the historical character of the narrative opinions have differed widely. Quite irrespectively of the miraculous features in the narrative, it must be admitted that there are indications that it is not strictly historical. The sudden conversion, on such a large scale as (without pressing single expressions) is evidently implied, of a great heathen population, is contrary to analogy ; nor is it easy to imagine a monarch of the type depicted in the Assyrian inscriptions behaving as the king of Nineveh is represented as acting in presence of the Hebrew prophet. It is remarkable also that the conversion of Nineveh, if it took place upon the scale described, should have produced so little permanent effect ; for the Assyrians are uniformly represented in the OT. as idolaters. But, in fact, the structure of the narrative shows that the *didactic purpose* of the book is the author's chief aim. He introduces just those details that have a bearing upon this, while omitting others which, had his interest been in the history as such, might naturally have been mentioned ; *e.g.* details as to the spot at which Jonah was cast on to the land, and particulars as to the special sins of which the Ninevites were guilty.

No doubt the materials of the narrative were supplied by tradition ; and these the author cast into a literary form in such a manner as to set forcibly before his readers the truths which he desired them to take to heart. The details are artistically arranged. The scene is laid far off, in the chief city of the great empire which had for long been Israel's formidable oppressor. Jonah, commissioned to proceed thither, seeks, with dramatic propriety, to escape to the furthest parts known to the Hebrews in the opposite direction. The ready homage done by the heathen sailors to the prophet's God is a significant omen of what is to follow. Jonah is represented (like those less spiritual of his [304] fellow-countrymen of whom he is the type) as wayward, unspiritually-minded, deficient in insight ; he does at last what he is commanded to do, but he does it with so little perception of a prophet's mission that he is disappointed with a result at which he ought clearly to have rejoiced : he has Elijah's despondency (1 Ki. 19⁴), without Elijah's excuse. It is in consistency with the prophet's character that in c. 4 he is led indirectly to make the confession from which the main lesson of the book is immediately deduced, by his love of self being painfully touched ; for his compassion upon the gourd is elicited only by the scorching effect of the sun's rays upon his own person. We learn nothing respecting the after-history either of Nineveh or of the prophet : the author, having pointed the moral of his story, has no occasion to pursue the narrative further.

The Psalm 2²⁻⁹ is not strictly appropriate to Jonah's situation at the time ; for it is not a *petition* for deliverance to come, but a *thanksgiving* for deliverance already accomplished (like Ps. 30, for instance). Hence, no doubt, the Book of Jonah was not its original place ; but it was taken by the author from some prior source.* The expressions in v.³· ⁵· ⁶ &c. may have been intended originally in a figurative sense (as in the Psalms cited above, from which they are mostly borrowed), but they may also have been meant literally (see v.⁵ᵇ· ⁶ᵃ, which are not among the phrases borrowed), and have formed part of a Psalm composed originally as a thanksgiving for deliverance from shipwreck, and placed by the author in Jonah's mouth on account of the apparent suitability of some of the expressions to his situation.

The allegorical view of the book is supported by Kleinert (in Lange's *Bibelwerk*), and in this country by Professor Cheyne and C. H. H. Wright [above, p. 299]. According to this view, Jonah does not merely represent the unspiritual Israelites, he symbolizes Israel as a nation, and the narrative is an allegory of Israel's history. Israel, as a nation, was entrusted with a prophetical commission to be a witness and upholder of Divine truth ; but Israel shrank from executing this commission, and often apostatized : it was in consequence "swallowed up" by the world-power Babylon (see esp. Jer. 51³⁴), as Jonah was swallowed by the fish ; in exile, however, like Jonah (c. 2), it sought its Lord, and thus was afterwards disgorged uninjured (cf. *ib.* v.⁴⁴) ; after the return from exile, there were many who were disappointed that the judgments uttered by the prophets did not at once take effect, and that the cities of the nations still stood secure, just as Jonah was disappointed that the judgment pronounced against Nineveh had been averted. Comp. F. W. Farrar, *The Bible, its Meaning and Supremacy* (1897), p. 233 ff.

[305]   § 6. MICAH

Micah was a younger contemporary of Isaiah's. This appears partly from 1⁶, which was evidently uttered prior to the fall of

---

* Cheyne (*Origin of the Psalter*, p. 106 f.) and Budde (*ZATW.* 1892, p. 42) suppose that the Psalm was introduced, not by the author of the Book, but by a later hand.

Samaria in 722, partly from the interesting notice in Jer. 26[17f.], from which we learn that 3[12] was spoken during the reign of Hezekiah. While Isaiah's home, however, was the capital, Micah was a native of a small town in the maritime plain, Moresheth, a dependency of Gath (1[1. 14]). As has been observed, the difference of position and surroundings is marked in the writings of the two prophets. Isaiah writes as one acquainted with the society and manners of the capital; Micah speaks as a "man of the people," who sympathized with the peasantry in their sufferings, and he attacks, not indeed with greater boldness than Isaiah, but with greater directness and in more scathing terms (see especially 3[2-4]), the wrongs to which they were exposed at the hands of the nobles and rich proprietors of Judah. Further, while Isaiah evinces a keen interest in the political movements of the time, Micah appears almost exclusively as an ethical and religious teacher: he mentions, indeed, the Assyrians, but as a *mere* foe, not as a power which might tempt his countrymen to embark upon a perilous political enterprise, and he raises no warning voice against the danger to Judah of Egyptian influence.

The Book of Micah falls naturally into two parts, c. 1–5 and c. 6–7.

I. In this part there is again a division at the end of c. 3: in c. 1–3 the predominant tone is one of reproof and denunciation; in c. 4–5 it is one of promise. The prophet begins (1[2-4]) by describing, in impressive imagery, the approaching manifestation of Jehovah for judgment, on account (v.[5]) of the transgression of the two kingdoms, which is centred in their respective capitals, Samaria and Jerusalem. In the first instance, v.[6-7], Micah declares the impending ruin of *Samaria*: the evil does not, however, rest there; he sees it (v.[9]) advancing upon *Jerusalem* as well, and utters his wail of lament as the vision of disaster meets his eye. His sympathy is in particular attracted by the district in which his own home lay; and he describes, in a series of characteristic paronomasiae, the fate of [306] different places situated in it, v.[8-16]. 2[1-11] the nature of the people's sin, and its punishment, are both more distinctly indicated. The people's sin is the high-handed conduct of its great men, who eject their poorer neighbours from lands and homes, in order that their own possessions may become the larger. The punishment is

in correspondence with the sin: ere long the nation will see
heathen conquerors dividing amongst themselves the inheritance
of Jehovah, 2^{1-5}. The people attempt to stop the prophet's
unwelcome harangue. He replies, It is not impatience on
Jehovah's part that prompts Him thus to threaten; neither is
punishment His chosen work: as long as His people "walk
uprightly," He responds to them with friendly words and acts,
v.$^{6-7}$; the cause of His present unwonted attitude lies in *you*,
who plunder mercilessly the unsuspicious and the unprotected:
as a just retribution for the expulsion of others, you, the ag-
gressors, shall be expelled yourselves, v.$^{8-10}$. V.^{11} Micah returns
to the thought of v.^{6}: the only prophets to whom the people will
listen are those who hold out alluring, but deceitful, promises of
material enjoyment and prosperity (cf. Isa. 30^{10}).

At this point there is an abrupt transition, and v.$^{12f.}$ consists
of a prophecy of the *restoration* of Israel. Assembled as a
thronging multitude at one centre, as sheep in a fold, the
Israelites prepare to re-enter their ancient home. The "breaker
up"* advances before them, forcing the gates of the prison in
which they are confined; the people follow, marching forth
triumphantly through the open way: their king, with Jehovah at
his side (Ps. 110^5), heads the victorious procession (Ex. 13^{21};
Isa. 52^{12}). The scene in these two verses is finely conceived;
and the past tenses represent it forcibly and vividly.

C. 3 is parallel in thought to 2^{1-11}; but the offences of the
great men are depicted in more glaring colours; and the punishment is announced with greater distinctness and finality. Judges,
priests, and prophets are alike actuated by a spirit of heartless
avarice and cupidity; and yet (v.^{11b}) they rely upon Jehovah to
defend them against calamity (cf. Jer. 7^4). And the prophet
closes with the startling announcement that on *their* account, on
[307] account, viz., of the misconduct of its great men, the capital
itself would be completely ruined (3^{12}).

In c. 1–3 the promise of *restoration*, $2^{12f.}$, interrupts the connexion, and
occasions difficulty. Such promises occur, no doubt, in the prophets after an
announcement of *disaster* (*e.g.* Hos. $1^{10}-2^1$; Isa. 4^{2-6}); but here the promise is

---

* *I.e.* either a leader, or a detachment of men, whose duty it was to break
up obstacles opposing the progress of an army. See more fully the *Expositor*,
Apr. 1887, p. 266 ff., where it is shown that the statement of Bp. Pearson and
others, that the Jews understood this term of the Messiah, is an error.

associated closely with a *denunciation of sin*, so that between v.[11] and v.[12] there is no point of connexion whatever. Ewald felt the difficulty of 2[12f.] so strongly that (like Ibn Ezra before him) he supposed the verses placed in the mouth of the false prophets, as an illustration of their deceptive promises of security (to be construed then with v.[11]: "he shall even be a prophet of this people (saying), I will surely assemble," &c.; comp. Isa. 5[19], Jer. 23[17]). The contents of the two verses are, however, too characteristic, and the thought is too elaborately drawn out, for this view to be probable ; moreover, as Caspari (p. 123) observes, they *presuppose* disaster, if not exile, which itself would not be granted by the false prophets (see 3[11]). The ordinary interpretation must thus be acquiesced in ; though it must be granted that the verses stand in no logical connexion with 2[1-11]. But their contents afford no sufficient ground for attributing them to an exilic (Stade, Kuen.) or (Wellh.) post-exilic hand. The idea of a scattering or exile is implied in 1[16] 2[4. 5] 3[12] ; the idea of the preservation of a "remnant" had been promulgated more than a generation before by Amos (9[8-9] ; comp. also Hos. 1[10. 11] 11[10. 11]) ; and the general thought of the passage is similar to that of 4[6f.]. The verses can scarcely, however, be in their original context : either they belong to another place in the existing Book of Micah (Steiner would place them after 4[8]), or—which may be a preferable alternative—the existing Book of Micah consists only of a collection of *excerpts*, in some cases fragmentary excerpts, from the entire series of the prophet's discourses, and the context in which 2[12f.] originally stood has not been preserved to us.

The picture of disaster and ruin with which c. 1–3 closes, is followed (in the manner of the other prophets, especially Isaiah) by a vision of restoration. Zion, no longer ruined and deserted, is pictured by the prophet as invested with even greater glory than before ; it has become the spiritual metropolis of the entire earth ; pilgrims flock to it from all quarters ; a "federation of the world" has been established under the suzerainty of the God of Israel, 4[1-5]. In that day the banished and suffering Israelites will be restored ; and Jehovah will reign over them in Zion for ever, v.[6f.]. V.[8] the prophet proceeds to contemplate the ultimate revival of the kingdom of David ; but v.[9f.] he returns to the present (or immediate future), and dwells on the period of distress which must be passed through before that revival can be consummated. "*Now*, why dost thou cry out aloud?" he exclaims ; for he hears in imagination the wail of despair and [308] pain rising from the capital at the approach of the foe (the Assyrian), v.[9] ; he takes up, v.[10], the figure used at the end of v.[9] : the painful process must continue till the new birth has been achieved ; the nation must leave the city, dwell in the field, and journey *even to Babylon* ; there will it be delivered and rescued from its foes. But *now*—*i.e.* as v.⁹, in the present (or immediate future)—many nations are assembled against Zion, eager to see her prostrate in the dust; they know not, however, Jehovah's purpose; He has assembled them only that they may be gathered themselves "as the sheaves into the floor," and there "threshed" by the triumphant daughter of Zion herself, v.$^{11\text{-}13}$. And yet, *now*, there is a siege imminent; and humiliation awaits the chief magistrate of Israel (the king): the ruler who is to be his people's deliverer will arise from another quarter, from the insignificant town of Bethlehem; and Israel will be "given up" —*i.e.* abandoned to its foes—until he appears and reunites the scattered nation, 5$^{1\text{-}3}$ (Heb. 4^{14}–5^{2}). Then will Israel dwell securely: when danger threatens, capable men will be at hand, in more than sufficient numbers ("seven . . . eight") to ward it off; when *the Assyrian* essays to invade the territory of Judah, under the leadership of its ideal king he will be triumphantly repelled, v.$^{4\text{-}6}$. Upon those of the nations who are disposed to welcome it, the "remnant of Jacob" will exert an influence like that of the softly-falling, beneficent dew; towards those who resist it, it will be as a fierce, destructive lion, v.$^{7\text{-}9}$. Finally, Micah points to the inward notes of the nation's changed state, destruction of warlike implements, which will be no longer needed, and of idolatry, in which it will no longer find its delight, v.$^{10\text{-}15}$.

In c. 4–5 the connexion of thought is so incomplete that again the question arises whether the text is in its original integrity. The two chief sources of difficulty are the clause in 4^{10}, *And shalt come even to Babylon*, and 4$^{11\text{-}13}$. In the abstract, to be sure, the mention of Babylon would not be inexplicable: as Mic. (5$^{5,\,6}$, cf. 1^{6}) views the *Assyrians* as the power which the Jews have to dread, Babylon would be named by him, not as the place to which, some 120 years afterwards, Judah was actually exiled, but as a principal city of the Assyrian empire, with which recently, it is probable, Judah had had dealings (Isa. 39), and to which, in accordance with the Assyrian custom (2 Ki. 15^{29}), Micah pictured the people as exiled by them (cf. also Isa. 39$^{6f.}$). But the clause does not harmonize with the context in which it actually stands: exile *to* Babylon is inconsistent with the victory promised to them in 4$^{11\text{-}13}$ (if these verses be Micah's) as well as with the general tenor of 5$^{2\text{-}6}$; redemption *in* Babylon (v.^{10} "there") is not less inconsistent with the context, besides being a singular and improbable idea in itself. But with this clause omitted, v.^{10} yields at once a clear and consistent sense: it then describes how the inhabitants, having been compelled to surrender their capital to the foe, encamp in the fields on the road for exile, when Jehovah interposes suddenly on their behalf, and *there* delivers them). No doubt, the clause in question is a gloss, written originally on the margin with the view of making the prophecy more definite, and introduced afterwards by error into the text. V.[11-13], if Micah's, must depict the manner in which the deliverance promised in v.[10] is effected, viz. by the nation being supernaturally strengthened in order to vanquish its foes (so Kuenen, in his defence of the integrity of Micah 4–5—except the Babylon-clause in 4[10]—in the *ThT.* 1872, p. 299 f.). It must, however, be admitted that there are parts in the two pictures which it is very difficult to reconcile. "According to v.[10] Zion shall be captured by the enemy, and this agrees with 3[12]. But in the following verses the besieging hosts of many nations are broken beneath the walls of Jerusalem" (W. R. Smith, *Proph.*[1] p. 428). Accordingly, W. R. Smith rejects 4[11-13] as a later insertion in the text of Micah, as does also Nowack, *ZATW.* 1884, p. 285 f. The reasons for this conclusion are forcible: but it ought at the same time to be remembered that the prophets, in their imaginative pictures of the future, are not always perfectly consistent (contrast, *e.g.* Isa. 3[25f.] with Isa. 29[5-8]), and that 4[11-13] may not have been uttered at the same time as 4[9-10] (and still less at the same time as 3[12]), and may consequently reflect a new phase in Micah's conception of his nation's future. *

Recent critics have, however, as in the case of Hosea and Amos, and upon similar grounds, gone considerably further in the rejection of parts, or even of the whole, of Micah 4–5. Thus Stade (*ZATW.* 1881, p. 165 ff.; cf. 1883, p. 1 ff., 1884, p. 291 ff.) treats 4[1-3] (both here and in Isa. 2[2-4]: above, p. 230) 4. [11-13] 5[1-4. 7-15] as a post-exilic addition, designed to supplement the dark picture of 3[12] with an outlook of hope, in which, upon the assumption that it was really Micah's work, were inserted at a yet later date 4[5-10] 5[5-6]. Kuenen (§ 74. 4–9) criticizes this view, admitting that the historical background is not the same throughout the two chapters, but contending that parts still presuppose the existence of the monarchy: accordingly, he assigns to an exilic or post-exilic hand only 4[6-8] (as presupposing the Babylonian exile), [10] (the Babylon-clause), [11-13] (which he now owns "has the Assyrian period far behind it," and recalls the defeat of ideal foes in Ez. 38-39, Zech. 12. 14), and *perhaps* the allusion to "pillars" and "Ashérahs" in 5[13. 14] (so Wildeboer, § 10, p. 181). Wellh. (in his *Minor Prophets*) regards c. 4–5 as an appendix attached to 3[12] by a later hand, including, however, in 5[10-14], and possibly also in 4[9-10] (except the Babylon-clause) 5[1], words of Micah. Cheyne (W. R. Smith, *Proph.*[2] p. xxiii) appears to agree with Wellh.

[310] II. C. 6–7. (1.) 6[1]–7[6]. Here the standpoint changes. It is no longer the *leaders* only, as in c. 1–3, whose misconduct the prophet denounces, the people as a whole are addressed, and the entire nation is represented as corrupt, not "a good

---

* Caspari (p. 190), Keil, and Kirkpatrick (pp. 216, 229) escape the contradiction between 4[11-13] and 4[9f.] by taking ועתה, 4[11], in the sense of *And then*, (*i.e.* after the deliverance of 4[10], when the nations who presume to assail Israel will be triumphantly dispersed). But according to usage ועתה would denote only either the *present*, or the *immediate* future, as contrasted with the more distant future indicated at the end of v.[10].

man" can be found in it (7^{1-2}). The prophecy is conceived dramatically, and may be headed (comp. Ewald) *Jehovah and Israel in controversy*: Jehovah, represented by the prophet, is plaintiff; Israel is defendant. V.$^{1f.}$ is the exordium: v.$^{3-5}$ *Jehovah* states His case: what has *He* done to merit Israel's ingratitude and neglect? V.$^{6-7}$. *The people*, admitting its sin, inquires how its God can be propitiated? will thousands of sacrifices, will even a man's first-born son, be sufficient to satisfy His demands? V.^{8}. *The prophet* gives the answer: Jehovah demands not material offerings, but justice, mercy, humility. V.$^{9-16}$. *Jehovah* speaks, addressing primarily the capital, denouncing with indignation the injustice, oppression, and violence rampant in it, and threatening condign punishment, in the shape of invasion, desolation, and disgrace. 7^{1-6}. *The prophet* is the speaker: he describes—with a passing glance at the day of retribution, v.^{4b}—the desperate condition of the nation,—anarchy, persecution, universal corruption of justice, the ties of society dissolved, even friendship and wedded love no longer to be trusted—"a man's enemies are the men of his own house."

The social condition thus depicted is darker than that which is either described or implied in any other part of the book. In their connexion with c. 6, the verses 7^{1-6} may be taken as exhibiting anew the necessity of the judgment held out in 6^{13-16} against a people which will listen neither to the admonition of 6^8, nor to the denunciation of 6^{9-12}.

(2.) 7^{7-20}. Here, though the literary form is still that of a dramatic dialogue, both the subject and the point of view are different. V.$^{7-13}$ may be headed *Israel and the prophet*: v.$^{14-20}$ *The prophet and his God*. V.$^{7-10}$ *the community* speaks,—not, however, the corrupt community of the present, as described in v.$^{1-6}$, but the *penitent* community of the future: the day of distress, v.^{4b}, is supposed to have arrived: the suffering and humiliation (here described as "darkness") involved in [311] it have brought the nation to a sense of its guilt; hence it is able to assert its confidence in the approach of a brighter future, and to triumph over its adversary's fall. V.$^{11-13}$. *The prophet* supposes himself to reply: he re-echoes the nation's hopes: the ruined fence of the vineyard (Isa. 5^{1-7}) will be rebuilt, and the banished Israelites will return, though, he adds, before this promise can be realised, judgment must take its course, and "the land" become desolate (cf. 6^{16b}).

V.[14]. *The prophet*, turning now to Jehovah, supplicates, in the name of the penitent people, for the fulfilment of the promise of v.[11f.]. V.[15]. *Jehovah* gives His reply, short but pregnant: at the restoration, the wonders of the Exodus will be re-enacted. V.[16-17] the words glide insensibly into those of *the prophet*: the effects of the spectacle upon the nations of the world, their terror and prostration, are powerfully depicted. The prophecy closes with a lyric passage, v.[18-20], celebrating the Divine attributes of mercy, compassion, and faithfulness, as manifested in the deliverance promised in the preceding verses.

C. 6–7 were assigned by Ewald to an anonymous prophet writing in the reign of Manasseh. The hope and buoyancy which Isaiah kindled, and which left its impress upon the pages of Micah, c. 1–5, have given way, he remarks, in c. 6–7 to despondency and sadness: Micah declaims against the leaders of the nation only, in c. 6–7 (as was already observed above) the corruption has extended to the entire people; and 6[16] ("the statutes of Omri, and all the works of the house of Ahab") points directly to the age of Manasseh as that in which the prophecy was written. It is true there is no chronological difficulty in supposing that Micah himself may have survived at least the commencement of the heathen reaction which marked the reign of Manasseh: but the difference in form and style between c. 6–7 and c. 1–5 is such, Ewald urges, as to be scarcely compatible with the opinion that both are by the same author. C. 6–7 is dramatic in structure; the prophecy is distributed between different interlocutors in a manner which is far from common in the prophets, and is altogether alien from c. 1–5: the "echoes of Isaiah's lofty eloquence" are here no longer audible; the elegiac tone of c. 6–7 already approaches closely to that of Jeremiah: the linguistic features which mark c. 1–5 are also absent.

Wellhausen (in Bleek's *Einl.*, ed. 4, 1878, p. 425 f.) advanced a step [312] beyond Ewald, accepting Ewald's judgment so far as related to 6[1]–7[6], but calling attention to the sharp contrast subsisting between 6[1]–7[6] and 7[7-20]—

"7[1-6] consists of a bitter lamentation uttered by Zion over the corruption of her children; and the day of retribution, though ready, is yet future, v.[4]. But with v.[6] the thread of the thought is broken, and the contents of v.[7-20] are of a wholly different character. Zion, indeed, is still the speaker; but here she has already been overpowered by her foe, the heathen world, which is persuaded that by its victory over Israel it has at the same time vanquished Jehovah, v.[10]. The city has fallen, its walls are destroyed, its inhabitants pine away in darkness, *i.e.* in the darkness of captivity, v.[8. 11]. Nevertheless, Zion is still confident, and though she may have to wait long, she does not question her final triumph over the foe, v.[7. 8. 10a. 11]. She endures patiently the punishment merited by her past sins, assured that when she has atoned for them, God will take up her cause, and lead her to victory, v.[9]. Then the leaf turns: Zion rules over the heathen, and these humbly proffer her their homage at Jerusalem.* Thus the situation in 7[7-20] is quite different from that in 7[1-6]. What was *present* there, viz. moral disorder and confusion in the existing Jewish state, is here *past*; what is there *future*, viz. the retribution of v.[4b], has here come to pass, and has been continuing for some time. What in v.[1-6] was still unthought of, viz. the consolation of the people, tempted in their trouble to mistrust Jehovah, is in v.[7-20] the main theme. Between v.[6] and v.[7] there yawns a century. On the other hand, there prevails a remarkable similarity between 7[7-20] and Isa. 40–66."

Accordingly Wellhausen's conclusion is that 7[7-20] was added to 6[1]–7[6] by a prophet writing during the Babylonian captivity † (or, as he prefers to suppose now, after the return).‡

Ewald's *date* for 6[1]–7[6] is exceedingly probable; though we cannot affirm with equal confidence that Micah is not the author. With such a small basis as c. 1–5 to argue from, we are hardly entitled to pronounce the dramatic form of 6[1ff.] inconsistent with Micah's authorship. At the same time, there is a difference of tone and manner in 6[1]–7[6], as compared with c. 1–5, which, so far as it goes, tell against, rather than in favour of, identity of author: instead of Micah's sharp and forceful sentences, we have here a strain of reproachful tenderness and regret (see esp. 6[3. 5] 7[1]); and, as Kuenen remarks (§ 74. 11), the prophecy does not, as would be natural if the author were the [313] same, carry on, or develop, lines of thought contained in c. 1–5. The point is one on which it is not possible to pronounce confidently; but internal evidence, it must be owned, tends to support Ewald's conclusion.

As regards 7[7-20] Wellh.'s characterisation of the passage, and exposition of the argument, are both eminently just. The

* Wellh. here interprets v.[12] (with Keil and others) of the heathen hastening to join themselves to Israel (as Isa. 45[14] &c.), not of the scattered Israelites returning (though in his *Minor Prophets* he adopts the latter explanation). And in v.[13] he takes הארץ, also as Keil, of the *earth*. The view adopted in the text (p. 331) is that of Caspari, Hitzig, and Ewald.

† So also Stade; Kuenen (§ 74. 14).

‡ So Giesebrecht, *Beitrage* (1890), p. 216 f.; Cornill.

question remains whether the inferences which he deduces from them follow.

It is true that a century or more elapsed *in fact* between the period alluded to in v.[6] and the period supposed to have commenced in v.[7] : but we can hardly measure the prophet's representations by the actual history ; to him, as to other prophets, future events may have seemed nearer than they were shown by the result to be : both Isaiah and Micah, for example, pictured the Messianic age as immediately succeeding the downfall of the Assyrian. The prophet who is here speaking may similarly have pictured calamity working its penitential effect upon the nation much sooner than the course of history actually brought about. The contradiction with 7[1-6] is really confined to v.[7-10] : the transition must be admitted to be abrupt ; but these verses may fairly be regarded as an *ideal* confession placed in the mouth of the people, whilst lying under the judgment which the prophet imagines (implicitly) to have passed over it : comp. Jer. 3[22b-25], the confession supposed to be spoken by the penitent nation in response to the prophet's invitation, v.[22a]. V.[11ff.] may be treated as consolations spoken from the prophet's standpoint, after the manner of Zeph. 3[14ff.]. As regards the resemblances with Isa. 40-66, it is true again that the thought is often similar ; * but there are no unambiguous references to the Babylonian exile, such as are frequent both in Isa. 40-66 and in other prophecies belonging to the same period. Thus Jer. 50[19] is remarkably parallel with v.[14] ; but it is preceded (v.[17f.]) by the express mention both of Babylon and of its king, Nebuchadnezzar, unlike anything to be found in Mic. 7[7-20], where, indeed, even the word *return* does not occur.† It is not clear, therefore, that the expressions here, which seem to imply that a state of exile is in the prophet's mind (as v.[11] "a day *to build up thy fences*"), are more than parts of the imaginative picture drawn by him of the calamity which he sees to be impending. Comp. Zeph. 3[14-20].

Elhorst (above, p. 300) defends Micah's authorship of the entire book (except 4[9]-5[1] 5[9]), escaping the difficulties which it presents in parts by an ingenious but complicated theory that the original order of the prophecies had been disarranged by a series of careless copyists.

[314] § 7. NAHUM.

The theme of the prophecy of Nahum is the fall of Nineveh. In a noble exordium, 1[2-6], Nahum depicts the appearance of Jehovah in judgment, and its effects upon the physical universe ; then, after briefly commemorating, v.[7], His faithfulness towards

---

* Comp. 7[8b. 9b] Isa. 42[16] 62[1b].—7[9a] 42[24. 25] 64[5b].—7[10] 49[25. 26] 51[23].—7[11] 58[12] &c.—7[12] 43[5f.] 49[12].—7[14] 63[17b] 64[9] 65[9. 10] [Jer. 50[19]].—7[15] 41[18] 43[16f.] 48[21].—7[16f.] 45[14] 54[15].—7[18-20] 43[25] 44[22] 54[8f.] 55[7b].

† The mention of *Assyria* in Mic. 7[12] rather than Babylon, and the name *Mazor* for Egypt (only besides in *Isaiah*, 19[6] 37[25] [=2 Ki. 19[24]]), do not favour the exilic (or post-exilic) date of 7[7-20].

those who are His true servants, he proceeds to describe the fall
and irretrievable destruction destined to overtake the Assyrian
capital, v.[8-12a], and the exultation which the news of the oppressor's fall will produce in Judah, v.[12b-15].* In c. 2 he depicts in
forcible and vivid language the assault upon Nineveh, the
entrance effected by her foes, the scene of carnage and tumult
in the streets, the flight of her inhabitants, the treasures plundered
by the captors, the city which hitherto had been the home of
brave intrepid warriors ("the den of lions," v.[11-12]) deserted and
silent. In c. 3 the theme of c. 2 is further developed and confirmed. The cruelty, the avarice (v.[1]), the crafty and insidious
policy (v.[4]) of the Assyrians, directed only to secure their own
aggrandisement, is the cause of Nineveh's ruin : and again
Nahum sees in imagination the chariots and horsemen of the
victor forcing a path through the streets, and spreading carnage
as they go (v.[2-3]). For Jehovah is against Nineveh (v.[5f.]),
and in the day of her desolation none will be there to comfort
her (v.[7]) : as little will she be able to avert her doom as was
No-amon (Thebes, in Upper Egypt), in spite of the waters that
encircled her, and the countless hosts of her defenders (v.[8-11]).
Nineveh's fortresses will give way : her men will be as women :
in vain will she prepare herself to endure a siege : the vast
multitude of her inhabitants will vanish as locusts : amid the
rejoicings of all who have suffered at her hands the proud empire
of Nineveh will pass for ever away.

Respecting the person of Nahum nothing is known beyond the statement
of the title that he was an *Elkoshite*. A place bearing the name of *Alkush*,
containing a grave which is shown as that of Nahum, exists at the present
day in the neighbourhood of Mosul (the ancient Nineveh) ; but the tradition
connecting this locality with the prophet cannot be traced back beyond the
16th cent. Far more ancient and credible is the tradition recorded by
Jerome in his commentary on Nahum, that the prophet was the native of a
[315] village in Galilee, which in Jerome's time bore the name of *Elkesi*. If
Nahum were of Galilæan origin, certain slight peculiarities of his diction
might be explained as provincialisms.

As regards the date of Nahum's prophecy, the *terminus a quo*
is the capture of Thebes in Egypt (alluded to in 3[8-10]) by
Asshurbanipal, shortly after 664 ; † the *terminus ad quem*, the

---

* V.[8-12a] is addressed to the people or city of Nineveh, v.[12b. 13] to Judah
or Jerusalem, v.[14] to Nineveh again, and v.[15] (expressly) to Judah.

† See Schrader, *KAT.*[2] p. 450 f.

destruction of Nineveh by the "Ummanmanda" (at the invitation of the Babylonians) * in 607. Within these limits it is difficult to fix the date more precisely. On the one hand, the freshness of the allusion to the fate of Thebes, and the vigour of style (which resembles that of Isaiah rather than Zephaniah's or Jeremiah's), may suggest that it belongs to the earlier years of this period ; on the other hand, as the fall of Nineveh is contemplated as imminent (*e.g.* 1^{13} "And *now*," &c.), and the Assyrians are represented as powerless to avert the fate which threatens them, it may be thought to belong to the period of the decadence of the Assyrian power, which followed the brilliant reign of Asshurbanipal (B.C. 668–626).

Kuenen (§ 75. 9, 10) suggests that the immediate occasion of the prophecy may have been the attack made upon Nineveh by Cyaxares, king of Media (Hdt. i. 103), *c.* 623 B.C., which, though it proved abortive, may have turned the prophet's thoughts towards the city, and the destiny which he saw to be in store for it. The terms of $1^{11.\ 13.\ 15}$ $2^{13\ end}$ seem to point to some recent invasion, or act of tyranny, on the part of the Assyrians, not recorded in the historical books. The determination of the *terminus a quo* makes it improbable that these verses allude to the invasion of Sennacherib, nearly 40 years before (B.C. 701) ; and, of course, altogether excludes a date immediately after Sennacherib's retreat (adopted formerly by some commentators). Prof. A. R. S. Kennedy (*Good Words*, Nov. 1891, p. 743), and Winckler (*Alttest. Unterss.* 1892, p. 124), argue in favour of a date (*c.* 645 B.C.) soon after the rebellion of Shamash-shumukin (*KAT*.[2] 368–370), for complicity with which, it is *conjectured*, Manasseh was taken captive to Babylon (2 Ch. 33^{11}) by Asshurbanipal. Prof. Davidson (pp. 14–18) criticises this and other views, and decides in favour of *c.* 608 B.C.

Nahum's poetry is fine. Of all the prophets he is the one who in dignity and force approaches most nearly to Isaiah. His descriptions are singularly picturesque and vivid (notice especially $2^{3-5.\ 10}$ 3^{2-3}) : his imagery is effective and striking (*e.g.* $2^{11f.}$ $3^{17.\ 18}$) ; the thought is always expressed compactly ; the parallelism is regular : there is no trace of that prolixity of style which becomes soon afterwards a characteristic of the prophets of the Chaldæan period. "The Book of Nahum is less directly spiritual than the prophecies of Hosea, Isaiah, and Micah : yet it forcibly brings before us God's moral government of the world, and the duty of trust in Him as the Avenger of wrong-doers, the sole source of security and peace to those who love Him" (Farrar).

* See Davidson, p. 137 f., with the references (esp. Messerschmidt, pp. 10–12).

In Nah. 1^2–2^2 (Heb.[3]) traces of an acrostich (below, p. 367 f.) seem to be discernible; and attempts have recently been made to restore, though not without violence, the supposed original alphabetical arrangement of half-verses; see Gunkel, *ZATW.* 1893, p. 223 ff.; Bickell, *Sitzungsberichte der kaiserl. Akad. der Wiss. in Wien* (phil.-hist. Classe), vol. 131, V. p. 1 ff.; Gunkel, *Schöpfung u. Chaos,* 1895, p. 102 f.; and the criticisms of Davidson, p. 19 f.

[316] § 8. HABAKKUK.

Habakkuk prophesied towards the beginning of the Chaldæan supremacy. His prophecy is constructed dramatically, in the form of a dialogue between himself and Jehovah (comp. Mic. 6–7; Jer. 14–15). The prophet begins, 1^{2-4}, by expostulating with Jehovah on account of the violence and injustice which prevails unchecked in the land. V.$^{5-11}$ Jehovah answers that the iustrument of judgment is near at hand—the Chaldæans, "that bitter and hasty nation, which march through the breadth of the earth to possess dwelling-places that are not theirs," whose advance is swift and terrible, and whose attack the strongest fortresses are powerless to resist. But the prophet is now perplexed by a difficulty from the opposite direction : will Jehovah, who has ordained the power of the Chaldæans as an instrument of judgment (comp. Is. $10^{5f.}$), permit the proud, idolatrous nation to destroy the righteous with the guilty, and to trample inhumanly, not upon Israel only, but upon all the nations of the earth ? v.$^{12-17}$. Habakkuk places himself in imagination upon his prophetic watch-tower (cf. Is. 21^6), and waits expectantly for an answer that may satisfy his "complaint," or impeachment, touching the righteous government of God, 2^1. Jehovah's answer, the significance of which is betokened by the terms in which it is introduced (v.$^{2,\,3}$), is this : *The soul of the Chaldæan is elated with pride ; but the righteous shall live by his faithfulness* * (v.^{4}). The different characters of the Chaldæan and of the righteous carry in them their different destinies. The pride of the former, it is implied in particular, will prove in the end his ruin ; and this the prophet, after dwelling somewhat more fully (v.^{5}) on the ambitious aims of the Chaldæan, develops at length, v.$^{6-20}$, in the form of a taunting proverb (מָשָׁל), which he imagines, with dramatic vividness and propriety, to be pronounced

---

* *I.e.* moral steadfastness and integrity ; see 2 Ki. 12^{16}, Jer. 5^1 9^3.

against him by the nations whom he has oppressed. The "proverb" consists of a series of five "Woes" (cf. Is. 5[8ff.]; also Jer. 22[13]), denouncing in succession the rapacious violence of the Chaldæans, the suicidal policy pursued by them in establishing their dominion, the dishonesty and cruelty by which the magnificence of their cities was maintained, the barbarous delight with which they reduced to a state of helplessness the nations that fell under their sway, their irrational idolatry. At the close of the last strophe the [317] prophet passes by contrast from the contemplation of the dumb and helpless idol to the thought of the living God, enthroned on high, before Whom the earth must stand in awe. V.[20] leads on to the theophany in c. 3.

The explanation of c. 1, given above, is the usual one ; but there are scholars who nevertheless do not deem it satisfactory. The great difficulty which has been found in the ch. is that, whereas in 1[5. 6] the establishment of the power of the Chaldæans appears to lie in the future, elsewhere (esp. 1[13-16] 2[8a. 10. 17]) the prophet describes their treatment of conquered nations, and reflects upon the moral problems to which it gave rise, in a manner which seems to imply that he and his countrymen were already perfectly familiar with it. Other difficulties which have been felt are : the inconsistency of emphasizing (1[2-4]) the injustice prevalent *in* Israel, in a prophecy the main theme of which is to set forth the injustice which Israel suffers, and to announce judgment upon its authors ; and the different sense which this explanation postulates for the complaint in 1[2] and 2[1], and for the "wicked" and the "righteous," respectively, in 1[4] and 1[13]. Giesebrecht (*Beiträge*, p. 197 f.) and Wellh. infer upon these grounds that 1[5-11] is an older, independent prophecy, written *before* the rest of c. 1–2, and not now in its original place, that 1[12] is the true sequel of 1[4], and that 1[2-4] describes the tyranny of the *Chaldæans* (v.[9b]), and its consequences in the relaxation of law and religion (v.[3c. 4a]) in Judah itself. It is true, 1[5-11] does seem to presuppose a different historical situation from the sequel, and, with 1[2-4] (as ordinarily understood), may well have been written down by Hab. at an earlier date : the book as a whole is "the fruit of religious reflection," and exhibits conclusions which doubtless were reached by the prophet not at once, but only "after a prolonged mental struggle" (Kirkpatrick, *Doctrine of the Prophets*, p. 268) ; so that in such a supposition there would be nothing unreasonable. On the other hand, it may be doubted whether the other difficulties mentioned are sufficiently serious to justify the conclusions founded upon them ; the sense proposed for 1[3-4] is, in particular, far from natural. Kuenen, § 77. 5, 6, and Davidson, p. 48, seek to harmonize 1[5-11] with its context by treating it as not in reality a prediction, but only as an explanation, cast in a dramatic form, of the appearance of the Chaldæans as the instruments of Providence, though the last-named scholar owns, pp. 49 f., 55, that this is not a satisfactory hypothesis. On Budde's too ingenious development of the view of Giesebr. and Wellh., see Davidson, pp. 50–55. Against the opinion

(Stade, *ZATW.* 1884, p. 154 ff.; Kuen. §§ 76. 4–7 ; 77. 9) that much of 2[9-20] is inapplicable to the Chaldæans, and that 2[6b-8] was the original close of Hab.'s prophecy, see Wellh. p. 163 ff., and Davidson, p. 55 ff.

C. 3 consists of a lyric ode, which, for sublimity of poetic conception and splendour of diction, ranks with the finest (Ex. 15 ; Jud. 5) which Hebrew poetry has produced. In this ode the prophet represents God as appearing Himself in judgment, and executing vengeance on His nation's foes : he longs (v.[2]) to see the work of judgment completed, yet prays that Jehovah in wrath will remember mercy. V.[3-7] depicts the theophany and its effects. God approaches—as Dt. 33[2], Jud. 5[4]—from the direction of Edom (Teman : cf. Jer. 49[20]) : the light of His appearing illumines the heavens ; the earth quakes, and nations flee in consternation. V.[8-15] the prophet states the *motive* of the theophany. Was Jehovah, he poetically asks, wroth with seas or rivers, that He thus came forth riding in His chariots of salvation? and once again he depicts, in majestic imagery, the progress of Jehovah through the earth, v.[8-12]. The answer to the inquiry follows, v.[13f.] : Jehovah's appearance was for the salvation of His people, to annihilate those who sought to scatter it, and whose delight it was to destroy insidiously the helpless people of God. The poet closes, v.[16-19], by describing the effect which the contemplation of Jehovah's approaching manifestation produced in his own heart : suspense and fear on the one side, but on the other a calm and joyous confidence in the God who, he is persuaded, will ensure His people's salvation.

The title of Hab. 3, and the musical notes (v.[3. 9. 13. 19]), both of which resemble closely those in the Psalter, suggest the inference that this ode was excerpted from a liturgical collection, and placed here by a compiler (Kuenen, § 76. 8 ; Cheyne, *Origin of the Psalter,* p. 157 ; Cornill, § 34. 3 ; Wellh. ; *al.*). The same critics consider further that the ode was originally an independent poem, unconnected with the Book of Hab. : to the circumstances of Hab.'s own age, so clearly reflected in 1[2]–2[8], there are here no allusions ; the community is the speaker (v.[14. 18. 19]), it trusts that Jehovah will interpose on its behalf, but the descriptions are general, there is no specific reference to the Chaldæans, it complains in part of other needs (v.[17]), and encourages itself upon other grounds, and in another way, than the prophet who speaks in 1[2]–2[8]. There is force in these arguments ; and we may agree with Prof. Davidson (p. 58 f.), that the conclusion to which they point may not improbably be correct. Of v.[10-15] there are evident reminiscences in Ps. 77[16-19] (Heb.[18-20]).

Internal evidence makes it tolerably clear that Habakkuk prophesied during the reign of Jehoiakim (B.C. 608–597); but the precise period of his reign is difficult to fix.   The descriptions in 1⁷⁻¹⁰· ¹⁴⁻¹⁶ 2⁵ᵇ· ⁶ᵇff· seem to show that the prophet is writing at a time when the character and aims of the Chaldæans were becoming patent, and conquests had been gained by them (2⁸ᵃ) ; but we are not sufficiently acquainted with the particulars of their movements to say confidently to what stage in their career the descriptions relate.   Most probably, however, Hab. wrote shortly before 600.   Nabopolassar had made Babylon the seat of an independent monarchy in 625 ; in 607, with the help of the Ummanmanda (p. 336), Nineveh had been destroyed ; in 604 Nabopolassar's son, Nebuchadnezzar, had gained a brilliant victory over Pharaoh Necho at Carchemish, the natural result of which, as Jeremiah at once saw (p. 248), could only be that the whole of W. Asia would fall into the hands of the Chaldæans. What, however, the Chaldæans were doing during the three following years, we do not know ; perhaps they were obtaining the successes which gave them the character that Habakkuk attributes to them.   They invaded Judah for the first time in 601 or 600 (2 Ki. 24¹).   The familiarity shown by the prophet with their treatment of subject nations, and the reflections which their threatened interference in Judah arouses in his mind, point to the latter part of this period rather than to the former.

[318] The different point of view in Hab., as compared with Jeremiah, should be observed.   "Jeremiah emphasizes throughout his people's sin, and consequently regards the Chaldæans almost exclusively as the instrument of punishment : Habakkuk, though not blind to Judah's transgressions (1²⁻⁴), is more deeply impressed by the violence and tyranny of the Chaldæans, and hence treats their chastisements as the first claim on Jehovah's righteousness " (Kuen. § 77. 8.   Comp. Cheyne, *Jeremiah*, p. 133 ; Farrar, p. 161 ff.).

Jeremiah teaches that wickedness in God's own people is doomed : Habakkuk declares that wickedness in the Chaldæans is doomed likewise.

§ 9. ZEPHANIAH.

Respecting Zephaniah's personality, nothing is known beyond what is recorded in the title to his book.   He is there described as the descendant, in the fourth generation, of " Hezekiah," and as having prophesied during the reign of Josiah.   Hezekiah is not a very common Israelitish name ; and it is supposed by some that the Hezekiah meant is the king of that name, so that the prophet would be a great-grandson of a brother of Manasseh. [319] From the allusions to the condition of morals and religion in Judah in 1⁴⁻⁶. ⁸. ⁹. ¹² 3¹⁻³. ⁷, it may be inferred with tolerable certainty that the period of Josiah's reign during which Zephaniah wrote was prior to the great reformation of his eighteenth year (B.C. 621), in which the idolatry attacked by the prophet was put down (comp. *e.g.* 1⁴. ⁵ with 2 Ki. 23⁴. ⁵. ¹²).

Zephaniah's prophecy may be divided into three parts: I. the menace, c. 1; II. the admonition, 2¹–3⁷; III. the promise, 3⁸⁻²⁰.

I. C. 1. Zephaniah opens his prophecy with an announcement of destruction, conceived apparently—to judge from the universality of its terms (1². ³. ¹⁸ ["earth," not "land"])—as embracing the entire world, v.²ᶠ., but directed in particular against the idolaters and apostates in Judah and Jerusalem, v.⁴⁻⁶. Let the earth be silent! for a "Day of Jehovah" (p. 208) is at hand, a day of sacrifice, in which the victims are the Jewish people, and those invited to partake in the offering are the heathen nations "sanctified" (see 1 Sa. 16⁵) for the occasion, v.⁷. Three classes are named as those upon whom the judgment will light with greatest severity, court officials, who either aped foreign fashions or were foreigners themselves, and who were addicted to corruption and intrigue; the merchants resident in Jerusalem; and Jews sunk in irreligious indifferentism, v.⁸⁻¹³. V.¹⁴⁻¹⁸ the prophet develops the figure of the "Day of Jehovah," describing the darkness and terror which are to accompany it, and the fruitlessness of the efforts made to escape from it.

II. 2¹–3⁷. Here Zephaniah urges his people to repent, v.¹⁻³, and thus to escape the threatened doom, which will engulph, he declares, in succession the Philistines, v.⁴⁻⁷, Moab and Ammon, v.⁸⁻¹¹, Ethiopia, v.¹², and even Nineveh, the proud Assyrian capital, itself, v.¹³⁻¹⁵. From Nineveh the prophet turns again to address Jerusalem, and describes afresh the sins rampant in her, especially the sins of her judges and great men, [320] and her refusal to take warning from the example of her neighbours, 3¹⁻⁷.

III. 3⁸⁻²⁰. Let the faithful in Jerusalem, then, wait patiently until the approaching judgment (cf. 1². ³. ¹⁸) is accomplished, v.⁸, the issue of which will be that the peoples who survive it will serve Jehovah "with one consent," and that the purged and purified "remnant of Israel" will cleave to God in sincerity of heart, and, trusting in Him, will dwell in safety upon their own land, v.[9-13]. With his eye fixed on this blissful future, the prophet, in jubilant tones, bids his people rejoice thankfully in the restoration of Jehovah's favourable presence in their midst, in the removal of the reproach and sorrow at present resting upon them, and in the honourable position which they will then hold among the nations of the earth, v.[14-20].

Though Zephaniah predicts the destruction of Nineveh (2[13-15]), he makes no allusion to the agents by whom it was brought about, the Chaldæans, who indeed at the time when the prophet wrote, while Asshurbanipal was still sitting on the throne of Assyria, or had but recently (626) died, had not yet appeared as an independent power. The early years of the reign of Josiah coincided, however, with the great irruption of Scythian hordes into Asia recorded by Herodotus (above, p. 252 f.); and it is not impossible that the prophet's language, and especially his description of the approaching Day of Jehovah, may reflect the impression which the news of these formidable hosts, advancing in the distance and carrying desolation with them, produced in Judah (comp. 1[2-3. 7b. 13. 16. 17b], from which it appears that Zephaniah pictures some invading foe as the agent in the coming disaster).

The authenticity of several parts of c. 2–3 has been questioned by recent critics. Stade (G. i. 644 n.) doubted 2[1-3. 11], and remarked that parts of c. 3 expressed the ideas and hopes of a later age than that of Zeph. Kuenen (§ 78. 5–8) defended 2[1-3. 11], but allowed—on account, chiefly, of the great difference both in tone and (v.[15a]) situation from 1[2]–3[13]—that 3[14-20] was a supplement, dating probably from shortly after B.C. 536. Wellh. rejects 2[8-11]; and treats c. 3 as an appendix added subsequently in two stages, first v.[1-7] (cf. Mic. 7[1-6]), and then v.[8-20] (cf. Mic. 7[7-20]). Budde (Stud. u. Krit. 1893, p. 393 ff.) argues that 2[1-3] 3[1-5. 7-8. 6. 11-13] forms a well-connected whole, in harmony with Zeph.'s historical situation, and forming an excellent sequel to c. 1 : 2[4-15] he rejects, as inconsistent with c. 1 (Israel no longer the perpetrator of wrong, but the victim of wrong, for which it is now to receive compensation); 3[9f.] interrupts the connexion of v.[8] with v.[11]; and 3[14-20] is a later lyrical epilogue to 3[11-13]. Cornill (Einl.[3] § 35. 3) agrees with Budde. There is certainly no sufficient reason for questioning 2[1-3] 3[1-13] : the exhortation in 2[1-3], and the promise addressed to the "remnant" in 3[11-13], are (to a prophet) the necessary complements of the denunciation in c. 1 (in 3[19] בת־פוצי is obscure, and probably corrupt). As regards 2[4-15], there is nothing surprising in a specification of particular nations upon whom the judgment (1[2. 3. 18]) is to alight ; and the promises are addressed not to the sinful Judah of c. 1, but to the "remnant," who are naturally pictured by the prophet (cf. 3[12f.]) as free from all sinful propensities (see further Davidson, p. 101 f.). Only 2[11] seems to be really out of place. 3[14-20] may be more doubtful (ib. p. 103 f.) : its buoyant tone forms a marked contrast to the sombre, quiet strain of 3[11-13], and the period of Israel's judgment seems to be past (cf. v.[15a]). Still, the picture is, of course, an imaginative one ; and the question remains whether it is sufficiently clear that it was beyond the power of Zephaniah's imagination to construct it. Cf. pp. 306, 307, and 334 (on Mic. 7⁷⁻²⁰).

Some interesting remarks on the prophetic representation of Zephaniah may be found in the article of W. R. Smith in the *Encycl. Brit.*⁹ *s.v.*

§ 10. HAGGAI.

Sixteen years had elapsed since the return of the Jewish exiles from Babylon, and no effort—or at least no successful effort—had been made to rebuild the national sanctuary. In the second year of Darius (B.C. 520), the prophets Haggai and Zechariah (cf. Ezr. 4²⁴ 5¹· ²) came forward, reproaching the people with their neglect, and exhorting them to apply themselves in earnest to the task, with the result that four years afterwards (*ib.* 6¹⁴· ¹⁵) the work was completed.

The prophecy of Haggai consists of four sections, arranged chronologically :—

(1.) C. 1. In the 2nd year of Darius, the first day of the 6th [321] month, Haggai appeals publicly to the people no longer to postpone the work of rebuilding the Temple : their neglect was not due to want of means, for they had built ceiled houses for themselves, and it had been followed, he points out, by failure of crops and drought, indicative of the Divine displeasure. His words produced such an effect upon those who heard them, that on the 24th day of the same month the people, headed by Zerubbabel and the high priest Joshua, began the work.

(2.) 2¹⁻⁹. On the 21st day of the 7th month, the prophet addresses words of encouragement to those who might have seen the Temple of Solomon, and compared the structure now rising from the ground unfavourably with it : the later glory of the Temple will exceed its former glory, by reason, viz., of the munificence of the Gentiles, who will offer their costliest treasures for its adornment (v.⁷ RV.; cf. Isa. 60⁵ᵇ· ¹¹ᵇ) ; and the blessing of peace is solemnly bestowed upon it.

(3.) 2¹⁰⁻¹⁹. On the 24th day of the 9th month, Haggai, by means of replies elicited from the priests on two questions respecting ceremonial uncleanness,* teaches the people, that, so long as the Temple continues unbuilt, they are as men who are unclean : their offerings are unacceptable ; and hence the

* See the explanation of the passage in Farrar, p. 193.

late unfruitful seasons.   From the present day, however, on which the foundation of the Temple was laid (v.[18f.]), Jehovah promises to bless them.

(4.) 2[20-23]. On the same day, Haggai encourages Zerubbabel, the civil head of the restored community, and representative of David's line (1 Ch. 3[19]), with the assurance that in the approaching overthrow of the thrones and kingdoms of the heathen (cf. v.[6f.]), he will receive special tokens of the Divine favour and protection.*

The style of Haggai, though not devoid of force, is, comparatively speaking, simple and unornate.   His aim was a practical one, and he goes directly to the point.   He lacks the imagination and poetical power possessed by most of the prophets; but his style is not that of pure prose: his thoughts, for instance, not unfrequently shape themselves into parallel clauses such as are usual in Hebrew poetry.

[322] § 11. ZECHARIAH.

The Book of Zechariah falls into two parts, clearly distinguished from each other by their contents and character, c. 1–8 and c. 9–14.   There is no question that c. 1–8 are the work of the Zechariah whose name they bear; but the authorship and date of c. 9–14 are disputed, and will be considered subsequently.

Zechariah, the son of Berechiah, the son of Iddo, prophesied, according to 1[1.7] and 7[1], in the 2nd and 4th years of Darius Hystaspis (B.C. 520 and 518).   He was thus a contemporary of Haggai's, and is unquestionably identical with the Zechariah, son of Iddo, who is named in Ezra 5[1] 6[14] as co-operating with Haggai in his efforts to induce the people to prosecute the work of rebuilding the Temple.

I. C. 1–8. This part of the book consists of three distinct prophecies: (1) 1[1-6], introductory; (2) 1[7]–c. 6; (3) c. 7–8.

(1.) 1[1-6].   A brief but earnest exhortation to repent, which Zechariah is directed to address to his fellow-countrymen, based upon the consequences which their forefathers had experienced

---

* See Jer. 22[24]: the honourable position from which Jehoiachin is there degraded, is here bestowed afresh upon Zerubbabel.

when they neglected the warnings of the "former prophets."
The 8th month of the 2nd year of Darius would fall between the
date of Hag. 2¹⁻⁹ and that of Hag. 2¹⁰⁻¹⁹.

(2.) 1⁷–6⁸ (24th day of the 11th month of the same year),
comprising *eight* symbolical visions, with an appendix, 6⁹⁻¹⁵, the
whole being designed for the encouragement of the Jews, and
especially of Zerubbabel and Joshua, respectively the civil and
religious heads of the community, in the work of rebuilding the
Temple. The significant features of each vision are pointed out
to the prophet by an angel.

(*a*) 1⁸⁻¹⁷. The Divine horses, which are Jehovah's messengers
upon earth (1¹⁰ᵇ; cf. Job 1⁷), report that there is no movement
among the nations (Hag. 2⁶ᶠ. ²¹ᶠ.), no sign of the approach of the
Messianic crisis : 70 years have passed (B.C. 586–520), and still
Jerusalem lies under the Divine displeasure ! Jehovah replies
with the assurance that the Temple shall now be rebuilt, and the
prosperity of His people be no longer delayed.

(*b*) 1¹⁸⁻²¹ [Heb. 2¹⁻⁴]. Four horns, symbolising the [323]
nations opposed to Israel, have their strength broken by four
smiths.

(*c*) C. 2. An angel with a measuring line goes forth to lay
out the site of the new Jerusalem : it is to have no walls, for its
population will be unlimited, and Jehovah will be its defence.
Judgment is about to break upon Babylon ; let those still in
exile, then, hasten to escape : ere long many nations will join
themselves to Israel : already Jehovah is stirring in His holy
habitation.*

(*d*) C. 3. Joshua, the high priest, appears, standing before
Jehovah, laden with the sins of the people : he is accused by
Satan, but is acquitted, and given rule over the Temple, with
the right of priestly access to Jehovah, v.¹⁻⁵. After this he
receives the further promise of the advent of the Messiah (v.⁸ᵇ :
see Jer. 23⁵ 33¹⁵), and the restoration of national felicity, v.⁶⁻¹⁰.

(*e*) C. 4. The vision of the golden candlestick and the two
olive trees, symbolising the restored community (the candlestick),
receiving its supply of Divine grace (the oil) through the two
channels of the spiritual and temporal power (the olive-branches,

---

* Former prophecies are here reaffirmed : see Isa. 54²ᶠ· 60¹⁸ᵇ· ¹⁹ 14², Ez.
43⁹, Isa. 14¹ 66⁶. Similarly with 1¹⁶· ¹⁷ cf. Isa. 52⁸ᵇ· ⁹ᵇ 58¹²; with 8⁴, Isa
65²⁰; with 8⁷ᶠ·, Isa. 43⁵, Ez. 36²⁴· ²⁸ ; with 8²²ᶠ·, Isa. 45¹⁴ &c.

v.[12], or "sons of oil," *i.e.* anointed ones, v.[14], viz. Joshua and Zerubbabel), v.[1-5. 11-14]. V.[6-10.] contains an encouragement addressed to Zerubbabel, who, it is said, will find the obstacles before him disappear, and, in spite of mockers (v.[10]), will himself finish the Temple which he has now begun.

(*f*) 5[1-4]. A roll, inscribed with curses, flies over the Holy Land, as a token that in future the curse for crime will of itself light upon the criminal.

(*g*) 5[5-11]. Israel's guilt, personified as a woman, is cast into an ephah-measure, and, covered by its heavy lid, is transported to Babylonia, where for the future it is to remain.

(*h*) 6[1-8]. Four chariots, with variously coloured horses, appear, for the purpose of executing God's judgments in different quarters of the earth. That which goes northwards is charged in particular to "quiet His spirit" (*i.e.* to satisfy His anger : cf. Ez. 5[13] 16[42]) on the north country, *i.e.* on Babylonia.

[324] 6[9-15] (historical appendix). The prophet is commanded to take of the gold and silver which some of the exiles had sent as offerings for the Temple, and to make therewith crowns (*or* a crown) for the high priest Joshua : * at the same time, he repeats (3[8]) the promise of the Messiah, who will rule successfully, and complete the building of the Temple.

(3.) C. 7-8 (4th day of the 9th month of the 4th year of Darius). C. 7. Zechariah, in answer to an inquiry put to him by the men of Beth-el, whether the fast of the 5th month (which had been kept during the exile in memory of the destruction of the Temple, Jer. 52[12-14]) should still be observed, declares that Jehovah demands no fasts, but only the observance of His moral commands, which their forefathers, to their cost, had neglected (cf. Isa. 58[3-12]). In c. 8 he draws a picture of the Messianic future, when the nation will be prosperous and the land yield its fruit, when the fast days † will become seasons of gladness, and the heathen will press forward to share the blessings of the Jews.

II. C. 9-14. These chapters contain two distinct prophecies :

---

* So in the existing text ; but v.[13b] speaks so clearly of *two* persons that many modern scholars are of opinion that the text has been altered, and that, as it originally stood, *Zerubbabel* was crowned, either as well as (Ew. Hitz. Marti), or (Wellh. Rothstein) instead of, Joshua (with v.[13a] comp. then 4[9]).

† V.[19] : see Jer. 52[6f. 12-14] 41[1-3] 52[4].

(1) c. 9–11, with which, it is probable, 13⁷⁻⁹ should be connected; (2) 12¹–13⁶ c. 14.

(1.) In c. 9 the prophet announces a judgment about to fall upon Damascus, Hamath, Tyre, and Sidon, and upon the chief cities of the Philistines in the South; a remnant of the Philistines is converted, and Jehovah encamps about His sanctuary as a protector, v.¹⁻⁸. The advent of the Messiah, as prince of peace, follows, v.⁹⁻¹⁰; the Israelites in captivity are invited to return to their own country, where Jehovah, after having enabled them to contend victoriously with their foes (the *Greeks*, v.¹³), will further bless and defend them, v.¹¹⁻¹⁷.

[325] C. 10. The people are exhorted by the prophet to seek help from Jehovah, not from teraphim and diviners, through whose baleful influence it is that they fall a prey to unworthy rulers,* v¹ᶠ.. But Jehovah will remove these unworthy rulers; and Judah, under new leaders, after His own heart (v.⁴) † will signally discomfit its foes, v.³⁻⁶; the banished Ephraimites will return; Egypt and Assyria will both be humiliated; and the restored nation will walk in obedience to its God, v.⁷⁻¹².

C. 11. A storm of war bursts over the North and East of the land, filling the people's unworthy rulers with consternation, v.¹⁻³.‡ An allegory follows, in which the prophet, representing Jehovah, takes charge of the people, whom their own selfish and grasping rulers had neglected and betrayed; but they resent his authority, so he casts them off in disdain, v.⁸⁻¹⁰: when he proceeds to demand the wages for his services, they offer him a paltry sum—the price of an ordinary slave (Ex. 21³²), which he flings contemptuously into the treasury (RV. *marg.*), after which he declares symbolically that the brotherhood between Judah and Israel is at an end, v.¹⁴.

The people having thus openly rejected the Divine guidance, the prophet now assumes the garb and character of a "foolish shepherd," to represent the manner in which Jehovah will permit them (or, perhaps, has already permitted them) to be treated by

* Figured as "shepherds": see p. 351, *n.*, at the end.

† So Stade, *ZATW.* 1881, p. 21 *n.* (*him* being Jehovah). But Wellh. and Kirkpatrick (*Doctrine of the Prophets*, p. 454) think the reference is to native rulers (*him* being Judah), taking the place of foreign oppressors (cf. Jer. 30²¹).

‡ Cf. Stade, p. 25, *note* 2. Stade himself, however, Wellh., and Kirkp. (p. 455), understand these verses as a symbolical description of the fall of heathen nations and princes.

their next ruler, v.[15f.], who will meet, however, eventually with a just retribution, v.[17]. The (unworthy) shepherd will be smitten by the sword, and his flock will be dispersed : two-thirds will perish immediately ; the remainder, purified by further trial, will constitute the faithful people of God, 13[7-9].

The section, 13[7-9], where it stands, is disconnected both with what precedes and with what follows : with c. 11 it is evidently connected by the similarity of the figure ; and, containing as it does a promise, it forms a suitable sequel to 11[15-17]. The suggestion that it forms the conclusion to c. 11 is due to Ewald, and has been treated as probable by many critics (Reuss, Wellh., Stade, Cheyne, Kuenen).

The date of this prophecy is difficult to determine ; and, in fact, the internal evidence points in different directions. On the one hand, there are indications which seem to show that the prophecy is *pre-exilic*. The kingdom of the ten tribes is spoken of in terms implying apparently that it *still* exists (9[10] [**326**] 11[14]) ; Assyria and Egypt are mentioned side by side (10[10. 11]), just as in Hosea (Hos. 7[11] 9[3] 11[11] 12[1]) ; the teraphim and diviners in 10[1f.] point to a date prior to the exile rather than to one after it ; the nations threatened in 9[1-7] are those prominent at the same time (cf. Am. 1[3. 6. 9]). The period to which, by those who acknowledge the force of these arguments, c. 9 is assigned, is towards the end of the reign of Jeroboam II., prior to the anarchy which broke out after his death, and to Tiglath-Pileser's conquest of Damascus in B.C. 732. C. 10 is placed somewhat later : v.[10] presupposes—not, indeed, the exile of the ten tribes in 722, but—the deportation of the inhabitants of N. and N.E. Israel by Tiglath-Pileser in 734 (2 Ki. 15[29]—observe that the districts to be repeopled are *Lebanon* and *Gilead*) ; 11[1-3] (somewhat earlier than c. 10) is a prediction of the same invasion of the Assyrian king ; 11[4-17] is understood as a symbolical description of the rejection of Jehovah by the kingdom of the ten tribes in the troubles which followed the death of Jeroboam II.,* and of His consequent abandonment of them (v.[10] ; cf. 2 Ki. 15[19. 20. 29]), v.[14-17] being aimed at the existing king of Ephraim, probably Pekah, under whom the previously amicable relations between Israel and Judah ceased. Upon this view, the author

---

* The "three shepherds" of v.[8] are supposed to be Zechariah, Shallum, who reigned for one month, and some usurper who attempted to succeed Shallum, but who in the brief narrative of 2 Kings is unnoticed.

is an early contemporary of Isaiah, and probably a native of the
kingdom of Judah.*

On the other hand, the prophecy also contains passages
which appear to imply a *post-exilic* date ; $9^{11f.}$ and 10^{6-9} seem to
presuppose the captivity at least of Ephraim (notice especially
" cast them off " in 10^6) ; and in 9^{13} the Greeks (" Javan," *i.e.* the
'Ιάϝονες) are mentioned, not as a distant, unimportant people,
such as they would be in the 8th century B.C., and even in the
days of Zechariah (*c.* 520), but as a *world*-power, and as Israel's
most formidable antagonist, the victory over whom (which is
achieved only by special Divine aid) inaugurates the Messianic
age. This position, however, was only attained by the Greeks
after the overthrow of the Persian empire at Issus by Alexander
the Great, B.C. 333.

[327] The double nature of the allusions in this prophecy
has greatly perplexed commentators, and obliged them to resort
sometimes to forced interpretations. Nevertheless, on the whole,
a post-exilic date for the prophecy is the most probable. Not only
is the manner in which the Greeks are mentioned in 9^{13} a grave
obstacle to a date before B.C. 722, but the portrait of the Messianic
king seems to be *original* in Isaiah, so that it is very doubtful
whether $9^{9f.}$ can be rightly treated as prior to Isaiah : moreover,
the style of representation often differs perceptibly from that of
the pre-exilic prophets ; and inasmuch as there are clear indications in some parts (as $9^{11. 12}$ 11^{4-17}) that the writer for some
reason intentionally veils his meaning, and speaks allegorically, a
presumption arises that he may do the same elsewhere. Hence
it is not impossible that the author may use " Ephraim " and
" the house of Joseph " as symbolical designations of the
Israelites still in exile (the Diaspora)—whose return was anticipated by the prophets long after B.C. 722 (Jer. 3^{12-18} $31^{4ff.}$, Ez.
$37^{16ff.}$)—and " Assyria," the name of the power which carried
Ephraim into exile, for Israel's present oppressors, whether the
Persians (cf. Ezr. 6^{22}), or—if the prophecy were written later—
the kingdom of the Seleucidae. Upon this view of the prophecy,
it is in part a re-affirmation, in a form adapted to the circumstances of the time, of older promises of victory over foes,

* So Abp. Newcome and others, Ewald, Bleek, Hitzig (slightly earlier),
Reuss, von Orelli, Briggs (*Mess. Proph.* p. 183 ff.), H. Schultz (*Old Test.
Theol.* i. 70), Riehm (*Einl.* ii. p. 156 f.).

restoration of exiles, and the advent of the Messianic age; *
but, in its most characteristic parts ($10^{3. 4}$ 11^{3}, and especially
11^{4-17}), it is a promise of deliverance from the "shepherds," *i.e.*
native rulers (? high priests), who misgovern Israel, and from the
"traffickers of the flock," † *i.e.* foreign powers (presumably the
Seleucidae or the Ptolemies), whose dealings with Israel are
prompted solely by the thought of their own aggrandizement
(so Wellh.).   The date of the prophecy will not (on account of
9^{13}) be earlier than B.C. 333.‡   Stade places it *c.* 280 B.C. §

11^{4-14} (and perhaps $11^{15. 16}$ as well) is to be understood, in all probability,
not as a prediction, but as a symbolical description of events which had
already taken place, the *significance* of which it is the object of the allegory
to point out.   These would be most naturally understood as events which
had happened recently when the prophet wrote ; but in our imperfect knowledge of much of the post-exilic period we are unable to say definitely
whether this view is correct or not.   Upon any view of the prophecy there
is much in it which is obscure, and much which may be differently interpreted
(as $10^{3. 4}$ $11^{1-3. 4ff.}$).   The "three shepherds," cut off "in one day" (11^{8}),
have often, for instance, been supposed to denote the three leading classes
of kings, priests, and prophets, the reference—according to Bred. and Kuiper
(p. 29)—being to the violent interruption of the national life occasioned by
the catastrophe of B.C. 586.   The obscurity of the allusions is much greater
than is usual in pre-exilic prophecies, and is a point in which the prophecy

---

* Hence, probably, the pre-exilic colouring which it in parts presents.
Kuiper (p. 145) and Eckardt (p. 101 f.), however, both agree with Cheyne
(*JQR.* 1888, p. 82) and Kuenen (§ 81. 10), that there are grounds for supposing actual fragments of pre-exilic prophecies to have been incorporated
by the author in parts of his work.

† כנעני הצאן ($11^{7. 11}$ LXX; Stade, p. 26 *n.*; Kirkp. p. 404 *n.*; Wellh.).

‡ Kirkp. indeed dates it "60–70 years after the Return" (p. 451) ; but
he is obliged for this purpose to reject the words *against thy sons, O Greece*,
as a gloss (p. 472 f.).

§ In 320 Ptolemy Lagi surprised Jerusalem on a Sabbath ; and Josephus
speaks of many Judahites taken captive by him afterwards to Egypt (cf.
Ewald, *Hist.* v. 226) ; and shortly afterwards invading armies passed through
Palestine more than once, viz. under Eumenes in 318, Antigonus in 315–314,
Seleucus in 301 and 295, and Antiochus in 281.   One of the last three
occasions might, Stade thinks (*ZATW.* 1882, pp. 302, 304), have suggested
the terms of 9^{1-8}.   Kuiper (p. 158 ff.) places c. 9–10 immediately after the
battle of Issus (B.C. 333), supposing 9^{1-8} (as also 11^{1-3}) to have been written
in anticipation of the advance of Alexander upon Egypt (in the course of
which he besieged and took Tyre and Gaza), B.C. 332, and understanding
the two chapters generally as giving expression to the hopes of restoration
raised by Alexander's successes ; c. 11 was written later, after these hopes
had been disappointed.

resembles Isa. 24–27. For *diviners* (10²) in the post-exilic age, cf. Mal. 3⁵.
Comp. further Wellh. *Minor Prophets*, p. 180 ff. ; Kirkp. pp. 443–447, 452–
458, 459–467.

Hengstenberg, Stade, and others seek to support the same conclusion as
to the date of Zech. 9–11, by pointing to passages in which the author is
dependent upon earlier prophecies (esp. those of Jer. and Ez.).* But the
argument is of doubtful cogency ; and that Stade, in particular, has greatly
overstated it, is generally allowed (Kuen. § 81. 7 ; Kirkp. p. 441 ; Kuiper,
pp. 116–120) : in some cases the expressions quoted as parallel are not so
similar, or of such an exceptional character, that one must necessarily have
been borrowed from the other ; and, where the resemblance is greater, it is
often uncertain (comp. above, p. 312 f.) which of two similar passages has
formed the model for the other, until it has been shown, upon independent
grounds, which of the passages was first written.

(2.) 12¹–13⁶. In c. 12 the prophet sees an assembly of
nations, including *Judah*, advancing against Jerusalem, 12¹⁻³ ;
but their forces are smitten with a sudden panic, v.⁴, and the
[329] chieftains of Judah, perceiving that Jehovah fights for
Jerusalem, turn their arms against the other nations, v.⁵ᶠ· ;
Jehovah, however, saves Judah first, in order that the capital,
elated by deliverance, may not triumph over it, v.⁷⁻⁹. After this,
Jehovah pours upon the inhabitants of the capital (who seem to
be represented as guilty of some murder) a " spirit of grace and
supplication " ; they mourn in consequence long and bitterly,
expressing thereby their penitence, v.¹⁰⁻¹⁴. Henceforth a fountain
of purification from sin is permanently opened (נִפְתָּח ... יִהְיֶה) in
Jerusalem ; idols are cut off ; and prophets (who appear to be
represented in an unfavourable light) cease, either being repudiated by their friends or disowning their vocation, 13¹⁻⁶.

C. 14. Another assault upon Jerusalem is here described.
The nations this time *capture* the city, and half of its population
is taken into captivity, v.¹ᶠ· ; Jehovah next appears in order to
rescue the remainder ; He stands upon the Mount of Olives,
which is rent in sunder beneath Him, and through the chasm
the fugitives escape, v.³⁻⁵. Thereupon the Messianic age commences : two streams issue forth from Jerusalem, E. and W., to

* Comp. 9²ᵇ⁻⁴, Ez. 28³· ⁴· ⁸ᵇ.—9⁵, Zeph. 2⁴.—9⁵ᵇ⁻⁷, Am. 1⁷⁻⁸.—9¹⁰, Mic.
5¹⁰ᶠ·.—9¹²ᵇ, Isa. 61⁷.—10³, Jer. 23²ᵇ, Ez. 34¹⁷ (the he-goats).—10⁵ᵃ, Mic.
7¹⁰.—10⁵ᵇ (riders on horses), Ez. 38¹⁵.—10⁸ᵇ, Jer. 23³ᵇ.—10⁹ᵃ, Jer. 31²⁷.—10¹⁰ᵃ,
Hos. 11¹¹.—10¹⁰ᵇ, Mic. 7¹⁴ᵇ.—11³ᵃ, Jer. 25³⁶.—11³ᵇ, Jer. 12⁵ (the " pride of
Jordan ").—11⁴ᵇ, Jer. 12³ (" flock . . . slaughter ").—11⁵ᵃ, Jer. 50⁷ᵃ.—11⁹· ¹⁶,
Ez. 34⁴. For the figure of the shepherd and the sheep, see also p. 275,
No. 1, Mic. 5⁶, Zeph. 3¹⁹, Ez. 34 (*passim*), and Isa. 56¹¹.

water the land, which becomes a plain, with the exception of Jerusalem (cf. Isa. 2²), which is rebuilt to its former limits (cf. Jer. 31³⁸ff.), v.⁸⁻¹¹. V.¹²⁻¹⁵ the prophet reverts to the period of v.³ in order to describe more fully the dispersion of the invaders, in which Judah is specially named as taking part (v.¹⁴ RV. *marg.*). The nations who escape do homage to Israel's God, and come annually to worship Him at the Feast of Tabernacles; if they neglect to do this, Jehovah withholds from them their rain, while the Egyptians (whose country was not dependent upon rain for its fertility) are punished in another manner, v.¹⁶⁻¹⁹; and all Jerusalem is consecrated to His service, v.²⁰ᶠ.

By many critics * this prophecy has been assigned to a prophet living shortly before the close of the kingdom of Judah, under either Jehoiakim, Jehoiachin, or Zedekiah. That the Northern kingdom no longer existed may be inferred from the fact that though the subject of the prophecy is said (12¹) to be Israel, Judah alone is mentioned, and is regarded as constituting the entire people of God; the promise, too, in 14¹⁰, includes Geba, the most northernly border town of Judah, but takes no notice of the territory of the ten tribes. That, further, it was written subsequently to the death of King [330] Josiah at Megiddo (B.C. 609), appears from 12¹¹, if it may be assumed (as is commonly done) that by the "mourning of Hadadrimmon in the valley of Megiddo" is meant the lamentation over the death of that king, alluded to in 2 Ki. 23²⁹ᶠ· 2 Ch. 35²²⁻²⁵. And the mention of the "House of David" (12⁷· ¹⁰· ¹² 13¹) appears to indicate a time when Judah was still ruled by kings. The idolatry noticed in 13², and the description of the prophets in 13²⁻⁶, would agree with the same date (Jer. 23⁹ff· &c.). The references in 12²ff· 14¹ff· are supposed accordingly to be to the approaching attack of the Chaldæans, to their capture of Jerusalem in 586, and to the escape, after severe trials, of a fraction of the inhabitants.

It is doubtful whether these reasons are conclusive. The prophecy is very different in character from the contemporary prophecies of Zephaniah and Jeremiah (see esp. 14¹⁻⁵); and the passages quoted, though sufficient to make it probable that it was written *after* the end of the Northern kingdom in 722 and the death of Josiah in 609, do not show with equal clearness that it was written *before* the destruction of Jerusalem in 586. The lamentation for Josiah remained, as 2 Ch. 35²²⁻²⁵ shows, in the memory of the people, long after the generation which witnessed it had died out. The terms in which the "House of David" is alluded to do not necessarily imply that it was the *ruling* family, though it is true that a pre-eminence is attached to

---

* Abp. Newcome, Knobel, Schrader, Bleek, Ewald, Riehm, von Orelli.

it ($12^{7.\ 8}$ 13^{1}): it is mentioned side by side with other families (12^{12-14}); and from 1 Ch. 3^{17-24}, Ezr. 8^{2} we know that the descendants of David were reckoned as a distinct family as late as the time of the Chronicler. Other indications favour the post-exilic date. The independent position assigned to the "House of Levi," as a whole, beside the "House of David," is unlike the representations of the earlier period (*e.g.* those of Jeremiah, who only names the priests as a class, and ranks them after the king's "princes," 1^{18} 2^{26} 4^{9} 8^{1} 13^{13} &c.); on the other hand, it would harmonize with post-exilic relations, when the family of David was reduced in prestige, and the tribe of Levi was consolidated. The allusions in 13^{2-6} are obscure; but prophets generally (not false prophets only) seem to be regarded with disfavour, and we are reminded of the age in which Shemaiah, Noadiah, and "the rest of the prophets," conspired against Nehemiah (Neh. 6^{10-14}). Sorcerers are alluded to in Mal. 3^{5}. One of the most remarkable features in the prophecy is the opposition between Judah and Jerusalem [331] (12^{7}, cf. 14^{14} *), of which there is no trace in pre-exilic writings, but which might arise in later times, when the central importance of the Temple had increased, when Jews of the Diaspora would turn their eyes naturally to Jerusalem, so that in comparison with it the country districts might be depreciated, and might readily be looked down upon by the inhabitants of the capital. It is to be observed that the "House of David" and the inhabitants of Jerusalem are repeatedly spoken of as associated together ($12^{7.\ 8}$ 13^{1}).

As regards the *occasion* of the prophecy it is impossible to do more than speculate. It is conceivable that in the post-exilic period where our history is a blank (B.C. 518–458; 432–300), the family of David assumed importance in Jerusalem, and supplied some of the leading judges and administrators, and that they had been implicated with the people of the capital in some deed of blood (12^{10-14}), on the ground of which the prophet depicts Jehovah's appearance in judgment. In the heathen invaders of $12^{2ff.}$ $14^{2f.}$ he perhaps has not in view any actual expected foe, but pictures an imaginary assault of nations, like Ezekiel (c. 38–39 †), from which he represents Jerusalem, though

---

* In 12^{2} it may be assumed that Judah fights against Jerusalem by compulsion; cf. v.$^{4b.\ 5.\ 6}$.

† Traits suggested by earlier prophecies are perhaps: 12^{1}, Isa. 51^{13}.—v.^{2} (the cup of reeling), Isa. 51^{22}.—v.^{4}, Dt. 28^{28}.—v.^{6b}, 14^{11b}, Joel 3^{20}.—v.^{9}, Ez. 39^{4-24}.—13^{1}, Ez. 36^{25}.—v.^{2}, Hos. 2^{17}.—14^{5}, Am. 1^{1}.—v.$^{6.\ 7.\ 9}$, Isa. 24^{23}.—v.^{8}, Ez. $47^{1ff.}$, Joel 3^{18b}.—v.^{10}, Jer. $31^{38f.}$—v.^{11}, Jer. 25^{9}, Isa. 43^{28} (the *herem* or "ban").—v.$^{12.\ 13}$, Ez. $38^{21.\ 22a}$.—v.^{16}, Isa. 66^{23}.—v.$^{20f.}$ Jer. 31^{40}, Joel 3^{17}.

not without severe losses, as delivered. In other features also the prophecy appears to be one of those (cf. Isa. 24–27) in which not merely the *figurative*, but the *imaginative* element is larger than is generally the case, especially in the pre-exilic prophets. But even when allowance has been made for this, many details in the prophecy remain perplexing ; and probably no entirely satisfactory explanation of it is now attainable.*

That the author of Zech. 1–8 should be also the author of either c. 9–11 or c. 12–14 is hardly possible. Zechariah uses a different phraseology, evinces different interests, and moves in a different circle of ideas from those which prevail in c. 9–14.

Thus Zech. is peculiarly fond of the confirmatory formula, "Thus saith the Lord" (1[3. 4. 14. 16. 17] 2[8] 3[7] 6[12] &c.); "came the word of the Lord unto . . ." 1[7] 4[8] 6[9] 7[1. 4. 8] 8[1. 18]; in c. 9–14 we have the former only in 11[4], the latter not at all : the parenthetic "Saith the [332] Lord" is also much more frequent in c. 1–8 than in c. 9–14 ; on the other hand, "in that day," which is specially frequent in c. 12–14 (12[3. 4. 6. 8 *bis*. 9. 11] 13[1. 2. 4 *bis*] 14[4. 6. 8. 9. 13. 20. 21]), occurs thrice only in c. 1–8 (2[11] 3[10] 6[10]), and only twice in c. 9–11 (9[16] 11[11]). In c. 9–14 (except in the narrative part of c. 11) poetic imagery and form prevail (the verses, as in the prophets generally, being composed largely of parallel clauses) : in c. 1–8 the style is unpoetical, and parallelism is uncommon.

That c. 1–8 consists largely of visions, of which there are none in c. 9–14, might not itself be incompatible with identity of author (cf. Am. 1–6 and 7–9); but the dominant ideas and representations of c. 1–8 are very different from those of either c. 9–11 or c. 12–14. In c. 1–8, the lifetime of the author and the objects of his interest—the Temple and the affairs of the restored community—are very manifest; but the circumstances and interests of the author, whether of c. 9–11 or of c. 12–14, whatever obscurity may hang over particular passages, are certainly very different. Zechariah's pictures of the Messiah and the Messianic age are coloured quite differently from those of c. 9–11 or c. 12–14 (contrast 3[8] 6[12f.] with 9[9f.], and c. 8 with the representation in c. 14): the prospects of the nation are also represented differently (contrast 1[21] 2[8-11] 8[7f.] with 12[2ff.] 14[2f.]; and observe that in c. 12–14 the *return* of Jewish exiles is not one of the events which the prophet looks forward to).

Similarities between c. 1–8 and c. 9–14 are few, and insignificant as compared with the features of difference. The only noteworthy one is the

---

* The post-exilic date of c. 12–14 is accepted by most critics, except those named p. 352, *note*.

phrase מעבר ומשב, 7¹⁴ 9⁸ (but see Ez. 35⁷): העביר =to remove 3⁴ 13² (in different connexions) occurs too often to be characteristic of a single writer (2 Sa. 12¹³ 24¹⁰, Job 7²¹: 1 Ki. 15¹², 2 Ch. 15⁸, Eccl. 11¹⁰); "daughter of Zion," 2¹⁰ 9⁹, is used constantly by the prophets; and the mention of Israel beside Judah in 1¹⁹ 8¹³, as in 9¹³ ("Ephraim"), 10⁶ ("the house of Joseph"), and 11⁴, forms a slender argument in favour of the unity of authorship, in view of the frequency with which the prophets, even after the fall of the northern kingdom, refer to both divisions of the people, and include both in their promises of restoration (cf. p. 291).

The position of c. 9–11, 12–14 is probably to be attributed to the compiler who united the writings of the "Minor Prophets" into a volume.

[333] This appears to follow from a comparison of the titles to Zech. 9–11, 12–14 and Malachi. We have, namely—

Zech. 9¹ משא דבר יהוה בארץ חדרך

12¹ משא דבר יהוה על ישראל

Mal. 1¹ משא דבר יהוה אל ישראל

As the combination משא דבר יהוה is a little remarkable, and does not occur besides, it is natural to seek some common explanation for the similarity of the three titles. In 9¹, now, these words form an integral part of the sentence that follows; in the other two cases they belong entirely to the title. It is a plausible conjecture therefore that, the three prophecies now known as "Zech." 9–11, 12–14 and "Malachi" coming to the compiler's hands with no authors' names prefixed, he attached the first of these at the point which his volume had reached, viz. the end of Zech. 8, arranging the other two so as to follow this, and framing titles for them (Zech. 12¹ and Mal. 1¹) on the model of the opening words of Zech. 9¹.

§ 12. MALACHI.

The prophecy of Malachi may be divided for convenience into six parts or paragraphs.

(1.) 1²⁻⁵ (Exordium). The love of Jehovah towards Israel (which was questioned by some of Malachi's contemporaries) is manifest in the contrasted lots of Israel and Edom: in vain may Esau's descendants expect a restoration of their ruined country.

(2.) 1⁶–2⁹. Israel, however, is unmindful of this love, and does not render to Jehovah the honour and reverence which are His due. Especially the priests are neglectful of their duties, allowing inferior or unclean offerings to be presented upon the altar: the service of Jehovah is in consequence brought into contempt, for which they are threatened, 2¹⁻⁹, with condign punishment: Jehovah will send a curse upon them, and make them contemptible before all the people.

(3.) 2[10-16]. A denunciation of those who had divorced their own wives and contracted marriages with foreign women.

(4.) 2[17]–3[6]. To those who questioned the Divine government of the world, and argued that righteousness secured no greater favour in God's sight than unrighteousness, the prophet announces the approach of a day of judgment, when Jehovah will appear "suddenly" for the purpose of purifying His unworthy priests, besides declaring Himself as a "swift witness" against the guilty members of His nation generally.

[334] (5.) 3[7-12]. The neglect of the people in paying tithes and other dues has been visited by Jehovah with drought, locusts, and failure of crops; but a blessing is promised upon the land if in the future these obligations are conscientiously discharged.

(6.) 3[13]–4[6]. The people complain that "it is vain to serve God"; no distinction is made between the evil and the good: the day is coming, replies the prophet, when Jehovah will own those that are His, and silence the murmurers, 3[13-18]: the workers of wickedness will be punished, and the righteous triumph over their fall, 4[1-3]. The prophecy concludes with an exhortation to obey the requirements of the Mosaic Law, and with a promise of the advent of Elijah the prophet, to move the people to repentance against the day of Jehovah,. and thus to avert, or mitigate, the curse which otherwise must smite the earth, 4[4-6].

Respecting the person of Malachi nothing is known. The name does not occur elsewhere; and it has even been questioned whether it be the personal name of the prophet. Already the LXX have strangely, in 1[1], ἐν χειρὶ ἀγγέλου αὐτοῦ (*i.e.* מלאכו for מלאכי); and the Targum has, "by the hand of Malachi [or, of my messenger], *whose name is called Ezra the scribe.*" The same tradition is mentioned by Jerome (who accepts it) and other writers. But had Ezra been the author of the prophecy, it is difficult to think that his authorship would have been thus concealed. From the similarity of the title, in form, to Zech. 9[1] 12[1], it is probable (p. 355) that it was framed by the compiler of the volume of the twelve prophets; and this, taken in conjunction with the somewhat prominent recurrence of the same word in 3[1], has led some modern scholars to the conjecture that the prophecy, when it came to the compiler's hands, had no author's name prefixed, and that he derived the name from 3[1], מלאכי being there understood by him either as an actual designation of the author, or as a term descriptive of his office, and so capable of being applied to him symbolically (Ewald, Kuenen, Reuss, Stade, Wellh.).

It is evident that the prophecy of Malachi belongs to the period after the Captivity, when Judah was a Persian province ("thy *governor*" פחתך 1⁸: cf. Hag. 1¹, Neh. 5¹⁴ 12¹⁶ &c.), when the Temple had been rebuilt (1¹⁰ 3¹), and public worship was again carried on in it. The three abuses which he mainly attacks are the degeneracy of the priesthood, intermarriage with foreign women, and the remissness of the people in the payment of sacred dues. These abuses, especially the second and third, are mentioned prominently in the memoirs of Ezra and Nehemiah, and are what those reformers set themselves [335] strenuously to correct (see Ezra 9² 10³. ¹⁶⁻⁴⁴, Neh. 10³⁰. ³²ff. 13⁴ff. ¹⁵ff. ²³ff. ²⁸f.). It may reasonably be inferred therefore that the prophecy dates from the age of Ezra and Nehemiah.

The only question open is whether its author wrote *before* the arrival of Ezra in Judah, B.C. 458 (Herzfeld, Bleek, Reuss, Stade), or somewhat later, viz. either shortly before or during Nehemiah's second visit there (Neh. 13⁶ff.), B.C. 432 (Schrader, Köhler, Keil, von Orelli, Kuenen). On the whole, the period of Nehemiah's absence at the Persian Court is the most probable : the terms of 1⁸ make it a little unlikely that Nehemiah himself was "governor" at the time when Malachi wrote.

The situation in Judah at the time when Malachi prophesied was one of depression and discontent. The expectations which earlier prophets had aroused had not been fulfilled; the restoration from Babylon had brought with it none of the ideal glories promised by the second Isaiah : bad harvests increased the disappointment : hence many among the people began to doubt the Divine justice; Jehovah, they argued, could no longer be the Holy God, for He was heedless of His people's necessity, and permitted sin to continue unpunished; to what purpose, therefore, should they concern themselves with His service? A spirit of religious indifference and moral laxity began thus to prevail among the people. The same temper appears even among the priests : they perform their offices perfunctorily; they express by their actions, if not by their words, their contempt for the service in which they are engaged. And the mixed marriages which were now the fashion threatened to obliterate altogether the distinctive character of the nation. Malachi seeks to recall his people to religious and moral earnestness : he insists on the importance of maintaining the purity of the public worship of God, and the distinctive character of the nation. His book is remarkable among the writings of the prophets on account of the interest which it evinces in ritual observances, and the grave light in which it views ritual laxity.   The explanation is to be found in the circumstances of the time.   Israel's preservation as the people of God could only be effectually secured by a strict observance of the ceremonial obligations laid upon it, and by its holding firmly aloof from the disintegrating influences to which unrestricted intercourse with its neighbours would inevitably expose it.   Malachi judged the times as the reformers Ezra and Nehemiah judged them.   But he is no formalist; his book [336] breathes the genuine prophetic spirit: ceremonial observances are of value in his eyes only as *securing* spiritual service; moral offences are warmly reprobated by him (3^5); and from the thought of the brotherhood of all Israelites, under one Father, he deduces the social duties which they owe·to one another, and the wrongfulness of the selfish system of divorce prevalent in his day.

The style of Malachi is more prosaic than that of the prophets generally: he has several peculiarities of expression (Köhler, p. 26); and his diction betrays marks of lateness, though not so numerous or pronounced as Esther, Chronicles, and Ecclesiastes.* He adopts also a novel literary form: first he states briefly the truth which he desires to enforce, then follows the contradiction or objection which it is supposed to provoke, finally there comes the prophet's reply, reasserting and substantiating his original proposition ($1^{2f.\ 6ff.}\ 2^{13f.\ 17}\ 3^{7.\ 8.\ 13ff.}$).   Thus "in place of the rhetorical development of a subject, usual with the earlier prophets, there appears in Malachi a dialectic treatment by means of question and answer.   We have here the first traces of that method of exposition which, in the schools that arose about this time, became ultimately the prevalent one" (Köhler, p. 26, after Ewald).

---

* *E.g.* נאל *to defile*, $1^{7.\ 12}$; כפי אשר 2^9; and the inelegant syntax of 2^{13}, which is quite in the style of the Chronicler.

CHAPTER VII.

THE PSALMS.

LITERATURE.—H. Ewald in the *Dichter des AB.s*,[2] 1866 (translated : also the basis of *The Psalms chronologically arranged*, by Four Friends, 1867) ; Justus Olshausen (in the *Kgf. Exeg. Handb.*), 1853 ; H. Hupfeld, *Die Psalmen*, 1855–62,[2] revised by W. Nowack, 1888 ; F. Hitzig, *Die Psalmen*, 1863, 1865 ; F. Delitzsch, 1867, [4] 1883 (translated : Hodder & Stoughton, 1887–89), [5](posthumous) 1894 ; J. J. S. Perowne, *The Book of Psalms: a new transl. with Introd. and Notes*, 1864–68, [6] 1886 ; W. Kay, *The Psalms with Notes*,[2] 1874 ; H. Grätz, *Krit. Komm. zu den Psalmen*, 1882–83 (alters the text much too freely) ; T. K. Cheyne, *The Book of Psalms : a new transl. with Comm.* 1888 (on the *text*, see esp. pp. 369–406) ; *The Historical Origin and Religious Ideas of the Psalter* (the "Bampton Lectures" for 1889), 1891 ; *Aids to the Devout Study of Criticism*, 1892, p. 129 ff. (chiefly sermon-studies on Ps. 8, 16, 24, 26, 28, 32, 51, 63, 68, 86, 87, 113–118) ; A. F. Kirkpatrick, in the *Camb. Bible for Schools*, 1891 (Bk. i.), 1895 (Bks. ii.–iii.) ; F. Baethgen (in Nowack's "Handkommentar"), 1892 ; J. Wellhausen (in Haupt's *SBOT.*), 1896. See also Lagarde, *Orientalia*, ii. (1880) p. 13 ff.; R. W. Church (Dean of St. Paul's) in *The Gifts of Civilisation*, 1880, p. 391 ff.; W. R. Smith, *OTJC.*[2] Lect. vii.; M. Kopfstein, *Die Asaph-Pss. untersucht*, 1881 ; A. Neubauer, *On the Titles of the Psalms according to early Jewish Authorities*, in *Studia Biblica*, ii. p. 1 ff. (Oxford, 1890) ; Montefiore, "Mystic Passages in the Psalms," *JQR.* Jan. 1889, p. 143 ff., and review of Cheyne's *Orig. of Ps.*, Oct. 1891, p. 129 ff.; A. Rahlfs, עני *und* עָנָו *in den Pss.*, 1892 ; B. Stade, "Die Mess. Hoffnung im Psalter," *Z. f. Theol. u. Kirche*, 1892, p. 369 ff.; W. T. Davison, *The Praises of Isr., an Introd. to the Study of the Pss.*, 1893, [2]1897 ; G. Beer, *Individual- u. Gemeindepsalmen*, 1894 ; W. Diehl, *Erklärung von Ps. 47*, 1894 ; B. Jacob, "Beiträge zu einer Einl. in die Pss." (on *Selah*, the titles, &c.), *ZATW.* 1896, pp. 129 ff., 265 ff., 1897, p. 48 ff.

The Book of Psalms (in most German MSS.,* which are followed in the printed editions of the Hebrew Bible) opens the third division of the Hebrew Canon, the כְּתוּבִים, or *writings* (also sometimes כתבי הקדש, Ἁγιόγραφα).

Hebrew Poetry.†—Hebrew poetry reaches back to the most

---

* In Spanish MSS., as in Massoretic lists, it is preceded by *Chronicles.*

† See Rob. Lowth, *De sacra poesi Hebraeorum praelectiones academicae*

[338] ancient recollections of the Israelites (Gen. 49, Nu. 21$^{17f.}$ $^{27-30}$, Jud. 5, &c.); probably, as with other nations, it was the form in which their earliest literary efforts found expression. Many poetical pieces are preserved in the historical books; and the Books of Psalms, Proverbs, Job (the Dialogue), Song of Songs, and Lamentations are entirely poetical. The line between poetry and elevated prose being, moreover, less sharply drawn in Hebrew than in Western languages, the prophets not un-frequently rise into a lyric or elegiac strain; and even the author of Ecclesiastes is led sometimes, by the moralizing character of his discourse, to cast his thoughts into the form of gnomic poetry.

Of the two forms of poetry in which the greatest masterpieces of the Aryan races have been cast, the epos and the drama, the former is entirely unrepresented in Hebrew literature, the latter is represented only in a rudimentary and imperfect form. As will be shown in its proper place, the Song of Songs is of the nature of a drama; and the Book of Job may be styled a dramatic poem. But the genius of the ancient Israelite was pre-eminently *subjective*; the Hebrew poet did not readily accommodate him-self to the presentation, in a poetical form, of the thoughts and emotions of others, such as the epos and the drama both require; it was his own thoughts and emotions for which he sought spontaneously to find forms of expression. Hence Hebrew poetry is almost exclusively *lyric* and *gnomic*.

In lyric poetry, the poet gives vent to his personal emotions or experiences—his joys or sorrows, his cares or complaints, his aspirations or his despair; or he reproduces in words the impres-sions which nature or history may have made upon him. The character of lyric poetry, it is evident, may vary widely according to the subject, and according to the circumstances and mood of the poet himself. *Gnomic* poetry consists of observations on human life and society, or generalizations respecting conduct and character. But the line between these two forms cannot always

(Oxon. 1753; transl. by G. Gregory 1847); J. G. von Herder, *Vom Geist der Ebr. Poesie*, 1782–83 (reprinted, Gotha, 1890); H. Ewald, *Die Dichter des AB.s*, i. 1 ("Allgemeines über die hebr. Dichtkunst, und über das Psalmenbuch"; only pp. 239–292, 209–233 translated, in the translation of the Psalms, i. p. 1 ff., ii. p. 328 ff.); Kuenen, *Onderzoek*,[2] iii. 1 (1893), 1–59, with the references.

be drawn strictly: lyric poetry, for instance, may assume a parenetic tone, giving rise to an intermediate form which may be called *didactic* (*e.g.* Ps. 15, 25, 37; Pr. 1–9); or again, a poem which is, on the whole, didactic may rise in parts into a lyric strain (Job 29–31, 38–39; Pr. 8¹²ff·).

Most of the Hebrew poetry that has been preserved is of a religious type: but poetry is the expression of a national character; and no doubt other [339] sides of the national life—*e.g.* deeds of warriors, incidents of domestic interest, love, wine, marriages, and deaths—were fully represented in it. Examples of poems, or poetic sayings, in the OT. of a purely secular character are Gen. 4²³f· (Lamech's song of triumph over the invention of metal weapons), Nu. 21¹⁷f· ²⁷⁻³⁰, Jud. 15¹⁶, 1 Sa. 18⁷, and even David's two elegies, 2 Sa. 1¹⁹⁻²⁷ 3³³f·. Allusions to songs accompanying banquets or other festal occasions occur in Gen. 31²⁷, 2 Sa. 19³⁵, Am. 6⁵, Isa. 5¹² 16¹⁰ 24⁹, Job 21¹², Ps. 69¹² (cf. Job 30⁹, Lam. 3¹⁴· ⁶³) 78⁶³, Lam. 5¹⁴, Eccl. 2⁸: cf. also Isa. 23¹⁶, Jer. 38²²ᵇ.

Poetry is distinguished from prose partly by the character of the thoughts of which it is the exponent,—which in Hebrew poetry, as a rule, either express or spring out of an emotion,— partly by its diction (the choice and order of words), but especially by its *rhythm*. The onward movement of emotion is not entirely irregular or unrestrained; it is *checked*, or interrupted, at particular intervals; and the flow of thought has to accommodate itself in a certain degree to these recurring interruptions; in other words, it is divided into *lines*. In most Western poetry these lines have a definite *metre* or measure: they consist, viz., of a fixed number of syllables (or of "feet"): in some cases all the lines of a poem being of the same length, in other cases lines of different length alternating, according to certain prescribed rules. To the modern ear, also, the satisfaction which the recurrence of lines of equable length produces, is often enhanced by that assonance of the corresponding lines which we term *rhyme*. But in ancient Hebrew poetry, though there was always *rhythm*, there was (so far as has yet been discovered) no *metre***** in the strict sense of the term; and rhyme appears

---

* On the attempts that have been made to discover metre (strictly so called) in the OT., see the study of C. Budde in the *Stud. u. Krit.* 1874, p. 747 ff., and in the *Theol. Lit.-zt.* 1888, No. 1. The cleverest of these attempts is that of G. Bickell in his *Carmina Vet. Test. metrice* (1882), where the poems of the OT. are transliterated in metrical forms analogous to those used by the Syriac poets (Ephrem, &c.). But the numerous alterations in the text, and the metrical licences, which are necessary for Bickell's system, form a serious

[340] to have been as accidental as it was with the classical Latin poets. The poetical instincts of the Hebrews appear to have been satisfied by the adoption of lines of *approximately* the same length,* which were combined, as a rule, into groups of two, three, or four lines, constituting *verses*, the verses marking usually more distinct pauses in the progress of the thought than the separate lines. The fundamental (and predominant) form of the Hebrew verse is the couplet of two lines, the second line either repeating, or in some other way reinforcing or completing, the thought of the first. In the verse of two lines is exemplified also the principle which most widely regulates the form of Hebrew poetry, the *parallelismus membrorum* — the parallelism of two clauses of approximately the same length, the second clause answering, or otherwise completing, the thought of the first. The Hebrew verse does not, however, consist uniformly of two lines; the addition of a third line is apt especially to introduce an element of irregularity : so that the *parallelismus membrorum*, though an important canon of Hebrew poetry, is not the *sole* principle by which its form is determined.

The significance in Hebrew poetry of the parallelism of clauses was first perceived by Rob. Lowth, who thus distinguished its principal varieties :—

1. *Synonymous* parallelism. In this kind (which is the most frequent) the second line enforces the thought of the first by repeating, and, as it were,

---

objection to it. At the same time, it is probable that in his search for a metre he has in reality been guided by a sense of *rhythm*, which has enabled him to discover imperfections due to corruption of the text. Prof. Briggs' system (*Biblical Study*, p. 279 ff.; *Hebraica*, 1887, p. 161 ff., 1888, p. 201 ff.; comp. Fr. Brown, *JBLit.* 1890, p. 71 ff.) is not one of strict metre, but of measurement by *accents* or rhythmical beats, the "foot" not necessarily consisting of the same number of syllables. The principle of Jul. Ley, *Leitfaden der Metrik der Heb. Poesie* (1887), is similar. Apart from conjecture, metre is only *known* to have been introduced into Hebrew poetry by the Jewish poets of the Middle Ages, in imitation of Arabic poetry. (Bickell's *Carmina* should be supplemented by his short papers in the Innsbruck *Z. für Kathol. Theol.* 1885, p. 717 ff.; 1886, p. 205 ff., 355 ff., 546 ff., 560 ff.; and his metrical edition of Prov. in the *Wiener Ztsch. f. d. Kunde des Morgenl.* v. 79 ff., 191 ff., 271 ff. (Nachträge, vii. 167 f.) ; Job, *ib.* vi. 137 ff., 241 ff., 327 ff., vii. 1 ff., 153 ff.; Lam., *ib.* viii. 101 ff.) See also Grimme, *ZDMG.* 1896, p. 529 ff.

* And approximately, also, each complete in itself, or coinciding with a pause in the thought,—another point of difference from Western poetry, in which the thought may generally move on continuously through two or more.

echoing it in a varied form, producing an effect at once grateful to the ear and satisfying to the mind : as—

Nu. 23[8] How shall I curse, whom God hath not cursed?
And how shall I defy, whom the LORD hath not defied?

Or the second line expresses a thought not indeed identical with that of the first, but parallel and similar to it—

Josh. 10[12] Sun, stand thou still upon Gibeon ;
And thou, Moon, upon the valley of Aijalon.

[341] 2. *Antithetic* parallelism. Here the thought of the first line is emphasized, or confirmed, by a *contrasted* thought expressed in the second. Thus—

Pr. 10[1] A wise son maketh a glad father,
But a foolish son is the heaviness of his mother.
Ps. 1[6] For the LORD knoweth the way of the righteous ;
But the way of the wicked shall perish.

This kind of parallelism is most frequent in gnomic poetry, where, from the nature of the subject-matter, antithetic truths are often contrasted.

3. *Synthetic* or *constructive* parallelism. Here the second line contains neither a repetition nor a contrast to the thought of the first, but in different ways supplements or completes it. The parallelism, therefore, is merely of *form*, and does not extend to the thought at all. *E.g.*—

Ps. 2[6] Yet I have set my king
Upon Zion, my holy hill.
Pr. 15[17] Better is a dinner of herbs where love is,
Than a stalled ox and hatred therewith.
26[4] Answer not a fool according to his folly,
Lest thou also be like unto him.
27[8] As a bird that wandereth from her nest,
So is a man that wandereth from his place.

A comparison, a reason, a consequence, a motive, often constitutes one of the lines in a synthetic parallelism.

4. A fourth kind of parallelism, though of rare occurrence, is still sufficiently marked to be noticed by the side of those described by Lowth, viz. *climactic* parallelism (sometimes called "ascending rhythm"). Here the first line is itself incomplete, and the second line takes up words from it and completes them—

Ps. 29[1] Give unto the LORD, O ye sons of the mighty,
Give unto the LORD *glory and strength.*
[8] The voice of the LORD shaketh the wilderness ;
The LORD shaketh the wilderness *of Kadesh.*
Ex. 15[16b] Till thy people pass over, O LORD,
Till the people pass over, *which thou hast purchased.*

This kind of rhythm is all but peculiar to the most elevated poetry : see Jud. 4[4b. 7. 19a. 23b], Ps. 29[5] 92[10] 93[3] 94[3] 96[13] 113[1] (cf. 67[4. 6]), Isa. 24[15] (Cheyne). There is something analogous to it, though much less forcible and distinct, in some of the "Songs of Ascents" (Ps. 121-134), where a somewhat emphatic word is repeated from one verse (or line) in the next, as Ps. 121[1b. 2] (help); v.[3b. 4]; v.[4b. 5a]; v.[7. 8a]; 122[2b. 3a] &c.

By far the greater number of verses in the poetry of the OT. consist of distichs of one or other of the types that have been illustrated; though naturally every individual line is not constructed with the regularity of the examples selected (which, [342] indeed, especially in a long poem, would tend to monotony). The following are the other principal forms of the Hebrew verse :—

1. Single lines, or *monostichs.* These are found but rarely, being generally used to express a thought with some emphasis at the beginning, or occasionally at the end, of a poem : Ps. 16[1] 18[1] 23[1] 66[1]; Ex. 15[18].

2. Verses of three lines, or *tristichs.* Here different types arise, according to the relation in which the several lines stand to one another. Sometimes, for instance, the three lines are synonymous, as—

> Ps. 5[11] But let all those that put their trust in thee rejoice,
> Let them ever shout for joy, because thou defendest them :
> And let them that love thy name be joyful in thee.

Sometimes *a* and *b* are parallel in thought, and *c* completes it—

> Ps. 2[2] The kings of the earth set themselves,
> And the rulers take counsel together,
> Against Jehovah, and against his anointed.

Or *b* and *c* are parallel—

> Ps. 3[7] Arise, Jehovah ; save me, O my God :
> For thou hast smitten all mine enemies upon the cheek-bone ;
> Thou hast broken the teeth of the wicked.

Or *a* and *c* may be parallel, and *b* be of the nature of a parenthesis—

> Ps. 4[2] Answer me, when I call, O God of my righteousness ;
> Thou hast set me at large when I was in distress :
> Have mercy upon me, and hear my prayer.

3. *Tetrastichs.* Here generally *a* is parallel to *b*, and *c* is parallel to *d* ; but the thought is only complete when the two couplets are combined ; thus—

> Gen. 49[7] Cursed be their anger, for it was fierce ;
> And their wrath, for it was cruel :
> I will divide them in Jacob,
> And scatter them in Israel.

So Dt. 32[21. 30. 38. 41], Isa. 49[4] 59[3. 4], &c.

Sometimes, however, *a* is parallel to *c*, and *b* to *d*—

> Ps. 55[21] His mouth was smooth as butter,
> But his heart was war ;
> His words were softer than oil,
> Yet were they drawn swords.

So Ps. 40[14] 127[1], Dt. 32[42], Isa. 30[16] 44[5] 49[2].

Occasionally *a* corresponds to *d*, and *b* to *c*; this is called technically "*introverted* parallelism," but is of rare occurrence; see Pr. 23¹⁵ᶠ·, Isa. 11¹³ (Cheyne), 59⁸.

[343] Or *a*, *b*, *c* are parallel, but *d* is more or less independent—

> Ps. 1³ And he is as a tree planted by streams of water,
> That bringeth forth its fruit in its season,
> And whose leaf doth not wither:
> And whatsoever he doeth he maketh to prosper.

Or *a* is independent, and *b*, *c*, *d* are parallel—

> Pr. 24¹² If thou sayest, Behold, we knew not this;
> Doth not he that weigheth the hearts consider it?
> And he that keepeth thy soul, doth not he know it?
> And shall not he render to every man according to his work?

Or it may even happen that the four members stand in no determinate relation to one another; see *e.g.* Ps. 40¹⁷.

4. and 5. Verses of 5 lines (*pentastichs*) occur but seldom in the OT., and those of six lines (*hexastichs*) are still rarer; see for the former, Nu. 24⁸, Dt. 32¹⁴·³⁹, 1 Sa. 2¹⁰, Ps. 39¹², Cant. 3⁴; for the latter, Nu. 24¹⁷, 1 Sa. 2⁸, Cant. 4⁸, Hab. 3¹⁷ (three distichs, closely united).

The finest and most perfect specimens of Hebrew poetry are, as a rule, those in which the parallelism is most complete (synonymous distichs and tetrastichs), varied by an occasional tristich (*e.g.* Job 28, 29–31, 38–39, Ps. 18, 29, 104, Pr. 8¹²ᶠᶠ·; and in a quieter strain, Ps. 51, 81, 91, 103 &c.).

Upon an *average*, the lines of Hebrew poetry consist of 7 or 8 syllables; but (so far as appears) there is no *rule* on the subject; lines may be longer or shorter, as the poet may desire; nor is there any necessity that the lines composing a verse should all be of the same length.* In Job and Proverbs lines of approximately the same length are of more frequent occurrence than in the Psalms; and the didactic and historical psalms are more regular in structure than those which are of a more emotional character. Where the line is much longer than 7–8 syllables, it is commonly divided by a *cæsura* (comp. Ps. 19⁷⁻⁹; Ps. 119): on the use of this form of line in the *elegiac* poetry of the Hebrews, see below, under Lamentations.

The prophets, though their diction is usually an elevated prose, manifest a strong tendency to enforce and emphasize their thought by casting it, more or less completely, into the

---

* Sometimes an exceptionally short line appears to be chosen for emphasis, Job 14ᵇ (לא אחר), Ps. 49¹⁵ᵇ (כי יקחני), 99⁸ᵇ ⁵ᶜ·.

form of parallel clauses (*e.g.* Isa. $1^{2. \ 3. \ 10. \ 18. \ 19. \ 20. \ 27. \ 29}$ &c.; $13^{10.}$ $^{11. \ 12. \ 13}$ &c.; Am. $6^{1. \ 2. \ 3. \ 4. \ 5. \ 6. \ 7}$ &c.).   And sometimes they adopt a distinctly lyrical strain, as Isa. 42^{10-12} [**344**] 44^{23} 45^8.   But with the prophets the lines are very commonly longer than is the case in poetry (in the technical sense of the word); and the movement is less bright and rapid than that of the true lyrical style.

Strophes or *stanzas.*   By the strophe of the ancient Greek choral ode, as by the stanza of modern European poetry, is meant a group of lines, each line possessing a determinate length and character, recurring regularly in the course of the same poem. In this sense there are no strophes or stanzas in Hebrew poetry. If, however, the term "strophe" be understood in the modified sense of a group of verses, connected together by a certain unity of thought, it is true that strophes of this kind are found in Hebrew poetry.   For that the Hebrew poets, at least sometimes, grouped together a certain number of verses, and marked consciously the close of such a group, may be inferred from the *refrains* which appear from time to time in the Psalms.*   The number of verses closed by a refrain is seldom, however, more than approximately uniform in the same poem; no importance therefore appears to have been attached to uniformity in the length of the Hebrew "strophe"; the poet placed the refrain where his thought came to a natural pause, without being anxious to secure perfectly regular intervals.   It may be assumed with probability that in other cases, especially if the poem be one of any length, the poet would mark the progress of his thought by *pauses* at more or less regular intervals; and the sections of the poem, closed by these supposed pauses, we may term "strophes."   And this conclusion is confirmed by the fact that many of the Psalms seem naturally to fall, logically as well as poetically, into groups of verses, two, three, or more, as the case may be.†   But often the divisions are less regular or [**345**]

---

* See Ps. $39^{5c. \ 11c}$; $42^{5. \ 11}$ 43^5 [the two Psalms forming originally one]; $46^{[3]. \ 7. \ 11}$; $49^{12. \ 20}$; $56^{4. \ 10f.}$; $57^{5. \ 11}$; $59^{6. \ 14}$ and $^{9. \ 17}$; $62^{1f. \ 5f.}$; $67^{3. \ 5}$; $80^{3.}$ $^{7. \ 19}$; $87^{4c. \ 6b}$; $99^{5. \ 9}$; $107^{6. \ 13. \ 19. \ 28}$ and $^{8. \ 15. \ 21. \ 30}$; $116^{13b-14. \ 17b-18}$; $136^{1b. \ 2b}$ &c. (26 times); $144^{7c-8. \ 11}$.   Comp. Isa. $9^{12b. \ 17b. \ 21b}$ 10^{4b}.   These refrains are not always expressed in quite identical terms; in one or two cases (Ps. 42^5 59^9) the variation is due probably to textual error; but elsewhere it appears to be intentional.

† *E.g.* Ps. $2^{1-3. \ 4-6. \ 7-9. \ 10-12}$; $3^{1f. \ 3f. \ 5f. \ 7f.}$; $13^{1f. \ 3f. \ 5f.}$; $68^{1-3. \ 4-6. \ 7-10. \ 11-14.}$ $^{15-18. \ 19-23. \ 24-27. \ 28-31. \ 32-35}$; $114^{1f. \ 3f. \ 5f. \ 7f.}$.

clearly marked; and in such cases the question arises whether they were really intended by the poet, and whether such sub-divisions as the articulation of the thought may appear to suggest are not to be regarded as *logical* rather than as poetical units, and as not properly deserving—even in its modified sense—the name of "strophes."

The Hebrew title of the Book of Psalms is תְּהִלִּים, *lit.* "praise-songs," a word which in the OT. itself occurs only in the forms תְּהִלָּה (*sing.*), תְּהִלּוֹת (*plur.*), and with the general sense of *praise, praises* (*e.g.* Ex. 15[11], Ps. 22[4]). The modern term "Psalms" is derived from the LXX rendering of תהלים, ψαλμοί.

In the Massoretic text the Psalms are in number 150; but Ps. 9 and 10, as the alphabetical arrangement shows (see below), must have formed originally a single whole (as they do still in the LXX and Vulg.); the same was also the case with Ps. 42 and 43 (notice the *refrain*, 42[5. * 11] 43[5]), which are actually united in 36 Hebrew MSS. On the other hand, there is reason to suppose that some Psalms, which now appear as one, consist of elements which have been incorrectly conjoined; this is certainly the case with Ps. 144 (where v.[12] is quite unconnected with v.[1-11]), and probably also with Ps. 19, 24, 27. The LXX adds, after Ps. 150, a Psalm, stated in the title to be ἔξω τοῦ ἀριθμοῦ, and ascribed to David, ὅτε ἐμονομάχησε τῷ Γολιαδ, which is undoubtedly spurious.

In the Hebrew Bible (as in the RV.) the Psalter is divided into five Books, Ps. 1–41; 42–72; 73–89; 90–106; 107–150. The end of each of the first four Books is marked by a doxology (Ps. 41[13]; 72[18f.]; 89[52]; 106[48]), of liturgical character, pointing, in all probability, to the fact that the collections were formed in the first instance for use in public worship; in Book 5 the place of such a doxology appears to have been taken by Ps. 150 itself. The second Book has in addition a special subscription (Ps. 72[20]), viz. "The Prayers of David, the son of Jesse, are ended." The division into five Books is older than the LXX translation, in which the doxologies are already found. The probable explanation of the division will be considered subsequently.

The following Psalms are *alphabetical, i.e.* successive verses, half-verses, or groups of verses begin with the successive letters of the Hebrew alphabet; Ps. 9–10 (two verses to each letter, the scheme, however, being [346] incompletely carried through); 25 (one verse to each letter, with an extra verse at

---

the end : the ו verse missing) ; 34 (also with an extra verse *) ; 37 (2 verses to each letter : the ע verse is missing through a corruption in v.²⁸ ; see the commentators) ; 111 (a half-verse to a letter) ; 112 (do.) ; 119 (8 verses to a letter) ; 145 (the נ verse missing).† The alphabetical order appears to have been sometimes adopted by poets as an artificial principle of arrangement, when the subject was one of a general character, that did not lend itself readily to logical development.

The Psalms, speaking generally, consist of reflexions, cast into a poetical form, upon the various aspects in which God manifests Himself either in nature, or towards Israel, or the individual soul, accompanied often—or, indeed, usually—by an outpouring of the emotions and affections of the Psalmist, prompted by the warmth of his devotion to God, though vary-ing naturally in character, according to the circumstances in which he is placed.   Thus, in some Psalms the tone is that of praise or thanksgiving, in others it is one of penitence or sup-plication, in others again it is meditative or didactic : not un-frequently also a Psalm is of mixed character ; it begins, perhaps, in a strain of supplication, and as the poet proceeds the confidence that his prayer will be answered grows upon him, and he ends in a tone of jubilant exultation (*e.g.* Ps. 6, 13, 22 (see v.²²ᶠᶠ.), 26, 31, 36, 64, 69, 71).   In the Psalter the *devotional* element of the religious character finds its completest expres-sion ; and the soul is displayed in converse with God, disclosing to Him its manifold emotions, desires, aspirations, or fears.   It is the surprising variety of mood and subject and occasion in the Psalms which gives them their catholicity, and, combined with their deep spirituality, adapts them to be the hymn-book, not only of the second Temple, but of the Christian Church.

Individual Psalms often present a mixed character, so that it is difficult to classify them in accordance with their subject-matter ; but the following out-line of the subjects which they embrace may be useful (comp. Hupfeld, pp. vii–ix) :—1. Meditations on different aspects of God's providence, as manifested in creation, history, &c.: Ps. 8 (man, how small, and yet how great !), 19¹⁻⁶ (God's glory in the heavens), 29 (Jehovah's majesty [347] seen in the thunderstorm), 33, 36, 65 (a harvest Psalm), 103 (the mercifulness of

---

* The פ verse here no doubt originally stood before the ע verse (giving a *subject* for " cried " in v.¹⁸), as in Lam. 2, 3, 4.

† The other alphabetical poems in the OT. are Lam. 1, 2, 3, 4 ; Prov. 31¹⁰⁻³¹ : cf. also p. 337.   The original Hebrew of Sirach 51¹³⁻³⁰, also, as Bickell has shown (in the Innsbruck *Z. f. Kathol. Theol.* 1882, p. 326 ff.), though his restoration is open in details to criticism, was alphabetical.

God), 104 (the poem of Creation), 107, 145–147 ; and with invocations of a liturgical character, 24$^{7-10}$ 47, 67, 95–100, 111, 113, 115, 117, 134–136, 148–150.

2. Reflexions on God's moral government of the world : Ps. 1, 34, 75, 77, 90, 92, 112 ; and of a directly didactic character, Ps. 37, 49, 73 ; or on the character and conduct that is pleasing in His eyes, Ps. 15, 24$^{1-6}$ 32, 40$^{1-12}$ 50.

3. Psalms expressive of faith, resignation, joy in God's presence, &c.: Ps. 11, 16, 23, 26, 27, 42 f., 62, 63, 84, 91, 121, 127, 128, 130, 131, 133, 139 (the sense of God's omnipresence) ; praise of the law, Ps. 19$^{7-14}$ 119.

4. Psalms with a more distinct reference to the circumstances of the Psalmist (including sometimes his companions or co-religionists), viz. (*a*) petitions for help in sickness, persecution, or other trouble, or for forgiveness of sins (often accompanied with the assurance that the prayer will be answered): Ps. 3–7, 9 f., 12, 13, 17, 22, and many besides ; (*b*) thanksgivings, Ps. 30, 40$^{1-12}$ 116, 138.

5. *National* Psalms :—consisting of (*a*) complaints of national oppression or disaster : Ps. 14 (= 53), 44, 60, 74 and 79 (desolation of the sanctuary), 80, 82, 83, 85, 94, 102, 108, 123, 137 ; (*b*) thanksgivings for mercies either already received, or promised for the future : Ps. 46, 47, 48, 66, 68, 76, 87 (Zion, the future spiritual metropolis of the world), 118, 122 (prayer for the welfare of Jerusalem), 124–126, 129, 144$^{12-15}$.

6. The *historical* Psalms, being retrospects of the national history with reference to the lessons deducible from it : Ps. 78, 81, 105, 106, 114.

7. Psalms relating to the king (*royal* Psalms), being thanksgivings, good-wishes, or promises, esp. for the extension of his dominion : Ps. 2, 18, 20, 21, 45 (on the occasion of a royal wedding), 72, 89 (a supplication on account of the humbled dynasty of David), 101 (a king's rule of life), 110, 132 ; cf. 28, 61, 63. These Psalms have often a Messianic import.

The line separating 4 and 5 is not always clearly drawn.

Most of the Psalms are provided with *titles*. The object of the titles is partly to define the character of a Psalm, partly to state the name of the author to whom it is attributed, and sometimes also the occasion on which it is supposed to have been composed, partly (as it seems) to notify the manner in which the Psalms were performed musically in the public services of the Temple. The terms describing the character and the musical accompaniment of a Psalm are frequently obscure : for the explanations that have been offered of them, reference must be made to the commentaries.

As *authors* of Psalms are named—

1. Moses, "the man of God" (Dt. 33^1) : Ps. 90.

2. David : in Book I. 37, viz. Ps. 3–9, 11–32, 34–41 ; in Book II. 18, viz. Ps. 51–65, 68–70 ; in Book III. 1, viz. Ps. 86 ; in Book IV. 2, viz. [348] Ps. 101, 103 ; in Book V. 15, viz. Ps. 108–110, 122, 124, 131, 133, 138–145, —in all 73.

3. Solomon : Ps. 72, 127.
4. Asaph : Ps. 50, 73–83,—in all 12.
5. Heman the Ezrahite : Ps. 88 (one of two titles).
6. Ethan the Ezrahite : Ps. 89.
7. The sons of Korah : Ps. 42, 44–49, 84, 85, 87, 88,—in all 11.

Asaph, Heman, and Ethan are the names of the three chief singers of David, often mentioned by the Chronicler, and referred by him to the three Levitical families of Gershonites, Kohathites, and Merarites respectively (1 Ch. 6$^{33-38.\ 39-43.\ 44-47}$; 15$^{17-18.\ 19}$). They were regarded as the founders of the families, or guilds, of singers, who assisted in the public worship of the second Temple.* The "sons of Korah" must be the descendants— actual or reputed—of the Korah, son of Jizhar, son of Kohath, son of Levi, who perished in the wilderness (Nu. 16$^{1ff.}$), but whose sons are stated (*ib.* 26^{11}) to have escaped, who are also, under the title "Korahites," described by the Chronicler as the gate-keepers of the Temple (1 Ch. 9^{19} 26$^{1-19}$); from 2 Ch. 20^{19} it may also be inferred that, if not in the time of Jehoshaphat, yet in the Chronicler's own time, they took part in the public worship of the Temple.

The following Psalms are referred by their titles—in terms borrowed generally, though not always, and sometimes with slight variations in detail, from the historical books—to events in the life of David : Ps. 3 (2 Sa. 15, &c.), 7 (allusion obscure), (18=2 Sa. 22), 34 (cf. 1 Sa. 21^{13}), 51 (2 Sa. 12), 52 (1 Sa. 22^9), 54 (1 Sa. 23^{19}), 56 (1 Sa. 21^{11} [or 27$^{2f.\ 7-12}$?]), 57 (1 Sa. 22^1 24$^{3ff.}$), 59 (1 Sa. 19^{11}), 60 (2 Sa. 8^{13} [cf. v.^{3} Zobah], 1 Ch. 18^{12}), 63 (1 Sa. 23$^{14ff.}$ 24^1 26^2), 142 (1 Sa. 22^1 24$^{3ff.}$). The title of Ps. 30, "at the dedication of the House [or Temple]," alludes, not to any event in the life of David, but to the occasion on which in later days the Psalm was publicly recited (see *Soferim*, c. 18, § 2), viz. on the anniversary of the Dedication of the Temple by Judas Maccabæus, 1 Macc. 4$^{52ff.}$ (τὰ ἐγκαίνια, John 10^{22}); the title of Ps. 92 "For the Sabbath day," is to be explained similarly.

In the LXX there are some additional titles. The anonymous Psalms 33, 43, 67, 91, 93–99, 104 are ascribed to David ; in cod. A also Ps. 42 ; and in a few MSS. Ps. 1, 2 as well. The title to Ps. 71 is τῷ Δαυείδ, υἱῶν Ἰωναδὰβ καὶ τῶν πρώτων αἰχμαλωτισθέντων ; to Ps. 138 (in cod. A) τῷ Δαυείδ [349] Ζαχαρίου ; and to Ps. 139 (in cod. A) τῷ Δ. Ζαχαρίου (with ἐν τῇ δια-σπορᾷ on the marg. and in cod. T). Ps. 146, 147$^{1-11}$ 147$^{12-20}$ (for the LXX treat this Psalm as two), 148 have each the title Ἀγγαίου καὶ Ζαχαρίου.

---

* See 1 Ch. 25$^{1ff.}$, 2 Ch. 5^{12} 29$^{13f.}$ 35^{15} (where it is generally allowed that Jeduthun [cf. Ps. 39, 62, 77 *titles*] is another name of Ethan). "Sons of *Asaph*" (who are especially prominent) are mentioned also 2 Ch. 20^{14}, Neh. 7^{44} 11^{22} *al.*

There are also references—sometimes obscure—to the occasion of the Psalm : Ps. 27 + πρὸ τοῦ χρισθῆναι ; Ps. 29 + ἐξοδίου σκηνῆς ; Ps. 31 + ἐκστάσεως [see v.²³] ; Ps. 66 + ἀναστάσεως ; Ps. 70 + εἰς τὸ σῶσαί με κύριον ; Ps. 76 + ᾠδὴ πρὸς τὸν Ἀσσύριον ; Ps. 80 + ψαλμὸς ὑπὲρ τοῦ Ἀσσυρίου ; Ps. 93 εἰς τὴν ἡμέραν τοῦ προσαββάτου, ὅτε κατῴκισται ἡ γῆ, αἶνος ᾠδῆς τῷ Δ. ; Ps. 96 ὅτε ὁ οἶκος οἰκοδομεῖται μετὰ τὴν αἰχμαλωσίαν, ᾠδὴ τῷ Δ. ; Ps. 97 τῷ Δ., ὅτε ἡ γῆ αὐτοῦ καθίσταται ; Ps. 143 + ὅτε αὐτὸν ὁ υἱὸς καταδιώκει ; Ps. 144 + πρὸς τὸν Γολιάδ ; as well as notices of the days on which certain Psalms were recited in public worship, viz. Ps. 24 τῆς μιᾶς σαββάτων ; Ps. 38 περὶ σαββάτου ; Ps. 48 δευτέρᾳ σαββάτου ; Ps. 93 εἰς τὴν ἡμέραν τοῦ προσαββάτου ; Ps. 94 τετράδι σαββάτων (cf. Ps. 92 in the Hebrew). So far as regards Ps. 24, 48, 92 (Heb.), 93, 94 these statements agree with the usage of the second Temple, according to which the Psalms referred to were sung, on the days mentioned, during the Drink-offering that accompanied the morning Burnt-offering.*

Arrangement of Psalms, and gradual formation of the Psalter.
That the Psalter is not the work of a single compiler, but was formed gradually out of pre-existing smaller collections of Psalms, appears from many indications. More than one Psalm occurs in a *double* recension, the two forms differing so slightly that both are not likely to have been incorporated by a single hand : thus Ps. 53 = Ps. 14 ; Ps. 70 = Ps. 40¹³⁻¹⁷ ; Ps. 108 = Ps. 57⁷⁻¹¹ + 60⁵⁻¹². The manner in which the Psalms ascribed to the same author are often distributed, viz. in independent *groups*, points in the same direction : and a collector, knowing that there were still 18 Davidic Psalms to follow, would scarcely have closed Book II. (72²⁰) with the words "The prayers of David, the son of Jesse, *are ended.*" The same conclusion follows from the remarkable manner in which the use of the Divine names varies in the different parts of the Psalter. In Book I. *Jehovah* occurs 272 times, *Elohim* (absolutely) 15 ; in Book II. *Jehovah* 30 times, *Elohim* 164 ; in Book III., in Ps. 73–83, *Jehovah* 13 times, *Elohim* 36 times, but in 84–89, *Jehovah* 31 times, *Elohim* 7 ; in Book IV. *Jehovah* only ; in Book V. *Jehovah* only, except in Ps. 108¹· ⁵· ⁷· ¹¹· ¹³ [repeated from Ps. 57, 60] and 144⁹. The exceptional preponderance of *Elohim* over *Jehovah* in Book II. (Ps. 42–72), and in Ps. 73–83, cannot be attributed to a preference of the authors of these Psalms for the former name ; for not only is [350] such a supposition improbable in itself, but it is precluded by the occurrence of the *same two* Psalms, in the double recension just spoken of, once with *Jehovah* (Ps. 14 ; 40¹³⁻¹⁷) and once with *Elohim* (Ps. 53 ; 70) : it must be due to

* Del. p. 26 f.: the Psalms for the 3rd and 5th days were 82 and 81.

the fact that Book II. and Ps. 73–83 have passed through the hands of a compiler, who *changed* "Jehovah" of the original authors into "Elohim." * The reason of this change probably is that at the time when this compiler lived there was a current preference for the latter name (comp. the exclusive use of the same name in Ecclesiastes, and the preference shown for it by the Chronicler).

It appears then that Ps. 42–83 formed once a separate collection, arranged by a special compiler. But how is the subscription 72^{20}, "the prayers of *David* are ended," to be accounted for, when Ps. 42–49 are ascribed to the sons of Korah, and Ps. 50 to Asaph? A conjecture of Ewald's, which has been generally accepted by subsequent critics, explains this plausibly. Ewald supposed that a transposition of the original order had taken place, and that Ps. 42–50 once stood after the Psalm now numbered 72. If this conjecture be accepted, the arrangement of the Psalms becomes at once intelligible. Book I. (Ps. 1–41), consisting almost wholly of Psalms ascribed to David, was the *first* collection; the *second* collection (Ps. 51–83) comprised, firstly, Ps. 51–72, consisting all but entirely of Davidic Psalms, with the subscription 72^{20} (which is now in an appropriate place); secondly, Ps. 42–49 a group of Korahite Psalms; and thirdly, Ps. 50, 73–83 a group of Asaph-Psalms (which now stand together, instead of being separated by Ps. 51–72); Ps. 84–89, consisting of four additional Korahite Psalms, one ascribed to David and one to Ethan, form an *appendix* to the previous collection, added to it by a different hand (for had Ps. 84–89 been collected by the same hand, the Korahite and Davidic Psalms contained in it would not, probably, have been separated from Ps. 42–49 and Ps. 51–72 respectively, nor would *Jehovah* have suddenly begun again to preponderate over *Elohim*). The *third* collection consists of Ps. 90–150. This differs from the two preceding collections in containing a far larger proportion of Psalms of a liturgical character, or Psalms composed with a view to use in the public worship of the Temple. It must have been [351] formed subsequently to the collection Ps. 42–83; for Ps. 108 is composed of two Psalms (57^{7-11} 60^{5-12}) with *Elohim*, in spite of the marked preference shown elsewhere in Ps. 90–150

---

* Hence the expression "God, my (thy) God" (for "Jehovah, my (thy) God") peculiar to these Psalms: Ps. 43^4 45^7 50^7.

for *Jehovah*, which shows that they must have been derived from a *collection* in which the use of "Elohim" was characteristic. Though no principle of arrangement is observed consistently throughout, this third collection seems in several parts to be based upon shorter, independent collections: thus Ps. 92–100 form a group, the Psalms in which, though assigned to no particular author, show much similarity in both subject-matter and expression; Ps. 111–118 (containing the *Hallel* Psalms); Ps. 120–134 (the 15 "Songs of Ascents"); Ps. 135, 136; 146–150; and the two groups of Psalms ascribed to David, Ps. 108–110; Ps. 138–145,—form respectively collections marked either by similarity of contents or by community of title. The *natural* division of the Psalter appears thus to be into *three* parts, Ps. 1–41, Ps. 42–89, Ps. 90–150: the division into *five* parts is generally supposed to have been accomplished later, in imitation of the Pentateuch, Ps. 42–89 being broken into two at Ps. 72, the subscription to which would form a natural point of division, and Ps. 90–150 being divided at Ps. 106, where v.[48] was adapted by its contents to mark also the conclusion of a Book.

The *order* of the individual Psalms appears often to have been determined by accidental causes: sometimes, however, the juxtaposition of two Psalms seems to be due to community of subject (*e.g.* Ps. 20, 21, both royal Psalms; 105 and 106, both historical Psalms), and sometimes also to the occurrence in them of some more or less noticeable expression (*e.g.* 1[6b] and 2[12a]; 3[5] and 4[8]; 16[11] and 17[15]; 32[11] and 33[1]; 34[7] and 35[5-6] [the only places in the Psalms where "the angel of J." is mentioned] &c.). Delitzsch would extend this principle of juxtaposition to the entire Psalter; but the expressions to which he points are often so insignificant (*e.g.* מִי in 14[7] and 15[1]) that it is not likely that a collector would have been guided by them.

Authorship of the Psalms. Were the titles—in the case of such Psalms as are provided with them—added by the authors themselves, or do they at least record authentic traditions respecting the authorship, or not? So far as regards the musical and liturgical notices, there is a decided presumption that their origin dates from the period when these subjects first become prominent in the OT., viz. the period of the second Temple: *

* The principal terms used occur elsewhere only in Isa. 38[20], Hab. 3, and 1 Ch. 15[17-21]; comp. 16[41f.], 2 Ch. 5[12f.] 7[6] &c.). The verb נצח (whence מְנַצֵּחַ "precentor"—only in the titles to Psalms, and Hab. 3[19]—is derived) is used otherwise only by the Chronicler (see the list of phrases at the end of Ch., No. 21). It is remarkable, if the word had been in use earlier, that it should

they were [352] added probably when the Psalms came generally into liturgical use. And the strongest reasons exist for supposing that the *historical* notices are of late origin likewise, and though they may embody trustworthy information respecting the source or collection whence the Psalms were derived by one of the compilers of the Book, that they contain no authentic tradition respecting the authorship of the Psalms, or the occasions on which they were composed. The grounds for this conclusion are briefly as follows :—

1. The titles are suspicious, from the circumstance that almost the only names of authors mentioned are David, and two or three prominent singers of David's age : except in the case of those attributed to the " Sons of Korah," *no* author is named of a date later than that of Solomon. But (amongst the anonymous Psalms) many, by common consent, are much later than the age of David and Solomon ; how comes it that their authors' names are not recorded ? If the names of earlier Psalmists were known, *à fortiori*, it would seem, those of later Psalmists would be preserved by tradition.

2. The titles are strongly discredited by internal evidence ; again and again the title is contradicted by the contents of the Psalm to which it is prefixed. Thus of the 73 ascribed to David, the majority, at least, cannot be his ; for (*a*) many are of unequal poetical merit, and instead of displaying the freshness and originality which we should expect in the founder of Hebrew Psalmody, contain frequent conventional phrases (*e.g.* Ps. 6, 31, 35, 40¹³ᶠᶠ·), and reminiscences of earlier Psalms,* which betray the poet of a later age. (*b*) Some have pronounced Aramaisms, the occurrence of which in an early poem of *Judah* is entirely without analogy, or other marks of lateness.† (*c*) Others have

---

not have occurred, at least in its more general sense, in pre-exilic writings ; but in 2 Ch. 2²ᵇ· ¹⁸ᵇ [Heb. ¹ᵇ· ¹⁷ᵇ] it is *substituted* for the older word רדה used in 1 Ki. 5¹⁶ [Heb.³⁰]. See more fully the writer's note in Prof. Sanday's *Oracles of God*, ed. 2, p. 146 ff.

* Ps. 86 is composed almost entirely of such reminiscences ; see W. R. Smith, *OTJC.* pp. 413–415 (ed. 2, pp. 435–437). Similarly 144¹⁻¹¹.

† כי- in the suff. of 2 ps. fem. 103³· ⁴· ⁵ (as in 116⁷· ¹²· ¹⁹ 135⁹) ; 109⁸ the *plur.* מעטים (only Eccl. 5¹ besides) ; 122³· ⁴·124¹· ²· ⁶ 133²· ³ 144¹⁵ שׁ- (for אשׁר, as in 123² 129⁶· ⁷ 135²· ⁸· ¹⁰ 136²³ 137⁸· ⁹ 146³· ⁵, and other late writings) ; 139² רע *thought*, v.³ רבע *lying down*, v.⁸ סלק, v.¹⁹ קמל (all Aram.) ; 144⁷· ¹⁰· ¹¹† פצה *to deliver* (Aram.), v.¹³ זן (2 Ch. 16¹⁴, and Aram.), 145¹⁴ זקף (Aram.).

stylistic affinities with Psalms which, upon independent grounds, must be assigned to an age much later than that of David: though the alphabetical arrangement (Ps. 9–10, 25, 34, 37, 145), [353] for instance, cannot be *proved* to have been unused as early as David's day, the known examples of it are much later (Lam. 1–4, Pr. 31¹⁰⁻³¹); and at least Ps. 25, 34, 37, 145 are shown by their general tone and style to belong to the later products of Hebrew poetry. (*d*) Many are unadapted to David's situation or character.

Thus some imply the existence of the *Temple* (Ps. 5⁷ᵃ 27⁴ 28² [see 1 Ki. 6⁵] 65⁴ 68²⁹ 138² *); and it is at least open to question whether the expression God's "holy hill," applied to Zion (3⁴ 15¹; cf. 24³ 26⁸ 27⁴ᶠ·), would have come into use until the sanctuary had been established upon it for a considerable time. Others again, when we proceed to reconstruct, from the allusions contained in the Psalm, the situation in which it was composed, are found to imply that the Psalmist is living in an evil time, when the wicked are established in the land, and the godly are oppressed, and suffer in silence from their tyranny and pride (Ps. 9–10, 12,† 14,† 35, 38, &c.),—a condition of things entirely out of harmony with the picture presented to us of any period of David's life in 1–2 Samuel. Often also the terms used do not suit the circumstances of David's life: let the reader examine carefully, for example, the following passages, and ask himself whether they correspond really to David's situation; whether they are not, in fact, the words of a man (or of men) in a different condition of life, surrounded by different companions, subject to different temptations, and suffering at the hands of a different kind of foe: Ps. 5⁸⁻¹⁰ 6⁷ᶠ· 12¹⁻⁴ 17⁹⁻¹⁴ 22¹¹ᶠᶠ· 26⁹ᶠ· 27¹⁰ ("For *my father and my mother have forsaken me*") ¹² 28³⁻⁵ 35¹¹⁻²¹ 38¹¹⁻¹⁴ 41⁵⁻⁹ 62³ᶠ· ⁹ᶠ· 64²⁻⁶.

To take some further illustrations: Ps. 11 is referred, by those who defend the title, to the occasion of Absalom's rebellion; but the situation which it implies is really very different: it implies a state of social disorder (v.³), in which the wicked shoot "in the darkness" (v.²) at the upright; the Psalmist

---

* It is exceedingly doubtful whether, as Keil and others contend, the term היכל (*palace*, Isa. 39⁷; *temple*, 1 Ki. 6³· ⁵· ¹⁷, and often) found in these passages could be used of the "tent" spread by David for the ark (2 Sa. 7²· ⁶). The היכל at Shiloh had folding-doors and door-posts (1 Sa. 1⁹ 3¹⁵).

† Implying an almost *national* defection. With 12¹ comp. Jer. 5¹ 9³⁻⁶, Mic. 7², Isa. 57¹.

is exhorted by his desponding companions to take refuge in flight [354] (v.[1]) ; instead of complying, he asserts his unabated confidence in God's justice (v.[4-7]). Ps. 20 and 21 contain good wishes for a king, who is either addressed in the 2nd pers., or spoken of in the 3rd : both evidently spring out of the regard which was entertained towards him by his subjects ; to suppose that David wrote for the people the words in which they should express their own loyalty towards him, is in the highest degree unnatural and improbable. A similar remark may be made with reference to Ps. 61 (see v.[6f.]). Ps. 55 is generally explained as referring (cf. v.[12-18]) to David's treacherous counsellor Ahithophel ; but the situation is again very unlike that of David during Absalom's rebellion ; the Psalmist lives among foes in a city, whose walls they occupy with their patrols : from the violence which they exercise within it he would gladly escape to the desert (v.[9b-11] ; v.[6f.]) ; one who had been his associate had treacherously abandoned him, for which he is bitterly reproached by the poet. The situation in its principal features recalls rather that in which Jeremiah found himself (Jer. 6[6f.] 9[2-6] 11[18-21] 20[10]), or the author of Mic. 7[5]. Ps. 58 is a denunciation of *unjust judges* ; the manner in which they are addressed, however, is not that of a king, who could remove them if he chose, but of one who was powerless to take action himself, though he desired (and expected) retribution to fall upon them from heaven. In Ps. 69, 86, 109, the singer is in great affliction and trouble ; his nearest relations and friends have forsaken him (69[8]) ; he is " poor and needy " (86[1] 109[22]), and is cruelly reproached (69[7-9] [for his *religion*] 19[f.] 109[1-5. 22-25]),—traits which are all inapplicable to David, and most insufficiently explained from 2 Sa. 16[5ff.].

The titles which assign Psalms to particular occasions of David's life are not more probable than the others. Ps. 35 is referred to the time when David feigned madness at the court of Achish (1 Sa. 21[13]) ; but there is not a single expression in the Psalm suggestive of that occasion ; the Psalm consists of religious reflexions and moral exhortations—much in the manner of Ps. 37—of a perfectly general kind, and expressed in the hortatory style of the later gnomic poetry (v.[11] ; comp. Pr. 4[1] 5[7] 7[24] 8[32]), entirely out of relation with the situation supposed. Ps. 52 is stated to refer to Doeg. In point of fact it speaks of some rich and powerful man, a persecutor of the righteous, in whose fall will be seen exemplified the Nemesis which overtakes the abuse of *riches* (v.[7]), while the Psalmist will flourish " like a spreading olive tree in the house of God." Is this consistent either with the picture of Doeg drawn in 1 Sa. 21[7] 22[9ff.], or with David's situation at the time ?

The occasions to which Ps. 56, 57 are referred are not less improbable. Ps. 59 is stated to have been composed by David when his house was watched by Saul's messengers (1 Sa. 19[11]) ; but the Psalm shows plainly that the poet who wrote it is resident in a city attacked by heathen or ungodly foes, whom he prays God to cast down, that His power may be manifest *to the ends of the earth* (v.[5-8. 11-13] ; notice esp. the " *nations* ")—both inconsistent with the feelings which David entertained towards Saul (1 Sa. 24[6] &c.), and implying relations with the "nations" which did not then exist. The titles in all these cases are palpably incongruous, and appear sometimes to have been merely suggested to the compiler by a superficial view of particular expressions (*e.g.* 52² supposed to point to Doeg ; [355] 54³ to the Ziphites ; 56² to the Philistines ; 57³ to Saul ; 59³ to Saul's messengers : so 63¹ᵇ to the wilderness of Judah). But the situation and circumstances implied by the Psalm, *as a whole*, are in each instance different from those of David. As W. R. Smith (*OTJC.*² p. 216) has well said, the titles, it is manifest, spring from an age " to which David was merely the abstract Psalmist, and which had no idea whatever of the historical conditions of his time."

(*e*) Not unfrequently also the Psalms ascribed to David presuppose the circumstances or character of a later age. Ps. 51¹⁸ᶠ· 69³⁵ᶠ· imply an approaching *restoration* of Jerusalem and Judah : * Ps. 68⁴ (" make a *highway* for him that rideth *through the deserts* ") points to the same historical situation as Isa. 40³ : Ps. 22²⁷⁻³⁰ 65² 68³¹ 86⁹ presuppose the prophetic teaching (Isa. 2²⁻⁴ &c.) of the acceptance of Israel's religion by the nations of the earth. Many also of the same Psalms, it is difficult not to feel, express an intensity of religious devotion, a depth of spiritual insight, and a maturity of theological reflexion, beyond what we should expect from David or David's age. David had many high and honourable qualities : he was loyal, generous, disinterested, amiable, a faithful friend, a just and benevolent ruler ; and the narrative in the Books of Samuel shows that his religion elevated and ennobled his aims, and, except on the occasion of his great fall, exerted a visible influence upon the tenor of his life.† Still, as we should not gather from the history that he was exposed to a succession of trials and afflictions *of the kind represented in the Psalms ascribed to him*, so we should not gather from it that he was a man of the deep and intense spiritual feeling reflected in the Psalms that bear his name. Every indication converges to the same conclusion, viz. that the " Davidic " Psalms spring, in fact, from many different periods of Israelitish history, from the time of David himself downwards ; and that in the varied moods which they reflect— despondency, trouble, searchings of heart, penitence, hope, confidence, thankfulness, exultation ; or the various situations which they shadow forth—distress, sickness, oppression or persecution, deliverance,—they set before us the experiences of many men, and of many ages of the national life.

---

* Notice also the " prisoners " of 69³³, and comp. 102¹⁶· ²⁰· ²⁸.

† Contrast the *Assyrian* kings (Farrar, *Minor Proph.* p. 147 f.) ; and see W. R. Smith in the *Encycl. Brit.*⁹ *s.v.* " David," p. 841. (On 2 Sa. 12³¹, comp. RV. *marg.*, and the writer's note *ad loc.*)

The majority of the " Davidic " Psalms are thus certainly not David's : is it possible to determine whether any are his ? It [356] being apparent, in many instances, that the titles are untrustworthy, it becomes a question whether they are more trustworthy *in the instances which remain*, whether, in fact, they record in *any* case a genuine tradition, or do more than reproduce an opinion which existed when they were framed, without supplying any guarantee that the opinion itself was well founded. It must be remembered that the close connexion of David with psalmody is first set before us in the *Chronicles*. All that we learn from the pre-exilic literature respecting David's musical and poetical talents is that he was a skilful player on the harp (1 Sa. 16^{18} &c.), and probably on other instruments as well (Am. 6^5) ; that he composed a beautiful elegy on Saul and Jonathan (2 Sa. 1$^{19ff.}$), and a shorter one on Abner (*ib.* 3$^{33f.}$) ; that he "danced and leapt" before the ark, when it was brought up into Zion (*ib.* 6$^{14. 16}$ *) ; and that in the appendix to 2 Sam. (p. 183) two sacred poems (c. 22, 23$^{1-7}$) are attributed to him. The poem 2 Sa. 1$^{19ff.}$, however, it is somewhat remarkable, possesses no religious character, but is the expression of a purely *human* emotion : and in Am. 6^5 David is alluded to, not as an author of sacred poetry, but as the inventor of musical instruments such as were used by the luxurious nobles of Samaria at their banquets.   The Chronicler, on the other hand, views David as the founder of Temple psalmody (1 Ch. 23^5 25$^{1-7}$, 2 Ch. 7^6 29$^{26. 27. 30}$ 35^{15}, Ezr. 3^{10}, Neh. 12^{36}), and while excerpting from 2 Sa. 6 the narrative of the transference of the ark to Zion, takes occasion to place in the king's mouth a Psalm (1 Ch. 16$^{7-36}$), which, remarkably enough, so far from being an original work, is composed of parts of three exilic, or post-exilic, Psalms, preserved still in the Psalter (Ps. 105$^{1-15}$ 96^{1-13a} 106$^{1. 47. 48}$) !   That David, skilled as he was in music, and zealous in his devotion to Jehovah, should have made arrangements for some musical services in connexion with the ark, is far from improbable ; though it can hardly be doubted that in the account which the Chronicler has given of them, he has transferred to David's age the institutions of the Temple in the fully developed form in

---

* V.^{5} he is mentioned also, in conjunction with the "house of Israel" generally, as playing and singing (see *QPB.*^{3} ; 1 Ch. 13^8) on the same occasion.

which they existed in his own day.* But most of the [357] Psalms ascribed to David are *not* of a liturgical character, or adapted (at least in the first instance) for public worship; they reflect the *personal* experiences and emotions of the singer. Hence David's presumed connexion with the services of the sanctuary would not account for his authorship of more than a very few of the Psalms ascribed to him by their titles.

We are thus thrown back upon internal grounds for the purpose of determining the Psalms which may be David's. Ewald, upon *æsthetic* grounds, referred to David Ps. 3, 4, 7, 8, 11, 15, 18, 19$^{1-6}$ 24$^{1-6}$ 24$^{7-10}$ 29, 32, 101; and the following fragments, embedded in later Psalms: Ps. 60$^{6-9}$ [Heb. $^{8-11}$] 68$^{13-18}$ [Heb. $^{14-19}$] 144$^{12-14}$: these, he argues, display an originality, dignity, and unique power which could have been found in David, and in David alone. In particular, Ewald points to the noble and kingly feelings which find expression in these Psalms,—the sense of inward dignity (כבוד), Ps. 3^3 4^2 7^5 18$^{43-48}$, 2 Sa. 23^1, the innocence and Divine favour of which the singer is conscious, 4^3 18$^{20-30}$ (cf. 2 Sa. 6^{21}), the kingly thoughts of 18$^{43-45}$ 101$^{1-8}$, the trust in God, the clear and firm sense of right, and the indications of a brave and victorious warrior, who had near at heart his people's welfare, contained in such passages as 3$^{7. 8}$ 18$^{34-42}$ 24^8 29^{11}, 2 Sa. 23$^{6-7}$.†

There is no doubt that the Psalms upon which Ewald's critical tact has thus fastened are marked by a freshness and poetic force and feeling, and a certain brightness of language and expression, which distinguish them from most of the others attributed to David; and if Davidic Psalms are preserved in the

---

* If the Temple psalmody was organised in the age of David and Solomon as the Chronicler represents, the absence of all allusion to it in the descriptions of sacred ceremonies in Sa. Kings is very singular. 2 Sa. 6^5, 1 Ki. 1^{40} speak of the *people* singing, but not of the authorized "singers" (משוררים), so frequently mentioned in Ezr. Neh. Chr. 1 Ki. 8 makes no mention of either singing or music (though the Chronicler, in his account of the same ceremony, excerpted by him from Kings, has *inserted* two notices respecting both, viz. 2 Ch. 5$^{11b-13a}$ and 7^6): the allusion in 1 Ki. 10^{12} (שרים, cf. 2 Sa. 19^{36} Heb., not the technical משוררים) is ambiguous. On the other hand, that there was some organization for music and song in the pre-exilic Temple may be justly inferred from Neh. 7^{44} (=Ezr. 2^{41}), where in the contemporary register of those who returned from Babylon in B.C. 536 are included 148 (128) "sons of Asaph, *singers*."

† The peculiarities of *expression*, cited by Ewald, are of slight weight.

Psalter, we may say safely that they are to be found among [358] those which Ewald has selected. At the same time, it must be admitted that the æsthetic criterion upon which Ewald relies is a *subjective* one : we have no standard outside the Psalter by which to determine David's poetical style except 2 Sa. 1[19-27], 3[33f.], and (assuming the author of the appendix 2 Sa. 21–24 to have been well informed *) 2 Sa. 22 (= Ps. 18), and 23[1-7] ; nor (in our ignorance of what other poets might have achieved) are we entitled to declare that certain Psalms could have been composed by no one but David himself. It is doubtful also whether some of the Psalms in Ewald's list do not contain expressions, or imply a situation, not consistent with David's age. On the other hand, if Deborah, long before David's time, had "sung unto Jehovah" (Jud. 5[3]), there can be no *à priori* reason why David should not have done the same ; and 2 Sa. 23[1] the expression "the sweet singer of Israel" implies that David was the author of religious songs.† On the whole, a *non liquet* must be our verdict : it is possible that Ewald's list of Davidic Psalms is too large, but it is not clear that none of the Psalms contained in it are of David's composition. The question, however, whether any of the Psalms are David's possesses in reality little but an antiquarian interest : David, it is certain, left his impress upon the religion of Israel not, like the prophets, directly, but *indirectly*, by establishing the monarchy upon a permanent basis, and laying the foundations for a national religious centre.

The titles assigning Psalms to other authors are often not more trust-worthy than those assigning Psalms to David. Ps. 90 in dignity and deep religious feeling is second to none in the Psalter : but it may be questioned whether it does not presuppose conditions different from those of Moses' age ; and had Moses been the author, it is natural to suppose that it would have been more archaic in style than it actually is. The Psalms assigned to Asaph, Heman, Ethan, and Solomon show, almost without exception, marks of a far later age than that of David and his successor : Ps. 74 and 79 are late in tone, and allude to the desolation of the sanctuary and of the city in terms certainly inapplicable to the plundering of Shishak (1 Ki. 14[25f.]), to which they have strangely been supposed to refer : Ps. 76 might be plausibly

---

* The *generality* of 2 Sa. 22[1] detracts considerably from its value : there was no "day" on which Jehovah delivered David "out of the hand of *all his enemies, and* out of the hand of *Saul*." Contrast 2 Sa. 1[17].

† זמירות, properly "songs of *praise*" ; see Isa. 24[16], Job 35[10], Ps. 95[2]; and comp. the verb in Jud. 5[3], Isa. 12[5] &c., and וְזִמְרָת in Ex. 15[2] (= Isa. 12[2] = Ps. 118[14]).

referred to the destruction of Sennacherib's army B.C. 701 ; the style and manner of Ps. 72, 78 indicate that they are not early ones : * Ps. 89 is clearly not earlier than the fall of the monarchy.

[359] The *origin* of the titles must remain matter of speculation. It is even possible that the sense in which the titles are now understood is not their primary meaning, but may be due to a misapprehension. The Psalms ascribed to the sons of Korah were derived, it is reasonable to suppose, from a collection of Psalms in the possession of the Levitical family, or guild, of that name, in the time of the Second Temple. Those ascribed to Asaph, Heman, and Ethan may have a similar origin : they may be taken from collections not necessarily *composed* by these three singers respectively, but *in the possession* of families or guilds claiming descent from them : the title לאסף, for instance, prefixed by a compiler to the Psalms extracted from one of these collections, as an indication of the *source* whence it was taken, and meant by him to signify *belonging to Asaph*, would be ambiguous, and would readily lend itself to be understood in the sense of *written by Asaph*. The explanation of לדוד may be similar. It is far from impossible that there may have been a collection known as "David's," the beginnings of which may date from early pre-exilic times, but which afterwards was augmented by the addition of Psalms composed subsequently : either the collection itself came ultimately to be regarded as Davidic, or a compiler excerpting from it prefixed לדוד as an indication of the source whence a Psalm was taken, which was afterwards misunderstood as denoting its author: in either case the incorrect attribution of Psalms to David upon a large scale becomes intelligible. In some instances, also (Ps. 51, 52, &c.), attempts were even made to fix the occasion of his life to which a Psalm belonged. Of course, in particular cases the title לדוד may be due to independent tradition, or to conjectures of readers or compilers. The musical and liturgical notices combine with other indications to show that the titles were only finally fixed when the Psalter came into general use in the Temple services during the period that began with the return from Babylon.

* Ps. 72 is probably ascribed to Solomon on account of the general resemblance of the picture of imperial sway which the Ps. presents with that of Solomon's empire in 1 Ki. 3–10 ; Ps. 127 on account of a supposed allusion in v.² ("his *beloved*" ידיד) to 2 Sa. 12²⁵ (ידידיה).

Is it possible, upon independent grounds, to fix the dates or occasions of any of the Psalms? The full discussion of this subject would occupy more space than can here be given to it: a brief notice of its more general aspects must therefore suffice. As a rule, the dates of the Psalms cannot be fixed otherwise than *approximately*. The only criteria which we possess are (1) the historical allusions; (2) the style; (3) the relation to other [360] writers whose dates are known; (4) the character of the religious ideas expressed.

(1.) The historical allusions are seldom definite enough to do more than fix the *general* period—within tolerably wide limits—to which a Psalm belongs: for instance, some Psalms allude to the king in terms which imply that the monarchy is still in existence, and are therefore presumably pre-exilic;* others appear to contain allusions to the condition of the people during the Exile; others again imply that the Exile is past, though to what *part* of the post-exilic period such Psalms are to be referred, the allusions contained in them often do not declare. The historical allusions, which *seem* to be more precise, are often not conclusive. Thus Ps. 46, 76 have been referred plausibly to the period of the overthrow of Sennacherib's army in B.C. 701; but the language used in these Psalms, though it is not unfavourable to such a reference, can hardly be said to *require* it. In Ps. 74, 79 it is disputed whether the desolation alluded to is that effected by the Chaldæans in 586, or that wrought by Antiochus Epiphanes in B.C. 169–168. Nor is it by any means certain what the national disasters or dangers alluded to in Ps. 60, 83 are. Ps. 118 has been referred to the occasions described in Ezr. 3$^{1-4}$ (Ewald); 3$^{10f.}$ (Hengstenberg); 6$^{16ff.}$ (Delitzsch); Neh. 8$^{16-18}$ (Perowne); 1 Macc. 4$^{52-56}$, B.C. 165 (Cheyne).

To determine the author is impossible; for the necessary standards of comparison fail us. The only author, known to us by name, with whose writings some of the Psalms display marked similarities, is Jeremiah (Ps. 31, 35, 69; comp. also Ps. 79^6, Jer. 10^{25}): but when we bear in mind how apt Hebrew writers are to borrow expressions from their predecessors, we cannot feel the requisite assurance that these similarities are due to identity of authorship; a later writer may have cast his thoughts into

---

* Unless, indeed (as some suppose), they can in some cases be referred to the *revival* of the monarchy under the Maccabees (1 Macc. 14$^{41-43}$ &c.).

phraseology suggested by his acquaintance with the prophecies of Jeremiah.* Ps. 46 is worthy of Isaiah; but this is not sufficient to prove that he was its author. (The Davidic Psalms have been considered above.)

(2.) As regards the criterion of style, the judgment of Hupfeld, endorsed by his editor, Nowack, is sound (i. p. xlii): "From [361] the linguistic and poetical character of the Psalms, it is not possible to do more than distinguish in general older Psalms from later, or those that are original from those that show marks of imitation: . . . such as are hard, bold, original, are, as a rule, the older; those of which the style is easy and flowing, and which are marked by the presence of conventional thoughts and expressions, are later. For older poets had to strike out their own paths, and thus appear often contending with language and thought: later poets, on the contrary, moved, as it were, upon accustomed tracks, and frequently found thoughts, figures, and language ready for their use; hence their compositions generally contain many reminiscences and standing phrases, and may even sometimes almost entirely consist of them. Such reminiscences and conventional phrases are most frequent in the Psalms of complaint, the alphabetical Psalms, and the doxological or liturgical Psalms. Aramaisms and non-classical idioms are likewise marks of a late age. But we cannot with equal confidence, from the poetical power or purity of diction which a Psalm may display, infer conversely that it is ancient, since Psalms that are unquestionably late have in these respects not unfrequently equalled the more ancient models." †

(3.) This criterion seldom carries us very far. In the case of two similar passages, the difficulty of determining which is the one that is dependent on the other, *when we have no other clue to guide us*, is practically insuperable (comp. p. 312 f.). Ps. 93, 96–100 appear to presuppose Isa. 40–66; and from the use made of Ps. 96, 105, 106, 130, 132 in 1 Ch. 16⁸⁻³⁶, 2 Ch. 6⁴⁰. ⁴¹⁻⁴², they seem clearly to be *earlier* than the age of the Chronicler (B.C. 300): Ps. 93, 97–100, moreover, are so similar in character to Ps. 96 that they can hardly belong to a different period. We thus obtain a group of six Psalms which may be assigned plausibly

---

* Cf. W. Campe, *Das Verhältnis Jeremias zu den Psalmen* (1891).

† On the language of the Psalms, see especially App. II. in Prof. Cheyne's *Origin of the Psalter*.

to B.C. 538–300; but even here the limits are sufficiently wide. And of other Psalms still less (on this ground) can be affirmed with certainty.

(4.) This criterion cannot be altogether repudiated, though it is to be applied with caution. There is undoubtedly a *progress*, both in the revelation contained in the OT., and also in the [362] feelings with which sacred things are viewed : prophets, for instance, arose, introducing new ideas as the centuries passed on; religious problems were more deeply and more frequently reflected upon; after the Temple was established, a growing attachment to it, as a centre of religious worship and of religious sentiment, would naturally form itself; and there was undeniably, especially in later times, an increasing devotion to the law. It is reasonable to suppose that Hebrew psalmody would stand in some sort of correlation with the phases of this progress under its various aspects. And when the Psalms are compared with the prophets, the latter seem to show, on the whole, the greater originality; the psalmists, in other words, *follow* the prophets, appropriating and applying the truths which the prophets proclaimed, and bearing witness to the effects which their teaching exerted upon those who came within range of its influence. The Psalms which presuppose a wide religious experience, and display a marked spirituality of tone, will hardly be among the earliest; while those in which liturgical interests are most prominent are probably among the latest.

It must be owned that these criteria are less definite than might be desired, and that when applied by different hands they do not lead always to identical results. Nevertheless some conclusions may be fairly drawn from them. It may be affirmed, for instance, with tolerable confidence that very few of the Psalms are earlier than the 7th cent. B.C. Of many Psalms the exilic or post-exilic date is manifest, and is not disputed : of others, it is difficult to say whether they are pre- or post-exilic. *Approximately* the Psalms may be dated somewhat as follows :— In Books IV. and V. (Ps. 90–150) Ps. 101 (the portrait of a righteous king), 110 * [363] may be presumed to be pre-exilic;

---

* This Psalm, though it may be ancient, can hardly have been composed by David. If read without *præjudicium*, it produces the irresistible impression of having been written, not by a king with reference to an invisible, spiritual Being, standing above him as his superior, but by a prophet *with*

Ps. 90, 91 may be so likewise ; Ps. 102 (see v.[13-16]) will be exilic ; **Ps. 93,** 96–99 (the keynote of which is struck by Isa. 52[7 end]) may date from the close of the exile, or the early years of the restoration : the rest in these two books will be post-exilic, some, perhaps, late in the post-exilic period—especially those Psalms in which Aramaisms, &c., are marked. In Book III. (Ps. 73–89) Ps. 76 may date from B.C. 701, Ps. 89 presupposes the fall of the monarchy ; Ps. 77, 78, 80, 81, 85, 86, 87 appear to be post-exilic ; Ps. 74, 79, and perhaps 83, belong (as it seems) to the period of the Maccabees ; the dates of Ps. 73, 75, 82, 84, 88 must remain undecided, but they will not be earlier than the age of Jeremiah. In Books I. and II. (Ps. 1–72), even though Ewald's list of Davidic Psalms be not accepted in its entirety, it may include several that are ancient ; the Psalms alluding to the king (Ps. 2, 18, 20, 21, 28, 45, 61, 63, 72) will presumably be pre-exilic, Ps. 72 (from its general style) being the latest ; *

reference to the theocratic king. (1) The title " My lord " (אדני), v.[1], is the one habitually used in addressing the Israelitish king (*e.g.* 1 Ki. 1-2 *passim*) ; (2) Messianic prophecies have regularly as their point of departure some institution of the Jewish theocracy—the king, the prophet, the people (Isa. 42[1] &c.), the high priest, the Temple (Isa. 28[16]) : the supposition that David is here speaking and addressing a superior, who stands *in no relation with existing institutions*, is—not, indeed, impossible (for we are not entitled to limit absolutely the range of prophetic vision), but—contrary to the analogy of prophecy ; (3) the justice of this reasoning is strongly confirmed by v.[3, 5-7], where the subject of the Psalm is actually depicted, not as such a spiritual superior, but as a *victorious Israelitish monarch*, triumphing through Jehovah's help over earthly foes. The Psalm is Messianic in the same sense that Ps. 2 is : it depicts the *ideal glory of the theocratic king*, who receives from a prophet (v.[1] נאם יהוה) the twofold solemn promise (1) of victory over his foes ; (2) of a perpetual priesthood (cf. Jer. 30[21b] : see p. 143). In the question addressed by our Lord to the Jews (Mt. 22[41-46] ; Mk. 12[35-37] ; Luke 20[41-44]) His object, it is evident, is not to instruct them on the *authorship* of the Psalm, but to argue from its *contents* : and though He assumes the Davidic authorship, accepted generally at the time, yet the cogency of His argument is unimpaired, so long as it is recognised that the Psalm is a Messianic one, and that the august language used in it of the Messiah is not compatible with the position of one who was a *mere* human son of David. Comp. von Orelli, *OT. Prophecy*, pp. 153–157.

* G. B. Gray, however, in "The references to the ' King' in the Psalter " (*JQR.* July 1895, p. 658 ff.), remarks that after the exile the theocratic attributes and privileges of the pre-exilic king became the inheritance of the nation (cf. Isa. 55[3-5]), and argues accordingly that as Israel was idealized as Jehovah's "son " (Hos. 11[1] *al.*), and (in II Isaiah) as Jehovah's "servant,"

Ps. 46 may date from B.C. 701; Ps. 47 is related closely to the group 93, 96–99; of the devotional and didactic Psalms (such as Ps. 1, 8, 15, 19$^{1-6}$ 24$^{1-6}$ 42–43), and those describing the sufferings or persecutions of the writers (which are numerous in these two books), it is difficult to say when they were written; though a few may be early Psalms, and some may have been written by a contemporary or companion of Jeremiah, many, it is probable, spring from different parts of the [364] Persian period (B.C. 536–333). To the exile, or somewhat later, will belong, in particular, Ps. 22, 51, 66–70; Ps. 19$^{7-14}$ 25, 33, 34, 37 will also be late ones. It is possible that future investigation, and especially a more systematic comparison of the Psalms with other parts of the Old Testament, may tend to reduce these somewhat wide limits; for the present, the writer's judgment on the *data* at his disposal does not enable him to speak more definitely.

From what has been said, it will be apparent that even Books I. and II. will not have been compiled until after the exile. This fact is important: it proves, namely, that the Psalter, in *all* its parts, is a compilation of the post-exilic age (cf. Davison, *Praises of Isr.* p. 30; Bäthgen, p. xxxv f.), and shows that the proper method of inquiry is to make this our starting-point, and arguing back from it to endeavour so to determine what Psalms in it may be of *pre*-exilic origin.

The Psalms attributed to Asaph and the sons of Korah respectively, in many cases (though not in all) have points of contact with one another which will hardly all be accidental. In the Asaph-Psalms God is often represented as *Judge* (Ps. 50, 75, 76, 82), and introduced as speaking (Ps. 50, 75, 81, 82); He is more constantly than elsewhere called אל and עליון; He is compared to a shepherd (74^1 * 77^{20} 78^{52} 79^{13} * 80^1); *Joseph* or *Ephraim* is alluded to (77^{15} 80^1 81$^{4, 5}$); the peculiar word רעה occurs only Ps. 50^{11} 80^{14}. In the Korahite Psalms God is often represented as *King* (Ps. 44^4 47$^{2, 6, 7}$ 84^3 [but also elsewhere, as 5^2 68^{24} 74^{12} 89^{18} 149^2]), and a warm affection is evinced towards the holy city or the Temple (Ps. 46, 47, 48, 87; 42–43, 84). In one or two instances, the Psalms with these peculiarities may have been the work of the same author; but this cannot be the case with most; and the similarities are perhaps to be accounted for by the Psalms having been composed by

---

so the nation could be idealized as His "anointed," or His "King"; and he applies this principle to Ps. 2, 18, 28, 84, 89 (v.$^{38, 44, 51}$), and even to Ps. 21, 61, 63, 72 (in which the "king," absolutely, is mentioned). Cf. Beer [above, p. 359], p. lix ff., and on Ps. 2, 28, 84, 89, 132. Hab. 3^{13} (see Davidson), and Ps. 105^{15} ("mine anointed ones," of the patriarchs), show at least that the term *anointed* might be applied figuratively to the people. But it is difficult to think that the "king" in Ps. 21, 61, 63, 72 can be so intended.

* Comp. Ps. 95^7 100^3. Probably dependent on Jer. 23^1; Ez. 34^{31}.

members of the same family, or guild, in which a type of representation, once set, may have been followed by the poets of successive generations.

On two questions connected with the Psalms the writer is obliged to touch more briefly than he had hoped to be able to do.

(1.) Do any of the Psalms date from the period of the Maccabees (B.C. 168 ff.)? Very many commentators—including even Delitzsch and Perowne—admit (on historical grounds) that *some* Psalms belong to this period : Ps. 44 (on account of the protestation of *national innocence*, which it is difficult to reconcile with any earlier stage of the nation's history) ; * 74 (on account of v.[8], which appears to allude to *synagogues*, and v.[9] [cf. 1 Macc. 4[46] 9[27] 14[41]]) ; 79 (similar to Ps. 74 : with v.[2b. 3] cf. 1 Macc. 7[17] ; with v.[1-3] 74[3-7], 1 Macc. 1[20-32. 37-39. 63] 2[7] [365] 12 3[45. 51f.] 4[38]). But some scholars, especially Olshausen (1853), and more recently Reuss and others,† have attributed a much larger number of Psalms, and even the majority, to the same period.

These scholars point to the frequency with which in the Psalms two *classes* of persons are opposed to one another—Israel and the nations (heathen), the godly ("saints," "the righteous," "they that fear Jehovah," "the upright of heart," &c.) and the godless ("the wicked," "transgressors," "violent men," "workers of wickedness," &c.), and to the question when this opposition was most pronounced, reply : in the times that began with the persecution of the Jews by Antiochus Epiphanes, when the loyal servants of Jehovah —the "meek" or the "afflicted," as they are termed—found themselves engaged in a struggle, not only with their heathen masters, but with a powerful party composed of their own renegade brethren. The phases of this struggle, it is said, are echoed in the Psalter : in Reuss' words (§ 481), for instance, "The breach of parties in the nation is described in Ps. 55, 94, 140 ; the varying fortunes of the war are reflected in songs of triumph (Ps. 76, 98, 116, 118, 138, cf. 75, 96–100, 148, 149), or in lamentations for defeats (Ps. 60, 89 &c.) ; the dark period before the revolt of Judas Maccabæus is brought before us (Ps. 54, 56–59, 62, 64, 71, 77, 86, 88, 90, 102, 142, 143)."

It is true, our knowledge of the circumstances under which either the Psalter was compiled, or the Canon of the OT. was

* Though Ewald thought it possible to refer these Psalms (together with Ps. 60, 80, 85, 89, 132) to the period shortly before Nehemiah, the terms of Neh. 1[3] 2[3] 4[2] seeming to him to point to some recent calamity which had befallen Jerusalem (*Hist.* v. 119–121).

† Olsh. *Die Psalmen*, p. 4 ff. ; Reuss, *Les Psaumes* (in his translation of the entire Bible), p. 55 ff. ; or *Gesch. der Heil. Schriften AT.s*, § 481.

completed, does not entitle us to deny peremptorily the presence of Maccabæan Psalms in the collection; and if it be the fact that Ps. 44, 74, 79 were introduced into the Psalter in (or after) this period, it is difficult to argue that other Psalms may not have been introduced into it likewise.   But there is no sufficient reason for supposing this to have been the case on the scale supposed by Olshausen and Reuss.   Had so many Psalms dated from this age, it is difficult not to think that they would have borne more prominent marks of it in their diction and style. Reuss' exegesis is arbitrary : Jeremiah is witness that the loyal worshippers of Jehovah were in a minority, and were often exposed to persecution and reproach, even in pre-exilic times (cf. Jer. 5^1 $7^{9\text{-}11}$ $9^{2\text{-}6}$ 15^{15} $17^{15\text{-}18}$ $20^{7\text{-}11}$).

The existence of Maccabee Psalms is maintained in this country by Prof. Cheyne (*Origin of the Psalter*), but within much more moderate limits.   He assigns to this period Ps. 16 (cf. v.^{4a} with Jos. *Ant.* xii. 5. 1), 20, 21, 33, 44, 60, 61, 63, 75 (?), 83, 86, 94 (?), 101, 108, 110, 115–118, 135–138, 144, 145–150.   Of the other Psalms, he treats one only as pre-exilic, viz. Ps. 18, which he assigns to the reign of Josiah : Ps. 47, 93, 95–100 belong to B.C. 516, when the Temple was completed : the remaining Psalms are distributed by him over the intermediate period, between the age of Ezra and Neh., and the pre-Maccabæan Greek period (B.C. 333–168), Ps. 74, 79 (*Introd. to Isaiah*, pp. 360–363), 89, 132, being assigned in particular to the occasion of the revolt under Artaxerxes Ochus (above, p. 222).   The grounds, how-ever, upon which *specific* dates can be assigned to individual Psalms are often exceedingly slender.   It may be readily granted that the Psalms date *mostly* from the exile or later (cf. Davison, *l.c.* p. 63) ; but it may be doubted whether only *one* Psalm is earlier than B.C. 516.   The existence of a sub-stantial, though not definitely ascertainable, pre-exilic nucleus in the Psalter, is maintained strongly by Budde, *Theol. Lit.-zt.* 1892, No. 10 (in a review of Cheyne's work) ; cf. also Kautzsch, *Stud. u. Krit.* 1892, p. 586 ff., *Abriss*, pp. 141, 206 f., ^{2}10, 127.   J. P. Peters (" The Development of the Psalter," in the *New World*, Boston, U.S.A., June, 1893), while calling attention to the various evidences of gradual growth which the Psalter presents, agrees that none of the " Books " was compiled until after the exile, but thinks that, esp. in Book I., there are probably Psalms, in origin pre-exilic, and even Davidic, but so modified, and adapted to the situation of a later age, as to be seldom recognisable as such.

W. R. Smith (*OTJC.*^{2} 201–208, 219 ff.) adduces independent grounds showing that Books I.–III. were not compiled till after the exile, and that they express on the whole (though not exclusively) " a religious life of which the exile is the presupposition.   Only in this way can we understand the conflict and triumph of spiritual faith, habitually represented as the faith of a poor and struggling band, living in the midst of oppressors, and with no strength or help but the consciousness of loyalty to Jehovah, which is the

fundamental note of the whole book " (p. 220). The compilation of Books
IV.–V. he places in the early years of the Maccabee sovereignty (pp. 208–
212), many of the Psalms in this collection belonging to the Greek period,
and some (as Ps. 113–118, 149) manifestly springing out of the enthusiasm
evoked by the great victories of the Maccabees, which culminated in the
re-dedication of the Temple B.C. 165. He finds, however, a difficulty in
accepting a Maccabæan date for Ps. 44, 74, 79, on account of their position
in the Elohistic Psalter (Ps. 42–83), the compilation of which, he urges,
must have been completed before the Maccabæan age. He is disposed
consequently (pp. 437–440) to refer these Psalms to the occasion of the revolt
under Ochus, when, it is *conjectured*, Jerusalem and the Temple may have
suffered in the manner alluded to in Ps. 74, 79. Cheyne (see above) accepts
now this date for Ps. 74 and 79. The conjecture is an attractive one ; but in
the scantiness of our information respecting this, as respecting many other
periods of post-exilic Judaism, the point is one on which we must be content
to remain in uncertainty. Had we fuller knowledge of the post-exilic
history of Judah, many obscure and difficult questions connected with the
later parts of the OT. would doubtless be cleared up.

(2.) The opinion has latterly gained ground that in many
[366] Psalms the speaker, who uses the first person singular,
though apparently an individual, is in reality *the community*.
This opinion is no new one : it was held, for instance, by the
old Protestant commentator Rudinger (1580–81) ; but it has
been revived, and defended anew, by Olshausen, Reuss (*Gesch.*
§ 478 ; *Les Psaumes*, p. 56), Stade (*Gesch*. ii. 214), to a certain
degree by Prof. Cheyne, and especially by Rud. Smend in the
ZATW. 1888, pp. 49–147. The Psalter, it is urged by these
writers, was confessedly the hymn-book of a *community* : this
being so, it is remarkable that so many of the Psalms thus used
in public worship should have a strongly marked *individual*
character, and owe their origin to *individual* experiences ; on the
other hand, these experiences, and the emotions to which they
give rise, are much more significant if regarded as felt and
expressed by the *community* as such, which was keenly conscious
both of the close relation in which it stood to its God, and of
the opposition subsisting between it and the heathen nations
around, or ungodly members within. And so, it is argued, we
hear constantly in the Psalter, not the voices of individuals, but
the voice of the *nation*, expressing its thankfulness, its needs, its
faith, or its triumph. This is the main argument ; for others,
the writers just referred to must be consulted. It is true, this
interpretation of the " I " of the Psalms is legitimate in principle ; for there is undoubtedly a strong tendency in the OT. to

treat groups of men, smaller or larger, as the case may be, and especially peoples or nations, as *units*, applying to them the first (or second) person singular, and speaking of them in terms properly applicable only to an individual. This custom is due, probably, partly to a sense of community of interests and sympathies pervading the entire group, partly to the love of personification. Examples: Ex. 14^{25} "Let *me* flee" (said by the Egyptians), Num. 20$^{18.\ 19}$ (sing. and plur. interchanging), Dt. 2$^{27-29}$, Josh. 9^7 (Heb.), 17$^{14f.\ 17f.}$, Jud. 1^3 20^{23} (and elsewhere *): in the prophets, Isa. 12$^{1.\ 2}$ 25^1 26^9 (in these passages, as the context shows, the subject that speaks is the people), Jer. 10$^{19.}$ $^{20.\ 24}$, Mic. 7$^{7-10}$, Hab. 3^{14}, Lam. [367] 1$^{11b-16.\ 18-22}$ c. 3,† Isa. 61$^{10f.}$ (the ransomed nation, or the prophet speaking in its name), 63$^{7.\ 15b.}$‡ At the same time, it is impossible not to feel that the applicability of the principle to the Psalms has been much exaggerated, especially by Smend.§ It is constantly the case in lyric poetry (cf. Beer, p. lxxix ff.) that the poet, while describing truly what he feels or has experienced himself, writes at the same time with a view to the public around him, and hence so generalizes the expressions which he uses that others, situated similarly, may feel that he speaks for themselves as well, and find themselves able to appropriate his words. Thus a Psalm describing the experiences of an individual may well possess traits fitting it for liturgical use by the community, even if it may not have been accommodated to general use by slight changes in the phraseology. It is but one step further to suppose (as is probably often the fact) that a Psalm has a *representative* character, and that the Psalmist speaks in it, not on behalf of himself alone, but on behalf of his godly co-religionists as well.

---

* As Gen. 34^{30}, 1 Sa. 5^{10b} (Heb. *me*, *my*), 30^{22} (Heb. *with me*). It is not, however, clear that these are all cases of true personification : in some, the individual rather speaks, as *representing* his companions or fellow-countrymen.

† See esp. Lam. 1$^{13.\ 14}$ 3$^{4.\ 13.\ 16.\ 20.\ 48-54}$, where the personification is so vivid as to include various bodily parts. Elsewhere, also, the *history* of the nation is viewed as that of an individual, as Isa. 44$^{2.\ 24}$ 46$^{3f.}$, Jer. 2^2 3$^{4.\ 24f.}$ 31^{19}, Hos. 11^1, Ps. 129$^{1-3}$.

‡ Comp. also the many places in the Pent., esp. Ex. (JE) and Dt., in which Israel is addressed in the 2nd pers. sing.: *e.g.* Ex. 23$^{20ff.}$, Dt. 28 : cf. Ps. 50$^{7ff.}$. In some of these passages the thought of the writer glides from the whole to the individual members in consecutive verses.

§ Cf. *OTJC.*^{2} p. 189 ; Beer, pp. xiv–xvii, lxxxvii–xcvi ; Cheyne *Origin of the Psalter*, p. 277.

It is, however, no doubt true that in more Psalms than is commonly perceived to be the case the speaker is the nation, as Ps. 44$^{4.\ 6.\ 15}$ 60^9 66$^{13ff.}$ (cf. " us," " our," v.$^{9\text{-}12}$), 74^{12} 89^{50} 94$^{16ff.}$ 102, 118; and perhaps in Ps. 65^3 51,* 71 (cf. v.^{20} " us "), and some others.

See further the study (from this point of view) of the Psalms *seriatim* in Beer, pp. 1–92. Beer points out (p. xii) that as in the " We "-Psalms the principal question is whether the first person plural refers to the nation as a whole, or to a particular party within it, so in the " I "-Psalms, it is not only whether the Psalmist speaks purely as an individual, but also whether he speaks in the name (*a*) of the nation, or (*b*) of a party within it. Beer does not recognise many Psalms in which the nation, as such, is the speaker ; but he recognises many of the *representative* character spoken of above, in which the Psalmist, while expressing truly his own experiences and emotions, expresses at the same time those of his godly compatriots (*e.g.* Ps. 7, 9–10, 28, 37, 42–43, 71, 92, 94, 109, 119, 120, 130, 140), or even of the nation as a whole (*e.g.* Ps. 44, 56, 57, 59, 60, 65, 66, 74, 86, 88, 102, 118, 138, 145), so that he speaks in their name, and on their behalf. He also thinks that there are several Psalms (5, 22, 31, 35, 38, 40, 51, 69) spoken in the name of the godly kernel of the nation, the *ecclesiola in ecclesia*, which feels itself called to be the future *ecclesia*, the historical representative of Deutero - Isaiah's " servant of Jehovah," conscious of suffering and disappointment, conscious of the guilt which, in virtue of the solidarity of the nation, rests upon it, but conscious also (22$^{22ff.}$) of the great future which in the providence of God is reserved for it (cf. Cheyne, *O.P.* p. 263 f.; Kirkpatrick on Ps. 22, p 114).

---

* A confession written on behalf of the nation, by one who had a deep sense of his people's sin, shortly after the exile (comp., from a *prophetic* point of view, Isa. 63^7–64^{12}). That the title, at any rate, cannot be correct appears partly from the inapplicability of v.^{4a} to David's situation (for however great David's sin against God, he had done Uriah the most burning wrong that could be imagined ; and an injury to a neighbour is in the OT. a " sin " against him, Gen. 20^9, Jud. 11^{27}, Jer. 37^{18} *al.*) ; partly from the general literary style of the Psalm, which points to an age much later than that of David ; partly from the fact that many of the ideas expressed in it " appear to belong to a later and more developed stage of the religious consciousness " (cf. Kirkpatrick, p. 286),—notice, for instance, the similarities of thought and expression with II Isaiah in v.^{1b} (Isa. 63^7), v.^{3a} (59^{12}), v.^{9b} (43^{25} 44^{22}), v.^{11b} (63$^{10.\ 11b}$: Jehovah's " holy spirit," represented also as dwelling in the nation, and an expression not found elsewhere in the OT.; had it been in use as early as David's time, would it not have been met with more frequently?), v.^{17} (57^{15b} 61^{1b} 66^{2b}). Comp. further W. R. Smith, *OTJC.* p. 440 ff., who observes that the assumption that the subject is the nation is the only one which neutralises the contradiction between v.^{18} and v.^{19} ; the complete restoration of Jerusalem would be the sign that God was reconciled to His people (Isa. 40^2), and would accept the sacrifices, in which now He had no pleasure. However, v.$^{18.\ 19}$ are regarded by many scholars as a liturgical addition to the original Psalm.

CHAPTER VIII.

THE BOOK OF PROVERBS.

LITERATURE.—H. Ewald, *Die Sal. Schriften erklärt*,[2] 1867, pp. 1-266; F. Hitzig, *Die Sprüche Salomo's*, 1858; F. Delitzsch, *Das Sal. Spruchbuch*, 1873; W. Nowack (in the *Kgf. Hdb.*), 1883; A. Kuenen, *Onderzoek*, iii. (1865) pp. 57-110 ([2]1893, p. 59 ff.); T. K. Cheyne, *Job and Solomon*, 1887, p. 117 ff. (where, p. 178, other literature is mentioned); H. L. Strack (in the *Kgf. Comm.*), 1888; also P. de Lagarde, *Anmerkungen zur Griech. Uebers. der Prov.* 1863; A. J. Baumgarten, *Étude critique sur l'état du texte du livre des Proverbes*, 1890; G. Bickell (p. 340 n.); H. Pinkuss, *Die Syr. Uebers. der Prov.*, *ZATW.* 1894, pp. 65 ff., 161 ff.; R. Smend, *Alttest. Rel.-gesch.* p. 508 ff.; W. T. Davison, *The Wisdom-lit. of the OT.* 1894.

THE Book of Proverbs introduces us to the *Chokhmah-* or Wisdom-literature of the Hebrews. Wisdom, among the ancient Hebrews, was a term which was used in special connexions, and hence acquired a special limitation of meaning. It was applied to the faculty of acute observation, shrewdness in discovery or device, cleverness of invention. The "wise" woman of Tekoa came before David (2 Sa. 14[2ff.]) with an apologue designed to rouse into action the king's longings for his absent son.* The wisdom of Solomon showed itself in the skill with which he elicited the truth in his judgment on the two infants (1 Ki. 3[16-28]), and in the answers which he gave to the "questions" —*i.e.* no doubt riddles (v.[1]) or other inquiries designed to test the king's sagacity—put to him by the Queen of Sheba (1 Ki. 10[3ff.]). Joseph's skill in interpreting dreams entitles him similarly to be termed "wise" (Gen. 41[39]). Of the nations around Israel, Edom was specially famed for "wisdom" in this sense (Ob.[8], Jer. 49[7]); Egypt † and the "children of the East" must also have been noted in the same way (1 Ki. 4[30]). Four celebrated "wise men," whom Solomon is stated to have excelled,

* Cf. the wise woman of Abel-Meholah, *ib.* 20[16].

† Cf. Gen. 41[8], Isa. 19[11. 12], Ex. 7[11].

are mentioned in 1 Ki. 4[31]. "Wise men" are alluded to in the OT. in terms which appear to show that they must have [369] formed, if not a school, yet a tolerably prominent class in ancient Israel (cf. Jer. 18[18]; Pr. 1[6] 22[17] 24[23], Job 15[18]). The interest of these "wise men," however, did not centre in the distinctively national elements of Israel's character or Israel's faith; and hence, for instance, the absence in the Proverbs of warnings against idolatry, and of most of the favourite ideas and phraseology of the prophets (as "Israel," "Zion," "my people," "saith Jehovah," &c.). The wise men took for granted the main postulates of Israel's creed, and applied themselves rather to the observation of human character as such, seeking to analyse conduct, studying action in its consequences, and establishing morality, upon the basis of principles common to humanity at large. On account of their prevailing disregard of national points of view, and their tendency to characterise and estimate human nature under its most general aspects, they have been termed, not inappropriately, the *Humanists* of Israel.* Their teaching had a practical aim : not only do they formulate maxims of conduct, but they appear also as moral advisers, and as interested in the education of the young (Pr. 1–9; cf. Ps. 34, 37).† The observation of human nature, however, naturally leads on to reflexion on the problems which it presents; hence Job and Ecclesiastes form part of the Hebrew *Chokhmah*-literature. Nor is the observation of nature, especially in so far as it affords evidence of providential arrangements or design, alien to the lines of thought which the wise men of Israel pursued : comp. Job 38–41, Pr. 30[24ff.]; and the comparisons instituted between animal and human life in Pr. 6[6ff.] and elsewhere. Solomon is stated (1 Ki. 4[33]) to have "spoken" of all known departments of the animal and vegetable kingdoms, presumably with reference to the instincts or habits displayed in them, but possibly also in fables, or apologues, in which trees (Jud. 9[8-15]; 2 Ki. 14[9]) or animals figured characteristically. From the consideration of nature, as evincing wise dispositions and arrangements,

---

* Cf. Delitzsch, p. 34; Cheyne, p. 119.

† Hence the "utilitarianism" of the Proverbs, which has sometimes been adversely criticised. The profit of wisdom, and the foolishness of folly, can only be *practically* demonstrated by pointing to the consequences to which each leads.

and of human society as benefited by the wise action of its individual members, would arise without difficulty the conception [370] of "wisdom" as a principle disposing the one, and regulating the other; and hence the step was not a far one to its *personification*, on the one hand, as a "master workman" (Pr. 8[30]) assisting the Almighty in His work of creation; on the other hand, as presiding over human affairs and directing men in the choice of means, whether to secure their individual happiness, or the well-being of society as a whole. This is the step taken in Pr. 1–9.*

The Hebrew term for "proverb" is *māshāl*, which, as Arabic seems to show, denotes properly a *representation*, *i.e.* a statement not relating solely to a single fact, but *standing for* or *representing* other similar facts. The statement constituting the *māshāl* may be one deduced from a particular instance, but capable of application to other instances of a similar kind, or it may be a generalisation from experience, such as in the nature of the case admits of constantly fresh application. The *māshāl* is by usage limited almost entirely to observations relative to human life and character, and is expressed commonly in a short, pointed form. Sometimes the *māshāl* includes a comparison, or is expressed in figurative or enigmatic language (cf. Pr. 1[6]): the different types preserved in the Book of "Proverbs" will be illustrated below.

The *māshāl* would also probably include fables, such as those of Jotham (Jud. 9[8-15]) and Joash (2 Ki. 14[9]), and parables, as those in 2 Sa. 12[1-6] 14[5-7], 1 Ki. 20[39f.], though the term is not actually used in these instances; but similar allegorical representations are so styled in Ez. 17[2] (see v.[3-10]), 20[49] (see v.[47]), 24[3-5]. (For certain other, secondary senses of משל, see the *Lexica*.) Examples of the *popular* "māshāl" are: "Is not Saul among the prophets?" (1 Sa. 10[12] 19[24]); the "proverb of the ancients, 'Wickedness proceedeth from the wicked'" (*ib.* 24[13]); "The fathers have eaten sour grapes," &c. (Ez. 18[2], Jer. 31[29]); see also Ez. 12[23] 16[44]. But the examples contained in the Book of Proverbs are not of this simple, popular kind: they are, at least mostly, "works of art," and bear the impress of the skilled hands which produced them.

Contents and character of the Book of Proverbs.—The Book of Proverbs consists of eight distinct parts, of very unequal length and character, and for the most part marked by separate titles or introductions.

* See more fully on the Hebrew "wisdom," and "wise men," Prof. Davidson's paper in the *Expositor*, May 1880, p. 321 ff., and his art. "Proverbs" in the *Encycl. Brit.*

(1.) C. 1–9. The "Praise of Wisdom" (Ewald, Cheyne). [371] The writer, speaking like a father (1^8 and repeatedly, "my son") to an imagined pupil or disciple, warns him against the dangers and temptations to which he is most likely to be exposed, invites him affectionately to listen to his precepts, and commends to him the claims of *Wisdom* to be his guide and friend. No definite arrangement can be traced in the subjects treated; nor is the argument logically articulated: the discourse flows on till the topic in hand is exhausted, and then it recommences with another.

1$^{1-6}$ is adapted to form the introduction both to the exhortations which follow and to the "Proverbs," properly so called, contained in c. 10 ff., the aim and value of which it points out.

The exhortations may be divided for convenience (nearly as is done by Delitzsch) into 15 paragraphs, each, in the main, dealing with a single aspect of the writer's theme, viz. (1) 1$^{7-19}$ a warning against the temptation to commit crimes of violence; (2) 1$^{20-33}$ Wisdom's denunciation of those who despise her; (3) c. 2 the pursuit of wisdom as the road to virtue and the fear of God; (4) 3$^{1-20}$ the blessings which attend devotion to God, and the prize which Wisdom proves herself to be to those who find her; (5) 3$^{21-26}$ Wisdom a protection to those who possess her; (6) 3$^{27-35}$ liberality and integrity commended; (7) 4^1–5^6 a father's counsels to his son; (8) 5$^{7-23}$ on fidelity to the marriage-tie; (9) 6$^{1-5}$ the imprudence of becoming surety for another; (10) 6$^{6-11}$ advice to the sluggard; (11) 6$^{12-19}$ warning against different evil machinations; (12) 6$^{20-35}$ warning against adultery; (13) c. 7 the same subject continued, the warning being pointed by an illustration; (14) c. 8 Wisdom speaks, proclaiming her august nature, and the gifts which she is ready to bestow upon men; (15) c. 9 Wisdom and Folly, each personified, contrasted with each other.

The form is throughout poetical, and the parallelism of members is, as a rule, carefully observed. The style is flowing, forming in this respect as strong a contrast as possible to that of the "proverbs" which follow (10$^{1ff.}$): instead of a series of thoughts, each forcibly expressed, but disconnected with one another, a thought is here developed at length and presented from different points of view. A general uniformity of tone pervades the whole discourse; and the same idea is often repeated with but slight variations of expression. The aim of the writer evidently was to provide the collection of proverbs, 10$^{1ff.}$, with a hortatory introduction, commending the wisdom of which he viewed them as the expression (cf. 1$^{1-6}$), and pointing to the dangers, prominent in his day, from which those who would listen to her teachings might be guarded. It is doubtful if the [372] writer is identical with the compiler of the collection of proverbs which follows, but he is familiar with them, and adopts several expressions from them into his vocabulary. The errors to which his hearers appear to be specially tempted are crimes of violence (1^{11-18} 4^{14-17}), and unchastity (2^{16} 5^{3-20} 6^{24-35} 7^{5-27} 9^{13-18}): other faults are warned against in 6^{12-19}. The imprudence of becoming surety for a friend is strongly insisted on, 6^{1-5}; the value of industry is exemplified, 6^{6-11}. The fine personification of Wisdom in c. 8 and 9^{1-6} is to be especially noticed. The unity of thought and efficiency operative in the world is here abstracted from God, the actual operator, and presented as a *personal* agent, the first-born child of the Creator, standing beside Him and giving effect to His creative design, afterwards, in history, inspiring kings and princes with their best thoughts, delighting in the sons of men (v.^{31}), and promising abundant reward to those who will commit themselves to her guidance. The representation in $3^{19f.}$ $8^{22ff.}$ is the prelude of the later doctrine of the Λόγος. 9^{1-6} Wisdom invites men to accept her gifts; and the discourse closes with the picture of her rival, "Madam Folly," sitting at the door of her house, and displaying her attractions to those who are simple enough to be tempted by them ($9^{13ff.}$).

Delitzsch has remarked—and other critics have agreed in the observation—on the similarity, partly in tone and warmth of feeling, and partly also in expression, between Pr. 1–9 and Deuteronomy. "As Dt. would have the rising generation lay to heart the Mosaic *Tôrāh*, so here the author would impress upon his hearers the *Tôrāh* of wisdom." In particular, with Dt. 6^{4-9} cf. the *Hear* of Pr. 1^8 $4^{1.\ 10}$ &c., and 3^3 $6^{20f.}$ 7^3 (*Bind, Write*); with 8^5, cf. Pr. 3^{12}; and with 4^{5-8}, Pr. $3^{9t.}$.

(2.) C. 10–22^{16}, with the title "The Proverbs of Solomon." This division of the Book is composed of proverbs, strictly so called. The proverbs exhibit great regularity of form: each verse contains a complete proverb; and each proverb consists of two members only (*i.e.* is a *distich*), each member containing, as a rule, (in the Hebrew) not more than three or four words. The one three-membered proverb which this division of the Book contains (19^7) is undoubtedly due to a defective text (cf. LXX, and the commentators); if the missing clause be supplied, the number of independent proverbs will be 376. The pro-

verbs [373] are arranged in no particular order,* though sometimes two or more dealing with the same subject (as $16^{10.\ 12-15}$
on kings, $18^{6f.}$ on the fool), or containing the same more or
less characteristic word (as $10^{6f.}$ *the righteous*, v.$^{11f.}$ *covereth*, v.$^{14f.}$
destruction, v.$^{16f.}$ v.$^{18f.}$ 12^{5-7} $15^{8f.}$ $15^{33}-16^{7.\ 9.\ 11}$ *Jehovah*) occur in
juxtaposition.† The two members stand usually, and in c. 10–
15 almost exclusively, in *antithetic* parallelism (p. 363), the
second confirming or enforcing the first by declaring some contrasted truth which forms, as it were, its counterpart. Instances
of *synonymous* (11^7 14^{19} *al.*) and "synthetic" parallelism (see
ibid.), however, also occur.

Thus the second member states a *reason* ($16^{12.\ 26}$) or *purpose* (13^{14} 15^{24} *al.*) ;
elsewhere, again, the thought is only *completed* by the second member, as
when this commences with the comparative *than* (מן), 12^{19} $15^{16.\ 17}$ $16^{8.\ 19}$ 17^{10}
19^1 21^{19}), or with *how much more* [or *less*] (אף כי), 11^{31} 15^{11} 17^7 $19^{7a.\ 10}$ 21^{27} ;
other cases in which the proverb is incomplete without the second clause only
become frequent towards the end of the collection (16^7 $17^{13.\ 15}$ $18^{9.\ 13}$ 19^{26}
$20^{7.\ 8.\ 10}$ &c.). Of proverbs containing a *comparison* there are only two
examples in this collection, viz. 10^{26} 11^{22}.

Both in this and in the subsequent divisions of the Book there occur
several cases in which a proverb, entirely or in part, is *repeated*. Thus
$14^{12}=16^{25}$; and with but slight changes of expression, the following pairs
also agree : 10^1 15^{20} ; 10^2 11^4 ; 16^2 21^2 ; $19^{5.\ 9}$; $20^{10.\ 23}$; $21^{9.\ 19}$. In the
following, one line is the same, or nearly the same : $10^{6b.\ 11b}$; 10^{8b} and 10^b
[but cf. LXX Pesh. RV. *marg.*] ; 10^{15a} 18^{11a} ; 11^{13a} 20^{19a} ; 11^{21a} 16^{5b} ; 12^{14a} 13^{2a}
18^{20a} ; 14^{31a} 17^{5a} ; 15^{33b} 18^{12b} ; 16^{18a} 18^{12a} ; 19^{12a} 20^{2a} ; comp. also 19^{12} with
$16^{14a.\ 15b}$: in 13^{14} 14^{27} ; 16^{28b} 17^{9b} ; 17^{15b} 20^{10b} the wording is very similar,
but the subject of the proverb is different : notice also the variety of objects
which are described as a *fountain* or *tree of life* 10^{11a} 13^{14a} 14^{27a} 16^{22a} ; 11^{30a}
13^{12b} 15^{4a}), or as *Jehovah's abomination* ($11^{1.\ 20}$ 12^{22} $15^{8.\ 9.\ 26}$ 16^5 17^{15} $20^{10.\ 23}$),
or the different persons who *come only to want* (11^{24} 14^{23} 21^5 22^{16}).

Where the contents are so miscellaneous, it is difficult to
indicate their characteristics, except in very general terms. But
of the present collection it may be said that, as compared with
the [374] subsequent collections, the proverbs are usually brighter
and more cheerful in tone : if good and bad, rich and poor meet
together (as they must meet in every society), nevertheless the
happier aspects of life are predominant : prosperity seems to

---

* Ewald supposed that the collection was divided into five parts by the
recurrence at intervals of a proverb pointing out to the young the advantages
of wisdom (10^1 13^1 15^{20} 17^{25} 19^{20}) ; but this is probably accidental.

† The groups 11^{9-12} 20^{7-9} 20^{24-26} 22^{2-4} are marked by the recurrence of the
same initial letter.

prevail, and virtue is uniformly rewarded. The collection includes some fine and elevated religious proverbs; but the generalizations are mostly drawn from secular life, and describe the fortune which may be expected to attend particular lines of conduct or types of character. The religious proverbs mainly emphasize Jehovah's sovereignty, or all-pervading omniscience; as $15^{3.\ 11}$ $16^{2.\ 4}$ 17^3 19^{21} ("Man proposes, but God disposes"; cf. 16^9) $20^{12.\ 24}$ $21^{2.\ 30f.}$ 22^2; others point out the blessings which flow from the fear of Him (*e.g.* $15^{16.\ 29}$), or describe who are His "abomination" (above, p. 397); the prophetic teaching, that righteousness is more acceptable to God than sacrifice, appears in 21^3 (cf. 15^8 16^6 21^{27}). The principle that men are rewarded (in this life) according to their works, pervades the entire collection ($10^{2.\ 3.\ 6.\ 7.\ 25.\ 27.\ 30}$ $11^{4.\ 5.\ 6}$, and repeatedly). The wise and fool, their different aims, and different lots, are contrasted with great frequency: other characters often mentioned are the rich and the poor, the diligent and the slothful ($10^{4.\ 5}$ $12^{24.\ 27}$ 13^4 &c.), and the scorner (13^1 14^6 15^{12} &c.). The "fool" is the man who, whether from weakness of character (the אֱוִיל) or from obstinacy (the כְּסִיל), lacks the perception necessary to guide him aright in the affairs of life, and remains consequently an object of satire or contempt to his fellow-men. Wealth is spoken of as an advantage to its owner (10^{15} 13^8 $14^{20.\ 24}$ 19^4 22^7), but not if amassed in unrighteousness (10^2), or if made the object of a blind confidence (11^{28}). Pride is the subject of 13^{10} $16^{18f.}$ 21^4 &c.; the care of the poor is commended in 14^{31} 17^5 19^{17}. A remarkably large proportion of the proverbs turn on the right use of the lips or tongue. The imprudence of becoming a surety is taught in 11^{15} 20^{16}. A good wife is described as God's best gift (12^4 18^{22} 19^{14}); on the other hand, an injudicious or quarrelsome woman is depicted satirically (11^{22} 19^{13} $21^{9.\ 19}$). The value of parental authority is recognised (13^{24} 19^{18} $22^{6.\ 15}$); and a want of respect for either parent is strongly condemned (13^1 15^5 19^{26} 20^{20}). The king is alluded to in terms of admiration, being praised for [375] his justice and love of righteousness (14^{35} $16^{10.\ 12.\ 13}$ 20^8 22^{11}), his wisdom (20^{26}), his mercy and faithfulness (20^{28}), his amenableness to the Divine guidance (21^1), though naturally regarded personally with some awe and deference ($16^{14.\ 15}$ 19^{12} 20^2); but his nation's prosperity is his glory (14^{28}), and that prosperity has its source in righteousness (14^{34}). The associations connected with the king in this collection are bright and happy; no dark shadows cross the picture of his character.

(3.) 22^{17}–24^{22}. Here 22^{17-21} forms an introduction, inviting attention to the admonitions which follow, and which are described as "words of the wise."

The form of the proverbs contained in this collection is, as a rule, much freer than is the case in No. 2. Distichs are exceptional (22^{28} 23^9 24^{7-10}), the thought generally extending over four members (tetrastichs), the second distich being sometimes synonymous with the first, sometimes stating the ground or purpose of it, or otherwise supplementing it ($22^{22f.}$ $^{24f.}$ $^{26f.}$ $23^{10f.}$ &c.). A tristich (22^{29}), several pentastichs ($23^{4f.}$ $24^{13f.}$), and hexastichs ($23^{1-3.}$ $^{12-14.}$ $^{19-21.}$ $^{26-28}$ $24^{11f.}$), a heptastich (23^{6-8}), and an octastich (23^{22-25}) also occur; and in 23^{29-35} (on wine-drinking) the thought is developed into a short poem; in these cases, though the individual verses are usually parallelistic, the terse, compact form of the original *māshāl* is entirely surrendered.

This division of the Book is less a collection of individual proverbs (as No. 2) than a body of maxims, in which proverbs are interwoven, addressed with a practical aim to an individual (to whom the expression *My son* * is applied, $23^{15.}$ $^{19.}$ ^{26} $24^{13.}$ ^{21}), and worked up usually into a more or less consecutive argument. The tone is hortatory, like that of No. 1; but No. 3 differs from No. 1, in that, while that is devoted in the main to a single subject, the commendation of wisdom, the advice proffered here relates to many different topics. From the terms of $22^{19f.}$ (notice esp. the emphatic *thee* in v.^{19}) it would almost seem to have been addressed originally to a particular individual: the 2nd pers. in c. 1–9 seems rather to be a poetic fiction. The maxims are mostly of a very practical character; *e.g.* against becoming surety for another, $22^{26f.}$ (cf. 11^{15} 20^{16}), against indulging to excess in unwonted dainties, 23^{1-3}, against the undue pursuit of riches, $23^{4f.}$, and especially against gluttony and drunkenness (which, it is rather remarkable, [376] is only commented on twice in the numerous proverbs contained in No. 2, viz. 20^1 21^{17}), $23^{20f.}$ $^{29-35}$.

(4.) 24^{23-34}, with the title, "These also are sayings of the wise." An appendix to No. 3, displaying similar variety of form: a hexastich v.$^{23b-25}$, a distich v.^{26}, a tristich v.^{27}, a tetrastich v.$^{28f.}$, and a decastich v.$^{30-34}$. In the decastich, the slothful man (who has more than once been satirized in No. 2) is made the subject

* As in No. 1; in No. 2, only once, 19^{27}.

of a short apologue, drawn professedly from the writer's experience (cf. 7^{6-23}, Ps. $37^{35f.}$, Job 5^{3-5}).

In Nos. 3 and 4, 24^{6a} is very similar to 20^{18b}; 24^{6b} has occurred before in 11^{14b}; 24^{20b} in 13^{9b}; and $24^{33f.}$ is all but identical with $6^{10f.}$. In the collection itself, the following repetitions occur: 22^{28a} 23^{10a}; 22^{23a} 23^{11b}; $23^{3a.\ 6b}$; 23^{17a} 24^{1a}; 23^{18} $24^{14b.\ c.}$

(5.) C. 25–29, with the title, "These also are Proverbs of Solomon, which the men of Hezekiah king of Judah copied out." An appendix to No. 2. In this collection, distichs reappear, though not with the same regularity as in No. 2, being accompanied by tristichs ($25^{8.\ 13.\ 20}$ $27^{10.\ 22}$ 28^{10}), tetrastichs ($25^{4f.}$ $9f.\ 21f.$ &c.), a pentastich ($25^{6f.}$), and, as in Nos. 3 and 4, a short poem (on the value of industry to the farmer), consisting of a decastich (27^{23-27}). The proverbs appear sometimes, as in No. 2, to be grouped by catch-words (as $25^{8f.}$ *debate*; v.$^{11f.}$ *gold*; $26^{1f.}$ *As . . . so*), but they are also, more frequently than in No. 2, grouped by real community of subject, as 25^{1-7} (on kings), 26^{3-12} (where each verse illustrates some aspect of the character of the "fool"), $^{13-16}$ (on the sluggard), $^{23-26.\ 28}$ (on false flattery). Another distinction between this collection and No. 2 is that while in No. 2 the predominant type of proverb is the antithetic, this is common here only in c. 28–29, while in c. 25–27 the *comparative* type prevails. In this type of proverb (which occurs but twice in No. 2) an object is illustrated by some *figure* derived from nature or human life, the comparison being sometimes expressed distinctly,* sometimes [377] left to the reader to be inferred from the mere juxtaposition of two ideas.†

The proverbs in this collection differ often in character from those in No. 2, though not so widely as is the case in Nos.

---

* 26^1 As snow in summer, and as rain in harvest;
    So honour is not seemly for a fool.
So $26^{2.\ 8.\ 18f.}$; 27^8; and before, 10^{26}. Without *so* 15^{13} 26^{11}. Or with the particle of comparison omitted—
    25^{12} An earring of gold, and an ornament of fine gold,
      Is a wise reprover upon an obedient ear.
So $25^{11.\ 14.\ 18.\ 19.\ 26.\ 28}$ $26^{17.\ 23}$ $28^{3.\ 15}$; and before, 11^{22}.

    † 25^{25} Cold water to a fainting soul,
      And good news from a far country.
I.e. the two resemble one another. On this "*Waw* of equality," which occurs also in Arabic, see Delitzsch, p. 9, *note*. So $25^{3.\ 20.\ 23}$ $26^{3.\ 7.\ 9.\ 14.\ 21}$; comp. 26^{20} $27^{3.\ 20}$.

3 and 4. The proverbs in c. 28–29 bear the greatest general resemblance to those in No. 2 ; but, on the whole, the proverbs in c. 25–29 appear to spring out of a changed state of society. The king is not presented in the same attractive or amiable light. If 25^2 represents him as searching out a matter for his subjects' weal, 25^3 associates him with the thought of what is arbitrary and mysterious. 25$^{4f.}$ speak of the removal of bad ministers before him, 28^2 alludes suggestively to calamities which rival claimants for a throne may inflict upon a land ; and 28$^{12.}$ $^{15f.}$ ^{28} 29$^{2. 4. 16}$ hint at sufferings experienced at the hands of unrighteous rulers. 25$^{6f.}$ 29^{14} are of more neutral character : one contains a maxim for behaviour in the king's presence ; the other promises a sure throne to a just king. 27^8 is not impossibly an allusion to exile, such as became familiar to the Israelites from the 8th cent. B.C. Religious proverbs are rare : see, however, 29^{13} (cf. 22^2), $^{25f.}$. The importance of the prophet, as an element in the state, is significantly expressed in 29^{18}. The "fool" (כסיל), who already in the collection No. 2 is represented with a touch of satire, is here the subject of a series of satirical attacks, 26$^{1. 3-12}$, cf. 27^{22}. In 26$^{13-16}$ the sluggard is held up to derision. Agricultural industry is inculcated in 27$^{23-27}$. Some of the proverbs are maxims for conduct (as in Nos. 3 and 4), e.g. 25$^{6f. 8. 9f. 16f. 21f.}$ (love of an enemy) : in these cases the advice is sometimes enforced by a prudential motive. The address *my son* occurs once, 27^{11}.

No. 5 is remarkable for the many proverbs identical, or nearly so, with proverbs in No. 2 : thus 25^{24} 21^9 ; 26^{8b} 10^{13b} ; 26^{13} 22^{13} ; 26^{15} 19^{24} ; 26^{22} 18^8 ; 27^{12} 22^3 ; 27^{13} 20^{16} ; 27^{15} 19^{13b} ; 27^{21a} 17^{3a} ; 28^6 19^1 ; 28^{19} 12^{11} ; 29^{13} 22^2 ; 29^{22a} 15^{18a} ; none is repeated from No. 3, and only one is substantially identical with one in No. 4, viz. 28^{21a} ; cf. 24^{23b}. In No. 5 itself, two proverbs occur, worded very similarly, but with a different subject, 26^{12} and 29^{20} ; comp. also 28^{12b} and 28^{28a}.

[378] (6.) C. 30. "The words of Agur, the son of Jakeh, the oracle." V.$^{1b-4}$ states, as it seems, the conclusion of a sceptic as to the impossibility of knowing God ; * v.$^{5-6}$ the poet gives the answer, an appeal *viz.* to God's revelation of Himself, followed, v.$^{7-9}$, by a prayer that he may never be tempted himself, by extremes of worldly fortune, to abandon or dishonour

* Introduced, v.^{1b} with some solemnity, as an oracular declaration, by נאם הגבר (cf. Nu. 24$^{3. 15}$, 2 Sa. 23^1, and the common נאם יהוה).

God. V.[10-33] consists of nine groups of proverbs, each of which describes some quality or character in terms of either warning or commendation, and in most of which the number *four* is conspicuous : viz. v.[10] a warning against slander ; v.[11-14] the four marks of an evil generation ; v.[15-16] the four insatiable things ; v.[17] the fate of the disobedient son ; v.[18-20] the four incomprehensible things ; v.[21-23] the four intolerable things ; v.[24-28] the four wise animals ; v.[29-31] the four things comely in their going ; v.[32-33] a warning against strife. The form in which most of these proverbs are cast is peculiar ; they are sometimes called "numerical" proverbs ; there is another example in 6[16-19].

30[1] is peculiar and enigmatic. Neither Agur nor Jakeh is named elsewhere : המשא, "the oracle," is introduced abruptly, and the term is elsewhere applied to *prophetic* utterances only (Isa. 13[1] &c.) : Ithiel and Ucal, also, as proper names, are very strange. In המשא there is probably an error. We may read (with Hitz., Mühlau,* Del., Nowack) מִמַּשָּׂא *of Massa*, or הַמַּשָּׂאִי *the Massaite*, in which case Agur would be described as belonging to the Ishmaelite tribe of Massa (Gen. 25[14]), whose home was probably in the north of the Arabian Peninsula, south-east of Palestine ; or (with Grätz, Cheyne) הַמֹּשֵׁל (Ez. 16[44] *al.*) *the proverb-writer* : 31[1] (see below) somewhat supports the former view. V.1[b] is probably to be read לָאִיתִי אֵל לָאִיתִי אֵל וָאֵכֶל (see RV. *marg.*), and treated as a confession, introductory to v.[2-4], of the writer's failure in his effort to reach the knowledge of the Most High. If the reading "of Massa" be correct, c. 30 will contain specimens of foreign "wisdom" (which may account for its somewhat peculiar character and vocabulary †), though the [379] Israelitish author who adopted them must have accommodated them to the spirit of his own religion (see esp. v.[5-9]). As regards the probable date of c. 30, Prof. Cheyne (p. 152) observes justly that the authors of both v.1[b-4] and v.[5-9] must have lived in an age of advanced religious reflexion and Scripture-study : the one is rather a philosopher (cf. Job and Eccl.), the other a Biblical theologian ; but both would be at home only in the exilic or post-exilic period. V.[5] is based upon Ps. 18[30b, c], the passage, by the addition of "every," and of v.[6] (from Dt. 4[1] 12[32]), being generalised so as to designate a collected body of revealed truth.

(7.) 31[1-9]. "The words of Lemuel, a king ; the oracle which his mother taught him." A series of very homely maxims, addressed to king Lemuel by the queen-mother, warning him against sensuality and immoderate indulgence in wine, and

---

* *De Proverbiorum quæ dicuntur Aguri et Lemuelis origine atque indole* (1869).

† 30[15] עֲלוּקָה ; הֵן אמרו לא ; v.[17] יקהה (also Gen. 49[10], but with Arabic affinities) ; v.[27] חצץ ; v.[31] אלקום (as it seems, a strong Arabism ; Cheyne, p. 175).

exhorting him to relieve the necessities and defend the cause of the poor.

31[1]. Another enigmatic title. The combination למואל מלך, "Lemuel, a king," is singular ; we should expect naturally either " King Lemuel " (המלך למואל, or, in *late* Hebrew, למואל המלך), or the addition of the country, or people, of which he was king. משא, a *prophetic* utterance, seems also to be as unsuitable here as in 30[1]. Both these anomalies are, however, removed together, if we simply connect מלך משא, and construe as in RV. *marg.*, "The words of Lemuel, *king of Massa*, which," &c. (so Hitz., Mühlau, Del., Nowack, Kuen.[2] § 95. 10). Here also, as in c. 30, some unusual expressions occur (v.[2] the strong Aramaism בר, *son* (thrice) ; v.[3] the Aram. plur. חלוף; v.[8] מחות; מלכין).

(8.) 31[10-31]. The description of a virtuous woman, without any title, the verses of which are arranged alphabetically.

The literary style of the Proverbs has some peculiarities of its own. Not only, especially in the principal collection (No. 2), are the individual Proverbs terse in statement and regular in form, but the vocabulary of the Book includes many words and expressions which are met with seldom or never in other parts of the OT., though here they recur with considerable frequency. Some of these are confined to one division of the Book, others are found in more than one.

Thus confined chiefly to No. 2 are—

מקור חיים *a fountain of life* (above, p. 397).

מְחִתָּה *destruction* : 10[14. 15. 29] 13[3] 14[28] 18[7] 21[15] (rare besides).

בֵּן מֵבִישׁ *a son that causeth shame* : 10[5] 17[2] 19[26].

סֶלֶף *perverseness* : 11[3] 15[4]↑ ; סלף *to subvert, ruin* : 13[6] 19[3] 21[12] 22[12] (only besides Ex. 23[8]=Dt. 16[19], Job 12[19]).

יד ליד *hand to hand* (a very peculiar idiom) : 11[21] 16[5]↑.

[380] אך למחסור (tendeth) *only to want* : 11[24] 14[23] 21[5] 22[16].

מפרי פי איש *from the fruit of a man's mouth* : 12[14] 13[2] 18[20].

התגלע *to show the teeth*, i.e. *to rail* or *quarrel* : 17[14] 18[1] 20[3]↑.

Jehovah's abomination : 11[1] &c. (see above, p. 397, and add 3[32]).

. . . יש *there is that* . . ., as a formula introducing a proverb : 11[24] 12[18] 13[7. 23] 14[12] 16[25] 18[24] 20[15]. (The use of יש in 3[28] 19[18] 23[18] 24[14] : 8[21] is evidently different.)

תחבולות *wise guidance* (lit. *steersmanship*, a met. from sea-faring life) : 11[14] 12[5] 20[18b] : also 1[5] 24[6a] (varied from 20[18b]), Job 37[12]↑.

עץ חיים *a tree of life* : see p. 397 ; also 3[18]. Cf. עץ החיים Gen. 2-3.

לא ינקה *will not go unpunished* (perhaps, as Ew. suggests, an echo of Ex. 20[7]) : 11[21] 16[5] 17[5] 19[5. 9] 28[20] : also 6[29]↑.

מרפא *healing* (in different applications) : 12[18] 13[17] 14[30] 15[4] 16[24] 29[1b] : also 4[22] 6[15b] (=29[1b]).

יפיח כזבים *breathes forth lies* : 14[5b. 25] 19[5. 9] ; also 6[19a] (=14[5b]) ; cf. 12[17] יפח אמונה *breathes forth faithfulness*, and Ps. 27[12].

מְרַדֵּף *a pursuer of* . . ., with different objects : 11¹⁹ רעה ; 12¹¹ and 28¹⁹ צדקה ; 15⁹ ריקים.

הפיק רצון מי' *to draw out favour from Jehovah* : 12² 18²²ᵇ (=8³⁵ᵇ) : the verb also (which is uncommon) 3¹³.

יגרה מדון *stirreth up strife* : 15¹⁸ 28²⁵ 29²².

נִרְגָּן *whisperer, talebearer* : 16²⁸ 18⁸=26²² 26²⁰.

מוסר *correction, instruction*, is also much more frequent in Pr. than else-where (30 times). The idea of life being a *discipline* is fundamental in the book. " God educates men, and men educate each other " (Holtzmann in the continuation of Stade's *Gesch.* ii. 297).

There are also some other terms chiefly used in, and perhaps, when they occur elsewhere, borrowed from, the Wisdom-literature : as תּוּשִׁיָּה, לֶקַח, אֲמָרִים, מַעְגְּלוֹת (cf. מַעְגָּל), תַּהְפֻּכוֹת ; and *my son*, used by the teacher in addressing his pupil. Other words occurring in the book with great frequency are due to the types of character, or qualities, described, as אויל the *weak fool* (13 times in No. 2, in other parts 4 times), אולת *folly* (16 times in No. 2, in other parts 6 times), כסיל the *obstinate fool* (30 and 19 times), לץ the *scorner* (1²² 3³⁴ 9⁷· ⁸ 13¹ 14⁶ 15¹² 19²⁵· ²⁹ 20¹ 21¹¹· ²⁴ 22¹⁰ 24⁹ : only besides Isa. 29²⁰, Ps. 1¹), פתי the *simple* (1⁴· ²²· ³² 7⁷ 8⁵ 9⁴· ⁶· ¹⁶ 14¹⁵· ¹⁸ 19²⁵ 21¹¹ 22³ 27¹² : elsewhere only Ez. 45²⁰, Ps. 19⁸ 116⁶ 119¹³⁰), the *void of heart* (i.e. *of understanding*), 6³² 7⁷ 9⁴· ¹⁶ 10¹³· ⁽²¹⁾ 11¹² 12¹¹ 15²¹ 17¹⁸ 24³⁰ (not elsewhere), the *sluggard* (14 times : not elsewhere), the *poor* (רש, ראש, not the usual word : 15 times), and *poverty* (ריש, ראש), 7 times (not elsewhere).

It is evident that there was a tendency to cast proverbs into particular types, and that when a given predicate had once been formulated, fresh proverbs readily arose by new subjects being [381] attached to it. Another way by which new proverbs were produced was by clauses being differently fitted together : this is illustrated by the occurrence of proverbs partially varied, of which the chief examples have been quoted in the account given above of the different collections in the Book.*

Age and authorship of the Book.—From the very different character of the various collections of which the Book is com-posed, it is apparent that the Book must have been formed gradually. According to the common opinion, the oldest col-lection is 10¹–22¹⁶.† At what date this collection was formed,

* Comp. 12¹¹ and 28¹⁹ ; 11¹⁴ 20¹⁸ and 24⁶ ; 10¹⁵ and 18¹¹.

† It is, not, however, certain that this opinion is correct. Prof. Davidson (in the *Encycl. Brit.*) adduces strong reasons tending to show that the oldest proverbs are those preserved in c. 25–29, especially c. 25–27. He remarks that the highly finished, regular form of the proverbs in c. 10 ff. is not such as to suggest a great antiquity, but rather an advanced stage of literary culture, and long use of the arts of the proverbialist : the proverbs in c. 25–27, on the other hand, while less regular in form, are more nearly what

cannot be determined with precision; but from the general picture of society which the proverbs seem to reflect, and especially from the manner in which the king is uniformly alluded to, it is generally referred to the golden days of the monarchy : Delitzsch thinks of the reign of Jehoshaphat; Ewald assigns it to the beginning of the 8th century. Of the other parts of the book, the first to be added were probably the introduction, 1^{1-6}, with the discourse that follows, 1^7–c. 9, and 22^{17}–24^{22}. The aim of the writer of c. 1–9 (as we have seen) [382] was to provide c. 10–22^{16} with a hortatory introduction : he was thus in any case the " editor " of this collection, and (if Prof. Davidson's view be correct) may have been its compiler as well. As regards the date of c. 1–9, Ewald, Davidson, Nowack, Cheyne (p. 168) agree in placing it shortly before the exile.* 22^{17}–24^{22} is not probably by the same author as c. 1–9 : for though a hortatory strain prevails in both, the style and manner are in many respects different: 22^{17-21}, for instance, does not

we should imagine the early popular proverb to be, as they are also in many instances more epigrammatic and forcible than those in c. 10 ff., and include most of those which have obtained currency among ourselves ($25^{20.\ 22.\ 25.\ 26.\ 28}$ $26^{2.\ 3.\ 11.\ 28}$ $27^{17.\ 19.\ 22}$). The title " These *also*," &c. (25^1) shows that when c. 25–29 was introduced into the book, it was preceded by another Solomonic collection, but not that such a collection existed when c. 25–29 was first compiled by the " men of Hezekiah." Individual proverbs in 10^1–22^{16} may be old, though the collection itself may be late (though not later than c. 600 B.C.). Other recent scholars have gone further, and arguing (chiefly) from the theology of c. 10-22^{16}, which seems to presuppose, and to have assimilated, the higher teaching of the prophets, and from the absence of all warnings against idolatry—so prominent in the pre-exilic literature—have supposed this collection to date (in the main) from the post-exilic period. So Kuen.², who, while not denying that particular proverbs are pre-exilic (§ 97. 19), holds that the collections of which the Book consists were all compiled after the exile (§ 97. 14-18), the Book as a whole being completed in its present form c. B.C. 350-300 (§ 97. 20). The arguments both for and against this view are stated with moderation in an interesting and suggestive paper by C. G. Montefiore, " Notes upon the Date and Religious Value of the Proverbs," in the *Jewish Quart. Rev.* July 1890, p. 430 ff.

* Now, however, Prof. Cheyne treats it as post-exilic (*Founders of OT. Crit.* p. 340) : so Kuenen² (§ 97. 21). Frankenberg (*ZATW.* 1895, p. 104 ff.), developing the view of Stade (*G.* ii. 216), and O. Holtzmann (*ib.* p. 296 f.), combated by Kuen.² (§ 97. 20), that Pr. 1-9 is a product of the Greek age, argues, chiefly on ground of the resemblances in the religious ideas, and social conditions presupposed, to the proverbs of Ben Sira (Ecclesiasticus), that it springs from substantially the same period, c. B.C. 200.

produce the impression of being by the same hand as 1^{1-6}.*
The injunction 24^{21}, "My son, fear thou the LORD and *the king*,"
authorises the inference that this collection also was formed
before the exile. 24^{23-34}, the appendix to $22^{17}-24^{22}$ was no
doubt added somewhat later: for the compiler of $22^{17\text{ff.}}$, had
these additional "words of the wise" come to his hand, would
probably have included them in his collection in preference to
appending them to it with a new title. C. 25–29 must have
been added *after* 22^{17}–c. 24 had been attached to c. $10-22^{16}$:
otherwise, it is natural to suppose, the supplementary "Proverbs
of Solomon" would have been made to follow the principal
collection $10^{1}-22^{16}$ immediately, instead of being placed after
the "words of the wise," 22^{17}–c. 24. It is thought by some,
on account of the similarity of the headings 24^{23} and 25^{1}
("*These also* are" . . .), that both appendices were added by
the same hand, the short passage 24^{23-34} being arranged in
juxtaposition with the other "words of the wise," and c. 25–29,
with the more formal title, pointing back to 10^{1}, being placed
after it. By the addition, at a still later date, of c. 30, 31^{1-9}
31^{10-21}, all doubtless of post-exilic origin, the Book of Proverbs
finally reached its present form.

What share in the Book, now, may reasonably be assigned
to Solomon? 22^{17}–c. 24, and c. 30–31 are not, by their titles
or otherwise, brought into any connexion with Solomon: the
question therefore need only be considered with reference to
c. 1–9, c. $10-22^{16}$, and c. 25–29. 1^{1} is not the title to the
Book, but consists of the opening words of a sentence (v.$^{1-6}$)
declaring the *value* of the "Proverbs of Solomon," and [383]
evidently (as "proverbs," properly so called, are to be found
only here and there in 1^{7}–c. 9) pointing forwards to the
collection which begins with 10^{1}. The introduction, c. 1–9,
is not therefore stated to be Solomon's; and, in fact, both its
style and contents point to a date considerably later, as that at
which it was composed. But even $10^{1}-22^{16}$ cannot, at least in
its entirety, be Solomon's work. Not only is the same proverb,
or part of a proverb, often repeated, and the same predicate

---

* Observe the contrast between the 3rd pers. in 1^{1-7} and the emphatic
2nd pers. in 22^{17-21}. There are also many favourite expressions used by the
author of c. 1–9 (*e.g.* תורה *teaching* or *law*) which do not occur in $22^{17\text{ff.}}$. See
Ewald, p. 53. Kuenen¹ (p. 105) and Nowack (p. xxxv) agree.

applied to many different subjects (above, p. 397), but there are also many other cases in which the same *thought* recurs, expressed in different words : it is not probable, however, that one and the same author would have adopted methods such as these for the formation of new proverbs, or have propounded a number of independent variations of the same theme. It is far more probable that in such cases we have before us the work of different wise men casting fresh generalisations into an old mould, or recording in slightly different phraseology the same observations of life and manners which another had made before them. Secondly, it is difficult not to feel that many of the proverbs are unsuitable to Solomon's character and position. The proverbs concerning the king seem rather to express the sentiments of the people than the reflexions of a king about either himself or other kings. The proverbs which speak in depreciation of wealth, or which praise monogamy, do not fall naturally from Solomon's lips : consider, for instance, 13^1 15^{16} 18^{22} $19^{13.\ 14}$ 21^{31} 22^{14} in the light of Solomon's character, as depicted in 1 Kings. The most probable view is that $10^{1ff.}$ consists of a collection of proverbs by different "wise men" living under the monarchy, including a nucleus, though we cannot determine its limits or ascribe particular proverbs to it, actually the work of the Wise King * (in accordance with the tradition, 1 Ki. 4^{32}). The proverbs in $10^{1ff.}$ exhibit great uniformity of type ; perhaps this type was set by Solomon, and was afterwards adopted naturally by others. *Mutatis mutandis*, the same remarks will apply to c. 25–29. The title (25^1), the accuracy of which there is no reason to question, is an indication that the proverbs which follow were reputed in Hezekiah's age to be ancient : it cannot be taken as a guarantee that all, or even a majority, were the work of Solomon himself.†

* So Ewald (p. 14) and Nowack.

† The Proverbs of Jesus the son of Sirach (Ecclesiasticus), written *c.* 200 B.C., deserve to be compared with the Book of Proverbs : cf. Cheyne, *Job and Solomon*, p. 179 ff.; Montefiore, *Jewish Quart. Rev.* 1890, p. 449 ff.

CHAPTER IX.

THE BOOK OF JOB.

LITERATURE.—H. Ewald in the *Dichter des AB.s,*[2] 1854 (translated); K. Schlottmann, *Das B. Hiob,* 1851; F. Delitzsch, 1864, [2]1876 [only the *first* ed. is translated]; A. Dillmann (in the *Kgf. Exeg. Handb.*), 1869, [2]1891; A. Merx, *Das Gedicht von Hiob,* 1871 (alters the text not always wisely); W. H. Green, *The Argument of the Book of Job unfolded* (New York, 1873); F. Hitzig, *Das B. Hiob,* 1875; E. W. Hengstenberg, *Das B. Hiob,* 1875; C. Budde, *Beiträge zur Kritik des B. Hiob,* 1876 (I. Die neuere Kritik u. die Idee des B. Hiob; II. Der Sprachliche Charakter der Elihu-Reden); S. Cox, *A Comm. on the Book of Job,* 1880; A. B. Davidson, in the *Camb. Bible for Schools,* 1884 (to be recommended), and in the *Encycl. Brit.*[9] *s.v.*; T. K. Cheyne, *Job and Solomon,* 1887, pp. 11–115; G. G. Bradley [Dean of Westminster], *Lectures on the Book of Job,*[2] 1888 [explanatory paraphrase]; C. Siegfried (in Haupt's *SBOT.*), 1893; Kuenen, *Onderz.*[2] iii. 1 (1893), pp. 105–167; G. Bickell, above, p. 362 *n.,* and *Das Buch Job nach Anleitung der Strophik und der LXX auf seine urspr. Form zurückgeführt, u. im Versmasse des Urtextes übersetzt,* 1894; G. Beer, *Der Text des B. Hiob,* part i. (c. 1–14), 1895; K. Budde (in Nowack's "Handkomm."), 1896, with Cheyne's critiques, *Expositor,* June and July, 1897, *JQR.* July 1897; also J. B. Mozley in *Essays Hist. and Theol.* 1878, ii. p. 164 ff.; J. A. Froude in *Short Studies on Great Subjects* (series 1, 1867), p. 266 ff.; A. M. Fairbairn, "The Problem of Job" in *The City of God,* 1886, p. 143 ff. See further Delitzsch,[2] p. 35 ff.; Cheyne, pp. 112–115; Dillm.[2] p. xxxix f.; Budde, *Komm.* p. lvi. On the LXX text of Job, G. Bickell, *De Indole Vers. Alex. Jobi,* 1863; and in the *Z. für Kath. theol.* (Innsbruck), 1886, p. 557 ff.; E. Hatch in *Essays in Biblical Greek,* 1889; A. Dillmann, "Textkritisches zum B. Ijob," in the *Sitzungsberichte* of the Berlin Acad. 1890, p. 1345 ff. [an elaborate criticism of Dr. Hatch's Essay]; G. Beer, "Textkritische Studien zum B. Job," *ZATW.* 1896, p. 297 ff., 1897, p. 97 ff. (specially on the additions and omissions in Jerome's transl. of the LXX).

The Book of Job recounts how the patriarch whose name it bears, a man of exemplary piety, was overtaken by an unprecedented series of calamities, and reports the debate between Job and other speakers, to which the occasion is supposed to have given rise.

The Book consists of five parts :—

1. The Prologue (c. 1–2), written in prose.
2. The Colloquies between Job and his three friends, Eliphaz, Bildad, and Zophar, written in poetry (c. 3–31).
3. The discourses of Elihu (c. 32–37), likewise poetical, except the introductory verses, 32$^{1-6}$.
4. Jehovah's reply to Job (38^1–42^6), also poetical.
5. The Epilogue, recounting Job's subsequent fortunes, in prose (42$^{7-17}$).

[385] The Book of Job is a product of the Wisdom-literature (p. 392 f.) : it deals with a problem of human life ; in modern phraseology it is a work of *religious philosophy.* The problem with which it deals is this : *Why do the righteous suffer?* and its principal aim is to controvert the theory, dominant at the time when it was written, *that suffering is a sign of the Divine displeasure, and presupposes sin on the part of the sufferer.* The doctrine that righteousness brings prosperity, while wickedness is the forerunner of misfortune, is often taught in the OT. : with regard to the nation, for instance, it is inculcated in the exhortations Ex. 23$^{20ff.}$, Dt. 28, Lev. 26 ; applied to individuals, it is the principle repeatedly insisted on in the Book of Proverbs.* Of course, in a large measure, this doctrine is true. Society being organised as it is, the habits which go to constitute righteousness are such as to win a man respect from his fellow-men, and to command success ; on the other hand, wickedness paralyses the moral energies, blinds an individual and a nation alike to the real conditions upon which prosperity depends, and often overreaches itself. The doctrine was deeply impressed on the ancient Hebrew mind ; and all exceptions were a source of great perplexity to it. The perplexity was the greater, because the Hebrews had an imperfect conception of *general laws,* whether in nature or in society : they were keenly sensible of God's omnipresence, and pictured Him as interposing actively in the course of the world : hence virtue overtaken by calamity, or vice flourishing unrebuked, seemed to them to cast a direct slur upon the justice of God's government of the world. But the laws governing nature and the constitution of society being *general* ones, it may happen that in individual cases their operation does not redound to the advantage of virtue or the punishment of sin : the forces of nature may combine to overwhelm the innocent ;

* Comp. Jer. 7$^{5-7}$ 17$^{5-8.\ 19-27}$, Isa. 58$^{7ff.\ 13f.}$, Ps. 1, &c.

men, in virtue of the society in which they live, being variously bound together, the innocent may suffer through the ill-deeds of the guilty; or wickedness may elude detection, and triumph unchecked. The problem is touched on in Jer. 12[1f.] 31[29f.], Ez. 18 (see p. 284), Hab. 1[13f.], Ps. 37, 49, 73. One solution which the Hebrew thinker found was that the prosperity of the wicked was shortlived, that it met with a sudden and ignominious fall (Ps. 37[20f. 36] 73[18-20]); while the righteous in [386] the end inherited the land (Ps. 37), or was conscious that he owned a higher and inalienable spiritual possession (Ps. 49, 73). In the case of the sufferings of the righteous, there was a tendency to invert the argument, and to conclude that *because* sin was followed by suffering, *therefore* suffering was necessarily a consequence of antecedent sin. That this conclusion is illogical, is, of course, obvious. Nevertheless, it was a conclusion that was widely drawn; it prevailed even to the days of Christ (Luke 13[1-5]; John 9[2]). And it was the conclusion which Job's friends drew. Job's sufferings, they argue, convict him implicitly of some grave antecedent sin, which they urge him to acknowledge and repent of. This conclusion Job controverts. He steadily refuses to admit that he is guilty of any sin adequate to account for his extraordinary sufferings.* And when his friends appeal to the evidences of God's retributive justice visible in the world, he retorts by pointing to the numerous instances which experience affords of the wicked prospering even to the day of their death.

The main aim of the Book is thus a negative one, to controvert the dominant theory that *all suffering proceeds from sin*: God's retributive justice is not the *only* principle by which men are governed. Positively the book teaches—1. (the dialogue being interpreted in the light of the prologue) that sufferings may befall the righteous, not as a chastisement for their sins, but as a trial of their righteousness, and that as such they have a tendency to strengthen and establish their faith. Eliphaz, also (5[17ff.]), and particularly Elihu (33[15-30]; 36[8-25]), insist, in addition, upon the *disciplinary* value of suffering. 2. The Book teaches the danger of conceiving too narrowly of God and His providence: by conceiving of Him *solely* as a dispenser of rewards and punishments,

---

* Job does not claim actual *sinlessness*: he only contends that he is punished out of all proportion to the magnitude of his sin (7[21] 13[26] 14[16f.]).

the friends charge Job unjustly with grave sin; and Job, conscious of his innocence, imputes injustice to God, and is tempted to cast off his fear of Him altogether.   3. Inasmuch as Job, in spite of his combined physical and mental suffering, does not succumb to this temptation, it teaches, in opposition to the insinuation of the Satan (1^9), that man is capable of real and disinterested goodness, and can love God for His own sake.   4. It teaches (c. 38-42) that the true solution of *moral* perplexities is to be found in a fuller and larger sense of God, in a conception of Him as the author of a vast and infinitely complex system of nature, in which it is unreasonable for the individual [387] to conceive of himself as isolated from the care of Providence, or to infer that his sufferings have no place in God's purpose. 5. It has also, probably, a *practical* aim, that of helping the author's contemporaries, who appear to have been in circumstances of national depression, to understand the situation in which they were placed, and of encouraging them to hope for a favourable issue (Davidson, p. xxvi).   In other words, Job is a type of the suffering godly Israelite.

In structure, the Book of Job is of the nature of a drama, and may be termed a dramatic poem.   Its principal parts are constructed in the form of a dialogue; and the action which it represents passes through the successive stages of entanglement, development, and solution.   The action is, however, for the most part internal and mental, the successive scenes exhibiting "the varying moods of a great soul struggling with the mysteries of fate, rather than trying external situations."

The Book cannot be supposed to recite a literal history.   This appears partly from the symbolical numbers, three, five, and seven, used to describe Job's flocks and children, and from the fact that after his restoration the latter are exactly the same in number as before, while the former are exactly doubled; partly from the ideal and dramatic character of his misfortunes, nature and man alternating in their endeavour to ruin him, and one only escaping each time to bring the tidings; but especially from the character of the dialogue, which contains far too much thought and argument to have been extemporised on the occasion, and is manifestly the studied product of the author's leisurely reflexion.

It is not, however, probable that the Book is throughout a work of the imagination: for in Ezek. 14^{14}, Job is alluded to in terms which seem to imply that he was a real person, whose piety was well known to Ezek.'s contemporaries by tradition.

And as the author of the Book comes forward clearly as a *teacher*, the ends which he had in view would be better secured if he set vividly before his people a history of which the outlines were popularly known, than if he took as his hero one with whose name they were unfamiliar. To determine precisely what elements in the Book belong to tradition, is, of course, no longer possible. But probably tradition told at least as much as that Job, a man of exceptional piety, was overtaken by unparalleled misfortunes, that he broke out into complaints against God's providence, and refused to be satisfied or calmed by the arguments of his friends, but that he never absolutely [388] discarded his faith in God, and was finally restored to his former prosperity. This history is made by the author of the Book the vehicle for expounding his new thoughts on the religious and ethical significance of suffering.

1. The Prologue (c. 1–2) acquaints us with the person of Job, and the occasion of the calamities which befell him. Job was a man of exemplary goodness, a non-Israelite, whose home was in the land of Uz : * Heaven's testimony to his piety might seem to be seen in the prosperity which attended him, and his great possessions. In the celestial Council, however (cf. 1 Ki. 22[19]), the disinterestedness of his virtue is called in question by "the Satan," or Adversary,† the angel whose office it is to test the sincerity of men, and oppose them in their pretensions to a right standing before God : it is insinuated that it is dependent upon the blessings lavished upon him by God; if these were withdrawn, he would disown God to His face. The Satan receives permission to test Job's piety as severely as may be, without touching his person ; and one after another his flocks, his servants, and his children are destroyed. But Job's piety stands the trial ; he is deeply moved, but receives his misfortunes with submission (c. 1).

A second time the celestial Council is held, and again the Satan is present : dissatisfied with the test which has been applied

---

* Probably near Edom, on the E. or N.E. : see Gen. 36[28], Lam. 4[21]. Teman, the home of Eliphaz, was a district of Edom (Ob. v.[8], Ez. 25[13] ; cf. Gen. 36[15]).

† See Zech. 3[1f.] and (without the article) 1 Ch. 21[1]. The idea conveyed by the word may be learnt from 1 Sa. 29[4], 2 Sa. 19[22] [H. [23]], 1 Ki. 11[14. 23. 25]. See more fully Prof. Davidson's note.

to Job, he receives permission to try the patriarch again. Forthwith Job is smitten with sore boils, the severe and loathsome form of leprosy called Elephantiasis. In spite of the miserable condition to which he is reduced, his piety still stands fast : he even repels, with some emphasis, the seductive counsel of his wife to "renounce God and die" (2^{1-10}). After an interval, as it seems (7^3; cf. $19^{13ff.}$), of some months, his three friends, having heard of his troubles, come to condole with him. Appalled at the spectacle of his misery, they sit with him mourning upon the ground, for seven days, without uttering a word (2^{11-13}). Moved by their deep unspoken sympathy, his feelings gather strength, and at length break forth in a passionate cry for death (c. 3).

[389] 2. (c. 3–31). Job's cry passes through three phases. In the first, 3^{3-10}, he curses bitterly the day of his birth, wishing himself unborn; in the second, 3^{11-19}, he asks why, if he must needs be born, did he not pass at once to the grave? in the third, 3^{20-26}, he expresses his mournful surprise that life should be prolonged to those who, in their misery, long only for death.

This outburst of feeling on Job's part gives occasion to his friends to speak, and so opens the debate. Job's language and demeanour shock them : he betrays impatience, and a sense of resentment at God's providence, which they cannot but reprobate. Eliphaz speaks first, the oldest (cf. 15^{10}), and also the most courteous and conciliatory of Job's friends.

First cycle of speeches (c. 4–14).

Eliphaz (c. 4–5). Eliphaz commences apologetically : he is surprised that one who had so often consoled others should, in his own trouble, thus yield to despair, forgetting that the righteous never perishes under affliction, 4^{1-11}. No man is so perfect in God's eyes as to be able to claim exemption from suffering; it is only the ungodly who resent the dispensations of Providence, $4^{12}-5^7$. Let Job remember that *goodness* is God's uniform principle of action; let him submissively regard his affliction as a chastening, and he may yet look forward to abundant blessings in the future, 5^{8-27}. The argument of Eliphaz is constructed with great delicacy and tact, and his speech "is one of the masterpieces of the book" (Davidson).

Job (c. 6–7). Eliphaz's words, however well-meant, do not meet Job's case. Job feels that his sufferings are of too exceptional a character to be deduced from the *general* imperfection of human nature; and of any special guilt, calculated to draw down upon him the Divine displeasure, he is unconscious. In his reply he first defends himself against his friend's remonstrances: little does Eliphaz realize (5^2) the force of his "vexation" (6^2), if he imagines him to be complaining without cause; his pains are intolerable, $6^{2\text{-}13}$. Next, $6^{14\text{-}30}$, he expresses his disappointment at the line adopted towards him by his friends, and demands (6^{24}) to be told what his sin is: thirdly, c. 7, he breaks out into a renewed cry of desperation at the thought of his sorrowful destiny; human life, his own especially, is short and evil; why does God "set a watch over him," as though he were a dangerous monster that needed to be subdued with [390] tortures? why ($7^{17f.}$)—with a bitter parody on the words of a well-known Psalm (Ps. 8^5)—does God occupy Himself with a being so insignificant as man, and make him the object of His unfriendly regard?

Bildad (c. 8). Job, in 6^{29}, had implied that he had right on his side as against God, and (c. 7) had further charged God with holding man generally enthralled in a cruel bondage. Bildad attacks these points, arguing in particular the *discrimination* of the Divine justice, and supporting his teaching by an appeal to the immemorial experience of the race. God cannot, as Job strangely imagines, be unjust; if Job's children have perished, it is because they have sinned; if Job himself is pure, let him turn to God, and seek mercy from Him, $8^{2\text{-}7}$. The experience of generations teaches that a sure retribution awaits the wicked, $8^{8\text{-}19}$; if thou art righteous, know that God will yet again cause thee to behold prosperity, $8^{20\text{-}22}$.

Job (c. 9–10). Ironically, in reply, Job concedes the premises of his friends: of course, no man can be just before God (4^{17}); for God, as all nature witnesses, is mighty—*so* mighty, indeed, that He is irresponsible, and no one, however innocent, could plead successfully before Him, $9^{1\text{-}21}$. So far from His justice being discriminating, He destroys the innocent and the guilty alike (9^{22}, in direct contradiction to 8^{20}); universal *in*justice prevails upon the earth, and God is its author! $9^{23f.}$. In a calmer strain, Job next laments the pitiful brevity of his life, and the hopelessness of every attempt, so long as his afflictions continue, to clear himself before God, $9^{25\text{-}35}$. In c. 10 he exerts himself to discover what secret purpose God may have had ın afflicting him : he offers different suggestions, each, of course, only to be rejected, 10$^{1-7}$. What a contrast is God's treatment of him now with the providential skill and care lavished upon him in the past! 10$^{8-12}$. And the desperate thought rises to his lips that this had been God's design with him from the first, and that He had bestowed upon him the apparent tokens of His favour only that in the end He might vex him with cruel torments, 10$^{13-17}$. If this was God's purpose with him, why did He give him life at all? at least, will He not have mercy on him now, and grant him a brief respite from his pain, before he passes for ever into the impenetrable blackness of Sheol? 10$^{18-22}$.

[391] Job, as well as his friends, believes sufferings to be a mark of God's displeasure for some grave sin. Job, however, is conscious that he has *not* so sinned ; hence the terrible dilemma in which he finds himself, and which forces him to the conclusion that God, though He *knows* him to be innocent (10^{7}), is determined to treat him as guilty, and that it is hopeless for him to attempt to clear himself. Hence the charge of injustice which he brings against God, and which, goaded on by what, in his present frame of mind, he feels to be the falsity of Bildad's position, 8^{20}, he formulates, 9$^{20-22}$, so as to make it embrace, not himself alone, but mankind generally. This is how it comes that in c. 9–10 he appears overwhelmed by the thought, not of a beneficent God, but of a cruel non-moral Force, ruling despotically in the world. At the same time, as 10$^{8-12}$ shows, his faith in God as a gracious, benevolent Being does not forsake him, and the two aspects of God's nature are, for the time, balanced one against another in his mind.

Zophar (c. 11). Job, in c. 9–10, had asserted more emphatically than before his innocence ; and this is the point to which Zophar addresses himself. He begins in a sharper, more impetuous tone than Eliphaz or Bildad had done. Job's flow of words must be stopped : if only God would speak, as Job had desired (9^{35}), it would quickly appear where the truth lay, 11$^{2-6}$. God's all-penetrating eye sees further than Job can comprehend ; it detects sin where man is unconscious of it, 11$^{7-12}$. Let Job put evil from him, and spread out his hands to God, and once more he shall enjoy the light of brighter days, 11$^{13-19}$. But a very different future awaits the impenitent, v.^{20}.

Job (c. 12–14). Zophar had appealed against the verdict of Job's conscience to the omniscience of God, and had alluded to Job's wisdom in terms of strong depreciation (11^{12}). Job keenly resents this assumption of insight into God's ways, 12$^{1-6}$; he points out that it is of a very ordinary character, 12$^{7-10}$; and proceeds to rival Zophar by showing, 12$^{11-25}$, that he has a wider knowledge of God's omnipotence than Zophar of His omniscience. Zophar had said, $11^{10f.}$, that God's action was directed by a moral purpose: Job draws a picture of great social and national catastrophes, which illustrate (so he implies) God's absoluteness rather than His moral discrimination. The method by which his friends seek to condemn him is indefensible: *in maiorem Dei gloriam*, as they imagine, they even dare to distort the truth, 13^{1-12}. But his own conscience gives him courage; and he bids them listen while he pleads his case with God, 13^{13-22}. His tone is calmer than in $7^{11ff.}$ or $10^{1ff.}$: an appeal for forbearance takes the place of his [392] former irony and defiance. Will God persecute a creature so shattered as he is, so imperfect and shortlived as is every child of man? Does the sadness of human life and the hopelessness of its close awaken in Him no pity? 13^{23}–14^{12}. Would only, he passionately exclaims, that the prospect of its close were different! Would only that *another life*, however long delayed, were possible for man! 14^{13-15} (RV.). And the blissful possibility entrances him; but the hope is too remote a one to be seriously entertained, and it dies away almost before it is distinctly expressed upon his lips, 14^{16-22}.

The friends have all failed to convince Job by dwelling upon the nature or attributes of God. Eliphaz's appeal to His universal goodness, Bildad's to His discriminating justice, Zophar's to His omniscient insight, have equally failed to dislodge Job from his position: he still maintains that his afflictions are unmerited. Accordingly the friends adopt now a different line. They turn from the nature of *God* to His government of *men*, drawing more distinctly than before (5^{3-5} 8^{22} 11^{20}) pictures of the vexations which, as experience shows, befall the sinner, in the hope thereby of awakening Job's conscience, and inducing him to see himself reflected in the mirror thus held up before him. Job, on the other hand, becomes more conscious of his isolation. Hitherto the alienation of God has been the burden of his complaint; now he is more keenly sensible of the alienation of men, to which, in his speeches in the second cycle, he often pathetically refers. God and man are both ranged against him. The only support which remains to him is his own sense of innocence, and to this he clings all the more tenaciously.

Second cycle of speeches (c. 15–21).

As before, Eliphaz (c. 15) opens the debate. He begins more severely than in c. 5 : Job's principles and conduct seem to him to cut at the root of all religion (v.⁴) ; he is displeased also at Job's assumption of superior wisdom, and at his rejection of the consolatory views of God's providence suggested by himself (v.¹¹, with reference to 5⁸ᶠᶠ. ¹⁷ᶠᶠ.). After repeating briefly, 15¹⁴⁻¹⁶, what he had urged before (cf. 4¹⁷ᶠ.), he proceeds to meet Job's contention (9²³ᶠ. 12⁶), that wickedness rules unchecked in the world, by pointing to the retribution which overtakes the sinner, —in particular, to the troubled conscience and presentiments of evil which haunt him during life, 15²⁰⁻²⁴, and to his **[393]** calamitous end, 15³⁰ᶠᶠ.. The picture of the evil conscience is drawn here with great force, and is without a parallel in the OT. (cf., however, Isa. 57²⁰).

Job (c. 16–17). After a few words of contempt for the empty solace of his friends, 16²⁻⁵, Job proceeds to draw a graphic but pitiable picture of the condition to which, in spite of the innocence of his life, he now finds himself reduced—God, his unrelenting adversary ; man, his too eager foe, 16⁶⁻¹⁷. Death is approaching with rapid steps,—death, which to Job means the reprobation of God, and the reproach and obloquy of men. Nevertheless, the conviction is strong within him that he has still a Witness in heaven, a witness to whom he accordingly appeals to uphold—at least after death—his right, and to grant him even now (17³) a pledge that in the end He will cause his innocence to appear, 16¹⁸–17⁹ (v.⁹ in direct contradiction to 15⁴). He ends, 17¹⁰⁻¹⁶, with repudiating as folly the counsel of his friends (8²⁰ᶠᶠ. 11¹³ᶠᶠ.), to hope for restoration in the present life.

Bildad (c. 18). Job's piteous expression of his mental con- flict wins no sympathy from Bildad ; rather, he shows himself (18²⁻⁴) deeply vexed by the hard terms which Job had applied to his friends (16². ²⁰ 17². ⁴. ¹⁰), and by his impious words respecting God (16⁹,—which 18⁴ is intended directly to meet). This is followed, as an answer to Job's protestation of innocence (16¹⁸), by a picture, more elaborated and pointed than the one drawn by Eliphaz (15²⁰ᶠᶠ.), of the misery in life, and the dishonour after death, which are the certain lot of the sinner, 18⁵⁻²¹. The figures used by Bildad are drawn largely from the commonplaces of moralists and prophets (*e.g.* 18[5a], see Pr. 13[9] 24[20]; v.[7a], opp. to Pr. 4[12]), though in several instances they seem to be selected with the view of suggesting the circumstances of Job himself; and no doubt it is Bildad's desire that Job should so apply them.

Job (c. 19). This application, however, Job disowns. Nevertheless, he is acutely pained by his friends' cruel insinuations, 19[2-6]; and he breaks out into a yet more agonized and pathetic description than he had given before of his sufferings,—assailed remorselessly by God, abandoned by his acquaintances, an object of aversion to his closest relations,—ending with a moving appeal to his friends to show him pity, 19[7-22]. But [394] from his friends he can expect nothing; and so with the wish that the protestation of his innocence might be inscribed in imperishable letters upon the rock, there passes from his lips the sublime utterance of his faith, his conviction that his Vindicator liveth, and that even though his human frame succumb to his disease, He will reveal Himself to him after death, and manifest his right, 19[23-27].

On 19[23ff.] see esp. Davidson, pp. 291–296. The stages in Job's brightening faith should be noticed. 7[12ff.] 9[15ff.] his attitude towards God is defiant: 10[8-12] he has the thought of a beneficent God, but it is immediately obscured under the frightful suggestion of 10[13-17]: 14[13-15] the vision of a reconciliation of God in a future life dawns momentarily upon him: 16[18f. 20f.] 17[3] his conviction that God in His real, inmost nature will ultimately own his innocence breaks forth: 19[25-27] the same conviction, combined with the thought that he will then himself *see* God, is expressed still more strongly. The thought of a future beatific life is *nascent* in the Book of Job; it is expressed, not as a generally accepted doctrine, but first as an aspiration, afterwards as a moral persuasion or conviction on the part of Job personally. Had it been a *dogma* at the time when the Book was written, it must have formed one of the premises of the argument, which is not the case. The term "redeemer," it will be noticed, is used here in a sense the very opposite of the Christian application, to denote, viz. a deliverer, not from sin, but from affliction and wrong *not* due to sin (RV. *marg.* vindicator).*

Zophar (c. 20). Zophar, like Bildad, is unmoved by Job's appeal; he had spoken before (c. 11) somewhat impetuously;

---

* גאל is *to assert* (by purchase) *a right*, Lev. 25[29ff.] 27[13. 15]; hence fig. *to reclaim, rescue*, esp. from servitude, oppression, &c. Ex. 15[13], Ps. 72[14], freq. in II Isaiah, as 41[14] 43[1] 44[23]: here, from unjust and cruel imputations. And so גאל הדם is the vindicator of the rights destroyed by bloodshed = the avenger of blood.

and now he declares that his spirit is roused by Job's perverse blindness to the teachings of experience (v.[4]). The general aim of his speech is similar to that of Eliphaz (c. 15), and of Bildad (c. 18), but he takes a different point for illustration. Emphasizing the *brevity* of the wicked man's prosperity, and the *dissatisfaction* which it brings him, Zophar draws the picture of a man of substance, whose riches, amassed by injustice, turn to wormwood within him, who is overtaken by sudden destruction in the midst of his days, and whose greed is satisfied at last with the fire of God's judgments.

Job (c. 21). Thrice have the friends sought to arouse Job's conscience by pointing to the retribution which in one shape or [395] another inevitably awaits the ungodly. Twice (c. 16 f. ; c. 19) Job has contented himself with reasserting his own innocence : he has made no attempt to controvert the principle of his friends' teaching. The third time he is impelled to do this, and in c. 21 he meets Zophar's closing words (20[29]) with a direct contradiction. The doubt is a terrible one ; as he says (v.[5f.]), it makes him tremble when he thinks of it. He arraigns, in its entirety, the justice of God's rule of the world (cf. 9[22-24]). The wicked prosper and die in peace ; they do *not*, as the friends maintain, meet with sudden and ignominious deaths, 21[2-26] ; the friends, in asserting that they do, deliberately pervert the truth, 21[27-34] (v.[30. 32f.] as RV. *marg.*).

Third cycle of speeches (c. 22–28).

All the means adopted hitherto by the friends to dislodge Job from his position have proved ineffectual, and they are reduced a second time (see p. 416) to alter their line of attack. Accordingly they now charge Job explicitly with the great sins which before they had only hinted at or imputed to him indirectly. This charge is laid against Job by Eliphaz (c. 22). Job had implied that God's dealings with men were dictated by arbitrary motives : Eliphaz answers that God deals with men according to their ways ; and as it is inconceivable that He should punish Job for his piety, the cause of his afflictions must lie in his sins, 22[2-5]. These sins Eliphaz does not scruple to enumerate,—they are chiefly those of inhumanity, avarice, and abuse of power, most commonly associated in the East with wealth and influence, all being, of course, merely *inferred* by him, on theoretical grounds, from the fact of Job's calamities, 22[6-20] (see the detailed reply to this charge in c. 31). In conclusion, he exhorts Job, in tones which show that he still (see 5[17ff.]) cherishes feelings of affection towards him, to reconcile himself with God, assuring him, if he will do so, of his restoration to both spiritual and material prosperity.

Job (c. 23–24). Job makes no direct reply to the imputations of Eliphaz; he is still absorbed in the painful thought of the mystery of God's providence, which had formed the theme of c. 21. The marks of a righteous providence he can discern, he says, neither in God's dealings with himself (c. 23), nor in His dealings with mankind generally (c. 24). Did he, indeed, *know* where he could find God, and gain a hearing from Him, he is [396] confident that he could establish his innocence before Him, 23[1-7]. But God, though He knows His servant's innocence, has withdrawn Himself from him, 23[8-12]; nor will He rescind the strange, inscrutable decree which He has passed against him, 23[13-17]. "Why," he exclaims, "are times" of retribution "not reserved by the Almighty" for the guilty? Why is the world abandoned to violence and wrong? And he illustrates by many examples the oppressions which reign unavenged even in the unsophisticated life of the country, and the crimes that prevail unchecked in the populous city, 24[1-17]. In vain do his friends repeat that the prosperity of the godless is but for a moment, 24[18-21]: experience shows that God only too often supports the oppressor through life, and brings him to a natural and painless death, 24[22-25].

Bildad (c. 25) makes no attempt to reply to the facts adduced in such abundance by Job; and his short speech is, in truth, an indication that the friends have exhausted their arguments. But he cannot avoid protesting against Job's presumption in imagining that he would be declared innocent at God's tribunal (23[3-7]), and in indicting the justice with which the world is administered. Accordingly, in words borrowed partly from Eliphaz (4[17] 15[14f.]), he restates the two main principles which have throughout underlain the arguments of the friends, viz. the majesty of God, and the imperfection in His eyes of all things human.

Job (c. 26). After a sarcastic allusion to the vain comfort afforded by Bildad's last speech, Job proceeds to meet Bildad's *first* contention (25[2f.]), by demonstrating that, if the explanation of his troubles is to be sought in a knowledge of God's greatness, he possesses that not less than he does (cf. 9^{4-13} 12^{13-25}). And he forthwith draws a picture, far more imposing than Bildad's, of the greatness of God as manifested in nature, ending with the sublime thought that the visible operations of God, majestic as they are, are but the "outskirts" of His real ways, and convey but a "whisper" of His full power. Job thus indirectly reminds his friends that the question at issue turns, not on God's *greatness*, but on His *justice*.

C. 27-28. Job's final words to his friends. Zophar fails to come forward; and Job accordingly, after a pause, resumes his discourse. 27^{1-6}, with reference specially to Bildad's *second* [397] contention (25^{4-6}), but implicitly at the same time to similar words on the part of his other friends, he enters a solemn protestation before God of his innocence: 27^{7-10} he describes, with great emphasis and feeling, the dreary, God-abandoned *mental* condition of the wicked man,—it is a fate which he could himself wish only for his *enemy!* 27^{11-23} he proceeds to instruct his friends at some length respecting the terrible *material* ruin which befalls the sinner at the hand of God.

C. 28. The wisdom of God unattainable by man. Man, says Job, pointing to the methods by which in ancient times mining operations were conducted, can wring from the earth its hidden treasures, 28^{1-11}; but wisdom has no place where it can be found; it cannot be purchased by gold or precious stones; it cannot be discovered either in the land of the living or in the realm of the dead, 28^{12-22}; it is known to God only, who was guided by it in His work of creation, and who prescribed to man, as *his* wisdom, the pursuit of a religious and virtuous life, 28^{23-28}.

The gist of this extremely striking and beautiful chapter is sometimes misunderstood. By *wisdom* is meant the intellectual apprehension of the principles by which the course of the physical world and the events of human life are regulated; and it is declared to belong—at least in its fulness—only to God, who has appointed for man, as its *substitute*, the practice of a righteous and holy life.

Hitherto the argument of the poem has been consistent and intelligible; but 27^{7-23} and c. 28 have been a source of great perplexity to commentators.* (1) 27^{7-10}. These verses appear to be inconsistent with Job's position. The

---

* See also Wellhausen in Bleek's *Einl.* (ed. 4), p. 540 f., and especially Budde, *ZATW.* 1882, p. 193 ff.

state of mind which he here denies to the ungodly, seems manifestly to be one *of which he has experience himself.* V. $^{8.\ 10}$ would not, indeed, be out of place in Job's mouth (cf. 16^{19} $19^{25f.}$ $23^{11f.}$); but v.^{9} is in direct contradiction with his repeated declarations that God refuses to hear him ($9^{15f.}$ 13^{24} 19^7 $23^{8f.}$). Two solutions are offered. The words being inconsistent with the condition of Job's mind as revealed in his speeches, it is supposed (*a*) that he has at last found his way to an assured trust in God, or that such a trust has suddenly, after the attacks of his friends are ended, flashed upon him, and filled his mind with the hope of a restoration to God's favour (Ewald, Dillm.). This altered frame of mind, however, though not in itself inadmissible, is difficult to reconcile with what follows; for in $30^{20.\ 23}$ Job expresses again the same thought, which *ex hypothesi* he would here have overcome: he denies, precisely as he has done throughout the debate, that God listens to his cry. And [398] similarly in 31^{35-37} he treats God *still* as his adversary. At the same time, it is conceivable that the author only intended to represent Job as having regained a *temporary* calmness of mind, which afterwards, as the contrast between his past and present position forces itself upon him (c. 30–31), he fails to maintain. The alternative (*b*) is to conclude that the implicit reference is to Job's *past* condition, and to suppose that the state of mind which Job denies to the ungodly is suggested by memories of his own former condition, as described in c. 29, when the tokens of God's friendship were abundantly bestowed upon him. Upon this view the words are considered to be introduced here as a *confirmation* of v.$^{2-6}$, as though to say: How could one have ever been tempted to sin, who knew so well the miserable mental state into which the sinner falls? (Hengstenberg partly, Budde, pp. 205–210, and in his *Comm.*).

(2) 27^{11-23}. Here it is remarkable (*a*) that Job should undertake to teach his friends what they had continuously maintained, viz. the evil fate which overtakes the wicked; (*b*) that he should himself affirm the opposite of what had been his previous position, viz. that an evil fate does *not* overtake the wicked (9^{22-24}: c. 21; c. 24);* (*c*) that while coinciding with his friends in opinion, he should reproach them with folly (v.^{12}); "to appropriate their sentiments, and cover the operation by calling them foolish persons, was not generous" (Davidson). The solution commonly offered of this difficulty is that Job is here modifying his former extravagant expressions respecting the prosperity of the wicked, and conceding that, *as a rule*, or *often*, a disastrous fate overtakes them. But, as Professor Davidson remarks, (α) the limitation "as a rule" has to be read into the passage, for the language is as absolute as that of any of his friends; (β) if the passage be a retractation of Job's previous language, it is a retractation which errs equally in extravagance on the other side; for it asserts a law of temporal retribution without any apparent qualification whatever; (γ) it is singular that in describing the fate of the wicked at God's hands, Job should use the same figures, and even sometimes the same words, which he employs when speaking of his own destruction by God (v.^{21}, cf. 9^{17} 30^{22}; v.^{22}, cf. 16^{13}; v.^{23}, cf. 17^6 30^{9-14}). Perhaps, however, this coincidence is accidental. A decidedly better ex-

---

* Contrast v.^{14} with $21^{8.\ 11}$; v.^{15} with 21^{32}; v.^{18} with 21^9 &c.

planation is that of Schlottmann and Budde (*ZATW*. p. 211 ff.), who suppose the passage to be spoken by Job *with an eye to his three friends*: v.[11] he ironically declares that he will "teach" them, which he does by forthwith turning their own weapons against them; they *know* (v.[12a]) what the fate of the wicked man is, and yet they strangely do not see that by their wicked insinuations against Job they are invoking it deliberately upon themselves! Job has spoken strongly before of the wrong done to him by his friends, 13[4. 7. 9] 19[2f.] 21[34], and has threatened them with Divine vengeance, 13[10f.] 19[29]; and here, upon this view, he holds up to them, if they will make the application, a more distinct warning.*

More violent remedies have been proposed. Kennicott, for instance, a [399] century ago, suggested that 27[13-23] should really be assigned to *Zophar*. But the brevity of Bildad's last speech (c. 25) seems a clear indication, on the part of the author, that the friends had exhausted their arguments, and that a third speech of Zophar—especially a longer one than Bildad's—is not to be expected; the terms of 27[11], moreover, show that 27[12] cannot be the *end* of a speech. Professor Cheyne (pp. 38, 114) conjectures that the text is dislocated, and rearranges it thus: c. 25, 26[5-14] (Bildad); 26[1-4] 27[1-7] (Job); 27[8-10. 13-23] (Zophar,—the opening verses being supposed to be lost); 27[11f.] c. 28 (Job).

(3) C. 28. As regards the relation of this chapter to what precedes, it might no doubt be supposed that Job, no longer irritated by the retorts of his friends, has reached a calmer mood; and abandoning the attempt to discover a *speculative* solution of the perplexities which distress him, finds man's wisdom to consist in the *practical* fulfilment of the duties of life. But a serious difficulty arises in connexion with what follows. If Job has risen to this tranquil temper, how comes it that he falls back (30[20-23]) into complainings, and dissatisfaction at not having been justified by God (31[35])? And, further, if he has reached by the unaided force of his own meditations this devout and submissive frame of mind, how is the ironical tone of the Divine speeches (c. 38 ff.) to be accounted for? If he is already resigned to the inscrutability of the Divine ways, how does it need to be again pointed out to him? The difficulty is analogous to that arising out of 27[7-9]: the changed frame of mind, which both appear to imply, is not preserved in the subsequent parts of the book. It is hardly possible that such a noble and characteristic passage can have been inserted into the poem by a later hand. May it be supposed, as was suggested above, on 27[7-10], that Job's tranquil state of mind was conceived by the author as temporary only? It must, however, be allowed that there is an imperfect psychological basis even for a temporary recovery of calmness: Job is unmoved by all the arguments of his friends; and no other independent influence (as in c. 38-39) has been brought to bear upon him. The truth, perhaps, is that the author's psychology must not be measured by the standard that would be applied to a Western poet; and that he represents Job, in this part of the book, as passing through moods of feeling without what, as judged by Western standards, would be deemed the necessary psychological motives.

According to Budde, Job's intellectual inability to reconcile his sufferings

---

* Against Delitzsch's solution, see Davidson, p. 190.

with his innocence having reached its climax in c. 27, he gives up the problem, explaining his incapacity from the fact that wisdom is reserved by God for Himself : what He has given to man under this name is a practical substitute for wisdom, not wisdom itself. Job, upon this view, accepts the ordinance of Providence, though not in a spirit of resignation, but (*Comm.* pp. xxvii, 156) in dissatisfaction and despair. This explanation brings the chapter into consistency with the context ; but it is open to the grave objection that (as Davidson, p. 201, already remarked) no trace of such a state of mind is discernible in the entire chapter : on the contrary, the writer seems to be stating, with an eloquence and warmth which surely cannot be misunderstood, the conclusions which satisfy himself. Cf. Dillm.[2] p. 238, who, however, owns that the chapter, so understood, cannot state the ground (v.[1] " For ") of what has immediately preceded, and is consequently obliged to assume that something different stood originally in the place of what is now 27[11-23] (p. 234).

C. 29–31. Job's final survey of the whole circumstances of his case. C. 29 Job draws a pathetic picture of his former prosperity, of the days when God's favour rested visibly upon him, and especially of the high respect which his benevolence, and philanthropy, and justice, won for him from his fellow-men. C. 30 there follows a contrasted picture of his present humiliation : he is derided by the meanest ; even the outcasts of society (v.[2-8]) hold him in disdain ; he is tormented by the anguish of his [**400**] disease : instead of sympathy such as he himself once extended to others, a painful and intolerable solitude is his portion. Such has been Job's strange change of fortune. And yet he is conscious that nothing that he has done can be the cause of it : accordingly in c. 31 he utters his final and solemn protestation of the innocence of his former life (cf. 27[1-6]). The chapter is a remarkable one ; it contains the portrait of a character instinct with nobility and delicacy of feeling, which not only repudiates any overt act of violence or wrong, but also disowns all secret impulses to impure or dishonourable conduct.

3. (c. 32–37). After Job's appeal to God, at the end of c. 31, it would seem that the crisis of the poem was at hand, and that God must appear to declare His award upon the struggle. Instead of this, however, Elihu, a speaker who has not been named or alluded to before, steps forward, and expresses his judgment upon the matter in dispute. Elihu is represented as a bystander who has listened to the course of the debate with some dissatisfaction at the line taken in it by both parties ; being younger, however, than any of the principal disputants, he has

waited until now before venturing to join in the discussion. He is introduced, like the other speakers (c. 2), in a few verses of prose : his own discourse is in poetry. It falls into five parts— the *first* is introductory ; in the *second*, *third*, and *fourth*, Elihu criticises Job's positions ; the *fifth* contains Elihu's positive contribution to the solution of the problem. (1) 32^{6-33}. In this rather long and laboured introduction, Elihu explains the reasons which prompted him to interpose ; he is vexed with Job, because he justified himself as against God ; he is vexed with his three friends, because they failed to refute Job. (2) C. 33. Turning now to Job, Elihu begs his attention : he addresses him as a fellow-man, not as a God who would overwhelm him with His might (v.^{7}, with allusion to 9^{34} 13^{21}). Thereupon, after quoting some of Job's words, he observes that Job is wrong in insisting that God is His enemy, and does not answer his cries : God speaks to man, if he will but listen, in many ways ; by visions of the night He withdraws the sinner from his evil purpose, or He sends upon him the chastening influences of sickness ; if His warnings are obeyed, He afterwards restores him to health, and fills his heart with grateful joy. (3) C. 34. Elihu protests against Job's complaint that God afflicts him unjustly, and that [401] it is no profit to a man to be righteous : injustice, he replies, is inconsistent with the very idea of God, 34^{10-12} ; as Author and Sustainer of the Universe, He can have no motive to injustice ; as its Supreme Ruler, He must be incapable of it, 34^{13-19}. And history confirms this judgment, for it abounds with instances in which He has struck down the wicked, and listened to the cry of the oppressed ; Job, in questioning God's principles of action, has displayed both ignorance and impiety, 34^{20-37}. (4) C. 35. Elihu here applies himself to meet Job's contention that righteousness does not profit a man : righteousness, he argues, must profit some one ; but God is too lofty to be affected by human conduct ; it follows that man's righteousness must benefit himself, 35^{1-8} : the reason why the cry of the oppressed often remains unanswered is that it is merely the animal cry of suffering, not the voice of trust and submission, 35^{9-16}. (5) C. 36–37. Elihu, having corrected Job's false ideas, now sets before him what he deems a truer and worthier conception of the Creator. For this purpose he points to different illustrations of the *greatness* of God, especially as exemplified in His providential dealings with men. (*a*) Afflictions are not, as Job had supposed, evidence of God's *wrath*, but of His *goodness* ; they are a *discipline*, designed for the warning and purification even of the righteous, 36^{1-15} ; let Job understand this, and refrain from rebelling under God's chastening hand, 36^{16-25}. (*b*) The incomprehensibility of the Divine nature is manifest in the wonderful phenomena of the skies, $36^{26}-37^{13}$; let Job learn the greatness of God, who is just as well as mighty, who afflicts none without cause, but who regards not those who are wise in their own understanding, 37^{14-24}.

4. (38^1-42^6). Here Jehovah intervenes, and answers Job out of the whirlwind. His answer consists of two parts, each followed by a few words from Job.

The aim of these speeches is to bring Job back into a right frame of mind towards God. Job has sustained the trial successfully ; for though he has sinned by impatient utterances under the weight of his afflictions, he has not, as the Satan predicted, cast off his religion ; in spite of the doubts by which he has been assailed, he has preserved his faith in a just and holy God (13^{16} 16^{19} 19^{25}), and in a righteous order of the world (17^9 27^{8-10}). Nevertheless, the cloud of discontent and doubt is not yet dispelled from his mind (30^{20-23} $31^{35f.}$; and while this remains, his trial cannot be said to be ended. What is [402] needed is thus, firstly, to convince him that in his demeanour toward God he has not been free from blame ; and secondly, to raise him effectually into peace of mind. For this purpose Jehovah, *firstly*, 38^1-40^2, in a series of questions, each of which admits of but a single humiliating reply, causes to pass before Job a "panorama of creation," exemplifying (*a*) the wonders of inanimate nature, both upon earth, 38^{4-18}, and in the heavens, 38^{19-38} ; (*b*) the astonishing variety of instincts and powers possessed by the animal creation, $38^{39}-39^{30}$. The effect of this brilliant display upon Job is indicated in his brief reply, $40^{4f.}$: he is overwhelmed by it : it brings home to him in a degree which, in spite of what fell from him in 9^{4-10} 12^{12-25} 26^{5-14} (esp. ^{14}), he had not before realized, the *comprehensiveness* and *infinite resource* of the Divine intelligence ; it fills him with a vivid and overpowering sense of the transcendent majesty of the Creator, in the presence of which his doubts vanish, and he owns his presumption in having dared to contend with God.

The aim of Jehovah's *second* speech, 40⁶–41³⁴, is to convince
Job of his error in charging God with injustice in His government of the world, and especially in His treatment of himself.
As Job had questioned the principles of God's rule, he is
ironically invited to assume the Divine attributes, and rule the
world himself, 40⁶⁻¹⁴. And, as a test of his capabilities, two
formidable creatures, the work of God's hand, like himself (40¹⁵),
are described to him at some length, and he is asked whether
he can even subdue *them*, 40¹⁵–41³⁴. Job's answer to these
demands follows in 42¹⁻⁶. He is keenly sensible of the folly of
his doubts, and he solemnly retracts his hasty and ill-considered
words.

The first speech of Jehovah transcends all other descriptions of the
wonders of creation or the greatness of the Creator, which are to be found
either in the Bible or elsewhere.   Parts of II Isaiah (*e.g.* c. 40) approach it ;
but they are conceived in a different strain, and, noble as they are, are less
grand and impressive.   The picturesque illustrations, the choice diction, the
splendid imagery, the light and rapid movement of the verse, combine to
produce a whole of incomparable brilliancy and force.   " The attempt which
is here made to group together the overwhelming marvels of nature, to
employ them for the purpose of producing an approximate impression of the
majesty of the Creator, though dependent upon the childlike, but at the same
time deeply poetical, view of nature prevalent in antiquity, still retains not
only its full poetical beauty, but also an imperishable religious worth.   For
though many of the phenomena here propounded as inexplicable are referred
by [403] modern science to their proximate causes, and comprehended under
the general laws of nature, yet these laws themselves by their unalterable
stability and potent operation only the more evoke our amazement, and will
never cease to inspire the religious mind with adoring wonder of the infinite
Power, Wisdom, and Love by which the individual laws, and forces, and
elements, are sustained and ruled " (Dillmann).

The long description of Behemoth and Leviathan (40¹⁵–41³⁴ [Heb. ²⁶]) is
considered by Ewald, Dillm., Cheyne (*Job and Sol.* p. 56), Kuenen (§ 101. 17),
and others, to be out of harmony with the idea of Jehovah's second speech,
as well as (in parts) poetically unworthy of the author of c. 38–39 ; and hence
it is regarded by these scholars as having been inserted in the original poem
by a later hand (see most fully Dillm.² p. 342 f. ; and cf. Dav. p. liv).
Budde, limiting the interpolated part to 41¹²⁻³⁴ [Heb. ⁴⁻²⁶] (which is certainly
the most laboured and prolix), retains the rest, supposing that 40¹⁵–41¹¹
[Heb. ³] formed originally the close of c. 38–39, being followed by 40¹⁻². ⁸⁻¹⁴.
³⁻⁵ 42². ³ᵇᶜ. ⁵⁻⁶. ⁷ff.. But 40¹⁵⁻²⁴ is conceived in a different style from c. 38–39
(the characteristic *questions*, addressed to Job, are, for instance, entirely
absent) ; so that it is difficult to think that it could ever have been the continuation of these chapters.

5. The Epilogue, 42⁷⁻¹⁷. The end of Job's trials. Having

thus regained a right frame of mind towards God, Job is restored to prosperity twofold as great as that which he enjoyed before. Job's friends are condemned for what they have said, and Job is commended (v.[7f.]).

Of course Job's friends had, in fact, said much that was just and true; their fault was that they had *misapplied* it; upon a limited basis they had framed *universal* theories of the methods of God's providence, and upon strength of them had imputed to Job sins of which he was innocent. Job, though he had said much that was blameworthy and false, had nevertheless adhered to the truth in the matter under dispute. The three friends " had really inculpated the providence of God by their professed defence of it. By disingenuously covering up and ignoring its enigmas and seeming contradictions, they had cast more discredit upon it than Job by honestly holding them up to the light. Their denial of its apparent inequalities was more untrue and more dishonouring to the Divine administration, as it is in fact conducted, than Job's bold affirmation of them " (Dr. W. H. Green, quoted by Prof. Davidson).

It is all but certain that the speeches of Elihu are not part of the original poem. This is the general opinion of commentators and critics, and rests (principally) upon the following grounds :—

1. Elihu is not mentioned in either the Prologue or the Epilogue. That he is not mentioned in the Prologue is indeed of slight weight : he does not join with the others in the debate ; and he is introduced with sufficient particulars in 32^{1-5}. But his non-mention in the Epilogue is remarkable. A definite judgment is passed on both Job and his three friends : if Elihu had been one of the original speakers, would not some verdict have been pronounced on what he had said ?

2. The speeches of Elihu are attached but loosely to the poem as a whole. They might be removed from it without any detriment to the argument, and without the reader being sensible of a lacuna. Not only, however, are these speeches loosely connected with the poem, they are a disturbing element in it. They interrupt the connexion between the words of Job (c. 29–31) and Jehovah's reply (for the terms of 38^2 naturally suggest that Job is almost in [404] the act of speaking when the reply begins), and weaken the force of the latter by anticipating (c. 36 f.), at least in part, its argument.

3. Elihu occupies substantially the same position as the three friends, especially Eliphaz : he explains Job's sufferings as arising from his sins (34^{37}) ; the only point in which he differs from the friends is in his emphasizing the *goodness* of God, as the principle determining His dealings with man, and in his laying greater stress than they did on the chastening character of affliction (33^{14-30} 36^{8-25}) : but this had already been taught in

effect by Eliphaz ($5^{8\text{ff. }17\text{ff.}}$) ; and Job had rejected the theory as inapplicable to his own case. Moreover, from both the Prologue and the Epilogue (42^{7-9}), as well as from the general tenor of Job's discourses, it is apparent that in the view of the author of the Book this principle, however just and true in itself, was *not* the explanation of the sufferings of righteous Job. No doubt Elihu censures the friends for not sufficiently developing these aspects of the case ; but as they *are* touched upon by Eliphaz, it is strange that the author should not have allowed Eliphaz to develop them, but should have introduced an independent speaker for the purpose.

4. The *style* of Elihu differs considerably from that of the rest of the Book. It is prolix, laboured, and sometimes tautologous ($32^{6\text{ end. }10\text{b. }17\text{b}}$) : the power and brilliancy which are so conspicuous in the poem generally are sensibly missing. The reader, as he passes from Job and his three friends to Elihu, is conscious at once that he has before him the work of a writer, not indeed devoid of literary skill, but certainly inferior in literary and poetical genius to the author of the rest of the Book. The language is often involved and the thought strained : these speeches are marked also by many peculiarities of expression, and by a deeper colouring of Aramaic than the poem generally. It is possible, no doubt, that these features have sometimes been exaggerated by critics ; and Budde, in his elaborate and interesting study on the subject (*Beitr.* p. 65 ff.), has shown that parallels, or analogies, to many of them, which had not previously been observed, may be found in other parts of the Book : but he does not by this process succeed in obliterating the differences: the peculiarities are not *aggregated* in other parts of the Book as they are here ; and the impression which the reader derives from a perusal of the entire group of speeches is unmistakably different from that which any other six chapters of the Book leave upon him. *

The most probable view of the Elihu-speeches is thus that they are an addition to the original poem, made by a somewhat later writer, for the purpose of supplementing certain points in which it appeared to him to be defective. He wished, in contrast with the spirit of Job's speeches, to insist on the reverence due to God : he wished, in contrast to the friends, to meet Job's positions by considerations drawn more directly from the essential character and attributes of God : he wished to

---

* Budde admits now (*Comm.* p. xix) that the more he fixes his attention on the whole rather than on individual details, "the stronger the impression upon him becomes that there remains nevertheless a great difference between the style of Elihu and that of the rest of the Book" ; and allows that he would be obliged to grant that these chapters were the work of a different hand, did he not think it possible to refer this difference to interpolation and corruption of the text : when the speeches of Elihu have been freed from interpolated ($32^{2-5. 11-12. 15-17}$ $33^{4. 15\text{b. }33}$ $34^{9. 10\text{a. }25-28. 29\text{c}}$ 35^{4} $36^{13-14. 17. 25-26. 29-30}$ $37^{13. 15-16}$) and corrupt passages, he claims that they are (from a literary point of view) worthy of the author of the rest of the Book.

emphasize, more fully than Eliphaz (c. 5) had done, the disciplinary function of suffering. These are all points which, it is difficult not [405] to think, the original author, had he desired so to notice them, would have introduced into the main debate, instead of leaving them to be dealt with, as it were, in an appendix, by a supernumerary speaker. Such an appendix is, however, the form that would naturally be chosen by a subsequent writer desirous of supplementing the poem as it stood. The resemblances, such as they are, in phraseology and general treatment are sufficiently explained by the supposition that the author was a student of the Book, and accommodated, so far as he was able, his tone and style to it. It is not, however, fair to describe the speeches of Elihu by a term of disparagement, as if, for instance, they were an unauthorised " interpolation" : though not part of the original plan of the Book, they are a valuable supplement to it ; they attach prominence to real and important truths which in the rest of the poem might seem not to have received their proper due.

A different view of the scope of the Book is taken by those who—as Schlottmann, Hengst., Riehm (*Einl.* ii. 263 f. 278 f.), and especially Budde —acknowledge the Elihu-speeches as an original part of the poem. These writers consider that what was indicated above (p. 410) as a collateral aim of the Book, viz. the doctrine of the *disciplinary* or *purifying* value of suffering, is in reality its main aim—or, at least (Riehm), its main positive aim. Thus Budde (*Comm.* pp. xxv, xxx ff. &c.) observes that Job, though righteous before the visit of his friends, in defending his righteousness against their silent reproaches (2^{18}) and (c. 4–5, &c.) open attacks, fell into sin : *spiritual pride*, a sin subtler even than the selfishness of his piety, which was what the tempter suspected, was latent in his nature from the first (cf. Riehm, p. 263) ; and the object of the suffering sent upon him was to bring this hidden sin to his consciousness, to lead him to confess it, as he does in 42^{2-6}, and so to purify and confirm his spiritual nature. The materials supplied by tradition did not, according to Budde, embrace more than 1^1-2^{10} (to *evil*), and 42^{10-17} (except v.$^{10a,\beta}$) ; these portions of the Prologue and Epilogue constituted substantially the original folk-tale (" das Volksbuch ") of Job, in which the question was, *Is Egoism the root of piety ? Is there such a thing as disinterested piety ?* This folk-tale the poet adopted as the framework for his thoughts. With him, however, the question becomes a deeper and broader one, *Can the righteous suffer ? and if so, why ?* and the trial of Job's righteousness (which is the theme of the Prologue) becomes the purification of his character, and the confirmation of his faith. The discussion of the problem which thus arises forms the subject of the dialogue which the poet has inserted between the two parts of the " Volksbuch " (*Comm.* p. xxii ff.). Consistently with this view of the general scope of the Book, the same writers consider not only that the Elihu-speeches are the work of the original author, but that they present his own solution of the problem. And so Budde remarks (pp. xxxv ff., 213) that Eliphaz (c. 4–5) explains suffering only as a punishment for *actual* sin : Job takes the same view of it ; Elihu, on the contrary, explains it as designed to make a man conscious of *latent* sin, and thereby to enable him to repent and overcome it. Budde defends his theory of the Book with marked skill and ability ; but it may be doubted whether a doctrine, which, however true and profound in the abstract, is so little developed by the poet himself, can have formed the *main* idea of his work. The doctrine of the disciplinary function of suffering is very subordinate in the Book ; even in Elihu, it does not stand out with the clearness and directness that would be expected, if the poet were there presenting his own solution of the problem, Nor, though it is true that Elihu sees in suffering a purpose of grace, is it at all clear that he views it as sent only (or even chiefly) for the correction of *latent* sin ; and pride is alluded to by him only in 33^{17} 36^9 (cf. further Dillm.[2] pp. xv, 274 ; Davidson, pp. xliv f., lii ; Kuen. § 101. 20).

With regard to the *text* of Job, it is to be observed that the genuine LXX text of the Book (which has been recovered lately from the Sa'idic (Coptic) version, published by Ciasca)* is shorter than the Hebrew text by nearly 400 στίχοι. The origin of these differences between the two texts is not in all cases apparent ; but the omission of the lines not expressed by the LXX does not relieve the logical difficulties presented in parts (*e.g.* 27^{13-23}) by the poem ; and there are no sufficient reasons for supposing—except, at most, here and there—that the LXX preserves a more original form of the poem than the Hebrew (see especially Dillm.'s *Abhandlung*, cited above, p. 408). Bickell's restoration (*ibid.* : it may be read in English in E. J. Dillon's *Sceptics of the OT.* 1895, p. 159 ff.), though clever in details, is, as a whole, exceedingly arbitrary : comp. the present writer's article in the *Contemp. Review*, Feb. 1896, p. 257 ff. ; and Budde, *Comm.* p. xlvi ff.

Date of the Poem.—Formerly, in days when the Book was commonly treated as a narrative of literal history, and the truth of a *progress* in the revelation and beliefs of the OT. had not been reached, its composition was assigned to the supposed age

---

* *Sacrorum Bibliorum fragmenta Copto-Sahidica*, vol. ii. (1889) : see the table of passages omitted, p. xxiii ff. Ordinary editions of the LXX (as well as the majority of MSS.) exhibit the text as it was corrected by Origen (who in his Hexapla supplied what to him seemed to be its deficiencies from Theodotion or other sources), the asterisks by which he himself marked the insertions having been neglected by transcribers, though they are preserved, more or less completely, in 5 MSS. (two Greek, viz. Colb. 1952 in the Paris Library, and Vat. 346 ; two of the Old Latin version, printed by Lagarde in his *Mittheilungen*, ii. 1887, p. 189 ff. ; and the Ambrosian MS. of the Syro-Hexaplar text of the LXX). The Sa'idic version was made from the uncorrected, pre-Hexaplar text of the LXX. See more fully Beer's studies, cited above, p. 408.

of the patriarch himself, and Moses was sometimes suggested as a possible author. But though the narrative of the Prologue and Epilogue is in the general style of parts of the Book of Genesis, and though Job is represented as a patriarch, surrounded by his dependants, rich in pastures and flocks, offering sacrifice as the head of his family, and attaining patriarchal longevity, these constitute very insufficient grounds for assigning the Book itself to such an early age. Indeed, a careful consideration of its contents brings to light unmistakable indications that it belongs to a far later and maturer stage of Israelitish history. The antique, patriarchal colouring of the portrait of Job in c. 1–2, 42 must be attributed to the skill of the author, who preserved the general features of the age that he was describing, aided no doubt by his own knowledge of the character of an Arab sheikh, which can hardly have differed materially from what it had been many centuries before.

It is not possible to fix the date of the Book *precisely* ; but it will certainly not be earlier than the age of Jeremiah, and most probably it was written either during or shortly after the Babylonian captivity.*

[406] The following, in the main, are the grounds on which this opinion rests :—

1. Though references to *distinctive* observances of Israel's religion (as in the Wisdom-literature generally, p. 393) are rare, an acquaintance with the *law* seems here and there to betray itself : *e.g.* 22^6 24^9 (pledges : Ex. 22$^{26f.}$, Dt. 24^{17}), 22^{27} (vows) 24^2 (landmarks ; Dt. 19^{14} *al.*), 31$^{9-11.\ 26-28}$ (*judicial* procedure against those guilty of adultery, or worship of the sun or moon ; cf. Dt. 22^{22} : 4^{19} 17$^{3-7}$), 31^{11} (זִמָּה : p. 49, No. 11).

2. The Book presupposes an advanced social state, and a considerable range and faculty of observation on the part of its author. A wide and varied experience lies behind him. His illustrations are abundant ; and they are drawn from many different departments of the natural world, from history (c. 12), from various grades and ranks of society (c. 24 ; 30$^{1-8}$). The "gate" (29^7 31^{21}), as the place of judgment, implies the settled life of Palestine (Am. 5^{10} &c.). The forensic terms in which Job's plea with God is regularly stated, imply an established system of judicature.

* Budde (p. xlv f.) places it about (but not later than) B.C. 400.

3. The Book presupposes much reflexion on the problems of life and society. The period of unquestioning faith has passed by : the laws of providence are no more *stated* merely, they are made the subject of doubt and discussion. " The very problem which the Book discusses, the riddle which vexes the soul of Job, is not one which springs into full life, or would form the subject of a long and studied, an intensely argued and elaborate discussion, in any early or simple stage of a nation's progress " (Bradley, p. 171). The Book exhibits a struggle between a traditional creed which taught that all suffering was a penalty for sin, all prosperity a reward for goodness, and the spectacle of undeserved suffering afforded by more complex social conditions ; it presents speculations on the relation subsisting between virtue and happiness, and on the compatibility of God's justice and benevolence with His sovereignty and greatness, which can hardly be conceived as arising in the infancy of a nation's life. Thinking men must have pondered often on moral problems before they could have been treated with the fulness and many-sidedness displayed in the Book of Job. Apart from Psalms of uncertain date (but which it is clear are not early ones—Ps. 37, 49, 73), the first [407] notice which such questions receive is in the age of Jeremiah (Jer. 12¹ &c.: p. 410).

4. A condition of disorder and misery forms the background of the poem (Davidson, p. lxiii; Dillm.² p. xvii f.). Passages such as 3²⁰ 7¹ 9²⁴ 12⁶ 24¹², seem to reflect something beyond the personal experiences of Job himself: 12¹⁷ff. points to nations overthrown, the plans of statesmen wrecked, kings, princes, and priests led into exile. Is not the author's eye fixed here on the great political changes wrought by the Assyrians or the Chaldæans among the principalities of Palestine and Syria (Isa. 10⁷· ¹⁸f.)? Have not the disasters involving the righteous with the wicked, which his own nation has experienced, forced upon men's attention the question of God's moral government of the world, and moulded in some degree the author's argument?

5. The great literary power of the poem, its finished form, and the ability which its author displays of not merely expounding a subject briefly (as in a prophecy or a Psalm), but of developing it under different aspects in a regularly progressing argument, implies that a mature stage of literary culture has been reached. The nearest parallel is Isa. 40–66; but Job, viewed as a work of

art, is more finished and powerful even than that great prophecy. Though the author's originality is very great, and though he displays singular freshness and independence in his mode of handling his subject, the points of view, the illustrations, the poetical figures, the terminology, must in many cases have been found by him ready to his hand (notice, for instance, the illustrations in 20^{19} 22^{27} $24^{2ff.}$ $29^{12ff.}$ $31^{11ff.}$, so familiar from the law and the prophets).

6. The developed form, both of the morality and the doctrine of God, points in the same direction. "The teaching of Eliphaz regarding human nature ($4^{17ff.}$), and the inwardness of the moral conceptions of Job (c. 31), are very surprising" (Davidson). The doctrine of God is expressed with a breadth and loftiness which are without parallel elsewhere in the OT., except in its later portions (as Isa. 40–66, Ps. 139). The "Satan" is named besides only in Zech. 3 and 1 Ch. 21^1: had the conception been familiar to the Hebrews in the days of Solomon, for instance, it is probable that it would have been mentioned elsewhere in the earlier literature (especially in 2 Sa. 24^1, the parallel passage to 1 Ch. 21^1).

7. The language of Job points likewise to a relatively late [408] date. The syntax is extremely idiomatic; but the vocabulary contains a very noticeable admixture of Aramaic words, and (in a minor degree) of words explicable only from the Arabic. This is an indication of a date more or less contemporary with II Isaiah; though it appears that the author came more definitely within the range of Aramaizing influences than the author of Isa. 40–66, and perhaps had his home in proximity to Aramaic- and Arabic-speaking peoples.*

8. The comparison of parallel passages in other books leads seldom to conclusive results, partly because the dates of the books referred to are often doubtful, partly from the frequent difficulty (p. 312 f.), even where the dates are clear, of determining on which side the dependence lies. The principal parallels presented by Job are with Amos, Isaiah (both parts), Jeremiah, Lamentations, Proverbs, and several Psalms (esp. Ps. 39, 88, 107).† Ps. 8^5

---

* The far south-east of Palestine has been suggested (Dillm.² p. xxxvii; Cheyne, pp. 75, 295). But doubtless it is only tradition that leads the author to represent both Job and his friends as non-Israelites; the thoughts expressed by them are thoroughly Hebraic, and the entire work is manifestly a genuine product of the religion of Israel.

† Comp. Cheyne, *Job and Solomon*, p. 83 ff.; *Isaiah*,³ ii. p. 259 ff.

is no doubt parodied in Job 7^{17}; but the date of the Psalm is uncertain. It appears, however, to be more probable that Isa. 19^5 is the original of Job 14^{11} than that the prophet is the imitator (cf. Davidson, p. lxii). With regard to the relation between Job 3^{3-10} and Jer. 20^{14-18} opinions differ. The former has been usually regarded as the original; but the argument that the passage in Job is more vivid and powerful is not decisive: the author of the poem possesses greater literary power than Jeremiah, and he may have adapted some of Jeremiah's artless phrases to his own more elaborate and finished picture. Both Pr. 10–22 and Pr. 1–9 appear to be anterior to Job: Pr. 13^9 is taken by Bildad ($18^{5,\ 6}$) as the text of his discourse; it is controverted by Job (21^{17}).* Job 15^{7b} (esp. taken in connexion with v.^{8b}) might seem to be an ironical allusion to Pr. 8^{25}: and Wisdom, who, in Pr. 1–9, offers herself to men as their guide, is represented in Job 28 as beyond the intellectual reach of man (contrast Pr. $3^{18-15}\ 8^{10f.}$ with Job 28^{15-19}).† Whether Isa. 53^9 is the original of Job 16^{17}, and Isa. $51^{9b,\ 10a}$ of Job $26^{12f.}$, or whether the reverse is the true relation, is uncertain: Kuenen (*Th. T.* 1873, p. 540 f.; *Onderz.* § 102. 6) decides in favour of the former alternative, Prof. Cheyne (*Job and Solomon*, pp. 75, 84) supports the latter. There are points of contact—in some cases subtle ones—between Job and Isa. 40–66, which make it probable that the authors of both, in Prof. Davidson's words (p. lxvi f.), "lived surrounded by the same atmosphere of thought."

---

* So Eliphaz (5^{17}) takes as his starting-point the teaching of Pr. 3^{11}.

† Comp. Budde, *ZATW.* 1882, pp. 241 f., 251; Davidson, p. lxi f.; Kuen. § 102. 4: on the other hand, Dillm.^{2} p. xxx.

CHAPTER X.

THE FIVE MEGILLOTH.

§ 1. The Song of Songs.

LITERATURE.—K. F. Umbreit, *Lied der Liebe*, ²1828; E. J. Magnus, *Krit. Bearb. u. Erkl. des Hohenlieds Sal.* 1842; F. Hitzig (in the *Kgf. Hdb.*), 1855; C. D. Ginsburg, *The Song of Songs, with a Comm., historical and critical*, 1857; H. Ewald in the *Dichter des A B.s* (²1867), iii. 333–426; F. Delitzsch, *Hoheslied u. Koheleth*, 1875; H. Grätz, *Shirha-Shirim*, 1871; W. R. Smith, art. "Canticles" in the *Encycl. Brit.*⁹; J. G. Stickell, *Das Hohelied in seiner Einheit u. dram. Gliederung*, 1888; S. Oettli in Strack and Zöckler's *Kgf. Kommentar*, 1889; W. E. Griffis, *The Lily among Thorns*, New York, 1890; C. Bruston, *La Sulammite*, 1891; D. Castelli, *Il Cantico dei Cantici, studio esegetico*, 1892; R. Martineau in the *Amer. Journ. of Phil.*, Oct. 1892, p. 307 ff.; J. W. Rothstein, *Das Hohe Lied. Ein Vortrag nebst einer mit Anmerkungen versehenen Übersetzung des Hohen Liedes*, 1893.

In the Jewish Canon the Song of Songs forms the first of the five *Megilloth*, or "Rolls," which are read publicly at certain sacred seasons in the synagogues.*

The Song of Songs is a poem, the subject of which is evidently love, though, as to the manner in which this subject is dealt with, opinions have differed. It is evident, from the change of number and (in the Hebrew) of gender, that different parts of the poem are spoken by, or addressed to, different persons, or, in other words, that the form is that of a dialogue; but who the speakers are, or how the poem is to be distributed between them, is not in all cases equally apparent. Some scholars (of whom the chief are Herder,† de Wette, Magnus, and Bleek) have,

---

* The Song of Songs at the Passover; Ruth at Pentecost; Lamentations on the 9th of Ab (the day on which Jerusalem was destroyed); Qoheleth at the Feast of Booths; Esther at the Feast of Purim.

† Herder, *Salomon's Lieder der Liebe, die ältesten und schönsten aus dem Morgenlande*, 1778 (in Müller's edition of Herder's works, vol. iv.), who displays, however, a high appreciation of the æsthetic value of the Song.

indeed, supposed that the Book consists of a number of independent songs, the only link binding them together being the [410] common subject, love; but the frequent repetition of the same words and phrases (including some remarkable ones)* and indications, not to be explained away, that the same characters are speaking in the latter as in the earlier parts of the poem, have convinced most modern commentators and critics that this view is not correct, and that the poem forms, in some sense or another, a real unity.†

As regards the sense, however, in which the poem is a unity, there exist two fundamentally different opinions. According to one of these, the traditional view, there are but *two* main characters by whom the dialogue is sustained, viz. King Solomon and a Shulamite ‡ maiden (6^{13}) of whom he is enamoured; and the poem describes how this maiden, who is endowed with surpassing grace and loveliness, is taken away from her rustic home by the king and raised to the summit of honour and felicity by being made his bride at Jerusalem (3^6–5^1). The dialogue, upon this view, § consists substantially of mutual expressions of love and admiration on the part of the two principal characters. According to the other view, propounded first in modern times by J. S. Jacobi, ‖ developed in a masterly manner by Ewald, and accepted by the majority of modern critics and commentators, there are *three* principal characters, viz. Solomon, the Shulamite maiden, and her shepherd lover: a beautiful Shulamite maiden, surprised by the king and his train on a royal progress in the north (6^{11-12}), has been brought to the palace at Jerusalem (1^4 &c.), where the king hopes to win her affections, and to induce her to exchange her rustic home for the honour and enjoyments which a court life could afford. She has, however, already pledged her heart to a young shepherd; and the admiration and blandishments which the king lavishes upon her are

---

* See Kuenen, *Onderzoek* (ed. 1), § 148. 3; or Oettli, p. 156.

† The marks of unity in the poem are well drawn out by W. R. Smith.

‡ Probably a by-form of *Shunammite* (1 Ki. 1^3; 2 Ki. $4^{8ff.}$), *i.e.* a native of Shunem, a town in Issachar (Josh. 19^{18}).

§ In modern times supported chiefly by Hengstenberg, Delitzsch, Keil, and Kingsbury in the *Speaker's Commentary.*

‖ *Das durch eine leichte u. ungekünstelte Erkl. von seinen Vorwürfen gerettete Hohelied* (1771). Ibn Ezra (12th cent.) had also distinguished the lover and the king: Ginsburg, p. 46 (cf. p. 56 f.).

powerless to make her forget him.   In the end she is permitted to return to her mountain home, where, at the close of the poem, [**411**] the lovers appear hand in hand (8^5), and express, in warm and glowing words, the superiority of genuine, spontaneous affection over that which may be purchased by wealth or rank (8^{6-7}).

The following synopses of the traditional view, as represented by Delitzsch, and of the modern view as represented by Ewald,* together with certain slight modifications, in some cases improvements, adopted by Oettli, the most recent commentator on the Book, will, it is hoped, assist the reader to estimate the two alternatives correctly.

In case some surprise should be felt at the amount which (upon either view) has, as it were, to be read between the lines, it may be pointed out that, if the poem is to be made intelligible, its different parts *must*, in one way or another, be assigned to different characters ; and as no names mark the beginning of the several speeches, these must be *supplied*, upon the basis of such clues as the poem contains, by the commentator.   The problem which is, if possible, to be decided is, which of the proposed schemes does fullest justice to the language of the poem, or to casual hints contained in particular passages.   The traditional view may seem to be the simpler and the more obvious, but this does not decide the question of its truth ; for, as it cannot be shown to reach back to the time when the poem was composed, it may, just on account of its simplicity, have been adopted, and have gained currency, at a time when the true view had been forgotten.

I. The scheme of the poem according to Delitzsch † :—

ACT I. (1^2–2^7).

The Lovers' Meeting.

Scene 1.—Ladies of the Court,‡ 1^{2-4} (praising Solomon, and desiring his caresses).—The Shulamite, 1^{5-7} (excusing her sunburnt looks, and inquiring where her lover [Solomon] is).—Ladies of the Court, 1^8 (in reply).

Scene 2.—Solomon (entering), 1^{9-11}.—The Shulamite, 1^{12-14}.—Solomon, 1^{15}.—The Shulamite, 1^{16}–2^1.—Solomon, 2^2.—The Shulamite, 2^{3-7}.

ACT II. (2^8–3^5).

Monologues of the Shulamite, relating two scenes from her past life.

Scene 1 (2^{8-17}).—The Shulamite relates how the king on an excursion had once visited her in her mountain home, and proposed to her to accompany

---

* With whom W. R. Smith substantially agrees.

† Short explanations of the drift of the speeches are inserted where necessary.

‡ The "daughters of Jerusalem" (see 1^5 2^7 &c.).

him on a lovers' walk through the fields, v.[10-14], repeating the words of a vinedresser's ditty which she had then sung to him, v.[15-16], and telling how she had invited him to return to her again in the evening, when his excursion was ended.

[412] *Scene 2* (3[1-5]).—The Shulamite narrates a dream, in which she had once seemed to go in search of her lover through the city till she found him.

ACT III. (3[6]–5[1]).

The Royal Espousals.

Scene 1. (*Jerusalem and the neighbourhood. A pageant seen approaching in the distance.*)—A citizen of Jerusalem, 3[6] (inquiring what the pageant is). —Another citizen, 3[7-8] (in reply).—A third citizen, 3[9-10].—The people generally, 3[11].
The procession is supposed to be conducting to the king his future bride.

Scene 2. (*Banqueting-hall of the palace.*)—Solomon, 4[1-5] (in praise of his beloved's charms).—The Shulamite, 4[6] (interrupting the king's commendations of her beauty, and proposing to withdraw till the evening).—Solomon, 4[7-15] (inviting the Shulamite to forsake her northern home, and to become his bride).—The Shulamite, 4[16] (accepting the king's invitation).—Solomon, 5[1] (a morning greeting to his bride).
(The bridal night is supposed to intervene between 4[16] and 5[1].)

ACT IV. (5[2]–6[9]).

Love lost and found again.

Scene 1. (*Jerusalem.*)—The Shulamite, 5[2-8] (narrating a dream in which she seemed to hear her beloved calling her, but upon rising to open to him, he had vanished, and she sought him vainly through the city).—Ladies of the Court, 5[9].—The Shulamite, 5[10-16] (praise of her beloved, elicited by the reply in 5[9]).—Ladies of the Court, 6[1].—The Shulamite, 6[2-3].
The dream is accounted for psychologically by the supposition that an *estrangement* had taken place between the newly-married pair.

Scene 2.—Solomon (entering), 6[4-9].

ACT V. (6[10]–8[4]).

The lovely, but modest Queen.

Scene 1. (*Solomon's park at Etam.*)—Ladies of the Court (meeting the Shulamite wandering in a nut-grove), 6[10].—The Shulamite, 6[11-12] (declaring that in her enjoyment of the country she had almost forgotten the rank to which she had been elevated).—Ladies of the Court, 6[13a, b].—The Shulamite, 6[13c] *.—Ladies of the Court, 6[13d]. (Here the Shulamite complies with the request expressed in 6[13d], and dances.)—Ladies of the Court (watching her as she dances, and admiring her beauty), 7[1-5].

---

* Rendering, "What would you see in the Shulamite?" "As it were the dance of Mahanaim."

Scene 2.—Solomon, 7⁶, (addressing the Shulamite) 7⁷⁻⁹ᵃ.—The Shulamite, 7⁹ᵇ· ᶜ· ¹⁰–8⁴ (interrupting the king, and inviting him to revisit with her her rustic home).

[413]   ACT VI. (8⁵⁻¹⁴).

The bridal pair together in the Shulamite's home.

Scene 1. (*A valley near Shulem. Solomon and the Shulamite enter, arm in arm.*)—A villager of Shulem, 8⁵ᵃ· ᵇ.—Solomon, 8⁵ᶜ· ᵈ· ᵉ * (pointing to the fruit tree under which he first aroused the Shulamite's love, and to a cottage hard by which was her birthplace).—The Shulamite, 8⁶⁻⁷.

Scene 2. (*The Shulamite's home.*)—The Shulamite, 8⁸ (speaking in the name of her family, and inquiring how her little sister, when she reaches marriageable age, is to be dealt with).—The Shulamite's brothers, 8⁹ (replying to their sister's question).—The Shulamite, 8¹⁰⁻¹² (recalling the care taken of herself formerly by her brothers, in consequence of which she was secured to her lover ; and commending them to the king's grateful regard for a *douceur*). —Solomon, 8¹³ (addressing his bride, and begging her to gratify the companions of her youth—who are now supposed to be thronging round her— and himself, with a song).—The Shulamite, 8¹⁴ (singing [cf. 2¹⁷], and inviting the king to join her over the hills).

II. The scheme of the poem according to Ewald :—

ACT I. (1²–2⁷).

Scene 1. (*The Shulamite and Ladies of the Court.*)—The Shulamite, 1²⁻⁷ (longing for the caresses of her absent shepherd-lover, complaining that she is detained in the royal palace against her will, and inquiring eagerly where he may be found).†—The ladies of the Court, 1⁸ (in reply—ironically).

Scene 2. (*Solomon enters.*)—Solomon, 1⁹⁻¹¹ (seeking to win the Shulamite's love).‡—The Shulamite, 1¹²§, (*aside*) ¹³⁻¹⁴ (parrying the king's compliments with reminiscences of her absent lover).—Solomon, 1¹⁵.—The Shulamite (*aside*), 1¹⁶–2¹ (taking no notice of the king's remark in v.¹⁵, and applying the figures suggested by it to her shepherd-lover).—Solomon, 2².—The Shulamite (*aside*), 2³⁻⁷ (applying similarly to her lover the comparison suggested by v.². In v.⁵ᶠ· she sinks down in a fit of half-delirious sickness ; in v.⁷ she reminds the ladies of the Court that love is an affection which arises spontaneously, and entreats them not to excite it artificially in Solomon's favour).

---

* Punctuating (with Pesh.) the pronouns as *feminines*. But the paraphrase of "aroused" or "awakened thee" is questionable.

† Oettli's distribution of 1²⁻⁷ is perhaps preferable : viz. a lady of the Court, 1²⁻³ (in praise of Solomon, endeavouring thereby to arouse in the Shulamite an affection for the king).—The Shulamite, 1⁴ᵃ· ᵇ (expressing her eagerness to be with her absent lover).—Ladies of the Court, 1⁴ᶜ· ᵈ· ᵉ (in praise of Solomon).—The Shulamite, 1⁵⁻⁷.

‡ Render 1⁹ &c. as RV. *marg.* (see Jud. 11³⁷) : " my love " is too strong.

§ *I.e.* while the king was *away from me*, at table with his guests, my love (for another) was active, and filled me with delicious memories.

[414] Act II. (2⁸–3⁵).

The Shulamite and Ladies of the Court.

Scene 1. (*The Shulamite's reminiscence of her lover's visit.*) — The Shulamite recounts a scene from her past life, 2⁸⁻¹⁵. The scene is of a visit which her shepherd-lover once paid her in her rural home, inviting her to accompany him through the fields, v.¹⁰⁻¹⁴; and she repeats the words of the ditty which she then sang to him, v.¹⁵. V.¹⁶⁻¹⁷ she declares her present unaltered devotion to him, and expresses the wish that the separation between them may quickly be at an end.*

Scene 2. (*The Shulamite's first dream.*)—The Shulamite narrates a dream which she had recently had whilst in the royal palace, 3¹⁻⁵: she had seemed to go in search of her absent lover through the city, and to her joy she had found him, v.¹⁻⁴. V.⁵ she repeats the refrain of 2⁷.

The dream reflects the waking feelings and emotions. In the economy of the poem it serves to explain to the chorus the state of the heroine's feelings; and the adjuration in 3⁵ follows appropriately: let them not seek to stir up an unwilling love; even in her dreams she is devoted to another.

Act III. (3⁶–5⁸).

Scene 1. (*Citizens of Jerusalem assembled in front of one of the gates. In the distance a royal pageant is seen approaching.*)—First citizen, 3⁶.†—Second citizen, 3⁷⁻⁸.—A third citizen, 3⁹⁻¹¹.

The intention of the spectacle is to dazzle the rustic girl with a sense of the honour awaiting her if she will consent to become the king's bride. In the palanquin is Solomon himself, wearing the crown of state which his mother gave him on his wedding-day.

Scene 2. (*In the Palace. Solomon, the Shulamite, and Ladies of the Court.*)—Solomon, 4¹⁻⁷ (seeking to win the Shulamite's love).

Scene 3. (*The Shulamite and Ladies of the Court. The Shulamite and her lover in ideal interview.*)—The Shulamite, 4⁸–5¹ (hearing in imagination her lover's impassioned invitation, 4⁸⁻¹⁵, giving him her reply, v.¹⁶, and seeming to hear again his grateful response, 5¹‡).§

---

* Oettli treats this interview with the lover as a *real* one, supposing the scene to lie in one of Solomon's summer residences, perhaps near Shulem itself, where her lover visits her at the window.

† Render "*What* is this . . . ?" see Gen. 33⁸ Heb.

‡ 5¹ᵉ·ᶠ the lover, in view of the anticipated bridal feast (Jud. 14¹²), inviting his guests to partake of it. But RV. *marg.* is perhaps right; in which case the words may be supposed to be spoken by the chorus, watching at a distance, or overhearing, the scene, and bidding the pair enjoy the delights of love.

The *perfects* in 5¹ describe the future imagined as already accomplished. Upon Delitzsch's view they are construed as actual pasts. Either interpretation is consonant with Hebrew usage.

§ Oettli, as before (2⁸⁻¹⁵), treats this as an actual visit made during the king's absence (v.⁶), in which the shepherd lover invites her to flee with him

[415] *Scene 4. (The Shulamite's second dream.)*—The Shulamite relates a dream of the past night, in which she had imagined herself to hear her shepherd-lover at the door, but upon rising to open to him, had found him vanished, and sought him in vain through the city, 5² ⁷. The memory of the dream still haunts her, and impels her, v.⁸, to make a fresh (2⁵) avowal of her love.

The dream of her lover visiting her, and of her *failing* to secure him, coming at the moment when the king's importunities are threatening to tear her from him for ever (and, upon Oettli's view, immediately after her lover's departure), is conceived with great psychological truth.

ACT IV. (5⁹–8⁴).

Scene 1. (The Ladies of the Court and the Shulamite. Dialogue respecting the lover.)—Ladies of the Court, 5⁹ (in surprise at the Shulamite's persistent rejection of the king's advances, and her devotion to one absent).—The Shulamite, 5¹⁰⁻¹⁶ (an enraptured description of her lover).—Ladies of the Court, 6¹.—The Shulamite, 6²⁻³.

Scene 2. (The king enters.)—Solomon, 6⁴⁻¹³ (renewed endeavour to win the Shulamite's affection by praise of her beauty, and description of the honour in store for her, v.⁴⁻⁹. V.¹⁰ the king's memory passes back to the occasion of his first meeting the Shulamite in the nut-orchard, and he repeats the words with which the ladies of the Court then accosted her, v.¹⁰, together with her reply, in which she excuses herself for having wandered there alone, and allowed herself to be surprised by the king's retinue, v.¹¹⁻¹² : v.¹³ᵃ⁻ ᵇ he quotes similarly the request which they then made to her to remain with them, with her reply, v.¹³ᶜ, and their answer, v.¹³ᵈ, that they desired to see her dance).*

Scene 3.—Solomon, 7¹⁻⁹ † (making a final endeavour to gain the Shulamite's heart by praising her charms in more effusive terms than before).‡

---

from her perilous position, and makes a fresh avowal of his passion for her. Oettli thinks that Ewald's "psychologically powerful" conception of an *imagined* interview is too violent ; and points out that the actual visit takes place dramatically at the right moment, when, after the king's withdrawal till the evening (4⁶), there is a pause in the progress of the action, and when the position of the Shulamite is on the point of becoming more critical.

* Oettli assigns 6¹¹⁻¹³ to the Shulamite, supposing Solomon's quotation of the ladies' exclamation in 6¹⁰ to elicit from her the excuse 6¹¹⁻¹² now ; 6¹³ he explains as Ewald, but treats it as containing her reminiscences, not Solomon's. (Ewald and Oettli render 6¹³ᶜ⁻ ᵈ as Delitzsch, p. 439, *note*.)

† Oettli assigns 7¹⁻⁶ to the chorus.

‡ Reading in 7⁹ᵇ "for lovers" (לדודים) in place of "for my beloved" (לדודי). But the existing text may be preserved, by assigning v.⁹ᵇ⁻ ᶜ to the Shulamite, supposing her to interrupt the king, by declaring that such delights are only for her true love. So Oettli. (V.⁹ᵇ⁻ ᶜ cannot be assigned to Solomon as it stands, "my beloved" being in the Heb. a masculine, so that it cannot be addressed to the Shulamite.)

[416] *Scene* 4.—The Shulamite, 7^{10}–8^4 (heedless of the king's admiration, declaring her unswerving devotion to her shepherd-lover, and her longing to be with him again in the open fields. The refrain, 8^4, slightly altered in form [see RV. *marg.*], as 2^7 3^5 7^{10} (where "*my beloved's*" should be pronounced with some emphasis) is her final repulse of the king).

ACT V. (8^{5-14}).

Shepherds. The Shulamite and her lover.

Scene 1.—Shepherds of Shulem (perceiving the Shulamite approaching, leaning on her lover's arm), $8^{5a. b.}$—The Shulamite, $8^{5c. d. e.}$ $^{6-7}$ (addressing her lover, and pointing to the apple-tree, under which she had once aroused him from his sleep, and the spot where he had first seen the light,* and declaring passionately the irresistible might of true love). 8^{8-12} (addressing all present, recalling, v.$^{8-9}$, words in which her brothers had planned formerly for her welfare,† and declaring how she had fulfilled their best expectations).‡—The lover, 8^{13} (asking his love for a song).—The Shulamite, 8^{14} (singing [cf. 2^{17}], and inviting her lover to join her over the hills).

Upon either view of its purport and scope it will be seen that though much of the poetry is lyrical in character, the Song, as a whole, is of the nature of a *drama*, with dialogue, and action, and character consistently sustained, constituting a rudimentary kind of plot. The action is not, however, as in the drama properly so called, represented in person throughout, or (in subordinate matters) related directly by one of the characters: in several passages, according to Ewald, and in at least one or two, according to Delitzsch and Oettli, the speakers acquaint the hearers with incidents of their previous life, by introducing passages supposed to have been spoken before the drama opens, forming, as it were, "a picture within a picture," out of perspective [417] with the main action of the piece. As *read*, the

* In $8^{5c. d. e}$ Ewald adheres to the Massoretic punctuation, according to which the pronouns are masculine : Oettli (with Pesh. Hitz. Del. and others) points them as feminines, assigning the three lines to the lover.

† $8^{8. 9}$ are assigned by Oettli to two of the Shulamite's brothers, who view their sister, returning after her absence, with some suspicion, which the poet makes them express by recalling their former plans for her welfare.

‡ V.^{10} means that in her resistance to Solomon's advances she had been as an impregnable fortress, and had secured from her assailant terms of peace. V.$^{11-12}$ she plays upon a double application of the term "vineyard": let Solomon, and his vineyard-keepers, receive the proceeds of the king's actual vineyard, if they please: her own vineyard—*i.e.* her person and charms (cf. 1^6)—is at her own disposal ("before me," Gen. 24^{51}) still ; neither he, nor they, will get *that* !

Song is so difficult of comprehension, that it would seem to have been originally designed to be acted, the different parts being personated by different characters, though even the varied gesture and voice of a single reciter might perhaps be sufficient to enable a sympathetic circle of hearers to apprehend its purport. The scene till 8^4 appears to be laid in the royal palace at Jerusalem, or (3^{6-11}) before one of the gates ; * but in 8^5 it evidently changes, and is supposed to be in the heroine's native place.

An attentive study of the poem can leave little doubt that the modern view is decidedly more probable than the traditional view. (1) It has several distinct advantages on the ground of *general* considerations. Thus, that Solomon should appear in the garb and character of a shepherd ($1^{7. 16f.}$† $6^{2f.}$), visiting a country girl in her home ($2^{8ff.}$), proposing to make her his bride ($3^{6ff.}$), and appearing with her in the closing scene, not in his own palace, which, *ex hypothesi*, was to be her future abode, but in her native village ($8^{5ff.}$), is improbable in itself, and inconsistent with all that we know respecting the king's character and tastes : on the other hand, if her lover really was a Shulamite shepherd, all these traits are natural and appropriate. The fine description of love in $8^{6f.}$, from its emphatic position, and the emotion which breathes in it, seems clearly to be intended by the poet to express the main idea of the poem : it is, however, thoroughly unsuitable in the mouth of one who could at most expect to be introduced into a harem of "threescore queens, fourscore concubines, and virgins without number" (6^8) : not only has a maiden who consents willingly to such a position no sense of womanly dignity, but the terms in which (in $8^{6f.}$) she describes her passion demand, and imply *that she expects to receive*, an *undivided* affection in return. But, addressed to a lover in her own position of life, the words are perfectly natural and true : and the allusion in v.^{7b} to the wealthy suitor whose love is despised has an evident force. Again, upon the modern view, the entire poem is far more significant than upon the traditional view : upon the traditional view it consists substantially of nothing but mutual declarations of admiration and affection which lead to no result (for the marriage is evidently [418] determined on when the poem opens), and all that follows

---

* Or (Oettli) in a summer residence of the king in Lebanon (till 8^4).

† Where the lovers' future *woodland* home is anticipated.

the Royal Espousals in 3^6–5^1 lacks dramatic justification; upon the modern view, the idea of the poem, the triumph of plighted love over the seductions of worldly magnificence, is one of real ethical value. And the plan corresponds with the idea—the heroine appears in the first chapter in a difficult and painful situation, from which the last chapter represents her as extricated; thus the interest culminates in its proper place, at the end, not in the middle of the poem. It is to be noted also that the admiration expressed in the poem is not (on either side) evoked by graces of character, but solely by the contemplation of physical beauty: and it is only relieved from being purely sensuous by the introduction of an ethical motive, such as is supplied by the modern view, giving it a purpose and an aim. The two dreams are much more expressive upon the modern than upon the traditional view: they are in evident contrast to one another, for in one ($3^{1\text{-}4}$) the heroine *finds* her lover, while in the other she fails to find him ($5^{2\text{-}7}$), and the distinction between them must have some psychological basis. The estrangement between Solomon and the Shulamite, almost on the morning after their marriage (5^1), assumed by the advocates of the traditional view, in explanation of the second dream, is extremely artificial and improbable; but that the Shulamite, after the vision of her lover (4^8–5^1)—whether this took place in reality or only in the vividness of her imagination—when the crisis of her resistance to the king was approaching, should experience such a dream, is in the highest degree true to nature.

(2) While there are many passages in the poem which may be accommodated without violence to either view, and which cannot consequently be quoted on one side or the other, there are certain crucial passages which, upon the view that the Shulamite and Solomon are the only principal characters, are deficient in point; whereas, if there be a *rival* to Solomon, they are at once forcible and significant.

Thus 2^7 Delitzsch supposes the heroine to sink into Solomon's arms, entranced by an "ecstasy of love," which she adjures the chorus not to interrupt or disturb. But עוּר, הֵעִיר, do not mean to *disturb* (so as to bring to an end) an emotion, but to *arouse it into activity* (Ps. 80³, Pr. 10¹², Isa. 42¹³), which exactly suits Ewald's interpretation that it is an adjuration to [419] the chorus not to excite in her the passion of love artificially (for Solomon). The repetition of the adjuration in 3^5 8^4 is also extremely forcible upon Ew.'s view of the poem.

3[4b]. Even in a dream it is more probable that the heroine would have thought of bringing a shepherd of her own rank into her "mother's house" than a king. So 5[2 *end*] suggests the picture of one who has the actual occupations of a shepherd (Gen. 31[40]).

4[6]. Is it probable that a bride, *on her wedding day* (Del.), would propose thus to withdraw herself from the company of her husband?

6[4c. 5]. Solomon's *dread** of the heroine's eyes is surely incredible if she were his *bride*; but it is intelligible if she is *resisting* his advances.

7[8. 12d] 8[1] all imply that the marriage is not yet consummated, and are thus inconsistent with Del.'s view.

6[12] is too difficult and uncertain to have much weight on either side; but Ew.'s explanation is at least preferable to Del.'s. Ew.: "I knew not that my soul (*i.e.* my desire [as often in Heb., *e.g.* Dt. 24[15], Eccl. 6[9]], viz. to roam about) had set me by the chariots of my noble people" (*i.e.* had led me unawares, as I wandered in the nut-orchard, to the neighbourhood of the king's retinue). Del.: "I knew not that my soul (*i.e.* my desire, viz. for Solomon) had set me on the chariots of my people, (even) of a noble (prince)," *i.e.* in the enjoyment of rambling through the royal park, she hardly remembered (?) that she had won the right to a seat beside the king on his chariots of state. שָׂם מֶרְכְּבוֹת in the sense *brought to* . . . is not an easy construction; but the sense *set on to*, as Hitzig remarks, would seem to be precluded by the absence of the preposition (1 Sa. 8[11] שָׂם בְּ *to set among*, which Del. refers to, is quite different).

The reader will find some other passages noted by Oettli.

Further, if the speeches ascribed to Solomon (1[9-11. 15] 2[2] 4[1-7] 6[4-10] 7[1-9]) † and to the lover (2[10-14] 4[8-15] 5[1] 8[13]) ‡ be compared, a difference may be observed, which, though it might not be sufficient to establish the distinction, nevertheless agrees with it when made probable upon other grounds: Solomon's speeches, though a progress is traceable in them, and 7[7-9] represents a climax, are, on the whole, cold in tone, and contain little more than admiration of the heroine's beauty: those ascribed to the lover are much warmer, and 4[8-15] 5[1] especially is an outburst of genuine passion (notice the warm response in 4[16]). §

[420] From an artistic point of view, it is to be observed that

* הִרְהִיב cannot mean "overcome" in the sense of *fascinate*: the sense *make proud* (Ps. 138[3]) being unsuited to the context, it must be the Syr. ܘܗܒܐ, Arab. أرهب (Ex. 15[6] Saad.), to *confuse*, *perturb* (of RV. *marg.*).

† According to Oettli 1[9-11] 2[2] 4[1-7] 6[4-10] 7[7-9a].

‡ According to Oettli 1[8. 15] 2[10-14] 4[8-15] 5[1] 8[5c. d. e. 13].

§ Solomon calls her only "my friend" [Jud. 11[37] Kt.] 1[9. 15] 2[2] 4[1. 7] 6[4] (also in the mouth of the lover 2[10. 13] 5[2]): the lover alone calls her "my sister, bride" (4[9. 10. 12] 5[1]), or "bride" 4[8. 11]. The term used by the chorus is "the fairest among women," 1[8] 5[9] 6[1].

the characters are clearly distinguished from one another, and are consistent throughout. The permanent element in the poem are the "Daughters of Jerusalem" (1^5 2^7 3^5 $5^{8.\ 16}$ 8^4)—*i.e.* no doubt the ladies of the Court, who play a part somewhat like that of the chorus in a Greek play: they watch the progress of the action; and their presence, or a question asked by them, is the occasion of declarations of feeling on the part of the chief actors (cf. $1^{6.\ 8}$ 2^7 $5^{8.\ 9}$ 6^1 8^4). The principal character is, of course, the Shulamite maiden, a paragon of modesty and beauty, who awakens the reader's interest in the first chapter, and engrosses it till the end: surrounded by uncongenial companions, amid the seductive attractions of the Court, her thoughts are ever with her absent lover; her fidelity to him enables her to parry time after time the king's advances; in the end her devotion triumphs, and she appears happy in the companionship of him whom her heart loves. Her lover is regularly termed by her דודי, "my love" ($1^{13.\ 14.\ 16}$ 2^3 &c.).* The speeches attributed to the king are somewhat stiff and formal; those of the lover, on the contrary, breathe a warm and devoted affection. The brothers are represented as having treated their sister with some brusqueness (1^6), and viewed her future behaviour with a suspiciousness which the event proves to be wholly unfounded (8^9). The poem can hardly be said to exhibit a "plot" in the modern sense of the term; the action is terminated, not by a favourable combination of circumstances, but by the heroine's own inflexible fidelity and virtue. Ewald considered that each act embraced the events of one day, the close of which, he observed, appeared in each case to correspond with a stage in the heroine's series of trials (2^7 3^5 5^8 8^4).

The poetry of the Song is exquisite. The movement is graceful and light; the imagery is beautiful, and singularly picturesque; the author revels among the delights of the country; one scene after another is brought before us—doves hiding in the clefts of the rocks (2^{14}) or resting beside the water-brooks [421] (5^{12}), gazelles leaping over the mountains (2^9) or feeding among the lilies (4^5), goats reclining on the sloping hills of Gilead (4^1 6^5): trees with their varied foliage, flowers with bright hues or richly-scented perfume are ever supplying the poet with a fresh picture or comparison: we seem to walk, with the

* Or "he whom my soul loveth," 1^7 $3^{1.\ 3.\ 4}$.

shepherd-lover himself, among vineyards and fig-trees in the balmy air of spring (2¹¹⁻¹³), or to see the fragrant, choicely furnished garden which the charms of his betrothed call up before his imagination (4¹³⁻¹⁵). The number of animals and plants, as well as works of human art and labour—many not mentioned elsewhere—which are named in the Song, is remarkable. The poet also alludes to many localities in a manner which usually shows him to have been personally familiar with them—Kedar, En-gedi, the Sharon, Bether (if this be a proper name), Lebanon (several times), the hills of Gilead, David's Tower in Jerusalem with its hanging shields (4⁴), Amana, Senir, Hermon, Tirzah (6⁴), Mahanaim, Heshbon (the pools by the gate Bath-rabbim), the "Tower of Lebanon looking out towards Damascus " (7⁴), Carmel, Baal-hamon : those with which he seems to be most familiar, and to which he turns most frequently being localities in *North* Palestine, especially in or near Lebanon.

Authorship and Date of the Poem.—It is improbable, even upon the traditional view, that the author is Solomon ; if the modern view be correct, his authorship is evidently out of the question. The diction of the poem exhibits several peculiarities, especially in the *uniform* use of the relative -שׁ (except in the title 1¹) for אֲשֶׁר, and in the recurrence of many words found never * or [422] rarely † besides in Biblical Hebrew, but

* נטר 1⁶ 8¹¹. ¹² for נצר (נטר in pure Heb. is used only of retaining *wrath*) ; איכה=*where*? 1⁷ as 2 Ki. 6¹³ Kt. (see p. 188)=ܐܟܐ ; שֶׁלָּמָה 1⁷ analogous to the Aram. ܠܡܟܐ, די למה Ezr. 7²³ ; ברות for ברוש 1¹⁷ ; קפץ 2⁸ ; חרכים 2⁹ ; כתל 2⁹ ; סתו 2¹¹ ; סמדר 2¹³. ¹⁵ ; פג 2¹³ ; לְכִי *ib.* Kt. as 2 Ki. 4² Kt. (ܟܒ܆) ; ‑שׁל 3⁷ (1⁶ 8¹²) after the suff., as in the Mishna, and like ܕܝܠܝ ; אחז 3⁸ construed as a *deponent* (Gen. 25²⁶, Jud. 5⁸ Targ.; ܐܚܕ) ; רסיסים 5² (Ps. 65¹¹ Targ. Pesh.) ; טנף 5³ ; הרהיב=*to perturb* 6⁵ (ܪܗܒ); אֹפֶן 7² (ܐܘܦܢܐ=Heb. חֶרֶשׂ, Ex. 28¹¹ Pesh., likewise of gems) ; מוג (elsewhere מסך, ממסך ; cf. the verb מסך) and סוגה 7³ ; סנסנים 7⁹ (cf. ܣܡܣܡܐ).

† טָעָה 1⁷ (Pesh. Symm. Vulg. RV. *m.*) as Ezek. 13¹⁰ ↑, and in Aram. (Gen. 21¹⁴ Onq.) ; קְוֻצּוֹת 5². ¹¹ ↑ (ܩܘܨܐ) Ez. 44²⁰) ; גֻנָּה 6¹¹ if the punctuation is to be trusted, as Est. 1⁵ 7⁷. ⁸ ↑ (Aram. גִּנָּא ; Heb. גַּנָּה) ; שלהבת 8⁶ as Job 15³⁰, Ez. 21³ ↑ (שלהוביתא): perhaps also מנד 4¹³. ¹⁶ 7¹⁴, Dt. 33¹³⁻¹⁶ ↑ (cf. ܣܓܝ). Words found besides only in late Hebrew are פרדס 4¹³, Neh. 2⁸, Eccl. 2⁵ ↑ ; איככה 5³, Est. 8⁶ ↑ ; נליל *rod* 5¹⁴, Est. 1⁶ ↑ ; שׁשׁ *marble* 5¹⁵, Est. 1⁶, 1 Ch. 29² (שׁישׁ) ↑.

common in Aramaic, which show either that it must be a late work (post-exilic), or, if early, that it belongs to *North Israel*, where there is reason to suppose that the language spoken differed dialectically from that of Judah.* The general purity and brightness of the style favour the latter alternative, which agrees well with the acquaintance shown by the author with localities of North Palestine, and is adopted by many modern critics. The foreign words in the poem, chiefly names of choice plants or articles of commerce, are such as might have reached Israel through Solomon's connexions with the East.† The title was probably prefixed, at a [423] time when the true origin of the poem had been forgotten, on account of Solomon being a prominent figure in it. The precise date of the poem is, however, difficult to fix. From the manner in which Tirzah and

---

* שׁ occurs in Deborah's Song (Jud. 5[7]), and in narratives seemingly of Ephraimite origin, Jud. 6[17] 7[12] 8[26]; 2 Ki. 6[11] (p. 188) ; elsewhere, only in exilic or post-exilic writings, as Lam. (4 times), Jonah (p. 301), Eccl. (often), late Psalms (p. 352 *n.*), Chr. and Ezr. (thrice) : Gen. 6[3], Job 19[29] are both uncertain. [Sayce (*Acad.* Aug. 2, 1890, p. 94), and Neubauer (*Athenæum*, Aug. 2, 1890, p. 164), thought that שׁל, exactly as in Cant. 3[7], was to be read on a hematite weight, found on the site of Samaria ; but the reading and interpretation are both doubtful : see W. R. Smith's very careful and minute description of the weight in the *Academy*, Nov. 18, 1893, p. 443 ff., reprinted in the *Quarterly Statement of the Palest. Explor. Fund*, July 1894, p. 225 ff. (The characters of the original, Prof. Smith observes, lend no support to Euting's reading (of the cast) נצף (for נצג), *ap.* König, *Einl.* p. 425).] It should be explained, to avoid misconception, that שׁ itself is not Aramaic ; but neither is it normal Hebrew. It seems that, as the language of Moab, while nearly identical with Judaic Hebrew, yet differed from it dialectically (see the writer's *Notes on Samuel*, p. lxxxv ff.) in one direction, so the language of North Israel differed from it slightly in another : especially in *vocabulary*, it showed a noticeable proportion of words known otherwise only, or chiefly, from the Aramaic, while in the use of שׁ it approximated to the neighbouring dialect of Phoenicia, in which the relative was שׁא.

† אהלות, ארגמן, קנמון (these three also occurring elsewhere), נרד 1[12] 4[13. 14], אפריון 3[19], כרכם 4[14], are probably Indian ; פרדס 4[13] is the Zend *pairidaêza*, properly *an enclosure* ; אגוז 6[11] is Persian ; שׁשׁ also is doubtless foreign ; אפריון (also in the Talmud, &c.) is foreign in appearance, and has no plausible Semitic etymology (those mentioned, or suggested, by Delitzsch being most precarious) : if it be not the Sk. *paryaṅka*, a couch-bed, whence Hind. *palki*, a "*palanquin*" (so W. R. Smith, *ap.* Yule, *Glossary of Anglo-Indian Words, s.v.*), it must be the Greek φορεῖον ; which would imply that the poem was a work of the Greek age. The origin of כפר = κύπρος (also in Syriac) 1[14] 4[13] calls for further investigation ; but it will, at least, not be the verb כפר.

Jerusalem are mentioned together in 6[4], it has been thought by many (Ew. Hitz. Oettli) that it was written during the time that Tirzah was the capital of the N. kingdom (1 Ki. 14[17]–16[23f.]), *i.e.* in the 10th cent. B.C.; but Tirzah is named afterwards, 2 Ki. 15[14. 16], so that this argument is not exactly decisive. Recollections of Solomon, and the pomp of his Court, appear, however, to be relatively fresh. The poem, it is possible, may be constructed upon a basis of fact, the dramatic form and the descriptive imagery being supplied by the imagination of the poet.

The linguistic character of the Song of Songs is certainly remarkable ; and it must remain doubtful whether the considerations just advanced are sufficient to neutralize the philological indications (esp. ע, של, פרדס, and אפריון) pointing to a late date. The tendency of recent critics has been to take this view of the poem. In 1890, Kuenen, in answer to an inquiry, wrote, " On the plan and scope of the Song of Songs, I still think much as I did 25 years ago [*i.e.* substantially as Ewald]. But about its age I am perplexed. I would gladly adhere to its pre-exilic origin. But the language of the book is too strong for me. However, before I revise the chapter of my *Onderzoek* relating to it, I must work through the question thoroughly." And it is known that, before his death, he left a lecture in which he assigned it to the Greek period (*JQR.* 1892, p. 595). The same view had been advocated before by Grätz ; and it has been adopted since by Cornill, Wildeboer, Cheyne (*Founders of OT. Crit.* p. 351 f.), Budde, Kautzsch, and others. The grounds for it are stated most fully (though with some exaggeration) by Grätz, p. 43 ff.; more briefly, and also more moderately, by Martineau (pp. 324–328), who follows Grätz in assigning the Song to the age of Ptolemy Euergetes, B.C. 247–221. In the philological argument, the element of uncertainty is our imperfect knowledge of the history and usage of ע (and של) prior to the age of Ecclesiastes (and the Mishnah) ; in other parts of the OT. its use is rare and sporadic (p. 449 *n.*) ; what, then, were the antecedents of its frequent appearance in Ecclesiastes? and to what stage in the history of the word does its *exclusive* use in the Song of Songs point? It must be owned that אפריון resembles φορεῖον more than it resembles *paryaṅka*, and that it is surprising to find in Hebrew, at a time long before either the Medes or the Persians had become an influential power, a word like פרדס, which could not even, like the name of a commodity, have travelled with the thing.

The *interpretation* of the Song has passed through many and strange phases, which are illustrated at some length in Dr. Ginsburg's learned Introduction. By the Jews it was largely interpreted as an allegory ; it is so expounded, for instance, in the Targum, where it is made to embrace the entire history of Israel, from the Exodus to the future Messiah. The same method was adopted by the early Christian Fathers, especially by Origen, Solomon and the Shulamite representing Christ and the Church respectively. But there is nothing in the poem to suggest that it is an allegory ; and the attempt to apply it to details results in great artificiality and extravagance. Bp. Lowth, though not abandoning the allegorical view, sought to free it from its extravagances ; and while refusing to press details, held that the [424] poem, while describing the actual nuptials of Solomon with the daughter of Pharaoh, contained also an allegoric reference to Christ espousing a Church chosen from among the Gentiles.* Among modern scholars also there have been several who, while refusing to allegorise, have nevertheless been unwilling to see in the poem nothing beyond a description of human emotions, and have adopted a view nearly identical with Lowth's modified allegorical view : they have regarded, viz., the love depicted in the poem as typical of a higher love, supposing it either (*a*) to represent the love of Jehovah to His people (Keil), or (*b*) that of the soul to God (Moses Stuart), or (*c*) to foreshadow the love of Christ to the Church (Delitzsch, Kingsbury). This is free from the vices which attach to the old allegorical method of interpretation ; but there is still nothing in the poem to suggest it : nor, if the poem, as is the case upon Ewald's theory, *contains an ethical motive*, is it necessary. Both the allegorical and the typical systems of interpretation owe their plausibility to the assumption that the poem exhibits only two principal characters ; in this case, if interpreted literally, it is destitute of ethical purpose, and a hidden meaning has to be postulated in order to justify its place in the Canon. Upon Ewald's view, the literal sense supplies the requisite ethical justification. At the same time, the typical interpretation is perfectly compatible with Ewald's view, and indeed, if combined with it, is materially improved ; the heroine's true love then represents God, and Solomon, in better agreement with his historical position and character, represents the blandishments of the world, unable to divert the hearts of His faithful servants from Him.

It cannot, of course, be pretended that there are no difficult passages in the Song, or none which may have been incorrectly understood by both Ew. and

---

* *Sacred Poetry of the Hebrews*, Lect. xxx.–xxxi. But the identification of the Shulamite with Pharaoh's daughter cannot be right.

Del. And some modern scholars, it is right to add, are not satisfied with either of the above explanations of the poem ; so *e.g.* Reuss in his translation, p. 51, &c. (who thinks that the *lover* speaks throughout, and merely represents his betrothed as addressing him by a graceful poetic fiction); and Grätz, p. 26 ff. (who thinks similarly that the Shulamite speaks throughout). But there are passages which it is impossible to accommodate to the theory of either Reuss or Grätz without great [425] exegetical liberties : notice, for instance, the violent rendering in both of 1^4, the artificial explanation of 3^{6-11}, &c.

Stickel, Bruston, Castelli, Martineau, and Rothstein (above, p. 436) all adopt the same general view of the poem as Ewald (Castelli, however, denying that it is a drama), with subordinate modifications designed to remove certain difficulties which, in their judgment, attach to his conception of it. Thus Stickel considers that 1^{7-8} $1^{15}-2^4$ 4^7-5^1 form three scenes in which a *second* pair of lovers appear, in designed contrast to Solomon and the Shulamite : Bruston holds that 3^1-5^1 represents the marriage of Solomon with a Tyrian princess ; Rothstein (whose presentation of the poem is an attractive one) assigns 4^{8-16} 5^1 to the King, 6^{4-9} 7^{7-9} to the lover, and $6^{10.\ 13a.b}$ 7^{1-6} to a chorus of peasants. Castelli and Martineau go further, both eliminating Solomon as a speaker, and the latter (whose view will appear shortly *in extenso* in Haupt's *SBOT.*) assuming also many transpositions and interpolations in the text.

The principal alternative explanation is that suggested by J. G. Wetzstein, for many years Prussian Consul at Damascus, in his Excursus on Syrian marriage-customs in Delitzsch, p. 172 *n.*, which has been accepted by Stade (*G.* ii. 197 *n.*), Kautzsch (*Abriss*, p. 210 f. [^{2}p. 134]), and esp. by Budde (*New World*, Boston, U.S.A., 1894, p. 56 ff.). The fullest account of these marriage-customs is that given by Wetzstein in an article in Bastian's *Ztsch. f. Ethnologie*, 1873, p. 270 ff., on "Die Syrische Dreschtafel," explaining the uses of it (which are more varied than might be imagined), and offering many illustrations of the OT. from customs still prevalent in the East. In modern Syria, the first seven days after a wedding are called "the King's Week"; the young pair play during this time king and queen ; the "threshing-board" is turned into a mock-throne, on which they are seated, while songs are sung before them by the villagers and others, celebrating them on their happiness, among which the *wasf*, or poetical "description" of the physical beauty of the bride and bridegroom, holds a prominent place. The first of these *wasfs* is sung on the evening of the wedding-day itself : brandishing a naked sword in her right hand, and with a handkerchief in her left, the bride dances in her wedding array, lighted by fires, and surrounded by a circle of guests, half men and half women, accompanying her dance with a *wasf* in praise of her charms. This sword-dance, with its concomitants, forms a striking scene (Wetzstein, *ap.* Del. p. 171). Other *wasfs* follow on the subsequent days. Wetzstein supposes the "Song of Solomon" to be a collection of such wedding-songs : according to his view, as developed by Budde (*l.c.*), the bridegroom is called King Solomon hyperbolically, the sixty valiant men who escort his litter ($3^{7f.}$) being the "companions of the bridegroom" (cf. Jud. 14^{11}); the bride is designated the Shulamite (6^{13}), as a term suggestive of the highest beauty (1 Ki. 1³; cf. Song 1⁸ 5⁹ 6¹: so first Stade, *G.* i. 292); the greater part of the poem consists of imaginative descriptions of love and wedded bliss, not actually sung by the royal pair themselves, but placed in their mouths by the men and women who sing before them; 7¹ᶠᶠ· might be the *wasf* of the sword-dance, 4¹⁻⁶ 6⁴⁻⁷ would correspond to the *wasfs* of the following days, here placed dramatically by the poet in the mouth of the bridegroom, 5¹⁰⁻¹⁶, the *wasf* of the bridegroom, is sung by the bride: in some places connecting links were added by the redactor. Wetzstein (*ap.* Del. p. 172 ff.) relates how at the marriage of the daughter of the Sheikh of Nawâ, a noted poet of the neighbourhood was called in, who composed a poem suited to the occasion ending with a *wasf*, or description of the bride's charms, which is quoted at length, and which, though longer and more ornate, is similar in character to those in the Song of Songs. Budde's view is criticised by C. Bruston in *Le Xᵉ Congrès des Orientalistes et l'Anc. Test.* (Paris, 1895), pp. 13-19, who points out that it cannot be carried through consistently without considerable violence to the text.

§ 2. RUTH.

LITERATURE.—The Commentaries of Bertheau and Keil on Judges (p. 160), at the end; Wellhausen, *Comp.* pp. 357-359; W. R. Smith, "Ruth" in the *Encycl. Brit.*⁹; S. Oettli in Strack and Zöckler's *Kgf. Komm.* (in the part entitled *Die Geschichtlichen Hagiographen*, 1889, p. 211 ff.).

The contents of this Book are too well known to need a detailed description. Elimelech, a native of Bethlehem in Judah, in the days of the Judges, goes with his wife, Naomi, and his two sons, Mahlon and Chilion, to sojourn in Moab. He dies there; and his two sons marry Moabitish wives, Orpah and Ruth respectively. After a while Mahlon and Chilion die likewise, and Naomi is left alone with her two daughters-in-law. She resolves upon returning to Bethlehem, but bids her daughters-in-law remain in their own country. Orpah accepts her mother-in-law's offer; Ruth expresses her determination to accompany Naomi back (c. 1). C. 2-4 narrate how it happened that after their return to Bethlehem, Ruth made the acquaintance of her kinsman Boaz, and how in the end he took her as his wife. The offspring of their union was Obed, father of Jesse, and grandfather of David. The narrative is told with much picturesque and graceful detail, and affords an idyllic glimpse of home life in ancient Israel.

Aim of the Book.—The Books of Samuel contain no particulars respecting the ancestry of David, merely giving the names of his father Jesse and of his brethren (1 Sa. 16¹⁻¹³ &c.); hence the aim of the Book appears to have been partly to fill up this deficiency, partly (and perhaps particularly) to show how Ruth, a daughter of Moab, and a native therefore of a country hostile theocratically to Israel, obtained an honourable position among Jehovah's people, and became an ancestor of the illustrious king, David.*   Has the writer, however, any ulterior aim, besides the one which is visible on the surface? Intermarriage with foreign women was one of the practices which Ezra (c. 9–10) and Nehemiah (13²³⁻²⁹) strove earnestly to suppress; and hence [426] it has been thought, from the favour with which Boaz's marriage with Ruth is regarded in the Book, that it was written as a protest against the line taken by these two reformers.   But this cannot be considered probable; nor can the present writer, at any rate, satisfy himself that the Book is as late as the 5th cent. B.C.   It is, however, not impossible, considering the prominence given to this subject in c. 3–4, that it is a collateral *didactic* aim of the author to inculcate the duty of marriage on the part of the next-of-kin † with a widow left childless.

Date of Composition.—Most modern critics consider Ruth to be exilic (Ew. *Hist.* i. 154 f.), or post-exilic (Berth. Wellh. Kuen. &c.); the chief grounds alleged being (1) the learned, antiquarian interest which is thought to manifest itself in 4¹⁻¹², pointing in particular to the time when the custom referred to in v.⁷ had become obsolete; and (2) the language, which exhibits some Aramaisms and other late expressions.

It is doubtful whether these grounds are decisive.   The general Hebrew style (the idioms and the syntax) shows no marks of deterioration; it is palpably different, not merely from that of Esther and Chronicles, but even from Nehemiah's memoirs or Jonah, and stands on a level with the best parts of Samuel.‡

---

* Keil, § 136; Bertheau, p. 283; Kuenen, *Onderzoek*, § 36. 9.   Notice 1¹⁶ᵇ 2¹²ᵇ.   This reception of Ruth appears to conflict with Dt. 23³.

† Not the duty of the *levirate*-marriage (Gen. 38; Dt. 25⁵).   Boaz is not Ruth's *brother-in-law*.

‡ The style in general is classical; but among particular idioms notice 1¹⁷ וג ל יִי כה יעשה (elsewhere only in Sam. Kgs.: p. 184); 1¹⁹ ותהם כל העיר יִי ל (1 Ki. 1⁴⁵); 2²¹ עד אם (only besides Gen. 24¹⁹ J, Isa. 30¹⁷); 4⁴ גלה אזן (as 1 Sa. 9¹⁵ 20². ¹². ¹³ 22⁸. ¹⁷, 2 Sa. 7²⁷); and esp. 2⁸ פה *here*, in the *local* sense, elsewhere only in JE (Gen. 22⁵ 31³⁷, Ex. 2¹², Nu. 11³¹ 23¹⁵) and 2 Sa. 18³⁰, which is not a trait likely to have been *imitated* by a later writer.   The suff. באנה 1¹⁹ is paralleled also in E (Gen. 21²⁹ 42³⁶).

The linguistic traits alluded to are the 2nd fem. sing. impf. in ןִ-, 2[8. 21] 3[4. 18] (elsewhere only Isa. 45[10], Jer. 31[22], 1 Sa. 1[14]), and the 2nd fem. sing. pf. in תִּי- 3[3. 4] (elsewhere only in Mic. 4[13]; Jer. [frequently]; Ez. 16 *): these, however, are in fact the original terminations, which may have remained in use locally (cf. אַתִּי, כִּי-, p. 188 *note*), and, as the parallels quoted show, are, at least, not confined to *post*-exilic authors. Further—

לָהֵן *therefore* 1[13] (as in Aram., Dan. 2[6. 9] 4[24]).

[427] נשא נשים *to take wives* 1[4] (for the usual לקח נ׳), as 1 Ch. 23[22], 2 Ch. 11[21] 13[21] 24[3], Ezr. 9[2. 12] 10[44], Neh. 13[25] (in Jud. 21[23] rather differently = *to carry away, secure* ; Budde, *Richter und Samuel*, p. 154).

עגן *to restrain* 1[13] (as *perhaps* in Aram. : but comp. Payne Smith, *s.v.*).

שׂבר *to hope* 1[13], as Isa. 38[18] (poet.), Ps. 104[27] 119[166] 145[15], Est. 9[1] ↑ (=Aram. סבר) : cf. the subst. שֵׂבר Ps. 119[116] 146[5] ↑ (late).

שׁדי *Almighty* 1[20f.] (without אל *God* : p. 127, *note*), as never elsewhere in prose, and in poetry chiefly in Job.

מרגלות *the parts about the feet* 3[4. 7. 8. 14], only besides Dan. 10[6].

לפת *to turn about* 3[8], only besides Job 6[18] (but Arab., not Aram.).

קִיַּם *to confirm* 4[7], as Ezek. 13[6], Ps. 119[28. 106], Est. 9[21. 27. 29. 31. 32], and in Aram. (Dan. 6[8])↑.†

Of these קים cannot be defended as old Hebrew ; but the word occurs in a verse which is not needed in the narrative, and has every appearance of being an *explanatory gloss* (cf. the gloss in 1 Sa. 9[9], *which begins similarly*). Of the others, מרגלות is formed in exact analogy with מראשׁות (1 Sa. 19[13] &c.); its not occurring elsewhere till Dan. may be due merely to its not being required. שׁדי (which occurs in poetry in Nu. 24[4. 16]) may be a poetical term (cf. 2[12b]) chosen intentionally by the author : poetical expressions occur from time to time in other pre-exilic historical books. In reference to the rest, it may be remembered that words, with Aramaic or late Hebrew affinities, occur, at least sporadically, in passages admittedly of early date (as תשׁורה, אוּל in 1 Sa. 9[1]–10[16]). לחן is the word which it is most difficult to reconcile with an early date ; but it is possible that the Book, in spite of its interest in Bethlehem and David, was yet written in the N. kingdom, and preserves words current there dialectically (p. 449).

It seems to the writer that the general beauty and purity of the style of Ruth point more decidedly to the pre-exilic period than do the isolated expressions quoted to the period after the exile. The genealogy, 4[18-22], which also appears to suggest an exilic or post-exilic date (הוֹלִיד [p. 134, No. 45] ; and comp. 1 Ch. 2[9ff.]), forms no integral part of the Book, and may well

---

* This very peculiar distribution of an anomalous form—in books neither specially early nor specially late, and in *one* chapter only of a long book— must be due, in some measure, to accidental causes.

† צבט (2[14]) is wrongly cited as an Aramaism. It is pure Heb. =Arab. ضبط =Aram. ܟܒܬ, according to the regular interchange of consonants (*Tenses*, § 178. 1). Nor is צבת (2[16]) an Aramaic word.

have been added long after the Book itself was written, in an age that was devoted to the study of pedigrees, in order to supply the missing links between Boaz and Perez (4^{12}).

That David had Moabite connexions is probable independently from 1 Sa. $22^{3f.}$. The basis of the narrative consists, it may reasonably be supposed, of the family traditions respecting Ruth [428] and her marriage with Boaz. These have been cast into a literary form by the author, who has, no doubt, to a certain extent idealised both the characters and the scenes. Distance seems to have mellowed the rude, unsettled age of the Judges. The narrator manifestly takes delight in the graceful and attractive details of his picture. His principal characters are amiable, God-fearing, courteous, unassuming; and all in different ways show how a religious spirit may be carried unostentatiously into the conduct of daily life.

§ 3. THE LAMENTATIONS.

LITERATURE.—H. Ewald in *Die Psalmen* (above, p. 359), p. 321 ff. (ii. 99 ff. of the translation); Otto Thenius (in the *Kgf. Hdb.*), 1855; Nägelsbach, Keil, Payne Smith, Cheyne, Plumptre, at the end of their Commentaries on Jeremiah (above, p. 247); W. R. Smith, art. " Lamentations" in the *Encycl. Brit.*[9]; S. Oettli in Strack and Zöckler's *Kgf. Komm.*; M. Löhr, *Die Klagelieder Jeremia's* (1891); and in Nowack's "Handkomm.," 1893; S. Minocchi, *Le Lamentazioni di Geremia* (Roma, 1897); G. Bickell (p. 340 *n.*).

In Hebrew Bibles the title of this Book, derived from its first word, is איכה *Ēchāh*; another name by which it is also known among the Jews is קינות, *i.e. Lamentations* or *Dirges* * (LXX θρῆνοι). The Book consists of five independent poems, all dealing with a common theme, viz. the calamities that befell the people of Judah and Jerusalem in consequence of the siege and capture of Jerusalem by the Chaldæans, B.C. 586. The poems are constructed upon an artificial plan; and though the details are varied, they are evidently all conformed to the same type. In the first four poems the verses are arranged *alphabetically* : in the first and second each verse consists of three members, and the verses begin severally with the successive letters of the Hebrew alphabet; in the third, the verses consist

* Cf. the writer's *Joel and Amos*, p. 184.

of single members, and three verses, each having the same initial letter, are assigned to each successive letter, so that the poem contains in all 66 verses ; the fourth is similar in structure to the first, except that each verse has two members only ; the fifth poem is not alphabetical, but consists nevertheless of 22 verses, each formed by two somewhat short members.*

The *rhythm* of the first four poems is peculiar. It was observed [429] long ago by Lowth † that the verses here were of unwonted length ; De Wette ‡ noticed that each member of a verse was marked by a *cæsura*, corresponding both with the accent and with the sense: afterwards Keil § made the further observation that the *cæsura* divided the verse into two *unequal* parts ; but the subject was only systematically investigated by C. Budde, professor (at that time) in Bonn, in an essay in the *ZATW.* 1882, pp. 1–52, entitled " Das Hebräische Klagelied." In this essay Budde showed that the form of verse characteristic of Lam. 1–4 recurred in other parts of the OT., written in an elegiac strain, and that it was in fact the rhythm *peculiar to Hebrew elegy.* The verse itself may consist of one or more members, but each member, which contains on an average not more than five or six words, is divided by a *cæsura* into two unequal parts, the first being usually about the length of an ordinary verse-member, the second being decidedly shorter, and very often not parallel in thought to the first. An example or two, even in a translation, will make the character of the rhythm apparent :—

Lam. 1¹ How doth the city sit solitary,—she that was full of people !
    She is become as a widow,—she that was great among the nations :
    The princess among the provinces,—she is become tributary.

2³ He hath hewn off in fierceness of anger—all the horn of Israel :
    He hath drawn back his right hand—from before the enemy :
    And he hath burned up Jacob as a flaming fire,—it devoureth round about.

---

* In c. 2–4 the ﬤ precedes the ﬠ (cf. p. 368, *note*) : it would seem either that when the Lamentations were composed the order of the Hebrew alphabet was not definitely fixed, or that different orders prevailed in antiquity.

† *Sacred Poetry of the Hebrews*, Lect. xxii.

‡ *Comment. zu den Psalmen* (ed. 4), 1836, p. 55 f.

§ In Hävernick's *Einleitung*, iii. (1849), p. 512.

3[1-3] I am the man that hath seen affliction—by the rod of his wrath :
Me hath he led and caused to go—in darkness and not in light :
Surely against me he ever turneth his hand—all the day.

Occasionally the first member may be abnormally lengthened
(as 2[13a] 3[56] 4[18b. 20a]), or if it consists of long and weighty words,
it may contain two only (as 1[1b. c] already quoted, 1[4c. 9b] &c.), or,
again (though this happens more rarely), there may be a slight
collision between the rhythm and the thought (as 1[10c. 13a] 2[8b]) :
but the general relation of the two members to one another
continues the same ; the first member, instead of being balanced
and reinforced by the second (as is ordinarily the case in Hebrew
poetry), is echoed by it imperfectly, so that it [430] seems, as it
were, to die away in it, and a plaintive, melancholy cadence is
thus produced. There are, however, particular verses in Lam.
1–4 which, even with the licences just noticed, cannot be
reduced to the type described : Budde himself supposes that
in these cases the text has not been transmitted intact ; * but
whether the corrections proposed by him be accepted or not, the
number of such verses is relatively small, and the *tendency* of the
poet of Lam. 1–4 to cast his separate verse-members into the
type in question cannot be denied.

The same scholar points to other parts of the OT. as exhibiting a similar
structure ; of which the principal are perhaps Isa. 14[4b-21] † (the elegy on the
king of Babylon), Ez. c. 19, 26[17] (from *How*)[-18] (see LXX, Corn.; or
QPB.[3]), 28[18f.], Jer. 9[9b] (from מעוף)[-10. 18. 20-21] ‡ 22[6] (from גלעד)[-7. 21-23], Am. 5[2] ;
in many of these passages a קינה, or " dirge," is expressly announced as about
to be sung ; it is, moreover, to be observed that the rhythm seems to be
chosen intentionally, for in the context the *ordinary* poetical rhythm, with
verse-members of equal length, is, as a rule, employed. In Jer. 9[16] מקוננות
women that chant dirges, in the parallel clause חכמות *wise* or *cunning women*,
are summoned to sound the strain of woe,—an indication that the קינה or
" dirge " was no simple spontaneous outburst of grief,§ but a work requiring
for its production some technical skill ; the women referred to evidently
belonged to a profession, and not improbably (to judge from the analogy of

---

* Budde has expressed most recently his view of the text of these chapters
in the *ZATW.* 1892, p. 264 ff.

† v.[4b] How hath the oppressor ceased,—the raging [מַרְהֵבָה] ceased !

   v.[5] Jehovah hath broken the staff of the wicked,—the sceptre of rulers, &c.

‡ י״י דבר כה נאם v.[21] being (with LXX, Ew. &c.) omitted (or disregarded,
as parenthetic). See also Jer. 38[22] (Budde, *ZATW.* 1883, pp. 1–8).

§ 1 Ki. 13[30], Jer. 22[18] 34[5] (the interjections).

what prevails in modern Syria*) knew by rote certain conventional types of dirge which they were taught how to apply in particular cases (cf. v.[19b]). Probably also the elegiac rhythm which has been described was accompanied by a corresponding plaintive melody, and in any case it was connected with mournful associations: hence its adoption by the prophets when they were anxious to make an unusually deep impression upon their hearers. Budde has developed and applied his theory further in the *ZATW.* 1891, p. 234 ff.: see also *ib.* 1892, pp. 31–33 (on Isa. 37[22ff.]); and "The Folk-song of Israel in the mouth of the Prophets," in the *New World*, March 1893.

Exquisite as is the pathos which breathes in the poetry of these dirges, they are thus, it appears, constructed with conscious art: they are not the unstudied effusions of natural emotion, they are carefully elaborated poems, in which no aspect of the common grief is unremembered, and in which every trait which might stir a chord of sorrow or regret is brought together, for the [431] purpose of completing the picture of woe. And hence, no doubt, the acrostic form of the first four dirges. As in the case of the Psalms (p. 368), the acrostic form is an *external* principle of arrangement, where the subject is one which does not readily admit of logical development; and here it secures the orderly and systematic expression of the emotions with which the poet's heart is filled.

Contents of the Poems.—The aspect of the common theme, which each poem develops, may be said to be indicated in its opening words.

I. *The desolation and misery of Jerusalem* ("How doth she sit solitary, the city that was full of people!"). The poet bewails the solitude and desertion of Jerusalem: her people are in exile; the enemy have laid violent hands upon her treasures; her glory is departed, v.[1-11a]. In the middle of v.[11] the city itself is supposed to speak, declaring the severity of her affliction, v.[11b-16]; v.[17] the poet speaks in his own person, but v.[18] the city resumes its plaint, though acknowledging Jehovah's righteousness, and prays that retribution may overtake its foes, v.[18-22].

II. *Jehovah's anger with His people* ("How hath Jehovah covered the daughter of Zion with a cloud in His anger!"). Here the stress lies on the *cause* of the country's sufferings; Jehovah has become its *enemy*, and has cast off His people, His land, His sanctuary, v.[1-9]; the agony of the residents in the

* Wetzstein, *ap.* Budde, pp. 25-28. See also Budde, "Die Hebräische Leichenklage," in the *Zeitschr. d. Deutschen Pal. Vereins*, vi. p. 180 ff.

capital, the famine in the streets, the contempt of the passers-by, the malicious triumph of the foe, are depicted, v.[10-17]. The nation is invited to entreat Jehovah on behalf of its dying children, v.[18f.]; and it responds in the prayer of v.[20-22].

III. *The nation's complaint, and its ground of consolation* ("I am the man that hath seen affliction by the rod of His wrath"). Here the poet, speaking in the name of the people—or the people itself personified (p. 390, *note*) *—bewails its calamities, v.[1-20]; v.[21-39] it consoles itself by the thought of God's compassion, and the purposes of grace which He may have in His visitation; v.[40-54] its members are invited to confess their guilt, and turn to God in penitence; v.[55-57] the tone becomes more hopeful; [432] and v.[58-66] the poem ends with a confident appeal for vengeance on the nation's foes.

IV. *Zion's past and present contrasted* ("How is the gold become dim! how is the most pure gold changed!"). The contrast between the former splendour and the present humiliation of Zion and its inhabitants, v.[1-11]; prophets and priests are so stained by guilt that they find no resting-place even among the heathen, v.[12-16]; in vain do the people seek to escape from their pursuers: the hopes fixed upon Egypt were disappointed, the protection which they looked for from "the breath of our nostrils," Jehovah's anointed (Zedekiah), failed them, v.[17-20]. But though for a while Edom (see Ps. 137[7]) may triumph, Israel's punishment will ere long be completed, and the cup of humiliation be passed on to its foe, v.[21-22].

V. *The nations appeal for Jehovah's compassionate regard* ("Remember, O Jehovah, what is come upon us"). The poet calls upon Jehovah to consider the affliction of His people, the nature and severity of which is indicated in a series of characteristic traits, v.[1-18]. But Zion's desolation brings to his mind by contrast (Ps. 102[27]) the thought of Jehovah's abiding power, on the ground of which he repeats his appeal for help, v.[20-22].

The poems all have a *national* significance, the poet speaking throughout in the name of the nation. From the historical references, it is evident that they were composed after the capture

---

* In 3[14] עמים *peoples* for עמי *my people* must doubtless be read, with the Peshitto, and many Heb. MSS., and modern authorities. Either a letter has fallen out, or a mark of abbreviation has been disregarded. Comp. Cheyne's crit. notes on Isa. 5[1], Ps. 45[10].

of the city, the people, including the king (2^9), being in exile.
C. 5 was perhaps written somewhat later than c. 1–4 : it dwells
less upon the actual fate of Jerusalem than upon the continued
bondage and degradation which was the lot of the survivors;
v.^{8} "servants rule over us" appears to allude to the subordinate
foreign officials holding command in Judah; and v.^{20} implies
that Jehovah's abandonment of Jerusalem has lasted for some
time. From a poetical point of view the second and fourth
poems are generally considered to be superior to the others.

Authorship. There is no statement in the OT. as to the
authorship of the Lamentations; but the tradition that they were
written by Jeremiah can be traced back to the LXX;* it is [433]
found also in the Targum,† and is alluded to in the Talmud
and by the Fathers. It cannot, however, be at once assumed
that this tradition has a genuine historical basis : an interval of
at least three centuries separated the LXX translators from the
age of Jeremiah; and the tradition *may*, for example, be merely
an inference founded on the general resemblance of tone which
the Lamentations exhibit with such passages as Jer. 8^{18}–c. 9,
c. 14–15, and on the reference assumed to be contained in
$3^{14. \ 53-56}$ to incidents in the prophet's life (20^7; $38^{6ff.}$).‡ The
question, therefore, which we have to ask is, Does the internal
evidence of the Book confirm the tradition or not? Most
modern critics § answer this question in the negative; Keil,
and especially Hornblower,‖ seek to maintain the tradition of
Jeremiah's authorship; Thenius adopts an intermediate position,
holding c. 2 and c. 4 to be Jeremiah's, but not more.

Some of the arguments advanced on both sides possess too
little of an objective character to have great value; *e.g.* the
improbability of the same writer dealing five times with the same
theme, or the different æsthetic worth of the different poems

---

* Who preface their translation of the Book with the words : "And it came
to pass, after Israel was led into captivity, and Jerusalem laid waste, that
Jeremiah sat weeping, and lamented with this lamentation over Jerusalem,
and said, . . ."

† "Jeremiah the prophet and chief priest, said, . . ."

‡ Though the expressions are, of course, really figurative; and 3^{54} (if taken
literally) is in express contradiction with Jer. 38^6 (*no* water).

§ Ewald, Schrader (*Einl.*), Nöldeke, Kuenen, Nägelsbach, Cheyne, &c.

‖ In notes appended to his translation of Nägelsbach's Commentary,
p. 19 ff.

(which leads Thenius, for instance, to regard only c. 2, 4 as worthy of Jeremiah's pen), or (on the other side) the improbability of different poets beginning with the same word *How*, c. 1, 2, 4 (which is a common elegiac exclamation, and might, moreover, have been suggested to one writer from another). Of more substantial arguments, there may be cited in support of the tradition :—

a. The same sensitive temper, profoundly sympathetic in national sorrow, and ready to pour forth its emotions unrestrainedly, manifests itself both in Lam. and in Jer. (*e.g.* c. 14–15).

b. The national calamities are referred to the same causes as in Jer. ; comp. *e.g.* the allusions to national *sin* in $1^{5. 8. 14. 18}$ 3^{42} (cf. v.^{39}) $4^{6. 22}$ $5^{7. 16}$ with Jer. 14^7 16^{10-12} 17^{1-3} &c. ; to the guilt of the prophets and priests in 2^{14} 4^{13-15} with Jer. $2^{7. 8}$ 5^{31} 14^{13} 23^{11-40}, c. 27, &c. ; to the people's vain confidence in the help of weak and treacherous allies in $1^{2. 19}$ 4^{17} with Jer. $2^{18. 36}$ 30^{14} 37^{5-10}.

c. Similar representations and figures occur in both Lam. and Jer., *e.g.* the [434] virgin daughter of Zion broken with an incurable breach, 1^{15} 2^{13}, Jer. $8^{21f.}$ 14^{17} ; the prophet's eyes flowing down with tears (below, *d*, 3), the haunting sense of being surrounded with fears and terrors (*d*, 7), the appeal for vengeance to the righteous Judge, 3^{64-66}, Jer. 11^{20}, the expectation of a similar desolation for the nations that exulted in the fall of Jerusalem, 4^{21}, Jer. 49^{12}.

d. Similarities of expression, of which the following are the most striking :—

LAMENTATIONS.	JEREMIAH.
1^2 (no comforter of all her lovers).	30^{14}.
1^{8b-9}.	$13^{22b. 26}$.
1^{16a} $2^{11a. 18b}$ $3^{48. 49}$ (eyes running down with tears, &c.).	$9^{1. 18b}$ 13^{17b} 14^{17}.
2^{11} 3^{48} 4^{10} (the breach of the daughter of my people) ; cf. 2^{13} (the breach great), 3^{47}.	6^{14} $8^{11. 21}$; cf. $4^{6. 20}$ 6^1 10^{19} 14^{17b} *al.*
2^{14} 4^{13} (sins of prophets and priests).	Cf. 2^8 5^{31} $14^{13f.}$ 23^{11}.
2^{20} 4^{10} (women eating their own children).	Cf. 19^9 (Dt. 28^{53}).
2^{22} ("*my terrors* round about ").	6^{25} 20^{10} ("*terror* round about ").
3^{14} (I am become a derision).	20^7.
3^{15} (wormwood) ^{19} (wormwood and gall).	9^{15} 23^{15} (Dt. 29^{17}).
3^{47} (fear and the snare).	48^{43} ("fear and the snare *and the pit* ").
3^{52} (they hunt me).	16^{16b}.
4^{21b} (the cup).	25^{15} 49^{12}.
5^{16}.	13^{18b}.

Against the tradition may be urged :—

a. The variation in the alphabetic order, which would tend at least to show that c. 2, 3, 4 were not by the author of c. 1.

b. The point of view is sometimes other than that of Jeremiah, viz. (1) 1²¹ᶠ· and 3⁵⁹⁻⁶⁶. It was Jeremiah's conviction that the Chaldæans were executing Jehovah's purpose upon Judah; this being so, would he, even when speaking in the nation's name, invoke, or anticipate, retribution upon them? (2) 2⁹ᶜ. Do these words read as if they were spoken by Jeremiah? do they not rather read as if they were spoken by one who was *not* himself a prophet? (3) 4¹⁷. The speaker here identifies himself with those who expected help from Egypt, which Jeremiah never did (37⁵⁻¹⁰); would not Jeremiah have written *Their* rather than *Our*? (4) 4²⁰. Considering Jeremiah's view of Zedekiah (24⁸⁻¹⁰ &c.), is it likely that he would have alluded to him in such laudatory terms as are here employed? *

[435] *c.* The phraseology varies from that of Jeremiah. Lam. contains a very large number of words not found in Jer.; and though the non-occurrence in Jer. of several of these must be due to accident (as לחי *cheek*, שבט *rod*, צפור *bird*), and the non-occurrence of others may be attributed to the peculiar character of Lam., and is thus of slight or no significance, yet others are more remarkable; † and, taken altogether, the impression which they leave upon an impartial critic is that their number is greater than would be the case if Jeremiah were the author.

d. It may perhaps be doubted whether a writer, who, in his literary style, followed, as Jeremiah did (p. 274), the promptings of nature, would subject

---

* 5⁷ is also pointed out as inconsistent with Jer.'s general teaching; but see Jer. 15⁴, and observe that the other side of the truth is expressed in v.¹⁶ᵇ.

† As עני *affliction* 1⁸· ⁷· ⁹ 3¹· ¹⁹ ; שומם 1⁴· ¹³· ¹⁶ 3¹¹ ; ינה 1⁴· ⁵· ¹² 3³²· ³³ ; הביט *to look* 1¹¹· ¹² 3⁶³ 4¹⁶ 5¹ ; ארני *Lord* (alone) 1¹⁴· ¹⁵ 2¹· ²· ⁵· ⁷· ¹⁸· ¹⁹· ²⁰ᵇ 3⁸¹· ³⁶· ³⁷· ³⁸ ; עולל (=*to do* something *to* a person) 1²² 2²⁰ 3⁵¹ ; בלע 2²· ⁵· ⁸· ¹⁶ ; ונח 2⁷ 3¹⁷· ³¹ ; ש (for אשר) 2¹⁵· ¹⁶ 4⁹ 5¹⁸ ; שאג 3⁸. (In one or two cases due to the acrostic.) In the matter of diction much that is irrelevant has been adduced on both sides. See further Löhr, *ZATW.* 1894, p. 31 ff., who has analysed very fully the diction of Lam., esp. in its relation to Jer., Ez., II Isa. and the Psalms. All the poems have literary affinities with the Psalms, esp. the Psalms of complaint: c. 2 (and to a less extent c. 4) has noteworthy affinities with Ez., which seem to be reminiscences from it; note 2⁴ כל מחמרי עין, cf. Ez. 24¹⁶· ²¹· ²⁵ [also 1 Ki. 20⁶]; 2¹⁴ חזה שוא (*to see vanity*), as Ez. 13⁶· ⁹· ²³ 21³⁴ 22²⁸†, cf. חזון שוא 12²⁴†, מחזה שוא 13⁷† ; 2¹⁴ תפל, cf. (also in connexion with *prophets*) Ez. 13¹⁰· ¹¹· ¹⁴· ¹⁵ 22²⁸ ; 2¹⁵ כלילת יפי Ez. 27³ (cf. כליל referring to יפי 16¹⁴ 28¹², and כללו יפי 27⁴· ¹¹ [but also מכלל יפי Ps. 50²]); 4¹¹ (of יהוה) כלה חמתו ב', as Ez. 5¹³ 6¹² 13¹⁵† (cf. with אפו 17⁸ 20⁸· ²¹†). The points of contact with II Isa. are slighter; they occur chiefly in c. 1, 3, 5. (Löhr's details are, however, not always exact—see *e.g.* p. 43 on מימי קרם [*never* in II Isa.], p. 44 פרק, p. 45 מבה, and דרך קשת [*not* in Dt. 32²³], p. 46 שרק : also מגורים pp. 44, 46, פרש יד p. 43, and גורה p. 48 have quite different senses in some (or all) the passages quoted; nor, in particular, does he always make it sufficiently clear—*e.g.* p. 46 under גוית חנר שקים and לא חמל, p. 48—whether the expressions quoted are *peculiar* to the two writers compared, or whether they are in fairly common use.)

himself to the artificial restraint implied by the alphabetical arrangement of c. 1–4.

On the whole, the balance of internal evidence may be said to preponderate against Jeremiah's authorship of the Book. The case is one in which the *differences* have greater weight than the resemblances. Even though the poems be not the work of Jer., there is no question that they are the work of a contemporary (or contemporaries); and the resemblances, even including those of phraseology, are not greater than may be reasonably accounted for by the similarity of historical situation. Many, in the same troublous times, must have been moved by the experience of the national calamities, as Jeremiah was moved by their prospect; and a disciple of Jeremiah's, or one acquainted with his writings, who, while adopting in some particulars (No. *b*) the general standpoint of his nation, agreed in other respects with the prophet, might very naturally interweave his own thoughts with reminiscences of Jeremiah's prophecies. When the general uniformity of Jeremiah's style is remembered, there is perhaps a presumption that, had he been the author, the number of expressions common to Lam. and his prophecies would have been greater than it is, and that those found in Lam., but not occurring in Jer.'s prophecies, would have been less abundant.*

The question whether or not all the poems are by one writer, is one which cannot be determined with certainty. The chief expressions common to more than one of the poems are the following : עֲנִי, שׁוֹמֵם, יִנָּה, הִבִּיט, אֲדֹנָי, [436] ; 3¹⁹ 1⁷ מְרוּדִים 4¹²; צָר 1⁵·⁷·¹⁰ 2⁶·⁷·²²; 1⁴·¹⁵ מוֹעֵר (p. 463, *note*), שׁ (p. 463, *note*), זֶנַח, עוֹלֵל; מַחְמַדִּים 1¹⁰·¹¹ Qrê (Kt. מַחֲמוֹרִים, as 1⁷) 2⁴; רוּחַ 1¹³ 5¹⁷; חִמַּרְמְרוּ מֵעַי 1²⁰ 2¹¹; לֹא ; 3⁴⁹ חֲפָנוֹת 2¹⁸ פּוּגָה 3⁴⁶ 2¹⁶; פָּצָה פֶּה עַל 2¹⁴ 4²²; נֻלָּה עַל עֹין 2²·¹⁷·²¹ 3⁴³; חֶמְלָ(ת) ; רֹאשׁ כָּל חוּצוֹת 2¹⁹ 4¹; נָגִינָה 3¹⁴ 5¹⁴ (otherwise applied). These (though the possibility of imitation cannot, it is true, be altogether excluded) would tend to show that the author was the same. Ewald insisted strongly that this was the case ; Prof. Smith was of the same opinion, remarking that the repeated treatment of the same theme, from different points of view, is in harmony with the aim that prevails in each individual poem, viz. to dwell upon *every* element and aspect of the common woe. Others (as Kuen.[1] § 147. 9) so estimate the poetical superiority of c. 2, 4, 5 above c. 1, 3, as to conclude even on this ground that it is not the same poet who speaks throughout. Æsthetic criteria are, however, often subjective and uncertain : Thenius declared that the author of c. 2, 4 could not have written c. 1, 3, 5 ; Budde, on the other hand (*ZATW*. 1882, p. 45), considers that c. 5 forms the climax to c. 1, 2, 4, and assigns only c. 3 to a different author : similarly Stade (*G.* i. 701). Either

---

* To the same effect Löhr, *l.c.* p. 40 f., *Comm.* (Nowack), p. xv.

opinion must be allowed to be tenable : the opinion that the author is throughout the same has perhaps, on the whole, probability in its favour ; but the
criteria at our disposal do not authorize us to pronounce dogmatically upon
either side. The poem which stands out most distinctly from the rest is c. 3 :
Löhr ascribes c. 2, 4 to one author, writing *c.* 570 B.C., c. 1, 5 to a second,
c. 530, c. 3 to a third, writing at about the same time as the second, or possibly
a little later.

§ 4. ECCLESIASTES (QOHÉLETH).

LITERATURE.—H. Ewald in *Die Dichter des AB.s,*[2] ii. 267–329 ; F.
Hitzig (in the *Kgf. Hdb.*), 1847,[2] by W. Nowack, 1883 ; C. D. Ginsburg,
Koheleth, London, 1861 (transl. and comm., with very full sketch of the history
of the interpretation of the book, pp. 27–243, 495 ff.) ; H. Grätz, *Kohélet
übersetzt u. kritisch erläutert,* 1871 (clever, but often arbitrary and forced :
see Kuenen, *Th. T.* 1883, pp. 113–144) ; T. Tyler, *Ecclesiastes,* 1874 ; Fr.
Delitzsch, *Hoheslied u. Koheleth,* 1875 ; E. H. Plumptre in the *Cambridge
Bible for Schools,* 1881 ; E. Renan, *L'Ecclésiaste,* 1882 (see Kuenen, *l.c.*) ;
C. H. H. Wright, *The book of Koheleth considered in relation to modern
criticism, and to the doctrines of modern pessimism, with a critical and
grammatical commentary and a revised translation,* 1883 ; G. Bickell, *Der
Prediger über den Wert des Daseins, Wiederherstellung des bisher zerstückelten
Textes, Übersetzung und Erklärung,* 1884 (see Cheyne, pp. 273–278) ; G.
G. Bradley [Dean of Westminster], *Lectures on Ecclesiastes,* 1885 (explanatory
paraphrase) ; T. K. Cheyne, *Job and Solomon,* 1887, pp. 199–285, 298–301 ;
W. Volck in Strack and Zöckler's *Kgf. Kommentar,* 1889 ; S. Cox in the
"Expositor's Bible," 1890 ; S. Euringer, *Der Masorahtext des Koheleth
kritisch untersucht,* 1890 ; A. Dillmann, " Über die griech. Übers. des Qoh.,"
in the *Sitzungsberichte der Kön.-Preuss. Akad. der Wiss.* 1892, p. 3 ff. [shows
that this is not, as Grätz and others had maintained, by Aquila, but is an
older version, revised on the basis of Aquila's translation] ; E. Klostermann,
De Libri Coh. Vers. Alex. 1892 ; Kuenen, *Onderzoek,*[2] iii. 1, p. 167 ff. See
further Cheyne, p. 285 ; Volck, p. 110.

The word קהלת *Qohéleth,* in the Book of which it forms the
title, is a name given to Solomon (1[1. 2. 12] 7[27] 12[8. 9. 10]) ; and the
Book itself consists of meditations on human life and society,
placed in the mouth of the wise king. In virtue of the subject
with which it deals, the Book forms part of the *Chokhmah-* or
Wisdom-literature of the Hebrews (p. 392). It is written, as a
[437] whole, in prose ; but when the thought becomes elevated, or
sententious, it falls into the poetical form of rhythmic parallelism.
The precise sense which the word *Qohéleth* was intended to
express is uncertain ; but it is most probable that it is applied to
Solomon, regarded as a public teacher of wisdom, a "preacher"
or "debater" (Plumptre) in an assembly, setting forth before his

listeners the conclusions to which experience or reflexion had brought him.

קֹהֶלֶת is manifestly connected with קָהָל *assembly*, and הִקְהִיל *to assemble* (*e.g.* Nu. 10[7]) ; and means probably (for the *Qal* conjug. קָהַל does not elsewhere occur) *one who takes part in an assembly*, or gathers a circle of hearers round him, LXX ἐκκλησιάστης, Jerome "concionator," AV. "The Preacher." But the word, though construed as a masculine,* has a *feminine* termination ; and of this two explanations are given.   According to some (Ewald, Hitzig, Ginsburg, Kuenen, Kleinert), the fem. alludes to חָכְמָה *Wisdom*, which is represented in Pr. 1[20f.] 8[1-4] as addressing men in the places of concourse ; and the name is given to Solomon, as the impersonation of wisdom.   It is an objection to this view that some of the meditations in the Book are un-suitable in the mouth of "Wisdom" (*e.g.* 1[16-18] 7[23f.]), and that where Wisdom actually speaks (as in Pr. 1-9), her discourse is in a widely different strain from that which prevails here.   According to others, the feminine is to be explained in a neuter sense, either, in a manner frequent in late Hebrew,† as denoting the holder of an office (properly "*that which* holds the office "),‡ or, as in Arabic, with an intensive force, the neuter gender exhausting the idea expressed by the word, and so, applied to an individual, denoting him as one who realises the idea in its completeness.§

The literary form of Qohéleth is imperfect.   Except in c. 1-2, where the author is guided by the course of his (real or imagined) experience, the argument is seldom systematically developed : the connexion of thought is often difficult to seize ; the subject is apt to change with some abruptness ; and the Book shows no clearly marked subdivisions.   Nor are the views expressed in it perfectly consistent throughout : evidently it reflects the author's changing moods, and these, for some reason (cf. p. 478), he has presented side by side without always bringing them into logical connexion with each other.‖

* In 7[27] אמר הקהלת must, no doubt, be read ; cf. 12[8].

† Comp. *has-Sophereth* "the scribe," Ezr. 2[55] ; *Pochereth-hazzebaim* "the binder of the gazelles," *ib.* v.[57] ; and see Strack and Siegfried, *Lehrb. der Neuhebr. Sprache*, p. 54.

‡ So Ges., Del., Nowack, Cheyne.

§ So Dr. W. Wright, *Arab. Gr.* i. § 233, Rem. *c* (who compares بَاقِرَة *a deep investigator*, جَمَّاعَة *a great collector*, &c.) ; C. H. H. Wright.   Hence RV. *marg.* "the great orator."

‖ Bickell supposes these defects to have arisen through the leaves of a MS. (the "Unfallshandschrift") having become accidentally disarranged, and being afterwards faultily put together ; and he rearranges the text in what he conceives to have been its original order.   His treatment of the book is clever and suggestive ; but the transpositions, additions, and other alterations, which

[438] The author states the conclusions to which his observations of life had brought him, in the two sentences with which his Book opens (1²ᶠ·): "All is vanity. What profit hath man of all his labour wherein he laboureth under the sun?" He establishes these conclusions by a survey of the different fields of human activity, and a demonstration of the fruitlessness of human effort upon each. 1⁴⁻¹¹ he shows that man's labour achieves nothing permanent: the course of human life is as monotonous and resultless as the operations of nature; the wind moves round in its circuits, as it seems, aimlessly, and human activity advances similarly, in a perpetual circle, without producing anything essentially new. He next recounts more particularly his own experience. He assumes the character of Solomon, the wise and powerful king of Israel, and identifies his experiences with his. He describes how he had sought happiness under many forms; and how his search had uniformly failed. The pursuit of wisdom had proved disappointing; increase of knowledge brought with it only fresh perplexities, and an increasingly painful sense of the anomalies of society (1¹²⁻¹⁸). From wisdom he had turned to pleasure; he had provided himself with all the enjoyments and luxuries which a king could command; but this also brought him no enduring satisfaction (2¹⁻¹¹). He turned to the study of human nature in its wisdom and its folly; but though he perceived wisdom to be better than folly, yet the advantage was of short duration; for death placed the wise and the fool upon the same footing; and from another point of view life again appeared to be unprofitable and vain (2¹²⁻¹⁷). Nor was the acquisition of riches more satisfactory: for none can tell who will inherit them (2¹⁸⁻²³). The only conclusion to which his quest brought him was that there was "nothing better for a man than that he should eat and drink," and enjoy such pleasure as God provides for him during the brief span of life that is his lot (2²⁴⁻²⁶).

Qohéleth next contemplates human activity under another

his theory obliges him to assume, are far too numerous and violent to be probable, and withal often do not enable him to secure the desired end (see esp. Budde, *Theol. Lit.-zt.* 1885, No. 3; and cf. Kuen. § 104. 7; Cheyne, *Job and Sol.* p. 274 f.). Bickell's theory is expounded at length in English (with a translation of his text) by E. J. Dillon, *The Sceptics of the O.T.* pp. 87 ff., 241 ff. (cf. the writer's critique, *Contemp. Rev.*, Feb. 1896, p. 265 ff.).

aspect. Every action in which man can engage has its allotted season; but who can be sure that he has found this season? God's plan can be known but partially by man (3^{11}); hence man's efforts to secure success are constantly liable to fail; and again nothing remains for him but to enjoy the present (3^{1-15}). He saw injustice usurping the place of justice; and if, for a [439] moment, the thought crossed his mind that wrong here might be redressed hereafter, it quickly vanished, for man, he argued, has no pre-eminence above a beast: the future of both is alike; and once more the conclusion follows that there is nothing better for man than the enjoyment of the present (3^{16-22}). He surveyed human society generally; and saw in it only trouble, failure, and disappointment: the evils of unredressed oppression (4^{1-3}), rivalry (4^{4-6}), isolation (4^{7-12}),—a king, for example, beginning his reign brightly, in popularity and favour, and ending it amid murmurings and discontent (4^{13-16}). 5^{1-9} he introduces a series of moral (v.$^{1-7}$) and prudential (v.$^{8f.}$*) maxims, intended, as it seems, to show how at least a part of the vexations of life may be escaped. 5^{10-17} he resumes his former moralising strain: riches also are too often but a source of anxiety and care; they are a blessing only when God grants the faculty to enjoy them (5^{18-20}); and it happens often that He does not do this (6^{1-6}). Men toil and toil, and are never satisfied; in this the wise and the fool resemble each other: still present enjoyment is better than insatiable desire (6^{7-9}). Man's fate was fixed long ago; he cannot contend with a power above him; and no one knows what the future will bring forth (6^{10-12}). The question "what is good for man in life" (6^{12}), suggests a series of reflexions on what it is "good" for a man to do in order to alleviate his vexations; to cultivate seriousness in preference to frivolity (7^{1-7}), patience and resignation rather than an over-anxious temper, ever brooding over the wrongs of life (7^{8-22}). Wisdom, if it could be found, would indeed be man's best guide: Qohéleth has in vain sought it; but his attempt to read the enigma of life convinced him strongly of one fact—and it is introduced with both abruptness and emphasis—that *woman* is one of the chief foes to human happiness—"whoso pleaseth God shall escape from her; but the sinner shall be taken by

---

* Under a government which is a hierarchy of corruption and oppression, be careful how you criticise the acts of its representatives.

her" ($7^{23\text{-}29}$). $8^{1\text{-}9}$ there follows another series of maxims, teaching how wisdom may display itself, and chiefly inculcating prudent demeanour towards kings and others in authority (v.$^{5\text{-}8}$ against hastily taking part in a revolution). The righteous are speedily forgotten, the wicked are honoured and rewarded; hence the best thing that a man can do is to enjoy life during the time that [440] God permits it ($8^{10\text{-}15}$). All man's endeavours to understand the work of God are unavailing; life is evil, even while it lasts; death comes and sweeps away all distinctions; and there is no assured hope of immortality ($8^{16}\text{-}9^6$): once more the old advice is repeated, "Go thy way, eat thy bread with joy, and drink thy wine with a merry heart; for God hath already accepted thy works": do thy pleasure and thy business while life permits; for nothing can be done when that is ended ($9^{7\text{-}10}$). Resuming his contemplation of society, Qohéleth is struck by the disproportion of the rewards which attend merit and exertion: "The race is not always to the swift, nor the battle to the strong." Wisdom does more than strength; and yet the poor wise man, who delivered his city, was afterwards forgotten ($9^{11\text{-}16}$). $9^{17}\text{-}10^{15}$ contains proverbs on wisdom, designed (as it seems) to teach at least its *relative* superiority, as a guide in life, above folly, intermingled with some bitter reflections on the anomalies which the author had witnessed in the course of his experience — misrule, which yet could not be remedied without peril, folly set in great dignity, and the rich sitting in low places: "I have seen servants upon horses, and princes walking as servants upon the earth" ($10^{4\text{-}7}$): $10^{16\text{-}20}$ carries on the strain of $10^{4\text{-}7}$, contrasting good and bad government, and closing with a significant warning of the danger of criticising the acts of a despot (cf. $5^{8\text{f.}}$).

$11^{1\text{-}3}$ the author counsels benevolence; for a time of misfortune may come, when friends thus won may prove serviceable. Hesitate not unnecessarily in thy daily work; for the issue rests in God's hand ($11^{4\text{-}6}$). Life, in spite of its trials, is a good, even though its enjoyment be haunted by the thought of the darkness that must follow it ($11^{7\text{-}8}$). Especially, let the young man rejoice in his youth, ere the decrepitude of old age overtakes him, yet not so as to forget his responsibility to his Maker. Man's life ends, as it begins, in vanity: "Vanity of vanities, saith the Preacher: all is vanity" ($11^9\text{-}12^8$).

The Book closes with an Epilogue : (a) 12^{9-10} describing
"the Preacher" as a wise man, whose aim in committing his
meditations to writing had been to communicate his wisdom to
others ; (b) 12^{11-12} counselling attention to the sayings of the
"wise," and exhorting the reader to be satisfied with the teaching which they contain ; (c) 12^{13-14} defining the one thing [441]
needful for man, viz. "Fear God, and keep His commandments."

In spite of the disconnected character of some of the author's
utterances, the general tone and drift of his meditations is unmistakable. Life under all its aspects is dissatisfying and disappointing : * the best that can be done with it is to enjoy—not
indeed in excess, but in a wise and well-considered moderation,
and as a gift intended by God to be enjoyed—such pleasures as
it brings with it.†

If the Book of Ecclesiastes is to be properly estimated, it
must be read in the light of the age in which it was written, and
the temper of the author. Of course Qohéleth is not really the
work of Solomon. The language (see below), the tone, the
social and political allusions, show that it is, in fact, the product
of a far later age. The tone is not that in which Solomon could
have spoken. The Solomon who speaks here is a different
character from the Solomon of history. It is not Solomon the
righteous judge, nor Solomon the builder of the Temple, nor
even Solomon confessing his declension from a spiritual faith.
There is no note of *penitence* in the entire Book. Nor are the
social and political allusions such as would fall from Solomon's
lips. The historical Solomon, the ruler of a great and prosperous
empire, could not have penned such a satire upon his own
administration as would be implied if 3^{16} (the place of judgment
filled by wickedness), 4^1 (the wrongs done by powerful oppressors), 5^8 (one corrupt ruler above another making appeal
for redress useless), were written by him. ‡ The author of
Qohéleth evinces no kingly or national feeling : he lives in a
period of political servitude, destitute of patriotism or enthusiasm. When he alludes to kings, he views them from
below, as one of the people suffering from their misrule. His

* The refrain, "All is vanity, and the pursuit of wind," 1^{14} 2^{11} &c.
† 2^{24} $3^{12.\,22}$ $5^{18f.}$ 8^{15} 9^{7-10} $11^{9f.}$
‡ Notice also the *anachronisms* in 1^{16} 2^9.

pages reflect the depression produced by the corruption of an Oriental despotism, with its injustice (3^{16} 4^1 5^8 8^9), its capriciousness ($10^{5f.}$), its revolutions (10^7), its system of spies (10^{20}), its hopelessness of reform.* He must have lived when the Jews had lost their national independence, and formed but a province of the Persian empire,—[442] perhaps even later, when they had passed under the rule of the Greeks (3rd cent. B.C.). But he adopts a literary disguise, and puts his meditations into the mouth of the king, whose reputation it was to have been the great sage and philosopher of the Hebrew race, whose observation and knowledge of human nature were celebrated by tradition, and whose position might naturally be supposed to afford him the opportunity of testing systematically in his own person every form of human pursuit or enjoyment.

The Book exhibits, in a word, the reflections of a spirit, manifestly not of an optimistic temperament, impelled to despair and distrust of its own future, as well as of its nation's (6^{12}), by the depressed and artificial circumstances in which the author lived. Qohéleth is not, like the prophets, animated by a great religious enthusiasm, enabling him to look beyond the present, or sustaining him by the thought of Israel's Divine election : he stands—like the " wise men " of Israel generally (p. 393)—on the footing of experience, and views human life in its sober reality. And the age was a darker one than that which is reflected in any part of the Book of Proverbs. Qohéleth recounts the experiences through which he had himself passed, and the conclusions which his observation of society forced upon him. He recounts, and as he recounts he generalises, the disappointments which had been his own lot in life. He surveys the life of other men ; but he can discover no enthusiasm, no energy, no faculty of grave and serious endeavour. He frames his conclusions accordingly. It is upon life, not absolutely, but as he witnessed and experienced it, that he passes his unrelenting sentence, " All is vanity." It was the particular age with which he was himself acquainted that wrung from his soul those melancholy moralizings on the uselessness of human exertion, and the inability of man to remedy the anomalies of society. He does not, however, stop here. He passes on to show what, under the existing conditions, is the highest good for man : and, as the

* Comp. Dean Bradley, p. 25.

ordinary enterprises of mankind are foredoomed to failure, he finds it in a wise and temperate enjoyment of the pleasures of life.

Of course, Qohéleth takes a false view of life. His aphorisms are indeed often pregnant and just : they are prompted by a keen sense of right ; and in his satire upon society he lays his finger upon many a real blot. But his teaching, as a whole, if followed consistently, would tend directly to paralyse human effort, to [443] stifle every impulse to self-denial or philanthropy, to kill all activity of an ennobling or unselfish kind. The circumstances of his age obscured for him the duty of man to his fellow-men. A life not circumscribed by merely personal ends, but quickened and sustained by devotion to the interests of humanity, is not "vanity," or the pursuit of wind. It follows that, whatever justification Qohéleth's conclusions may have, it is limited to the age in which he himself lived.

No doubt he would have judged human nature less despairingly had he possessed a clear consciousness of a future life. But the revelation of a future life was only accomplished gradually ; and though there are passages in the prophets which contain this great truth in germ, and though the intuition of it is expressed at certain sublime moments by some of the Psalmists (Ps. 16, 17, 49, 73), yet these passages altogether are few in number, and the doctrine formed no part of the established creed of an ancient Israelite.* Qohéleth shares only the ordinary old Hebrew view of a shadowy, half-conscious existence in Sheol ($3^{19f.}$ 6^6 $9^{5.10}$): he does not believe in a life hereafter in the sense in which the apostles of Christ believed it.† Even at the end of his book the description of the decay of the body in old age, until "the dust returns to the earth as it was, and the spirit returns to God who gave it" is followed, not by any thought of the beatific vision which may there await it, but by the refrain which is the keynote of the book, "Vanity of vanities, saith the Preacher : all is vanity." Not life in the body merely, the life of the spirit even, including

---

* Comp. the writer's *Sermons on the OT.* p. 72 ff.

† In the Targum to Qohéleth (which is very paraphrastic), as if to counteract what seemed to a later age the negative teaching of the Book, a reference to a future life and retribution (רינא רבא ,עלמא ההוא ,עלמא דאתי) is introduced with great frequency, and the pessimistic utterances of the author are expressly limited to the present life (עלמא הדין). Cf. *ibid.* pp. 92, 98.

its return to God, appears thus to be counted by him as "vanity." *

Nevertheless the author is no "pessimist," in the sense in which the word is used in modern times. He does not believe that the world is growing worse and worse, and hastening to its ruin. Nor is he ever tempted to abandon his theistic faith. He [444] retains his belief in God : he is conscious of a moral order in the world, though its operation is often frustrated : he is aware of cases in which the man who fears God has an advantage over others (see 2^{26} 5^7 $7^{18.\ 26}$ $8^{12f.}$). He holds that it is man's duty to enjoy the gifts of God, and also to fear Him. His fear is indeed a "pale and cheerless" fear ; but it nevertheless exerts a constraining power over him. The contradictions in his book spring out of the conflict between his faith and his experience,— his faith that the world is ordered by God, and his experience that events often do not fall out as he would have expected God to order them. His theory of life is imperfect, because it is one-sided. But the Bible contains not only the record of a history ; it exhibits also, as in a mirror, the most varied phases of human emotion, suffused and penetrated in different degrees by the Spirit of God. And so there is a mood of melancholy and sadness to which, in one form or other, the human soul is liable ; and this has found its most complete expression in Ecclesiastes. It would seem that "in the great record of the spiritual history of the chosen and typical race, a place has here been kept for the sigh of defeated hopes, for the gloom of the soul vanquished by the sense of the anomalies and mysteries of human life" (Dean Bradley, p. 39).

Linguistically, Qohéleth stands by itself in the OT. The Hebrew in which it is written has numerous features in common with the latest parts of the OT., Ezra and Nehemiah, Chronicles, Esther, but it has in addition many not met with in these books, but found first in the Mishnah (which includes, no doubt, older elements, but received its present form *c.* 200 A.D.). The characteristic of the Hebrew in which these latest parts of the OT. are written is that while many of the old classical words and

---

* The limitation of "all is vanity" in 12^8 to man's earthly life, *as opposed to a higher life that is not vanity*, adopted by some commentators, is arbitrary, and introduces a distinction of which the author does not show that he is conscious. Comp. the just remarks of Bickell, pp. 37–45.

expressions still continue in use, and, in fact, still preponderate, the syntax is deteriorated, the structure of sentences is cumbrous and inelegant, and there is a very decided admixture of words and idioms not found before, having usually affinities with the Aramaic, or being such as are in constant and regular use in the Hebrew of post-Christian times (the Mishnah, &c.). And this latter element is decidedly larger and more prominent in Ecclesiastes than in either Esther or Ezr. Neh. Chron.*

Thus the following expressions occurring in Qohéleth—in some cases new words, in others new or extended applications of old words—are not found [445] besides in Biblical Hebrew, but are common either in Aramaic or in the Mishnah (or in both) † :—

1. אָבַד=to lose : 3⁶.—2. אִי Woe ! 4¹⁰ 10¹⁶.—3. בטל to cease : 12³.—4. נומץ a pit : 10⁸.—5. בּן־חוֹרִים lit. a son of nobles=free-born : 10¹⁷.—6. חוץ מן outside of, except : 2²⁵.—7. חוש to enjoy (prop. to feel) : 2²⁵.—8. חסרון deficiency : 1¹⁵.—9. חפץ (usually desire) in the weakened sense of business, matter : 3¹· ¹⁷ 5⁸ [Heb. ⁷] 8⁶ [there is an approximation to this sense in Isa. 58³· ¹³].—10. יצא to go out of, in the sense of to fulfil, discharge : 7¹⁸.—11. יתרון advantage, preference, profit : 1³ 2¹¹· ¹³ bis 3⁹ 5⁸· ¹⁵ 7¹² 10¹⁰· ¹¹.—12. כבר long ago : 1¹⁰ 2¹²· ¹⁶ 3¹⁵ 4² 6¹⁰ 9⁶· ⁷.—13. לוה to accompany : 8¹⁵.—14. מלאה in the sense pregnant : 11⁵.—15. משך to indulge, cheer (peculiar sense) : 2³.—16. נהג to act, behave [RV. wrongly "guiding (me)"] : 2³.—17. נסכן to be endangered : 10⁹.—18. עָבָד deed, work : 9¹ (= ܟ̇ܒ̇ܕ).—19. ערן, ערנה yet : 4²· ³.—20. ענין trouble, business : 1¹³ 2²³· ²⁶ 3¹⁰ 4⁸ 5²· ¹³ 8¹⁶.—21. פשר interpretation : 8¹ (as in Aram., Dan. 2⁴ &c.: in older Hebrew פתרון).—22. שׁ as the relative sign. This in itself occurs elsewhere in the OT. (p. 449) ; but in Qoh. its use is widely extended, and it appears in many combinations, unknown otherwise to Biblical Hebrew, but common in the Mishnah, as שֶׁל־כּל all that which : 2⁷· ⁹ 11⁸ ; כּשׁ as, when [normal Hebrew כּאשׁר] : 5¹⁴ 9¹² 10³ 12⁷ ; מִשּׁ than that [normal Hebrew מאשׁר] : 5⁴ ; and esp. מַה־שׁ that which [=? ما] : 1⁹

---

* The recently discovered Hebrew original of Ecclus. 39¹⁵–49¹¹ (see A. E. Cowley and Ad. Neubauer's edition, Oxford, 1897) stands linguistically in a different category from any of the books named in the text. Ben Sira, it is true, makes use of a considerable number of New Hebrew or Aramaic words (see the glossary, ibid. p. xxxi ff.) ; but the predominant character of the recovered text is nevertheless classical : it contains none of the peculiar New Hebrew idioms found in Qoh. and the Mishnah ; and in syntax and general style, it stands upon a much higher level than either Qoh. or Est. Ezr. Neh. Chron. The newly recovered text shows that in the quotations preserved in the Talmud, &c. (ibid. p. xix ff.), Rabbinical idioms (as שׁמא for פן, ibid. p. xxvii, No. LXI : see 42⁹· ¹⁰) had sometimes been substituted for the more classical expressions used by Ben Sira himself.

† For particulars, see the glossary in Delitzsch's commentary (abbreviated and much spoilt in the translation), or in Wright's Ecclesiastes, p. 488 ff.

3¹⁵ 6¹⁰ 7²⁴ 8⁷ 10¹⁴; -שׁ מֶה 3²²; בְּשֶׁל אֲשֶׁר *because that*, 8¹⁷, is modelled on the Aram. דְּ בְּדִיל (Gen. 6³ Onq. &c.).*—23. שכח in the *Hithp.*: 8¹⁰ (elsewhere in Biblical Hebrew the passive is always expressed by the Nifal).—24. תקיף *strong*: 6¹⁰.—25. תקן *to be straight*: 1¹⁵; תִּקֵּן *to make straight, arrange*: 7¹⁰ 12⁹.

The following expressions, common in either Aramaic or post-Bibl. Hebrew (or in both), are found besides in Biblical Hebrew only in the passages cited, being mostly from admittedly post-exilic books, though in one or two instances the word occurs *in isolation* somewhat earlier : —

1. אִלּוּ *if*: 6⁶, Est. 7⁴.—2. בְּהַל in the sense *to hasten* (intrans.): 5¹ 7⁹: cf. Est. 2⁹, 2 Ch. 35²¹ (trans.), and in the Pual Est. 8¹⁴, Pr. 20²¹; the Hif. Est. 6¹⁴, 2 Ch. 26²⁰ (ordinarily in Heb. the word means *to terrify*).—3. בכן *then, thus*: 8¹⁰, Est. 4¹⁶.—4. . . . . הוא זה 1¹⁷, 1 Ch. [446] 22¹ (see the author's *Hebrew Tenses*, § 201. 3).—5. זמן *time*: 3¹ Neh. 2⁶, Est. 9²⁷·³¹.—6. חשבון = *reckoning, account*: 7²⁵·²⁷ 9¹⁰ 7²⁹ ("devices"), 2 Ch. 26¹⁵ (in the derived sense of "engine" [=ingenium]).—7. יותר in an adv. sense, *exceedingly, more*: 2¹⁵ 7¹⁶ 12⁹ (*moreover*); יותר מן *more than*: 12¹² as Est. 6⁶.—8. כְּאֶחָד lit. *as one*, in the weakened sense of *together*: 11⁶ Ezr. 2⁶⁴ (=Neh. 7⁶⁶) 3⁹ 6²⁰, 2 Ch. 5¹³, Isa. 65²⁵ (Aram. כחדא, ‎ܐ‎: כאחד is common in the same sense in the Mishnah).—9. כנס (in *Qal*) *to gather*: 2⁸·²⁶ 3⁵, Ps. 33⁷ 1 Ch. 22², Neh. 12⁴⁴, Est. 4¹⁶.—10. כשר *to be good, prosperous*: 10¹⁰ 11⁶, Est. 8⁵; כשרון 2²¹ 4⁴ 5¹⁰ (כּוּשָׁרָה) in Ps. 68⁷ = ‎ܟܫܪ‎).—11. סוף *end*: 3¹¹ 7² 12¹³, 2 Ch. 20¹⁶, Joel 2²⁰.—12. פתגם *edict*: 8¹¹ Est. 1²⁰ (a *Persian* word).—13. שלט *to rule over*: 2¹⁹ 8⁹, Neh. 5¹⁵, Est. 9¹; השליט 5¹⁸ 6² Ps. 119¹³³; שלטון 8⁴·⁸.—14. תקף *to be strong, prevail*: 4¹² Job 14²⁰ 15²⁴ (common in Aram.).—15. זה *this* (fem.) for זאת: 2²·²⁴ 5¹⁵·¹⁸ 7²³ 9¹³, 2 Ki. 6¹⁹ (N. Palest. [p. 188]), Ez. 40⁴⁵.

Another Mishnic usage is the constant use of the perf. with simple *waw* for the classical impf. with *waw* consec. (which occurs but thrice in Qoh., 1¹⁷ 4¹·⁷): this appears with increasing frequency in the later books of the OT., but in none so regularly as in Qohéleth (cf. *Tenses*, § 133). There are also many finer points of style and construction, which cannot well be tabulated, but which confirm the evidence afforded by the vocabulary. The linguistic peculiarities of Qohéleth are very different in character from those of the Song of Songs (p. 448 ff.): the latter, treated as dialectical usages, seem, at least in most cases (so far as can be judged), to be compatible with an early date: the phraseology of Qohéleth bears throughout the stamp of lateness. (In the recovered text of Ben Sira, the impf. with *waw* consec. occurs repeatedly. The relative שׁ is not found in it.)

The *precise* date of Qohéleth cannot be determined, our knowledge of the history not enabling us to interpret with any

---

* בשל אשר cannot be called Hebrew: like באשר למי Jon. 1⁸ (cf. בדיל מן Jon. 1⁷ Targ.; בדיל מא Jud. 8¹ Targ.), or אשר למה Dan. 1¹⁰ (=‎ܕܠܡܐ‎), it is the phrase of an author who *thought* in Aramaic, and translated the Aramaic idiom, part by part, into unidiomatic Hebrew.

confidence the allusions to concrete events which it seems to contain.* But the general political condition which it presupposes, and the language, make it decidedly probable that it is not earlier than the latter years of the Persian rule, which ended B.C. 333 (Ewald, Oehler, Ginsburg, Delitzsch, Cheyne, Volck); and it is quite possible that it is later. Nöldeke, Hitzig, Kuenen, Tyler, Plumptre (p. 34), and Cornill, place it *c.* 200 B.C., partly on the ground of language (which *favours*, even though our knowledge is not sufficient to enable us to say that it *requires*, a date later than that assigned by Ewald), partly (Kuenen) on the ground of an absence of national feeling, and religious enthusiasm (*e.g.* 5²), in which the author seems to be a forerunner of the later Sadduceeism, and of the indifferentism characteristic of a particular [447] Jewish party in the time of the Maccabees, partly (Tyler, Plumptre) on the ground of traces which the Book is supposed to contain of Greek influences, especially of Epicurean and Stoic teaching. It is true, a knowledge of Greek speculation may sometimes have influenced the writer's thought. There is force in Kuenen's arguments; but the paucity of independent *data* respecting the condition of the Jews in the 3rd cent. B.C. does not enable us to say whether they are decisive, or whether the characteristics referred to may not have shown themselves earlier. Nowack (p. 196 f.) hesitates between the two dates proposed, considering that the allusions are not decisive in favour of either, but allowing that the language, if its testimony, in the absence of more definite standards of comparison, be rightly interpreted, supports the later date. On the whole, a date during the Greek period, and approaching B.C. 200, may be said to be the most probable.†

The question whether Greek influences are traceable in Ecclesiastes is treated with discrimination by P. Kleinert, *Stud. u. Krit.* 1883, p. 761 ff., who argues that, although the general intellectual atmosphere to which the later systems of Greek philosophy owe their origin no doubt breathes in it, the specific resemblances which have been pointed to are not sufficiently close, or distinctive, to justify the opinion that they were derived from any of these systems. A. Palm, *Qoheleth und die nach-Aristotelische Philosophie,* 1885 (who gives an interesting collection of parallels from the later classical

---

* 4¹³⁻¹⁶; 6² (perhaps); 8¹⁰; 9¹³⁻¹⁶; 10¹⁶; 10¹⁷.

† Against the views of Grätz (who assigns the Book to the age of Herod the Great, and supposes it to be a satire on his administration), and of Renan (*c.* 125 B.C.), see Kuenen, *Th T.* 1883, p. 129 ff., *Onderz.* § 104. 3, 105. 5.

writers), and Kuenen (§ 105. 9, 3), think that the book shows clearer traces of the impression which Greek speculation had made upon the author, and consider that, though he never abandoned his distinctively Jewish standpoint, or adopted, as such, the tenets of a particular school, he was often guided in his line of thought by his knowledge of the questions that were being debated by contemporary Greek thinkers. Similarly Cornill, § 42 [³45]. 4. Stated in this moderate form, the hypothesis is not an improbable one. P. Menzel, *Der Griechische Einfluss auf Prediger und Weisheit Salomos* (1889), pp. 1–38, criticises chiefly the attempt of Edm. Pfleiderer, in his work on Heraclitus, to trace the influence of that philosopher in Qohéleth.

Integrity of Qohéleth. (1) It has been questioned whether the Epilogue, 12⁹⁻¹⁴, is the work of the author of the Book. The author's meditations end evidently at 12⁸ : and 12⁹⁻¹⁴ has been regarded as a "commendatory attestation," added by an editor, or perhaps by those who admitted the Book into the Canon, justifying its admission (v.⁹⁻¹²), and pointing out (v.¹³⁻¹⁴) what was the true moral of its preaching (Plumptre). (2) It has further been questioned* whether certain passages, not in harmony with the general tenor of the Book, may not be later insertions in it, viz. 3¹⁷ 11⁹ᵇ 12¹ᵃ· ⁷ᵇ. (1) There does not appear to be any sufficient reason for doubting that 12⁹⁻¹² is by the author of the Book ; it is true, these verses contain [448] some unusual expressions ; but their general tone and strain is quite that of the Book generally (with v.¹²ᵇ cf. 1¹⁸). 12¹³⁻¹⁴ stands upon a different footing, and must be considered in connexion with (2). The difficulty which these passages present is this. It is clear that Qohéleth, as a whole, knows nothing of a future life : and 3¹⁹⁻²¹ (RV.) the doctrine is expressly treated as unproven. 3¹⁷ 11⁹ᵇ 12¹⁴, however, *seem* to teach it. The attempt to reconcile them with the rest of the Book by the supposition that there are "Two Voices"† in Qohéleth cannot be sustained. The author's aphorisms are no statements of the arguments for and against future retribution ; nor is the higher faith (if it can be so termed) of c. 12 in any way the outcome of a previous train of reflection. It thus differs from the poem of Tennyson. In the poem there is a real debate : and the voice of doubt, having shown itself powerless in argument, is finally silenced by a particular observation of the poet. No such debate is, however, traceable in Qohéleth : the passages in question are introduced abruptly, and stand isolated. But 3¹⁷, by the punctuation בְּ ("for *he hath appointed* a time for," &c.) for שָׁם "*there*," adopted by Delitzsch and others, is referred quite naturally to temporal judgments. 11⁹ᵇ 12¹⁴, as they stand, may be interpreted similarly.‡ 12⁷ expresses just

---

* See Cheyne, pp. 211, 232 ff., 238 f.

† Cf. Cheyne, pp. 245, 301 ; Dean Plumptre, pp. 53, 211 f., 224 f.

‡ If, however, it be thought that these two verses can be reasonably interpreted only of judgment hereafter, there seems to be no alternative but to treat them as later insertions. Had this truth been a *certainty* to Qohéleth ("and *know* that for all these things," &c.), as it was, for instance, to the author of the Book of Wisdom, it seems impossible but that the allusions to it would have been more frequent and distinct, and, indeed, that the general tenor of the Book would have been different.

the reversal of Gen. 2[7] : the question of the continued consciousness of the "spirit" does not appear to be before the author.* 12[1a. 13] are not so readily explained. These passages *emphasize* godliness in a manner foreign to the general spirit of Qohéleth, whose *summum bonum* is the discreet and temperate *enjoyment of life*. The context of 12[1a] (cf. 11[10]) would point to the same *summum bonum* being inculcated here, viz. the enjoyment of life while the powers are fresh, rather than the importance of beginning the service of God in youth. And if 12[1a] (to *youth*) be treated as a subsequent insertion, this is the sense which the original text will have expressed ("or ever," &c. connecting with 11[10]). 12[13] similarly lays stress upon a thought *implicit* in the teaching of the Book (2[24] &c.: p. 470), [449] but disregards that which is *explicit*. Hence the conjecture (which would also account for the unfinished form of parts of the Book) that the author's meditations were left by him at his death in an incomplete state (Cheyne, pp. 204, &c.), and that 12[1a. 13-14] were added by an editor for the purpose of stating distinctly what he conceived to be the true moral of the Book, and disarming possible objections which the general tenor of its teaching might provoke. The conjecture, especially as regards 12[13-14], must be allowed to be a plausible one. At the same time, the thought is in other parts of Qohéleth not entirely consistent, or logically developed ; and the author himself may have appended the two closing verses with the same purpose in view as his supposed editor.†

§ 5. ESTHER.

LITERATURE.—H. A. C. Hävernick, *Einl. in das AT.* ii. 1 (1839), p. 328 ff.; Ewald, *History of Israel*, i. p. 196 f., v. p. 230 ff.; E. Bertheau in *Die Bb. Esra, Nech. und Ester* (in the *Kgf. Hdb.*), 1862,[2] (revised by V. Ryssel), 1887 ; C. F. Keil in the *Bibl. Commentar über die Chronik, Esra, Neh. u. Ester*, 1870 ; S. Oettli in *Die Gesch. Hagiographen*, in Strack and Zöckler's *Kgf. Komm.* 1889, p. 227 ff.; Dieulafoi, "Le Livre d'Esther et le palais d'Assuérus," *Rev. des Études Juives*, 1888 (*Actes et Conférences*, p. cclxv ff.) ; B. Jacob, "Esther bei den LXX," *ZATW.* 1890, p. 241 ff.

The Book of Esther relates how Esther, a Jewish resident in the Persian capital, Susa, rose to be queen of Ahasuerus, *i.e.* Xerxes (B.C. 485–465), and how, in virtue of her position, she

---

* Notice that in Ps. 104[29] the "spirit" (רוח) of *animals* is "gathered in" by God at their death.

† Grätz's conjecture on 12[1a] (*ap.* Cheyne, pp. 225 f., 300) is infelicitous. The originality of the entire Epilogue is elaborately defended by Kuenen (*Onderz.*[2] iii. pp. 179–191). But he saves 12[13-14] (p. 189 f.) only by understanding it to express, not the highest end of man absolutely, but the *condition* under which enjoyment, which Qohéleth regards as the chief end of life, is attainable. This makes Qohéleth's teaching consistent ; but the limitation is scarcely compatible with the terms of the text. The truth is, 12[13-14] can be vindicated for the author only at the cost of an inconsistency.

succeeded in rescuing her countrymen from the destruction which Haman, the king's favourite courtier, had prepared for them.

The story may be told briefly as follows :—Ahasuerus, in the third year of his reign, gave a great feast, first, for 180 days, to the principal men of his kingdom, and then for 7 days to all the people of Shushan (Susa) ; on the last day, he ordered his seven eunuchs to bring in his queen Vashti, in order that she might display her beauty in presence of his guests. Upon her refusing to comply with this request, the king, fearing that her example might encourage other wives to disregard their husbands' wishes, resolved to put her away by a royal edict ; and, further, sent [450] instructions into all parts of his empire that every man was to be master in his own house (c. 1). The king, after his wrath had subsided, took measures to supply Vashti's place. Accordingly, all the most beautiful virgins in Persia were collected at Susa, and after 12 months' preparation, presented to the king. His choice fell, in the 7th year of his reign, upon Esther, the cousin and adopted daughter of Mordecai, a Benjaminite resident in Susa, who was forthwith installed formally in the palace as queen. Shortly afterwards, Mordecai was enabled, through Esther, to give information concerning a plot which two of the royal chamberlains had formed against the king's life ; the conspirators were hanged, and Mordecai's good deed was inscribed in the archives of the kingdom (c. 2).

After this Ahasuerus promoted a certain Haman above all his other nobles, and directed his servants to do obeisance to him. As Mordecai refused, Haman, deeming himself slighted, conceived against both him and his people a violent hatred ; and persuaded the king, in the 12th year of his reign, on the 13th day of the 1st month, to issue an edict, which was published throughout the empire, that 11 months hence, on the 13th day of the 12th month, Adar, the Jews, in every province, young and old, should be massacred, and their goods confiscated (c. 3). This decree aroused naturally the greatest alarm among the Jews ; Mordecai, however, contrived to inform Esther of it, and induced her to intercede with the king on behalf of her nation (c. 4). Accordingly, having gained the king's favour, and obtained from him a promise to grant her what she desired, " even to the half of his kingdom," she, in the first instance,

merely invited him and Haman to a banquet. At the banquet
the king repeated his promise ; but Esther merely begged them
to come again on the morrow to another banquet. Haman,
highly elated at the honour done to him, and hoping next day
to obtain from the king an order for Mordecai's punishment, at
his wife's suggestion had a gallows erected, 50 cubits high, for
his rival's execution (c. 5).

That night it happened that the king, being unable to sleep,
ordered the archives of the kingdom to be read before him.
Among the contents that were read out was the record of the
plot of the two chamberlains, and of the manner in which it had
been frustrated by Mordecai's timely information. Upon learning that no reward had been conferred upon Mordecai for [451]
his good deed, the king asked Haman, when he arrived in the
morning, what should be done to the man whom the king
delighted to honour. Haman, imagining that the king could
be thinking only of himself, named the very highest marks of
royal approval, which, to his intense mortification, he was directed
at once personally to bestow upon Mordecai. Having carried
out these instructions, Haman hastened back home, greatly
dejected ; and his wife predicted yet worse things for him in
the future (c. 6).

At the banquet, upon the king's repeating once more his
previous offer, Esther now answered plainly, and begged him to
save her and her people from the destruction with which they
were threatened. The king, apparently surprised, asked who
had brought this danger upon them, and was told in reply that
it was Haman. He instantly rose in great wrath, and left the
banqueting-hall. Haman fell down upon his knees to crave the
queen's intercession ; the king returning, and finding him at
her feet, imagined that he was insulting her ; and a courtier
observing 'opportunely that the gallows prepared for Mordecai
was ready outside, he ordered his immediate execution upon
it (c. 7).

Mordecai was now installed in Haman's position ; and Esther
set herself to frustrate, if possible, the decree against the Jews.
As the Persian laws did not permit this decree to be directly
revoked, Ahasuerus, on the 23rd day of the 3rd month, authorised
Mordecai to issue an edict, which, like the previous one, was
transmitted to every part of the empire, permitting the Jews, on

the day appointed for their destruction, to defend themselves against their assailants (c. 8). Accordingly, when the 13th of Adar arrived, the Jews in every place acted in concert together, and prevailed against their enemies. In Susa they slew 500 men, including the ten sons of Haman; and as Esther, in answer to the king, expressed a desire that the Jews might be permitted to act similarly on the next day, they slew on the 14th 300 more. In the provinces of the empire the Jews slew, on the 13th, 75,000 of their enemies, and observed the following day, the 14th, as a day of rejoicing. In the capital, as two days were occupied with the slaughter, the 15th was celebrated as the day of rejoicing. To commemorate this deliverance from their enemies, Mordecai and Esther sent letters to the Jews dispersed throughout the empire, instructing them to observe annually the 14th and 15th of Adar " as days of feasting and gladness, and of [452] sending portions one to another, and gifts to the poor "— the 14th in the country, and the 15th in cities (9^{19}). The days were called the days of *Purim*, with allusion to the " lot " (Pur) which Haman had originally cast (3^7) for the purpose of fixing the day of the massacre (c. 9).

The Book closes with an account of the might and greatness of Mordecai, which it is stated stood recorded in the royal archives of Media and Persia (c. 10).

The aim of the Book of Esther is manifest : it is to explain the origin of the Feast of Purim, and to suggest motives for its observance. The first subsequent allusion to the feast is in 2 Macc.,—written probably about the time of the Christian era, —where it is said (15^{36}) that the Jews resolved to celebrate their victory over Nicanor (B.C. 161) on Adar 13, πρὸ μιᾶς ἡμέρας τῆς Μαρδοχαικῆς ἡμέρας. This "day of Mordecai" is evidently the day appointed by Mordecai to be observed by the Jews in commemoration of their deliverance, viz. Adar 14.* In later times the Book of Esther, recording, as it did, a signal national triumph, acquired great popularity among the Jews ; and was even ranked by them as superior both to the writings of the prophets and to all other parts of the Hagiographa.

That a young Jewess, resident in Susa, may have been taken into the harem of the Persian king, and there, with the assist-

---

* But the passage only *proves* that the day was observed when the author of 2 Macc. lived ; there is no similar allusion in 1 Macc. $7^{43.\ 49}$.

ance of a relative, may have been the means of averting from a portion of her fellow-countrymen the ruin which some high official, whom they had offended, had devised against them, is fully within the limits of historical possibility.* The historical character of the narrative, as we possess it, has, however, been very differently estimated by different writers. To some the narrative has appeared to teem with improbabilities; by others it has been defended in every particular as thoroughly possible and credible. It may be admitted that it contains details which it is difficult to find a standard for estimating objectively. But putting aside trivial or inconclusive criticisms, and also disregarding such details as may reasonably be attributed to the capricious character of Xerxes (which is attested independently by Herodotus), it can still hardly be pronounced altogether free from improbabilities.

[453] Thus 1, Esther cannot, it seems, have been Ahasuerus' *queen*. Between the 7th and the 12th years of his reign (2^{16} 3^7) Xerxes' queen was Amestris, a superstitious and cruel women (Hdt. 7, 114. 9, 112), who cannot be identified with Esther, and who leaves no place for Esther beside her. Esther may have been one of the women in the king's harem; but the narrative represents her consistently as queen, and as sole queen (2^{17} &c.). Moreover, the manner in which she was selected is in conflict with the law by which the Persian monarch, in his choice of a queen, was limited to seven noble families of Persia (cf. Hdt. 3, 84). Again, the public notification of the decree for the destruction of the Jews *eleven* months before it was to take effect seems scarcely probable—the assumption that it was Haman's object to induce the Jews indirectly to leave the Persian dominion being countenanced by nothing in the narrative, which, in fact, implies distinctly that their actual ruin was contemplated (3^9 $4^{1-3.\ 13f.}$). It is remarkable, also, that though the courtiers (in spite of the admonition $2^{10.\ 20}$) are manifestly aware of Esther's relationship to Mordecai, and Mordecai is known to be a Jew ($3^{4.\ 6}$ &c.), Haman seems not to suspect the relationship; and Ahasuerus, although he had himself (3^{9-11}) authorized the decree, not only (6^{10}) honours the Jew Mordecai (which might be excused on the ground of his good deed), but is surprised to be told of its existence (7^{5-7}).

2. To many critics, moreover, the narrative as a whole seems to read as a romance rather than as a history: the incidents at each stage seem laid so as to prepare for the next, which duly follows without hitch or interruption. It is true, certainly, that considerable art is shown in the composition of the Book. Mordecai and Haman stand in manifest contrast to each other: the two edicts and the circumstances of their promulgation (3^{12-15}; 8^{10-17}) are similarly contrasted; the climax of difficulty and danger for the Jews is reached, from which, by an unexpected turn of events, they are suddenly

---

* Comp. Ewald, v. 231; Nöldeke, *AT. Lit.* p. 85.

released : the double banquet ($5^{4,\ 8}\ 7^1$) allows scope in the interval for the contrasted pictures, first of Haman's exultation (5^{9-14}), then of his vexation (6^{11-13}),—a prelude and omen of the greater humiliation that is to follow (c. 7). Fact, however, is proverbially sometimes stranger than fiction : so that it is somewhat precarious to build a far-reaching argument upon appearances of this nature. At the same time, it must be allowed that incidents thus mutually related are *accumulated* in Esther ; and they, at least, authorize the inference that, whatever materials the narrator may have had at his disposal, he has elaborated them with the conscious design of exhibiting vividly the dramatic contrasts which they suggested to him.

On the other hand, the writer shows himself well informed on Persian manners and institutions ; he does not commit anachronisms such as occur in Tobit or Judith ; and the character of Xerxes, as drawn by him, is in agreement with history. The conclusion to which, on the whole, the facts point, and which is adopted by most modern critics (*e.g.* Oettli, p. 233), is that [454] though the narrative cannot reasonably be doubted to have a substantial historical basis, it includes items that are not strictly historical : the elements of the narrative were supplied to the author by tradition, and, aided by his knowledge of Persian life and customs (for he cannot have lived long after the Persian empire reached its close), he combined them into a consistent picture : in some cases the details were coloured already by tradition before they came to the author's hand, in other cases they owe their present form to the author's love of dramatic effect. An evident collateral aim of the narrative is to magnify the importance and influence of the Jews. Of all the maidens collected at Susa, it is a Jewess who is the fortunate one, and who, throughout, is successful in all that she essays to obtain from the king. Not the Jews only, but the inhabitants of Susa generally are troubled by the first edict, as they are delighted by the second ($3^{15}\ 8^{15}$). Haman, the Jews' enemy, is disgraced, and consigned to the fate which he had prepared for Mordecai ($5^{14}\ 7^{10}$) : Mordecai succeeds to his position ($8^{2,\ 15}$; cf. $3^{1,\ 10}$), issues the decree which is to neutralise his ($8^{9ff.}$; cf. 4^{12}), and is represented finally as invested with even greater authority and importance ($9^{3b,\ 4}$; c. 10). The Jews themselves find favour with the Persians (8^{16}), are regarded with awe ($8^{17b}\ 9^{2b-3}$), and secure an unexampled triumph over their foes.* It is in some

---

* Notice, also, the second speech of Haman's wife (6^{13}), which is both in pointed contrast with her first (5^{14}), and also plainly reflects the *narrator's*

of the details connected with his picture of the Jews that the author's narrative is most open to the suspicion of exaggeration. It is probable in fact that the danger which threatened the Jews was a local one, and that the massacre which they wrought upon their foes was on a much smaller scale than is represented.*

Materials do not exist for fixing otherwise than approximately the date at which the Book of Esther was composed. Xerxes is described ($1^{1f.}$) in terms which imply that his reign lay in a somewhat distant past when the author wrote. By the majority of critics the Book is assigned either to the early years of the [455] Greek period (which began B.C. 332), or to the 3rd cent. B.C.† With such a date the diction would well agree, which, though superior to that of the Chronicler, and more acommodated to the model of the earlier historical books, contains many late words and idioms, and exhibits much deterioration in syntax.

The character of the Hebrew style of Esther may be inferred from the remarks on p. 505. Words or idioms peculiar to Esther, or occurring otherwise (in Biblical Hebrew) only in the passages cited, are—בִּיתָן, שִׂיחָה 1^8 (cf. for the form שְׁחִימָה 2 Ch. 30^{17}, יְנִיעָה Eccl. 12^{12} ‡), מַאֲמַר, כֶּתֶר, אֹנֶס (cf. פ×|×ב), הַבְזֹה (hif.), בָּיוֹן, נוּר = to decree (2^1, Job 22^{28}), הֲנָחָה (Ges.-Kautzsch, § 72, R. 7), נִשָּׂא חֵן ($2^{15. 17}$ 5^2 †), for the earlier מָצָא חֵן, which occurs here only in the stereotyped phrase 5^8 7^3 8^5), נִדְחַף, רָחוֹק, שָׁוֶה (2 Ch. 26^{20} †), הוֹשִׁיט, פַּרְשָׁה, אֶבֶן, נֹזֶק (as Eccl. 12^3, and in Aram:), בְּקֻשָּׁה, הַצָּלָה (Ezr. 7^6), וֵּיו 5^9 שַׁרְבִיט, (= ×|ב), עַל כָּכָה, הַתִּיהַד, תַּכְרִיךְ (9^{26}). Several of these are of Aramaic origin.

---

point of view. It is singular that no motive is assigned for Mordecai's disregard of Persian etiquette : obeisance to a superior was quite usual in ancient Israel ; and there is nothing to suggest that Haman claimed *Divine* honours.

* Sayce, who defended formerly (*Introd. to Ezr. Neh. and Est.*, 1885, p. 98 ff.) the historical credibility of the Book of Esther, is of opinion now (*Monuments*, p. 469 ff.) that it contains improbable and unhistorical representations ; and considers it to be "an example of Jewish Haggadah,"—*i.e.* moralizing tale or romance [on the original signification of the term, see below, p. 487 *note*], attached mostly to historical names or events,—"which has been founded upon one of those semi-historical tales, of which the Persian chronicles seem to have been full."

† Ewald, Bleek, Nöldeke, Dillmann, Bertheau, von Orelli (in Herzog's *Encycl.* ed. 2), Oettli.   Against the strange views of Grätz and Bloch on the date and aim of the Book, see Kuenen, § 38. 14, 15.

‡ And elsewhere ; but in an *abstract* sense the form is chiefly late : cf. **Strack and Siegfried**, *Lehrb. der Neuhebr. Spr.* § 47^b.

ראוי=*suitable*, 2⁹, is a Mishnic sense: Zunz (*ZDMG.* 1873, p. 685) notes also as recalling the style of the Mishnah עבר מצוה 3³ (cf. 9²⁷ᴸ·, 2 Ch. 24²⁰), עשה יום טוב 9¹⁹, and מה ראו, 9²⁶. See also the citations from Esther, pp. 475, 506 f., 535 ff. The principal *Persian* words are: פרתמים, 1³ 6⁹ (also Dan. 1³); כרפס *cotton* (or *fine linen*), 1⁶; פתגם *decree* (p. 475, No. 12); אחשדרפנים *satraps* (also Dan.); פתשגן (also in Ezr. in the form פרשגן); דת *law* (also Ezr. 8³⁶, and in the Aram. of Ezr. and Dan.), רמכים 8¹⁰ (also in Syr.), אחשתרנים (8¹⁰· ¹⁴), אגרת *letter* (also 2 Ch. 30¹· ⁶, and in Neh. Ultimately Assyrian).

Whether the name "Purim" is rightly explained (9²⁶) is open to doubt. The incident with which the term is connected (3⁷) is altogether subordinate in the narrative, and not likely to have given its name to the festival. There is also a more serious difficulty. No Persian word resembling *Pur*, with the meaning "lot," is known to exist.* Lagarde attempts an explanation based on the reading of the LXX φρουραι, in Lucian's recension φουρδαια; but this can hardly be right: whatever the etymological difficulties attaching to the term, the form "Purim" is supported *by the tradition of the feast itself*.

[456] Much fault has been found with the temper displayed in the Book of Esther: it is said, for instance, to breathe a spirit of vengeance and hatred, without any redeeming feature; and to be further removed from the spirit of the gospel than any other Book of the OT. It is impossible altogether to acquit it of this accusation. In the first place (looking at the narrative as it stands), the Jews had been brought into a position of mortal danger through no fault of their own, but by the irrational malice of a foe; and it was both natural and right that Mordecai and Esther should do what lay in their power to extricate them from it. In what is narrated in c. 4–7 no blame can be attached to them. The terms of the second decree were, however, dictated by Mordecai and Esther themselves (8⁸ "as it liketh you"); and if all that it authorized the Jews to do was to *act in*

* Lagarde, *Purim, ein Beitrag zur Gesch. der Religion* (1887), pp. 18–28. The Pers. *pāre* means "part, portion" (μέρος, pars); but though a word meaning "lot" may acquire the derived sense of *allotted portion* (as κλῆρος, גורל Jud. 1³), it is manifestly an unsound argument to infer that a word meaning properly "portion" would acquire the meaning *lot*. Lagarde shows that "lot" is expressed in Persian by altogether different words. Zimmern (*ZATW.* 1891, p. 157 ff.) derives "Purim" from the Bab. *puchru, assembly* (viz. of the gods, under the presidency of Marduk, on New Year's day, Nisan 1 [cf. Est. 3⁷], to fix the destinies for the coming year), and thinks that the Feast of Purim is in its origin a Jewish adaptation of the Babylonian festival of the New Year, which was celebrated annually with great pomp in the first days of Nisan.

self-defence against any who assailed them, it would be perfectly legitimate. Unfortunately, it seems to do more than this. It authorizes the Jews to take the lives of those who surely must have been harmless to them, the "little ones and the women": we are told, further, that when the terms of this decree became known, the people everywhere either actually rejoiced or stood in awe of the Jews (8[15b-17]); but this being so, it is scarcely credible that as many as 75,000 persons would take the aggressive against them: it seems consequently impossible to acquit Mordecai of permitting, and the Jews of engaging in, an *unprovoked* massacre. Nor, as it seems, can the request in 9[13] be excused. Not satisfied with the death of Haman's ten sons, Esther here demands their public exposure on the gallows; and obtains permission, besides, for a second massacre in Susa, where 500 persons (as she knew, v.[12]) had been massacred already. If all these measures were necessary *in self-defence*, they need no justification; but the terms of the narrative itself make it extremely difficult to think that this was the case. Mordecai and his compatriots can be completely justified only at the cost of the perfect accuracy of the narrative. And this an impartial historical criticism entitles us happily to doubt (cf. p. 482 f.).

Turning now from the facts narrated to the narrative, and the spirit in which it is written, it is remarkable that whereas generally in the OT. national and religious interests are commingled, they are here divorced: the national feeling being extremely strong, and the religious feeling being practically [457] absent altogether. In Ewald's words, in passing to Esther from other books of the OT., we "fall from heaven to earth." Not only does the name of God not occur in the Book, but the point of view is throughout purely secular: the preservation of the race as such, and its worldly greatness, not the perpetuation or diffusion of its religion, are the objects in which the author's interest is manifestly centred.* This peculiarity is probably to be explained from the circumstances under which the Book arose. The Feast of Purim, the observance of which it was intended to inculcate, had no religious character: even in its origin, no hint is dropped of its having been an occasion of thanksgiving to God: it was merely a season of mutual congratulation, and of

---

* The only religious observance mentioned is that of fasting. Providence is alluded to in 4[14].

sending gifts to the poor (9$^{17-19.}$ ^{22} &c.). Thus the feast itself was the expression of a purely national interest; and the Book reflects the same spirit. It is possible, moreover, that the author's temper was to some extent moulded by the age in which he lived. The depressed condition of the nation, which filled the brooding soul of Qohéleth (p. 471) with thoughts of despair, might well arouse in a mind differently constituted feelings of antagonism to foreign nations, and exaggerate in it the sentiment of race. The national name, the pride inseparable from it, the ambition to assert it against all traducers, might readily, under long continued depreciation, assume an unhealthy prominence. Even the author's representation, as well as his tone, seems sometimes to reflect the associations of his own age. He pictures the Jews, for instance, as surrounded by their "haters" (9$^{1.}$ $^{5.}$ ^{16} &c.); but no overt act is attributed to them: the only real enemy of the Jews is Haman. It must be admitted that the spirit of Esther is not that which prevails generally in the Old Testament; but we have no right to demand, upon *à priori* grounds, that in every part of the Biblical record the human interests of the narrator should, in the *same* degree, be subordinated to the Spirit of God.

Note on the word " Haggadah."—" Haggādāh " is in form an Aramaizing infin. *Hiph.*, from הִגִּיד *to tell* (of the same type as הַצָּלָה Est. 4^{14}, above, p. 484; cf. חֲנֻחָה 2^{18}, חֲנֻפָּה Isa. 30^{28}), used as a subst.* It is commonly explained as signifying properly *tale, narration*; but W. Bacher, one of the most learned and competent of living students of Rabbinical literature, points out (*JQR.* April 1892, p. 406 ff.) that *higgīd* is *to tell* in the sense of *declaring* some particular fact (see *e.g.* Gen. 3^{11}), not in that of *recounting* or *narrating* a tale, and that even in post-Biblical Hebrew it is not found in the latter sense: on the other hand, he observes that in the oldest Jewish exegesis (as in the *Mechilta*, a Midrashic commentary on Exodus), allegorical or Midrashic expositions are constantly introduced by the phrase מַגִּיד הַכָּתוּב " the text *declares*," and infers accordingly, very plausibly, that the subst. *Haggādāh* was derived from this usage, the term meaning properly simply *declaration*, but acquiring by custom the sense of an *imaginative development* of a thought supposed to be contained in, or intimated by, the text in question.†

---

* A softened Palestinian form is *Aggādāh* (אַגָּדָה): see Bacher, p. 429.

† For illustrations, see Schürer, *Gesch. des Jüd. Volkes*, ii. 278 ff. [Eng. transl. II. i. p. 339 ff.]; and cf. in the N.T. Acts 7$^{22.}$ ^{53}, 1 Cor. 10^4 (see the writer's note in the *Expositor*, Jan. 1889, p. 15 ff.), Gal. 3^{19} 4^{79} (see Lightfoot's note), Heb. 2^2, 2 Tim. 3^8, Jude^9.

CHAPTER XI.

DANIEL.

LITERATURE.—F. Hitzig (in the *Kgf. Handb.*), 1850; H. Ewald in *Die Proph. des AB.s* [2] (1868), iii. 298 ff. (in the transl., v. 152 ff.) ; E. B. Pusey, *Daniel the Prophet*, 1865, [3] 1869 ; C. F. Keil (in the *Bibl. Comm.*), 1869; O. Zöckler (in Lange's *Bibelwerk*), 1869 ; J. M. Fuller in the *Speaker's Commentary* (philology to be often distrusted); F. Delitzsch, art. "Daniel" in Herzog's *Real-Encyklopädie*, [2] vol. iii. (1878) ; J. Meinhold in Strack and Zöckler's *Kgf. Komm.* (in the part entitled *Die Gesch. Hagiographen*, 1889, p. 257 ff.) ; also *Die Compos. des B. Daniel*, 1884, and *Beiträge zur Erkl. des B. Dan.* 1888 ; A. A. Bevan, *Comm. on Dan.* 1892 ; G. Behrmann (in Nowack's "Handkomm."), 1894 ; F. A. Farrar (in the "Expositor's Bible"), 1895 ; A. Kamphausen, *Das B. Dan. u. die neuere Geschichtsforschung* (ein Vortrag), 1893, and in Haupt's *SBOT.* 1896 ; A. Bludau, *De Alex. Interpr. Libri Dan. indole*, 1891 ; A. Freiherr von Gall, *Die Einheitl. des B. Dan.* 1895 ; M. Löhr, "Textkrit. Vorarb. zu einer Erkl. des B. Dan.," *ZATW.* 1895, pp. 75 ff., 193 ff., 1896, p. 17 ff.; C. von Orelli, *OT. Prophecy*, p. 454 ff.

The Book of Daniel narrates the history of Daniel (c. 1–6), and the visions attributed to him (c. 7–12). It is written partly in Hebrew, partly in Aramaic, viz. from 2^{4b} (from "*O king*") to the end of c. 7.

C. 1 (introductory). In the 3rd year of Jehoiakim (B.C. 605), Nebuchadnezzar lays siege to Jerusalem : part of the vessels of the Temple, and some Jewish captives, fall into his hands. Daniel, and three other Israelitish youths of noble blood, Hananiah, Mishael, and Azariah, are instructed at Nebuchadnezzar's command in the language and learning of the Chaldæans, and educated for the king's service ; they refrain, however, studiously from defiling themselves in any way by partaking of the meat and drink of the king. At the expiration of three years their education is completed ; all are distinguished for wisdom and knowledge, Daniel in a pre-eminent degree, being gifted in particular with "understanding in all visions and dreams."

C. 2. Nebuchadnezzar, in his second year (B.C. 603–2), has a disquieting dream, which the wise men of the Chaldæans are unable to interpret to him. Daniel, the secret being revealed to him in a vision of the night (v.¹⁹), interprets it successfully. The king in gratitude exalts Daniel to great honour; he is made [459] "chief governor over all the wise men of Babylon," and has a permanent home at the Court, while his three companions are appointed administrators of the province of Babylon.

Neb.'s dream was of a colossal image, the head of gold, the breast and arms of silver, the body of brass, the legs of iron, the feet of iron and clay mixed; a stone "cut out without hands" suddenly fell, smiting the feet of the image, which thereupon broke up, while the stone became a mountain, filling the whole earth. The image symbolizes the anti-theocratic power of the world; and its principal parts are interpreted to signify four empires (or their rulers), the head of gold being Nebuchadnezzar himself. The empires intended (except the first) are not mentioned by name; and it is disputed which are meant. According to the traditional view they are: (1) the Chaldæan; (2) the Medo-Persian (Cyrus); (3) (the belly) the Macedonian (Alexander), followed by the empires of the Seleucidæ at Antioch, and the Ptolemies in Egypt (the thighs); (4) the Roman, afterwards (the mingled clay and iron of the feet) divided into East and West (Constantinople and Rome), and ultimately further subdivided. According to many modern interpreters, the empires meant are: (1) the Chaldæan; (2) the Median; (3) the Persian; (4) the Macedonian, issuing in the often externally allied, but yet inwardly disunited, empires of the Diadochi (the Seleucidæ and Ptolemies).* As the vision in c. 7 is generally allowed to be parallel in import to the dream here, if the fourth kingdom there be rightly interpreted of the empire of Alexander, the second interpretation will be the correct one. In any case, the "stone cut out without hands" represents the kingdom of God, before which all earthly powers are ultimately to fall.

C. 3. Nebuchadnezzar erects in the plain of Dura, near Babylon, a colossal golden image, and assembles for its dedication the high officials of his kingdom, all being commanded, under penalty of being cast into a burning fiery furnace, to fall down and worship it at a given signal. Daniel's three companions refusing to do this, are cast into the furnace; but, to the king's surprise, are wonderfully delivered from the power of the

* So Eichhorn, v. Lengerke, Ewald, Bleek, Westcott (Smith's *Dict. of the Bible*, *s.v.* "Daniel"), Delitzsch, Meinhold, Kuenen. In favour of the Median and Persian empires being reckoned separately, it is remarked that in the Book itself they are distinguished (6⁸ &c.; 8³), and the rule of "Darius the Mede" (5³¹ 6²⁸) precedes that of Cyrus the Persian. Others (Bertholdt, Zöckler, Herzfeld) understand less probably: (1) the Chaldæan; (2) the Medo-Persian; (3) the Macedonian; (4) the Diadochi.

flames. Thereupon Nebuchadnezzar solemnly acknowledges the power of their God, issues a decree threatening death to any who presume to blaspheme Him, and promotes the three men in the province of Babylon.

[460] C. 4. The edict of Nebuchadnezzar, addressed to all peoples of the earth, in which he extols (v.[1-3. 34-37]) the power and greatness of the God of Israel. The occasion of the edict is explained in v.[4-33]. Nebuchadnezzar had a dream of a mighty tree, the head of which towered to heaven, while its branches sheltered the beasts and fowl of the earth : as he watched it, he heard the command given that it should be hewn down to the earth. This dream, which the Chaldæans were unable to interpret, was explained to him by Daniel. The tree represented the great king himself, in the pride and splendour of his empire ; but the time should come when he would be humbled, and his reason would leave him for seven years, that he might learn that the Most High was the disposer of the kingdoms of the earth. At the end of twelve months, as the king was contemplating from his palace the city which he had built, Daniel's words were suddenly verified, and Nebuchadnezzar was bereft of his reason for seven years. In gratitude for his recovery, he now issued his present edict.

C. 5. Belshazzar's feast. While Belshazzar and his lords are at a feast, impiously drinking their wine from the golden cups which had belonged once to the Temple at Jerusalem, the fingers of a man's hand appear writing upon the wall. The king, in alarm, summons the wise men of the Chaldæans to interpret what was written ; but they are unable to do so. At the suggestion of the queen, Daniel is called, who interprets the words to mean that the days of Belshazzar's kingdom are numbered, and that it is about to be given to the Medes and Persians.* Daniel is invested with purple and a chain of gold, and made one of the three chief ministers in the kingdom (v.[7. 29] : see QPB.[3] and RV. marg.). The same night Belshazzar is slain, and " Darius the Mede " receives the kingdom.

C. 6. Daniel being promoted by Darius above the other princes, the latter in envy seek an opportunity to ruin him. They accordingly persuade the king to issue a decree forbidding any one to ask a petition of God or man, except the king, for 30

* On v.[25] see QPB.[3] ; and esp. Nöldeke, Zeitschr. f. Assyriol. i. 414 ff.

days. Daniel, however, continues as before to pray three times a day at his open window towards Jerusalem. The king, upon information being brought to him, reluctantly yielding obedience to the law, orders Daniel to be cast into a den of lions, Next [461] morning he is overjoyed to find him uninjured, and publishes a decree enjoining men, in all parts of his dominion, to honour and revere the God of Daniel, who had given such wonderful evidence of His power.

In the following chapters of the Book of Daniel, Antiochus Epiphanes, the persecutor of the Jews in the 2nd cent. B.C., is such a prominent figure, that a synopsis of the chief events of his reign will probably be of service to the reader * :—

B.C. 176. Accession of Antiochus to the throne of Syria (1 Macc. 1[10]), Dan. [7[8. 11. 20]] 8[9. 23] 11[21].

,, 175. Jason, intriguing against his brother, Onias III., purchases the high-priesthood for himself from Antiochus. Rise of a powerful *Hellenizing* party in Jerusalem, which is patronized and encouraged by Jason (1 Macc. 1[11-15], 2 Macc. 4[7-22]).

,, 172. Menelaus, outbidding Jason, gets the high-priesthood conferred upon himself. Onias III., having rebuked Menelaus for sacrilege, is murdered, at his instigation, by Andronicus, deputy of Antiochus (2 Macc. 4[32-35]), Dan. [9[26a]] 11[22b].

,, 171. *First* expedition of Antiochus against Egypt (1 Macc. 1[16-19]), Dan. 11[22-24].

,, 170. *Second* expedition of Antiochus against Egypt (1 Macc. 1[20]), Dan. 11[25-27]. Antiochus on his return from Egypt enters the Temple, carries off the sacred vessels, and massacres many Jews (1 Macc. 1[21-28], 2 Macc. 5[11-21]), Dan. 8[9b-10] 11[28].

,, 169. *Third* expedition of Antiochus against Egypt. When in sight of Alexandria, the Roman legate, Popilius Lænas, obliges him to retire, and evacuate the country (Polyb. 29, 1 ; Livy, 44, 19. 45, 12), Dan. 11[29-30a].

,, 169-8. Fresh measures against Jerusalem. The capital surprised by Apollonius on the Sabbath day, and many of the inhabitants either captured and sold as slaves, or slain. A Syrian garrison commanding the Temple established in the citadel ; flight of the God-fearing Jews from Jerusalem, and prohibition of all practices of the Jewish religion. The Temple-worship suspended, and on 15 Chisleu, B.C. 168, the "abomination of desolation " † (a small

---

* The references in Dan. are appended (those in c. 11 according to Meinhold), such as are disputed being enclosed in brackets.

† Cf. Dan. 9[27] 11[31] 12[11] LXX and Theod. In explanation of the Heb. שִׁקּוּץ מְשֹׁמֵם (11[31]) or שִׁקּוּץ שֹׁמֵם (12[11]), see esp. Nestle, *ZATW.* 1884, p. 248, or in Bevan or Behrm. *ad locc.* (a contemptuous punning designation of בַּעַל שָׁמַיִם = Zeὺs 'Ολύμπιος, 2 Macc. 6[2], the favourite Deity of Antiochus).

heathen altar) erected on the altar of Burnt-offering. Books of
the law burnt, and women who had had their children circum-
cised put to death (1 Macc. 1[29-64]; 2 Macc. 6-7), Dan. [7[21. 24b. 25]]
8[11f. 13b. 24. 25] [9[26b. 27a]] 11[30b-35.* [36-39]] [12[1. 7. 11]].

[462] B.C. 167. Revolt against the persecuting measures of Antiochus, organized
  by Mattathias and his five sons (the Maccabees), (1 Macc. 2),
  Dan. 11[34] (the "little help").

,, 166. After the death of Mattathias, the war of independence is carried
  on by his son Judas, who slays Apollonius and Seron (1 Macc.
  3[1-24]). Antiochus sends Lysias with a large army to suppress
  the rebellion in Judæa; his generals, Nicanor and Gorgias, are
  defeated by Judas near Emmaus (1 Macc. 3[25]-4[27]).

,, 165. Lysias himself defeated by Judas at Beth-zur, between Hebron and
  Jerusalem (1 Macc. 4[28-35]); the Temple purified, and public
  worship in it re-established, on 25 Chisleu, just *three years* after
  its desecration. The dedication of the altar continued during
  eight days. The Temple hill and Beth-zur fortified by Judas
  (1 Macc. 4[36-61]). Offensive measures of Judas against Edom,
  Ammon, Philistia, &c. (1 Macc. 5). In the following year (164),
  Antiochus, after an abortive attempt to pillage a temple in
  Elymais in Persia, dies somewhat suddenly (1 Macc. 6[1-16]; but
  see also Polyb. 31, 11), Dan. [7[11. 26]] 8[14b. 25 *end*] [9[26b. 27b] 11[45b]
  12[7 *end*. 11 *end*. 12. 13]].†

The reader ought to consider whether, in view of the parallelism which
appears generally to prevail between the passages of Daniel quoted, the
bracketed ones are legitimately separated from the rest.

C. 7. A vision, seen by Daniel in a dream, in the first year of
Belshazzar. The vision was of four beasts emerging from the
sea, a lion with eagle's wings, a bear, a leopard with 4 wings and
4 heads, and a fourth beast, with powerful iron teeth, destroying
all things, and with 10 horns, among which another "little horn"
sprang up, "speaking proud things," before which three of the
other horns were rooted out. Hereupon a celestial assize is
held: the Almighty, figured as an aged man, with hair white like
wool, and snow-like raiment, appears seated on a throne of
flame, and surrounded by His myriads of attendants: the beast
whose horn spake proud things is slain; and one "like unto a
son of man"—*i.e.* a figure in human form—comes with the
clouds of heaven into the presence of the Almighty, and receives

---

* V.[30b-32a] alluding to the renegade Jews (1 Macc. 1[15. 43. 52]), v.[32b-35] to those
who remained faithful, including some who were martyrs (*ib.* v.[57. 63]).

† See further the monograph of J. F. Hoffmann, *Antiochus IV. Epiphanes*,
1873 (who explains some parts of c. 11 differently). In illustration of the
character of Antiochus, see especially Polybius, 26, 10. 31, 3-4.

from Him a universal and never-ending dominion, v.[1-15]. In v.[16-28] the vision is interpreted to Daniel: the four beasts are explained to signify four kingdoms; and after the destruction of the fourth, "the people of the saints of the Most High" will receive the dominion of the entire earth.

[463] The vision, as remarked above, is generally agreed to be parallel to the dream in c. 2 (the only material difference being that the symbolism of the fourth kingdom is more developed); and there is a corresponding divergence of interpretation. On the one hand, the ten horns are supposed to be the European kingdoms into which the Roman empire ultimately broke up, the "little horn" being an anti-Christian power destined to arise out of them in the future; on the other hand, the ten horns are interpreted to represent the successors of Alexander, in particular (as is commonly held) the Seleucidæ, the "little horn" being Antiochus Epiphanes. The latter view is somewhat strongly supported by the sequel of the Book. The terms in which the "little horn" is here spoken of—his arrogance, his impiety, his persecution of the people of God (7[20f. 25])—are closely analogous to those used in 8[9-13. 23-25], likewise with reference to a "little horn," which is admitted to signify Antiochus Epiphanes, who is also prominent in c. 10-12; the time, v.[25], during which his ambitious purposes are to take effect ($3\frac{1}{2}$ years) agrees likewise very nearly with the event. According to Ew., Del., Meinhold (who adopt this view), the ten horns are: (1) Seleucus Nicator (B.C. 312-280); (2) Antiochus Soter (279-261); (3) Antiochus Theos (260-246); (4) Seleucus Callinicus (245-226); (5) Seleucus Ceraunus (225-223); (6) Antiochus the Great (222-187); (7) Seleucus IV. Philopator (186-176); (8) Heliodorus (treasurer of Seleucus IV., who murdered his master, but who was prevented by two of the courtiers, in the interests of Seleucus' brother, Antiochus Epiphanes, from securing the throne); (9) Demetrius Soter (son of Seleucus, and so, after his father's murder, legitimate heir to the crown, but detained at Rome as a hostage, whither his father had sent him to release Antiochus from the same position); (10) Ptolemy VI. Philometor, who claimed the throne of Syria through his mother, Cleopatra, sister of Seleucus IV. and of Antiochus Epiphanes. (A slightly different reckoning in Kuen. § 89. 4.) It is objected to this explanation that Heliodorus, Demetrius, and Ptolemy VI., whom Antiochus is regarded as having supplanted, were not all strictly "kings" (7[24]); but we do not, perhaps, know how they were viewed by those living at the time.

C. 8. A vision of Daniel in the third year of Belshazzar. A ram with two horns appeared, pushing towards the West, North, and South, until a he-goat, with "a notable horn" between its eyes, emerged from the West, and, drawing nigh, smote the ram, and brake its two horns; after this the he-goat increased in strength; but ere long its horn was broken: and in place of it there rose up four other horns towards the four quarters of the earth. Out of one of these came forth a little horn, which waxed exceedingly great towards the South, and the East, and the land of Judah: it even exalted itself against the host of heaven, and against its Prince (God), destroying His sanctuary, and interrupting the daily sacrifice for 2300 "evenings, mornings." The meaning of this vision is explained to Daniel by the [464] angel Gabriel: the ram with two horns is the Medo-Persian empire; the he-goat is the empire of the Greeks, the "notable horn" being its first king (Alexander), whose conquests are significantly indicated in v.[7]; the four horns which follow are the four kingdoms which arose out of the empire of Alexander at his death (*i.e.* those of the Seleucidæ at Antioch, of the Ptolemies in Egypt, of Lysimachus in Thrace, and of Cassander in Macedonia). The name of the king symbolized by the "little horn" is not stated; but the description given of him (v.[9-14. 23-25]) leaves no question that it is Antiochus Epiphanes, which, indeed, is not here disputed.

In v.[14] the expression "evenings, mornings" is peculiar; and it seems impossible to find two events separated by 2300 days (= 6 years 4 months) which would correspond with the description in v.[14f.]. The terms of v.[14f.] appear plainly to indicate the interval from the time when the sanctuary was first profaned to its purification on 25 Chisleu, B.C. 165. As this was approximately three years, it is supposed by many that the peculiar expression in v.[14] is intended to denote 2300 half-days (= 3 years 2 months). In point of fact, it is true, just 3 years had elapsed since the heathen altar was set up (p. 492); but the sanctuary may well have been first "trodden under foot" two months previously (cf. 1 Macc. 1[37-39]). In 7[25] the tribulation of the saints is to last 3½ years (cf. 12[7]); in 12[11] from the time that the daily offering is suspended 1290 days are counted; in 12[12] the trial is to terminate after 1335 days. It is difficult not to think that the same period of 3–3½ years is intended in all these passages. Did we know the history of the time more accurately, it would probably appear why a slightly different *terminus a quo* (or *ad quem*) was fixed in the several cases.

C. 9. In the first year of Darius the Mede, Daniel, considering that the 70 years of desolation prophesied by Jeremiah (25[11] 29[10]) for Jerusalem were drawing to their close, implores God to forgive His people's sin, and to look favourably upon His ruined sanctuary, v.[1-19]. The angel Gabriel explains to Daniel that it would be, not 70 years, but 70 weeks of years, before the iniquity of the people would be entirely atoned for. This entire period is then divided into three smaller ones, 7 + 62 + 1; and it is said (*a*) that 7 weeks (= 49 years) will elapse from the going forth of the command to restore Jerusalem to "an anointed one, a prince"; (b) that for 62 weeks (=434 years) the city will be rebuilt, though in straitened times; (c) that at the end of these 62 weeks "an anointed one" will be cut off, and the people of a prince that shall come will desolate the city and the sanctuary : he will make a covenant with many for one [465] week (=7 years), and during half of this week he will cause the sacrifice and oblation to cease, until his end come, and the consummation decreed arrest the desolator, v.[20-27].

Of the passage 9[24-27] no entirely satisfactory interpretation appears yet to have been found. As commonly understood, it is a prediction of the death of Christ, and the destruction of Jerusalem by Titus. But this view labours under serious difficulties. (1) If the 490 years are to end with the Crucifixion, A.D. 29, they must begin c. 458 B.C., a date which coincides with the decree of Artaxerxes and the mission of Ezra (Ezra 7). But this decree contains no command whatever "to restore and build Jerusalem"; nor was this one of the objects of Ezra's mission. (2) In the 490 years, the first 49 are distinguished from those that follow, their close being marked by a break, as though some epoch were signalized by it; but no historical importance is known to attach in Jewish history to the year 409 B.C. (3) Christ did not " confirm a covenant with many for one week " (=7 years): His ministry lasted at most somewhat over 3 years; and if, in the years following, He is regarded as carrying on His work through the agency of His apostles, the limit, " seven years," seems an arbitrary one; for the apostles continued to gain converts from Judaism for many years subsequently. (4) If the RV. of v.[27] ("for half the week," &c.) be correct—and it is at least the natural rendering of the Heb.—a reference to the death of Christ would seem to be precluded altogether.

The view taken by many modern scholars is represented in its most probable form by Bleek (" Die Mess. Weiss. im B. Daniel " in the *Jahrb. f. Deutsche Theol.* 1860, p. 45 ff.: see also the synopsis in the *Speaker's Comm.* p. 360 ff.) and Meinhold. V.[25] the command (lit. " word ") is the Divine promise given through Jeremiah (31[38ff.]) for the rebuilding of Jerusalem, c. B.C. 588 ; the anointed prince is Cyrus (see Isa. 45[1] 44[28]), B.C. 538 ; v.[25b] alludes to the relatively depressed state of the restored community, B.C. 538–172 ; v.[26a] the "anointed one " is the High Priest Onias III., deposed in 175, assassinated in 172 ; v.[26b-27] alludes to the attacks made by Antiochus Epiphanes on the Holy City, to the willing allies whom he found among the renegade Jews, to his suspension of the Temple services, and the destruction which finally overtook him (B.C. 164). V.[24] describes the Messianic age, to succeed the persecutions of Antiochus (comp. c. 12), "to anoint the most holy " alluding to the re-dedication of the altar of Burnt-offering, B.C. 165 (it is doubtful if קרש קדשים is ever applied to a person, see 1 Ch. 23[13] RV.: it is applied to the altar of Burnt-offering, Ex. 29[37] 40[10]). That some of the expressions in this verse describe what was only in fact accomplished by Christ, is but natural : though the author pictured the consummation as relatively close at hand, it was actually postponed, and in its fulness only effected by Him. The chief objection to this interpretation is that the period from B.C. 538 to 172 is 366 years only, not 434 (=62 weeks); but, in reply, it is urged that we do not know what chronology the author followed, or how his years were computed.* The general parallelism of v.²⁶ᵇ⁻²⁷—especially [466] the suspension of the Temple services for 3½ years—with 7²⁵ and other passages of the Book where the persecutions of Antiochus are alluded to, and the fact that elsewhere in c. 7–12 Antiochus is the prominent figure, may be said to favour the second explanation. It ought to be understood that the issue is not between one interpretation which is clear and free from difficulty, and another that is the reverse of this, but between two (or perhaps more than two) interpretations, to both of which objection may be taken. On which side the difficulties are least grave, it must be left to the reader to decide for himself.† The two most recent monographs on 9²⁴ᶠᶠ· are by J. W. van Lennep, *De 70 jaarweken van Daniel*, Utrecht, 1888, and C. H. Cornill, *Die siebzig Jahrwochen Daniels*, 1889; cf. Kamphausen's *Vortrag*, p. 32 ff.

C. 10–12. A vision of Daniel in the third year of Cyrus, by the Hiddekel (the Tigris). Daniel had fasted for 21 days, when an angel appears to him, and tells him that he had been prevented from coming before by the opposition of the "prince" (*i.e.* the guardian-angel) of Persia, but being at length assisted by Michael, the "prince" (guardian-angel) of the Jews, he had been able to do so, and was now come in order to give Daniel a revelation concerning the future, 10¹⁻¹⁹. The angel that speaks and Michael will have a long contest on behalf of Israel, first with the "prince" (guardian-angel) of Persia, then with the "prince" of Greece, 10²⁰–11¹. The details of the contest form the subject of 11²–12³. Here, under veiled names, are described, first, briefly, the doings of four Persian kings, v.², and of Alexander the Great (v.³), with the rupture of his empire after his death (v.⁴); afterwards, more fully, the leagues and conflicts between the kings of Antioch ("the kings of the north") and of Egypt ("the kings of the south"), in the centuries following (v.⁵⁻²⁰); finally, most fully of all, the history of Antiochus Epiphanes (v.²¹⁻⁴⁵), including his conflicts with Egypt, and the measures adopted by him for suppressing the religion of the Jews (v.³⁰ᵇ⁻³⁹). The death of Antiochus is followed by the resurrection (of Israelites), and advent of the Messianic age, 12¹⁻³. The revela-

* Comp. the somewhat curious parallels quoted by Schürer, *Gesch. des Jüd. Volkes im Zeitalter Jesu Christi*, ii. 616 (Engl. transl. II. iii. p. 54).

† See more fully Pusey, p. 166 ff.; J. Drummond, *The Jewish Messiah*, 1877, p. 243 ff.; and comp. Schultz, *OT. Theology*, ii. 437 ff.

tion is designed for the encouragement of those living "in the time of the end," *i.e.* under the persecution of Antiochus,* 12⁴⁻¹³, the close of which (v.¹¹ᶠ·) appears to [467] be placed 1290 (or 1335) days after the suspension of the daily sacrifice in B.C. 168 (with 12¹¹ᵃ cf. 11³¹ and 8¹¹·¹³).

The allusions in 11⁵ᶠᶠ· to the Ptolemies and the Seleucidæ are explained in the Commentaries. V.¹⁸ the "captain" (RV. *marg.*) is Lucius Cornelius Scipio, who defeated Antiochus the Great with severe loss at Magnesia, B.C. 190 : v.²⁰ the "exactor" is Heliodorus (see 2 Macc. 3), treasurer of Seleucus IV. Philopator. On v.²¹ᶠᶠ· see the Synopsis above. Some of the older interpreters supposed that at v.³⁶ there was a transition from Antiochus to the future Antichrist. But whatever typical significance may attach to the *whole* character of Antiochus, it can hardly be legitimate, in a *continuous* description, with no apparent change of subject, to refer part to the type and part to the antitype.† V.⁴⁰⁻⁴⁵ occasion difficulty. They seem to describe a fourth Egyptian expedition, on which, however, our chief authorities are silent : several of the other details also do not agree with what is known independently of the closing events of Antiochus' life. Hence, many understand these verses as giving a *summary* of Antiochus' career, a view not favoured by their position in the chapter. See Meinhold, and Hoffmann, pp. 74 ff. 101 ff. (who points out that, in view of a statement of Porphyry's, we are not quite in a position to deny a fourth expedition against Egypt). C. 12 is to be taken in close connexion with c. 11.

Authorship and date. In face of the facts presented by the Book of Daniel, the opinion that it is the work of Daniel himself cannot be sustained. Internal evidence shows, with a cogency that cannot be resisted, that it must have been written not earlier than *c.* 300 B.C., and in Palestine ; and it is at least *probable* that it was composed under the persecution of Antiochus Epiphanes, B.C. 168 or 167.

(1.) The following are facts of a historical nature which point more or less decisively to an author later than Daniel himself :—

(*a*) The position of the Book in the Jewish Canon, not among the prophets, but in the miscellaneous collection of writings called the *Hagiographa*,

---

* The "end" in this Book (spoken from Daniel's standpoint) means regularly the close of the present age, the "time of the end" coinciding with the persecution—or in 11⁴⁰ (upon one view) with the entire reign—of Antiochus : 8¹⁷·¹⁹(see v.²³⁻²⁶) 11³⁵·⁴⁰ 12⁴·⁹·¹³ ; cf. 9²⁶ᵇ 11⁴⁵ᵇ. The Messianic age (12²ᶠ· &c.) is represented as beginning immediately after the death of Antiochus, the future (as often in prophecy) being foreshortened (Delitzsch, p. 478 f.).

† Such a transition is "wholly unfounded and arbitrary" (Westcott).

and among the latest of these, in proximity to Esther. Though little definite is known respecting the formation of the Canon, the division known as the " Prophets " was doubtless formed prior to the Hagiographa ; * and had the Book of Daniel existed at the time, it is reasonable to suppose that it would have ranked as the work of a prophet, and have been included among the former.

(*b*) Jesus, the son of Sirach (writing *c*. 200 B.C.), in his enumeration of [463] Israelitish worthies, c. 44–50, though he mentions Isaiah, Jeremiah, Ezekiel, and (collectively) the Twelve Minor Prophets, is silent as to Daniel.

(*c*) That Nebuchadnezzar besieged Jerusalem, and carried away some of the sacred vessels in "the *third* year of Jehoiakim " (Dan. 1¹ᶠ·), though it cannot, strictly speaking, be disproved, is highly improbable : not only is the Book of Kings silent, but Jeremiah, *in the following year* (c. 25, &c.: see v.¹), speaks of the Chaldæans in a manner which appears distinctly to imply that their arms had not yet been seen in Judah.

(*d*) The " Chaldæans " are synonymous in Dan. (1⁴ 2² &c.) with the caste of wise men. This sense " is unknown to the Ass.-Bab. language, has, wherever it occurs, formed itself after the end of the Babylonian empire, and is thus an indication of the post-exilic composition of the Book " (Schrader, *KAT*.² p. 429). It dates, namely, from a time when practically the only "Chaldæans" known belonged to the caste in question (comp. Meinhold, *Beiträge*, p. 28).

(*e*) Belshazzar is represented as *king* of Babylon ; and Nebuchadnezzar is spoken of throughout c. 5 (v.². ¹¹. ¹³. ¹⁸. ²²) as his *father*. In point of fact, Nabonidus (Nabu-nahid) was the last king of Babylon ; he was a usurper, not related to Nebuchadnezzar, and one *Belsharuzur* is mentioned as his son.† Belsharuzur's standing title is the "king's son,"—something like the " Crown Prince " (see the contract-tablets translated by Sayce, *Records of the Past*, second series, iii. 125–127). In the Nabu-nahid-Cyrus-chronicle, now,‡ the "king's son"—*i.e.* as may fairly be assumed, Belsharuzur—is mentioned repeatedly (in Nabu-nahid's 7th, 9th, 10th, and 11th years) as being " with the nobles and the soldiers in the country of Akkad " (North Babylonia) : it thus seems that he acted as his father's general. In the year in which Cyrus marched against Babylon (Nabu-nahid's 17th year), we read (obverse, line 14 ff.) that on Tammuz (June) 14 Sippar was taken without fighting, and Nabu-nahid fled ; on the 16th Ugbaru — no doubt the prototype of the "Assyrian" Gobryas, who is mentioned by Xenophon in his (unhistorical) account of the capture of Babylon (*Cyrop*. vii. 5. 8, 24–32 ; cf. iv. 6, v. 2,

---

* Cf. Ryle, *Canon of the OT*. p. 121 f. (² p. 131 f.).

† Schrader, *KAT*.² on Dan. 5¹. The succession is : Nebuchadnezzar, B.C. 604–561 ; Evilmerodach (Avil-Marduk), 561–559 ; Neriglissar, 558–555 ; Laborosoarchod (Lâbashi-Marduk), 555 (9 months) ; Nabu-nahid, 555–538. Nabu-nahid names as his father Nabû-balatsu-iḳbi (*KB*. iii. 2, pp. 97, 119, 121).

‡ Schrader, *KB*. iii. 2, p. 128 ff.; more exactly Hagen in Delitzsch and Haupt's *Beiträge zur Assyriologie*, ii. (1891), p. 215 ff. (The translation in *Records of the Past, ib*. v. 158 ff., is in many respects antiquated.)

viii. 4)—governor of Gutium,* and the troops of Cyrus, "entered Babylon without fighting," after which Nabu-nahid was taken prisoner in Babylon. The soldiers of Gutium guarded the great temple of Esakkil. On the 3rd of Marchesvan (October) Cyrus entered Babylon, and proclaimed peace to the inhabitants ; and Gubaru appointed governors in the city. On the 11th of the same month during the night "ging Gubaru drauflos (?) und tödtet den Sohn (?) des Königs."† From the 27th of Adar (Feb.) to the 3rd of Nisan (March) the people publicly lamented, &c. The inscriptions thus lend no support to the hypothesis that Belsharuzur was his father's viceroy, or was entitled to be spoken of as "king" : according to the best accredited reading of the passage just quoted, he was called "the king's son" to the day of his death. Further, when the Persians (as the same inscription shows) had been in peaceable possession of Babylon for *four months*, how could Belshazzar, even supposing (what is not in itself inconceivable) that he still held out in the palace, and was slain afterwards in attempting to defend it, promise, and dispense ($5^{7.\ 16.\ 29}$), honours in his kingdom, and what need could there be for the solemn announcement (5^{25-28}), as of something new and unexpected, that his (or his father's) kingdom was to be given to the Medes and Persians, when it must have been patent to every one that they were already in posses-sion of it? As regards Belshazzar's relationship to Nebuchadnezzar, there remains the *possibility* that Nabu-nahid may have sought to strengthen his position by marrying a daughter of Nebuchadnezzar, in which case the latter might be spoken of as Belshazzar's father (=grandfather, by Hebrew usage). The terms of c. 5, however, produce certainly the impression that, in the view of the writer, Belshazzar was actually Neb.'s son. The historical pre-suppositions of Dan. 5 are inconsistent with the evidence of the contemporary monuments. Belshazzar may have distinguished himself, perhaps more than his father Nabu-nahid, at the time when Babylon passed into the power of the Persians ; and hence in the recollections of a later age he may have been pictured as its last king: but he was not styled "king" by his contem-poraries (cf. Schrader on Dan. $5^{1.\ 2}$).

(*f*) Darius, son of Ahasuerus—elsewhere the Heb. form of *Xerxes* (Pers. *Khshayârshâ*),—a *Mede*, after the death of Belshazzar, is "made king over the realm of the Chaldæans" ($5^{31}\ 6^{1ff.}\ 9^1\ 11^1$). There seems to be no room for such a ruler. According to all other authorities, Cyrus is the immediate successor of Nabu-nahid,‡ and the ruler of the entire Persian empire. It has been conjectured that Darius may have been an under-king—perhaps either

---

* Probably the region N. of Babylonia, between the upper Adhem and the Dijâlâ (Delitzsch, *Paradies*, p. 234).

† So Hagen, Pinches (now), and Delitzsch. The tablet is slightly mutilated. Schrader also agrees now that this reading is probable. See Hagen, pp. 247, 256 ; and Whitehouse, *Critical Review*, Apr. 1893, p. 136.

‡ This is particularly clear from the contract-tablets, which, bearing date at this period almost continuously, pass from 10 Marchesvan, in the 17th year of Nabu-nahid, to the 24th of the same month in the accession-year of Cyrus (Sayce, *Monuments*, pp. 522 f., 528 ; Strassmaier, *Bab. Texte*, i. 1887, p. 25, vii. 1890, p. 1).

identical with the Cyaxares II. of Xenophon, or a younger brother of Astyages—whom Cyrus may have made governor of [469] Babylon. In 6^1, however, where he organizes the empire in 120 satrapies, and in 6^{25}, he seems to be represented as absolute ruler of the Babylonian empire, without any such limitation to his jurisdiction. And in 6^1 the temptation to suspect a confusion with Darius *Hystaspis*—who actually organized the Persian empire into "satrapies," though much fewer than 120 *—is strong. Tradition, it can hardly be doubted, has here confused persons and events in reality distinct (Behrm. p. xix): "Darius the Mede" must be a reflection into the past of Darius Hystaspis, father—not *son*—of Xerxes, who had to reconquer Babylon in B.C. 521, and again in 515, and who established the system of satrapies, combined, not impossibly, with indistinct recollections of Gubaru (or Ugbaru), who first occupied Babylon on Cyrus' behalf, and who, in appointing governors there (see the inscription cited under *e*), appears to have acted as Cyrus' deputy.†

(g) In 9^2 it is stated that Daniel "understood by *the books* (בספרים) " the number of years for which, according to Jeremiah, Jerusalem should lie waste. The expression used implies that the prophecies of Jeremiah formed part of a *collection* of sacred books, which nevertheless, it may safely be affirmed, was not formed in 536 B.C.

(h) Other indications adduced to show that the Book is not the work of a contemporary, are such as the following :—The improbability that Daniel, a strict Jew, should have suffered himself to be initiated into the class of Chaldæan "wise men," or should have been admitted by the wise men themselves (c. 1; cf. 2^{13}); Nebuchadnezzar's 7 years' insanity ("lycanthropy"), with his edict respecting it ; the absolute terms in which both he and Darius ($4^{1-3.\ 34-37}$ 6^{25-27}), while retaining, so far as appears, their idolatry, recognise the supremacy of the God of Daniel, and command homage to be done to Him. On these and some other similar considerations our knowledge is hardly such as to give us an objective criterion for estimating their cogency. The circumstances alleged will appear improbable or not improbable, according as the critic, upon *independent* grounds, has satisfied himself that the Book is the work of a later author, or written by Daniel himself. It would be hazardous to use the statements in question in *proof* of the late date of the Book ; though, *if* its late date were established on other grounds, it would be not unnatural to regard some of them as involving an exaggeration of the actual fact.

Of the arguments that have here been briefly stated, while

---

* Herodotus (iii. 89) gives the number as 20 ; the Behistun Inscription (col. I, par. 6) enumerates 23 ; the later (sepulchral) Inscription of Naksh-i-Rushtan (l. 7–19), 29.

† Comp. Sayce, *Monuments*, pp. 524–537, who also shows that the representations in the Book of Daniel are inconsistent with the testimony of the inscriptions, and considers that the aim of the author was not to write history, in the proper sense of the word, but to construct, upon a historical basis, though regardless of the facts as they actually occurred, edifying religious narratives (or " Haggadah ").

h should be used with reserve, the rest all possess weight. They do not, however, except *b* (which, standing alone, it would be hazardous to press), show positively that the Book is a work of the 2nd cent. B.C. ; they only tend to show that it reflects the traditions, and historical impressions, of an age considerably later than that of Daniel himself.

(2.) The evidence of the *language* of Daniel must next be considered.

(*a*) The number of *Persian* words * in the Book (especially in [470] the Aramaic part) is remarkable. That such words should be found in books written after the Persian empire was organized, and when Persian influences prevailed, is not more than would be expected ; several occur in Ezr. Neh. Est. Chr., and many were permanently naturalised in Aramaic (both Syriac and the Aramaic of the Targums) ; but that they should be used as a matter of course by Daniel under the Babylonian supremacy, or in the description of Babylonian institutions *before* the conquest of Cyrus, is surprising.†

(*b*) Not only, however, does Daniel contain Persian words, it

---

* Probably at least 15 : *viz.* פרתמים (p. 506) ; פתבג *portion of food, dainty* ; אזרא *certainly* (Nöldeke, in Schrader, *KAT.*[2] p. 617) ; הדם *limb* ; דת *law* ; רז *secret* (Gesenius-Buhl, *s.v.*; Nöldeke, *Mand. Gramm.* p. xxxi) ; אחשדרפן *satrap* ; אדרגור *counsellor* (Nöldeke, *Tabari*, p. 462) ; דתבר *law bearer, judge* ; זן *kind* (Nöld. *Syr. Gr.* § 146) ; פתגם *message, order,* and even in the weakened sense of *word* ; הדבר *lawyer* ; סרך *president* ; נדן *holder, sheath*, 7[15] (Nöld. *GGA*. 1884, p. 1022,—unless, indeed, בְּגִין דְּנָה is to be read, with Marti and Buhl) ; אפרן (p. 507) ; cf. also המינכא, נבובה, סרבל, הפתיא, in the Glossary in Marti's *Gramm. der Bibl.-Aram. Sprache* (1896) ; גדבר 3[2, 3] is uncertain ; it *may* be a textual corruption, or a faulty pronunciation, of the Persian גזבר *treasurer* (as in Ezr.) ; it *may* have arisen by dittography from the following דתבר, as Lagarde, *Agathangelus*, p. 158, supposes ; LXX and Theod. express in 3[2, 3] only *seven* titles of officers. Some of these describe offices or institutions, and are not found elsewhere, or only in Ezr. Neh. Est. ; others (as פתגם, רז, הדם) are used exactly as in the later Aramaic, and are of a kind that would not be borrowed by one people from another unless intercourse between them had subsisted for a considerable time. The argument is confirmed by the testimony of the Inscriptions. The numerous contract-tablets which have come down to us from the age of Nebuchadnezzar and his successors, and which represent the everyday language of commercial life, show no traces of Persian influence : and if the language of Babylonia was uninfluenced by Persia, that of Israel would be far less likely to be so influenced (Sayce, *Monuments*, p. 493 f.).

† The same point is urged by Meinhold, *Beiträge*, pp. 30–32. The words cannot be Semitic, as the *Speaker's Comm.* (in some cases) seeks to show.

contains at least three *Greek* words : קיתרם *kītharos*, 3⁵· ⁷· ¹⁰· ¹⁵
= κίθαρις ; פסנתרין *psantērīn*, 3⁵· ⁷ (פסנטרין) ¹⁰· ¹⁵ = ψαλτήριον ; *
סומפניה *sūmpōnyāh*, 3⁵· ¹⁵ (AV. dulcimer) = συμφωνία.† Whatever may be the case with κίθαρις, it is incredible that ψαλτήριον
and συμφωνία can have reached Babylon *c.* 550 B.C. Any one
who has studied Greek history knows what the condition of the
Greek world was in that century, and is aware that the arts and
inventions of civilized life streamed then into Greece from the
East, not from Greece eastwards.‡ Still, if the instruments
named were of a primitive kind, such as the [471] κίθαρις (in
Homer), it is *just* possible that it might be an exception to the
rule, and that the Babylonians might have been indebted for
their knowledge of it to the Greeks ; so that, had קיתרם stood
alone, it could not, perhaps, have been pressed. But no such
exception can be made in the case of ψαλτήριον and συμφωνία,
both *derived* forms, the former used first by Aristotle, the latter
first by Plato, and in the sense of concerted music (or, possibly,
of a specific musical instrument) first by Polybius.§ These
words, it may be confidently affirmed, could not have been
used in the Book of Daniel unless it had been written *after the
dissemination of Greek influences in Asia through the conquests of
Alexander the Great.*∥

   (*c*) The *Aramaic* of Daniel (which is all but identical with that

  * -ιον = ין-, as in *Sanhedrin* = συνέδριον, אפופורין = ὑποπόδιον, &c.

  † Cf. in New Heb. סומפניה and סימפון (see Levy's *Neuhebr. Wörterb.*),
double flute. The form סיפוניה in 3¹⁰ is remarkably illustrated by ספון =
σύμφωνοι, in the sense *agreed*, in the great bilingual inscription from Palmyra
of A.D. 137 : *ZDMG.* 1883, p. 569 ; 1888, p. 412 (cf. the New Heb. סימפון,
i.e. σύμφωνον, *agreement*). Behrmann (p. ix f.), very needlessly, has recourse
to an imaginary σιφώνια.

  ‡ Comp. Sayce in the *Contemp. Review*, Dec. 1878, p. 60 ff.

  § And singularly enough, in his account of the festivities in which
Antiochus Epiphanes indulged (26. 10, 5 ; 31. 4, 8). The context does not
make it *certain* that an instrument is denoted ; though in the light of the
fact that the word undoubtedly appears with that sense afterwards (see
Du Cange, *s.v.* symphonia), and of the usage in Daniel, that is very
probable.

  ∥ The note on these words in the *Speaker's Comm.* (p. 281 ff.) throws
dust in the reader's eyes. None of them can be Semitic. Meier's attempted
derivation of סומפניה from סוף is not possible : even granting that a musical pipe
could be constructed out of the marine or fluvial growth which the Hebrews
called סוף (see Dillm. on Ex. 13¹⁸), סיפניה and סומפניה would both be forma-
tions philologically illegitimate, whether in Heb. or Aram.

of Ezra) is a *Western* Aramaic dialect, of the type spoken in and about *Palestine.** It is nearly allied to the Aramaic of the Targums of Onkelos and Jonathan; and still more so to the Aramaic dialects spoken E. and SE. of Palestine, in Palmyra and [472] Nabatæa, and known from inscriptions dating from the 3rd cent. B.C. to the 2nd cent. A.D. In some respects it is of an earlier type than the Aramaic of Onkelos and Jonathan; and this fact was formerly supposed to be a ground for the antiquity of the Book. But the argument is not conclusive. For (1) the differences are not considerable,† and largely orthographical: the Targums of Onkelos and Jonathan did not probably receive their present form before the 4th cent. A.D. : ‡ and we are not in a position to affirm that the transition from the Aramaic of Dan. and Ezra to that of the Targums must have required 8–9 centuries, and could not have been accomplished in 4–5 ; (2) recently discovered inscriptions have shown that many of the forms in which it differs from the Aramaic of the Targums

---

* Nöldeke, *Encycl. Brit.*[9] xxi. 647ᵇ–8ᵃ = *Die Semit. Sprachen* (1887), pp. 30, 32. The idea that the Jews forgot their Hebrew in Babylonia, and spoke in "Chaldee" when they returned to Palestine, is unfounded. Haggai and Zechariah and other post-exilic writers use Hebrew : Aramaic is exceptional. Hebrew was still normally spoken *c.* 430 B.C. in Jerusalem (Neh. 13²⁴). The Hebrews, after the Captivity, acquired gradually the use of Aramaic *from their neighbours* in and about Palestine. See Nöldeke, *ZDMG.* 1871, p. 129 f. ; Kautzsch, *Gramm. des Bibl. Aram.* § 6 ; Wright, *Compar. Gramm. of the Semitic Languages* (1890), p. 16 : "Now do not for a moment suppose that the Jews lost the use of Hebrew in the Babylonian captivity, and brought back with them into Palestine this so-called Chaldee. The Aramean dialect, which gradually got the upper hand since 5–4 cent. B.C., did not come that long journey across the Syrian desert ; it was *there*, on the spot ; and it ended by taking possession of the field, side by side with the kindred dialect of the Samaritans." The term "Chaldee" for the Aramaic of either the Bible or the Targums is a misnomer, the use of which is only a source of confusion.

† They are carefully collected (on the basis, largely, of M'Gill's investigations) by Dr. Pusey, *Daniel,* ed. 2, pp. 45 ff., 602 ff. (an interesting lexical point is that the vocabulary agrees sometimes with Syriac against the Targums). But when all are told, the differences are far outweighed by the *resemblances* ; so that relatively they cannot be termed important or considerable. (The amount of difference is much exaggerated in the *Speaker's Comm.* p. 228. The statement in the text agrees with the judgment of Nöldeke, *l.c.* p. 648ᵇ.)

‡ Deutsch in Smith's *DB.* iii. 1644, 1652 ; Volck in Herzog,² xv. 366, 370. Cf. Dalman, *Gramm. des Jüd.-Pal. Aramäisch,* pp. 9, 11 (5th cent. A.D.).

were actually in use in neighbouring countries *down to the 1st cent. A.D.**

Thus the final ה (for א) in verbs ל״א, and in חרה, מה, אנה, &c., occurs often in Nab. ; the Hofal, and (probably) the passive of Pe'al, in the Palm. Tariff (Sachau, *ZDMG.* 1883, p. 564 f. ; Wright, *Comp. Gr.* p. 224 f. ; cf. Dalman, p. 202 *note*) ; note also עבידת *was made* in the Madabah Inscr. ; the א in the impf. of verbs ל״א (not changed to י) repeatedly in Nab. and the Tariff ; מראנא (with א) Dan. 4[16. 21] Kt., Nab. 48 27[13] ; איתי (Tg. אית) Nab. 3[7] 4[7] &c. ; די (Tg. ר) and דנה (Tg. רין), both regularly in Palm. Nab. ; אנוש Dan. 4[13. 14] Kt., as Nab. 2[7] 9[8. 5] &c. ; נ retained in the impf. of verbs פ״נ, Nab. 2[2] ינפק, 2[6] ינתן, 3[5] &c. ; the 3 pl. pf. *fem.* in ן-, as Dan. 5[5] 7[20] Kt., Nab. 3[2] 8[1]. For the suff. of 3 ps. pl., Nab. has -הום (the more original form), Palm. -הון ; Dan. agrees here with Palm., Jer. 10[11] with Nab. ; Ezr. has both forms.

It is remarkable that, to judge from the uniform usage of the inscriptions from Nineveh, Babylon, Têma, Egypt, and even Cilicia,† at present known, in the Aramaic used officially (cf. p. 255 ; Isa. 36[11]) in the Assyrian and Persian empires, [473] the relative was זי,‡ not, as in Dan. Ezr., and Aram. generally, די (ר). See the *Corp. Inscr. Sem.* Pars II. Tom. i. *passim* (from c. 725 to the 5th cent. B.C.; Nos. 65, B.C. 504, 69–71, B.C. 418, 407, 408, being contract-tablets from Babylon) ; and the seal in Levy, *Phön. Studien*, ii. 24. זנה and זא (not רא, דנה) are found also in the same inscriptions.

The difference just noted certainly constitutes an argument against the opinion that the Aramaic of Daniel was that spoken at Babylon in Daniel's age. Its character in other respects (apart from the Persian and Greek words which it contains) cannot be said to lead to any definite result. Its resemblance with the Aramaic of Ezra (probably *c.* 400 B.C.) does not prove it to be contemporary ; but at present we possess no independent evidence showing actually how long afterwards such a dialect continued in use. The discovery of fresh inscriptions may enable us in the future to speak more positively.

(*d*) In order properly to estimate the *Hebrew* of Daniel, it must be borne in mind that the great turning-point in Hebrew

* See (chiefly) De Vogué, *La Syrie Centrale* (1868), with inscriptions from Palmyra, mostly from 1–3 cent. A.D. ; *ZDMG.* 1888, 370 ff., the bilingual Tariff of tolls from Palmyra, of A.D. 137 ; Euting, *Nabatäische Inschriften* (1885), with inscriptions (largely of the reign of חרתת ='Ἀρέτας, 2 Cor. 11[32]) from B.C. 9 to A.D. 75, and the *Z. f. Assyriol.* 1890, p. 290 (a Nabatæan inscription from Madabah in Moab, of the 46th year of Aretas, kindly pointed out to the writer by Prof. Nöldeke, now also to be found in the *CIS.* II. i. No. 196).

† See the interesting inscription on certain coins of the satrap Mazæus (362–328 B.C.) חלך=Κιλικία (מורי זי על עבר נהרא וחלך) : Halévy, *Mél. d'Epigr. Sém.* 1874, pp. 65, 67 ; Six, *Numismatic Chronicle*, 1884, pp. 97 f., 130.

‡ So also in the Zinjirli inscriptions (above, p. 255 *n.*) : see D. H. Müller, *l.c.* p. 56.

style falls in the age of *Nehemiah*.* The purest and best Hebrew prose style is that of JE and the earlier narratives incorporated in Jud. Sam. Kings : Dt. (though of a different type) is also thoroughly classical : Jer., the *latter* part of Kings, Ezekiel, II Isaiah, Haggai, show (though not all in the same respects or in the same degree) *slight* signs of being later than the writings first mentioned ; but in the "memoirs" of Ezra and Nehemiah (*i.e.* the parts of Ezra and Neh. which are the work of these reformers themselves, see p. 544), and (in a less degree) in the contemporary prophecy of Malachi, a more marked change is beginning to show itself, which is still more palpable in the Chronicles (*c.* 300 B.C.), Esther, and Ecclesiastes. The change is visible in both vocabulary and syntax. In vocabulary many new words appear, often of Aramaic origin, occasionally Persian, and frequently such as continued in use afterwards in the "New Hebrew" of the Mishnah (200 A.D.), &c. ; old words also are sometimes used with new meanings or applications. In syntax, the ease and grace and fluency of the earlier writers (down to at least Zech. 12–14) has passed away ; † the style is often laboured and inelegant : sentences constantly occur which a pre-exilic, or even an *early* post-exilic writer, would [474] have moulded differently : new and uncouth constructions make their appearance.‡ The three books named do not, however, exhibit these peculiarities in equal proportions : Ecclesiastes (p. 474) has the most striking *Mishnic* idioms : the Chronicler (p. 535 ff.) has many peculiarities of his own, and may be said to show the greatest uncouthness of style ; but they agree in the possession of many common (or similar) features, which differentiate them

---

* And not, as is sometimes supposed, the Captivity. This appears with especial clearness from Zech., the style of which, even in the parts which are certainly post-exilic, is singularly pure. The diction of Zech. 12–14, for instance, very much resembles that of Amos ; and has fewer expressions suggestive of lateness than even Joel or Ruth, or the prose parts of Job.

† This judgment is meant generally : *particular* sentences still occur, which are thoroughly classical in style.

‡ Another feature often observable in Hebrew of the same age is the *frequent* occurrence in it of a word or construction which occurs only *exceptionally* in the earlier Hebrew. The characteristics noted in the text do not, however, belong to the syntax of "New Hebrew," properly so called. This, though different (in many particulars) from that of the old classical Hebrew, has an ease and naturalness of its own, which is not shown by Hebrew of the intermediate stage (Chr. Eccl. Est. Dan.).

from all previous Hebrew writers (including Zech. Hagg. Mal.), and which recur in them with decidedly greater frequency and prominence than in the memoirs of Ezr. and Neh. And the Hebrew of Daniel is of the type just characterized : in all distinctive features it resembles, not the Hebrew of Ezekiel, or even of Haggai or Zechariah, but that of the age *subsequent to Nehemiah.*

The following list of words and idioms in Daniel, though it does not contain all that might be adduced, may be sufficient to substantiate this statement :—

1. מלכות 1[1. 20] 2[1] 8[1. 22. 23] 9[1] 10[13] 11[2. 4. 9. 17. 21], as regularly in Ezr. Chr. Est. (see p. 536, No. 9). The phrase in 1[1] 2[1] 8[1] . . . בשנת שלוש למלכות, as 1 Ch. 26[31], 2 Ch. 15[10. 19] 16[1] 35[19] : the earlier language, in similar sentences (Kings, *passim*), dispenses with מלכות.

2. מקצת 1[2. 5] = *some of*, where older Hebrew would use simply מן ; a common Rabbinical idiom. Elsewhere in the OT. only Neh. 7[70], in a verse to which nothing corresponds in Ezr. 2, and which there are independent reasons (Stade, *Gesch.* ii. 108) for supposing not to be part of the original document.

3. אמר ל' 1[3. 18] 2[2] = *to command to* . . ., where the older language would prefer the *direct* narration : 1 Ch. 13[4] 15[16] 21[18] [contrast 2 Sa. 24[11b-12a]] 22[2], 2 Ch. 14[3] 29[21b. 27. 30] 31[4. 11] 33[16], Neh. 8[1] 9[15], Est. 1[17] 4[13] 9[14].

4. פרתמים *nobles* (lit. *first ones*) 1[3], Est. 1[3] 6[9] †. Persian (Zend *fratema,* Sk. *prathema* = πρῶτος).

5. מדע *knowledge* 1[4. 17], 2 Ch. 1[10. 11. 12], Eccl. 10[20] †. Aramaic.

6. מנה *to appoint* 1[5. 10. 11], 1 Ch. 9[29]. The earlier language would use צוה or הפקיר. Elsewhere in Heb. only Ps. 61[8], Job 7[3], Jon. 2[1] 4[6. 7. 8] (p. 322). Common in Aramaic.

[475] 7. 1[5. 12. 14. 15] 9[24. 25. 26] 12[12], the numeral *after* the subst., as constantly in Chr. (sometimes even *altered* from Kgs.), Ezr. &c. Very rare in earlier Heb., except in enumerations, where different objects have to be contrasted, as Gen. 32[15f.].

8. אשר למה = *lest* 1[10] †. Not properly Hebrew at all : see p. 475 *n.*

9. חיב *to inculpate* 1[10]†. Aram. (חַיָּב, ܢܚܒ) and Talm.

10. גיל *age* 1[10]†. Also in Samaritan and Talmudic.

11. 1[21] 8[1] the *order* כורש המלך. So often in post-exilic writings. The older Heb. has nearly always the order המלך (דוד) : cf. *Notes on Samuel,* p. 236.

12. 8[8b] . . . וכעצמו, 8[18] . . . ובדברו : similarly 10[9b. 11b. 15. 19b] 11[2. 4] 12[7b]. A type of sentence common in Chr., very rare earlier (see *ib.* on 1 Sa. 17[55] ; and below, p. 538, No. 37).

13. החמיד 8[11. 12. 13] 11[31] 12[11]† of the continual Burnt-offering, as in the Mishnah, &c., constantly. In the older Heb. the full phrase עולת החמיד is always used, Nu. 28[10] &c., Neh. 10[34].

14. (עמדי) על עמדי lit. *on my (thy) standing* 8¹⁸ (cf. v.¹⁷) 10¹¹, Neh. 8⁷ 9³ 13¹¹, 2 Ch. 30¹⁶ 34³¹ 35¹⁰↑.

15. נבעת *to be afraid* (not the ordinary word) 8¹⁷, 1 Ch. 21³⁰, Est. 7⁶. בעת in the *Nif.* occurs only in these passages.

16. עמד *to stand up*, where the earlier language would use קום, 8²². ²³ 11²⁻⁴· ⁷· ²⁰ᶠ· ³¹ 12¹ᵃ (prob. also 12¹³), as Ezr. 2⁶³, Eccl. 4¹⁵ (contrast Ex. 1⁸), 1 Ch. 20⁴ (contrast Ps. 27³): with על *against* 8²⁵ 11¹⁴, as 1 Ch. 21¹, 2 Ch. 20²³ 26¹⁸ (contrast Dt. 22²⁶): in the sense of *to be established* 11¹⁷ᵇ (contrast Isa. 7⁷). Cf. Sir. 47¹· ¹².

17. אבל 10⁷· ²¹ with an *adversative* force, as Ezr. 10¹³, 2 Ch. 1⁴ 19³ 33¹⁷. Not so elsewhere.

18. עצר כח *to control power* = *to be able* 10⁸· ¹⁶ 11⁶, 1 Ch. 29¹⁴, 2 Ch. 2⁵ 13²⁰ 22⁹ ; and without כח 14¹⁰ 20³⁷↑. A somewhat peculiar phrase.

19. צפיר *he-goat* 8⁵· ⁸· ²¹, Ezr. 6¹⁷ (Aram.) 8³⁵, 2 Ch. 29²¹↑. Aramaic: in the Targums for the Heb. שעיר.

20. רשם *to inscribe* 10²¹. Only here in Biblical Hebrew. Aramaic.

21. העמיד 11¹¹· ¹³· ¹⁴, not lit. *to station*, as in the earlier books, but in the weakened sense *appoint, establish*: see p. 535, No. 4.

22. תקף *strength* 11¹⁷, Est. 9²⁹ 10². Not elsewhere in Biblical Hebrew. Aramaic. Comp. p. 475, Nos. 24 and 14.

23. בזה *prey* 11²⁴, Ezr. 9⁷, Neh. 3³⁶, Est. 9¹⁰· ¹⁵· ¹⁶, 2 Ch. 14¹³ 25¹³ 28¹⁴↑. The older language uses בז (Ezek. often).

24. אפדן *palace* 11⁴⁵↑. A Persian word. Also in Syr. and the Targ.

25. הזהיר *to shine* 12³. So only here. An Aramaic sense. Cf. Sir. 43⁹.

Comp. also הרשיע *intrans.* 9⁵ 11³² 12¹⁰, Neh. 9⁸³, Ps. 106⁶, 2 Ch. 20³⁵ 22³, Job 34¹² (Elihu)↑ ; נתן לב 10¹², 1 Ch. 12¹⁹, 2 Ch. 11¹⁶, Eccl. 1¹³· ¹⁷ 7²¹ 8⁹· ¹⁶ ; היך 10¹⁷, 1 Ch. 13¹²↑ ; [476] התחוק עם 10²¹, 1 Ch. 11¹⁰, 2 Ch. 16⁹ ; החזיק *intrans.* 11⁷· ³², 2 Ch. 26⁸↑ ; the *plural* פלאות 12⁶, Ps. 119¹²⁹↑ (cf. Sir. 43²⁵). חתך 9²⁴↑ *to decree* is a Talmudic term. See also p. 535, No. 4, p. 553n.

For instances of sentences constructed in the later, uncouth style, see 8¹²ᶠᶠ· ²⁴ᶠᶠ· 9²⁵ᶠᶠ· 10⁹ᵇ 12¹¹, and the greater part of c. 11. *Some* of the idioms quoted, standing by themselves, might not be decisive ; but the accumulation admits of but one interpretation. The only part of the Book in which late idioms are all but absent, is the prayer of 9⁴ᶠᶠ· ; but here the thought expresses itself almost throughout in phrases borrowed from the Pent. (esp. Dt.) and other earlier writings (cf. Neh. 1⁵⁻¹¹ 9⁶⁻³⁷). Evidently the style of the Book as a whole must be estimated from its more original and characteristic elements.*

In case the reader should desire a corroborative opinion, the judgment of Delitzsch may be quoted. The Hebrew of Daniel, writes Delitzsch (Herzog, p. 470), "attaches itself here and there to Ezekiel (cf. עת קץ 11³⁵· ⁴⁰ 12⁴ 8¹⁷,

* The supposition that Daniel may have unlearnt in exile the language of his youth does not satisfy the requirements of the case : it does not explain, viz., how the new idioms which he acquired should have so exactly agreed with those which appeared in Palestine independently 250 years afterwards. Daniel himself, also, it is probable, would not (unlike both Jer. and Ez.) have uniformly written the name Nebuchadnezzar incorrectly (p. 272).

with עַת עֵין קֵץ Ez. 21[30, 34] 35[5]; בֶּן אָדָם in the address to the seer, 8[17], as regularly in Ezekiel [above, p. 297],[*] and also to Habakkuk (cf. 11[27, 29, 35] with Hab. 2[3]); in general character it resembles the Hebrew of the Chronicler, who wrote shortly before the beginning of the Greek period [B.C. 333], and, as compared either with the ancient Hebrew or with the Hebrew of the Mishnah, is full of singularities (*Sonderbarkeiten*) and harshnesses of style."

The verdict of the language of Daniel is thus clear. The *Persian* words presuppose a period after the Persian empire had been well established: the Greek words *demand*, the Hebrew *supports*, and the Aramaic *permits*, a date *after the conquest of Palestine by Alexander the Great* (B.C. 332). With our present knowledge, this is as much as the language authorizes us definitely to affirm; though συμφωνία, as the name of an instrument (considering the history of the term in Greek), would seem to point to a date somewhat advanced in the Greek period.

[477] (3.) The *theology* of the Book (in so far as it has a distinctive character) points to a later age than that of the exile. It is true, this argument has sometimes been stated in an exaggerated form, as when, for instance, it is said that the doctrine of the resurrection, or the distinction of rank and office in the angels, is due to the influence of Parseeism, or that the asceticism of Daniel and his companions, and the frequency of their prayers, &c., are traits peculiar to the later Judaism. For exaggerations such as these there is no adequate foundation: nevertheless it is undeniable that the doctrines of the Messiah, of angels, of the resurrection, and of a judgment on the world, are taught with greater distinctness, and in a more developed form, than elsewhere in the OT., and with features approximating to (though not identical with) those met with in the earlier parts of the Book of Enoch, *c.* 100 B.C. Whether or not, in one or two instances, these developments may have been *partially* moulded by foreign influences, they undoubtedly mark a later phase of revelation than that which is set before us in other books of the OT.

---

* Delitzsch means that the writer borrows particular expressions from Ezek. He might have added one or two more: as הַצְּבִי 8[9] and אֶרֶץ הַצְּבִי 11[16, 41] (cf. v.[45]) of Canaan (comp. Jer. 3[19], Ez. 20[6, 15]); נְחֻשַׁת קָלָל *burnished brass* 10[6], Ez. 1[7]; לְבוּשׁ הַבַּדִּים *clothed in linen* 12[6f.], Ez. 9[3]. The statement in Smith's *Dict. of the Bible* (ed. 1) and the *Speaker's Comm.* (p. 227), that the language of Dan. bears "the closest affinity" to that of Ezek., appears to be due to a misunderstanding of Del.'s expression in Herzog (ed. 1). It is totally incorrect.

And the conclusion to which these *special* features in the Book point is confirmed by the *general* atmosphere which breathes in it, and the tone which prevails in it. This atmosphere and tone are not those of any other writings belonging to the period of the exile : they are rather those of a stage intermediate between that of the early post-exilic and that of the early post-Biblical Jewish literature.

A number of independent considerations, including some of great cogency, thus combine in favour of the conclusion that the Book of Daniel was not written earlier than *c.* 300 B.C. More than this can scarcely, in the present state of our knowledge, be affirmed *categorically*, except by those who deny the possibility of predictive prophecy. Nevertheless it must be frankly owned that grounds exist which, though not adequate to *demonstrate*, yet make the opinion a *probable* one, that the Book, as we have it, is a work of the age of Antiochus Epiphanes. The interest of the Book manifestly *culminates* in the relations subsisting between the Jews and Antiochus. Antiochus is the subject of 8[9-14. 23-25].* The survey of Syrian and Egyptian history in c. 11 leads up to a detailed description of his reign (v.[21-45]) : 12[1.] [478] [7. 11-12] reverts again to the persecution which the Jews experienced at his hands. This being so, it is certainly remarkable that the revelations respecting him should be given to Daniel, in *Babylon*, nearly four centuries previously : it is consonant with God's general methods of providence to raise up teachers, for the instruction or encouragement of His people, *at the time when the need arises.* It is remarkable also that Daniel—so unlike the prophets generally—should display no interest in the welfare, or prospects of his contemporaries ; that his hopes and Messianic visions should attach themselves, not (as is the case with Jer. Ez. Isa. 40–66) to the approaching return of the exiles to the land of their fathers, but to the deliverance of his people in a remote future. The minuteness of the predictions, embracing even special events in the distant future, is also out of harmony with the analogy of prophecy. Isaiah, Jeremiah, and other prophets unquestionably uttered predictions of the future ; but their predictions, when definite (except those of Messianic import, which stand upon a different footing), relate to events of

---

* And, it can hardly be doubted, of 7[8ff. 20ff.], as well. 9[24-27] is not here taken into account.

the proximate future only; when (as in the case of Jeremiah's prediction of 70 years' Babylonian supremacy) they concern a more distant future, they are general and indefinite in their terms. And while down to the period of Antiochus' persecution the *actual* events are described with surprising distinctness, after this point *the distinctness ceases* : the prophecy either breaks off altogether, or merges in an *ideal* representation of the Messianic future. Daniel's perspective, while thus true (approximately) to the period of Antiochus Epiphanes, is at fault as to the interval which was actually to follow before the advent of the Messianic age.

On the other hand, if the author be a prophet living in the time of the trouble itself, all the features of the Book may be consistently explained. He lives in the age in which he manifests an interest, and which needs the consolations which he has to address to it. He does not write *after* the persecutions are ended (in which case his prophecies would be pointless), but *at their beginning*,* when his message of encouragement would have a value for the godly Jews in the season of their trial. He thus utters genuine predictions; † and the advent of the [479] Messianic age follows closely on the end of Antiochus, just as in Isaiah or Micah it follows closely on the fall of the Assyrian : in both cases the future is foreshortened. The details of the Messianic picture are different from the representation of the earlier prophets, because they belong to a later stage of revelation : so the representations of Jeremiah, II Isaiah, or Zechariah differ similarly; in each case, the shape and colouring of the representation being correlated with the spiritual movements of the age to which it belongs.

It by no means follows, however, from this view of the Book, supposing it to be accepted, that the narrative is throughout a pure work of the imagination. That is not probable. Delitzsch, Meinhold, and others—most recently Behrmann—insist rightly that the Book rests upon *a traditional basis*. Daniel, it cannot be doubted, was a historical person,‡ one of the Jewish exiles

---

* So Ewald, p. 155 f.; Delitzsch, p. 479, &c.

† Comp. especially 8²⁵ *end* with the event.

‡ Whether, however, he is alluded to in Ez. 14¹⁴· ²⁰ 28³ is uncertain : the terms in which Ezek. speaks in c. 14 seem to suggest a patriarch of antiquity, rather than a younger contemporary of his own.

in Babylon, who, with his three companions, was noted for his staunch adherence to the principles of his religion, who attained a position of influence at the court of Babylon, who interpreted Nebuchadnezzar's dreams, and foretold, as a seer, something of the future fate of the Chaldæan and Persian empires. Perhaps written materials were at the disposal of the author: it is, at any rate, probable that for the descriptions contained in c. 2–7 he availed himself of some work, or works, dealing with the history of Babylon in the 6th cent. B.C.* These traditions are cast by the author into a literary form, with a special view to the circumstances of his own time. The motive underlying c. 1–6 is manifest. The aim of these chapters is not *merely* to describe who Daniel was, or to narrate certain incidents in his life: it is also to magnify the God of Daniel, to show how He, by His providence, frustrates the purposes of the proudest of earthly monarchs, while He defends His servants, who cleave to Him faithfully in the midst of [480] temptation. The narratives in c. 1–6 are thus adapted to supply motives for the encouragement, and models for the imitation, of those suffering under the persecution of Antiochus. In c. 7–12, definiteness and distinctness are given to Daniel's visions of the future; and it is shown, in particular, that the trial of the saints will reach ere long its appointed term.

It remains to notice briefly some features in which the Book of Daniel differs from the earlier prophetical books. Its view of history is much more *comprehensive* than that of the earlier prophets. Certainly there is a universal element observable in the writings of the earlier prophets (as when they contemplate the future extension of Israel's religion to the Gentiles); but it does not occupy the principal place: in the foreground are the *present* circumstances of the nation, social, religious, or political, as the case may be. Daniel's view is both wider and more definite. He takes a survey of a continuous *succession* of world-empires; points out how their sequence is determined before by

---

* Thus there are good reasons for supposing that Nebuchadnezzar's lycanthropy rests upon a basis of fact (Schrader, *KAT.*² p. 432 f.). Berosus, a learned Chaldæan priest, compiled his history of Babylonian dynasties *c.* 300 B.C.; and other sources of information, which have since perished, may naturally have been accessible to the author. But whatever elements of fact may be contained in the book, the inscriptions leave no doubt that they are mingled with much that is unhistorical.

God; declares that, when the appointed limit has arrived, they are destined to be overthrown by the kingdom of God; and emphasizes the precise moment when their overthrow is to take place. No doubt the motive of such a survey is in part suggested by the course of history, and the wider and more varied relations which it opened to the Jews. From the time of the exile, the Jews were brought into far closer contact with the great world-empires than had previously been the case; and as they witnessed one empire giving place to another, the problem of their own relation to the powers of the world pressed upon them with increasing directness and cogency. The older prophets had promised to the restored nation ideal glories; but the reality had proved very different: their promises had remained unfulfilled; and under Antiochus Epiphanes, the very existence of the theocracy was threatened, as it had never been threatened before, by a coalition of heathen foes without with false brethren within. Hence the question *when* the heathen domination would cease was anxiously asked by all faithful Jews. And the answer is given in the Book of Daniel. Not writing as a historian, but viewing comprehensively, in the manner just indicated, the past, the present, and the future, as parts of a predetermined whole, the author places himself at the only epoch from which this would be visible in continuous perspective: upon the basis [481] supplied him by tradition, he represents Daniel, whose age had coincided with the last great turning-point in the history of his people, when Israel became permanently dependent upon the great powers of the world, as surveying from the centre and stronghold of heathenism the future conflicts between the world and the theocracy, and declaring the gradual degeneration of the former ($2^{32ff.}$), and the final triumph of the latter. The prophets do not merely foretell history; they also *interpret* it (*e.g.* Gen. 9^{25-27}; Isa. 10^{5-7}). And the Book of Daniel does this on a more comprehensive scale than any other prophetical book. It outlines a religious philosophy of history. It deals, not with a single empire, but with a succession of empires, showing how all form parts of a whole, ordained for prescribed terms by God, and issuing in results designed by Him. The type of representation is artificial; but it is adapted to the purpose required, and is borrowed from the forms employed by the older prophets. As is common in the case of dreams or visions, it is largely symbolical, the symbolism being not of the simple kind found usually in the earlier prophets (*e.g.* Am. 7–8), but more elaborate and detailed, and being, moreover, sometimes interpreted to the seer, or even altogether set forth to him (c. 10–12), by an angel (comp. Ez. 40$^{3\text{ff.}}$; Zech. 1^8–6^8). That the past (to a certain point) is represented as future, is a consequence of the literary form adopted by the author for the purpose of securing the unity of his picture (comp. Delitzsch, p. 469). "In warmth of religious feeling, and in the unflinching maintenance of Divine truth, the Book resembles closely enough the writings of the older prophets: but also—what is here most important of all—the course of events in the immediate future, the fall of the tyrant after 3½ years, and the triumph of the saints of God, is defined beforehand by the author as certainly as by any prophet of the olden time. Upon this account chiefly he has obtained recognition in the Jewish Church, if not as a prophet, at least as a man inspired of God.* It is, moreover, exactly in virtue of this true perception of the present and of the immediate future, that his book is distinguished, very much to its advantage, from the later Jewish Apocalypses" (Dillmann).

[482] On the characteristics of "apocalyptic" literature, see further Lücke, *Versuch einer vollst. Einl. in die Offenb. des Johannes*, 1852, pp. 34–55; A. Hilgenfeld, *Die Jüd. Apokalyptik*, 1857, pp. 1–16, 34–50; A. Dillmann in Schenkel's *Bibel-Lexicon*, iii. (1872), art. "Propheten," p. 626 f.; E. Schürer [p. 496 *n.*], ii. p. 609 ff. [Eng. tr. II. iii. p. 44 ff.]; R. Smend's essay, "Über jüdische Apokalyptik," *ZATW.* 1885, p. 222 ff.; H. Schultz, *OT. Theol.* i. 421 f. The Book of Daniel determined the form assumed by subsequent writings of the same kind; and these ought properly to be compared with it. Some account of such of them as are extant will be found in J. Drummond, *The Jewish Messiah*, 1877, pp. 1–132; in Schürer, *l.c.* p. 616 ff.; or, more briefly, in the *Encycl. Brit.* art. "Apocalyptic Literature." The standard edition of the Book of Enoch is that of Dillmann (text, 1851; transl. and notes, 1853: see also "Über den neugefundenen griech. Text des Henoch-Buches," in the *Sitzungsberichte* of the Berlin Academy, 1892, pp. 1039 ff., 1079 ff.); but R. H. Charles' translation (Oxford, 1893), with notes (less full than Dillm.'s), is based on new and better MSS. (Abp. Laurence was the first to publish the Ethiopic text; but his edition and translation are both antiquated.)

In estimating the critical view of Daniel, it is to be remembered that we have no right to argue, upon *à priori* grounds, if a passage or book proves

---

* The author, it may be noticed, does not claim to speak with the *special* authority of the "prophet"; he never uses the prophetical asseverations, "Thus saith Jehovah," "Saith Jehovah."

not to contain the predictive element so largely as we had been accustomed to suppose, that, therefore, it can have no place in the economy of revelation. Prediction is one method, but by no means the only method, which it pleased God to employ for the instruction and education of His people. Hence, whether, or to what extent, a particular part of Scripture is predictive, cannot be determined by the help of antecedent considerations : it can be determined only by the evidence which it affords itself respecting the period at which it was written. In interpreting the prophets, it is, moreover, always necessary to distinguish between the *substance* of a prophecy and the *form* under which it is presented ; for the prophets constantly clothe the essential truth which they desire to express in imagery that is figurative or symbolical (*e.g.* Isa. 11[15f.] 19[16ff.] 23[17f.] 66[23]). And the elements in the Book of Daniel which, upon the critical view of it, are predictive in appearance but not in reality, are just part of the *symbolic imagery* adopted by the writer for the purpose of developing one of the main objects which he had in view, viz. the theocratic significance of the history.

Why the Book of Daniel is written partly in Aram., partly in Heb., is not apparent, upon any theory of its authorship. The transition to Aramaic in 2[4b] might indeed be accounted for by the fact that it was, or was assumed to be, the language used at the Court of Babylon ; but this does not explain why the Aramaic part should include c. 7. Meinhold (reviving the view of some older scholars) holds that 2[4b]-c. 6 is earlier in date than has been generally supposed by critics, having been written, he considers, in Aramaic *c.* 300 B.C., and incorporated by the later author of the rest of the book in his work ; and he points to certain differences of scope and representation in support of this opinion. Not only, however, would 2[4b]-c. 6 be unintelligible without the introductory particulars contained in 1[1]-2[4a], but c. 7, though added by the author who (*ex hyp.*) otherwise uses Hebrew, is in *Aramaic* ; it is, moreover, so connected, on the one hand with c. 2, on the other with c. 8-12, that it seems to forbid the distribution of the Aramaic and Hebrew parts of the book between different writers. (Comp. further [483] Budde, *Theol. Literaturzeitung*, 1888, No. 26 ; Kuenen, §§ 87. 5, 6 ; 90. 11, 12 ; Behrm. pp. i, ii ; and esp. von Gall [above, p. 488].)

No conclusion of any value as to the date of Daniel can be drawn from the LXX translation. (1) The date of the translation is quite uncertain ; the grounds that have been adduced for the purpose of showing that it was made in the time of Antiochus Epiphanes himself being altogether insufficient. (2) The "Septuagint" translation of different books (or, in some cases, of groups of books) is of course the work of different hands ; but in all parts of the OT. the translators stand remarkably aloof from the Palestinian tradition— often, for instance, not only missing the general sense of a passage, but showing themselves to be unacquainted with the meaning even of common Hebrew words. Thus the errors in the LXX translation of Daniel merely show that the meaning of particular words was unknown in *Alexandria* at the time, whatever it may have been, when the translation was made ; they do not, as has sometimes been supposed, afford evidence that the meaning was unknown in *Palestine* in the 2nd cent. B.C. The Greek translator of the Proverbs of Jesus, son of Sirach, though a grandson of the author himself, nevertheless often misunderstood the Hebrew in which they were written.

It was argued formerly by Prof. Margoliouth (*Expositor*, April 1890, p. 300 f.), partly on the strength of the quotations of Ben Sira preserved in Rabbinical writers, partly upon the ground of his own hypothetical restorations, from the Versions, of the original text of Ecclesiasticus, that the language spoken in Jerusalem *c.* 200 B.C. was the fully developed Rabbinical idiom ; and hence it was inferred by him that the Hebrew of the Book of Daniel must date from a period considerably earlier than that to which modern critics assigned it. The discovery (above, p. 474) of ten chapters of the original Hebrew of Ecclus. has shown, however, that Prof. Margoliouth's theories, both of the "metre" and of the language of Ben Sira's proverbs, were mistaken, and has more than justified those who at the time expressed their distrust of the principles upon which his restorations were based. It is not any longer possible to maintain that the Hebrew of the Book of Daniel is incompatible with a date in the 2nd century B.C.

That the Book of Daniel, as we have it, whatever basis of tradition it may rest upon, is a work of the age of Antiochus Epiphanes, is a conclusion accepted by even the most moderate critics, *e.g.* not only by Delitzsch and Riehm (*Einl.* ii. 292 ff.), but also by Lücke, p. 41 ; Strack, *Einleitung in das AT.,*[4] 1895, § 63 ; K. Schlottmann, *Compendium der ATlichen Theologie,* 1889, § 87 ; Schürer, *l.c.* p. 613 ff. [Eng. tr. *ib.* p. 49 ff.] ; C. A. Briggs, *Mess. Proph.* p. 411 f.; &c.

It may interest the philological student to know that the pron. אֱלֵךְ (Dan. Ezr.) occurs in the *Corp. Inscr. Sem.* II. i. No. 145 B ; הִמּוֹ (Ezr.) *ib.* Nos. 137 B (as a *suffix*), 145 B, 149 A ; הלו *ib.* Nos. 137 A, B, appears to be a variant of אֵלּוֹ (Dan.). The inscriptions quoted are all from Egypt.

CHAPTER XII.

CHRONICLES, EZRA, AND NEHEMIAH.

§ 1. CHRONICLES.

LITERATURE.—Ewald, *Hist.* i. p. 169 ff. ; E. Bertheau in the *Kgf. Hdb.*
1854, ² 1873 ; K. H. Graf in *Die Gesch. Bücher des AT.s*, 1866, pp.
114–247 (" Das B. der Chr. als Geschichtsquelle ") ; C. F. Keil (see p. 478) ;
Wellhausen, *Hist. of Israel*, pp. 171–227 ; C. J. Ball in Bp. Ellicott's *Comm.
for English Readers* (1883) ; Kuenen, *Onderzoek*,² i. (1887), p. 433 ff.; S.
Oettli in Strack and Zöckler's *Kgf. Komm.* 1889 ; R. Kittel in Haupt's
SBOT.

The Books of Chronicles—in the Hebrew canon one book—
with their sequel, the Books of Ezra and Nehemiah—in the
Hebrew canon similarly one book, " Ezra " *—form the second
great group of historical writings preserved in the Old Testament
(above, p. 4). It is plain, from many indications, that these
books form really a single, continuous work. Not only is their
style—which is very marked, and in many respects unlike that
of any other Book of the OT.—closely similar, but they also
resemble each other in the point of view from which the history
is treated, in the method followed in the choice of materials, as
well as in the preference shown for particular topics (genealogies, statistical registers, descriptions of religious ceremonies,
details respecting the sacerdotal classes, and the organization of
public worship). Moreover, the Book of Ezra-Neh. begins
exactly at the point at which the Book of Chronicles ends, and
carries on the narrative upon the same plan to the time when
the theocratic institutions under which the compiler lived were
finally established through the labours of Ezra and Nehemiah.

* The division into two books, in modern editions of the Hebrew Bible,
arises from the same cause as the division of 1–2 Sam. and 1–2 Kings, viz.
the influence of the LXX operating through the Christian Bible.

In ordinary Hebrew texts (cf. p. 359, *note*), Ezr.-Neh., contrary to [485] the chronology, *precedes* the Chronicles : in the LXX, and versions influenced by it, the books are arranged in accordance with chronological propriety. It will be convenient to follow the same order here.

The entire work, of which the Chronicles form thus the first part, comprises, though, of course, not with the same amount of detail throughout, the period from Adam to the second visit of Nehemiah to Jerusalem, B.C. 432. Although, however, the narrative embraces a wide period, the aim with which it is written is a limited one ; it is that, viz., of giving a history of *Judah*, with special reference to the institutions connected with the *Temple*, under the monarchy, and after the restoration. The author (who seems to be the same throughout) begins, indeed, after the manner of the later Semitic historians, with Adam; but the genealogies in I 1 have merely the object of exhibiting, relatively to other nations, the position taken by the tribe of Judah, to which I 2 is wholly devoted, as I 3 is devoted to the descendants of King David. In I 4–8, dealing with the other tribes, it is the priestly tribe of Levi (I 6) that is treated at greatest length. Incidentally in these chapters, more decidedly in 9^{1-34}, the interest of the writer betrays itself : his notices have constantly a bearing, direct or indirect, upon the organization and ecclesiastical institutions of the *post*-exilic community. The introduction (I 1^1-9^{34}) ended, the history proper begins. The reign of Saul is past over rapidly by the compiler : I 9^{35-44} his genealogy is repeated from 8^{29-38}; I 10 (excerpted from 1 Sa. 31) contains the narrative of his death. Thereupon the narrator proceeds to David's election as king over all Israel at Hebron (= 2 Sa. 5^{1-10}), omitting as irrelevant to his purpose the incidents of David's youth, his persecution by Saul, the reign of Ishbosheth, &c. He omits similarly events in David's reign of a personal or private nature (*e.g.* the greater part of 2 Sa. 9–20). The account of Solomon's reign is excerpted from 1 Kings with tolerable fulness. After the division of the kingdom no notice is taken of the history of the N. kingdom, except where absolutely necessary (as II 22^{7-9}); on the other hand, the history of Judah is presented in a series of excerpts from 1–2 Kings, supplemented by additions contributed by the compiler. Though secular events are not excluded from the record, the writer, it is plain, dwells with the greatest satisfaction upon the *ecclesiastical* [486] aspects of the history. The same interest is not less apparent in Ezr.-Neh.; and hence the entire work (Chr. Ezr.-Neh.) has been not inaptly termed by Reuss the "Ecclesiastical Chronicle of Jerusalem."

The Hebrew name of the Chronicles is דברי הימים, lit. *words* (or *affairs*) *of the days*, a term which, as explained above (p. 197), is used to denote an official *diary*, containing minutes of events, lists of officers, &c. Its application in the present case is due probably to the fact that a large proportion of the contents, especially towards the beginning (I 1-27), are of a *statistical* character. In the LXX the two books are called παραλειπόμενα, a name no doubt suggested by the observation that they contain numerous particulars not found in the Books of Samuel and Kings (cf. Bacher, *ZATW.* 1895, p. 305 ff.). The title *Chronicles* is derived from Jerome, who used *chronicon* to express the Hebrew דברי הימים.

Date of Composition.—The only positive clue which the book contains as to the date at which it was composed is the genealogy in I 3[17-24], which (if v.[21] be rightly interpreted) is carried down to the *sixth* generation after Zerubbabel. This would imply a date not earlier than *c.* 350 B.C. 3[21] is, however, obscurely expressed; and it is doubtful if the text is correct.* More conclusive evidence is afforded by the Books of Ezra and Neh., which certainly belong to the same age, and are commonly assumed to be the work of the same compiler. As will appear below, these books contain many indications of being the compilation of an author living long subsequently to the age of Ezra and Nehemiah themselves,—in fact, not before the close of the Persian rule. A date shortly after B.C. 333 is thus the earliest to which the composition of the Chronicles can be plausibly assigned; and it is that which is adopted by most modern critics.† From the character of his narrative it is a probable in-

---

* LXX, Pesh. Vulg. read בנו, four times for בני, and at the end of the verse before ובני v.[22] ("And the sons of Hananiah: Pelatiah, and Jesaiah his son, Rephaiah his son, Arnan his son, Obadiah his son, Shecaniah his son" —of the same type as v.[10-14]), yielding at once a sense consistent with the context, but bringing down the genealogy to the *eleventh* generation after Zerubbabel. It is quite possible that this is the true reading: the later date which it would—not merely permit, but—necessitate for the Chronicles being no objection to it. Keil, wishing to uphold Ezra's authorship, disputes the integrity of the text in the opposite direction; but the opinion that the Chronicles are Ezra's composition is certainly incorrect.

† Ewald, i. 173; Bertheau, p. xlvi; Schrader, § 238; Dillmann in Herzog,²

ference [487] that the author was a *Levite*, perhaps even a member of the Temple choir.

The *basis* of the Chronicles consists of a series of excerpts from the earlier historical books, Gen.–2 Kings, with which are combined materials derived by the compiler from other sources. These excerpts are not made throughout upon the same scale. In the preliminary chapters (I 1–9) they are often condensed, and consist chiefly of genealogical notices: in I 10–II 36 (which is parallel to 1 Sa. 31–2 Ki. 25) passages are generally transferred *in extenso* with but slight variations of expression, due, probably, in a few cases (as they exist in our present text) to textual corruption, but more commonly originating with the compiler. Not unfrequently, however, the excerpted narratives are *expanded*, sometimes remarkably, by the insertion either of single verses or clauses, or of longer passages, as the case may be. Minute particulars can naturally only be learnt from a word-for-word collation of the text of Chr. with the original passages of Sam. Kings, which the reader is strongly recommended to make for himself; but the following synopsis has been arranged so as to exhibit both the passages excerpted from the earlier narratives, and the more important additions introduced by the compiler. The omissions in the third column will indicate the parts of Gen.–2 Kings which he has passed over:—

I. *Preliminary history* (I 1¹–9³⁴).
C. 1–2. *The pedigree of Judah:*—

The patriarchal period, ...	c. 1.	{ See Gen. 5, 10, 11, 25, 36.
The 12 sons of Israel, ...	2¹⁻².	Gen. 35²³⁻⁶.
The 5 sons of Judah (Perez, Zerah, &c.),	2³⁻⁴.	{ 38³⁻⁷·²⁹ᶠ·, Nu. 26¹⁹ᶠ·.
The sons of Perez, viz. Hezron and Hamul, ... }	2⁵.	{ Gen. 46¹², Nu. 26²¹.
The sons of Zerah, ...	2⁶⁻⁸.	Josh. 7¹; 1 Ki. 4³¹.
The descendants of Hezron—(*a*) through Ram, leading down to *David*, v.¹⁰⁻¹⁷; (*b*) through Chelubai (=Caleb), v.¹⁸⁻²⁴; (*c*) through Jerahmeel, v.²⁵⁻⁴¹, . . }	2⁹⁻⁴¹.	{ With v.⁵·⁹⁻¹² comp. Ru. 4¹⁹⁻²¹; with v.¹³⁻¹⁷, 1 S. 16⁶⁻⁹, 2 S. 2¹⁸ 17²⁵.

---

s.v. p. 221; Ball, p. 210; Oettli, p. 101 Kuenen is disposed to adopt a some-what later date, § 29. 7, 8, 10 (*c*. 250): Nöldeke, *AT. Lit.* p. 64, one later still, *c*. 200. The language, not less than the general style and tone, favours a date subsequent to B.C. 300 rather than one prior to it.

[488] An appendix, largely geographical, relating to localities inhabited by descendants of Caleb, (a) directly, v. $^{42-49}$; (b) through his son Hur, v. $^{50-55}$, . } I 2^{42-55}. *

C. 3. *The family and descendants of David* :—

David's children, ...	3^{1-9}.	2 S. 3^{2-5} 5^{14-16}.
David's descendants—		
(a) The kings of Judah, . . .	3^{10-16}.	1-2 Kings.
(b) The descendants of Jeconiah (Jehoiachin), extending to some generations after the return, . . . }	3^{17-24}.	

C. 4–7. *Notices respecting the genealogies, history, and military strength of the several tribes* :—

Judah (including particulars respecting *localities*, esp. those prominent after the exile), ... } 4^{1-23}.

Simeon, ... {
4^{24}. { Gen. 46^{10}, Ex. 6^{15}, Nu. $26^{12f.}$.
4^{25-27}. ......
4^{28-33}. Josh. 19^{2-8}.
4^{34-43}. ......
}

Reuben, Gad, and the E. half of Manasseh, ... } 5^{1-26}. { V. ^{3}: Gen. 46^9, Nu. $26^{5f.}$.

Levi—

High priests from Zadok to Jehozadak (B.C. 586), with their pedigree from Aaron,† . . . . . . } 6^{1-15}. { V. $^{1-3}$: Gen. 46^{11}, Ex. $6^{16.\ 18.\ 20}$, Nu. 3^2 &c.

Genealogies : viz. (a) two parallel, but in part divergent, pedigrees, connecting David's three chief singers, Heman, Asaph, and Ethan, with the three Levitical families of Gershon, Kohath, and Merari, v. $^{16-30}$ and $^{31-48}$; (b) the line of chief priests to the time of Solomon, v. $^{49-53}$ (= v. $^{4-8}$), ... } 6^{16-53}. { V. $^{16-19.\ 22}$: Ex. 6 $^{16-24}$ V. $^{26-28.\ 33-35}$: 1 S. 1^1 8^2.

---

* The names in these chapters are frequently those, not of individuals, but of families and localities. Wellhausen in his Dissertation *De Gentibus et familiis Judæis quæ* 1 *Chr* 2. 4. *enumerantur* (1870)—cf. more briefly, *Hist.* p. 216 ff.—has shown that in c. 2 v. ^{9} (the words "and Ram") $^{10-24.\ 34-41.\ 50-55}$ do not form part of the original scheme of the chapter, but are subsequent insertions ; and that while v. $^{42-49}$ describes the pre-exilic abodes of the Calebites (about Hebron and the S. of Judah), v. $^{50-55}$ enumerates the more northerly districts (about Beth-lehem) occupied by them after the Captivity (cf. Meyer, *Die Entstehung des Judenthums*, pp. 116 f., 164).

† Several of the persons here named are not mentioned in the historical

books. On the other hand, the old and famous line which held the priesthood under Samuel and David—Eli, Phinehas, Ahitub, Ahimelech, Abiathar
—is not noticed.

* Expanded.   † With alterations.

Exploits of David's heroes, . . .	I 20$^{4-8}$.	2 S. 21$^{18-22}$.
David's census of the people : the pestilence : his purchase of the threshing-floor of Araunah, . . .	21^{1-4a}. 21^{4b}; 5. 21$^{6-7}$. 21$^{8-27}$. 21^{28}–22^1.	24^{1-4a}. 24^{4b-8}; * 9. .... 24^{10b-25}. ....

[490] 22^2–c. 29. *David's arrangements for the construction of the Temple and the maintenance of public service, and for his army :—*

Instructions to Solomon, . .	22$^{2-19}$.	......
Numbers (38,000), families, and duties of the Levites, ...	c. 23.	......
The 24 courses of priests, . .	24$^{1-19}$.	......
Heads of the families of Kohathites and Merarites enumerated in 23$^{16-23}$, . .	24$^{20-31}$.	......
The 24 courses of singers (4 referred to the sons of Asaph, 6 to the sons of Jeduthun, 10 to the sons of Heman), .	c. 25.	......
The courses of the gate-keepers, . .	26$^{1-19}$.	......
Overseers of Temple-treasuries, . .	26$^{20-28}$.	......
Levitical officers engaged outside the Temple, ...	26$^{29-32}$.	......
The 12 divisions of the army, . . .	27$^{1-15}$.	......
Princes of the tribes (Gad and Reuben not named), ...	27$^{16-24}$.	......
The 12 superintendents of David's personal possessions, and his ministers, .	27$^{25-34}$.	......
David's last instructions to his people and to Solomon, . . .	c. 28.	......
Offerings made in response to his invitation, ...	29$^{1-9}$.	......
David's prayer of thanksgiving : Solomon confirmed as king : death of David, .	29$^{10-22}$. 29$^{23a.\ 27}$. I K. 2$^{12a.\ 11}$. 29^{23b-26} 29$^{28-30}$. }	...... } ......
Solomon's offering at Gibeon : his dream,	II 1$^{1-2}$. 1^{3a}. 1^{3b-6a}. 1^{6b-13}.	...... 3^{4a}. ...... 3^{4b-13}.† 15b 4^1.
Solomon's horses and chariots, . .	1$^{14-17}$.	10$^{26-29}$.
Preparations for building the Temple, and correspondence with Hiram, .	2$^{1-2}$. ‡ 18. 2$^{3-16}$. { 2^{17}.	5$^{5a.\ 15f}$. 5$^{2-9}$; § cf. 5^{11} 7^{14}. ......

---

* Abridged.   † With omissions and alterations.
‡ In 2^{1b} (cf. 7^{11}) a brief allusion only to the Palace, 1 K. 7$^{1-12}$.
§ With considerable alterations and additions, esp. in v. 4-7. 13f.

	II	I K.
The Temple, with the two pillars in front of it, ...	3^{1-13}. 3^{14}. 3^{15-17}.	$6^{1-3.\ 5-35}$. * ...... 7^{15-21}.
The sacred vessels, and the court. The Temple completed, . . .	4^{1}. 4^{2-5}. $4^{6}-5^{1}$.	...... 7^{23-26}. 7^{38-51}.
[491] The Ark taken into the Temple, .	5^{2-11a}. $5^{11b-13a}$. 5^{13b-14}.	I K. 8^{1-10a}. ...... 8^{10b-11}.
The prayer of dedication, . . .	6^{1-39}. 6^{40-42}.	8^{12-50a}. ......
Conclusion of the ceremony, . . .	7^{1-3}. $7^{4-5.\ 7-10}$. 7^{6}.	...... 8^{62-66}. ......
Jehovah's answer to Solomon, . .	$7^{11-12b\alpha}$. $7^{12b\beta-16}$ (to chosen). 7^{16-22}.	9^{1-3a}. ...... 9^{3c-9}.
Particulars respecting the organization of Solomon's empire, ...	8^{1-2}. $8^{3.\ 4b.\ 11b}$. $8^{4a.\ 5-11a}$. 8^{12-16}. 8^{17-18}.	cf. 9^{10-11}. ...... $9^{17b-24a}$. 9^{25}.† 9^{26-28}.
Visit of the Queen of Sheba. Solomon's magnificence and wealth, . . .	9^{1-24}. 9^{25-26}. 9^{27-28}. 9^{29}. 9^{30-31}.	10^{1-25}. $10^{26b}\ 4^{26.\ 21a}$. 10^{27-28}. ...... 11^{42-43}.
Revolt of the Ten Tribes, . . .	c. 10.	12^{1-19}.
Hostilities stopped by Shemaiah, . .	11^{1-4}.	12^{22-24}.
Rehoboam's reign, ...	$11^{5}-12^{1}$. 12^{2a}. $12^{2b-9a\alpha}$. $12^{9a\beta-11.\ 13}$. $12^{12.\ 14-15a}$. $12^{15b.\ 16}$.	...... 14^{25}. ...... $14^{26-28.\ 21}$. ...... $14^{30.\ 31a.c}$.
Abijah, ...	13^{1-2}. 13^{3-22}.	$15^{1-2.\ 7b}$. ......
Asa, ...	$14^{1a.\ 2}$. 14^{3-5}. $14^{6}-15^{15}$. $15^{16}-16^{6}$. 16^{7-11}. 16^{12-14}.	$15^{8.\ 11}$. 15^{12}.‡ ...... 15^{13-22}. ...... $15^{23b-24a}$.†

---

* Abridged.   † Expanded.   ‡ With alterations.

[492] Jehoshaphat, ...	II 17^{1a}.	1 K. 15^{24b}.
	17^{1b-19}.	......
	c. 18.	22^{1-35a}.
	19^1-20^{30}.	......
	20^{31-33a}.	22^{41-43a}.
	20^{33b-34}.	
	$37a.b\alpha.$ }	......
	20^{35-36}.	
	$37b\beta.$ }	22^{48-49}.
Jehoram, ...	21^1.	22^{50}.
	21^{2-4}.	......
	21^{5-10a}.	2 K. 8^{17-22}.
	21^{10b-19}.	......
	21^{20}.	$8^{17.\ 24a.}$ *
Ahaziah, ...	22^{1-6}.	8^{24b-29}. *
	22^{7-9}.	c. 9–10. †
Athaliah, ...	$22^{10}-23^{21}$.	11^{1-20}. *
Joash, ...	24^{1-14a}.	$11^{21}-12^{14}$. *
	24^{14b-22}.	......
	24^{23-26}.	$12^{17f.\ 20f.}$*
Amaziah, ...	25^{1-4}.	14^{2-6}.
	25^{5-11a}.	......
	25^{11b}.	14^{7a}.
	25^{12-16}.	......
	$25^{17-20a\alpha.}$	
	25^{21-24}. }	14^{8-14}.
	$25^{25.\ 27a\beta-28}$.	$14^{17.\ 19f.}$
Uzziah, ...	26^{1-4}.	$14^{21f.}\ 15^{2f.}$.
	$26^{5-20b\alpha.}$	......
	$26^{20b\beta-21.\ 23}$.	$15^{5.\ 7.}$
Jotham, ...	$27^{1-2a\alpha.\ 3a.}$	$15^{33-34.\ 35b.}$
	$27^{2a\beta b.\ 3b-7}$.	......
	27^8.	15^{38}.
Ahaz, ...	28^{1-4}.	16^{2-4}.
	28^{5-15}.	16^5. ‡
	$28^{16.\ 17.\ 20-25.}$	cf. 16^{6b-17}. *
	28^{18-19}.	......
	28^{27}.	16^{20}.
[493] Hezekiah.	29^{1-2}.	18^{1b-3}.
	29^3-31^{21}.	18^{4-7a}. ‡
	32^1.	cf. 18^{13}.
	32^{2-8}.	......
	32^{9-21}.	$18^{17}-19^{37}$. †
	32^{22-23}.	......
	32^{24-33}.	c. 20. * †

* With alterations.   † Abridged.   ‡ Expanded.

Manasseh,	.	.	.	.	$\left\{ \begin{array}{l} \text{II } 33^{1\text{-}10.\ 20}.\quad 2\text{ K. } 21^{1\text{-}10.\ 18}. \\ 33^{11\text{-}19}.\qquad\qquad \ldots\ldots \end{array} \right.$

Amon,	.	.	.	.	.	$33^{21\text{-}25}.$	$21^{19\text{-}24}.$

Josiah, ... $\left\{ \begin{array}{ll} 34^{1\text{-}2}. & 22^{1\text{-}2}. \\ 34^{3\text{-}7}. & [23^{4\text{-}20}.\,*]\dagger \\ 34^{8\text{-}12a.}\!+\ & 22^{3\text{-}6.\ 7b}. \\ 34^{12a\text{-}14}. & \\ 34^{15\text{-}31}. & 22^{8}\text{-}23^{3a}. \\ 34^{32\text{-}33}. & \ldots\ldots \\ 35^{1\text{-}19}. & 23^{21\text{-}23}.\,\S \\ 35^{20\text{-}25}. & 23^{29\text{-}30a}.\,\S \end{array} \right.$

Jehoahaz,	.	.	.	.	.	$36^{1\text{-}4}.$	$23^{30b.\ 31.\ 33f.}.\,*$
Jehoiakim,	.	.	.	.	.	$36^{5\text{-}8}.$	$23^{36}\text{-}24^{6}.\,*$
Jehoiachin,	.	.	.	.	.	$36^{9\text{-}10}.$	$24^{8\text{-}17}.\,*$
Zedekiah,	.	.	.	.	.	$36^{11\text{-}21}.$	$24^{18}\text{-}25^{21}.\,*$
Decree of Cyrus,	.	.	.	.	$36^{22\text{-}23}.$	Ezra $1^{1\text{-}3a}.$

Character of the additions. The additions contributed by the compiler consist partly of altogether fresh matter,—whether statistical information, or incidents recounted at length, partly of detailed accounts of what is mentioned but briefly in the earlier sources, partly of particulars occupying one, two, three verses, or even a part of a verse, introduced into a narrative borrowed otherwise from Sam. or Kings. All, long and short alike (except, indeed, such as comprise merely lists of names), show the peculiar diction and mannerisms of the compiler, and are either his own composition, or (the diction being not merely peculiar, but *late*) must be derived from *a contemporary writing.*‖ In respect of contents and aim, the following features may be noticed in the additions :—

[494] (1.) They consist often of *statistical* matter, genealogies, lists of names, &c.

(2.) Very frequently they relate to the organization of public worship, or describe religious ceremonies, especially with reference to the part taken in them by Levites and singers.¶

* Abridged.

† Referred in Kings to Josiah's *eighteenth* year (22^{9} 23^{23}).

‡ To *faithfully*. § Expanded.

‖ The former alternative is decidedly the more probable ; but the latter cannot be absolutely excluded. The author of the "Midrash of the Book of the Kings" (p. 529) *may*, for instance, have used a style and diction similar to those of the Chronicler.

¶ *E.g.* I $13^{1\text{-}5}$ $15^{1\text{-}24}$ $16^{4\text{-}42}$, most of c. 22-29, II $8^{13\text{-}15}$ $20^{14.\ 19.\ 21.\ 29}$ $29^{30f}.$

(3.) In many cases they have a *didactic* aim : in particular, they show a tendency to refer events to their *moral* causes,—to represent, for instance, a great calamity or deliverance as the punishment of wickedness or the reward of virtue.   This feature is especially noticeable in the case of discourses attributed to prophets.   The prophets in the Chronicles are far more frequently than in the earlier historical books brought into relation with the *kings*, to whom they predict good or ill success, in accordance with their deserts, with much uniformity of expression, and in a tone very different from that of the prophets who appear in the Books of Samuel or Kings.

Thus notice I 10¹³ᶠ· (the cause assigned for Saul's death) ; 15¹³ (cause of Uzzah's death) ; II 12²ᵇ (cause of Shishak's invasion) ; 17¹⁰ ; 21¹⁰ᵇ ; 22⁷· ⁹ ; 24²³⁻²⁵ (cf. v.¹⁸⁻²²) ; 25²⁰ᵇ (cause of Amaziah's defeat) ; 26¹⁶⁻²⁰ (only the *fact* of Uzziah's leprosy is stated in 2 Kings) ; 28⁵· ¹⁹· ²²· ²³ (Ahaz's troubles attributed to his idolatry) ; 33¹¹⁻¹³ (Manasseh's repentance followed by his restoration) ; 35²¹ᶠ· (Josiah's death at Megiddo explained by his rejection of a Divine warning) ; 36¹²ᵇ.

Examples of prophets : II 12⁵⁻⁸ (Shemaiah announces Shishak's invasion, and the mitigation of its consequences after the king's repentance) ; 15¹⁻¹⁵ Asa's prosperity is ascribed to his obedience to Azariah's exhortations ; 16⁷⁻¹⁰ Hanani declares to Asa the ground of his imperfect success against the Syrians ; 19¹⁻³ Jehu, son of Hanani, reproves Jehoshaphat ; 20¹⁴⁻¹⁷ Jahaziel, a Levite, promises victory to the same king ; 20³⁷ᵃ Eliezer, son of Dodavah, predicts the ruin of Jehoshaphat's shipping on account of his league with Ahaziah king of Israel ; 21¹²⁻¹⁵ the letter of Elijah announcing Jehoram's sickness as a punishment for his idolatry : see also 24²⁰ (Zechariah son of Jehoiada) ; 25⁷⁻⁹ (the "man of God" who warns Amaziah) ; 25¹⁵ᶠ·; 26⁵ ; 28⁹⁻¹⁵ (Oded).

Attention should also be directed to the *short insertions*, introduced into the narratives excerpted from Sam. or Kings. These appear commonly to be designed with the view of filling up some point in which the earlier narrative appeared to be deficient : thus they state a reason or add a reflexion, usually from the points of view which have been just illustrated.

[495] Comp., for instance, the notices relating to ritual, or the part taken by the Levites, singers, &c., in I 15²⁷ᵃ· ²⁸ᵃᵦᵇ ; II 5¹¹ᵇ⁻¹³ᵃ ; 6¹³ ; 7⁶ ; 8¹³⁻¹⁵ ; 23⁶· ⁸ᵇ· ¹³ *middle*· ¹⁸ (from ביר) ⁻¹⁹ ; 34⁹ (in parts) ¹² (from *and the*) ⁻¹³ ; and the explanations, or reflections, in I 21⁶ ; II 8¹¹ᵇ ; 12¹²· ¹⁴ ; 18⁸¹ᵇ (from *and Jehovah*) ; 22¹ᵃᵦ· ³ᵇ· ⁴ᵇ ; 26²¹ᵃᵦ· ²³ᵃᵦ ; 27⁶ ; 28²⁷ᵃᵦ ; 32²²ᶠ·   The aim of the

31²¹ 35¹⁻¹⁷ &c : cf. II 13¹²· ¹⁴ (the priests with חצצרות in battle), 17⁸ᶠ· (the Levites teaching) ; and in speeches II 2⁴ᵃᵦ· ᵇ·⁶ᵇ (Heb. ³ᵃᵦ· ᵇ·⁵ᵇ) 13¹⁰ᶠ· 35³⁻⁶.

addition in I 21²⁹ᶠ· is evidently to justify David's sacrifice on Zion, as that of II 1³ᵇ⁻⁶ᵃ (cf. I 16³⁹ᶠ·) is to legalise the worship at the high place of Gibeon.

Sources of the Chronicler. One main source of the Chronicler has been sufficiently indicated, viz. the earlier historical books from Gen. to Kings.* It remains to consider the sources of the additional matter which the Chronicles contain. The notices— chiefly relating to tribes and families—incorporated in the earlier part of his work (I 1–9) were derived by him in some cases, perhaps (4²²ᶠ· ³⁹⁻⁴³ 5¹⁰· ¹⁹⁻²²), from general tradition; in other cases more probably from written documents. It seems that the returned exiles felt an interest in reviving as far as possible the old *status quo* of the community, and with this end in view paid careful attention to such genealogical records as existed, and took steps to complete and restore them.† It is probable that lists drawn up now with this object were at the disposal of the compiler (comp. I 5¹⁷ 9¹). But from the time of David (inclusive) the Chronicler, like the compiler of Kings, refers, as a rule,‡ at the end of each reign, to some definite source or sources where further particulars are to be found ("the rest of the acts § of . . . behold, they are written in," &c.). The sources thus referred to are:

(*a*) "The Book of the Kings of Judah and Israel" II 16¹¹ (Asa), 25²⁶ (Amaziah), 28²⁶ (Ahaz): cf. below, *k*.

(*b*) "The Book of the Kings of Israel and Judah" II 27⁷ (Jotham), 35²⁷ (Josiah), 36⁸ (Jehoiakim).

[496] (*c*) "The acts ‖ of the Kings of Israel" 33¹⁸ (Manasseh).¶

(*d*) "The Midrash of the Book of the Kings" 24²⁷ (Joash).

---

* It cannot be shown that the Chronicler used the *sources* (p. 186 f.) of Kings. Not only does he never quote them as his authorities, but (see below) he quotes other authorities instead; and many of the passages common to Chr. and Kings—*e.g.* the judgments on the kings—are palpably the work of the compiler of the Book of Kings. See, for instance, II 7¹²ᵃᵇᵅ· ¹⁶⁻²² 14¹⁻² 15¹⁷ 20³¹⁻³³ᵃ 25¹⁻⁴ 26¹⁻⁴ 28¹⁻⁴ 29¹⁻² 33⁷⁻⁹ &c.

† Comp. (in B.C. 536) Neh. 7⁵· ⁶¹· ⁶⁴, and (later) 12²³.

‡ The exceptions are II 21²⁰ 22⁹ 23²¹ 33²⁴ᶠ· 36⁴· ¹⁰· ²¹.

§ Sometimes with the addition of the words "first and last" I 29²⁹, II 12¹⁵ *al.*, or with other slight variations or additions (the longest is in I 29³⁰, II 24²⁷ 33¹⁸· ¹⁹ 36⁸). (*Acts* is lit. "words": see the next note.)

‖ Lit. *words*; hence *affairs, things*,—in so far ,as they are done, "acts," in so far as they are narrated, "history."

¶ In I 9¹ either *b* or *c* will be referred to, according as the verse is construed with LXX., AV., Kuen., Meyer, or with Berth., Keil, RV., Oettli.

(*e*) "The words (*or* acts ; RV. history) of Samuel the seer, and the words (history) of Nathan the prophet, and the words (history) of Gad the seer" I 29²⁹ (David).

(*f*) "The words (RV. history) of Nathan the prophet, and the prophecy of Ahijah the Shilonite, and the vision of Iddo the seer respecting Jeroboam the son of Nebat" II 9²⁹ (Solomon).

(*g*) "The words (history) of Shemaiah the prophet and of Iddo the seer for reckoning by genealogies" 12¹⁵ (Rehoboam).

(*h*) "The Midrash of the prophet Iddo" 13²² (Abijah).

(*i*) "The words (history) of Jehu, son of Hanani, which are inserted in the Book of the Kings of Israel" 20³⁴ (Jehoshaphat).

(*j*) "The rest of the acts (*lit.* words) of Uzziah, first and last, did Isaiah the prophet, the son of Amoz, write" 26²².

(*k*) "The vision of Isaiah the prophet, the son of Amoz, in the Book of the Kings of Judah and Israel" 32³² (Hezekiah).

(*l*) "The words (history) of Hozai" [or "of the seers," LXX, Berth., Kuen., Oettli, Kautzsch : see v.¹⁸] 33¹⁹ (Manasseh).

Allusion is made also (*m*) in I 5¹⁷ (in the account of Gad) to a genealogical register compiled in the days of Jotham and of Jeroboam II.; (*n*) in I 23²⁷ to "the later acts (*or* history) of David;" (*o*) in I 27²⁴ to "the chronicles of king David," into which the census taken by Joab was not entered ; and (*p*) in II 35²⁵ to a collection of "lamentations."

It is generally allowed that the first three of these titles, *a*, *b*, *c*, and the "Book of the Kings of Israel" referred to under *i*, are different names of one and the same work, which embraced a history of *both* kingdoms, and of which the full title was "The Book of the Kings of Israel and Judah" (or "of Judah and Israel"), but which was sometimes referred to more briefly, the term "Israel" being understood in its wider sense as denoting the entire nation.   It seems clear that the compiler means to refer to *one* book, and not to two; for (1) the book under its full title "of the Kings of *Israel* and Judah" is mentioned as the authority for the reigns of Josiah and Jehoiakim, after the N. kingdom had ceased to exist; and (2) the book under its shorter title "Kings of *Israel*" alone is referred to for the reigns of two kings of Judah, Jehoshaphat and Manasseh (Nos. *i*, *c*). That this book is not the existing Book of Kings is clear from the fact that the compiler cites it for particulars respecting matters not mentioned in that book.*   Nor was it identical with [**497**] either of the books cited as authorities in the Book of Kings : for these were *two* distinct works (p. 187 f.), in which the

---

* As I 9¹ genealogies ; II 27⁷ the wars of Jotham ; 33¹⁸ the prayer of Manasseh ; 36⁸ acts and "abominations" of Jehoiakim.

history of each kingdom was treated separately. Whether *d*
("the Midrash of the Book of the Kings") is also the same as *a*,
b, *c* is uncertain; on the one hand, the peculiar title would
suggest a distinct work; on the other hand, it is not apparent
why, if (as its title shows) it was a comprehensive work, dealing
with the kings generally, it should be cited for one reign only.
Whether it be the same work * or not, it may be inferred from
its title that its aim was to develop the religious lessons deducible
from the history of the kings.

The term *Midrash* † occurs only here and 13³² in the OT. though it is
common in post-Biblical literature. דרש is to *search out, investigate, explore*
as applied to Scripture, to discover or develop a thought not apparent on
the surface,—for instance, the hidden meaning of a word, or the particulars
implied by an allusion (*e.g.* what Abraham did in Ur of the Chaldees, what
Eldad and Medad said when they prophesied, the circumstances of Moses'
death, &c.). The Midrash may be defined as an imaginative development of
a thought or theme suggested by Scripture, especially a didactic or homiletic
exposition, or an edifying religious story (Tobit and Susannah are thus
"Midrashim"). To judge from the title, the book here referred to will
have been a work on the Book of Kings, developing such incidents as were
adapted to illustrate the didactic import of the history. And this seems in
fact to be the motive which prevails in many of the narratives in the
Chronicles: they are pointed illustrations of some religious or moral truth.
Haggadah (above, pp. 484, 487) is a synonym of *Midrash*.

The "words" (*or* histories) of the several prophets referred
to in *e*, *f*, &c., have been supposed to point to independent
historical monographs, written by the prophets with whose names
they are connected. But it is observable that the "words (*or*
history) of Jehu" (*i*) and the "vision of Isaiah" (*k*) are cited,
not as independent works, but as sections *incorporated* in the
"Book of the Kings of Israel" (or "Judah and Israel"): and if
the more probable reading in II 33¹⁹ be adopted, the same will
be true of the "words (*or* histories) of the seers," cited as an
authority for the reign of Manasseh (see v.¹⁸). This being so,
the question arises whether the other "words" (*or* histories) of
prophets (*e*, *f*, *g*) were not also portions of the same historical
work. For, except in the passages quoted, where the "words"

---

* So Ewald, *Hist.* i. 187; Wellh. *Hist.* p. 227; Kuenen, p. 493. Berth.
p. xxxi, Schrader, § 232⁸, Dillm. p. 223, Ball, p. 212, Oettli, p. 7, think them
distinct.

† *Commentary* (RV.) suggests a wholly false idea of the kind of work
meant.

(histories) are referred to as part of the "Book of Kings," it [498] is the compiler's habit to quote but *one* authority at the end of the reign of each king, which is always *either* the "Book of Kings" *or* the "words" (*or* history) of some prophet; and hence, in view of the express statement respecting the "words" (*or* history) of Jehu and the "vision" of Isaiah, it is supposed by most critics that the other prophetic histories referred to were really integral parts, or sections, of the same great historical compilation, which embraced the history of particular prophets, and was hence familiarly quoted under their names.* However, this conclusion, though not an improbable one, does not follow necessarily from the premises; and it must be admitted that the compiler may have meant, in *e*, *f*, and *g*, to refer to independent writings.† In *j* the terms of the citation are different; and it is, on the whole, more probable that an independent work is referred to : for, as Ew. (*l.c.*) remarks, a section of a prophetical work dealing with the reign of Uzziah would hardly be named after Isaiah, as he came forward as a prophet only in the last year of that king (Isa. 6¹).‡ Once (*h*) the "Midrash" of a prophet, Iddo, is cited : this will have been either a particular section of the "Midrash of the Book of the Kings" (*d*), or, more probably, a separate work of the same character, which was either attributed to Iddo as its author, or in which the prophet Iddo played a prominent part.

The question arises whether the parts peculiar to Chr. are *excerpts* from any of these works, in the same sense in which other parts are excerpts from Sam. and Kings. If they are, as their style is not only peculiar, but *late*, the work, or works, from

* So Ewald, i. 185; Berth. p. xxxi f.; Dillmann, p. 223; Kuen. p. 487; Ball, p. 212*b*; Oettli, p. 8.

† The existence of which is allowed also by Ewald and Dillmann, *ll.cc.*

‡ The existing Book of Isaiah, of course, cannot be meant; for neither in 6¹ nor in any other part of it are particulars of the life or reign of Uzziah recorded. In II 12¹⁵ the words "for reckoning by genealogies" probably indicate that the section referred to either began with, or included, some genealogical notices. The opinion—adopted, for instance, by Lumby, *Comm. on Kings*, p. xii f.—that the books cited as authorities by the compiler of Kings were compilations from the prophetical writings cited in Chronicles is destitute of all probability : the books cited in Kings are referred to (above, p. 187 *n.*) for the *political* doings of the kings, those cited in Chr.—if there is any reason for supposing the matter peculiar to Chr. to have been derived from them—will have been of a *didactic* character.

which they are taken must have been composed at a date scarcely earlier than that of the Chronicles itself, and by an author writing in a similar style and with a similar aim. The style is conclusive evidence that no part of the additions can be an excerpt from the autograph of any pre-exilic prophet:* if such autographs were accessible to the compiler, the information derived from them must have been entirely recast by him, and [499] presented in his own fashion.† The *speeches* contained in the additions form no exception to what has been said : these also, even the shortest,‡ are shown by the numerous points of contact which they display, both in thought and expression, with the post-exilic narratives peculiar to the Chronicles, to be one and all the Chronicler's own composition.

The most important of the sources cited appears to have been the Book of the Kings of Israel and Judah. The contents and character of this book can be determined only inferentially. It follows, of course, from the title, that it must have contained a history of both kingdoms : from I 9^1 it would seem that genea-logies were included in it, and that a part at least of the statis-tical information contained in I 1–8, and perhaps also in other parts of the book, was derived from it. The narratives peculiar to the Chronicles are often thought to be based upon this work ; though whether they were presented in it nearly in the form in which we now read them, or how far they were recast by the Chronicler, cannot be readily decided. The most probable view of the "Book of the Kings of Israel and Judah" is that it was a *post*-exilic work, incorporating statistical matter, and dealing generally with the history of the two kingdoms in a spirit con-genial to the temper and interests of the restored community. A book thus constituted would supply materials which a writer, having the aims of the Chronicler in view, could at once utilise,

* Mr. Girdlestone's hypothesis (*Foundations of the Bible*, pp. 31, 32, 34, 119, 120) that they were "extracted" from "the original and comprehensive work from which our Books of Kings were condensed," would thus be an untenable one, even granting that there were sufficient grounds for supposing that such a work ever existed.

† The statement in the *Speaker's Comm.*, that the language of much of I 16^{4-42} is "remarkably archaic," is the very reverse of the fact.

‡ As I Ch. 12^{18} $13^{2f.}$ $15^{12f.}$ 22^5, 2 Ch. $19^{6f.}$ $30^{18b\beta-19}$. See more fully, in support of this description of the speeches in the Chronicles, two articles by the present writer in the *Expositor*, Apr. 1895, p. 241 ff., Oct. 1895, p. 286 ff.

and would also provide to some extent a model on which he
might work himself.

The relation of the Chronicles to the canonical Book of Kings on the one
hand, and to this "Book of the Kings of Israel and Judah" on the other, is
generally represented by the following scheme : *—

    1. The Book of the Chronicles of the Kings of Israel (*a*).
    2. The Book of the Chronicles of the Kings of Judah (*b*).

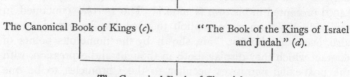

The Canonical Book of Kings (*c*).   "The Book of the Kings of Israel
and Judah" (*d*).

The Canonical Book of Chronicles.

This scheme is, of course, only approximate.   It takes no account of the
elements in the existing Kings or Chronicles derived from other sources—in
[500] the former, for instance, from prophetical narratives (p. 188 f.), in the
latter from genealogical or other records.   It must be admitted also that we
do not *know* that *a* and *b* were used in the compilation of *d* ; the materials
used may have been obtained from other sources, even including (as Kuen.
supposes) *c*.

It does not fall within the province of the present work to
examine the relation of the narrative of Chronicles to that of
Samuel and Kings, except so far as may serve to illustrate the
method or point of view of the compiler.   The following general
remarks must therefore suffice.   It does not seem possible to
treat the additional matter in Chronicles as strictly and literally
historical.   In many cases the figures are incredibly high : † in
others, the scale or magnitude of the occurrences described is
such that, had they really happened precisely as represented, they
could hardly have been passed over by the compiler of Samuel
or Kings ; elsewhere, again, the description appears to be irreconcilable with that in the earlier narrative ; while nearly always
the speeches assigned to historical characters, and the motives
attributed to them, are conceived largely from a point of view

* Graf, *Gesch. B.* p. 192 ; Berth. pp. xl–xli ; &c.

† It is illegitimate to explain these as due to textual corruption ; the numbers in the Chronicles are systematically higher than in other parts of the
OT.; and no reason exists for supposing the text of these books to have been
specially subject to error in transmission.   Besides, numbers written in full
would not be readily corrupted : the supposition that *letters* were used for
numerals in the sacred autographs is destitute of foundation (comp. the
writer's note on 1 Sa. 13¹).

very different from that which dominates the earlier narrative, and agreeing closely with the compiler's. The peculiarities of the historical representation which prevails in the Chronicles are to be ascribed, no doubt, to the influences under which the author lived and wrote. The compiler lived in an age when the theocratic institutions, which had been placed on a new basis after the return from Babylon, had long been in full operation, and when new religious interests and a new type of piety—of course with points of contact with the old, but, at the same time, advancing beyond it—had been developed, and asserted themselves strongly. The Chronicler reflects faithfully the spirit of his age. A new mode of viewing the past history of his nation began to prevail: pre-exilic Judah was pictured as already in possession of the institutions, and governed—at least in its greater and better men—by the ideas and principles, which were in force at a later day; the empire of David and his successors [501] was imagined on a scale of unsurpassed power and magnificence; the past, in a word, was *idealised*, and its history, where necessary, rewritten accordingly. Thus the institutions of the present, which, in fact, had been developed gradually, are represented as organized in their completeness by David; the ritual of the Priests' Code is duly observed; the Passovers of Hezekiah and Josiah (the former of which is not mentioned in the Book of Kings at all, the latter only briefly) are described with an abundance of ceremonial detail, suggested no doubt by occasions which the compiler had witnessed himself; David organizes a vast military force, and amasses for the Temple enormous treasures; his successors have the command of huge armies, and are victorious against forces huger even than their own. In these and similar representations there is certainly much that cannot be strictly historical; but it was not the Chronicler's intention to pervert the history; he and his contemporaries did not question that the past was actually as they pictured it, and the Chronicler simply gives expression to this persuasion. It is not necessary to deny—on the contrary, it is highly probable—that a traditional element lies at the basis of his representations; but this element has been developed by him, and presented in a literary form, with the aim of giving expression to the ideas which he had at heart, and of inculcating the lessons which he conceived the history to teach.

There is, for instance, no improbability in the statement that David amassed materials for a Temple, though the details as recorded in Chr. must be greatly exaggerated (in I 22^{14} David states that he has accumulated 100,000 talents of gold and 1,000,000 talents of silver ; contrast the very much more moderate estimate of even Solomon's revenue in I Ki. 10$^{14f.}$) ; and the manner in which David expresses his aims and wishes is entirely that of the compiler and his age. In 2 Sa. 6' we appear to possess a tolerably circumstantial account of the transference of the ark from Kirjath-jearim to Zion, and if the ground of Uzzah's misfortune was really at the time attributed to the Levites not having borne the ark as (according to the Priests' Code) they should have done, and if afterwards they and the singers took the prominent part in the ceremony ascribed to them in 1 Ch. 15–16, the silence of the earlier narrative is inexplicable. But the Chronicler appears just to have constructed a picture of the ceremony which, in his eyes, was worthy of the occasion, and to have inserted it into the narrative excerpted by him from Samuel (comp. p. 378). In 1 Ki. 8^3 the ark is borne by priests (in accordance with the general pre-exilic practice) ; but in 2 Ch. 5^4 "Levites" is substituted to bring the passage into conformity with the later Levitical law : 1 Ki. 8$^{65f.}$ is similarly altered in 2 Ch. 7$^{9f.}$ so as to harmonize with the custom of the Second Temple. In cases such as these it is clear [502] that the representation has been modified in details so as to accord with the conceptions of the Chronicler's own age.* Elsewhere traits have been altered, or added, for the purpose of inculcating more pointedly the author's doctrine of retribution : see some good examples of this in W. R. Smith, *OTJC.*^{2} p. 140 ff. In 2 Ch. 23, 24$^{4-14}$, 28$^{22f. 24f.}$, the older narrative has been so transformed that a new complexion has been given to the whole occurrence : cf. Berth. *ad locc.*; Kuen. §§ 30. 21, 31. 2 ; Wellh. *Hist.* pp. 194–200.† In 2 Ch. 2$^{3-16}$ the correspondence between Hiram and Solomon (1 Ki. 5$^{2-9}$) has been rewritten by the Chronicler (with reminiscences from other parts of Kings) in his own style.‡ On the historical value of the *lists of names* found in the Chronicles, see especially G. B. Gray, *Studies in Hebrew Proper Names* (1896), pp. 170–190, 211–241.

We are, of course, very imperfectly informed as to the *precise* nature of the sources used by the Chronicler ; but it has been supposed,§ not improbably, that the new point of view from which the history is regarded, and its didactic treatment, had

---

* The singers, who, in the register of B.C. 536, and even by Neh., are *distinguished* from the Levites, and named after them (Ezr. 2$^{40f. 70}$; Neh. 7^1 10^{28}) are, in Chr., classed as *belonging to them* (I 9^{33} 15$^{16ff.}$ &c.). It seems as though in the interval the singers had come to be reckoned as Levites ; and the new point of view is represented by the Chronicler.

† On 2 Ch. 23–24, see also F. W. Farrar, *Expositor*, Aug. 1894, p. 81 ff.

‡ Prof. Sayce also does not question that in the Chronicles we have frequently "Haggadah" rather than history in the modern sense of the term (*Monuments*, p. 467 ; cf. p. 465).

§ *E.g.* by Berth. p. xxxvii ; Dillm. p. 224 ; cf. above, p. 531.

already appeared in the "Book of the Kings of Israel and Judah." Nor should it be forgotten that two of the sources quoted by him are expressly termed *Midrashim* (p. 529 f.). From what has been said, the importance of the Chronicles as evidence respecting the *ideas and institutions* of the period, *c.* 300 B.C., in which the compiler himself lived, will be apparent.

The style of the Chronicles is singular. Not only does it display the general novelties of vocabulary and syntax indicated on p. 505 f., showing either that the language itself is in decadence, or that the author has an imperfect command of it; but it has in addition numerous peculiarities and mannerisms of its own, not found in other post-exilic writings, which are often, if the Book be read carefully, perceptible even in a translation. It is impossible to exemplify here all the characteristics of the Chronicler's style : the following are some of those which are the most striking and of most frequent occurrence. In some instances they appear in germ, or *occasionally* (cf. p. 505 *n.*), at an earlier period of the language; in others, they consist of a peculiar application of old words. The occurrences in Ezr.-Neh. are included in the list.

1. התְיַחֵשׂ *to be reckoned genealogically* : I 4³³ 5¹· ⁷· ¹⁷ 7⁵· ⁷· ⁹· ⁴⁰ 9¹· ²², II 12¹⁵ 31¹⁶· ¹⁷· ¹⁸· ¹⁹, Ezr. 2⁶² (=Neh. 7⁶⁴) 8¹· ³, Neh. 7⁵†. יַחַשׂ *genealogy*, Neh. 7⁵†. A late word found only (in the OT.) in these books.

2. לרב *abundantly* : I 4³⁸ 12⁴⁰ 22³ *bis.* ⁴· ⁵· ⁸· ¹⁴· ¹⁵ 29²· ²¹, II 1¹⁵ (=9²⁷= I Ki. 10²⁷) 2⁸ 4¹⁸ 9¹· ⁹ 11²³ 14¹⁴ 15⁹ 16⁸ 17⁵ 18¹· ² 20²⁵ 24¹¹· ²⁴ 27³ 29³⁵ 30⁵· **[503]** ¹³· ²⁴ 31⁵ 32⁵· ²⁹. So Neh. 9²⁵, Zech. 14¹⁴. In the earlier books the usage *here and there* approximates; but generally לרב occurs in them only in a *comparison = in respect of multitude* (as Jud. 6⁵). The earlier language, where the Chr. has לרב, would use, as a rule, רבים or הרבה.

3. מעל *trespass* (subst. and verb) : I 5²⁵ 9¹ 10¹³, II 12² 26¹⁶· ¹⁸ 28¹⁹· ²² 29⁶· ¹⁹ 30⁷ 33¹⁹ 36¹⁴, Ezr. 9²· ⁴ 10²· ⁶· ¹⁰, Neh. 1⁸ 13²⁷. A favourite term with Chr.: see also p. 134, No. 43. (In I 2⁷, from Josh. 7¹ P.) Cf. Dan. 9⁷ (prob. from Lev. 26⁴⁰ : but see also I Ch. 10¹³, Ez. 17²⁰ 18²⁴).

4. העמיד metaph. *to establish, appoint* (a weakened sense : in earlier books lit. *to station*): I 6¹⁶ [AV. ³¹] 15¹⁶· ¹⁷ 16¹⁷ (=Ps. 105¹⁰) 17¹⁴ 22², II 8¹⁴ 9⁸ 11¹⁵· ²² 19⁵· ⁸ 20²¹ 24¹³ (cf. Ezr. 2⁶⁸) 25⁵· ¹⁴ 30⁵ 31² 33⁸ [2 Ki. נחתי] 35², Ezr. 3⁸, Neh. 4³ 6⁷ 7³ 10³³ 12³¹ 13¹¹· ³⁰, Dan. 11¹¹· ¹³· ¹⁴. Cf. Ps. 107²⁵. (Also II 34³² used specially. In II 23¹⁰· ¹⁹ 29²⁵ 33¹⁹, Ezr. 3¹⁰, Neh. 4⁷ 13¹⁹ the lit. sense is more prominent : in Neh. 3¹ff· 6¹ 7¹, of setting up *doors*.) An approximation to the weaker sense occurs in I Ki. 12³² 15⁴.

5. בית האלהים *house of God* : I 6³³ [AV. ⁴⁸], and 33 times besides, as well as often in Ezr. and Neh. So Dan. 1² (in Kings, &c., always

"house of Jehovah," which also occurs frequently in Chr.). Comp. above, p. 21 *note*.

6. הבין *to establish, prepare*, in different applications : I 9^{82} 12^{39} 15^1 &c. (about 40 times in all), and Ezr. 3^3 ; esp. with לב *to set* or *fix* the heart, I 29^{18}, II 12^{14} 19^3 20^{33} 30^{19}, Ezr. 7^{10}.

7. דרש *to seek to, enquire of* (God), in a general sense, of seeking Him in the various exercises and offices of religion : I 13^3 15^{13} 16^{11} (from Ps. 105^4), 21^{30} (at altar), 22^{19}, II 1^5 (obj. the altar), 12^{14} $14^{4.\ 7}$ [Heb. $^{3.\ 6}$] $15^{2.\ 12.\ 13}$ 16^{12} 17^3 (to the Baals), ^{4} 19^3 20^3 22^9 $25^{15\ and\ 20}$ (foreign gods), 26^5 30^{19} 31^{21} 34^3, Ezr. 4^2 6^{21} ; cf. 7^{10}. (A weakened sense of the Heb. word. In the earlier historical books very much rarer, and only of a *special* inquiry, esp. by a prophet, as 1 Ki. 22^5, 2 Ki. 22^{13}.)

8. התחזק *to strengthen oneself* : I 11^{10} 19^{13} (=2 Sa. 10^{12}), II 1^1 12^{13} $13^{7.\ 8.\ 21}$ 15^8 16^9 17^1 21^4 23^1 25^{11} 27^6 32^5 ; cf. Dan. $10^{19\text{-}21}$. Use in earlier books both rarer and more distinctive.

9. מלכות *kingdom* : I 11^{10} and nearly 30 times besides. Ezr. 1^1 $4^{5.\ 6}$ 7^1 8^1, Neh. 9^{35} 12^{22}. Regularly also in Est. Dan. Very rare in the older language : which prefers ממלכה, or מלוכה.

10. עזר *to help*, in connexion with God : I 12^{18} 15^{26}, II 18^{31b} (in a half-verse *inserted* into the narrative of 1 Ki. 22) 26^7 ; cf. 14^{10} 25^8 32^8 : in the passive, I 5^{20}, II 26^{15}.

11. קבּל *to receive* : I 12^{18} 21^{11} (in a passage *inserted* into 2 Sa. 24^{13}), II $29^{16.\ 22}$ Ezr. 8^{30}. A common Aramaic word. Elsewhere only Pr. 19^{20}, Job 2^{10}, Est. 4^4 $9^{23.\ 27}$; and in the Aram. of Daniel.

12. נקבו בשמות *to be expressed by names* : I 12^{31} 16^{41}, II 28^{15} 31^{19}, Ezr. 8^{20}, Nu. 1^{17} (P)†.

13. למעלה *upwards*=exceedingly : I 14^2 22^5 23^{17} $29^{3.\ 25}$, [504] II 1^1 16^{12} 17^{12} 20^{19} 26^8. This metaph. use of *upwards* as a mere intensive= "exceedingly" is exclusively a late one, and confined to these passages. (Ezr. 9^6 the use is different.)

14. ארצות *lands* (see p. 297, No. 4) : I 14^{17} 22^5 29^{30}, II 9^{28} 12^8 13^9 15^5 17^{10} 20^{29} $32^{13\ bis.\ 17}$ 34^{33}, Ezr. 3^3 $9^{1.\ 2.\ 7.\ 11}$, Neh. 9^{30} 10^{29} : even " *lands* of Israel and Judah," I 13^2, II 11^{23}.

15. מבין *understanding*, of those technically skilled : I 15^{22} $25^{7.\ 8}$ 27^{32}, II 34^{12}, Ezr. 8^{16}. Comp. (*a*) II 26^5 ; (*b*) more generally, Neh. $8^{2.\ 3}$ 10^{29} ; (*c*) transit., II 35^3, Neh. $8^{7.\ 9}$.

16. הורות והלל I 16^4 23^{30} 25^3, II 5^{13} 31^2, Ezr. 3^{11}, Neh. 12^{24}.

17. חדוה *joy* : I 16^{27} [substituted for תפארת Ps. 96^6], Neh. 8^{10}, Ezr. 6^{16} (Aram.)†. An Aramaic word. The cognate verb Ex. 18^9 (E), Ps. 21^7, Job 3^6†.

18. נכנע *to humble oneself* or *be humbled* (esp. morally*) : I 20^4, II 7^{14*} $12^{6*.\ 7\ bis.*}$ ^{12*} 13^{18} 30^{11*} 32^{26*} $33^{12*.\ 19*.\ 23}$ *$34^{27\ bis*}$ (first time= 2 Ki. 22^{19}), 36^{12*} : cf. *to humble* I 17^{10} 18^1 (=2 Sa. 8^1), II 28^{19}. Observe how this word appears frequently in a *short insertion* introduced into an excerpt from Kings.

19. אשמה *guilt* : I 21^3 (*altered* from 2 Sa. 24^3), II 24^{18} $28^{10.\ 13}$ 33^{23}, Ezr. $9^{6.\ 7.\ 13.\ 15}$ $10^{10.\ 19}$. Uncommon.

20. רכוש *substance* : I 21¹⁷ 27³¹ 28¹, II 20²⁵ 21¹⁴ 31³ 32²⁹ 35⁷, Ezr. 1⁴· ⁶ 8²¹ 10⁸, Dan. 11¹³· ²⁴· ²⁸. The use of this word is somewhat peculiar : see p. 132, No. 17.

21. נצח *to oversee* : (*a*) generally I 23⁴, II 2¹· ¹⁷ 34¹²· ¹³, Ezr. 3⁸· ⁹↑ ; (*b*) in music, *to lead* : I 15²¹. (Only so besides in the titles to Psalms and Hab. 3¹⁹ : למנצח, AV. *to the precentor*.)

22. שמעוני *Hear me* (esp. at the beginning of a speech) : I 28² (David), II 13⁴ (Abijah), 15² (Azariah), 20²⁰ (Jehoshaphat), 28¹¹ (Oded), 29⁵ (Hezekiah). One of the many marks which the speeches in Chr. contain of the compiler's hand. No other speech in the OT. so begins : cf., however, Gen. 23⁶.

23. התנדב *to show oneself ready* in sacred gifts or services : I 29⁵· ⁶· ⁹· ¹⁴· ¹⁷, II 17¹⁶, Ezr. 1⁶ 2⁶⁸ (in a passage *inserted* into the text of Neh. 7⁷¹, after "fathers' houses"), 3⁵ 7¹³· ¹⁵· ¹⁶ (Aram.), Neh. 11². Only besides Jud. 5²· ⁹ (of warriors).

24. *Riches and honour* : I 29¹²· ²⁸, II 1¹¹· ¹² 17⁵ 18¹ 32²⁷. The example shows how a combination of *ordinary* words may be a favourite with a particular writer.

25. המון *multitude* : II 11²³ (strangely : read probably with F. Perles, *Analekten zur Textkritik des AT.s*, 1895, p. 47, וישאו להם נשים) 13⁸ 14¹⁰ 20²· ¹²· ¹⁵· ²⁴ 32⁷, Dan. 11¹⁰⁻¹³. Only used *exceptionally* in early prose.

26. *And the fear of Jehovah was upon* . . . II 14¹⁴ [Heb. ¹³] 17¹⁰ (19⁷) 20²⁹ : cf. I 14¹⁷ᵇ.

The following are chiefly instances of singular *syntactical* usages :—

27. Sentences expressed peculiarly (without a *subject*, or sometimes without a *verb*) : I 9³³ᵇ (cf. Ezr. 3³), 15¹³ᵃ, [505] II 11²²ᵇ 15³ 16¹⁰· ¹²ᵃ· ᵇ 18³ ᵉⁿᵈ (altered from I Ki. 22⁴), 19⁶ᵇ 21¹⁵ 26¹⁸ᵇ 28²¹ᵇ 30⁹· ¹⁷ᵇ 35²¹ ; and some of the cases with לא in No. 40. Comp. Ew. § 303ᵇ.

28. The inf. constr. used freely, almost as a subst. : I 7⁵· ⁷· ⁹· ⁴⁰ 9²² (all החתחשם), 23³¹, II 3³ 24¹⁴ (cf. Ezr. 3¹¹), 33¹⁹, Ezr. 1¹¹, Neh. 12⁴⁶ : cf. Est. 1⁷. Cf. Ewald, *Lehrb.* § 236ᵃ.

29. יום ביום : I 12²² (לעת יום ביום), II 8¹³ 24¹¹ (ליום ביום), 30²¹, Ezr. 3⁴ 6⁹ (Aram.), Nch. 8¹⁸↑.

30. The relative omitted (very rare in prose : see *Notes on Samuel*, 1 Sa. 14²¹) : I 9²²ᵇ 12²³ 15¹²ᵇ 29¹· ³ᵇ, II 13⁹ (poet. : cf. Jer. 5⁷), 14¹⁰ (poet. : cf. Isa. 40²⁹), 15¹¹ 16⁹ 20²² 24¹¹ 28⁹ 29²⁷ 30¹⁸ᵇ⁻¹⁹ᵃ 31¹⁹ᵇ, Ezr. 1⁵· ⁶, Neh. 8¹⁰ 13²³.

31. לָמֶ (very strangely) : I 15¹³, II 30³↑.

32. ל with the inf. at the end of a sentence : I 15¹⁶ להרים בקול, ¹⁹· ²¹ 22⁵ (להגדיל) 25⁵, II 5¹³ 22³ᵇ 25¹⁹ (varied curiously from 2 Ki. 14¹⁰) 36¹⁹ ᵉⁿᵈ, Ezr. 3¹².

33. אמר ל = *to purpose*, or *promise, that* . . . (in preference to quoting the words used) : I 21¹⁷ 27²³, II 1¹⁸ (as I Ki. 5¹⁹), 6¹ (as I Ki. 8¹²), ²⁰ (altered from I Ki. 8²⁹), 13⁸ 21⁷ (as 2 Ki. 8¹⁹), 28¹⁰· ¹³ 32¹ 35²¹, Neh. 9²³. See also p. 506, No. 3. So *sometimes* also in early Heb. (cf. p. 505 *n*.). Cf. I 17²⁵ (*altered* from 2 Sa. 7²⁷).

34. על ידי = *at the direction* or *appointment of* : I 25[2. 3. 6 *bis*], II 23[18b] 29[27], Ezr. 3[10]. (An unusual sense : Jer. 5[31] 33[13].)

35. Combinations of the type שער ושער, עיר ועיר, יום ויום, often with כל prefixed, to express every *several gate, city, day,* &c. : I 26[13] 28[14 *bis*], II 8[14] 11[12] 19[5] 28[25] 31[19] 32[28] 34[13] 35[15], Ezr. 10[14], Neh. 13[24], Est. 1[8. 22 *bis*] 2[11. 12] 3[4. 12. 14] 4[3] 8[9. 11. 13. 17] 9[21. 27. 28] (דור ודור), Ps. 87[5]. The phrase in which this idiom appears to have first come into use is דור ודור Dt. 32[7] ; but even this occurs mostly besides in passages not earlier than the close of the exile, Lam. 5[19], Isa. 13[20] 34[17] 58[12] 60[15] 61[4], Jer. 50[39], Joel 2[2] 4[20], and often in the Psalms, esp. those which appear to be late. Except in this phrase, the idiom is a distinctively late one, being found only in the passages quoted. It is common (especially with כל) in post-Biblical Hebrew.

36. ה for the relative I 26[28] 29[8] (unless this be analogous to the Arabic المولود له, Ewald, *gr. arab.* ii. p. 242 f.), [17], II 1[4] (בַּהֵכִין לוֹ), 29[36] (עַל הַהֵכִין הָאֱלֹהִים), Ezr. 8[25] 10[14. 17]. Very singular, and of doubtful occurrence elsewhere (see Ew. § 331[b] ; Ges.-Kautzsch, § 138. 3[b] ; and the writer's note on 1 Sa. 9[24]).

37. . . . . וכבלות : II 7[1] 29[29] 31[1], Ezr. 9[1]. The same *order* constantly in these books, as 12[7] 15[8] 20[20. 22. 23] 24[14. 25] &c. The older language in such cases would either prefix ויהי (so Josh. 8[24] 10[20], 1 Ki. 8[54] [omitted in 2 Ch. 7[1]] 9[1], and constantly), [506] or place the infin. *later* in the sentence (as Gen. 19[16] 34[7] &c.). Cf. p. 506, No. 12 ; and the author's note on 1 Sa. 17[55].

Prepositions used in combinations either entirely new, or occurring with much greater frequency than in earlier writings :—

38. עד ל' (where the older language would find עד or ל alone sufficient) : (*a*) before a *subst.*, I 4[39] 12[22] 23[25] עד לעולם (so 28[7]), II 14[12] עד לנגד 16[12] עד למעלה (so 17[12] 26[8]), 16[14] עד למאר, 26[15] עד למרחוק (so Ezr. 3[13]), 28[9b] עד לשמים (so Ezr. 9[6b]), 29[30] 36[16] עד לאין מרפא, Ezr. 9[4b] עד למנחת העֶרב, 10[14] עד לרבר הזה ; (*b*) before an *inf.*, I 28[20] עד לכלות (so II 29[28]), II 24[10] 26[16] 31[1. 10] 32[24] עד למות (2 Ki. 20[1] למות), Ezr. 10[14]. Only before in the phrase . . . עד לבוא Josh. 13[5]=Jud. 3[3], as also I 5[9] 13[5], II 26[8] ; and in עד לעלות המנחת 1 Ki. 18[29].

39. ל as the mark of the accus. :—(*a*) in general, as 1 Ch. 16[37] 22[19] and often ; (*b*) after a preceding verbal suffix, in the Syriac fashion : I 5[26] 23[6], II 25[5. 10] 28[15] (cf. Neh. 9[32]) ; (*c*) introducing the definite obj. after the indef., I 29[18], II 2[12] 23[1], so Ps. 135[11] 136[19. 20] (=the earlier את Gen. 26[34], Jud. 3[15] &c.) ; (*d*) carrying on the suff. of a *noun*, II 31[18], Ezr. 9[1b] (cf. 10[14a]). ל also denotes the goal after a verb of motion much more frequently in Chr. than in the earlier prose (in which it is chiefly confined to certain phrases, as לְאָהֳלָיו, לביתו, לדרכו, למקומו,—naturally, also, with other suffixes).

40. ל with the inf., expressing *necessity, purpose, intention* (much more freely and frequently than by earlier writers, and sometimes very peculiarly) : I 9[25] 10[13] 22[5], II 8[13] 11[22] 19[2] 31[21] 36[19] (cf. 26[5]), Ezr. 10[12] (Hahn, but not Baer), Neh. 8[13b] : esp. after אין or לא I 5[1] 15[2]

23²⁶, II 5¹¹ 7¹⁷ 12¹² 20⁶ 22⁹ 30⁹ 35¹⁵, Ezr. 9¹⁵ ; cf. 2 Ch. 28²¹. Comp. the writer's *Hebrew Tenses*, §§ 202–206.

41. ב expressing concomitance (*without* a verb) : I 15¹⁹˙ ²⁰˙ ²¹˙ ²² 16⁶ 25⁶ᵃ, II 5¹²ᵃ 7⁶ 13¹⁰ end and 35¹⁴, Ezr. 3¹²ᵇ.

42. לדבר יום ביומו : I 16³⁷, II 8¹⁴ 31¹⁶†. (In the earlier language, without ל ; *e.g.* Ex. 5¹³.)

43. . . . לאין *in the condition of none* . . . =*without* : I 22⁴, II 14¹² 20²⁵ 21¹⁸ (לאין מרפא : cf. 36¹⁶ עד לאין מרפא), Ezr. 9¹⁴. Cf. ללא II 15³ *ter*. (Peculiar. Not elsewhere.)

44. להרבה : II 11¹² 16⁸, Neh. 5¹⁸†.

45. לכל *as regards all* . . . (=*namely, in brief* : Ew. § 310ᵃ) : I 13¹, II 5¹² 25⁵ 31¹⁶ 33⁸ᵇ, Ezr. 1⁵. (Comp. p. 132, No. 14.) ל is also used peculiarly in Chr. in other ways, as the ל of "introduction," I 5² 7¹ 28¹ᵇ˙ ²¹ 29⁶ᵇ, II 7²¹ (1 Ki. 9⁸ כל only), Ezr. 7²⁸, *al.*, which the reader must observe for himself, or which he may find noted by Bertheau (see also ל in the *New Heb. Lex.*).

46 The following four technical expressions occur only in these books, the first, second, and fourth with great frequency : משוררים *singers*, I 6¹⁸ 9³³ &c.; שוערים *gate-keepers* or *porters* (of the Ark or Temple), I 9¹⁷˙ ¹⁸ &c.; מצלתים *cymbals*, I 13⁸ (*altered* from 2 Sa. 6⁵), 15¹⁶ &c.; מחלקת *division*, of the *courses* of the [507] priests, &c. I 23⁶ 24¹ &c. (שוער and מחלקת are also found elsewhere, but not in these applications).

In addition to the idioms that have been noted, hardly a verse occurs, written by the Chronicler himself, which does not present singularities of style, though they are frequently of a kind that refuses to be tabulated. Amongst these may be noticed the heavy combined sentences, such as would be avoided in the earlier language by the use of two clauses connected by אשר : *e.g.* 1 Ch. 11³ [כדבר יי ביד שמואל [contrast 1 Ki. 15²⁹ᵇ 16¹²ᵇ], v.¹⁰ 25⁵ᵃ 28¹⁹ᵃ 29²⁵ᵇ, 2 Ch. 1⁹ 8¹⁵ 13⁸ᵃ 20¹⁷ ורב המשא עליו יי עמכם, 24⁹˙ ¹¹ᵃ˙ ²⁷ 26¹¹ 28⁹ 29¹⁵ 30¹²ᵇ 32²² 33⁸ᵇᵝ 34¹⁴ᵇᵝ 35⁶˙ 36¹²ᵇ˙ ²¹˙ ²² Ezr. 3⁷ כרשיון כורש מלך פרס עליהם ; *al.* For examples of strangely-worded sentences, see 1 Ch. 12¹⁸ יהיה לי עליכם, 23 13² 15¹³ᵃ 22⁵ 28²¹ᵇ 29³˙ ¹¹˙ ¹⁷ᵇ, 2 Ch. 5¹³ 12¹²ᵃᵝ 14¹² 16⁹ 19²˙ ⁶ᵇ 26¹⁸ (לכב ליחד 28¹³ &c. The Chronicler also sometimes uses words or constructions which otherwise are only *poetical*, as 1 Ch. 2³⁰˙ ³² לא בנים (Ges.-K. § 152. 1 *h*, Rem.), 28⁹ לעד, 2 Ch. 13⁹ ללא א', 14¹⁰ בין רב לאין כח (see Isa. 40²⁹ᵇ, Job 26²˙ ³), 16¹⁰ 26¹⁹ 28⁹ ועף (cf. Jon. 1¹⁵), 20¹⁵ 33¹⁰ הקשיב, 32¹⁵ (the *sing.* אלוה, as Neh. 9¹⁷, Dan. 11³⁷˙ ³⁸˙ ³⁹), 32¹⁸ בהל. The following are words found either (*a*) only in Chr., or (*b*) only in Chr. and other late writings, esp. Ezr. Neh. Est. Dan., many also being common in Aram. or New Heb. :—(*a*) הוניח ; נגוד ; גופה ; בירניות (*hiph.*) ; שש (שיש, 4 times in Job) ; כבש, 2 Ch. 9¹⁸ ; מכרבל (cf. כרבלא Dan. 3²¹) ; כרמיל *crimson* (prob. Pers.) ; הלעיב (*ethp.* in Syr. and Targ.) ; הלעיג *hiph.* (as NH.) ; ספר 2 Ch. 2¹⁶ ; ערד *to arrange* 1 Ch. 12³⁴˙ ³⁹ (text dub.) ; עתיק *ancient* (1 Ch. 4²²† ; in Aram., Dan. 7⁹ &c.) ; פטר=*to free from service* (1 Ch. 9³³, 2 Ch. 23⁸) ; פרדר *an open portico* (1 Ch. 26¹⁸ : Persian, properly *lighted* (by the sun) ; cf. פרורים 2 Ki. 23¹¹) ; צרך *need* (2 Ch. 2¹⁵†) ; שחיטה (2 Ch. 30¹⁷ : cf. p. 484 *n*.) ; חלמיד *scholar* (1 Ch. 25⁶) ; (*b*) אנוד (p. 485) ; ארדכון (1 Ch. 29⁷, Ezr. 8²⁷† : cf. דרכמון Neh. 7⁶⁹˙ ⁷⁰ [=Ezr. 2⁶⁹] ⁷¹†) ; בירה

1 Ch. 29[1. 19], בְּרוּרִים chosen, choice (lit. separated), 1 Ch. 7[40] 9[22] 16[41], Neh. 5[18] ; נרחף 2 Ch. 26[20], Est. 6[12]↑ (cf. רחוף Est. 3[15] 8[14]) ; זְנִים 2 Ch. 16[14], Ps. 144[13] (זָן), and Aram. ; כְּפוֹר 1 Ch. 28[17], Ezr. 1[10] 8[27]↑ ; גְּרֶן sheath 1 Ch. 21[27], Dan. 7[15]↑ (p. 501) ; נְכָסִים 2 Ch. 1[11. 12] (p. 112 n.) ; נֹשָׂא נֹשִׂים (p. 455) ; לחם המערכת 1 Ch. 9[32] 23[29], Neh. 10[34] (for the earlier לחם הַפָּנִים : שׁ (p. 449 ; but only 1 Ch. 5[20] 27[27], Ezr. 8[20]) ; שֶׁלַח weapon 2 Ch. 23[10] 32[5], Neh. 4[11. 17], Job 33[18] 36[12], Joel 2[8]↑ ; נִשְׁלָה 2 Ch. 29[11] (p. 188 n.) ; פְּעַל 2 Ch. 32[19], Ps. 119[14] (differently Isa. 59[18] 63[7])↑ ; see also p. 475, Nos. 2, 4, 6, 8, 9, 11, and p. 506 f., Nos. 5, 6, 7, 14, 15, 16, 17, 18, 19, 23, with the note at the end of the same list. Comp. further the idioms noted by Prof. Francis Brown, in Clark's *Bible Dictionary*, *s.v.* CHRONICLES.

§ 2. EZRA AND NEHEMIAH.

LITERATURE.—Ewald, *Hist.* i. 189 ff. ; E. Bertheau in the *Kgf. Hdb.* 1862,[2] by V. Ryssel, 1887 ; C. F. Keil (see p. 478) ; Eb. Schrader, "Die Dauer des zweiten Tempelbaues. Zugleich ein Beitrag zur Kritik des B. Esra," *Stud. u. Krit.* 1867, pp. 460–504 (important ; pp. 494–498 to be qualified by *KAT.*[2] p. 374 f.) ; Rud. Smend, *Die Listen der Bb. Esra u. Nehemia* [tabulated synoptically, and discussed] ; S. Oettli (see p. 516) ; A. Kuenen, *Onderzoek*, ed. 2, §§ 29, 33–35, and *De Chronologie van het Perzische tijdvak der Joodsche geschiedenis*, Amsterdam, 1890 (tr. in *Gesammelte Abhandlungen*, 1894, pp. 212–251) ; P. H. Hunter, *After the Exile : a Hundred Years of Jewish History and Literature*, 1890 ; H. E. Ryle in the *Camb. Bible for Schools*, 1893 ; C. C. Torrey, *The Composition and Hist. Value of Ezra-Neh.*, Giessen, 1896 ; Ed. Meyer, *Die Entstehung des Judenthums*, 1896.

Chronological Table.

B.C.		B.C.	
536.	Cyrus.	425.	Xerxes II. (2 months).
529.	Cambyses.	425.	Sogdianus (7 months).
522.	Pseudo-Smerdis (Gaumâta), for 7 months.	424.	Darius II. (Nothus).
522.	Darius Hystaspis.	405.	Artaxerxes II. (Mnemon).
516.	*Completion of the Temple.*	359.	Artaxerxes III. (Ochus).
485.	Xerxes.	351–331.	*Jaddua, high priest* (Neh. 12[11]).
465.	Artaxerxes I. (Longimanus).		
458.	*Mission of Ezra.*	339.	Arses.
444.	*Nehemiah's first visit to Jerusalem* (Neh. 2[1]).	336.	Darius Codomannus.
		333.	Persian empire overthrown by Alexander the Great.
432.	*Nehemiah's second visit to Jerusalem* (Neh. 13[6f.]).		

As remarked above (p. 516), Ezra and Nehemiah form in the Jewish canon a single book, "Ezra." This book embraces the period from the return of the exiles under Zerubbabel, B.C. 536, to the second visit of Nehemiah in B.C. 432 ; but the history is not told continuously: it is confined chiefly to certain periods or occasions of importance, viz. the return, and events immediately following it (B.C. 536), the rebuilding of the Temple (B.C. 520–16), and the visits of Ezra and Nehemiah in B.C. 458, 444, and 432. [508] Parts of the Book of Ezra are written in Aramaic (4^8–6^{18} ; 7^{12-26}).

Contents. I. Ezr. 1–6. Events issuing in the restoration of the Temple. C. 1. The edict of Cyrus (B.C. 536), granting the Jews permission to return to Jerusalem, and to take back with them the sacred vessels which Nebuchadnezzar had removed to Babylon. C. 2. A register of the numbers and families of those who availed themselves of this permission. C. 3. The altar of Burnt-offering is set up, and the feast of Booths observed ($v.^{1-7}$) ; in the 2nd month of the 2nd year (B.C. 534) the foundations of the Temple are laid amid the mingled rejoicings and regrets of the people ($v.^{8-13}$). C. 4. The "adversaries of Judah and Benjamin" (chiefly, as the context shows, Samaritans) ask permission to assist in the task of rebuilding the Temple, which is refused by Zerubbabel and Jeshua : they exert themselves consequently with success to stop the further progress of the restoration till the second year of Darius (B.C. 520), $v.^{1-5.\ 24}$. $V.^{6.\ 7-23}$ deal with a different matter, viz. the interruption of the work of rebuilding the *city walls,* caused by misrepresentations made by the enemies of the Jews at the Persian court, under *Xerxes* (B.C. 485–465), and *Artaxerxes* (B.C. 465–425). C. 5. B.C. 520, at the instigation of the prophets Haggai and Zechariah, the restoration of the Temple is resumed : Tattenai, the Persian governor of the provinces west of Euphrates, and Shethar-bozenai, in doubt whether it should be permitted to proceed, make a formal application to Darius for instructions (5^{3-17}) ; a favourable answer is returned by him (6^{1-12}) ; the work in consequence advances rapidly ; and the restored Temple is solemnly dedicated in the 6th year of Darius, B.C. 516 (6^{13-18}). There follows a brief notice of the Passover of the following year (6^{19-22}) ; and with this the first part of the Book of Ezra ends. Between 6^{22} and 7^1 there is an interval of nearly *sixty years.*

II. Ezr. 7–10. The journey of the scribe and priest Ezra to Jerusalem in the 7th year of Artaxerxes (458 B.C.), and the reforms introduced by him upon his arrival there. C. 7, after stating who Ezra was, and mentioning briefly how he obtained leave to return to Jerusalem with such of the Jews as were disposed to accompany him (v.[1-10]), recites (in Aramaic) the edict of Artaxerxes, defining the terms of Ezra's commission, and authorizing the different Persian officers west of the Euphrates to afford him (within certain specified limits) such assistance as he might need (v.[12-26]). The edict ended, Ezra speaks in the *first* person to the end of c. 9. First, after an expression of thankfulness (7[29f.]) to the God of his fathers for having thus put it into the [509] heart of the Persian king to benefit his nation, he states (c. 8) the numbers of his countrymen who accompanied him to Jerusalem, and describes the journey thither: afterwards (c. 9) he relates how he learnt that the Jews in Judah had contracted numerous foreign marriages, for which he makes solemn confession to God in the name of his people (v.[4-15]). In c. 10 the narrative is resumed in the *third* person. Certain of the leading Jews express their willingness to reform the abuse : Ezra, having exacted a promise from them to abide by their word, summons a general assembly of the people, and expostulates with them on their dereliction of duty; they undertake to put away their foreign wives; and the chapter closes with a list of the offenders.

The Book of Nehemiah falls into three main divisions, c. 1–7, c. 8–10, c. 11–13. I. In Neh. 1–7 the narrative is told in the *first* person. In c. 1–2 Nehemiah relates the occasion of his visit to Jerusalem. Tidings reached him in Shushan of the ruined condition of the walls of Jerusalem; being cup-bearer to Artaxerxes, the grief manifest on his countenance attracted the notice of the king, and he succeeded in obtaining permission to visit Jerusalem for the purpose of effecting their restoration. Upon his arrival there he induced a number of the leading Jewish families to co-operate with him; and successfully defeated the efforts made by the Jews' enemies, Sanballat the Horonite, Tobiah the "servant," and Gashmu the Arabian to interfere with the progress of the work (c. 3–4). C. 5 he relates how he persuaded the wealthier of his fellow-countrymen no longer to treat their impoverished brethren as slaves (viz. by holding them in bondage for debt); and describes his own solicitude not to be chargeable to the people during the time that he held the office of governor among them. C. 6 he narrates the fresh efforts made by Sanballat, Tobiah, and

Gashmu to hinder the completion of the walls, and the series of unsuccessful attempts made by them to allure him to a personal conference. Provision having been made, 7^{1-3}, for the safe custody of the gates, Nehemiah determines, $7^{4f.}$, to take measures to augment the number of residents in the city. Before, however, describing how he does this, he inserts in his narrative the list found by him of the exiles who returned with Zerubbabel 90 years previously, 7^{6-73}. This list agrees [510] (except for verbal alterations, which, however, are somewhat numerous) with Ezra, c. 2.

II. Neh. 8–10. In this division of the book, Nehemiah no longer speaks in the first person; and *Ezra*, assisted by the Levites, appears as the chief actor. The people, on the 1st day of the 7th month, assembled on "the broad space before the water-gate," express a desire to have the Law read to them. Ezra, supported by the Levites, responds to their request; and they are deeply impressed by the words which they hear, 8^{1-12}. On the following day the reading is continued; and finding the observance of the feast of Booths inculcated (Lev. $23^{40, 42}$), they celebrate it solemnly in accordance with the instructions, 8^{13-18}. Two days after the close of the feast, on the 24th of the 7th month, the people assemble again in order publicly to acknowledge their sins, 9^{1-3}, the Levites—or, more probably, Ezra (see v.[6] LXX)—leading their devotions in the long confession, v.$^{6-37}$. At the end, v.^{38}, the confession passes into a covenant, which is solemnly sealed by Nehemiah and other representatives of the people, 10^{1-27}, the terms of the covenant, reciting the obligations taken by the people upon themselves, being afterwards stated in detail, v.$^{28-39}$.

III. Neh. 11–13, of miscellaneous contents. (1) C. 11 : *a.* v.$^{1-24}$ (the sequel to 7^4) the names of those men (one in ten) taken by lot to reside in Jerusalem; * *b.* v.$^{25-36}$ a list of the villages and towns in the neighbourhood which were occupied by the returned Israelites. (2) 12^{1-26}: *a.* v.$^{1-9}$ a list of the priests and Levites who returned with Zerubbabel in 536; *b.* v.$^{10-11}$ the series of high priests from Joshua to Jaddua (536–331 B.C.); † *c.* v.$^{12-21}$ the heads of families of the priests in the time of the high priest Joiakim, son of Jeshua (499–463 B.C.); *d.* v.$^{22-26}$

---

* V.$^{4-18a}$ is repeated in 1 Ch. 9^{9-17a}.

† Forming the sequel, for the *post*-exilic period, to 1 Ch. 6^{9-15}.

chief Levitical families to the time of Johanan (383–351). (3) 12²⁷⁻⁴³ Nehemiah's own account (in the *first* person) of the dedication of the walls. (4) 12⁴⁴⁻⁴⁷ the appointment, at the same time, of officers to collect the dues of the priests and Levites; and the liberality shown by the community for the maintenance of the porters and singers. (5) C. 13. Nehemiah's narrative (in the *first* person) of his second visit (12 years later) to Jerusalem, of his removal of the heathen Tobiah from the [**511**] precincts of the Temple v.⁴⁻⁹, and of the measures taken by him to secure the payment of their dues to the Levites v.¹⁰⁻¹⁴, to ensure the observance of the Sabbath v.¹⁵⁻²², and to prevent marriages with foreign women v.²³⁻³¹.

Structure.—The Books of Ezra and Nehemiah are a compilation made by an author (to all appearance identical with the Chronicler) writing long after the age of Ezra and Nehemiah themselves, on the basis, partly, of the authentic "memoirs" (as the parts written in the first person are generally termed) of those two reformers, and partly of other materials.* The compilatory character of the two books is apparent from many indications:— (1) The change, in both, from the 1st to the 3rd person, and *vice versâ*, which one and the same writer might make, as Thucydides does, at wide intervals in his work,† but which is not probable in nearly contiguous sections. (2) The unevenness in the treatment of the history. There are long periods on which the narrative is silent: in one case especially (Ezr. 6²²–7¹), an interval of sixty years, *immediately before Ezra's own time*, being passed over by the words, "After these things," in a manner not credible if the writer were Ezra himself, but perfectly natural if the writer lived in an age to which the period B.C. 516–458 was visible only in a distant perspective. (3) The style and language differ. In certain parts of the two books the *personality* of the writers is very prominent; it is conspicuous both in their tone and manner and in their phraseology: other parts show much less force and originality, and at the same time exhibit close affinities with the style of the Chronicler.

* So also now Prof. Sayce (*Monuments*, pp. 537, 538, 548), abandoning his former view (*Introd. to Ezr. Neh. Est.*, 1885, p. 29 f.) that the Book of Ezra is the work of Ezra himself.

† The change from the 3rd person to the 1st in Thuc. 5, 26 arises manifestly from the nature of the fact to be narrated.

Passages bearing the impress of Ezra's and Nehemiah's personality hardly need to be quoted: some illustrations of Nehemiah's style will be found below. The phraseology of the Chronicler is especially noticeable in Ezr. 1, 3, 6^{16-22} 7^{1-10}, Neh. $12^{22-26. 43-47}$.

(4) The books contain internal marks of having been compiled in an age long subsequent to that of Ezr. and Neh. Thus notice :—

(*a*) The phrase "King *of Persia*," Ezr. $1^{1. 2. 8}$ 3^7 $4^{3. 5. 7. 24}$ 7^1 : the addition would, during the period of the Persian supremacy, be at once unnecessary and contrary to contemporary usage (see p. 546, *n.*): the expression used by Ezr. and Neh., when speaking in their [512] own person (Ezr. $7^{27f.}$ $8^{1. 22. 25. 36}$, Neh. 1^{11} $2^{1ff. 18f.}$ $5^{4. 14}$ 6^7 13^6), or in passages extracted from sources written under the Persian rule (Ezr. $4^{8. 11. 17. 23}$ $5^{6f. 13f. 17}$ $6^{1. 3. 13. 15 *}$ $7^{7. 11. 21}$, Neh. $11^{23. 24}$), is simply "the king" (so Hag. $1^{1. 15}$, Zech. 7^1). The observation is due to Ewald, *Hist*. i. 173.

(*b*) Neh. $12^{11. 22}$ Jaddua, three generations later than Eliashib, the contemporary of Nehemiah, high priest B.C. 351–331, is mentioned.†

(*c*) Neh. 12^{22} "Darius the Persian" must (from the context) be Darius Codomannus, the last king of Persia, B.C. 336–332: and the title "the Persian" could only have become a distinctive one after the Persian period was past.

(*d*) Neh. $12^{26. 47}$ the "days of Nehemiah" are spoken of in terms clearly implying that the writer looked back upon them as past.

(*e*) Other indications of the same fact will appear below ; *e.g.* the position of Ezr. 4^{6-23} (which, referring, as it does, to what happened under Xerxes and Artaxerxes, could not possibly have been placed where it now stands by Ezra, a *contemporary* of the latter), the contents and character of 7^{1-10}, &c.

The two books may now be considered briefly in detail.

Ezr. 1–6, which, even if written by Ezra, would not be the work of a contemporary, consists only partially of extracts from earlier documents ; other parts are shown by their style to be the work of the Chronicler, such materials, whether written or traditional, as were at his disposal being (in accordance with his custom) considerably expanded. In c. 1 the edict of Cyrus (to judge from its Jewish phraseology and Jewish point of view) is, no doubt, recited only in general terms, not reproduced with

---

* In 6^{14b} the words "and Artaxerxes, king of Persia," can hardly (on account of the context) be part of the original narrative.

† It is sometimes supposed that both this genealogy and the one in 1 Ch. $3^{21ff.}$ may have originally ended at an earlier stage, the later names being filled in subsequently. But even supposing this to have been the case, the other marks of late composition which the books contain would still remain.

literal exactness.* The interest of the writer (as in the [513] Chronicles) centres evidently in the Temple; hence he dwells more on the restoration of the sacred vessels than on the particulars of the journey homewards (contrast Ezra himself, 8¹⁵ff.).† The register in c. 2 has every appearance of being a nearly contemporary document,‡ but it must have been derived immediately by the compiler from Neh. 7, where it was incorporated by Nehemiah — who states that he found it himself — in his memoirs.

The passage Ezr. 2⁶⁸f· (on the offerings to the treasury and for the priests' vestments) differs considerably from the parallel Neh. 7⁷⁰⁻⁷²; and in neither, probably, is it quite in its original form (cf. Kuen. § 34. 3; Stade, *Gesch.* ii. 108; Meyer, p. 195). In Ezr. 2⁶⁸⁻⁶⁹ᵃ there is an insertion in the text of Neh. 7⁷¹, which shows marks of the compiler's hand (*e.g.* התנדב, העמיד, p. 535 ff., Nos. 23, 4; cf. also v.⁶⁸ᵃ with 1³ᵇ· ⁴ᵇ). The introduction to the sequel of the list in Neh. was borrowed by the compiler of Ezra at the same time (for the "seventh month" belongs, in Neh., to a year previously stated, whereas here no year to which it can be referred has been named): hence the remarkable similarity of Ezr. 3¹ (to *as one man to*) and Neh. 7⁷³ᵇ–8¹ᵃ.

3¹–4⁵ is similar in literary character to c. 1, c. 3 in particular displaying throughout marks of the compiler's style, and being

* Comp. Ewald, *Hist.* v. 48 f.; Ryssel, p. 4 ff.; Schrader, *KAT.*² p.372 f.; Meyer, p. 49. Persia was absorbed and lost in the wider empire of which, by Cyrus' conquest of Babylon, the Achæmenidæ became the heirs; hence after that date their standing official title is not "King of Persia," but "King of Babylon" (*Records of the Past*, 1st series, ix. 67; cf. 2nd series, v. 166, and comp. Ezr. 5¹³), or, more commonly, "the King," "the great King," "King of kings, "King of the lands," &c. (often in combination): see the series of inscriptions of Persian kings in *Records*, 1st series, i. 111 ff. (Behistun), v. 151 ff., ix. 67–88; also the Aramaic funereal inscription found at Saqqarah, near Memphis, in 1877 (*CIS.* II. i. No. 122), dated the 4tʜ year of [מלכיא וי מלכא חשיארש, *i.e.* of "Xerxes, King of k[ings]"; and βασιλεὺς βασιλέων Δαρεῖος ὁ 'Υστάσπεω Γαδάται δούλωι τάδε λέγει, in the interesting decree cited by Meyer, p. 19: comp. Ezr. 7¹². ("King of Persia" is used of Cyrus only *before* his conquest of Babylon, *Records*, 2nd series, v. 160; and of Darius only exceptionally, in the midst of other titles, *ib.* 1st series, i. 111. By their subjects the Persian kings are also styled "King of Babylon," or "King of the lands" (often in combination): see the numerous contract-tablets belonging to the reigns of Cyrus, Cambyses, and Darius, published in Schrader's *Keilinschr. Bibliothek*, iv. 259–311.)

† In the language of c. 1, notice *e.g.* v.¹ (=2 Ch. 36²²) ⁵ העיר רוח, as 1 Ch. 5²⁶, 2 Ch. 21¹⁶ [also Jer. 51¹¹, Hag. 1¹⁴↑]; v.⁶ מגרנות, 2 Ch. 21³ 32²³ [also Gen. 24⁵³ J]; and see the list, p. 535 ff., Nos. 9, 20, 23, 28, 30, 45.

‡ Cf. Meyer, p. 190 ff.; also Wellh. *Gött. gel. Anz.*, 1897, p. 94 (where he qualifies what he had said in *Die Rückkehr*, &c. [below, p. 552], p. 11 ff.).

manifestly his composition, constructed, it may be reasonably supposed, upon a traditional basis.

Notice, for instance, $3^{2\,end}$, to offer וג' כבתוב, 2 Ch. 23^{18b}, cf. 31^3 $35^{12.\ 26}$, Ezr. 6^{18} (Aram.), Neh. $10^{34.\ 36}$ [Heb. $^{35.\ 37}$], 1 Ch. 16^{40}; *the man of God*, as 1 Ch. 23^{14}, 2 Ch. 24^9, esp. 30^{16} (likewise of Moses: of David 2 Ch. 8^{14}, Neh. $12^{24.\ 36}$); v.^{3} the strange sentence כי באימה עליהם, 2 Ch. 16^{10} כי בועף עמו (cf. p. 535 ff., No. 27); עלות לבקר ולערב 1 Ch. 16^{40}, 2 Ch. 2^3; v.^{4} יום ביום (*ib.* No. 29); כמשפט *according to the ordinance*, cf. 1 Ch. 23^{31} במספר כמשפט עליהם (also 1 Ch. 15^{13}, 2 Ch. 4^{20} 35^{13}, Neh. 8^{18}); v.^{5} התנרב *to offer freely* (*ib.* No. 23); v.$^{8.\ 10}$ העמיד *to appoint* (No. 4); v.^{8} נצח על *to preside over* (No. 21: esp. 1 Ch. 23^4 על ידי דוד; v.^{10} לנצח על מלאכת בית יהוה (No. 34: esp. 2 Ch. 23^{18}); v.^{11} בהלל ובחורות (No. 16, and for the inf., No. 28: cf. also 2 Ch. 5^{13} generally); v.^{12b} the use of ב (No. 41); להרים קול (phrase as 2 Ch. 5^{13}: constr. with ל as No. 32); v.^{13} עד ל (No. 38; esp. 2 Ch. 26^{15}). See further on this chapter Schrader, *l.c.* p. 481 ff.; Ryssel, p. xxi.

[514] The account, $3^{2f.}$, of the erection of the *altar* is confirmed independently by the allusion in Hag. 2^{14}: but in connexion with 3^{8-13} a difficulty arises; and Schrader, in his study on Ezr. 1-6 in the *St. u. Krit.* 1867, adduces strong reasons (p. 460 ff.) for supposing the foundation of the *Temple* to have been ante-dated by the compiler (comp. Steiner, *Comm. on Hagg.* p. 322, and Kuenen, § 34. 4). The *earlier* narrative of 5^2 speaks of Zerubbabel and Jeshua as "beginning to build the house of God," not in 535, but in 520; Hag. $2^{15.\ 18}$ names expressly the 24th day of the 9th month in Darius' second year (520) as that on which the foundations of the Temple were laid (comp. Zech. 8^9); and the terms of 5^{16b} appear to preclude the idea of any interruption having occurred since the work was begun. Thus all contemporary sources mention only a foundation of the Temple in the 2nd year of Darius; a foundation in the 2nd year of the return appears to have no better authority than a tradition committed to writing some 200 years subsequently. It is difficult, however, to think that this tradition can have arisen without some historical basis; and the truth probably is that the ceremony described in Ezr. 3^{8-13} was one of a purely *formal* character, such as Haggai could afford to disregard altogether (cf. Stade, ii. 122 f.; Ryle, p. xxxiii f.; Meyer, p. 44 f.; and on the other side, König, *Einl.* p. 281 ff.).

The sequel of 4^5 is 4^{24}. The section 4^{6-23}—containing the notice of the letter to "Ahasuerus," and the correspondence with Artachshasta—relates to a different and subsequent period, and is here out of place: it relates, viz., to the interruptions caused by the Samaritans and other enemies of the Jews to the project of rebuilding—not the Temple, but—the *city walls* (cf. Neh. 1^3), probably shortly before the 20th year of Artaxerxes (B.C. 444), when Nehemiah (Neh. 2^1) succeeded in impressing the Persian king favourably on behalf of his nation; and helps to fill up the gap between Ezra 10 and Neh. 1.

This is apparent from two independent considerations. (1) *Achashwêrosh* and *Artachshasta* in v.[6. 7] are elsewhere regularly the Hebrew forms of the names which we know as Xerxes * and Artaxerxes † respectively; these two kings, however, reigned long after the age of Cyrus or Darius (v.[5]), viz. 485–465, and 465–425; (2) in 4[1-5] all that the Jews are represented as contemplating is the rebuilding of the *Temple*; so in the sequel, 4[24], only the Temple is referred to; ‡ in the two letters, on the contrary, mention is made throughout of nothing but the rebuilding of the *city walls* (v.[12. 13. 16. 21]). [515] This, however, was the work which, as we know from Neh., the Jews took up in the days of Artaxerxes. The allusion in v.[12] appears to be to the Jews who had returned in 458 with Ezra.

All recent writers on Ezra agree in this view of the *contents* of 4[6-23]: they differ only in their explanation of the disregard of chronological sequence shown here by the compiler. Bertheau, Keil, Oettli suppose that, though aware in fact that the section related to occurrences some 80 years later than the period he was describing (4[1-5] c. 5–6), he inserted it here "episodically," or with the view of "giving a synopsis of the entire series of hostilities experienced by the Jews at the hands of their neighbours." But this explanation cannot be deemed a probable one; it is difficult to think that a method which could only mislead and confuse the reader would have been adopted by the compiler intentionally. It is far more natural to suppose that, for some reason, the true reference of the section was not perceived by him; and that he referred by error to troubles connected with the restoration of the Temple what related in fact to the restoration of the city walls (so also Ryle, p. 66; Meyer, p. 14 ff.).

The letter to Artaxerxes, and his reply, 4[8-23], are taken by the compiler from an *Aramaic* source; 4[24] is generally thought to have been added by him partly as a comment on his interpretation of their contents (Schrader, p. 474; Ryssel; Kuenen; Meyer, p. 14), partly for the purpose of connecting 4[1-5] with 5[1ff.].

5[1]–6[18] is another extract from an Aramaic source, the same, probably, as that from which 4[8-23] is derived.

* In the Persian inscriptions *Khshyârsha* or *Khshayârshâ*, with which the form used in *contemporary* Aramaic (p. 546, *note*) closely agrees.

† In the Persian inscriptions *Artakhshathrâ*.

‡ The case is the same in c. 5–6; in 5[3. 8. 9] the words rendered "walls" are different from the one in 4[12. 13. 16] (שור = Heb. חומה; *e.g.* 2 Sa. 11[20] Targ.), and do not denote the walls of a *city* (5[3. 9] אשרנא of uncertain meaning; 5[8] כחל = Heb. קיר; *e.g.* 1 Ki. 6[5. 6] Targ., of the Temple, and Dan. 5[5] of Belshazzar's palace).

What the nature of this Aramaic source may have been, can, of course, only be conjectured ; Bertheau, p. 6 (=Ryssel, p. xiii), supposes it to have been a narrative of the troubles which arose between the returned exiles and their neighbours, down to the period of Artaxerxes. Stade (ii. 188) thinks it may have been a more comprehensive history of the restored community. It certainly appears to have been a thoroughly trustworthy document (cf. Stade, ii. 100), though the edicts contained in it, so far as their *form* is concerned, [516] are open to the suspicion of having been coloured by their transmission through Jewish hands. Notice in 6⁹. ¹⁰ the technical expressions of the Jewish law ; in v.¹²ᵃ a phrase characteristic of Dt. (p. 101, No. 35) ; and cf. pp. 537, No. 29, 553 (Kuenen, § 34. 9). The dialect in which it is written (including the edicts) is the Western, or *Palestinian*, Aramaic (p. 503).*

6¹⁹⁻²² (where the Hebrew recommences) the compiler (as is plain from the phraseology) speaks again in his own person.†

The second section of the book, c. 7–10, dealing with Ezra's own age, there is no reason to doubt, is throughout either written by Ezra or based upon materials left by him. 7²⁷–9¹⁵— with the exception, as it seems, of occasional glosses or slight additions made by the compiler—is thus an extract from Ezra's own memoirs. But 7¹⁻¹⁰ is certainly not Ezra's work, though doubtless composed on the basis of Ezra's materials ; it is mani- festly a summary account of Ezra, prefixed by the compiler as an introduction to the excerpt from Ezra's memoirs which follows.

In 7¹⁻¹⁰ notice (*a*) the omission of Ezra's immediate ancestors (for Seraiah was contemporary with Zedekiah, 2 Ki. 25¹⁸. ²¹, 130 years previously to Ezra's time) ; (*b*) the fact that v.⁷⁻⁹ *anticipates* c. 8 ; (*c*) the expressions of the com- piler in v.¹⁰ (p. 536, Nos. 6, 7 ; esp. 2 Ch. 12¹⁴ 19³ 30¹⁹). The phrase in v.⁶ ᵉⁿᵈ. ⁹ ᵉⁿᵈ will have been taken naturally from Ezra's memoirs (see 7²⁸). In 7²⁷–9¹⁵, the clause in 8²⁰ "whom," &c., for instance, reads like an explanatory gloss ; notice also *v*, never besides in Ezr. Neh., and only twice

---

* Meyer (pp. 8 ff., 41 ff.) defends the authenticity of the letters and edicts (4¹¹⁻²² 5⁷⁻¹⁷ 6³⁻¹² 7¹²⁻²⁶) in their existing form (except 6¹²ᵃ), supposing the Jewish colouring of the latter to be due to the fact that they were drawn up in the first instance by Ezra and other Jews possessing influence at the Persian court, and were then accepted without material modification by the king. Cf. the criticism of Wellh., *Gött. gel. Anzeigen*, 1897, No. 2, p. 89 ff.; and Meyer's reply, *Julius Wellhausen u. meine Schrift, Die Entstehung des Judenthums*, 1897 (see, briefly, the *Expos. Times*, 1897, Apr. p. 320 ff., June, p. 415 f.).

† Probably, indeed (Schrad. p. 477 ; Ryssel, pp. xiv, xix ; Kuen. § 34. 9 ; Meyer, p. 13), v.¹⁶⁻¹⁸ are also due to the compiler, who, designing them as the conclusion of the *Aramaic* narrative of the building of the Temple, may have written them in the same language. Wellh. [below, p. 552], p. 13, remarks on the appearance in v.¹⁶ of בני הגולה, a favourite expression of the compiler's (4¹ 6¹⁹. ²⁰ 8³⁵ 10⁷. ¹⁶).

in Ch. (I 5^{20} 27^{27}); the last clause of the verse includes a phrase of the compiler's (p. 536, No. 12). And $8^{35f.}$ (unlike the context) is written without reference to Ezra himself; it is not improbable therefore that it may have been condensed by the compiler from Ezra's own more detailed and personal description. The decree of Artaxerxes, 7^{12-26}, as is evident from the terms of 7^{27}, must also have stood in Ezra's memoirs, though it may have been cast into its present form by one familiar with the terminology of the Jewish sacred books (see v.^{13b} [p. 537, No. 23] $^{15.\ 16.\ 17.\ 24.\ 26}$; comp. Ewald, i. 191). The dialect, as before, is the Palestinian Aramaic. In *substance*, it is undoubtedly genuine (Stade, ii. 153).

C. 10, though the immediate sequel of c. 9, is distinguished from it by the use of the third person, and also by being in parts considerably less circumstantial (see especially the brief and incomplete notices in v.$^{15.\ 16f.}$) : at the same time, in other [517] respects the particulars are full and graphic (v.$^{9b.\ 13}$); so that in all probability the narrative has merely been somewhat altered in form, and abridged, from the memoirs of Ezra.*

Neh. 1^1–7^{73a} is an excerpt, to all appearance unaltered, from the memoirs of Nehemiah,—the register, 7^{6-73a} (relating to the time of Zerubbabel), being expressly stated in v.^{5b} to have been an earlier document, found by Nehemiah, and incorporated by him in his memoirs.

In Neh. 7^{73b}–c. 10 *Ezra* reappears ; and both Ezra and Nehemiah are mentioned in the third person (8^{1-6} &c.: in 8^9 10^1 alone Nehemiah receives the Persian title, " the Tirshatha " [cf. $7^{65.\ 70}$, Ezr. 2^{63} of Zerubbabel]). The connexion of the section with 1^1–7^{73a} is also imperfect: for 7^{73b} c. 8 is not the sequel to 7^{4-5} (Neh.'s purpose to class the people genealogically), but relates to an entirely different matter, viz. the people's engaging to observe the Mosaic law. It cannot therefore be regarded as a continuation of Nehemiah's narrative, though it is not questioned that it is based upon a well-informed, contemporary source, perhaps here and there modified by the compiler : by many critics this source is supposed to have been the memoirs of Ezra.

So Ewald, *Hist.* i. 192 ; Berth. p. 8 ; Schrader, *Einl.* § 237 ; Ryssel, pp. xvi, xx ; Oettli, p. 150 ; and at least for 9^6–10^{40} (except the list of names, 10^{3-14} [$^{2-13}$]) Stade, *Gesch.* ii. 153, 178, 179, who points to the great similarity of the prayer in c. 9 with that in Ezr. 9 (in Neh. 9^6 the words *And Ezra*

---

* Keil's explanation (*Einl.* § 146. 3) of the change of person is most inadequate.

spake should very possibly be restored from the LXX : so Berth., Ryssel, Stade). It is true, the section exhibits *some* affinities with the style of the compiler ; but they are not here sufficiently numerous or marked to indicate identity of author : they are rather (as in the case of Ezr. 7^{27} c. 9) due to the fact that the theme is in part similar (the functions of the Levites, theocratic ordinances, &c.), and that some of the expressions used by the Chronicler were already current in Ezra's time. It is remarked justly by Kuenen, that in point of grammar and literary style Neh. 7^{73b}-c. 10 stands on a much higher level than the narratives which proceed from the pen of the Chronicler : so the prayer in c. 9, for instance, shows no traces of his peculiar mannerisms. For details of the style, see Kuenen, § 34. 13.

To c. 11, on the other hand, the remark in 7^4 forms a natural introduction,* though the narrative is hardly continued *uno* [518] *tenore*, for no allusion is made to the " assembly " mentioned in 7^5, and the absence of all notice of Nehemiah's initiative, so prominent in 7^{1-5}, is remarkable. In all probability, the particulars contained in c. 11 are based upon materials left by Nehemiah himself, or dating from his time, but not strictly a continuation of the memoirs of 1^1-7^{73a}.

In c. 12 f., 12^{27-43} 13^{1-31} (in the first person) are two additional extracts from Nehemiah's memoirs, the former probably in the introductory and concluding verses ($12^{27-30. 42f.}$) somewhat altered in form, or glossed, by the compiler.† The lists in $12^{1-7. 8f. 12-21}$ may be regarded as derived from other, older sources, accessible to the compiler : it is a plausible conjecture of Wellh.'s that the " Book of Chronicles " mentioned in 12^{23} is one of them : $12^{10f. 22-26}$ (relating to circumstances *after* the age of Nehemiah), and 12^{44-47} (in which " the days of Nehemiah " are referred to as past), will be due to the compiler.‡

It is manifest that we possess the memoirs neither of Ezra nor of Nehemiah in their integrity. Those of Ezra, besides showing in parts (see above) marks of condensation, end (as it seems) in the midst of the narrative of his reforms (cf. Kuenen, *Ges. Abhandlungen*, p. 245 ff.) : in those of Neh., 7^{5a} promises what is not described, and the account of the dedication of the walls is introduced abruptly, and without mention of the date or other circumstances

---

* So Ew. v. 159 *note*; Kuen. § 29. 9 ; Smend, p. 23 ; Stade, ii. 98, 174 ; Ryssel, p. xix ; Meyer, p. 99.

† Comp. 12^{43} with 2 Ch. 20^{27}, Ezr. 6^{22} (also 3^{13}) ; and cf. Meyer, p. 103 f.

‡ Notice also the resemblance of 12^{24b} with 2 Ch. 5^{13} 8^{14} 29^{25}, and with 1 Ch. 26^{16} (" ward against ward " ; cf. v. ^{12}) : the absence of the verb in 12^{44b} (p. 537, No. 27) ; 12^{45b}, 2 Ch. 35^{15} (also 8^{14} 35^{4b}) ; 12^{46} the infin. as subst. (p. 537, No. 28), and 2 Ch. 29^{30} 35^{15}. Cf. Meyer, pp. 94, 97 *n*.

which Neh.'s generally careful and methodical style would entitle us to expect. The connexion of 13¹ (or 13⁴) with what precedes is also imperfect ; comp. Ryssel, pp. xvii, 346 ; Kuen. § 33. 13.*

It does not fall within the scope of the present volume to discuss the different views that have been held of recent years respecting the *history* of the restoration-period ; though, as they have some bearing on the narrative of Ezr.-Neh., a brief notice of them may not be out of place. The controversy has been carried on chiefly between van Hoonacker, Kuenen, Kosters, Wellhausen, and Ed. Meyer. Van Hoonacker (*Néhémie et Esdras, nouvelle hypothèse*, &c., 1890) places the mission of Ezra *after* Neh., in the 7th year of Artaxerxes *II*. (B.C. 397) ; his view was criticised at length by Kuenen, *Ges. Abhandlungen*, p. 212 ff.; and he replied in *Néhémie en l'an 20 d'Artax. I.*, &c., 1892 ; *Zorob. et le second Temple*, 1892, and *Nouvelles études sur la restauration*, &c., 1896. W. H. Kosters (*Het herstel van Israël in het Perzische tijdvak*, 1894 ; Germ. tr. by Basedow, 1895) argues that *no* exiles returned from Babylon in 536, the list in Ezr. 2 relates really to the time of Neh., the temple was built by the Jews left behind in the land (2 Ki. 25¹². ²²⁻²⁶), Ezra was the first to lead back a body of exiles from Babylon, which he did, not before, but *after*, Neh., *c*. 433 ; it was the Chronicler who first ascribed the rebuilding of the Temple to the returned exiles (the " Gola "), the founder of the later spiritual aristocracy of Judaism, whom he represents (unhistorically) as actuated from the first (Ezr. 1–3) by anxiety for the restoration of the Temple-worship (cf. Wildeboer, *Die Litt. des AT.s*, pp. 411 f., 419 f.; Cheyne, *Introd. to Is.* pp. xxxv–xxxvii). The difficulties attaching to Kosters' view (though he makes some concessions to him) are pointed out by Wellh. in *Die Rückkehr der Juden aus dem bab. Exil* (from the Göttingen *Nachrichten* for 1895, No. 2). Kosters has replied to Wellh. in the *Th. T.* 1895, p. 549 ff. Meyer (above, p. 540) discusses at length the contents of Ezr.-Neh.: he defends (against Kosters) the ordinarily accepted view of the history of the restoration-period, and (against Wellhausen, who, though he does not question the general course of events as told in Ezr. 1–7, regards the documents quoted as free compositions of the writer) the genuineness of the documents quoted in Ezr. 4–7 (cf. A. R. S. Kennedy in the *Expository Times*, March 1897, p. 268 ff.; and see also above, p. 549 *n*.). Although, however, Meyer holds that in these cases the Chronicler has preserved genuine documents, his general estimate of him as a historian is highly unfavourable, and he refers frequently to his representations as unhistorical and imaginative (*e.g.* pp. 1, 13 (Ezr. 6¹⁶⁻²²; cf. p. 130), 49 (the terms of the edict of Cyrus, Ezr. 1²⁻⁴), 72 (Ezr. 1⁹⁻¹¹), 73 (Ezr. 3), 92 *n.*, 97 *n.* 2, 106 (Neh. 11²⁵⁻³⁶), 124 (Ezr. 4¹⁻⁵; cf. pp. 14, 44, 74, 204), 140, 161, 164, 189 f. (Neh. 11³⁻¹⁹. ²¹⁻²⁴), 203). Meyer considers that the sole authority which the Chronicler had for the period between the return and Ezra (Ezr. 1–6) was the " book of Chronicles " mentioned in Neh. 12²³, from which Ezr. 5³–6¹⁴ᵃ. ¹⁵ 4⁶⁻²³ are excerpted, but which narrated the circumstances of the

---

* That 13¹⁻³ is not to be referred to the compiler, appears both from the general difference of tone and from אשר v.¹, and " our God " v.² (see p. 553). With v.¹ᵇ comp. 8¹⁴ᶠ.

return only in the briefest possible terms : all other details in Ezr. 1–6, except 2¹–3¹ (derived from Nehemiah's memoirs, Neh. 7¹–8¹ᵃ), and 5¹⁻² (based upon Hag. and Zech.), are due simply to the Chronicler's "*sehr ergiebige Phantasie*" (pp. 13, 74 f., 104, 203 f.).

On the style of Ezra and Nehemiah much need not be said. From a literary point of view, Nehemiah's memoirs are superior to other parts of the two books. Nehemiah writes Hebrew easily and naturally. As might be expected, his memoirs contain examples of late words and idioms ; * but they are much less numerous and marked than those which occur in the writings of [519] the Chronicler ; his syntax also is more classical than his. Ezra's style approaches slightly more than Neh.'s does to that of the compiler ; this may be partly due to modifications which the compiler has allowed himself to introduce into his extracts from Ezra's memoirs : partly it may be due to the fact that Ezra was a priest, and consequently used more words belonging to the priestly terminology than Nehemiah did.

Examples of recurring phrases in the memoirs of Neh.:—

My God, 2⁸· ¹²· ¹⁸ 5¹⁹ 6¹⁴ 7⁵ 13¹⁴· ²²· ²⁹· ³¹.

החרים והסגנים *nobles and deputies*, for the magnates of Judah : 2¹⁶ᵇ 4¹⁴· ¹⁹ 5⁷ 7⁵ : cf. *the nobles of Judah* 6¹⁷ 13¹⁷ : † the "deputies" 2¹⁶ᵃ 5¹⁷ 12⁴⁰ 13¹¹. (סגנים only Ezr. 9² in this sense besides.)

His נערים *young men* are mentioned : 4²³ 5¹⁰ 13¹⁹.

Remember unto me, O my God, for good (or similar phrases): 5¹⁹ 6¹⁴ 13¹⁴· ²²· ²⁹· ³¹.

God of heaven 1⁴· ⁵ 2⁴· ²⁰ is a post-exilic expression often used in converse with heathen, or placed in their mouth : Ezr. 1² (= 2 Ch. 36²³) 5¹¹· ¹² 6⁹· ¹⁰ 7¹²· ²¹· ²³, Jon. 1⁹, Dan. 2¹⁸· ¹⁹· ³⁷· ⁴⁴. Only once earlier, Gen. 24⁷ J (where, however, "and God of the earth" has perhaps fallen out : so LXX, cf. v.³).

Neh. is also fond of אשר = *that* (כי), which is found also in Dan. Eccl. Est., and *occasionally* in pre-exilic writings, but is used very rarely (2 Ch. 2⁷) by the Chronicler. See Neh. 2⁵· ¹⁰ 4⁶ 7⁶⁵ (= Ezr. 2⁶³) 8¹⁴· ¹⁵ 10³¹ 13¹· ¹⁹· ²².

Our God is an expression occurring frequently in the parts assigned above to the memoirs of both Ezr. and Neh.: it is never used by the Chronicler when speaking in his own person.

NOTE.—In the Greek Bible, the Book of Ezra appears in two forms :

---

* As 2⁶ זמן ; 4²³ (Heb. ¹⁷) אין with the *nomin.*; 5⁷ נמלך = *to consult*, as in Aram. (Dan. 4²⁴) ; 5¹⁵ שלם ; 13⁶ לקץ (2 Ch. 18², Dan. 11⁶· ¹³. In early Hebrew, מקץ) ; 13²⁴ עם ועם (p. 538, No. 35) ; 13²⁵ (ונשים) נשא (p. 455).

† חרים is an Aramaic word, used in *North* Israel (p. 188 *n.*), but never applied to the nobles of Judah, except Jer. 27²⁰ 39⁶, in two passages not in the LXX, and probably of later origin than Jer.'s own time (cf. pp. 264, 270). Elsewhere only Isa. 34¹² (of Edom), and Eccl. 10¹⁷ (בנחרים).

2 Esdras representing—of course with the textual variations usual in LXX—the Hebrew "Ezra"; and 1 Esdras* incorporating the Hebrew "Ezra" (with variations) with other matter, as exhibited in the following table :—

1 Esdr. 1	=	2 Ch. 35^1–36^{21}.
,, 2^{1-14}	=	Ezr. 1.
,, 2^{15-25}	=	,, 4^{7-24}.
,, 3^1–5^6	=	* * *
,, 5^{7-70}	=	,, 2^1–4^5.
,, c. 6–9^{36}	=	,, c. 5–10.
,, 9^{37-55}	=	Neh. 7^{73b}–8^{13a}.

[520] The termination is abrupt ; probably the concluding parts of the book have been lost.   The section 3^1–5^6 has been borrowed by the compiler from some independent source ; it describes how three of the guards of Darius agreed to test their wisdom by writing three sentences and placing them under Darius' pillow, to be read and adjudicated on by him in the morning. One wrote, " Wine is the strongest " ; another, " The king is the strongest " ; the third, " Women are the strongest ; but, above all things, truth beareth away the victory."   In the morning, each defends his thesis at length before the king ; the conclusion of the third, whose name was Zorobabel (4^{13}), that "truth endureth, and is strong for ever," is greeted by the people with applause.   Darius bids him ask what he will ; and he seizes the opportunity to remind the king of a vow made by him at his accession to restore the Jews.   Darius thereupon issues a decree, permitting the Jews to return from exile, taking back with them their sacred vessels, and to rebuild the Temple, and granting them many other privileges.   This representation, attributing the restoration of the Jews to *Darius*, is evidently in direct conflict with Ezra 1.   The position assigned to Ezr. 4^{7-24} is also thoroughly unsuitable.   Different motives have been assigned for the compilation : probably the writer wished partly to stimulate his countrymen to a more zealous observance of the Law (note the transition from Ezr. 10 to Neh. $7^{73ff.}$), partly by the example of the munificence of Cyrus and Darius to gain for them the favour of some foreign ruler—perhaps one of the Ptolemies.†   The parts which correspond with the Heb. Ezra are translated in a freer and more flowing style than in the LXX ; but the translation is important for the criticism of the Hebrew text of Ezra, which in some cases may be restored by its aid.

---

* So in the English Apocrypha ; in the Vulgate 3 Esdras.   (1 Esdras = our Ezra ; 2 Esdras = Nehemiah ; 4 Esdras = the Engl. 2 Ezra.)

† Comp. Ewald, *Hist.* v. p. 126 f. ; Lupton, in the *Speaker's Comm. on the Apocrypha*, i. p. 10.

INDEX I.

—o—

Subjects.

INDEX II.

—o—

*Select list of words or phrases commented
upon or cited.*

מעטים *few*, 374 n.

מעל, מעל *a trespass, to trespass*, 134 No. 43, 146, 535 No. 3.

מצלתים *cymbals*, 539 No. 46.

מקנה *purchase, purchased possession*, 133 No. 24.

מקצת *some of*, 506.

מקרב and מתוך *from the midst of*, 49, 146.

מרפא *healing*, 403.

משא *oracle*, or name of country *Massa?* (Prov. 30^1 31^1), 402, 403.

משא דבר יהוה *the oracle of Jehovah's word*, 355.

משובה *turning back, backsliding*, 275.

משוררים *singers* (official term), 379 n., 539.

משל *proverb*, 395 (cf. 337).

משתין בקיר = *every man - child*, 185, 194.

נאם הגבר, 401 n.

נדן *holder, sheath* (Persian), 501, 540.

נטר *to keep* (a vineyard), *retain* (anger), 448 n.

נכסים *riches*, 112 n., 540.

נמלך *to consult*, 553 n.

נפש *soul* in the sense of *person*, 132 No. 19.

נצח *to preside over, lead* (in music), מנצח *precentor*, 373 n., 537.

נקבו בשמות *to be expressed by name*, 536 No. 12.

נרד *nard* (Indian), 449 n.

נשא חן *to obtain favour*, 484.

נשא נשים *to take wives*, 455, 537 No. 25, 553 n.

נתן דרך בראש *to put a person's way upon his head* (i.e. to requite him), 298.

נתן לב ל' *to set the heart to*, 507.

נתן לפני *to set before* (i.e. *deliver up to*), 101 No. 29.

סגנים *deputies* (of the magnates of Judah), 553.

סומפניה — συμφωνία, 502.

סוף *end* (Aram.), 313, 475.

סלף, סלף *perverseness, to subvert*, 403.

ספינה *ship*, 322.

סרבל *hosen* (?), 501 n.

סרך *president* (Persian), 501 n.

עד אם, 454 n.

עד ל' prep. *until, unto* (pleonastic combination), 538, 547.

ערף *to remain over*, 134 No. 37.

עול *iniquity*, 144, 146.

עזר *to help* (in connexion with God), 536 No. 10.

עלי ידי *at the direction of*, Introd. vii n., viii n., 538, 547.

על עמרי (עמרך) lit. *on my (thy) standing*, 507.

עלה על לב *to come up upon the heart*, 275 No. 6.

עם סגלה *a people of special possession*, 99 No. 7a.

עמד in late Heb. = קום, 507.

עמים *kinsfolk* 133 No. 25, 148 n.

עמית *neighbour*, 49, 56, 57, 148 n.

ענין *trouble, business*, 474.

עצור ועזוב "*the fettered and the free*," 194, 201 No. 28,

עצם היום ההוא *the self-same day*, 132.

עצר כח *to control power* = *to be able*, 507.

ערץ *to be affrighted*, 105.

עשתי עשר *eleven*, 156 n.

פאר, התפאר *to deck, to deck oneself*, 239 f.

פסנתרין (פסנטרין) = ψαλτήριον, 502.

פצה *to deliver* (Aram.), 374 n.

פצח *to break out into singing*, 238.

פרבר *open portico* (Persian), 539 bottom.

פרדם *enclosure, park, "paradise"* (Zend), 448 n., 449 n., 450.

פרך *rigour*, 133 No. 28.

פרתמים *nobles* (Persian), 485, 501, 506.

פשט *to spread out, deploy*, 185.

פשר *interpretation* (= פתרון), 474.

פתבג *portion of food, dainty* (Persian), 501 n.

פתגם *message, edict, word* (Persian), 475 No. 12, 485, 501 n.

פתשגן *counter-word, copy* (Persian), 485.

566 INDEX II

צאצאים *offspring*, 239.
צבאות *hosts* (of the Israelites), 133
No. 31.
צבט *to hold out, reach*, 455 n.
צבי *beauty*, the *delightsome* land (of
Canaan), 508 n.
צלח *to come mightily* (of a spirit), 184.
צמח *to shoot forth* (fig.), 238 No. 3.

קבל *to receive*, 536.
קים *to confirm*, 455.
קיתרם=κιθαρις, 502.
קצוצי פאה *corner-clipt* (of certain Arab
tribes), 276.
קשיטה *a piece of money*, 126 n.

ראוי *suitable* (Mishnic use), 485.
רגם and סקל *to stone* (as used by different writers), 134 No. 45, 146
bottom
רז *secret* (Persian), 501 n.
רכש, רכוש *amassed substance, to amass*,
132, 537.
רמך *herd* (of horses), *stud* (Persian),
485.
רע *thought* (Aram.), 374 n.
רק אם *if only*, 200 *bottom*.
רָאשׁ, רָשׁ *the poor*, רִישׁ *poverty*, 404.

שׁ for אשר, rel. particle, 188 n., 322,
374 n., 448, 449 n., 450, 463 n.,
474 No. 22, 540, 549 f.
שׁוּט, שָׁאט *contempt, to contemn*, 298.

שְׁאֵר *flesh=next of kin*, 49 No. 10.
שׂבר *to hope*, שֶׂבֶר *hope*, 455.
שבתון *deep rest*, 134 No. 40.
שגגה *error, inadvertence* (in P), 112.
שוערים *gate-keepers, porters* (official
term), 539.
שור *wall* (Aram.=Heb. חומה), 548 n.
שְׁחִיטָה *slaying* (form of word), 484.
שֶׁל (relat. and prep.), 188 n., 448 n.,
449 n., 475 with n.
שלהבת *flame*, 448 n.
שלח *weapon*, 313, 540.
שלט, שליט, שלמון *to rule, ruler, rule*,
475 No. 13, 553 n.
שְׁלָמָה *for why?=lest*, 448 n.
שפטים *judgments*, 133 No. 29, 297
No. 6.
שפק *to suffice*, 188 n.
שש *marble*, 448 n., 449 n.

תולדות *generations*, 10 n., 131 No. 7.
תור and רגל *to spy* (as used by different
writers), 110, 134 No. 45.
תורה *direction, law*, 31, 153 n., 372.
תושיה *sound wisdom* or *success*, 404.
תחבלות *wise guidance* (lit. *steersmanship*), 403.
תי- term. of 2nd fem. sing. pf., 455.
תנין *reptile*, 24 n.
תֹּפֶל, 463 n.
תקף, חקף *to be strong, prevail, strength*
(Aram.),* 475 Nos. 24, 14, 507
No. 22.

---

* See the writer's *Hebrew Tenses* (ed. 3, 1892), Appendix III. "On Arabic as
illustrative of Hebrew," p. 228, n. 5.

INDEX III.

—o—

Texts.*

---

* Passages occurring in their natural place, or in accordance with the arrangement of the work, are not, as a rule, included in the Index. The case is the same with passages cited in the lists of words and phrases characteristic of particular writers.

Ecclesiasticus.

S. R. Driver

Samuel Rolles Driver was born in 1846 in England of Quaker parents. A fellowship and then a tutorship followed his undergraduate years at New College, Oxford. The first attempt in English to expound principles of Hebrew syntax in philosophical and scientific terms was his *Use of the Tenses in Hebrew* (1874), the foundation for all modern study of Hebrew. His reputation as a Hebraist gained him a seat on the Old Testament revision committee (1875-1884). His numerous scholarly works include commentaries on nearly one-half of the Old Testament. For thirty-one years he was Regius Professor of Hebrew and Canon of Christ Church, Oxford. He died in 1914.

MERIDIAN BOOKS

Art, Architecture, and Music

BARZUN, JACQUES *Berlioz and His Century.* M30
BERENSON, BERNARD *The Italian Painters of the Renaissance.* M40
BIKEL, THEODORE *Folksongs and Footnotes.* MG27
FRY, ROGER *Vision and Design.* M33
GILSON, ETIENNE *Painting and Reality.* M79
HUXLEY, ALDOUS *On Art and Artists.* M99
KAUFMANN, EDGAR, AND RAEBURN, BEN (EDS.) *Frank Lloyd Wright: Writings and Buildings.* MG22
NOSS, LUTHER (ED.) *Christian Hymns.* LA38
PACK, ROBERT, AND LELASH, MARJORIE (TRS.) *Mozart's Librettos.* M80
PANOFSKY, ERWIN *Gothic Architecture and Scholasticism.* M44
PATER, WALTER *The Renaissance.* M124
PHILIPSON, MORRIS (ED.) *Aesthetics Today.* M112
READ, HERBERT *The Grass Roots of Art.* M108
READ, HERBERT *The Philosophy of Modern Art.* M7
SMITH, G. E. KIDDER *The New Architecture of Europe.* MG33
STEINBERG, SAUL *The Catalogue.* M147
TOVEY, DONALD FRANCIS *The Forms of Music.* M36
TOVEY, DONALD FRANCIS *The Main Stream of Music and Other Essays.* M74

Fiction

BABEL, ISAAC *The Collected Stories.* MF3
BEDFORD, SYBILLE *A Legacy.* MF4
BELLOW, SAUL *Dangling Man.* MF9
BUECHNER, FREDERICK *A Long Day's Dying.* MF7
CURVERS, ALEXIS *Tempo di Roma.* MF15
DE BEAUVOIR, SIMONE *The Mandarins.* MF1
DENNIS, NIGEL *Cards of Identity.* MF13
DREISER, THEODORE *An American Tragedy.* MF21
GADDIS, WILLIAM *The Recognitions.* MF20
GASCAR, PIERRE *Beasts and Men* and *The Seed.* MF10
GOLD, HERBERT *Love and Like.* MF16
HOWE, IRVING, AND GREENBERG, ELIEZER (EDS.) *A Treasury of Yiddish Stories.* MG13
JARRELL, RANDALL *Pictures from an Institution.* MF2
MACAULAY, ROSE *The Towers of Trebizond.* MF8
PALEY, GRACE *The Little Disturbances of Man.* MF14

POWELL, ANTHONY *The Acceptance World.* MF11
RENAULT, MARY *The Charioteer.* MF19
ROSENFELD, ISAAC *Passage from Home.* MF18
ROTH, PHILIP *Goodbye, Columbus.* MF5
SPARK, MURIEL *Memento Mori.* MF12
STERN, RICHARD G. *Golk.* MF17
WILSON, ANGUS *The Middle Age of Mrs. Eliot.* MF6

Literature, Criticism, Drama, and Poetry

AIKEN, CONRAD *Ushant.* M148
AUBERBACH, ERICH *Scenes from the Drama of European Literature.* M63
BELLOW, SAUL; BOTSFORD, KEITH; AND LUDWIG, JACK (EDS.) *The Noble Savage 1.* M88
BELLOW, SAUL; BOTSFORD, KEITH; AND LUDWIG, JACK (EDS.) *The Noble Savage 2.* M102
BELLOW, SAUL, AND BOTSFORD, KEITH (EDS.) *The Noble Savage 3.* M113
BELLOW, SAUL, AND BOTSFORD, KEITH (EDS.) *The Noble Savage 4.* M125
BELLOW, SAUL, AND BOTSFORD, KEITH (EDS.) *The Noble Savage 5.* M136
BERDYAEV, NICHOLAS *Dostoevsky.* LA15
BERRYMAN, JOHN *Stephen Crane.* M131
BRADLEY, A. C. *Shakespearean Tragedy.* M20
BRENAN, GERALD *The Literature of the Spanish People.* MG9
BROOKS, VAN WYCK *The Ordeal of Mark Twain.* M14
BROWNE, E. MARTIN (ED.) *Religious Drama 2: Mystery and Morality Plays.* LA20
BURNSHAW, STANLEY (ED.) *The Poem Itself.* M142
EISENSTEIN, SERGEI *Film Form* and *The Film Sense.* MG10
EMPSON, WILLIAM *Seven Types of Ambiguity.* M11
FIEDLER, LESLIE A. *Love and Death in the American Novel* MG43
FOWLIE, WALLACE *Dionysus in Paris: A Guide to Contemporary French Theater.* M92
FOWLIE, WALLACE *A Guide to Contemporary French Literature.* M48
GRIGSON, GEOFFREY (ED.) *The Romantics.* M132
HALL, DONALD, AND PACK, ROBERT (EDS.) *New Poets of England and America: Second Selection.* M135
HALL, DONALD; PACK, ROBERT; AND SIMPSON, LOUIS (EDS.) *New Poets of England and America.* M50

Social Sciences, Psychology, and Anthropology

HUTCHINS, ROBERT M. *Freedom, Education, and the Fund.* M31
JUNG, C. G. *Answer to Job.* M86
JUNG, C. G. *Two Essays on Analytical Psychology.* M28
KARDINER, ABRAM, AND OVESEY, LIONEL *The Mark of Oppression: Explorations in the Personality of the American Negro.* M141
LASSWELL, HAROLD *Politics: Who Gets What, When, How.* M58
LEKACHMAN, ROBERT (ED.) *The Varieties of Economics, Vol. I.* MG46A
LEKACHMAN, ROBERT (ED.) *The Varieties of Economics, Vol. II.* MG46B
LERNER, DANIEL (ED.) *The Human Meaning of the Social Sciences.* M64
MACDONALD, DWIGHT *Memoirs of a Revolutionist.* M56
MALINOWSKI, BRONISLAW *Sex and Repression in Savage Society.* M15
NELSON, BENJAMIN (ED.) *Freud and the 20th Century.* M45
PIAGET, JEAN *The Language and Thought of the Child.* M10
ROSE, H. J. *Gods and Heroes of the Greeks.* M59
ROVERE, RICHARD H. *Senator Joe McCarthy.* M98
SCHUMPETER, JOSEPH *Imperialism and Social Classes.* M4
SWADOS, HARVEY (ED.) *Years of Conscience: The Muckrakers.* M129
WILLIAMS, CHARLES *Witchcraft.* M62
WILSON, WOODROW *Congressional Government.* M27
ZIMMER, HEINRICH *The King and the Corpse.* M93

History

ACTON, LORD *Lectures on Modern History.* M109
BOORSTIN, DANIEL J. *America and the Image of Europe.* M89
COULTON, G. G. *Medieval Panorama.* MG2
D'ARCY, M. C. *The Meaning and Matter of History.* M110
DAWSON, CHRISTOPHER *The Making of Europe.* M35
DILL, SAMUEL *Roman Society in the Last Century of the Western Empire.* MG31
DILL, SAMUEL *Roman Society from Nero to Marcus Aurelius.* MG48
FINLEY, M. I. *The World of Odysseus.* M68
GEYL, PIETER *Debates with Historians.* M57
GEYL, PIETER *Encounters in History.* M114
GLATZER, NAHUM N. (ED.) *Jerusalem and Rome: The Writings of Josephus.* M106

GRANET, MARCEL *Chinese Civilization.* MG14
HASKINS, C. H. *The Renaissance of the 12th Century.* M49
History 1. M72
History 2. M83
History 3. M95
History 4. M117
HUIZINGA, JOHAN *Men and Ideas.* M61
KIRKPATRICK, F. A. *The Spanish Conquistadores.* M146
LUETHY, HERBERT *France Against Herself.* MG8
MAYER, J. P. (ED.) *The Recollections of Alexis de Tocqueville.* M82
MOMMSEN, THEODOR *The History of Rome.* MG32
PIRENNE, HENRI *Mohammed and Charlemagne.* M42
ROEDER, RALPH *The Man of the Renaissance.* MG17
RUNCIMAN, STEVEN *Byzantine Civilization.* M23
SAUNDERS, DERO A. (ED.) *The Autobiography of Edward Gibbon.* M111
SEYFERT, OSCAR *Dictionary of Classical Antiquities.* MG34
STERN, FRITZ (ED.) *The Varieties of History.* M37
TARN, W. W. *Hellenistic Civilisation.* M121
TOYNBEE, ARNOLD *Civilization on Trial* and *The World and the West.* M52
WOODCOCK, GEORGE *Anarchism: A History of Libertarian Ideas and Movements.* M133

Meridian Documents of American History

BARCK, OSCAR THEODORE, JR. (ED.) *America in the World.* M127
DIVINE, ROBERT A. (ED.) *American Foreign Policy.* M91
KIRWAN, ALBERT D. (ED.) *The Confederacy.* M76
KLINGBERG, FRANK W. (ED.) *A History of the United States: From 1865 to the Present.* M115
LEFLER, HUGH T. (ED.) *A History of the United States: From the Age of Exploration to 1865.* M101

Philosophy

BABBITT, IRVING *Rousseau and Romanticism.* M3
BOSANQUET, BERNARD *A History of Aesthetic.* MG36
BURKE, KENNETH *A Grammar of Motives* and *A Rhetoric of Motives.* M143
BURNET, JOHN *Early Greek Philosophy.* MG30
CLIVE, GEOFFREY *The Romantic Enlightenment.* M85

Religion (General)

Of Catholic Interest

Of Protestant Interest (Living Age Books)

OTTO, RUDOLF *Mysticism East and West.* LA14
ROWLEY, H. H. *The Unity of the Bible.* LA16
SAYERS, DOROTHY L. *The Mind of the Maker.* LA2
TALON, HENRI A. *God's Knotty Log: Selected Writings of John
   Bunyan.* LA31
THOMPSON, BARD (ED.) *Liturgies of the Western Church.* LA35
TILLICH, PAUL *The Religious Situation.* LA6
TROELTSCH, ERNEST *Christian Thought.* LA12
VISSER 'T HOOFT, W. A. *Rembrandt and the Gospel.* LA30
WHITEHEAD, ALFRED NORTH *Religion in the Making.* LA28
WILLIAMS, CHARLES *The Descent of the Dove.* LA5

Of Jewish Interest (Jewish Publication Society Series)

ABRAHAMS, ISRAEL *Jewish Life in the Middle Ages.* JP4
ASCH, SHOLEM *Kiddush Ha-Shem* and *Sabbatai Zevi.* JP9
BAECK, LEO *Judaism and Christianity.* JP23
BARON, SALO W. *Modern Nationalism and Religion.* JP18
BEIN, ALEX *Theodore Herzl.* JP30
BUBER, MARTIN *For the Sake of Heaven.* JP1
DUBNOW, SIMON *Nationalism and History: Essays on Old and
   New Judaism.* JP20
FINKELSTEIN, LOUIS *Akiba: Scholar, Saint and Martyr.* JP25
GINZBERG, LOUIS *On Jewish Law and Lore.* JP26
GINZBERG, LOUIS *Students, Scholars and Saints.* JP2
GRAYZEL, SOLOMON *A History of the Contemporary Jews.* JP16
HA-'AM, AHAD *Selected Essays.* JP29
HERBERG, WILL *Judaism and Modern Man.* JP10
HERTZBERG, ARTHUR (ED.) *The Zionist Idea.* JP17
HESCHEL, ABRAHAM JOSHUA *God in Search of Man.* JP7
HESCHEL, ABRAHAM JOSHUA *The Earth Is the Lord's* and *The
   Sabbath.* JP28
HUSIK, ISAAC *A History of Mediaeval Jewish Philosophy.* JP3
KORN, BERTRAM W. *American Jewry and the Civil War.* JP24
LEWY, HANS; ALTMANN, ALEXANDER; AND HEINEMANN, ISAAK (EDS.)
   Three Jewish Philosophers. JP13
LIPTZIN, SOLOMON *Germany's Stepchildren.* JP19
MARCUS, JACOB R. *The Jew in the Medieval World.* JP14
MARGOLIS, MAX, AND MARX, ALEXANDER *A History of the Jewish
   People.* JP6

MODDER, MONTAGU FRANK *The Jew in the Literature of England.*
JP15
PARKES, JAMES *The Conflict of the Church and the Synagogue.*
JP21
ROTH, CECIL *A History of the Marranos.* JP12
SAMUEL, MAURICE *Prince of the Ghetto.* JP11
SCHECHTER, SOLOMON *Studies in Judaism.* JP5
SPIEGEL, SHALOM *Hebrew Reborn.* JP27
STRACK, HERMANN L. *Introduction to the Talmud and Midrash.*
JP8
TRACHTENBERG, JOSHUA *The Devil and the Jews.* JP22

Natural Sciences

DANTO, ARTHUR, AND MORGENBESSER, SIDNEY (EDS.) *Philosophy of Science.* M90
DAMPIER, WILLIAM CECIL *A Shorter History of Science.* M47
GALTON, FRANCIS *Hereditary Genius.* M134
IRVINE, WILLIAM *Apes, Angels, and Victorians.* M78
KÖHLER, WOLFGANG *The Place of Value in a World of Facts.*
MG19
NORTHROP, F. S. C. *The Logic of the Sciences and the Humanities.*
M71
PEARSON, KARL *The Grammar of Science.* ML7

General and Reference

BOLTIN, LEE *Jail Keys Made Here and Other Signs.* MG21
ELAM, SAMUEL MILTON *Hornbook for the Double Damned.* MG47
JEFFERY, GRANT *Science & Technology Stocks: A Guide for Investors.* MG41
KIRSCHBAUM, LEO *Clear Writing.* MG38
The Meridian Compact Atlas of the World. M126
SEYFFERT, OSCAR *Dictionary of Classical Antiquities.* MG34
SIMON, KATE *New York Places & Pleasures: Revised Edition.*
MG18R
Webster's New World Dictionary of the American Language (Concise Edition). MG25

Meridian Books are published by The World Publishing Company, Cleveland and New York. For a free Meridian catalogue please write to Department AM, Meridian Books, 119 West 57th Street, New York 19, New York.